SURVIVAL WISDOM & KNOW-HOW

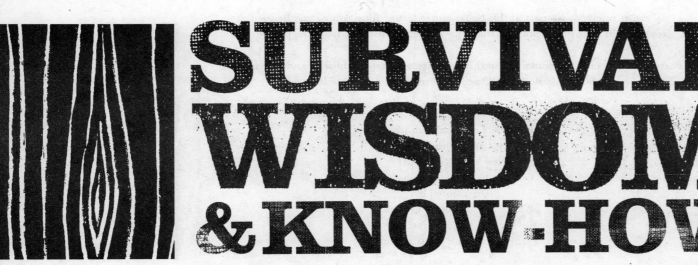

SURVIVAL WISDOM & KNOW-HOW

Everything You Need to Know to Subsist in the Wilderness

From the Editors of Stackpole Books

Compiled by Amy Rost

BLACK DOG
& LEVENTHAL
PUBLISHERS
NEW YORK

Published by
Black Dog & Leventhal Publishers, Inc.
151 West 19th Street
New York, NY 10011

Distributed by
Workman Publishing Company
225 Varick Street
New York, NY 10014

Manufactured in the U.S.A.
Cover and interior design by Ohioboy Design

Cover illustration: clipart.com
ISBN-13: 978-1-57912-753-4

t s r q p o n

Library of Congress Cataloging-in-Publication Data available on file

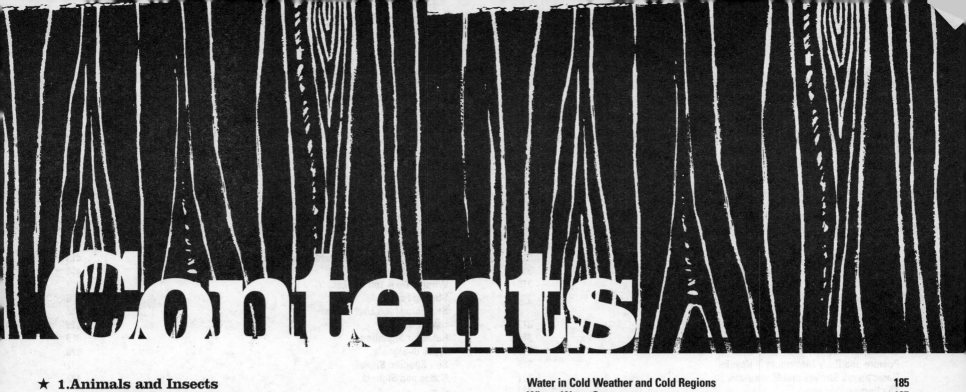

Contents

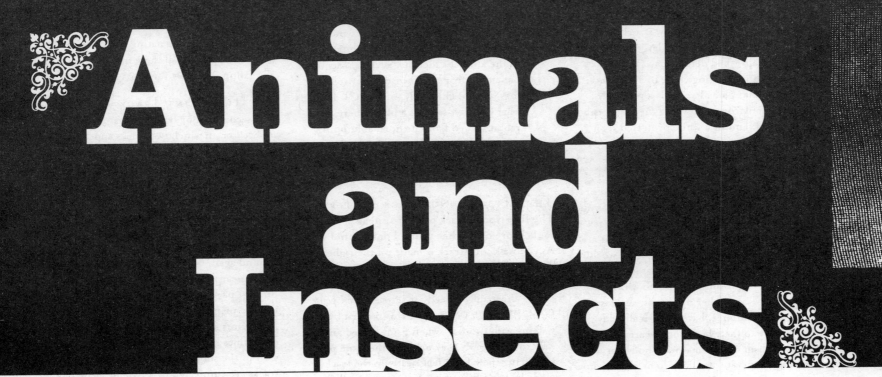

Animals and Insects

The Basics of Tracking Animals

Louise R. Forrest
Illustrations by Denise Casey

Many people assume that in winter wild animals, like so many of us, escape the difficulties of traveling, feeding, and keeping warm by migrating or hibernating. This is true of cold-blooded animals and of many warm-blooded birds and mammals. However, a surprising number of birds and mammals conduct business as usual, and whenever they move, rest, feed, hunt, or behave in other ways on the ground, a record is impressed in the snow. Indeed, without the use of sophisticated equipment, snow offers one of the best opportunities to learn about the lives of animals in winter.

But why, you may ask, would anyone want to follow an animal around in the winter? Imagine a bright, sunny morning after a snow storm—air crisp, snow sparkling—a perfect day for a ski, a walk, or a snowmobile ride. Traveling into the woods or across the fields, you suddenly intersect a winding trail interrupting the snow's smooth surface. With a little imagination, you envision the trail-maker walking, waddling, or trotting along. You follow the trail and find numerous clues that reveal this animal's daily activities.

Perhaps the trail leads to the scene of a successful hunt where the two-print trail of a weasel slowed, disappeared under the snow, and then reappeared, accompanied by tiny drag marks of a hapless vole. It may lead to a spot marking the swoop of an unlucky hawk and the scurry of a luckier mouse; to a place where two coyotes met and continued on together; to a mysterious dead-end where a grouse took off in flight; to a small depression where a moose gently touched its nose to the snow to sniff for food; or to a hill that proved irresistible to sliding otters or mink. The trail itself, whether it meanders or strikes out straight ahead, reflects the behavior of the animal in motion and provides substantial amounts of biological data. More important, following it is fun! But please be aware that in winter animals are generally operating on very strict energy budgets. If you frighten them excessively or harass them, either by pursuing too closely on foot or following on a snowmobile, you may tip the scale between survival and death.

Why a book on snow-tracking when so many fine tracking books exist? During my first winter tracking efforts, I often found it difficult to match the tracks I saw in the snow with the detailed shape and toe counts of my track book illustrations. So often, snow obscured these foot details that are useful when identifying tracks in mud, sand, and sometimes in shallow snow. After several winters studying animals in the field, I decided to compile that information, gathered from my own experiences and from other track books, which proved most helpful for identifying tracks in snow.

I learned that the first rule of snow-tracking is to identify the animal's track pattern, the trail left in the snow, which is often identifiable even when the tracks are windblown and obscured. Consequently, this book emphasizes track patterns, although print details are always important tracking clues whenever visible.

Mammals are the prime focus of this book because their tracks are the ones most likely to be found in winter. Tracks of birds and domestic mammals are also discussed. The North American animals included in this book are primarily those that are active in winter in areas that commonly receive snow.

Continued →

About Snow

How animals have adapted to life in snow country is fascinating. Let's take a closer look at that snow environment. Snow is not just snow. Arctic natives have a surprisingly large vocabulary to describe the various forms of snow and its structure within the snowpack. While some of these variations are caused above the snow by environmental conditions like wind and cold; others, more important to many animals, are caused from below.

In areas where a persistent snow cover occurs, the temperature of the ground surface closely parallels the outside air temperature until snow cover is deeper than 6 inches. With snow cover comes an insulating blanket that retards the natural loss of the earth's heat. As a result, the bottom of the snowpack becomes warmer than the top (which is exposed to cold air), and a thermal gradient is created in which heat and moisture flow upward. Snow crystals near the soil break down, and their water molecules migrate either to larger crystals or to those above.

Eventually, the bottom snow structure becomes a fragile latticework of large, coarse, granular crystals called depth hoar. This weak layer, often an underlying cause of avalanches, also provides many small animals a relatively warm, stable environment where they can easily burrow, travel, and nest while protected from the cold temperatures above. A dark, silent "undersnow" world is created with intricate systems of runways, tunnels, and burrows. Above, you trod along unaware of the world of activity below you! But if you are observant, you can find holes by trees or shrubs or openings near downed logs, brush piles, or rocks that are entryways to this subnivean (undersnow) world.

Of the animals that do not migrate or hibernate, only the larger ones are able to withstand extreme cold. The smaller mammals, such as shrews, voles, and mice, have such small body masses relative to their body surface area that their metabolism cannot maintain body warmth in freezing temperatures. They go below the snow where it rarely drops below 15°F. Even some spiders can remain active in this environment.

The subnivean air is saturated with moisture—a boon to shrews, which have poor mechanisms to control their body moisture. It is also ideal for scent communication in the hunting efforts of small predators. The difficult times for these small animals are spring and fall when temperatures are cold and the snowpack is beginning or ending.

Small weasels spend much of their time under the snow hunting rodents and using rodent runways and nests for their own. Besides the fact that most of their prey live under the snow, these weasels must also seek shelter here because they have high rates of metabolism, small bodies, little fat, and fur of only moderate insulating value.

Red squirrels are also confined to the subnivean world at times. They make tunnels and runways to reach their cone caches near the soil, and nest under the snow when temperatures reach below about −25°F.

Large mammals have adapted to snow travel through modifications of the feet or legs. For example, the feet of the snowshoe hare and the lynx are large relative to body size. Other examples are the rounded, splayed hoofs of the caribou and the long, stiltlike legs of the moose. The moose's rear legs articulate so they can be inserted in snow and retracted at nearly the same angle.

When you travel on snow, it's fascinating to speculate on the ways animals manage to stay active in the winter and to look for clues to where and how they do it.

Steps to Track Identification

Step One: Identify the animal's track pattern

Taking a walk in the snow, you come upon a series of foot prints or tracks ahead of you. This series of tracks is the animal's trail. Looking more carefully, you notice that the trail has a track pattern, a distinctive arrangement of the tracks.

- First, you need to identify which of the three main track patterns the trail resembles. To do this, follow the trail for at least several yards in one or both directions to get a feel for the animal's most typical track pattern and to find additional clues to the animal's identity, such as scats (or pellets or droppings) or distinctive behaviors (does it climb, fly, or swim?). Perhaps what you first saw was a place where a rabbit slowed from its normal hopping gait to walk and explore a shrub. *When in doubt, follow the trail!* Here are the main track patterns.

THE ALTERNATING TRACK PATTERN

The first type of track pattern animals make looks more or less like yours. Look behind you. As you walk, one track is made on the right, then another on the left, right, left, and so on. What you see are two parallel rows of tracks with the prints alternately spaced—*an alternating track pattern* (a, b). Although we produce this pattern by walking with two feet, when four-footed animals walk or trot slowly they produce the same pattern by placing their hind feet neatly in the tracks made by their front feet. Sometimes in shallow snow, an animal's hind feet fall slightly ahead, behind, or to the side of its front-foot prints, making an *offset alternating track pattern* (b). However, in deep snow, the animal saves energy by placing its hind feet in its front-foot tracks. Think about following a friend's tracks in deep snow.

It's much easier to step in those tracks than to make your own.

All mammals and most birds *walk*, but more often mammals travel in other movement patterns or *gaits*. Other gaits include, in general order of increasing speed, *trotting*, *loping* (a slow gallop), *jumping* (a bounding or hopping gait), and *galloping*. Jumping is different from loping or galloping because movement off the feet occurs simultaneously and with equal force.

Some animals that commonly walk in snow, making an alternating track pattern, are the members of the bear, dog, and cat families, and the ungulates (hoofed mammals)—all of which are long-bodied and thus take long steps. Those walkers that are short-bodied (and take short steps) include opossums, beavers, muskrats, porcupines, badgers, skunks, lemmings, and ground-dwelling birds. Marmots, prairie dogs, and voles also fall in this group; however, they often move in a jumping gait. (Group members drag their bodies in soft, relatively shallow snow.) Members of the dog family and the ungulates sometimes trot when snow is shallow, maintaining the alternating track pattern but with longer steps. All these mammals occasionally gallop, but only for short stretches in snow.

THE TWO-PRINT TRACK PATTERN

The second major track pattern is the *two-print track pattern*, in which two tracks appear close together followed by a distinct space, then two more tracks (c, d, e). One type of two-print track pattern is made by members of the weasel or mustelid family (except badgers and skunks) when they lope (c). They move by leaping forward off their hind feet and landing with their front feet. Then the front feet leave the ground again before the hind feet finally land—on or near the front-foot prints (see illustration on next page). Usually, but not always, one of the two prints falls slightly behind the other. The prints are usually spaced close together, sometimes making a single two-lobed impression in the snow. Occasionally two pairs of tracks are connected by a trough made by the animal's body.

In soft snow, mice, voles (d), chipmunks, tree squirrels, and tree-dwelling birds (e) make a two-print pattern in which the tracks are typically paired side by side. Except for birds, these short-bodied animals actually jump as they

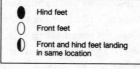

An elk walking. Note how the hind foot lands where the opposing front foot previously stepped (drawn from Muybridge, 1979).

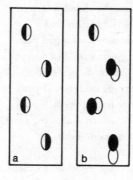

Key to identifying front and hind feet in track patterns described below.

Left: Alternating track pattern. a. Alternating track pattern with hind-foot prints neatly registering on front-foot prints. b. Offset alternating track pattern with hind feet landing close to front-foot prints.

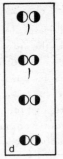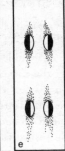

Some two-print track patterns. c. Two-print loping track pattern made by most members of the weasel or mustelid family. d. and e. Paired two-print track patterns made by voles and mice (d) and chipmunks and tree squirrels (e). This occurs when their four-print group merges in soft snow.

Short-tailed weasel loping. Its hind feet land together in the location previously occupied by the front feet (drawn from Gambaryan, 1974).

ments and leaving a clustered four-print track group. (Much of this discussion on mammal gaits is taken from James Halfpenny's excellent book, *A Field Guide to Mammal Tracking in Western America.*)

• A final note on track patterns: Consider the character of the animal's movements. Does it travel erratically, moving in different directions (a weasel energetically investigating every spot)? Does it move purposefully forward, largely unconcerned with cover or habitat (a wolf or coyote on the move)? Do its movements lead from tree to tree (a tree squirrel, porcupine, or marten) or from burrow to burrow (a ground squirrel, prairie dog, or perhaps a black-footed ferret)? Or does it wander from shrub to shrub nibbling winter stems (a hare, elk, or moose)? An animal's trail holds many different clues to the animal's identity. These clues are described in the species accounts.

would to make a four-print pattern (described below) in shallow snow; however, the tracks merge to form a two-print pattern. Their bodies may also make troughs linking two sets of tracks. In the case of voles, this is a particularly common pattern. Tree-dwelling birds usually hop on the ground with their feet together.

Raccoons and opossums, short-legged and wide-bodied, make a two-print walking pattern in which the hind feet are placed next to the tracks of the opposing front feet (f). Thus, each two-print group contains prints of two sizes—one the print of the larger hind foot. The opossum's hind-foot track is particularly distinctive because it shows a backward-pointing "thumb."

Some of the long-bodied walking mammals, particularly ungulates and dogs, make two-print track patterns when trotting in shallow snow. When the trot is fast, ungulates, especially, may completely overstep the front-foot prints with their hind feet, making a two-print track pattern (g), really a very offset alternating track pattern. Another trotting pattern typical of the dog family shows a two-print pattern with the front-foot prints on one side of the imaginary center-line and the hind foot prints on the other side, behind, next to, or ahead of the front print, depending on speed (h).

Common four-print track patterns. i. Four-print track patterns made by most rabbits and rodents when hopping; ground dwellers place their front feet on a diagonal (top), while tree dwellers place theirs side by side (bottom). j. Three-print variations of the four-print track pattern where a front-foot print merges with a hind-foot print or the front-foot prints merge together.

front-foot prints leaving only three or two prints showing (see two-print track patterns), or the two front feet land close together merging into one print (j). In the case of larger rodents and rabbits, both front prints rarely merge with the hind prints to form the two-print pattern made by small rodents in deep snow.

Four-print track patterns are also made when a mammal lopes or gallops, as shown; but, because of the energy it takes to move in snow, they are uncommon and typically seen only for short stretches. Those mammals that already jump in a four-print pattern merely extend their feet, maintaining the same pattern as speed increases. Basically, other mammals gallop by leaping off their hind feet, landing forward with their front feet, and then taking off from their front feet to create an airborne phase before the hind feet land again. A galloping track pattern is sometimes an indication that the animal was frightened—perhaps by you!

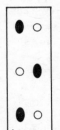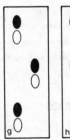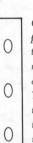

Other two-print track patterns. f. Walking two-print track pattern made by raccoons and opossums. g. and h. Two-print trotting track patterns typical of the ungulates (g) and the dog family (h).

The Four-print Track Pattern
The third major track pattern is the *four-print track pattern*, where four footprints are grouped together followed by a space and then four more prints (i and j). The most common type of four-print pattern is made by rodents and rabbits as they jump or hop. The animal jumps forward off its large muscular hind legs and lands on its front feet, placing them either side by side or slightly on a diagonal. Then it places its hind feet around the outside and ahead of its front-foot prints (see illustration). Tree dwellers place their front feet side by side most often (i, bottom), while ground dwellers usually place their front feet on a diagonal (i, top). This rule applies to mammals as well as to most birds.

During a four-print jump, the hind feet sometimes fall on top of one or both of the

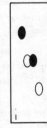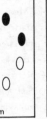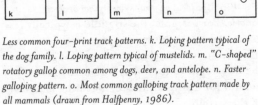

Less common four-print track patterns. k. Loping pattern typical of the dog family. l. Loping pattern typical of mustelids. m. "C-shaped" rotatory gallop common among dogs, deer, and antelope. n. Faster galloping pattern. o. Most common galloping track pattern made by all mammals (drawn from Halfpenny, 1986).

Loping and galloping four-print patterns vary, depending on the species of animal and its speed. The accompanying illustrations show slower lopes (k and l), and faster gallops (m, n, o). Lope k is typical of the dog family, while lope l is typical of mustelids. The C-shaped rotatory gallop (m) is common among the dog, deer, and antelope families. Dogs, mustelids, and ungulates commonly make gallop n. Gallop o is the most common galloping print made by almost all families of mammals. Mule deer exhibit their own variation of a jump called a "stot," jumping off all four legs at once in pogo-stick-like move-

Tassle-eared squirrel hopping. Note how the hind feet are brought around and ahead of the front feet (drawn from Gambaryan, 1974).

Step Two: Decide in which type of habitat the animal lives
• While identifying the basic track pattern of your mystery animal, think about where you are. Are you deep in a New England forest? A Minnesota riparian area (near a lake, pond, or stream)? Or maybe an "edge" between different habitat types? Some animals, such as prairie dogs and ground squirrels, are lovers of open, western prairies, while others, such as tree squirrels, require forest habitats. Still others, like coyotes, travel long distances through all types of terrain. Are you in the suburbs or the wilderness? A wolverine rarely visits the suburbs. When you look at the species accounts, make sure you look at both the habitat information and the range map that tell you which part of the country is home to each animal.

Step Three: Identify the animal
• Now is the time to move in on the track (but don't push snow over it!) and take a closer look. Look for additional clues (are there pads or claws?) and take a few measurements. When out in the woods or mountains in winter I often carry a small cloth tape measure, a notebook, and a camera for recording tracks. You may want to carry a ruler or use the one on the back cover of this guide, or you may prefer standby rulers—a hand or fingers. The stretch between my thumb and little finger across my palm measures about 8 inches. The tip joint of my index finger measures an inch. This often gives me the ballpark estimate I need to confirm a track or give me a general ideal about which one to look up in a track book later. More often than

Continued ➡

not, I recognize a certain track by its relative size compared to my hand or finger than by actual numbers I have memorized.

TRACK SHAPES AND OTHER HINTS

• Although an animal's footprint is rarely perfectly detailed in snow, you often see the general foot shape, the overall track size and hints of toes, foot pads, or claws. It is important to remember that all the toes rarely register in a snow track, both because soft snow does not hold a print well and because the hind foot often falls where the front foot landed. Toe count is a major key to identifying tracks in many track books, and it can be useful in old or shallow snow as well as in dirt substrates, *but don't count on it.* For example, among three groups that walk making similar track patterns—dogs, cats and ungulates— the dogs can be distinguished by their elliptically shaped feet and traces of pad prints and claws. Cats have round feet with retractile claws, and ungulates have hoofs. In particularly soft, deep snow, even these features may be obscured, in which case you must look for other tracking clues or follow the trail to an area of shallower snow, for example under a tree branch.

TRACK SIZES

• Keep three things in mind before measuring tracks. First, tracks in snow are slightly larger than the actual foot size and sometimes larger than the actual foot size and sometimes larger than tracks of the same animal in mud or sand. Also, when the hind-foot print registers on the front-foot print, this track composite is slightly larger than you would expect a single footprint to be. The range of track measurements given in this book for each species group reflects these facts.

• Second, *prints in snow change size with age.* A print exposed to warm sun may melt out to twice its original size after a couple of days. Gravity, freezing, and thawing break apart tracks; blowing snow or new snow fills in tracks. Use your own footprints to judge a track's freshness. Follow the trail to find tracks made in the shelter of trees or rocks, or on a different snow surface, to get a better idea of the real track size. Keep in mind that track sizes can vary with age of the track as well as with age and sex of the animal, and use the other clues— habitat, range, and associated signs—to help identify the track.

• Finally, keep in mind that the depth of the print is a good indicator of an animal's size and weight. For example, lynx and mountain lion tracks are similar in size, but the lynx, very light for its large feet, rarely sinks deeply into snow. Look around your neighborhood to see the depth and size of the prints made by a local cat, dog, or other resident animal for a frame of reference.

• Track measurements given in this book include: (1) length and width of *single prints,*

a track made by one foot or, in the alternating or two-print track patterns, by two feet when the hind foot registers on the front foot; (2) the length and width of the *print group,* the tracks made when each foot has touched down once, generally applicable to the two- and four-print track patterns (the print group in the alternating pattern does not occur as a distinct cluster); (3) the distance between each single print or print group, called the *intergroup* distance or length; and (4) the *straddle,* the width between the outermost prints or the width of the trail (*p* and *q*). (The distance from the trailing end of one print group to the trailing end of the next group, one full step cycle, is commonly called a stride.)

When measuring single prints or print groups, measure between the widest or longest points and just where the animal's foot stepped down (the flat part of the track), excluding the outer edges of the track or places where the foot slid through the snow before or after it stepped down. When claw marks are visible, include them in the print length measurement. To measure the intergroup distance, measure the distance between any two consecutive print groups. Note that in the alternating pattern, the print group can be a set of any two prints. In this case, consider the distance between any two prints as the intergroup distance.

The straddle indicates the width of the animal and is often a good way to distinguish between two members of a family that move in the same manner, such as between deer, elk, and moose. In general, as an animal increases speed, the print group length increases and the straddle decreases. However, the straddle often increases when an animal moves into deep snow. The intergroup distance may actually decrease when some animals increase their gait.

Always take several measurements, averaging them until you obtain a general range of measurements to compare with the range of sizes for each measurement in the book. Measuring one or two unusually long leaps made by a tree squirrel or only one or two fox prints could prove puzzling, but measuring several tracks along the trail will give a more accurate picture of which animal you are tracking. *When in doubt, follow the trail.*

Finally, *focus on measurements that are least variable.* For example, the straddle is typically less variable than the intergroup distance. Look in the section introducing each mammal group for the discussion of those measurements most helpful for distinguishing between the mammals in that group.

ASSOCIATED SIGNS

• The signs an animal leaves along its trail are excellent clues to the animal's identity. These signs include *scats* or pellets; resting *beds* where the animal lay down to rest during the day or night; *evidence of feeding* where the animal stopped to browse or perhaps feed on another animal; *scent marks* where the animal rubbed or scratched, often in association with *urination*; and *hair.* The signs found most often in winter for each species or species group are described in the species accounts. In many cases, signs are frequently seen along trails, and they enliven the story of the animal you are tracking.

Direction of Travel

People often wonder how to determine which way an animal is going—something that may be important if you wish to observe (or perhaps avoid!) an animal. Look for partial toe or claw prints, which point in the direction of travel. The shape of the foot can help you tell where the front of the track is. For example, the hind foot of most weasels and rodents is broadest across the front, tapering down to a narrower heel. The snow is often more compressed at the front of the track where more weight is placed. Foot placement is also important. When rabbits and rodents bound, they usually place their hind feet ahead of their front feet, so that the hind feet are actually leading the tracks.

Finally, when an animal walks either on the flat or downhill, it often slides its feet into the print trough, steps, and then lifts them out. The result is a trough in the snow, longer and shallower where the foot entered, and steeper and more abrupt where the foot was lifted out—or toward the direction the animal was traveling. The movement pattern uphill is often reversed because the animal lifts its legs high to step into the snow and then drags them out as it moves forward. This movement may throw snow forward, too.

Preserving Tracks

Besides making various field notes about tracks, I generally preserve tracks with photographs. Tracks are best photographed in direct sunlight with the print an inch or more deep. Position yourself so the sun casts shadows in the print, adding depth and contrast against the snow. On

Single print measurements
length
width
Four-print group measurements
group
straddle
Two-print group measurements
group
straddle
p

Alternating pattern
Two-print pattern
q

Intergroup distance
Straddle
Print group
Four-print pattern

Standard track measurements. (Note: in the alternating pattern, use the distance between any two prints as the intergroup distance.)

Continued ➡

a bright day, I sometimes use a polarizing filter to help cut the glare from the snow, or I under-expose the photo a little. Shoot at a couple of exposure readings to see what works best with the particular film you are using. (Make sure you have some scheme to remember which shot was which.) Including a pencil, lens cap, notebook, foot, body, or ruler in the photo helps give scale to the tracks. Shoot at least one photo aiming straight down at the print and scale item if possible. This alleviates any distortion caused by shooting at an angle and allows you to take measurements from your slide later. Your camera should be as close to the print as your focus will allow, filling the frame.

It's also possible to make plaster casts of tracks in snow. You will need: temperatures below freezing; a spray bottle (such as that used to humidify plants); plaster of paris; a mixing container; and water. Spray the track with a mist of water (if the water doesn't come out in a fine mist, it will break apart the track). Allow it to freeze. Mix some plaster of paris with water to the consistency of a slightly thick pancake batter. Be careful not to make it too thick, otherwise it will set up too quickly, preventing a good flow into all the nooks and crannies of the track. If it's too thin or too warm, it will break through your ice mold. If the water has warmed up, mix it with snow to cool it down as much as possible. You may need to form a barrier of snow or to use a cardboard ring held together with a paper clip to prevent the plaster from flowing out of the track. After you fill the print with plaster, overflowing it slightly, let it set for a good ten minutes or more before removing the cast. Heavy, wet snow provides the bese chance for good track detail, while soft, powder snow proves frustrating to casting efforts.

—Excerpted from *Field Guide to Tracking Animals in the Snow*

Common North American Mammals: Tracks, Behavior, and Ranges

Small Rodents

Louise R. Forrest
Illustrations by Denise Casey

Chipmunks
Tamias species

Description: Varying in color from gray to brown to red, the sprightly chipmunks have alternating dark and light stripes along their backs and the sides of their heads. They have larger hind feet than front feet and tails of moderate length. Total length ranges from 7 to 11 inches with the tail 3 to 5 inches long. Weights range from 1 to 4.5 ounces.

Habits: Chipmunks live in partially wooded or brushy habitats and are primarily terrestrial, although they will climb trees. Generally solitary, they are active by day and make small, shallow burrows in the ground in which they nest and store seeds and other plant material for winter.

Track Pattern: Chipmunks retire to their burrows and become torpid from October or November to February or March depending on species and area, except least chipmunks (*Tamias minimus*), which retire from September or October to April or May. They arise occasionally to feed on stores and may emerge in warm spells. They jump in a four-print track pattern with diagonally placed front feet (*a*). The large eastern chipmunks (*Tamias striatus*) may make tracks slightly larger than shown. Note variations in soft snow (*b*, *c*).

Associated Signs: If you see chipmunk tracks, you are likely to glimpse the chipmunk itself perching alertly on a fallen log or streaking toward its small—about 2-inch-wide—burrow. Other signs are rarely seen in winter.

Large Tree Squirrels
Sciurus species

Description: This group contains gray squirrels (*Sciurus carolinensis*, colored gray or black); fox squirrels (*S. niger*; red, gray, or black); western gray squirrels (*S. griseus*, gray); and tassle-eared squirrels (*S. aberti*, gray with red dorsal stripe). Total length is 17 to 27 inches with bushy tails 8 to 13 inches. Weight is 0.8 to 3 pounds.

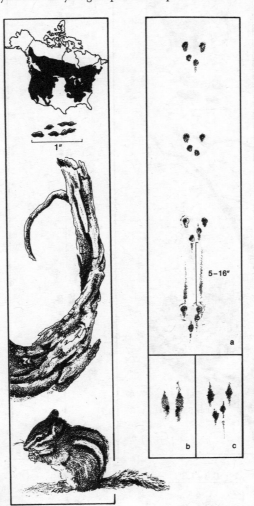

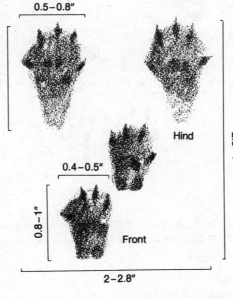

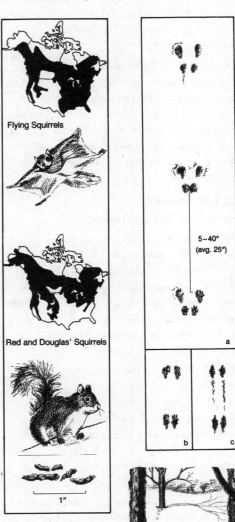

Flying Squirrels

Red and Douglas' Squirrels

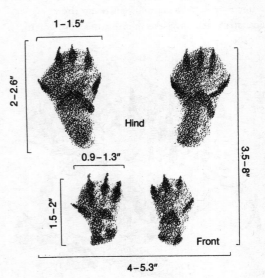

Continued ➡

Habits: Gray squirrels live in deciduous forests, fox squirrels in open forests or forest edges, western gray squirrels in oak and open conifer woodlands, and tassle-eared squirrels in open conifer forests. Gray and fox squirrels also live in cities. In fall, all but tassle-eared squirrels bury food for winter, mainly nuts, usually one item per cache. All are arboreal, diurnal, and somewhat solitary.

Track Pattern: These squirrels are active all winter and make a four-print hopping track pattern in which their front feet land side by side (*a*). The tracks may merge to form a two-print pattern when slowing down (*b*) or in deep snow (*c*). Squirrel trails typically run from one tree to another.

Associated Signs: Aside from spotting a scampering or chattering squirrel, you may find leafy nests on tree branches, although nests are usually in tree hollows, or excavated nut or seed stores. Like porcupines, squirrels gnaw on trees and saplings, but the damage and the tooth marks are usually smaller. Scats are occasionally found on snow.

Small Tree Squirrels
Tamiasciurus and *Glaucomys* species

Description: This arboreal group includes red squirrels (*Tamiasciurus hudsonicus*, colored red-brown); Douglas' squirrels or chickarees (*T. douglasii*, dark-brown); and flying squirrels (*Glaucomys* species, brown or gray and white) with prominent fur-covered membranes along their sides. Total length is 9 to 15 inches; tail is 3 to 7 inches; weight is 2 to 9 ounces.

Habits: Red squirrels live in conifer or mixed forests, Douglas' squirrels in dense conifer forests, and flying squirrels in deciduous and conifer forests. The diurnal and solitary *Tamiasciurus* species store large conifer seed caches on the ground for winter, while the more social, nocturnal flying squirrels may store nuts and seeds in tree holes.

Track Pattern: Squirrels in this group hop making a squarish four-print track pattern with their front feet landing side by side (*a*). Front prints may merge (*b*). In deeper snow, hind and front prints merge into a two-print pattern showing foot drag marks (*c*). Flying squirrels seldom glide to the ground, but when they land, they may make a sitzmark showing their outstretched winglike membranes. Trails run

between trees. All these squirrels den up in stormy weather, but only flying squirrels become torpid for short periods.

Associated Signs: *Tamiasciurus* species scold intruders with loud chattering. They tunnel through snow to nests and food caches near which may be found piles of castoff cone scales and cores (middens) and some scats. They also

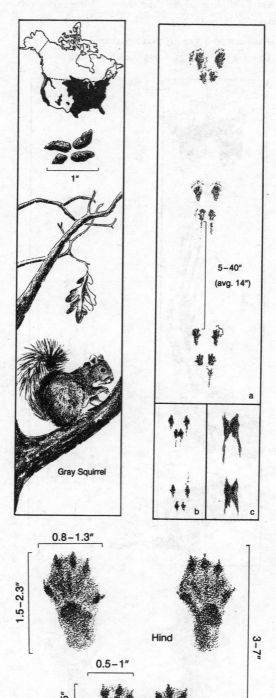

Gray Squirrel

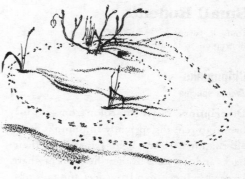

0.8–1.3"

1.5–2.3"

Hind

3–7"

0.5–1"

0.8–1.5"

Front

3.5–4.5"

make leafy tree nests. Flying squirrels leave few signs, maybe a few gnawed nuts below their tree cavity nests.

Mice
Cricetidae and Muridae

Description: Most mice are dark above and light below and generally have long tails (naked for the introduced house mouse, *Mus musculus*), slender bodies, and relatively large hind feet. Total length ranges from 4 to 10 inches with tails from 1 to 6 inches. Weight is 0.2 to 1.4 ounces.

Habits: Most mouse species prefer grasslands, others rocky and brushy areas or wooded and

semiwooded areas. Some are tolerant of human habitation, especially the house mouse. Most are gregarious seed eaters and semiarboreal, except the solitary, carnivorous grasshopper mice (*Onychomys* species). All are largely nocturnal and active year-round.

Track Pattern: Mice make a tiny four-print hopping track pattern (*upper a*). Their front feet usually land side-by-side, but sometimes they land diagonally for a few prints. One exception—James Halfpenny found that ground-dwelling grasshopper mice regularly place their front feet diagonally. In soft snow, the track often merges to a two-print pattern with a tail drag mark (*lower a*),

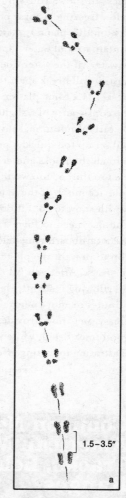

0.5"

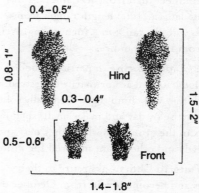

Deer Mouse

1.5–3.5"

a

0.4–0.5"

0.8–1"

Hind

0.3–0.4"

1.5–2"

0.5–0.6"

Front

1.4–1.8"

Continued ➤

resembling a small, linked chain. The relatively short intergroup distances help to avoid confusion with a vole's two-print track.

Associated Signs: You may trail a mouse to its burrow openings (1.5–1.8" wide) in snow or to natural entryways leading under the snowpack. There, they share subnivean runways made by other small rodents. Small, dark scats are rarely seen on the snow, but more often in an invaded cabin.

Rats
Rattus species

Description: Rats arrived in North America with our founding fathers and are commonly associated with humans, particularly the Norway, or brown, rat (*Rattus norvegicus*). This brown to black rat has a long, naked tail and hind feet larger than the front feet. Total length is 12.5 to 18.5 inches with the tail 5 to 8.5 inches. Weight is 7 to 10 ounces.

Habits: Rats are largely restricted to human habitats, especially cities, farms, and dumps, but Norway rats may also live ferally in extensive burrow systems in the ground. Rats are colonial, highly omnivorous, and active year-round, day or night.

Track Pattern: The rat track pattern is similar to that of the woodrat, a four-print hopping track pattern with diagonally placed front feet (*a*), except that you're most likely to find it in a city park, dump or farm grain storage area. Sometimes the track slows to an alternating walking pattern (*b*), or the four-print merges into a two-print pattern (*c*). Tails drag in soft snow.

Associated Signs: Rat trails may lead to small burrows (about 2" wide) under tree roots and rocks, and scats may be found in a variety of places where rats and humans live. Destruction of food and fabric also signals the presence of a rat.

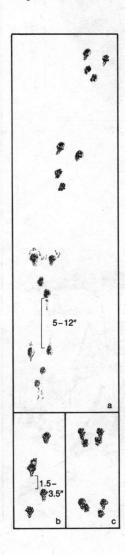

RANGE: Rats share human habitation in the lower U.S., southern Canada, and coastal western Canada and Alaska.

Woodrats
Neotoma species

Description: Woodrats, alias pack rats, have long, fur-covered tails, gray to brown pelage, and hind feet larger than front feet. Total length ranges from 11 to 19 inches with a tail 3 to 9 inches long. They weigh 7 to 20 ounces.

Habits: Solitary and nocturnal, woodrats prefer rugged, rocky terrain in woodlands or shrublands where they make large, bulky nests and feed on nearby vegetation. The name "pack rat" derives from the woodrat habit of trading dull nest materials they happen to be carrying for brighter, more attractive ones (e.g., jewelry, small utensils, garbage).

Track Pattern: Woodrats are active year-round, although they restrict their activity in severe weather. They usually hop in a four-print track pattern with diagonally placed front feet (*lower a*), similar to that of the chipmunk and rat. Their tails drag in soft snow. They may also walk in an alternating pattern (*upper a*) and tunnel under the snow. Woodrat trails are sometimes seen near rural hay stacks and backyards.

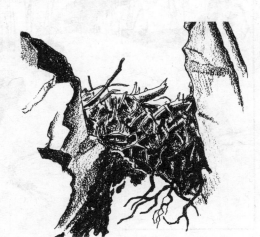

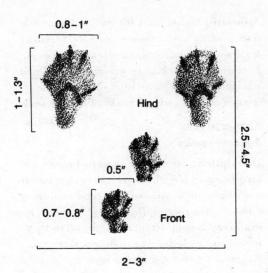

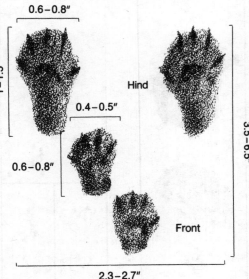

Associated Signs: Woodrats make conspicuous nests—elaborate piles of twigs, foliage, bones, rocks, feathers, dung, or garbage, often added to by subsequent generations. Below those nests located on rock ledges or crevices, you sometimes see a rank, slimy accumulation of urine and feces. Piles of dry scats are also found near nests.

Voles and Lemmings
Subfamily Microtinae

Description: Voles and lemmings are small rodents with chunky bodies, short tails, and hind feet larger than front feet. All are dull-colored, except for collared lemmings (*Dicrostonyx* species), the only rodents which turn white in winter. Total length is 4 to 10 inches with the tail 0.5 to 3.5 inches. Weight is 0.5 to 6 ounces.

Habits: Often colonial, these mostly terrestrial herbivores prefer moist habitats in woodlands,

Continued →

grasslands, brush, and tundra, although some species prefer drier areas. One species is semi-aquatic. They may be active any time during the year, day or night, and they huddle together in nests for warmth when resting.

Track Pattern: Voles (*Phenacomys*, *Microtus*, *Clethrionomys*, and *Lagurus* species) and bog lemmings (*Synaptomys* species) jump making a four-print pattern with diagonally placed front feet (unlike mice) (*b*). This often merges to a two-print pattern for voles (*upper a*). In soft snow, feet drag, but tails drag only rarely (unlike mice). The gait may slow periodically to a walk (may be scurrying trot) in an alternating pattern (*lower a*). Like voles, lemmings (*Lemmus* and *Dicrostonyx* species) walk in snow but may also make a four-print loping track pattern (*c*).

Associated Signs: Look for vole and lemming trails leading under snow to nests and feeding areas amidst subnivean tunnels and runways. Spring snow melt exposes grassy, globular nests, scat piles, and extensive litter-lined runways, vestiges of a busy winter world under the snow.

Kangaroo Rats
Dipodomys species

Description: Tan above and white below with long tails and large hind feet, kangaroo rats are not commonly associated with snow country; however, one species, *Dipodomys ordii*, ranges into southern Canada. Its total length is 8 to 13.5 inches and includes a 4- to 8-inch-long tail. Weight is 1.5 to 2.5 ounces.

Habits: Kangaroo rats live in arid to semiarid regions with sparse shrubs or grasses and soft or sandy soil into which they dig burrows. They eat mainly seeds, which they store in winter, and are nocturnal, terrestrial, and solitary.

Track Pattern: In winter, kangaroo rats travel on snow during warm weather but stay below ground for extended periods in severe weather. Like kangaroos, they hop on their hind feet when traveling long distances or moving quickly (*a*). Otherwise, they make a four-print hopping pattern with diagonally placed front feet (*upper a*). Their two-footed leaping prowess is impressive—several feet at a bound! Their trails run

from burrows to feeding areas and often include tail drag marks.

Associated Signs: Look for the "K" rat's large, mounded burrows (entrances 4 to 5 inches wide) in the sand. Inside these burrows, it nests and stores seeds and root sections. Scats may be found near burrows.

Prairie Dogs
Cynomys species

Description: These medium-sized squirrels are light brown in color and have short legs, hind feet larger than front feet, and short black or white-tipped tails. Total length is 12.5 to 16.5 inches with a tail 1.5 to 4.5 inches. Weight is 1.5 to 3 pounds.

Habits: Colonial plains dwellers and ground burrowers, prairie dogs are diurnal herbivores. Historically, they were widely poisoned because of their suspected competition with western livestock for forage. Open grass and shrublands are where you'll find their colonies or "towns." One species, the Utah prairie dog (*Cynomys parvidens*), is listed as endangered.

Track Pattern: White-tailed prairie dog species hibernate from late summer or fall to February, March, or April, depending on location and age. Conversely, the black-tailed species only reduces its activity in winter. Track patterns vary

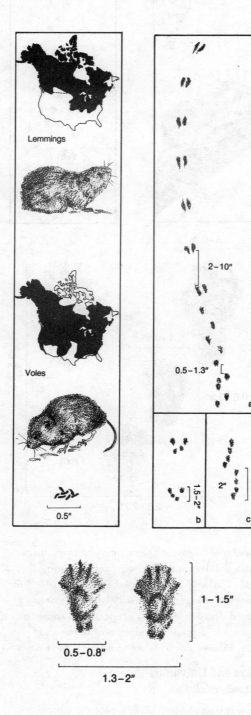

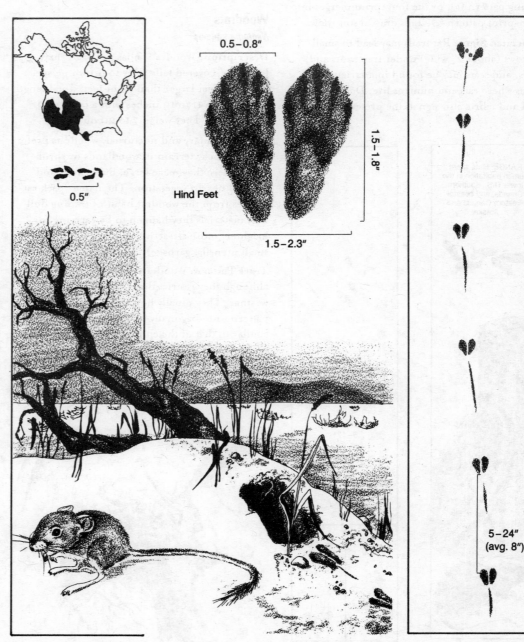

Continued →

includes most of the eastern, southern, and midwestern United States, except Maine and the northern portions of Michigan, Wisconsin, and Minnesota. Opossums are found in parts of California, Oregon, Washington, Arizona, and New Mexico, too.

Porcupines

Porcupines walk pigeon-toed with footprints pointed inward. Both feet have large, oval-shaped pads that are slightly larger on back feet. Front feet have four toes, with an extra one present on each of the hind feet. Imprints of the rough surface of pads are sometimes visible in tracks. Drag marks from feet and tail may be visible in the snow. Tail drags are sometimes visible in sand. In deep, soft snow, porkies leave furrows where they walk.

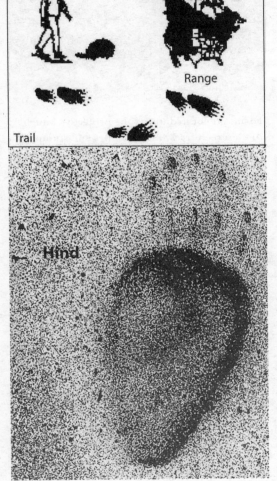

PORCUPINE

Range

Trail

Hind

The appearance of these quill-covered animals should be familiar to most people. They are generally black in color, with white on quills, and can weigh up to 30 pounds or more, but the average is probably somewhere around 15 pounds. Porkies are most often found in wooded areas, but I have seen them above timberline in the Rockies and far out in grassy fields where their armor would protect them from most predators. Fishers are the only animal known to prey on porcupines with consistent success, although bobcats succeed in killing them occasionally.

Porcupines are not the favorite animal of lumbermen due to their habit of gnawing bark from trees to eat, sometimes removing bark completely from around tree trunks, which kills the trees. Trees with large patches of missing bark on limbs and trunk are obvious porky

signs. Hemlock and white cedar are favored winter foods. Snow that is littered with small pieces of hemlock or cedar under one of these trees is an indication of a porcupine dining above. I have seen porkies break off aspen branches in the spring and eat the buds and eat leaves from aspen saplings in the summer. Droppings and urine-stained snow will usually be present at the base of trees occupied by porcupines.

Their scat is in pellet form that resemble those of deer in shape, although porky pellets are longer. They are brown in color, too, as opposed to deer pellets that are more often black, at least when fresh. Den sites used by porcupines in hollow stumps or trees usually have large accumulations of pellets present.

Porcupines range across the entire western United States, the upper Great Lakes and north-east states, all of Canada, and most of Alaska. These animals are sluggish enough that they can be killed with a club, if a person becomes lost and is desperate for food.

—Text from *Animal Tracks and Signs of North America*
Illustrations from *Track Pack: Animal Tracks in Full Life Size*

Rabbits and Hares

Richard P. Smith
Illustrations by DeCourcy L. Taylor, Jr.

The track pattern of rabbits and hares is roughly triangular in shape, consisting of oval to oblong hind feet prints planted side by side, with the smaller, almost circular prints of front feet appearing behind them, usually one in front of the other. Major differences of tracks from one species to another is in size of imprints left by feet, but there are some other variations.

Rabbit or hare tracks most closely resemble those left by squirrels. However, there should not be much difficulty distinguishing between the two, if for no other reason than squirrel tracks go from tree to tree while rabbit tracks seldom lead to trees larger than saplings, unless they have fallen or their base is associated with ground cover where a rabbit might seek shelter. Beyond that, footprints left by squirrels show both front and back feet paired, whereas prints of front feet of rabbits are seldom paired. Where toes of the hind feet are visible in squirrel tracks, five are present. Four toes show in rabbit tracks when visible.

Rabbits

The two primary species of so-called rabbits in North America are cottontails and jackrabbits, with the snowshoe or varying hare the most common representative of that species, although there are Arctic hares in the far northern reaches of Canada and Alaska. Cottontails are actually the only true wild rabbit native to North America. The difference between rabbits and hares is that the young of rabbits are born naked with their eyes closed, whereas hares are furred when born and have their eyes open. The young of "jackrabbits" fall into the latter category.

COTTONTAILS

Measurements of the length of the track pattern (from the base to the tip of the imaginary triangle) of cottontails vary from 7 to 12 inches in length. Tracks of hind feet themselves average

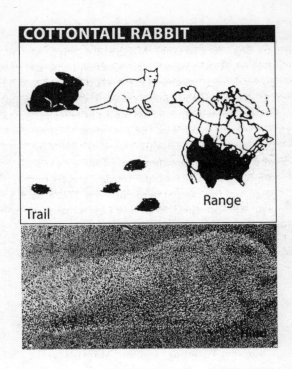

COTTONTAIL RABBIT

Trail

Range

about 3 inches in length, twice as long as front footprints. There are at least eight relatives of the cottontail, some of which are subspecies; including eastern, mountain, New England, brush, desert, swamp, marsh and pygmy rabbits. They vary in weight from less than a pound to at least 3 pounds, obviously resulting in variations in track size.

Distance between normal cottontail hops is 10 to 14 inches. When hopping, hind feet are fairly uniform in width from front to back. However, the four toes on hind feet will usually be spread when running, increasing track width at the front. Rabbit tracks are not observed regularly until snow covers the ground, except in sandy or muddy areas the animals might hop across.

These rabbits have relatively short ears and are basically brown in color, except for their cottonball-like tails that are prominent as they run, although the tail is not white on several close relatives such as pygmy, marsh, swamp, and brush rabbits. Sign other than tracks to look for are droppings, feeding activity, and forms. Rabbit scats are circular, pill-shaped, and pill-sized pellets that are brown in color. It is difficult to mistake them for anything else.

When feeding, rabbits clip twigs neatly, leaving a clean-cut diagonal edge. They choose twigs close to the ground. Deer also feed on tips of brush, but they *break them off* rather than bite through the stem because deer do not have teeth on top in front, only on the bottom. Consequently, twigs deer feed on have rough, uneven edges. Cottontails also gnaw the bark from saplings and fallen trees, leaving the light-colored inner wood visible where they have fed. The snow or ground where they feed is normally covered with droppings. When snow is present, it is packed down where rabbits have stopped and eaten.

Cottontails typically seek shelter under brushpiles or in patches of brushy cover. This is where forms will be found, which are nothing more than nests or beds where rabbits rest and hide for the day, and are marked by shallow depressions. Rabbits have a tendency to circle back toward their forms when jumped from them and tracked or trailed by hounds. Cottontails are also at home in woodpiles, lumber piles, in

Continued ➡

burrows, and under buildings. That is why they are often seen in cities. Marsh and swamp rabbits, as their name implies, search out wetter, lower-lying habitat than their relatives.

Combined ranges of the eastern and mountain cottontails encompass most of the lower forty-eight states, with the exceptions of Maine, Vermont, New Hampshire, most of California, and the westernmost portions of Oregon and Washington. The mountain variety resides in the west, and the eastern in the midwest, south, and east with some overlap along a jagged line from northeast New Mexico to northwest North Dakota. The New England variety is established in Vermont, New Hampshire, Massachusetts, New Jersey, Rhode Island, Connecticut, eastern New York, most of Pennsylvania, and parts of the Virginias and Carolinas.

Desert cottontails are at home in the southwest, but are found northward through Colorado, Wyoming, and into Montana, and south into Mexico. The belt-shaped range of brush rabbits extends south along the coast from Oregon into Mexico. Pygmy rabbits dwell in northern Nevada, southwestern Idaho, eastern Oregon, and into small parts of Washington and California. Southeastern states of Arkansas, Mississippi, Alabama, Louisiana, and eastern Texas are the home of the swamp rabbit. Marsh rabbits have established themselves throughout Florida, and north along the coast into parts of Georgia and the Carolinas.

Jackrabbits

The two most common jackrabbits are white and black-tailed, with the blacktail being the smaller of the two. Hind foot tracks of blacktails measure about $2^1/2$ inches in length when hopping, as opposed to $3^1/2$ inches for whitetails. Only prints from the front portion of hind feet register while hopping, unlike cottontails and snowshoes. When the animals stop, heels are lowered and also leave imprints. So tracks made by hind feet of resting whitetail jacks will be longer, about 6 to 7 inches, than when hopping. Similar tracks of the blacktail will be slightly shorter.

Track patterns of blacktails are 9 to 12 inches deep, and hops of 10 inches are average. Whitetails have track patterns that measure about 17 inches, with distance between tracks ranging from 1 to 2 feet.

As their names suggest, these jackrabbits can be distinguished by the color of their tails. Blacktails also have longer ears than their cousins and do not change color in the winter. In the northern part of their range, whitetails turn white in the winter and their ears become black. Their legs are too long, their size too big, and their habitat too open to be mistaken for snowshoe hares.

Whitetails weigh from 6 to 8 pounds or more, and blacktails may weigh as much as 7 pounds, but are generally around 5 or 6 pounds, sometimes less. It would take an exceptionally large varying hare to weigh 6 pounds.

The larger variety of jackrabbit is found over a much greater area than the blacktail, residing in all of the western states and some in the midwest—the Dakotas, plus parts of Minnesota, Iowa, and Wisconsin. They do best on open plains. Blacktails occupy more arid regions and are commonly found in sagebrush. They are distributed throughout Kansas, plus portions of Oklahoma, Colorado, Utah, Idaho, Nevada, Oregon, and Washington.

Jackrabbit droppings are similar to those from cottontails, only a little larger. Feeding sign is similar when they eat brush, although jacks feed on cactus plants in desert areas, too. Jackrabbit forms can be found under bushes, next to rocks, or in the open.

Whitetail jacks use the same form day after day during the winter and are continually forced to dig out after a snowfall. Snow tunnels develop as a result that are sometimes marked by dirt at the entrance. Jackrabbit forms can sometimes be spotted from a distance by looking for patches of dirty snow.

Hares

Snowshoe hare tracks are the most familiar to me among members of the rabbit family. Their big hind feet leave prints that average 6 inches in length. In deep snow the animals spread their toes to better support their weight, leaving tracks that are wide at the front and taper down toward the heel. The snowshoe's track pattern is 10 to 11 inches in length, and normal hops cover 10 to 14 inches.

These hares most often weigh between 3 and 4 pounds. They are brown during the summer and gradually turn white, except for black-tipped ears, from fall to winter. However, there is a hare in Washington state, related to the snowshoe, that remains brown year round. Ear length on snowshoes is intermediate between that of cottontails and jackrabbits. They inhabit lowland swamps and evergreen thickets during the winter, but can be found in upland habitat at other times of the year.

Their range includes northernmost states in the lower forty-eight, but extends south in the west in correspondence with mountain ranges and evergreen forests, and as far south as Tennessee in the east. Most of Canada and Alaska and their abundant northern forest are also home to these hares.

Scats and feeding sign of the snowshoe are very much like those of cottontails, eating bark of saplings and fallen trees, especially aspen, and twigs. However, droppings are slightly larger.

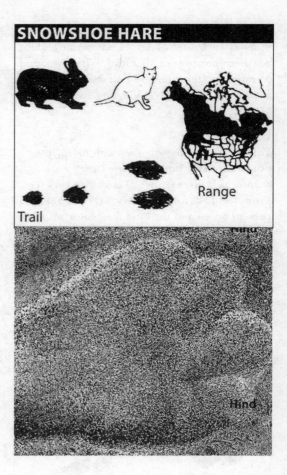

SNOWSHOE HARE

Trail

Range

Hind

Forms are located under the protective boughs of evergreen trees, in brushpiles and stumps and other dense cover The animals will burrow into the snow for protection from the elements during inclement weather, although they spend far less time in such hideouts than cottontails. Where both cottontails and snowshoes occur together, the size of their tracks usually differentiates between the two.

Varying hares pack down trails over routes they travel regularly. Outdoor people who find themselves in a rough survival situation in northern forests where snowshoes occur can catch hares by setting a snare with a shoelace, fishing line, or piece of wire on such a trail. Urine from snowshoes often stains the snow orange and is sometimes mistaken for blood.

These hares are as apt to circle when trailed as cottontails, perhaps even more so. I have spent many days tracking them and it is not unusual to have them follow the same circle time and time again. Hunters or photographers who are familiar with this tactic can often get a look at the animals by cutting across the circle or starting after a hare, then quickly backtracking to the starting point to wait for the rabbit's return.

Hare populations, including jackrabbits, are subject to extreme highs and lows that sometimes occur on regular cycles of so many years. The reasons for these population cycles are not fully understood. The animals become so abundant at times they all but eliminate their food supply, then disease and parasites take over and dramatically reduce populations. Such dramatic highs and lows are less common where the animals are routinely hunted, which is not only better for the hares themselves, but their habitat as well.

—Text from *Animal Tracks and Signs of North America*
Illustrations from *Track Pack: Animal Tracks in Full Life Size*

JACKRABBIT

Trail

Range

Hind

Weasel Family

Richard P. Smith
Illustrations by DeCourcy L. Taylor, Jr.

Most members of the weasel family have a distinctive track pattern in the snow, which is the medium their prints are most often visible in. More often than not, their tracks consist of two depressions side by side. Weasels themselves, plus many of their relatives, are bounders and when more than a skiff of snow is present on the ground, their front and back feet leave impressions one on top of the other, or practically so.

Prints of all four feet will sometimes be visible in wet snow, and the pattern will resemble those of tree squirrels. However, the feet of members of the weasel family are not as consistently paired as those of squirrels, and there are five toes on each of the weasel's feet, although all of the toes are seldom visible in the prints of weasels themselves, as opposed to four visible toes in front footprints of squirrels. Some members of the weasel family climb trees like squirrels, so that trait alone is not always reliable in differentiating between tracks of the two families.

Members of the weasel family regularly travel underneath the snow's surface, as well as on top, when it is deep and fluffy. Tracks on the snow may suddenly disappear and reappear some distance away. This past winter I noticed some weasel tracks that could be puzzling to individuals not familiar with this habit. The animal would come up from under the snow and make one bound, then disappear under the snow again for a matter of feet, reappear and make another bound, then dive into the snow again.

The two prints left on the snow's surface were connected by drag marks from the animal's feet. It appeared as though the animal was finding travel easier under the snow than on top because of the lack of support on the snow's surface.

In mud or a skiff of snow, the track pattern spreads out into a diagonal string of four individual footprints. The above information applies to long and shorttail weasels, mink, pine martens, and fishers. Other members of the tribe, including skunks, badgers, and wolverines, are walkers, too, and leave correspondingly different track patterns. Skunks and badgers are not suited for tree climbing either. Since tracks differ among wolverines, skunks, and badgers, their characteristics will be discussed individually further on in this chapter. Otters are also members of the weasel family, but are discussed in the chapter on aquatic mammals.

Longtail and Shorttail Weasels

Tracks of the feet of longtail and shorttail weasels are less than an inch in length, as a rule. The animals have long, slender bodies that are brown with white extending from the chin all the way along the underside during spring and summer months. Weasels turn all white with the exception of a black-tipped tail during late fall and remain that color during the winter, except in locations where snow is uncommon. Weasels stay brown all year in snowless regions. White weasels are sometimes referred to as ermine, especially the shorttail.

Weasels are both curious and bold, at least longtails are, which is the variety I have had the

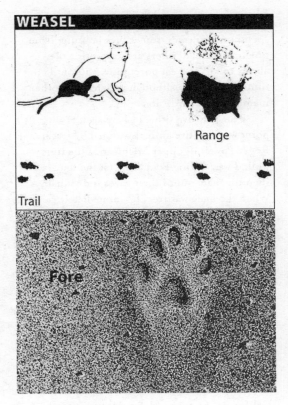

WEASEL

Range

Trail

Fore

most experience with. They feed on small mammals such as mice primarily, but occasionally kill a rabbit or hare. When observing weasels I sometimes make a squeak with my mouth like a mouse would and have had them come right up to me to investigate. If meat is placed before them or a hole they have recently entered, the animals often reappear to eat it or drag it off with a person standing only a matter of feet away.

On one occasion during the winter, I saw a longtail dash across a road nearby, and I quickly went after it hoping to photograph the animal. Since the animal was out of sight in seconds, I followed its tracks in the snow and was surprised to find them end abruptly at the base of a tree. At the time, I was not aware that weasels climb trees, so I was surprised to see the animal perched on a limb in the jack pine tree above me.

Weasels occupy a wide variety of habitat and can be seen almost anywhere in woodlands, brush, wetlands, rocks, and fields. I have seen them above timberline in the Rockies and in an open field in Montana where the animal had a den under a boulder, as well as in swamps and forests. The longtail ranges over most of the lower forty-eight states and well into Canada. About the only state in the lower United States where the weasel is absent is Oklahoma. They are also not normally found in northern Texas, most of Arizona and Utah, and parts of southern Nevada and California. Shorttails are distributed over most of Canada and all of Alaska, the Great Lakes states, the northeastern United States, and roughly the northern two-thirds of the western United States.

Mink

Mink are nothing more than a large weasel, weighing between 1 and 3 pounds. Large weasels may weigh half a pound, but are generally lighter. Mink and their tracks are closely associated with water—streams, rivers, lakes, and ponds—where their footprints can be seen in mud along banks or shoreline. Mink tracks usually measure just over an inch from their five toenails to heel.

These animals are brown in color year-round, not turning white like the weasel in the northern part of its range. They do have a spot of white on their chins, but this coloration does not extend down the chest and along the underside like weasels.

Mink are at home in the water and are excellent swimmers. Their prey consist of fish, muskrats, frogs, and other aquatic creatures, plus small land mammals, birds, and insects. Scats are not an important sign. The animals are distributed across North America, with the exception of northernmost Canada and Alaska, plus a band of states in the southwestern United States where water is scarce.

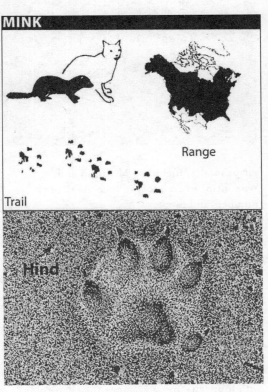

MINK

Trail

Range

Hind

Pine Martens

Pine martens are similar in size to mink, but average a little larger, between 2 and 4 pounds. The hind feet of martens are about 1 1/2 inches in length, but may leave prints 2 inches or more in the snow. Only four of five toes on feet usually register in tracks when they are visible at all. Marten tracks may be found near water like those of mink, but the animals do not usually spend as much time directly associated with water and do not often actually go in.

The body of these animals is brown in color, usually lighter than mink, with an even lighter colored face that appears tan. Martens have a throat patch that varies in color, but in many cases is yellow to orange. Trees play a major role in the pine marten's life, generally more so than other members of the weasel family discussed thus far. They prey on squirrels and birds in trees, as well as occupying cavities in them. Small mammals, including hares, make up the bulk of the marten's diet.

I saw a marten in a tree in Ontario last fall that I detected when hearing a low growl-like noise it made. The animal jumped from tree to tree via limbs in much the same manner squirrels do. Most of Canada and Alaska is home to the pine marten. They also reside in the Great Lakes region, the northeast, and mountainous regions of the west in the lower United States. Martens have been transplanted from Canada to

Continued ➡

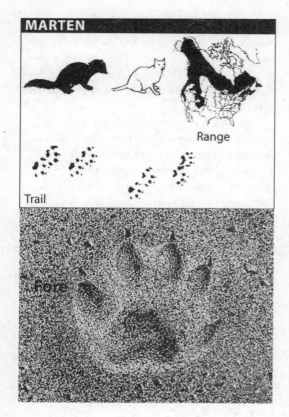

Range

Trail

Fore

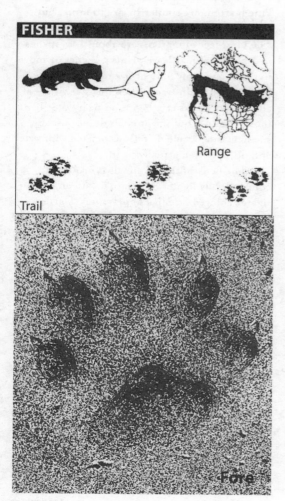

Trail

Fore

FISHER

Range

Trail

Fore

body. And also like their close relative, fishers spend time in trees, sometimes jumping from one to another. Fishers are known for their ability to kill and eat porcupines without being injured by quills, although they feed on other mammals and birds, too.

The only live fishers I have seen at this point were captive animals studied by researcher Roger Powell in upper Michigan. One time while I was visiting Powell, he let the female, then the male out of their cages individually. When the male was free, he immediately came up to me, climbed my pantlegs and clamped my right wrist between its jaws in an apparent show of dominance. The animal did not bite down, so no damage was done. Rather than aggravate the situation, I remained motionless while Roger pried the fisher's jaws open.

Fishers are presently on the increase in my home region of Michigan's Upper Peninsula and neighboring northern Wisconsin where I hope to see a fisher in the wild someday. The animals are also found in northern Minnesota, from northern New York to Maine, and parts of California, Oregon, Idaho, Montana, and Wyoming in the United States. Their primary range is from east to west across much of Canada in the northern forests they prefer.

Wolverines

Wolverine tracks measure 3 1/2 to 5 inches in length, and can be confused with those of wolves. However, five distinct toes should show in wolverine tracks, whereas wolf prints have four, and foot pads are shaped differently between the two as well. Front feet of wolverines have small, oval-shaped heel pads separated from the main pad that may show in prints. Wolves have one main foot pad in addition to four toe pads. Wolverines both walk and bound and leave corresponding track patterns.

The animals are brown in color, with contrasting stripes of light brown, yellow, or orange on sides of the body that join at the tail, and another band across the top of the head. Their tails are bushy and short in relation to the length of the body, although much longer than the tails of bears, which they resemble somewhat, depending on the angle and distance from which they are viewed. Wolverines weigh from 15 to 25 pounds, with both lighter and heavier weights on record.

Wolverines occupy open terrain such as the tundra and mountain regions above timberline, although they do enter forests, too. Their primary range is northern Canada and Alaska, but they are found throughout British Columbia and range south from there into portions of the western United States. States where their presence has been recorded are Montana, Idaho, Washington, Wyoming, Colorado, Utah, California, and Oregon.

Badgers

Badgers are diggers like some members of the squirrel family, leaving tracks of front feet with noticeable claw marks. They walk somewhat pigeon-toed like the porcupine, but have five toes per foot, and shorter claws of hind feet do not normally show in prints. Porkies have four toes on front feet and claws register in prints of both front and back feet. Badger tracks are 3 to

various states, including Michigan and Wisconsin, in an effort to increase their numbers and range.

Fishers

Fishers leave prints which show all five toes. Tracks of hind feet measure from 2 inches to more than twice that in the snow. Presence of five toes and toenails are usually enough to distinguish their tracks from those of bobcats and fox or coyote. Fishers sometimes walk in addition to bounding like other weasels.

The animals weigh from 4 1/2 to 10 pounds, on the average. They are dark brown in color with long tails, but may appear black in color. Like the marten, the face is lighter than the

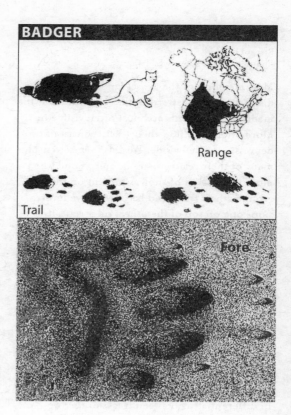

Range

Trail

Fore

3 1/2 inches in length and lead to a burrow or will be found in sand where the animals are hunting.

Fairly large pieces of ground are dug up by badgers when trying to catch ground squirrels and other small mammals they feed on. Badgers walk low to the ground on short legs and are gray in appearance with white and brown visible in some places. Their tails are short and stubby. Faces have distinct black and white markings that are broken. These animals weigh between 12 and 20 pounds, with some individuals weighing more. Due to their short legs, badgers make furrows when walking in the snow.

I have heard reports of badgers claiming deer shot by hunters that fell near their dens. In at least one case, an animal had a deer almost completely underground before the hunter that shot the deer came along and found it.

Badgers inhabit fields, pastures, farmland, grasslands, and open terrain above timberline. They are found in all of the western and midwestern states and range northward into the plains and farmbelt of Canada.

Skunks

There are two major species of skunks in North America—the striped and spotted. Their tracks are similar. Markings of the striped skunk are similar to those of the wolverine, except their bodies are black and the stripes along sides and markings on the head are white. Bushy, long-haired tails are similar in appearance between wolverines and skunks, too.

Skunks are walkers primarily, but when striped skunks run, they leave a track pattern characteristic of members of the weasel family—prints arranged in a diagonal line, one in front of the other. Running tracks of spotted skunks more often resemble those of a squirrel. When walking, feet are usually placed one ahead and slightly to the side of the other and leave impressions roughly oval in shape. Short strides are characteristic of this animal. Five toes are present on each foot and claw marks are usually present in tracks, especially the longer ones of front feet. Tracks measure from 1 1/4 inches to almost 2 inches.

Continued ➡

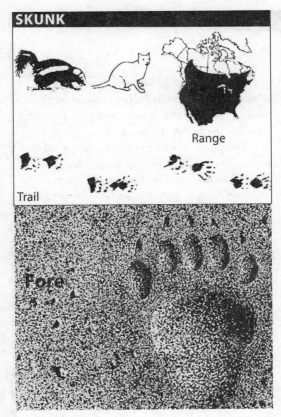

SKUNK

Range

Trail

Fore

The skunk is well known for its defense mechanism, which is the ability to spray offensive-smelling liquid from its anal scent glands. Musk glands that produce strong, usually objectionable odors are what link members of the weasel family together. Few representatives of the weasel tribe are recognized for this other than the skunk, with the possible exception of the wolverine, which leaves scent in cabins and along traplines that they invade.

Color variations are common among striped skunks, with some individuals mostly to all black and others mostly white. Spotted skunks actually wear a number of broken white stripes, giving them a spotted appearance. Spotted skunks are smaller than the striped variety averaging between 1 and 3 pounds. Striped skunks weigh from 5 to 10 pounds.

Striped skunks are distributed in each of the lower forty-eight states and well north in Canadian provinces, which is an indication they are found in a wide variety of habitats. Spotted skunks do not have a range quite as large, being absent from much of the midwest and northeast, including an area along the east coast south to Florida. They are also largely absent from Montana, North Dakota, and most of Canada.

Many skunks live in or near cities and towns, venturing forth at night to search for insects and food scraps discarded by people. Their tracks are commonly seen at or near garbage dumps. Dead skunks are a common sight along highways where they are killed by cars. One of the major predators of skunks are great horned owls, but other birds of prey and predatory mammals such as badgers also kill and eat them.

In connection with their search for larval insects or grubs, skunks dig shallow, cone-shaped holes in lawns, fields, and openings. Skunks also eat bird and turtle eggs and scavenge on road- or winter-killed animals. Broken egg-shells littering a sandy area near a lake is a sure sign a skunk raided a nest of turtle eggs there.

—Text from *Animal Tracks and Signs of North America*
Illustrations from *Track Pack: Animal Tracks in Full Life Size*

Aquatic Mammals

Richard P. Smith
Illustrations by DeCourcy L. Taylor, Jr.

There is no uniform track pattern among aquatic mammals such as beavers, otters, muskrats, and nutria. Furthermore, tracks may be the least obvious sign left by members of this group. The beaver is a perfect example.

Beavers

Last fall I was in several areas where beavers were abundant and looked carefully for their tracks, but found none. However, I did see several types of more obvious sign, one of which was tree-cutting activity. The animals were working on aspen or poplar trees situated near water in one particular area. Several trees had been felled, and the trunks of others were partially gnawed through.

Beavers fell trees by biting chunks of wood evenly all the way around the trunk, although some animals work only from one side. Chips of wood that are bitten out are dropped at the base of the trees. Partially gnawed trunks will often have an even band of wood removed all the way around. The animals continue away until the gnawed trunk becomes too weak to support the tree and it topples over.

Once a tree is down, beavers often cut it into lengths, at least the limbs, that they can carry or drag into the water to feed on later. They eat the bark. In the fall, beavers in northern parts of the country store as much food as possible in a central location called "feed beds" for their use during the winter when ice covers their pond. Tips of freshly cut tree branches can sometimes be seen protruding above the water in beaver ponds, marking the location of feed beds. The animals may eat the bark from tree trunks themselves where they fall.

Wide paths marked by flattened vegetation and furrowed banks usually develop along routes beavers follow from the water to their cutting operation. These paths are sometimes referred to as beaver slides, and the animals may indeed slide into the water on them where they lead down steep banks. The print of a big webbed hind foot may appear in the mud or snow near slides, but not often. The reason beaver tracks are not frequently seen is that their big, flat tail dragging behind them erases the prints as they walk.

Sometimes beavers start to work on a tree and never finish, evident by dark, dried-out wood where the tree was gnawed. I have seen a number of trees in this condition and can only guess why the job was never finished. Perhaps the animal was killed by a predator or trapped before the cutting could be completed. Or maybe the animal found a tree of a more desirable species to work on. There is also the possibility that beavers are absent-minded and may occasionally forget where they were working. ...

Light-colored chunks of wood varying in size on which the bark has been completely gnawed off are common along the banks of rivers and lakes frequented by beavers. These chewed pieces of wood are also used in the construction of dams, another prominent beaver sign. Dams are nothing more than walls of sticks and mud that slow the flow of water on streams and rivers, forming beaver ponds. These dams sometimes flood roads, causing damage in some cases. Dams on streams with fast water and heavy spring runoff are sometimes washed out, leaving remnants of the structure along banks. Old beaver ponds may eventually fill in and form meadows over a period of many years.

Beaver houses or lodges are large, dome-shaped structures that the animals live in. The outside is often covered with barkless pieces of wood and mud, like dams. These houses have an underwater entrance that leads into a chamber situated above the water's surface. Some beavers also live in holes or burrows along the banks of rivers.

Another sign beavers leave is scent posts that can usually be detected by smell as well as sight. The animals place a pile of mud and grass or other debris that can be as much as a foot in height, on the bank on which they secrete a sweet-smelling liquid from their castor glands located near the base of tails. The smell of this oil is so pleasing to humans (as it probably is to beavers) it is used in perfume.

I spotted a beaver on the bank of a stream from a Michigan highway on one occasion, and I stopped to try to photograph the animal. As I neared the location, the strong smell of castor was obvious. My nose led me to the scent post the animal was in the process of making when I saw it.

Beaver scats are deposited underwater. The animals are generally brown in color, but may be blonde or black. Their scaly, paddlelike tail is their most distinctive feature, which they use to slap the water when alarmed. The animals weigh between 20 and 50 or 60 pounds, on the average, but weights over 100 pounds have been recorded. These important furbearers are found

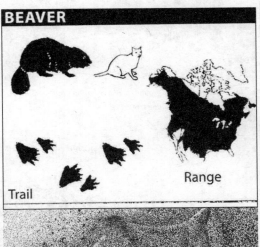

BEAVER

Range

Trail

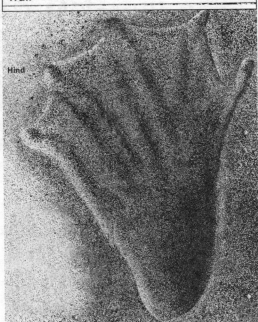

Hind

Continued ➡

BEAVER DAMS AND LODGES

Elizabeth P. Lawlor   Illustrations by Pat Archer

Beavers are best known for their ability to create ponds, which are their major defense against predators. To make one, beavers must first build a dam across a stream or rivulet. This floods the area upstream of the dam. Choosing a suitable site for the dam is critical. Beavers sometimes pick the wrong location, and the water washes around the dam or flows off in a new direction instead of forming a shallow pond. Other times, the pond may block a road, causing problems for the beaver's human neighbors.

After the dam site is chosen, the job of felling trees begins. The beaver selects a tree, then perches on its hind feet and, grasping the trunk with its front paws, bites into the tree with two long, orange, chisel-shaped upper teeth. The beaver then uses its lower front teeth to gnaw away the wood. The two upper teeth remain jammed into the wood until it has been removed by the lower teeth.

Tail braced against the ground, a beaver has no problem quickly cutting down even a young tree.

The next bite puts the upper teeth deeper into the wood. The beaver thus digs a V-shaped notch deeper and deeper into the tree, until it completely encircles the tree and the tree begins to sway. Although beavers are masters at cutting trees, they cannot judge the direction the tree will take as it falls. Amazingly, most beavers can waddle away fast enough to get out of the way, but there are sometimes accidents.

Aside from their use as building material, another reason for cutting down trees is for food. The tender, growing wood tissue just beneath the bark is an important food supply for the beaver. Beavers are primarily bark eaters, eating the bark from tender twigs and the new growth (cambium layer) that lies between the old outer bark and the wood. In the summer, beavers forage for plants along the pond's muddy bottom, where they are safe from land-based predators. Nonwoody foods there include roots and rhizomes of aquatic plants, such as lily, watercress, but reed, and arrowhead. Beavers' front paws are excellent tools for digging up these delicacies. A beaver eats about one and one-half to two pounds of food a day.

The trees cut down are usually about three to five inches in diameter, and the beaver can fell them in a matter of minutes. A record for beavers was established in British Columbia, where they cut down a 110-foot-tall cottonwood with a diameter of about seven inches.

Once they've constructed a dam, the next project for the beavers is to build a lodge. The beavers usually build their lodge in the pond that develops on the downstream side of the dam. The pond surrounding the lodge acts as a moat that effectively keeps away most predators most of the time, although an occasional mink has been known to cross the pond and slip undetected into the lodge to capture a young beaver for dinner. They may also build their lodge in a mudbank or in an existing shallow

pond, lake, or marsh, but wherever the lodge is built, the water must be four feet or more deep so the beavers can come and go without exposing themselves to danger.

The pond also helps beavers survive the winter. Even though beavers store a supply of tender branches and saplings in the lodge, they may need to gather more food before the end of the cold season. If the pond is partially frozen, they can swim under the ice, where they can breathe oxygen from air trapped in a layer between the ice and the water. If water freezes to the bottom of the pond, however, the beavers would be trapped in the lodge. Beavers can protect themselves from this when they construct the dam. The higher the dam, the deeper the pond, and the less likely the water will be to freeze throughout its depth.

The lodge is constructed from small logs, branches, and twigs, with mud holding it all together. Sometimes the beavers also include wet vegetation. Lodges vary in size, but they generally don't exceed seven feet in height and forty feet in diameter.

A beaver colony is a family group consisting of a pair of beavers mated for life, plus yearlings and newborn kits. Thus the beaver work crew during the construction of a new dam and lodge can be a considerable size. The usual size of the litters is two to four, although they may range in size from one to nine. Males may leave the lodge following the birth of a new litter, but they return later in the year. Kits mature in one and one-half to two years, at which time they are encouraged to leave the lodge.

Beavers' expertise at building extends far beyond the construction of a dam and a lodge. When the supply of timber for the dam along the banks of the stream is exhausted, they need to find suitable supplies elsewhere. This often requires the beavers to dig canals deep into the woods. In these water-filled trenches, beavers float the timber downstream to the construction site. During this period, beavers can be exposed to dangers, so to avoid becoming the next meal of a hungry predator, they dig a temporary living space in the mud along the banks. In certain areas within their range, beavers may live permanently in such bankside lodges.

—From *Discover Nature in Water and Wetlands*

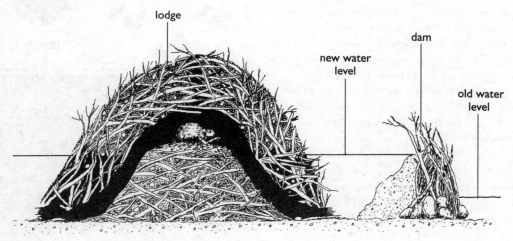

Cross section of a beaver dam and lodge

Continued ➔

throughout North America with the exception of most of Florida and areas along the east coast, parts of California, Arizona, Nevada, and north-central Texas.

Muskrats

Muskrat tracks are seen more often than those of beaver in mud near water. Their long hind feet are not noticeably webbed, and may measure about 3 inches long. Five toes are present. The smaller front feet show four distinct toes. A much smaller thumb on the inside usually is not visible in tracks. One of the most distinct features about the muskrat track is a wavy line between prints, which is a drag mark left by the tail.

Their tail is naked like other rats, but is not round. It has flat sides from top to bottom which propel the animals while swimming. Muskrats sometimes leave water to head cross-country during the fall and winter, and their tracks or the animals themselves, may show up some distance from water as a result.

Muskrat houses are generally obvious in marshes occupied by these animals. They are dome-shaped like those built by beavers, but are much smaller, usually less than four feet in height, and are constructed with aquatic vegetation. Houses or huts used by muskrats may be numerous and situated close to one another where the animals are abundant. These furbearers burrow into banks, too, like beavers. Holes leading into burrows are normally underwater and not visible unless water levels drop.

Muskrats feed mostly on vegetation, although, I once saw one eating a fish, and they also eat mussels. The animals dig in mud along banks for roots and bulbs, leaving signs of their activity. Stalks of bank-growing vegetation are also cut by muskrats. Mats of cut vegetation mark feeding beds in favored dining areas.

Scats are common in clusters on logs and rocks in the water, and other frequently used resting places. The droppings are elongated pellets and measure about a half-inch in length.

These animals are brown in color and much smaller than beavers, averaging between 2 and 4 pounds, a little less in some locations. Florida water rats are closely related to muskrats. They are smaller in size and have round, instead of flat, tails. They leave sign identical to muskrats, and are only found in the Okefenokee Swamp, shared by Georgia and Florida, where muskrats do not occur. The range of muskrats is similar to that of beavers, although they are not found as far north in Canada and Alaska, and they are largely absent from Texas.

Nutria

Nutria exhibit characteristics similar to both beavers and muskrats and, in fact, could pass as a hybrid between the two. Bodily, they look like beaver, but their tail is ratlike and round. The nutria's large hind feet are webbed, but webbing only includes four toes. The fifth toe on the outside of the foot is independent of the others. That characteristic along should help differentiate between beaver and nutria tracks. Prints left by nutria are more commonly seen than those of beaver because they do not possess a large flat tail to erase them.

These furbearers construct feed beds similar to muskrats, only larger. Nutria normally weigh less than 20 pounds, but more than 15. They burrow into banks along bodies of water they occupy. Native to South America, nutria were introduced in the United States and are found in Louisiana, east Texas, Arkansas, southern Mississippi, and into Florida. Populations have also been established in scattered locations in states such as North Carolina, Virginia, Kentucky, Ohio, Idaho, Washington, and Oregon.

Otters

River otters are actually members of the weasel family, but since they spend much of their time in and around water, they deserve mention in this chapter. All four feet are webbed, although the front feet are more lightly webbed than the rear, with five toes on each foot. Webbing is not always visible in their tracks, especially front footprints.

I recently saw the tracks of a pair of otters in the snow that were traveling together cross-country. Both animals left continuous furrows in the snow with paired tracks at regular intervals. The webbing on hind feet was visible in many prints, but not in impressions left by front feet. I have seen similar tracks made by otters, usually single animals, during other winters as well. Webbing may not be visible in any tracks when otters tread on sand and ice.

Long, narrow bodies coupled with short legs are why otters generally plow their way through the snow. Hind legs are longer than front ones. Even in shallow snow, the animals seem to slide along as much as they bound. Look for otter tracks in mud along rivers, streams, lakes, and ponds during snowless seasons. Webs usually show in tracks made in mud. Hind feet average less than 3 inches in length with front feet smaller.

It is not unusual to see the tracks of two or three otters traveling together. The times I have seen otters in the fall they appeared to be in family groups. I also observed and photographed a pair

together in the spring that were sunning themselves on the ice of a pool at the Seney National Wildlife Refuge in upper Michigan. When they got hungry, they entered the water through a hole in the ice and were only gone short periods of time before reappearing with fish. The animals appear to be excellent fishermen.

Otter scats are watery, not holding together well and the mass measures 3 to 5 inches across. Fish scales and bones, plus remains of crayfish may appear in their scats. Droppings I have noticed are black in color and may be found on logs, rocks, beaver dams, or in the snow when they travel overland.

These animals are generally brown in color, but may look black. They have long, fully-haired tails that are thick at the base and taper to a point at the end. Their primary range includes much of Canada and Alaska, plus northern states in the west, Great Lakes region, and northeast. Otters are also found in a block of states in the southeastern United States.

—Text from *Animal Tracks and Signs of North America*
Illustrations from *Track Pack: Animal Tracks in Full Life Size*

Felines

Richard P. Smith
Illustrations by DeCourcy L. Taylor, Jr.

Cat tracks, whether made by the domestic variety or one of the three species of wild cats in North America—bobcat, lynx, and mountain lion—are basically circular in shape, exhibit four toes and do not, as a rule, leave marks from toenails in their prints. This is because cats walk with their

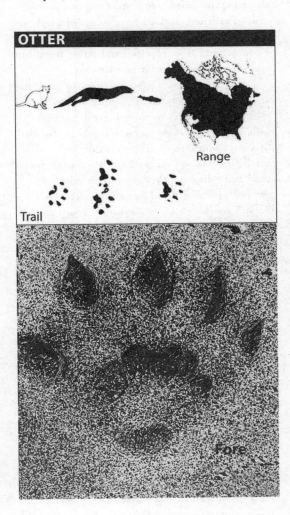

OTTER
Range
Trail
Fore

Continued ➡

claws sheathed, having the ability to extend them when needed for climbing or catching prey.

Clearly defined prints left by a member of the cat family are not likely to be mistaken for those of other species of wildlife. However, confusion may arise in situations where powdery snow or soft sand fails to register a distinct imprint of feet. Under these circumstances, it can be difficult at times to distinguish between bobcat and coyote or fox tracks. Spoor left by these animals are similar in size.

In situations where there is a question about whether a canine or feline made a track, look closely at the front edge of prints for any sign of marks left by toenails. The nails in the middle of the foot are often most pronounced in coyote and fox tracks. If deep snow is involved, toenails may leave narrow grooves in front of toes as they sink in the snow. Evidence of toenails is enough proof that a fox, coyote, or other animal of similar size with nonretractable nails planted a foot on the spot, not a cat.

Follow the tracks for a short distance frontwards, backwards, or both to look for a more distinct print if the ones encountered initially are impossible to distinguish. Under sandy conditions the animal may step in a spot where the soil is more compact and conducive to recording an accurate imprint of the bottom of the animal's foot. In the snow, check tracks where the animal walked under an evergreen tree or heavy brush where snow will be shallower than in the open.

There are other clues to look for, too, if a clear view of the tracks themselves is impossible. Bobcats, for example, regularly walk up on and along logs or fallen tree trunks and even on the rails of railroad tracks. I once followed a bobcat that walked on a rail for at least a quarter mile. Coyotes and foxes cross logs and fallen trees, but seldom walk on them for any distance.

And if any scat is present, check to see if the animal attempted to cover it. Members of the cat clan customarily try to cover their droppings with front feet, leaving scratch marks in the soil or snow around the scat, unless the soil is too hard. Coyotes and foxes do not attempt to cover their scat, although they sometimes rake the ground with their hind feet after defecating. Scratch marks left by wild canines are usually off to one side of the scat.

Cats generally place one foot in front of the other when walking in snow, leaving a neat row of tracks. Hind feet are slightly smaller than the front ones. When running, footprints are bunched together or in a staggered line with at least 2½ feet separating impressions. Members of the cat family are not as prone to trot or run when traveling or chased as wild canines are. If increased speed is called for cats simply walk fast whenever possible. However, this is not necessarily true when it comes to securing prey.

Tracks left by domestic cats measure from 1 to 1½ inches in length and width, with from 5 to 8 inches between tracks. When running, house cats leave tracks about 2 ½ feet apart, sometimes a little more. House cat tracks are most often seen in residential areas or near farms in rural settings. However, feral cats are found in some areas and their tracks may show up miles from human habitations. Populations of feral cats sometimes become established at garbage dumps.

Bobcats

Bobcat tracks range from 1 3/4 to 3 1/2 inches in width and 1 3/4 to 2 1/2 inches long. Width measurements of tracks from one animal can vary considerably depending upon the type of material they are imprinted in. When walking in deep snow, for example, cats spread their toes for support, leaving tracks wider than normal. Distance between bobcat tracks while walking range from 9 to 14 inches. A distance of 3 to 3½ feet separates running tracks.

A trait of bobcats to keep in mind during the winter is they sometimes cross roads in the same place time after time. If deep snow is present, an animal may step in exactly the same depressions left during the previous crossing.

Bobcats are generally solitary animals, but the tracks of a female with her kittens may be seen into the fall. I have also encountered the tracks of mated pairs traveling together during late winter and into spring. The larger prints are usually those of the male. Bobcats range between 15 and 30 pounds in weight, but weights of 60 pounds or more have been recorded. The animals breed from February through April.

They have the widest distribution of any of the North American wild cats. Their range includes most of the United States. The largest vacancy in their range is in the lower midwest where there are few, if any, in Ohio, Indiana, Illinois, Iowa, the northern two-thirds of Missouri, eastern South Dakota, plus the southern portions of Minnesota, Wisconsin, and Michigan. Portions of Kentucky, North Carolina, Virginia, Maryland, Pennsylvania, New Jersey, Massachusetts, and New York are void of bobcats, too, in addition to all of Connecticut and Delaware. In Canada, the bobcat is established in southern portions of British Columbia, Alberta, Saskatchewan, Manitoba, Ontario, Quebec, and all of New Brunswick.

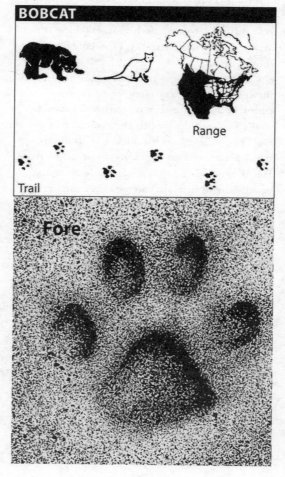

BOBCAT

Range

Trail

Fore

In the east and midwest, bobcats commonly inhabit lowland swamps with thick cover, but they can also be found in hilly country with rock caves. Rugged terrain that is rocky and mountainous, or that has thick brush is favored in the west, although these bob-tailed cats frequent the arid southwest where none of these conditions exist. Bobcats frequently travel along the course of rivers and creeks and may walk river ice in the winter to escape deep snow on the banks. Heavy cover surrounding some lakes is attractive to bobcats, too.

Bobcats vary widely in color from one part of their range to another, but their bobbed tail is a good identifying feature. The tail has a black spot on top near the end, but is white at the tip. A tuft of black hair sticks up from the tip of each ear. Growths of hair called ruffs grow out of the sides of the head and extend downward below the chin.

Due to the bobcat's habit of covering its scat, this type of sign is not seen often, except in parts of the west where the ground is too hard to permit the practice. Droppings that are not covered are normally 4 to 5 inches long and can be confused with those from coyotes, although constrictions in several places along its length are characteristic of bobcat dung. Scats may be broken into segments due to these constrictions. Some bobcats have favored locations for depositing waste.

Lynx

Lynx tracks are noticeably larger than those of the bobcat even though the animals average weights are similar (20 to 30 pounds for lynx). This is due to extra padding on the lynx's feet in the form of hair to increase their surface area for walking on snow like snowshoes. Prints left by lynx can even be as large as, and sometimes larger than, those of mountain lions. In snow, lynx sink less than mountain lions, and the width of their trail is generally narrower. Lynx leave a trail 6 to 8 inches wide, with a width of 8 to 13 inches typical for lions. Mountain lions sometimes leave a drag mark from their tails in deep snow, too, whereas this is impossible for lynx since their tails are shorter than those of bobcats.

Measurements of lynx tracks are 3 to 4 1/2 inches in width and 4 to as much as 7 inches long in deep snow. Strides are from 7 to 14 inches when walking and about the same as a bobcat when running. Lynx sometimes take shorter steps than bobcat when walking in deep snow.

Lynx range throughout most of Canada and Alaska, and a few find their way into northern Minnesota, Michigan, New Hampshire, Vermont, and Maine. The principal range of this cat in the lower forty-eight is in mountainous regions of the west including parts of Colorado, Utah, Wyoming, Idaho, Montana, Washington, and Oregon. Since the lynx's primary prey is the snowshoe hare, it spends much of its time in thick, lowland habitat and mountain thickets that hares also frequent.

Ear tufts and ruffs are longer and more pronounced on lynx than bobcat, and the tip of the tail is black. Lynx appear larger than bobcats due to longer legs and hair, even though they may weigh the same. These animals breed during late winter into spring like bobcats.

Continued →

DOMESTIC CAT AND DOG TRACKS

Elizabeth P. Lawlor   Illustrations by Pat Archer

Dogs

A way to begin exploring your neighborhood for animal tracks is to first examine the front and hind feet of a friendly dog. The black pads you see on the bottom of the dog's foot are shock absorbers for the dog when jumping and provide friction when running. Feel them. Describe their texture. How many pads are there on the front foot? Are they all the same shape? Describe their shapes. What is the relationship between the toes and pads? Do the claws grow beyond the tips of the pads? Compare your nails with those of a dog. How are they different? Compare the front and hind paws and the front and back legs of the dog. How are they similar and how are they different? Write your observations in your field notebook.

Dogs and other members of the canid group of mammals, such as wolves, coyotes, and foxes, walk on their toes. These animals have four toes that generally leave their mark in the snow. The fifth toe, or dew claw, on each front paw, about an inch or so up the inside of the leg, is analogous to our thumb. Unlike our very valuable thumbs, however, the dew claws do not have much practical use, except that wild canids use them to grasp large prey. The dew claws will sometimes show up in the track if the animal is in a high-speed gallop.

The prints made by all members of the canid group have similar characteristics. Both front and rear paws usually will show four claws and four toe pads, one behind each claw. Each print will be longer than it is wide. The next time there is a fresh cover of snow, walk around your neighborhood—along sidewalks, through backyards (get permission from the owners), park lawns, school grounds, public golf courses, and fields—and look for dog prints. When you find a set of tracks, determine how many dogs there were and in what direction the dog or dogs were traveling. How many different sets of prints did you find on your walk? Measure the length and width of a print in each set. What was the range in size (length and width) of local dog prints?

Cats

Another neighborhood animal is the domestic cat. Although much smaller in size, these cats belong to the same family of mammals (Felidae) as the bobcat, tiger, lion, and leopard. If you don't own a cat, ask a friend if you may examine the paws of his or her cat. Look at the claws and pads. Compare these structures with those you found on the dog. How are they similar and how are they different? Would you expect to find clawmarks in a print left by a cat? ... Does a cat also walk on its toes? What is the general shape of a cat's paw? How does its shape differ from that of a dog? The print left in the snow by a domestic cat is very similar to but smaller than those left by bobcats or other larger cats in the wild. A round, clawless print is a clue that it was made by a feline.

—From *Discover Nature in Winter*

Typical domestic dog tracks have an overall round appearance, especially the larger front track, where the four toes splay outward in different directions.

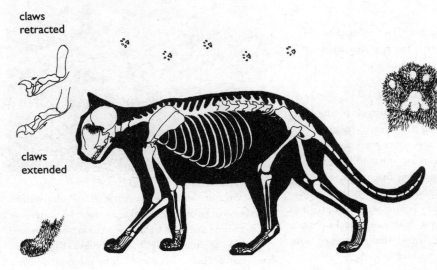

claws retracted

claws extended

All cats have four toes in a circular print, with no claws showing. Large, protruding cheekbones, forward-facing eye sockets, and a short muzzle give the cat a round, flat face.

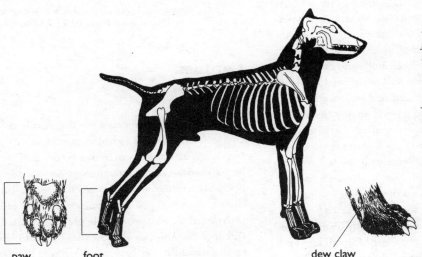

paw   foot   dew claw

If we compare dogs' feet to human hands and feet, dogs walk on their four "fingers" and toes. On the front foot, they have a fifth toe, called the dew claw, an inch or so up the inside of the leg; this is equivalent to the human thumb.

Continued ➡

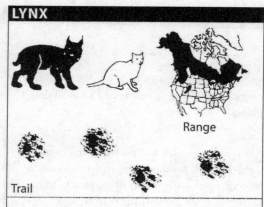

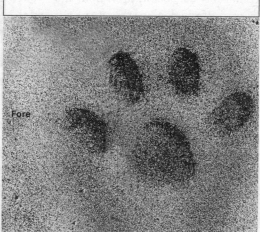

Mountain Lions

Mountain lion tracks are 3 to 4½ inches wide and as much as 4 inches long, with a stride of 12 to 22 inches. Lions are capable of bounds of at least 5 feet when running.

Residents of the western United States and Canada have a better opportunity of seeing lion tracks than those living in the eastern half of either country, although there are a few locations in the east where mountain lions still live such as Arkansas, Florida, and New Brunswick in Canada. The animals have also been seen in Mississippi, Louisiana, Tennessee, the Carolinas, the Virginias, Vermont, Maine, Massachusetts, and New Hampshire. Unverified reports of lions have come from other states as well.

Mountain lions are most common in the following states: Washington, Oregon, Idaho, Nevada, Utah, Arizona, Wyoming, the western halves of Montana and New Mexico, southern Texas, and much of California. In Canada, they roam through much of British Columbia and Alberta, plus parts of Manitoba and Saskatchewan. The large cats are also well established in Mexico.

Like its short-tailed relatives, mountain lions inhabit rugged, rocky, brushy country where its prey is most abundant. Large animals such as deer are the lion's favorite prey, although they do feed on smaller mammals, too. When a large animal is killed, lions commonly cover portions of the carcass they do not eat with leaves, twigs, grass, and other debris.

Mountain lions can be easily distinguished from other wild cats by their long tail and large size. Their overall length is from 7 to 8 feet, including 2½ to 3 feet of tail. And they range in weight from 100 to 175 pounds, with males over 200 pounds on record. Like the other cats, females are smaller than males. There is no distinct breeding season among mountain lions like the short-tailed cats.

Scats of mountain lions are similar to those left by bobcats, only larger in diameter, and are often buried. Droppings average about 5 inches in length with constrictions at various points along the length, or they may be in smaller segments.

Lions frequently scrape up mounds of soil to create scent posts they urinate on. Scratch marks are usually visible near these mounds and indicate which way the lion was traveling. As a rule, the animal continues in the direction it was facing when making the scent post. Dirt will be pulled backward when scratching.

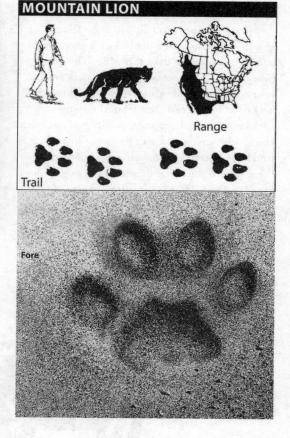

Another sign characteristic of mountain lions is claw marks on tree trunks. Lions rake their claws along the bark to sharpen them. Bobcats and lynx do the same thing, but claw marks they leave are not as obvious as those left by mountain lions. Scratch marks left on trees by lions are not as deep as those made by black bears.

–Text from *Animal Tracks and Signs of North America*
Illustrations from *Track Pack: Animal Tracks in Full Life Size*

Canines

Richard P. Smith
Illustrations by DeCourcy L. Taylor, Jr.

Tracks made by members of the dog family are characteristically oval or oblong in shape with toenails usually visible in prints. Front feet are larger than back feet. Anyone who owns a dog is probably familiar with the pattern. Clear prints show a large heel pad with four smaller toe pads in front of it. The two middle toes are situated side by side, with the outside ones opposite one another and further back. Nails on middle toes register in tracks most often.

Toe pads are arranged in a different pattern than those on the feet of cats. Cat toes are arranged in a neat, semi-circular row in front of heel pads. This characteristic can help distinguish between canine and feline tracks. For more information on differentiating between cat and dog tracks refer to the section on cats.

There is a way to determine the approximate weight of a dog, coyote, fox, or wolf using measurements of a track from a front foot. Multiply the width times the length then multiply the resultant figure by 5.

I tried this on my dog, which is a big hound, and the results were close. A front foot measured 4 x 3½ inches. The calculations produced a weight of 70 pounds. Charlie tipped the scales at 80 pounds the last time I weighed him.

Wild members of the dog family include four species of foxes (red, gray, kit, and arctic), plus coyotes and wolves. In rural settings where free roaming domestic dogs are found, it is sometimes difficult to tell the difference between tracks left by pets and their wild relatives, although the size of prints can be helpful. Large farm dogs such as collies, shepherds, and mongrels have larger feet than coyotes or foxes. Where tracks of dogs are similar in size to those of wolves, coyotes, or foxes, behavior of the individual animals can help differentiate between them.

Dogs frequently walk along rural roads, for example, urinating on trees or brush at regular intervals, and may walk or run off the road for a short distance, then quickly return. This sign is most obvious when snow is covering the ground, of course. Coyotes, foxes and wolves, on the other hand, seldom spend much time on roads that receive much traffic. They either cross directly from one side to the other, sometimes on the run, or walk a short distance down the road before crossing. Occasionally, they will leave a road on the same side they entered.

This trait applies to roads that receive regular vehicular traffic where homes are located that domestic dogs would come from. Coyotes, foxes, and wolves regularly follow lightly used roads and trails that penetrate their home territory. Dogs are not normally seen along these thoroughfares, except possibly during hunting seasons when hunting dogs would be accompanied by their masters.

Foxes

RED FOXES

Red fox tracks are 2 to 2½ inches long, depending on whether front or back foot is measured. Distance between tracks when walking to trotting ranges from about 12 to 18 inches. The trail they leave in the snow is generally no wider than 4 inches. Reds are known for leaving tracks in a straight line, but this is not always true. Pads may not leave distinct impressions, if any at all, in the snow due to covering hair. … [T]he feet of red foxes are completely covered with hair during the winter. A unique feature of heel pads of red foxes (where clear prints are visible) is a raised bar across the pad that is roughly shaped like an inverted V.

Neither coyote nor gray fox feet have this feature. Coyote tracks are generally larger than those of red fox and those of gray fox are smaller. Marks from toenails are also more pronounced in coyote and especially gray fox tracks than those of red fox, during the winter at least, due to the amount of hair that grows on the bottom of red's feet then. In addition, coyotes sink further in the snow than lighter red foxes.

Continued ➡

Red foxes mate during January, and the tracks of a male and female traveling together are common then.

This species of fox has a wider distribution than any of the other foxes, making itself at home in most of North America, including Alaska. However, there are a few areas where they are generally not found including most of Arizona and Montana, parts of California, New Mexico, Texas, Colorado, Oklahoma, Kansas, Nebraska, Wyoming, South Dakota, and Florida.

These foxes are often associated with agricultural areas where there is a mixture of fields and woodlands, but they are adaptable enough to survive in country that tends toward either extreme. They generally inhabit denser cover in the winter than other times of the year.

Even though this animal's coat is usually red in color, it can vary from yellowish to orange, and may be partially gray or even black on occasion with silver-tipped hairs. What are referred to as silver foxes are simply color mutations of the red. All "red" foxes have a white-tipped tail regardless of what color their coat actually is. Their feet and lower legs are black. Reds vary in weight from 7½ to 13 pounds, with females being smaller than males.

No effort is made to cover droppings, which may be seen along two-track roads or wooded trails red foxes often travel. An accumulation of scats may be deposited one on top of the other. Scats are generally from 2 to 3 inches long and pointed at the ends. They are usually smaller in diameter (about a half-inch) than coyote droppings.

Red fox dens are another sign to look for. They are usually located in the open with more dirt around the opening than woodchuck dens. Tracks may be visible in excavated soil. Fur, feathers and bones from prey may be seen near the den, too.

GRAY FOXES

Tracks of gray foxes are a little more than an inch to 1½ inches long. This animal's stride is generally 10 to 12 inches. Unlike other foxes, grays sometimes climb trees, where their long toenails come in handy. Pairs of grays travel together on a regular basis. Mating takes place in the winter.

Gray foxes range over much of the United States and into Mexico. They are largely absent from an area in the northcentral to northwest United States that extends as far south as Kansas. These foxes are more at home in thick brush and other cover than reds.

Grays have red coloration on their face and ears, but are largely gray in color. A black streak runs along the top of the tail, including the tip. Average weights of gray foxes range from 5 or 6 to 11 pounds.

Scats are deposited along wooded trails much the same as with red fox. Droppings from grays are usually smaller than those from reds with tapered ends. Gray fox dens are normally well hidden.

KIT FOXES

Swift and kit foxes leave prints a little over an inch to 1¾ inches in length and can be confused with those of gray fox where their ranges overlap. When walking, they place their feet 8 to 10 inches apart. Kit foxes are the least common species, being found only in the southwestern United States and northern Mexico in dry, desert-type habitat. The kit and swift foxes are actually separate species, although the names are sometimes used interchangeably. They are similar in appearance with one variety having longer ears than the other. These small foxes are light in color and have black-tipped tails. Droppings are very similar to those of the gray fox.

ARCTIC FOXES

Tracks of the arctic fox overlap those of the red in size, but average larger, with lengths up to 2¾ inches. However, the animals themselves are seen as readily as their tracks, unlike other species of foxes. These animals are curious and not generally afraid of man. Their range is in the northern reaches of Canada and Alaska on the tundra.

Arctic foxes have a white or blue coat in the winter that changes to a brownish color for summer months. Their dens are marked by soil spread about the entrance. These animals weigh from 8 to 12 pounds.

Coyotes

Coyotes or brush wolves leave prints that measure from 2 to 2¾ inches long, with walking strides ranging from 13 to 15 inches apart. When running, tracks may be separated by 3 to as much as 8 or 10 feet, depending on snow depth or the lack of it. Trails left by walking coyotes in the snow are generally 4 to 6 inches in width. Brush wolves do not grow as much hair on the bottoms of their feet as red foxes do, so their pads normally show in tracks.

Like the red fox, coyotes mate in the winter (January and February), although that is not the only time the animals travel together. The tracks of family groups or packs containing a number of individuals are sometimes encountered.

Coyotes enjoy a wide distribution, ranging south into Mexico and as far north as Alaska. The southeastern United States and northeastern portions of Canada are the only locations where these animals are not firmly established. As might be guessed, coyotes are adaptable, occupying a variety of habitats from remote woodlands to the suburbs of large cities.

Color variations are common among coyotes like other wild dogs, although they generally appear gray in color, with a bushy tail tipped in black. Coyotes are much larger than gray foxes, weighing from 20 to 40 pounds. They carry their tails down when running as opposed to wolves, which carry theirs straight out or at an upward angle.

Coyote droppings are deposited in locations similar to those used by foxes. In fact, coyote and fox scats may be found on top of each other where their ranges overlap. Scats measure about 3 inches in length and up to an inch in diameter. Dens are well hidden like those of the gray fox.

Wolves

Timber or gray wolves have the largest tracks among wild canines, measuring from 4 to more than 5 inches in length. Alaskan wolves are larger than their relatives in Canada and the northern United States, leaving correspondingly larger tracks. Family groups and packs are common among wolves, so tracks of a number of wolves may be seen together. In the winter, packs often walk in single file leaving a well defined trail. Mating takes place in February. As a rule, only dominant members of a pack breed, not all adults as is the case among coyotes and foxes.

Canada and Alaska are the timber wolves' primary ranges, but they also roam in northern Minnesota, Wisconsin, Michigan, and Montana. Their habitat consists of barren tundra and expansive woodlands where rivers and lakes abound. Some wolves look like coyotes, only they

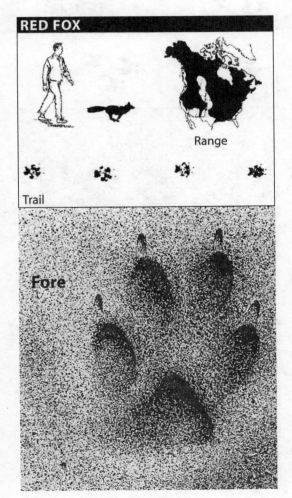

RED FOX

Range

Trail

Fore

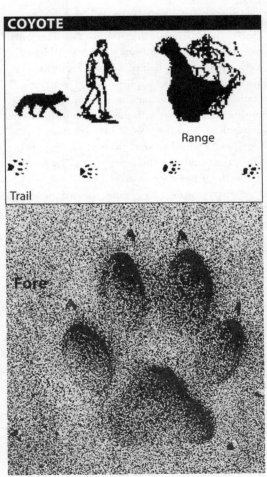

COYOTE

Range

Trail

Fore

Continued ➡

WOLF

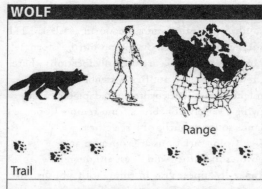

Range

Trail

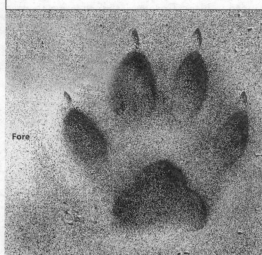

Fore

are larger with weights ranging from 60 to well over 100 pounds. Some wolves are black and others are white.

Scats measure from 3 to 6 inches in length and an inch in diameter. Dens have large entrances and may have remains of prey nearby.

—Text from *Animal Tracks and Signs of North America*
Illustrations from *Track Pack: Animal Tracks in Full Life Size*

Deer

Richard P. Smith
Illustrations by DeCourcy L. Taylor, Jr.

Unlike other animals discussed so far, deer only have two toes on each foot, which form hooves. Each toe makes up half of a hoof. Front hooves are larger than those on hind feet. Deer tracks made by a walking animal may resemble an upside-down heart, with the bottom of the heart being the tips of the toes, if toes are close together. And, of course, there is a line running down the middle of the heart-shaped tracks that marks the inner edge of each toe.

When trotting or running, toes will be spread and small marks from dew claws, which can be considered a deer's heels, often appear directly behind each toe. Impressions from dew claws may also appear in walking tracks made in mud, soft sand, or snow an inch or more deep. The dew claws simply increase the surface area of feet for added support. Dew claws are further from toes on hind feet than they are on front feet.

This characteristic can be helpful in differentiating between front and back feet in running deer tracks. Whitetail deer characteristically leave imprints from hind feet in front of forefeet when running. Mule deer and blacktail deer, on the other hand, leave running prints with front feet ahead of hind feet. The reason for this is differences in their gait.

Whitetails run like most other animals with their front feet striking the ground as they bring hind feet forward to touch down ahead of them to kick off with a powerful forward bound or leap. Muleys and blacktails, which are closely related, generally keep their legs stiff when running and bounce from one spot to the next like they have pogo sticks for legs. The only circumstance under which mule deer and whitetail tracks can reliably be distinguished from one another is when they are running, due to this fundamental difference in how they run.

The ability to tell the difference between the tracks of different species of deer is not necessary in most areas because there is not a lot of overlap in their ranges. Where two species do share the same range, the different animals normally occupy distinct types of habitat. In some western states where both mule deer and whitetails are found such as Montana and Wyoming, whitetails spend much of their time in lowland river bottoms and agricultural areas with woodlots. Muleys inhabit timbered slopes and meadows at higher elevations, for the most part.

Track patterns left by running deer may appear in one of two forms. The four footprints are sometimes bunched together, with both front and rear feet slightly offset from one another rather than side by side. Prints of front feet may be closer together than those of hind feet in patterns left by mule deer or blacktails. A more elongated running track pattern exhibits tracks of individual feet farther apart, almost in a line. However, each print is usually to the right or left of the center of the track pattern.

The length of footprints in running tracks, including dew claws, ranges from 3½ to 4½ inches for most adult deer. Tracks of walking deer range from 2½ to more than 3 inches in length. Keep in mind that there is a tremendous variation in track size among deer from one part of the country to another, even within the same species. Whitetails tend to be smaller in the southern portion of the United States, for instance, than in the north.

Two of the smallest subspecies of whitetails are found in the south. The key deer is the smallest and lives in the Florida Keys. Coues deer inhabit desert regions in parts of the southwestern United States. Tracks made by adults of these subspecies may be similar in size to prints made by fawns from Wisconsin, Pennsylvania, New York, Maine, or Michigan in the fall.

It is not unusual to see the tracks of two or more deer traveling together at any time of the year. In fact, the animals are sometimes seen in groups or herds, especially in feeding areas. One or two sets of small tracks with those of a noticeably larger animal are obviously made by a doe and her fawns. Two or more sets of adult-size prints may be those of a buck and does, especially during late fall breeding seasons, or simply does traveling together.

When deer travel over the same route time and time again, or many animals follow the same course, trails develop. Heavily used trails are usually void of vegetation, and numerous tracks can be seen in them. These may lead to favored feeding areas or mark migration routes used by some deer during late fall into winter and

WHITETAIL DEER

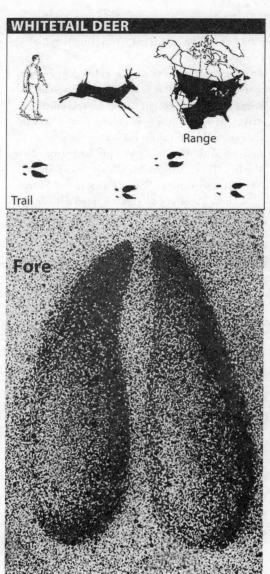

Range

Trail

Fore

MULE DEER

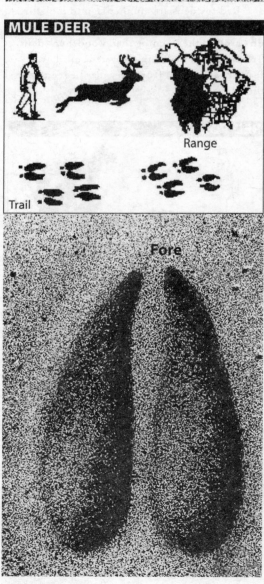

Range

Trail

Fore

Continued ➜

DISTINGUISHING DEER SPECIES
Allan A. Macfarlan   Illustrations by Paulette Macfarland

Distinguishing the Mule Deer from the Whitetail

The mule deer, usually larger than the whitetail, has branched antlers. Since the main beam of an antler forks equally, and the two forks branch again, the normal number of points on a mature mule deer's rack is generally four on each side. When there are additional points, they usually branch off this main structure. The whitetail's main beam sweeps outward, then curves forward, and all the points branch off the main beam. The

mule deer got his name because of his enormous ears, much larger than a whitetail's, but there are other differences that can be used as field marks. This is sometimes very important, because the range of the whitetail and the mule deer overlap in a wide area and in some places the season on one animal may be closed while the other may be legal game.

The whitetail's large white flag is characteristic. The mule deer has a long, ropelike tail with a black tip. When the mule deer is

going away, his tail is carried low, pressed against his rear. The whitetail's flag is carried high when the deer is running, with the white underside plainly visible.

Identifying the Columbia Blacktail

The Columbia blacktail deer is smaller than a mule deer. It resembles the whitetail in both habits and appearance. Again, the tail is a field mark for the hunter. The tail is not as large as a whitetail deer's, though the shape is similar. When the blacktail is not alarmed, the tail is down; so its rear surface is almost entirely black. There is only a thin white margin around the edges.

Range of the Columbia Blacktail

The Columbia blacktail is confined to the western slope near the Pacific from Sitka, Alaska to Southern California; therefore the blacktail's range barely overlaps that of the whitetail in very few places.

The blacktail deer is an animal of forest margins, low scrub, swamps, and thickets. Because he inhabits much the same kind of country, hunting methods for the blacktail closely resemble those used when hunting whitetail deer.

—From *Exploring the Outdoors with Indian Secrets*

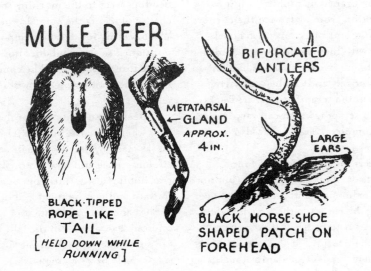

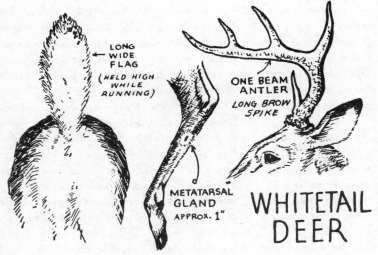

Distinguishing Features of Mule Deer and Whitetail Deer.

Distinguishing Features of Columbia Blacktail Deer.

spring. The course of less used trails can usually be determined by a line of scuffed leaves or flattened vegetation. Trails are easiest to see in sand and snow.

One fairly reliable way to tell the tracks of a buck from those of a doe, if there is an inch of snow or less on the ground, is to look for drag marks. Bucks do not generally lift their feet as high as does do, dragging their feet in the snow from one step to the next. When snow gets deeper, deer of either sex may drag their feet.

Big bucks make tracks that are both longer and wider than those of most does. So an exceptionally large track like the one I measured last

fall that was 4 inches long and 3¾ inches wide across the rear of the print, are often made by bucks. However, this is only true in areas where big bucks live. Bucks in some locations with heavy hunting pressure seldom live longer than 2½ years, not long enough to attain large size. Does in the same area may live longer and grow larger, leaving tracks bigger than those of most bucks.

Measurements of the feet of more than 100 blacktail deer from Oregon showed that adult bucks definitely do have wider and longer feet than adult does. The feet of adult bucks averaged 73 millimeters or 2.874 inches in length, with

the shortest being 71 millimeters or 2.795 inches. Adult doe feet averaged 66 millimeters or 2.598 inches, with 68.5 millimeters or 2.697 inches the longest, so there was no overlap. There was some overlap in foot size among yearling bucks and does, but the length of feet among males averaged longer even in that age class (68 millimeters or 2.677 inches versus 64 millimeters or 2.52 inches).

The same was true for width of feet measured one-third of the way back from tips of toes. Feet of yearling bucks averaged wider, 15 millimeters or .591 inches versus 13.8 millime-

Continued →

ters or .543 inches. There was a clearcut difference in width of feet among adult bucks and does, averaging 17 millimeters or .669 inches for bucks and 14 millimeters or .551 inches for does. The widest adult doe track measured 14.5 millimeters or .571 inches and the narrowest buck foot was 16.5 millimeters or .65 inches.

This sample also showed that foot size of both bucks and does were comparable as fawns. The same information probably applies to whitetail and mule deer, too, but it would be better if similar studies had been done of their feet to confirm it.

If a track is thought to have been made by a mature buck due to its size, one way to confirm those suspicions, at least during fall and early winter months, is to follow the animal's tracks and look for other signs. A blanket of snow on the ground is necessary to make this possible, of course. Look for locations where the deer stopped to feed on items close to or on the ground. In locations where acorns and other types of nuts are found, the animals will paw up leaves on the ground, sometimes in large patches, to get at the nuts. Antler tines from bucks with decent size antlers (six points or better) will sometimes leave impressions in the snow as they feed an acorns. All tines will not necessarily show in the snow. Small antlered bucks usually will not leave any marks in the snow from their headgear.

Black bears and raccoons will also paw through patches of leaves like deer to feed on nuts. So when seeing this type of sign, especially when no snow is on the ground, look for droppings or tracks in the soil to better determine what was responsible for the activity.

Deer also graze on grass or eat fallen apples in openings or fields where these items are found, and signs of antlers may sometimes be discovered in the snow at these locations. The first time I noticed round holes in the snow from antler tips on either side of a spot where a buck had been feeding, the animal had been eating fallen apples. Two or three punctures were visible on each side and they were widespread, so it appeared as though the buck had a respectable set of antlers. I followed the animal in an effort to find out just how big they were, but never did get a glimpse of its head.

Deer are browsers, too, breaking off the tips of limbs, saplings, and low-growing stems. Look for evidence of tines in the snow where a deer browses on stems growing close to the ground. Because deer do not have teeth on top in the front of their mouths, they must break off bits of woody browse rather than biting them off cleanly. As a result, ragged edges will be visible on the ends of plants, brush, and trees where deer have browsed. Rabbits clip twigs off cleanly, at a slant, where they feed. . . .

There are other signs that can confirm whether tracks were made by a buck in the fall. That is the time of year when the "rut" or breeding season takes place. Mature bucks leave two types of signs in conjunction with the rut—antler rubbings and ground scrapes. Antler rubs are made on trees of various sizes, but most often on saplings. Bucks rake their antlers along the trunks of selected trees, sometimes so aggressively that the sapling is broken.

The bark is rubbed off on tree trunks worked over by bucks, some of it left hanging in ragged stripes. Light-colored inner wood on fresh rubs can usually be spotted from some distance away. Antler rubs made by deer are normally only a foot or two off the ground. Bits of bark and wood can generally be seen at the bases of rubbed trees. Rubs on full-fledged trees are made by bucks with larger antlers, as a rule. Since the bases of both beams are rubbed on trees, the antlers have to be at least as wide as the damaged tree to fit around it.

Scrapes are patches of ground, most often located underneath an overhanging limb, that bucks paw free of leaves and other debris exposing bare soil. Bucks often leave scent on the overhanging branch by nibbling on it or rubbing a secretion from a gland at the corners of their eyes on them. Bucks may also attack these branches with their antlers. As a result, many such limbs are broken and left hanging or broken off entirely and can be seen laying on the ground in the scrape or near it. Bucks often urinate in scrapes, which can vary in size, once they are complete. Tracks may also be visible in scrapes.

Rubs and scrapes are sometimes found together, or at least in the same vicinity, but not always. Scrapes help bucks and receptive does get together during the rut when the time is right. Once does are ready to be bred, they visit a scrape to leave their scent. For this reason, bucks usually check their scrapes (each animal makes a series of these markers) on a regular basis. When a scrape has been visited by a doe, the buck trails her from there until he finds her.

All deer make rubs and scrapes, but whitetails make more scrapes than mule deer or blacktails. In fact, scrapes are not as important to mule deer as whitetails. Due to the whitetail buck's habit of revisiting scrapes during the rut, anyone who finds a series of them in a small area can usually see the animal that made them by waiting in the vicinity.

Deer tracks that lead up to a freshly made rub or scrape are those of a buck. If they are fresh, rubbed bark and pawed soil will be on top of the snow. A second set of tracks leading to a scrape could be those of a doe, or of another buck in the area. Bucks will visit scrapes made by other males, and may even add their scent to them.

Deer beds are oval-shaped depressions in grass, moss, leaves, or snow where the animals lay down to chew their cud or rest. Animals that are traveling together may bed down in the same locality. Large and small beds together usually represent those of a doe and fawns. Marks from antlers can sometimes be seen at the head end of beds in the snow made by bucks. During the rut, the tracks of a buck will frequently lead to the beds of other deer in their search of does ready to be bred.

If one rutting buck encounters another of equal size, a fight sometimes takes place, and the evidence of such a contest is unmistakable. The ground will usually be trampled, with turf torn up, trees and bushes will be knocked over, and clumps of hair will be visible on the ground. I saw signs left by a pair of fighting whitetails last fall that were impressive. It appeared as though their antlers may have been locked for a time

because there was a continuous trail of devastation for a good 50 yards where they pushed, pulled, and shoved one another. The antlers of fighting bucks sometimes become inseparably locked and they die.

Beds in fields usually mark locations where animals laid down to chew their cud or rest during hours of darkness. Beds in thick cover are usually daytime resting places. An accumulation of deer beds in a location that has been used over a period of time, some old, some fresh, is indicative of a preferred bedding area. Anyone interested in intercepting deer between bedding and feeding areas should post as close to bedding areas as possible without alerting the animals in the evening. Persons who beat deer to bedding areas in the morning stand a good chance of seeing the animals when they arrive. When waiting for deer it is important to be positioned so the wind does not carry your scent in the direction deer will be coming from. Deer that smell people generally will not show themselves.

Deer may urinate and/or defecate in their beds when they arise at their leisure. Urine marks made by does are usually smaller in circumference and between or slightly behind rear hoofprints. Urine from bucks falls further forward and may be splattered over a wider area because they often urinate over glands located on hind legs, at least in the fall. Drops of urine can sometimes be seen in the snow between tracks made by a walking buck.

Deer droppings consist of groupings of pellets of a half-inch to an inch in length that are usually black or brown in color, but they may have a greenish cast. Deer pellets are cylindrical in shape with rounded ends, as a rule, but one end of some pellets may be concave with the other possessing a nipple-shaped projection. In the summer, deer scats may appear as individual clumps of fecal material rather than pellets.

Deer hair is another sign the animals sometimes leave, although it is not one of the more important ones. Long, brownish, hollow deer hairs can be found in narrow places along trails where they rub or bump against trees and brush. Hairs are also left on strands of barbed wire where the animals crawl under fences. Deer hair can serve as an important sign for hunters that an animal was hit, if found on the ground where the deer was standing when shot at. Both bullets and arrows cut hair from deer when striking them, even though there may be no blood at that point.

Concentrations of bleached, white antlers shed by bucks are sometimes seen in locations where deer winter, especially the open terrain mule deer favor. Deer are usually only abundant in these areas during the winter when deep snows push them down from higher elevations. Most bucks shed their antlers during the winter, but some may lose them late in the fall or retain them until spring. Healthy bucks usually have antlers longer than undernourished or injured males. Mule deer antlers characteristically have branched tines. Typical whitetail antlers have tines that do not branch, but nontypical antlers exhibited by some whitetails do have branched tines.

Continued

Another deer sign common in wintering areas with too many deer are browse lines. These distinct lines visible on trees and other vegetation are created by the animals eating everything edible within reach.

In appearance, the three major types of deer under discussion here are easy to tell apart. Whitetails have large tails that are white on the underside and brown on top. When alarmed, these deer raise their tails and they resemble a white flag waving as they run. This serves as a warning to other animals in the vicinity.

Mule deer tails are much narrower than those of whitetails and consequently, do not cover their rump. The tails are black at the tip, with the rest being white. Blacktails are a subspecies of mule deer, and as their name implies, tails are black on top, not on the underside. The tails of blacktails are similar in size and shape to those of whitetails.

All of these deer have coats that are brown to gray during fall, winter, and spring months. Summer coats are reddish brown. Whitetails average between 100 to 150 pounds, with smaller subspecies usually weighing under 100 pounds. Some enormous whitetails have been recorded that weighed more than 300 pounds. Average weighs of blacktails are similar to those for whitetails. Muleys average between 150 and 200 pounds, with larger animals reaching weights of 300 to 400 pounds or more.

Blacktail deer are only found along the west coast of North America, with sitka blacktails found in southern Alaska and into British Columbia. Columbian blacktails are distributed along the coast of British Columbia, Washington, Oregon, and northern California. Mule deer are found in all western states and western Canada. The eastern limit of their range is on a line with western portions of Nebraska and the Dakotas.

Whitetail deer reside in all of the lower forty-eight states, but few are found in California, Nevada, and Utah. Parts of other states such as northern Arizona, western Colorado, southwestern Wyoming, and southern Idaho are also without whitetails. All of southern Canada, with the exception of most of British Columbia, is home to whitetails, as well.

—Text from *Animal Tracks and Signs of North America*
Illustrations from *Track Pack: Animal Tracks in Full Life Size*

Elk, Moose, and Caribou

Richard P. Smith
Illustrations by DeCourcy L. Taylor, Jr.

Elk and Moose

The tracks of elk and moose are similar to those of deer since the animals are closely related, except elk and moose tracks are much larger. Elk tracks measure 4 inches in length, with some variation either way, and usually have more rounded toes than those of moose, which measure 5 inches or more in length. The length of running moose tracks may be as much as 10 inches, including the dew claws, with running elk tracks shorter.

Footprints of elk can be confused with those of cattle at times, although adult cattle usually leave tracks slightly larger and more rounded than those of adult elk. Young cattle make tracks intermediate in size, about 3 inches, between those of adult and calf elk (2 inches). Look for droppings if in doubt as to which animal made tracks. Elk scat may resemble those of cattle (flat patties) in the summer, but are much smaller, only 5 or 6 inches in diameter. However, elk scats are often in pellet form.

Elk pellets are elongated like those of deer and can be rounded on the ends or concave and pointed. Scat from elk measure 3/4 of an inch to twice that in some cases. Moose pellets are sometimes shaped the same as those of elk, but may resemble large marbles in shape, and are generally an inch to 13/4 inches long. Moose will also void larger quantities of scat than elk, averaging a quart, in one location.

Moose commonly travel alone, although a cow may have a calf with her. And during the fall rut, the tracks of a bull and cow may be seen together. However, moose are sometimes gregarious with groups often visible in small areas. I have seen two or three bulls and a cow together in Wyoming. Elk are herd animals, but bulls sometimes wander off on their own.

Elk are grazers primarily, so look for their tracks and droppings in meadows surrounded by timber. When they do browse, willow is a preferred species. Patches above timberline are most often visited by elk during the summer and early fall. Aspen bark is also eaten during winter. Elk gouge out pieces of bark from tree trunks with their canine teeth. Old scars from this type of feeding activity blacken. Light-colored inner wood can be seen where bark was recently removed.

Moose chew bark from aspen trees, too, so either animal may be responsible if both are present where this sign is noticed. I have also seen where a moose ate bark from maple trees. Willows browsed by moose frequently have stems broken by the animals as they pull the tops down to get at tender tips in tops. Other species of small trees moose browse on may be damaged in a similar fashion. Moose commonly feed on water plants during summer months, so look for their tracks along shores of lakes, ponds, or rivers at that time of year. In the winter, moose browse on some evergreen trees such as balsams, sometimes leaving noticeable browse lines.

Like deer, elk and moose rub their antlers on trees during the fall prior to and during the rut. Both elk and moose rubs are on larger trees than deer use and higher off the ground than deer normally rub. Males of both species sometimes fight during the rut. Moose antlers sometimes lock like those of deer, and then the animals die.

There are a few moose where I live in upper Michigan, although they are abundant on Isle Royale in Lake Superior, but their primary range is further north in all of Canada and Alaska. Moose are common in Maine and more numerous in Minnesota (the northern part) than Michigan. The animals also range into Vermont and New Hampshire. Western states that have moose are Utah, Colorado, Wyoming, Idaho, Montana, and Washington. Shira's moose, the smallest subspecies, reside in western states. Canadian moose are larger, and Alaskan moose are the largest subspecies.

The smaller subspecies of moose range in weight from 800 to at least 1,200 pounds. Alaskan moose reach weights of 1,800 pounds.

In weight, elk are lighter than moose, but there is some overlap. Six hundred to 1,000 pounds is the weight scale for elk. The elk's primary range includes Montana, Idaho, Wyoming, Colorado, Utah, New Mexico, Arizona, Washington, Oregon, and California, in the United States. Pockets of the animals are also found in South Dakota, Texas, Arkansas, Virginia, and Michigan. In Canada, they are distributed in parts of Manitoba, Saskatchewan, Alberta, and British Columbia.

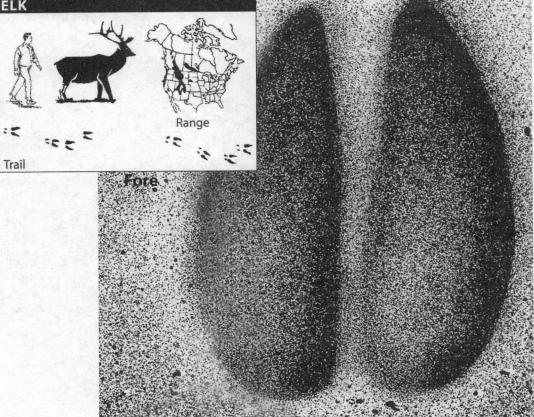

ELK

Trail

Range

Fore

Continued →

Elk and moose beds are much larger than those made by deer, with vegetation and snow being flattened under the animals where they lay. Beds may be found singly or in clusters. Both animals also make and use wallows in conjunction with the breeding season. Elk wallow in moist, black soil along the edges of meadows, and moose do the same although the location may be different. The animals often urinate in wallows then roll in the odorous mud.

Due to their size, these animals are not likely to be mistaken for anything else. Moose are dark brown to black. Bulls have palmate or flat antlers and an appendage hanging under their chins called bells. Their antlers are shed annually.

The bodies of elk are tan in color, with much darker, longer hair on the neck. Their rumps are light in color, cream to yellow, and sometimes give the animals' presence away because this part of their anatomy contrasts with their surroundings and is easy to spot. Mature bulls grow tall antlers with long tines, which are shed every year and replaced with a new set. While developing, all antlers of members of the deer family are covered with velvet. The velvet is shed early in the fall, exposing hardened antlers.

Caribou

Caribou tracks are unlike those of any other member of the deer family. The sharply curved toes form two halves of an incomplete circle. Prints would be perfectly circular if toes came together, but there is usually wide spacing between the toes, more so in the center of tracks

than at tips of toes. Dew claws are almost always visible in caribou tracks, even when the animals are walking.

These animals spend a lot of time on wet, spongy ground, and the design of their hooves help support their weight when walking or running. Many caribou inhabit treeless terrain or tundra in Canada and Alaska where their primary food is lichen, a type of moss, although they also graze on grasses and browse on woody plants. One subspecies of caribou, the woodland variety, is more often found in association with forested areas than their relatives.

Caribou are nomadic, traveling long distances during the course of a year, especially on spring and fall migrations. Their migration routes are marked by heavily used trails that wind their way across the tundra. Once snow covers the ground, caribou dig down through it, sometimes more than a foot, to reach lichen and grass it covers. I have seen signs left by whitetail deer doing the same thing to reach grass, as well as apples.

Scat left by these animals is not an important sign. It closely resembles dung deposited by other members of the deer family, as well as sheep.

Both male and female caribou grow antlers, which is unusual among members of the deer family. In fact, caribou are the only antlered animals in North America with females that grow antlers, although this characteristic is common among horned big game. The difference between antlers and horns is that antlers are shed annually. Horns are not shed, and they grow continuously as a result.

Antlers grown by cow caribou are generally spindly and small. Mature bulls grow large antlers with long beams that are sometimes palmate on the ends like those of moose. Auxiliary beams often project upward near the base of main beams and flat "shovels" may also extend forward from the base of antlers. Caribou antlers, like the animals themselves, are different.

Caribou are also known as reindeer, which most children and adults would recognize as the animals that are supposed to pull Santa Claus' sleigh on Christmas. The bodies of these animals are dark brown, with much lighter-colored hair on their necks. They also have white rump patches. Barren ground caribou generally weigh between 300 and 400 pounds, but the woodland subspecies weigh upwards of 600 pounds or more.

The range of caribou includes much of Canada and Alaska, with the animals being absent from southern portions of most provinces.

—Text from *Animal Tracks and Signs of North America*
Illustrations from *Track Pack: Animal Tracks in Full Life Size*

Other Hooved Animals

Richard P. Smith
Illustrations by DeCourcy L. Taylor, Jr.

Pronghorn Antelope

The tracks of pronghorn antelope are similar to those of deer, although they tend to be wider at the rear than deer tracks and the inside of toes are slightly concave toward the tips. This results in the front of the toes being spread wider in antelope tracks than is typical of deer tracks. One distinct difference between deer and pronghorn feet is antelope do not have dew claws, so they will not be visible in running antelope tracks.

Pronghorn tracks average just under 3 inches to a little more than 3 inches in length. Antelope themselves are often easier to see than their tracks because they occupy open plains and grasslands where they can be spotted a long way off. The animals' upper bodies are brown with white on the rump, sides, chest, and throat. Their white markings normally stand out against their surroundings. Antelope are often seen in herds. The animals range between 80 and 125 pounds or more.

Both male and female pronghorns grow black horns that have curled ends and prongs on each horn, usually closer to the bases than tips. Horns grown by does seldom grow as long as those of bucks, with 3 to 4 inches being normal. The horns of bucks can be as much as 20 inches long, but are usually less. Antelope do not shed their horns each year like deer do, although the outer sheath is replaced annually. The inner core of horns remain intact continuously.

In locations where both mule deer and antelope occupy the same habitat, their tracks can be confused, especially where clear prints are not visible. Scats of antelope also resemble those of mule deer. However, a type of sign characteristic of pronghorns associated with their scat is a depression pawed in the ground for depositing both droppings and urine. These are referred to as scrapes, but do not have any connection with mating like those made by whitetail deer.

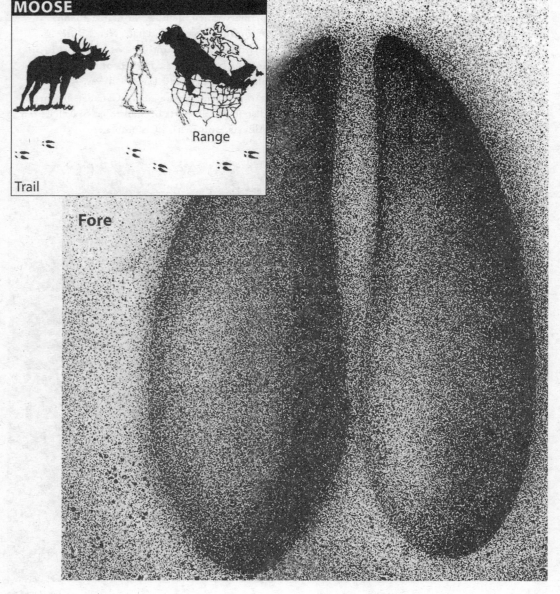

MOOSE

Range

Trail

Fore

Continued ➡

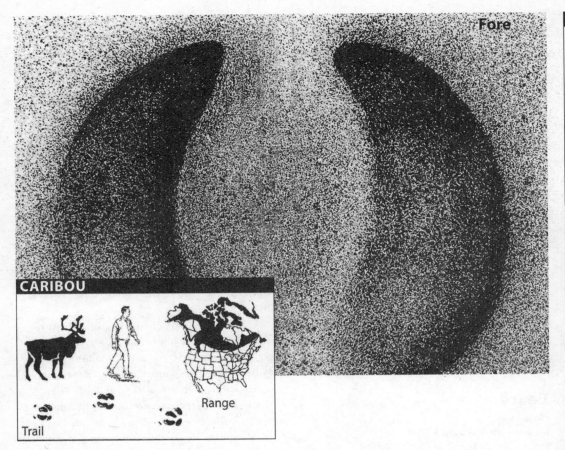

Fore

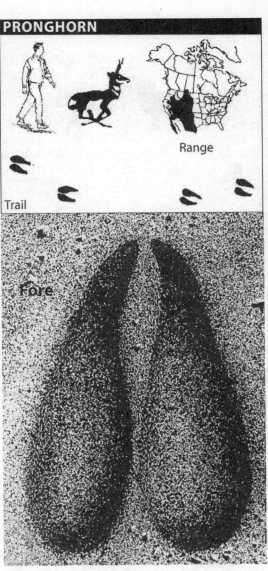

PRONGHORN

Trail

Range

Fore

CARIBOU

Trail

Range

The distribution of pronghorn antelope is more spotty than deer, due primarily to the occurrence of their preferred habitat. They are found in most western states and into the Dakotas, with good numbers in states such as Wyoming, Montana, Colorado, and South Dakota. In Canada, these animals are found in parts of Alberta and Saskatchewan just north of the United States border.

Mountain Goats

Mountain goats make tracks that are shaped like a square. Prints are about as wide at the front as they are at the back, although there is generally as indentation where the toes are separated at the front. Adult goat footprints average more than 3 inches in length, with 3½ inches typical.

Like pronghorns, mountain goats can be easier to see than their tracks in areas where they are found. They usually occupy rocky, mountainous regions. The animals are totally white and have short, black horns that come to a point. Both sexes grow horns, which are not shed, and the horns of females can be as long as those of males. Patches of long white, shaggy hair they shed during the summer can sometimes be found on trees and brush in areas they occupy.

The scats of mountain goats are more irregularly shaped than those of deer when in pellet form, but they do resemble deer droppings in some cases. However, many times goat pellets tend to be more bell shaped than those of deer, with pointed tops and flat, widened bottoms. Droppings may also be round like marbles. Summer dung may appear as conglomerations of pellets clinging together or soft masses of feces that harden when dry.

Mountain goat beds are usually located on slopes where they have good visibility, but may also be seen in caves and other protected areas where the animals go to escape inclement weather. These animals average much larger than deer and antelope, with billies (males) attaining

weights of up to 300 pounds. These wild goats are distributed from Washington State northward through British Columbia and into parts of the Yukon and Alaska. They also range from Idaho and Montana into British Columbia and Alberta. Scattered populations of the animals brought about through releases are in Colorado, Wyoming, and South Dakota.

Wild Sheep

The tracks of wild sheep are similar to those of mountain goats, being squared, although the inner edges of toes on goats tend to be straighter than those of sheep. The inner edges of the toes of sheep are slightly concave and this shows in some tracks. Tracks of the front feet of sheep range between 3 and 3½ inches, with back footprints shorter.

There are two species of wild sheep—*bighorns* and *Dalls*. Bighorns are generally tan to brown in color with light-colored rumps. They are commonly found in mountainous regions of the western United States and Canada, but a smaller variety referred to as desert bighorns, reside in desert regions in the southwestern United States southward into Mexico. Desert Bighorns may attain weights of 200 pounds, usually less, while some of their alpine relatives reach weights of 300 pounds.

Dall sheep are pure white, but there are color variations with some black to gray evident. A subspecies called Stone sheep are gray to black in color, with the exception of white rumps, bellies, and backs of legs. Dall sheep average smaller than bighorns, with weights in the 200-pound range, give or take 25 pounds, common.

Both rams and ewes grow horns, but the ewes' horns are pointed and curved backward. Mature rams grow massive horns that curl back around to or past their eyes.

Sheep scats closely resemble those of mountain goats, tending to be bell shaped when in pellet form. Bighorns and Dalls have a habit of

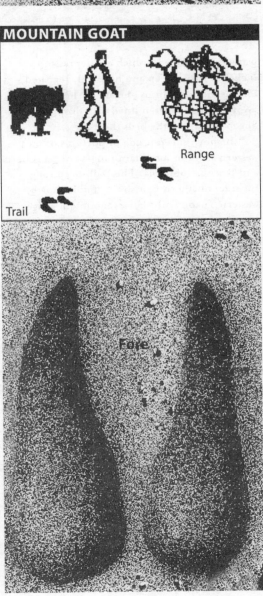

MOUNTAIN GOAT

Trail

Range

Fore

Continued ➡

BIGHORN SHEEP

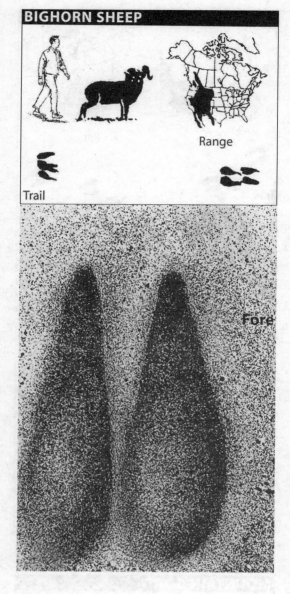

Trail

Range

Fore

using the same beds, which are depression 6 inches to a foot deep and bare soil, repeatedly as long as they remain in one area. The edges of favored beds are often lined with droppings. Sheep urinate in the beds themselves.

Bighorn sheep reside in portions of most western states in mountain ranges and in Alberta and British Columbia. The Dall sheep range includes northern British Columbia, northwestern Yukon and Alaska's mountain ranges.

Representatives of the Stone sheep subspecies are most common in northern British Columbia and southern Yukon.

Buffalo

Another hooved animal of the open plains is the buffalo. Their tracks resemble those of domestic cattle and can be confused with them, although buffalo tracks are generally larger. The prints of adult buffaloes measure 5 inches or more, both in length and width. Cow tracks are usually less than 5 inches in length.

Tracks left by buffaloes are circular in shape and could pass for those of a horse if it were not for the two toes. Horses only have one toe on each foot. The outside of each toe on the feet of buffalo are semicircular and the insides are concave.

Buffaloes are brown in color with horns that curve to the sides and upward. Both bulls and cows have horns. The animals weigh between 900 and 1,800 pounds, but some bulls are heavier and some cows lighter.

Dung from buffalos look exactly like cow patties and can be confused for the same. Other sign made by these animals include tree rubs and wallows. Even though buffalos spend a lot of time on open grasslands, they also enter stands of trees, usually pines. Trunks of trees where buffalo roam are rubbed and gouged with horns, forming a light band of scarred bark. Long, brown, kinky buffalo hairs are usually visible on rubs.

Wallows are enlarged beds worn down to the soil where buffalos roll in the dust. A number of wallows may be seen close together. The large patches of bare soil stand out against green grass making them easy to see. Tree rubs and wallows are numerous in South Dakota's Custer State Park, which has one of the largest herds of free-roaming buffalos in the country. Buffalo herds are also located in southern Oklahoma, eastern Utah, northwest Wyoming, southeast Montana, plus a couple of locations in Alberta and Alaska.

—Text from *Animal Tracks and Signs of North America*
Illustrations from *Track Pack: Animal Tracks in Full Life Size*

Bears

Charles Fergus
Illustrations by DeCourcy L. Taylor, Jr.

American Black Bear
(*Ursus americanus*)

The range of the American black bear stretches from Newfoundland to Florida in the east and from Alaska to Mexico in the west. It takes in all or part of thirty-eight states, much of northern Mexico, and every Canadian province except Prince Edward Island. Black bears live in a variety of wooded and partially wooded settings, including mountains, lowlands, swamps, deserts, and the fringes of the arctic tundra. Biologists estimate the population of *Ursus americanus* at 400,000 to 750,000 continentwide, with the greatest concentrations in the forests of the Northeast, the Upper Midwest, and the Pacific Northwest.

Most black bears are black in color. Some individuals have a white V or blaze on the chest, and many have brown or tan muzzles. The nose is black, and the eyes are dark brown to almost black. Because the first bears encountered by settlers in North America were black, the species was given the name black bear. But not all black bears are black: coat color in bears is influenced by as many as ten separate genes, yielding many possible shades and color patterns, and perhaps the greatest color variation of any carnivore species.

The black color phase predominates in the East, Midwest, Pacific Northwest, Canada, and Alaska, with the occasional brown or cinnamon-colored individual showing up in those areas. In the drier regions of the West, an increasing percentage of black bears are a tawny or cinnamon color; one study in Colorado found that more than 80 percent of black bears were brown. The pale coat picks up less solar heat than a black pelt, which may prevent an animal from overheating in the more open western woodlands. Some scientists suggest an alternate reason for the pale coloration: it mimics the grizzly bear's fur, a pattern that may have evolved to bluff away potential predators.

In three areas of British Columbia resides the Kermode bear (named after Canadian zoologist Francis Kermode), which comes in a spectrum of colors: black, creamy, chestnut, yellow, bluish gray, and orangish. Southeastern Alaska is home to the glacier bear, whose bluish white coat blends in with its icy home. In the past, these different color phases were classified as separate species, but today they are considered subspecies, or races, of *Ursus americanus*.

The muzzle of the black bear is relatively narrow and straight compared with the broader, slightly upturned snout of the grizzly bear. The ears are rounded, and they are larger than a grizzly's ears. Biologists believe that the black bear has prominent ears so that individuals can send social signals to one another in the wooded, low-light settings where *Ursus americanus* lives.

Black bears vary greatly in size. A mature female in an area where food is scarce may weigh less than 100 pounds. In autumn, having laid on fat before winter, a large, older male in a rich habitat can top 800 pounds—heavier than grizzly bears in many locales. In August 2001, a fifteen-year-old boar was killed by a car in Manitoba; he weighed 856 pounds, and biologists speculated that the bruin might have weighed 900 or even 1,000 pounds by the time he went into hibernation in November. But it's unusual for a male black bear to weigh in excess of 600 pounds. The following are average sizes and weights: 2 to 3 feet tall at the shoulders, when standing on all fours; 4½ to 6 feet long, including a 4- to 5-inch tail; and 150 to 400 pounds. In general, males are 33 to 50 percent larger than females.

BLACK BEAR

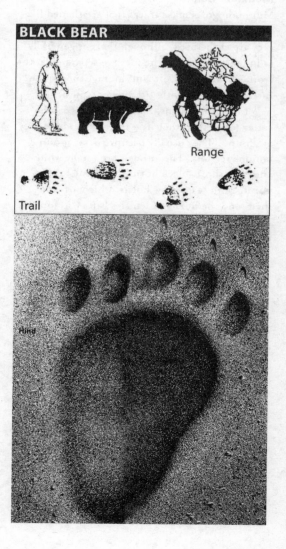

Range

Trail

Hind

Continued ➤

Black bears are often characterized as adaptable, and of all the North American bear species, they have proven the most capable of living alongside humans and in habitats modified by human activities. Perhaps because there were so many huge, fierce predators around during the Pleistocene epoch—everything from lions to dire wolves to short-faced bears the size of ponies—black bears evolved to be somewhat timid, inclined to flee from any potential danger or shinny up a tree when threatened. Black bears, particularly young and lightweight ones, climb up trees in a series of quick, humping bounds; they almost run up the trunks. And since *Ursus americanus* inhabits forested settings, this avenue of escape almost always remains open.

Black bears live in a host of habitats: dense rain forests in the Pacific Northwest; the sparse montane woodlands of the Desert Southwest; cypress swamps in the Deep South; the fertile hardwood forests of the Mid-Atlantic states and New England; lodgepole pine woodlands in the Rockies; redwood forests in California and Oregon; and along the edge of the tree line in northern Canada and Alaska.

Black bears have even begun colonizing the treeless tundra, perhaps in places where grizzlies once occurred but have been extirpated by humans. One such area is northern Labrador and the Ungava Peninsula in northern Quebec east of Hudson Bay. There are historical records of grizzlies inhabiting the region (though not all scientists believe in the validity of the records), and in the 1970s, an anthropologist unearthed a grizzly skull while excavating an eighteenth-century Inuit site on the Labrador coast. What's certain is that in this wild area, black bears have established a population more than 200 miles out onto the "barren ground," as the treeless tundra is known. There they have become more predatory, feeding on caribou—perhaps like the grizzlies that may have ruled the area in the past.

Despite the black bear's great adaptability and recent expansion into certain areas, in the last three centuries the species' range and population have shrunk. In the South and Midwest, much land has been cleared for agriculture, and fewer bears exist in those regions than in the past. In Florida and Louisiana, black bears have become increasingly rare in the wake of urban sprawl and habitat fragmentation. States with no black bears include Illinois, Indiana, Iowa, Kansas, North Dakota, and South Dakota. Recently, black bears have begun spreading from Virginia into Kentucky and from Arkansas into Oklahoma. The Northeast has more bears today than it did a century ago. Several factors have contributed to this increase: Many abandoned farms have grown back into forest, creating excellent bear habitat. State and national parks and forests now safeguard many wooded acres. In the past, people considered bears vermin or dangerous creatures and shot them on sight; today black bears are valued as game animals, and state wildlife biologists manage their populations to remain stable or increase.

No longer persecuted so consistently, black bears have become less shy, and many now venture around rural dwellings and even into towns and the fringes of cities, where they find new and nutritious foods such as garden crops, birdseed, and garbage—foods that can increase the bears' survival and reproduction rates. But rubbing shoulders with people also puts bears in jeopardy. Many are killed by automobiles, and "nuisance bears" are trapped and relocated to more remote settings, placed in zoos, or in some cases euthanized.

Grizzly Bear
(*Ursus arctos*)

With a scientific name that means "northern bear," *Ursus arctos* is found across the Northern Hemisphere in the largest distribution of any bear on earth. In Europe and Asia *Ursus arctos* is known as the brown bear. Most Americans call it the grizzly, a colloquial name describing a pattern of fur coloration—brown with a grayish, or grizzled, tinge—occurring on many bears in the western United States and Canada. Genetic studies have shown that the grizzly bear (*Ursus arctos horribilis*) is actually the same creature as the so-called Alaskan brown bear or Kodiak bear (*Ursus arctos middendorffi*), as well as the brown bears of Europe and Asia. Any and all of those members of the various subspecies or races of Ursus arctos could interbreed and produce fertile young. Up to ten subspecies are recognized worldwide. ... Paleontologists believe that the black bear (*Ursus americanus*) has inhabited North America for several million years, whereas the brown bear is a much more recent immigrant, having crossed the Bering land bridge from Asia to Alaska as recently as 30,000 years ago. In North America, grizzlies thrived in open, treeless habitats created by the retreating glaciers during the ice ages. *Ursus arctos* once ranged from northern Alaska and Canada south through California to Mexico, east to the Mississippi River, and possibly as far east as Labrador and the Ungava Peninsula in northern Quebec. Biologists estimate that from 100,000 to as many as 250,000 grizzlies inhabited the continent in 1800, with 50,000 to 100,000 of them south of Canada. Over the next two centuries, people eliminated many of the bears by shooting, trapping, and poisoning them, and by destroying or changing their habitat—turning it into farmland, housing developments, and highways. The great bears were gone from the Great Plains by 1900. California once had 10,000 grizzlies and was known as the Golden Bear State, but the species was extirpated there by the 1920s. Grizzlies had vanished from Oregon and the Southwest by the mid-1930s.

Today around 50,000 grizzlies remain in North America, most of them in the wilder parts of Canada and Alaska. In the lower forty-eight states, 900 to 1,200 grizzlies survive on less than 1 percent of the species' original range. The two largest populations live in the Greater Yellowstone Ecosystem, a 9,500-square-mile area centered on Yellowstone National Park in northwestern Wyoming, with 400 to 600 individuals, increasing by 2 to 4 percent yearly; and along the Continental Divide in northern Montana, including Glacier National Park, with 400 to 500 bears, thought to be stable or increasing. Other, smaller populations exist in the Cabinet-Yaak Ecosystem in northwestern Montana and northern Idaho, with 30 to 40 bears; the Selkirk Ecosystem in northern Idaho and northeastern Washington, with 40 to 50 bears; and the Northern Cascades Ecosystem in north-central Washington, with fewer than 20 bears.

The words bear and bruin derive from an old Germanic word meaning *brown*, and most grizzly bears are basically brown, but often their pelage shows additional tones of blond, auburn, silver, or black. From a distance, a grizzly's legs may look darker than the animal's sides and back. Like black bears, grizzlies molt during the summer, shedding their old fur and replacing it with a new pelt. When the new fur grows in, the outer guard hairs, which are longer than the insulating underfur, will be darker than the old, bleached-out hairs that they're replacing. So a freshly molted bear will wear a darker pelt than it did before its molt.

A grizzly bear's head is large. Its face has a "dished," or concave, appearance, with the muzzle ending in a broad, upturned snout. The grizzly possesses massive forelegs and a huge chest. A hump of muscle between the front shoulders provides power to the forelegs, for digging out food or excavating dens. (Black bears lack this muscular hump, although under some conditions, and depending on how an individual happens to be standing, a black bear may appear to have a hump.) A grizzly's front claws—digging tools par excellence—are longer than its rear claws and may be 3 to 4 1/2 inches or more in length. The claws are usually pale in color. If a bear's claws are prominent enough that you can see them while the bear is walking, you are probably looking at a grizzly rather than a brown-phase black bear. The rear track of a big grizzly can be 14 inches long and 8 inches wide.

In coastal areas such as Kodiak Island in Alaska, where grizzlies feast on rich marine foods, mature males can weigh 1,000 to 1,500 pounds. These impressive creatures stand almost 5 feet tall at the shoulder when on all fours and approach 10 feet tall when standing on their hind legs. Among inland grizzlies, most adults weigh between 350 and 700 pounds. Individuals living north of the tree line on the arctic tundra are smaller, as are many brown bears of Europe.

Large and sturdy though they may be, grizzlies are also agile and quick. They can sprint over short distances to catch prey as large as elk. They can dart this way and that to nab small, nimble creatures such as ground squirrels. Good swimmers, grizzly bears are able to catch salmon and other fish in the water; in the far north of their range, some of the bears hunt seals by swimming in the sea, much like polar bears. A grizzly's jaws are extremely powerful. When naturalist Terry Domico photographed a large male that researchers had caught in a leg snare, he watched the bruin vent its frustration on a 4-inch-diameter pine, snapping it off with a single bite. The bear had also chewed through several 6- and 8-inch-diameter trees nearby.

Continued ➡

BEAR ATTACKS
Charles Fergus

In recent decades, hiking, birding, fishing, foraging, backpacking, and wilderness canoeing have put more and more people into bear country. Human settlements have expanded to include areas frequented by bears, and bears have been drawn to suburbs and rural dwellings, where food sometimes can be more plentiful than in natural settings, particularly in years when crops of wild nuts and berries fail. Each year, people and bears are coming into increasing contact with each other.

Most bears could kill humans easily if they wanted to. But the fact is that bears rarely harm people. Several factors probably account for this restraint. First, both black and grizzly bears had many other, more-powerful carnivores to contend with during the Pleistocene epoch, which ended only around 10,000 years ago, and that situation built a healthy amount of caution into their temperaments. Second, thanks to our sophisticated weaponry, people are deadlier than bears. We have killed so many bears for so many years that a fear of humans has been passed down through the generations, to the point that it likely has become embedded in their genes. And third, by eliminating aggressive bears, humans have selected far more timid ones; to a certain extent, we have molded the bears that exist in subpolar North America today.

When a bear kills a human, the event often becomes national news. Outdoor magazines regularly print photographs and paintings of snarling, slavering bears—usually grizzlies—pandering to people's fears of large predators. Dramatic films play up the potential for mayhem while ignoring the fact that humans and bruins generally coexist. How dangerous are bears, really? How often do they attack humans?

According to Canadian biologist Stephen Herrero, in an introduction to the 2002 revised edition of *Bear Attacks* (a minor best-seller, with more than 82,000 copies sold since it was first published in 1985), bears killed 29 people in the United States and Canada during the 1990s. Of these, grizzlies killed 18; blacks 11. In comparison, every year in the United States, dogs cause the death of around 15 people and injure 800,000 to the extent that they seek medical attention. Statistics show that while engaged in outdoor recreation, a person is much more likely to be struck by lightning than attacked by a bear. And a person is far more apt to be killed in a car accident while traveling to enjoy the outdoors, en route to a trailhead or trout stream, than to run afoul of a bruin. Each year, bears kill an average of

3 people in North America. Each year, more than 15,000 people are murdered in the United States and 44,000 perish in motor vehicle accidents.

Usually when a bear sees, hears, or smells a human, it runs away—fast. Some bears, however, give ground less readily. A bear that has become used to people—through eating garbage, being fed by folks who like to watch bears, or living in an area crisscrossed by hiking trails—is less likely to flee, because experience has taught it that humans are not an immediate, dangerous threat. Some bears learn that by approaching people, they can sometimes get a free meal. A few garbage-eating bears completely lose their fear of humans. They become dangerous animals, ones that may at some point attack a person. Writes Herrero, "In developed areas where black bears have become habituated to human food or garbage, there is evidence of increased danger from females with cubs."

Bears vary in temperament. One bear may be aggressive—toward both bears and humans. Another may be meek and docile. A bear may behave aggressively when it finds itself in a certain condition or situation, such as a sow that believes her cubs are in danger; a ravenous bear that has just killed a prey animal or found a carcass in springtime and begun feeding on it, only to be confronted suddenly by a person; or a bear that has been startled or hemmed in and concludes that it has no escape route.

In general, black bears are much less aggressive than grizzlies. Since they stay mainly in wooded areas, black bears of all ages can usually climb a tree to escape from danger. In contrast, grizzlies evolved as creatures of open terrain, where trees are few or absent; because their claws are straight, they generally cannot climb trees unless there are conveniently placed, ladderlike limbs. During the Pleistocene, in the grizzly's open, high-plains habitat, females had to be fiercely aggressive to protect their cubs against the many other predators that abounded. Today, when confronted by a potentially dangerous predator—which is probably how most bears view humans—most grizzly sows display that fierceness in defense of their young.

A lot of bears' social behavior amounts to posturing and bluffing. When a bear meets a human, it may behave toward the human as it would toward another bear, particularly if the bear has become habituated to people through feeding on garbage or being fed directly for the humans' entertainment. When a person gets too close to such a bear, the bruin may protect its own personal space by scratching, cuffing, or biting the human—just the sort of behavior it would display toward another bear. That sort

of bear-human interaction is particularly apt to take place in a campground where bears have gotten used to being fed by people—and where the bears have pushed things a bit further and begun appropriating people's food. Sometimes bears bluff-charge people to scare the humans away from their food, a behavior akin to one bear chasing another away from a productive berry patch or a carcass.

In a confrontation with a bear that has been habituated to humans, people have two options. They can abandon their food and supplies, which is usually the best option—and the only sane choice to make when the bear is a grizzly. Or, in the case of a marauding black bear, people can advance toward it, yelling or otherwise making a lot of noise; they can throw sticks and stones, trying to persuade the bruin that the food reward is not worth the pain it may have to suffer to obtain those extra calories. Groups of people are more likely than single humans to be able to drive off a bear trying to steal food.

Bears may also bluff humans in other situations, such as when a sow interprets people's presence or actions as a threat to her cubs. Often people wrongly interpret bluff charges as actual attacks, resulting in bears getting shot unnecessarily. Because they are so powerful, bears try to avoid physical clashes with each other, and the same holds true when bears square off against humans. Herrero notes that "an ability to recognize high- and low-intensity threats by black or grizzly bears" may help a person deduce "when a bear is sufficiently agitated that attack may follow if you do the wrong thing." A bear expresses aggression—also called agonistic behavior—in the way it holds its head, how it positions its mouth and ears, whether it moves forward or retreats, and the sounds it makes. Before traveling in bear country, you should study Herrero's excellent book *Bear Attacks*. You also may want to view videos he helped produce, which illustrate specific components of bears' agonistic behaviors and the correct responses to those behaviors.

Attacks on people by bears that are not habituated to humans may be either defensive or predatory. When humans get too close to a female with cubs, the sow may launch a defensive attack. Often such attacks happen when people surprise bear families. If you learn to identify bear habitat and fresh sign, you can stay away from places where bruins are likely to be feeding or resting, minimizing the odds that you will come in contact with a sow and her young. In grizzly areas, to avoid startling the animals, many hikers announce their presence

Continued ➨

well in advance by talking loudly, singing, or using noisemakers, especially when traveling on trails that curve around slopes or lead through dense vegetation.

If you round a corner and happen upon a bear, watch what the animal does. If it bluffs a charge and then stops, you can probably back away slowly. Do not stare at the bear, because a direct stare is perceived as a threat. Do not run away, as that may trigger a charge. Sometimes you can frighten off a bear by yelling, but the bear may interpret such behavior as aggression and attack. If the bear is a grizzly and a tree is handy, you may be able to climb to a safe height.

If a bear actually attacks you in defense of its cubs or itself, the best tactic is to play dead. Fall on your stomach and clasp your hands behind your head and neck to protect those areas from a damaging bite. (If you are carrying a backpack, it may afford additional protection.) Draw your knees up to your chest to shield your vital organs. Do not move or make a sound, even if the bear bites you or rakes you with its claws. Some hikers have remained so cool during an attack that they have gotten off with injuries no more severe than a few scratches; others have not been so fortunate. In the aftermath of an attack, wait until you are certain that the bear has gone away before moving.

In extremely rare instances, bears attack humans as they would prey. Very few grizzly attacks are predatory in nature; almost all of them are defensive, aimed at keeping the bear safe. In recent years, most, if not all, human deaths and major injuries caused by black bears have resulted from predatory attacks. A black bear living in a remote region may never have seen a human and may look upon a hiker or angler as a potential meal. Some people attacked by predatory black bears have played dead and, as a result, suffered terrible injuries or death. The correct response when attacked by a predatory bear is to fight back. Gouge the bear in the eyes and punch it in the nose. Kick it. Scream at it. If you have an actual or potential weapon, such as a knife or hiking staff, jab it into the bear's face. Try to inflict as much pain as you can.

Many hikers in bear county carry capsaicin spray, derived from extracts of red chili pepper. When pepper spray is shot directly into a bear's eyes, it will usually repel an aggressive or an overly curious bruin. Though it deters both blacks and grizzlies, Herrero points out, "pepper spray is not a substitute for the normal precautions [you should take] when traveling or camping in bear country."

Avoiding Dangerous Encounters

Here are some rules to follow that will minimize your chances of having a bad experience with a bear:

• Ask park personnel or local resource managers if bears in the area where you intend to camp or travel have become habituated to humans, and whether "garbage bears" frequent the area.

• When hiking in grizzly country, use binoculars to scan the terrain ahead of you. If you spot a bear, either retreat or carefully detour far downwind of the animal.

• Continually make noises to let hidden bears know that you are approaching. This is especially important in brush and other areas where visibility is limited.

• Travel in a group of four or more people. Grizzlies have been known to attack lone hikers, pairs, and groups of three, but no attack has been documented on four or more humans.

• Do not camp near a game trail.

• Do not camp in an area where bear droppings or tracks are present.

• Avoid campsites that have trash strewn around—good evidence that bears have gotten into the habit of visiting the site to find garbage or steal food.

• Clean any fish well away from camp. If regulations allow it, dispose of entrails by dumping them in high-volume streams or rivers, which can absorb this detritus without becoming polluted.

• Do your cooking at least 100 yards downwind of where you place your tent.

• Store food away from camp, by hanging it in a tree (this may not effectively deter black bears, which are good at climbing), locking it in a bear-proof plastic cylinder, or placing it inside two or three layers of airtight plastic bags and hiding the bags in vegetation.

• Always sleep in a tent. A bear is much less apt to harm a camper inside a tent than one out in the open.

• Learn as much as you can about bear behavior and ecology by reading books and articles. Your goal should be to enjoy yourself and remain at ease in bear country. Keep in mind that your odds of having a bad experience with a bear are very low indeed. If you do encounter a bear, you want to be able to interpret its behavior and react in ways that minimize any danger.

—From *Bears*

Grizzly bears, particularly females with cubs, are at least as famous for their ferocity as for their strength. The grizzly probably evolved from a forest-dwelling existence to a life on open, treeless terrain. Natural selection favored an animal with longer claws and a musculature that helped it dig for food. It also favored females that aggressively defended their young from other predators, since the bears had taken up residence in an environment offering no trees to climb. Today the grizzly is more apt than the black bear to attack other creatures, including people, particularly when it thinks they're a threat to its young. In his book *True Grizz*, the author and biologist Douglas Chadwick compares grizzlies to humans, both of which, he avers, "possess a lively intelligence and inquisitive nature along with the potential for monstrous behavior."

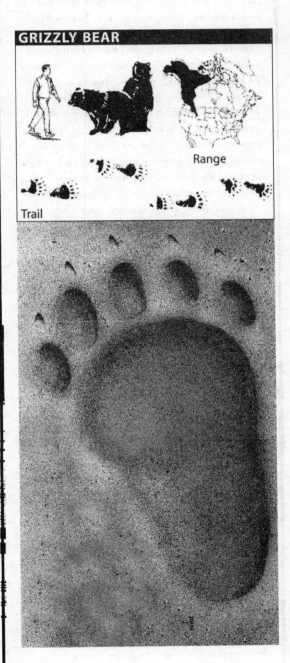

GRIZZLY BEAR

Trail

Range

BEAR SIGN
Charles Fergus

Even if you never see a bear in the wild, you can learn about these intelligent omnivores—and feel their presence in nature—by finding signs of their activities. Based on the evidence at hand, you may be able to deduce what the bear was up to. Biologists refer to this sort of evidence as field sign, while hunters have traditionally called it simply sign. The traces that bears leave in the environment spring from five general categories of ursine behavior: feeding, defecating, resting, traveling, and communicating.

Feeding

Walk along a trail—even a well-used human hiking trail—in bear country, and sooner or later you will probably encounter evidence of bears feeding. Early in the year, before berries ripen and nuts mature, bears eat many insects, particularly grubs, beetles, and ants. Rotten stumps and logs are often broken apart by bruins in search of these insects and their larvae; look for bright, newly exposed yellowish or reddish wood contrasting with the gray, weathered wood that commonly covers logs and stumps. Bears use their powerful shoulders and forelimbs and their claws to get at insect colonies in rotting wood; such colonies occur both in mature forests and in clear-cut areas with abundant slash and stumps. Both black and grizzly bears feed in this manner. You can often find several logs ripped apart in a fairly small area. Pieces of rotten wood several feet away from a log indicate bear work; raccoons and skunks, which also dig for insects in rotten wood, usually do not scatter chips to such a distance.

Check out overturned logs and displaced stones. If you can manage it, push a stone or log back into its original resting place. This may take a fair bit of effort, providing you with a practical demonstration of just how strong a bear is. Claw marks on wood or stone often show where a bear started to pull a log free or dislodge and overturn a stone.

Bears use their paws to scoop open the tops of anthills. They dig out nests of ground wasps, including yellow jackets; look for the nests' gray-brown paper and six-sided honeycombs lying on the ground, in or near the excavation. It can be difficult to distinguish between the workings of raccoons and bears, but holes dug by bears are generally larger and, in areas where wasps are abundant, more numerous. . . .

When black bears climb into trees to feed on flowers, leaves, fruit, and nuts, they may leave sign that remains for years. Beech is a common forest tree in eastern North America, occurring from Nova Scotia south to Florida and west to Wisconsin and Texas. Beech bark is smooth and gray—a perfect surface for recording the claw marks of bruins, which often clamber into beeches to feed on the trees' sweet-tasting nuts. Aspens are also smooth-barked trees; when bears climb into aspens to eat flowers and new foliage in spring, their claw marks show up as black linear scars on the pale greenish gray

bark. The scars may persist for the life of the tree, becoming scablike and expanding as the tree's trunk diameter increases. Deep claw marks and broken branches in oak, sassafras, apple, shadbush, and other food-providing species signify the foraging of bears.

Bears use their strength and weight to break down trees with spindly trunks, as well as shrubs such as highbush blueberry and autumn olive, giving them better access to fruits, nuts, and berries. You may also find a branch or stem that is not broken but has simply been bent down to ground level by a bruin. In late fall, before black bears enter hibernation, they often search for mast in forested areas; using their paws, they sweep aside the leaves covering the ground to expose fallen nuts. Evidence of this sort of feeding is particularly noticeable after a light snowfall.

Bears bite and pull away strips of outer bark from both hardwood and softwood trees to eat the sweet-tasting inner bark: basswood, pine, spruce, tamarack, and fir are species that bears like to feed on. Look for bark strips lying on the ground at the bases of trees. Vertical gouges from bears' teeth may be visible in the exposed wood tissues.

In the high country of the American West, look for holes where grizzlies have dug out roots, tubers, and ground squirrels. Diggings can be as small and subtle as a single divot, or they can be extensive and prominent—as if, according to [biologist, Olaus] Murie, "someone had been sporadically digging a garden plot." Excavations may cover hundreds of square feet. Sometimes a bear rips free and peels back a patch of sod to feed on the roots of grass plants. If hiking in grizzly country, you will want to figure out how recently such an excavation was made: lift up the displaced sod to see whether the vegetation beneath it remains fresh or has become yellow. In habitats edging marine areas in the Pacific Northwest and Alaska, look for places where bears have dug for clams and other shellfish at low tide. . . .

A disturbing and all-too-common sign of a feeding bear is an overturned garbage can in a park or campground, its contents scattered about as the bruin searched for something edible in the trash.

Defecating

A significant percentage of what goes into one end of a bear ultimately comes out the other end. Bears process large quantities of food to fuel their large bodies; a black bear will defecate approximately six to eight times per day. Look for droppings on hiking trails, in wildlife corridors, along logging roads, and in areas where you have found bears' feeding sign.

Biologists have learned much about what bears eat by closely examining their droppings, usually referred to as scats. Wildlife technicians employ forceps and scanning microscopes when studying scats. You don't have to be so systematic; carry along rubber gloves or use a pair of sticks to tease the droppings apart. According to Stephen Herrero in *Bear Attacks*, "Even a superficial examination of the composition of a scat may give you important information." Although he notes that "bear scats seldom smell bad and

probably don't contain parasites transmittable to people," Herrrero recommends against letting them come in contact with the skin. It's always best to take such precautions. A friend of mine once found a dead black bear carcass decomposing in a small pond in Pennsylvania and retrieved the very large skull, which indicated that the bear had been a mature male. From handling the remains, my friend developed a skin infection that took weeks to clear up.

Bear scats vary greatly in size, diameter, and form, depending on the size of the bear that deposited them and what the bruin had been eating. Cubs leave small scats that may look like the droppings of raccoons. Mature bears have the potential to produce large scats—unless the bear was eating certain types of fruits or animal flesh. Blueberries and strawberries, for example, usually result in a shapeless mass, and meat, including fish, generally produces a dark-colored, amorphous scat. Typical adult black bear scats are $1^1/4$ to $2^1/2$ inches in diameter and 5 to 12 inches long. Grizzly bears leave scats that are $1^1/4$ to almost 3 inches in diameter and 7 to 20 or more inches long. These figures are approximations, and scats of the two species are difficult and sometimes impossible to tell apart, even by trained technicians.

Bear scats often break up into segments as they are deposited and may show blunt, broken ends. Observers have compared them to horse droppings and human feces, although horse manure usually forms a more copious pile, is lighter in color, and contains smaller plant fragments, and human feces tend to be smaller and less abundant than bear droppings.

The remains of plant items often can be distinguished in bear scats, including grasses, roots, bulbs, nuts, corn, seeds, and fruit pits. Bears are adept at plucking berries from bushes, so you probably won't find many twigs or stems in their droppings. Scats may contain insect remains such as shiny red and black body parts of ants, black-and-yellow wasp parts, or beetle carapaces. Lab technicians regularly find and identify items as small as ant antennae and earthworm bristles. If a bear has been feeding on carrion, its droppings may contain the remains of fly larvae or scavenger beetles. Indigestible parts of prey, such as hair, feathers, claws, teeth, bones, or beaks may show up in scats.

Meat scats usually stink, particularly when fresh. Vegetation scats lack a foul odor. Some foods, such as mushrooms, leave no identifiable traces. Bits of aluminum foil and plastic embedded in dung signify a bear getting into garbage.

Resting

During spring, summer, and fall, black bears may locate their day beds at the bases of substantial, climbable trees, particularly conifers with tall, straight trunks. Mother bears leave their young cubs beneath trees while going off to forage. The cubs rest beneath the trees, which they can quickly climb to escape danger. Vermont tracking expert Susan Morse has dubbed these "baby-sitter trees." Adults' beds show up as oval depressions about 2 feet wide by

Continued ➡

3 feet long in leaves, grass, or fallen needles.

Bears also rest out of sight in shrub thickets, including mountain laurel and rhododendron, and in stands of young conifers. Grizzlies loaf among dense willows and alders. Black bears site their day beds on high ground in swamps and on exposed knolls in steep areas. In chilly weather, both black and grizzly bears may build beds. They tear or bite limbs off trees and shrubs and gather them into a pad that elevates the resting bear above the ground; sometimes grasses and conifer boughs are added to the mattress. Along salmon rivers in Alaska, grizzlies rake moss into piles to form beds. A concentration of scats may indicate a bedding area, and bear hairs may be wedged into the bark of nearby trees, against which bears purposely rub.

Bear dens are some of hardest types of sign to find, but they are among the most exciting to locate. Grizzlies often den on steep, south-facing slopes above timberline. A bear may begin several dens before deciding to complete one and hibernate in it. These "den starts" show up as sizable holes in open terrain, with accompanying fringes or piles of dirt. Grizzlies may begin these digs in early autumn; try scanning for them at this time, using binoculars or a spotting scope.

Entrances to black bear dens vary greatly in size, but many are between 18 and 24 inches tall and approximately as wide. In late autumn, dens may be marked by heaps of newly excavated soil. Black bears are fairly unaggressive animals, but humans still should not go too close to suspected dens at times of the year when the lairs may be occupied. Bears disturbed or startled out of their dens during hibernation burn up calories that their bodies need to survive winter. In summer, when bears are not inside their winter dens, peek into rock crevices and hollows in large logs and at the bases of trees. Look for hairs snagged on rough edges of den entrances. Claw marks may be visible on large trees with cavities partway up heir trunks.

Traveling

In moving from place to place, bears leave sign in the form of tracks and trails. As Herrero suggests in *Bear Attacks*, "Seeing bear tracks can be better than actually seeing the bear"—particularly true where grizzlies are concerned. Bears move about on paths, game trails, woods roads, stream banks, and wetlands edges. A good time to look for their sign is a day or two after a rain, when you are most likely to find fresh, sharp examples impressed in mud. Grizzlies and black bears make similar tracks, although there can be noticeable differences between the two species. A simplified description of bear tracks follows; for more information, consult a field guide of animal tracks and sign.

A bear track usually includes three components: toes (with or without marks made by the claws), front pads, and heel pads. The front feet differ somewhat from the back feet and are slightly smaller. When a bear is walking, its back feet often come down directly on top of the prints made by the front feet on the animal's same side. When a bear moves at a rate faster than a walk, its rear feet print ahead of its front feet.

The following information on size and stride of bear tracks is drawn from Mark Elbroch's *Mammal Tracks and Sign*:

In adult black bears, front tracks are 3 3/4 to 8 inches long by 3 1/4 to 6 inches wide; rear tracks are 5 3/8 to 8 7/8 inches long by 3 1/2 to 6 inches wide. In grizzlies, front tracks are 7 to 13 1/2 inches long by 5 to 8 3/4 inches wide; rear tracks are 8 1/4 to 14 inches long by 4 5/8 to 8 1/2 inches wide. Records exist, however, of grizzly tracks 16 inches long. In black bears, the stride, or distance between tracks, varies from 17 to 25 inches while walking to 24 to 60 inches during a full gallop. Track groups, the area where all four feet print close together, can be as far apart as 75 inches if a bear was galloping. In grizzlies, the stride varies from 19 to 29 inches while walking to 30 to 35 inches at a gallop. Track groups of galloping grizzlies can be 95 inches (almost 8 feet) apart. The trail width—essentially the distance from the outside edges of the left and right tracks—is 6 to 14 inches in blacks and 10 to 20 inches in grizzlies.

In general, grizzlies leave larger tracks than blacks, which can be important to know in areas where both species occur. A female grizzly may leave a track about the same size as that of a male black bear, however.

Bears walk slightly up on their front toes, which often prevents the round heel pad of the front foot from registering. Bears have five toes on each foot, but not all of them may be represented in a track, depending on the firmness of the surface, such as sand, mud, packed dirt, or snow, into which the track was pressed. In bears, the "big toe" is the outer one on each foot, not the inner one as in humans. Sometimes the innermost "little toe" leaves only a faint mark, or no mark at all, making a footprint that appears to be four-toed. In grizzlies, the claws may make small, round holes in the ground well in front of the toe marks. The claw marks of black bears, which have shorter claws, print closer to the ends of the toes.

Both black and grizzly bears have a curious habit of placing their feet in the same spot each time when walking on established trails. This results in a series of shallow pits or worn circles that zigzag down the path. Videos made of bears using such trails show the bruins walking stiff-legged and twisting their feet while in contact with the ground, as if intentionally deepening the trail pattern. Elbroch writes, "Many researchers believe that these trails are a marking behavior, whereby bears leave scent from the glands on their feet and rub it into the earth."

Depending on where it is made, a trail can become quite prominent over time and with repeated use. Traditional bear trails show up dramatically in moss. Grizzlies often create highly visible trails through brush along salmon streams in western Canada and Alaska. Grizzlies wear deep paths into tundra and high mountain areas above the tree line, trails that are often visible from the air. Over the years, a trail may become a pair of parallel furrows, like a miniature wagon trail. Writes Murie, "I have walked in such bear trails but found it awkward, for the brown bear's hips and shoulders are much greater than a man's, and I found it necessary to spraddle widely to keep in the ruts." In wooded terrain, a bear trail often will go under obstructions, such as leaning trees or low branches, that a large grazing animal—an elk, for instance—would be forced to detour around.

Communicating

Bears bite and rub against trees and shrubs to leave social messages. Bears want other bears to read those messages, so they intend for the signposts to be conspicuous. When biologists searched for bear trees in Tennessee, they found them on ridgelines, in valley bottoms, and along game trails, hiking paths, and dirt roads. In Minnesota, researchers located bear trees in forest openings and at the edges of the openings. Both the Tennessee and Minnesota studies were conducted in black bear habitats; in northern and western North America, grizzlies mark trees in similar ways and settings.

A bear tree is very different from a tree that a bear has fed on, climbed into, or scrambled up to find denning shelter or escape danger. Often a bear tree is situated next to a well-used trail, where it can be easily seen. A side trail made by bears visiting the tree may loop off from another, larger trail. Sometimes distinct pits made by bears setting their feet in the same spots, year after year and generation after generation, lead up to a bear tree.

A bear creates a marker tree by taking a bite out of the bark. Most bites are made about 5 feet above the ground (though they can be lower or higher than that) and face a trail or an open area. Over the years, other bears may enlarge the breach. Often a considerable chunk of bark is removed—up to 3 feet in length, in some cases. If the tree is a softwood, it will ooze resin from the gash; if a hardwood, a raised callus may form around the bite as the tree tries to close off the wound with its bark. Look for tooth and claw marks on marker trees.

Bear trees vary in size. Some are only a few inches in diameter, whereas others have trunks several feet wide. Some marker trees end up bitten almost entirely through. When bears girdle trees, the trees will die; spotting a dead or dying tree near a trail can lead you to an old marker tree. Bears also mark utility poles, trail signs, and human structures such as sheds and porch posts.

As they rub their backs, necks, and shoulders against objects, bears often leave fur sticking to resin or hooked into upraised splinters or chips. Bear hair looks like thin human hair; it is not coarse, like the hair of an elk or moose. The hair matches the coat color of the bear, although it may bleach out over time. Grizzly hairs often have silver or white tips.

Bears also use their jaws to snap off saplings and shrubs in travel corridors, feeding habitats, and areas where females are raising cubs, perhaps as a type of communication. Elbroch speculates that bears may also bite trees as a form of displacement behavior that alleviates frustration or sends a warning. Twice he came face-to-face with cornered black bears that had no obvious escape route. "Both bears stood up," he writes, "and repeatedly raked their claws on tree bark, leaving impressive and unmistakable signs while staring me down, vocalizing, and jaw-popping."

—From *Bears*

Continued ➡

Polar Bear
(*Ursus maritimus*)

Polar bears differ from other bears so markedly, in form, habits, and habitat, that it's hard to believe they are closely related to brown bears—so closely related, in fact, that polar bears and brown bears have mated in captivity and produced fertile offspring. Although the definition of a single species is a group of animals that can mate and produce fertile young, scientists nevertheless classify the polar bear as a species all its own. Paleontologists believe that *Ursus maritimus* branched off from *Ursus arctos* only 250,000 to 100,000 years ago, in the Pleistocene, perhaps in Siberia during a period of intense glaciation when the advancing ice cut off a northern population of brown bears, which then evolved separately. Should their divergent evolution continue, at some point polar bears will differ enough from brown bears that the two will not be able to produce offspring. In nature, brown bears and polar bears live in separate areas and have developed completely different reproductive behaviors and timing, so that the two types never mate.

The polar bear is considered to be the largest and most powerful land predator on earth. It is twice the size of a Siberian tiger and three times as large as an African lion. Adult males weigh 650 to more than 1,750 pounds. A large male can reach 5 feet tall at the shoulders while on all fours and 10 feet long from the nose to the tip of the tail; standing on its back legs, it towers 11 feet tall. Females are one-half to three-quarters the size of mature males and weigh an average of 330 to 700 pounds.

The pure white coat of the polar bear provides camouflage against ice and snow. The whiteness is interrupted by black eyes and a black nose and lips. As the arctic explorer Vilhjalmur Stefansson wrote, "No stone, no bare spot in the snow, no dark shadow is as black as the polar bear's nose." The fur is extremely dense. The long outer guard hairs are hollow, providing better insulating value. These hairs are clear, lacking in pigment altogether; they look white because they reflect and scatter visible light. Beneath that pale blanket, the skin is black, maximizing solar heat gain. In addition to its fur, a polar bear is insulated by a layer of fat, or blubber, up to 2 to 4 inches thick and lying just beneath the skin.

The hollow, air-filled fur, along with its blubber, help buoy a polar bear up in the water. The fur insulates when dry, but when the fur gets soaked, it is the blubber that provides a warm barrier against the cold. The name *Ursus maritimus* means "sea bear," and polar bears are strong swimmers. They can dive as deep as 15 feet and stay submerged for more than two minutes. They have been spotted swimming many miles out to sea.

The polar bear is almost exclusively a meat eater. It has long, sharp canine teeth. The carnassials—the flesh-shearing teeth between the canines and molars—are pointed and sharp-edged, in contrast to the flattened ones of brown and black bears. The polar bear has a proportionally smaller head than other bears, which it extends through holes in the ice to catch seals.

Its long neck increases the polar bear's reach and allows the animal to hold its head above water while swimming. The front paws are huge—up to a foot in diameter. With partial webbing between the toes, they serve as paddles when the bear swims.

Dense fur pads the soles of the feet, improving traction on ice. The exposed skin on the bottom of the feet, in areas that contact the ground directly, is resistant to frostbite. The skin is also studded with numerous pliable, microscopic bumps that keep the feet from slipping. The external ears are small to minimize heat loss. Polar bears are believed to have fairly sharp vision; studies suggest that they may be somewhat farsighted. Their eyes appear to be sensitive to low light levels, important to an animal that hunts during the arctic winter. There is no evidence that polar bears ever suffer from snow blindness, so perhaps some as-yet-unknown adaptation shields their retinas from damaging ultraviolet rays reflected from snow and ice.

Polar bears live on the ice that covers the polar sea to the north of Alaska, Canada, Greenland, Norway, and the former Soviet Union. They do not occur at the South Pole. Many of the white bears come onto land during summer, when the sea ice melts. On land, they generally do not eat much food; in an adaptation not dissimilar to the hibernation of bears in more southerly latitudes, they enter a period of inactivity that some scientists call "walking hibernation." Some bears enter caves in the permafrost where they can keep cool and escape from biting flies.

Biologists recognize six core populations around the fringes of the Polar Basin, each centered on a traditional seal-hunting and denning area. A separate group of bears lives farther south, on and adjacent to Hudson and James Bays in Canada. Canada has 15,000 polar bears, most of them in the Northwest Territories. An estimated 25,000 to 40,000 polar bears exist worldwide, twice what the population is thought to have been in the 1960s, when the five nations where *Ursus maritimus* lives began cooperating to limit hunting and safeguard critical habitats.

Polar bears are vulnerable to oil spilled by tankers and discharged from ships. The oil can cause a bear's fur to clump together, reducing its insulating properties. Bears groom themselves by licking their fur, and if they accidentally ingest oil, it can poison them. Scientists have found that oil has caused intestinal ulcers, lung collapse, anemia, and kidney failure in polar bears. The increase in offshore drilling for oil in the Arctic could have significant effects on the white bears and their prey. Climate change is another environmental threat. Today global warming—which most scientists agree is caused largely by humans' burning of fossil fuels—is spurring an earlier breakup of sea ice in the spring and thinner ice year-round. These changes have great potential for disrupting the annual cycle of polar bear life.

—Text from *Bears*
Illustrations from *Track Pack: Animal Tracks in Full Life Size*

Armadillos
Richard P. Smith

The only category I could think of to label armadillos under is miscellaneous. They are so unlike any other animal in North America, and the same goes for their tracks. There are five stubby, long-nailed toes on rear feet and four on the shorter front feet. Toenail marks are usually visible in tracks of all feet because the animals are diggers and their claws are well developed.

Toes on front feet are paired, with the two middle ones noticeably longer than the toes on the outside. There is a distinct V formed between the equal-lengthed middle toes. The other two toes are positioned opposite one another on either side of front feet, but those on the inside are slightly shorter than those on the outside. The location of these toes reminds me of the positioning of dew claws on pigs' feet.

On rear feet, the three middle toes are grouped together with two much shorter toes back behind those on either side of the feet. As on front feet, small toes on the inside of hind feet are slightly shorter than those on the outside. The two outside toes of the group of three in front are paired, with a slightly longer toe between them.

Front feet range in length from a little under 2 inches to a little over. Hind feet are slightly longer. Since the armadillo's legs are short, the animal may drag its tail, partially brushing out tracks when walking in sand.

Armadillos cannot be mistaken for any other animal in appearance. They literally wear a coat of armor and try to curl up for protection when attacked. Their shells have nine bands around them and are brown to gray in color. Armadillos average about the size of domestic cats, weighing up to 17 pounds.

These animals are primarily insect eaters, but also eat lizards, scorpions, eggs, and berries. They sometimes dig in anthills or elsewhere in the ground while feeding and may uproot small trees in the process. Rooting in the ground by armadillos may be confused with that of other animals, so look for tracks to confirm what animal was responsible. Burrows dug by these animals are conical in shape, between 7 and 8 inches in diameter and up to 15 feet in length, but may be much shorter.

Front

Hind

Armadillo track. (Sketch courtesy of Sue Adams.)

Armadillos are presently in the process of extending their range. They are found in states between and including New Mexico and Florida, with Kansas now the northern limit of their range. Like skunks, armadillos are commonly killed by cars on highways, and are considered pests to some degree. Mothballs are an effective repellent.

—From *Animal Tracks and Signs of North America*

Calls of the Wild: Sounds of Common Mammals

Lang Elliott

Mammals are distinguished by their covering of hair or fur as well as the mammary glands that nourish their young. Over 350 species inhabit North America. Most are nocturnal, secretive, and silent. However, a small number of species regularly produce loud and obvious night sounds that are among the most fascinating and human-like of all animal sounds.

Coyote: A grayish, doglike mammal with erect, pointed ears and a drooping tail carried low when running. Up to 4 feet long; weighs 18 to 30 pounds, with some individuals up to 50 pounds. Timid and wary. Inhabits deserts, prairies, and open woodlands in the West, and brushy forest in the East. Hybridizes with dogs and wolves. Vocalizes at night and at dusk and dawn. Produces outbursts of high-pitched and vibrant yips, yaps, and yapping howls that often end with a shrill, broken scream.

Raccoon: Common and widespread. Recognized by black mask over its eyes and alternating rings of yellow and black on its bushy tail. About 24 inches long; weighs up to 35 pounds. Chiefly nocturnal in habits. Dens in hollow trees, sometimes as a family group. In the wild, feeds mostly along the shorelines of streams and lakes. Also common in suburban areas where it raids trash cans for garbage. During fights, raccoons growl, bark, whine, and produce snarling screams that many people confuse with sounds made by quarreling housecats. Also make garbled, twittering sounds.

American Beaver: A widespread aquatic mammal with a broad, flat, hairless tail. About 28 inches long with 10-inch tail; adults weigh 30 to 60 pounds. Makes dams of sticks and mud and lives in conical houses made of same. Chiefly nocturnal, but active at dusk and dawn. Feeds on the bark of living trees. Gnaws through limbs and trunks with huge front teeth and strips away the bark. An alarmed beaver slaps its tail against the water and then dives. The loud gnawing sounds of a feeding beaver can be heard several hundred feet away on a quiet night. Young make plaintive moaning sounds, usually from inside the den.

Porcupine: Heavy-bodied and clumsy-looking, with a lumbering walk. Recognized by sharp spines or quills emerging from fur on head, back, and tail. Up to 2 feet long with 10-inch tail; weighs 10 to 25 pounds. Prefers coniferous and mixed woods that grow in the West and Northeast and throughout Canada. Strips bark off trees and also eats buds, roots, and so forth. Readily climbs trees; primarily nocturnal in habits. Porcupines are seldom heard, but make a variety of grunts, groans, and cries, especially during the fall breeding season. Expressive, whining squeals are made by agitated porcupines during aggressive encounters.

River Otter: A sleek, streamlined mammal with webbed toes and a heavy, rounded tail tapering to a point; excellent swimmer. Dark brown above, pale below. Over 2 feet long, with 15-inch tail. Associated with rivers, lakes, and streams, where it feeds on fish, frogs, crayfish, and so on. Principally nocturnal in habits. Gregarious and playful; often travels in family groups. Otters are usually silent, but they do make a variety of chirps, grunts, barks, and low growls. A prominent sound is a loud snort, given upon surfacing and periodically when feeding.

White-tailed Deer: The most widespread and familiar deer of North America. Adults about 6 feet long, with weights of 100 to 300 pounds or more (males are larger than females). Males grow and shed antlers annually. Prefers woodland edge habitats and thrives in agricultural areas with abundant forest cover. Most active at dusk and dawn. Whitetails are usually silent, but alarmed individuals respond with loud, airy snorts, sometimes accompanied by foot-stomping: *WHIEW!* They may then bound away excitedly with white-bottomed tail held erect.

—From *A Guide to Night Sounds*

Mammals to Avoid

Bears

Greg Davenport
Illustrations by Steven A. Davenport

Polar Bears

DESCRIPTION
Polar bears are large, white, four-footed carnivores (meat eaters) that range in size from 350 to 1,100 pounds. The adult male is larger (8 to 11 feet long) and appears leaner than the smaller, stocky female (6 to 8 feet long). In addition, the male has a longer neck and higher rump than the female. These bears can be found in Alaska, Canada, Russia, Greenland, and Norway. Polar bears are very nomadic and can be seen on pack ice, coastal islands, coastlines, and even out in arctic waters. Around November, pregnant female polar bears dig dens and hibernate, emerging in late March or early

Polar bear.

April with their newborn cubs.

WHAT YOU SHOULD KNOW
As a carnivore, a polar bear's primary diet consists of seals, but when hungry, they have been known to prey on humans. They have an acute sense of smell, so when you're in polar bear country, make every effort to eliminate or reduce odors on yourself and in your camp.

BEFORE YOU GO
The best advice I can give is to avoid polar bear country. If you intend to travel in one of these areas, however, ask park or forest rangers about possible bear activity in the area where you are headed, and take time to research seasonal bear sightings there. If you are unfamiliar with an area or information is scarce, you should consider hiring a local guide.

ONCE YOU GO
Always be on the lookout for polar bears, and avoid traveling when visibility is poor. Avoiding areas where polar bears concentrate can reduce the potential for aggressive interaction. These areas include boulders, pressure ridges, coastlines, icebergs, islets just offshore, maternal den sites, summer retreats, and fall staging sites where bears congregate to wait for ice to form. Since polar bears are curious creatures with an acute sense of smell, keep food and garbage in bearproof containers, and stay away from carcasses. Menstruating females should use tampons instead of pads, placing used ones in a bearproof garbage container. Since polar bears rarely do a bluff charge, a rapidly approaching bear should be interpreted as aggression that will end in physical contact. With this in mind, protect your camp by using a warning system, trained alert dogs, or both to warn of a polar bear's approach. If a bear is spotted, go immediately to a safe and secure location, like a building. If this is not possible, deterrents like pepper spray and loud noises are sometimes helpful, as long as you know how to use them. If a polar bear attacks, use any weapon to try to dissuade it from continuing its aggressive behavior.

Brown Bears

DESCRIPTION
Brown bears, called grizzlies in the Lower 48, are four-footed omnivores, meaning they eat both vegetation and animals. They range in size from 300 to 850 pounds, with an average height of 3.5 to 4 feet at the shoulder when on all four legs, and 6 to 7 feet when standing upright. Its distinctive shoulder hump, color, and long snout distinguish the brown bear from other bears. These bears can be found in Alaska, Wyoming, Montana, Idaho, and Washington, as well as Canada, eastern and western Europe, northern Asia, and Japan. The brown bear lives in a variety of environments that include dense forests, subalpine meadows, and arctic tundra. The brown bear's diet varies greatly; it has been known to eat grasses, sedges, roots, berries, insects, fish, carrion, and small and large mammals. Brown bears hibernate during winter months, until April or May, usually five to eight months.

Brown bear.

WHAT YOU SHOULD KNOW
Contrary to popular legend, encounters with grizzly bears are infrequent, and grizzlies do not naturally behave aggressively toward humans. As

Continued ➡

solitary animals, these bears actually try to avoid contact with other bears and people. The rage grizzly attack occurs when the bear has been surprised, it feels the need to protect its cubs or food, it is sick or wounded, or a human is acting in an aggressive fashion. The importance of keeping grizzlies out of human food and garbage cannot be stressed enough. Once a bear becomes accustomed to these food sources, it will lose its natural fear of close contact with humans. The brown bear uses its acute sense of smell, keen eyesight, and excellent hearing to stay abreast of its surroundings and can often be seen standing on its hind legs to obtain more information from these senses. A grizzly bear can run and climb a tree faster than you can.

Before You Go
Talk to park or forest rangers about possible bear activity in the area where you are headed, and take time to research seasonal bear sightings there. Let someone know where you are going and when you plan to return.

Once You Go
To avoid sudden encounters, stay on well-established trails, be aware of your surroundings, and make noise by occasionally yelling, clapping, or wearing a bear bell. Watch for bear signs like tracks, scat, torn-up logs, and turned-over rocks. If you have children with you, keep them close by. Do not let them wander off-trail and into the wilderness. Since bears have an acute sense of smell, always cook away from your campsite, and sleep in different clothes than those you cooked in. Should you encounter a grizzly bear, stay calm, and determine the potential risk before deciding what to do. A calm, curious bear often stands on its hind legs, sniffing the air. If a bear is looking in your direction, avoid direct eye contact, speak in a soft monotone, and slowly back away. Never turn your back and run, as this may precipitate a bear attack. Before backing away, if you have a hat or bandanna (a good thing to have when in bear country), drop it on the ground. An approaching bear will often stop to sniff the object, which gives you more time to distance yourself from it. If a bear charges, stand your ground. Bears often "bluff charge" several times before leaving. If the bear is not bluffing and makes contact with you, play dead by curling into a ball or lying flat, while covering your neck with your hands and arms. Since your backpack adds protection, leave it on. During the attack, stay facedown, and don't move or make a sound until the bear is gone. When prepared in advance and used correctly, a deterrent like bear pepper spray can be effective at repelling an approaching bear.

Black Bears

Description
Black bears are four-footed omnivores, eating both vegetation and animals. They range in size from 100 to 300 pounds. In addition to being smaller than the brown bear, black bears do not have a shoulder hump, and their snout is shorter and less pointed. American black bears are found in thirty-two states, as well as Mexico and Canada. Black bears are primarily found in forested areas, including the tundra, and wetlands. The bear's diet primarily consists of nuts and berries but can also include other plants, insects, small mammals, carrion, salmon,

and an occasional young deer or moose calf. Most black bears hibernate during the winter months. In areas of warmer weather and an available food supply, however, black bears have been known not to hibernate at all. Like the grizzly, a black bear can run and climb a tree faster than you can.

What You Should Know
Encounters with black bears are infrequent, and black bears do not naturally behave aggressively toward humans. As solitary animals, these bears actually try to avoid contact with other bears and people. The rare attack occurs when the bear has been surprised, it feels the need to protect its cubs or food, it is sick or wounded, or a human is acting in an aggressive fashion.

Black bear.

Once You Go
Black bears are rarely a threat to the backcountry traveler, since they often turn and run away when startled by a human. Should a black bear attack, however, deterrents like pepper spray and loud noises are sometimes helpful, as long as you know how to use them. If deterrents don't work and an attack appears imminent, use any weapon to try to dissuade the bear from continuing its aggressive behavior.

—From *Surviving Cold Weather*

Pumas

Greg Davenport
Illustration by Steven A. Davenport

Description
The puma is also known as cougar, mountain lion, panther, and catamount. Pumas average 3.5 to 5.5 feet in length and can weigh up to 225 pounds. They are found throughout the Western Hemisphere, from Canada to Argentina, residing in coniferous forests, swamps, grasslands, and tropical forests. The puma's diet primarily consists of large mammals, such as deer, but they have also been known to eat smaller game, including beavers, rabbits, squirrels, and mice.

What You Should Know
Encounters with pumas are infrequent, and pumas do not naturally behave aggressively toward humans. As solitary animals, these cats

Puma.

actually try to avoid contact with other cats and people. The rare puma attack occurs when the cat has been surprised, it feels the need to protect its cubs or food, it is sick or wounded, or a human is acting in an aggressive fashion.

Before You Go
Talk to park or forest rangers about possible puma activity in the area where you are headed, and take time to research seasonal puma sightings there. Let someone know where you are going and when you plan to return.

Once You Go
To avoid sudden encounters, stay on well-established trails, be aware of your surroundings, and avoid hiking alone or at dawn and dusk, when pumas are most active. If you have children with you, keep them close by. Do not let them wander off-trail or into the wilderness. Should you encounter a puma, stay calm, and try to make yourself appear bigger by opening your coat or standing close to another person while slowly backing away. If the cat continues to act in an aggressive manner, throw stones or sticks at it. Should it attack, protect your neck, and aggressively fight back using anything at your disposal.

—From *Surviving Cold Weather*

Gray Wolves

Greg Davenport
Illustration by Steven A. Davenport

Description
The gray wolf is a four-footed carnivore that ranges in size from 55 to 150 pounds and stands approximately 26 to 32 inches at the shoulder. Gray wolves are found in Alaska, Idaho, Michigan, Minnesota, Montana, Wisconsin, and Wyoming, as well as Canada, Europe, Asia, the Middle East, and Russia. They are primarily located in forests, tundra, deserts, plains, and

Gray wolf.

mountains. The wolf's diet mainly consists of large, hoofed mammals, such as deer and elk, though on occasion they also prey on smaller animals, such as beavers or rabbits.

What You Should Know
Encounters with wolves are infrequent, and wolves do not naturally behave aggressively toward humans. Wolves live in packs, which include a dominant alpha male and female, along with their offspring, and they communicate by scent marking, vocalizing, facial expressions, and body postures.

Once You Go
To avoid sudden encounters, stay on well-established trails, be aware of your surroundings, and avoid hiking alone or at dawn and dusk, when wolves are most active. If you have children with you, keep them close by. Do not let them wander

Continued ➡

Animals and Insects

off-trail or into the wilderness. Wolves are generally shy and timid, and the likelihood of an attack is extremely remote.

—From *Surviving Cold Weather*

Moose

Greg Davenport
Illustration by Steven A. Davenport

DESCRIPTION

Moose are four-footed vegetarians that can weigh as much as 1,600 pounds and stand as tall as 6.5 feet at the shoulder. They are found in the northern United States, Canada, Europe, and Asia, usually in forested areas. A moose's

Moose.

WHY THE MOOSE IS DANGEROUS

Allan A. Macfarlan

Some hunters say that there are two dangerous kinds of game in North America—the big western bears and the moose. Many hunters and other outdoorsmen have been killed by moose; sometimes the bull is so driven by the frenzy of the rut that he will charge anything that annoys him. When moose first see a human being, they often stand and stare at the man for a while before running off. Some observers say that this is due to a low-level nervous system that reacts slowly. Others believe that the bull is contemplating an attack. Most of the time, the moose tries to fade away, but sometimes, especially during the rut, the animal will make an all-out charge. Cows are less belligerent, but if a cow has young nearby, she can be nearly as dangerous as the bull.

Like all other North American deer, the moose uses his antlers in fights with rival males. Since his long legs give him a long reach, when fighting wolves, man, and other predators, the moose uses his sharp-pointed front hoofs, which can disembowel a man in one stroke.

—From *Exploring the Outdoors with Indian Secrets*

diet primarily consists of new tree growth (aspen, poplar, willow, birch, dogwood, and balsam fir) and underwater vegetation. Although moose can run fast, a large percentage of yearlings fall prey to wolves and bears.

WHAT YOU SHOULD KNOW

Moose are generally solitary animals and are not normally aggressive toward humans. The rare moose attack occurs during mating season, when the animal believes its calf or food is threatened, it is tired of walking in deep snow, or it is being harassed by people.

ONCE YOU GO

To avoid sudden encounters, stay on well-established trails, and be aware of your surroundings. Should you encounter a moose and it begins walking toward you, stay calm, back away, and look for a tree or other object to put between you and the animal. Like brown bears, moose will often do a bluff charge. Unlike your behavior with the bear, however, you should run and look for a tree or other obstacle to get between you and a charging moose. If a moose should knock you down, curl up into a fetal position, and use your arms and hands to protect your neck and head. Do not move until the moose has left and is a safe distance away from you.

—From *Surviving Cold Weather*

Skunks

Elizabeth P. Lawler
Illustrations by Pat Archer

Striped Skunk
(*Mephitis mephitis*)

Although skunks are considered nocturnal animals, they often begin foraging during the late afternoon or early evening hours. They have a fine sense of smell and very good hearing, important since they hunt at night. Striped skunks are nearsighted, however, which makes it relatively easy for us to get close to them. If you move quietly and slowly toward a grazing skunk, you can usually get within ten feet of it without disturbing it. If this makes you nervous, you can make accurate observations from as far away as twenty feet. The skunk will use its warning system to tell you if you get too close. Remember, the skunk does not want to spray you, so back away when you see it raise its tail. ...

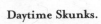

Daytime Skunks. Although skunks are generally nocturnal, you may find one foraging during the day, especially during warm winter days. You also can expect to see newly weaned skunks foraging in cornfields, hay fields, pastures, fencerows, and along waterways in daylight. Although nocturnal animals that have the disease rabies are often seen out of their dens during the day, they usually exhibit more

The striped skunk (Mephitis mephitis) assumes its infamous U posture before spraying musk.

than one behavioral abnormality such as aggression toward other animals. If unusual behavior raises questions about the health of a particular skunk, call a wildlife specialist. Do not harm the skunk or approach it. ...

Voice. Skunks are quiet animals. They hunt and play in silence, although when a fight breaks out between two skunks you will hear a barrage of growls, squeals, and hisses. When foraging or when tending their pups, you may hear soft grunts, growls, barks, and churrings. Snarls and twitters that resemble those made by birds and squirrels are also in the skunk vocabulary. ...

The Warning. It is well known that skunks will not discharge a blast of musk without ample warning, so it is a good idea to learn how to recognize it. An unconcerned, relaxed striped skunk ambles along with its tail nearly touching the ground. As the first signal in the warning system the skunk may stamp its front feet. It does this rapidly and loudly enough that you can hear it several yards away. You may also hear growls or hissing sounds at this time. Many skunks omit this first step and proceed directly to the tail-raising signal. In this stage the major portion of the tail is held erect, but the tip may flop over to one side. The long guard hairs along the entire length of the tail stick out at right angles to it. This makes the tail look extremely large. Immediately before musking, the skunk assumes its infamous U posture, at which time its head and tail directly face the intruder. If you are still considered a threat at this point, the skunk will probably spray you.

Myths. Like other creatures of the night, many myths surround the lives and habits of skunks. Following is a list of some of them:

- *Musk can damage your eyes.* The truth is that although musk can cause intense burning, it does not cause permanent damage to the eyes.

- *Skunks spray musk with their tails.* Scientists know that they spray with nipples that are connected to anal sacs.

- *Musk is made of urine.* Musk has its own chemical composition that is very different from skunk urine.

- *Skunks are aggressive.* They are not. They are among the peaceable animals in the forest. ...

Spotted Skunk
(*Spilogale putorius*).

This little skunk is smaller than its cousin the striped skunk. Its weight ranges from a mere three-fourths of a pound to two and three-fourths pounds, and its total length can be from about fourteen inches to twenty-two inches. Generally, the spotted skunk doesn't venture from its den until after nightfall, and it is more secretive than the striped skunk. ...

Alarm Display. The spotted skunk has a fasci-

The spotted skunk performs its famous handstand before musking.

Continued →

043
Survival Wisdom & Know-How

nating alarm display. Like the striped skunk, its gives its first warning by stamping its feet and then raising its tail. If these signs do not deter the intruder, the spotted skunk displays its famous handstand. When raised up on its two front feet it looks larger than it really is, and its agility in this position rivals that of a high-wire performer. There is no doubt that the spotted skunk can spray in this position; it does not have to have four feet on the ground in order to do so. …

Antidote for Musk. There are as many antidotes for removing skunk musk as there are people who have been sprayed by it. One large can of tomato juice, perhaps two, is usually sufficient to neutralize the musk sprayed on one small boy and a dog.

Although it may seem inconceivable for those who find the smell of skunk musk offensive, there are those who find the odor quite pleasant, at least in small doses. The tolerance for this odor appears to be genetic.

—Excerpted from *Discover Nature at Sundown*

Bats

Elizabeth P. Lawlor
Illustrations by Pat Archer

[B]ats are mammals. They have body hair and mammary glands and give birth to live young, but unlike any other mammal, bats can fly. Their "hand" and forearm bones are similar to those found in other mammals but they are adapted to accommodate the bat's continuous wing membranes. This thin, double layer of skin encloses its somewhat elongated forearm; long, tapered fingers; and hind limbs. In some bat species, the tail is also enclosed by this membrane. A bat's fingers have great dexterity, so they can manipulate the wings to form umbrella shapes that trap insects, as well as hover in midair like hummingbirds. In all species of bats, the clawlike thumbs of their extraordinary hands remain free outside the wing. Bats use this fine tool for clinging to the walls of caves, hanging from tree branches, and manipulating food and other objects. The wings are designed so that a bat can fold them close along its side like a collapsed umbrella. This feature lets the bat crawl along a flat surface without getting tangled in folds of skin.

Bats belong to the order Chiroptera, which comes from the Greek word *chiro*, meaning "hand," and *petra*, meaning "wing," references to the unique structure of the "hand-wing." Bats come in a variety of sizes and colors including dark brown, orange, yellow-gray, black, red, gray, and white. Bats have adapted to such a variety of climates that you can find them anywhere in the world except in the polar regions. A few red bats (*Lasiurus borealis*) have been found as far north as Southampton Island in the Canadian Arctic, but most species of bats live in the tropics because food is available there year-round.

The order Chiroptera is divided into two groups: large bats, or megabats (Megachiroptera), and small bats, or microbats (Microchiroptera). Megabats, often called flying foxes because of their foxlike faces, live in the tropics of Africa, Australia, and Asia and have wingspans up to six feet. Unlike their smaller relatives, many megabats are active during daylight hours and have large eyes and good vision. This feature, coupled with their finely tuned sense of smell, leads them to nutrient-rich flowers and ripe fruits, the staples of their diet. Their pointed, doglike snouts and long tongues allow them to reach into flowers for protein-rich pollen and sweet nectar, pollinating the flowers in the process. Some bats also help propagate tropical plants by eating their fruit and later depositing the seeds some distance from the parent. Bats in some regions of the world feed on fish, lizards, and mice, and the vampire bat that lives in the tropics eats the blood of cattle. This preference for blood has led the bat to occasionally inflict a pinprick wound in humans and has contributed to the superstition that all bats drink blood.

The smallest microbat is the bumblebee bat of Thailand, which weighs less than an average paper clip. All of the bats that live in the United States and Canada are microbats. These bats spend the day in dark places and hunt for food—usually flying insects—at night. Filling this nighttime niche permits them to be active when most predatory animals are at rest. Microbats do not see well in dim light, but their well-designed sonar systems more than compensate for that deficit. With this tracking capability, called echolocation, a bat can determine the size and shape of an object, how far away it is, and whether it is moving. To do this, the bat emits a stream of high-pitched clicks and squeaks that are inaudible

to humans. When the sound waves hit an obstacle, they are returned to the bat as an echo. The bat "reads" the echo and acts accordingly. You can observe this sonar system at work if you watch a bat rapidly fly through a grove of trees. It never hits a single branch or twig as it pursues its next meal. The sending of the pulses and their return as echoes happens in a fraction of a second. We can hear sounds that are within the range of 20 to 20,000 cycles per second, or hertz. The pulses produced by bats are above 20,000 Hz (also expressed as 20 kilohertz or 20 KHz).

Only microbats echolocate by producing the high-frequency tones in the larynx. Some echolocation calls, such as those of the North American *Nyctinomoas*, are audible to humans, but most of the gentle squeaks we hear are not the vibrations of the tracking system but communication among the bats. One species of macrobat produces high-frequency calls with its tongue, a more primitive form of echolocation than the laryngeal technique of the microbats. Leafnose bats, of which four species live in North America, release sound from megaphone-shaped mouths or queer-looking folds of skin on their noses.

Most microbats have a spearlike growth called the *tragus* that stands upright inside each ear. The tragus is somehow part of the echolocation system, but scientists have yet to discover its exact function. Ridges inside the fleshy part of the bat's ear are also part of the sonar system. Echolocation is an advanced strategy for navigating and hunting in the dark shared by dolphins, whales, some shrews, and a few species of South American birds.

Throughout the warm months of spring and summer, insect populations explode. As the numbers of these pests increase, so do the numbers of electric bug zappers in suburban neighborhoods. This human invention can't equal the work of bats, however. Scientists have estimated that a little brown bat (*Myotis lucifugus*) eats at least one-third of its body weight in insects in a half hour of foraging. At this rate, a population of Mexican freetail bats in Texas would eat 12,000 tons of insects per night. The insect diet of North American bats makes them our most important allies in insect control.

As summer fades into autumn, the supply of insects begins to dwindle and the nights grow cool. Soon freezing temperatures will cover the ponds with ice and the land will be in winter's

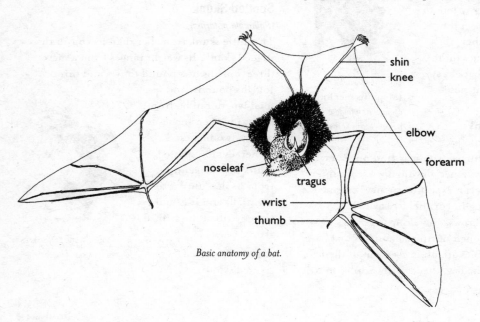

Basic anatomy of a bat.

shin
knee
elbow
forearm
noseleaf
tragus
wrist
thumb

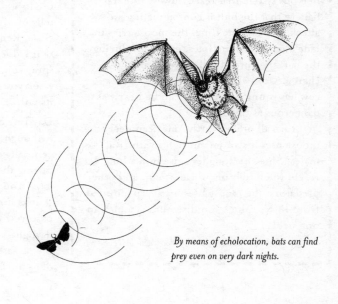

By means of echolocation, bats can find prey even on very dark nights.

Continued ➡

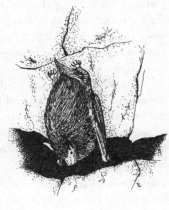

*Above: A young Mexican freetail bat (*Tadarida brasiliensis*) is carried by its mother.*

*Right: The little brown bat (*Myotis lucifugus*) is one of America's most abundant bats.*

grip. So in July, some species of microbats begin migrating to the warmer latitudes of Central and South America. By August, most migratory bats are on the move. Some species of bats that spend the summer in Canada and the northern United States migrate to certain areas of the American South to hibernate. The Mexican freetail bats migrate to Mexico and Central America, where they remain active. ...

During the warmer months, many bats use their winter hibernation caves as daytime roosts. They leave these roots at dusk to feed on night-flying insects and to drink by skimming water surfaces while flying. A colony of Mexican freetail bats leaving a cave often looks like a huge, black cloud; observers frequently compare the emerging bats to the whirling spiral of a tornado. Other bat species are solitary and may roost in tree hollows or hang upside down from branches. Bats in this position often resemble dead leaves or are camouflaged by the foliage. Solitary bats sometimes find the space behind window shutters or under loose tree bark to their liking. They look for a snug spot that is secluded and dark. ...

Bats are not dangerous, but when you find one leave it alone. Your touch might startle it and it may respond like any other frightened animal by snarling, biting, and scratching. Scientists who study bats usually wear heavy work gloves when handling bats.

Where to Find Bats

Except for the nectar-drinking, pollen-eating long-nosed bats (*Leptonycteris*) of the southwestern United States, which forage during the day, most North American bats wait until twilight to begin hunting for insects. Although large roosts are easier to find than small ones, locating any of these daytime hangouts can be very difficult. Some species of bats gather in rock crevices where they are protected from the burning rays of the summer sun. Others snuggle in the crannies of bell towers or attics, and still others prefer to dangle from barn rafters. Sometimes bats like to recuperate from a night of hunting in the close spaces behind window shutters. The big brown bat (*Eptesicus fuscus*), also known as the house bat, is especially fond of shelter.

Bats that roost in churches, houses, barns, and other buildings generally give away their presence by a brown stain caused by their droppings running down the side of the building. Another sign of bats is the whitish guano that collects on the ground below a roost. If you are a patient and persistent observer, you may discover some bat roosts in your community. Another good way to locate bats is to ask a naturalist at a nature center about local bat populations. Some of the North American bats that prefer group living and congregate in buildings are the evening bat (*Nycticeius humeralis*), the big brown bat, the little brown bat, and the pallid

bat (*Antrozous pallidus*). Although the Mexican freetail bat (*Tadarida brasiliensis*) gathers in huge colonies, it prefers to assemble in caves rather than in buildings.

Communal living is not for all bats. Some bats shun both buildings and caves and seek the solitude offered by a hollow tree, or simply hang from tree branches. Asleep in the cool shadows of the foliage, these bats usually go unnoticed because they resemble dead leaves. Young bats, still hugging their mothers, also find safety in trees. Hunting for solitary bats can exhaust the patience of the most skilled field worker. The eastern pipistrel (*Pipistrellus subflavus*), the most abundant bat in the eastern United States, prefers to roost in sycamore trees, but they're extremely difficult to find. The red bat, the silver-haired bat, and the hoary bat (*Lasiurus cinereus*) also like to hide in trees and shrubs.

Many people who live in or visit the southwestern United States know that millions of Mexican freetail bats roost in the caves of Texas and New Mexico, where they are featured as a tourist attraction. Unlike most bats that live in the eastern part of the United States, western bats generally roost in caves and deserted mines.

Listed below are some of the bats you are likely to find in and around your community. Although these are the bats we see most often, little is known about their habits and their haunts.

Little brown bats. Widely distributed across the United States and Canada, this is our most abundant bat, often found with the big brown bat. Look for it in buildings, behind shingles or siding, or in attics.

Big brown bats. These bats range from Alaska and Canada south through the United States into Mexico. Their roosts include attics, barns, and other buildings; behind window shutters; in expansion joints beneath bridges; and occasionally in tree hollows. These bats hang around with the mouse-eared bats such as the little brown bat

Silver-haired bat.
(Lasionycteris noctivagans)

Red bat.
(Lasiurus borealis)

Hoary bat.
(Lasiurus cinereus)

Pallid bat.
(Antrozous pallidus)

Evening bat.
(Nycticeius humeralis)

Big brown bat.
(Eptesicus fuscus)

BATS AND SAFETY

Despite the legends, bats (*Desmodus* species) are a relatively small hazard to the survivor. There are many bat varieties worldwide, but you find the true vampire bats only in Central and South America. They are small, agile fliers that land on their sleeping victims, mostly cows and horses, to lap a blood meal after biting their victim. Their saliva contains an anticoagulant that keeps the blood slowly flowing while they feed. Only a small percentage of these bats actually carry rabies; however, avoid any sick or injured bat. They can carry other diseases and infections and will bite readily when handled. Taking shelter in a cave occupied by bats, however, presents the much greater hazard of inhaling powdered bat dung, or guano. Bat dung carries many organisms that can cause diseases. Eating thoroughly cooked flying foxes or other bats presents no danger from rabies and other diseases, but again, the emphasis is on thorough cooking.

—From *Survival* (*U.S. Army Field Manual 21–76*)

Continued ➡

and its western cousin Yuma myotis (*Myotis yumanensis*). You also can find it with the Mexican freetail bat, with the pallid bat, and in close association with people.

Evening bat. Found from Pennsylvania south to the Gulf Coast, this bat avoids caves but prefers buildings, where large nursing colonies are often found. Smaller groups of these bats will roost behind tree bark or in tree hollows. It commonly roosts with the Mexican freetail bat.

Mexican freetail bats. On the West Coast and in the Southeast, this bat prefers to roost in buildings. In Texas, Arizona, Oklahoma, and New Mexico, however, its preference for caves is well known by visitors and locals. Because these bats have been studied so extensively, we probably know more about them than any other kind of bat. They share buildings in the West with the pallid bat, the big brown bat, and the Yuma myotis. In the Southeast you can find them with southeastern myotis (*Myotis austroriparius*) and the evening bat.

Pallid bat. These desert bats of the Southwest prefer rocky ledges and outcroppings where scrub vegetation such as mesquite grows. They are also found in Oregon and Washington, and a few colonies flourish in southern Kansas and Oklahoma.

The remaining bats prefer to spend the day in trees, and because of their solitary nature, they are extremely difficult to find.

Hoary bat. The most widespread of North American bats, the hoary bat is not yet found in Alaska. Its capture in the mist nets of bat banders suggests that there may be more of these rare bats than previously thought. This bat spends its days hidden in tree foliage, where it can be well concealed from above but have enough open space in the foliage below that it can drop down and begin its flight.

Red bat. Ranging from southern Canada and the eastern United States into Mexico and Central America, this tree-roosting bat prefers to hide beneath the leaves of sycamore trees, although the lush foliage of any board-leaved tree will suffice. Infrequently they dangle like dead leaves from a branch or twig. Female bats roost with their young.

Silver-haired bat. Found primarily in the North but appearing in all states except Florida, these bats spend their days roosting behind loose tree bark or in abandoned woodpecker holes or bird nests. Sometimes they find solitude in outbuildings such as tool sheds and garages. Infrequently they have been found in small nursing groups. …

Bats on the Wing

Although an occasional bat can be found flying about during the day, most bats take to the sky during the twilight hours. On a summer evening you can observe them in a dance of twists, spirals, and loops that is choreographed by the insects they pursue. Although it's difficult to identify a flying bat, the following are some points to keep in mind as you make your observations.

Describe its flight path. Is it straight and steady? Is is circular? Describe the habitat. Is there water nearby? Is the bat flying over a pasture? Was it flying close to the treetops? Did the bat spend most of its flying time higher or lower than the trees? Was it flying over a lawn or around lampposts? Was it alone, or were other bats flying nearby?

The following focuses on the flight pattern, wingspans, flight patterns, and foraging habits of the bats you will most likely see. Keep a record of bat sightings. Don't forget to include the date and time of your observations in your field notebook.

Little brown bat. A medium-sized bat with a wingspan of about eight inches (222–269 mm.), this mouse-eared bats prefers to forage over water, but if none is available it will hunt for food over pastures and lawns and among trees. They fly their zigzag flight ten to twenty feet above the ground. Look for their foraging pattern, which is often a repeated circular path around a cluster of houses or trees and often includes the entrance to their roost.

Big brown bat. A large bat with a wingspan of thirteen inches (325–350 mm.), this is the most familiar bat of the summer night. It begins foraging at dusk and flies in a steady, somewhat straight path about twenty to thirty feet above the ground. A big brown bat's flight pattern is often broken as it zips off course to capture insects. In a pattern similar to that of other kinds of bats, big brown bats fly over and over the same path each night. If you become familiar with some of these feeding paths, you will probably see the same bat flying there each night. These bats frequently are seen flying around the lights that line city streets.

Evening bats. The wingspan of these small bats is about ten inches (260–280 mm.). They begin foraging early in the evening and are plentiful around southern communities. Their slow flight and steady course make them easy to recognize after you have had some experience observing bats in flight. Not much is known about the feeding habits or the seasonal movements of these bats.

Mexican freetail bats. The span of their narrow wings is about eleven inches (290–325 mm.). When they leave their caves in Texas and New Mexico about fifteen minutes after sunset, they form a huge black cloud in the sky, and a roar like that of rushing water accompanies their departure from the roost. The flight is spectacular. Soon after leaving the cave, the bats go off in separate directions. These colonies are so large that some bats are just leaving as the first to exit begin to reenter the cave. They feed on small moths.

Pallid bat. Its wingspan is about fifteen inches (360–390 mm.), and it flies low, about three or four feet above the ground as it forages. Unlike other bats, these large-eyed bats hunt the ground for beetles and other insects.

Hoary bat. This is a large bat with a wingspan of about sixteen inches (380–410 mm.). Look for their straight and fast flight as they emerge late in the evening. Little is known about the eating habits of these attractive bats.

Red bat. The long, pointed wings that span about eleven inches (290–332 mm.) and its long tail in silhouette against the darkening sky are clues that you may be seeing this lovely reddish orange bat. These fast fliers have been clocked at forty miles per hour. When foraging, they fly low over treetops but will frequently hunt only a few feet above the ground. Red bats look for flies, true bugs, beetles, cicadas, and crickets. Although not much is known about their diets, the few known food preferences lead scientists to believe the little red bat hunts for some of its food on the ground. Not much is known about their habits.

Silver-haired bat. This medium-sized bat has a wingspan of about ten inches (270–310 mm.). Its flight is leisurely, and it cruises close to the ground and not above twenty feet. These bats may appear singly but are frequently found foraging in pairs. Because they are so difficult to find during the day, these bats, like so many others, have not been studied extensively, and most of their habits remain a mystery.

Is It a Bat or a Bird?

Although swallows are active during the day, you may see them in the twilight as they skim the surfaces of ponds and streams. At this time, they are often mistaken for bats.

Common nighthawks (*Chordeiles minor*) are adept at catching insects while in flight. These avian fliers lead reclusive lives during the day but appear in the night sky in search of insects. These birds forage over open country, but you may see their silhouettes against the night sky in cities and towns. Scientists have found that bats and birds feast on caddisflies (trichopterans) and other insects, whereas both avoid midges (chironomids).

Whippoorwills feed extensively on moths and other insects caught on the wing. You may see these nightjars flying over woodlands that are close to open fields. When caught in the beam of automobile headlights, the birds' eyes reflect ruby red. Chuck-will's-widow flies over fields and low to the ground in its hunt for beetles, moths, winged ants, and termites. Look for these competitors in the evening sky.

With the help of the silhouettes below, try to identify the nighthawk, whippoorwill, and swallow while in flight. Compare their flight patterns with those of bats. Which of these night fliers do you think is most agile?

Battling Bats

Occasionally bats get into squabbles with one another. Although these confrontations are seldom serious, bats have been known to die as a result of them. If you should find a pair of battling bats, observe the strategies each uses to outwit the other. How do they use their arms? Do they make any noise?

swallow   whippoorwill   nighthawk

Continued ➡

Hanging

Most scientists believe that hanging upside down lets bats use spaces not inhabited by other animals, such as cave ceilings, undersides of tree limbs, and rock crevices. It may be an adaptation that protects them from predators.

Do Bats Really Want to Dive into Your Hair?

Bats don't really want to tangle with you or your hair. How close do you predict a bat will come to you before veering off? To find out, you will need some courage and a friend to help you. When you see a bat coming in your direction, remain still. Your friend can observe the flying bat to determine how close it gets. Try it again. Why do you think the bat doesn't hit you?

—Excerpted from *Discover Nature at Sundown*

The birds are partly obscured by distance, shade, and vegetation.

Birds

Birding: An Introduction
Kurt Rinehart

Lots of great birders take their guides with them into the field, but I'm more of a general naturalist than a dyed-in-the-wool birder. Faced with the prospect of taking six or more guides with me into the field, I choose to take none. In the field I concentrate on observations, often taking notes on a small pad. This forces me to spend lots of time with the books at home. Ultimately, spending time paging through your guides and imagining encounters with those birds are the best things you can do to improve your birding skills.

I recommend that you start birding without binoculars. At first, you just need to be able to spot birds—birds that quietly sneak off into the brush or zip into distant trees as you approach. The more birds you see, the more you will identify, so try to see lots of birds. Once you start to get the hang of seeing the birds, begin noticing the landscape and the birds' behaviors. Keep your mind and your eyes wide open to changes in habitat; see where the birds are within the habitat and how they act. Spend some time, wherever you are, observing bird behavior. My memories of watching House Sparrow mothers feed their fledgling young at a bus stop in New Jersey are just as precious as my memory of going to that one magical spot glimpse some exotic species and check it off my list. Due attention to the familiar will build your skills and usher in new mysteries.

The Situation

There is a park in Southern California that I used to visit almost every day when I was really learning my birds. I had been interested in natural history for a while, but I was channeling a lot of energy into building my skills as a naturalist. Let's suppose that you are walking through this park along the Creek Trail, which runs along a small creek in a wooded ravine. The trail starts off open to your right, but ahead the trees close in and cover both sides of the trail.

As you near the oak canopy, you see a couple of birds up ahead. Both are on the ground in the shadows. One is to the left of the trail near some trees and brush, and the other is a little deeper

in the woods under the trees to the right. You stop when you see them and watch for a few moments. You want to get a better look, but as you approach, they both fly away. All you could see for sure was that they were both medium sized, about the size of a robin, and both brown. The shadows made it hard to tell, but neither had any obvious or bold markings. You're pretty sure that they were two different species, however, because one seemed to have a longer tail and was a little lighter color than the other.

In the moment that you see a bird, you strive to observe all you can, but there is often little time. Sometimes there are obvious details of appearance that make identification easy, but it takes practice to see them. In this case, you didn't see anything that would distinguish one bird from another. Given that you saw little of the two birds' plumage and field marks, even if you could find some possible matches by flipping through every page in your field guide, you still couldn't be confident of an identification. There will always be sightings that stump you or leave you feeling a little confused, but let's look at this situation again. Was it really so ambiguous? What else could you have noticed?

Taking a Closer Look

It's important to notice where the birds are within the habitat, or the natural setting where they live. I call this location within the habitat the "microhabitat." With birds, this generally refers to where they are in relation to the ground and what they are perching on. Since they can fly, birds' microhabitat can be anywhere from on the ground to thousands of feet up in the air.

Most birds are observed when they are foraging, so we can assume that both the birds you saw are ground feeders, but they were doing so differently. The first bird scratched in the leaves with its feet. It used an odd double-scratch technique, like short foot-dragging hops backward. The other bird scooted along by running, one foot in front of the other, inter-

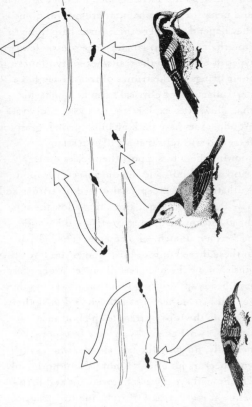

Microhabitat and behavior clearly identify woodpeckers, nuthatches, and creepers as trunk feeders. Broad arrows show flight paths. Small arrows show trunk foraging paths.

mittently picking through the leaves with its beak. The manner of the first bird was what I call high-strung; its movements were sharp and jerky. The other bird was more fluid, almost sneaky. The posture of the two birds was similar, generally stooped forward. But the first bird held its tail and often its head up a bit, whereas the second bird's tail was angled down and it kept its head hunched down, at least while it was looking for food.

This may seem like too much to have noticed with such a brief glimpse, but the more you practice paying attention, the more you'll see. But how is this useful? You can't look up behavior in a field guide. The point is, behavior can provide other information that will help identify these birds from a book.

For instance, we are guessing that these

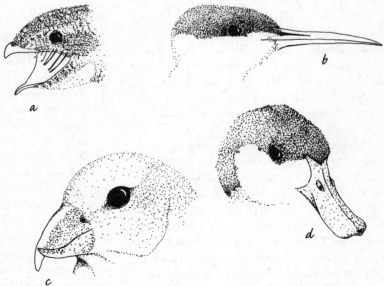

Bills for eating insects on the wing (a), diving on fish (b), opening conifer cones (c), and dabbling in pond mud (d).

Continued ➡

birds are ground feeders based on microhabitat and behavior. Microhabitats are not random; they depend on where these birds have to be to find the right food. For instance, only a few types of birds have the traits necessary to make their livings on the trunks of trees. Each has a particular mix of physical form and behavior that allows it to exploit tree trunks for survival. Woodpeckers have pecking bills; strong, grasping feet; and stiff tails that act like kickstands, allowing them to support themselves on tree trunks and limbs and dig out insects for food. Nuthatches and creepers also feed on trunks and have their own unique traits that allow them to do so. So any bird on a tree trunk is a wood-pecker, a nuthatch, or a creeper. The behavior of these three kinds of birds allows you to distin-guish among them at great distances. Woodpeckers feed head-up, working their way upward as they go. Nuthatches feed head-down and work their way from the tops of trees to the bottoms. Creepers work their way upward but move stealthily, hugging the tree closely, whereas woodpeckers jut out and move about noticeably. The human eye registers movement and form before it registers color, so by the time you see the plumage, your job is narrowed down to identifying the species of woodpecker, creeper, or nuthatch. Since we have a sense of what is available to eat on the ground here—seeds and invertebrates—we should be able to make some guesses about the birds' beaks. The beak is the primary tool for foraging. It has other func-tions, such as grooming feathers, but feeding ecology has a major influence on the form of the beak. Even though both birds you saw are ground feeders, I would guess that they have different beaks based on their different foraging behaviors.

Woodpecker beaks are stout, straight, and sharp for pecking into wood. Nuthatches have fine, straight, sharp bills that are good for picking insects and spiders from bark crevices and are capable of hacking into tough seeds and nuts. Creepers move slowly up trees and limbs using their fine, downward-curving bills to pluck bugs from the bark. In addition to insect-eating bills like these, there are beaks designed for eating every other kind of available food.

Suppose you were a bird picking through leaves to find your food. Would you want a long beak or a short beak? Consider the people who pick up trash in parks and on roadsides. They usually carry a pincerlike grabber with a 3-foot handle. Imagine trying to pick up trash with a pair of pliers. If you had to use pliers, you might change your tactics. Maybe instead of picking up each piece of trash individually, you would kick a bunch of it together in a pile and then pick it up all at once.

These birds (their ancestors, actually) have had to grapple with these same issues of effort and efficiency. Because of this, I would guess that the bird picking through the debris with its beak has a longer beak than the other bird. But why would a bird feeding in debris have a short beak at all? The answer has to do with leverage. A 3-foot-long trash grabber is good for picking up litter, but I would rather have pliers for loos-ening a nut on my car—or for cracking a nut, for that matter. Many ground-feeding birds that eat

seeds have short, stout bills like pliers that allow them to crack or husk hard seeds. If your preferred food was seeds, you wood be better off with a stout, seed-cracker bill. And if you had a bill like that, you probably wouldn't use it to dig through leaves; you would use your feet, like a chicken. It's efficient, and it's the behavior that fits the tool. I would guess that the longer-billed bird probably doesn't eat seeds, or at least not as its main diet. It probably eats invertebrates, using its longer, tweezerlike bill to grab and hold bugs hiding in the leaves.

The other thing you saw both birds do was fly. Both birds had a fluttery flight. The scratcher didn't fly far, just farther along the trail. If you had kept walking, you probably would have seen it again. The bill picker, when it flushed, flew over the low ridge to the left and out of sight; it seemed to be headed to another patch of woods about 50 yards away. It flew low and straight in an even line. The manner, how readily, and where a bird flies to are clues about its ecology and its identity. Maybe next time you'll only need to see the trajectory of a distant bird's flight to accurately identify it. This is exactly what experienced birders do when they seem to magically identify birds from mere glimpses.

Taking a Broader Look

Recall the moment that you first saw the birds. Just by noticing them, you gathered critical information about their identities. The location of the sighting eliminates all those birds whose ranges and habitats don't include that area. This particular park is just east of a sharp point sticking out into the Pacific above the westward sweep of the Southern California coast. It is on the seaward edge of some high, chaparral-covered mountains.

The majority of California is hot and dry and could never naturally support the palm trees and exotic tropical plants associated with the Golden State. Much of central and southern California is dominated by drought-resistant oak woodlands and a scrub woodland called chaparral. Lack of moisture limits chaparral to a profusion of prickly, scratchy shrubs that form an almost impenetrable thicket spreading over the poor, rocky soil. In this park, oak woods fill the creek bottoms between chaparral-covered hills. Open fields consisting of dry meadows maintained by mowing add some diversity to the landscape.

So, you know that these birds include Southern California in their ranges. You also know that they can tolerate the chaparral habitat. Species ranges are influenced by the extremes of climate, particularly temperature, and the kind of ecosystem. Some birds suited to woodland ecosystems could never survive in a desert either because they couldn't find the food (and water) they need or because the heat itself would prove fatal. Each species has to be able to find the right food, water, and shelter and, for residents, suit-able nesting sites and materials. The particular ecosystems that meet these needs describe the habitat that a species can occupy. Predators, birds, and other animals competing for the same foods can influence a bird's habitat as well. It's also important to consider the season of the

sighting, since some birds are present in their North American ranges for only part of the year—something that is clearly noted in good filed guides.

You know that these two birds can inhabit oak woods and chaparral and perhaps other habitats as well. In a field guide covering all of North America, there are over nine hundred species listed. A little over two hundred species are found on land in this part of California and less than half of those live in dry, wooded, or brushy areas like these. So, in that first instant of the sighting, you gained critical information for making the identification. You'll definitely want to file it away under this bird's name when you get to that.

Taking a Look at the Bird Itself

Finally, what did the bird actually look like? In reality, your mind processes all this information together, but in terms of imposing a logical pattern and structure on your observations, save these details for last. When observing birds, look at their component shapes: beak, wings, tail, and even feet, if possible. These are the characteris-tics by which ornithologists define species, not coloration. You should be able to note these features fairly quickly when they're visible, and you'll still be able to notice the plumage colors and other aspects. The above list of possible species can be reduced to five or six based on size and shape.

Note the overall size of the bird. We called the birds in this example robin sized, denoting a medium-sized bird. As you learn a few birds, you can use them as relative sizes, such as warbler and crow sized. This makes it easy to remember and to communicate to others. Your field guide is the best teacher of which details deserve atten-tion—things such as wing bars, mustachial lines, and eye lines. First, spend some time with the "bird topography" diagram somewhere in the front of your guide so that you'll know what the various parts are called. Make sure that you're familiar with these features, because they are the basis of the species descriptions you will ulti-mately be relying on. Eventually, you'll begin to see family patterns emerge. For instance, wing bars are important when differentiating sparrows but not tanagers.

So far, we've been able to mine quite a bit of information from that quick sighting, although the details of appearance are still largely lacking. We've been engaging in a dialogue with the object of our attention, but that object isn't just the bird; it's the bird and landscape, the bird as it evolved and continues to survive as part of a dynamic community. We're going to get to the names of these birds eventually. But your goal should not be just the name; it should be to know the thing for which the name is a symbol.

Names are the keys to unlocking the volumes of experience and information that others have collected in books and images. But that information will have meaning only if those names are invested in a rich impression of the bird as a living being interacting with a complex ecological community. At this point, we've made the observations and drawn what conclusions we can. Now it's time to go to the field guide.

Continued ➔

Making the Identification

The ultimate objective when using a field guide for identification is to find a picture that looks just like what you saw. One of my primary goals is to save you the tedium of flipping through every page in your guide to find a match. The result of the previous steps—looking at what the bird is doing and where it is and then thinking about its physical features—can narrow your search and deepen your knowledge.

Many guides also include a little information on microhabitat in the picture. In my guide, ground-feeding birds are pictured on the ground in appropriate settings, shore-birds are on rocks or sand, woodpeckers are on trees, and sparrows are on the ground or in low vegetation. Even the species of trees included in the drawings are appropriate to the bird species' range. When you look at the picture, you are seeing the posture, structure, and appearance of the birds, plus their microhabitat.

If you flip through your guide looking for the two birds observed—the scratcher and the bill picker—you'll notice that there are large sections filled with birds that look nothing like them. All the gulls and terns are grouped together, as are the ducks and geese, owls, and hummingbirds. Thus, you can essentially disregard most of the book.

Many field guides are arranged phylogenetically, which means that the families are depicted in the order in which they evolved. For example, the loon family has been around the longest of all modern birds, so it comes first. The finch family was the most recent on the scene, so it comes last. So if you know the family of the bird you're looking for, you can narrow your search. The good news is that you already know a number of bird families, because the common terms for birds usually correspond to their family names. For example, in a field guide, the birds we collectively call owls will be located together as a family, with the individual owl species displayed on consecutive pages. Once you're familiar with the key characteristics of a family, it's not hard to categorize a new species on the first try. Most field guides help by giving brief descriptions of family characteristics at the beginning of each section. The best way to familiarize yourself with bird families is to make the family a vital part of the basic information you learn about any bird you identify in the field or read about in a book.

Based on our interpretation of the behaviors observed, the birds seen along the Creek Trail are in two different families. Start by flipping through the field guide and looking not necessarily for the specific bird but for a family of birds that resembles what you saw. Read the family descriptions as you do this. Once you find the probable family, search for a bird that matches not just the appearance but also the range and habitat of what you saw. Look at the graphics *and* read the text. Flycatcher bills might look right, but the description will tell you that flycatchers generally hunt insects in the air from an exposed perch, which is clearly not what you saw.

The bill picker likely has a longish bill that is straight or down-curved, the typical pattern for ground-feeding, insect-eating birds. As you go through your guide, thinking about tails and bills, a number of possibilities will catch your eye, but most will not stand up to scrutiny. A liberal list for the bill picker might be Mourning Dove, Hermit Thrush, California Thrasher, and maybe even Wrentit.

The Mourning Dove is long and low with a long tail. Mourning Doves feed on the ground and have longish bills. The Hermit Thrush is a ground feeder that can be found in the area, but it has a stubby tail, and the illustrated posture is very upright. The Wrentit has the right body shape and dimensions, and it is a chaparral bird. It's rather small, though, unless we overestimated the size of the bird sighted. Finally, the thrasher looks right in body structure and dimension and has the ideal bill for the foraging behavior we observed.

A simple reference that provides a little more natural history than the typical field guide would likely clarify the picture. Of all the birds listed, only the California Thrasher is uniformly dark brown, has a long tail, picks through leaf litter with its bill ("thrashing"), and is common in chaparral. This is exactly why a good natural history reference is an important tool for building your skills in the field. It's also helpful to look at the photos or paintings of birds in several guides, seeing them in different poses.

The first thrasher I ever identified was a California Thrasher in just this situation. What clinched it for me was knowing that thrashers "thrash" and having an impression of their long shapes from time spent poring over a field guide. After the bird flew off, I followed it over the hill, found it again (I heard it in the leaves), and snuck up for a closer view. I just needed a good look at that bill to positively identify the bird in the guide. Only much later was I able to watch a few of them closely enough to pick up all their other field marks.

Working on identifying the scratcher, only the emberizid, cardinal, and finch families exhibit the ideal "conical" seed-cracking beak we presume that it has. However, most of the species in these families are small, colorful, or

Brownish overall and resident in chaparral, the California Towhee forages mostly on the ground, sometimes scratching among the leaf litter.

Drab-colored and common in chaparral-covered foothills, the California Thrasher uses its large, curved bill to flip leaf litter aside as it forages on the ground.

Hermit Thrush (a), Mourning Dove (b), Wrentit (c), and California Thrasher (d).

Some Southern California members of the family Emberizidae—the sparrows and allies. Junco (a), Rufous-capped Sparrow (b), California Towhee (c), Spotted Towhee (d).

Continued ➡

found outside of this location. The most likely matches are among the emberizids—the sparrows and allies. These birds are a little more similar than the short list for the thrasher. Identifying this bird will ultimately depend on plumage color and pattern, because all these birds fit the structural, range, and habitat criteria. If we can be sure that it was a medium-sized bird that lacked streaking and patterning, that leaves only the California Towhee with the necessary traits. In order to settle on a single bird, you need to have a sense of why it couldn't have been something else.

Note that if you had seen a smaller, streaky bird in that same scenario, your job would have been much harder. Species identification often rests on the details, and in those cases, you may not walk away from a sighting with a positive identification. You would, however, be much better prepared to get it right the next time.

Now you know the names of the birds you saw, but that's just the beginning. When you visit that spot again and see a bird in the shadows, you might think, "That bird sure isn't acting like a California Towhee." Even better, now you can read up on these birds in your field guide and other resources. If you do, you'll learn—like I did, after my first sighting—that the California Towhee commonly gives a metallic *chink!* as a call note. The next time I was out for a walk, my mind suddenly registered that I had been hearing these notes almost constantly without even realizing it. Suddenly I was identifying California Towhees everywhere simply by this sound and a quick rustle in the brush.

Birding by Ear

Birdsong and other vocalizations are valuable tools for birders. In addition to songs, many birds make distinctive calls throughout the year that are fantastic aids for identification. Using vocalizations is easiest when you prepare ahead of time. Choose a few common species on which to concentrate, and review and learn their songs and calls before going into the field. When you're adept at recognizing those first few, tackle a few more.

There are some good resources for songs

and calls, but the best way to learn birdsong is to use those resources to make your own recordings. For example, if you want to learn the robin, record its vocalizations from a commercial tape or CD several times over. Then do another repetitive recording for, say, the mockingbird. When you listen to the recording, you'll hear the robin song five or six times in a row, followed by similar repetitions of the mockingbird. You can do four or five species this way. This will familiarize you with their songs much faster than if you simply listened to an entire CD of all the birds in the east or west over and over.

A friend of mine spent one summer surveying breeding birds in his hometown as part of a statewide research project. He admitted that he had to relearn all the songs each year because, for some reason, they never stuck with him. In addition to doing some good focused preparation of the sort mentioned above, he shared a new technique that I hadn't thought of. He carries an iPod into the field so that he can play through the candidate songs on site and compare them to the actual songster. The key to this handy trick is that he has a base of knowledge about the songs of certain families or groups of species, making his in-the-field recording search narrow and efficient.

Looking Deeper

Approaching your field observations from an ecological perspective prepares you to see patterns that were previously invisible. Your field guide can tell you how things look. I want you to think beyond mere appearances—in terms of the underlying patterns of ecological life. Form, function, and environment are interacting parts of a whole organism. As you apply this perspective, you will learn to recognize a bird's family or even subfamily at the first sighting. As you saw, simply noticing where the bird is in the habitat can imply family through traits such as feeding behavior or beak shape.

I once asked myself why so many chaparral birds have long tails. There seemed to be a pattern in the wings of many species, too. Scrub Jays, for example, have long tails and broad, stubby wings that make a fluttery sound when

Microhabitat can provide clues to how a bird might look or act. Here, a Western Wood Peewee (a), an Orange-crowned Warbler (b), and a Golden-crowned Sparrow (c) are shown at the relative heights where they are seen in oak woodlands or chaparral.

they fly. Why this shape? This is the question I began carrying in my head as I walked and watched. It was a simple question, but it deepened the impact of my daily observations.

One day I followed the Creek Trail into the high meadow. I was sitting in the stubble of the recently mowed field watching nothing in particular when I saw a Red-tailed Hawk soaring above me. As I watched, another bird came up over the lip of the hill beside me. This second hawk shot right over my head about 20 feet off the ground. I had a great view of it as it sailed away and disappeared deep into the opposite wood line. I knew what kinds of hawks might be in the area, and I had seen enough to be sure that it was a Cooper's Hawk that shot over my head. Seeing that Cooper's Hawk answered my question about why I was seeing so many birds with long tails.

A Red-tailed Hawk hunts by soaring high

A Cooper's Hawk flaps to a new perch while a Red-tailed Hawk soars overhead.

Flight silhouettes of the (a) Cooper's Hawk (woodlands pursuer), (b) American Kestrel (open-country perch diver), and (c) Red-tailed Hawk (open-country soarer).

Continued ➡

above the ground and looking down for prey. It spends many hours each day circling and drifting without flapping its wings. When a redtail soars, it spreads its long, broad wings and flares its tail into a short wedge. It makes its body into a wide paraglider, allowing it to catch rising currents of warm air and ride them all day long. If you watch a redtail soar in unstable air, its tail is constantly angling this way and that, balancing the airflow over its body. The tail is the steering mechanism, and the wings provide the lift. The spread of the primary feathers on the ends of the wings decreases drag and lets the hawk soar at very slow speeds without stalling and falling from the sky. Redtails are often seen hunting from perches along highways. Whether hunting or roosting, they often perch in the uppermost part of a tree for better access to their primary element, the open sky. Redtails rise from their roosts slowly, with heavy wing beats. Those long, broad wings that are so excellent for soaring are tiresome to flap—a trade-off in efficiency between soaring and active flying.

In contrast, a Cooper's Hawk has short wings. It spends less time soaring, preferring to hunt from a roost within the woods. The Cooper's Hawk perches under the upper canopy and watches for prey, usually small birds, which are pursued and captured in the air. Its short, broad wings are more efficient for flapping than a redtail's are. They catch a lot of air, allowing the Cooper's to fly quickly and with great agility. The long tail gives it even more power in its maneuvering, a critical capability for aerial pursuit in canopied woodlands.

All hawks and their close relatives have the same basic features—grasping talons, tearing beaks, flying wings, and steering tails—but in each species, those features are molded to suit a particular prey and habitat. The Cooper's Hawk is a hawk built in the bird-chasing woodland mold. The Red-tailed Hawk soars high over open country as it hunts for small rodents and rabbits. The American Kestrel, a small falcon, hunts from an exposed perch in open territory. It doesn't need broad wings or a long tail for bursts of speed and maneuverability, but it must be able to drop quickly from a perch when it spots a grasshopper. Accordingly, kestrels have narrow, pointed wings.

Members of the flycatcher family are calm, stately birds. They usually sit on mid- to high-elevation perches from which they fly out and catch insects on the wing. Their bills are broad at the base, open wide, and have "whiskers" and a hooked tip to help catch and hold prey. Warblers are small, often brightly colored, "nervous" birds that pick soft insects off the foliage of trees and bushes with their small pointed beaks. Sparrows generally have stout bills, thick from top to bottom, for leverage in cracking seeds. They are found mostly on the ground and often in flocks.

These aren't hard-and-fast rules, but they are valuable. Even if you can say that a bird is warblerlike, you are well on your way to identifying its family and maybe even the bird itself—and you are learning a deeper story about the living landscape. Ecological and family traits give you a place to start. Then you can search for the details that distinguish one species or another

within that group. Those field marks illustrated in your field guide that used to seem like an endless parade of obscure details will now fit easily into a rich and expanding picture of birds and bird life.

—From *A Naturalist's Guide to Observing Nature*

Basic Bird Identification

Elizabeth P. Lawlor
Illustrations by Pat Archer

Identifying Birds

There are many excellent guides to bird identification from which to choose, and they are available in most bookstores. You will find some of the most widely used field guides listed in the Bibliography. If you are a beginner at bird identification, you might prefer to use a guide that covers only your region rather than a more inclusive guide that describes the birds that live in all of North America. Expert birders and teachers at nature centers can be extremely helpful to you as you sort through the large selection of available bird guides. As you become more proficient in bird identification, you may find that your first guide does not provide all of the information you would like to have at your

fingertips. Seasoned birders own several field guides and use them regularly.

Once you have selected your field guide, read the introduction and skim through the rest of it. You will notice that the birds are grouped according to families. What kinds of information are given about the bird families? If the guide has range maps, what do the maps tell you? Why are the loons at the beginning of the guide and the passerine or perching birds at the back of the book? Get to know your guide; read through it whenever you have some extra time. The more you use your guide, the easier it will be for you to identify that mysterious bird that visits your feeder.

A good way to learn to identify birds is to go on bird walks. Look in your local newspaper for bird walks sponsored by a local bird club or a local chapter of the National Audubon Society. Nature centers and museums also sponsor walks.

The early stages of bird identification can be the most confusing and discouraging. This diagram of a bird will help you focus on the features that are commonly used to distinguish one kind of bird from another. Birders refer to these features as field marks.

Your first task when you see an unfamiliar bird at your feeder is to pay attention to the most general features of the bird—its size, shape,

SONGBIRD ANATOMY

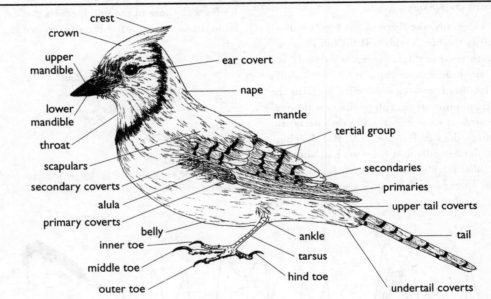

crest, crown, upper mandible, lower mandible, throat, scapulars, secondary coverts, alula, primary coverts, belly, inner toe, middle toe, outer toe, ear covert, nape, mantle, tertial group, secondaries, primaries, upper tail coverts, tail, ankle, tarsus, hind toe, undertail coverts

FAMILIAR BIRD SILHOUETTES

shrike, mourning dove, cardinal, blue jay, starling, flicker, house sparrow

Continued ➔

and color or color pattern. Next, observe specific details, such as the bird's bill, tail, head, wings, and feet. The bird's flight pattern can be another clue to its identity.

Size. Nearly everyone is familiar with the crow (seventeen to twenty-one inches), a robin (nine to eleven inches), and the sparrow (five to seven inches). These birds can be used as a mental measuring tape for determining the approximate size of your "mystery" bird. Is it smaller than a crow but bigger than a robin? Larger than a sparrow but smaller than a robin?

Shape. Birds can be plump or slender, chunky or sleek. What is the bird's general shape? Is it sleek like a crow? Chunky like a grosbeak? Stout like a nuthatch? Learning to recognize bird silhouettes against the gray of a winter sky or other drab background can be very helpful. Starlings, for example, differ from other birds of their size in that they have very short tails.

Color (Pattern). What color is the bird? Is there more than one color? Where are the colors? On the bird's back, breast, belly, rump, wings, or tail? Does it have wing bars? Does the color appear carelessly splashed on the bird, like the speckles on a starling? Or is it clearly defined, like the dignified black and white pattern of a hairy of downy woodpecker? A bird's name is often a reflection of its color. Blue jay, American goldfinch, purple finch, and redpoll are a few of the birds that sport their colors in their names.

Bill. Generally, the shape of the bird's bill identifies the bird's family. Is the bill long or short, thick or slender, curved or straight? Is there anything unique about it? The crossbill's beak is twisted, making it effective is prying the seed from pine cones. You probably will not see these birds at your feeder, since they prefer to remain in the coniferous woods. Warblers have short, slender bills, but sparrows have short, thick bills. Warblers are primarily insect eaters, but the sparrows' thicker bills are good for

cracking the hard coats of seeds. The curved bills of brown creepers are effective probing tools for picking out grubs from between the cracks in tree bark.

Tail. What is the shape? Color and pattern? Is it long like the tail of a mockingbird or short like the tail of a sparrow? Is it forked, notched, rounded, or squared off? How does the bird hold its tail (see silhouette for shape)? Does the tail droop or is it held upright like a wren's? (The "tail up" image comes from the standard guidebook picture of a wren, but they often sing, a spring behavior, with tail pointed straight down.)

Head. What is the color? Is it a solid color or patterned? Are there eye stripes, as in a Carolina wren? Eye rings, as in a tufted titmouse or ruby-crowned kinglet? Does the bird have a crest like a cardinal? A hood or a cap like a chickadee?

Wings. Look for wing bars (thin lines) or wing patches of a lighter color than the wing. The wing bars or patches may have a dark margin that sets them off. The red-winged blackbird shows red wing patches with a yellowish margin when it flies.

Feet. The birds that visit backyard feeders are the perching birds and woodpeckers. The illustration show the difference in the feet of these two types of birds. How does the design of the feet help the birds when they eat? Compare the feet of the perching birds that come to the feeder with those of the woodpeckers that eat from the suet cakes affixed to the tree trunk.

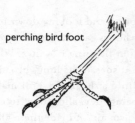

Passerine birds have a single hind toe, which helps them grip a branch when perching.

Flight Pattern

Frequently birds will fly away from the feeder before you have an opportunity to get a good look at them, but you can get some information about the bird before it disappears. How does it fly? Does its flight pattern resemble a roller coaster, such as woodpeckers and finches? Does it flap, flap, glide? Does the bird fly in a straight line? It might be a mourning dove. Are the wingbeats slower than those of other birds? Perhaps your bird is the slow-flapping mockingbird. You might hear a whistle as the bird files away. This tells you the bird is probably a mourning dove. Woodcocks also whistle as they take off, but you won't find these birds of moist woodlands and marshes at your feeder.

Certain birds will display additional colors and color patterns only when they are in flight. The slate-colored junco reveals white feathers on the outer margins of its tail when in flight. The towhee will show patches of white on the corners of its tail, and yellow-shafted flickers flash a white rump when in flight.

One Way to Begin

There are birds that are familiar to most people. When one of these familiar birds visits your feeder, observe it carefully. Make a list of the characteristics that helped you determine what it was. In doing this exercise, you will be applying the criteria needed to identify other birds. Try it. Learning to distinguish one bird from another takes patience, time, and more patience.

—From *Discover Nature in Winter*

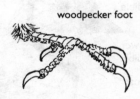

woodpecker foot

The feet of most woodpeckers have two toes pointing forward and two pointing backward, which helps anchor them as they chisel wood.

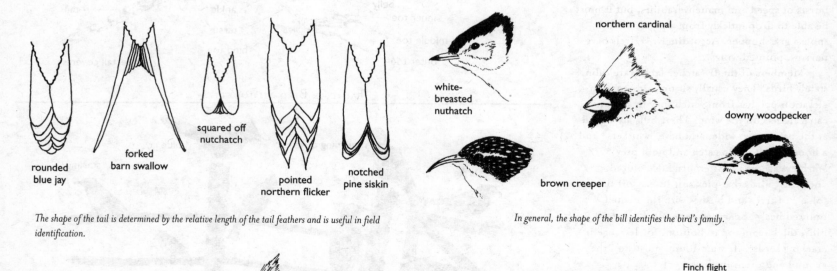

rounded
blue jay

forked
barn swallow

squared off
nutchatch

pointed
northern flicker

notched
pine siskin

white-breasted nuthatch

brown creeper

northern cardinal

downy woodpecker

The shape of the tail is determined by the relative length of the tail feathers and is useful in field identification.

In general, the shape of the bill identifies the bird's family.

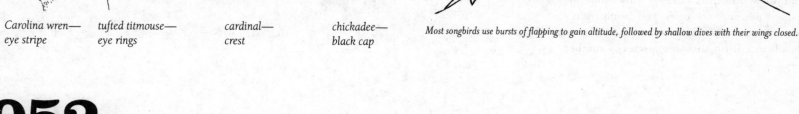

Carolina wren—
eye stripe

tufted titmouse—
eye rings

cardinal—
crest

chickadee—
black cap

Finch flight

Most songbirds use bursts of flapping to gain altitude, followed by shallow dives with their wings closed.

Bird Nests

Elizabeth P. Lawlor
Illustrations by Pat Archer

You can expect to find abandoned bird nests in the winter, since they are no longer hidden by a thick curtain of leaves. Winter nests are usually vacant, but if you find one covered with leaves, it might be a temporary shelter for a mouse or some other weary traveler; do not disturb it.

Warning: It is against the law to take nests apart or to remove them from trees, shrubs, or any other place you may find them. You may, however, take photographs or make sketches of the nests in your field journal. Also write your observations in your journal. Include any questions you may have so that you can research them later.

Sparrow nests are neatly cupped grass nests in low shrubs or on the ground.

Goldfinch nests are formed of downy materials that show as gray or white in the nest foundation.

Baltimore oriole nests, woven of yarn, plant fibers, and hair, are found hanging from drooping branches of elms, maples, willows, or apples.

Chickadees, woodpeckers, titmice, nuthatches, and brown creepers nest in excavated cavities in dead trees.

Birds do not use their nests in the same way that we use our homes. For the birds, a nest is a place to lay their eggs, incubate them, feed the hatchlings, and serve as a jumping-off point when the young begin their flight lessons. After the young have learned to fly, the family breaks up, and for most bird species, the nest is no longer used. Some birds raise more than one brood in a season. These birds will build a new nest for each brood.

To find nests, search the trees and shrubs around your home and in your neighborhood. Walk along the edges of fields, look in thickets, on the ground, and in clearings. Look for dark clumps at various levels in the trees. Do not mistake the large, leafy summer nests (dreys) of squirrels for bird nests. When you spot a nest, record its location in your notebook. If the nest is in a limb, how high is it? Is it in the crotch of a limb, near the end of a branch, or close to the trunk? How many nests are there in the same tree? Include in your description the type of tree or shrub where the nest was found so that you can find it again.

Make a chart that shows the distribution of nests in your neighborhood. Have a friend make similar observations in his or her neighborhood and compare your charts.

About 77 percent of the birds in North America build open nests, and they come in a variety of sizes and shapes. The remaining birds raise their young in holes or in structures with rooflike tops. Blue jays prefer to build their bulky but well-hidden nests in conifers, generally ten to twenty-five feet off the ground. The nests are made of thorny twigs, bark, moss, string, and leaves. Robins build nests with weed stalks, strips of cloth, string, and grasses woven into soft mud. Robins and blue jays will build nests close to human habitation, so look for them in trees in neighborhood yards and along the roadside. Baltimore orioles build their pouchlike nests of plant fibers, hair, and yarn high in the trees, generally twenty-five to thirty feet above the ground. The rose-breasted grosbeak prefers to nest in moist, deciduous thickets and suburban trees and shrubs. It builds its flimsy nest of twigs six to twenty-five feet above the ground. The red-eye vireo's delicate nest of bark, grasses, vine tendrils, and paper is decorated on the outside with lichens. You can find these nests five to ten feet above the ground, suspended in the forked branches of saplings. Wood thrushes build compact nests of grasses, bark, moss, and paper, held together with mud. Their preferred sites are in deciduous trees, usually ten feet above the ground in parks or gardens. Wood thrushes appear to be growing more tolerant of human presence.

Because of the regulations against taking nests from the places where the birds built them, you may not have the opportunity to see many nests up close. Museums, nature centers, and other educational facilities may have collections of bird nests for you to examine. Compare those nests with the nests you found. What are the similarities and differences?

Take photographs wherever possible. You can add the photos to your filed notebook or build a special notebook just for birds.

—From *Discover Nature in Winter*

Birds and Winter

Elizabeth P. Lawlor
Illustrations by Pat Archer

During the millions of years that birds have been on earth, they have developed several strategies that help them survive the rigors of winter. One of these strategies is to migrate south from their northern breeding grounds to more hospitable lands. By late summer, birds that thrive on flying insects, such as orioles, flycatchers, thrushes, and warblers, are on their way south. Although their favored food is more readily available there, life in the land of sunshine has its own problems. The new arrivals must compete with native birds not only for a share of the bounty but also for territorial space in the rapidly diminishing woodlands and rain forests.

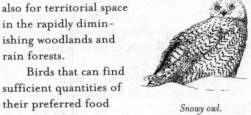

Rough-legged hawk.

Snowy owl.

Birds that can find sufficient quantities of their preferred food remain in their northern breeding grounds throughout the cold months. Others that winter in the North simply change their diet. Instead of foraging for active insects, these birds find high-energy substitutes in such fare as dormant insects and seeds.

Sometimes there is not enough food in a region to support the huge numbers of birds that survive a very successful breeding season. Such a sudden population increase is known as an irruption. In response to this crisis, generally in late autumn, massive numbers of birds begin to flock into our northern states from Canada, where they have bred and where they usually spend the winter. It is not unusual for such birds to travel thousands of miles in search of scarce food.

Such movements by raptors like rough-legged hawks and snowy owls can be predicted because they are directly related to food supply, such as the number of lemmings available in the far north. At such times, snowy owls have been reported foraging on the beaches of Cape Cod and Long Island. Similar movements of northern shrikes depend on the abundance of mice in the birds' northern breeding grounds. Every three to five years the prey populations decline, and by November bird-watchers who live in the

Northern cardinal fluffing its feathers on a cool winter day.

Continued ➡

northern states such as Maine, Vermont, New Hampshire, New York, and Michigan report an increase in predaceous shrikes.

The mass movements of seed-eating birds are less predictable. They usually remain in their northern breeding grounds over the winter. Seeds from deciduous trees such as birch and aspen and the seed-laden cones of conifers normally sustain them throughout the winter. Movements of these birds into more southerly areas are difficult to predict because seed production depends on the vagaries of the weather—a warm spring and a warm autumn are necessary for a large crop of seeds. A bumper crop in one year does not mean a similar harvest the following year. In years of poor seed production, birds from the boreal forests descend across the Canadian border. At such times, residents of the northern states may see unusual winter visitors, such as redpolls, evening grosbeaks, pine grosbeaks, pine siskins, and red-breasted nuthatches, foraging with familiar winter birds such as cardinals, tufted titmice, and blue jays.

Migration and movements due to population surges are strategies for winter survival that are related to food supply. Except for those that migrate to tropical or semitropical climates, most birds must still cope with the frigid days and nights of winter.

Birds have evolved several strategies for surviving in cold weather. Some strategies cost very little in terms of energy use; others are extremely expensive. One of the least expensive survival techniques involves the birds' feathers. As the temperature goes down, birds fluff up their feathers through the workings of tiny muscles located in their skin. The fluffing action traps and holds the air surrounding the skin, which has been warmed by the birds' internal temperature (102 to 107 degrees F.).

Another, more expensive, strategy is to grow a more dense cover of feathers. Birds that winter in the cold climates have relatively more feathers than migrating birds. Tiny birds such as chickadees, kinglets, and creepers have more feathers relative to their size than the larger birds.

Most warm-blooded animals have devised a natural defense against life-threatening cold: They huddle. The smaller the animal, the more beneficial this strategy can be. Many birds use this strategy to keep warm, huddling together in trees, nest boxes, or any place where there is protection from ice storms or chilling winds. This roosting behavior helps minimize the difference between the body temperature of each bird and that of the surrounding air. When groups of birds huddle together, the heat lost from the group as a whole is similar to that lost from one large animal. Large animals have a smaller surface area relative to their size than smaller animals, thus they lose relatively less heat than smaller animals. The huddled "big bird" in the roost stays warmer than each of the little birds could if left alone in the cold. Scientists have learned that a cluster of house sparrows huddling in a nest box can save about 13 percent of the energy required to keep warm at night. Some birds, such as ruffed grouse and common redpolls, use the insulative properties of snow to protect them from the bone-chilling night air.

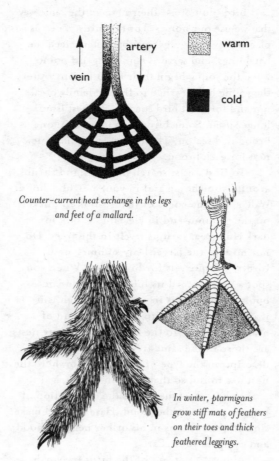

Counter-current heat exchange in the legs and feet of a mallard.

In winter, ptarmigans grow stiff mats of feathers on their toes and thick feathered leggings.

Shivering is another strategy birds use to keep warm. Because this method of getting warm has a high energy price tag, birds must eat large quantities of high-energy (high-fat-content) food to pay the debt. American goldfinches, for example, increase their body weight by 15 percent after a day of foraging. The payoff for the birds is that they can convert food into heat energy four to five times faster when shivering. They could not maintain the shivering if they had not eaten so vigorously. With their engines running at top speed, these birds can endure temperatures as low as minus 40 degrees F. The ability to increase their metabolic rate is believed to be triggered by the diminished light of winter. In the summer, when the days are longer, the birds can metabolize at such a high rate for only an hour. During the short days of winter, they may need to metabolize rapidly for many hours at a time.

Some birds use an opposite strategy, reducing their body temperature during periods of inactivity. When resting, chickadees can reduce their body temperature by about 50 degrees F., which slows their metabolism by 23 percent. This conservation strategy safely carries them through the night with sufficient reserve to fuel early-morning foraging activities. Hibernating animals usually have very low metabolic rates for long periods of time. Although we do not ordinarily associate hibernation with birds, poor-wills and possibly swifts are known hibernators in the bird world.

Most birds' legs are covered with scales, which do not protect from the cold. Those staying the winter in cold climates have shorter legs than their relatives living in warmer regions. This is a structural strategy that helps them conserve heat. Some birds have developed a protective behavior, frequently tucking one leg under the breast feathers to reduce heat loss. Look for these one-legged balls of feathers in

RESOURCES FOR BIRDERS

Elizabeth P. Lawlor

1. Local chapters of the National Audubon Society are listed in the telephone book. If there is no listing for this group in your area, you can write to the national headquarters at 700 Broadway, New York, NY 10003, or call (212) 979-9009.

2. The Cornell Laboratory of Ornithology is a university-based education and field-research facility that has programs of interest for the general public. You can write to the facility at 159 Sapsucker Woods Rd., Ithaca, NY 14850, or call (607) 254-2400.

3. Bird rescue groups can be contacted through your local conservation officer, animal control center or the humane society.

4. The Bird Banding Laboratory, U.S. Fish and Wildlife Service, Laurel, MD 20708 will provide information about this activity that benefits both the birds and us.

—From Discover Nature in Winter

trees and shrubs during the next cold spell.

Something called counter-current heat exchange also helps birds reduce heat loss through their legs and feet. It works in an interesting way. As in other animals, blood flows through arteries from a bird's heart to its extremities, while blood returning to the heart flows through veins. In birds' legs, arteries and veins are close to each other so that warm arterial blood passes some of its heat to the cooler blood in the veins. When the cooled arterial blood reaches the feet, considerably less heat is lost to the environment. In addition, this system decreases the potential shock to the birds' bodies from cold blood returning from the extremities.

A few winter-adapted birds have feathers that protect their legs from the cold. Ptarmigans wear feathered leggings and dense mats of stiff feathers on their feet. The legs of snowy owls are also sheathed in feathers.

Even with these adaptations for cold weather, mortality is high among birds that winter in cold climates. As many as 50 percent of chickadees wintering in the North do not live to sing the next spring. Scientists believe that many of these deaths are among the first-year birds, which may not have had access to good roosting sites or feeding grounds. Fierce winters are not as damaging to bird populations as are early freezes and unseasonable bad weather. Many strategies birds use to carry them through the winter are controlled by shorter days, so an early autumn can do as much damage as a severe winter.

If you live in Vermont, you may find that only about twenty species of birds spend the winter in your neighborhood, but if you live in Maryland, there may be over a hundred species. It is truly amazing that any of these tiny creatures can survive the low temperatures, snow, ice, and killing winds. Winter is certainly a challenge for birds.

—From Discover Nature in Winter

Bird Tracks

Richard P. Smith
Illustrations by DeCourcy L. Taylor, Jr.

Unlike mammals, birds only walk on two feet and they normally have four toes on each foot, three facing forward and one back, although the fourth toe does not always show in tracks. The rear toe is usually the shortest of the four.

There are exceptions to this pattern, though. The long-tailed, brown, crest-headed roadrunner of the arid southwest is a perfect example. This relatively large predatory bird of cartoon fame that feeds on snakes and lizards, among other things, has two toes forward and two backward. The tracks from one of these birds measured as much as 3 inches in length.

The flicker is another bird with toes that do not fit the normal pattern. There are two toes forward and two backward like the rest of the woodpecker family that flickers belong to. One toe facing each direction is smaller than its mate. Unlike other woodpeckers, I have seen flickers feeding on the ground on a regular basis, so there is a possibility of seeing their tracks. The length of one flicker track along the longest toes was 1 3/4 inches.

Flickers have prominent red patches on the backs of their heads and are brown on their backs with black-spotted white breasts. A black, biblike marking is on the chest forming the upper margin of the spotting.

Getting back to bird tracks in general, there are two basic types of track patternsæhopping and walking. Birds that hop will make tracks with both feet side by side. A series of single tracks, one ahead of the other, are made by walking birds. Birds that spend most of their time perched in trees such as songbirds have a tendency to hop, while birds that spend a lot of time on the ground like quail, grouse, and pheasant walk or run.

For the most part, songbirds leave slim-toed tracks showing four toes, with the rear toe at least as long as the other three. Their tracks measure between 1 and 2 inches in overall length. Quail tracks like the bobwhite and California variety leave prints about 2 inches long, with much thicker toes than songbirds. If the rear toe is visible, it is short and angled off to one side, rather than facing straight back like the footprints of songbirds.

Quail

I remember flushing large coveys of California quail with my father and brother in Southern California as a boy. Some coveys contained upwards of fifty birds or more. They occupied brushy valleys and foothills. The males are a blue-gray in color, with large dark patches outlined in white starting under the eyes and covering the throat. Patches of rust coloration are on the lower breast. Males and females have fingerlike top-knots curved forward on their heads. Females are brown in color. Gambel and mountain quail are similar to the California variety. Scaled quail are brown to gray in color with a band of what looks like fish scales on the breast and back of the neck. They also have crests on top of their heads.

The California quail's original range included the southernmost portion of Oregon,

BOBWHITE QUAIL

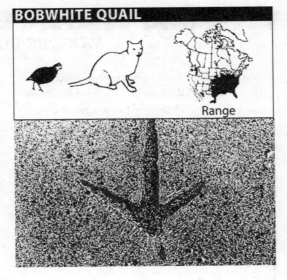

Range

most of California and Mexico. They have since been introduced into much of Oregon and parts of Washington, Idaho, Nevada, and Utah. The gambel quail's stronghold is Arizona and adjacent portions of Utah, Nevada, California, New Mexico, and Colorado in arid regions. Mountain quail, as the name implies, are typically found at higher elevations than the other quail in California, Oregon, Washington, and Idaho. Scaled quail inhabit western Texas, most of New Mexico, and nearby portions of Oklahoma, Kansas, Colorado, and Nevada.

Grouse

Grouse tracks are similar to those of quail, but toes are noticeably thicker and longer. * Tracks are between 2 and 3 inches in length. Some of the birds that fall in this group are ruffed, sharptail, spruce, blue, and ptarmigan. Pheasant tracks are very similar.

The habitat and part of the country where these types of tracks are found are indicative of what species made them, although there is some overlap in the ranges of these birds. *Ruffed grouse* are birds of woodlands and are common in the Great Lakes Region, the eastern United States, and parts of the south, plus states in the northwest. They are also distributed throughout most of Canada and into central Alaska.

As an adaptation for walking in snow, ruffed grouse grow scales along each toe in the fall and shed them in the spring. Tracks of a number of birds can be seen together at times. Ruffed grouse are brown and gray in color with light breasts that have dark bars across them. They got their name from a collar of black feathers usually extended by males when displaying for a female. The rear margin of tail feathers have bands across them producing a continuous band across the tail when it is fanned.

Spruce grouse are found primarily in spruce and jackpine forests. Females are sometimes mistaken for ruffed grouse, being a mottled brown. Males are black. Spruce grouse are also known as "fools hens" due to their habit of letting people approach close enough to kill

*Pigeon tracks could pass for those of quail or grouse, except the toes are slimmer and the rear toe projects straight back and is longer than those of grouse or quail. The prints of these birds are most common in cities or near barns where they reside. The tracks of a pigeon in the snow in my front yard were 2 1/2 inches long.

them with rocks or sticks in some cases. On one occasion I watched Dr. William Robinson, who has studied the birds for years and wrote a book on them aptly titled *Fool Hen*, catch one of these birds by hand, and it was not the first time he had done it.

The distribution of spruce grouse is similar to that of ruffed grouse, except they have a more limited range in the United States (restricted to northernmost states) and is established across a wider area in Canada and Alaska.

Sharptail grouse prefer open country with few trees, although they do spend some time in groves of trees near openings. Flocks of sharptails are common. These birds are tan in color with white breast feathers and short, pointed tails. Both sexes look alike. Their range includes most of the Dakotas, northwest Nebraska, eastern Colorado, eastern Montana, the upper Great Lakes Region, plus much of central Canada and Alaska.

Blue grouse inhabit mountainous regions and the coniferous forests associated with them. The birds are blue-gray in color. They are found primarily in the northwestern United States and Canada, with largest populations in Colorado, Utah, Wyoming, Idaho, Montana, California, Oregon, and Washington. Blue grouse are distributed throughout British Columbia and into the Yukon, plus southwestern Saskatchewan.

Ptarmigan are also mountain grouse, usually living in treeless habitat above timberline or on the tundra, and occur in small flocks. They grow feathers on their feet for the winter. These birds are generally gray to brown in color in the summer and turn white for the winter. Either one of the three species of ptarmigan (rock, willow, and white-tailed) range throughout western and northern Canada and Alaska, and southward in some western states including Washington, Montana, Idaho, Wyoming, Colorado, and New Mexico.

RUFFED GROUSE

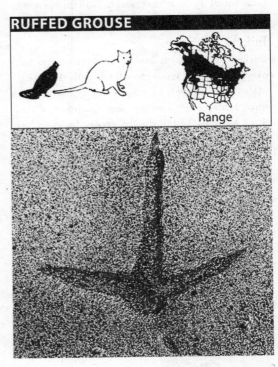

Range

Pheasants

Pheasants are often associated with agricultural areas, with groups of birds present in some fields. Males are colorful, having copper-

Continued ➡

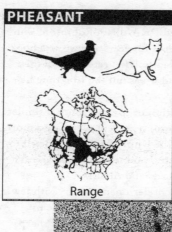

PHEASANT

Range

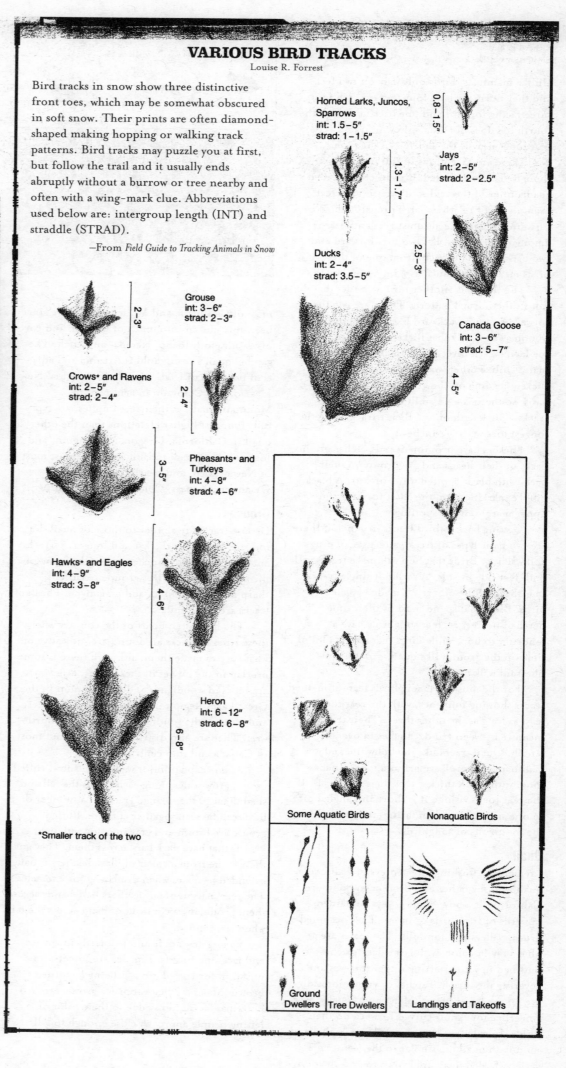

VARIOUS BIRD TRACKS
Louise R. Forrest

Bird tracks in snow show three distinctive front toes, which may be somewhat obscured in soft snow. Their prints are often diamond-shaped making hopping or walking track patterns. Bird tracks may puzzle you at first, but follow the trail and it usually ends abruptly without a burrow or tree nearby and often with a wing-mark clue. Abbreviations used below are: intergroup length (INT) and straddle (STRAD).

—From *Field Guide to Tracking Animals in Snow*

Horned Larks, Juncos, Sparrows
int: 1.5–5"
strad: 1–1.5"

0.8–1.5"

Jays
int: 2–5"
strad: 2–2.5"

1.3–1.7"

Ducks
int: 2–4"
strad: 3.5–5"

2.5–3"

Canada Goose
int: 3–6"
strad: 5–7"

4–5"

Grouse
int: 3–6"
strad: 2–3"

2–3"

Crows* and Ravens
int: 2–5"
strad: 2–4"

2–4"

Pheasants* and Turkeys
int: 4–8"
strad: 4–6"

3–5"

Hawks* and Eagles
int: 4–9"
strad: 3–8"

4–6"

Heron
int: 6–12"
strad: 6–8"

6–8"

*Smaller track of the two

Some Aquatic Birds

Nonaquatic Birds

Ground Dwellers | Tree Dwellers

Landings and Takeoffs

colored bodies, iridescent blue-green heads, red around each eye, and white rings around their necks. Females are a mottled brown. Both sexes have exceptionally long, pointed tail feathers. Though these birds are now found in a band of states from the northeast to Montana, and in the southern portions of several Canadian provinces (Alberta, Saskatchewan, and British Columbia), they are not native to North America.

Pheasants were introduced here from China many years ago. The band of states the pheasant's range includes in the United States is narrowest in the northeast and is widest at mid-continent, going as far south as the northern-most tip of Texas at that point. Some birds are also distributed in parts of every western state.

Turkeys

Turkey tracks will measure 4 or more inches in overall length in correspondence with their size. Males reach weights of 20 pounds or better while females weigh in the neighborhood of 10 to 15 pounds. To tell the difference between hen and gobbler tracks measure only the length of

TURKEY

Range

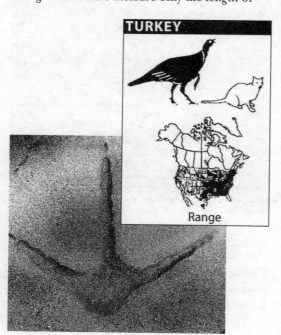

Continued ➡

the middle toe. Those toes are more than 2¹/2 inches on adult toms and less than that for hens. A distance of at least 8 inches separates tracks made by gobblers and the stride of hens is just over 7 inches.

Male turkeys possess beards that grow out of the chest. Wattles, which are normally red, are on the head. The head itself may be red or blue when aroused. Gobblers appear black in color while hens look brown and have naked, dull-colored heads. Hens occasionally grow beards.

Wild turkeys are distributed all across the southern half of the United States from Texas and Oklahoma eastward, with populations established further north in New York, Pennsylvania, Michigan, along the borders of Wisconsin, Minnesota, and Iowa, and in the Dakotas. West of Texas, turkeys are established in parts of Nevada, New Mexico, Arizona, Colorado, Wyoming, Montana, Idaho, Oregon, Washington, and California.

Sandhill Cranes

Tracks of the sandhill crane can be confused with those of turkeys. However, the toes of sandhills are slimmer, have relatively straight edges and are smoother on the underside than turkey toes. Jointed, callous-type pads are on the bottom of turkey feet, and this characteristic sometimes shows in clear prints. Sandhill tracks resemble turkey prints in size, measuring 4 inches or less.

There are two major subspecies of sandhills—*greater* and *lesser*. Greater sandhills are much larger than their relatives. The birds have long legs and are gray to brown in color with the tops of their heads being red. Both males and females look the same. Interestingly, the birds are named after horses, with females referred to as mares, males as roans. And, of course, their young are called colts.

Sandhills nest in the upper Great Lakes Region, plus a group of states in the northwest, and most of Canada and Alaska. Since the birds are migratory and winter in the south, they can be seen virtually anywhere. They nest in bogs, but feed in fields, both noncultivated and agricultural.

Great Blue Herons

Great blue herons leave longer tracks than turkeys and sandhills because their fourth toe shows in prints. One track measured between 6 and 7 inches in length. Even without the rear toe, blue heron tracks are distinctive. Two toes on the inside of each foot are close together with a noticeable gap between them and the toes on the outside.

These migratory birds are blue-gray in color with light-colored breast and head. Long feathers on the chest hang down away from the body and there is a crest or top-knot on the head. Herons are long-legged like cranes. They build colonies of large nests called rookeries in trees over or near water. Blue herons are always associated with water where they feed on fish, frogs, and other items.

Shore Birds

Shore birds such as sandpipers, yellowlegs, and snipe make narrow-toed tracks. Short rear toes may or may not be visible in prints. Small shore-bird tracks are less than an inch long, with those of larger varieties approaching 2 inches. The middle toe is noticeably longer than those on the sides in the tracks of larger shore birds. Their tracks are sometimes abundant in the mud or sand along oceans, lakes, ponds, or rivers. Small round holes left by long, pointed beaks may also be visible where the birds were probing the mud for insects or worms.

Woodcock

Woodcock, a bird of the uplands resembling snipe, make similar tracks, only their prints will be visible in the mud of woods roads most often, although they do feed along the shores of rivers and ponds, too. Incidentally, I have seen some snipe in upland habitat with woodcock, so snipe are not "shore-birds" exclusively. Woodcock tracks are about 13/4 inches in length on the average and probing holes may be visible nearby. Snipe tracks may be smaller, measuring about 1¹/2 inches.

Snipe are white and black in color. Woodcock are brown and black, with bulging eyes that are larger than those of snipe well suited for seeing at night. The winter and summer ranges of woodcock encompass the eastern half of the United States and southern Canada. Snipe are distributed throughout North America.

Waterfowl

Web-footed birds include ducks, geese, swans, and gulls. Webbing may not be visible in all tracks though. Only three toes are usually present. Waterfowl tracks usually have marks from toenails visible at the ends of toes. Duck tracks range from less than 2 inches in length for small teal to 3 inches for mallards. The prints of herring gull I measured were 2¹/2 inches long and a glaucous gull left prints measuring a little over 3 inches. One Canada goose track was 3 inches long, but smaller subspecies have duck-size feet. Swan tracks are largest, taping 7 inches or more.

Look for waterfowl tracks in the mud or snow along lakes, ponds, and rivers. However, those are not the only locations where their tracks will appear. Both ducks and geese feed on grain and grass in fields where imprints may be left in mud. I have also seen goose tracks in sand and gravel pits where they have stopped to rest.

Scavengers

Scavengers such as crows, ravens, and magpies make four-toed tracks. The three forward-facing toes of ravens and crows leave impressions closer together than most other bird tracks I have seen. This is because the outside toes face forward more than to the sides like those of other birds. The tracks of magpies are about 2 inches long, with crow prints ranging between 2¹/2 and 3 inches, and raven feet leave prints from 3¹/2 to 4¹/2 inches in length.

Look for their tracks in the sand or snow around the carcasses of dead animals, especially those killed by cars. However, ravens have also clued me in to the locations of both hunter-killed and winter-killed deer. Magpies have long, narrow, black tails with bodies that are black and white. They are seen most often in western North America. Both ravens and crows are totally black, with ravens being the larger of the two. Ravens have slower wingbeats than crows and tails that are more rounded on the corners as opposed to the squared off tails of crows. Ravens are found primarily in the northern United States and into Canada, while crows enjoy a wide distribution in North America.

—From *Animal Tracks and Signs of North America*

Frogs

Elizabeth P. Lawlor
Illustrations by Pat Archer

Today, there are 3,800 known species of frogs worldwide, 82 of which live in North America. Frogs are amphibians, which means that in the course of their lifespan they lead a "double life," first in water and then on land. As eggs and larvae they are bound to a watery existence in freshwater ponds, streams, lakes, or even puddles, but then as adults they adapt to life on land. Scientists place frogs in a special group of amphibians called *anurans*. The word means "without tail" and distinguishes frogs from salamanders and caecilians. …

Some frogs live for as long as nine years, but most live about four. Therefore, frogs living in cold climates need some strategies for surviving the winter. American and spadefoot toads sleep in burrows beneath the earth; wood frogs and gray tree frogs (*Hyla versicolor*) prefer to overwinter on the forest floor or in rock crevices covered by leaf litter. Green frogs find shelter on the bottoms of ponds, lakes, or streams, whereas northern leopard frogs snuggle into the soft ooze of streambeds, lakes, and ponds. Scientists know a great deal about the breeding life of many frog species but little about the way they spend the rest of their year. …

Adult frogs must live near water to reproduce, thus water remains essential to the success of the species. During the breeding season they need to mate and deposit their eggs in water because frog eggs are wrapped in a gelatinelike material that easily dries out, rather than a calcium case or leathery shell like bird or turtle eggs.

Although most adult frogs do not drink, all frogs absorb water through their permeable skins, especially the abdominal skin. Some frogs sit for some time during the day in small puddles to replace the water lost through their skin or used in metabolism. Frogs of one species counter water loss by secreting a waxy substance and rubbing it on themselves. Tree frogs have evolved another strategy: they spend the hottest part of the day with their abdomens pressed against the bark of a tree, which minimizes water loss through their permeable abdominal skin. It could be that the problem of water loss is a factor in making frogs creatures of the night, because the night is cooler and more moist. The daytime sun can make it dangerous for frogs to be out.

Herpetologists—those who study the life and times of frogs—are becoming more and more concerned about the amphibians' future. The reports from 1989 and 1990 conferences held by the World Congress of Herpetology and by the Biology Board of the National Research Council cite an alarming worldwide decline in some frog species. Though scientists agree that frogs have had to cope with predators and variations in rainfall, they point out that because frogs absorb

Continued ➡

moisture through their skin, they are susceptible to pollutants dissolved in the water such as insecticides and pesticides. These chemicals are leached from the land as rain and melting snow drains into frog breeding ponds. Frogs are also gravely affected by acid rain. Habitat destruction through the draining of wetlands for homes and agriculture by humans is another cause of their decreasing numbers, and frogs are killed by cars, generally on roads that separate breeding pools from winter resting places.

Frog voices calling from bogs and swamps as soft rains fall on the still-cold earth stir a sense of hope and of regeneration every spring, but there may come a time when we won't hear those magical sounds. Frogs, like the birds, are warning us that there is a problem with the environment; these beautiful creatures are telling us that something is very wrong in the frog pond.

Putting Anurans in Order

People tend to lump all frogs into a few simple categories—pond frogs versus toads, big frogs versus little frogs—but the world of nature is much more complicated than that. Even in the world of the frogs it is beautifully diverse. Scientists have organized frogs into several groups: tailed frogs, narrow-mouthed toads, spadefoot toads, true toads, cricket frogs, chorus frogs, tree frogs, and true frogs. The activities in this chapter focus on a few of the most available frogs in each major group, as follows:

- Spadefoot toads—eastern spadefoot toad (*Scaphiopus holbrooki*)
- True toads—American toad (*Bufo americanus*)
- Tree frogs—spring peeper (*Pseudacris crucifer*), gray tree frog (*Hyla versicolor*)
- True frogs—eastern wood frog (*Rana sylvatica*), northern leopard frog (*Rana pipiens*), green frog (*Rana clamitans*), bullfrog (*Rana catesbeiana*)

These representative frogs have a wide range east of the Rocky Mountains. You can find other species in your locality by consulting a field guide to amphibians. The specific habitats preferred by these frogs are outlined in the chart that follows.

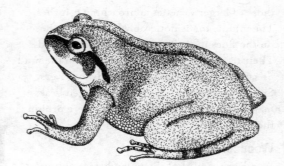

Pacific tree frog (Hyla regilla)

Rain and humidity bring out the frogs. If the night is windless, so much the better. Listen early in the spring for the calling that marks the beginning of the frogs' annual trek from winter hideouts to their breeding places. Once this migration begins, you can expect the calling to continue into summer. Throughout this period you may see hundreds of frogs hopping across country roads because these roadways cut through the bogs, swamps, and other inland wetlands frogs use for breeding.

If you are not able to locate any frog ponds, ask the naturalists at a local nature center or museum or contact a local group such as the Audubon Society. Members of your local or regional herpetological society are also excellent resources.

Frog Calls

The most accurate way to identify a frog call is to see the vocalist in action, but this is not always possible. A good substitute is to listen to recordings. With the help of modern technology, scientists have recorded frog calls in the field and you can use these at home. Sometimes your local library will have a tape or will get it if you request it.

The following table describes frog calls as compiled by field investigators. It is very difficult to put animal sounds into print, but perhaps this listing will help you.

There are those who say that frog calls lack melody, but all agree that the calls have character. Make a tape recording of frog calls to help you decide. ...

Is It a Frog or a Toad?

It's easy to tell frogs and toads from other amphibians such as salamanders and newts. What is not so easy is to separate frogs from their closer relatives, the toads, as the terms *frog* and *toad* often cause some confusion. It is easiest to make the distinction if you remember that *frog* is an umbrella term that includes all hopping or leaping amphibians, including toads. In other words, toads are a type of frog. ...

Did you find the critter in a moist habitat such as a marsh, pond, or swampy area? Is it slim with smooth skin and long slender legs? Does it move quickly and leap great distances (greater than its body length)? Did you find it near others of its kind? If you have answered yes to these questions, you probably have caught a frog.

If you found the animal by itself in a drier habitat, such as woodland, meadow, or suburban yard, and thick, bumpy skin covers its plump body, it's a safe guess that you have captured a toad. Prominent bony ridges on top of their heads (cranial crests) and conspicuous swelling behind their eyes (parotid glands) are other marks of toads.

Toads also are known for their sluggish movements, and with stubby legs they hop rather than leap as frogs do. Some frog species such as the gray tree frog have rough skin, which may lead you to believe they are toads, and other frog species may even look like toads—but their long legs and moist skin are good clues to their identity.

Additional Observations

Almost everyone knows a frog when he sees one, and even small children can tell us that frogs have bulging eyes, wide mouths, and front legs shorter than their hind legs. What may not be so widely known is the way their tongues work. The long, sticky tongue of a frog is attached at the front of its mouth rather than the back, which allows it to do a remarkable thing. Like a fly fisherman casting his line, the frog can flip its tongue into the air and snare a passing insect with amazing speed and efficiency. ...

Frogs have eardrums, or tympanic membranes, which are round and often a different color than the frog's skin. Look for them behind the eyes. In some frog species you can distinguish the males from the females by the size of the eardrum relative to the eye. If the eardrum is larger than the eye, the frog is a male; if the eardrum is about the same size as the frog's eye, then the frog is a female.

Look at the area behind the frog's eyes. Do you see a conspicuous swelling behind each eye? These are the parotid glands, which toads use to produce toxic chemicals that are distasteful to predators. When threatened, a toad will lower its head to the level of its abdomen, so that when the predator attacks, it will grab the parotids, thus getting a mouthful of foul-tasting, toxic chemicals. Some frogs, such as the northern leopard frog, similarly secrete acidic fluids that irritate the mucous lining in the predator's mouth....

Spadefoot toads are equipped with a special hard, crescent-shaped spade at the heel of each hind foot, an adaptation the toad uses for

FROG	HABITAT
Eastern spadefoot toad (*Scaphiopus holbrooki*)	Gravelly, sandy, or loamy soils of dunes, farmlands, forests, and meadows
American toad (*Bufo americanus*)	Diverse, dry habitats including meadows, suburban backyards, mountain forests
Spring peeper (*Pseudacris crucifer*)	Low-growing shrubs near temporary pools and inland wetlands, floodplains
Gray tree frog (*Hyla versicolor*)	Trees and shrubs near temporary woodland wetlands
Eastern wood frog (*Rana sylvatica*)	Damp woodlands, shaded wooded hillsides, meadows
Northern leopard frog (*Rana pipiens*)	Damp meadows, fields, orchards, brackish marshes
Green frog (*Rana clamitans*)	Wetlands, along the edges of streams and ponds
Bullfrog (*Rana catesbeiana*)	Permanent bodies of water, ponds, lakes

Continued ➡

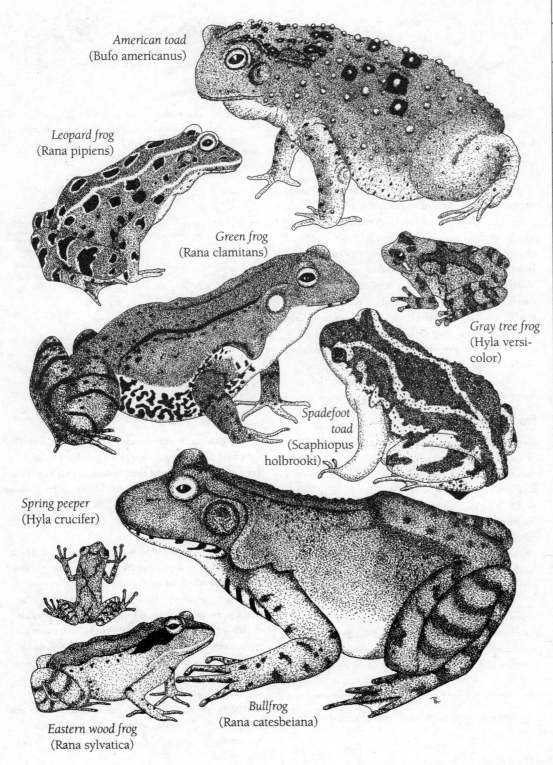

American toad
(Bufo americanus)

Leopard frog
(Rana pipiens)

Green frog
(Rana clamitans)

Gray tree frog
(Hyla versi-color)

Spadefoot toad
(Scaphiopus holbrooki)

Spring peeper
(Hyla crucifer)

Eastern wood frog
(Rana sylvatica)

Bullfrog
(Rana catesbeiana)

FROG IDENTIFICATION

TREE FROGS (*Hyla spp.*): Swollen discs on tips of toes, toes not webbed

Spring peeper (H. crucifer)	Has "x" on its back *1 inch long* Light ash gray to light brown
Gray tree frog (H. versicolor)	Ash gray Yellow-white spot below eye Rough skin

TRUE FROGS (*Rana sp.*): Seldom found far from water. Many have two ridges (dorsolateral folds) of skin that begin behind the eye and run down on either side of the back. All have webbed toes.

Bullfrog (R. catesbeiana)	Largest frog, 6–8 inches long Large mouth Color dusky, mottled Bars of dark color on legs No dorsolateral folds
Green frog (R. clamitans)	Small Leaps widely into water when disturbed, often "screaming" Dorsolateral folds Bright green head and shoulders Shades to dusty brown olive on back
Wood frog (R. sulvatica)	Small, slender Very long hind legs Pronounced dorsolateral folds Chocolate brown or fawn colored Wears a "face mask" Spends a lot of time away from water
Northern leopard frog (R. pipiens)	3–5 inches long Hunts insects in grassy meadows Eardrum (*tympanum*) almost size of eye Dorsolateral folds Head somewhat pointed Large light-bordered spots on back

FROG CALLS

FROG	SOUNDS
Bullfrog (*Rana catesbeiana*)	Deep hum or drone, "burr woom," "jug-o-rum," "ooohoom"
Spadefoot toad (*Scaphiopus holbrooki*)	Deep, explosive, nasal "waank" or "waagh"
Green frog (*Rana clamitans*)	Banjolike, explosive single note or a series of plunks descending in scale
Spring peeper (*Pseudacris crucifer*)	Whistlelike, high peep, slurred, higher pitch at the end, 1-second intervals.
Gray tree frog (*Hyla versicolor*)	Brief, hoarse, 2–6 seconds long
American toad (*Bufo americanus*)	High-pitched and musical, 5–30 seconds, has a distinct flutelike quality
Eastern wood frog (*Rana sylvatica*)	"Quack," like a duck
Northern leopard frog (*Rana pipiens*)	Snorelike croaks

The hind feet of tree frogs have adhesive discs on toes, which help them cling to twigs and bark.

The hind feet of bullfrogs have extensive webs; fourth toe protudes well beyond other toes.

Continued ➡

digging backwards into its burrow beneath the sandy soil. Young spadefoot toads must make their burrows in very soft, crumbly soil because their spades are soft.

What is its general body shape? How is this an advantage for a creature that spends a great deal of time in the water?

Compare the frog skeleton with a human skeleton. You will notice that frogs don't have ribs. Look for other differences and similarities.

The frog has a long, sticky tongue attached to the front of the mouth. When an insect flies by, the frog's tongue is propelled out for an instant to grab it.

Frogs do not have exterior ears. The eardrum lies on the surface behind the frog's eyes. Many times eardrums of males are larger than those of females.

Getting to Know a Frog

One of the most rewarding aspects of frog watching is that you can learn to identify individuals. This kind of identification is important to scientists because it helps them find out such things about a frog as how far it roams, what its territorial boundaries are, and how long it lives. One investigator discovered that an American toad (*Bufo americanus*) lived in his backyard for nine years.

Although frogs and toads of the same species will look similar to each other, you can learn to recognize individual difference in color and pattern design. With practice you will know whether the frog in the garden on one night is the same frog that appears there on other occasions. To do this, you will need to make careful records of each of the frogs you find. Look carefully and record the pattern of color on each frog that you are observing. …

Observing Food Chains and Webs

Frogs and toads eat invertebrates. Most of these are insects, but spiders, ants, and even earthworms have a place in the anuran diet. Thus, adult frogs and toads are predators. The prey need to be moving in order to activate the feeding response in frogs. You can observe this if you sit quietly beside a frog pond in the twilight. Watch carefully, and you may witness a frog capture a dragonfly or other large insect with its tongue.

Frogs and toads are also delicacies for many other animals. As you spend time around the frog "hot spots," look for the creatures that prey on them. You may be on hand to see some food chains at work. Some frog predators include skunks, turtles, hognosed snakes, garter snakes, wading birds such as green herons, fish, and small mammals such as weasels, raccoons, and muskrats. Even domestic cats and dogs may help themselves to a frog or two.

While you are observing the food chains that involve frogs, look for those in which tadpoles are among the players. Newts, fish, water beetles, and water scorpions are a few tadpole predators. …

Frog Calls

Calling is the most expensive activity in the life of an adult male frog in terms of the energy it requires. During the breeding season, male frogs call hundreds or thousands of times each night. The calling behavior of frogs can cost more than calories, as predators often use the calls to find tasty meals. The life of a frog is often the price a species pays for successful mating and the subsequent arrival of a new generation of frogs.

To produce calls, frogs take air into their lungs through their nostrils and pump the air rapidly back and forth from the lungs to a resonating chamber called the vocal sac. In its journey the air passes over the vocal cords,

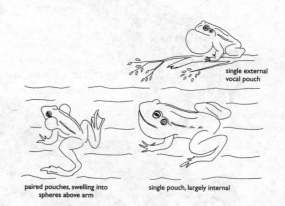

Three types of vocal sacs in frogs.

causing them to vibrate and produce the familiar "croak." If you have ever tried to sleep near a frog pond, you know that croaking can continue throughout the night. When calling, a frog never needs to open its mouth. …

Eyelids

Since frogs live both in water and on land, their eyes must be able to function both when exposed to air and when submerged. The biggest problem for an eye in open air is that it might dry up; to prevent this, frogs have thick eyelids. A thin, transparent fold called the nictitating membrane passes over the eye from bottom to top and serves to moisten and protect the eye by washing it with a thin film of tearlike liquid secreted by glands in the eye. This liquid contains lysozyme (an enzyme found in tears and in egg whites), which protects the eyes from bacteria, viruses, and fungi that sneak in under the eyelids.

Frogs cannot turn their heads as we do. To compensate for this lack of neck motion, frogs' bulging eyes provide them with a wide range of vision. This helps them find food and spot predators. You need only to sneak up on a frog to find out how well this design works. Frogs see well in twilight, and their night vision is extremely good. When frogs slip beneath the water's surface, the nictitating membrane rises to cover the eye. As tadpoles, their eyes are suited to life in the winter. During this phase of their life, frog's eyes more closely resemble those of fish than those of adult frogs.

Camouflage

Frogs have lightly colored underparts that contrast sharply with their darker tops. This is called countershading and is part of the frog's camouflage. The light coloring along the underside of the frog makes it difficult for a deep-swimming predator looking toward the surface of the water to see its prey as it swims along the

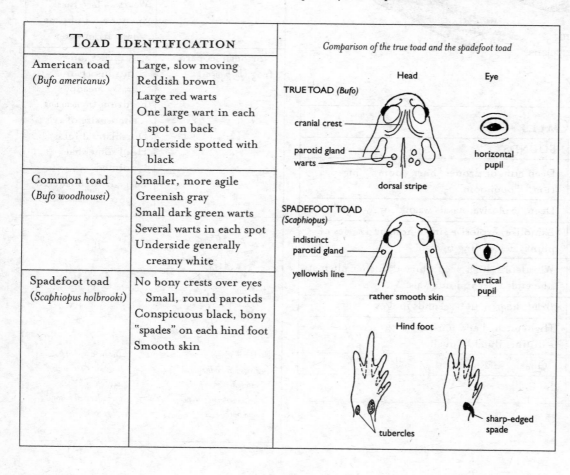

Toad Identification	
American toad (*Bufo americanus*)	Large, slow moving Reddish brown Large red warts One large wart in each spot on back Underside spotted with black
Common toad (*Bufo woodhousei*)	Smaller, more agile Greenish gray Small dark green warts Several warts in each spot Underside generally creamy white
Spadefoot toad (*Scaphiopus holbrooki*)	No bony crests over eyes Small, round parotids Conspicuous black, bony "spades" on each hind foot Smooth skin

Comparison of the true toad and the spadefoot toad

Head — Eye

TRUE TOAD (*Bufo*)

cranial crest

parotid gland
warts

horizontal pupil

dorsal stripe

SPADEFOOT TOAD (*Scaphiopus*)

indistinct parotid gland

yellowish line

rather smooth skin

vertical pupil

Hind foot

tubercles

sharp-edged spade

Continued ➡

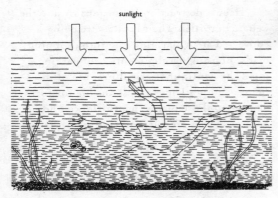

Viewed through the water, the dark dorsal surface of the frog is difficult to see against the dark bottom of the pond.

surface. It is equally difficult to see the dark upper surface of the frog against the dark background of the pond bottom when looking down through the water.

The mottled pattern found on frogs also serves to make the frog difficult to see because the irregular outline breaks up the form of the frog's body. When looking for frogs, your eyes see the disruptive pattern as part of the vegetation in the frog's habitat.

Eye Shine

In the dark, our pupils become large black circles. Their size is controlled by the muscular irises, which contract as light diminishes. This process allows the maximum amount of available light to reach the rods of the retina; however, not all the light that passes through the pupil reaches the rods. Some of it is absorbed by surrounding tissues and is not available to illuminate our way in the dark.

Other critters have evolved different strategies for night vision. Owls, known for their nocturnal activity, have eyes that contain only rods, and their night vision is far superior to ours. The eyes of cats and water-bound dolphins contain many thousands more rods than our eyes do, and they see very well in the dark.

Another device developed by night-wandering animals is a layer of specialized cells called the *tapetum* that lies behind the retina. These mirrorlike cells reflect light back through the retina where it has a second chance to stimulate vision cells. You can see the tapetum when the eyes of skunks, raccoons, cats, and other animals are caught in the beam of light from a flashlight or the headlight of a car. Look for the red, yellow, or green eyeshine in our common night stalkers. You can learn to identify some animals by the color of their eye shine.

—Excerpted from *Discover Nature in Water and Wetlands*

Turtles

Elizabeth P. Lawlor
Illustrations by Pat Archer

Much remains unknown about the origin of turtles. Scientists believe that their forebears may date as far back as 250 million years ago, to a primitive two-foot-long reptile. This ancestor carried a row of unfused bony plates over its back and tail. The plates eventually fused and spread out over the body to form a primitive, tubelike shell. This armor protected the animal from predators, as well as from extremes in temperature, but did not interfere with its stout walking legs. Over time, there were further changes in the reptilian ancestor, until it eventually looked much like the turtle we know today. Those early but fully formed turtles differed somewhat from those we see today, however. They were unable to pull their heads into the neck fold of skin, and they had tiny teeth, but they did possess a shell, the unmistakable hallmark of the turtle. Across eons of time, this basic characteristic has remained unchanged.

The new blueprint of the turtle's shell shows several modifications in the animal's body plan. Unlike the shell of the ancestral turtles, the bony upper shell, or carapace, is firmly attached to the flattened ribs that support it. The bony portion of the shell is now covered by close-fitting horny sections called scutes, which vary in color and design and aid in identifying different species of turtles. Like the rafters in the roof of a house, the pitch of the ribs determine the shape of the carapace; some turtle shells are dome shaped, while others are relatively flat.

The carapace and plastron are made of bony plates, or scutes, that fit closely together. The scutes are covered with a horny material that resembles our fingernails. This outer layer is sometimes shed or worn off, but as the turtle grows in size, it cannot shed its shell to accommodate the increasing size of the bones and other organs that underlie it. Instead, new material grows beneath the older horny material and covers the constantly enlarging bone of the shell. The new growth extends beyond the old shield and produces a ring around its edges. Like the concentric rings found in tree trunks, each ring on a shield represents a year of growth. Because the rings are easier to see on young turtles, the technique is most accurately used on turtles up to about the age of eight. In warm climates, growth continues throughout the year, so it is difficult to determine the age of the turtles.

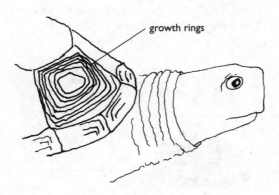

growth rings

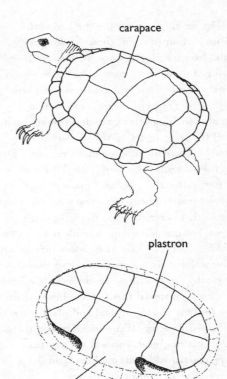

carapace

plastron

bridge

Turtles have an upper shell, or carapace, and a lower shell, or plastron, connected by a bony bridge.

GENERIC TURTLE

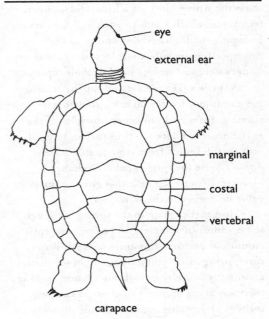

eye
external ear
marginal
costal
vertebral
carapace

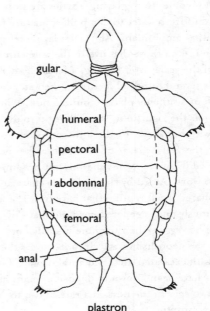

gular
humeral
pectoral
abdominal
femoral
anal
plastron

Continued →

The development of the shell required additional modifications in turtle design. Turtles have lungs, but since the ribs are fused to the ridged shell, chest muscles like ours would not help them inhale and exhale air. Instead, they have three sets of special muscles that control their lungs. Two muscles, one on each side of the body, increase the size of the body cavity. This activity pulls air into the lungs. The air is forced out of the lungs by a third muscle pushing against the internal organs. When you observe a turtle, it may seem that muscles in the animal's throat are involved in the breathing process, but the movement actually is a result of breathing, not the cause of it. Some turtles can survive without air for an amazing six months.

Turtles are toothless. Their jaws are covered with a horny material that forms a beak, which is a fine tool for tearing animal and plant material into bite-size pieces. If you watch turtles in captivity eat raw meat, you will see that this arrangement works well for them, and the absence of teeth is not a handicap.

What turtles eat depends primarily on where they live. Those that spend most of their time on land are generally herbivores, tending to eat only plant material. Some aquatic turtles feed on the plants or animals they find in the ponds and quiet streams where they live. Some dine on carrion, and others eat only small animals. Because turtles are slow moving and cannot chase their prey, they use a hide-and-pounce technique, which seems to work well for them. Snapping turtles have been known to grab unsuspecting ducks by their legs, drag them underwater, and make a meal of their captives.

A turtle's skin is scaly and tough, helping prevent injury from attacks by predators or abrasion from rocks or other obstacles in the environment. There is a thin surface layer of cells that flakes off from time to time. This doesn't cause the turtle's color to change, however, because the cells that give the turtle its color lie deeper in the skin.

Most turtles mate in the spring, although some wait until summer, and a few even until autumn to perform this annual ritual. From early spring into autumn, you might see turtles crawling resolutely through woodlands, making their way along roadside ditches, or slogging through the muddy realm of ponds and swamps. When it comes to egg laying, turtles are not bound to fresh water to damp places, as are frogs and other amphibians. All turtles lay their eggs on land, even those that live in the water for the rest of the year. After mating, a female generally travels several hundred feet from the water in search of a suitable place to build a nest. When she finds the right spot, she will begin to dig a hole with her sharp-toed front feet. After excavating the surface layer of earth, which has been softened by spring rains, she will put her hind legs to work. Aided by sharp claws, a characteristic shared by all reptiles that have feet, she will laboriously dig a deeper inner hole that will cradle her eggs. When the hole is sufficiently deep, she deposits her eggs into it, covers the hole with excavated dirt, and ambles away. Large turtles have been known to deposit as many as fifty-two eggs in the nest, at a rate of two to three a minute. ...

In all animals, heat production and regulation of internal temperature are essential for metabolic activity to take place. In birds and mammals, the source of body heat and the mechanism for control of that heat are internal, and the temperatures produced are stable within a given range. These animals are referred to as endotherms. In turtles, the body heat produced is conducted to the outside environment faster than they can replace it. Thus, the turtle's internal body temperature is controlled mostly by external factors, such as the daily fluctuations of temperature and seasonal variations. Turtles and other animals that function this way are called ectotherms. (The terms "cold-blooded" and "warm-blooded" are old-fashioned and have fallen into disuse, since they do not provide a realistic idea of the metabolic differences between these two groups of animals.)

As the ambient temperature falls, turtles cannot generate enough body heat to maintain a constant internal temperature. Without a sufficiently high internal temperature, turtles cannot keep their vital processes, such as circulation, respiration, and digestion, working effectively. By the end of August, shorter days and cooler nights herald the coming of autumn. The turtles instinctively know that these events signal a cooling trend that leads to frigid winds and icy landscapes. They know that it's time to prepare now for the cold season. As the temperature drops, turtles become increasingly inactive. When the temperature is about 50 degrees F., turtles will seek protection beneath piles of leaf litter. But when the temperature drops below freezing, many species, including painted, musk, and snapping turtles, return to the ponds that fed them during warmer weather and crawl beneath blankets of mud. While beneath the mud in a state of suspended animation, a turtle's internal functions are slowed considerably. A painted turtle, for example, reduces its heartbeat to a mere one beat in ten minutes. In the reduced metabolic state brought on by the cold, turtles can go without food and air for a very long time.

Different turtle species have various ways of surviving the cold weather. Painted turtles that hatch from their eggs in early autumn remain throughout the winter about four inches below their earthen cover. They will surface sometime in May, after the spring sun has warmed the air. The eastern box turtle digs a den about three to four feet into the soil and remains there tightly closed inside its "box."

During winter's milder days, turtles are often seen sunning themselves on fallen logs, rocks, clumps of dead grass, and rafts of sphagnum moss, where they may pile up two or three deep. You can observe turtles basking even in the winter on warm days.

The eastern box turtle digs a den about 3 to 4 feet down and backfills with leaves and soil to cover itself. Snug in its shell, it is protected from the winter's chilling cold.

Habitat destruction is a major threat to the welfare of turtles. Their habitats are being converted at an alarming rate into shopping malls, housing developments, and parking lots. The continued agricultural use of insecticides and pesticides is responsible for further damage to those places that turtles call home. Several species are currently on the protected list....

Turtle Types

Wood and Pond Turtles. These turtles are adapted for living both on land and in the water. Their legs are strong enough for walking on land, and they have webbed toes that make them effective swimmers. Their cumbersome shells do not interfere with their ability to swim. They are omnivores, eating both plant and animal material.

Land Tortoises. These turtles have heavy, bulky shells and move more slowly than wood and pond turtles. Their front legs are adapted for shoveling soil and sand aside. The front edge of the bottom shell is curved upward so that it doesn't get hung up on obstacles but instead helps the turtles slide up and over obstacles, like the upcurved front of a sled. With their heavy armor, they don't need to run from predators, and this, combined with their diet of plant materials, makes life in the slow lane possible.

Soft-shelled Turtles. These turtles seldom leave their watery world, where they live partly buried in the mud. The soft-shelled turtle has a thin, leathery shell that resembles a pancake and a flat body adapted to wiggling into the mud for protection, leaving only the head projecting. This turtle is colored to look like mud or muddy stones.

Turtle Anatomy

The ideal way to observe a wild creature is to avoid anything that interferes with it or disturbs its normal routine. When you are observing turtles, be very careful to do no harm, both to

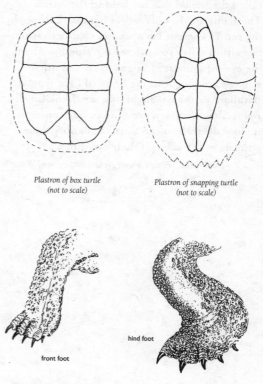

Plastron of box turtle
(not to scale)

Plastron of snapping turtle
(not to scale)

hind foot

front foot

The webbing on the turtle's hind feet is more highly developed.

Continued ➡

the creature and to its habitat. Some turtles, like the box turtle, withdraw into their shells if you pick them up, but others have long, agile necks and may reach back to bite you, so be careful both for your sake and for the turtle's.

Since many turtle species tend to retract their legs, head, and tail when picked up, this is a good time to look at the suit of armor it wears. The top shell, or carapace, derived from the Spanish word for "shield," adheres to the turtle's backbone and ribs. In many turtles, this shell has a dome shape. The steepness of the dome varies and is dependent on the curve of the turtle's ribs that lie beneath it. In some species, the carapace is almost flat. In others, it is high and boxy. The bottom shell, which adheres to the breastbone, is called the plastron, from the Italian word for "breastplate," a piece of armor that soldiers strapped across the chest to deflect arrows and blows from swords. …

The diagrams of the box turtle and the snapping turtle illustrate two extremes in plastron design. The crosslike shape of the snapping turtle's lower shell allows greater freedom of movement, but protection of limbs, head, and neck from below has been sacrificed. The snapping turtle's head, neck, and limbs are extremely agile, and it can be dangerous unless you are very careful and know how to handle it. In contrast, the box turtle has given up agility for complete protection from its shell.

People often think they see a snake in a pond, only to find out they were looking at the head and neck of a turtle. …

Turtle Identification

The outline and illustrations below include some of our more common turtles and will help you identify the turtles you find.

1. Spotted Turtle
(*Clemmys guttata*)

Habitat. Shallow ponds, marshes, small woodland streams, and rain-filled pools in wooded areas, along dirt roads, and in rain-soaked pastures.

Field marks. The blue-black to black top shell is smooth and low. It's handsomely decorated with

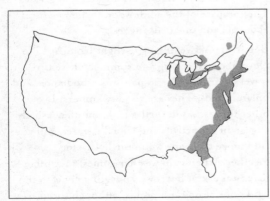

Range of the spotted turtle.

Spotted turtle (Clemmys guttata), 3¹/₂ to 5 inches.

randomly placed lemon yellow spots. The polkadot pattern differs for each individual. Head and limbs are similarly spotted but are gray to black. The dark pigment melanin increases with age, so the top shells of older turtles are frequently spotless. The underside edges of the upper shell are marked with yellow. The female has a yellow chin and orange eyes; the male has a tan chin and brown eyes. The male's tail is almost twice as long as the female's tail, and the male's carapace grows to about five inches.

Behavior. Look for spotted turtles during the daylight hours, when they sun themselves on floating logs, rocks, or clumps of grasses and reeds near water's edge. They may bask in the company of painted turtles. You may see them hunting for food as well. These turtles don't engage in aimless wandering. With darkness, they burrow under vegetation, into muddy bottoms of wetlands, where they remain until dawn.

Food preferences. Feed on grasses and green algae underwater. Also eat live or dead aquatic insect larvae, small crustaceans, snails, and tadpoles.

Predators. Bald eagles, skunks, and raccoons.

Breeding and nesting. Early March, when water temperatures reach 46 degrees F. and the air reaches 54 degrees F. Dry, sandy fields and the margins of hayfields are choice nest spots. Vegetation such as bluestem grasses or sweet ferns generally shelters a nest.

Other remarks. Spotted turtles have keen senses of smell and sight. These turtles may live into their twenties.

2. Painted Turtle
(*Chrysemys picta*)

Habitat. Permanent shallow waters with muddy bottoms and plenty of vegetation, such as partially overgrown ponds.

Field marks. A handsome small turtle with a flat top shell that is olive with yellow or red markings along its edge. The carapace colors blend with the patterns and colors of shade, plants, and earth, camouflaging the turtle, but you may see the scarlet rim of the shells when it dips beneath the surface of the pond. The plates on the upper shell sides are bordered with yellow. The lower shell is bright yellow-orange. The head and neck are adorned with yellow streaks behind the eye. Yellow stripes of uniform length become red as they extend to throat. Limbs and tail are also speckled and streaked with red. There are four subspecies of the painted turtle, each of which sports its own characteristic pattern of red and yellow. Adults measure six to eight inches in length.

Behavior. In the northern part of their range, look for them from March into November. They often are seen basking on logs, rocks, and amid clumps of floating grasses early in the morning and again in the afternoon. You may also be able to see these turtles swimming beneath winter ice. Farther south, they emerge sooner and begin hibernation later. Be careful if you want to observe them for details; the slightest movement may send them spilling into the water and out of sight. At night they sleep on the muddy sheets that line their ponds. They don't ever stray far from their watery homes.

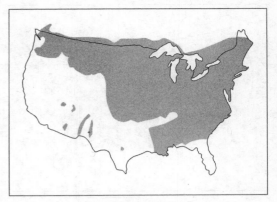

Range of the painted turtle.

Painted turtle (Chrysemys picta), 6 to 8 inches.

Food preferences. Animal or plant material of any type, living or dead, including earthworms, leeches, slugs, snails, crayfish, spiders, water striders, beetles, dragonflies, springtails, damselflies, and dead fish. Forage in the morning and late in the afternoon, along the bottom of ponds and among algae. Eat underwater and seem unable to swallow their food if out of water.

Predators. Primarily raccoons, but chipmunks, skunks, badgers, foxes, garter snakes, fish crows, and humans also destroy nests.

Breeding and nesting. Nests may be found along the tree-lined margins of fields, a few feet to several yards away from the tree line, along roadsides, and in gravel pits. Only females leave the pond, and they do so when ready to lay their eggs.

Other remarks. One of the most numerous turtles in North America. One reason for its success is that it is able to live in ponds close to our homes in the suburbs and in cities. May live some twenty years.

3. Eastern Box Turtle
(*Terrapene carolina*)

Habitat. Primarily woodland turtles, you may find them in neglected pastureland and marshy meadows. Although considered a land turtle, they will take to water. They will soak in mud for hours to wash away the dust and to escape hot summer air.

Field marks. Unique hinged lower shell that can be closed tightly by strong muscles against the upper shell, protecting the turtle against all predators. The seal is so tight that even a thin knife blade cannot be wedged between the shells when they are closed. Easily recognized high, domed, brownish top shell with yellow or orange rays, and spots or bars in each plate. Tan to brown lower shell that may or may not be patterned. Black to reddish skin streaked or spotted with red, yellow, or orange. There are four subspecies that differ somewhat in color. Males can be distinguished from females by eye coloræred or pink in males, and generally

Continued ➔

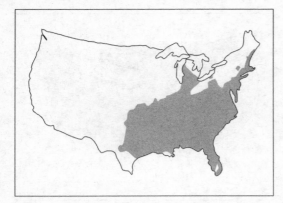

Range of the eastern box turtle.

Eastern box turtle (Terrapene carolina), 4 to 6 inches.

brown, but sometimes purple or gray, in females. Adults measure four to six inches in length.

Behavior. From April through October, you may find them sunning themselves at the edges of fields or roads or in forest groves. They avoid the heat of the day by hiding under logs, in clumps of decaying leaves, vacant mammal burrows, or holes they dig into the mud. Box turtles have fairly well-defined home territories that are usually less than 750 square feet, which they wander freely. Because they have a strong sense of direction, they seldom get lost.

Food preferences. Forage on land or in shallow water. The young are carnivorous, but as they grow older, box turtles prefer a more vegetarian diet, including mushrooms, blueberries, elderberries, wild grapes, strawberries, tomatoes, mayapples, wintergreen, and mosses. Blackberries are their favorite food, and box turtles have been known to gorge on them. Animal foods include insects, snails, slugs, earthworms, and spiders.

Predators. Badgers, foxes, skunks, barn owls, crows, and snakes destroy many nests and feed on young. Adults are often attacked by carnivores such as raccoons, skunks, coyotes, and dogs. Box turtles found with mutilated legs are usually victims of such attacks.

Breeding and nesting. Nests may be found in sandy fields and meadows, cultivated gardens, along roadsides, and in ditches. The female digs a flask-shaped nest in three to five hours, lays up to eight elliptical eggs, and covers them with the excavated dirt.

Other remarks. Can live more than 120 years and are the longest-lived vertebrates in North America.

4. SNAPPING TURTLE
(*Chelydra serpentina*)

Habitat. Almost every kind of shallow freshwater habitat, especially slow-moving streams with soft, muddy bottoms. Although these are water turtles, you have a good chance of finding one on land, and during the early spring, you might

see one roaming through a roadside ditch, along a streambank, or in a salt marsh.

Field marks. A snapping turtle looks like a prehistoric animal that wandered into present geologic time. It has a large, pointed head and a strong beak that is excellent for tearing meat. Its tail is as long as or longer than the carapace and has three rows of bumps down its length. The huge, bumpy top shell is brown or deep gray to black, providing camouflage, and each plate is generally patterned with radiating lines. The rear of the top shell is notched. The cross-shaped bottom shell is much smaller than the top shell and does not protect an overturned turtle. Webbed toes and heavy claws indicate a good swimmer and efficient digger. The snapper's design is fitting for the life of a bottom dweller. Snappers generally weigh twenty-five to thirty pounds, although adults can reach forty pounds and a length of three feet.

Behavior. The snapper spends most of its time on the bottom of a pond or buried in the mud, with only its eyes and the tip of its nose visible. It must extend its neck to raise its nostrils above the water from time to time to breathe. The snapper may also hide in tangles of roots and under tree stumps. It can anchor itself to an object by wrapping its strong tail around it. A swift walker, it can also lunge and jump. The snapping turtle can move its head with surprising speed, and its sharp beak tears very well—a compensation for the loss of protection from its abbreviated shells. It is aggressive on land but docile in the water.

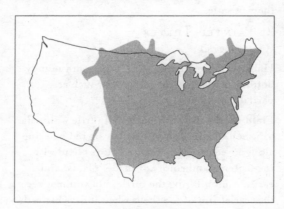

Range of the snapping turtle.

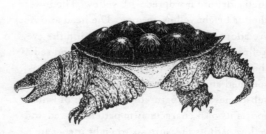

Snapping turtle (Chelydra serpentina), 18 to 32 inches.

Food preferences. Plants and animals, including salamanders, small turtles, frogs, snakes, and birds. Forages along weedy and muddy bottoms, where it eats almost anything its powerful hooked jaws can rip into bite-size pieces.

Predators. Hognose snakes, mink, crows, bears, foxes, wolves, and raccoons eat snapper eggs. Hatchlings and young turtles provide food for herons, egrets, bitterns, shrikes, large hawks, bald eagles, bullfrogs, and water snakes.

Breeding and nesting. Nests are dug in loose,

sandy soil or loam along railroads, roadside ditches, and beaches. Sometimes make their nests in beaver lodges. Females lay their eggs at night.

Other remarks. Do not treat these fast-moving turtles casually. When handled improperly, they can inflict serious wounds. It is best to leave them alone.

5. WOOD TURTLE
(*Clemmys insculpta*)

Habitat. The wood turtle wanders far from water in late spring and summer, when you may find them lumbering through pastures and woodlands. In early spring and in the autumn, the turtles prefer the wetter environs of swamps, brooks, and ponds, because they spend the winter in the muddy bottoms of these damp places.

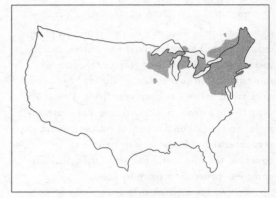

Range of the wood turtle.

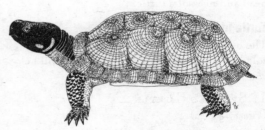

Wood turtle (Clemmys insculpta), 5¹/₂ to 7¹/₂ inches.

Field marks. The roughly sculptured concentric ridges on the plates of the gray-brown carapace make this turtle easy to identify. Head and feet are rusty brown to black, and the limbs, neck, and tail are a muted brick red—ideal for camouflaging the turtle among dead leaves and grasses. The carapace of the adult wood turtle measures about six and one-half inches.

Behavior. Active during daylight from April to November. In spring and summer, these turtles travel far from water to pastures, woodlands, and upland fields. They are good swimmers. Like other turtles, wood turtles bask, but they usually engage in the activity individually; rarely will you find more than one wood turtle basking together. When cold weather comes, they hibernate in muskrat burrows, snuggling beneath the banks of streams and ponds, although they have been seen swimming under the ice during the winter.

Food preferences. When on land, eat the same fare as ground-nesting birds, including strawberries, blackberries, and leaves of various wildflowers, but seem to prefer mushrooms. In water, eat aquatic insects and animals.

Predators. Raccoons, rodents, and striped skunks eat wood turtle eggs. Feral cats, dogs, and opossums feed on young wood turtles.

Continued ➡

Breeding and nesting. The nesting season is from May to July. Well-drained, moist sand or soil provides good nest material. Female digs a hollow in fields, along sunny roadsides, or in gravelly ditches, where she deposits about twelve eggs.

6. MUSK TURTLE
(Sternotherus odoratus)

Habitat. Shallow ponds with clear water. Spends an inactive winter at the bottom of a pond or in a muskrat den. Comes on land only to lay eggs. In general, keeps a low profile.

Field marks. Highly arched, smooth, brown carapace provides good camouflage for a turtle that spends a great deal of time on muddy pond bottoms. The carapace is frequently covered with algae, which makes it difficult to distinguish the turtle from rocks or chunks of wood on the muddy bottom. Two yellow lines, one above and one below the eye, extend along each side of the head and neck. Mature musk turtles measure about four to five inches in length.

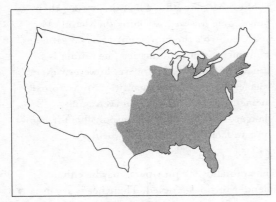

Range of the wood turtle.

Musk turtle (Sternotherus odoratus), 4 to 5 inches.

Behavior. Most active after sunset. Live and feed on the bottoms of ponds, reservoirs, lakes, and slow-running streams. Musk turtles snap, and with their strong beaks, they can inflict a serious wound.

Food preferences. Small fish, worms, insects, and tadpoles.

Predators. Raccoons, foxes, and skunks eat the eggs. Snakes, frogs, herons, and fish feed on hatchlings.

An important part of the day for many turtles is the time spent basking in the sun.

Breeding and nesting. Visit land in late June only to lay their eggs. Egg laying in May and June seems to be a haphazard affair. The females deposit their eggs in shallow nests on the surface of the ground, in leaf litter, tucked into rotting logs, or in muskrat lodges.

Other remarks. The musk turtle is nicknamed stinkpot, for the odor that is secreted from musk glands near the base of the limbs.

—Excerpted from *Discover Nature in Water and Wetlands*

Dangerous Animals

Animals rarely are as threatening to the survivor as the rest of the environment. Common sense tells the survivor to avoid encounters with lions, bears, and other large or dangerous animals. You should also avoid large grazing animals with horns, hooves, and great weight. Your actions may prevent unexpected meetings. Move carefully through their environment. Do not attract large predators by leaving food lying around your camp. Carefully survey the scene before entering water or forests.

Smaller animals actually present more of a threat to the survivor than large animals. To compensate for their size, nature has given many small animals weapons such as fangs and stingers to defend themselves. Each year, a few people are bitten by sharks, mauled by alligators, and attacked by bears. Most of these incidents were in some way the victim's fault. However, each year more victims die from bites by relatively small venomous snakes than by large dangerous animals. Even more victims die from allergic reactions to bee stings. For this reason, we will pay more attention to smaller and potentially more dangerous creatures. These are the animals you are more likely to meet as you unwittingly move into their habitat, or they slip into your environment unnoticed.

Keeping a level head and an awareness of your surroundings will keep you alive if you use a few simple safety procedures. Do not let curiosity and carelessness kill or injure you.

—From *Survival (U.S. Army Field Manual 21–76)*

Poisonous Snakes
U.S. Army

There are no infallible rules for expedient identification of poisonous snakes in the field, because the guidelines all require close observation or manipulation of the snake's body. The best strategy is to leave all snakes alone. Where snakes are plentiful and poisonous species are present, the risk of their bites negates their food value. Apply the following safety rules when traveling in areas where there are poisonous snakes:

- Walk carefully and watch where you step. Step onto logs rather than over them before looking and moving on.
- Look closely when picking fruit or moving around water.
- Do not tease, molest, or harass snakes. Snakes cannot close their eyes. Therefore, you cannot tell if they are asleep. Some snakes, such as mambas, cobras, and bushmasters, will attack aggressively when cornered or guarding a nest.
- Use sticks to turn logs and rocks.
- Wear proper footgear, particularly at night.
- Carefully check bedding, shelter, and clothing.
- Be calm when you encounter serpents. Snakes cannot hear and you can occasionally surprise them when they are sleeping or sunning. Normally, they will flee if given the opportunity.
- Use extreme care if you must kill snakes for food or safety. Although it is not common, warm, sleeping human bodies occasionally attract snakes.

Snake-Free Areas

The polar regions are free of snakes due to their inhospitable environments. Other areas considered to be free of poisonous snakes are New Zealand, Cuba, Haiti, Jamaica, Puerto Rico, Ireland, Polynesia, and Hawaii.

Poisonous Snakes of the Americas
- American Copperhead *(Agkistrodon contortrix)*
- Bushmaster *(Lachesis mutus)*
- Coral snake *(Micrurus fulvius)*
- Cottonmouth *(Agkistrodon piscivorus)*
- Fer-de-lance *(Bothrops atrox)*
- Rattlesnake *(Crotalus species)*

Poisonous Snakes of Europe
- Common adder *(Vipers berus)*
- Pallas' viper *(Agkistrodon halys)*

Poisonous Snakes of Africa and Asia
- Boomslang *(Dispholidus typus)*
- Cobra *(Naja species)*
- Gaboon viper *(Bitis gabonica)*
- Green tree pit viper *(Trimeresurus gramineus)*
- Habu pit viper *(Trimeresurus flavoviridis)*
- Krait *(Bungarus caeruleus)*
- Malayan pit viper *(Callaselasma rhodostoma)*
- Mamba *(Dendraspis species)*
- Puff adder *(Bitis arietans)*
- Rhinoceros viper *(Bitis nasicornis)*
- Russell's viper *(Vipera russellii)*
- Sand viper *(Cerastes vipera)*
- Saw-scaled viper *(Echis carinatus)*
- Wagler's pit viper *(Trimeresurus wagleri)*

Poisonous Snakes of Australia
- Death adder *(Acanthophis antarcticus)*
- Taipan *(Oxyuranus scutellatus)*
- Tiger snake *(Notechis scutatus)*
- Yellow-bellied sea snake *(Pelamis platurus)*

Ways to Avoid Snakebite

Snakes are widely distributed. They are found in all tropical, subtropical, and most temperate regions. Some species of snakes have specialized glands that contain a toxic venom and long hollow fangs to inject their venom.

Although venomous snakes use their venom to secure food, they also use it for self-defense. Human accidents occur when you don't see or

Continued →

hear the snake, when you step on them, or when you walk too close to them.

Follow these simple rules to reduce the chance of accidental snakebite:

- Don't sleep next to brush, tall grass, large boulders, or trees. They provide hiding places for snakes. Place your sleeping bag in a clearing. Use mosquito netting tucked well under the bag. This netting should provide a good barrier.

- Don't put your hands into dark places, such as rock crevices, heavy brush, or hollow logs, without first investigating.

- Don't step over a fallen tree. Step on the log and look to see if there is a snake resting on the other side.

- Don't walk through heavy brush or tall grass without looking down. Look where you are walking.

- Don't pick up any snake unless you are absolutely positive it is not venomous.

- Don't pick up freshly killed snakes without first severing the head. The nervous system may still be active and a dead snake can deliver a bite.

Fangs

The proteroglypha have, in front of the upper jaw and preceding the ordinary teeth, permanently erect fangs. These fangs are called fixed fangs.

The solenoglypha have erectile fangs; that is, fangs they can raise to an erect position. These fangs are called folded fangs.

Venom

The fixed-fang snakes (proteroglypha) usually have neurotoxic venoms. These venoms affect the nervous system, making the victim unable to breathe.

The folded-fang snakes (solenoglypha) usually have hemotoxic venoms. These venoms affect the circulatory system, destroying blood cells, damaging skin tissues, and causing internal hemorrhaging.

Remember, however, that most poisonous snakes have both neurotoxic and hemotoxic venom. Usually one type of venom in the snake is dominant and the other is weak.

Poisonous versus Nonpoisonous Snakes

No single characteristic distinguishes a poisonous snake from a harmless one except the presence of poison fangs and glands. Only in dead specimens can you determine the presence of these fangs and glands without danger.

VIPERIDAE

The viperidae or true vipers usually have thick bodies and heads that are much wider than their necks. However, there are many different sizes, markings, and colorations.

This snake group has developed a highly sophisticated means for delivering venom. They have long, hollow fangs that perform like hypodermic needles. They deliver their venom deep into the wound.

The fangs of this group of snakes are movable. These snakes fold their fangs into the roof of their mouths. When they strike, their fangs come forward, stabbing the victim. The snake controls the movement of its fangs; fang movement is not automatic. The venom is usually hemotoxic. There are, however, several species that have large quantities of neurotoxic elements, thus making them even more dangerous. The vipers are responsible for many human fatalities around the world.

CROTALIDAE

The crotalids, or pit vipers, may be either slender or thick-bodied. Their heads are usually much wider than their necks. These snakes take their name from the deep pit located between the eye and the nostril. They are commonly brown with dark blotches, though some kinds are green.

Rattlesnakes, copperheads, cottonmouths, and several species of dangerous snakes from Central and South America, Asia, China, and India fall into the pit viper group. The pit is a highly sensitive organ capable of picking up the slightest temperature variance. Most pit vipers are nocturnal. They hunt for food at night with the aid of these specialized pits that let them locate prey in total darkness. Rattlesnakes are the only pit vipers that possess a rattle at the tip of the tail.

India has about 12 species of these snakes. You find them in trees or on the ground in all types of terrain. The tree snakes are slender; the ground snakes are heavy-bodied. All are dangerous.

China has a pit viper similar to the cottonmouth found in North America. You find it in the rocky areas of the remote mountains of South China. It reaches a length of 1.4 meters but is not vicious unless irritated. You can also find a small pit viper, about 45 centimeters long, on the plains of eastern China. It is too small to be dangerous to a man wearing shoes.

There are about 27 species of rattlesnakes in the United States and Mexico. They vary in color and may or may not have spots or blotches. Some are small while others, such as the diamondbacks, may grow to 2.5 meters long.

There are five kinds of rattlesnakes in Central and South America, but only the trop-

SNAKE GROUPS

Snakes dangerous to man usually fall into two groups: proteroglypha and solenoglypha. Their fangs and their venom best describe these two groups.

GROUP	FANG TYPE	VENOM TYPE
Proteroglypha	Fixed	Usually dominant neurotoxic
Solenoglypha	Folded	Usually dominant hemotoxic

DESCRIPTIONS OF POISONOUS SNAKES

There are many different poisonous snakes throughout the world. It is unlikely you will see many except in a zoo. This manual describes only a few poisonous snakes. You should, however, be able to spot a poisonous snake if you learn about the two groups of snakes and the families in which they fall.

GROUP	FAMILY	LOCAL EFFECTS	SYSTEMIC EFFECTS
Solenoglypha Usually dominant **hemotoxic** venom affecting the circulatory system	Viperidae True vipers with movable fangs	Strong pain, swelling necrosis	Hemorrhaging, internal internal organ breakdown, destroying of blood cells
	Crotalidae Pit vipers with movable fangs in front Trimeresurus		
Proteroglypha Usually dominant **neurotoxic** venom affecting the nervous system	Elapidae Fixed front fangs		
	Cobra	Various pains, swelling, necrosis	Respiratory collapse
	Krait	No local effects	Respiratory collapse
	Micrurus	Little or no pain; no local symptoms	Respiratory collapse
	Laticaudinae and Hydrophidae Ocean-living with fixed front fangs	Pain and local swelling	Respiratory collapse

Note: The venom of the Gaboon viper, the rhinoceros viper, the tropical rattlesnake, and the Mojave rattlesnake is both strongly hemotoxic and strongly neurotoxic.

Continued →

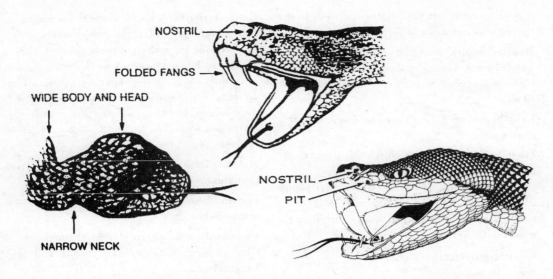

Positive identification of vipers.

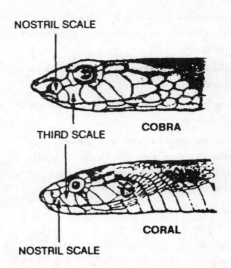

Positive identification of cobras, kraits, and coral snakes.

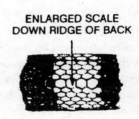

ical rattlesnake is widely distributed. The rattle on the tip of the tail is sufficient identification for a rattlesnake.

Most will try to escape without a fight when approached, but there is always a chance one will strike at a passerby. They do not always give a warning; they may strike first and rattle afterwards or not at all.

The genus Trimeresurus is a subgroup of the crotalidae. These are Asian pit vipers. These pit vipers are normally tree-loving snakes with a few species living on the ground. They basically have the same characteristics of the crotalidae—slender build and very dangerous. Their bites usually are on the upper extremities—head, neck, and shoulders. Their venom is largely hemotoxic.

ELAPIDAE

A group of highly dangerous snakes with powerful neurotoxic venom that affects the nervous system, causing respiratory paralysis. Included in this family are coral snakes, cobras, mambas, and all the Australian venomous snakes. The coral snake is small and has caused human fatalities. The Australian death adder, tiger, taipan, and king brown snakes are among the most venomous in the world, causing many human fatalities.

Only by examining a dead snake can you positively determine if it is a cobra or a near relative. On cobras, kraits, and coral snakes, the third scale on the upper lip touches both the nostril scale and the eye. The krait also has a row of enlarged scales down its ridged back.

You can find the cobras of Africa and the Near East in almost any habitat. One kind may live in or near water, another in trees. Some are aggressive and savage. The distance a cobra can strike in a forward direction is equal to the distance its head is raised above the ground. Some cobras, however, can spit venom a distance of 3 to 3.5 meters. This venom is harmless unless it gets into your eyes; then it may cause blindness if not washed out immediately. Poking around in holes and rock piles is dangerous because of the chance of encountering a spitting cobra.

LATICAUDINAE AND HYDROPHIDAE

A subfamily of elapidae, these snakes are specialized in that they found a better environment in the oceans. Why they are in the oceans is not clear to science.

Sea snakes differ in appearance from other snakes in that they have an oarlike tail to aid in swimming. Some species of sea snakes have venom several times more toxic than the cobra's. Because of their marine environment, sea snakes seldom come in contact with humans. The exceptions are fisherman who capture these dangerous snakes in fish nets and scuba divers who swim in waters where sea snakes are found.

There are many species of sea snakes. They vary greatly in color and shape. Their scales distinguish them from eels that have no scales.

Sea snakes occur in salt water along the coasts throughout the Pacific. There are also sea snakes on the east coast of Africa and in the Persian Gulf. There are no sea snakes in the Atlantic Ocean.

There is no need to fear sea snakes. They have not been known to attack a man swimming. Fishermen occasionally get bit by a sea snake caught in a net. The bite is dangerous.

COLUBRIDAE

The largest group of snakes worldwide. In this family there are species that are rear-fanged; however, most are completely harmless to man.

They have a venom-producing gland and enlarged, grooved rear fangs that allow venom to flow into the wound. The inefficient venom apparatus and the specialized venom is effective on cold-blooded animals (such as frogs and lizards) but not considered a threat to human life. The boomslang and the twig snake of Africa have, however, caused human deaths.

Poisonous Snakes of the Americas

AMERICAN COPPERHEAD
Agkistrodon contortrix

Description. Chestnut color dominates overall, with darker crossbands of rich browns that become narrower on top and widen at the bottom. The top of the head is a coppery color.

Characteristic. Very common over much of its range, with a natural camouflage ability to blend in the environment. Copperheads are rather quiet and inoffensive in disposition but will defend themselves vigorously. Bites occur when the snakes are stepped on or when a victim is

Viperidae	Crotalidae	Elapidae	Hydrophlidae
Common adder	American copperhead	Australian copperhead	Banded sea snake
Long-nosed adder	Boomslang	Common cobra	Yellow-bellied sea snake
Gaboon viper	Bush viper	Coral snake	
Levant viper	Bushmaster	Death adder	
Horned desert viper	Cottonmouth	Egyptian cobra	
McMahon's viper	Eastern diamond	Green mamba	
Mole viper	back rattlesnake	King cobra	
Palestinian viper	Eyelash pit viper	Krait	
Puff adder	Fer-de-lance	Taipan	
Rhinoceros viper	Green tree pit viper	Tiger snake	
Russell's viper	Habu pit viper		
Sand viper	Jumping viper		
Saw-scaled viper	Malayan pit viper		
Ursini's viper	Mojave rattlesnake		
	Pallas' viper		
	Tropical rattlesnake		
	Wagler's pit viper		
	Western diamondback		
	rattlesnake		

Continued ➡

lying next to one. A copperhead lying on a bed of dead leaves becomes invisible. Its venom is hemotoxic.

Habitat. Found in wooded and rocky areas and mountainous regions.

Length. Average 60 centimeters, maximum 120 centimeters.

Distribution. Eastern Gulf States, Texas, Arkansas, Maryland, North Florida, Illinois, Oklahoma, Kansas, Ohio, New York, Alabama, Tennessee, and Massachusetts.

BUSHMASTER
Lachesis mutus

Description. The body hue is rather pale brown or pinkish, with a series of large bold dark brown or black blotches extending along the body. Its scales are extremely rough.

Characteristics. The world's largest pit viper has a bad reputation. This huge venomous snake is not common anywhere in its range. It lives in remote and isolated habitats and is largely nocturnal in its feeding habits; it seldom bites anyone, so few bites are recorded. A bite from one would indeed be very serious and fatal if medical aid was not immediately available. Usually, the bites occur in remote, dense jungles, many kilometers and several hours or even days away from medical help. Bushmaster fangs are long. In large bushmasters, they can measure 3.8 centimeters. Its venom is a powerful hemotoxin.

Bushmaster.

Habitat. Found chiefly in tropical forests in their range.

Length. Average 2.1 meters, maximum 3.7 meters.

Distribution. Nicaragua, Costa Rica, Panama, Trinidad, and Brazil.

CORAL SNAKE
Micurus fulvius

Description. Beautifully marked with bright blacks, reds, and yellows. To identify the species, remember that when red touches yellow it is a coral snake.

Characteristics. Common over range, but secretive in its habits, therefore seldom seen. It has short fangs that are fixed in an erect position. It often chews to release its venom into a wound. Its venom is very powerful. The venom

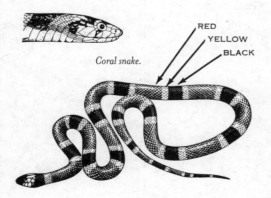
Coral snake.
RED
YELLOW
BLACK

is neurotoxic, causing respiratory paralysis in the victim, who succumbs to suffocation.

Habitat. Found in a variety of habitats including wooded areas, swamps, palmetto and scrub areas. Coral snakes often venture into residential locations.

Length. Average 60 centimeters, maximum 115 centimeters.

Distribution. Southeast North Carolina, Gulf States, west central Mississippi, Florida, Florida Keys, and west to Texas. Another genus of coral snake is found in Arizona. Coral snakes are also found throughout Central and most South America.

COTTONMOUTH
Agkistrodon piscivorus

Description. Colors are variable. Adults are uniformly olive brown or black. The young and subadults are strongly crossbanded with dark brown.

Characteristics. These dangerous semiaquatic snakes closely resemble harmless water snakes that have the same habitat. Therefore, it is best to leave all water snakes alone. Cottonmouths often stand their ground. An aroused cottonmouth will draw its head close to its body and open its mouth showing its white interior. Cottonmouth venom is hemotoxic and potent. Bites are prone to gangrene.

Habitat. Found in swamps, lakes, rivers, and ditches.

Length. Average 90 centimeters, maximum 1.8 meters.

Distribution. Southeast Virginia, west central Alabama, south Georgia, Illinois, east central Kentucky, south central Oklahoma, Texas, North and South Carolina, Florida, and the Florida Keys.

EASTERN DIAMONDBACK RATTLESNAKE
Crotalus adamanteus

Description. Diamonds are dark brown or black, outlined by a row of cream or yellowish scales. Ground color is olive to brown.

Characteristics. The largest venomous snake in the United States. Large individual snakes can have fangs that measure 2.5 centimeters in a straight line. This species has a sullen disposition, ready to defend itself when threatened. Its venom is potent and hemotoxic, causing great pain and damage to tissue.

Habitat. Found in palmettos and scrubs, swamps, pine woods, and flatwoods. It has been observed swimming many miles out in the Gulf of Mexico, reaching some of the islands off the Florida coast.

Length. Average 1.4 meters, maximum 2.4 meters.

Distribution. Coastal areas of North Carolina, South Carolina, Louisiana, Florida, and the Florida Keys.

EYELASH PIT VIPER
Bothrops schlegeli

Description. Identified by several spiny scales over each eye. Color is highly variable, from bright yellow over its entire body to reddish-yellow spots throughout the body.

Characteristics. Arboreal snake that seldom comes to the ground. It feels more secure in low-hanging trees where it looks for tree frogs and birds. It is a dangerous species because most of its bites occur on the upper extremities. It has an irritable disposition. It will strike with little provocation. Its venom is hemotoxic, causing severe tissue damage. Deaths have occurred from the bites of these snakes.

Habitat. Tree-loving species found in rain forests; common on plantations and in palm trees.

Length. Average 45 centimeters, maximum 75 centimeters.

Distribution. Southern Mexico, throughout Central America, Columbia, Ecuador, and Venezuela.

FER-DE-LANCE
Bothrops atrox

These are several closely related species in this group. All are very dangerous to man.

Description. Variable coloration, from gray to olive, brown, or reddish, with dark triangles edged with light scales. Triangles are narrow at the top and wide at the bottom.

Characteristics. This highly dangerous snake is responsible for a high mortality rate. It has an irritable disposition, ready to strike with little provocation. The female fer-de-lance is highly prolific, producing up to 60 young born with a dangerous bite. The venom of this species is hemotoxic, painful, and hemorrhagic (causing profuse internal bleeding). The venom causes massive tissue destruction.

Habitat. Found on cultivated land and farms, often entering houses in search of rodents.

Length. Average 1.4 meters, maximum 2.4 meters.

Distribution. Southern Mexico, throughout Central and South America.

JUMPING VIPER
Bothrops nummifer

Description. It has a stocky body. Its ground color varies from brown to gray and it has dark brown or black dorsal blotches. It has no pattern on its head.

Characteristics. It is chiefly a nocturnal snake. It comes out in the early evening hours to feed on lizards, rodents, and frogs. As the name implies, this species can strike with force as it actually leaves the ground. Its venom is hemotoxic. Humans have died from the bites inflicted by large jumping vipers. They often hide under fallen logs and piles of leaves and are difficult to see.

Habitat. Found in rain forests, on plantations, and on wooded hillsides.

Length. Average 60 centimeters, maximum 120 centimeter.

Distribution. Southern Mexico, Honduras, Guatemala, Costa Rica, Panama, and El Salvador.

MOJAVE RATTLESNAKE
Crotalus scutulatus

Description. This snake's entire body is a pallid or sandy odor with darker diamond-shaped markings bordered by lighter-colored scales and black bands around the tail.

Continued ➡

RATTLESNAKES
Tod Schimelpfenig Illustrations by Joan Safford

Rattlesnakes have triangular heads, thick bodies, and pits between the eyes and nostrils. Coloring and length vary with the species. Most are blotched and colored in earthy browns, grays, or reds. Four feet is an average length, although large eastern diamondback rattlesnakes have reached 6.5 feet in length. The number of rattles varies with the snake's age and stage of molt. Often the rattles do not rattle before a strike. Rattles are thought to have evolved as a warning device to prevent hoofed mammals from stepping on the snake.

Rattlesnake fangs retract when the mouth is closed and extend during a strike. Rattlesnakes periodically shed their fangs. At times, two fangs are present on each side. One is potent, the other not. Venom release is under the snake's control. A rattler can apparently adjust the volume of venom injected to match its victim's size. The age, size, and health of the snake affect venom toxicity. The same factors affect the victim's response to the venom.

Multiple strikes are possible, and depth of the bite varies, as does the amount of venom injected. Fang marks are not a reliable sign of envenomation, as 20 to 30 percent of bites do not envenom. Pain at the site with rapid swelling and bruising is a better sign that venom has been injected.

—From *NOLS Wilderness Medicine*

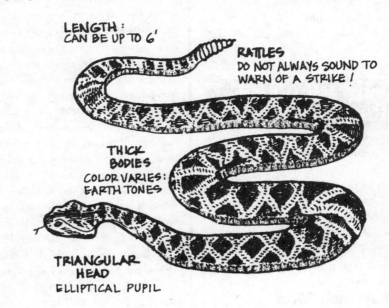

LENGTH: CAN BE UP TO 6'

RATTLES DO NOT ALWAYS SOUND TO WARN OF A STRIKE!

THICK BODIES
COLOR VARIES: EARTH TONES

TRIANGULAR HEAD
ELLIPTICAL PUPIL

MECHANISMS OF A RATTLESNAKE BITE:

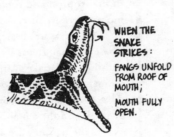

WHEN THE SNAKE STRIKES:
FANGS UNFOLD FROM ROOF OF MOUTH;
MOUTH FULLY OPEN.

FANG MOTION
SNAKES TEND TO HOLD THEIR HEAD LEVEL WHEN THEY STRIKE, SO EVEN IF THE FANGS PENETRATE FULLY THE WOUND MAY BE SLANTING and FAIRLY SHALLOW.

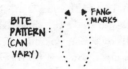

BITE PATTERN: (CAN VARY)
FANG MARKS

SYMPTOMS:
• IMMEDIATE BURNING PAIN;
• SWELLING, DISCOLORATION;
• BLOOD OOZING FROM WOUND.

Characteristics. Although this rattlesnake is of moderate size, its bite is very serious. Its venom has quantities of neurotoxic elements that affect the central nervous system. Deaths have resulted from this snake's bite.

Habitat. Found in arid regions, deserts, and rocky hillsides from sea level to 2400-meter elevations.

Length. Average 75 centimeters, maximum 1.2 meters.

Distribution. Mojave Desert in California, Nevada, southwest Arizona, and Texas into Mexico.

TROPICAL RATTLESNAKE
Crotalus terrificus

Description. Coloration is light to dark brown with a series of darker rhombs or diamonds bordered by a buff color.

Characteristics. Extremely dangerous with an irritable disposition, ready to strike with little or no warning (use of its rattle). This species has a highly toxic venom containing neurotoxic and hemotoxic components that paralyze the central nervous system and cause great damage to tissue.

Tropical rattlesnake.

Habitat. Found in sandy places, plantations, and dry hillsides.

Length. Average 1.4 meters, maximum 2.1 meters.

Distribution. Southern Mexico, Central America, and Brazil to Argentina.

WESTERN DIAMONDBACK RATTLESNAKE
Crotalus atrox

Description. The body is a light buff color with darker brown diamond-shaped markings. The tail has heavy black and white bands.

Western diamondback rattlesnake.

Characteristics. This bold rattlesnake holds its ground. When coiled and rattling, it is ready to defend itself. It injects a large amount of venom when it bites, making it one of the most dangerous snakes. Its venom is hemotoxic, causing considerable pain and tissue damage.

Habitat. It is a very common snake over its range. It is found in grasslands, deserts, woodlands, and canyons.

Length. Average 1.5 meters, maximum 2 meters.

Distribution. Southeast California, Oklahoma, Texas, New Mexico, and Arizona.

—From *Survival (Field Manual 21–76)*

Dangerous Lizards
U.S. Army

The Gila monster and the Mexican beaded lizard are dangerous and poisonous lizards.

Gila Monster
The Gila monster (*Heloderma suspectrum*) of the American southwest, including Mexico, is a large lizard with dark, highly textured skin marked by pinkish mottling. It averages 35 to 45 centimeters in length and has a thick, stumpy tail. Unlikely to bite unless molested, it has a poisonous bite.

Gila monster.

Mexican Beaded Lizard
The Mexican beaded lizard (*Heloderma horridum*) resembles its relative, the Gila monster. It has more uniform spots rather than bands of color (the Gila monster). It also is poisonous and has a docile nature. You find it from Mexico to Central America.

Continued ➡

Komodo Dragon

This giant lizard (*Varanus komodoensis*) grows to more than 3 meters in length and can be dangerous if you try to capture it. This Indonesian lizard can weigh more than 135 kilograms.

—From *Survival (Field Manual 21—76)*

Dangerous Fish and Mollusks

Fish and mollusks will present a danger in one of three ways: by attacking and biting you, by injecting toxic venom into you through its venomous spines or tentacles, and through eating fish or mollusks whose flesh is toxic.

The danger of actually encountering one of these dangerous fish is relatively small, but it is still significant. Any one of these fish can kill you. Avoid them if at all possible.

Fish That Attack Man

The shark is usually the first fish that comes to mind when considering fish that attack man. Other fish also fall in this category, such as the barracuda, the moray eel, and the piranha.

Sharks

Sharks are potentially the most dangerous fish that attack people. The obvious danger of sharks is that they are capable of seriously maiming or killing you with their bite. Of the many shark species, only a relative few are dangerous. Of these, four species are responsible for most cases of shark attacks on humans. These are white, tiger, hammerhead, and blue sharks. There are also records of attacks by ground, gray nurse, and mako sharks.

Sharks vary in size, but there is no relationship between the size of the shark and likelihood of attack. Even the smaller sharks can be dangerous, especially when they are traveling in schools.

Sharks

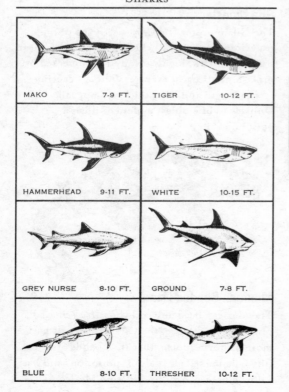

MAKO	7-9 FT.	TIGER	10-12 FT.
HAMMERHEAD	9-11 FT.	WHITE	10-15 FT.
GREY NURSE	8-10 FT.	GROUND	7-8 FT.
BLUE	8-10 FT.	THRESHER	10-12 FT.

SHARKS
U.S. Army

Whether you are in the water or in a boat or raft, you may see many types of sea life around you. Some may be more dangerous than others. Generally, sharks are the greatest danger to you. Other animals such as whales, porpoises, and stingrays may look dangerous, but really pose little threat in the open sea.

Of the many hundreds of shark species, only about 20 species are known to attack man. The most dangerous are the great white shark, the hammerhead, the mako, and the tiger shark. Other sharks known to attack man include the gray, blue, lemon, sand, nurse, bull, and oceanic white tip sharks. Consider any shark longer than 1 meter dangerous.

There are sharks in all oceans and seas of the world. While many live and feed in the depths of the sea, others hunt near the surface. The sharks living near the surface are the ones you will most likely see. Their dorsal fins frequently project above the water. Sharks in the tropical and subtropical seas are far more aggressive than those in temperate waters.

All sharks are basically eating machines. Their normal diet is live animals of any type, and they will strike at injured or helpless animals. Sight, smell, or sound may guide them to their prey. Sharks have an acute sense of smell and the smell of blood in the water excites them. They are also very sensitive to any abnormal vibrations in the water. The struggles of a wounded animal or swimmer, underwater explosions, or even a fish struggling on a fishline will attract a shark.

Sharks can bite from almost any position; they do not have to turn on their side to bite. The jaws of some of the larger sharks are so far forward that they can bite floating objects easily without twisting to the side.

Sharks may hunt alone, but most reports of attacks cite more than one shark present. The smaller sharks tend to travel in schools and attack in mass. Whenever one of the sharks finds a victim, the other sharks will quickly join it. Sharks will eat a wounded shark as quickly as their prey.

Sharks feed at all hours of the day and night. Most reported shark contacts and attacks were during daylight, and many of these have been in the late afternoon. Some

of the measures that you can take to protect yourself against sharks when you are in the water are—

- *Stay with other swimmers*. A group can maintain a 360-degree watch. A group can either frighten or fight off sharks better than one man.

- *Always watch for sharks*. Keep all your clothing on, to include your shoes. Historically, sharks have attacked the unclothed men in groups first, mainly in the feet. Clothing also protects against abrasions should the shark brush against you.

- *Avoid urinating*. If you must, only do so in small amounts. Let it dissipate between discharges. If you must defecate, do so in small amounts and throw it as far away from you as possible. Do the same if you must vomit.

If a shark attack is imminent while you are in the water, splash and yell just enough to keep the shark at bay. Sometimes yelling underwater or slapping the water repeatedly will scare the shark away. Conserve your strength for fighting in case the shark attacks.

If attacked, kick and strike the shark. Hit the shark on the gills or eyes if possible. If you hit the shark on the nose, you may injure your hand if it glances off and hits its teeth.

When you are in a raft and see sharks—

- Do not fish. If you have hooked a fish, let it go. Do not clean fish in the water.

- Do not throw garbage overboard.

- Do not let your arms, legs, or equipment hang in the water.

- Keep quiet and do not move around.

- Bury all dead as soon as possible. If there are many sharks in the area, conduct the burial at night.

When you are in a raft and a shark attack is imminent, hit the shark with anything you have, except your hands. You will do more damage to your hands than the shark. If you strike with an oar, be careful not to lose or break it.

—From *Survival (Field Manual 21—76)*

If bitten by a shark, the most important measure for you to take is to stop the bleeding quickly. Blood in the water attracts sharks. Get yourself or the victim into a raft or to shore as soon as possible. If in the water, form a circle around the victim (if not alone), and stop the bleeding with a tourniquet.

Other Ferocious Fish

In salt water, other ferocious fish include the barracuda, sea bass, and moray eel. The sea bass is usually an open water fish. It is dangerous due to its large size. It can remove large pieces of

flesh from a human. Barracudas and moray eels have been known to attack man and inflict vicious bites. Be careful to these two species when near reefs and in shallow water. Moray eels are very aggressive when disturbed.

In fresh water, piranha are the only significantly dangerous fish. They are inhabitants of the tropics and are restricted to northern South America. These fish are fairly small, about 5 to 7.5 centimeters, but they have very large teeth and travel in large schools. They can devour a 135-kilogram hog in minutes.

Continued ➡

Venemous Fish and Invertebrates

There are several species of venomous fish and invertebrates, all of which live in salt water. All of these are capable of injecting poisonous venom through spines located in their fins, tentacles, or bites. Their venoms cause intense pain and are potentially fatal. If injured by one of these fish or invertebrates, treat the injury as for snakebite.

FEROCIOUS FISH

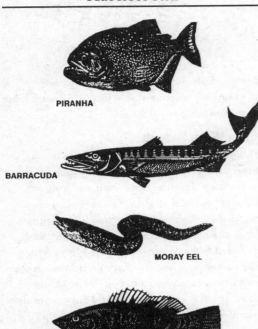

PIRANHA

BARRACUDA

MORAY EEL

SEA BASS

STINGRAYS
Dasyatidae species
Stingrays inhabit shallow water, especially in the tropics and in temperate regions as well. All have a distinctive ray shape but coloration may make them hard to spot unless they are swimming. The venomous, barbed spines in their talls can cause severe or fatal injury.

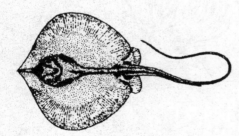

RABBITFISH
Siganidae species
Rabbitfish are found predominantly on reefs in the Pacific and Indian oceans. They average about 30 centimeters long and have very sharp spines in their fins. The spines are venomous and can inflict intense pain.

SCORPION FISH OR ZEBRA FISH
Scorpaenidae species
Scorpion fish or zebra fish live mainly in the reefs in the Pacific and Indian oceans. They vary from 30 to 90 centimeters long, are usually reddish in coloration, and have long, wavy fins and spines. They inflict an intensely painful sting.

SIGANUS FISH
The siganus fish is small, about 10 to 15 centimeters long, and looks much like a small tuna. It has venomous spines in its dorsal and ventral fins. These spines can inflict painful stings.

STONEFISH
Synanceja species
Stonefish are found in the tropical waters of the Pacific and Indian oceans. Averaging about 30 centimeters in length, their subdued colors and lumpy shape provide them with exceptional camouflage. When stepped on, the fins in the dorsal spine inflict an extremely painful and sometimes fatal wound.

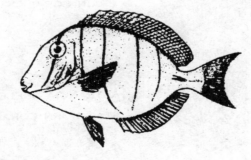

TANG OR SURGEONFISH
Acanthuridae species
Tang or surgeonfish average 20 to 25 centimeters in length, with a deep body, small mouth, and bright coloration. They have needlelike spines on the side of the tail that cause extremely painful wounds. This fish is found in all tropical waters.

TOADFISH
Batrachoididae species
Toadfish are found in the tropical waters off the coasts of South and Central America. They are between 17.5 and 25 centimeters long and have a dull color and large mouths. They bury them-selves in the sand and may be easily stepped on. They have very sharp, extremely poisonous spines on the dorsal fin (back).

WEEVER FISH
Trachinidae species
The weever fish is a tropical fish that is fairly slim and about 30 centimeters long. All its fins have venomous spines that cause a painful wound.

BLUE-RINGED OCTOPUS
Hapalochlaena lunulata
This small octopus is usually found on the Great Barrier Reef off eastern Australia. It is grayish-white with iridescent blue ringlike markings. This octopus usually will not bite unless stepped on or handled. Its bite is extremely poisonous and frequently lethal.

JELLYFISH
Jellyfish-related deaths are rare, but the sting they inflict is extremely painful. The Portuguese man-of-war resembles a large pink or purple balloon floating on the sea. It has poisonous tentacles hanging up to 12 meters below its body. The huge tentacles are actually colonies of stinging cells. Most known deaths from jellyfish are attributed to the man-of-war. Other jellyfish can inflict very painful stings as well. Avoid the long tentacles of any jellyfish, even those washed up on the beach and apparently dead.

Continued ➡

SEA SNAKES

Venomous sea snakes are not found in the Atlantic, but occur in large numbers off the shores of the Indian Ocean and the southern and western Pacific. They usually are encountered in tidal rivers and near the coast but may be seen far out at sea. They do not disturb swimmers, so

there is little danger of being bitten. They are identified by their flat, vertically compressed paddle tail.

CONE SHELLS

Conidae species

These cone-shaped shells have smooth, colorful mottling and long, narrow openings in the base

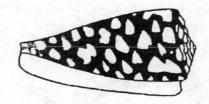

of the shell. They live under rocks, in crevices or coral reefs, and along rocky shores of protected bays in tropical areas. All have tiny teeth that are similar to hypodermic needles. They can inject an extremely poisonous venom that acts very

swiftly, causing acute pain, swelling, paralysis, blindness, and possible death within hours. Avoid handling all cone shells.

TEREBRA SHELLS

Terebridae species

These shells are found in both temperate and tropical waters. They are similar to cone shells

but much thinner and longer. They poison in the same way as cone shells, but the venom is not as poisonous.

Other Water Hazards

Dangerous water animals listed above by no means exhaust the list of hazards you may encounter. Tropical bone shell and long, slender, pointed terebra snails are also poisonous. Handle big conchs with caution; large abalones and clams can be dangerous if gathered by hand instead of pried loose with a bar or wedge. They may clamp onto your fingers and hold you under until you drown. Coral, dead or alive, can inflict painful cuts; seemingly harmless sponges and sea urchins can slip fine needles of lime or silica into your skin, which will break off and fester.

DANGERS IN RIVERS
U.S. Army

Common sense will tell you to avoid confrontations with hippopotami, alligators, crocodiles, and other large river creatures. There are, however, a few smaller river creatures with which you should be cautious.

Electric Eel

Electric eels (*Electrophorus electricus*) may reach 2 meters in length and 20 centimeters in diameter. Avoid them. They are capable of generating up to 500 volts of electricity in certain organs in their body. They use this shock to stun prey and enemies. Normally, you find these eels in the Orinoco and Amazon River systems in South America. They seem to prefer shallow waters that are more highly oxygenated and provide more food. They are bulkier than our native eels. Their upper body is dark gray or black. With a lighter-colored underbelly.

Piranha

Piranhas (*Serrasalmo* species) are another hazard of the Orinoco and Amazon River systems, as well as the Paraguay River Basin, where they are native. These fish vary greatly in size and coloration, but usually have a combination of orange undersides and dark tops. They have white, razor-sharp teeth that are clearly visible. They may be as long as 50 centimeters. Use great care when crossing waters where they live. Blood attracts them. They are most dangerous in shallow waters during the dry season.

Turtle

Be careful when handling and capturing large freshwater turtles, such as the snapping turtles and soft-shelled turtles of North America and the matamata and other turtles of South America. All of these turtles will bite in self-defense and can amputate fingers and toes.

Platypus

The platypus or duckbill (*Ornithorhyncus anatinus*) is the only member of its family and is easily recognized. It has a long body covered with grayish, short hair, a tail like a beaver, and a bill like a duck. Growing up to 60 centimeters in length, it may appear to be a good food source, but this egg-laying mammal, the only one in the world, is very dangerous. The male has a poisonous spur on each hind foot that can inflict intensely painful wounds. You find the platypus only in Australia, mainly along mud banks on waterways.

—From Survival (*Field Manual 21–76*)

SHELLS AND CORAL

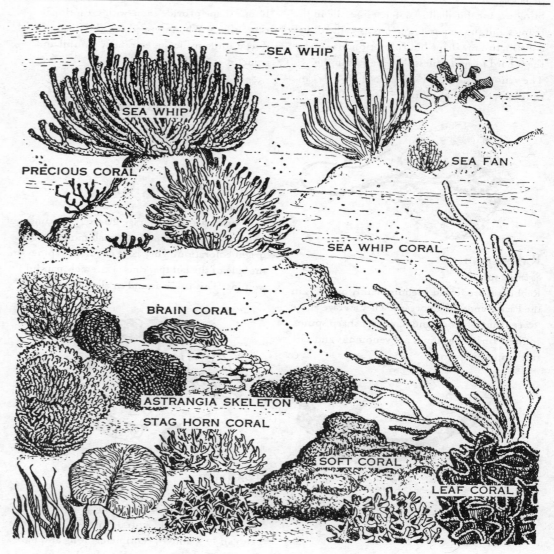

Continued ➡

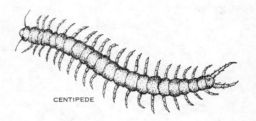

In areas where seas and rivers come together, there are dangers associated with both fresh and salt water. In shallow salt waters, there are many creatures that can inflict pain and cause infection to develop. Stepping on sea urchins, for example, can produce pain and infection. When moving about in shallow water, wear some form of footgear and shuffle your feet along the bottom, rather than picking up your feet and stepping.

Stingrays (*Dasyatidae* species) are a real hazard in shallow waters, especially tropical waters. The type of bottom appears to be irrelevant. There is a great variance between species, but all have a sharp spike in their tail that may be venomous and can cause extremely painful wounds if stepped on. All rays have a typical shape that resembles a kite. You find them along the coasts of the Americas, Africa, and Australasia.

—From Survival *(Field Manual 21–76)*

Dangerous Insects and Arachnids

U.S. Army

You recognize and identify insects, except centipedes and millipedes, by their six legs while arachnids have eight. All these small creatures become pests when they bite, sting, or irritate you.

Although their venom can be quite painful, bee, wasp, and hornet stings rarely kill a survivor unless he is allergic to that particular toxin. Even the most dangerous spiders rarely kill, and the effects of tick-borne diseases are very slow-acting. However, in all cases, avoidance is the best defense. In environments known to have spiders and scorpions, check your footgear and clothing every morning. Also check your bedding and shelter for them. Use care when turning over rocks and logs. See Appendix D for examples of dangerous insects and arachnids.

Scorpions

You find scorpions (*Buthotus* species) in deserts, jungles, and forests of tropical, subtropical, and warm temperate areas of the world. They are mostly nocturnal in habit. You can find desert scorpions from below sea level in Death Valley to elevations as high as 3,600 meters in the Andes. Typically brown or black in moist areas, they may be yellow or light green in the desert. Their

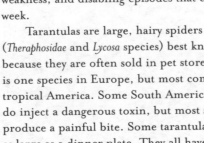

Scorpion.

average size is about 2.5 centimeters. However, there are 20-centimeter giants in the jungles of Central America, New Guinea, and southern Africa. Fatalities from scorpion stings are rare, but they can occur in children, the elderly, and ill persons. Scorpions resemble small lobsters with raised, jointed tails bearing a stinger in the tip. Nature mimics the scorpions with whip scorpions or vinegarroons. These are harmless and have a tail like a wire or whip, rather than the jointed tail and stinger of true scorpions.

Spiders

You recognize the brown recluse or fiddleback spider of North America (*Loxosceles reclusa*) by a prominent violin-shaped light spot on the back of its body. As its name suggests, this spider likes to hide in dark places. Though rarely fatal, its bite causes excessive tissue degeneration around the wound and can even lead to amputation of the digits if left untreated.

You find members of the widow family (*Latrodectus* species) worldwide, though the black widow of North America is perhaps the most well-known. Found in warmer areas of the world, the widows are small, dark spiders with often hourglass-shaped white, red, or orange spots on their abdomens.

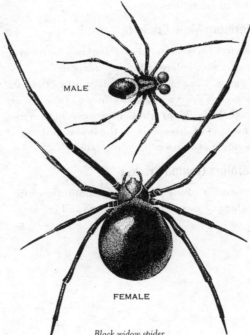
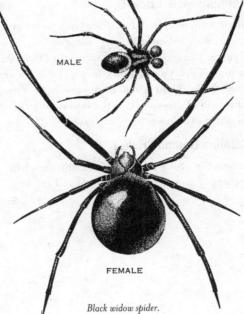

MALE

FEMALE

Black widow spider.

Funnelwebs (*Atrax* species) are large, gray or brown Australian spiders. Chunky, with short legs, they are able to move easily up and down the cone-shaped webs from which they get their name. The local populace considers them deadly. Avoid them as they move about, usually at night, in search of prey. Symptoms of their bite are similar to those of the widow's—severe pain accompanied by sweating and shivering, weakness, and disabling episodes that can last a week.

Tarantulas are large, hairy spiders (*Theraphosidae* and *Lycosa* species) best known because they are often sold in pet stores. There is one species in Europe, but most come from tropical America. Some South American species do inject a dangerous toxin, but most simply produce a painful bite. Some tarantulas can be as large as a dinner plate. They all have large

fangs for capturing food such as birds, mice, and lizards. If bitten by a tarantula, pain and bleeding are certain, and infection is likely.

Centipedes and Millipedes

Centipedes and millipedes are mostly small and harmless, although some tropical and desert species may reach 25 centimeters. A few varieties of centipedes have a poisonous bite, but infection is the greatest danger, as their sharp claws dig in and puncture the skin. To prevent skin punctures, brush them off in the direction they are traveling, if you find them crawling on your skin.

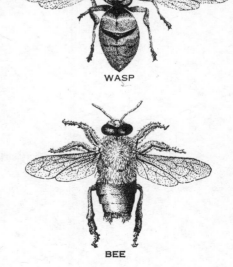

CENTIPEDE

Bees, Wasps, and Hornets

We are all familiar with bees, wasps, and hornets. They come in many varieties and have a wide diversity of habits and habitats. You recognize bees by their hairy and usually thick body, while the wasps, hornets, and yellow jackets have more slender, nearly hairless, bodies. Some bees, such as honeybees, live in colonies. They may be either domesticated or living wild in caves or hollow trees. You may find other bees, such as carpenter bees, in individual nest holes in wood, or in the ground, like bumblebees. The main danger from bees is their barbed stinger located on their abdomens. When the bee stings you, it rips its stinger out of its abdomen along with the venom sac, and the bee dies. Except for killer bees, most bees tend to be more docile than wasps, hornets, and yellow jackets that have smooth stingers and are capable of repeated attacks.

Avoidance is the best tactic for self-protection. Watch out for flowers or fruit where bees may be feeding. Be careful of meat-eating yellow jackets when cleaning fish or game. The average person has a relatively minor and temporary reaction to bee stings and recovers in a couple of hours when the pain and headache go away.

WASP

BEE

Continued ➜

Those who are allergic to bee venom have severe reactions including anaphylactic shock, coma, and death. If antihistamine medicine is not available and you cannot find a substitute, an allergy sufferer in a survival situation is in grave danger.

Ticks

Ticks are common in the tropics and temperate regions. They are familiar to most of us. Ticks are small round arachnids with eight legs and can have either a soft or hard body. Ticks require a blood host to survive and reproduce. This makes them dangerous because they spread diseases like Lyme disease and Rocky Mountain spotted fever.

—From *Survival (Field Manual 21–76)*

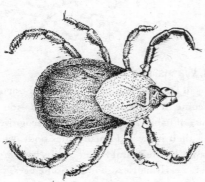

HARD TICK

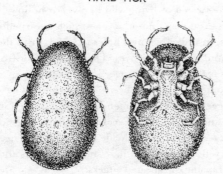

Sounds of Common Night Insects

Lang Elliott

The majority of night-active insect soundmakers belong to the order Orthoptera, which includes the crickets, grasshoppers, and katydids. In these groups, breeding males produce calls with specialized "stridulating" organs located on their wings. These consist of a "file and scraper" mechanism that is used to produce chirps, trills, and grating chatters. Other insect groups also produce sounds, but these may have little to do with breeding. For instance, the bark-eating grubs of certain long-horned beetles produce distinctive chewing sounds as they feed, both day and night.

Snowy Tree Cricket

About 3/4 inch long. Pale-green cricket with delicate, lacy wings and long antennae. Stridulating male produces melodic chirps from shrubs, often near the ground. He raises his wings straight up when singing and exposes a gland that secretes a glutinous liquid that the female devours prior to copulation. Often referred to as "temperature cricket" because the number of chirps occurring in 15 seconds plus 40 yields a close approximation of the temperature in Fahrenheit.

Northern Mole Cricket

About 1 inch long. An odd-looking, burrowing cricket with enlarged forelegs adapted for digging. Common throughout most of the East in muddy areas along shorelines or in other wet areas. Male chirps from entrance to his burrow. The song of this species is the lowest-pitched of all our native insect breeding calls.

Carolina Ground Cricket

A member of the subfamily Nemobiinae which includes a variety of different ground crickets.

About 1/2 inch long and brownish-black in color. Ranges across most of the Unites States. Sings from the ground in pastures, lawns, and moist ditches. The song of the male is a high-pitched buzzing trill that often has a pulsating or jerky quality.

Northern True Katydid

About 1 1/2 to 2 inches long; dark green with gauze-like wings and long antennae. Katydids are members of the Long-horned Grasshopper family (*Tettigoniidae*), named for their long antennae. The Northern True Katydid is common throughout most of the East. Male's harsh call sounds like *ch-ch* or *ch-ch-ch*, given about once every second with rhythm of words *ka-ty* or *ka-ty-did*. Neighboring individuals and large choruses sometimes call in almost perfect unison.

Sword-bearing Cone-headed Grasshopper

Another member of the Long-horned Grasshopper family. About 2 inches long. Slender and green, with long antennae and conical head. Commonly found in tall grass or weeds in the Northeast and upper Midwest, often along roads and highways. Song is composed of very high-pitched, lispy notes given in rapid succession.

Pine Sawyer

Member of Cerambycidae, the Long-horned Beetle family. Adults about 1 inch long, elongated, with long antennae. Larvae of certain species, such as *Monochamus notatus*, the Northeastern Sawyer, bore into the trunks of dead or dying pines to feed on the inner bark, hence the name "Pine Sawyer." Larvae are white grubs with dark mouthparts; they grow to about 13/4 inch long. Pine Sawyer larvae make scraping and chewing noises when feeding. These sounds can be heard over 100 feet away on a quiet night.

—From *A Guide to Night Sounds*

Flowers, Trees, Other Plants, and Mushrooms

Getting Acquainted with Flowers

William Carey Grimm

The Parts of a Flower

Many of us who would like to know more about the wild flowers and be able to recognize them have had little or no training in the subject of botany. For this reason it is well to present here a brief introduction to the structure and arrangement of flowers.

Most of the flowers that we ordinarily see are what the botanist would call a *complete flower*: one which has four sets of flower parts or organs—sepals, petals, stamens, and one or more pistils.

The outermost of these sets of organs are the *sepals*. Very often they are green in color and they cover the parts of the flower in the bud stage. Collectively the sepals are known as the *calyx* of the flower. In some flowers the sepals are more or less united and they may form a sort of cup or tube. In this case it is usually spoken of as the *calyx tube*. Usually it has lobes on its rim which represent the free tips of the individual sepals

Continued ➡

and they are called the *calyx lobes*. The number of calyx lobes therefore tells us how many sepals have been united to form the calyx tube.

The next series of flower parts is made up of the *petals*. They are usually the showy and brightly colored parts of the flower. Collectively the petals are known as the *corolla* of the flower. As in the case of the sepals, the petals may be joined to one another to form a *corolla tube*. The free ends of the individual petals which were united to form the corolla tube are usually seen as *corolla lobes* on its rim. Often at the bases of petals there are glands which secrete a sweet substance called nectar, from which bees make their honey. The petals actually serve as billboards to attract bees or other insects to the flower.

Sepals and petals taken together are usually spoken of as the *floral envelopes* or the *perianth* of the flower. While the sepals and petals are quite distinct and differently shaped and colored in most flowers, this is not universally true. In most members of the Lily Family, the Amaryllis Family, and in many plants belonging to the Iris Family, the sepals and petals are very much alike in size and color. It is therefore quite convenient just to speak of them as the *perianth parts*. Some flowers actually have but one set or series of floral envelopes, the sepals. In many members of the Buttercup Family these sepals are white or variously colored and look very much like petals. The sepals, in this case, have taken over the usual role of the petals in attracting insects to the flowers.

Stamens and pistils are the only flower parts that are actually involved in the production of the fruits and seeds. They are the *sexual organs* of flowers. The *stamens* are the organs just inside of the petals when petals are present. They usually have a slender stalk which is called the *filament* and a box-like compartment at the summit which is known as the *anther*. The anthers contain the grain-like, powdery, and usually yellow or yellowish pollen. Stamens are the male organ of a flower.

In the center of the flower there is a *pistil* or sometimes several pistils. Usually the pistil has a somewhat swollen part at its base which is called the *ovary*, inside of which are one to many small bodies known as *ovules*. The summit of the pistil is commonly enlarged, often knob-like or branched, and usually quite sticky. This part of the pistil is the *stigma*. Between the stigma and the ovary there is usually a stalk-like portion called the style. Pistils are the female organs of a flower.

Several things must happen before the flower can produce seeds. First of all, some of the pollen must get from the stamens to the sticky stigma of the pistil. This transfer of the pollen is known as *pollination* and in plants with showy flowers bees or other insects usually perform the task. That is why their flowers have attractive petals, alluring odors, and produce the sweet nectar. Following pollination each pollen grain sends a tube down through the style and into the ovary. There it seeks out one of the ovules. A sperm from the pollen goes down this tube and unites with an egg cell within the ovule, a process which is called *fertilization*. Thereafter the egg cell develops into a tiny plant or *embryo* and the ovule becomes a *seed*. The ovary of the pistil (sometimes with other parts attached) matures into what botanists call a *fruit*.

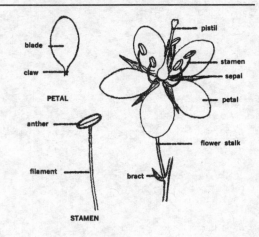

PETAL

STAMEN

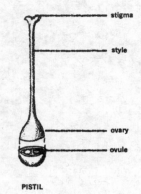

PISTIL

PARTS OF A COMPLETE FLOWER

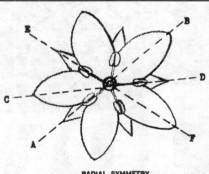

RADIAL SYMMETRY

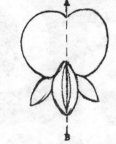

BILATERAL SYMMETRY

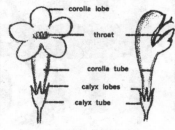

UNITED SEPALS AND PETALS

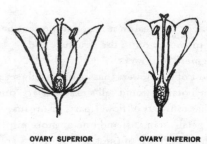

OVARY SUPERIOR   OVARY INFERIOR

Various devices are frequently employed to assure that pollen from the stamens will not pollinate the pistil of the same flower. In some flowers the anthers will have shed their pollen before the stigma of the pistil is ready to receive the pollen, or vice versa. In some plants the stamens and pistils are found in separate flowers, or the stamen-bearing and pistil-bearing flowers may even be on separate plants.

The Forms of Flowers

Flower structure is of primary importance in the identification of plants. In fact, botanists base the classification of plants into species, genera, and families on the basis of their flower structure. While color is sometimes useful in making an identification, it is by no means a reliable characteristic. The same species of plant may have flowers in two or more different colors, and the colors of flowers sometimes change with age. Size, too, is quite variable. A plant may vary considerably in size depending upon environmental factors, especially in the case of annuals.

In the simpler types of flowers all of the flower parts are attached to the *receptacle* or enlarged tip of the stem, and they are all separate and distinct. Good examples are seen in members of the Buttercup Family. A flower in which the ovary of the pistil is free from the surrounding parts is said to be a *superior ovary*. In many flowers the ovary is more or less surrounded by and united with the calyx tube or the receptacle. Such flowers are said to have an *inferior ovary*. The filaments of the stamens in many flowers are attached to the petals or the corolla tube rather than the receptacle.

In many flowers all of the flower parts radiate from the center of the flower and those in each series are more or less alike in size and shape. Like a pie, such a flower could be divided in any number of directions through the center into quite identical halves. Such a flower is said to have a *radial symmetry*. It is often called a *regular flower*.

It should take but one look at a flower of a pea, mint, violet, or orchid to see that it could be divided into two similar halves by cutting it in but one direction—vertically through the center. A flower of this type has a *bilateral symmetry*. It is often called an *irregular flower*. Often when the sepals or petals of a flower are joined together, the calyx or the corolla will be two-lipped. Such flowers are common among the members of the Mint Family but they also occur in many of the other flower families.

Flower Clusters or Inflorescences

Flowers may be solitary but more often they are arranged in various types of flower clusters or *inflorescences* as shown diagramatically on page 77. A *spike* is a simple inflorescence of stalkless flowers which are arranged along a stem. A *raceme* is similar except that the flowers are stalked. A *head* is a dense cluster of stalkless or very short-stalked flowers at the tip of a stem. In an *umbel* the flowers are on stalks which all arise from the summit of a stem. It is the typical

Continued ➡

inflorescence of the Parsley Family but it also occurs among the members of other flower families. A *panicle* is a branching flower cluster which may be likened to a compound raceme. The *cyme* is also a branching flower cluster, a more or less forking one in which the central flowers open first, and it tends to be flat-topped. Another flat-topped inflorescence is the *corymb* but in this one it is the outer or marginal flowers which open first.

It is very easy to be fooled unless one is very observant, and what is usually taken to be a flower may really be a flower cluster. In the Arum Family the flowers are quite small and

seated on a thick and somewhat fleshy stem called a *spadix*. Usually the spadix is more or less surrounded by a large and often colorful bract called a *spathe*. The "flowers" of the familiar Jack-in-the-pulpit and the cultivated calla-lilies are good examples.

The sunflower or a daisy is not a flower in the ordinary sense, but rather a dense cluster—a head—of many small flowers. What may be mistaken for petals are the marginal *ray flowers* which have a strap-shaped corolla. In the center of the head is a prominent *disk* which contains a large number of small flowers (*disk flowers*) which have a tubular corolla. The entire head is surrounded by an involucre made up of greenish bracts which may be mistaken for sepals. Sunflowers, daisies, asters, goldenrods, and many other common flowers are called *composites*. They are members of the very large Compositae Family.

Types and Arrangements of Leaves

Leaves show a marked variation in size, shape, and arrangement on the stems. In a few cases plants have leaves which are so distinctive that

they may be identified by the leaves alone. Many of the features of leaves are shown on page 14 and it would be well to become acquainted with them.

Most leaves have a flattened and more or less broad portion which is called the *blade*. In a great many there is a prominent central vein or *midrib* from which the veins branch off like the barbs from the shaft of a feather. Such a leaf is said to be *pinnately-veined*, or feather-veined. Other leaves have several main veins which radiate from the base or from the summit of a leaf stalk. This type of leaf is *palmately-veined*. The margin of the leaf blade may be untoothed or *entire*, or it may have teeth of various sizes or shapes. Sometimes a leaf blade is deeply cut or cleft, or it may be divided into smaller leaf-like parts which are called *leaflets*. A leaf in which the blade is in one piece is known as a *simple leaf*. One in which the blade is divided into leaflets is called a *compound leaf*. A leaf may be pinnately divided or *pinnately* compound or *palmately* divided or palmately compound. In many leaves there will be a pair of appendages or *stipules* at the base of the leaf stalk.

—From *The Illustrated Book of Wildflowers and Shrubs*

TYPES OF INFLORESCENCES

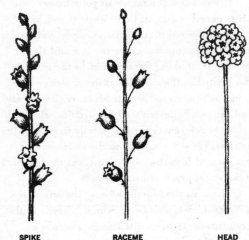

SPIKE   RACEME   HEAD

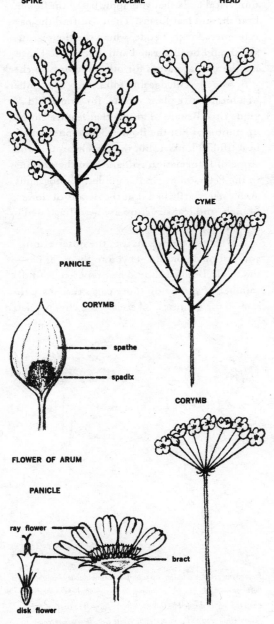

CYME

PANICLE

CORYMB

CORYMB

spathe

spadix

FLOWER OF ARUM

PANICLE

ray flower

bract

disk flower

COMPOSITE (HEAD)   UMBEL

LEAF PARTS AND TYPES OF LEAVES

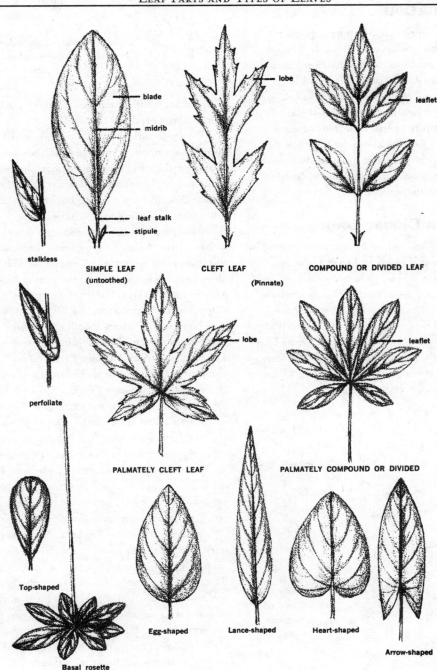

blade

midrib

lobe

leaflet

leaf stalk

stipule

stalkless

SIMPLE LEAF (untoothed)   CLEFT LEAF (Pinnate)   COMPOUND OR DIVIDED LEAF

perfoliate

lobe

leaflet

PALMATELY CLEFT LEAF   PALMATELY COMPOUND OR DIVIDED

Top-shaped

Basal rosette

Egg-shaped

Lance-shaped   Heart-shaped

Arrow-shaped

Wildflowers are the nonwoody, or herbaceous, plants. This includes what are also known as weeds, those wildflowers that have no idea they are mocking our desire for order and control.

I remember when wildflowers first sprang into my consciousness. I was walking along an old woods road in West Virginia when I noticed a solitary white flower blooming. I was beginning to take an interest in wild things and had been studying trees. I knew many of the common tree names, such as oak, pine, and maple, from my childhood, but I had only recently started to look into what those names meant. In the instant I saw that white bloom in the woods, the term *flower* took on a new meaning. It no longer meant all the cultivated varieties that had blocked my view of the myriad flowering plants that grew according to their own schedules and needs. Once my mind accepted the possibility of wild-flowers and all that they implied, my under-standing of plants started to change. That little white flower—I have no idea what it was—was the catalyst that changed my whole relationship to the plant world.

The Situation

Imagine that we're walking along a quiet, rural dirt road. This road runs alternately through tunnels of woods and along small lawns and wide open pastures. At one point, the road is bordered on the right by a rocky, wooded slope and on the left by a pasture. A casual glance into the bright pasture reveals hundreds of small yellow flowers floating above the lengthening grass. Perhaps by chance, or maybe after some close looking, we also notice some fascinating red flowers on the wooded slope.

Taking a Closer Look

Your observations will necessarily be informed by the guide that you're using, but at a minimum, pay attention to flower, branching pattern, and leaf type. A good guide should clearly illustrate and define all the terms used. Most commonly, the front and rear endpapers are filled with illus-trations of flower, branch, and leaf forms. These may take a little getting used to, but it's critical that you become familiar with the terms used in

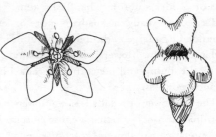

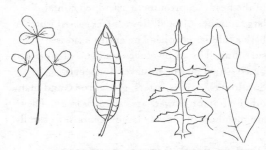

This regular flower can be divided into symmetrical halves along five different axes. An irregular flower has only one axis of symmetry.

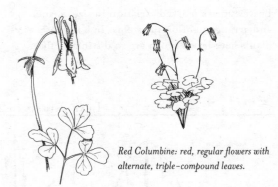

Compound, simple, dissected, and lobed leaves.

Tall Buttercup: yellow, regular flowers with five parts; alternate, five-lobed, dissected leaves.

Red Columbine: red, regular flowers with alternate, triple-compound leaves.

your guide. A little attention to this in the beginning will pay off down the road.

The yellow flowers we found are small and numerous on tall, spindly plants. They look like shallow dishes, slightly cupped. Each has five shiny petals. The flower is a *regular* flower, which means that, like a pie, it can be divided along any radius into symmetrical halves. The branching form is *alternate*, meaning that the points where the leaves grow from the main stem alternate sides as they go up the stem. The leaves show deep divisions, and all the pointy lobes radiate from a central point, like fingers extending from the palm of a hand. This form may be called palmately lobed, compound, divided, or dissected, depending on your guide. Lobed leaves are like a simple round leaf that has some chunks cut out of it, making baylike areas in the outline. Dissected means the same sort of thing, but with lots of fine cutting. Compound or divided leaves are actually groups of smaller leaflets, serving together as a leaf. In this case, I favor the term dissected or lobed. The terms to use depend on the terms your guide uses. If you are unsure which of two terms in your guide apply to a flower at hand, try each in turn until you get a satisfactory identification.

Whereas the yellow flower is plain and ordi-nary, the red flower seems outlandish at first. But on closer inspection, they're not so different. The red flower is regular, with five main parts, and has alternate, palmate leaves. The similarity in form is a clue that these two flowers may be in the same family. This simple outline of traits closely follows family traits, which is why it's helpful to start your closer look there.

Making the Identification

The great thing about most plants is that you can identify them right away based on just a closer look. With these few traits firmly in mind, you can begin to sift through the species presented in your find guide to find the one you are looking at. The Peterson guides, which have regional volumes covering all of North America, are arranged by color. So in the section on yellow flowers, you'll have to search for the illus-tration of the pasture flower. These guides group species with similar flower and leaf shapes together within their respective colors. Page headings describe the key traits illustrated on the facing page, so you can quickly scan these as you also look for plants that resemble yours.

If you know the family of your flower, you can proceed in one of three ways. If you know that the flower is orchid, for example, you can go to the appropriate color section and flip through it, looking for the icon in the margin that identifies the orchid family. A more effi-cient way is to go to the introductory chapter and find the family description for orchids, along with page references for that family in each of the sections. Or you could go to the index entry for orchids and find the pages that cover those plants in the appropriate color section.

Those in the Northeast have the advantage of *Newcomb's Wildflower Guide*, which is keyed to the very traits we've been discussing. There is a numerical code that you apply based on flower, branch, and leaf forms. Then you find the page references for that code, where the flower you saw should be illustrated and described. There may be similar guides for other regions, so check with some knowledgeable folks, such as members of a local native plant society, for some field guide tips. Beware of guides that feature close-up photos of just the flower. These photos are beautiful to look at, but they rarely capture the scope of information contained in the drawings in the Peterson or similar guides. Photographs aren't necessarily bad, but the details of flower, branch, and leaf structure are best illustrated by an artist's hand.

Whatever guide you use, the observations you just made should get you to the right part of the book. But you should be prepared to find a number of species on those pages that share the same basic qualities. These are the closely related

Four members of the buttercup family (Ranunculacae). Two are true buttercups. All have regular, five-part flowers and compound or dissected leaves divided by threes or fives. Top left to bottom right: Yellow-flowered Water Buttercup, White Baneberry, Creeping Buttercup, Dwarf Larkspur.

Continued ➤

species, most likely of the same genus as the plant you hope to identify. If this is the case, you'll probably need to draw on a few additional observations to be completely sure of the identification. A species may be distinguished from its relatives by fine hairs on the stem or petals, the relative length and width of leaflets, the way the leaf attaches to the stem, or other details that you are unlikely to consider without the prompting of your guide. Such fine details are rarely captured in photographs.

The yellow pasture flower—with its five petals and its deeply lobed, palmate, alternate leaves—will be found among the yellow buttercups. Once you get to that section of your guide, the height of the plant marks it as the Tall Buttercup (*Ranunculus acris*). Although the Tall Buttercup is rather distinctive, there are other similar yellow Ranunculus species. The Bulbous Buttercup, for example, differs in having reflexed sepals under the open flower and swelling at the base of the stem.

The red flower turns out to be the Red Columbine (*Aquilegia canadensis*). Its five long spurs and divided leaves are unmistakable, resembling only the cultivated variety of columbine. The columbine is so striking and fantastic in appearance that it might be easy to overlook its essential similarities to the Tall Buttercup. As it is, the two plants are of the same family, Ranunculaceae, the Buttercups. Typical members of this family have flowers with five main parts and a bushy button of stamens and pistils in the center; the leaves are divided in groups of either threes or fives.

You'll get to know the families as you identify individual species. Use each new species as an opportunity to figure out its family, and soon you'll be able to place unknown flowers in the right families and identify them. Luckily, plants sit still, so you can go through this process slowly and deliberately with the plant right in front of you. For the most part, if you can reexamine the flower based on questions prompted by the guide, you'll be able to identify it. Concentrating on structural traits and searching in family terms will make the process go more smoothly. These structural, family traits are the signature of how a plant manages pollination and seed dispersal. It is these processes that give the flower "meaning."

The buttercup, for example, has small flattish flower disks. They smell good and are upward-facing, with small bees crawling about inside them. These bees are feeding on nectar and collecting pollen, but as they do so, they carry pollen from one flower to another, fertilizing them and allowing seeds to develop. Every flower needs some way to move pollen from the stamen of one flower to the pistil of another. Since the plants can't move, they must rely on either wind or animals to do the work for them. The structure of a flower is a mix of the original family traits and adaptations to a certain scheme of pollination.

The columbine is a wonder. Its downward-facing flowers look like a bundle of long, red funnels. Each funnel has a long spur that extends backward from the opening and ends in a small bubble. These long, tubular flowers are adapted to specialized nectar-feeding birds and

Birds and bees are active pollinators of different kinds of flowers.

long-tongued insects such as moths. The columbine is clearly animal pollinated. The bubbles at the ends of the spurs store the nectar that the pollinators are searching for. When a hummingbird pokes into a flower for some nectar, it gets pollen on its face. When it visits the next flower, it brings the pollen with it. Transferring pollen from one place to another is incidental to the hummingbird, which is simply trying to feed itself, but the next generation of flowers depends on it.

When a seed germinates at the foot of the parent plant, parent and offspring become competitors for space, light, water, and nutrients. (This might sound familiar to some of you with grown or growing children.) It's in the interest of both to get the seeds away from the parent plant. Almost everyone has had experience with the milkweed, which, like the familiar dandelion, relies on the wind to disperse its seeds. This accounts in part for its ability to colonize almost any patch of open ground. Seeds of

Milkweed seeds are dispersed by the wind. The seeds of violets are dispersed by ants.

other plants have Velcro-like prickles that allow them to cling to fur and be carried to new sites. Fruits with sweet flesh, such as berries, encourage birds and bears and other animals to eat them and disperse the seeds in their droppings. Violets rely on ants to disperse their seeds. Violet seeds have fruitlike nuggets attached to them. The ants eat the fruits and discard the seeds in their underground nests. The seeds sprout from where they were "planted" by the ants.

The physical tools that correspond to the ecological functions of pollination and seed dispersal define the plant families. Each family demonstrates some collection of structural traits and associated behaviors that distinguishes it from other families. With birds, we look at the bill, wing, and tail; when tracking mammals, we consider feet and legs. With plants, we look at flower, fruit, leaf, and branch.

The problem with plants is that in any one area, there are more plant families represented

by wildflowers than there are bird and mammal families combined. Many people apply only the family name to many plants—such as with milkweed, cattail, grass, reed, mint, and violet—never going any further in identification. My field guides for the northeastern United States list thirty-one and thirty-nine species of violet, respectively. *The Flora of the State of Vermont* lists twenty-seven species in that state alone. One summer, I had a great time learning to identify violets down to the species. Even some of my naturalist friends thought I was crazy (again). For many plants, knowing the family or perhaps a few major groups, or tribes, within the family will be enough. For instance, most folks probably know only the most common species of goldenrod, aster, and sunflower, the tribes of the Compositae family. Regardless of how you proceed, you can start by using these core traits to narrow your search.

Representatives of the sunflower tribe of the Compositae Family and the violet, lily, and mint families.

Ecological factors can be a shortcut to separating species within a family. What are the odds of seeing a Yellow-Flowered Water Buttercup growing out in that pasture? About zero. But look at the illustration a few pages back and notice that it has a typical buttercup flower and five-part, divided leaves. Note the thready leaves, which are similar to those of other water-living plants. You might have guessed that it lives inundated in water just from the illustration in your guidebook.

A good species description should include reference to the habitats or microhabitats where you would expect to find the plant. These big-picture concerns might consist of only a word or two in the text, but they capture 90 percent of your experience of the plant in the field. The most difficult aspect of learning about plants is not identifying them but taking the abundance and profusion of plants you could learn about and putting them together in your head in a meaningful way. Most people fail to remember what they see in the woods because they fail to understand, to contextualize. They overlook the larger story weaving the facts together and bringing them to life.

Taking a Broader Look

Our example is set in the spring. Buttercups and columbines bloom early, and by late summer, their flowers are long gone; only their green parts and maybe the dried fruit bodies remain. These flowers were just two of a host of wildflowers blooming around that time, many of which have completely disappeared. In late summer, goldenrods and then asters dominate the pasture. Only a few flowers can be found on the rocky, shady slope. Those plants flourish (which means "to flower") in the early spring, before the canopy above has matured and

Continued ➡

robbed them of most of their sunlight. When the flowers are gone, a thick cover of green leaves remains.

As you get to know species and families, you'll be able to identify some plants from the dried structures—dead stalkes and fruit pods—that remain visible throughout the nonblooming season. For the most part, though, as you look through your guide to identify a flower, be sure to consider the blooming season as listed in the species accounts. Although the timing of the bloom can vary somewhat, depending on local conditions, the overall range is a handy rule. It can make a real difference in which plant you choose in the end.

As always, the range of the plant is important to consider. Ranges for most of the flowering plants are rather large and are not as clearly delineated as those of mammal species, but range information can still help exclude some closely related species from consideration. Is the site where the plant is growing wet or dry? Is it open and sunny, or a dense thicket? Is the site "disturbed" or a "waste place"? Perhaps the most important big-picture consideration with plants is the character of the site. The most important site qualities are soil nutrients and moisture, openness, and disturbance. These are the essential factors that affect plant survival.

Soil nutrients and moisture are complementary characteristics, since adequate moisture aids in breaking down leaves and other debris, returning nutrients to the soil. The underlying geology influences the nutrients available in the soil, as does the topography. A high, rocky ridge has thin, poor soil relative to the rich soil of low valleys. Openness, and therefore access to sunlight, has an obvious effect on growing conditions. Disturbed sites or waste places include roadsides, abandoned fields or lots, or riverbanks—anywhere activity has upset the natural vegetation and broken up the soil.

Some species of wildflowers and trees are able to establish themselves quickly in disturbed sites. Other species take longer to eventually establish themselves in stable sites, such as woodlands that have been spared logging for a few decades. Sites with recent or frequent disturbance favor quick-growing plants that channel most of their growth into seed production. These tend to be annual herbs and trees that rely on wind for pollination and seed dispersal. Had the site not been disturbed, a different collection of plants would dominate. In stable woodlands, the wildflowers tend to be perennials that produce few seeds but grow large roots, allowing the plant to persist from season to season. Wind is less reliable for pollination under the forest canopy, so understory plants there tend to rely on insects or other animals for pollination and seed dispersal.

In our example, the pasture with the buttercups slopes gradually down to a low area of mostly shrubs and cattails. This is a wet, marshy spot where water seeps up from a spring and flows along the ground to the pond below. The buttercups are crowded into the lower half of the pasture, where the soil is obviously moister. The pasture is open, and it is also subject to regular disturbance from rotational grazing and hay cutting. The grazing and cutting make the

pasture inhospitable for any trees that might want to sprout there, but there is ample opportunity for the buttercups to grow and thrive between cuts. In contrast, no buttercups can be found growing in the lawns of the nearby farm, where the mowing is finer and more frequent.

The columbine is growing under the canopy of the woods, in a site that is both darker and rockier than the open, moist meadow. I would guess that this site is nutrient poor. It's a stable site, as evidenced by the relatively few flowers the columbine produces compared with the buttercup, which can have dozens of flowers per plant.

Why worry about the site if you can identify a plant based strictly on its physical appearance? Site conditions can help separate species, such as the Smooth and Downy Wood Violets. Site preferences are also a clue to abundance. If a plant grows in disturbed sites, it's likely to have spread throughout most of the continent. Finally, there are many species that may be mentioned in your guide but not illustrated due to lack of space. Site conditions are often the best way to recognize these.

—From *Naturalist's Guide to Observing Nature*

Why Plants have Scientific Names

William Carey Grimm

Have you ever wondered why plants have scientific names, or why common names are not good enough?

To begin with, and this may amaze you, most of our wild plants actually have no common names at all. They never have been given any. On the other hand, every known kind of plant does have a scientific name.

Common names are frequently very confusing. In some instances the same name is used for two or more entirely different plants. Button-snakeroot, for example, is used as a common name for plants in both the Parsley and Compositae families. Samson's-snakeroot may be either a gentian or member of the Pea family. A fireweed may be a plant belonging to either the Evening primrose or the Compositae Families; and a loosestrife could be either a true loosestrife or an entirely plant of the Primrose Family.

To make things a bit more confusing, a plant may be known by more than one common name. Thus the little member of the Lily Family which bears the scientific name *Erythronium americanum* is variously known as the Trout-lily, Fawn-lily, Yellow Adder's-tongue, and even Dog's-tooth Violet. Often a plant is known by one common name in one part of its range and by other names elsewhere. It is obvious, too, that common names are often misleading in that they do not show the true relationship of a plant. The little lily-like plant just mentioned is most certainly not a violet, nor even remotely related to the true violets.

Scientific names have several advantages. First there can be but one plant known as *Erythronium americanum*. It cannot therefore be confused with any other plant. The first part of its scientific name tells us that it belongs to the genus *Erythronium*. It is the generic name of the

plant and this particular genus is a member of the Lily Family. Its relationship is thus firmly established beyond a doubt. The second part of the name—*americanum*—is the Latin adjectival name, the two together comprising the name of the species. In this case it means "American." Scientific names are always in Latin and are the same throughout the world, regardless of language differences in the various countries.

In some cases two or more varieties of the same species of plant may be recognized. *Cypripedium calceolus* is the Yellow Lady's-slipper of the Old World. Botanists now recognize our American plants as a variety of this wide-ranging species. Thus our Yellow Lady's-slipper is known as *Cypripedium calceolus var.* (or variety) *pubescens*.

Naturally the question is going to arise as to why the scientific names do not always agree in even the technical manuals. The rule is that the first published name, accompanied by a valid description of the plant, becomes its scientific name. Thus a great many of the scientific names of our plants have remained the same for a long time, even for more than two centuries. Often, however, researchers find that a plant was given a valid scientific name before one in current usage was given; and in such a case it becomes necessary to make a change in its name. Research is constantly continuing in the taxonomy of plants and for other reasons a name may become invalid. As we learn more about the true relationship of species, a change often becomes necessary in the name. Thus botanists no longer accept *Ascyrum* and *Hypericum* as two distinctly different genera of plants. All species formerly placed in the genus *Ascyrum* are now regarded as species of *Hypericum*. Someday such matters will, of course, be definitely decided, but right now they are in a state of flux.

Scientific names are actually not as dreadful as they may at first seem. We use many of the generic names of plants—names such as *Trillium*, *Hepatica*, *Anemone*, and *Chrysanthemum*—without ever thinking, or perhaps even knowing, that they are scientific names. Others such as *Lilium* (lilies), *Viola* (violets), and *Rosa* (roses) come very close to the English equivalents of the generic names. With a little practice one could soon become adept at using scientific names of plants and appreciate their advantages.

How Plants Are Named

Our modern method of naming plants was devised by the Swedish botanist Linnaeus in 1753. The first part of the scientific name is that of the genus to which a plant belongs, and it is always written with a capital letter. The second part is the name of the particular species, and it is customary to write this in lower case, even though it may be a geographical name or name of a person. Sometimes varieties, forms, or subspecies are recognized, and these names follow the species name. In this book only some of the more outstanding or distinct varieties or forms are recognized. Following the name of the plant it is customary to give the name of the author, or person who described the plant. In most cases these names are abbreviated.

Scientific names are derived from various

Continued ➡

sources. Sometimes the generic names are simply the ancient Greek or Latin names for groups of plants: *Rosa* for the roses, *Vitis* for grapes, *Prunus* for the plums and cherries, etc. In quite a few cases the names signify some characteristic of the plant: *Xanthorhiza*, for example, means "yellow root." Again, the name may honor some person, as *Lyonia* for John Lyon; or some character from mythology, such as *Andromeda*. Specific names, too, often tell us of some distinctive characteristic: *acerifolium* means "with leaves like a maple," *macrocarpon* means "large-fruited," and *pubescens* tells us that perhaps the leaves, at least, are downy.

—From *The Illustrated Book of Wildflowers and Shrubs*

The Study of Trees

William Carey Grimm
Revised by John Kartesz

The serious student of trees should first become familiar with their general structure. ... Identifications, in most instances, have been based on characters that are evident for long periods of time; principally on leaves and fruits in summer identifications and twig and bark characteristics in winter identifications. The accompanying plates have been planned to show the leaves, twigs, fruits, and detailed characteristics of the buds. In some instances, particularly where the flowers are conspicuous, drawings of the flowers have also been included.

Trees are, of course, woody plants, but so are the so-called shrubs. We often recognize a tree as being larger than a shrub, and usually think of trees as having a solitary stem or trunk. Actually the differences between trees and shrubs are purely relative ones. There is no real line of demarcation between trees and shrubs. The gray birch, for instance, often has several stems in a clump, and it could, therefore, just as logically be called a large shrub as a tree. Frequently a species will be merely shrubby in one portion of its range and be quite large and treelike somewhere else. The great-laurel and the mountain-laurel are usually only shrubs in the mountains of Pennsylvania, yet they grow to be nearly 40 feet in height and assume treelike proportions in the Great Smoky Mountains of North Carolina and Tennessee. In a work on trees it is often doubtful just which borderline species should be included and which ones should be omitted. Many species very properly belong both in a work on trees and also in one on shrubs. For some of the more shrubby tree species, refer to *The Illustrated Book of Wildflowers and Shrubs* (Stackpole 1993).

How Trees Grow

Trees, like all other green plants, are able to make their own foods out of raw materials derived from the soil and from the air. The roots serve the very important function of anchoring the trees to the earth; the very youngest portions of the roots also absorb water and dissolved mineral nutrients from the soil. The water passes upward through the *sapwood*, the lighter-colored outer wood in the trunks and larger branches of the tree, and finally reaches

How a Tree Grows

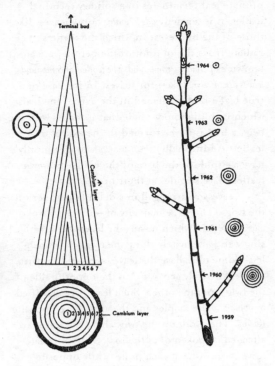

the leaves. The leaves of the tree are, in a sense, food factories. It is within the leaves that sugars and starches are made from water and nutrients from the soil and from the gas carbon dioxide, which is derived from the air. The machines utilized in this process of foodmaking, or *photosynthesis*, are microscopic bodies called *chloroplasts*, which are green because they contain a green pigment known as *chlorophyll*. The energy necessary to run this food-making machinery comes from the sunlight. Much more water passes into the leaves than is actually needed in the food-making and other life processes, so the leaves pass off this excess water into the atmosphere in the form of an invisible vapor. Oxygen, another important waste product of food making, also is returned to the air.

The food materials that are manufactured within the leaves of the tree must be transported to all the growing parts of the tree, even to the very tips of the roots. The sap containing this food material is distributed through the inner bark of the branches, trunks, and roots. Thus if a tree is girdled, or the layer of inner bark is completely severed throughout the circumference of its trunk, the tree will not die immediately, but it will gradually starve to death because the food materials made within the leaves cannot be transported to its roots.

Nearly everyone at some time has observed the *annual rings*, or rings of growth, in some sawed-off tree trunk. Between the innermost layer of the bark and the outermost layer of the wood there is a very thin layer of actively growing cells called the *cambium layer*. It is within this layer that all of the growth in diameter takes place. Each growing season the cambium layer adds a new layer of wood on the outside of the older wood, and a new layer of bark on the inside of the older bark. Because trees grow most rapidly soon after their growth begins in the spring, the cells of the *spring wood* are larger and thinner walled than those in the *summer wood* developed later, when the growth slows down. The differences in these cells are responsible for the annual rings. Catastrophes such as extreme heavy

freezes or ice storms may temporarily interfere with growth processes and result in false annual rings, but a reasonably accurate estimate of the tree's age can be obtained by counting the annual rings very close to its base. Naturally the number of annual rings decreases when the count is made higher on the trunk, for the upper portions are actually not as old as the base. The diagram above will make this more apparent. As the trunk or branches grow in diameter, the older layers of the sapwood die, and they generally become darker in color due to the accumulation of various waste products within the cells. This darker interior portion, called the *heartwood*, merely serves to give the trunk or branch structural strength. We have seen hollow trees that go on living year after year. They are able to do so because the living tissue is all within the outer few inches of the trunks; unless they are broken off by a violent wind, such trees might go on living for many years in spite of the fact that the trunks are entirely hollow.

Growth also takes place within the *buds* that occur on the younger branches, or *twigs*. Contrary to popular belief, buds do not appear on the twigs in the spring; they develop during the growing season and are fully developed before autumn. The buds contain rudimentary branches and leaves, or in some cases flowers, which are simply modified branches and leaves. They remain in a dormant condition throughout the winter months. When growth is resumed in the spring, some of the buds expand rapidly, due primarily to the intake of water. It is then that most people say that the trees are "budding." All growth in length, in the tree's height, in the lengthening of its branches, and in the formation of new branches takes place in the growth tissues, which emanate from the buds. A spike driven into the trunk of a tree six feet above the ground will always be six feet above the ground, but it will gradually be buried within the expanding layers of wood laid down by the tree's cambium layer.

Tree Identification

Summer Characteristics

- Leaves

The leaves of trees are used much in making summer identifications. Unlike flowers or fruits, leaves or leaflike structures are present on all living trees during the summer months, and are available for study for a comparatively long period of time. Small trees often do not have the characteristic bark of older specimens, but they do have leaves by which they may be identified. In attempting to identify any tree by its leaves, or leaflike structures, care should be taken to procure *normal or typical leaves at all times*. As a rule, the leaves found on sprout growth are seldom characteristic of the species, and in many cases may prove to be very confusing. Such leaves are frequently much larger than normal leaves, often differing markedly in shape and other characteristics. The keys and the descriptions in this book are all based on normal leaves and other normal characteristics. Do not collect the first specimen

Continued ➡

you find. Look carefully at the tree, or preferably several trees; then select a branch that has average-looking or normal leaves.

On pages 83 and 84 an attempt has been made to illustrate most of the important characteristics that are used for the identification of trees by means of their leaves. There are other important things such as leaf texture, the presence or absence of hairiness, or pubescence, the color, and the odor or taste. These characteristics cannot be illustrated, but such characteristics are often mentioned in both the keys and the text.

The leaves of firs, larches, pines, and spruces are long, narrow, and needlelike; in fact, they are commonly referred to simply as *needles*. In the case of the larches and the pines the needles are arranged in clusters or bundles, usually with a sheath about the base of the cluster. The needles of the firs and the spruces are arranged singly along the branchlets or twigs. The leaves of the hemlock and of the balsam fir are also narrow, but they are distinctly flattened and have almost parallel margins. Such leaves are said to be *linear*. If one were to examine the branchlets of the northern or Atlantic white-cedars, it would be obvious that the leaves are quite small and *scalelike*, with their edges overlapping each other like the shingles on a roof. The red-cedar also has scalelike leaves, which are closely pressed against the branchlets, but on the more vigorous growth the leaves are awl-like, or spreading, stiff, and very sharp-pointed.

The majority of our trees are classified as *broad-leaved* trees. Their leaves have a distinctly flattened portion called the *blade*. They also usually have a distinct leafstalk, or *petiole*. Some trees such as maples, aspens, and basswoods have relatively long petioles, while the petioles of the elms and most birches are rather short. The petioles are usually rounded, but sometimes they are grooved, and in the case of most poplars and aspens they are distinctly flattened. At the very base of the petioles there is often a pair of *stipules*. In most trees the stipules are small or they soon disappear, but in some instances they are leaflike and persistent. Such stipules are often conspicuous on certain willows, the American sycamore, and the tuliptree. The paired thorns at the bases of the leaves of the black locust are actually modified stipules.

In many leaves the petiole is extended through the leaf blade to its tip as the midrib. Conspicuous primary veins are arranged along both sides of this *midrib*, much like the barbs along the shaft of a feather; these leaves are said to be *pinnately veined*. The leaves of oaks, chestnuts, beeches, elms, birches, and many other trees are pinnately veined. In other leaves several primary veins appear to radiate from the summit of the petiole, like the spread fingers of one's hand; these leaves are described as *palmately veined*. Our maples are excellent examples of the latter type. When the leaf blade appears as a single piece without divisions, the leaf is known as a *simple* leaf. Sometimes, however, the leaf blade is divided into smaller leaflike sections that are called *leaflets*. Such leaves are said to be *compound*. In locusts, sumacs, and ashes, the leaflets are arranged along the prolongation of the petiole, which is termed the *rachis*; they are said to be *pinnately compound* or *pinnate*, and with two leaflets

at the apex they are termed *even-pinnate*. If a pinnate leaf terminates in a solitary terminal leaflet, it is termed *odd-pinnate*. Some leaves, like those of the buckeyes, in which the leaflets radiate from the summit of the petiole, are known as *palmately compound. The leaflets of compound leaves are often mis*taken for leaves. In the case of a true leaf a bud is formed in the axil of the leaf, which is in the upper angle that it makes with the twig, a bud is never formed in the axil of a leaflet. Additionally, true leaves will commonly have a stipule at the base of the blade; however, leaflets have stipules at their bases.

Leaves are arranged in a definite manner on the twigs. The large majority of our trees have *alternate* leaves, which means the leaves are arranged singly and alternately along the twigs or branchlets. Some trees have the leaves arranged in pairs, one leaf directly across or on the opposite side of the twig from the other. Such leaves are classified as *opposite*. The maples and the ashes have opposite leaves. The point on the twig where the leaves are attached is spoken of as the *node*. Thus alternate leaves occur one at each node, while opposite leaves occur two at each node. Sometimes, as in the catalpas, there are three leaves at a node; in this arrangement leaves are termed *whorled*.

Shapes of leaves must, of course, be taken into consideration in making identifications. In some instances the shapes of the leaves are so unique that they may be readily identified by shape alone, such as the leaves of the tuliptree and the sweet-gum. The common shapes of leaves and the terms that are used in describing them are shown on page 83. This same page also illustrates the various types of leaf tips, leaf bases, and leaf margins.

The student of trees should become familiarized with the more common terms applied to leaves, for they are quite convenient as well as necessary in an accurate description. Many leaves have teeth on their margins. They may be so fine as to be almost obscure, or they may be very large and conspicuous. Often these teeth on the leaf margins are forwardly pointed and sharp, resembling the teeth on a saw; this type of margin is defined as *serrate*, versus teeth that are not forwardly pointed and resemble the canine teeth in your mouth, which are defined as *dentate*. In some cases the larger teeth have smaller teeth on them; then the margins are said to be *double-serrate* or *doubly toothed*. Not infrequently the teeth may be blunt, and sometimes they end in bristle-tips. Some leaves have deep indentations that may extend halfway or more to the midribs. Such leaves are said to be *lobed*. The projecting portions of these leaves are spoken of as the *lobes*, while the deep indentations that separate them are called the *sinuses*. The pattern of lobing follows the pattern of venation. Most of our oaks have *pinnately lobed* leaves, while those of the maples are *palmately lobed*. Leaves that have neither teeth nor lobes on their margins are known as *entire*.

FLOWERS

A few of our trees have complete, showy flowers, as, for example, the apples, the locusts, and the magnolias. The majority of our trees, however, have relatively inconspicuous flowers. A *complete flower* is one that has all four sets of floral organs: a *calyx*, which is composed of the *sepals*; a *corolla*, composed of the *petals; stamens*; and in the center,

one or more *pistils*. The principal function of the sepals is to protect the other organs when the flower is in the bud stage. The corolla is generally the showy part of the flower, often attracting insects at flowering time. Only the stamens and the pistils are absolutely essential in the reproductive process, as they constitute the sexual elements of the flower. The stamens are the male element, producing the male germ cells or *pollen* within the *anthers*, which are often borne on slender stalks called the *filaments*. The pistil is the female organ, commonly consisting of three parts: the *ovary* at the base, which contains the ovules, or egg cells; the *stigma*, which receives the pollen; and the *style*, which connects the stigma and the ovary. A flower that contains both of these sexual elements, stamens and pistils, is known as a *perfect flower*. The majority of our trees have *imperfect* or unisexual flowers, the stamens and pistils occurring in separate flowers and very often on separate trees. Flowers that contain only stamens are called *staminate flowers*; those that contain only pistils are *pistillate flowers*. The portion of a flower to which the various organs are attached is called the *receptacle*.

In order to produce fruits and seeds it is absolutely essential that the pollen from the staminate flowers reaches the stigmas of the pistillate ones. This transfer of the pollen is known as *pollination*. Insects, particularly the bees, are a highly efficient agency for transferring the pollen from one flower to another. *Insect pollination* is the most certain and economical method of pollination, but it involves the necessity of attracting insect visitors to the flowers; consequently, those flowers that are insect-pollinated generally secrete *nectar*, the sweet fluid from which bees make their honey. Such flowers advertise the fact that nectar is present by having showy corollas or by broadcasting enticing odors, or often by using a combination of both. One need only stand beneath a flowering tuliptree or basswood and listen to the all-pervading hum of bees to realize just how effectively alluring such flowers can be.

In spite of the fact that *wind pollination* entails many risks and is extremely wasteful of pollen, the majority of our native trees depend entirely upon this method of pollination. To assure any degree of success, the pollen must be produced in prodigious quantities, and then the tree must depend upon the mercies of the winds to carry it to its intended destination. Of course wind pollination entails no necessity for showiness, nor the production of alluring odors or nectar. In fact, the simpler the flower structure the better. For this reason, most wind-pollinated tree flowers are stripped to the bare essentials, and most persons would not recognize many of them as flowers at all. Inasmuch as foliage would interfere materially with the wind-borne pollen reaching the stigmas of the pistillate flowers, the flowers are usually produced early in the spring before the leaves appear or at least before they are fully developed.

The flowers, like the buds, which will provide for the future growth of leafy branches, are sometimes formed on trees long before the flowering season. On the winter twigs of birches one will note long, cylindrical, scaly objects that we call *aments*, or *catkins*. These catkins are really well-developed staminate flowers. Each of the

Continued ➡

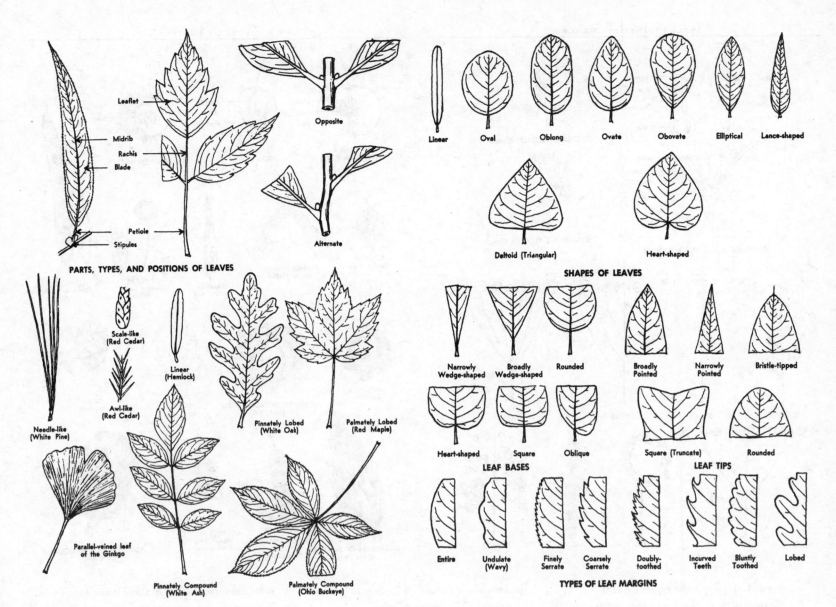

PARTS, TYPES, AND POSITIONS OF LEAVES

Leaflet · Midrib · Rachis · Blade · Petiole · Stipules · Opposite · Alternate

Scale-like (Red Cedar) · Linear (Hemlock) · Awl-like (Red Cedar) · Needle-like (White Pine) · Pinnately Lobed (White Oak) · Palmately Lobed (Red Maple)

Parallel-veined leaf of the Ginkgo · Pinnately Compound (White Ash) · Palmately Compound (Ohio Buckeye)

SHAPES OF LEAVES

Linear · Oval · Oblong · Ovate · Obovate · Elliptical · Lance-shaped · Deltoid (Triangular) · Heart-shaped

LEAF TIPS

Narrowly Wedge-shaped · Broadly Wedge-shaped · Rounded · Broadly Pointed · Narrowly Pointed · Bristle-tipped

LEAF BASES

Heart-shaped · Square · Oblique · Square (Truncate) · Rounded

TYPES OF LEAF MARGINS

Entire · Undulate (Wavy) · Finely Serrate · Coarsely Serrate · Doubly-toothed · Incurved Teeth · Bluntly Toothed · Lobed

flowers is subtended by a rather large *bract*, which is in reality a modified leaf. Similarly, on the winter twigs of the red maple there are clusters of buds that contain flowers, giving the tree a running start on the spring season. Sometimes flowers are borne solitary, but more often they are borne in some kind of clusters. These flower clusters are spoken of as *inflorescences*. Some of the more common types of these inflorescences are illustrated diagrammatically on page 84, along with the terms that are used in describing them.

Flowers differ markedly in their general structure, and our system of plant classification is based largely on this fact. The pistil is the portion of the flower that ordinarily develops into the fruit following the *fertilization* of the *egg cell* within the ovule by a *sperm cell* from the pollen grain. After fertilization the ovules develop into seeds. A *simple pistil* is one that has a solitary chamber or *cell* within its ovary, although it may contain one or many seeds. Sometimes the pistil is actually composed of two or more pistils that are united, and we call this kind of pistil a *compound pistil*. The ovary of a compound pistil, in a cross section, will show as many chambers or cells as the number of pistils composing it. The term *carpel* is applied either to a simple pistil or to one of the units of a compound pistil. Thus a pistil with five carpels is a compound pistil, which is composed of five united pistils. Often the styles of a compound pistil will be separate and distinct, in spite of the fact that the ovaries are united and appear as one. In some instances, as in the apple and its relatives, the ovary is

united with the receptacle and the calyx, and the latter parts of the flower also develop and become an integral part of the mature fruit.

Fruits

After the flowering season, the fruits begin to develop on the trees. The fruits are usually available for study for a much longer period than are the flowers. In some species the fruits mature in the autumn, but they persist on the trees throughout part or all of the winter season. Even in those cases of fruits dropping from the trees, one may often find remnants of them on the ground. Of course not all trees bear fruits, and some species do not produce fruits until they are many years old, or at least not until they attain a rather large size. In many of our trees the staminate and pistillate flowers are borne on different trees; only those individuals that produce pistillate flowers will ever bear fruits. The fruits of trees are often very helpful in arriving at an identification, and in a few instances the specific identifications are very largely based on fruit characteristics.

Following fertilization, the ovary of the pistil begins to develop into a fruit. Sometimes accessory parts, such as the receptacle and the calyx, also become a part of the mature fruit. The edible portion of the apple, for instance, is an enlarged and fleshy receptacle, for in this instance the pistil becomes the core of the apple. The seeds that are found in fruits develop from the fertilized ovules, which are normally found in the interior of the ovary. The coniferous

trees, pines, spruces, hemlocks, etc., do not, however, have their seeds enclosed within ovaries. In these cases the seeds are borne simply on the upper surfaces of the cone scales; such trees are said to be *naked-seeded*. Botanically they are classified as *gymnosperms*; all of our other trees, which have their seeds enclosed within ovaries, are classified as *angiosperms*.

Many of the commoner types of tree fruits are illustrated on page 84. The following is a classification of the important types of tree fruits arranged in outline form.

I. **Simple fruits**: Fruits derived from a single pistil, which may be either simple or compound (composed of two or more carpels).

  1. Dry and indehiscent fruits:

    a. **Achenes.** These are small 1-seeded fruits that are wingless but are commonly supplied with plumelike hairs, which aid in their dispersal by the winds (American sycamore).

    b. **Samaras.** These are 1-seeded fruits that are provided with winglike projections for wind dissemination (maples, ashes, and elms).

    c. **Nuts.** Nuts are 1-seeded fruits that have a hard shell. Most nuts are entirely surrounded by a husk or bur that may or may not split open at maturity (walnuts, hickories, chestnuts, beeches).

Continued ➡

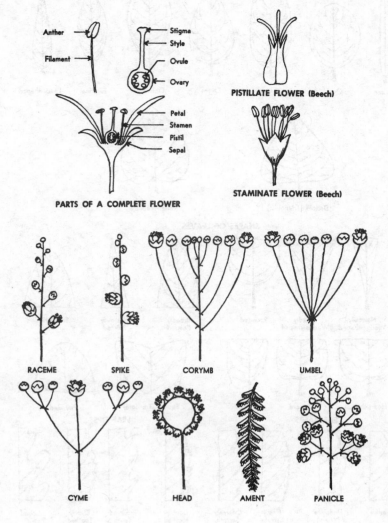

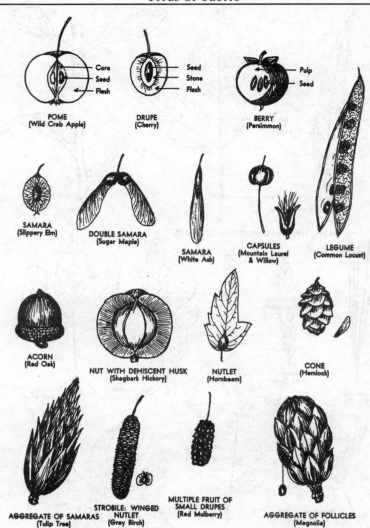

d. **Acorns**. This specific type of nut is characteristic of the oaks. The nut is seated within a cup that is covered with scales.

e. **Nutlets**. These are diminutive nuts. In the birches they have a pair of thin wings that aid in dissemination by the wind. In the hophornbeam the nutlets are enclosed within a bladderlike or baglike bract.

2. Dry and dehiscent fruits:

a. **Legumes**. Pods that result from a simple pistil. At maturity they split completely into two halves (black locust, honey-locust, redbud).

b. **Follicles**. These are podlike fruits that also result from a simple pistil, but at maturity they split down only one side (magnolias).

c. **Capsules**. Podlike fruits that result from a compound pistil. At maturity they split into two or more parts that correspond to the number of carpels of which they are composed (willows, mountain-laurel, great-laurel).

3. Fleshy fruits:

a. **Pomes**. Fruits that are derived from a compound pistil surrounded by, and united with, the enlarged calyx and the receptacle. The latter forms the fleshy portion of the fruit; the former forms the "core," which contains the seeds (apples, service-berries, mountain-ashes).

b. **Drupes**. Commonly known as "stone fruits." The inner portion of the ovary, which contains the seed, is hard and bony. The outer portion is fleshy and often very juicy (cherries, plums, nanny-berry).

c. **Berries**. Fruits that are fleshy or pulpy throughout, with the seeds embedded within the fleshy portion (common persimmon, common pawpaw).

II. **Compound fruits**: These fruits are derived from a number of separate pistils.

a. **Aggregate** fruits. Fruits that result from separate pistils, which were borne in the same flower. The cone-shaped fruit clusters of the tuliptree are aggregations of samara-like fruits. Those of the magnolias are aggregations of follicles.

b. **Multiple fruits**. These fruits result from the pistils of several flowers. The ball-like heads of the sycamore are composed of numerous achenes. The "berries" of the red mulberry are actually composed of many small drupes. The *strobili* or conelike fruits of the birch are also multiple fruits.

Winter Characteristics

The leaves of most trees are shed annually, at some time during the autumn. We say that the leaves of such trees are *deciduous*, and often refer to such trees as *deciduous* trees. Most of our common broad-leaved trees, or *hardwoods*, have deciduous leaves. A few, like the rhododendron and the mountain-laurel, retain their leaves for two or more years and are known as *evergreens*. Most *coniferous* or cone-bearing trees, such as pines, hemlocks, and spruces, are also evergreens. The coniferous trees are also known as *softwoods*.

TWIGS

The smallest branchlets of trees are commonly known as the *twigs*. Twigs afford perhaps the best means of identifying trees in the winter season. They vary widely in such important characteristics as size, shape, color, and general appearance. The twigs of some trees, like the black locust and the Osage-orange, are armed with prickles or thorns. Those of the stag-horn sumac are coated with a dense, velvety hair. The twigs of the stag-horn sumac, the buckeye, and the Kentucky coffeetree are stout, while those of the birch, the American hornbeam, and the willow are very slender. The twigs of some trees are more or less hairy, while others may be decidedly glabrous or even lustrous.

When the leaves fall, they leave scars on the twigs, which we know as the *leaf scars*. Naturally the position of these scars corresponds to the position of the leaves. Trees like maples, ashes, and buckeyes, which have opposite leaves, will have opposite leaf scars; those that have alternate leaves, like birches, oaks, and willows, will have alternately arranged leaf scars. The tubes, or *fibrovascular bundles*, which served to conduct water into the leaves and food materials from the leaves back into the branches, are ruptured when the leaf falls. The broken ends of these fibrovascular bundles, in many cases, are very distinctly seen within the leaf scars, and they are known as

Continued ➡

the *bundle scars*. Some trees have but a solitary bundle scar within each of the leaf scars, but the majority of our trees have three or more bundle scars within each of the leaf scars. When they are numerous, the bundle scars may be scattered throughout the leaf scars; but often they are arranged in definite groups, in curved lines, or in a circle. The number and the arrangement of these bundle scars is often important in making winter identifications. The leaf scars also show considerable variation from one genus to another, and sometimes vary in the different species of a single genus. They vary not only in size but also in shape: round, semiround, crescent-shaped, 3-lobed, heart-shaped, etc. As a rule the larger twigs have the largest and most prominent leaf scars.

Twigs are also often marked by the stipule scars, scars that are made by the stipules at the bases of the leaf petioles. These stipule scars are very prominent on the twigs of the magnolia and the tuliptree, where they completely encircle the twigs at the nodes. They are also quite prominent on the twigs of the American Beech. The lenticels are little porelike openings within the epidermis of the twigs, which permit the interexchange of gases with the atmosphere. On the twigs of many trees they are quite prominent and appear as little rounded or slightly elongated dots. The lenticels vary not only in degree of prominence, but also in their density and color.

In the very center of the twig there is a column of pith, which may be either lighter or darker in color than the surrounding wood. Some trees have a very large and conspicuous pith, while in others it may be very small. The pith may be continuous, or in a longitudinal section of the twig it may be chambered, with intervening hollow places, as in the black walnut and the butternut. That of the black gum, in a longitudinal section, shows intervening hard, woody diaphragms. The shape of the pith, in a cross section of the twig, is often used in making winter identifications; it may be rounded, angled, triangular, or even somewhat 5-pointed or star-shaped. The color of the pith is likewise often diagnostic for it may be white, pale brown, dark brown, greenish, or sometimes salmon pink.

The important twig features that can be illustrated are shown on page below. Twigs may have other unique features however, that are extremely useful in making winter identifications. For instance, many twigs possess very characteristic odors or tastes. One may very easily identify the sassafras by its odor and taste even when the tree is dead. The twigs of the magnolia and the tuliptree also have a spicy and aromatic odor. Those of the black birch and the yellow birch possess a very characteristic odor and taste of oil of wintergreen. Many of the cherries have an awful, pungent, cherrylike or bitter almondlike odor. And there are some trees, like the tree-of-heaven, which have a very disagreeable or fetid odor. The twigs of the slippery elm and the basswood are mucilaginous when chewed. As one gets acquainted with our trees, he or she will learn to use many of these things in identifying them when the leaves are not available.

Buds

The buds, of course, are located on the twigs, and they are very important in making winter identifications. In many trees a bud is formed at the very tip of the season's growth, thus terminating the growth for the season. Such buds are referred to as *terminal buds*. There is but one terminal bud, and in most trees it is usually larger than the other buds on the twig. Other buds are formed along the sides of the twigs, and we usually refer to them as the *lateral buds*. These buds usually occur solitary in the axils of the leaves, or in the upper angle that the leaf makes with the twig; they are also known as *axillary buds* for that reason. In a few species more than one bud occurs at each *node*, or place where a leaf was attached to the twig; we call these buds *accessory buds*. In the red maple and the silver maple additional buds occur on each side of many of the true axillary buds. In some other trees, like the black walnut and the butternut, other buds occur on the twigs above the true axillary buds; they are said to be superposed, being termed *superposed buds*.

Most buds are covered with one or more *bud scales*, which are in reality modified leaves. Their function is to protect the delicate growing point within the bud from drying out, or from mechanical injury that may result from too sudden changes in the temperature of the air. The number of scales, and particularly the number of visible scales, varies with the different kinds of trees. Such characteristics as the number of scales on the buds and their arrangement, color, etc., are very useful in winter identification. A few of our native trees have buds that are not covered with scales at all; they are said to have *naked buds*. Additional protection to the growing point within the buds is sometimes present in the form of hairs, or coatings of waterproof gums or resins.

The twigs of many trees do not develop true terminal buds at all. Growth in such species is more or less indefinite. It finally slows down, however, and the tip of the growth dies and is sloughed off just above one of the lateral or axillary buds, leaving a little scar at the tip. Thus the topmost lateral bud assumes the position of the terminal bud, but it is usually not any larger than the other buds beneath it. Sometimes this bud is called a *false terminal bud*. Excellent examples of this kind are found on the twigs of the staghorn sumac, the elm, and the basswood.

Buds that contain rudimentary stems and leaves are usually called the *leaf buds*, while those that contain only partially developed flowers are called the *flower buds*. The accessory buds of the red maple and the silver maple are flower buds. The large terminal buds on the twigs of the sassafras, and the flattened, biscuitlike terminal buds found on many of the twigs of the flowering dogwood, are likewise flower buds. The twigs of a few trees, like the birch and the Eastern hop-hornbeam, have partially developed staminate flowers on the twigs all winter in the form of aments, or catkins.

Buds vary greatly in size, shape, color, etc. The buds of some trees are rather minute, while others have very large and conspicuous buds. Those of the black locust, the honey-locust, and a few other species are embedded within the twigs, and they are scarcely recognizable as buds at all. The cigar-shaped buds of the American beech are so long, slender, and sharp-pointed that they are unmistakable for those of any other tree. The buds of the striped maple and the mountain maple, as well as the alders, are evidently stalked. Most of the common types of buds are illustrated on page below.

Bark

The bark of trees has a protective function, covering the trunks and the branches of the tree. Many trees can be readily identified at any

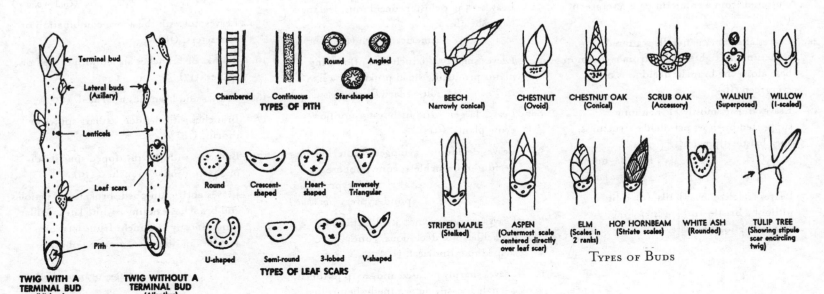

TWIG WITH A TERMINAL BUD (Hickory) — TWIG WITHOUT A TERMINAL BUD (Ailanthus) — Terminal bud — Lateral buds (Axillary) — Lenticels — Leaf scars — Pith

Chambered — Continuous — Round — Angled — Star-shaped — TYPES OF PITH

Round — Crescent-shaped — Heart-shaped — Inversely Triangular — U-shaped — Semi-round — 3-lobed — V-shaped — TYPES OF LEAF SCARS

BEECH (Narrowly conical) — CHESTNUT (Ovoid) — CHESTNUT OAK (Conical) — SCRUB OAK (Accessory) — WALNUT (Superposed) — WILLOW (1-scaled)

STRIPED MAPLE (Stalked) — ASPEN (Outermost scale centered directly over leaf scar) — ELM (Scales in 2 ranks) — HOP HORNBEAM (Striate scales) — WHITE ASH (Rounded) — TULIP TREE (Showing stipule scar encircling twig)

Types of Buds

Continued ➡

season of the year by bark characteristics alone. The bark of trees varies in color and general appearance, not only among the various species but often on the same tree. Often the color of the younger trunks and branches, as well as the appearance of their bark, will be much different from that of the older trunks. Yet most trees have some outstanding characteristic, as far as their bark is concerned, which enables those familiar with them to base their identification on bark characteristics alone. Even the novice can identify the American sycamore by the strikingly mottled appearance of the bark of its branches; or the American beech by the persistent smoothness of its light gray trunk; or the shag-bark hickory by the shaggy appearance of its trunk, from which the bark exfoliates in long, loose plates. Cherries and birches have very conspicuous, horizontally elongated lenticels on the bark of their trunks and branches.

Some trees never develop a thick bark, while in others the bark may attain a thickness of several inches. As trees grow, they normally shed the outer layers of bark. The bark of the yellow birch and the paper birch peels off in very thin filmlike, or papery, layers. In most trees the bark sooner or later develops cracks called *fissures*, or *furrows*, which separate the more elevated portions called *ridges*. These furrows and ridges assume various patterns that are often so distinctive that the identification of the tree may be safely based upon them. In some trees the ridges of the bark are broken into distinct blocks forming the alligator bark, which may be seen on the flowering dogwood, the black gum, and the common persimmon.

Key Based on Summer Characteristics

[Editor's note: Use this key as a flow chart. If, for example, the description under I is true, then, proceed to description 2. If the description for I is not true, proceed to Ia. If Ia is true, proceed to I2. And, so on, until you come to the name of the tree.]

I. Leaves linear, needlelike, scalelike, or awl-like, <3/16 inch wide. (go to 2)

Ia. Leaves with a flat blade, >3/16 inch wide. (12)

2. Leaves opposite or whorled, not tightly clustered from a common base, evergreen. (3)

2a. Leaves alternate, generally scattered or sometimes in tight clusters from a common base along the branch, deciduous or evergreen. (6)

3. Leaves linear, mostly >1 inch long, supported by short petiolelike structures; apex bristle-tipped . . . . Florida-nutmeg (*Torreya taxifolia*)

3a. Leaves scalelike or awl-like (or if linear without a bristle-tip), <1 inch long; without petiolelike base. (4)

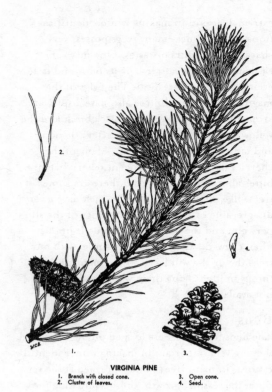

VIRGINIA PINE
1. Branch with closed cone.   3. Open cone.
2. Cluster of leaves.   4. Seed.

4. Leaves both scalelike and awl-like; fruits bluish and berrylike . . . . eastern red-cedar (*Juniperus virginiana*)

4a. Leaves all scalelike; fruit a small, dry cone. (5)

5. Branchlets flattened; scale leaves usually >1/8 inch long; cones egg-shaped with thin scales . . . . northern white-cedar (*Thuja occidentalis*)

5a. Branchlets not flattened; scale leaves much smaller; cones roundish and with shield-shaped scales . . . . Atlantic white-cedar (*Chamaecyparis thyoides*)

6. Leaves mostly densely clustered from a common base with 2 to many leaves per cluster. (7)

6a. Leaves scattered individually along the stems, not at all clustered. (8)

7. Leaves 2–5 per cluster, evergreen, basally enclosed by a conspicuous membranous sheath . . . . pines (*Pinus*)

7a. Leaves >5 per cluster, deciduous, lacking a basal sheath . . . . American larch (*Larix laricina*)

8. Leaves small, <1/16 inch long; flowering plants producing small pinkish flowers . . . . salt-cedar (*Tamarix ramosissima*)

8a. Leaves larger, >1/16 inch long; nonflowering plants. (9)

9. Leaves deciduous, arranged featherlike on deciduous branchlets; cones globose . . . . bald-cypress and pond-cypress (*Taxodium*)

9a. Leaves evergreen, not at all featherlike, branchlets not deciduous; cones egg-shaped to cylindrical. (10)

10. Leaves sharply pointed and sharp to touch, 4-angled, easily determined when rolled

between thumb and index finger; cones drooping . . . . spruces (Picea)

10a. Leaves soft and flexible, soft to touch, flat; cones drooping or erect. (11)

11. Leaves with persistent, short, woody stalks; cones drooping, <2 inches long . . . . hemlocks (*Tsuga*)

11a. Leaves stalkless, leaving round scars on twigs when shed; cones erect, 2–3 inches long . . . . firs (Abies)

12. Plants palmlike; leaves fan-shaped, 2 feet or more across . . . . palmettos (*Sabal*)

WHITE OAK
1. Branch with mature leaves.   4. Winter twig.
2-3. Acorns.   5. Details of bud and leaf scar.

12a. Plants not palmlike; leaves otherwise or if fan-shaped, <2 feet across. (13)

13. Leaves alternate. (14)

13a. Leaves opposite or whorled. (122)

14. Leaves simple. (15)

14a. Leaves compound. (105)

15. Leaves with nearly perfectly parallel veins and 2-lobed margins . . . . maidenhair-tree (*Ginkgo biloba*)

15a. Leaves not with the above combination of characters. (16)

16. Trunks or branches armed with thorns or spines. (17)

16a. Trunks and branches unarmed. (20)

17. Branches with slender, axillary spines or thorns. (18)

17a. Branches with sharply tipped spur shoots or sharp, pinlike branches. (19)

18. Leaves entire, unlobed; broken leaf petioles and branches exuding a white latex; axillary spines mostly <1/2 inch; fruits large, up to 4 inches in diameter, green, globose syncarp . . . . osage-orange (*Maclura*)

Continued ➡

18a. Leaves toothed and mostly lobed; broken leaf petioles and branches exuding a clear sap; axillary thorns mostly >1/2 inch; fruits much smaller, <1 inch in diameter, red or orange, pome . . . . hawthorns (Cretaegus)

19. Leaves with bristle-tipped lobes; buds clustered at branch apex; fruit an acorn . . . . oaks (Quercus)

19a. Leaves lacking bristle-tipped lobes; buds not clustered apically; fruit an apple . . . . apples and crabapples (Malus)

20. At least some leaves with toothed or lobed margins. (21)

20a. Leaves with entire or merely wavy margins. (70)

21. Leaf margins lobed, or both toothed and lobed. (22)

21a. Leaf margins toothed but not lobed. (34)

22. Leaf margins lobed but not toothed. (23)

22a. Leaf margins both lobed and toothed. (28)

23. Leaves palmately veined. (24)

23a. Leaves pinnately veined. (25)

24. Twigs and bark not grass-green; petioles with a pair of red glands on upper side . . . . tung-oiltree (Vernicia fordii)

24a. Twigs and bark grass-green; petioles without glands . . . . Chinese parasol-tree (Firmiana simplex)

EASTERN COTTONWOOD
1. Branch with mature leaves. 3. Winter twig.
2. Fruits. 4. Details of winter bud and leaf scar.

Member of the poplar family

25. Leaves and twigs not aromatic. (26)

25a. Leaves and twigs aromatic. (27)

26. Leaves nearly as long as broad; buds naked, shaped like a deer hoof, not clustered at twig apex; flowers with yellow, straplike petals . . . . witch-hazels (Hamamelis)

26a. Leaves >2 times long as broad; buds scaled, clustered at branch apex; flowers apetalous . . . . oaks (Quercus)

27. Leaves broadly V-shaped or notched apically, bases truncate, 4- to 6-lobed, long-petioled . . . . .tuliptree (Liriodendron tulipifera)

27a. Leaves more or less pointed apically, bases not truncate, mitten-shaped or 3-lobed, rather short-petioled . . . . sassafras (Sassafras albidum)

28. Leaves star-shaped, 5-pointed, aromatic . . . . sweet-gum (Liquidambar styraciflua)

28a. Leaves not at all star-shaped or aromatic. (29)

29. Bases of the leaf stalks swollen and covering the buds; bark exfoliating on trunk and branches exposing much lighter areas . . . . sycamores (Platanus)

29a. Bases of the leaf stalks otherwise; bark not as above. (30)

30. Leaf stalks exuding a milky sap if broken. (31)

30a. Leaf stalks otherwise. (32)

31. All leaves alternate; petioles and seasonal twigs glabrous or short-hairy; buds with 3–6 scales; female inflorescence cylindrical; stigmas 2 . . . . mulberries (Morus)

31a. Leaves either alternate, opposite, or whorled; petioles and seasonal twigs long-hairy; buds with 2–3 scales; female inflorescence globose; stigma 1 . . . . paper-mulberry (Broussonetia papyrifera)

32. Leaves palmately veined . . . . poplars (Populus)

32a. Leaves pinnately veined. (33)

33. Leaf margins double-serrate . . . . European white birch (Betula pendula)

33a. Leaf margins not double-serrate . . . . oaks (Quercus)

34. Trunks or branches armed with thorns. (35)

34a. Trunks and branches unarmed. (37)

SWEET BIRCH
1. Branch with mature leaves and fruits. 4. Details of bud and leaf scar.
2. Mature strobiles. 5. Scale from strobile.
3. Winter twig with catkins. 6. Winged nutlet.

35. Twigs or branches with slender axillary thorns . . . . hawthorns (Crataegus)

35a. Twigs or branches with sharply tipped spurlike shoots. (36)

36. Upper surface of leaves wrinkled-veiny, leaf stalks often with a pair of glands at the summit; fruit plumlike. . . . . plums (Prunus)

36a. Leaf surfaces and leaf stalks not as above; fruit applelike . . . . apples (Malus)

37. Leaves spicy-aromatic, with yellow resin dots at least beneath . . . . .southern bayberry (Morella cerifera)

37a. Leaves without the above combination of characters. (38)

38. Bark of young saplings and branches of trees with horizontally elongated lenticels; broken twigs often with either a pleasant, conspicuous wintergreen or foul cherrylike odor. (39)

38a. Bark and twigs otherwise; broken branches with or without a conspicuous odor. (41)

39. Leaves, leaf scars, and axillary buds 2-ranked; twigs odorless or often with a wintergreen odor . . . . birches (Betula)

39a. Leaves, leaf scars, and axillary buds > 2-ranked; twigs often with a fetid, cherrylike odor. (40)

40. Leaf blades 1 1/2 times or less long as wide; broken twigs without a fetid odor; fruits apples . . . . apples (Malus)

40a. Leaf blades 2 times or more as long as wide; broken twigs often with a fetid odor; fruits, cherries or peaches . . . . peaches, plums, cherries (Prunus)

41. Petioles flattened laterally, above and below . . . . aspens and poplars (Populus)

41a. Petioles rounded, at least below. (42)

42. Leaf stalks exuding a milky juice if broken . . . . mulberries (Morus)

42a. Leaf stalks otherwise. (43)

43. Leaves narrowly lanceolate, 4 or more times as long as wide . . . . willows (Salix)

43a. Leaves broader, <4 times as long as wide. (44)

44. Leaf margins with only an occasional large tooth above the middle . . . . black gum and tupelos (Nyssa)

44a. Leaf margins regularly or evenly toothed throughout. (45)

45. Leaf margins with 4 or fewer large teeth to the inch. (46)

45a. Leaf margins with smaller and finer teeth. (52)

Continued ➡

46.   Teeth with hard, sharp, and conspicuous spine tips . . . . hollies (*Ilex*)

46a. Teeth without hard, sharply spined tips. (47)

47.   Teeth sharply pointed and often incurved. (48)

47a. Teeth blunt, rounded, or leaf margin merely wavy. (50)

48.   Leaves more or less crowded toward the tips of the branchlets; buds in terminal clusters . . . . oaks (*Quercus*)

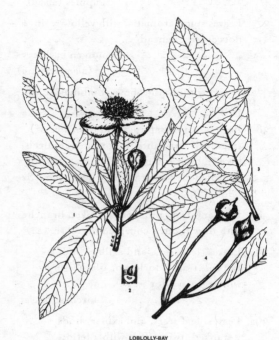

LOBLOLLY-BAY
1. Branch with leaves and flowers.   3. Typical leaf.
2. Detail of bud and leaf scar.   4. Fruiting branch.

48a. Leaves rather distantly and evenly spaced; buds not terminally clustered. (49)

49.   Leaves egg-shaped or oval; buds long and taper-pointed, cigar-shaped . . . . American beech
(*Fagus grandifolia*)

49a. Leaves broadly lanceolate or elliptical; buds plump and egg-shaped . . . . chestnuts (*Castanea*)

50.   Leaf stalks at least 1/3 as long as the leaf blades . . . . poplars (*Populus*)

50a. Leaf stalks much less than 1/3 as long as the leaf blades. (51)

51.   Leaves asymmetrical or lopsided at the base, rather distantly spaced along the branchlets . . . . American witch-hazel
(*Hamamelis virginiana*)

51a. Leaves symmetrical at the base, tending to be crowded toward the tips of the branchlets . . . . oaks (*Quercus*)

52.   Leaves thick and leathery in texture. (53)

52a. Leaves otherwise. (54)

53.   Most leaves >3 inches long, obscurely toothed; flowers large and showy . . . . loblolly-bay
(*Gordonia lasianthus*)

53a. Most leaves smaller, margins either bluntly toothed or minutely toothed and spine-tipped; flowers small, inconspicuous . . . . hollies (*Ilex*)

54.   Leaf margins with rather minute or inconspicuous teeth. (55)

54a. Leaf margins conspicuously toothed. (60)

55.   Twigs green and with a conspicuously foul odor when broken; individual marginal leaf teeth extremely thin and fine, appearing as ciliate hairs . . . . .sourwood
(*Oxydendrum arboreum*)

55a. Twigs variously colored, but lacking a foul odor; marginal teeth not as above. (56)

56.   Pith diaphragmmed, bark vertically striped; hairs on leaves stellate; fruits 2- or 4-winged; flowers white, showy, petals 4 . . . . silverbells (*Halesia*)

56a. Pith continuous, bark not vertically striped; hairs on leaves not stellate; fruits unwinged; flowers without the above combination. (57)

57.   Leaf margins conspicuously long ciliate, nearly entire, leaf tip strongly acuminate; leaves 2-ranked; flowers large and showy (not discussed in text) . . . . silky-camellia and mountain-camellia
(*Stewartia spp.*)

57a. Leaf margins eciliate, entire or not; leaves more than 2-ranked; flowers small, not showy. (58)

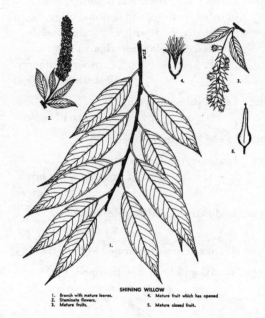

SHINING WILLOW
1. Branch with mature leaves.   4. Mature fruit which has opened
2. Staminate flowers.   5. Mature closed fruit.
3. Mature fruits.

58.   Most leaves not more than twice as long as wide; branchlets very slender and zigzag; leaf scars with 1 bundle-scar . . . . tree sparkle-berry
(*Vaccinium arboreum*)

58a. Most leaves 2–4 times as long as wide; branchlets moderate and not zigzag; leaf scars with 3 bundle-scars. (59)

59.   Buds naked and densely hairy, terminal bud present; leaves large, 2–6 inches long, 1–2 inches wide; leaf blades with conspicuously straight and parallel veins; fruit a fleshy drupe; petals 5 . . . . .Carolina false buckthorn
(*Frangula caroliniana*)

59a. Buds with a solitary, glabrous, or hairy scale, terminal bud lacking; leaves mostly narrower, shorter or both; leaf blades

without conspicuously straight and parallel veins; fruit a dry capsule; petals absent . . . . willows (*Salix*)

60.   Leaf margins with simple teeth. (61)

60a. Leaf margins doubly serrate. (68)

61.   Leaves lopsided or asymmetrical at the base. (62)

61a. Leaves symmetrical or nearly so at the base. (64)

62.   Leaves conspicuously and strongly heart-shaped at base, nearly as long as broad . . . . American basswood
(*Tilia americana*)

62a. Leaves not heart-shaped at base; clearly longer than broad. (63)

63.   Leaves with 3 prominent veins arising from the summit of the leaf stalk; pith at nodes chambered; bark commonly warty or corky-ridged, but otherwise smooth; fruit a fleshy drupe, but not burlike . . . . hackberries
(*Celtis*)

63a. Leaves merely with one prominent midrib; pith not chambered at nodes; bark rough and furrowed, but without warts or corky ridges; fruit a dry, burlike drupe . . . . planertree
(*Planera aquatica*)

64.   Leaves often arranged in clusters on short lateral spurs; hairs often black . . . . hollies (*Ilex*)

64a. Leaves never as above. (65)

65.   Branchlets with chambered pith; leaves with small branched hairs on the lower surface; bole or main stem often vertically striped . . . . silverbells
(*Halesia*)

65a. Branchlets with continuous pith; leaves otherwise; bole striped or not. (66)

66.   Most leaves > 2 inches wide, broadly oval or heart-shaped to triangular, often hairy beneath; bole not vertically striped . . . . poplars
(*Populus*)

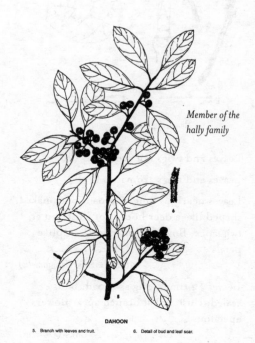

Member of the holly family

DAHOON
5. Branch with leaves and fruit.   6. Detail of bud and leaf scar.

Continued ➔

66a. Most leaves <2 inches wide, oval or obovate, usually glabrous beneath at maturity, or merely with scattered hairs; bole vertically striped. (67)

67. Leaf blades basally long-tapered, conspicuously clustered on branch tips; flowers solitary, large, 2 1/2 to 3 1/3 inches across, with numerous, conspicuous, yellow stamens at the centers; plants known originally only from the Altamaha River, in Georgia, now thought to be extirpated in the wild . . . . Franklintree
(*Franklinia alatamaha*)

67a. Leaf blades cordate to rounded, not long-tapered basally, nor conspicuously clustered on branch tips; flowers numerous and smaller, without a yellow cluster of stamens at the centers; plants from various locations . . . . service-berries (*Amelanchier*)

68. Leaves asymmetrical at the base . . . . elms (*Ulmus*)

68a. Leaves symmetrical at the base. (69)

69. Mature leaves glabrous above, hairs in axils of veins below, lateral veins of the leaves extending into the marginal teeth without forking; fruits enveloped by the base of 3 lobed, leaflike bracts; bark very tight, fluted or musclelike; bud scales not vertically striate . . . . American hornbeam
(*Carpinus caroliniana*)

69a. Mature leaves with some hairs above and hairy throughout below, lateral veins forking within the margin of the leaf; fruits enclosed in baglike bracts arranged in hoplike clusters; bark loose and flaking; bud scale minutely vertically striate . . . . .eastern hop-hornbeam
(*Ostrya virginiana*)

70. Young twigs and leaf undersurfaces covered with scurfy scales and brown dots . . . . Russian-olive
(*Elaeagnus angustifolia*)

70a. Young twigs and leaf undersurfaces lacking scurfy scales and brown dots. (71)

71. Leaves, bark, and/or twigs with a characteristic unpleasant or noticeably pleasant odor when bruised. (72)

71a. Leaves, bark, and/or twigs otherwise. (79)

72. Branchlets ringed at the nodes by stipule scars . . . . magnolias (*Magnolia*)

72a. Branchlets otherwise. (73)

73. Leaves with tiny, pale, glandular dots beneath, blades evergreen (not discussed in text) . . . . Florida anisetree
(*Illicium floridanum*)

73a. Leaves lacking glandular dots beneath, blades evergreen or not. (74)

74. Odor of broken twigs or leaves rank and fetid. (75)

74a. Odor of broken twigs or leaves pleasantly spicy. (76)

Member of the magnolia family

SWEET-BAY

1. Branch with leaves.
2. Leaf.
3. Flowering branch.
4. Fruit.
5. Detail of bud and leaf scar (enlarged).

75. Leaves conspicuously broadest above the middle and gradually tapers to base; pith diaphragmmed or chambered; buds naked . . . . common pawpaw
(*Asimina triloba*)

75a. Leaves broadest at or near the middle; pith continuous; buds scaled . . . . alternate-leaf dogwood
(*Cornus alternifolia*)

76. Leaves deciduous, blades blunt at the tip, paler and glabrous or slightly hairy beneath; some leaves usually lobed. (77)

76a. Leaves evergreen, blades sharply pointed at the tip, glabrous, whitened or rusty-hairy beneath; never lobed. (78)

77. At least some of the leaf blades lobed, but notched apically; pith white . . . . sassafras
(*Sassafras albidum*)

77a. Leaf blades unlobed; leaf apex conspicuously notched; pith tan . . . . smoketree
(*Cotinus obovatus*)

78. Petioles >7/8 inch long; leaves with only 2 large veins arising from the midrib near base, vein angles on upper leaf with yellow calluslike growths (callosities) . . . . camphortree
(*Cinnamomum camphora*)

78a. Petioles <7/8 inch long; leaves with veins evenly distributed along midribs or scarcely evident; leaves lacking callosities . . . . bays (*Persea*)

79. Leaves thick and leathery in texture. (80)

79a. Leaves otherwise. (87)

80. Leaf blades with a small but conspicuous apical notch . . . . buckwheat-tree
(*Cliftonia monophylla*)

80a. Leaf blades lacking a notch. (81)

81. Branchlets ringed at the nodes by stipule scars . . . . magnolias (*Magnolia*)

81a. Branchlets otherwise. (82)

82. Branchlets with chambered pith . . . . common sweetleaf
(*Symplocos tinctoria*)

82a. Branchlets with continuous pith. (83)

83. Most leaves 4–5 inches or more long, 1 1/2–3 inches wide; large egg-shaped flower buds usually present at branch tips . . . . .great-laurel and catawba rosebay
(*Rhodedendron*)

83a. Most leaves smaller or if as large, lacking the large egg-shaped flower buds at branch tips. (84)

84. Branch tips with multiple buds; leaf scars with several bundle-scars; fruit an acorn . . . . oaks (*Quercus*)

84a. Branch tips with single buds; leaf scars with but 1 bundle-scar; fruits otherwise. (85)

MOUNTAIN-LAUREL

1. Branch with leaves and flowers.
2. Branch with leaves and fruits.
3. Winter branch with leaves and flower buds.
4. Detail of fruit.

85. Leaves spine-tipped, or spined along margin, often stiff . . . . hollies (*Ilex*)

85a. Leaves not spined, rather flexible. (86)

86. Most leaves broadest above the middle, not apically verticillate; flowers in small racemes . . . . swamp titi (*Cyrilla racemiflora*)

86a. Most leaves broadest at the middle; conspicuously apically verticillate; flowers large and showy . . . . mountain-laurel
(*Kalmia latifolia*)

87. Petioles with bright red glands at their summit; broken petioles exuding a white latex; leaf blade cordate or truncate basally . . . . tung-oiltree
(*Vernicia fordii*)

87a. Petioles and blades lacking the above combination. (88)

88. Leaves conspicuously and strongly heart-shaped at base; leaf blades nearly as long as wide; fruit flat, beanlike . . . . eastern redbud
(*Cercis canadensis*)

88a. Leaves not strongly and conspicuously heart-shaped; fruits not as above. (89)

Continued ➡

89. Leaves with 3 prominent veins arising from the summit of the leaf stalk, leaf base often asymmetrical . . . . hackberries (*Celtis*)

89a. Leaves merely with 1 prominent midrib, leaf base symmetrical or nearly so. (90)

90. Branchlets with spines; petioles with milky sap if broken. (91)

90a. Branchlets lacking spines; milky sap present or not. (92)

91. Leaves narrow, blunt-pointed or rounded apically, usually clustered on lateral spurs . . . . bullies (*Sideroxylon*)

91a. Leaves broad, long-pointed apically, never clustered on lateral shoots . . . . osage-orange
(*Maclura pomifera*)

92. Petioles and branches with milky sap if broken; introduced tree . . . . Chinese tallowtree
(*Triadica sebifera*)

92a. Petioles and branches lacking milky sap if broken; plants native or introduced. (93)

93. Leaves with veins curving and strongly paralleling the leaf margins . . . . alternate-leaf dogwood
(*Cornus alternifolia*)

93a. Leaves otherwise. (94)

94. First-year branches conspicuously winged or strongly 4-angled below the nodes . . . . crape-myrtle
(*Lagerstroemia indica*)

94a. First-year branches rounded below nodes. (95)

95. Leaf scars with but 1 bundle-scar. (96)

95a. Leaf scars with 3 or more bundle-scars. (101)

96. Leaves strongly mucronate; blades long-hairy beneath; plants restricted to Georgia and adjoining South Carolina (not discussed in text) . . . . Georgiaplume
(*Elliottia racemosa*)

CRAPE-MYRTLE

1. Branch with leaves and fruits.   2. Detail of fruit.

96a. Leaves not mucronate; blades not long-hairy beneath; plants of various locations. (97)

97. Leaves 2-ranked, margins conspicuously long ciliate, apex long acuminate; flowers large and showy; plants mostly shrubby (not discussed in text) . . . . silky-camellia and mountain-camellia
(*Stewartia spp.*)

97a. Leaves more than 2-ranked, margins and apex various; flowers small, not showy; plants shrubby or not. (98)

98. Leaves 1 1/2 inches or more wide, long-acuminately pointed at the tip; leaf blades with irregularly placed dark spots below; petioles >1/2 inch long; large tree . . . . common persimmon
(*Diospyros virginiana*)

98a. Leaves narrower, short-pointed or rounded at the tip; leaf blades not black spotted below; petioles shorter; short, shrubby trees or shrubs. (99)

99. Leaves less than twice as long as wide, deciduous, membranous, margins minutely toothed; branchlets very slender and zigzag; fruit a black berry . . . . tree sparkle-berry
(*Vaccinium arboreum*)

99a. Leaves 2 or more times as long as wide, leathery, evergreen or persisting, margins completely entire; branchlets and fruits otherwise. (100)

100. Most leaves <2 inches long, with a tiny but conspicuous apical notch . . . . buckwheat-tree
(*Cliftonia monophylla*)

100a. Most leaves >2 inches long, without an apical notch . . . . swamp titi
(*Cyrilla racemiflora*)

101. Branchlets with a pleasant fruity odor and resinous sap; leaves mostly rounded or notched apically . . . . American smoketree
(*Cotinus obovatus*)

101a. Branchlets and leaves otherwise. (102)

102. Pith of the branchlets with transverse woody partitions . . . . black gum and tupelos
(*Nyssa*)

102a. Pith of the branchlets otherwise. (103)

103. Buds with a solitary scale; branches extremely narrow at tips . . . . willows (*Salix*)

103a. Buds with 2 or more scales; branches moderate thick to thick at tips. (104)

104. Leaves bristle-pointed at the tip; branchlets with a small, 5-angled pith . . . . oaks (*Quercus*)

104a. Leaves merely long-pointed at the tip; branchlets with a large, round white pith . . . . corkwood
(*Leitneria floridana*)

105. Plants armed with thorns, spines, or prickles. (106)

BLACK LOCUST

1. Branch with mature leaves.   4. Winter twig.
2. Cluster of flowers.   5. Detail of leaf scar and imbedded buds.
3. Fruits.

105a. Plants unarmed. (110)

106. Leaflet margins entire; short and broad-based; spines paired at the nodes, thorns lacking. (107)

106a. Leaflet margins toothed; thorns or spines present. (108)

107. Leaves bipinnatly compound; spines narrow at base and quite long, to 2 inches; barely reaching our area in Louisiana . . . . honey mesquite
(*Prosopis glandulosa*)

107a. Leaves 1-pinnately compound; spines broad at base and short, <1 inch long; plants throughout our range . . . . black-locust
(*Robinia pseudoacacia*)

108. Leaflets < 1 1/2 inches long; branchlets moderately stout; thorns often branched. . . . . honey-locust and water-locust
(*Gleditsia*)

108a. Leaflets longer; branchlets exceptionally stout with short prickles or broad-based spines. (109)

109. Branchlets 3/4 inch or more thick, with scattered spines or prickles and some in rows beneath the leaf stalks; most leaves 2 feet or more long, divided into a number of leaflets, not aromatic . . . . devil's-walkingstick
(*Aralia spinosa*)

109a. Branchlets more slender, with broad-based scattered and axillary spines; most leaves < 1 1/2 feet long, merely pinnate, aromatic . . . . Hercules'-club
(*Zanthoxylum clava-herculis*)

110. Leaflets entire or with a few large teeth at base only. (111)

110a. Leaflets regularly and prominently toothed. (118)

111. Leaf stalks winged between the leaflets . . . . sumacs (*Rhus*)

Continued ➡

111a. Leafstalks not winged. (112)

112. Leaflets with 1 or 2 large, basal, glandular teeth . . . . tree-of-heaven
(*Ailanthus altissima*)

112a. Leaflets without 1 or 2 large, basal, glandular teeth. (113)

113. Leaves with 3 leaflets, with a disagreeable odor . . . . common hoptree
(*Ptelea trifoliata*)

AMERICAN MOUNTAIN-ASH
1. Branch with mature leaves and fruits.   3. Detail of bud and leaf scar.
2. Winter twig.

113a. Leaves with >3 leaflets. (114)

114. Main vein of leaflet noticeably off center, much closer to one margin than the other . . . . silktree
(*Albizia julibrissin*)

114a. Main vein of leaflet near or at center of leaflet. (115)

115. Leaves doubly compound with >20 leaflets; branches >1/4 inch thick . . . . Kentucky coffeetree
(*Gymnocladus dioicus*)

115a. Leaves merely pinnate with fewer leaflets; branches more slender. (116)

116. Bark with horizontally elongated lenticels; leaflets always opposite; fruits berrylike, glaucous, in drooping clusters; plants of swamps and other wet habitats . . . . poison-sumac
(*Toxicodendron vernix*)

116a. Bark otherwise; leaflets commonly alternate; fruits beanlike pods; plants not of wet habitats. (117)

117. Shoots and branchlets remaining green; terminal leaflet more than twice as long as wide; fruits a rounded pod, conspicuously constricted between the seeds . . . . eve's necklacepod
(*Sophora affinis*)

117a. Shoots maturing to gray or brown, branches not remaining green; terminal leaflet less than twice as long as wide; fruits flat . . . . yellow-wood
(*Cladrastis kentukea*)

118. Leaf stalks exuding a milky sap if broken . . . . sumacs (*Rhus*)

118a. Leaf stalks otherwise. (119)

119. Leaves doubly pinnate or more . . . . china-berry
(*Melia azedarach*)

119a. Leaves singly pinnate. (120)

120. Leaflets not fragrant if crushed; leaf stalks usually red; buds usually gummy, if not, then leaflets rounded apically. . . . . mountain-ashes
(*Sorbus*)

120a. Leaflets fragrant if crushed; leaf stalks green; buds not gummy, leaflets pointed apically. (121)

121. Branchlets with chambered pith; twigs easily broken by hand; fruit husk indehiscent; nut surface rugose . . . . walnuts (*Juglans*)

121a. Branchlets with continuous pith; twigs extremely difficult to break by hand; fruit husk splitting into segments; nut surface not rugose . . . . hickories (*Carya*)

122. Leaves simple. (123)

122a. Leaves compound. (133)

BLACK MANGROVE
1. Branch with leaves and flowers.   2. Mature fruit.

123. Leaves with multiple primary veins from base. (124)

123a. Leaves with single, primary, basal vein. (127)

124. Twigs of previous year hollow except at nodes and occasionally elsewhere within the twig; flowers blue; fruits oval-shaped capsules . . . . princesstree
(*Paulownia tomentosa*)

124a. Twigs of previous year with continuous pith; flowers not blue; fruits not oval-shaped capsules. (125)

125. Twigs of current year densely hairy, with milky sap; fruits fleshy . . . . paper-mulberry
(*Broussonetia papyrifera*)

125a. Twigs of current year glabrous or nearly so, with or without milky sap; fruits dry. (126)

126. All leaf blades opposite, palm-shaped, conspicuously 3- to 7-lobed (rarely unlobed), 2–7 inches long, margins entire or toothed; fruit, a winged samara . . . . maples (*Acer*)

126a. Leaves often whorled or opposite, heart-shaped, unlobed or not conspicuously lobed, margins entire, 4–12 inches long; fruit an elongated, wingless capsule . . . . catalpas
(*Catalpa*)

127. Leaf margin entire and unlobed. (128)

127a. Leaf margin toothed or lobed. (132)

128. Leaves evergreen, leathery in texture. (129)

OHIO BUCKEYE
1. Branch with mature leaves.   4. Seed.
2. Portion of flower cluster.   5. Winter twig.
3. Fruit.

128a. Leaves deciduous, not leathery. (130)

129. Leaf blades finely hairy below, upper surface minutely glandular-dotted; fruit a flattened, dry capsule; plants restricted to coastal Florida . . . . black mangrove
(*Avicennia germinans*)

129a. Leaf blades glabrous below, upper surface not minutely glandular-dotted; fruit a fleshy drupe; plants throughout much of the Southeast . . . . devilwood
(*Osmanthus americanus*)

130. Leaves with the veins curving conspicuously and tending to parallel the leaf margins; leaf margins eciliate and twigs lacking conspicuous warty lenticels . . . . dogwoods (*Cornus*)

130a. Leaf veins otherwise; margins either ciliate or twigs with conspicuous warty lenticels. (131)

131. Branchlets, leaf stalks, and lower leaf surfaces densely tawny-hairy; twigs lacking conspicuous warty lenticels; leaf margins ciliate . . . . fevertree
(*Pinckneya bracteata*)

Continued ➡

131a. Branchlets, leaf stalks, and lower leaf surfaces glabrous or merely a little hairy; with conspicuous warty lenticels on twigs; leaf margins eciliate . . . . fringetree
(*Chionanthus virginicus*)

132. Leaves palmately lobed. . . . . maples (*Acer*)

132a. Leaf margins toothed but not lobed . . . . arrow-woods and blackhaws
(*Viburnum*)

133. Leaves palmately compound; leaflets radiating from the summit of the leaf stalk . . . . buckeyes and horse-chestnut
(*Aesculus*)

133a. Leaves ternately to pinnately compound, arranged along the side of the leaf stalk. (134)

134. Leaflets 3–5, the margins with irregular, large teeth or shallow lobes; fruits fused in pairs . . . . maples (*Acer*)

134a. Leaflets 5 or more, the margins entire or with fine and sometimes inconspicuous teeth; fruits separate . . . . ashes (*Fraxinus*)

Key Based on Winter Characteristics

[Editor's note: Use this key as a flow chart. If, for example, the description under 1 is true, then, proceed to description 2. If the description for 1 is not true, proceed to 1a. If 1a is true, proceed to 30. And, so on, until you come to the name of the tree.]

1. Leaves evergreen. (2)

1a. Leaves deciduous or, if persisting, not remaining green. (30)

2. Leaves with distinctly broad or flattened blades. (3)

2a. Leaves linear, needlelike, scalelike or awl-like. (23)

3. Plants palmlike; leaves 2 feet or more across, fan-shaped . . . . palmettos (*Sabal*)

3a. Plants not palmlike; leaves otherwise. (4)

4. Leaves opposite. (5)

4a. Leaves alternate. (7)

5. Most leaf blades 1/2–2 inches long, sessile or nearly so . . . . blackhaws
(*Viburnum*)

5a. Most leaf blades 3–9 inches long, clearly stalked. (6)

6. Leaves finely hairy beneath, upper surface minutely glandular-dotted; fruit a flattened, dry capsule; plants restricted to coastal Florida . . . . black mangrove
(*Avicennia germinans*)

6a. Leaves completely glabrous beneath, upper surface not glandular-dotted; fruit a fleshy drupe; plants found throughout areas of the Southeast . . . . devilwood
(*Osmanthus americanus*)

7. Leaves and twigs with a characteristic unpleasant or noticeably pleasant odor when bruised. (8)

7a. Leaves and twigs otherwise. (13)

8. Leaves and stems strongly aromatic with a pleasant camphor odor, dorsal surface of blades with conspicuous yellow callosities

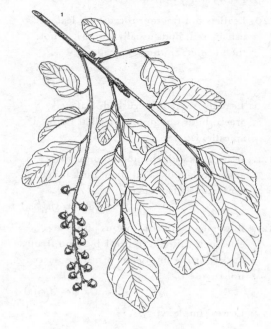

ALABAMA BLACK CHERRY

1. Branch with leaves and fruits.

within principal vein angle . . . . camphortree
(*Cinnamomum camphora*)

8a. Leaves without a camphor odor, dorsal surface not as above. (9)

9. Leaves with yellow resin dots beneath; catkinlike buds often present on the twigs . . . . southern bayberry
(*Morella cerifera*)

9a. Leaves and twigs otherwise. (10)

10. Leaf blades glandular-dotted beneath; petioles reddish; plants mostly shrubby (not discussed in text) . . . . Florida anisetree
(*Illicium floridanum*)

10a. Leaf blades not glandular-dotted beneath; petioles not reddish; plants treelike. (11)

11. Twigs ringed at the nodes by stipule scars . . . . .magnolias
(*Magnolia*)

11a. Twigs otherwise. (12)

12. Leaves entire, with a pleasant spicy odor; bundle-scar solitary . . . . bays (*Persea*)

12a. Leaves often with a few teeth, with fetid, cherrylike odor; bundle-scars 3 . . . . cherries (*Prunus*)

13. Twigs zigzag, <1/8 inch in diameter; leaf apex with a noticeable mucro, margins with minute, nearly microscopic teeth throughout; mostly small trees or tall shrubs . . . . tree sparkle-berry
(*Vaccinium arboreum*)

13a. The combination of characters not as above. (14)

14. Leaf margins toothed or lobed. (15)

14a. Leaf margins entire. (17)

15. Leaves tending to be clustered toward the tips of the twigs; buds scaled . . . . oaks (*Quercus*)

15a. Leaves more distantly and evenly spaced along twigs; buds scaled or naked. (16)

16. Most leaves >3 inches long; twigs somewhat clubby; buds naked . . . . .loblolly-bay
(*Gordonia lasianthus*)

16a. Most leaves <3 inches long; twigs slender; buds with 1 or more scales . . . . hollies (*Ilex*)

17. Twigs usually spiny; leaves clustered on lateral spurs . . . . bullies (*Sideroxylon*)

17a. Twigs and leaves otherwise. (18)

18. Twigs with chambered pith . . . . common sweetleaf
(*Symplocos tinctoria*)

18a. Twigs with continuous pith. (19)

19. Most leaf blades 4–5 or more inches long; twigs 1/4 inch or more in diameter; large egg-shaped terminal buds usually present . . . . great-laurel and catawba rosebay
(*Rhododendron*)

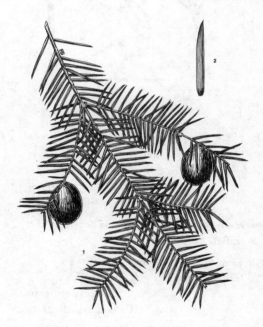

FLORIDA-NUTMEG

1. Branch with mature arils. 2. Detail of leaf.

19a. Most leaf blades smaller; twigs more slender; large egg-shaped terminal bud lacking. (20)

20. Leaves with a tiny, yet conspicuous, apical notch . . . . buckwheat-tree
(*Cliftonia monophylla*)

20a. Leaves lacking an apical notch. (21)

21. Stipule scars present; leaf scars with several bundle-scars; mostly single-stemmed trees; fruit an acorn . . . . oaks (*Quercus*)

21a. Stipule scars absent; leaf scars with a solitary bundle-scar; multiple-branched, tall shrubs; fruit a capsule. (22)

22. Leaves conspicuously verticillate apically, blades broadest at or near the middle . . . . mountain-laurel
(*Kalmia latifolia*)

Continued ➡

22a. Leaves clustered apically, but not verticillate, blades broadest above the middle . . . . swamp titi (*Cyrilla racemiflora*)

23. Leaves appearing opposite or whorled, not tightly clustered from a common base. (24)

23a. Leaves appearing alternate, or scattered in tight clusters from a common base along the branch. (27)

24. Leaves mostly >1 inch long, linear, supported by short petiolelike structures; apex bristle-tipped; plants restricted in the wild to northwestern Florida and adjacent Georgia . . . . Florida-nutmeg (*Torreya taxifolia*)

24a. Leaves mostly < 1 inch long, scalelike or awl-like (or if linear without a bristle-tip); without a petiolelike base; plants from various locations. (25)

25. Leaves both scalelike and awl-like; fruits bluish and berrylike . . . . eastern red-cedar (*Juniperus virginiana*)

25a. Leaves all scalelike; fruit a small, dry cone. (26)

26. Branchlets flattened; scale leaves usually > 1/8 inch long; cones egg-shaped with thin scales . . . . northern white-cedar (*Thuja occidentalis*)

26a. Branchlets not flattened; scale leaves usually much smaller; cones roundish and with shield-shaped scales . . . . Atlantic white-cedar (*Chamaecyparis thyoides*)

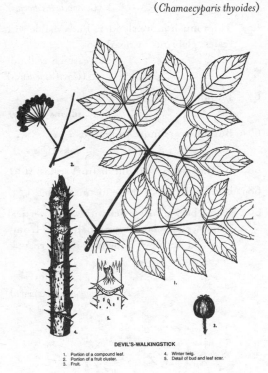

DEVIL'S-WALKINGSTICK
1. Portion of a compound leaf. 4. Winter twig.
2. Portion of a fruit cluster. 5. Detail of bud and leaf scar.
3. Fruit.

27. Leaves mostly densely clustered from a common base, ours having 2 to many leaves per cluster . . . . pines (*Pinus*)

27a. Leaves scattered individually along the stems, not at all clustered. (28)

28. Leaves sharply pointed and sharp to touch, 4-angled (easily determined by rolling between thumb and index finger); cones drooping . . . . spruces (*Picea*)

28a. Leaves soft and flexible, soft to touch, flat; cones drooping or erect. (29)

29. Leaves with persistent, short, woody stalks; cones drooping, <2 inches long . . . . hemlocks (*Tsuga*)

29a. Leaves stalkless, leaving round scars on twigs when shed; cones erect, largest ones 2–3 inches long . . . . balsam firs (*Abies*)

30. Leaf scars and buds alternate. (31)

30a. Leaf scars and buds opposite or whorled. (111)

31. Twigs with conspicuous silvery scales . . . . Russian-olive (*Elaeagnus angustifolia*)

31a. Twigs lacking silvery scales. (32)

32. Trunks, branches, or twigs armed with thorns, prickles, or spines. (33)

32a. Trunks, branches, and twigs unarmed. (42)

33. Stems with thorns, spines, or scattered prickles. (34)

33a. Stems with sharply tipped twigs or spur-shoots. (41)

34. Twigs very clubby, often 3/4 inch or more thick, nonaromatic when crushed, with scattered spines or prickles, some in rows beneath the leaf scars; leaf scars halfway encircling the twig . . . . devil's-walkingstick (*Aralia spinosa*)

34a. Twigs more slender, aromatic or not when crushed; leaf scars otherwise. (35)

35. Twigs exuding a milky juice when cut. (36)

35a. Twigs otherwise. (37)

36. Twigs with leaf scars crowded on short lateral spurs; buds rustywoolly, not imbedded in the bark. . . . . bullies (*Sideroxylon*)

36a. Twigs without lateral spurs; buds glabrous, brown, partially sunken in the bark . . . . osage-orange (*Maclura pomifera*)

37. Spines or prickles broad-based, mostly 1/2 inch or less long. (38)

37a. Thorns not noticeably broad-based, often >1/2 inch long. (39)

38. Twigs noticeably and conspicuously aromatic if broken; thorns scattered, becoming elevated on corky cushions; a southeastern coastal pain species . . . . Hercules'-club (*Zanthoxylum clava-herculis*)

38a. Twigs not noticeably and conspicuously aromatic; thorns in pairs at the nodes, becoming buried within the bark; a species found throughout our area . . . . black locust (*Robinia pseudoacacia*)

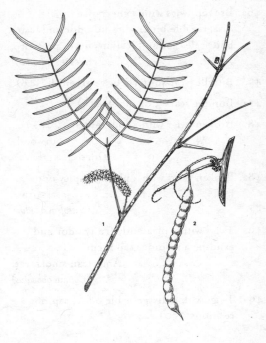

HONEY MESQUITE
1. Branch with bipinnate (having two pinnae) leaves and flower. 2. Fruit.

39. Bud scales sticky with elongated tips; barely reaching our area in Louisiana . . . . honey mesquite (*Prosopis glandulosa*)

39a. Buds not as above; bud scales not sticky; plants found throughout much of our area. (40)

40. Buds prominent, several-scaled, roundish-ovoid, often red; thorns simple, 1–2 inches long . . . . hawthorns (*Crataegus*)

40a. Buds sunken in the bark or hidden by the leaf scars; thorns often branched and several inches long . . . . honey-locust and water-locust (*Gleditsia*)

41. Terminal bud absent . . . . plums (*Prunus*)

41a. Terminal bud present . . . . apples (*Malus*)

42. Twigs with a characteristic odor if broken, pleasant or foul. (43)

42a. Twigs otherwise. (53)

43. Twigs ringed at the nodes by stipule-scars. (44)

43a. Twigs otherwise. (45)

44. Terminal bud flattened, somewhat 2-edged, 2-scaled, resembling a duck's bill . . . . tuliptree (*Liriodendron tulipifera*)

44a. Terminal bud not flattened, with a solitary scale . . . . magnolias (*Magnolia*)

45. Bark with conspicuous horizontally elongated lenticels. (46)

45a. Bark lacking conspicuous horizontally elongated lenticels. (47)

46. Broken twigs with an oil of wintergreen odor and taste; bud scales 2 or 3; catkins commonly present . . . . birches (*Betula*)

Continued ➡

46a. Broken twigs with a cherrylike or disagreeable bitter almond odor and taste; bud scales about 5, catkins never present . . . . cherries (*Prunus*)

47. Bundle-scar solitary; twigs greenish. (48)

47a. Bundle-scars 3 or more. (49)

48. Broken twigs with a foul odor . . . . sourwood (*Oxydendrum arboreum*)

48a. Broken twigs with a pleasant spicy odor . . . . sassafras (*Sassafras albidum*)

49. Twigs with a pleasantly fruity odor and exuding a resinous sap if cut . . . . American smoketree (*Cotinus obovatus*)

49a. Twigs with a disagreeable odor; sap not resinous. (50)

SALT-CEDAR
1. Branch with scalelike leaves.   2. Flowering branch.

50. Twigs extremely clubby with an exceptionally foul odor . . . . tree-of-heaven (*Ailanthus altissima*)

50a. Twigs without the above combination of characters. (51)

51. Terminal bud absent; buds partly surrounded by U-shaped leaf scars . . . . common hoptree (*Ptelea trifoliata*)

51a. Terminal bud present; buds otherwise. (52)

52. Buds naked, rusty-hairy, appearing featherlike, the terminal one elongate; bundle-scars 5; pith with transverse, greenish plates . . . . common pawpaw (*Asimina triloba*)

52a. Buds scaly, glabrous, the terminal one egg-shaped; bundle-scars 3, pith without plates . . . . alternate-leaf dogwood (*Cornus alternifolia*)

53. True leaf scars lacking. (54)

53a. True leaf scars with one or more bundle-scars present. (55)

54. Pith brown or tan; large nonflowering gymnosperms, often growing in water with pneumatophores protruding above water . . . . bald-cypress and pond-cypress (*Taxodium*)

54a. Pith white; mostly shrubby, flowering angiosperms that lack pneumatophores, not growing in standing water . . . . salt-cedar (*Tamarix ramosissima*)

55. Leaf scars very numerous, crowded on stubby spur shoots or closely spaced along the twigs; buds rounded; nonflowering gymnosperms. (56)

55a. Leaf scars comparatively few and more widely spaced; spur shoots present or not; buds various; flowering angiosperms. (57)

56. Twigs slender; cone-scales persistent . . . . American larch (*Larix laricina*)

56a. Twigs moderate; cone-scales absent . . . . maidenhair-tree (*Ginkgo biloba*)

57. Bole and branch bark conspicuously grass-green in color, branches thick and clubby; buds velvety red-brown . . . . Chinese parasol-tree (*Firmiana simplex*)

57a. Plants without the above combination of characters. (58)

58. Twigs commonly with more than one bud above each leaf scar. (59)

58a. Twigs with only one bud above each leaf

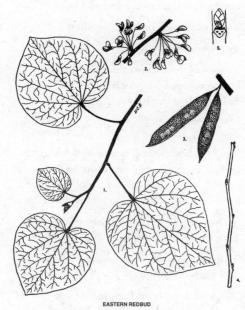

EASTERN REDBUD
1. Branch with mature leaves.   4. Winter twig.
2. Flowering branch.   5. Details of bud and leaf scar.
3. Fruits.

scar. (68)

59. Twigs with the accessory buds above the usual axillary bud. (60)

59a. Twigs with the accessory buds on either or both sides of the usual axillary bud. (67)

60. Twigs with chambered pith. (61)

60a. Twigs with continuous pith. (62)

61. Trunks not vertically striped; twigs clubby, up to 1/4 inch or more thick, with a brown pith . . . . walnuts (*Juglans*)

61a. Trunks often vertically striped; twigs more slender, with a white pith . . . . silverbells (*Halesia*)

62. Terminal bud present. (63)

62a. Terminal bud absent. (64)

63. Twigs 1/4 inch or more thick, very difficult to break; leaf scars large and with several bundle-scars . . . . hickories (*Carya*)

63a. Twigs much more slender, easily broken; leaf scars small with single bundle-scars . . . . hollies (*Ilex*)

64. Buds almost encircled by the leaf scars. (65)

64a. Buds distinctly above the leaf scars. (66)

65. Nodes not swollen; pith white; twigs brown or red-brown; bundle-traces 3–7; stipule-scars lacking . . . . yellow-wood (*Cladrastis kentukea*)

65a. Nodes swollen; pith pale green; twigs usually greenish then turning brownish; bundle-traces 3; stipule-scars small but present . . . . eve's necklacepod (*Sophora affinis*)

66. Twigs clubby, 1/4 inch or more thick; buds hidden within sunken, hairy pits . . . . Kentucky coffeetree (*Gymnocladus diocius*)

66a. Twigs much more slender; buds visible with scales, glabrous or nearly so . . . . eastern redbud (*Cercis canadensis*)

67. Bundle-scars 3 . . . . plums (*Prunus*)

67a. Bundle-scars more numerous . . . . oaks (*Quercus*)

68. Buds naked or without distinct scales. (69)

68a. Buds with one or more distinct scales. (72)

69. Trunk bark nearly black with white, vertical stripes; plants known originally only from Georgia, but now thought to be extirpated in the wild . . . . Franklintree (*Franklinia alatamaha*)

CAROLINA FALSE BUCKTHORN
1. Branch with leaves and fruit.   2. Detail of lateral winter bud.

Continued ➡

69a. Trunk bark not as above; plants from various locations. (70)

70. Terminal bud absent; leaf scars with several bundle-scars and partly to nearly surrounding the buds . . . . .sumacs (*Rhus*)

70a. Terminal bud present; leaf scars with 3 bundle-scars, not at all surrounding the buds. (71)

71. Buds stalked, tawny to rusty-hairy, appearing as a deer hoof . . . . American witch-hazel (*Hamamelis virginiana*)

71a. Buds not stalked, not appearing as a deer hoof, brownish to grayish and woolly . . . . Carolina false buckthorn (*Frangula caroliniana*)

72. Buds with but one visible scale. (73)

72a. Buds with 2 or more visible scales. (74)

73. Buds nearly surrounded by the leaf scars, conical, divergent; twigs ringed at the nodes by stipule-scars; bark exfoliating on larger branches and trunk . . . . .sycamore (*Platanus*)

73a. Buds above the leaf scars, more or less flattened and appressed; twigs not ringed by stipule-scars; bark not exfoliating . . . . willows (*Salix*)

74. Bark with horizontally elongated lenticels. (75)

74a. Bark otherwise. (76)

75. Leaf scars inversely triangular or heart-shaped with numerous bundle-scars; sap becoming black when exposed; fruits white, berrylike, occurring in drooping clusters; twigs clubby, nearly 1/4 inch thick . . . . poison-sumac (*Toxicodendron vernix*)

75a. Leaf scars half-round with 3 bundle-scars; sap not becoming black when exposed; fruits not as above; twigs much more slender . . . . birches (*Betula*)

76. Buds with 2–4 visible scales. (77)

76a. Buds with >4 visible scales. (99)

77. Leaf scars with a solitary bundle-scar. (78)

77a. Leaf scars with 3 or more bundle-scars. (86)

78. Terminal bud absent. (79)

78a. Terminal bud present. (82)

79. Branchlets 4-angled or winged; buds elongated, 2–3 times longer than wide, with the 2 bud scales ciliate on margins . . . . crape-myrtle (*Lagerstroemia indica*)

79a. Branchlets not 4-angled, nor winged; buds round or egg-shaped, length less than twice the width, bud scales not as above. (80)

80. Buds about 1/8 inch long, egg-shaped, pointed, with 2 overlapping scales; pith often chambered . . . . common persimmon (*Diospyros virginiana*)

80a. Buds smaller, roundish, with 3–4 scales; pith continuous. (81)

81. Twigs about 1/8 inch thick, very foul smelling if broken, not conspicuously zigzag; bud scales blunt-pointed; fruit a small woody capsule . . . . sourwood (*Oxydendrum arboreum*)

81a. Twigs more slender, not foul smelling, conspicuously zigzag; bud scales long-pointed; fruit a lustrous black berry . . . . tree sparkle-berry (*Vaccinium arboreum*)

COMMON PERSIMMON
1. Branch with mature leaves and fruit.   3. Detail of bud and leaf scar.
2. Winter twig.

82. Twigs with chambered pith . . . . common sweetleaf (*Symplocos tinctoria*)

82a. Twigs with continuous pith. (83)

83. Buds orangish-brown; pith brown; stipule-scar lacking; plants mostly shrubby and restricted to Georgia and South Carolina (not discussed in text) . . . . georgiaplume (*Elliottia racemosa*)

83a. Buds not orangish-brown; pith white; stipule-scars present or lacking; tree or shrublike; common throughout much of our area. (84)

84. Buds silvery, silky-hairy, narrowly elongate, appearing knife-blade-like (not discussed in text) . . . . silky-camellia and mountain-camellia (*Stewartia spp.*)

84a. Buds not as above (85)

85. Twigs more or less 3-sided, lustrous brown; leaf scars triangular; terminal bud about 1/4 inch long; stipule-scar lacking . . . . swamp titi (*Cyrilla racemiflora*)

85a. Twigs roundish, dull, grayish to reddish-brown; leaf scars crescent-shaped to half-round; buds all smaller; stipule-scars tiny, but present . . . . hollies (*Ilex*)

86. Leaf scars with 3 bundle-scars. (87)

86a. Leaf scars with >3 bundle-scars. (93)

87. Terminal bud present. (88)

87a. Terminal bud absent. (89)

88. Outer or lower bud scale centered directly above the leaf scar; pith uniform and continuous . . . . aspens and poplars (*Populus*)

88a. Outer bud scale not so centered; pith with transverse woody partitions . . . . black gum and tupelos (*Nyssa*)

89. Twigs moderate to very thick and clubby. (90)

89a. Twigs thin, not at all clubby. (91)

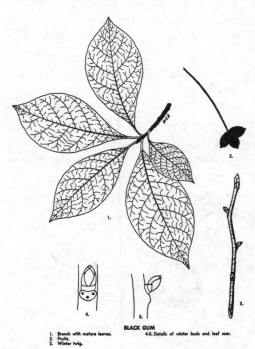

BLACK GUM
1. Branch with mature leaves.   4-5. Details of winter buds and leaf scar.
2. Fruits.
3. Winter twig.

90. Branches with short but conspicuous white, vertical stripes throughout . . . . .silktree (*Albizia julibrissin*)

90a. Branches lacking white vertical stripes . . . . China-berry (*Melia azedarach*)

91. Leaf scars minutely fringed on the upper margin; twigs noticeably zigzag, pith continuous, often with fine red streaks; buds not triangular . . . . eastern redbud (*Cercis canadensis*)

91a. Leaf scars otherwise; twigs not noticeably zigzag, pith continuous or chambered at the nodes, not reddish streaked; buds triangular. (92)

92. Bark and branches often with corky or warty outgrowths; pith finely chambered at the nodes; pseudoterminal bud conspicuously cocked; native species . . . . hackberries (*Celtis*)

92a. Bark and branches without corky outgrowths; pith continuous at nodes; pseudoterminal bud not conspicuously cocked; introduced species . . . . Chinese tallowtree (*Triadica sebifera*)

93. Broken twigs with milky sap . . . . paper-mulberry (*Broussonetia papyrifera*)

93a. Broken twigs without milky sap. (94)

Continued ➡

94. Terminal bud absent; leaf scars half-round. (95)

94a. Terminal bud present; leaf scars otherwise. (96)

95. Twigs rather zigzag, mucilaginous if chewed; pith round and white; buds appearing to be hooded with one scale atop a second . . . . American basswood (*Tilia americana*)

95a. Twigs rather straight, not mucilaginous; pith star-shaped or 5-angled; buds with >2 scales, not one atop another . . . . chestnuts (*Castanea*)

96. Leaf scars narrowly crescent-shaped; buds usually sticky . . . . .mountain-ashes (*Sorbus*)

96a. Leaf scars more or less heart-shaped; circular or 3-lobed; buds otherwise. (97)

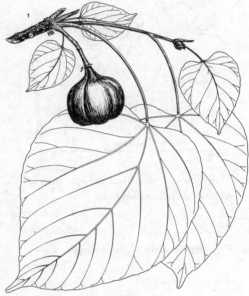

TUNG-OILTREE
1. Branch with leaves and fruit.

97. Leaf scars circular, or very broadly ovate; branches with milky sap (sometimes not apparently so in winter) . . . . tung-oiltree (*Vernicia fordii*)

97a. Leaf scars heart-shaped or 3-lobed; branches without milky sap. (98)

98. Twigs with continuous pith; twigs tough, difficult to break; fruit husk usually dehiscent . . . . hickories (*Carya*)

98a. Twigs with chambered pith; twigs breaking rather easily; fruit husk indehiscent . . . . walnuts (*Juglans*)

99. Leaf scars with 3 bundle-scars. (100)

99a. Leaf scars with > 3 bundle-scars. (108)

100. Terminal bud present. (101)

100a. Terminal bud absent. (105)

101. Outer or lower bud scale centered directly above the leaf scar . . . . aspens and poplars (*Populus*)

101a. Outer bud scale not so centered. (102)

102. Terminal bud about 1/8 inch long, the lateral ones smaller; large catkinlike buds present toward end of twig . . . . corkwood (*Leitneria floridana*)

102a. Terminal bud 1/4 inch or more long; catkinlike buds lacking. (103)

103. Buds egg-shaped, fragrant when crushed; twigs green, developing corky ridges the second season . . . . sweet-gum (*Liquidambar styraciflua*)

103a. Buds narrow, elongated and pointed, not fragrant; twigs otherwise. (104)

104. Buds with 8 or more chestnut-brown scales, placed to one side of the leaf scars; stipule-scars almost encircling the twigs . . . . American beech (*Fagus grandifolia*)

104a. Buds with about 6 greenish to reddish scales, placed directly above the leaf scars; stipule-scars not evident . . . . service-berries (*Amelanchier*)

105. Bud scales in 2 longitudinal rows. (106)

105a. Bud scales otherwise. (107)

106. Twigs dark red to reddish-brown, dotted with minute, whitish lenticels; buds about 1/16 inch long . . . . planertree (*Planera aquatica*)

106a. Twigs otherwise; buds larger . . . . elms (*Ulmus*)

FRINGETREE
1. Branch with mature leaves and fruits.   3. Winter twig.
2. Flower cluster.   4. Detail of bud and leaf scar.

107. Buds divergent; scales about 6, minutely grooved; catkins often present; bark scaly . . . . eastern hop-hornbeam (*Ostrya virginiana*)

107a. Buds nearly appressed; scales about 8–12, not grooved; larger flower buds often present; bark smooth . . . . American hornbeam (*Carpinus caroliniana*)

108. Terminal bud absent; twigs exuding a milky juice when cut. (109)

108a. Terminal bud present; twigs otherwise. (110)

109. Leaf scars 2-ranked; twigs glabrous; bud scales >3 . . . . mulberries (*Morus*)

109a. Leaf scars not 2-ranked; twigs hirsute; bud scales 2 or 3 . . . . paper-mulberry (*Broussonetia papyrifera*)

110. Buds clustered toward twig tips, 1/2 inch long or shorter; stipule-scars not evident . . . . oaks (*Quercus*)

110a. Buds all widely spaced along the twigs, very elongate, cigar-shaped, >1/2 inch long, taper-pointed; twigs almost ringed by stipule-scars . . . . American beech (*Fagus grandifolia*)

111. Terminal bud absent. (112)

111a. Terminal bud present. (113)

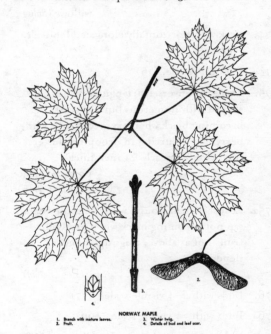

NORWAY MAPLE
1. Branch with mature leaves.   3. Winter twig.
2. Fruit.   4. Details of bud and leaf scar.

112. Twigs of previous year hollow except at nodes and occasionally in scattered areas between nodes . . . . princesstree (*Paulownia tomentosa*)

112a. Twigs of previous year with continuous pith . . . . catalpas (*Catalpa*)

113. Leaf scars with a solitary bundle-scar. (114)

113a. Leaf scars with 3 or more bundle-scars. (115)

114. Terminal bud conical, mostly 1/4 inch or more long; twigs densely tawny-hairy, lacking conspicuous warty lenticels . . . . fevertree (*Pinckneya bracteata*)

Continued ➜

114a. Terminal bud egg-shaped, most <1/4 inch
 long; twigs with conspicuous warty lenticels
 but otherwise glabrous . . . .
 . . . . fringetree
 (*Chionanthus virginicus*)

115. Buds striate; pith with a green diaphragm
 at the nodes . . . .
 . . . . paper-mulberry
 (*Broussonetia papyrifera*)

115a. Buds not striate; pith without a diaphragm
 at nodes. (116)

116. Lateral buds concealed by the persistent
 petiole bases; terminal (flower) buds often
 biscuitlike . . . .
 . . . . dogwoods
 (*Cornus*)

116a. Lateral buds otherwise; terminal (flower)
 buds never biscuitlike. (117)

117. Leaf scars with the opposing tips meeting.
 (118)

117a. Leaf scars otherwise. (119)

118. Twigs green or purplish-green, often
 glaucous . . . .
 . . . . maples (*Acer*)

118a. Twigs otherwise . . . .
 . . . . arrow-woods and blackhaws
 (*Viburnum*)

119. Buds with only 2 visible scales. (120)

119a. Buds with >2 visible scales. (122)

120. Terminal bud flanked by a pair of
 persistent petiole bases . . . .
 . . . . dogwoods (*Cornus*)

120a. Terminal bud otherwise. (121)

121. Twigs and buds greenish or light red; buds
 egg-shaped, evidently stalked . . . .
 . . . . maples (*Acer*)

121a. Twigs and buds brownish or grayish; buds
 narrow and without evident stalks . . . . . .
 . . . . arrow-woods and blackhaws
 (*Viburnum*)

122. Leaf scars with 6–8 bundle-scars . . . .
 . . . . maples (*Acer*)

122a. Leaf scars with more numerous
 bundle-scars. (123)

123. Terminal bud sharply pointed, mostly 1/2
 inch or more long; buds with many scales.
 . . . . buckeyes
 (*Aesculus*)

123a. Terminal bud blunt, <1/2 inch long;
 buds with about 4–6 visible scales . . . . . .
 . . . . ashes
 (*Fraxinus*)

—From *The Illustrated Book of Trees*

Identifying Trees in Winter: A Brief Guide

Elizabeth P. Lawlor
Illustrations by Pat Archer

Most people identify trees by their leaves. This makes tree identification a special challenge in winter. This may not be a disadvantage, because it forces you to observe the more subtle differences among trees.

Branch Patterns

Deciduous trees are those that shed their leaves in the fall. Without their leaves, you can see the trees' various shapes. This is an ideal time to learn about branching patterns. The diagrams will help you determine which pattern each tree illustrates.

1. Whorled branches grow out of the trunk in threes. This occurs rarely, but you can find it easily in larches (pine family), a deciduous gymnosperm.

2. The branches, twigs, and leaves are paired in some trees. Look for this pattern, called opposite, in maple, buckeye, ash, dogwood, and horse chestnut.

3. The third pattern of branch arrangement is called alternate. The branches and twigs grow in spiral steps.

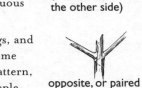

whorled
(third branch on
the other side)

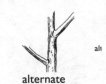

opposite, or paired

alt

alternate

Branching as seen in winter

 If you would like to learn more about patterns in nature, read *Fascinating Fibonaccis*, by Trudi Garland.

Tree Shape

Within the parameters of a tree's genetic code, its shape is determined by its environment. A tree growing in an open space will develop a different shape than will a tree of the same type growing in more cramped quarters such as woods or an urban park. A tree that grows close to its neighbors will have normal-sized limbs only near its top, with perhaps a few underdeveloped limbs along the length of its trunk. Look for this kind of stunted development.

 The shape of a tree aids in its identification. For example, a sugar maple is shaped like an egg standing on its broad end. An elm looks like an open umbrella or an upside-down bud vase. To see the distinct shape of a tree, you will need to observe the tree from a distance. You can easily do this in an open field or on a golf course.

 Find a tree that interests you. Describe its shape in your notebook. Draw an outline of the tree or photograph it. Do the branches droop like those of a weeping willow? Do they spread out from the trunk like a white oak, or do they grow close to the trunk like a hickory? Are the branches growing in any particular direction? Besides the prevailing winds, what might cause the tree to grow in a particular direction?

Identifying Trees by Their Bark

It is difficult to determine the identity of many trees by examining only the bark. One reason for this is that as a tree ages, its bark changes. Nevertheless, there are some trees that have very distinctive bark and are easily recognizable throughout their lives.

 The sycamore (*Platanus occidentalis*) is easily identified by its mottled and flaking bark. It is frequently planted as a shade tree, and you can find it in parks and along urban and suburban streets.

 A clue to the nature of the bark of shagbark hickory (*Carya ovata*) lies in the tree's name. Strips of bark scroll away from the trunk and give the tree a shaggy appearance.

 The bark of the American beech (*Fagus grandifolia*) is smooth and gray or blue-gray.

 The bark of the American hornbeam (*Carpinus caroliniana*) is often described as resembling flexed arm muscles.

WINTER TREE SILHOUETTES

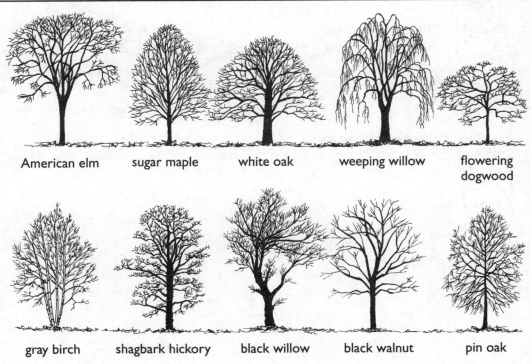

American elm   sugar maple   white oak   weeping willow   flowering dogwood

gray birch   shagbark hickory   black willow   black walnut   pin oak

Continued ➡

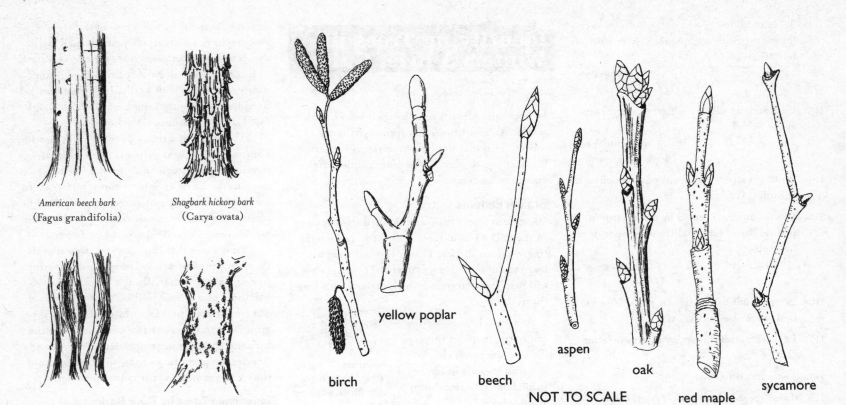

American beech bark
(Fagus grandifolia)

Shagbark hickory bark
(Carya ovata)

American hornbeam bark
(Carpinus caroliniana)

Sycamore bark
(Platanus occidentalis)

yellow poplar

birch

beech

aspen

oak

NOT TO SCALE

red maple

sycamore

Twigs and buds are especially useful in identifying trees in winter.

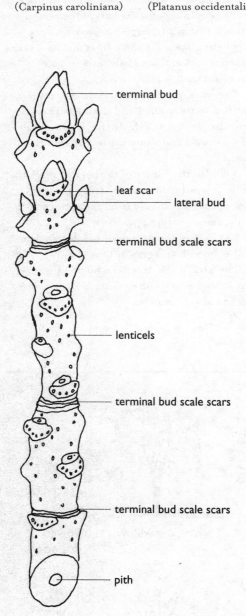

terminal bud

leaf scar

lateral bud

terminal bud scale scars

lenticels

terminal bud scale scars

terminal bud scale scars

pith

Green ash twig with terminal bud.

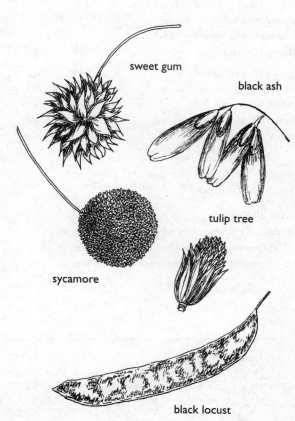

sweet gum

black ash

sycamore

tulip tree

black locust

Many deciduous trees retain some seed containers throughout the winter.

Clues from Twigs

Twigs come in a variety of colors, shapes, and sizes. Make a collection starting with beech, oak, shagbark hickory, and maple, if you can find them. How many colors are there among your twigs? Are they straight, zigzag, or curved? Study the additional twig traits described below. The illustrations will help you match twig with tree.

First look at the buds. The bud at the tip of the twig is called the terminal bud. As it develops, it adds length to the twig. The buds that grow along the side of the twig are called lateral buds. They produce flowers, leaves, or new branches. Each bud is covered by overlapping scales that protect the developing tissue.

The characteristics of the terminal bud can help you identify the tree. Is the bud single or in a cluster? Is it large or small? Pointed or rounded? Hairy? Sticky? What color is it? Oak twigs have clusters of three or four terminal buds protected by brown or reddish brown scales. Beech tree twigs have only one terminal bud. Like the lateral buds, it is shiny tan and cigar shaped. Red maple twigs have a single round, dark red terminal bud. The terminal bud of shagbark hickory is elongated with blunt tips, hairy, and usually dark brown.

Now look at the lateral buds along the sides of the twigs. How do they resemble the terminal buds?

The small dots you see on new or young twigs are lenticels. These are openings in the outer layers of the stem and root tissues that allow the exchange of oxygen into and carbon dioxide out of the plant. Is there a pattern to the arrangement of lenticels? How far back on the twig can you find them?

Twigs will also show leaf scars. During the summer, the tree produces a layer of cork between the leaf stem and the point where it attaches to the twig. When this layer is complete, the leaf falls, and the mark left on the twig is called the leaf scar. The shape of the leaf scar is

Continued ➡

unique for each type of tree. If you look closely at a bare twig, you will see tiny dots in the leaf scar. These dots mark where the transport tubes of the twig joined those of the leaf and are called the vascular bundle scar. The illustrations on page 100 show lateral buds and leaf scars on selected twigs. You will notice that they come in a variety of shapes and sizes. The color of the buds also will vary according to the type of tree.

The terminal bud scar is the point where the bud scales of the terminal bud were attached. The space between rings, which look like rubber bands around the twig, mark each year's growth. In what year did your twig grow the most? Look at other twigs the same age on the same tree. Do they also show the most growth during that same year?

If you cut into a twig, you will find a sponge-like substance called pith. When placed in a growth medium, pieces of pith grow into new plants. Cut a cross section of twig and examine the pith. If it is star-shaped, it is probably an oak, poplar, or hickory twig. If the pith is circular, it is probably an elm twig.

Seed Containers

Many deciduous trees retain some seed containers throughout the winter. You can easily see the button balls, or seed clusters, of the sycamore dangling from the zigzag twigs. If you live in an area where sweet gum (*Liquidambar styraciflua*) thrive, look for the spiked seed balls. Clusters of winged seeds that hang from branches announce the ash. The yellow poplar or tulip tree (*Liriodendron tulipifera*) produces seed clusters that resemble a tulip blossom. Ash trees (*Fraxinus spp.*) retain bunches of winged seeds. See if you can find these and other trees that retain some seed containers throughout the winter.

—From *Discover Nature in Winter*

Ferns: An Introduction

Elizabeth P. Lawlor
Illustrations by Pat Archer

When you first walk into the forest on a hot summer day, you are relieved to feel the cool, moist shade. As you walk along the path, you notice the small trees and bushes that thrive in the sun-mottled shade, as well as dense patches of ferns. Ferns are especially abundant in the wet areas near streams.

These common woodland plants have an exotic, ancient aura to them, like prehistoric relics. Ferns and their close relatives actually did flourish in the steamy forests of the dinosaur ages in the Carboniferous period, about 350 million years ago. The stable climate of that time encouraged their growth. Flat, marshy land and vast inland seas contributed to the success of these early land-dwelling plants. The forests of ferns they created flourished over a large portion of the earth, including what are now the icy polar regions. The cooling climate that followed this period resulted in the evolution of the ferns we see today, which are adapted to changing sets of environmental conditions. Today there are some twelve thousand fern species, about four hundred of which live in the United States, and about one hundred of those in the Northeast. Ferns of various sizes and

shapes live in a diversity of habitats, ranging from tropical rain forests to the arctic tundra. Robust, eighty-foot-tall fern trees thrive in the tropics, and dainty, two-inch leaves of curly grass fern (*Schizaea pusilla*) grow in the acid soils of southern New Jersey bogs. You also can find ferns in such unlikely places as the marshlands of northern Alaska and even Antarctica. However, few grow in arid deserts.

Ferns were the first plants with vascular systems. These systems carry minerals and water to the food factories in the leaves and the manufactured nutrients from the leaves to all parts of the plant. They also provide support so that these plants can stand upright.

Ancient mythology often attributed magical qualities to ferns. People noticed that ferns did not possess obvious structures related to reproduction, such as flowers, fruits, and seeds, but the plants continued to appear year after year. Compared with other plants, the ferns were a strange anomaly.

A rudimentary understanding of how ferns reproduce dates back only three hundred years, to 1669, when spores were discovered. But at that time, scientists were unable to make the connection between these tiny structures and fern reproduction. It was not until the mid-eighteenth century that this relationship became clear. However, the scientific explanation itself is quite an intricate tale filled with strange terminology.

Spores are tiny cells that do not contain a baby plant or embryo. Therefore, spores do not become new ferns, but if they fall on suitable soil and have adequate water, they will divide and produce a tiny structure called a prothallium (*plural, prothallia*). These flat, often heart-shaped structures lack leaves, stems, roots, and vascular systems. Prothallia get their nutrients directly

from the surrounding water, which doesn't have to be more than a thin film over the ground. The prothallia are small, growing only to about one-fourth inch in diameter, and are only about one cell thick except near the center. In this slightly thicker region, on the underside, two small structures develop. One of these is the archegonium, which contains an egg, and the other is the antheridium, which contains antherozoids or sperm. Spores need moisture for fertilization to take place, as the antherozoids must swim to the archegonium. The fertilized egg that develops from this union eventually becomes the plant we recognize as the fern. During this development, the prothallium withers, and the young fern becomes self-supporting. Often referred to as the private life of the fern, this phase in the two-part life cycle of a fern is called the gametophyte generation.

The self-supporting fernlets have tightly coiled, bright green heads, called crosiers, or fiddleheads, which poke their way through the soil in the spring. As the fern matures, the coils straighten into leaves, or fronds. With the unfurling of its young fronds, the fern enters

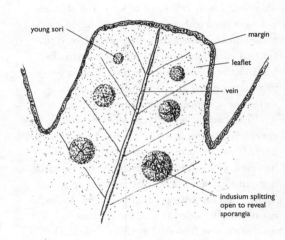

LIFE CYCLE OF FERNS

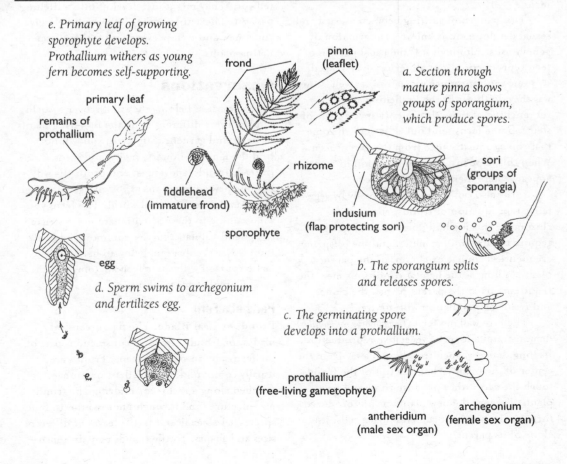

e. Primary leaf of growing sporophyte develops. Prothallium withers as young fern becomes self-supporting.

primary leaf

remains of prothallium

frond

pinna (leaflet)

a. Section through mature pinna shows groups of sporangium, which produce spores.

rhizome

sori (groups of sporangia)

fiddlehead (immature frond)

indusium (flap protecting sori)

sporophyte

egg

d. Sperm swims to archegonium and fertilizes egg.

b. The sporangium splits and releases spores.

c. The germinating spore develops into a prothallium.

prothallium (free-living gametophyte)

antheridium (male sex organ)

archegonium (female sex organ)

Continued ➡

another stage of its life cycle. Now its job is to produce spores. Some ferns produce hundreds of thousands of spores, and other, more prodigious ferns produce millions.

Individual fern species have their own unique patterns of spore production, but generalizations about this process can be made. In the spring, tiny green bumps appear on the undersides of the leaves. As the season progresses toward summer, these bumps turn brown, and the leaves may look as though they are growing fungi. These dark brown spots are called sori, and they contain spore cases, or sporangia. Sometimes the sporangia are covered with a thin protective membrane called an indusium.

When the sportes are mature, they are released from the sporangium. The method of release varies among species. In some ferns, the spores are shot into the air by a slingshot-like mechanism. In other species, the spore cases simply open, and the spores are caught in air currents and drift away from the parent fern. Whatever the discharge mechanism, the spores of all ferns become airborne with the slightest breeze, even by an imperceptible movement of air.

Relatively few spores come to rest on suitable soil. Those that land in warm, shady, moist places at the right time of year will begin to grow. If conditions are not appropriate at the time of their landing, the spores remain alive but inactive for as long as a year. This spore-producing phase in the life cycle of a fern is called the sporophyte generation.

The complete life cycle of a fern is even much more complicated than has been outlined here. If you keep in mind the following, however, you can easily remember the essential steps in the cycle: I. Fronds produce spores. 2. Spores develop into prothallia. 3. Prothallia manufacture gametes. 4. Gametes fuse to produce a new fern (the sporophyte). In the [Observations] section, you will have an opportunity to explore this process in some specific ferns.

This pattern of shifting between asexual and sexual development is known as alternation of generations. Although it is the usual pattern of fern reproduction, not all ferns are restricted to it; some can reproduce vegetatively as well. One way they do this is by the branching and rebranching of their rhizomes (a special type of stem). Some ferns send out a "feeler" rhizome that roots some distance from the parent fern. When this happens, a new population of ferns appears where there were none before.

Ferns also can reproduce asexually by vegetative reproduction of fronds, roots, or rhizomes. This method does not use spores or require the union of gametes, and the offspring are identical copies, or clones, of the parent plant. As long as the habitat conditions meet the requirements of the parent plants, the clones and resulting population will survive.

The rare walking fern (*Camptosorus rhizophyllus*) demonstrates a form of vegetative reproduction. Its long, lance-shaped fronds arch away from the center of the plant. When the tips of the fronds touch the earth, they produce roots and new plants. Because the new plant was not produced through the union of gametes or sex cells, it is a clone of its parent.

The Boston fern (*Nephrolepis exaltata bostoniensis*), used frequently as an interior decoration, reproduces vegetatively through the use of runners, stringlike leafless stems that develop among the fronds. These runners will sprout roots wherever they touch soil.

Buds on the roots of the staghorn fern (*Platycerium sp.*) develop into fernlets. Some less familiar ferns develop clones on the upper surfaces of their fronds. Eventually the new ferns will leave the parent fern, develop roots and rhizomes, and become independent ferns.

Most ferns are perennials. When it turns cold at the end of the growing season, the fronds of these ferns turn brown and become brittle. Their life above the ground is over, but the rhizomes continue to live throughout the winter. When spring arrives, new shoots will sprout from the rhizomes. If you feel around a clump of ferns in the autumn, you may feel some hard, round forms. These are the beginnings of the fiddleheads that will appear next spring.

Some ferns are evergreen and, along with pines, cedars, and hollies, provide a splash of color to the winter landscape. The common Christmas fern (*Polystichum acrostichoides*), which gets its name from the eared, stocking-shaped lobes of its fronds, is an evergreen fern you might find along wooded sloping streambanks, near stone walls, and in rocky, wooded areas. The marginal wood fern (*Dryopteris marginalis*) and the rare hairy lipfern (*Cheilanthes lanosa*) are frequent members of the rocky slope community.

Wherever they grow, ferns lend a subtle feeling of wildness to their habitat. Compared with the cheery spring blooms of wildflowers, ferns are subdued and are easily ignored. However, there is great diversity and beauty to be found. Find some ferns. Make a commitment to spend a season with them, observe them, ask questions, and learn what they have to tell you. They might just develop into a lifelong passion. The activities that follow will help give you a new and rich perspective on these fascinating plants.

Observations

In the activities below, you will discover a world of plants very different from the flowering plants of fields and gardens. On ferns, you will not find the familiar flowers, fruits, and seeds. Instead, fronds, sporangia, and prothallia will be your new companions as you navigate through this complex yet beautiful world. The ferns you will examine in these activities are not restricted to wetland habitats, but are common and easily found. Use the diagram below to help familiarize yourself with some fern anatomy and the vocabulary that goes with it.

Parts of a Fern

Frond, or Leaf Blade. The flat, green leaf blades, or fronds, the most conspicuous part of the fern, vary in size and shape. Fronds are usually compound, with leaflets, or pinnae, attached along a rachis, or midrib. The fronds manufacture food through photosynthesis. Some species have sterile and fertile leaves of different sizes and shapes. Fertile fronds contain repro-

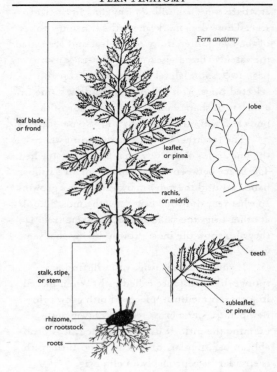

Fern anatomy

ductive spores. Fronds vary in size and shape in different species.

Stipe, or Stalk. The stipe, or stalk, is the leaf support below the rachis and above the root. It is covered with hairs or scales, rounded in back and concave or flat in front, and green, brown, tan, silver, or black in color.

Rachis. The rachis is the backbone of the frond and is the continuation of the stalk supporting the leaflets. It corresponds to the midrib of a simple leaf. Until the lobes in a fern are cut to the midrib, there is no rachis.

Leaflet, or Pinna (*Plural, Pinnae*). Leaflets are divisions of a compound leaf.

Subleaflet, or Pinnule. Subleaflets are subdivisions of leaflets.

Lobe, or Pinnulet. Lobes are the subdivision of a pinnule.

Teeth. Teeth are serrations along the edges of the pinnae, pinnules, or pinnulets.

Rhizome. Rhizomes are horizontal stems that lie on the surface of the soil or just below it.

Roots. Roots are thin, threadlike, sometimes wiry structures that anchor the plant and absorb water and minerals from the soil. They grow from the rootstock, or rhizomes.

Fern Identification

The shape of a frond will help you identify an unfamiliar fern. Is the frond triangular and broadest at the base, does it become narrow at both ends, or is it tapered only at the base?

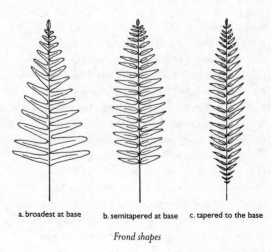

a. broadest at base   b. semitapered at base   c. tapered to the base

Frond shapes

Continued ➡

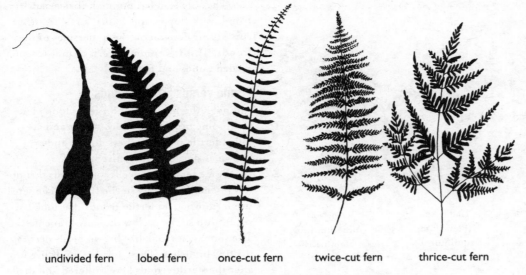

undivided fern   lobed fern   once-cut fern   twice-cut fern   thrice-cut fern

Fronds come in many shapes and may be undivided, somewhat divided, or much divided into smaller parts.

Ferns vary in appearance. Some are extremely delicate; others are more substantial. There are differences in the lobes, leaflets, and subleaflets. Ferns are organized into groups having similar leaf patterns, which makes fern identification somewhat easier. Botanists who specialize in ferns use an even more detailed system than the one presented here to help them categorize these beauties.

Undivided Ferns. These ferns are very unlike the typical fern. The simple leaves are straplike and lack the feathery appearance of most ferns. These include the rare walking fern and the bird's nest fern (*Asplenium nidus*), often grown as a houseplant.

Simple Ferns, or Lobed Ferns. Fronds of these ferns are divided by cuts on either side of the midrib but do not touch the midrib. The common polypody (*Polypodium virginianum*) has this design.

Compound Ferns. These ferns are cut into distinct leaflets to the midrib.

Once-cut ferns. Each leaflet, or pinna, is cut to the midrib. Ferns in this group are the sensitive fern (*Onoclea sensibilis*) and Christmas fern.

Twice-cut ferns. In these ferns, not only are the fronds cut into leaflets, but the leaflets are also cut into subleaflets, or pinnules. They include the marsh fern (*Thelypteris palustris*), cinnamon fern (*Osmunda cinnemomea*), ostrich fern (*Matteuccia struthiopteris*), and marginal wood fern.

Thrice-cut ferns. In these, the laciest of ferns, the fronds are cut into leaflets (pinnae), which are cut into subleaflets (pinnules), which are cut again into pinnulets. The common bracken fern (*Pteridium aquilinum*) of open fields and woods and the lady fern (*Athyrium filix-femina*) of moist, shaded woods are thrice-cut ferns.

Unfernlike Ferns. There are a few rare ferns that, in spite of their unfernlike appearance, are classified as ferns because they are vascular plants that reproduce by spores rather than seeds. The walking fern (*Camptosorus rhizophyllus*) prefers the northern face of moist limestone outcrops. The Hartford climbing fern (*Lygodium palmatum*) has vinelike fronds that climb and twist over shrubs and other obstacles in the partial or deep shade of low thickets and along streambanks in moist, wet, acid soil. It prefers sun, but the rhizomes must be wet. Curly grass fern (*Schizaea pusilla*) grows in wet, very acid soil, such as that found in cranberry bogs and cedar swamps. It is found in New Jersey, Nova Scotia, and Newfoundland.

Finding Ferns

Ferns are easier to find than you might think. You will find them to moist, shaded areas, along riverbanks, around ponds, and in the woods. Here are brief descriptions of three common ferns you are likely to find growing in swampy areas and in wet woodlands.

The cinnamon fern has twice-cut fronds and a separate cinnamon-colored fertile frond growing from the rhizome that bears club-shaped sporangia. The tall, pointed sterile fronds grow in a circular pattern.

The ostrich fern has tall, plumelike, twice-cut sterile fronds that are wider in the middle and taper toward the base and the top of the frond.

The fertile frond is also plume shaped, and its tough pinnae clasp dark brown clusters of sori.

The marsh fern also has twice-cut fronds. You can distinguish between sterile and fertile fronds by the presence of sori on the fertile fronds, which are also taller and thinner than the sterile fronds.

You need not limit yourself to ponds to discover the fascinating world of ferns. Other ferns grow in habitats such as roadside ditches, meadows, and damp, cool forests, and some even grow out of brick walls.

The sensitive fern is a very common fern with once-cut fronds, found in open fields and swamps. The wavy, lobed fronds do not produce sori, which means that they are sterile. A separate fertile frond appears during the fall. It contains small, brown, bead-shaped clusters containing sori that persist throughout the winter.

The common polypody grows in rock crevices in woodlands. The sori develop on the undersides of the upper lobes. The fronds are once-cut.

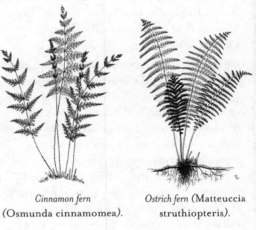

Cinnamon fern (Osmunda cinnamomea).   *Ostrich fern* (Matteuccia struthiopteris).

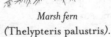

Marsh fern (Thelypteris palustris).   *Sensitive fern* (Onoclea sensibilis).

The Christmas fern has leathery, evergreen, once-cut fronds with a tough stipe and rachis. The fertile pinnae are limited to the top third of the frond, where there are reddish brown sori on the underside.

The marginal wood fern has large, leathery, evergreen, twice-cut fronds and scaly stipes. The sori are located on the margin of each pinnule. Look for this common fern on rocky woodland slopes.

The bracken fern is common in woodlands and fields. It has very large, leathery, thrice-cut, triangular fronds. Look for sori around the edges of the undersides of pinnules that are folded under.

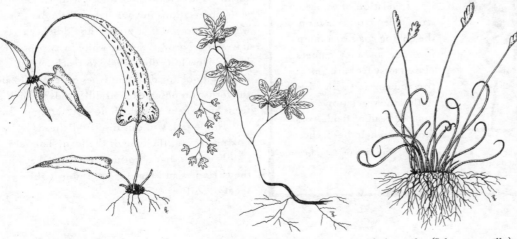

Walking fern (Camptosorus rhizophyllus).   *Hartford climbing fern* (Lygodium palmatum).   *Curly grass fern* (Schizaea pusilla).

Continued ➡

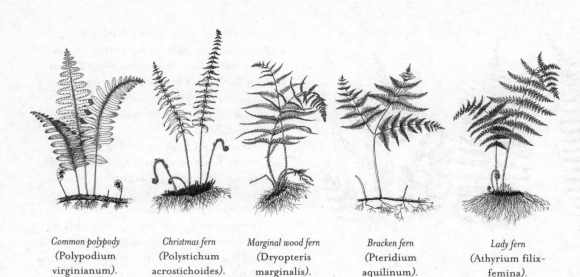

Common polypody (Polypodium virginianum).

Christmas fern (Polystichum acrostichoides).

Marginal wood fern (Dryopteris marginalis).

Bracken fern (Pteridium aquilinum).

Lady fern (Athyrium filix-femina).

THE MEDICINAL FERN

Bradford Angier   Illustration by Arthur J. Anderson

Bracken Fern (Pteridium aquilinum)

Family: Fern (*Polypodiaceae*)

Common Names: Brake Fern, Brake, Pasture Brake, Hogbrake, Hog Brake, Western Brake, Western Bracken, Western Brake Fern, Eastern Brake, Eastern Bracken.

Characteristics: Its vigor, fertility, and coarse ruggedness make the bracken fern the most familiar of North America's ferns, especially as it is among the first to poke its way up through the ground in the springtime and as it continues to produce new fronds until freezing temperatures interfere.

The rugged, stiff, darkly green fronds, reddish at their bases, vary from about 1 to 4 feet tall; unlike most of this continent's usually shade- and moisture-seeking ferns, they reach across many a sunny, dry stretch.

When they expire in the autumn, their wind-rattling brown expanses, when not flattened be heavy snows, stay to pinpoint the whereabouts of the highly edible fiddleheads when they arise the next growing season. These peculiar entities—each coming into being singly from the usually long, prolific root which extends horizontally underground, where it tends to branch over a sometimes considerable area—curl in such a way that they look something like the tuning end of a violin. After some 4 to 10 inches of edibility, depending on the region, they uncoil in a tough, stiff, toxic—darkening into the familiar, broadly triangular, erect, some 1 to 4 inches tall—fanlike verdancies that spring up green many a burnt area.

The brown fruiting bodies are grown on the undersurface of the fronds. The ferns are among the first great group of plants that develop an independent sporophyte—the asexual phase of the plant's life circle, whereby the fertilized egg with true roots, stems, and leaves is retained for some time in the female sex organs. This happens to be one of the most important steps in the evolution of the plant kingdom. The development of a vessel system, which allows water and food to be conducted rapidly through stems, roots, and leaves, was mainly responsible for this advance in the earth's destiny.

Area: There is only one species of the bracken fern (*Pteridium aquilinum*), and this grows widely across this continent, from Labrador to Alaska southward.

Uses: Although poisonous in large-enough amounts, especially to grazing cattle, the fronds of the bracken fern boiled with water and sugar were adjudged to be a good medicine, especially for those with lung ailments. The fronds were also boiled with a syrup of this sort, in small proportions, for liver troubles.

The roots or actually rhizomes, when boiled into a stronger tea than usual, were used for worms, for the relief of digestive gas, and to quell diarrhea. Root tea was also advocated to soften caked breasts, although that brewed from the fronds was widely held to be dangerous for this purpose.

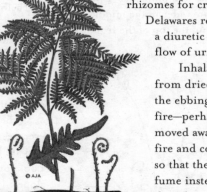

Bracken fern (pteridium aquilinum)

Ojibwa squaws were among those using the tea prepared from rhizomes for cramps, while the Delawares recommended it as a diuretic to increase the flow of urine.

Inhalation of smoke from dried fronds laid on the ebbing coals of a campfire—perhaps a few embers moved away from the main fire and covered with ashes so that the vegetation would fume instead of flame—was thought to help headache.

—From *Field Guide to Medicinal Plants*

The lady fern has pointed, thrice-cut fronds with floppy tips. Short, straight, or curved sori develop on the undersides of the fronds. This is a common fern of moist, semi-shaded woods and fields.

Fertile versus Sterile Fronds

Although the fronds of most ferns look identical, some of them produce spores and are called fertile fronds; others do not and are known as sterile or vegetative fronds.

Some ferns produce fertile fronds that do not resemble the leafy sterile fronds. The sensitive fern produces fertile fronds that look like small, thin sticks, each with many branchlets. The spore cases look like brown beads decorating the tiny branches. These fertile fronds live long after the sterile fronds have withered and died. The fertile fronds of the cinnamon fern look like cinnamon-colored sticks standing erect in the middle of a clump of bright green sterile fronds.

As you observe your ferns throughout the growing season, look for signs of fertile fronds. When do the fronds first appear? Do they all appear at once? If not, how long is the delay between frond appearance? When do the sori first appear? Are all the look-alike fronds on your fern fertile or are some sterile? When do the fronds, sterile and fertile, die back? On average, what is the lifespan of a frond? How many fronds does one fern produce in a season? Record your findings in your field notebook.

Fiddleheads

In the spring, bright green young ferns begin to poke up through the soil. As each emerges, you will see a coil of green called a fiddlehead, or crosier. These names refers to the coil's shape, the first for its resemblance to the head of a violin, and the second for a bishop's ceremonial staff also called a crosier, which is a stylized shepherd's staff with a crook at the top.

The fiddleheads are coiled because the upper and lower surfaces of the fronds grow at different rates. As the fern grows, the fiddlehead unrolls and expands, revealing tiny new fronds. Sometimes the fiddlehead has a cover of fuzzy, brown scales. Some ferns have a cover of silky hairs on the rachis when the young fiddlehead unrolls. Before the development of synthetic materials, these hairs from large tropical tree ferns were used for upholstery stuffing.

Locate a patch of ferns during the summer months, and return there the following spring to observe the fiddleheads poke through the soil, unfurl, and release their folded leaflets. Record your observations in your field notebook. On what date do you first notice the fiddlehead? Is it wearing a brown, tan, or white fuzzy protective hood? How long does it take to reach its full height? Look for different types of ferns. Do all the ferns you observe have fiddleheads? Which ferns have them and which do not?

In the fall, you can find fiddleheads by poking around the base of the fern. They are tightly coiled, hard, round structures that hug the rhizomes and may be covered by a thin sheet of soil.

Continued ➡

Some people relish fiddleheads as tasty vegetables, reminiscent of asparagus. The fiddlehead of commerce is the ostrich fern, great quantities of which are collected in the spring and shipped to markets or canneries. If you would like to investigate this gourmet aspect of ferns, try the following. (*Caution: Do not eat fiddleheads you pick in the wild. Use only those you buy from a grocer.*)

Select fiddleheads that are newly arrived to the grocer's shelves, choosing only those that are bright green and tightly coiled. Cut off the long tails. Between your palms, rub away the fuzzy or brown, papery covering, and wash the fiddleheads well. Steam them until fork-tender, and rinse in cool water. Dry them thoroughly, then toss with a favorite salad dressing. Or if you

prefer, stir-fry them in oil with ginger to taste for about two minutes. Add two cloves of garlic, salt, and one-quarter cup of chicken broth. Cover and simmer for about five minutes.

If eating fiddleheads does not appeal to you, you can still buy a few and unfurl them to examine how the leaves are packaged.

EDIBLE FERNS
Bradford Angier

Pasture Brake
(*Pteridium*)

When I attended college in Maine, we used to see fiddleheads regularly displayed for sale in the spring in the Lewiston markets. Later, I used to feast on them while spring bear hunting in New Brunswick. We have relished them many times, more recently, in the West and Far North. They are the young, uncoiled fronds of the fern family's brakes, so called because in this emerging state they resemble the tuning ends of violins. They are also known in many localities as croziers because of their resemblance to the shepherd's crook-like staffs of bishops, abbots, and abbesses.

Although some other similar fronds are edible, it is the fiddleheads from the widely familiar and distributed pasture brake, *Pteridium aquilinum*, that are most commonly enjoyed. These grow, often luxuriantly, through the Northern Hemisphere, in Europe and Asia as well as in North America. They are found, sometimes in waving acres that

Pasture brake

brush your knees as you ride through on horseback, from Alaska across Canada to Newfoundland, south through the states to California and Mexico.

These are edible, however, only while still fiddleheads and therefore young. They are then good both raw and cooked. Later, the full-grown fronds toughen and become poisonous to cattle as well as humans. While still in the uncurled state, on the other hand, they are found very acceptable by some of the wildlife, including the mountain beaver.

Pasture brake is known to different people as just plain brake, bracken, hog brake, bracken fern, eagle fern, brake fern, and Western bracken. It decorates often shady roadsides, dry open woods, pastures, clearings, and may often be seen adding welcome green to recently burned forests.

It is a coarse, perennial fern with a blackish root, so favored by the Japanese for thickening and flavoring soups that laws had to be passed there to prevent its extinction. Early in the spring, these roots send up scattered fiddleheads. These later uncoil and stretch into long, erect stalks with typically fernlike leaflets, whose greenness takes on a straw to purplish-brown color with maturity.

The widely triangular fronds, which may be from one to three feet across, are distinctively separated into three usually broadly spreading branches.

The fiddleheads, too, are noticeably three-forked. They are easily recognized, also, because of the fact that they are often found near the tangled previous year's bracken, perhaps flattened by snows. They are best when not more than five to eight inches high, while still rusty with a woolly coating. Break them off with the fingers as low as they will snap easily, remove the loose brown coatings by rubbing them between the hands, and they're ready for eating. If you like vegetables which, like okra, are mucilaginous, you'll probably enjoy a few of these raw.

The rather pleasant ropy consistency of this delicately glutinous juice is changed to a certain extent by cooking, but the sweetish fiddleheads are still reminiscent of okra. One way to enjoy fiddleheads is simmered in a little salted water until tender, then salted and peppered to taste, and eaten hot with plenty of melting butter or margarine.

Or bedeck them with a mayonnaise, perhaps homemade. You can very satisfactorily prepare this in a soup plate, if you don't happen to have a flat-bottomed bowl, by dropping in 2 egg yolks and stirring them vigorously with a fork. Then add a cup of oil, preferably olive, although any good cooking oil will do, pouring it in bit by bit and continually mixing with a fork until both ingredients, thoroughly mixed, stiffen. Blend in a tablespoon of good wine vinegar, then salt and pepper to taste. Spoon liberally over the hot fiddleheads.

A supper of fiddleheads on hot buttered toast sets just right for people who don't feel like eating much. When served this way, the little wild vegetables retain more of their delicate flavor when steamed. After they are cleaned and washed, drop them into 2 tablespoons boiling water in the top of a double boiler. Cover the utensil, place over boiling water, and cook for 30 minutes. The best way to keep on retaining the distinctive flavor is just to salt each serving lightly to individual taste, then top with a generous slab of butter or margarine.

Tender young fiddleheads can also add a lot to a mixed green salad. Oil seems to bring out the taste more in these, and we like it mixed 4 to 1 with preferably a wine vinegar, although lemon juice is good, too.

In cold regions such as Alaska, fiddleheads are often canned for opening as a winter vegetable. They delectably thicken soups. It may be well to remember, too, in case of a possible

emergency, that the long rootstocks can be roasted, peeled, and if you want, powdered Indian fashion, after which the nourishingly starchy insides may either be eaten as is or used as flour.

Sweet Fern
(*Myrica*) (*Comptonia*)

The fragrant leaves of the sweet fern were used as a tea as far back as the American Revolution. This plant is actually a shrub, partial to open fields and upland slopes where trees are sparse or absent, often forming solid stands in such habitats. It is also found to a lesser degree in open woods. Deer browse on it, and game birds and rabbits sometimes seek it out for food. It grows from the Maritimes to Saskatchewan and Minnesota, south to North Carolina, Georgia, Tennessee, and Indiana.

This sweet-scented shrub, growing from one to three feet tall, has fernlike leaves that give it its name. These are deeply divided into many roundish sections, the edges of which are usually sparingly toothed. The male flowers, about an inch in length, grow in clusters at the ends of the slim branches in catkins approximately one inch long. The female flowers grow in egg-shaped catkins. The resulting bristly round burrs envelop hard, glossy, brown little nuts. If you don't mind getting your thumbnail yellow, these are easily exposed and enjoyed, especially during June and early July while they are still tender.

The dried aromatic leaves of the sweet fern, a teaspoon to each cup of boiling water, make a very pleasant tea. When you use them fresh, just double the amount.

We've also brewed this in the sun by filling a quart bottle with cold water, adding 8 teaspoons of the fresh leaves, covering the glass with aluminum foil, and setting in the sun. The length of time required depends, of course, upon how hot the sunlight is. The several times I tried this in New Hampshire, about 3 midday hours were needed before the brew became sufficiently dark. Made this way, wild teas have no bitterness of acrid oils extracted by other methods. You can then strain it, dilute it to individual taste, and serve it with ice.

Sweet fern
Left: branch with leaves.
Right: burr.

—From *Feasting Free on Wild Edibles*

Continued ➡

Sori and Spores

Summer is the best time to look for ripe spores. You can tell which spores are ripe by the color of the sori, which will be a shiny dark brown. If the sori are white or green, the spores contained within the sporangia are immature. Withered or torn sori indicate that the spores have been dispersed.

On some ferns, the sori are covered with a thin membrane called an indusium, which can be curved, round, or long and narrow. These characteristics of the indusium vary among species and are used to help identify them. The size, shape, color, and location of the sporangia are also important clues in fern identification. The cinnamon fern has clusters of sori on separate stalks. On the ostrich fern, the sori are enveloped by leaflets with curved margins. On the bracken fern, the sori form a continuous line at the frond's edge. The wood fern has scattered rows of sori and a kidney-shaped indusium. The marsh fern has sori near the margins and a kidney-shaped indusium.

When did the spores on your fern mature? Are they on all the green leafy fronds or only on some of them? Where on the frond are they located? Are they confined to the margins of the frond, or are they along the midrib? Are they on a distinctly different fertile frond? Are the sori covered with an indusium? Describe the sporangia. Make a drawing or take a photograph of your fern, perhaps from several different angles. Keep a record of your findings in your field journal.

Remove a mature frond with shiny brown sori and place it between sheets of white paper. In a day or two, remove the top sheet carefully and pick up the frond. Spores should be present on the bottom sheet.

—From *Discover Nature in Water and Wetlands*

Plants as Food
U.S. Army

In a survival situation you should always be on the lookout for familiar wild foods and live off the land whenever possible.

You must not count on being able to go for days without food as some sources would suggest. Even in the most static survival situation, maintaining health through a complete and nutritious diet is essential to maintaining strength and peace of mind.

Nature can provide you with food that will let you survive any ordeal, if you don't eat the wrong plant. You must therefore learn as much as possible beforehand about the flora of the region where you will be operating. Plants can provide you with medicines in a survival situation. Plants can supply you with weapons and raw materials to construct shelters and build fires. Plants can even provide you with chemicals for poisoning fish, preserving animal hides, and for camouflaging yourself and your equipment.

Note: You will find illustrations of the plants described in this chapter in Appendixes B and C.

Edibility of Plants

Plants are valuable sources of food because they are widely available, easily procured, and, in the proper combinations, can meet all your nutritional needs.

Warning

The critical factor in using plants for food is to avoid accidental poisoning. Eat only those plants you can positively identify and you know are safe to eat.

Absolutely identify plants before using them as food. Poison hemlock has killed people who mistook it for its relatives, wild carrots and wild parsnips.

At times you may find yourself in a situation for which you could not plan. In this instance you may not have had the chance to learn the plant life of the region in which you must survive. In this case you can use the Universal Edibility Test to determine which plants you can eat and those to avoid.

It is important to be able to recognize both cultivated and wild edible plants in a survival situation. Most of the information in this chapter is directed towards identifying wild plants because information relating to cultivated plants is more readily available.

Remember the following when collecting wild plants for food:

- Plants growing near homes and occupied buildings or along roadsides may have been sprayed with pesticides. Wash them thoroughly. In more highly developed countries with many automobiles, avoid roadside plants, if possible, due to contamination from exhaust emissions.

- Plants growing in contaminated water or in water containing *Giardia lamblia* and other parasites are contaminated themselves. Boil or disinfect them.

- Some plants develop extremely dangerous fungal toxins. To lessen the chance of accidental poisoning, do not eat any fruit that is starting to spoil or showing signs of mildew or fungus.

- Plants of the same species may differ in their toxic or subtoxic compounds content because of genetic or environmental factors. One example of this is the foliage of the common chokecherry. Some chokecherry plants have high concentrations of deadly cyanide compounds while others have low concentrations or none. Horses have died from eating wilted wild cherry leaves. Avoid any weed, leaves, or seeds with an almondlike scent, a characteristic of the cyanide compounds.

- Some people are more susceptible to gastric distress (from plants) than others. If you are sensitive in this way, avoid unknown wild plants. If you are extremely sensitive to poison ivy, avoid products from this family, including any parts from sumacs, mangoes, and cashews.

- Some edible wild plants, such as acorns and water lily rhizomes, are bitter. These bitter substances, usually tannin compounds, make them unpalatable. Boiling them in several changes of water will usually remove these bitter properties.

- Many valuable wild plants have high concentrations of oxalate compounds, also known as oxalic acid. Oxalates produce a sharp burning sensation in your mouth and throat and damage the kidneys. Baking, roasting, or drying usually destroys these oxalate crystals. The corm (bulb) of the jack-in-the-pulpit is known as the "Indian turnip," but you can eat it only after removing these crystals by slow baking or by drying.

Warning

Do not eat mushrooms in a survival situation! The only way to tell if a mushroom is edible is by positive identification. There is no room for experimentation. Symptoms of the most dangerous mushrooms affecting the central nervous system may show up after several days have passed when it is too late to reverse their effects.

Plant Identification

You identify plants, other than by memorizing particular varieties through familiarity, by using such factors as leaf shape and margin, leaf arrangements, and root structure.

The basic leaf margins are toothed, lobed, and toothless or smooth.

These leaves may be lance-shaped, elliptical, egg-shaped, oblong, wedge-shaped, triangluar, long-pointed, or top-shaped.

The basic types of leaf arrangements are opposite, alternate, compound, simple, and basal rosette.

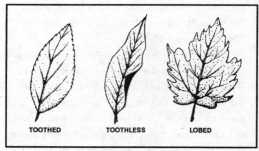

Leaf margins.

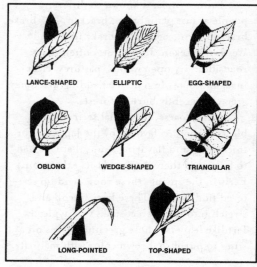

Leaf shapes.

Continued ➡

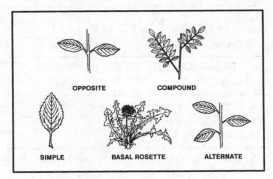

Leaf arrangements.

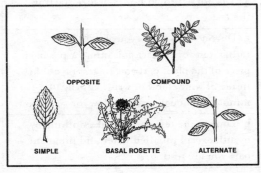

Root structures.

The basic types of root structures are the bulb, clove, taproot, tuber, rhizome, corm, and crown. Bulbs are familiar to us as onions and, when sliced in half, will show concentric rings. Cloves are those bulblike structures that remind us of garlic and will separate into small pieces when broken apart. This characteristic separates wild onions from wild garlic. Taproots resemble carrots and may be single-rooted or branched, but usually only one plant stalk arises from each root. Tubers are like potatoes and daylilies and you will find these structures either on strings or in clusters underneath the parent plants. Rhizomes are large creeping rootstocks or underground stems and many plants arise from the "eyes" of these roots. Corms are similar to bulbs but are solid when cut rather than possessing rings. A crown is the type of root structure found on plants such as asparagus and looks much like a mophead under the soil's surface.

Learn as much as possible about plants you intend to use for food and their unique characteristics. Some plants have both edible and poisonous parts. Many are edible only at certain times of the year. Others may have poisonous relatives that look very similar to the ones you can eat or use for medicine.

Universal Edibility Test

There are many plants throughout the world. Tasting or swallowing even a small portion of some can cause severe discomfort, extreme internal disorders, and even death. Therefore, if you have the slightest doubt about a plant's edibility, apply the Universal Edibility Test before eating any portion of it.

Before testing a plant for edibility, make sure there are enough plants to make the testing worth your time and effort. Each part of a plant (roots, leaves, flowers, and so on) requires more than 24 hours to test. Do not waste time testing a plant that is not relatively abundant in the area.

Remember, eating large portions of plant food on an empty stomach may cause diarrhea, nausea, or cramps. Two good examples of this

are such familiar foods as green apples and wild onions. Even after testing plant food and finding it safe, eat it in moderation.

You can see from the steps and time involved in testing for edibility just how important it is to be able to identify edible plants.

To avoid potentially poisonous plants, stay away from any wild or unknown plants that have—

- Milky or discolored sap.
- Beans, bulbs, or seeds inside pods.
- Bitter or soapy taste.
- Spines, fine hairs, or thorns.
- Dill, carrot, parsnip, or parsleylike foliage.
- "Almond" scent in woody parts and leaves.
- Grain heads with pink, purplish, or black spurs.
- Three-leaved growth pattern.

Using the above criteria as eliminators when choosing plants for the Universal Edibility Test will cause you to avoid some edible plants. More important, these criteria will often help you avoid plants that are potentially toxic to eat or touch.

An entire encyclopedia of edible wild plants could be written, but space limits the number of plants presented here. Learn as much as possible about the plant life of the areas where you train regularly and where you expect to be traveling or working. Listed below and on the following pages are some of the most common edible and medicinal plants.

TEMPERATE ZONE FOOD PLANTS

- Amaranth (*Amaranthus retroflexus* and other species)
- Arrowroot (*Sagittaria* species)
- Asparagus (*Asparagus officinalis*)
- Beechnut (*Fagus* species)
- Blackberries (*Rubus* species)
- Blueberries (*Vaccinium* species)
- Burdock (*Arctium lappa*)
- Cattail (*Typha* species)
- Chestnut (*Castanea* species)
- Chicory (*Cichorium intybus*)
- Chufa (*Cyperus esculentus*)
- Dandelion (*Taraxacum officinale*)

ALL PARTS EDIBLE

Dandelion

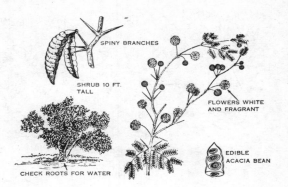

Acacia

- Daylily (*Hemerocallis fulva*)
- Nettle (*Urtica* species)
- Oaks (*Quercus* species)
- Persimmon (*Diospyros virginiana*)
- Plantain (*Plantago* species)
- Pokeweed (*Phytolacca americana*)
- Prickly pear cactus (*Opuntia* species)
- Purslane (*Portulaca oleracea*)
- Sassafras (*Sassafras albidum*)
- Sheep sorrel (*Rumex acetosella*)
- Strawberries (*Fragaria* species)
- Thistle (*Cirsium* species)
- Water lily and lotus (*Nuphar, Nelumbo,* and other species)
- Wild onion and garlic (*Allium* species)
- Wild rose (*Rosa* species)
- Wood sorrel (*Oxalis* species)

TROPICAL ZONE FOOD PLANTS

- Bamboo (*Bambusa* and other species)
- Bananas (*Musa* species)
- Breadfruit (*Artocarpus incisa*)
- Cashew nut (*Anacardium occidentale*)
- Coconut (*Cocos nucifera*)
- Mango (*Mangifera indica*)
- Palms (various species)
- Papaya (*Carica* species)
- Sugarcane (*Saccharum officinarum*)
- Taro (*Colocasia* species)

DESERT ZONE FOOD PLANTS

- Acacia (*Acacia farnesiana*)
- Agave (*Agave* species)
- Cactus (various species)
- Date palm (*Phoenix dactylifera*)
- Desert amaranth (*Amaranthus palmeri*)

Seaweeds

One plant you should never overlook is seaweed. It is a form of marine algae found on or near ocean shores. There are also some edible freshwater varieties. Seaweed is a valuable source of iodine, other minerals, and vitamin C. Large quantities of seaweed in an unaccustomed stomach can produce a severe laxative effect.

Continued ➡

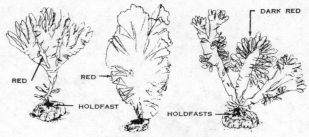

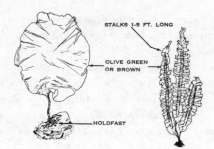

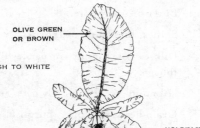

RED

RED

HOLDFAST

HOLDFASTS

DARK RED

THREE FORMS OF DULSE

Dulse.

STALKS 1-5 FT. LONG

OLIVE GREEN OR BROWN

HOLDFAST

Sugar wrack.

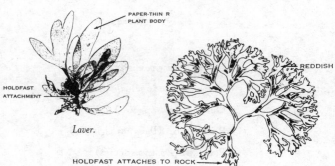

PAPER-THIN R PLANT BODY

HOLDFAST ATTACHMENT

Laver.

HOLDFAST ATTACHES TO ROCK

Irish moss.

OLIVE GREEN OR BROWN

REDDISH TO WHITE

HOLDFAST

Kelp.

When gathering seaweeds for food, find living plants attached to rocks or floating free. Seaweed washed onshore any length of time may be spoiled or decayed. You can dry freshly harvested seaweeds for later use.

Its preparation for eating depends on the type of seaweed. You can dry thin and tender varieties in the sun or over a fire until crisp. Crush and add these to soups or broths. Boil thick, leathery seaweeds for a short time to soften them. Eat them as a vegetable or with other foods. You can eat some varieties raw after testing for edibility.

Seaweeds

- Dulse (*Rhodymenia palmata*)
- Green seaweed (*Ulva lactuca*)
- Irish moss (*Chondrus crispus*)
- Kelp (*Alaria esculenta*)
- Laver (*Porphyra* species)
- Mojaban (*Sargassum fulvellum*)
- Sugar wrack (*Laminaria saccharina*)

Preparation of Plant Food

Although some plants or plant parts are edible raw, you must cook others to be edible or palatable. Edible means that a plant or food will provide you with necessary nutrients, while palatable means that it actually is pleasing to eat. Many wild plants are edible but barely palatable. It is a good idea to learn to identify, prepare, and eat wild foods.

Methods used to improve the taste of plant food include soaking, boiling, cooking, or leaching. Leaching is done by crushing the food (for example, acorns), placing it in a strainer,

---

The Berry Rule

Greg Davenport
Illustration by Steven A. Davenport

In general, the edibility of berries can be classified according to their color and composition. The following is a guideline (approximation) to help you determine if a berry is poisonous. In no way should the berry rule replace the edibility test. Use it as a general guide to determine whether the edibility test needs to be performed upon the berry. The only berries that should be eaten without testing are those that you can positively identify as nonpoisonous.

Aggregate berries are 99 percent edible.

- Green, yellow, and white berries are 10 percent edible.
- Red berries are 50 percent edible.
- Purple, blue, and black berries are 90 percent edible.
- Aggregate berries such as thimbleberries, raspberries, and blackberries are considered 99 percent edible.

—From *Wilderness Living*

How to Eat Bark

U.S. Army

The inner bark of a tree—the layer next to the wood—may be eaten raw or cooked. You can even make flour from the inner bark of cottonwood, aspen, birch, willow, and pine tree by pulverizing it. Avoid the outer bark because of the presence of large amounts of tannin.

Pine bark is rich in vitamin C. Scrape away the outer bark and strip the inner bark from the trunk. Eat it fresh, dried, or cooked, or pulverize it into flour.

—From *Survival (U.S. Army Field Manual 21–76)*

Universal Edibility Test

U.S. Army

1. Test only one part of a potential food plant at a time.

2. Separate the plant into its basic components—leaves, stems, roots, buds, and flowers.

3. Smell the food for strong or acid odors. Remember, smell alone does not indicate a plant is edible or inedible.

4. Do not eat for 8 hours before starting the test.

5. During the 8 hours you abstain from eating, test for contact poisoning by placing a piece of the plant part you are testing on the inside of your elbow or wrist. Usually 15 minutes is enough time to allow for a reaction.

6. During the test period, take nothing by mouth except purified water and the plant part you are testing.

7. Select a small portion of a single part and prepare it the way you plan to eat it.

8. Before placing the prepared plant part in your mouth, touch a small portion (a pinch) to the outer surface of your lip to test for burning or itching.

9. If after 3 minutes there is no reaction on your lip, place the plant part on your tongue, holding it there for 15 minutes.

10. If there is no reaction, thoroughly chew a pinch and hold it in your mouth for 15 minutes. **Do not swallow.**

11. If no burning, itching, numbing, stinging, or other irritation occurs during the 15 minutes, swallow the food.

12. Wait 8 hours. If any ill effects occur during this period, induce vomiting and drink a lot of water.

13. If no ill effects occur, eat 0.25 cup of the same plant part prepared the same way. Wait another 8 hours. If no ill effects occur, the plant part as prepared is safe for eating.

Caution

Test all parts of the plant for edibility, as some plants have both edible and inedible parts. Do not assume that a part that proved edible when cooked is also edible when raw. Test the part raw to ensure edibility before eating raw. The same part or plant may produce varying reactions in different individuals.

—From *Survival (Field Manual 21–76)*

Continued ➡

and pouring boiling water through it or immersing it in running water.

Boil leaves, stems, and buds until tender, changing the water, if necessary, to remove any bitterness.

Boil, bake, or roast tubers and roots. Drying helps to remove caustic oxalates from some roots like those in the *Arum* family.

Leach acorns in water, if necessary, to remove the bitterness. Some nuts, such as chestnuts, are good raw, but taste better roasted.

You can eat many grains and seeds raw until they mature. When hard or dry, you may have to boil or grind them into meal or flour.

The sap from many trees, such as maples, birches, walnuts, and sycamores, contains sugar. You may boil these saps down to a syrup for sweetening. It takes about 35 liters of maple sap to make one liter of maple syrup!

—From *Survival (Field Manual 21–70)*

EDIBLE PARTS OF A PLANT
Gregory J. Davenport

Some plants are completely edible whereas others have both edible and poisonous parts. Unless you have performed the edibility test on the whole plant—only eat the parts that you know are edible. A plant can be broken down into several distinct components (underground; stems and leaves; flowers, fruits, nuts, and seeds; and grains). In addition, some plants provide gums, resins, and saps that are edible.

Underground (Tubers, Roots and Rootstocks, and Bulbs)
Found underground these plant parts have a high degree of starch and are best served baked or boiled. Some examples of these are potatoes (tuber), cattail (root and rootstock), and wild onion (bulbs).

Stems and Leaves (Shoots/Stems, Leaves, Pith, and Cambium)
Plants that produce stems and leaves are probably the most abundant source of edible vegetation in the world. Their high vitamin content makes them a valuable component of our daily diet.

Shoots grow like asparagus and are best when parboiled (boiled five minutes, drained off, and boiled again until done). Some examples are bracken fern (only to be eaten in moderation), young bamboo, and cattail. Leaves may be eaten raw or cooked but they provide the highest nutritional value when eaten raw. Dock, plantain, amaranth, and sorrel are a few examples of edible leaves. Pith, found inside the stem of some plants, is often very high in food value. Some examples are sago, rattan, coconut, and sugar. Cambium is the inner layer found between the bark and the wood of a tree. It can be eaten raw, cooked, or dried and then pulverized into flour.

Flowers (Flowers, Buds, and Pollens)
Flowers, buds, and pollens are high in food value and are best when eaten raw or in a salad. Some examples include hibiscus (flower), rose hips (buds), and cattail (pollen).

Fruits (Sweet and Nonsweet)
Fruits are the seed-bearing part of a plant and can be found in all areas of the world. Best when eaten raw (retaining all their nutritional value), they may also be cooked. Examples of sweet fruits are apples, prickly pears, huckleberries, and wild strawberries. Examples of nonsweet fruits include tomatoes, cucumbers, plantains, and horseradishes.

Nuts
Nuts are high in fat and protein and can be found around the whole world. Most can be eaten raw but some, like acorns, require leaching with several changes of water to remove their tannic acid content.

Seeds and Grains
The seeds and grains of many plants—such as grasses and millet—are a valuable food resource and should not be overlooked. They are best eaten when ground into flour or roasted.

Gums and Resins
Gums and resins are sap that collects on the outside of trees and plants. Their high nutritional value makes them a great augmentation to any meal. Examples can be found on pine and maple trees.

Plants are an abundant food source that should be a major part of your daily diet. If you don't know if it's edible, however, don't eat it without either positively identifying it or performing an edibility test on one or all of its various parts. Become familiar with plants indigenous to your area.

Caution:
If unable to identify a plant DO NOT eat it without first performing the edibility test.

—From *Wilderness Living*

A Selection of Edible Plants
Bradford Angier

Acorns

(*Quercus*)

There is no need for anyone to starve where acorns abound, and from 200 to 500 oaks (botanists differ) grow in the world. Some eighty-five of these are native to the United States. Although some of the latter species are scrubby, the genus includes some of our biggest and most stately trees. Furthermore, except in our northern prairies, oaks are widely distributed throughout the contiguous states, thriving at various altitudes and in numerous types of soil.

Abundant and substantial, acorns are perhaps this country's most important wildlife food. The relatively tiny acorns of the willow oak, pin oak, and water oak are often obtainable near streams and ponds, where they are relished by mallards, wood ducks, pintails, and other waterfowl. Quail devour such small acorns and peck the kernels out of the larger nuts.

Pheasants, grouse, pigeons, doves, and prairie chickens enjoy the nuts as well as the buds. Wild turkeys gulp down whole acorns regardless of their size. Squirrels and chipmunks are among the smaller animals storing acorns for off-season use. Black-tailed mule and white-tailed deer, elk, peccaries, and mountain sheep enjoy the acorns and also browse on twigs and foliage. Black bears grow fat on acorns.

Acorns probably rated the top position on the long list of wild foods depended on by the Indians. It has been stated, for example, that acorn soup, or mush, was the chief daily food of more than three-quarters of the native Californians. The eastern settlers were early introduced to acorns, too. In 1620 during their first hungry winter in Plymouth, the Pilgrims were fortunate enough to discover baskets of roasted acorns which the Indians had buried in the ground. In parts of Mexico and in Europe, the natives today still use acorns in the old ways.

All acorns are good to eat. Some are less sweet than others, that's all. But the bitterness that is prevalent in different degrees is due to tannin, the same ingredient that causes tea to be bitter. Although it is not digestible in large amounts, it is soluble in water. Therefore, even the bitterest acorns can be made edible in an emergency.

Oaks comprise the most important group of hardwood timber trees on this continent. A major proportion of our eastern forests is oak. Its dense, durable wood has many commercial uses. Furthermore, oaks are among the most popular shade trees along our streets and about our dwellings.

The oaks may be separated into two great groups: the white oaks and the red oaks. The acorns of the former are the sweet ones. They mature in one growing season. The inner surfaces of the shells are smooth. The leaves typically have rounded lobes, but they are never bristle-tipped. The bark is ordinarily grayish and is generally scaly.

Among the red oaks, the usually bitter acorns do not mature until the end of the second growing season. The inner surfaces of the shells are customarily coated with woolly hair. The leaves have distinct bristles at their tips or at the tops of their lobes. The typically dark bark is ordinarily furrowed.

Indians used acorns both by themselves and in combination with other foods. For example, the Digger Indians roasted their acorns from the western white oak, *Quercus lobata*, hulled them, and ground them into a coarse meal which they formed into cakes and baked in crude ovens. In

Eastern white oak.

Continued ➡

the East, the acorns of the white oak, *Quercus alba*, were also ground into meal but then were often mixed with the available cornmeal before being shaped into cakes and baked. Roasted and ground white oak acorns provide one of the wilderness coffees.

Indians leached their bitter acorns in a number of ways. Sometimes the acorns would be buried in swamp mud for a year, after which they would be ready for roasting and eating whole. Other tribes let their shelled acorns mold in baskets, then buried them in clean freshwater sand. When they had turned black, they were sweet and ready for use.

Some tribes ground their acorns by pounding them in stone pestles, many of which are found today, and then ran water through the meal by one method or another for often the greater part of a day until it was sweet. The meal might be placed in a specially woven basket for this purpose, or it might just be buried in the sandy bed of a stream.

To make the familiar, somewhat sweetish soup or gruel of the results, all that is necessary is to heat the meal in water. The Indians generally used no seasoning. As a matter of fact, until the white man came they ordinarily had no utensils but closely woven baskets. These were flammable, of course, and the heating had to be done by putting in rocks heated in campfires. Still showing how little one can get along with, the tribe then ate from common baskets, using their fingers.

It's an easy thing to leach acorns today. Just shell your nuts and boil them whole in a kettle of water, changing the liquid every time it becomes yellowish. You can shorten the time necessary for this to as little as a couple of hours, depending of course on the particular acorns, if you keep a teakettle of water always heating on the stove while this process is continuing. The acorns can then be dried in a slow oven, with the door left ajar, and either eaten as is or ground into coarse bits for use like any other nuts or into a fine meal.

To make acorn cakes, mix 2 cups of the meal with 1/2 teaspoon salt and 3/4 cup of water to form a stiff batter. This will be improved if you let it stand at room temperature for about an hour before turning it into the skillet.

Heat 3 tablespoons cooking oil in a large frypan until a test drop of water will sizzle. Drop the batter from a tablespoon, using a greased spatula to shape cakes a bit over 3 inches in diameter. Reduce the heat and tan the cakes slowly on each side. They are good either hot or cold.

For acorn pancakes for two, combine a cup of acorn meal and a cup of regular flour with 2 tablespoons sugar, 3 teaspoons double-action baking powder, and 1/2 teaspoon salt. Beat 2 eggs, 1 1/2 cups milk, and 2 tablespoons liquid shortening. Get your preferably heavy frypan or griddle hot, short of smoking temperature, and grease it sparingly with bacon.

When everything is ready to go, mix the whole business very briefly into a thin batter. Overmixing will make these tough. For this reason, a slightly lumpy batter is preferable to one that's beaten smooth. Turn each hotcake only once, when the flapjack starts showing small bubbles. The second side will take only half as long to cook. Serve steaming hot with butter or margarine and sugar, maple syrup, or one of the wild jellies.

We think of antibiotics as modern developments, but some of the Indian tribes used to let their acorn meal accumulate a mold. This was scraped off, kept in a damp place, and used to treat sores and inflammations.

Birch
(*Betula*)

The nutritious bark of the black birch is said to have probably saved the lives of scores of Confederate soldiers during Garnett's retreat over the mountains to Monterey, Virginia. For years afterward, the way the soldiers went could be followed by the peeled birch trees.

The black birch may be identified at all times of the year by its tight, reddish-brown, cherrylike bark, which has the aroma and flavor of wintergreen. Smooth in young trees, this darkens and separates into large, irregular sections as these birches age. The darkly dull green leaves, paler and yellower beneath, are two to four inches long, oval to oblong, short-stemmed, silky when young, smooth when mature, with double-toothed edges. They give off an odor of wintergreen when bruised. The trees have both erect and hanging catkins, on twigs that also taste and smell like wintergreen.

Black birch.

In fact, when the commercial oil of wintergreen is not made synthetically, it is distilled from the twigs and bark of the black birch. This oil is exactly the same as that from the little wintergreen plant, described earlier.

Black birches enhance the countryside from New England to Ontario, south to Ohio and Delaware, and along the Appalachian Mountains to Georgia and Alabama.

A piquant tea, brisk with wintergreen, is made from the young twigs, young leaves, the thick inner bark, and the bark from the larger roots. This latter reddish bark, easily stripped off in the spring and early summer, can be dried at room temperatures and stored in sealed jars in a cool place for later use. A teaspoon to a cup of boiling water, set off the heat and allowed to steep for 5 minutes, makes a tea that is delicately spicy. Milk and sugar make it even better. As a matter of fact, any of the birches make good tea.

You can make syrup and sugar from the sap, too, as from the sap of all birches. I'll never forget my first introduction to this. It was our first spring in the paper birch country of the Far North, and Vena and I were bemoaning the fact that there were no maples from which to tap sap for our sourdough pancakes.

"Birch syrup you can get here in copious amounts," Dudley Shaw, a trapper and our nearest neighbor, informed Vena. "Heavenly concoction. It'll cheer Brad up vastly."

"Oh, will you show me how?"

"I'll stow a gimlet in my pack when I prowl up this way the first of the week to retrieve a couple of traps that got frozen in," Dudley agreed. "Noble lap, birch syrup is. Glorious in flippers."

Dudley told us to get some containers. Lard pails would do, he said, or we could attach some wire bails through nail holes in the tops of several tomato cans. He beamed approval when he arrived early Tuesday morning. The improvised sap buckets, suspended on nails driven above the small holes Dudley bored with his gimlet, caught a dripping flow of watery fluid.

"You'd better ramble out this way regularly to see these don't overflow," Dudley cautioned. "Keep the emptied sap simmering cheerfully on the back of the stove. Tons of steam have to come off."

"Will it hurt the trees any?" Vena asked anxiously.

"No, no," Dudley said reassuringly. "The plunder will begin to bog down when the day cools, anyway. Then we'll whittle out pegs and drive them in to close the blinking holes. Everything will be noble."

Everything was, especially the birch syrup. It wasn't as thick as it might have been, even after all that boiling. There was a distressingly small amount of it, too. But what remained from the day's work was sweet, spicy, and poignantly delicious. What we drank beforehand, too, was refreshing, sweet, and provocatively spicy.

All the birches furnish prime emergency food. Two general varieties of the trees grow across the continent, the black birch and those similar to it, and the familiar white birches whose cheerful foliage and softly gleaming bark lighten the northern forests. Layer after layer of this latter bark can be easily stripped off in great sheets, although because of the resulting disfigurement this shouldn't be done except in an emergency, and used to start a campfire in any sort of weather.

The inner bark, dried and then ground into flour, has often been used by Indians and frontiersmen for bread. It is also cut into strips and boiled like noodles in stews. But you don't need to go even to that much trouble. Just eat it raw.

Burdock
(*Arctium*)

This member of the thistle family marched across Europe with the Roman legions, sailed to the New World with the early settlers, and the now thrives throughout much of the Unites States and southern Canada. A topnotch wild food, it has the added advantages of being familiar and of not being easily mistaken.

The somewhat unpleasant associations with its name are, at the same time, a disadvantage when it comes to bringing this aggressive but delicious immigrant to the table. Muskrats are sold in some markets as swamp rabbits, while crows find buyers as rooks. But unfortunately in this country burdock is usually just burdock, despite the fact that varieties of it are especially cultivated as prized domestic vegetables in Japan and elsewhere in the Eastern Hemisphere.

Burdock is found almost everywhere it can be close to people and domestic animals—along roads, fences, stone walls, and in yards, vacant lots, and especially around old barns and stables.

Continued ➔

Its sticky burrs, which attach themselves cosily to man and beast, are familiar nuisances.

Burdock.

The burdock is a coarse biennial weed which, with its branches, rapidly grows to from two to six feet high. The large leaves, growing on long stems, are shaped something like oblong hearts and are rough and purplish with veins. Tiny, tubular, usually magenta flowers appear from June to November, depending on the locality, the second year. These form the prickly stickers, which actually, of course, are the seed pods.

No one need stay hungry very long where the burdock grows, for this versatile edible will furnish a number of different delicacies. It is for the roots, for instance, that they are grown by Japanese throughout the Orient. Only the first-year roots should be used, but these are easy to distinguish as the biennials stemming from them have no flower and burr stalks. We get all we can use from the sides of our horses' corral, where they are easily disengaged. When found in hard ground, however, the deep, slender roots are harder to come by, although they are worth quite a bit of effort.

The tender pith of the root, exposed by peeling, will make an unusually good potherb if sliced like parsnips and simmered for 20 minutes in water to which about 1/4 teaspoon baking soda has been added. Then drain, barely cover with fresh boiling water, add a teaspoon of salt, and cook until tender. Serve with butter or margarine spreading on top.

If caught early enough, the young leaves can be boiled in 2 waters and served as greens. If you're hungry, the peeled young leaf stalks are good raw, especially with a little salt. These are also added to green salads and to vegetable soups and are cooked by themselves like asparagus.

It is the rapidly growing flower stalk that furnishes one of the tastier parts of the burdock. When these sprout up the second year, watch them so that you can cut them off just as the blossom heads are starting to appear in late spring or early summer. Every shred of the strong, bitter skin must be peeled off. Then cook the remaining thick, succulent interiors in 2 waters, as you would the roots, and serve hot with butter or margarine.

The pith of the flower stalks has long been used, too, for a candy. One way to make this is by cutting the whitish cores into bite-size sections. Boil these for 15 minutes in water to which 1/4 teaspoon baking soda has been added. Drain. Heat what you judge to be an approximately equal weight of sugar in enough hot water to dissolve it, and then add the juice of an orange. Put in the burdock pieces, cook slowly until the syrup is nearly evaporated, drain, and roll in granulated sugar. This never lasts for very long.

The first-year roots, dug either in the fall or early spring, are also used back of beyond as a healing wash for burns, wounds, and skin irritations. One way to make this is by dropping 4

teaspoons of the root into a quart of boiling water and allowing this to stand until cool.

Butternut

(Juglans)

Confederate soldiers and partisans were referred to as butternuts during the Civil War because of the brown homespun clothes of the military, often dyed with the green nut husks and the inner bark of these familiar trees. Some of the earliest American settlers made the same use of them. As far back as the Revolution, a common laxative was made of the inner bark, a spoonful of finely cut pieces to a cup of boiling water, drunk cold. Indians preceded the colonists in boiling down the sap of this tree, as well as that of the black walnut, to make syrup and sugar, sometimes mixing the former with maple syrup.

The butternut thrives in chillier climates than does the black walnut, ranging higher in the mountains and further north. Otherwise, this tree, also known as white walnut and oilnut, closely resembles its cousin except for being smaller and lighter colored. Its wood is comparatively soft, weak, and light, although still close-grained. The larger trees, furthermore, are nearly always unsound.

Butternuts grow from the Maritime Provinces to Ontario, south to the northern mountainous regions of Georgia and Alabama, and west to Arkansas, Kansas, and the Dakotas. They are medium-sized trees, ordinarily from about thirty to fifty feet high, with a

Butternut.

trunk diameter of up to three feet. Some trees, though, tower up to ninety feet or more. The furrowed and broadly ridged bark is gray.

The alternate compound leaves are from fifteen to thirty inches long. Each one is made up of eleven to seventeen lance-shaped, nearly stemless leaflets, two to six inches long and about half as broad, with sharply pointed tips, sawtoothed edges, and unequally rounded bases. Yellowish green on top, these are paler and softly downy underneath. The catkins and the shorter flower spikes appear in the spring when the leaves are about half grown.

The nuts are oblong rather than round, blunt, about two to two and a half inches long, and a bit more than half as thick. Thin husks, notably sticky and coated with matted rusty hairs, enclose the nuts whose bony shells are roughly ridged, deeply furrowed, and hard. Frequently growing in small clusters of two to five, these ripen in October and soon drop from the branches.

The young nuts, when they have nearly reached their full size, can be picked green and used for pickles which bring out the flavor of meat like few other things and which really attract notice as hors d'oeuvres. If you can still easily shove a large needle through the nuts, it is not too late to pickle them, husks and all, after they have been scalded and the outer fuzz rubbed off.

Put them in a strong brine for a week, changing the water every other day and keeping them tightly covered. Then drain and wipe them. Pierce each nut all the way through several times with a large needle. Then put them in glass jars with a sprinkling of powdered ginger, nutmeg, mace, and cloves between each layer. Bring some good cider vinegar to a boil, immediately fill each jar, and seal. You can start enjoying this unusual delicacy in two weeks.

A noteworthy dessert can be made with butternuts by mixing 1/2 cup of the broken meats with 1 cup diced dates, 1 cup sugar, 1 teaspoon baking powder, and 1/8 teaspoon salt. Beat 4 egg whites until they are stiff and fold them into the above mixture. Bake in a greased pan in a slow oven for 20 minutes. Serve either hot or cold with whipped cream. This is also good, particularly when hot, with liberal scoops of vanilla ice cream.

Butternut and date pie is something special. Chop a cup apiece of dates and nuts. Roll a dozen ordinary white crackers into small bits, too. Mix with 1 cup sugar and 1/2 teaspoon baking powder. Then beat 3 egg whites until they are stiff. Sometimes, if the nuts are not as tasty as usual, we also add a teaspoon of almond extract. In either event, fold into the nut mixture and pour into a buttered 9-inch pie pan. Bake 1/2 hour, or until light brown, in a moderate oven. Cool before cutting. Ice or whipped cream is good with this, too, but it is also delicately tasty alone.

Butternut brownies, eaten by the nibble and washed down with draughts of steaming black tea, are one of the ways I like to top off my noonday lunches when hunting in the late fall. Just blend together 1 cup sugar, 1 teaspoon salt, 1/2 cup melted butter or margarine, 2 squares bitter chocolate, 1 teaspoon vanilla, and 3 eggs. When this is thoroughly mixed, stir into it 1 cup finely broken butternuts and 1/2 cup flour. Pour into a shallow greased pan and bake in a moderate oven 20 minutes.

Cattail

(Typhaceae)

Who does not know these tall strap-leaved plants with their brown sausagelike heads which, growing in large groups from two to nine feet high, are exclamation points in wet places throughout the temperate and tropical countries of the world?

Although now relatively unused in the United States, where four species thrive, cattails are deliciously edible both raw and cooked from their starchy roots to their cornlike spikes, making them prime emergency foods. Furthermore, the long slender basal leaves, dried and then soaked to make them pliable, provide rush seating for chairs, as well as

Cattail
Left: leaves, head, and flower spike.
Right: basal leaves and root.

Continued →

tough material for mats. As for the fluff of light-colored seeds, which enliven many a winter wind, these will softly fill pillows and provide warm stuffing for comforters.

Cattails are also known in some places as rushes, cossack asparagus, bulrushes, cat-o'-nine-tails, and flags. Sure signs of fresh or brackish water, they are tall, stout-stemmed perennials with thin, stiff, swordlike, green leaves up to six feet long. These have well-developed, round rims at the sheathing bases.

The branched rootstocks creep in crossing tangles a few inches below the usually muddy surface. The flowers grow densely at the tops of the plants in spikes which, first plumply green and finally a shriveling yellow, resemble long bottle brushes and eventually produce millions of tiny, wind-wafted seeds.

These seeds, it so happens, are too small and hairy to be very attractive to birds except to a few like the teal. It is the starchy underground stems that attract such wildlife as muskrat and geese. Too, I've seen moose dipping their huge, ungainly heads where cattails grow.

Another name for this prolific wild edible should be wild corn. Put on boots and have the fun of collecting a few dozen of the greenish yellow flower spikes before they start to become tawny with pollen. Husk off the thin sheaths and, just as you would with the garden vegetable, put while still succulent into rapidly boiling water for a few minutes until tender. Have plenty of butter or margarine by each plate, as these will probably be somewhat roughly dry, and keep each hot stalk liberally swabbed as you feast on it. Eat like corn. You'll end up with a stack of wiry cobs, feeling deliciously satisfied.

Some people object to eating corn on the cob, too, especially when there is company. This problem can be solved by scraping the boiled flower buds from the cobs, mixing 4 cups of these with 2 cups buttered bread crumbs, 2 well-beaten eggs, 1 teaspoon salt, 1/8 teaspoon pepper, and a cup of rich milk. Pour into a casserole, sprinkle generously with paprika, and heat in a moderate oven 15 minutes.

These flower spikes later become profusely golden with thick yellow pollen which, quickly rubbed or shaken into pails or onto a cloth, is also very much edible. A common way to take advantage of this gilded substance, which can be easily cleaned by passing it through a sieve, is by mixing it half and half with regular flour in breadstuffs.

For example, the way to make pleasingly golden cattail pancakes for 4 is by sifting together 1 cup pollen, 1 cup flour, 2 teaspoons baking powder, 2 tablespoons sugar, and 1/2 teaspoon salt. Beat 2 eggs and stir them into 1 1/3 cups milk, adding 2 tablespoons melted butter or margarine. Then rapidly mix the batter. Pour at once in cakes the size of saucers onto a sparingly greased griddle, short of being smoking hot. Turn each flapjack only once, when the hot cake starts showing small bubbles. The second side takes only about half as long to cook. Serve steaming hot with butter and sugar, with syrup, or with what you will.

It is the tender white insides of about the first 1 or 1 1/2 feet of the peeled young stems that, eaten either raw or cooked, lends this worldwide delicacy its name of cossack asparagus. These highly eatable aquatic herbs can thus be an important survival food in the spring.

Later on, in the fall and winter, quantities of the nutritiously starchy roots can be dug and washed, peeled white still wet, dried, and then ground into a meal which can be sifted to get out any fibers. Too, there is a pithy little tidbit where the new stems sprout out of the rootstocks that can be roasted or boiled like young potatoes. All in all, is it any wonder that the picturesque cattails, now too often neglected except by nesting birds, were once an important Indian food?

Chokecherry

(*Prunus*)

Perhaps the most widely distributed tree on this continent, the chokecherry grows from the Arctic Circle to Mexico and from ocean to ocean. Despite their puckery quality, one handful of the small ripe berries seems to call for another when you're hot and thirsty. The fruit, which is both red or black, also makes on enjoyable tart jelly.

Often merely a large shrub, the chokecherry also becomes a small tree up to twenty-five feet tall with a trunk about eight inches through. It is found in open woods, but is more often seen on streambanks, in thickets in the corners of fields, and along roadsides and fences. Although the wood is similar to that of the rum cherry, it has no commercial value because of its smallness.

Chokecherry leaves, from two to four inches long and about half as wide, are oval or inversely ovate, with abrupt points. They are thin and smooth, dull dark green above and paler below. The edges are finely indented with narrowly pointed teeth. The short stems, less than an inch in length, have a pair of glands at their tops. The long clusters of flowers blossom when the leaves are nearly grown. The red to black fruits, the size of peas, are frequently so abundant that the limbs bend under their weight.

Chokecherry
Left: flowering branch. Center: branch with leaves and fruit. Right: winter twig

An attractive and tasty jelly is made by adding 2 parts of cooked applejuice to 1 part of cooked chokecherry juice and proceeding as with rum cherry jelly. Too, a pure version can also be prepared with the help of commercial pectin.

Any of these tart wild cherry jellies can be used to flavor pies. Start by lightly beating 3 eggs. Mix 1 cup sugar, 1/4 teaspoon salt, and 1/4 teaspoon nutmeg, and add slowly to the eggs, continuing to beat. Melt 1/2 cup of butter or margarine and add that, too. Then thoroughly stir in 1 tablespoon of your jelly. Pour into an unbaked pie crust. Place in a preheated moderate oven for 10 minutes. Then reduce the heat to slow for 15 minutes, or until it firms.

Chufa

(*Cyperus*)

Chufa was so valued as a nutriment during early centuries that as long as 4,000 years ago the Egyptians were including it among the choice foods placed in their tombs. Wildlife was enjoying it long before that. Both the edible tubers of this plant, also known as earth almond and as nut grass, and the seeds are sought by waterfowl, upland game birds, and other wildlife. Often abundant in mud flats that glisten with water in the late fall and early winter, the nutritious tubers are readily accessible to duck. Where chufa occurs as a robust weed in other places, especially in sandy soil and loam, upland game birds and rodents are seen vigorously digging for the tubers.

Abounding from Mexico to Alaska, and from one coast to the other, this edible sedge also grows in Europe, Asia, and Africa, being cultivated in some localities for its tubers. Sweet, nutty, and milky with juice, these are clustered about the base of the plant, particularly when it grows in sandy or loose soil where a few tugs will give a hungry man his dinner. In hard dirt, the nuts are widely scattered as well as being difficult to excavate. Except for several smaller leaves at the top of the stalk supporting the flower clusters, all the light green, grasslike leaves of the chufa grow

Chufa.

from the roots. These latter are comprised of long runners, terminating in little nutlike tubers. The numerous flowers grow in little, flat, yellowish spikes.

Chufa furnishes one of the wild coffees. Just separate the little tubers from their roots, wash them, and spread them out to dry. Then roast them in an oven with the door ajar until they are rich brown throughout, grind them as in the blender, and brew and serve like the store-bought beverage. So prepared, chufa tastes more like a cereal "coffee" than like the regular brew. But it is wholesome, pleasant, and it contains none of the sleep-retarding ingredients of the commercial grinds.

All you have to do is wash and eat chufas, but if you are going to have a wild-foods dinner for guests, why not go one step further and have some really different chips to serve with your dip during the cocktail hour? The chufas first have to be very well dried, as in a slow oven, then ground to powder as in the ubiquitous blender. This powder can be mixed with regular wheat flour for all sorts of appetizing vitamin-and-mineral-rich cakes, breads, and cookies.

For these chips, which resemble fat little pillows, sift together a cup of powdered chufa, a cup of all-purpose flour, 3 teaspoons baking powder, and a teaspoon of salt. Then cut in 2 tablespoons of shortening with a pastry blender or a pair of knives. Not wasting any time, work in 3/4 cup of cold water bit by bit to make your dough. Roll this out as thinly as you can. Cut

Continued ➡

into 2-inch squares and fry these one by one in hot fat. They'll puff as they bronze. If you'll turn them, the other side will expand, too. Drain the some 30 resulting chips on paper toweling. They are particularly tasty, by the way, in an avocado and tomato dip touched up with grated wild onion.

The Spanish make a refreshing cold drink from the chufa, enjoyed both as is and as a base for stronger concoctions. A popular alcoholic drink is made by partially freezing this beverage in the refrigerator, then adding an equal volume of light rum to make a sort of wild frozen Daiquiri. The Spanish recipe calls for soaking $^1/_2$ pound of the well-washed tubers for 2 days. Then drain them and either mash them or put them through the blender along with 4 cups of water and $^1/_3$ cup sugar. Strain the white, milky results, and you're in business.

Europeans in the Mediterranean area, northward as far as Great Britain, used to make a conserve of chufa that is still very much worth the trouble. Again, begin by soaking the scrubbed tubers for 2 days in cold water. You'll need a quart of the drained vegetables for this recipe.

Make a syrup by boiling together a cup of sugar, a cup of corn syrup, and 1 $^2/_3$ cups of water for 10 minutes. Add the drained chufas. Simmer, stirring occasionally, until the tubers are tender and the syrup thickened. Then take off the stove. Cover and let stand overnight. The next day, reheat to boiling. Pack the chufas in hot, sterile pint jars. Bring the liquid once more to a boil and pour it over the chufas, filling the jars to within $^1/_2$ inch of their tops. Seal at once, cover if necessary to protect from drafts, allow to cool, label, and store.

Clover

(*Trifolium*)

Everyone who as a youngster has sucked honey from the tiny tubular florets of its white, yellow, and reddish blossoms, or who has searched among its green beds for the elusive four-leaf combinations, knows the clover. Some seventy-five species of clover grow in this country, about twenty of them thriving in the East.

Clovers, which are avidly pollinated by bees, grow from an inch or so to two feet high in the fields, pastures, meadows, open woods, and along roadsides of the continent. Incidentally, when introduced into Australia, it failed to reproduce itself until bumblebees were also imported.

The stemmed foliage is usually composed of three small leaflets with toothed edges, although some of the western species boast as many as six or seven leaflets. This sweet-scented member of the pea family provides esteemed livestock forage. Red clover is Vermont's state flower. White clover is all the more familiar for being grown in lawns. Quail are among the birds eating the small, hard seeds, while deer, mountain sheep, antelope, rabbit, and other animals browse on the plants.

Bread made from the seeds and dried blossoms of clover has the reputation of being very wholesome and nutritious and of sometimes being a mainstay in times of famine. Being so widely known and plentiful, clover is certainly a potential survival food that can be invaluable in an emergency.

The young leaves and flowers are good raw. Some Indians, eating them in quantity, used to dip these first in salted water. The young leaves and blossoms can also be successfully boiled, and they can be steamed as the Indians used to do before drying them for winter use.

Clover

If you're steaming greens for 2 couples, melt 4 tablespoons of butter or margarine in a large, heavy frypan over high heat. Stir in 6 loosely packed cups of greens and blossoms, along with 6 tablespoons of water. Cover, except when stirring periodically, and cook for several minutes until the clover is wilted. Salt, pepper, and eat.

The sweetish roots may also be appreciated on occasion, some people liking them best when they have been dipped in oil or in meat drippings.

Clover tea is something you may very well enjoy. Gather the fullgrown flowers at a time when they are dry. Then further dry them indoors at ordinary house temperatures, afterwards rubbing them into small particles and sealing them in bottles or jars to hold in the flavor. Use 1 teaspoon of these to each cup of boiling water, brewing either in a teapot or in individual cups, as you would oriental tea.

Cowslip

(*Caltha*)

The glossy yellow flowers of the cowslip, also known as marsh marigold and by over two dozen other common names, are among the first to gleam in the spring along stream banks and in marshy coolnesses from Alaska to Newfoundland and as far south as Tennessee and South Carolina. This wild edible is also eagerly awaited in Europe.

One reason this member of the crowfoot family gained its name of cowslip is that you often see it growing in wet barnyards and meadows and in the trampled soggy ground where cattle drink. Few wild blossoms are more familiar or beautiful, and New Englanders find few wild greens that boil us so delicately so soon after the long, white winters.

The bright golden blossoms, which grow up to an inch and a half broad and which somewhat resemble large buttercups, have from five to nine petal-like divisions which do not last long, falling off and being replaced by clusters of seed-crammed pods. These flowers grow, singly and in groups, on slippery stems that lift hollowly among the leaves.

Cowslips, growing up to one and two feet tall, have crisp, shiny, heart-shaped lower leaves, some three to seven inches broad. These grow on long, fleshy stems. On the other hand, the upper leaves appear almost directly from the smooth stalks themselves. The leaf edges, sometimes wavy, frequently are divided into rounded segments.

There are two things to watch out for if you are going to enjoy the succulent cowslip. First, this plant must be served as a potherb, as the raw leaves contain the poison helleborin, which is destroyed by cooking. It is, therefore, a good idea to gather cowslips by themselves to avoid the mistake of mixing them with salad greens. Secondly, ordinary care must be taken not to include any of the easily differentiated poisonous hellebore or water hemlocks that sometimes grow in the same places.

The two poisonous plants are entirely different in appearance from the distinctive cowslip. The water hemlock plant superficially resembles the domestic carrot plant but has coarser leaves and a taller, thicker stem. The white hellebore, which can be mistaken for a loose-leaved cabbage, is a leafy

Cowslip

plant which somewhat resembles skunk cabbage, one reason why that not altogether agreeable edible has been omitted from these pages.

The dark green leaves and thick, fleshy stems of the cowslip are at their tastiest before the plant flowers. The way many know them best is boiled for an hour in 2 changes of salted water, then lifted out in liberal forkfuls and topped with quickly spreading pads of butter.

For a change, you can cream them, too. Tear the cowslips into small pieces and boil for an hour in 2 changes of salted water. Then drain. In the meantime, be melting 3 tablespoons of butter or margarine, either in a saucepan over low heat or in the top of a double boiler. Stir in 3 tablespoons of flour and cook a minute. Then gradually add $^1/_2$ cup of cream. Salt and pepper to taste, and stir until thickened. Add the cooked greens, mix well, and serve.

Parmesan cheese also goes well with cowslips on occasion. Just use the above recipe, adding 3 tablespoons of grated cheese after the flour and other ingredients have started to thicken. Then stir until the Parmesan has melted and the sauce is creamy.

The leaves and stems aren't the only deliciously edible portions of this bright little harbinger of spring. You can make pickles from the buds, soaking them first for several hours in salted water, draining, and then simmering them in spiced vinegar, whereupon they take on the flavor of capers.

Dandelions

(*Taraxacum*)

Gathering wild greens is a happy way to sharpen a satisfactory hunger, even if you go no farther than to collect a bagful of common dandelions. Actually, this familiar vegetable, all too well known because of the way it dots many a lawn, is among the best of the wild greens.

Continued ➡

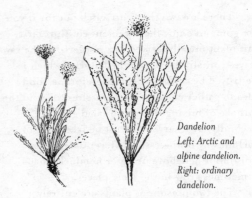

Dandelion
Left: Arctic and
alpine dandelion.
Right: ordinary
dandelion.

The well-known dandelion of flower beds, lawns, pastures, meadows, roadsides, and other moist, open places, boasts some three species in this country and about twenty-five in the civilized world, over which it is widespread. The green leaves are long and narrow, spreading in a rosette at the bottom. Their coarse edges, irregularly lobed and toothed, give this wild edible its name, which means "lion's tooth."

The flowers are yellow, maturing into full white ovals of plumetailed seeds that later scatter in the wind to make dandelions plentiful and persistent. The hollow and leafless flower stems discharge a bitterish milky juice when bruised or severed, as do the roots when the greens are cut free. These roots are generally thick and deep. Such wildlife as mule and white-tailed deer relish the green foliage, while grouse and pheasant find the seeds delectable.

The tender young leaves, available in the early spring, are among the first wild edibles I gather while bear hunting, trout fishing, or just plain hiking or horseback riding through the greening wilderness. At first they are excellent in salads. Later, when the plants begin blossoming, they develop a toughness and bitterness. Changing the first boiling water into which they are crammed will remove much of this bitter taste if you want, but we find it clean and zestful. Incidentally, when you can, include as many buds as possible, as they liven both the color and the flavor.

Young, tender dandelion greens can be used to add character and vitamins to scrambled eggs. Mix 4 eggs and 4 tablespoons cold water with salt and pepper to taste. Add a cup of shredded dandelions. Heat 2 tablespoons of butter, margarine, or bacon grease in a frypan just hot enough to sizzle a drop of water. Pour in the egg and dandelion mixture and reduce the heat. When the eggs have started to harden, begin stirring them constantly with a fork. Remove them while they're still soft and creamy.

Although they contain a laxative, taraxacum, the roots, when young, are often peeled and sliced, like carrots or parsnips, for boiling as a vegetable. To remove the characteristic tinge of bitterness, you may choose to change the salted water once. Serve with melting butter or margarine. Being particularly nourishing, these roots are a famous emergency food, having saved people from starving during famines.

Although the woods afford a multitude of teas, they are short on coffees. The dandelion will provide one of the latter. Roast the roots slowly in an open oven all afternoon until, shriveling, they resemble miniature dragons and will snap crisply when broken, revealing insides as brown as coffee beans.

Grind these roots and keep tightly covered for use either as regular coffee or for mixing to extend your normal supplies. Dandelion roots may be used the year around for this purpose. Because I generally roast my grind shortly before freezeup in the fall when the roots are near their strongest, I find I only have to use a level tablespoon of this homemade mixture per cup, whereas I prefer a heaping tablespoon of store coffee.

Dandelion wine is famous. If you'd like to make your own, pick a gallon of the flowers early on a dry morning, making sure that no parts of the bitterish stems are included. Press these into a 2-gallon crock. Pour a gallon of boiling water over them and leave for 3 days. Then strain through a cloth, squeezing all the liquid from the blossoms.

Add the juice and the thinly sliced rind and pulp from 3 oranges and 3 lemons. Stir in 3 pounds sugar. Add I ounce yeast. Cover the crock with a cloth and let it stand, out of the way, for 3 weeks while the mixture ferments. Then strain, bottle, and cork or cap tightly.

Giant Kelp

(*Nereocystis*)
If you live or vacation where giant kelp grows, this abundant marine alga, which often thrives in beds acres wide, makes unusual and excellent pickles.

Giant kelp has round, hollow stalks up to about seventy-five feet long, gradually widening from less than one-half inch at the base to perhaps four inches at the top and ending in a floating round bulb which may be up to eight inches in diameter. Two rows of narrow, leathery, leaflike blades, ten to thirty feet long, stem from the bulbs. These blades float on the ocean surface, and on the Pacific Coast from Mexico to Alaska you can often watch sea lions, whales, and sometimes sea otters swimming among them.

The long, hollow stalks, used by the Indians of southeastern Alaska as fishing lines for deep-sea angling, may be collected during June, July, and August, when they are at their prime. Although it is preferable to use only the ones rooted to the bottom, fresh stalks are also common along the beaches, especially after storms.

Giant kelp.

The kelp is washed, peeled, and used the same as green cucumbers or tomatoes for relish and pickles. It may also be used like watermelon rind for preserving.

For some memorable sweet sea pickles, you'll need 4 pounds giant kelp, 3 1/2 cups sugar, 2 cups white vinegar, I cup salt, 1/2 teaspoon alum, 1/2 teaspoon oil of cloves, 1/2 teaspoon oil of cinnamon, and water.

Cut the stalks into 12-inch lengths and split the bulbs. Using a vegetable parer, remove the dark surface layer and discard. Keep the pieces covered in a brine solution, I cup of salt to 2

gallons of water, for 2 hours. After the giant kelp is taken out of the brine, wash it thoroughly with cold water.

Then cut it into I-inch cubes. Soak these in a solution of 1/2 teaspoon of alum to 2 quarts of cold water for 15 minutes. Drain, wash in cold water, and redrain. Drop the cubes into an enamel kettle and cover them with boiling water. Simmer only until a few test cubes can be easily pierced with a fork. Then drain again.

Combine the sugar, vinegar, and oils. Simmer this for 2 minutes and then pour over the cooked kelp. Let stand overnight in the enamel kettle or in a crock. In the morning, drain and save the syrup. Reheat the kelp to the boiling point with just enough water to prevent sticking, pour off the water, recover with the syrup, and allow to set another 24 hours. On the third morning, heat both kelp and syrup to the boiling point, and seal immediately in 3 hot, sterilized pint jars.

Whole spices, tied in small bags, may be used instead, but the cubes will not then remain so nearly transparently clear. A conservative amount of green food coloring may be put in to make the pickles brighter. If you don't mind sacrificing a certain amount of crispness, omit the salt and alum solutions, merely soaking the kelp in cold water, rinsing, and then cooking until tender.

Hawthorn

(*Crataegus*)
It is fortunate that it's easy to distinguish the hawthorn from other shrubs and small trees. Even the professionals find it difficult to identify the separate species, the number of which in the United States is estimated to run all the way from about 100 to as high as 1,200. They grow from one coast to the other, making them valuable when survival is a problem. Taste varies considerably, and the only way to determine the edibility of hawthorn you've come across is by sampling. The better of them are delicious raw and when turned into jelly require very little sugar.

These cousins of the domestic apple are also known as thorn apples, thorn plums, thorns, mayhaws, red haws, scarlet haws, haws, cockspur thorn,

Hawthorn.

etc. Wood ducks eat the fruit. Pheasants, grouse, pigeons, and turkeys relish both buds and fruit. Black bears, rabbits, beavers, raccoons, and squirrels include both fruit and bark in their diets. Deer browse on the foliage and the applelike pomes. In addition to all this, hawthorns provide almost impregnable nesting places.

You can readily identify a hawthorn even in winter, particularly as the long, sharp, usually straight, occasionally slightly curved thorns, ranging in length up to about five inches, are not shared by any of our other native trees and shrubs.

Showy when blossoming in the spring and attractive when colorful with fruit, especially against the snow, hawthorns thrive in sunny

Continued ➡

locales in clearings, pastures, abandoned fields, and along roads and fences. The white and occasionally pinkish flowers, which have five petals, grow in terminal clusters. The fruit, which is usually red but sometimes greenish or yellowish, looks like tiny apples. Each contains one to five bony, one-seeded nutlets.

The part of the fruit that isn't seed is somewhat dry, and you'll need a lot of it, but the jelly made from hawthorns is golden and intriguing. Cover the berries with water and simmer them until they are soft, stirring them occasionally to prevent their sticking. Add more hot water if they start to run dry. Then put the results in a jelly bag, squeezing this to get out the last drop of juice. Depending on the particular fruit, it will take about 2 pounds of the berries to make the following recipe.

Stir a package of pectin into 4 cups of the juice. Continuing to stir, bring to a boil over high heat. Add 6 cups of sugar and stirring, bring to a full rolling boil for 2 minutes. Then remove from the heat, skim off the foam, and pour to within $1/4$ inch of the tops of hot, sterilized jelly glasses that are standing on a towel away from drafts. Seal with a thin layer of melted paraffin, carefully tilting each of the glasses so that this will adhere evenly to the sides. When it has cooled, add a second coating. Cool gradually, cover with regular caps or with aluminum foil, label, and store in a cool, dry place.

Hemlock

(*Tsuga*)

Hemlock tea is famous in northern New England and Canada. Drunk hot and black, its taste is reminiscent of the way a Christmas tree smells. More important for trappers, prospectors, and other outdoorsmen, this tea contains the vital Vitamin C.

Of the seven to nine species of hemlocks recognized in the world, four are native to North America. These tall, straight evergreens are typical of cool, damp slopes, ravines, and swamps, generally in northern regions and in the higher mountains. They also spring up after tree-cutting operations, their low dense foliage affording fine winter cover for grouse, turkey, deer, and other wildlife.

The needles grow in spirals, although they often seem to be attached in two ranks. The hanging cones have thin segments which hide a pair of tiny winged seeds that are important food for birds and red squirrels. Hemlocks in New England and the Maritimes are often killed by porcupines eating the bark.

Hemlock.

Incidentally, these conifers are no relation whatsoever to the poison hemlock from which Socrates and other ancients brewed their deadly draughts. Those entirely different plants are members of the parsley family.

It doesn't really make too much difference if you mistake one of the other conifers for hemlock. All these members of the pine family provide aromatic and beneficial tea. The bright green young tips, when they appear in the springtime, are best. These are tender and starchy at this time and can also be enjoyed raw. Older green needles will do, too. I just put a handful in a receptacle, cover them with boiling water, and let them steep until the tea tastes strong enough. If you prefer this black as I do, there's no need of any straining. Just narrow your lips on the rim and quaff it down.

The hemlocks and other members of the great pine family, which includes the numerous pines themselves, the spruces, firs, balsams, and all the others, have another feature which, if one is ever lost or stranded, can mean the difference between life and death. The inner bark can be cut off and eaten, either raw or boiled, to provide strength and nourishment.

Hickory

(*Carya*)

Hickories are probably our most important native nuts. The Indians used them in great quantities for food, and the settlers soon followed suit, even tapping the sweet sap in the spring for syrup and sugar. Today the nuts are familiar in the stores of this country.

The shellbark hickory, also called the shagbark, is the leader of the clan, although there are from twenty to twenty-two other species, depending upon the botanist. All are edible, although the taste of some is not appealing. There are the sweet hickories, including the above, in which the husk splits into 4 parts when the nuts are

Hickory.
1 Shagbark. 2 Pignut.
3 Bitternut.

ripe. There are the pignuts, often bitter but sometimes delicious, in which the thin husk splits only above the middle, or, sometimes late in the season, all the way to the base. There are also the familiar pecans.

The stout twigs and the gray bark which loosens in shaggy narrow strips, attached at the middle, distinguishes the shellbark and the shagbark, actually two different species, from all other trees. The leaves, from seven to fourteen inches long, are composed of usually five but sometimes seven leaflets. Dark yellowish green above, these are lighter and often downy beneath, with fine sharp teeth marking the edges.

Hickories grow slowly, and the shellbark does not produce nuts until about eighty years old. It becomes a large stately tree, reaching a height of up to 180 or more feet and a trunk diameter of one to three feet. Its wood is used for such things as bows, skiis, and ax handles, while hickory-smoked hams and bacon are famous. Wood duck, ring-necked pheasant, bobwhite, and wild turkey compete with man for the nuts. Black bear, raccoon, squirrel, and rabbit eat both nuts and bark, while the white-tailed deer relishes both these and the younger twigs.

The shellbark, which leafs out later than most other trees and sheds its bronze foliage earlier, ranges from Maine and Quebec west to the Great Lakes and Minnesota, and south to northern Florida and eastern Texas. The fruits, varying a great deal in size, are on the average from one to two inches in diameter, nearly round or somewhat oblong, and depressed at the top. The husks, which are about a quarter inch thick, split into four pieces at maturity. The familiar white or tawny nuts are a bit flattened with four ridges, an easily cracked thin shell, and large sweet kernels.

You can have an enjoyable time with just a heap of hickory nuts and a stone or hammer. But the pleasant, slightly aromatic meats also excel in the kitchen.

They can even be cooked with vegetables. Sometimes when you have gathered a bushel or so of nuts, probably from a noble tree in an open field or along the rim of a wood where its branches can stretch far into the sunlight, try cooking some with corn. Whip 2 eggs to a froth. Stir in a teaspoon salt, a tablespoon flour, and a cup of chopped hickory nuts. Add a cup of milk and 2 cups corn, fresh, canned, or frozen. Bake the mixture in a greased dish in a moderate oven until it is firm.

It is in the desserts, though, that the sweetmeat members of the clan are surpassingly good. For instance, it is difficult to outdo the following simple cookies. Just whip the whites of 2 eggs until they are stiff. Beat 2 cups of brown sugar into this. Then add 2 cups nuts that have been broken into small pieces. Drop from a teaspoon, about $1^1/2$ inches apart, onto a shallow greased pan or a greased baking sheet. Bake in a slow oven for 35 to 45 minutes or until light brown.

When we are in hickory country, nut balls have become traditional with us for the Christmas season, when neighbors are always dropping in to exchange cheer. You have to crush 2 cups of nuts for this by pounding, rolling, or, most easily, by running through a food grinder. Then blend a cup of butter or margarine with 4 tablespoons sugar and 3 teaspoons vanilla until creamy. Thoroughly mix the nuts with 2 cups sifted flour and stir into the preceding mixture. Shape the dough into little balls slightly larger than marbles. Place on a greased shallow pan or cookie sheet. Bake in a slow oven 45 minutes. Frost by rolling in confectioners' sugar while hot and again when cool. Store those that aren't snatched up immediately in a closed container.

The following pie is delectable with pecans but even better with shellbark hickories. Beat 3 eggs until light. Add 1 cup sugar, 1 cup white corn syrup, a melted $1/4$ pound stick of butter or margarine, $1^1/2$ teaspoons vanilla, and finally, 1 cup shopped nuts. Bake in an uncooked 9-inch pie shell in a moderate oven for about 40 minutes. We don't know of a tastier way to usher in the nutting season.

Jack-in-the-Pulpit

(*Arisaema*)

Many Indians relied on the dried and powdered roots of the familiar jack-in-the-pulpit for flour. Today, however, this edible has its principal value as an emergency food, especially for

Continued ➡

people stranded in one place for a long time. Widely known and easily recognizable, it can then be a lifesaver.

Indian turnip, wake-robin, and dragonroot are among the local names for this North and South American member of the great Arum family, used for food by people the world over. Both the leaves and the bright red fruit are eaten by the ring-necked pheasant and the wild turkey.

In the moist, sequestered woodlands of April and May, the jack-in-the-pulpit preaches his silent sermon to a congregation of wild violets and other spring neighbors. Unmistakable, the brown, green, and purplish "pulpit" is a striped two- to four-inch spathe terminating with a hood over the top. The "preacher" is a clublike spadix, two or three inches long, with small greenish yellow flowers, occasionally varying greatly in hues and in brightness, near its base.

The plant, growing in rich woods from the Maritime Provinces to Florida, west to Minnesota and Louisiana, becomes from one to three feet high. The two leaves, growing on long stems, are each composed of three egg-shaped, sometimes lobed, pointed leaflets. Green clusters of berries become handsome scarlet masses that brighten the dark woods in late August.

Jack-in-the-pulpit.

All parts of the plant, especially the round roots, will burn the mouth like liquid fire if eaten raw. Many youngsters used to have a standard ceremony for initiating newcomers to town, and perhaps still do. This consisted of offering the tenderfoot the tiniest morsel of what they claimed was the finest delicacy their woods had to offer. At first contact, this innocent-looking tidbit was palatable enough. But then the taste became as bitingly hot as a teaspoon of red pepper. This burning sensation, which was followed by inflammation and tenderness, seemed to permeate every part of tongue, mouth, and throat and to linger for hours, although cold milk did appear to allay it some.

The wonder is that aborigines the world over have learned to rid Arum roots of this corrosive acridness and thus capitalize upon their nutritious, delicate, white starchiness. Boiling won't do it! Drying will. The fastest way to do this is by roasting. The simplest method is just to cut the fresh roots into very thin slices, then set these aside in a dry place for upwards of three months. They then provide pleasant snacks, either as is or with a potato chip dip. Or you can crumble the crisp slices into flour and use it in regular recipes, preferably half and half with wheat flour.

Jack-in-the-pulpits and hazelnuts, often growing in the same habitats, go together in the following cookies which always seem to call for seconds and thirds whenever guests get their first samples of them. Beat 2 egg yolks until thick. Add, bit by bit, a cup of brown sugar and beat

that in well. Then mix in a cup of chopped hazelnuts and a scant 1/8 teaspoon salt.

Beat the 2 egg whites until they form peaks and fold them in. Sift together 3 tablespoons jack-in-the-pulpit flour and 3 tablespoons all-purpose flour. Stir that in. Distribute by the teaspoonful on cooky sheets or heavy foil, press gently flat with a spatula, transfer to a preheated 350-degree [F] oven, and bake about 7 minutes or until firm. After they have cooled, keep the 4 dozen or so cookies in a closed container for as long as they last, which isn't likely to be long.

Once the fire had been taken out of them, jack-in-the-pulpit roots were also held to be medicinally valuable. One prescription for spasms of asthma consisted of a handful of the dried and chipped roots, aged for three days in a quart of whisky. Even then, the dosage was conservative. It was a single tablespoonful twice a day.

Jerusalem Artichoke

(*Helianthus*)

Jerusalem artichokes, distinctively flavored tubers of a native wild sunflower, were cultivated by Indians and much used by early settlers. Besides still growing wild, they are also raised for today's markets, all of which indicates how well worth finding they are.

They have no connection with the Holy City. Soon introduced into Europe following Columbus' voyages to the New World, they became popular along the Mediterranean and were called *girasole* in Italian and *girasol* in Spanish. These words, denoting sunflower, became corrupted in English to *Jerusalem*. The artichoke part of the name stems from the fact that even centuries ago the flower buds of some of the edible sunflowers were boiled and eaten with butter like that vegetable.

About ninety species of sunflowers occur in the world. Some two-thirds of these grow in the United States, among them these tall perennials whose roots are such a delicacy. You have to like them, of course. We've learned to prepare them so that we do.

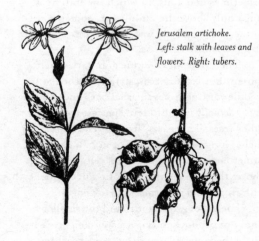

Jerusalem artichoke. Left: stalk with leaves and flowers. Right: tubers.

Wild Jerusalem artichokes, which should be harvested no sooner than fall, are native to the central parts of the United States and Canada. Their popularity among Indians and arriving Europeans, plus their cultivation in different parts of the country, helps explain why this native has long since escaped its original bounds and is now often found in abundance elsewhere—such as east of the Appalachians, where it has moved to usually moist soil along ditches,

streams, roadways, fence rows, and in vacant fields and lots.

These perennial sunflowers grow with thin stalks commonly five to ten feet tall. The rough leaves, whose tops are hairy, develop sharp points from oblong or egg-shaped bodies that are broadest near their bases. The frequently numerous flowers are yellow. From two to three inches broad, and maturing on slender stems that rise from where the higher leaves meet the stalk, these blossoms lack the purplish and brownish centers of those sunflowers that yield edible, oil-rich seeds. But the tubers, which are attached to the thickly creeping roots, more than make up for this deficiency.

History is all in favor of these delicacies whose somewhat sweetish juiciness, however, may take a bit of getting accustomed to. On the other hand, Jerusalem artichokes are nutritious and easily digestible enough to be regarded as a favored food for invalids. Here are a couple of hints that may help along your enjoyment. Dig them late in the year, even in winter if the ground is not too frozen, previously noting their whereabouts when they are conspicuously in bloom. Secondly, take care that they are not cooked too long nor at too high temperatures, as both toughen them.

Your cooking efforts may be as simple or as elaborate as you want them to be. The long, somewhat flat tubers are good just scrubbed, simmered in their skins in enough water to cover until just tender, and then peeled and served like potatoes, either with salt and butter or margarine or with a cream sauce. They then afford a by-product, too. When cold, the water in which they were boiled becomes jellylike, providing a flavorful and substantial foundation for soup.

Or, if you want everything all ready when mealtime arrives, wash and scrape the Jerusalem artichokes. As you finish with each one, drop it into acidulated water, made by stirring 1 teaspoon vinegar with a quart of cold water, to prevent it from darkening in the air. Slice or dice. Then cook, covered, in a small amount of boiling salted water 15 to 30 minutes, or until tender. Drain well. Serve with salt, pepper, and butter or margarine, or cream.

The non-starchy Jerusalem artichokes also make memorable salads. One way is to boil them first, then mix 4 cups with 1 finely diced small onion, 1 cup chopped celery, 1/2 teaspoon salt, a sliced cucumber, and a cup of mayonnaise. Stir together lightly, lifting from the outside in, season, and serve cold.

However, we usually prefer the crisp sweetness of the peeled tubers, which have somewhat the same texture as that of cabbage stalks, just sliced raw and added liberally to tossed salads.

Although not mealy like potatoes, Jerusalem artichokes can be substituted in many recipes for that common vegetable. For instance, fried slices of the wild edible have a flavor and consistency of their own. When in a hurry I've frequently cooked them in camp this way, sauteing them 8 to 10 minutes with bacon drippings in an already warm frypan and turning them several times during the process. When you have more leisure, they're even better rubbed with oil and baked. Or just add them to a mulligan when it's about half an hour from being done.

Continued ➡

When someone in the household is a little under the weather, they may especially enjoy Jerusalem artichokes simmered in milk. Peel about a pound of these healthful tubers and dice them. Drop these small pieces into 1/4 cup hot milk, stirring to moisten them well. Cover and cook just below the boiling point for 10 minutes. Then mix in 1 teaspoon salt and 2 tablespoons ground parsley. Sprinkle with paprika and serve while still steaming.

Juniper

(*Juniperus*)

Black bear, quail, and band-tailed pigeon are among the game dining on the fruit of the juniper. These evergreen shrubs and shrubby trees with their compact branches, thin shreddy bark, and scalelike leaves pressed closely to the twigs grow from Alaska to Labrador, south as far as New Mexico and California. The usually sprawling evergreens prefer exposed dry slopes and rocky ridges, and many a hunter has lounged in them to glass the country or to watch a game trail. The not unpleasant sharpness of some of their short needles makes one feel warmer on a brisk day.

The fruit, whose flavor and aroma is familiar to anyone who has had contact with gin, is dark blue and has a bloom to it. Growing in large numbers on the shoots of the female shrubs, these berries are to be found the year around. They are the size of peas. The flesh surrounding the large seed is sweetish and resinously aromatic.

Juniper.

Indians used to dry and grind juniper berries and use them for cakes and for mush. The principal individual use today is as a nibble and as a woodsy seasoning. A few will take the edge off hunger. Too many, though, are irritating to the kidneys. In fact, a diuretic is made of the berries, a teaspoon of them to a cup of boiling water, drunk cold, a large mouthful at a time, one or two cups a day.

Juniper tea, quaffed in small amounts, is one of the decidedly pleasant evergreen beverages. Add about a dozen young berryless sprigs to a quart of cold water. Bring this to a boil, cover, reduce the heat, and allow to simmer for 10 minutes. Strain and serve like regular tea.

Kentucky Coffee Tree

(*Gymnocladus*)

Roasted and ground, the seeds of the Kentucky coffee tree were used by early settlers in the New World as a substitute for coffee. Some of the Indians roasted them and ate them like nuts. The trees, often planted today for shade and for landscaping, range from New York to southern Minnesota, south to Tennessee and Oklahoma.

Usually a medium-sized tree, reaching a height of forty to ninety feet and a trunk diameter of from one to three feet, the Kentucky coffee tree ordinarily branches a few feet above the ground into three or four limbs which climb almost vertically to form a narrow crown.

The dark green leaves, which remain on for only about half of the year, are sometimes almost three feet long and two feet wide. They are composed of up to forty or more short-stemmed leaflets. Long clusters of greenish-white flowers appear in June. These develop into reddish-brown pods from four to ten inches long and from one to two inches wide. Each contains six to nine large, oval, flat, hard brownish seeds encased in a dark sweetish pulp.

You can roast these seeds slowly in the oven, grind them, and brew them like coffee. They have none of the caffeine of regular coffee, and the resulting beverage agrees with some people better.

Kentucky coffee tree.

Lamb's Quarter

(*Chenopodium*)

In a lot of homes the acknowledged pick of the edible greens is lamb's quarter. The tender tops of this wild spinach, which has none of the strong taste of market varieties, are delicious from early spring to frost-withering fall.

The entire young plant is good from the ground up. Even from the older ones a quantity of tender leaves can usually be stripped. However, the pale green leaves with their mealy-appearing underneaths and the slim stalks are not the only taste-tempting components of this green, also widely known as pigweed and goosefoot.

Indians long used the ripe seeds, 75,000 of which have been counted on a single plant, for cereal and for grinding into meal. These tiny gleaming discs, which develop from elognated dense clusters of small green flowers, are also handy for giving a pumpernickel complexion to biscuits and breads.

Some twenty of the sixty or more species in this genus, which belongs to the same family as beets and spinach, grow in the United States, thriving in nearly every part of the country. Lamb's quarter is a very common annual which grows from two to seven feet tall. By searching, you can usually find plenty of young plants up to about twelve inches high, and these are best for the table. These young plants have a mealy whiteness to them, but they do not require parboiling.

Lamb's Quarter.

Later, the tender tips alone are excellent. The alternate leaves, which are fleshy and tasty, have long stems and angular margins.

Along with other of the more tender leafy greens, lamb's quarter can be given a bit more taste on occasion with the help of a vinegar sauce. Such a flavorful acid also tends to preserve the vitamins C and A in such vegetables. Alkalies, on the other hand, such as the commonly but inadvisedly used baking soda, destroy an unnecessary proportion of these food values.

For 4 cups of loosely packed greens, take 1 small onion, 4 slices bacon, 1/4 cup vinegar, 1/4 teaspoon salt, and pepper to taste. Shred the greens if they are large. Dice the onion. Mix. Then chop up the bacon and fry it until the bits become brown and brittle. Put in the vinegar, salt, and pepper and bring to a simmer.

You now have 2 choices. You may pour the sauce over the raw greens. Or you may add the greens to the sauce and cook over low heat until they are limp. In either case, serve immediately. And see what the family's idea is for vegetables for the rest of the week.

May Apple

(*Podophyllum*)

Springtimes these attractive plants poke up like miniature forests of little opening umbrellas. Preferring moist rich woods and banks, their creamy-white flowers are later familiar from southeastern Canada to Florida and west to Minnesota and Texas. These produce sweetly scented, lemon-yellow fruits which, when delectably ripe, are relished by many.

This native perennial, a member of the barberry family, is also known as mandrake, wild lemon, and raccoon berry. Only the fruit is edible. The root, which Indians collected soon after the fruit had ripened and used in small quantities as a cathartic, is poisonous. So are the leaves and stems.

Each spring the long horizontal roots, which stay alive year after year, shoot up single-stemmed plants twelve to eighteen inches high. These roots, incidentally, are dark brown, jointed, and very fibrous. Internally yellow, they are mostly about half the size of a finger.

The solitary stems bear either one or two large leaves which open like tiny parasols. It is the latter plants that produce the single flowers which nod on short stems that rise from the fork of the leaves. About two inches wide, these oddly scented blossoms have from six to nine waxy white petals and twice that number of golden stamens.

*May apple.
Left: stem with flower and leaves. Right: fruit.*

The sweet yellow fruit, the size and shape of small eggs, ripens from July to September, depending on the climate, generally when the dying plants have dropped to the ground. Despite numerous seeds and a tough skin, it is very enjoyable in moderation raw, although there are those who, as in the case of serviceberries, prefer the May apple cooked.

The raw juice, however, really touches up sweet lemonade and other fruit drinks, while in some parts of the country there are those who add it and sugar to wine.

You can make a luscious, thick, pulpy jam from May apples. Clean about 2 quarts of fully ripe fruit, being sure to remove all stems. Place a layer in the bottom of a kettle. Crush them with a potato masher, repeating this process until all the fruit has been mashed. Add 1/2 cup water and heat short of simmering for 20

Continued ➡

minutes, stirring now and then. Then press the fruit through a colander. To 4 cups of the resulting juicy pulp, add a package of powdered pectin and a pinch of salt. Put back on the heat. When it starts to bubble, stir in 4 cups of sugar. Bring to a full boil, remove from the heat, skim, and seal in hot sterilized jars.

The heat does alter the delicate flavor of the fruit, although many think this is for the better, there are those who prefer the natural taste of May apples. For these, here is an uncooked jam that will keep for several months in the refrigerator. Clean and crush 2 quarts of ripe May apples as before, add 1/2 cup water, and heat to lukewarm only—100°F, on your thermometer. Press through a colander. Stir a package of powdered pectin into the still warm juice and pulp and let stand 20 minutes. Add 1 cup light corn syrup to prevent the sugar from crystalizing in the cold. Then thoroughly mix in 4 cups of sugar and a pinch of salt. Pour immediately into sterilized containers and store in the refrigerator.

Milkweed

(*Asclepias*)

Although milkweed grows from coast to coast and was long used by the Indians, it is the common milkweed, *Asclepias syriaca*, with which many are most familiar. This native perennial, thriving from the Maritimes to Saskatchewan and south to Kansas and the Carolinas, has stout stems reaching from two to five feet high.

This milkweed is abundant in meadows, old fields, marshes, and along roadsides, where in the fall its seeds with their familiar parachutes waft away by the thousands into the wind. These, plus a milky juice—latex, the subject of numerous experiments seeking a native rubber—are the plant's two predominant characteristics. However, these edibles should never be identified by this milky sap alone.

The leaves of this branchless edible grow in opposite pairs. Their short stems, like the stalks, are stout and sturdy. From four to nine inches long, and about half as wide, these oblong to ovate leaves taper at both top and bottom. They have wide central ribs.

The clusters of numerous tiny flowers have a memorable fragrance. They vary in color from greenish lilac to almost white. Each of the components of the delicate blossoms, which are deadly traps to many of the insects that seek their nectar, is divided into five parts. They eventually produce large green pods, some three to five inches long. The warty coverings of these finally split, exposing silk-tufted seeds.

Young milkweed sprouts, when up to some eight inches tall, are excellent asparagus substitutes, especially when cooked with a small piece of salt pork—if "substitute" is the right word, their being so regally satisfying in their own right. Then the young leaves provide cooking greens. The flower buds are a delicacy. Running the sprouts a close second, and even surpassing them in some estimations, are the firm, young pods. If they are at all elastic in your fingers, however, the silken wings of the seeds have developed too far to make for good eating.

There is one thing to keep in mind, however. All parts of the plant are bitter with the pervasive latex. However, this is readily soluble in water. Put your milkweed—whether sprouts, young leaves, flower buds, or seed-pods—all ready for cooking, in a saucepan. Cover it

Milkweed.

with boiling water, bring again to a boil over high heat, and pour off. Do this at least once again, maybe more times, depending on your palate. To some, a slight bitterish tinge is invigorating. In any event, finally recover with boiling water, add a bit of salt, and simmer until tender. This may require a bit longer than expected, as milkweed takes more cooking than most other greens. Serve with margarine or butter melting on top.

I've also used the similar *Asclepias speciosa* with its purplish flowers on the western side of the continent, from British Columbia to California.

The tough fibers of the mature stalks of this milkweed were employed by the Indians for making string and rope and for coarse weaving. The milky juice was applied to warts and to ringworm infections, as well as to ordinary sores and cuts. The exquisitely packed ripe seeds were gathered just before soaring and skittering over the landscape, their hairy protuberances burned off, and the remainder ground into a salve for sores. These seeds were also boiled in a minimum of water and the concentrated liquid applied to draw the poison out of rattlesnake bites.

Besides serving as a cough medicine, a hot beverage made by steeping the roots was taken to bring out the rash in measles. Externally, it was supposed to help rheumatism. The root, mashed with water, was applied as a poultice to reduce swelling.

Once the shoots are more than eight inches tall and too old to eat, the bottom leaves can no longer be used but the young top leaves are still tender and tasty before the green flowers. These are fine mixed with young dandelion leaves, although they are good by themselves, too. Then there are the buds themselves, prepared and cooked the same way. Finally, the young pods are fine served on the side with roast or steak, or you may like what they can do for a stew.

Getting back to the blossoms, the Indians are supposed to have used them for sweetening on summer mornings, shaking the dew-laden nectar onto their foods before this dampness evaporated in the heat of the day. This has never worked for me, however, perhaps because I've become too lazy too soon.

Mountain Sorrel

(*Oxyria*)

Mountain sorrel is a green we've enjoyed in such diverse places as New Mexico, British Columbia, and the green-sloped White Mountains of New Hampshire. This member of the buckwheat

family, which grows from Alaska and Greenland to Southern California, is also widely enjoyed in Europe and Asia. It is known in different parts of this country as sourgrass, scurvy grass, and Alpine sorrel.

The perennial mountain sorrel springs from a few inches to two feet high from a large, thick, deep, fleshy root. The small leaves, growing one or two on stems that for the most part rise directly from the root-stock, are smooth and either round or broadly kidney-shaped. Scarcely noticeable greenish or crimson flowers grow in rising clusters on long, full stems that extend above the mostly basal leaves. These blossoms turn into tiny reddish capsules.

The juicy leaves, which are at their best before the plant flowers, have a pleasantly acid taste which somewhat resembles that of rhubarb. In fact, mountain sorrel looks to some like miniature rhubarb, although it so happens that the leaves of domestic rhubarb, whether raw or cooked, are poisonous. Those of mountain sorrel, on the other hand, are delicious for salads, potherbs, and purees. Where this wild edible grows in the Arctic, Eskimos both in America and Asia ferment some of it as a sauerkraut. The tender young leaves will also give a zip to sandwiches.

Mountain sorrel.

Mountain sorrel leaves can be turned into a puree by simmering them for 20 minutes, then pressing them through a colander or mashing them, and adding butter or margarine, salt, and pepper. You'll save vitamins, flavor, and time, though, if you use a meat grinder or kitchen blender on these juicy greens, then quickly cook and add them to a piping hot base.

For a memorable cream soup, pour a quart of rich milk into a pan and set over low heat. When it starts to bubble, add 3 cups of mountain sorrel puree and salt and pepper to taste. Simmer for 5 minutes, stirring. Then gradually pour 3 beaten egg yolks into the mixture, stirring energetically until the color is even. Remove from the heat and, using a fork, blend in 4 tablespoons of butter or margarine. Serve immediately.

You can capitalize on the excellent way mountain sorrel combines with the delicate flavor of fish by making a thick fish stock, slowly bringing the heads, tails, bones, fins, and even the scales, if any, to a boil in cold water to cover, and simmering all afternoon along with a chopped onion and, if you want, a kernel of garlic. You'll need about 1/3 pound of such remnants for each individual, so wait until the fishing has been good.

Just before you're ready to sit down to the table, heat in proportional amounts for each diner 1 cup strained fish stock, 1/4 teaspoon salt, and a sprinkling of black pepper. Stir in an equal amount of mountain sorrel puree, simmer for 5 minutes, and serve hot with a liberal pat of butter or margarine spreading atop.

Continued ➡

Mountain sorrel adds a pungency to green salads, especially when about one-fourth as much watercress is added to contrast with its flavorsome sourness. We usually prefer a plain oil dressing, carefully touched up with a very little salt to taste. It's doubtful if you'll want any vinegar. Such salads go especially well with fish, crabs, and lobsters.

Boiled, mountain sorrel combines well with other greens, its acidity giving them added flavor. Because of this acidness, it is best to season gradually to taste and, in most cases, to omit the usual vinegar or lemon juice. A complement of hard-boiled eggs and crisp bacon, both thinly sliced, goes well with these greens.

Always welcome is this robust soup, individually seasoned. For 4 fishermen, the procedure is to start it by dicing about 1/2 pound bacon and, starting with a cold frypan, slowly bringing this to a sputter. Let the bits become crisp by tilting the pan so that the grease will run to one side. Then spoon them temporarily onto a plate.

Have 8 medium-sized potatoes, 2 onions, and 4 cups of mountain sorrel leaves chopped and mixed. Add these to the bacon fat and stir occasionally until the potatoes start to tan. Then return the bacon, flatten out everything in the pan, cover with water, stir, and simmer until a fork penetrates the potatoes easily. By this time none of us has ever been able to wait any longer.

Mustard

(Brassica)

Mustard, which flourishes wild over most of the globe, is universally recognizable because of its brilliant yellow flowers that become almost solid gold across many a field and hillside. Five species are widely distributed over the United States. Most important of these is black mustard, an immigrant from Europe and Asia, which has become so much at home on this continent that it now grows over most of the United States and southern Canada.

This annual ordinarily grows from two to six feet tall, although in California I have seen it as tall as a telephone pole. A relative of cabbages, turnips, cauliflowers, radishes, brussel sprouts, and similar cultivated vegetables, black mustard grows erect with widely spreading branches. The leaves on the young plants, which are the ones to pick, are rather fuzzy and feel stiffly hairy. The finely toothed lower leaves are deeply indented at the bases of the stalks and less indented as they ascend. These lobes do not appear on the upper, small, extremely bitter leaves that grow, nearly stemless, from the flower stalks.

The sunny yellow flowers are small but numerous. Typically for mustard, each has four petals and six little upright stamens, four long and two shorter. The blossoms mature during the summer into small, short pods. These are filled with dark, minute, zestfully pungent seeds.

One way this pleasantly edible plant can really start the mouth tingling is in a cream of wild green soup—especially when you come in dehydrated from a day of fishing or spring bear hunting and get that first sniff of it, all steaming and savory. To go with 2 cups of chopped or

scissored young mustard greens, start slowly heating a quart of milk, not allowing it to boil.

Mustard.

Meanwhile, melt 2 tablespoons of butter, margarine, bacon drippings, or any other edible fat in a saucepan over low heat. Gradually stir in 1 1/2 teaspoons salt, 1/8 teaspoon pepper, and 2 tablespoons flour. Add a finely minced small onion. Then pour in the hot milk bit by bit. Cook gently for 5 minutes.

Drop in the greens and, stirring occasionally, continue to heat just below the boiling point until these are just tender. To be at its best, mustard requires more cooking than most greens, something like a half hour. You'll need a lot, too, as it shrinks considerably. When the soup is ready, sprinkle with paprika. Serve at once.

Mustard, whether used in soup or elsewhere, is most agreeable when it first appears. The young stalks are not hard to identify, particularly as older mustard is often standing in the same patch. The slightly peppery young leaves are enjoyable raw. So are the young flowers with their then subtle pungency. The entire young plant goes well cooked with fish and meat.

Later on, the profusion of golden flowers can be capitalized upon to make a broccolilike dish. When you pick these over, it is best to eliminate any of the small upper leaves because of their bitterness. The blossoms boil up quickly in salted water. Bring them to a rapid boil, then let them stand away from the heat, tightly covered, for 5 minutes. Drain, spread with melting butter or margarine, and sprinkle with a little vinegar. Besides being colorful and delicious, this repast is full of vitamins and protein.

The easily gathered seeds of wild mustard, even after it has grown old and tough, are hard to equal for garnishing salads, adding to pickles and such for that extra seasoning, giving a final authority to barbecue sauces, and lending a wisp of zip and zest to stews. Mustard's very name comes from its seeds, being a corruption of must seeds, which harks back to ancient Roman-occupied Britain, where these were processed by saturating them in a solution of grape juice, or must, as it was sometimes called.

Table mustard can be made by finely grinding wild mustard seeds, between two stones, if you're in camp, or in the family food chopper, if you're at home, and adding enough water or vinegar to make a paste. After that, it's up to you. Commercially prepared condiments often contain such additional ingredients as flour, salt, turmeric, and other spices. If you choose to modify your raw mustard with up to an equal bulk of flour, brown this latter slowly and lightly in an oven first to take away the starchy taste. The vinegar may be diluted, depending on its strength, up to half and half with water. Occasionally, the blender likes the added flavor of horseradish. This white-flowered

member of the mustard family, with the pungent white roots, likewise grows wild.

A lot of us remember, back when we were growing up, the application of mustard plasters to cold-congested chests and sore backs. These famous old remedies, still highly regarded in many households, can be easily homemade. Just mix ground mustard seeds with an equal bulk of ordinary flour, then stir in enough tepid water to make a paste. Sandwich this sparingly between two cloths and tape into position while still warmly wet. Leave some 20 minutes, or until the recipient, with skin that starts to redden in about 5 minutes, begins to complain too vociferously of the increasing warmth.

Nettles

(Urtica)

Don't overcook your wild vegetables. Even with such a formidable green as young nettles, which, like prickly pears, are best gathered with leather gloves and a knife, once the salted water has reached the boiling point and the dark green nettles have been dropped in, they'll be tender almost immediately and ready for that crowning pat of butter or margarine as soon as they are cool enough to eat.

Nettles, which regrow in the same places year after year across Canada and the states, are for the most part erect, single-stemmed greens which sometimes grow up to seven feet tall. The opposite leaves are coarsely veined, egg-shaped to oblong, with heartlike bases, and roughly and sharply toothed. Both stem and leaf surfaces bristle with a fuzz of numerous, fine prickles containing irritating formic acid. Very small green flowers, which, like those of plantain, are easy to overlook, appear in multibranched clusters between leaves and stalk.

Nettle leaves may be gathered in the spring and early summer. These unlikely but delectable edibles are among the first wild vegetables available near our log cabin when greenery begins thrusting up like spring fire, but even so early in the season the presence of stinging bristles makes it necessary to wear gloves while harvesting them. If the skin should be irritated, maybe at the wrists, alcohol can be administered. The Indians of southeastern Alaska, several hundred miles west of our home-site, relieve the stinging by rubbing the irritated skin with the dryish, rusty, feltlike material that covers young ferns or fiddleheads.

Nettle.

When young, nettle leaves and the small entire plants quickly lose their stinging properties when boiled. They have such a delicate flavor that they are good by themselves. Topped with butter or margarine, they are far more subtly delicious than spinach and are excellent sources of vitamins A and C and some of the minerals.

Continued ➡

Because they are so easily and positively identified, nettles may be an important emergency food. Too, in a pinch, the stems of the older plants will yield a strong fiber, useful for fish lines.

Papaw

(*Asimina*)

This fruit so relished by raccoons and possums, sometimes called "false banana" because of its appearance, is also widely known as "custard apple" in deference both to its deliciousness and its family. Like the highbush cranberry, papaws usually call for an acquired taste. But once you come to like their creamy sweetness, they can become one of your favorite fruits. They are sometimes found in city markets, but they are at their best harvested when ripe, which in the North may mean after the first frost.

This hardy cousin of similar tropical fruits is native from New York southward to Florida and west to Nebraska and Texas. Preferring ground that is moist and fertile, it is most often seen in stream valleys and on the lower adjoining hills. It grows, too, in small clearings and along shaded roadsides. Papaws planted during landscaping often turn out to be doubly valued for their decorativeness as well as for their fruit.

A big shrub or a small tree, the papaw occasionally grows some forty feet high in the South, with a trunk perhaps as much as a foot in diameter. Northward, however, even the taller trees are often fifteen to twenty feet high, with trunks only a few inches thick. The papaw's large and often drooping leaves, which give it a tropical appearance, are from six to twelve inches long and, growing on short stems, are dark green above and paler beneath.

In early spring, just as these first leaves are starting to open, it blossoms with greenish flowers that later turn to a brownish or reddish purple. Growing from where the branches are met by the stems of the previous year's leaves, these are unusual in that they have six petals in two sets of three. The inner trio bunch together in a little chalice around which the outer three are outstretched like a saucer. About one and one-half inches wide, these produce slender fruits that look like short bananas, from several to about five inches long, with smooth, greenish-yellow hides that become brown a day or two after the papaws are plucked.

Papaw.
Left: bud and leaf scar. Center: branch with flowers and leaves. Right: fruit.

Despite the nuisance of several large dark seeds, the papaw has a wealth of bright yellow pulp whose mellow sweetness makes it really something to feast on outdoors, as the hungry members of the Lewis and Clark expedition discovered on their homeward journey. They are quickly gathered, often from the ground. You can also pull them slightly green and put them out of the way in a dark and dry place to ripen.

The custardlike consistency of the ripe fruit, whose odor is also fragrant, blends well with a number of desserts. For 2 people, make a sauce by beating the yolks of 3 eggs briefly, then stirring in 2 cups of milk and 1/2 cup sugar. Cook in the top of a double boiler until it thickens slightly. Then mix with a cup of papaw pulp that has been strained through a colander. Allow to cool, and then put in the refrigerator. Serve chilled, snowily topped with the beaten whites of 3 eggs into which, after they have become stiff, 6 tablespoons of sugar have been whipped.

Frozen papaw will also make you hope that no unexpected company drops in at the last moment. It's easy to make, although you have to go at it in stages, with everything at the same temperature to begin with. Start by separating 3 eggs. Beat the yolks until thick, add 1/2 cup sugar, and whip until creamy. Beat the whites until they form peaks, pour in 1/2 cup sugar, and continue beating until stiff. Then beat 1 cup of heavy cream until it, too, is stiff. Gently combine all these ingredients and fold in a cup of strained papaw pulp. Then just freeze.

Piñon

(*Pinus*)

The soft little nuts from the pinecones of millions of low-spreading conifers in the western United States and Mexico are not only pleasantly sweet by themselves, but they also afford prime flavoring for salads of the edible greens often seen flourishing nearby.

Roast the piñons first, after shelling them with the help of pliers or hammer, by spreading them in a single layer in a pan and placing it for 5 minutes in a moderate 350-degree [F] oven. Shake the pan several times during the process.

Coarsely chop 1/2 cup of the toasted piñons. Mix these with 1/4 teaspoon each of grated lemon peel, tarragon, and salt, and with 1/8 teaspoon cinnamon. Shake well with 1/2 cup salad oil and 1/4 cup vinegar. This salad dressing can be stored, tightly covered, in the refrigerator. Use only about 1 1/2 teaspoons for every cup of greens. As exciting as a honking wedge of geese undulating across the blue evening sky, it will make everything taste new.

Piñon pines have needlelike leaves in clusters of from two to five which persist for two, three, or more years. The flowers appear in the spring, producing an abundance of yellow, sulphurlike pollen which enlivens the wind. Once this fertilizes the pistillate flowers, which are scattered among the new shoots, there develop the familiar cones which take two and occasionally three years to reach maturity and disperse their winged seeds on the breezes. It is only on the innumerable small, low-growing pines in the vast drier mountainous regions of the West that these seeds become large enough to bother with. They are regularly available in stores.

However, if the cones' seeds, no matter how greatly relished by squirrels, turn out to be small, at least there will be nothing unwholesome about them. Romanian cooks grind entire young pinecones and use them to flavor game sauces. Some Indians used to roast the soft centers of green cones by the fringes of their campfires and feast on the syrupy results.

The settlers early learned to gather the inner bark of the pines in the spring, dry it throughout the summer, and then grind it and mix it with regular flour. Next to devouring it raw, though, the easiest way to eat this sweet cambium is first to cut it into thin strips, then cook it like spaghetti. The bland flavor goes well with meat simmered at the same time.

Some of the tribes went to more elaborate preparations, even to making a sort of bread. The squaws mashed the cambium to a pulp in water, then molded this into big cakes. In the meantime, a rousing fire was kindled in a rock-lined hole. The coals were then removed, the cakes set in on green leaves, and the embers raked back over a thick layer of leaves on top. Damp

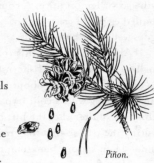

Piñon.

moss covered everything, which was left to smolder for upwards of an hour. The cakes were then placed on pole frames and smoked for a week, after which they could be carried as trail rations. The results were so hard that before use the cake was customarily broken into bits and boiled until soft.

Even pine needles, when they are new and starchy, are pleasantly nutritious to chew on. Some Indians boiled the still firm, spikelike flower clusters, in which the petalless blossoms grow in circular rows on slender stalks, to flavor their meats.

The piñons have also long been important medicinally. Hot pine tea, made by steeping the needles or by boiling gum or pitch, was one of the earliest cold remedies. Chewing the gum was considered soothing to sore throats. Too, the resin was dried, powdered, and applied to sore throats by swabs.

The piñon resin was also used by various Indians, and later by white adventurers and settlers, as a cure for everything from rheumatism and flu to indigestion. Heated, it was applied as a poultice to draw out splinters and to bring boils to a head. This hot resin dressing was also smeared on cuts, burns, sores, abrasions, and insect bites. Applied liberally to a hot cloth, it was used like mustard plasters in treating pneumonia, neuralgia, and general muscular soreness and stiffness.

The pines as a whole hold a position near the peak in importance to wildlife, partly because many birds and mammals feast on the seeds and to some extent because of the year-around cover the trees afford game birds, fur bearers, and both large and small game animals. Grouse, pigeons, doves, quail, prairie chickens, and turkeys eat the needles as well as the seeds. Deer, elk, moose, and mountain sheep browse on the foliage.

If you've ever lived in New Mexico, you'll remember the fragrance of burning piñon enlivening the air, as it has been doing in this country for centuries. The piñon and its cousins, such as the Parry pine and the Digger pine, have long been the most important trees to

Continued ➜

the Indians in the Southwest. The women still use the nuts in all kinds of cooking, from soups to salads, and a pocketful of their almost airy evergreen flavor goes well at any time.

Incidentally, when you're foraging for piñons in high country, don't overlook the ungainly nests of the pack rat. Indians customarily break each of these rough, large retreats apart, often finding as much as several pints of nuts stored for winter use.

These rich little nuts found in the hearts of pinecones add a subtle sweetness to the already piquant flavor of young dandelions. To go with enough of these greens to serve four, get 3 tablespoons of salad oil sizzling in a frypan. Then stir in 1/2 cup of piñons, 1/2 cup of diced black olives, 1/4 cup seedless raisins, and a small mashed clove of garlic. After 3 minutes, put in the greens that have been torn to bite size, including a reasonable number of buds if possible. Reduce the heat, cover, and cook only until warm and tender. Season to taste with salt and, if you want, with a dusting of black pepper. Serve hot.

A delicious green sauce, flavorsome over steaming noodles or spaghetti, can be made with piñons and watercress. Start with 1/2 cup of chopped watercress, 1/4 cup piñons, a large chopped garlic clove, and 1/8 teaspoon of salt in the blender. When this pureed, add 1/2 cup of freshly grated Parmesan cheese. Conclude by slowly blending in 1/4 cup salad oil and 1/2 stick of butter or margarine. With fruit and perhaps a dry red wine, this makes a perfect meal.

When the Indians taught the early frontiersmen how to obtain nuts from the piñons and related low-spreading pines, they began an adventure in good eating that continues to this day. Piñon cakes are unique and delicious, both hot and cold. You can make them in camp, perhaps where you're gathering the nuts, or at home. In either event, the shelled nuts first must be chopped or crushed, as with a rolling pin, to a coarse meal. The easiest way to go about this, of course, is in the home blender.

If you're cooking over an open fire, just mix each cup of piñon meal with 1/4 teaspoon of salt and about 1/3 cup of lukewarm water to make a stiff batter. Get a tablespoon of shortening warming in a large, preferably heavy frypan until it is just short of smoking. Drop the batter from a tablespoon, flattening it into cakes with a spatula. Reduce the heat and tan the cakes slowly on one side before turning them to brown the other.

If you are at home, you can make a little less primitive cake by stirring each cup of piñon meal, then 1/4 cup of all-purpose flour, into a well-beaten egg. Drop on a greased baking tin with a teaspoon. Bake in a moderate 375-degree [F] oven about 10 minutes until lightly browned. The flavor of these is even more delicate.

For about three dozen piñon bread sticks of unusual crunchiness and distinctive flavor, stir a package of yeast into a cup of lukewarm water. Once it has dissolved, pour into a mixing bowl. Add 1/4 cup olive oil, 1/4 cup salad oil, a tablespoon sugar, 1 1/2 teaspoons salt, a slightly beaten egg, and a cup of all-purpose flour. Beat until smooth.

Then add 3/4 cup piñons and enough additional flour, about 2 1/4 cups, to make a stiff dough. Using a floured board or square of plastic, knead this about 5 minutes until it is smooth and elastic, adding flour if necessary. Cover with a damp cloth and place in the refrigerator overnight or, if you are in a hurry, for at least 2 hours. In any event, plan your cooking so that the dough can later rise for another 2 hours, starting this recipe early in the afternoon if you plan to serve the hot bread sticks for dinner.

Divide the chilled dough into 3 parts. Cut each portion into a dozen equal slices. Using your palms, roll each piece into an 8-inch crayon-like strip. Place about 1/2 inch apart on greased baking sheets, brush with melted butter or margarine, and let rise until about double size. Salt lightly. Bake in a preheated moderate 325-degree [F] oven for about a dozen minutes until crisp and barely golden. Either warm or cold, such crusty tidbits, their outdoorsy flavor becoming more evident with each bite, will really arouse the appetite.

Piñon crops vary in different years, but if you happen to run into a bountiful harvest, you may like to try some cookies. These are simply made in any desired quantity by mixing each cup of chopped piñons with a cup of brown sugar and the beaten white of an egg. Drop small blobs from a teaspoon onto a greased pan or cooky sheet. Bake in a slow 300-degree [F] oven until lightly browned.

Or you can bake more elaborate cookies. In any event, piñon cookies will fill the house with a tantalizing aroma. Start the preparations for these by finely grinding 2 cups of blanched almonds. Lightly beat 2 egg whites. Mix these thoroughly with the almonds and with a cup of sifted confectioners' sugar. You may choose to omit this next step, but we now like to blend in 2 tablespoons of crème de cacao.

Shape the dough into cookies about 1 1/2 inches in diameter. Place apart on a well-greased cooky sheet. Brush the top of each with lightly beaten egg white. Arrange a half-dozen or so toasted piñons atop each cooky. Leave at room temperature all afternoon. Just before dinner, heat your oven to a moderate 350 degrees [F] and cook the delicacies, which will number between 3 and 4 dozen, for about 10 minutes or until they are a light brown.

One of the most splendiferous edibles ever concocted by man in piñon torte. Beat 1/4 cup of sugar and a stick of melted butter or margarine into 2 egg yolks. Add 2 tablespoons milk and 3/4 cup toasted piñons. Mix together 1/2 cup all-purpose flour and 1/2 teaspoon salt, and fold that in. Whip 2 egg whites until they form short peaks. Gradually beat in 1/4 cup of sugar and fold that, too, into the batter.

Bake in 2 deep, well-greased, 8-inch layer cake pans in a slow 300-degree [F] oven for 50 minutes. In the meantime whip a cup of heavy cream, sweetened to taste with sugar. Put the cooled layers together with half the whipped cream. Spoon the remaining whipped cream over the dome and garnish it with 1/4 cup of the toasted nuts, perhaps arranged in a pine tree pattern.

The flavor of chilled piñons soup is so satis-fyingly piquant that this luxury is particularly refreshing on a hot fall evening. The soup is also excellent while still steaming. Because it is better appreciated when served in small portions, the following recipe will make enough for four.

Bring 2 cups of milk, a cup of game bird or chicken stock, a cup of raw piñons, a small diced onion, 1/8 teaspoon dried mint, and 1/8 teaspoon of black pepper, preferably freshly ground, to a simmer. Stirring occasionally, cook for half an hour over heat so low that only an occasional bubble dances to the surface. Then process in the blender until smooth. Either reheat for immediate use or refrigerate for serving cold. A palmful of minced chives scattered on just before bringing to the table helps bring out the savor.

Plantain

(*Plantago*)

Plantain is almost as good as lamb's quarter. Furthermore, plantain is as well known to most of us as are the similarly prepared and eaten dandelions, although not usually by name.

It is the short, stemless potherb whose broadly elliptic green leaves rise directly from the root about a straight central spike. This singular spike blossoms, although possibly you've never noticed it, with minute greenish flowers that later turn into seeds. At any rate, plantain is found all over the world, even growing through sidewalks in New York, San Francisco, and Boston.

Some nineteen kinds of plantain thrive in the United States. One of the more widely distributed of these is the seaside plantain, also known as goosetongue, which grows along such widely separated coasts as those of Quebec, Nova Scotia, New England, Alaska, British Columbia, and California. The natives in Alaska boil this fresh both for eating on the spot and for canning for winter.

Plantain leaves make excellent greens. Fact is, the greener they are, the richer they are in vitamins A and C and in minerals. They are good boiled. What holds for plantain, when it comes to this common if often murderous method of cookery, goes for the other wild greens as well. Unless it means standing over a riled cook with a cleaver, try to see that all these are cooked only until just tender and still slightly crisp. This usually takes a surprisingly brief time.

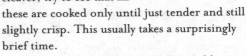
Plantain.

The simple gimmick with these wild vegetables is to start them in a minimum amount of boiling water and to cook them, covered, as rapidly and briefly as possible. Young plantain and such can be lifted directly from the rinse to the saucepan and cooked without added water.

For two liberal servings of slightly older greens, 1/2 cup water and 1/2 teaspoon salt will do the job. When the greens become tougher, a full cup of water may be required. Any of the vitamin- and mineral-rich fluid remaining

Continued ➜

should be used, as in soups, gravies, sauces, and the like, unless there's some reason against this such as unusual bitterness. Me, I drink it.

Plantain, also called ribwort and soldiers herb, is mildly astringent. During pioneer times, and even today in some backwoods localities, the fresh leaves are mashed and applied to cuts, scratches, and wounds. The leaves are also used for tea, 1/2 handful being dropped into a cup of boiling water and allowed to steep for 1/2 hour.

Pokeweed

(Phytolacca)

The first wild greens of the spring in many a happy household, pokeweed flourishes in the eastern half of the country except along the Canadian border, west to Texas and south to the tropics. The Indians found it delicious, and some of the first European adventurers on these shores were in such agreement that they took the seeds back to France and southern Europe, where the vegetable became popular. Today pokeweed finds its way into many of our stores as a springtime delicacy. Some devotees like it so well that they even grow it in their cellars.

Also known as pokeberry, poke, scoke, pigeonberry, garget, coakum, and inkberry, this wild vegetable has a huge perennial root often as large as a man's forearm. Fibrous and covered with a thin tannish bark, this can be easily broken to size and planted in garden soil in a deep, flat box. Best are the medium-size roots, some three or four inches in diameter, broken or cut into six-inch lengths, dug and replanted indoors after the first heavy freeze of fall. Kept in a dark, warm cellar and regularly watered, these will regularly send up shoots for months. For a family of three, you'll want about a dozen such roots.

The fat young sprouts, especially when they are some six to eight inches high, are the only part of pokeweed that is good to eat. The bitter roots—cathartic, emetic, and somewhat narcotic—are poisonous. So are the mature stalks when they take on a purplish cast. You may have seen birds get tipsy on the berries.

You'll want to be able to recognize the full-grown plants, however, as in the spring it is near their dried remains that the tender young shoots will arrow upward. These annuals grow into round stalks, about an inch in diameter, which reach and branch upwards from four to nine feet. The leaves, which are shaped like rounded lances, have stems on one end and points on the other. Scattered, smooth on both sides, and wavy-margined, they are up to about ten inches long.

Both flowers and fruit grow in long clusters on short stems. The numerous, small flowers are a greenish white. The round, ripe berries are a deep purple and are an important source of food for the mourning dove. Their reddish purple juice, as boys sometimes used to confirm in the fall when school classes were first resuming, will serve as an ink for steel pen points.

Gather your small, tender pokeweed shoots when they are no more than about eight inches tall. Remove skin and leaves, saving the latter for greens. Simmer the whole stems in a small amount of lightly salted water for 10 minutes or until tender. Serve on hot buttered toast, steaming with sauce.

One sauce whose flavor really brings out the springlike deliciousness of young pokeweed is started by finely chopping 2 slices of a medium-size onion, then tanning the bits in 2 tablespoons of butter or margarine. Then blend in 3 tablespoons flour. Slowly add a cup of milk, stirring vigorously. Mix in a teaspoon of chopped watercress. Salt and pepper to taste, sprinkle with 1/8 teaspoon nutmeg, and simmer gently for 5 minutes, stirring occasionally. Add 1/4 cup of heavy cream, bring again to a bubble, and serve.

Pokeweed.

A tantalizing cheese sauce to touch up the flavor of such pokeweed on toast can be made by slowly melting 2 tablespoons of butter or margarine in a saucepan over moderate heat, not allowing it to brown. Then smoothly stir in an equal volume of flour. Stirring vigorously, gradually add 1 1/4 cups of milk and bring to a bubble. Season with 1/4 teaspoon salt and 1/8 teaspoon pepper. Still stirring, simmer for 5 minutes to take away the raw taste of the flour. Now remove from the heat for several minutes. Add a bit at a time, stirring energetically until each portion has melted before adding more, 3/4 cup of good grated American cheese. Return to low heat but do not allow to boil. Spoon over each serving, dust with paprika and with parsley flakes, and see what everyone's idea is for vegetables the next day.

Pokeweed is also good with eggs. For this dish, skin the shoots but leave on the little unfurled leaves at the top. Wash well. Then boil whole for 8 minutes in salted water until nearly tender. Drain, saving 1/4 cup of the fluid. Mix this liquid with 3 beaten eggs, 3 tablespoons salad oil, a halved clove of garlic, and salt and pepper to taste. Add to the pokeweed and, stirring occasionally, cook about 2 minutes or until the latter is ready for the table. Remove the garlic and serve.

For a rich, aromatic soup, simmer 2 cups of pokeweed shoots until soft and then put either through a sieve or the blender. Bring 2 cups of milk to a bubble along with a halved clove of garlic. Then discard the garlic and add the pureed vegetable. Mix 3 tablespoons flour smoothly with a small amount of cold water. Stir that, along with 3 tablespoons of butter or margarine, into the soup. Season to taste with salt and pepper. Bring again to a bubble, add a tablespoon of chopped watercress and a cup of heavy cream, sprinkle with paprika, and serve steaming.

Those times when bachelors are doing the cooking they sometimes go in a lot for one-dish meals, and this wild vegetable is one of those lending itself well to such production. Simmer until tender in a minimum amount of salted water enough young pokeweed for four. In the meantime, be preparing a white sauce by melting 1/2 stick of butter or margarine in a saucepan, smoothly stirring in 1/4 cup flour, and then, still

stirring, slowly add 2 cups milk. Season to taste with salt and pepper. Stir in 2 tablespoons of finely diced green pepper. Bring to a simmer.

Also be simmering 4 eggs, completely covered with water, for 8 to 10 minutes depending on their size. Then remove them from the heat and plunge them into cold water. Crack the shells slightly before the eggs cool, so that peeling will be easier. Slice.

Spread a base of pokeweed over the bottom of a well-greased casserole. Cover with white sauce, then with sliced egg. Repeat until all the ingredients are used. Top with 1/2 cup of buttered white bread crumbs. Bake in a moderate 325-degree [F] oven for half an hour. Serve hot. Just a whiff of this will have your customers waiting eagerly.

Poplar

(Populus)

The poplar's sweetish, starchy sap layer is edible both raw and cooked. This lies between the wood of trunks, branches, and twigs and the outside bark, the latter being intensely bitter with salicin, which for some reason is relished by moose, beaver, and rabbit and is an ingredient in some tonics concocted for the benefit of mankind.

All three animals chaw poplar bark, and poplar trunks and branches are common in beaver dams and houses. Deer, elk, and mountain sheep browse on the twigs and foliage. Grouse, prairie chickens, and quail are among the game birds relying on buds, catkins, and seeds.

One of the most common trees on the continent, the life-giving poplar grows about as far north as any other on the great barrens of Canada. Cottonwoods as well as aspens are poplars. On the other hand, the so-called yellow poplar of the Southeast is not a polar at all. In numerous northern areas, poplars quickly spring up in burns and clearings.

The poplars, members of the great willow family which has saved more than one man from starving, have alternate leaves with toothed and sometimes lobed edges. The stems are long and slender, occasionally being definitely flattened. The branches are characteristically brittle

Poplar.

and, breaking easily from trunks and big limbs, make excellent firewood for lone campfires, burning with a clean, medicinal odor.

Pollen fills the wind when the flowers, growing in drooping spikelike clusters, appear in the first warm weather of spring before the light green leaves blaze forth, like pale green fire crowning the forest. The cottony aspect of the later splitting capsules of seeds, each with its long, fibrous hairs, has brought the name "cottonwood" to some species.

The soft formative tissue between wood and bark can be scraped off and eaten on the spot. One of the modern ways of obtaining such nour-

Continued ➡

ishment is in tea. It can also be cut into strips or chunks and cooked like noodles in soups and stews. Dried and powdered, it is a flour additive and substitute. No matter how it is eaten, however, it can by itself keep you going for weeks.

Prickly Pear

(Opuntia)

There is also the unlikely prickly pear—the little thorny knobs, ranging from the size of apricots to the size of large lemons, that bulge from the padlike joints of cactus. Actually, the spine-bristling skin of this fruit of the cactus is so unmistakable that any difficulties lie not in identifying but in picking. It's best to go about this with leather gloves and a knife.

Depending on the kind of cactus, the ripened colors of prickly pears vary from tawny green and purplish black to the choicest of them all—the big red fruits of the large *Opuntia megacantha* of the continental Southwest. To eat any of these Indian figs, as they're also known, slice off the ends, slit the hide lengthways, and scoop out the pulp.

Purslane

(Portulaca)

Purslane, although commonly unnoticed except as a weed, is sometimes the tastiest crop in the home gardens where it widely occurs. This annual also frequently becomes troublesome in fields and waste places throughout the contiguous forty-eight states, in the warmer parts of Canada, and even in Mexico where it is sold in the markets.

The reason for this distribution, which is worldwide, is its tremendous production of seeds, relished by birds and rodents. Although purslane does not become large, 52,300 seeds have been counted on a single plant. Indians in our Southwest used these for making bread and mush.

The trailing, juicy plant which is familiar to almost everyone who has ever weeded a yard, is native to India and Persia, where it has been a food for more than 2,000 years. An early mover to Europe, it has been eaten there for centuries. Introduced to the New World back in colonial days, it has spread into almost every American city and town.

"I learned that a man may use as simple a diet as the animals, and yet retain health and strength. I have made a satisfactory dinner off a dish of purslane which I gathered and boiled," Henry Thoreau noted in Massachusetts over a century ago. "Yet men have come to such a pass that they frequently starve, not for want of necessaries but for want of luxuries."

The semisucculent purslane, also sometimes called pusley, prefers fertile sandy ground over which it trails and crawls, sometimes forming mats. It seldom reaches more than an inch or so into the air, although it often spreads broadly. The jointed stems, purplish or greenish with a reddish tinge, are fleshy and forking. The narrow, thick leaves, scattered in nearly opposite positions, grow up to about two inches long.

Unfolding their six or seven petals and some eleven stamens only on bright mornings, the small yellow flowers peek out from stems lifting from the forkings of the stalk. They produce tiny round seed vessels whose tops, when ripe, lift uniquely off like lids.

There's a trick, incidentally, to gathering purslane for the table. If you'll just nip off the tender leafy tips, they'll rapidly sprout again. This way just a few plants will furnish you with greens from late June until frost.

Purslane makes excellent salads. However, after its usual grittiness is removed by washing, it has most frequently been enjoyed as a potherb wherever we've lived. Just drop it into salted boiling water, simmer for about 5 minutes or until tender and serve with melted butter or margarine. A little purslane goes surprisingly far, as it loses little bulk in cooking.

You can capitalize a little more on its mildly acid taste, though, by first cutting 4 slices of bacon into small shreds and frying them until crisp. Then pour in 1/2 cup vinegar and 1/2 cup hot water, along with 2 teaspoons brown sugar and salt and pepper to taste. Mix these thoroughly, bring to a bubble, and pour over a large heap of tender young purslane tips. Fork the greens gently about until they are all well coated. Garnish with chopped, hard-boiled eggs, sprinkled with paprika.

Individuals who don't like okra frequently object to purslane's mucilaginous quality, which can be an advantage, however, for lending consistency to soups and stews. It can be counteracted, on the other hand, by rolling each young tip, still slightly damp from washing, in flour, then dipping it in beaten egg, and finally rolling it in bread crumbs. Fry in deep, hot fat for about 8 minutes, or until brown.

People who like pickles may be interested to know that purslane has been furnishing these for centuries. As might be expected, methods have varied widely over the years, but you won't go far wrong by just substituting tender young purslane stems for cucumbers in your favorite recipe.

Here's one that works well. Mix 1 cup salt, 2 cups sugar, and 1 cup ground mustard. Gradually moistening and vigorously stirring at first, mix with 2 quarts vinegar. Pour over as many freshly picked and washed young purslane stems as it will cover. If you have a large crock, fresh purslane and pickling brine may be added day by day until the crock is full. Then cover with a weighed-down plate and leave for at least several weeks. These really stimulate enthusiastic conversation when friends stop by.

Rose

(Rosa)

Delicious wild foods grow everywhere. For example, there is familiar berry that, although you've maybe never sampled it, has the flavor of fresh apples. More important, its juice is from six to twenty-four times richer in Vitamin C than even orange juice. Throughout much of the continent you can pick all you want the greater part of the year, even when temperatures fall a booming 60° below zero. As for recognizing the fruit, no one with a respect for brambles and a modicum of outdoor knowledge is going to get the wrong thing by mistake. It is the rose hip, the ordinary seed pod of roses everywhere.

Some thirty-five or more varieties of wild roses thrive throughout the United States, espe-cially along streams, roadsides, fences, open woods, and in meadows, often forming briary thickets. The hips or haws, somewhat roundly smooth and contracted to a neck on top, grow from characteristically fragrant flowers, usually pink, white, or red. Remaining on the shrubs throughout the winter and into the following spring, they are available for food in the North when other sources of nourishment are covered with snow.

These rose hips have a delicate flavor that's delectable. They're free. They're strong medicine, to boot. Studies in Idaho found the scurvy-preventing vitamin in the raw pulp running from 4,000 to nearly 7,000 milligrams a pound. Daily human requirements, estimated to be 60 to 75 milligrams, provide a yardstick for this astonishing abundance.

Three rose hips, the food experts say, have as much Vitamin C as an orange. We don't pay much attention to these gratuitous vitamins in the United States and Canada. But in England during World War II, some five million pounds of

Rose hips, leaves, and stems.

rose hips were gathered from the roadsides and put up to take the place of then scarce citrus fruits. Dried and powdered, rose hips are sold in Scandinavian countries for use in soups, for mixing with milk or water to make hot and cold drinks, for sprinkling over cereals, etc., all of which they do admirably.

This cousin of the apple, one of the many members of the rose family, is nutritious whether eaten off the bushes, cut up in salad, baked in cake or bread, or boiled into jam or jelly. As a matter of fact, plain dried rose hips are well worth carrying in a pocket for lunching on like raisins. To prepare them for this latter use, just cut each in half. Remove the central core of seeds. Dry the remaining shell-like skin and pulp quickly in a cool oven or in a kettle suspended above the fringes of a small campfire.

One good way to use rose hips is turn them into syrup. Snip the bud ends from a freshly gathered batch. Then cover the fruit with water and boil rapidly until soft. Strain off the juice. Return the pulp to the kettle, add enough water to cover, and make a second extraction. For every 2 cups juice, add 1 cup sugar. Boil until thick. Pour into sterilized bottles. That's all. Poured over steaming sourdough pancakes on blue-black mornings when the Northern Lights are still ablaze, this syrup never lasts long.

Here's an extra hint. Don't throw away the pulp. Press it through a sieve to remove seeds and skins. Add one half as much sugar as pulp. Put in clove, cinnamon, and any other spices or flavoring agents to taste. Heat covered until the sugar is dissolved. Then uncover and cook slowly until thick, stirring to prevent sticking. Pack in sterilized jars and seal. Voilà! Fruit butter.

With rose hips up to sixty times richer in Vitamin C than lemon juice—and richer in iron, calcium, and phosphorus than oranges—you

Continued ➔

EDIBLE DESERT PLANTS
Greg Davenport   Illustrations by Steven Davenport and Ken Davenport

Hot, dry deserts, such as the Sahara and Middle Eastern Deserts, have little vegetation, whereas cooler, wetter deserts, such as the Great Basin and Gobi Deserts, are often relatively productive. Plants derive food from sunlight, and thus desert plants rarely have a starvation problem. Obtaining water, on the other hand, can be difficult for desert plants, and the presence or lack of desert vegetation is a direct result of water availability.

Survival strategies
In order to survive on limited water, the three basic desert plants employ different strategies.

Annual or ephemeral plants
Annual or ephemeral plants take root and grow when moisture is plentiful following a rainfall, and they die or become dormant when the drought returns. The dormant seeds are heat- and drought-resistant and remain in the soil until the next year's annual rains.

Phreatophytes
Phreatophytes, a term meaning water-loving plants, often have taproots extending deep enough to reach the water table. Mesquite is a phreatophyte with a deep root system that is an adaptation to the hot desert.

Xerophytes
Xerophytic plants, such as sagebrush, mesquite, yucca, and saguaro and prickly pear cactus, have the ability to extract water from extremely dry soil and adapt to decrease water vapor loss from the leaves. Leaves may possess surface hairs to reflect light and to slow wind flow; have a reduced surface area; roll or curl under hot, dry conditions; or drop during extreme drought. Succulents such as cactus have a highly efficient water-gathering root system and the ability to store water in a spongy tissue at the center of the stem or root.

Edible Desert Plants
Each of the numerous deserts around the world has edible vegetation unique to it. Although food is a lower priority than water, you should still become familiar with edible plants indigenous to your area of travel before departing. A few plant food sources common in most deserts include the following.

Prickly pear cactus
There are many species of prickly pear, but most are characterized by flat, fleshy, oval-shaped pads covered with spines. Most produce yellow, red, or purple flowers. Both the fruit and pads are edible. Before eating the pads, you should use a fire or hot coals to scorch the spines off and soften the outer skin. If you cannot build a fire, then carefully attempt to peel the skin away with a knife.

Grasses
Grasses can often be found in meadows, drainages, and dry riverbeds. The stems, roots, and leaves may be eaten raw or cooked,

Prickly pear cacti

and grass can be boiled in water to make a good broth or tea. Do not eat black or purple grass seeds, which indicate a fungal contamination that, if eaten, could cause severe illness or death.

Sotol
Sotol can be found on rocky slopes in many desert grasslands. The plant has hundreds of 3-foot-long ribbonlike leaves that shoot up from a central rounded ball core. Although similar in appearance to yucca, sotol's light green leaves have small teeth along the sides. Each year in early summer, the sotol plant produces a flower stalk that can grow up to 12 feet tall and has thousands of greenish white flowers that grow in a dense cluster. The rounded ball's heart is the edible part of sotol. It can be procured using a digging stick or similar device. To prepare, cook in a rock-lined baking pit until it no longer tastes bitter, which usually takes several days. The leaf bases can be eaten in the same manner as an artichoke. The stalks can also be used for building material and the leaves for making baskets, mats, and cordage.

Century plant
Similar to sotol, century plant is often found on rocky slopes in many desert grasslands. The plant has spine-tipped leaves that are about 18 inches long and 3 inches wide and crop up from a woody heart, and it produces a flower stalk that can reach up to 15 feet high. The heart of the century plant is edible and should be prepared in the same fashion as sotol. The stalks can also be

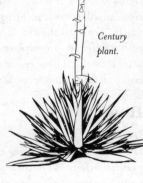
Century plant.

used for building material and the leaves for making baskets, mats, and cordage.

Yucca
Like the century plant and sotol, yucca is found on rocky slopes in many deserts. There are many species of yucca, most with stiff-pointed sword-like leaves and towering stalks with creamy white, waxy flowers. The plant may have one or several stalks that range in height from 3 to 10 feet tall. Yucca flower petals can be eaten raw or cooked, or dried for later consumption. The fruit can be

boiled until very soft, peeled, and seeded before eaten. The stalks can be used for building material and the leaves for making baskets, mats, and cordage. In addition, the roots of the soap-tree yucca plant have a high content of saponins, a soaplike compound, making it a favorite shampoo and soap for indigenous peoples.

Yucca.

Desert amaranth
Amaranth grows in most desert climates. Although there are many species of amaranth, most are short-lived annual herbs with green leaves and thick, erect fleshy stems. The young shoots and leaves can be eaten raw or cooked, or dried for later use. After removing the chaff from the seeds, they can be cooked like popcorn or ground into flour for use in breads.

Desert amaranth.

Date palm
The date palm is found in the deserts of North Africa and the Middle East. This tall tree has deep roots and is supported by a trunk growing from the woody leaf base. The feather-shaped leaves are about 15 feet long and support clusters of flowers or dates. The

Date palm.

ripened reddish brown date provides an excellent and abundant nutritious fruit. The branches of the date palm can be used for shade and roofing materials and to improvise containers. Date trees are a source of food for the inhabitants of the Arabian Peninsula, and their leaves provide shade from the intense desert sun.

Acorns
Acorns are found on many oaks and are edible when leached. Acorns collected from the tree are less prone to have insect, heat, or drying

Continued ➡

damage than those on the ground. An acorn is ready to pick when it can easily separate from its cap without tearing the seed coat. If you pick a green acorn, keep it—it will brown quickly. Leaching is necessary to remove the tannins from the acorn. To properly leach acorns, remove the meat from the shell (this may require boiling it for ten to fifteen minutes in order to soften the shell), and place the meat in a container. Cover the shelled acorns with water, bring the water to a boil, and drain. Repeat the process three or four times, or until the water is clear and the acorns are no longer bitter. If you can't boil water but a stream is close, place the acorns in a porous material and let them soak in a running stream for one to two days. Acorns can be eaten raw or dried, or ground into flour for use in pancakes or bread.

Acorn.

Cattails

Although cattails are found in moist, swamp-like areas, you may discover them in the desert around a natural spring or some other underground water source. Cattails provide several edible portions, including the roots, sprouts, shoots, flower spikes, seeds, and pollen. Cattails are easy to recognize when the stalks are topped with the dense, brown, oblong-shaped seed clusters that appear after the flowers have fallen off. Long, slender, sword-shaped leaves branch off the stalks that can reach up to 8 feet high. Cattail roots are best from late fall through early spring, when they have a high starch concentration, and can be eaten raw or cooked. Sprouts grow from the roots and can be gathered from late summer to winter. They are often cooked like potatoes. The green shoots are best when gathered during the spring before they reach 2 feet in height. Peel away the shoot's outer layer until you reach the white tender core, and eat it raw or steamed. The immature green flower spikes are gathered during late spring before they begin to produce pollen. To prepare, husk and cook the shoot like corn. Seeds are found in the lower section of the pod and are present during the summer. These high-protein seeds can be mashed into flour and used in any number of recipes. Pollen is found on the upper section of the pod and is present during early summer. To procure the yellow pollen, rub, shake, or strip it off into a container or bag. This yellow powder is very high in protein and can be eaten raw, cooked as a cereal, or used with flour.

Cattail.

Cattail.

—From *Surviving the Desert*

---

might as well get the most good out of them while insuring maximum flavor. The best way to do this is to use the rose hips the day they are picked and to gather them while they are red but slightly underripe on a dry, sunny day.

But even after frost or later in the winter when they are shriveled and dry, rose hips are still worth picking. Earlier in the season, the petals themselves, varying in flavor like different species of apples, are delicious if you discard the bitterish green or white bases. Dark red roses are strong-tasting, the flavors becoming more delicate as colors become subdued through the light pinks.

Even the seeds are valuable, being rich in Vitamin E. Some backwoods wives grind them, boil in a small amount of water, and then strain through a cloth. The resulting vitamin-rich fluid is used in place of the water called for in recipes for syrups, jams, and jellies.

The flowers make a rather tasty tea, if each heaping teaspoon of dried petals, twice that amount of fresh petals, is covered with a cup of boiling water, then steeped for five minutes. A little honey or sugar helps bring out the fragrance. Leaves, roots, and the rose hips themselves are also occasionally used for tea.

Sassafras

(*Sassafras*)

There is just one species of the familiarly fragrant sassafras that is native to North America. Ours is a small or medium-sized tree, growing from New England to Ontario, Iowa, and Kansas, south to the Gulf of Mexico.

This member of the laurel family, which also includes several trees whose bark is powdered to provide cinnamon, is found along fences and roads, in abandoned fields, in dry woods, and in other open and semi-open places. Thickets often spring up from the roots. Famous for its supposed medicinal qualities soon after Columbus voyaged here, sassafras is now employed commercially mainly as a flavor. Privately, though, it is still widely used for everything from jelly to gumbo.

The very limber twigs and young shoots of the easily recognized sassafras are bright green and mucilaginous. The leaves, aromatic when crushed, grow in three shapes as shown in the drawing, all varieties sometimes stemming from the same twig. Also mucilaginous, they oxidize in the autumn to beautiful reds and oranges. Greenish-gold flowers, which have a spicy odor, appear with the leaves in the spring, the sexes on separate trees. Birds flock to the dark bluish fruits, nearly half an inch long, when they ripen on their thick red stems in the fall.

Sassafras tea, famous for centuries on this continent, where many people still drink it as a spring tonic, can be made by putting a palmful of preferably young roots into a pot with cold water and boiling them until the rich red color that you've learned by experience you like best is reached. Second and third extractions can be made from the same roots.

For drying and storing some of the makings, use just the bark of the young roots. Older roots can be employed, too, but it is best to scrape off the usual hard, rough covering first.

We like this tea sweetened. Only moderate amounts should be used, in any event, as an overdose of the oil may have a narcotic effect. But you can drink too much ordinary tea, too.

With the help of lemon juice, commercial pectin, and sugar, spicy jellies are made of strong sassafras teas. The dainty green winter buds are delicious, and later the young leaves will add flavor to a salad.

In the South, soups are flavored and thickened by the dried leaves, the veins and hard portions of which are first discarded. If you like the wholesome thickness and smoothness of gumbos, why not try this for yourself? The easiest way to go about it is by drying the young tender stems and leaves, grinding them to a fine powder, sifting this through a sieve to remove the hard parts, and pouring the remainder into a large saltshaker for everyone at the table to use according to his own pleasure.

Shepherd's Purse

(*Capsella*)

Shepherd's purse is valuable to wild food seekers in that it is one of the more common of the wayside weeds, being found throughout most of the year in gardens, lawns, vacant lots, cultivated fields, and paths throughout most of the world where civilization has moved. It is quickly recognizable, and the tender young leaves, which, like others of the mustard family, are pleasingly pepper, may be enjoyed either raw or cooked. Indians even made a nutritious meal from the roasted seeds.

Sassafras.
Left: flowers. Right: twig with leaves and fruit.

This wild green is familiar because of its flat triangular or heart-shaped seed pods which, their broad bases uppermost, ascend the top parts of the stalks on short stems. A favorite food of blue grouse, these diminutive pouches develop from long clusters of tiny white flowers, each with twin pairs of opposite petals. Long green leaves, both smooth-edged and roughly toothed, grow in a rosette near the ground.

Growing so near to the earth and in such accessible places, these leaves are apt to pick up a lot of dust and grit, so it is best to gather them young and then wash them well, afterwards drying them in a towel. Otherwise, the dressing will slip off and form a pool in the bottom of the salad bowl. Tear, don't cut, these greens into bite-size pieces and toss them lightly with enough oil and vinegar, mixed 4 parts to 1, to coat them thoroughly. Arrange contrasting red tomato slices for trim. Incidentally, these tomatoes tend to become too watery if tossed with the greens. Serve without delay.

These young greens, which vary considerably in size and succulency according to the richness of the soil where they grow, can also be carefully gathered, washed, and then placed in a frypan where a little bacon has been cut fine and partly fried. Some sour cream is added, but the cooking is slight; just enough to wilt the leaves.

Continued ➡

Spoon out hot and divide the sauce over the servings.

Although the concentration of vitamins is greater in the green leaves, some people prefer the delicately cabbagelike flavor shepherd's purse takes on when blanched. Where, as so often happens, these edibles grow profusely near your home, you can experiment with blanching by anchoring paper bags over small groups of the young plants to exclude the sunlight.

The leaves, so bursting with vitamins but so low in calories, toughen as shepherd's purse matures. They then can be relegated to a small amount of boiling salted water, cooked until just tender, and dished out with the usual butter, margarine, vinegar, oil, hard-boiled egg, or other supplements.

Shepherd's purse.
Top: stalk with leaves and
flowers. Bottom: rosette.

Shepherd's purse, sometimes known as shepherd's heart and as pick-pocket, is also used as a tea, 1 teaspoon to a cup of boiling water, 2 cups of which daily are said to stimulate sluggish kidneys. Too, pioneers sometimes soaked a handful of the leaves in water and used the latter to wash painful bruises.

Slippery Elm

(*Ulmus*)

Pour a cup of boiling water over a teaspoon of the shredded inner bark of the slippery elm. Cover and allow to steep until cool. Then add lemon juice and sugar to taste, and you'll have some of the famous slippery elm tea of pioneer days, still highly regarded as a spring tonic and as a plain pleasant drink in some parts of the country.

The slippery elm—also known as the red, gray, moose, and rock elm—abounds on bottomlands and on rich, rocky inclines in company with other hardwoods. A medium-sized tree, generally some forty to seventy feet tall with a trunk diameter from about one to three feet, it grows from Maine and southern Quebec to North Dakota, south to eastern Texas and northern Florida. Spreading branches provide broad, open, flattish crowns.

The sharply toothed leaves, scratchy above and downy beneath, grow on short, hairy, stout stems. Growing from woolly, egg-shaped, blunt buds about one-quarter of an inch long, the leaves become unsymmetrical, four to eight inches long, and from two to three inches across the middle, where they are usually broadest. Dark green and dull, lighter on their under portions, they turn to beautiful masses of golden yellow in autumn. The bark is either grayish or dark reddish brown, becoming divided by shallow fissures and mottled by large, loose scales. The hairy twigs, incidentally, turn out to be mucilaginous when chewed.

The inner bark of branches, trunk, and root is extremely mucilaginous. Thick and

fragrant, it is still widely gathered in the spring, when because of the rising sap, trees peel more readily. This whitish inner bark is then dried as in a garret or a warm, half-open oven, then powdered as in the kitchen blender. It has demulcent and emollient, as well as nutritive, properties. Medically, it is still sometimes used for dysentery, diseases of the urinary passeges, and bronchitis. For external application, the finely ground or powdered bark is mixed with enough hot water to make a pasty mass and used as a poultice for inflammations, boils, etc., and also in the form of both rectal and vaginal suppositories. More simply, the tea described in the first paragraph is sometimes used for coughs due to colds, one or two cupfuls a day, several cold sips at a time.

Slippery elm.

Many boys chew this intriguing bark. The Indians used it for food, some of them boiling it with the tallow they rendered from buffalo fat. In an emergency, it will provide life-saving nourishment today, and not at all unpleasantly, either raw or boiled.

Sumac

(*Rhus*)

Sumac "lemonade" is just the thing to take the edges off a hard afternoon. Pick over a generous handful of the red berries, drop them into a pan and mash them slightly, cover with boiling water, and allow to steep away from any heat until this is well colored. Then strain through 2 thicknesses of cloth to remove the fine hairs. Sweeten to taste, and serve either hot or cold.

Some Indian tribes liked this acid drink so much that they dried the small one-seeded berries and stored them for winter use. Many settlers followed suit.

The rapidly growing staghorn sumac, also called the lemonade tree and the vinegar tree, is one of the largest species of the cashew family, commonly teaching ten to twenty feet in height. It is easily recognized at any season because of the close resemblance of its stout and velvety twigs to deer antlers while these are still in velvet. It ranges from the Maritime Provinces to Ontario, south to Georgia and Missouri.

The bark of these shrubs or small trees, which often form thickets, is smooth. The satiny and often streaked wood, sometimes used commercially for such small objects as napkin rings, is green to orange in color. The fernlike leaves, about fourteen to twenty-four inches long, are composed of eleven to thirty-one pointed leaflets from two to five inches in length. Dark green and smooth above, pale and sometimes softly hairy beneath, these flame into brilliant red in the fall.

The tiny, tawnily green flowers grow in loosely stemmed clusters, one sex to a shrub or tree. The male clusters are occasionally ten to

twelve inches long. The female blossoms are smaller and extremely dense, producing compact bunches of berries. These are erect and so startlingly red that sometimes I've come upon a lone cluster suddenly in the woods and thought it was a scarlet tanager perched on a branch.

The hard red fruits are thickly covered with bright red hairs. These hairs are tart with malic acid, the same flavorsome ingredient found in grapes. Since this is readily soluble in water, the berries should be gathered for beverage purposes before any heavy storms, if possible.

Incidentally, the berries of the poisonous sumacs are white. However, there are other sumacs in the United States and Canada with similar red berries that provide a refreshing substitute for pink lemonade. All these red-fruited species are harmless.

One of them is the smooth or scarlet sumac, *Rhus glabra*, which grows from the Maritimes to Minnesota, south to Florida and Louisiana. This closely resembles the staghorn sumac, except that it is entirely smooth, with a pale bluish or whitish bloom coating the plump twigs.

Another is the dwarf, shining, or mountain sumac, *Rhus copallina*, which grows

Staghorn sumac
Left: winter twig. Right: branch
with leaves and fruit cluster.

from New England and Ontario to Florida and Texas. Although similar to the aforementioned species, it can be distinguished from all other sumacs because of peculiar winglike projections along the leaf stems between the leaflets.

Indians made a poultice of the bruised leaves and fruit of the red-berried sumacs and applied it to irritated skin. An astringent gargle, made by boiling the crushed berries in a small amount of water, is still used for sore throats.

—From *Feasting Free on Wild Edibles*

Plants for Medicine

Plants for Medicine U.S. Army

In a survival situation you will have to use what is available. In using plants and other natural remedies, positive identification of the plants involved is as critical as in using them for food. Proper use of these plants is equally important.

Terms and Definitions

The following terms, and their definitions, are associated with medicinal plant use:

- **Poultice**. The name given to crushed leaves or other plant parts, possibly heated, that you apply to a wound or sore either directly or wrapped in cloth or paper.

- **Infusion or tisane or tea**. The preparation of medicinal herbs for internal or external application. You place a small

Continued ➡

EDIBLE ARCTIC PLANTS
Greg Davenport

Plants in an arctic area are normally small and stunted, due to the long-term effects of permafrost, low temperatures, and a short growing season. In the *open tundra*, a wide range of edible plants are available. During summer months, you can find Labrador tea, fireweed, dwarf arctic birch, willow, and an abundance of various other plants and berries. During winter months, you'll find roots, rootstalks, and frozen berries under the snow. Lichens can be found year-round, but be sure you can identify them and that you prepare them correctly, as some can be poisonous (see below). In *bog or swamp regions*, water sedge, cattail, dwarf birch, and berries are available. In *wooded areas*, trees such as birch, spruce, poplar, and aspen, along with many berry-producing plants, such as huckleberries, cranberries, raspberries, cloudberries, and crowberries, can be found. In addition, wild rose hips, Labrador tea, alder, and various other shrubs are very abundant. In cold environments, spruce, birch, and lichens are often the only available vegetation.

Spruce
Spruce, both black and white, is a common northern evergreen. It has short, stiff singular needles and cones that are small with thin scales. The resinous-flavored buds, needles, and stems are rich sources of vitamin C when eaten raw. The inner bark can be collected in the spring and early summer and eaten raw or dried and pounded into flour for later use.

Dwarf arctic birch
Dwarf arctic birch is a shrub that has thin, tooth-edged leaves and bark that can be peeled off in sheets. The fresh buds and leaves can be eaten raw and are rich sources of vitamin C. The inner bark can be collected in the spring and early summer and eaten raw or dried and pounded into flour for later use. A young shoot of dwarf arctic birch is edible, as are its roots, and both can be eaten raw or cooked.

Lichens
Lichens can be found in almost all cold-weather climates, and most species are edible. Some examples include Iceland moss, peat moss, reindeer lichen, and beard lichen. Beard lichen, which grows on trees, may contain a bitter acid that causes stomach and intestinal irritation. However, if it is boiled, dried, and powdered, the acid is removed, and the powder can be used as flour.

—From *Surviving Cold Weather*

quantity of an herb in a container, pour hot water over it, and let it steep (covered or uncovered) before use.

- **Decoction**. The extract of a boiled down or simmered herb leaf or root. You add herb leaf or root to water. You bring them to a sustained boil or simmer to draw their chemicals into the water. The average ratio is about 28 to 56 grams (1 to 2 ounces) of herb to 0.5 liter of water.

- **Expressed juice**. Liquids or saps squeezed from plant material and either applied to the wound or made into another medicine.

Many natural remedies work slower than the medicines you know. Therefore, start with smaller doses and allow more time for them to take effect. Naturally, some will act more rapidly than others.

Specific Remedies
The following remedies are for use only in a survival situation, not for routine use:

- **Diarrhea**. Drink tea made from the roots of blackberries and their relatives to stop diarrhea. White oak bark and other barks containing tannin are also effective. However, use them with caution when nothing else is available because of possible negative effects on the kidneys. You can also stop diarrhea by eating white clay or campfire ashes. Tea made from cowberry or cranberry or hazel leaves work, too.

- **Antihemorrhagics**. Make medications to stop bleeding from a poultice of the puff-ball mushroom, from plantain leaves, or most effectively from the leaves of the common yarrow or woundwort (*Achillea millefolium*).

- **Antiseptics**. Use to cleanse wounds, sores, or rashes. You can make them from the expressed juice from wild onion or garlic, or expressed juice from chickweed leaves or the crushed leaves of dock. You can also make antiseptics from a decoction of burdock root, mallow leaves or roots, or white oak bark. All these medications are for external use only.

- **Fevers**. Treat a fever with a tea made from willow bark, an infusion of elder flowers or fruit, linden flower tea, or elm bark decoction.

- **Colds and sore throats**. Treat these illnesses with a decoction made from either plantain leaves or willow bark. You can also use a tea made from burdock roots, mallow or mullein flowers or roots, or mint leaves.

- **Aches, pains, and sprains**. Treat with externally applied poultices of dock, plantain, chickweed, willow bark, garlic, or sorrel. You can also use salves made by mixing the expressed juices of these plants in animal fat or vegetable oils.

- **Itching**. Relieve the itch from insect bites, sunburn, or plant poisoning rashes by applying a poultice of jewelweed (*Impatiens biflora*) or witch hazel leaves (*Hamamelis virginiana*). The jewelweed juice will help when applied to poison ivy rashes or insect stings. It works on sunburn as well as aloe vera.

- **Sedatives**. Get help in falling asleep by brewing a tea made from mint leaves or passionflower leaves.

- **Hemorrhoids**. Treat them with external washes from elm bark or oak bark tea, from the expressed juice of plantain leaves, or from a Solomon's seal root decoction.

- **Constipation**. Relieve constipation by drinking decoctions from dandelion leaves, rose hips, or walnut bark. Eating raw daylily flowers will also help.

- **Worms or intestinal parasites**. Using moderation, treat with tea made from tansy (*Tanacetum vulgare*) or from wild carrot leaves.

- **Gas and cramps**. Use a tea made from carrot seeds as an antiflatulent; use tea made from mint leaves to settle the stomach.

- **Antifungal washes**. Make a decoction of walnut leaves or oak bark or acorns to treat ringworm and athlete's foot. Apply frequently to the site, alternating with exposure to direct sunlight.

Miscellaneous Uses of Plants

Make dyes from various plants to color clothing or to camouflage your skin. Usually, you will have to boil the plants to get the best results. Onion skins produce yellow, walnut hulls produce brown, and pokeberries provide a purple dye.

Make fibers and cordage from plant fibers. Most commonly used are the stems from nettles and milkweeds, yucca plants, and the inner bark of trees like the linden.

Make fish poison by immersing walnut hulls in a small area of quiet water. This poison makes it impossible for the fish to breathe but doesn't adversely affect their edibility.

Make tinder for starting fires from cattail fluff, cedar bark, lighter knot wood from pine trees, or hardened sap from resinous wood trees.

Make insulation by fluffing up female cattail heads or milkweed down.

Make insect repellents by applying the expressed juice of wild garlic or onion to the skin, by placing sassafras leaves in your shelter, or by burning or smudging cattail seed hair fibers.

Plants can be your ally as long as you use them cautiously. The key to the safe use of plants is positive identification whether you use them as food or medicine or in constructing shelters or equipment.

—From *Survival (Field Manual 21–76)*

Bradford Angier

Amaranth (*Amaranthus*)

Family: Amaranth (*Amaranthaceae*)

Common Names: Spleen Amaranth, Palmer's Amaranth, Red Amaranth, Redroot, Wild Beet, Red Cockscomb, Green Amaranth, Green-Opened Amaranth, Prostraite Amaranth, Prostrate Amaranth, Slim Amaranth, Hybrid Amaranthus, Prince's Feather, Pigweed, Slender Pigweed, Prostrate Pigweed, Keerless, Careless, Careless Weed, Love-Lies-Bleeding, Floramor, Flower Gentle, Velvet Flower, Flower Velure.

Characteristics: Amaranth is an erect annual, some 1 to 6 feet high, and branched above. The stemmed leaves, about 3 to 6 inches long, are dully green, rough, hairy, ovate or rhombic, with wavy rims. The small flower clusters end in pyramidical, loosely branched, reddish or greenish inflorescences. The fleshy taproots, lengthy and pinkish to red in color, give the medicinal some of its local names.

It is an easy thing to mistake amaranth for pigweed (*Chenopodium*), which makes little difference to the food gatherer, as both are about equally delicious. But the leaves and stalks of the amaranth are ordinarily softly fuzzy, whereas those of the *Chenopodium* are smooth with a loosely attached whitish bloom. Also, the *Amaranthus* has noticeably strong veins. It has picked up its deceptive common name of pigweed in some locales because it likes the rich soil found in and about pigpens.

The Zunis believed the rain gods brought the bright and shiny black seeds from the underworld and dispersed them over their lands. Minute, these seeds are numerous—some 28,000 per ounce—and are widely distributed by the wind. They emerge as plants within fourteen to twenty-one days at temperatures from 65 to 75°F. Department of Agriculture scientists have found that if water does not reach them, those of the A. retroflexus are still living and capable of reproduction after forty, but not fifty, years in the soil.

Area: Except where thwarted by frozen ground and too much cold, the amaranth thrives throughout most of the United States and Canada where there is enough dampness.

Amaranth (Amaranthus).

Uses: Containing, despite a water content of nearly 90 percent, 3.9 milligrams of iron per 100 grams (more than any green vegetable except parsley listed in the U.S.D.A. *Composition of Foods*), amaranth is extremely important to anyone with a deficiency in this mineral, including most women. It is also a vital antiscorbutic, the same 100-gram portion boasting 80 milligrams of vitamin C. Yet countless tons of this unusually nutritious and delec-table vegetable, considered by most to be just another weed, go to waste annually.

Amaranth used to be considered helpful in treating mouth and throat inflammations and sores, and in quelling dysentery and diarrhea; one dose was a teaspoonful of dried leaves steeped in a cup of bubbling water, although stronger dosages were considered more valuable. It was also thought to stem abnormally profuse menstrual flows as well as internal hemorrhaging. Taken internally, too, it was supposed to help quiet and eventually cure ulcers in the digestive tractk.

Flowers, leaves, and roots were sought because of their astringent quality for external wounds, sores, and ulcers. They were simmered to make a mouthwash for cankers, sore throats, ulcerated gums and to strengthen gums that bled too freely after ordinary tooth brushing. Amaranth was even said to be useful in the care of venereal diseases. At the other extreme, it was one of the remedies for a nosebleed.

Because of its ability to produce a soapy lather, the leaf of the A. retroflexus was used in the washing of bandages and other fabrics from the sickroom.

Indians made poultices from it to reduce ordinary swellings and to soothe aching teeth. A tea made from the leaves by some of the tribes to allay stomachache was also used to wash arthritic parts of the body. Strong decoctions were thought to kill and expel intestinal worms.

Arrowhead (*Sagittaria*)

Family: Water Plantain (*Alismaceae*)
Common Names: Arrowhead, Broad-Leaf Arrowhead, Duck Potato, Swan Potato, Swamp Potato, Tule Potato, Marsh Potato, Wapato, Wapatoo, Katniss.

Characteristics: The arrowhead, as its name suggests, has a pointed arrowheadlike leaf with the two barblike continuations, one on either side, as well as a stout green stem which might well be the shaft of the medicinal replica of this part of the Indians' arsenal—which also included bows, tomahawks, and lances. Just as they used the bow and arrow, Indians from one coast to the other relied on this wild vegetable as food and medicine. All leaves are not the same, especially when the plants grow submerged and ribbonlike foliage is formed, but there are generally enough in a group for sure identification.

Three-petaled white flowers, with numerous pistils and yellow clusters of stamens, grow on their own single stems from June to September. Papery thin leaves extend directly below in the form of attractive clusters of subtending bracts. They mature into fruits with two-winged, round-topped, generally flattish seeds.

The tubers are the important parts, and those on the nearly three dozen different species of arrowhead in North America are all edible. Inasmuch as none is harmful, there is little need to try to segregate them botanically, although only about half a dozen produce the big, starchy corms which wading squaws ordinarily located with their toes, then loosened so that they would float. Long sticks can also be used to release them from mud and roots.

Area: Growing commonly in wet places, the arrowhead can be seen in damp locations throughout the southern parts of Canada and where it is damp enough in the original forty-eight states.

Uses: In addition to being considered a valuable and easily digestible food for invalids and convalescents, the corms were used as a diuretic.

Arrowhead (Sagittaria).

Juice pressed from them by the Indians, later by the newcomers from the Old World, was thought both to increase the flow of urine and to multiply the amount of the discharge of other waste ingredients in the process. The quickest action was found to take place when this juice, or the concentrated liquid from boiled tubers, was drunk on an empty stomach, preferably while the patient remained inactive and particularly if he stayed lying down in a comfortable place.

Birch (*Betula*)

Family: Birch (*Betulaceae*)

Common Names: Silver Birch, Golden Birch, Yellow Birch, Red Birch, Black Birch, Gray Birch, White Birch, American White Birch, European White Birch, Blueleaf Birch, Mahogany Birch, Mountain Mahogany Birch, Paper Birch, Mountain Paper Birch, Canoe Birch, Lady Birch, Swamp Birch, River Birch, Tundra Dwarf Birch, Newfoundland Dwarf Birch, European Weeping Birch, Northern Birch, Virginian Birch, Cherry Birch, Spicy Birch, Sweet Birch, Oldfield Birch, Minor Birch, Water Birch, Poverty Birch, Wirefield Birch, Poplar Birch, Low Birch.

Characteristics: Historically, the birch probably derives its name from a somewhat similar Sanskrit word translated as "that which is written upon." Numerous letters and journals have been inscribed on thin sheets of the multilayered bark of the white birches, so durable and pliable that many an Indian canoe was made of it.

There are two distinct types of birches growing on this continent—the well-known white birches and the so-called black birches with their black to reddish brown bark. The former grow up to about 100 feet high, with papery bark, flutters of which can be pulled off without disfiguring the trunks for easily and quickly starting campfires, even in the rain. The black birches can be differentiated from some of the wild cherries in that the broken twigs of the former have the smell of wintergreen, whereas those of the cherries are characterized by a bitter-almond odor.

Area: The familiar white birches, both trees and shrubs, thrive over the majority of Canada and the United States with the exception of a wide band down the central western portion of this country, along the lower Pacific Coast except where they have been transplanted as bright and cheerful decorations, and in the Southwest in general.

Continued ➡

The black birches grow largely in higher, chillier, and not so fertile eastern regions of this country, where they became historically important when their nutritious bark was credited with saving the lives of numerous Confederate soldiers at the time of Garnett's retreat across the mountains before regrouping at Monterey, Virginia. For decades the path of the soldiers could be traced by the peeled birch trees. Black birches grow from Ontario to New England, south to Delaware and Ohio, and along the Appalachian range to Alabama and Georgia.

Uses: Before the commercial oil of wintergreen was manufactured synthetically, it was distilled from the bark and twigs of the black birch, this process being easier and less expensive than obtaining it from the spicy little wintergreen plant (*Gaultheria procumbens*), as was done previously on a large scale for such uses as a flavoring agent for toothpastes and other medicinals. The active principle here is methyl salicylate. Wintergreen tea, made by steeping a large handful of the freshly gathered, green leaves, was drunk, 1 or 2 cups a day, by the Indians and

PLANT MEDICINE: A QUICK REFERENCE
U.S. Army, Marine Corps, Navy, Air Force

Tannin

Medical uses. Burns, diarrhea, dysentery, skin problems, and parasites. Tannin solution prevents infection and aids healing.

Sources. Found in the outer bark of all trees, acorns, banana plants, common plantain, strawberry leaves, and blackberry stems.

Preparation
(a) Place crushed outer bark, acorns, or leaves in water.
(b) Leach out the tannin by soaking or boiling.
   • Increase tannin content by longer soaking time.
   • Replace depleted material with fresh bark/plants.

Treatments
(a) Burns.
   • Moisten bandage with cooled tannin tea.
   • Apply compress to burned area.
   • Pour cooled tea on burned areas to ease pain.
(b) Diarrhea, dysentery, and worms. Drink strong tea solution (may promote voiding of worms).
(c) Skin problems (dry rashes and fungal infections). Apply cool compresses or soak affected part to relieve itching and promote healing.
(d) Lice and insect bites. Wash affected areas with tea to ease itching.

Salicin/salicylic acid

Medical uses. Aches, colds, fever, inflammation, pain, sprains, and sore throat (aspirin-like qualities).

Sources. Willow and aspen trees.

Preparation
(a) Gather twigs, buds, or cambium layer (soft, moist layer between the outer bark and the wood) of willow or aspen.
(b) Prepare tea.
(c) Make poultice.
   • Crush the plant or stems.
   • Make a pulpy mass.

Treatments
(a) Chew on twigs, buds, or cambium for symptom relief.
(b) Drink tea for colds and sore throat.
(c) Use warm, moist poultice for aches and sprains.
   • Apply pulpy mass over injury.
   • Hold in place with a dressing.

Common plantain

Medical uses. Itching, wounds, abrasions, stings, diarrhea, and dysentery.

Source. There are over 200 plantain species with similar medicinal properties.

Preparation.
(a) Brew tea from seeds.
(b) Brew tea from leaves.
(c) Make poultice of leaves.

Treatments
(a) Drink tea made from seeds for diarrhea or dysentery.
(b) Drink tea made from leaves for vitamin and minerals.
(c) Use poultice to treat cuts, sores, burns, and stings.

Papain

Medical uses. Digestive aid, meat tenderizer, and a food source.
Source. Fruit of the papaya tree.

Preparation
(a) Make cuts in unripe fruit.
(b) Gather milky white sap for its papain content.
(c) Avoid getting sap in eyes or wounds.

Treatments
(a) Use sap to tenderize tough meat.
(b) Eat ripe fruit for food, vitamins, and minerals.

Common Cattail

Medical uses. Wounds, sores, boils, inflammations, burns, and an excellent food source.

Source. Cattail plant found in marshes.

Preparation
(a) Pound roots into a pulpy mass for a poultice.
(b) Cook and eat green bloom spikes.
(c) Collect yellow pollen for flour substitute.
(d) Peel and eat tender shoots (raw or cooked).

Treatments
(a) Apply poultice to affected area.
(b) Use plant for food, vitamins, and minerals.

—From *Survival, Evasion, and Recovery: Multiservice Tactics, Techniques, and Procedures*

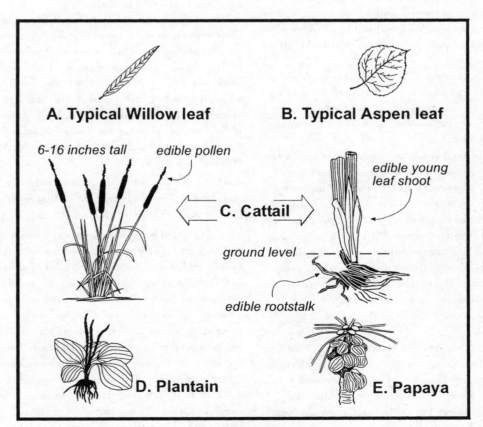

A. Typical Willow leaf

B. Typical Aspen leaf

6-16 inches tall   edible pollen

C. Cattail

edible young leaf shoot

ground level

edible rootstalk

D. Plantain

E. Papaya

Useful plants.

Continued ➡

pioneers as a remedy for rheumatism and for headaches, its inherent salicylic acid being the prime ingredient of the aspirin that doctors prescribe today.

Birch (Betula).

Some tribes, passing their lore along to frontiersmen, made a tea of the dried bark and leaves of the birches by steeping a teaspoonful to a cup of boiling water until the infusion cooled and then drinking it, strained, for the above and for a fever reducer to a stimulant and for relief from the pain of kidney stones. It was also used to relieve the cramps and discomfort caused by gas in the digestive system. The early Americans utilized it as a disinfectant and as a mouthwash, especially for sour mouths.

This infusion was also thought to be useful in stimulating the flow of urine, in purifying blood after the long cold winters, in expelling worms from the alimentary canal, and as a treatment for gout.

The maple-syruplike sap of the white birch—obtained in the spring as I have done by boring an inch or two into the lower tree trunk with an auger, fashioning a spout from a hollowed elderberry branch from which the pith has been poked or from a bent top of a tin can, and catching the drippings in a clean can whose wire bail is hung from a twig—may be boiled down in an uncovered pot for the hours needed to thicken it to a syrup which may then be mixed with cough syrup or drunk as is to relieve stomach cramps. (The hole in the tree was later plugged with wood.)

Some Indians brewed a tea from the leaves of the white birches, and made a poultice of the boiled bark for the treatment of burns, wounds, and bruises. The ashes they utilized to soften and eventually remove scabs.

The sap secured from the black birch was applied externally to help heal sores and boils or carbuncles.

Skin troubles such as eczema sometimes seemed to respond to an all secured from white birches by boiling the wood and bark in water, leaving enough moisture to make an ointment which was rubbed onto the afflicted part.

The small conelike structures formed by the maturing of the fruits of the low birch (*Betula pumila*), long central spikes to which innumerable tiny dry scales adhere, were steeped in boiling water to make a tea which women sipped during painful menstruation and as a tonic following childbirth. The cones of this birch were also roasted on the coals of an almost expired campfire and the fumes inhaled for chronic nasal infections such as catarrh, an inflammation of the mucous membranes of the nose and air passages.

The Catawbas simmered the buds of the black birch to make a syrup to which sulphur was added to provide a salve for ringworm and for sores in general. Indians in Texas boiled the bark of this tree for use in healing sore hooves on their horses.

Many early Americans recognized the efficacy of the vitamin C in the sap of the white birch in preventing and curing scurvy. In writing of the use of enema among aboriginal North Americans, Robert F. Heizer said in 1686 that the Ojibwas used steeped paper birch bark for this.

The sweet black smoke given off by burning white birch bark was believed efficacious in fumigating the air in dwellings where patients with contagious diseases had been confined.

The sap of the white birches was also credited with being laxative and diuretic. The bark and leaves of these widespread trees were applied externally by some of the tribes to cleanse ulcers and carbuncles, to combat gangrene, and to act as a general disinfectant in skin diseases.

Blackberry–Raspberry (*Rubus*)

Family: Rose (*Rosaceae*)

Common Names: Highbush Blackberry, Running Blackberry, Tall Blackberry, Sand Blackberry, Creeping Blackberry, Mountain Blackberry, Swamp Blackberry, California Blackberry, Blackcap, Black Raspberry, Purple Raspberry, Purple-Flowering Raspberry, White-Flowering Raspberry, American Red Raspberry, Wild Red Raspberry, Virginia Raspberry, Western Raspberry, Arctic Raspberry, Flowering Raspberry, Rocky Mountain Raspberry, Salmonberry, White-Flowered Salmonberry, Cloudberry, Wineberry, Nagoonberry, Red Nagoonberry, Dewberry, Thimbleberry, Western Thimbleberry, Baked-Apple Berry, Bake-Apple, Plumboy, Flymboy, Gout Berry.

Characteristics: Being the most valuable wild fruit in North America, both because of the money made from it and because of its eminence as a summer food for birds and animals, the blackberry-raspberry family is known to all. The facts that some plants are thorny and others thornless, that a few grow only a couple of inches and others taller than a man can reach, and that there is a wide variation in color and even taste makes little difference in their worth as a wild medicine.

The simplest method of identifying them is their likeness to market varieties. Rapidly gathered in heartening amounts, the ripe berries—each made up of innumerable tiny, fleshy, and juice-rich little globes, in the middle of each of which is a seed—detach readily from their light-colored, stem-attached centers and five-petaled hulls, coming off in the hand in a fragile, hollow completeness in which each part has rounded from its own ovule.

Area: At the very least, fifty distinct species of blackberries and raspberries thrive throughout all fifty states. They also abound in Canada.

Uses: Juice and wine made from the berries is still used in Appalachia to combat diarrhea. The berries and their juice were long used by many Indian tribes to rid their members of chronic stomach trouble and to allay vomiting and retching. It was considered effective in preventing miscarriage. It is astringent and believed generally beneficial to digestion, being thought mild enough to control diarrhea and dysentery even among infants and young children. In fact, early Americans sometimes combined it with honey and alum to tighten loose teeth. The settlers also came to use the juice to dissolve tartar on the teeth. It was

turned to by numerous tribes to cure cankers of the mouth, gums, and tongue.

A few of the berries, or their strained juices, were added to other wild medicines to make them less disagreeable. The juice, held to be extremely soothing and tension-relieving, was turned to by many of the Indians and pioneers to lessen the menstrual flow without suddenly ending it entirely. When the bowels were loose, it was drunk instead of tea or coffee. It was thought to ease nausea, to be an antacid, and to act as a parturient.

Many a colonial deemed his medicine chest incomplete if it did not contain blackberry brandy or cordial. Not only were mixtures of the juice and sugar fermented, but juice boiled down with a few spices for flavor was bottled with regular brandy to make a thick, sweet cordial, handy for unexpected digestive upsets. Too, black-berry brandy was considered to be a rapidly acting remedy for diarrhea. So, in

Top: Raspberry (Rubus); Bottom: Blackberry (Rubus).

fact, was the eating of a large quantity of the ripe berries.

The young leaves of these plants were gathered after the dew was off them on a dry morning, dried at no more than ordinary room temperature—not in the sun—and stored throughout the fall and winter in tightly capped jars in dark, dry cupboards for use like the regular Chinese tea whose taste the resulting beverage resembles, especially when served with a little sugar but no cream or milk. Like commercial tea, it is rich in tannin and similar substances and is therefore astringent, being considered in Appalachia and other places useful in controlling diarrhea.

The amount of dry leaves easily pinched by the fingertips of one hand, dropped into a warmed teapot, then covered with a quart of boiling water, and steeped for up to ten minutes, depending on individual tastes, was used to make four pleasantly steaming cups that were held to be an enjoyable blood purifier and spring tonic. A more precise measurement, recommended by many, was and is a level teaspoon of the dried leaves to a cup of bubbling water, steeped until it cools, and then drunk cold, 2 cups a day. It was thought to help mothers in childbirth and was given as a refreshing drink during delivery. The leaf tea, brewed so as to be particularly potent, was also applied to severe sores. Used as a gargle and mouthwash, it was also recommended for bad breath.

Such a tea was similarly made from the roots and rhizomes. This was also held to be effective against diarrhea and, in strong doses, even as an antidote against some poisons. The root tea was thought to be useful for drying up runny noses. The astringency and apparent healing properties of the roots resulted in their flavor as a gargle

Continued ➡

for sore throats and mouths, for cankers, and as a medication for bleeding cuts and wounds.

There are reports that some 500 Oneida Indians, beset by dysentery in one season, all recovered when treated with blackberry root, at the same time when many of their white neighbors, not using this primitive native medicine, fell before the ailment.

Other Indians used blackberry roots and vines for a tea taken internally by members of the tribe who were vomiting and expelling blood. Others utilized a solution made by soaking blackberry roots for bathing sore eyes and also for moistening compresses for use as poultices. Ojibwas simmered the branches for increasing the flow of urine and steeped the roots to make an infusion for stopping trouble with loose bowels.

The dried bark of the roots and rhizomes of the species were long officially recognized by the medical world both as an astringent and as a tonic. They were marketed as a diarrhea cure well before the Civil War. One prescription was for an ounce of blackberry roots boiled down from 6 cups to 4 cups, then drunk by the half cup about every two hours as long as the trouble persisted. A bigger dosage of this astringent tea was said to be useful in helping those suffering from whooping cough.

A tea made of the bark of these plants was used to control dysentery.

Raspberry stems powdered between two smooth rocks, or with mortars and pestles which the Indians also used, were applied dry to cuts.

The leaves were steeped in water, without boiling, and given to pregnant women to ease delivery. This infusion, the subject of later experiments in its ability to relieve labor pains, seemed to act principally to relieve muscular tension about the uterus.

In the desert and on the dusty plains, often when such expanses were scoured by savage winter winds, the Indian use of tea steeped from *Rubus* leaves to increase the flow of urine was adopted gratefully by the white newcomers. Bark scraped from the branches and vines of these species was also favored in a decoction for upset stomachs.

Bulrush *(Typha)*

Family: Cat-tail *(Typhaceae)*

Common Names: Rushes, Flags, Cat-tail, Cat-tail Flag, Narrow-Leaved Cat-tail, Broadleaf Cat-tail, Reed Mace, Cossack Asparagus, Cat-o'-Nine-Tails.

Characteristics: Although our ancestors used these favored tall, strap-leaved plants for floor coverings, woven mats and rugs, and seats and backs for chairs, they are now largely neglected except for the wild food seekers and the birds. They are easily recognizable both for their long, tapering, pointed, ribbonlike green leaves and for the wienielike plumpnesses which grow on separate, substantial, round stalks. These hot-dog-shaped protuberances are crowded with initially green feminine flowers. Above these later are shriveling, microspore-crammed tops which, when maturing, drop their male cells of their own accord to fertilize their sisters, even-

tually producing golden pollen and hoards of tiny, white-tufted seeds that the winds disperse over the landscape.

Almost every part of the bulrush, from the large starchy roots to the cornlike buds and later the flourlike pollen, is healthfully edible.

Area: Except in the permafrost of the Far North, bulrushes grow almost everywhere where there is fresh water and dampness in Canada and the United States.

Uses: The mature brown bulrush cobs used to be kept in closed dry places during the winter and their soft, alleviating down was spread antiseptically over burned, scalded, and chafed portions of the body. The roots were also crushed into a pulp, mixed with some wholesome fat such as black bear lard, and applied as a salve in such instances.

Bulrush (Typha).

The cut, sliced, and chopped stems were spread upon wounds, burns, and sores. They were also hopefully taken internally to quell diarrhea, kill and expel worms, and for gonorrhea.

Chickweed *(Alsine) (Stellaria media)*

Family: Pink *(Caryophyllaceae)*

Common Names: Common Chickweed, Indian Chickweed, Star Chickweed, Great Chickweed, Starwort, Scarwort, Starwirt, Stitchwort, Adder's Mouth, Tongue Grass, Satin Flower, White Bird's Eye, Pamplinas, *Mouron des Oiseaux.*

Characteristic: As the meekest sometimes turn out to be the strongest, so is it with chickweed, which is an apparently feeble member of the pink group but is actually a lusty annual with matted to upright green stems that take over many an area. Commencing its growth in the fall, it vigorously thrives through the sleet and snowstorms of winter even in the Far North, survives most weed killers, starts blooming while the snow is often still on the ground, and many times finishes its seed production in the springtime. It is so abundantly fruitful, however, that it flowers throughout most of the country every month of the year.

Growing to a foot high in matted to upright trailing stems, it has egg-shaped lower and median leaves and stemless and highly variable upper leaves. In the star chickweed or great chickweed (*Stellaria pubera*), the characteristic blossoms, brightly white and about $1/2$ inch across, have such deeply notched petals that their five appear more like ten, the number of the stamens. Usually gathering themselves together at night and on cloudy or foggy days, they unfurl under the brilliant sun.

Area: Growing the year around from Alaska to Greenland southward, chickweed is generally blooming in some area in every state, province, and territory in the United States and Canada throughout the year.

Uses: Far from being just a troublesome weed, chickweed is a valuable antiscorbutic and medicinal, as well as a low-calorie spinach-treated food more tender than the majority of wild greens.

Gathered fresh and dropped into enough bubbling water to cover, it is still regarded in numerous regions as an excellent warm poultice for inflammations and otherwise irritated skin, abscesses, swellings, wounds, cuts, sores, and even erysipelas, infections, hemorrhoids, inflamed eyes, ulcers that have been difficult to heal, boils, and carbuncles. Used on loose bandages, it was renewed at short intervals, the cooled water in which it had been steeped often being utilized on the trouble spot as a wash.

In fact, there were not many such troubles for which chickweed was not used, including swollen testicles and venereal diseases. It was also so utilized fresh, dried, powdered, and made into salves.

Believed to soothe and heal anything it came in contact with, it was taken internally for bronchitis, coughs, cold symptoms, hoarseness, arthritis, and such.

For blood poisoning, the affected part was treated by the usual poultice, and the chickweed also taken internally. For severe constipation, one prescription was for 3 tablespoonfuls of the fresh plant to be boiled in a quart of water until only 2 cups remained; then a warm cupful of this was taken at least every three hours—in badly blocked cases oftener—until evacuation was successful.

Chickweed was also credited with being a refrigerant, an alternative, and an expectorant.

Chickweed (Alsine) (Stellaria media).

It was considered to be rich in potash salts and therefore fine for the undernourished, especially children, whom it was claimed it rapidly strengthened—all this with a weed now considered merely pesky by many gardeners and enthusiastic lawn growers.

Chicory *(Chichorium intybus)*

Family: Composite *(Compositae)*

Common Names: Blue Dandelion, Blue Daisy, Blue Sailors, Ragged Sailors, Blowball, Succory, Wild Succory, Wild Endive, *Barbe de Capuchin*, Wild Bachelor Button, Witloof.

Characteristics: Chicory blues roadsides and fields with its large prominent flowers, usually blooming from May to October and also occasionally showing white or pink. Although on cloudy days the flowers often remain open, they ordinarily close in the noontime sun and then resemble small blue stalks. The daisylike rays have five square-rimmed straps at their tips. Many times in clusters but usually twins, the blooms are generally about 1 to $1 1/2$ inches wide.

As it had accompanied the Roman legions, the chicory came to the New World with the first settlers and was quickly adopted by the Indians. The perennial, resembling the dandelion except in color, forms a similar rosette of multifari-

Continued ➡

ously lobed, indented, and toothed leaves that taper into lengthy stalks. Those growing upward on the stem have clasping bases and are not so big.

Chicory
(*Cichorium intybus*).

Chicory grows from a large, deep taproot, erectly and rigidly angular, up to about a yard high, resembling the dandelion most when young, although it always remains bitter and exudes an acrid white juice when broken, cut, or bruised like its cousin, likewise a member of the extensive composite family.

It is now produced commercially in the western states, particularly in California and Idaho. With the *Cichorium intybus*, which tolerates cool soil, there are approximately 27,000 seeds per ounce, each requiring some five to fourteen days to germinate at temperatures from 68 to 86°F.

Area: The alien chicory has spread from the Maritime Provinces and New England west to the plains, then in the West from British Columbia to California.

Uses: A pound of chicory leaves, despite being a bit more than 95 percent water, contains 82 milligrams of calcium, 95 of phosphorus, 2.3 of iron, 32 of sodium, and 826 of potassium, plus vitamins A and C, thiamine, riboflavin, and niacin. The roots for centuries have been roasted and ground for making into a coffeelike beverage and as a stretcher, flavorer, and adulterant of the familiar coffee bean.

A medicinal infusion for upset or overacid stomachs was made by adding a teaspoonful of the dried, chopped root to 2 cups of boiling water, sipped cold several times a day. It has also been brought to a boil like regular coffee, in smaller amounts since it is stronger, set off the heat to steep, strained, and then drunk like coffee to increase the flow of urine, as a mild laxative, and as a tonic. An ounce of the powdered root to 2 cups of water was sometimes tried for the allaying of yellowish pigmentation of the skin, tissues, and body fluids caused by the deposition of bile pigments.

Being one of the first greens of spring, it was used raw when young, simmered when older, as a bitterish source of vitamin C to prevent and to cure scurvy. A reputedly healthful tea was steeped from the dried leaves.

Crushed chicory leaves were turned to as poultices for ordinary swellings, inflammations, irritations, rashes, and even for smarting and inflamed eyes, the patient lying down in the latter case with moist and cooling bruised leaves laid over the ailing eyes.

The root beverage was used by some for difficulties with the liver, spleen, gallbladder, and urinary system.

Common Burdock (*Arctium lappa*)

Family: Composite (*Compositae*)

Common Names: Burdock, Great Burdock, Woolly Burdock, Bur, Burrs, Bur Weed, Clot-

bur, Clotbur, Beggar's Buttons, Gobo, Wild Gobo, Happy-Major, Personata.

Characteristics: Everyone knows the burdock, which can scarcely be mistaken, particularly because its ever-clinging burrs, the seedpods which followed the Roman legions and other warriors across the Old World, came with the first ships to America and soon spread with the trappers, the pioneers, the settlers with their wagon trains, and the gold seekers to every part of the continent.

One of the coarser cousins of the thistle, the common burdock, for example, first has young leaves that are smooth and velvetlike, if a bit furry, giving a hint of their edible qualities that are so marked that we have watched farmers cultivating the plant in the Orient. The prickly ovule carriers further spread themselves by separating when one tries to pick them off of clothing, animals, and other possessions, additionally extending their range, although they generally do not grow at elevations above some 800 feet.

Common Burdock
(Arctium lappa)

The initial flowers differ in color from purplish amethyst to white. They burst from stout stalks, sometimes over an inch in diameter. The leaves, varying somewhat among the species, grow alternately on their rapidly lifting stems. They are large, vein-ridden, dark green, and a bit shaggy, a number of them a foot wide by twice that long. The flower stalks, whose rapidity of growth is astonishing, often shoot up several feet in a brief time.

For medicinal and eating uses, the roots should be gathered the first year of growth, at least by fall but perferably in early summer. What to look for is easy to determine, for the first-year burdock does not then have flowers or burs. Reaching a foot or more in length and perhaps an inch in diameter, with a grayish white covering and a creamy pith, they are ordinarily difficult to excavate. An especially slim spade or even a post-hole digger is not an out-of-the-ordinary tool to use in this task. The roots should be judiciously and completely peeled before any usage.

The long, obese flower stalks should, for most favorable results, be picked while the leaves are unfurling, in advance of the time when the flower buds would be starting to expand. The extremely bitter rind should be completely peeled and cut off and the remainder cooked in two waters. The young leaves are also ordinarily cooked in two waters to remove their extreme bitterness.

Area: Prospering throughout most of the United States and southern Canada where people and their animals have ventured, except for a southern region from California eastward, the burdocks are prominent along roads, trails, paths, and throughways, walls and fences, yards and fields. They spring up in profusion about

old farm buildings and yards, sawmills, logging regions, and abandoned mines, stamping mills, diggings, placer operations, and the like.

Uses: A teaspoon of the chopped roots was steeped in each cup of boiling water for a tea of many uses, having been, for one thing, considered to be an excellent urinary remedial; for another, it was considered to have been a general tonic, drunk cold, 2 cups a day, a few sips at a time. It was another of the arthritic palliatives. The tea was believed to help pleurisy, as well as to reduce the swelling of glands. It was given to women in labor. It was also used to reduce fever by increasing perspiration. In fact, the roasted and ground roots were often seen for sale for use as a so-termed healthful coffee substitute.

Interestingly, in the case of the burdocks it was the settlers who instructed the Indians in their various uses common in those early days. The red men, however, soon adapted it to their own usages; young medicine men, fasting for days at a time in their search for purity and wisdom, occasionally imbibed the bitter beverage of the plant in an effort to make what they had discovered mentally remain in their minds.

The settler and Indians alike made a wash by boiling the roots to bathe skin ailments and diseases. Root tea was even believed helpful, when taken internally, for syphilis and chronic skin ailments. The root tea was drunk by the jiggerful. Treatments to be effective were considered to be necessarily continued for at least several weeks.

The young leaves were believed to be both cooling and dehydrating and therefore were used for lingering ulcers and other sores. Juice from the leaves, taken internally perhaps with a little sweetening because of its natural bitterness, was said both to increase the flow of urine and to rid one of kidney pain.

A salve made from burdock roots was used in an effort both to decrease swelling on wounds and sores and to bring about general healing of infections. Such a salve was also used to soothe and cure burns and scalds.

Some settlers obtained seeds from the mature burrs and started them soaking in brandy for dosage by the teaspoonful for more severe skin diseases.

Another old-fashioned way to make burdock tea was to add an ounce of the root, first year as always, to 3 cups of water and to bring it to a bubble in an open pan, keeping up the simmering until but 2 cups of fluid remained. It was then strained and taken in 4-ounce potions several times every twenty-four hours. Besides the usual diuretic, diaphoretic, aperient, and alternative uses, it was supposed to be generally healthful and strengthening.

In Appalachia a tea of the roots is still used for rheumatism. In the seventeen hundreds in the New World it was prescribed as a cure for syphilis and gonorrhea. A poultice made of the leaves was also used for snakebites.

Elderberry (Sambucus)

Family: Honeysuckle (*Caprifoliaceae*)

Common Names: American Elderberry, Canadian Elderberry, Common Elderberry, Red-Berried Elderberry, Blue-Berried Elderberry, Mountain Blue Elderberry, Black

Continued ➡

Elderberry, Red Elderberry, Scarlet Elder, Florida Elderberry, Elder, American Elder, Common Elder, Black Elder, Blackbead Elder, Sweet Elder, Dwarf Elder, Elder Flowers, Elder Blows, Boor Tree, Boutry, Boretree, Tree of Music.

Characteristics: Elderberries differ considerably in form and taste, growing from bushy shrubs a few feet high to trees close to 50 feet in height. Their usual clusters of aromatic, star-shaped white flowers vary from flat-topped bunches to globular arrays, maturing to berry-like, limb-sagging fruits that differentiate in color from blue, amber, red, to black and also changing considerably in taste.

The Indians used the long, straight, hollow stems that became woodier with age for arrows and especially selected some in the springtime, dried them with their leaves on, pushed out all the soft and poisonous pith with hot sticks, and made either spouts for gathering maple and other sap or bored holes in them to fashion flutes; this gave the medicinal its additional name of tree of music. I've bugled in elk with an elderberry whistle.

The red-berried elderberry (*Sambucus pubens*), to describe one, is a 3- to 10-foot shrub preferring rich woods on rocky slopes and in cool and moist ravines. The limbs are obese, tan, with warty pores. The opposite leaves are compound with some five to seven parts, 2 to 6 inches long, with fine, sharp teeth and smooth green tops and paler, generally fuzzy undersides, with lance-head shapes and sharply pointed tips. The small creamy blossoms grow with five petals joined and with three to five stamens, an inferior ovary with from three to five chambers and a three-lobed style at the tip, in pyramid-formed terminal clusters blooming from June to August. These mature into round, bright red, berrylike fruits, usually slightly less than 1/4 inch in diameter. This particular species thrives from Alaska to Newfoundland, south to Iowa, the Great Lakes, Indiana, and Georgia.

Area: Elderberries, liking rich and moist soil, grow from Alaska to Newfoundland and throughout most of the continent from California to Florida.

Uses: Stomach upsets have followed the eating of too many of some of the red drupes, and not even all the bluish and blackish fruit is pleasant raw, although dried or cooked they are better, particularly when mixed with tastier berries. The wild fruit is among this continent's most potent in vitamin A, thiamine, calcium, and niacin, while having close to 450 calories per pound and about 9 grams of protein in the same amount. Indians and settlers used it widely.

The fruit was believed to have cooling, gentle laxative, and urine-increasing properties. Wine made from it was thought to be tonic, as well as a cooling lotion when washed over the bodies of those suffering with fever and, taken internally, to promote sweating both to reduce fever and to promote good general health. The berries, eaten regularly, were said to help arthritis, as well as gout. They were also taken to enable one to cough up phlegm.

The juice, simmered uncovered until thick, was used as cough syrup and for other cold symptoms. The Choctaws mashed the berries with salt for a headache poultice. Some boiled honey and the fruit juices together to make a medicine that, dropped into the ears, was thought to ease earache.

The rest of the medicinal was usually used with great caution and some parts of it were occasionally avoided entirely.

Elderberry
(*Sambucus*).

The white flowers were steeped into a tea that, drunk hot, was used to produce perspiring in an effort to reduce fever. It was also drunk hot, sometimes steeped for seven or eight minutes with sprigs of wild mint, *Mentha*, to relieve stomach trouble. Hot, it was also believed useful for sore throats and other cold symptoms. The cold tea had the reputation of increasing urine flow when this had been scanty. The flowers, dried and stored, were also used by some tribes when needed to control fever.

The flowers and the young fruit together, besides being utilized as a diuretic and to promote sweating for health and for fevers, were also used in ointments and balms for burns, sores, and swollen and paining joints. The properties of the flowers included those of a mild stimulant. The dried blossoms of the blue-berried *S. canadensis* were steeped for use as skin lotions and antiseptic washes. Those of the *S. cerulea* were thought to be an even more potent remedy and were also used as remedies for broken blisters, sores, rashes, pimples, acne, and hemorrhoids.

Some pioneer women mixed a strong tea made half from elderberry flowers and half with their apple vinegar for both healing and cooling purposes. The flower tea was also used to help digestion by preventing the formation of gas and the expelling of that already present. An infusion of the dried flowers was especially sought for tonsillitis, since it was thought to be stimulating to the mucous membranes. Elderberry flower water, used for sunburn, was even thought to help bleach freckles.

One ointment made from the flowers mixed all the blossoms possible with the pure white lard produced by warming black bear fat in open pans and draining off the cracklings. Once the flowers were well browned, the whole was strained through fine cloth and stored in jars for use as a skin cream, a sore healer, and, incidentally, a fly and mosquito repellent.

A fresh infusion of elderberry flowers in boiling water was, upon cooling, said to be a most excellent wash for sore eyes. In a number of areas the steeped dried flowers were used as a general help in cases of fever. It was also held to be valuable for treating consumption or any bleeding from the lungs.

The inner bark of the stems was removed, dried, and kept for use in very small amounts as a purgative. In larger doses it served as an emetic. The bark of the roots acted so drastically that it was generally regarded as too dangerous to experiment with. Some of the Indians gathered the spotted and lenticellate bark of the elderberry to mix with bear lard for an ointment with which to treat rashes, inflammations, irritations, sores, and other skin troubles. The bark also had the property of acting, when steeped, both as a purgative and an emetic, depending on the dosage; in very small amounts it was but a gentle laxative.

For instance, a tablespoon sipped several times a day was depended on to act as a purgative, while for an emetic the doses were 3 tablespoons every five minutes until vomiting resulted. Again, a large number of Indians and pioneers found the bark so potent that they would use it only in an emergency. Small amounts of the tea were believed to help in cases of water retention.

Still, women drank very small amounts of elderberry bark tea for cramps during menstruation and later to ease the pain of birth and to help labor along. Sometimes when the child was born dead, the mother was given a few sips of the bark decoction in an effort to ease her pain, although it is difficult to explain how it could do this. It was also sipped to assist in phlegm expectoration from the lungs.

Externally, the bark found favor in a number of different ways. The Iroquois boiled the inner bark of the *S. canadensis* and applied it to that part of the cheek over a throbbing toothache, apparently with good results. The bark, simmered in lard, provided an ointment used to treat ulcers, boils, carbuncles, burns, and such lesser irritations as abrasions, chafing, rashes, blistering, and so forth. The bark was mashed, steeped, and so used by itself for poultices and the like to treat arthritis and similar troubles. The cooled liquid in which the bark had been boiled or steeped was used liberally as a wash in various skin afflictions. The inner bark was used too as a febrifuge and a diuretic.

The leaves, also poisonous both in mature and bud form, were carefully used by some as a potent cathartic when constipation was particularly troublesome. Tea extracted from them was also cautiously administered for dropsy, as well as for a stimulating diaphoretic.

Externally, the crushed leaves were rubbed on the skin as a mosquito and fly repellent. Beaten with oats or cream, they formed a lotion and ointment said to be valuable for burns, scalds, contusions, and more severe skin difficulties.

Some tribes turned to the crushed leaves as a poultice for headaches. Others used them thus with salt added. They were also so used just warmed and laid or tied on the forehead. The leaves were also pressed and crushed to give a juice valued by some as an eyewash. They were applied, too, to stop itching. They also made one of the poultices used for aching joints.

The Creeks mashed the more tender roots, agitated them with hot water, and bound them on squaws troubled with sore breasts. Scrapings from the stalks were sometimes used as a substitute when the proper roots could not be located.

The wood and buds were boiled to provide what was said to be a remedy for agues as from malaria and for inflammations.

Continued ➡

Indian Fig (*Opuntia ficus indica*)

Family: Cactus (*Cactaceae*)

Common Names: Prickly Pear, Eastern Prickly Pear, Western Prickly Pear, Prickly Pear Cactus, Plains Cactus, Opuntia, Devil's Tongue, Tuna, Beavertail, Nopal, Slipper Thorn.

Characteristics: Indian figs are the cacti with the flat-jointed stems. Those members of the same *Cactaceae* family with round-jointed stems are called chollas and are fibrous and dry. On the other hand, the Indian fig family, protecting their bitterish moisture by having spines instead of leaves and by being layered with a thick covering of wax, have long been a source of emergency drinking water for the desert Indians and for those who followed them. This juice is so mucilaginous that it is still sometimes used in making mortar.

The pale, oval seeds are about 5 millimeters in diameter and have a depressed center and margin. The dramatically lush red and golden flowers that grow on the padlike joints of the Indian fig during the late spring and early fall evolve into the fruit that gives the genus its name. Ranging in size from that of small plums to oranges, the mature colors extend from golden green and dark purple to the red of the big delicious prickly pears, as they are also called, of the *Opuntia megacantha* of the Southwest.

The family is much more easily recognized than harvested, which, because of its sharp spines, is best accomplished with substantial leather gloves and a knife.

Area: Distribution of these cacti has been extended throughout North America because of their popularity as garden and house plants, from which domesticity many have escaped to the wilds. Native only in the Americas, these cacti thrive best in Mexico, where you see the cattle eating them. Within the United States and Canada they grow from California to British Columbia in the West, extending well eastward into the interior. In the East one finds them from New England to Florida.

Uses: The Indians, and the plainsmen, mountain men, prospectors, trappers, and settlers following them often in dusty wagon trains, long peeled the stems of the Indian figs, dampened bandages and compresses

Indian fig (Opuntia ficus indica).

with their rather acrid, sticky juice, and bound these on abrasions and other wounds to promote healing.

Poultices were also prepared from the mashed pulp and applied to suppurating sores on man and domestic animal alike, being especially useful among horses, mules, and burros for the treatment of saddle sores. Too, the peeled stems were bound over wounds like bandages. The young joints were also secured before the spines had time to grow, roasted or boiled, and used as compresses for arthritis. The carefully despined and peeled lobes were, and in

some cases still are, regarded as efficacious for the alleviation of arthritic swelling, redness, heat, and pain. These so-prepared, warmed pads were even applied to the breasts of new mothers to increase the flow of milk.

The split joints, care being taken with the spines, were roasted and applied to help heal ulcers. Roasted over campfire coals, they were bound over the swelling of mumps. The stems were also boiled in water to provide a wash to relieve sore eyes, headaches, rheumatism, and even insomnia. Even regarding the Indian fig as useful against gout, the Indians found relief, and in New Mexico, for instance, claim they still do with the split baked joints.

The fuzz of the young Indian fig plant was rubbed into warts with the idea of both removing them and guaranteeing their not recurring.

The arduously peeled Indian figs themselves were used as a fever-reducing agent in cases of pleurisy, mental disorders, and chills. They were believed to abate and cool arthritic pain. The fruit, from which candy is commercially made today, was used to treat everything from asthma and diarrhea to gonorrhea. It was believed to increase the flow of urine—a useful phenomenon in the hot regions.

A tincture made from the flowers and stems was prescribed to ease spleen disorders and diarrhea. A tea brewed from the flowers alone was imbibed to increase the flow of urine.

Western frontiersmen simmered the well-washed roots in milk and drank this to relieve dysentery. Slaves infected with severe diarrhea, in which mucus and blood were passed, often drank only half a cup of milk simmered with 8 cups of water, to which a little Indian fig root was added, both to stop the diarrhea and to restore mucus to the intestinal tract.

The Navajos made enclosed shelters and arranged steam baths by pouring infusions of Indian fig, sage, juniper, and piñon over heated stones to treat rheumatism, eye trouble, insomnia, and headache.

Maple (*Acer*)

Family: Maple (*Aceraceae*)

Common Names: Red Maple, White Maple, Chalk Maple, Silver Maple, Black Maple, Carolina Red Maple, Scarlet Maple, Scarlet-Flowering Maple, Virginia Ash-Leaved Maple, Ashleaf Maple, Striped Maple, Stripe-Leaved Maple, Drummond Red Maple, Sugar Maple, American Sugar Maple, Black Sugar Maple, White-Barked Sugar Maple, Rock Maple, Hard Maple, Soft Maple, Common Maple, Goosefoot Maple, Ivy-Leaved Maple, Bigleaf Maple, Vine Maple, Hedge Maple, River Maple, Water Maple, Mountain Maple, Rocky Mountain Maple, Mountain Maple Bush, Florida Maple, Montpelier Maple, Siberian Maple, Italian Maple, Norway Maple, Japanese Maple, Tartarian Maple, Spiked Maple, Sycamore Maple, Shoe-Peg Maple, Moose Maple, Moosewood, Box Elder.

Characteristics: Being the emblem of Canada, the maple leaf is recognized by nearly everyone. Coloring with oxidation as it does magnificently at the end of summer, it is a principal cause for

the unforgettable fall beauty of New Hampshire, Vermont, Maine, and the Bay State of Massachusetts.

The seeds also are distinctive, composed of a tan duo of wings in whose center bulge a plump pair of edible seeds.

The sugar maple, to pick the most famous member of the family, is a large tree 60 to more than 100 feet high which thrives in fertile, moist, to well-drained and frequently rocky soils. Three- to 6-inch-wide leaves, generally with a quintet of pointed and frugally wavy-toothed lobes which are divided by broadly U-formed sinuses, are deep green above, paler and many times somewhat whitened below, and smooth or almost so, making the tree seem more beautiful.

The blossoms, forming from April to June, are yellowish green, clustered on lengthy and sagging hairy stems. The paired fruits, centered between wings about an inch long to form a brownish U, ripen from June until September.

Certain of the maples develop mature seeds in no more than two months after flowering, whereas the bigtree (*Sequoia gigantea*), to note a contrast, requires about 125 years. The familiar winged seeds of the sugar maple (*Acer saccharum*), for example, disperse from October to December. They average 380 seeds per ounce.

Area: The maple family, which includes numerous refugees from elegant landscaping, grows as a whole throughout southern Canada and the contiguous states except for the Great Plains and the lower Rockies. The sugar maple, valuable for its hardwood and the major source of maple syrup and sugar, prospers from Newfoundland to North Carolina, northern Georgia, and northern Louisiana, west to southern Ontario and Minnesota.

Uses: A wash decocted from the soaked pith of a twig of the mountain maple (*Acer spicatum*) was often cupped in a hand and used to bathe an eye to remove such foreign matter as dust. A calming, moderating, and tranquilizing douche for the uterus was also brewed from this particular tree. The bark from the mountain maple was used, too, for the treatment of general eye infections, of worms in the alimentary canal, as poultices for abrasions, and, incidentally, to tone the appetite.

Maple (Acer).

In fact, the Indians often turned to the various maples in general for getting rid of intestinal worms, for treatment of eye trouble from minor irritations to infections, and for increasing the appetite.

An extract obtained by boiling both leaves and bark was said to strengthen liver activity, as well as to open obstructions there and in the spleen, at the same time relieving pain from such disorders.

The gathering of maple syrup, having been common on this continent since pre-Columbian centuries, produced a liquid and sugar far more important medically in B vitamins, phosphorus, calcium, and enzymes than

Continued ➡

today's commercial products, from which they are now largely refined. Scarce and expensive as these maple delicacies are today, it is a commentary on the times that colonists apologized for serving maple sugar in lieu of the then-costly, difficult-to-obtain, inferior, manufactured brown sugar.

Mint (*Mentha*)

Family: Mint (*Labiatae*)

Common Names: Peppermint, Brandy Mint, Apple Mint, Orange Mint, Corsican Mint, Lamb Mint, Lammint, Spearmint, Brown Mint, Curly Mint, Common Mint, Garden Mint, Canada Mint, Mackerel Mint, Lady's Mint, Scotch Mint, Scotch Spearmint, Lemon Mint, Squaw Mint, Water Mint, Horsemint, Moon Mint, American Mint, Wild Mint, Fieldmint, Pennyroyal, American Pennyroyal, Western Pennyroyal, Mountain Pennyroyal, Giant Hyssop, Sage of Bethlehem, Wild Bergamot, Beebalm, Yerba Buena, Horehound, Oswego Tea.

Characteristics: The numerous wild mints have been well known to us from ancient days to the present as medicines, scents, flavorings, and foods. Although there are numerous varieties, all have square stems, opposite leaves, and a pleasing familiar aroma. This fragrance may not permeate the surroundings if just a few mints flourish together, but you only have to rub or crush a leaf in your hand to recognize it.

Area: The wild mints, a number of them escapees from gardens, are broadly distributed from the southern half of Canada throughout the contiguous United States down into Mexico. They prefer damp soils.

Uses: For giving a sickroom a clean, agreeable odor, introduce the steam of mint leaves boiled in water. Otherwise, to conserve the highly volatile aromatic aroma of the oil-filled cells of these plants, as well as to save most of the abundant and medicinally valuable vitamins A and C, plunge a large amount of the freshly gathered green leaves into bubbling water, cover tightly, and let them steep overnight before straining and using. The highest available counts of these two invaluable vitamins are, of course, secured by eating the newly picked, tender young leaves raw. For out-of-season use, young mint leaves are best gathered on a dry morning, dried at room temperature, and then kept in a cool dark place in closely covered jars.

Mint tea, made the same way and in the same proportions as a regular tea, has long been considered a pleasant palliative for both colic and indigestion, partly because it tends to relieve the digestive system of gas.

Peppermint (*M. piperita*), held by many of the Indians and colonists to be the most effective of the mints, was believed to increase bile secretion. This mint, with its distinctive odor, grows about a yard high, has dark green and toothed leaves which are somewhat rough beneath, unlike the smooth spearmint leaves, and produces spikelike groups of purplish blossoms at the tops of the stalks and in the angles between the leaves and the stems.

The leaves were and are chewed to sweeten the breath. The newly plucked leaves were also bound over painful areas for relief. Peppermint

tea, a teaspoon of the leaves and flowering tips to a cup of bubbling water, was drunk cold for headache, heartburn, digestive gas, colic, indigestion, and as a sedative. The crushed, freshly gathered leaves, said to have mild anesthetic properties, were sometimes rubbed into the skin to relieve headaches and local pain. Peppermint has also been among those ingredients recommended as a seasickness preventative.

Mint (Mentha).

The milder spearmint, also recognized as a distinctive flavoring agent and, like peppermint, brought to the New World by the colonists, grows unbranched in thick clumps from heights of about 1 foot to 1 1/2 feet, with bright, smooth, oblong or lance-head-shaped, unevenly toothed leaves and whitish to deep violet flowers. A handful of the fresh leaves to a cup of boiling water, steeped for no longer than five minutes and then strained, makes a pleasant tea that some of our older family members still regard as a prompt remedy for nausea, indigestion, chills as well as even colds and influenza, and both as a sedative and as an inducement to sleep.

Our forefathers also prepared for the long, cold winters by gathering in dry weather the fresh, young, green leaves of their preferred mints, drying them at room temperatures until they were brittle enough to crumble, and storing them in cool dry places in tightly closed jars to preserve the volatile aroma, then measuring, timing, and using them exactly like Oriental tea. Because there were no English taxes on them, mint teas were popular during the American Revolution, while they were also resorted to during the Civil War, when importation of orange pekoes, Formosa oolongs, and the like were curtailed. Mint teas were enjoyed in the various ways that regular tea was imbibed, one favorite being with a bit of lemon and sugar.

The other mints, none of them harmful but having a variety of odors and flavors, were also widely used by the Indians and settlers. For instance, the horsemint (*Monarda Punctata*) which has other names such as wild bergamot, beebalm, and lemon mint—with unbranched square stalks growing up to about 3 feet tall, a general hairiness, and bright rather than dullish opposite green leaves, with distinctive pink to purple round flowers heads from about 1 to 3 inches in diameter—was regarded as the most potent of the mints, giving relatively the greatest amount of pungent and aromatic oil.

This extract, when applied to the skin as a liniment, produced redness and had to be used with care to prevent blistering. It was regarded professionally in the old days as useful externally in typhoid fever, arthritis, and even deafness. It was served by the Dakotas and the Winnebegos both internally and externally as a treatment for Asian cholera and was later used by white doctors. Other tribes bruised the fresh green leaves and let them soak in cold water, which was

later drunk to ease backache. This was believed to be stimulating. The Creeks, members of a confederacy of Indians mainly of Muskogean stock who formerly occupied most of Georgia and Alabama as well as parts of Florida, steeped and soaked the entire plant to extract an aromatic solution for bringing on sweating.

It was boiled with the familiar red willow for use, both internally and externally, for swollen legs and for dropsy in general. Some Indians sought the tops of the plants to alleviate chills and fever. It was also used in combination with other wild plants as a drink to reduce delirium and as a snuff for headaches.

The U.S. medical profession from the early to the latter part of the nineteenth century prescribed the leaves and tops of the horsemint to check vomiting, to induce perspiring, to alleviate arthritis, and to relieve gassy colic. It was also taken internally for the expulsion of general gas from the alimentary canal and for the increase of sweating for such purposes as breaking up a fever. Externally it was used in liniments as a stimulant, to produce superficial inflammation with the aim of reducing inflammations in deeper adjacent parts of the body, and to produce blistering.

Another derivative still used, thymol, is available from this wild medicinal. This aromatic antiseptic, used as a fungicide and as a preservative and today largely made synthetically, was officially listed in *The Pharmacopoeia of the United States* from 1820 to 1882 and in the *National Formulary* since 1950. Besides being utilized as an antiseptic, it was long found effective against various fungi and especially against hookworm.

With as much vitamin C as the same weight of oranges and about the same amount of vitamin A as carrots, the freshly gathered mints have long been valuable in preventing and curing scurvy and in aiding night blindness and dull-looking eyes, as well as imparting a glossiness to the hair.

Mullein (*Verbascum thapsus*)

Family: Figwort (*Scrophulariaceae*)

Common Names: Common Mullein, Great Mullein, Mullein Dock, Flannel Mullein, Mullen, Feltwort Flannel Leaf, Flannelleaf, Flannel Plant, Old Man's Flannel, Adam's Flannel, Blanket Flannel, Blanket Leaf, Feltwort, Velvet Plant, Velvet Dock, Torch-Wort, Cow's Lungwort, Bullock's Lungwort, Crown's Lungwort, Hare's Beard, Lady's Foxglove, Peter's Staff, Juniper's Staff, Jacob's Staff, Shepherd's Club, Aaron's Rod, Hedge Taper, Candlewick, Ice Leaf, Indian Tobacco, Wild Tobacco, Big Tobacco.

Characteristics: Mullein is a tall, weedy, unbranched biennial, hairy and soft, that grows up to about 8 feet high. It lifts strikingly from a basal rosette about 2 feet wide with winged stems and a soft, downy or woolly foliage. The leaves are single, alternate, and widely oblong or lancelike, 2 inches to a foot long, with smooth unlobed rims.

The high, clublike seed spike does not form until the second year, when, from late June until September, yellow flowers become dense along it, each with a five-part calyx, five-lobed corolla,

Continued ➡

and the same number of stamens, eventually forming a fruit that is a pod or seed-filled capsule. Incidentally, even after 70 years the seeds of the *Verbascum blattaria* are still able to germinate.

Mulleins seek old meadows and pastures that have been overgrazed, rocky or gravelly banks, wastelands, roadsides, and embankments. They also grow in Europe where the ancient Greeks and Romans dipped the dried stems into wax to make wicked candles.

Area: Mullein grows throughout southern Canada and the United States.

Uses: The reason for some of its names is that it was smoked in pipes and cigarettes to help throat congestion. Also, the Navajos blended it with ordinary tobacco and smoked it in the hope of straightening out mild mental disorders. The Mohicans were among the tribes smoking the dried leaves to relieve asthma. Some Indians made a smudge over the dwindling coals of their campfires and inhaled the smoke for catarrh and other pulmonary troubles. The fumes were also used in efforts to revive an unconscious patient.

The leaves and flowers were classed as astringent, cough-relieving, as a sedative to the respiratory system, as a fungus inhibitor, and as a pain reliever. They were supposed to contain a mucilaginous substance whose protective coating prevented added irritation to the digestive system and, externally, softened and soothed the skin.

Mullein was used to ease coughs and the ejection of unusually heavy phlegm. For this, one prescription was for an ounce of the dried leaves to be simmered in either water or perhaps milk for some ten minutes, strained to remove the hairs and other solids, and sipped warm, with

Mullein (Verbascum thapsus).

honey or possibly maple sugar added for smoothness and flavor. The same infusion was utilized for diarrhea.

The dried flowers were soaked in some edible oil for several weeks, then used to treat earaches, hemorrhoids, sunburn, rashes, inflammations, and even bruises and contusions. The flowers were also thought to be diuretic and were credited with curing coughs and lung and chest trouble, both they and the leaves being listed as official medicines in the *National Formulary* for twenty years up to 1936.

Mullein oil was considered to be effective against disease germs in the old days as what we would now consider to be an antibiotic.

Mullein roots were boiled to relieve convulsions, and the decoction was also reputed to be antispasmodic and an aid for nervous indigestion. Tea from the roots was regarded as an aid to liver trouble. Inflammations of the digestive and urinary systems were said to be relieved by steeping about an ounce of the dried leaves in 2 cups of boiling water, straining, and then drinking it cold.

Indians suffering from gout often turned to a decoction of mullein. Poultices made from it were put on sprains. A tea brewed from the heart of the young plant was believed to relieve spasmodic intestinal pain.

An Indian device to relieve foot pain was to soften a large leaf on a hot stone, fold it, and bind it to the sole of the foot.

Oak (*Quercus*)

Family: Beech (*Fagaceae*)

Common Names: Georgia Oak, Oregon White Oak, Western White Oak, California Black Oak, Spanish Oak, Red Spanish Oak, Oglethorpe Oak, Durand Oak, Chinquapin Oak, Gambel Oak, Black Oak, Scarlet Oak, Red Oak, Southern Red Oak, Northern Red Oak, Yellow Oak, Blackjack Oak, Blackjack, Bluejack Oak, Swamp Oak, Swamp White Oak, Swamp Chestnut Oak, Northern Pin Oak, Willow Oak, Valley Oak, Water Oak, Live Oak, Scrub Oak, Low Oak, Post Oak, Bur Oak, Basket Oak, Mossycup Oak, Tanner's Oak, Iron Oak, Rock Oak, Corkoak, Chestnut Oak, Cherrybark Oak, Laurel Oak, Shingle Oak, Bear Oak, Cow Oak, Turkey Oak.

Characteristics: Everyone knows the fruit of the oak, the acorn, likely both the Indians' and our wildlife's principal food. Acorns are divided into two main groups, the sweet and the bitter. The bitterness of the latter is due to tannic acid, the acid in our tea and injurious to the human digestive system only in large amounts; but once the substance is leeched out as in water, these acorns, too, are nutritious.

Oaks, furnishing about half the hardwood lumber milled in this country and being a favorite shade and landscaping tree, are also familiar to all.

The single, deeply lobed leaves that grow from short stems alternately on the limbs generally oxidize beautifully in the fall and clatter down to cluster on the ground, although a few shrivel and rattle on the trees throughout most of the winter. There are also smaller-leaved evergreen oaks like the live oak.

Maturing in a single season, the acorns of the white oaks, which have a characteristic scaly gray bark, are sweet and the insides of their saucerlike shells smooth.

The nuts of the red oaks, their shallow cuplike shells' inner surfaces being hairy, take two growing seasons to become ripe, and they are ordinarily bitter. The leaves are bristled, and the bark is darkly furrowed.

Area: Close to fifty species of oaks thrive throughout the original forty-eight states except in the northern prairies, as well as through southern Canada.

Uses: The Indians had their own antibiotics, one of them being the mold that collected on the bitter acorns during the sweetening process, which was carefully collected, stored in a cool and damp spot, and eventually utilized on sores, wounds, infections, and the like.

It is the bark of the oaks that has been most widely used medicinally. Being so rich in tannin, oak bark is exceedingly astringent and was therefore, after being soaked or simmered in water, valuable as one of the aborigines' antiseptics and astringents. The decoction was given for piles.

Indians in New England drank it for

Oak (Quercus).

bleeding and for internal hemorrhaging in general. The Ojibwas, for one, boiled the inner bark of trees and the root bark for diarrhea. Other tribes steeped the inner bark and imbibed it sparingly, as too much would disrupt the digestive system, for loosening phlegm in the lungs and deep respiratory passages and allowing it to be coughed up. Other tribes used the infusion in enemas for piles.

One formula called for a pound of pounded oak bark, boiled with a gallon of water until but 2 quarts remained. This was then strained. Among its other uses was that of bathing a feverish patient to bring down his temperature. It was used as a wash, too, for ulcers, gonorrhea, and general inflammations. It was given internally to anyone spitting blood, and was used as a vaginal douche.

The white oak (*Quercus alba*) was considered to be particularly valuable as an astringent, tonic, and hemostatic, as well as a medicine for a long list of ailments that included dysentery, cholera, hemoptysis, leukorrhea, phthisis, intermittents, and gonorrhea. Poultices made from it were even used for gangrene. Powdered, the dried inner bark became the basis for gargles and tooth powder.

Oak bark, soaked in alcoholic beverages, was considered useful as a liniment for arthritis and the like.

Powdered acorns, mixed with water, were an old remedy for diarrhea.

The inner bark of the red oak (*Q. rubra*), first chewed and then soaked in water, provided a wash that was said to be good for sore eyes, even those of long duration. The bark of this tree was also thought to help heart trouble.

The bark of the black oak (*Q. nigra*) was also steeped and crushed, as between two smooth stones or with a mortar and pestle, and boiled to make another bath for sore eyes.

The inner bark of the bur oak (*Q. macrocarpa*) was used to make a gargle for sore throats, especially for tonsillitis, and as a general astringent. Interestingly, the bark of this tree was stripped off for use as primitive bandages to hold broken bones in place, particularly those of the legs, feet, and arms.

The inner bark of the oaks was scraped or cut off, after the heavy outer bark had been stripped away, and steeped in more water than usual to make a mild medicine for children with intestinal troubles.

The inner bark of both the white oak and the bur oak were among those boiled to make douches for vaginal inflammations and infections. Decoctions of white oak bark were also used by Indians and colonials alike to quell dripping sinuses and chronic mucous discharges.

The galls found growing on the oaks were strong with tannic acid and a smaller amount of gallic acid and were used by the red men and the immigrants in attempts to heal skin diseases, including inflamed sores and ulcers of long standing, and to check bleeding.

Continued ➡

One reason some Indians particularly relished acorns for food was that they brought on thirst; their belief was that drinking a lot of water was healthful.

Pine (*Pinus*)

Family: Pine (*Pinaceae*)

Common Names: Eastern White Pine, Western White Pine, White Pine, Black Pine, Red Pine, Eastern Yellow Pine, Yellow Pine, Gray Pine, Alaska Pine, Norway Pine, Oregon Pine, North Carolina Pine, Monterey Pine, Scotch Pine, Austrian Pine, Jersey Pine, Virginia Pine, Cambria Pine, Walter Pine, Parry Pine, Oldfield Pine, Table Mountain Pine, Digger Pine, Rosemary Pine, Jack Pine, Loblolly Pine, Sand Pine, Bank Pine, Marsh Pine, Swamp Pine, Pond Pine, Mountain Pine, Stone Pine, Pocosin Pine, One-Leaved Pine, Four-Leaved Pine, One-Leaved Nut Pine, Shortleaf Pine, Longleaf Pine, Scrub Pine, Northern Scrub Pine, Giant Pine, Slash Pine, Poverty Pine, Prickly-Cone Pine, Hard Pine, Nut Pine, Blister Pine, Pitch Pine, Sugar Pine, Bur Pine, Lodgepole Pine, Tamarack, Larch Piñon, Ponderosa, Hackmatack.

Characteristics: The North American genus of pines includes the trees and shrubs collectively known as the evergreen conifers, embracing the two or three dozen pines themselves, depending on which school of thought the botanist doing the counting follows—the arbor vitae (literally the Tree of Life, so named because it saved a group of early explorers from dying of scurvy), the great hemlocks (the poison hemlock; any of the small poisonous herbs of the carrot family having finely cut leaves and tiny white blossoms differ vastly and visibly and are no relation), the prolific spruces, the tamaracks, the larches, the bald cypresses, the sequoias, the life-giving junipers (which one winter saved Jacques Cartier and his crew in the frozen St. Lawrence River, which they had discovered), the true and the false firs, and the numerous cedars.

If you make an error between a pine and the Christmas-tree fir or the more similar spruce, they will be the same medicinally. All have a life-sustaining edible inner bark and the all-important vitamin C, without which one painfully dies, since the human system cannot accumulate it. All too often we hear of the occupants of small downed planes starving to death or succumbing to scurvy when lost amid the innumerable pines that clad this continent. Medically, it is all so useless. The cambium, that coating that lies between the outer bark and the wood, can be scraped or sliced off and eaten for sufficient nourishment, raw or cooked, in any way that's handy. An even more pleasant tea, steeped by soaking a handful of needles in any convenient container of water, will provide the antiscorbutic. Or the greenest, newest needles, themselves tender enough to eat in the spring, can be chewed. The Christmaslike aroma makes the whole procedure memorable.

The pines flower in the spring, coating everything with thick yellow pollen. Once this overabundance fertilizes the female stigmas of the pistillate blossoms, the common cones commence forming. Very edible when young, these require a couple and sometimes three years to mature and let fly their own winged seeds, the commonest food of the chattering squirrel.

Most of the vast pine family is evergreen, but native conifers like the deciduous tamaracks, larches, and the bald cypresses drop their needles in the autumn.

Area: Pines green much of the United States and Canada up to timberline except in the tundras, the deserts, and the central plains.

Uses: In addition to the two lifesaving characteristics too important not to cover earlier, the pines have numerous medicinal uses. For instance, the Indians simmered the bark of the younger pines to draw the heat and inflammation out of burns and scalds and to guard against infection.

The bark of the white pine particularly, easily recognizable because its bluish green foliage—needlelike, flexible, soft, and generally curved 4 to 8 inches long—grows in bundles of three, was so treated by a number of the tribes. The fact that its sticky and fragrant resin becomes a white crust early gave the white pine and the eastern and western white pines their names.

The dried cambium of this particular species, having the property of ejecting mucus from the lungs and throat by coughing or hawking and expectorating, was adopted from the Indians by several manufacturers for this purpose. The steeped cambium of the young white pines especially was also resorted to internally for pains in the chest.

Some tribes ground and hammered the inner bark to a paste which they applied to ulcers and carbuncles, as well as to wounds and everyday sores, regarding it as one of their prime medicinals. Indians who pitched their wigwams around Lake Superior crushed the trios of needles and spread them over the foreheads of supine patients, or tied them there with deerskin bands, to ease headaches. For pain and discomfort in the back, they breathed in the hot fumes emitted from the same needles warmed over the fringes of their campfires, often on hot rocks. The pitch oozing from these and other pines was spread on sores and inflammations as salves.

Pine (Pinus).

Another use for the three-leaved bundles was simmering them for a drink regarded efficacious for treating sore throats arising from colds and even for consumption. The aborigines in what is now Connecticut steeped the bark and took the solution internally in the belief that it eased cold symptoms. The bark was also crushed into a poultice for piles and ulcers, as well as boiled to make a potion for bringing boils to a head. Some Indians just soaked the bark of this eastern white pine and, as soon as it was soft, used it on sores of all sorts.

The cambium of saplings, though, they boiled for drinking to quell dysentery. A drink made of the steeped buds was held to be laxative. The Indians and settlers made poultices by simmering the scrubbed roots of these evergreens.

The amber-colored resin seeping and solidifying from the pines was plastered over parts where there was muscular soreness, as after games or hard work and from arthritis. This resin, easily picked and scraped from the trees where it exuded prolifically from cuts and lacerations, is brittle at first but soon chews into a soft and pleasantly flavored pink gum which had many uses: sweetening the breath, increasing or quickening menstrual flow, treating kidney disorders and tuberculosis, smearing on the body to ease localized swellings, curing itching and even ulcers, and internally for treating sore throats.

The colonists dissolved it in brandies and other alcoholic beverages to wash inflammations, itchy spots, scalds, and burns.

This resin, found on all the pines, was heated and smeared on the chest for pneumonia, for helping rheumatism and muscular soreness, for bringing boils to a climax, for taking the soreness and inflammation out of wounds and cuts, and even for treating annoying mosquito and other insect bites.

One tribe burned and damped pine wood to charcoal, encompassed this in a wet cloth or strip of deerskin, and tied the whole around the throat for laryngitis.

Pine oil and tar was widely used as a disinfectant, insecticide, antiseptic, parasiticidal agent, expectorant, and deodorant; a number of these uses it still enjoys in modern times.

The tips of the dense, scalelike foliage of the arborvitae, so important in vitamins, were used for gout, fever, and lingering coughs. Half an ounce of the young leaves, steeped or soaked overnight in a cup of water, then sipped a tablespoon at a time, was relied on by some to produce menstruation, as well as to increase the flow of urine. Externally, it was used in an effort to eradicate wars and to cure athlete's food and ringworm.

Then there is the piñon. Indians in New Mexico simmered its needles in water, added sugar to the decoction, and tood it internally as a remedy for syphilis. Whether or not this had any beneficial effect, there are definitive reports from Department of Agriculture scientists that just a 100-gram portion of the pleasant little nuts boasts 635 calories, 60.5 grams of fat, 20.5 of carbohydrates, 13 of protein, in addition to a great 604 milligrams of phosphorus, 5.2 of iorn, 4.5 of niacin, 1.28 of thiamine, and 0.23 of riboflavin, all in a medically important, pleasantly piquant package.

Poke (*Phytolacca*)

Family: Pokeweed (*Phytolaccaceae*)

Common Names: Pokeweed, Pokeberry, Virginia Poke, Poke Root, Pocan, Pocan Bush, Scoke, Skoke, Caokum, Coakum, Cucum, Cokan, Inkberry, Red-Ink Plant, Redwood, Red Wood, Garget, Pigeonberry, Chongras, Jalap, American Nightshade.

Characteristics: The ripe, deeply purple, reddish purple, or orangish purple berries, growing in racemes some 4 to 7 inches in length (each fruit being a bit more than 1/4 inch in diameter) has a red juice that was one of the first natural inks of the New World, so enduring that it is still to be seen in museums. They also

Continued ➡

produce multitudes of bright, long, black seeds. Birds become intoxicated when eating these berries—another distinctive sign.

Beside the withered remains of the former season's plants spring the fat young sprouts that, up to some 7 inches in height, are the only part of the plant that, unless used very carefully, is not poisonous. The shoots proved so popular to the first mariners and explorers in the New World that they took the sprouts back to Europe, where they were equally regarded as delicious.

The mature, then poisonous stalks take on a purplish hue in place of the lush, appealing greenness of the young plants. The annuals mature into roundish stalks that soar upward for some 3 to 9 feet. They have multitudinous, tiny, greenish white flowers which grow on long, fat separate stems in lengthy clusters. The leaves, known botanically as ovate-lanceolate, grow in the form of rather stout lance heads with individual stems at their bases and sharp points at their tips. Scattered except for a little cluster at the top, and sometimes other small clusters on the stalks, they are some 10 inches in length. The leaves, smooth both top and bottom, have slightly undulating rims.

All in all, the perennials are plump and strong-smelling, not at all difficult to recognize.

Area: The poke, native to tropical America and a hearty perennial especially in the South, now is common in the eastern part of the country except along the Canadian border, west to Minnesota and the Lone Star State of Texas, southward through Mexico.

Uses: First, it should be reemphasized that except for the stout young shoots which grow to some 6 to 7 inches high, and the leaves growing from these sprouts, poke can be very harmful if not used with extreme caution. As for the shoots, they are so popular that they are regularly grown domestically, in such places as cellars, and they are sold in some grocery stores. Cut off just where they emerge from the ground, they are cooked like asparagus, rich in vitamin C.

Poke (Phytolacca).

The large, poisonous roots used to be collected in the fall by the pharmaceutical industry, as affirmed by the U.S. Department of Agriculture, and utilized in small portions as an emetic, for which it was favored because of its slow and harmless behavior, and for treating arthritis. The poisonous berries contain a strong laxative. The Indians and colonists, using those roots, mainly cut them into small pieces and steeped a level tablespoonful with 2 cups of boiling water, then dosed themselves sparingly by the tablespoon. The roots, like the berries, also have a narcotic action.

The poke's major medicinal component is said to parallel the action of cortisone in stimulating the complete glandular network, which would account for its help with rheumatism, for

one thing. But, again, caution was always the governing principle.

Poke was believed to be extremely useful as an alternative, perhaps the most effective in this respect of all wild medicinals; that is, a drug used empirically to alter favorably the course of an ailment. For this purpose, a tea prepared by steeping a tablespoon of the cut root or ripe berries with 2 cups of boiling water was taken by the tablespoonful.

The dried root is still used in Appalachia, according to the Department of Agriculture, for the treatment of hemorrhoids. The dried berries are used in some regions as poultices to bring boils and other sores to a head.

A number of tinctures and ointments have also been made of this powerful medicinal and used to reduce glandular swelling and to help chronic arthritis and stiffness of the joints. It was also regarded by some as being efficacious externally in such skin diseases as scrofula, eczema, and even syphilis. A decoction made from the roots was washed over the skin to do away with itching. Apparently it could be applied externally as often as necessary without undue risk, and it was believed to be very helpful in reducing such annoyances.

A number of tribes used the cut roots on the soles and palms of Indians suffering with fever, and the pioneers followed suit. The fresh leaves were made into poultices for scabs of long standing. They were also dried for application to swellings, ulcers, carbuncles, and wounds of one sort or another.

Pusley (*Portulaca oleracea*)

Family: Purslane (*Portulacaceae*)

Common Names: Purslane, Low Pigweed, Purslance.

Characteristics: The earth-embracing pusley, whose shoots seldom stretch more than an inch or two toward heaven, is a sprawling annual whose stems and tendrils creep over many a yard where, spurned by most as a lowly weed, it does not usually gain the attention it should, since it is unusually rich in medically important minerals and vitamins. Native and widely used in Persia and India long before the birth of Christ, it spread early to Europe and was one of the plants widely adopted by the Indians after its immigration to the New World with the first settlers. It spread quickly and widely because of its profusion of tiny seeds, well more than 50,000 having been counted on a single plant.

The corpulent, narrow, paddlelike, 1/2- to 2-inch-long leaves, growing almost opposite, prosper in rosettes lifting from fleshy, forking stems. Each disk of leaves, which have a lovely reddish to regal purplish green tinge to them, centers a tiny golden medallion of a flower which reveals itself only in warm, bright sunlight. These stemless delicacies have some five to seven yellow petals and about eleven elegant stamens that mature into small round pods whose tops lift off like crowns when the tiny seeds are ready to be revealed.

Area: Preferring as it does sandy fertile soil, pusley reigns from the balmier provinces of Canada throughout the continent to each of our southern states.

Uses: As a medicine, pusley is important because of the fact that, according to U.S. Department of Agriculture tests, a 100-gram portion has been found—despite the fact that it is more than 92 percent water raw and more than 94 percent water following boiling—to boast 2,500 international units of vitamin A raw and 2,100 cooked, 0.1 milligram of riboflavin raw and 0.06 simmered and drained, 25 milligrams of vitamin C raw, and a robust 3.5 milligrams of iron. Although the Indians did not know of vitamins and minerals, any more than did the colonists, they recognized the health-giving qualities of pusley, and where we once lived in Taos several of the women in the towering pueblo there canned quantities each year to give to their growing families.

The seeds, which U.S. government scientists have found will stay alive in the ground for more than forty years until moisture comes along to start their growth, were made into a tea by the Indians, who also used the tender stems and tips for the same purpose, to bring about relaxation and sleep.

Pusley (Portulaca oleracea).

Pusley tea had many uses among the American aborigines who, of course, passed along their particular findings to the Europeans who, knowing some of the virtues of the wild medicinal from the Old World, had been using it particularly for lightning and gunpowder burns.

The Indians found the decoctions useful in cases of gout, for reducing agitation and nervousness just as we use sedatives today, for gonorrhea, as a diuretic, for headaches, particularly those arising from exposure to the sun and weather, and for stomach, intestinal, and liver ailments.

The decoctions, not made so potent as usual, were considered mild enough to be safe in killing intestinal worms in children. Brewed stronger, it was considered effective for adults with the same problem.

The juice, gained by crushing and straining the plant, was stirred into wild honey for a cough medicine. It was also used externally as is for bathing inflamed generative organs. Mixed with oil, sometimes that rendered from grizzly fat, it was rubbed into stiff necks. It also seemed to help piles, used both internally and externally, the latter particularly when the ailment caused soreness of the skin.

Mixing it with wild honey or with maple sugar was claimed to help shortness of breath and immoderate thirstiness except when this arose from diabetes.

Bathing the body with cool, crushed pusley was resorted to in cases of fever and, less critically, for inflammation.

The multitudinous small black seeds, which the Indians and hungry pioneers crushed, sieved, and used for flour, were steeped for tea which some of the tribes looked to for help with painful urination, as a bath for eye irritations,

Continued ➧

and for stomach trouble. Boiled in wine, it was given in small doses to children to kill and pass worms.

Juice from the crushed and strained plant, used externally, was esteemed many centuries ago for ulcers and other sores in the generative parts, for inflammations in general, for soaking compresses which were laid where the head ached, for easing other aches and pains, for gout and fever, for trouble with the genitourinary organs and functions, and as a generally accepted antiseptic.

Sassafras (Sassafras)

Family: Laurel (Lauraceae)

Common Names: Saxifrix, Saxifras, White Sassafras, Red Sassafras, Common Sassafras, Silk Sassafras, Tea Tree, Mitten Tree, Gumbo, Cinnamonwood, Smelling Stick, Saloop.

Characteristics: Christopher Columbus is said to have been helped in his successful efforts to quell mutinous seamen, who feared to sail any farther westward, by the sudden sweet smell of the sassafras tree, which indicated the nearness of land. Sassafras even exceeded tobacco during the early days as a North American export to Europe. In fact, special ships were carrying cargoes of sassafras from this continent back to the Old World before any other New World product made an impression on medicine there.

The distinctive and agreeably aromatic odor and flavor of this small- to medium-sized tree, varying in height from about 10 to nearly 50 feet, is as pleasant as it is characteristic. Even the roughly furrowed grayish to reddish brown bark has this fragrance both in taste and smell. The leaves, which unfurl before the golden greenish blossoms appear in latter April and early May, are of three shapes even on the same tree—a thumbed mitten, a three-fingered glove, and a smooth egg shape. The spiceness of darkly blue, one-seeded berries, up to about $1/2$ inch in diameter but mostly of pea size, attract birds to the female trees in the autumn when they mature on their reddish stalks.

Area: The majority of our sassafras trees grow from Iowa, Indiana, Illinois, Michigan, southern Ontario, Ohio, Pennsylvania, New York, and Massachusetts, south to Texas and Florida, thriving mainly along roads and fences, in thickets on the edges of woods, and within pastures and cleared lands which have been deserted.

Uses: Wine made from sassafras berries was frequently imbibed for colds. During the flowering period from March to April, the blossoms were simmered to make a tea to lessen fevers. An old-fashioned idea, still adhered to in many parts of the country, is that the blood should be thinned and purified in the spring, and among the roots used to prepare brews for this were and are those of the sassafras.

Also, a tea made of the root bark is still utilized in Appalachia for such general and varied purposes as to increase the flow of urine, to treat kidney troubles, to ease the discomfiture of a gassy and upset stomach, to produce an increase in perspiration, to help dysentery, and to relieve respiratory troubles. About two centuries ago the tea was believed to slow the milk flow in nursing mothers when this seemed expedient. The tea has also been used as a stimulant and for the treatment of bronchitis.

The bark has been made into a poultice for sore eyes. Pioneers thought that chewing it would help break the tobacco habit, a problem even then.

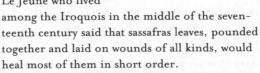

Sassafras (Sassafras).

Jesuit priest Paul Le Jeune who lived among the Iroquois in the middle of the seventeenth century said that sassafras leaves, pounded together and laid on wounds of all kinds, would heal most of them in short order.

Other early Europeans spoke of beating the bark of the root and using it to cleanse ulcers; also of applying it to swellings or contusions to ease the pain and to heal the parts. It was generally used along the eastern seaboard as an ointment for bruises. The leaves were chewed and laid on wounds to stop bleeding. Teas made from the sassafras were thought beneficial in the treatment of venereal diseases. Even years ago, the roots were distilled to make an oil for flavoring beverages such as ginger ale, sarasaparilla, cream soda, and root beer, as well as toothpaste and the like. It was used in such concoctions as Kickapoo Oil, featured at old-time medicine shows. The bark was favored as an insect repellent. Tea made from it was thought to be effective in helping the passage of gravel and kidney stones.

The fragrant and mucilaginous southern soups which have varied little since Indian times still are considered by many to be very healthful and beneficial.

The Rappahannocks made a tea from sassafras roots to bring out the rash to reduce fever in measles—a disease which in modern times has been determined to be much more dangerous than was previously thought.

The Catawbas showed the white man how to treat lameness by abrading the spot where the lameness lay, bathing it both during and after the bleeding with warm water, then drying some sassafras roots in the coals of a campfire, scraping off the thus-loosened bark, pounding it well between two smooth stones, spreading it over the afflicted part, and bandaging it there for several days, after which the patient was often adjudged cured.

One way to making sassafras tea was to put two roots, each a couple of inches long, in 3 pints of water, first scrubbing the roots vigorously with a stiff brush, rinsing them, and then scraping away the bark, which was included with the roots in a pot. Bring this to a boil, then reduce the heat, simmer for fifteen minutes, and finally remove from the heat, cover, steep for ten minutes, strain, and serve. Another dosage, especially used as a spring tonic, was made by cutting or grinding a teaspoon of the bark, steeping this in a cup of boiling water for ten minutes, then drinking cold, a few sips at a time, throughout the day. Still another formula called for dropping several roots into a quart of bubbling water, setting this off the heat, and steeping five minutes.

Or, you can use the entire root, first scrubbing and cutting it into pieces that will easily fit into a pot holding a gallon of water. A pound of roots will thus make 4 quarts of tea and can be used several times before they lose their strength. Merely simmer until the tea has a yellowish red hue, a rich smell, and a pleasing taste. Then you can treat it like Oriental tea, drinking it as is, or thinning with milk or cream and, if you wish, sweetening it.

Some scientists have been warning lately that the sipping of sassafras as a spring tonic is, like the alleged cumulative dangers of cranberries and Red Dye No. 2, dangerous to the health. But it has been added that the Red Dye No. 2 which proved dangerous to laboratory mice would have to be consumed at a rate of 1,200 pounds per day to pose a threat to human beings. Perhaps this proves that using sassafras tea to put spring into your spring is one of the few age-old customs that bureaucrats shouldn't mess with.

Sassafras was also used to make a mouthwash, held to be as beneficial as many of the commercial products now on the market.

Slippery Elm (Ulmus fulva)

Family: Elm (Ulmaceae)

Common Names: Elm, Indian Elm, Moose Elm, Rock Elm, Soft Elm, Sweet Elm, Red Elm, Tawny Elm, Gray Elm, American Tree.

Characteristics: The important slippery elm is a medium-sized tree, ordinarily about 60 to 70 feet high, and well known for centuries to many a youngster who has chewed its alluring mucilaginous and aromatic bark. The twigs, too, have the same qualities. The medicinal variety does best in rich soil, especially if the soil is impregnated with limestone, along stream banks, river terraces, flood plains, and bottomlands. However, it is also to be found on occasion in dry and poor sites. The slippery and pleasantly fragrant inner bark, once smelled and sampled, is unforgettable.

The rough and abruptly toothed leaves, intensely and darkly dull green on top, as well as somewhat abrasive—soft, fluffy, and lighter colored below—grow from brief, fuzzy, obese stems. Unfurling from downy, stubby, dully pointed, ovoid buds that in winter are an especially deep brown, the oblong to ovate, simple and alternate leaves, doubly serrated on the margins, are generally an uneven 4 to 7 or 8 inches in length and from 2 to 3 inches wide. The buds at the branch ends ordinarily have orange tips.

Interestingly, the slippery elm leaves, with their straight parallel veins from the midribs, are scratchy when rubbed either back or forth, while those of their cousin elms are scratchy only in one direction. In autumn they take on a rich golden hue with oxidation, not frost. The branches stretch out into wide, airy, relatively smooth and even crowns; hence this is one of America's most popular shade and decorative trees.

Small, greenish flowers in short-stacked assemblages enhance the slippery elm from February to April. They mature into winged seeds, dispersed from April to June by the

Continued ➡

winds, that are samaroid—that is, they resemble the small, dry, winged, seedlike fruits of the maples (considered elsewhere in this book). There are an average of 2,500 slippery elm seeds per ounce, the range being from 2,180 to an astonishing 3,370. The commercial age bearing

Slippery elm (Ulmus fulva).

of this elm's seeds is from 15 to 200 years, those in the open usually bringing these forth earlier and more abundantly than those in stands.

Area: Slippery elms, still regarded as extremely valuable medicinals in Appalachia, are distributed from the Canada–United States St. Lawrence River to the Dakotas, south to the Lone Star State of Texas, east along the Gulf of Mexico to Florida.

Uses: In Appalachia people still soak the inner bark of this tree in warm water to produce a mucilage that is used as a protective, as a soothing agent for an abraded mucous membrane, as an alleviative substance, too, for injured skin, and for healing wounds. There and elsewhere a tea made by steeping a teaspoon of the powdered inner bark to a cup of boiling water, still, as it did back in pre-Columbian times, provides a laxative. Softening the skin, this still is also believed to help prevent chapping.

The Indians mashed the bark and used the pulp both for gunshot wounds and to ease the painful removal of the lead. Poultices made from such bark has been lightly pressed over burns to assist in keeping them antiseptic and to hasten their healing. The Indians, as they showed the settlers, also used it to help infections concerned with the lungs and their allied channels and organs. It was another of the wild medicines relied on for diarrhea.

Tea brewed from the roots was trusted to assist pregnant women at the time of their giving birth. In fact, the slipperiness of the bark, or of the sap and juice, was depended on by midwives to ease the births themselves. Indeed, it was considered useful when anything had to be expelled from the body, even phlegm, when this viscid mucus became secreted in abnormal quantities in the respiratory passages.

Soaking from 1 to 2 ounces of the inner bark in 2 cups of water kept below the boiling point for at least an hour, preferably longer, then straining it, gave an extract that had many uses—for enemas, diluted for vaginal douches, and in small sips for digestive troubles. When it came to enemas for constipation, some wholesome oil and warm milk were often also combined with the decoction.

The powdered inner bark was often the major ingredient in suppositories. For the sick and convalescent the powdered and apparently easily digestible product was frequently flavored with honey or maple syrup and eaten as a strengthening gruel, a practice still often followed in some backwoods communities with the present-day common addition of cinnamon or nutmeg.

Stinging Nettle (*Urtica*)

Family: Nettle (*Urticaceae*)

Common Names: Nettle, Ground Nettle, Forest Nettle, Slender Nettle, Dwarf Nettle, Great Nettle.

Characteristics: These perennials, notable for their stinging qualities which disappear, however, after they have been simmered slightly, are generally single-stalked greens that are among the first to appear in snowy regions in the springtime. Filled with chlorophyll, vitamin C, many indispensable trace minerals, and protein, nettles, being some 7 percent nitrogen on a dry-weight count, are wealthier in this essential plant food than some commercial fertilizers. Where they luxuriate, there is rich, fertile ground.

Area: Nettles grow across the northern portions of the continent, south through Canada and much of the United States.

Uses: Nettles can be amply cooked with only the water clinging to the plants when they are washed free of dust, and none of this should be wasted because of human-health reasons. In fact, a pleasant beverage is thus provided which the colonists believed helped the pains, aches, and twinges of those growing old. The entire food, one of the most palatable greens nature has to offer, was at one time thought to be a potent medicinal, good for a wide variety of ills—diabetes, fever marked by paroxysms of recurring chills and fever and perspiring, asthma, bronchitis, poor blood, consumption, bites and stings of poisonous pests, and even as a poison antidote. It was also believed valuable in weight-losing. Incidentally, only the tender tips of young plants or those not more than a foot tall should be used.

In addition to its high vitamin C content, which wards off scurvy, for which it is particularly valuable in the Far North after the long white winter, the stinging nettle is rich in vitamin A, which assists night vision, gives a sparkle to the eyes, and makes the hair more glossy. In this latter connection, applied several times daily as a hair tonic, it had the reputation of lessening falling hair, reducing dandruff, and helping bring about a generally healthy scalp.

The stalks, the stems of the leaves, and the leaves themselves bristle with a fine stinging fuzz in which formic acid is a major irritant. They are best gathered with knife or scissors and disposable paper bags, with one's hands protected by

Stinging nettle (Urtica).

impermeable leather, rubber, or plastic gloves. Indians, not having these, counteracted the resulting itch both with crushed green dock leaves and with the rusty feltlike sheaths of young ferns.

Slim, lengthy, branched, inconspicuous bunches of small verdant blossoms grow rather late in the summer in some localities, in angles between stalks and leaf stems.

The juice from the simmered greens was believed to kill and expel worms in children, to aid diarrhea, to help purify blood as a spring tonic, to increase the flow of urine, and to act as an astringent. Claims were made for its checking hemorrhaging of the lungs, bowels, and kidneys. Stirred into a small portion of honey, this decoction gained the reputation of helping to relieve asthma, of mitigating bronchitis, and of soothing coughs.

In efforts to stop nosebleeds, pressing a leaf against the root of the mouth with the tongue was said to be effective. Crushed nettles were also stuffed sparingly into the nostrils for the same reason.

Stinging nettles were widely used as an agent applied locally to produce superficial inflammation with the object of reducing inflammation in deeper adjacent regions. For instance, stinging the skin with nettles was used in treating arthritis. They were believed helpful in stanching wounds. Ground nettles were important to the nomadic Indians for treating numb feet. In all such cases, the innumerable little injections of formic acid may have been a helpful factor. Striking paralyzed limbs with nettles was credited many times with restoring healthier circulation and even movement. Neuralgia and rheumatism were also treated with heated poultices of the crushed leaves.

The flowers and seeds of stinging nettles were gathered and put in wine, then later drunk for ague. A sweetened preserve of the flowers and seeds was given for kidney stones. Wine in which nettle leaves had been soaked was also resorted to in some instances for starting menses.

Nettle roots were boiled and the decoction used as a mouthwash or gargle, as a bath for painful parts such as those caused by rheumatism, and for saturating compresses for application to both new wounds as well as old and festering sores. It was taken internally for jaundice. Mixed with honey and dry sugar, it was used to assist the expulsion of matter from the lungs and throat by causing coughing and expectorating, thereby also helping to cure wheezing and shortness of breath.

Tansy (*Tancetum vulgare*)

Family: Compositae (*Compositae*)

Common Names: Common Tansy, Double Tansy, Bachelor's Buttons, Bitter Buttons, Golden Buttons, Yellow Buttons, English Cost, Ginger Plant, Stinking Willie, Scented Fern, Parsley Fern, Hind Heal, Hindheal.

Characteristics: The perennial tansy grows in clumps of erect, unbranched stems 2 to 3 feet high. It has pungent, strongly aromatic, fernlike foliage, some 4 inches wide and about 7 inches long, with jagged, toothed leaflets. Its flowers, green and inconspicuous, top the handsomely hardy plant and develop from July to September into clustering heads of flat, round, tubular, buttonlike, organish yellow flowers that live several weeks and then dry into a dark golden beauty.

Area: Tansy grows throughout much of Canada and the United States.

Continued ➡

Uses: Tanacetin oil, distilled from tansy, has been used as an insect repellent. Taken internally in an effort to induce abortion, it has sometimes proved to be fatal. Toxic to man and animals when eaten, tansy concoctions taken internally had to be used sparingly and with great caution. The flowering tops were also employed to make a tea to promote menstruation.

In small doses the decoctions of the blossoms and leaves were used to kill and expel worms, as a tonic and narcotic both, as a stomachic to strengthen the digestive system and to increase appetite, for inducing perspiration on the dry skin of fever patients, to quiet hysteria, to assist convalescents in regaining strength, to encourage sleepiness, to help in kidney disturbances, to cleanse the lower intestines, for a number of female complaints, to help gallbladder sufferers, and even for jaundice.

It was also used as a substitute for pepper, in the making of the liqueur chartreuse, and sparingly, because of its strong aroma, to flavor such dishes as salads and omelets.

The plants were once hung in colonial kitchens to dry for such usages and also to help keep away insects. They were also strewn on floors for the latter reason.

Applied externally to sexual organs, tansy was reputed to aid fertility. Decoctions were applied to skin eruptions and sores. The tender young leaves, soaked in buttermilk for about ten days, provided a skin lotion. Infusions of the plant were used for bruises, sprains, sore muscles, arthritic conditions, as a bath to cool feverish patients, and as a general liniment.

Crushed leaves were used as poultices for everything from sprains and contusions to stomachache. They were bound around many an Indian head for headache. The Catawbas relied on the authoritatively aromatic tansy in steam baths for sore, bruised, and swollen feet, ankles, and lower legs.

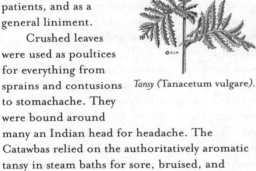

Tansy (Tanacetum vulgare).

Walnut *(Juglans)*

Family: Walnut *(Juglandaceae)*

Common Names: Black Walnut, Common Black Walnut, Walnut Tree, American Walnut, Eastern Black Walnut, Texas Walnut, California Walnut, Nogal.

Characteristics: Particularly valuable for its wood, which is used for paneling and furniture, and for its nuts, the native walnut is a strong, straight, stately tree, averaging between 50 and 100 feet in height and sometimes soaring to as much as 150 feet, with a tightly knit trunk some 2 to 5 feet in diameter. Nogales, where Arizona borders Mexico, has taken its name from the Spanish word for walnuts, nogal. The dark brown, nearly black bark is divided into rounded dullish ridges by deep, slim furrows.

The stems are topped with a single leaf, the other alternative leaflets growing opposite one another, some dozen to twenty-two a branch. They give off a distinctive spicy odor when crushed between the fingers. Sharply tipped and finely toothed, formed something like slim arrowheads, they vary from a few to 2 dozen inches in length. Green, with often a yellow tinge on top, they are more lightly colored and generally hairy beneath.

Frequently mistaken for its close relative the butternut, walnuts have light tan pitch, whereas the butternut emits a dark brown, viscous substance. A hairy fringe is found about the leaf scars of the butternut, whereas none occurs on its cousin.

The roundish walnuts mature to from 1 1/2 to about 3 inches in diameter by the time they are ready to drop from the broadly spreading branches about October, depending on the locality. Then the difficulty is getting off the thick, fleshy, warty, greenish husk—a job calling for waterproof gloves unless you don't mind staining your hands with a long-lasting brown dye. A knife is frequently used for the task, which the pioneers found easier if the damp walnuts were first spread in the sun until they became drier.

In turn, the at first wettish nuts underneath, each encased in its familiar sculptured bony shell, were also kept in the sunlight for a few days to dry and to lose some of their bitterness before being channeled open, or split into two halves with a thumbnail, to reveal their deeply indented, definitely delectable, four-celled nuts.

Area: Half of the world's dozen species of *Juglans* are native to the United States. They grow throughout a large part of the East and into the prairie states. A pair of different walnuts exists in California and another pair, growing up to more than a mile in altitude, elsewhere in the Southwest. Many walnuts are planted as shade trees.

Uses: Walnut meats boast a rugged 628 calories per 100 grams, as revealed by U.S. Department of Agriculture tests, which have shown this portion to have over 20 beneficial grams of protein, over 59 of fat, and almost 15 of carbohydrates. The same healthily edible volume was found to harbor phosphorus, 460 milligrams of potassium, 300 international units of the eye-benefiting vitamin A, 22 milligrams of thiamine, 0.7 of niacin, and 0.11 of riboflavin.

Walnut (Juglans).

The Apaches used the juice of the hulls to divest their horses and cattle of such parasites as lice. It was also believed effective in ridding any wounds of maggots. Dogs were wormed with 1 or 2 tablespoonfuls. For humans, the same long-lasting juice was rubbed into graying hair to make it brown. Aside from this cosmetic use, the juice was thought helpful for passing intestinal worms in human beings and for treating ulcers, boils, carbuncles, syphilis, as well as ringworm and fungus infections. It was also believed to be a medicine for diphtheria. The same juice of the green husks was simmered with honey for use as a soothing gargle and cough syrup, as well as for irritated stomachs.

The depressant characteristic of the crushed green hulls was long ago evidenced by their now illegal and unsporting use, except in survival situations, in stupefying fish for easy catching by hand, their use then for eating not being at all impaired.

The bark of the trees was both boiled and steeped in bubbling water to make a wash that the Indians believed lessened the aches and pains of arthritis. This bark is very astringent.

The inner bark of the tree, the cambium which lies between the outer bark and the wood, was boiled for use as a physic, its immediacy depending on its strength. The inner bark of the root was also so used, especially for dysentery where it seemed to work mainly as a cleansing laxative. It was also gathered in the fall and so used as a cathartic. Furthermore, it was regarded as a remedy when, as was fashionable in colonial America, one felt "liverish."

A leaf infusion is still used in Appalachia both as an astringent and as a remedy against bedbugs.

The oil extracted from the ripe kernels—by boiling them in water, skimming the oil from the top, and then drying the nuts for eating—was adjudged good for colic. It was also believed that it helped in the expelling of tapeworms. This oil used to be recommended as a palliative for various skin troubles.

Wild Clover *(Trifolium)*

Family: Pea *(Leguminosae)*

Common Names: Common Clover, Common Red Clover, Red Clover, Purple Clover, Purple Prairie Clover, White Clover, White Sweet Clover, Yellow Clover, Yellow Sweet Clover, Strawberry Clover, Sweet Clover, Prairie Clover, Meadow Clover, White Prairie Clover, Foothill Clover, Ditch Clover, Longstalk Clover, Broadleaved Clover, Pinpoint Clover, Bighead Clover, Clammy Clover, Hop Clover, Low Hop-Clover, Smaller Hop-Clover, Large Hop Clover, Buffalo Clover, Rabbitfoot Clover, Cow Clover, Tomcat Clover, Tick Clover, Beggar's Ticks, Tick Trefoil, Clever Grass, Trefoil, Bee-Bread, Fourleaf Clover.

Characteristics: There are a number of different species of this plant on this continent, but everyone knows the common varieties, mainly those with red, white, and occasionally yellow blossoms—everyone, that is, who has ever successfully sought as a youngster the so-called lucky four-leaved oddities among the vast stretches of trefoil masses of green foliage or who has sucked honey from one of the individual minute tubelike flowers forming the fragrant heads.

Red clover, *T. pratense*, is the official flower of the New England State of Vermont. It is a biennial or perennial legume with long-stemmed, trifoliate leaves, each ordinarily with three oval-shaped leaflets. The globular to ovate flower heads are dense and roseate.

Continued ➡

White clover, *T. repens*, is selected by many a home owner for his lawn, as, being a low, white-flowered, creeping perennial with glabrous runners and usually long-stemmed leaves, it does not need constant mowing. Bread made from its seed-replete dried flowers, being healthful and nourishing, has saved peoples from starvation.

Too, clover is widely known as an important food crop for all kinds of livestock at every time of the year, whether green or dry. It attracts large numbers of bumblebees, which serve to fertilize it, the genus not being successful in Australia until bees were brought in, too.

Areas: Clovers, some of them going wild from introduced species, prosper in all sorts of conditions and soils throughout much of the United States and Canada.

Uses: The red clovers, known by a number of different common names, depending on the locality, are regarded as antispasmodics, good for nervous indigestion and allied troubles. The flowers have been used therapeutically also as an expectorant, sedative, and for healing wounds and sores.

An ointment was made from them for spreading over ulcers, and a poultice made by crushing a handful of blossoms and steeping them in a small amount of water for four hours, then putting the mixture on while it was still warm. It is also soothing to irritated mucous membranes, and

Wild clover (Trifolium).

therefore is used for coughs. For youngsters, rashes were washed with a strong decoction of the flowers and water.

In fact, a syrup was made for whooping cough by simmering 2 ounces of blossoms to a quart of thick sticky solution of sugar and water, straining and then sipping this several times daily, especially when the coughing became particularly irritating.

The dried and ground flowers of the red clover were, according to the *U.S. Dispensatory*, used in some antiasthma cigarettes. Tea brewed from the flowers was also used to improve sluggish appetites, regulate digestive functions, and to treat liver ailments.

The blossoms of both the red and white clovers had the reputation of being blood purifiers and a strong tea steeped from them individually was applied externally to boils, ulcers, and other skin disorders. They were also drunk to cleanse the system and were furthermore taken as alternatives.

Some of the Indians ate the tender young leaves, especially raw but also sparingly simmered to prevent and cure scurvy, characterized by such symptoms as roughening of the skin, congestion about the hair follicles, large bruiselike areas of hemorrhaging, pain in the joints and muscles, and often swelling of the joints.

Wild Onion (*Allium*)

Family: Lily (*Liliaceae*)

Common Names: Nodding Onion, Nodding Wild Onion, Sickle-Leaved Onion, Swamp Onion, Marsh Onion, Tree Onion, Shortstyle Onion, Sierra Onion, Sierra Garlic, Wild Garlic, Eastern Wild Garlic, Meadow Garlic, Field Garlic, Siberian Garlic, Wild Chive, Wild Leak.

Characteristics: The one thing to watch out for is to use only those plants and bulbs that have the familiar odor and flavor of the onion family. None are poisonous. However, some domestic and wild plants, and bulbs especially, have an onionlike *appearance* only and are among the most insidious poisons in the plant world although, because of familiarity with them as flowers, you and children particularly may regard them as edible. Beware of them and keep them out of youngsters' reach as much as possible—admittedly a difficult thing to do in gardens. But try to drill into them the fact that all parts of such plants should be left strictly alone, and keep them out of reach when they are not in the ground.

The typical wild onion has slim, awllike, often hollow leaves similar to those of the vegetable garden species. Underground, it is a layered bulb with a distinctive odor and taste. Flowers appear at the tops of otherwise naked stems.

There are, as always, exceptions. With the *Allium canadense* or eastern wild garlic or meadow garlic, bulbs grow at the top. When Père Jacques Marquette, seventeenth-century Jesuit missionary and explorer, went from Wisconsin in 1674 to the present vicinity of Chicago, he and his party existed mainly on wild onions, likely this species. In the Menominee language, the word *Cigaga-Wuni* (to spell it phonetically) was the name of the wild leek, *A. tricoccum*, or skunk place, the first part of which name was given this region where so many of these plants thrived and were also probably eaten by the Marquette party.

The continent-crossing expedition of Rogers and Clark was introduced to the wild medicinals by the Indians, there being some fifty varieties in the Rocky Mountain region alone.

Wild onion (Allium).

Area: These numerous, pungent members of the lily family—the wild onions, leeks, chives, scallions, shallots, and garlics—grow throughout North America except in the land of the permafrost in the Arctic and Far North. The withered stems and seedpods of a number of the varieties stick up above the winter snows and indicate the presence of usable bulbs in the ground below.

Uses: For centuries, according to no less an authority than the U.S. Department of Agriculture, a medicinal oil has been extracted from the *A. sativum*, or wild garlic, and has been used to treat such ailments as bronchitis. The crushed bulbs were made into a poultice applied to the chest of those suffering from pneumonia.

The old people among the Indians and the settlers were brought up making cough syrups by cooking the sliced bulbs and dissolving the juice into some sweetness which might well have been maple sugar. Such syrup was used to treat cold symptoms and to help such afflicted children drift off to sleep. The same syrup was also used to attack hives.

Incidentally, the odor which is repellent to many people after someone has been eating garlic and the like can easily be eradicated. Just brushing the teeth, tongue, and gums thoroughly, so that no bits of the medicinal remains, will leave a fresh-smelling mouth.

These wild medicinals have long been what often seemed to be a miraculous cure for scurvy. When Maximilian, Prince of Wied, was weak with the vitamin deficiency at Fort Clark in 1834, it was the Indians who got the green leaves and bulbs of wild garlic (*A. reticulatum*), which cured him when his plight seemed hopeless. On Major Stephen Long's large expedition to the Rockies in 1819 and 1820, 300 of his men were laid low with scurvy, a third of them fatally, and it was likely the wild garlic brought in by the Indians which saved the remainder. On General George Crook's so-called Starvation March down the Yellowstone River in 1876, wild onions were credited with helping the men avoid scurvy.

The Cheyennes were among the Indians crushing the bulbs and stems of wild garlic, applying this as a poultice to carbuncles and boils, and then, when the sore burst or was opened, washing out the pus with a strong tea simmered from the same medicinal.

The Dakotas and the Winnebagos were among the Indians who crushed the wild onion and applied it to bee, wasp, hornet, and other insect bites with what was said to have been marked success in reducing the swelling and pain. Some Indians used it in an effort to draw the poison out of snakebites.

Many of the early Americans, both Indians and pioneers, simmered the juice of the wild onion family down to a heavy syrup which was used for coughs, tickling throats, and other cold symptoms. Some of the Indians and settlers used the juice expressed from roasted wild onions and wild garlic for infants with croup. Wild onion poultices are so used in parts of Appalachia today. The juice was also dropped in to the ear to relieve aching and the ringing noise that individuals sometimes notice.

Crushed members of the family were applied to scalds and burns, even those caused from too much exposure to ultraviolet rays, as well as to sores and even unsightly blemishes. It was also said to help digestion, to keep away disease germs in some instances, and to aid piles and hemorrhoids. The Indians and sourdoughs moistened clean, heavily steam-sterilized sphagnum moss, which covers thousands of miles of our continental North, with wild onion juice diluted with sterile water for antiseptic applications to wounds and suppurating sores.

The meadow garlic, *A. canadense*, has been used to rid the digestive system of gas, to increase the flow of urine, and to help patients relieve their respiratory systems of phlegm.

Continued ➜

Other members of the wild onion family have also been so utilized.

Water in which sliced or crushed wild onions had been steeped for at least twelve hours was drunk on empty stomachs to rid the system of worms.

Willow (Salix)

Family: Willow (Salicaceae)

Common Names: White Willow, European White Willow, Snow Willow, Black Willow, Pussy Willow, Swamp Willow, Blue Willow, Shining Willow, Canada Willow, Quebec Willow, Prairie Willow, Tall Prairie Willow, Coastal Plain Willow, Weeping Willow, Drummond's Willow, Glaucous Willow, Glossy Willow, Crack Willow, Sandbar Willow, Silky Willow.

Characteristics: The above is only a sampling of the names, for some 200 to 300 willows grow throughout the world, depending on which school of thought the botanist who is doing the counting follows; at least a third of them grow in this country. They range from large attractive trees, to shrubs and bushes, to small shoots in the Arctic and mountains, which are important for many times being at first spring source of vitamin C and, incidentally, of plant food, Being seen most frequently near water, they also grow in lofty stony country.

Particularly when some species become snowy with the widely known pussy willows, which I've seen growing from beaver houses on still-frozen ponds, it is not hard to recognize them, especially as most varieties have narrow and long smooth or toothed leaves, or oblong lancelike leaves, with short stems. Partly because they are the first growth to leaf in the spring-time, they are the favorite browse of moose and other members of the deer family.

To pick a few individual species, the black willow, *S. nigra*, is the largest American willow, stretching 50 and sometimes nearly 100 feet high in damp bottomlands and along water, although some remain bushes. The branches are reddish, smooth, brittle where they leave the trunks, which lift largely in clumps. The fruits are narrow, vaselike, closed receptacles containing innumer-able silky tufted seeds which run approxi-mately 150,000 to the ounce, one reason why they are so widely spread through New Brunswick west to Ontario and South Dakota, south to Texas.

The sandbar willow (*S. interior*), on the other hand, is a shrub from some 1 to nearly 3 yards tall, growing in thickets on sand and gravel along streams and other spots where there is often flooding. Again, the branchlets are reddish and mostly smooth. The characteristic willow leaves are narrowly lancelike, sharp-tipped at either end, and smoothly green on both sides and sometimes silky silver, growing on extremely short stalks. They grow from the Maritimes to

Willow (Salix).

gold-panning Alaska, south to Maryland and New Mexico.

Area: As can be surmised, the willow family grows in quantity in Canada and the United States from the Arctic to Mexico.

Uses: The bitterness in the leaves and the thin inner bark of the majority of the willows comes from salicylic acid, which gives the common aspirin its own bitterness, making this general species one of natures's most important natural gifts to mankind. The North American Indians soon discovered that tea decocted and steeped from the cambium of the majority of the willows (a very few of the shoots turn out to be sweet when eaten for nourishment and vitamin C—a fact which makes them more palatable but less important medically) was important for arthritis and for reducing fever and many pains—this centuries before the isolation and marketing of the drug aspirin. In fact, the willow's name of *Salix* comes from salicylic acid.

The ashes of burned willow twigs were blended with water and used for gonorrhea. Willow roots were powdered with stones and turned to in an effort to dry up sores resulting from syphilis. The settlers joined the Indians in using potent teas brewed from the thin cambium or inner bark of the bitter willows to treat vene-real diseases.

The dried and powdered bitter bark, astrin-gent and detergent, was applied to the navels of newly born babies. It was utilized to stop severe bleeding, as were the crushed young green leaves, the bark, and the seeds, also stuffed up the nostrils to stop bad nosebleeds. These were also used for toothache, the salicin in them here being the important component. They were steeped in water or wine as a dandruff controller and preventative.

Some tribes turned to the simmered bark and roots of the black willow, *S. nigra*, for weak-ness and lack of vigor that they attributed to poor blood. The inner bark of the black willow was brewed into a strong tea for keeping moist compresses over ulcers and gangrene.

The Mohicans were among the Indians soaking the inner bark of the red willow (*S. lucida*), to get bile out of the stomach and allow vomiting. The Chickasaws used the roots this way and for nosebleeds, as well as in small amounts for headache. Some of the Indians of New England used a weaker solution of the scraped bark of the red willow for cold symptoms and smoked the scraped and cut cambium for asthma. Other Indians, the settlers following, steeped the bark of the Red Willow and imbibed it for headache and lumbago.

To fend off fevers, the Creeks washed them-selves in a boiled solution of the roots. Some crushed the bark and bandaged it around the head to ease headaches. The Ojibwas turned to the inner bark for external use on wounds and sores; other tribes to check bleeding—a use also made of the root bark of the pussy willow, *S. discolor*, as well as other willows. Some bands utilized root tea in an enema for severe diar-rhea.

As if all this were not enough, the roots were used to kill and expel worms. Willow tea was used by the drop to relieve inflamed eyes.

The settlers soon adopted the Indian prac-tice of steeping willow roots for spring tonic, adjudged all the better for being bitter. And some tried many of the tribes' use of pussy willow catkins as an aphrodisiac.

Witch Hazel (Hamamelis virginiana)

Family: Witch Hazel (Hamamelidaceae)

Common Names: Common Witch Hazel, Wych Hazel, Southern Witch Hazel, Eastern Witch Hazel, White Hazel, Snapping Hazel, Snapping Hazel-Nut, Hamamelia, Spotted Alder, Striped Alder, Tobacco Wood, Wood Tobacco, Winterbloom, Pistachio, Long Boughs.

Characteristics: The plant has nothing to do with witches. The usual name is derived from an Old English word meaning "pliable" and related to "weak," not exactly a comedown when one considers that although the medicine is an offi-cial drug, there has never been any complete agreement as to its efficiency despite the fact that the public buys it by the millions of gallons.

Witch hazel is a crooked tree or shrub, usually 8 to 15 feet tall, although it sometimes reaches 25 feet in height. The twisting stem and long, forking branches with brown, smooth bark are characteristic, as is the balsamic fragrance of the bruised parts. It produces new shoots from the base. A peculiar feature, except in the springflowering species, is the late appearance of the threadlike, yellow flowers, their not appearing until late in the autumn or in the early winter after the leaves, smooth above and paler and smooth or almost so beneath, have fallen.

As for the urnlike, downy seed capsule, this does not mature until the following season, when it bursts open, scattering the shining, hard, black seeds with great force and to a considerable distance. These grow from a two-celled ovary, composed of a pair of pistils united below, forming a double-beaked, two-celled woody capsule, the one ovule suspended from the apex of each chamber becoming a bony entity. There are eight stamens, half of them perfect and the other half scalelike and sterile.

The twigs are mostly hairy, bearing the fruits in long clusters. The leaves are simple, 3 to 5 inches long, thick, scalloped along their margins, with an obtuse apex and curved to a tapering base, roundish to round-oval, borne on short stalks. Both the twigs and the buds are rough with a rusty or tawny pubescence.

Area: Used in land-scaping and growing in moist light woods

*Witch hazel
(Hamamelis virginiana).*

and along rocky banks and streams throughout most of the United States except in the Far West, this North American plant thrives especially from the Maritimes and Quebec to Florida, westward to Minnesota and Texas.

Uses: The twigs, leaves, and bark are all used to prepare witch hazel extract, which has been used for everything from shaving lotions and vaginal

Continued ➡

douches to treating contusions, sprains, insect bites, and piles. The fresh leaves especially contain a high concentration of tannin which make them very astringent. Indians taught the settlers to apply them to bruises and swellings.

The tannin, gallic acid, and the volatile oils are strongly hemostatic, and therefore a tea steeped from the leaves and bark has long been considered effective for bleeding in the stomach, as for ulcers, and in an enema for inwardly bleeding piles. The Iroquois also used a tea made from the steeped leaves, sweetened to taste with maple sugar, as both a pleasant and beneficial tea with meals. One recipe for the tea was a teaspoonful of the granulated or finely chopped leaves and bark added to a cup of bubbling water and steeped for five minutes. It was believed, incidentally, that the oils were more potent if the components were gathered in the late autumn and winter.

Compresses and bandages, kept wet with witch hazel, were applied to varicose veins and to burns, rashes, skin irritations, and infections. A small amount of alcohol was often added if available, and a steam extract from the twigs was what was often used. Cold compresses were also used for headaches and for sore and inflamed eyes. A decoction prepared from the inner bark was considered by many Indians as being especially efficacious for bathing the eyes.

The entire moistened herb was spread over hot rocks in enclosed places and water poured atop it for steam baths, which were believed to bring about speedy relief from feverish colds, catarrah, coughing, and abnormally heavy phlegm discharges.

The extract was used in massages for overexertion and muscular strain, for arthritis, and for general conditioning. It was applied manually, sometimes with a bit of moistened cotton, to insect bites, hemorrhoids, scalds, burns, and swellings.

Witch hazel was also relied upon as a rinse and gargle for irritated throats, sore gums, cankers, and general mouth irritations.

When one was traveling where water was scant, he often chewed the bark, which was first bitter and astringent but left a pleasantly lingering sweetish, pungent taste.

Yarrow (*Achillea millefolium*)

Family: Compositae (*Compositae*)

Common Names: Common Yarrow, Milfoil, Knight's Milfoil, Milfoil Thousand-Leaf, Soldier's Woundwort, Soldier's Wound-Wort, Bloodwort, Sanguinary, Nosebleed, Devil's Plaything, Green Arrow, Thousand-Leaf, Thousand-Seal, Thousand-Leaved Clover, Gordaldo, Gordoloba, Cammock, Old Man's Pepper, Carpenter Grass, Carpenter's Grass, Dog Daisy, Woolly Yarrow.

Characteristics: Once smelled, the aromatically lacy foliage and flat-topped terminal flowers of the yarrow will ever after be recognized. The almost always white blossoms are very rarely yellow and even more occasionally purple. They are small, developing in spring and summer into sometimes convex clusters. The complex leaves are made up of very small entities on small stems branching off of single stalks. Growing alternately, they are also many times clustered at the bottom of the usually less than

3-foot-high central stems. Finely dissected, they are linear to narrow-spatulate or lanceolate. The foliage as a whole often seems grayish from numerous small hairs.

Gathered in the late summer of early fall, many still scent the cabins where they are hung high to dry for later use.

Yarrow is widely known in England as tansy, an entirely different important medicinal plant here in the New World (covered elsewhere in this volume).

Area: The fragrant lacy and distinctive plants from coast to coast over most of Canada and the United States.

Uses: Yarrow roots are still the traditionally used local anesthetic of many of the western Indians, as revealed by two cases recorded by the Research Service of the U.S. Department of Agriculture.

Yarrow
(*Achillea millefolium*).

One involved a Nevada Indian who was suffering acutely from a deep thigh wound in which foreign substances had entered the cut. Fresh, scrubbed yarrow roots were crushed to a soft spongy mass and applied gently to the spot. Within half an hour the anesthetic had so dulled the pain that it was possible to expand and clean the wound. The second concerned a deeply sunk splinter that, following soaking in a solution of yarrow roots, was similarly opened and removed. This was accomplished by members of the family.

Not only fresh poultices, but washes in which the leaves and stems were also sometimes boiled were used in similar cases after battles and accidents. The entire plant was often reduced to a paste, spread over newly set fractures, and bound in place with fresh dandelion leaves or sterilized cloths.

The yarrow had the additional quality of acting as a coagulant and therefore was used for everything from a gashed toe to a speartorn side. The leaves of the yarrow, steeped in water, thus became in numerous regions the most commonly employed herb to stem the flow of blood. They were even soaked and stuffed up the nostrils to quell nosebleed.

Yarrow poultices were resorted to for common bruises and abrasions. In cases of burns and scalds, yarrow was crushed as between two smooth rocks, combined with water, and spread over the injury before perhaps wild onions were bruised, salted, and applied both in an effort to withdraw the heat and to prevent blistering.

The styptic characteristics of the yarrow were resorted to for all kinds of nicks and cuts, even those from the pioneer's razor. The leaves were even reported to heal inflammations, eczema, rashes, infections, and the like.

Yarrow tea was applied to sore nipples. Boiled yarrow leaves were used as a wash for eyes irritated from dust, glare, and snow blindness. It

was tried in eruptions such as those arising from measles and chicken pox. Swellings were bathed in the tea, as were regions irritated by poison ivy and poison oak and by general itching. It was a natural wash for fevers.

Bits from freshly cut yarrow roots were inserted in aching tooth cavities. It was even believed that the constant chewing of yarrow root or continual applications of root tea would kill the nerve of an ulcerated tooth.

Indians suffering from the gout took decoctions of yarrow. It was turned to for sciatica. It was resorted to for neuralgia. The Chicakasaws took an infusion of yarrow for cramps in the neck. It was given warm as a soothing agent in cases of hysteria. It was used to combat tuberculosis.

Yarrow was even used in attempted abortions. Dr. Charles F. Millspaugh reported in his 1892 book on *Medicinal Plants* that the use of yarrow was no more limited to the Indians than the age-old practice of abortion elsewhere in the world. The dosage suggested was 10 drops or more of the oil of the herb. The doctor recorded that yarrow was "one of the most frequently used abortives among ignorant people—not so dangerous generally as that following the use of nutmeg but very often serious." Too, yarrow tea, made from fresh leaves, was widely favored for suppressed menstruation.

Some of the tribes resorted to a yarrow poultice for spider bites, and, of course, after the sucking of the wound, it was used for poisonous snakebites.

The leaves of the yarrow were also favored for fevers. Hot yarrow tea, made from the dried leaves, was sought to induce perspiring, regarded as effective in breaking a fever. This was also used for chills. The feverish patient was bathed, too, in cold yarrow tea . . .

A poultice of bruised yarrow leaves was laid or bound over the forehead for headaches.

A weak brew of the entire plant was pressed into service as an astringent gargle and mouthwash. It was believed to be successful as a vaginal douche for leukorrhea. Indians injected it as an enema for hemorrhoids. It was generally relied on to adjust malfunction of the kidney, liver, and the genitourinary systems. Even today, yarrow is steeped in an effort to help a diseased condition in the stomach and intestinal system.

A small amount of the roots or preferably the whole plant was steeped in a small amount of water as a tonic for someone who was run down. A chilled infusion was recommended for convalescents. It was, as might have been suspected, another of the spring tonics. Tea made from the plant was given twice daily as a blood builder following childbirth.

The entire plant, including the roots, was boiled and taken mornings and nights to help one retain his strength during a cold. In fact, the chewing of yarrow root was supposed to help break up a cold.

Yarrow baths were favored for arthritis, and a solution served as a favored liniment for overexerted joints and muscles.

Leaves were soaked and a wad of them pressed into an aching or infected ear. The juice dropped into the eyes was believed to stop redness and inflammation.

Continued ➔

The dried and powdered herb was steeped with plantain tea to stem internal bleeding.

Generally, the herb is an aromatic with diaphoretic and emmenagogue activity that seemed to work out well as a general vulnerary. Leaves of both the common yarrow (A. mille-folium), and the woolly yarrow (A. lanulosaw), were picked for numerous difficulties with the reproductive organs.

Yucca (Yucca).

An ointment for wounds was made by blending yarrow leaves with a pure edible lard such as those made from wild-animal fat.

Yucca (*Yucca*)

Family: Lily (*Liliaceae*)

Common Names: Datil Yucca, Broad-Leaved Yucca, Spanish Bayonet, Spanish Dagger, Dagger Plant, Date Fruit, Datil, Soap Weed, Soapweed, Small Soapweed, Bear Grass, Joshua Tree, Our Lord's Candle, Adam's Needle, Eve's Darning Needle.

Characteristics: Not really a cactus, the yucca nevertheless grows in desert and desertlike areas and includes the well-known Joshua tree, which soars up to some 40 feet in height and has leaves up to about 7 inches long.

There are two general types of yucca—one with fleshy, moist fruit and the other with dry fruit, both at maturity. They produce big, flat-tish, black, wind-carried seeds in abundance that are freed by the splitting of the ripened ovaries.

The Spanish bayonet, *Yucca baccata*, grows with ferociously pointed, stiff, obese leaves from about 1 to 4 feet long. They do not bloom annually, but when this happens pyra-midical, loosely branched flower clusters arise from the mass of daggerlike leaves—2 or 3 feet long and some 2 inches wide, with a few coarse fibers wavering from their edges—with many white or creamy, bell-like, fleshy blossoms that can be shredded and enjoyed in salads. The big, pulpy, seed-filled fruit of those that are left mature into a some 3- to 6-inch-long delicacy that resembles a stubby banana, good roasted and peeled while still somewhat green, which can mature into a blackish purple or somewhat yellowish sweet, thick, adhesive, and sticky delicacy that the Spanish Americans use like a date.

The flowers are generally numerous each spring. However, successful pollination carried on by small yucca moths, that often remain in the closed blooms all day and do not visit the stigmas of surrounding plants until darkness, is not annually successful.

Area: The various yucca grow on dry plains and rocky slopes from California to South Dakota, Montana, and Kansas, to Maryland and Tennessee, south to Florida, Louisiana, Texas, and New Mexico.

Uses: Soapy and detergentlike suds result from the agitation of the roots with water, which was and still is in some regions used medicinally for cleaning purposes and for externally arising skin eruptions, rashes, and other such disorders, as well as for ulcers that have proved difficult to heal. The saponin ingredient responsible for this does not have the usual acrid flavor nor the sneeze-arousing qualities of other saponins. It is good for general skin care and for abrasions and the like. Some particularly seek it for healthful shampooing.

The pounded roots of the Joshua tree, *Y. brevifolia*, used to be boiled in water to provide a tea taken internally for gonorrhea. The fruit of this tree has been used as an emetic.

Yucca leaves contain salicylic acid, and therefore teas brewed from them have the same arthritis-helping, headache- and muscular-pain-relieving, and temperature-reducing qual-ities of aspirin.

The fruit of the datil yucca (*Y. baccata*) is reportedly laxative to a certain degree, especially if one is not used to it.

—From Field Guide to Medicinal Plants

Poisonous Plants

U.S. Army

Successful use of plants in a survival situation depends on positive identification. Knowing poisonous plants is as important to a survivor as knowing edible plants. Knowing the poisonous plants will help you avoid sustaining injuries from them.

How Plants Poison

Plants generally poison by—

- **Ingestion.** When a person eats a part of a poisonous plant.
- **Contact.** When a person makes contact with a poisonous plant that causes any type of skin irritation or dermatitis.
- **Absorption or inhalation.** When a person either absorbs the poison through the skin or inhales it into the respiratory system.

Plant poisoning ranges from minor irrita-tion to death. A common question asked is, "How poisonous is this plant?" It is difficult to say how poisonous plants are because—

- Some plants require contact with a large amount of the plant before noticing any adverse reaction while others will cause death with only a small amount.
- Every plant will vary in the amount of toxins it contains due to different growing conditions and slight variations in subspecies.
- Every person has a different level of resist-ance to toxic substances.
- Some persons may be more sensitive to a particular plant.

Some common misconceptions about poisonous plants are—

- *Watch the animals and eat what they eat.* Most of the time this statement is true, but some animals can eat plants that are poisonous to humans.
- *Boil the plant in water and any poisons will be removed.* Boiling removes many poisons, but not all.
- *Plants with a red color are poisonous.* Some plants that are red are poisonous, but not all.

The point is there is no one rule to aid in identifying poisonous plants. You must make an effort to learn as much about them as possible.

All About Plants

It is to your benefit to learn as much about plants as possible. Many poisonous plants look like their edible relatives or like other edible plants. For example, poison hemlock appears very similar to wild carrot. Certain plants are safe to eat in certain seasons or stages of growth and poisonous in other stages. For example, the leaves of the pokeweed are edible when it first starts to grow, but it soon becomes poisonous. You can eat some plants and their fruits only when they are ripe. For example, the ripe fruit of mayapple is edible, but all other parts and the green fruit are poisonous. Some plants contain both edible and poisonous parts; potatoes and tomatoes are common plant foods, but their green parts are poisonous.

Some plants become toxic after wilting. For example, when the black cherry starts to wilt, hydrocyanic acid develops. Specific preparation methods make some plants edible that are poisonous raw. You can eat the thinly sliced and thoroughly dried corms (drying may take a year) of the jack-in-the-pulpit, but they are poisonous if not thoroughly dried.

Learn to identify and use plants before a survival situation. Some sources of information about plants are pamphlets, books, films, nature trails, botanical gardens, local markets, and local natives. Gather and cross-reference information from as many sources as possible, because many sources will not contain all the information needed.

Rules for Avoiding Poisonous Plants

Your best policy is to be able to look at a plant and identify it with absolute certainty and to know its uses or dangers. Many times this is not possible. If you have little or no knowledge of the local vegetation, use the rules to select plants for the "Universal Edibility Test." Remember, avoid—

- *All mushrooms.* Mushroom identification is very difficult and must be precise, even more so than with other plants. Some mushrooms cause death very quickly. Some mushrooms have no known anti-dote. Two general types of mushroom poisoning are gastrointestinal and central nervous system.
- *Contact with or touching plants unnecessarily.*

Continued ➡

Contact Dermatitis

Contact dermatitis from plants will usually cause the most trouble in the field. The effects may be persistent, spread by scratching, and are particularly dangerous if there is contact in or around the eyes.

The principal toxin of these plants is usually an oil that gets on the skin upon contact with the plant. The oil can also get on equipment and then infect whoever touches the equipment. Never burn a contact poisonous plant because the smoke may be as harmful as the plant. There is a greater danger of being affected when overheated and sweating. The infection may be local or it may spread over the body.

Symptoms may take from a few hours to several days to appear. Signs and symptoms can include burning, reddening, itching, swelling, and blisters.

When you first contact the poisonous plants or the first symptoms appear, try to remove the oil by washing with soap and cold water. If water is not available, wipe your skin repeatedly with dirt or sand. Do not use dirt if blisters have developed. The dirt may break open the blisters and leave the body open to infection. After you have removed the oil, dry the area. You can wash with a tannic acid solution and crush and rub jewelweed on the affected area to treat plant-caused rashes. You can make tannic acid from oak bark.

Poisonous plants that cause contact dermatitis are—

- Cowhage.
- Poison ivy.
- Poison oak.
- Poison sumac.
- Rengas tree.
- Trumpet vine.

Ingestion Poisoning

Ingestion poisoning can be very serious and could lead to death very quickly. Do not eat any plant unless you have positively identified it first. Keep a log of all plants eaten.

Signs and symptoms of ingestion poisoning can include nausea, vomiting, diarrhea, abdominal cramps, depressed heartbeat and respiration, headaches, hallucinations, dry mouth, unconsciousness, coma, and death.

If you suspect plant poisoning, try to remove the poisonous material from the victim's mouth and stomach as soon as possible. Induce vomiting by tickling the back of his throat or by giving him warm saltwater, if he is conscious. Dilute the poison by administering large quantities of water or milk, if he is conscious.

The following plants can cause ingestion poisoning if eaten:

POISON SUMAC, IVY, AND OAK
William Carey Grimm

Poison Sumac (*Toxicodendron vernix*)

Caution: All parts of this plant contain a dangerous skin irritant.

Field marks. A shrub or small tree 4 to about 15 feet high; growing in swamps, bogs, and other wet places. Branchlets moderately stout, smooth, the end bud present. Leaves alternate, compound, 6 to 12 inches long; the 7 to 13 leaflets short-stalked, elliptic or egg-shaped, broadly pointed at base, pointed at tip, margin untoothed, rather lustrous above, paler beneath, smooth, 2 to 4 inches long; leafstalks usually reddish. Flowers small, greenish, in axillary clusters; blooming May to July. Fruits roundish, smooth, waxy white, about 3/16 inch in diameter, in rather loose and drooping clusters; ripening August or September and persisting.

Range. Southwestern Maine to Ontario and Minnesota, south to Florida and Texas.

Poison-Ivy (*Toxicodendron radicans*)

Caution: All parts of this plant contain a dangerous skin irritant.

Field marks. An erect or trailing leaf-losing shrub, or a woody vine climbing by means of aerial rootlets on the stems; growing in wooded areas, thickets, clearings, or along fence rows and roadsides. Leaves alternate, long-stalked, compound, 4 to 12 inches long; the 3 leaflets oval or egg-shaped, rounded or broadly pointed at base, pointed at tip, usually with a few coarse teeth on margin, often lustrous above, paler and slightly downy beneath, 1 1/2 to 8 inches long; the end leaflet rather long-stalked, the side ones almost stalkless. Flowers small, yellowish green, in axillary clusters; blooming May to July. Fruits roundish, waxy white, about 3/16 inch in diameter; maturing August to October and persisting.

Range. Nova Scotia to British Columbia; south to Florida, Texas, and Arizona.

Poison-Oak (*Toxicodendron pubescens*)

Caution: All parts of this plant contain a dangerous skin irritant.

Field marks. A stiffly erect, simple or sparingly branched, leaf-losing shrub 1 to 2 1/2 feet high; growing in dry sandy pine and oak woods and clearings. Leaves alternate, long-stalked, compound, 3 to 8 inches long; the 3 leaflets often broadly egg-shaped, pointed at base, blunt at tip, with 3 to 7 often deep lobes, somewhat downy above, more densely so and paler beneath, 2 to 5 inches long; the end leaflet rather long-stalked, the side ones almost stalkless; leafstalks downy. Flowers and fruits similar to those of Poison-ivy but usually more downy.

Range. Chiefly coastal plain; New Jersey and Maryland south to Florida; Tennessee to eastern Oklahoma south to Alabama and Texas.

—From *The Illustrated Book of Wildflowers and Shrubs*

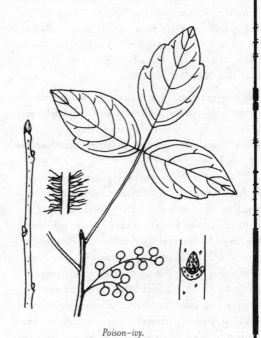

Poison-ivy.

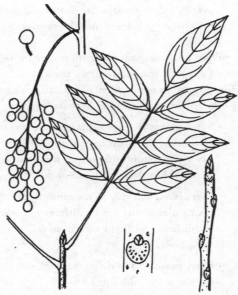

Poison sumac.

Poison-oak.

Continued ➡

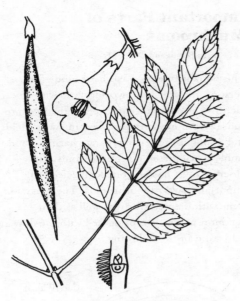

Trumpet vine or trumpet creeper*.

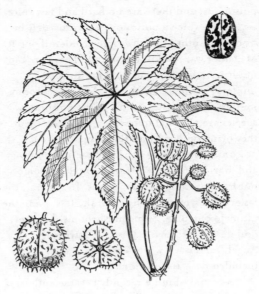

Castor bean (castor oil plant).

Pangi.

- Castor bean.
- Chinaberry.
- Death camas.
- Lantana.
- Manchineel.
- Oleander.
- Pangi.
- Physic nut.
- Poison and water hemlocks.
- Rosary pea.
- Strychnine tree.

—From *Survival (Field Manual 21–76)*

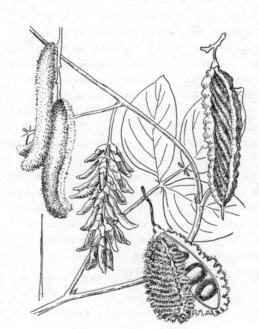

Cowhage.

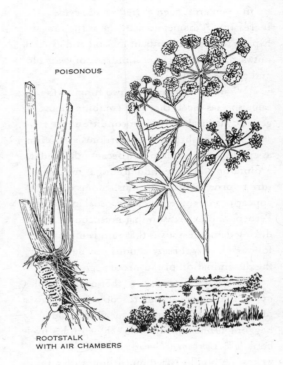

POISONOUS

ROOTSTALK
WITH AIR CHAMBERS

Water hemlock.

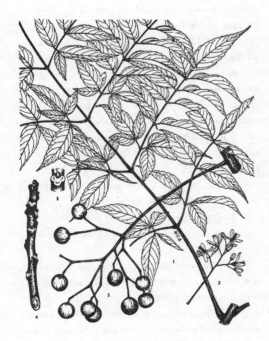

Chinaberry*.

Physic nut.

* by William Carey Grimm, from The Illustrated Guide to Wildflowers and Shrubs
* by William Carey Grimm, from The Illustrated Guide to Trees

Mushrooms

C. Leonard Fergus and Charles Fergus

A mushroom, no matter its shape or color or size, is a fruiting body of an organism known as a *fungus* (plural, *fungi*). The fungi have an entire kingdom to themselves in the taxonomic system, separate from the plants. While resembling plants in their immobility, fungi lack the green pigment chlorophyll and obtain essential carbon compounds not by manufacturing them, as plants do through photosynthesis, but by gleaning them from living or dead matter. Fungi break down and consume plants: grasses, leaves, wood, fruit, and other plant parts. The fungi—which include molds, yeasts, smuts, and mildews—are key decomposers of vegetation, and without them, life on earth would be utterly different than we know it.

In the past, people thought mushrooms emerged spontaneously out of rotting matter or grew where lightning struck the ground. Not

Continued ➡

until the eighteenth century did humans discover that fungi exist as *hyphae*, strands of living tissue that spread through square yards or even acres of earth. We see their gossamer filaments when we turn over a clump of rotten leaves, dig in the upper layers of the soil, or break apart an old log. In the soil, fungal hyphae often infiltrate the fine outer rootlets of trees, helping the trees take in minerals and other nutrients by linking them to the vast network of fungal filaments. Some trees cannot survive without their mycorrhizal (*myco* for fungi, *rhizal* for root) partners. In return, the fungi receive carbon compounds that the trees make through photosynthesis. This symbiotic relationship explains why many fungi are found in forests.

Some mushrooms fruit in "fairy rings," so named because people once believed that fairies danced around the rings and sat on the mushrooms to rest. Fairy rings mark the outer edge of an underground fungus. The rings often show up in open areas such as fields and lawns, increasing in diameter each year as the fungal hyphae use up nutrients in the soil and expand outward. Some rings are hundreds of years old and cover several acres.

When the hyphae from two fungi of the same species meet, they may combine their genetic material and, when conditions are right, send forth mushrooms. Mushrooms are to fungi as apples are to apple trees. Because the underground or otherwise hidden fungus needs moisture to produce its fruit, mushrooms often appear two or three days after a soaking rain. Perhaps another reason that mushrooms arise during damp periods is that rain is often followed by dry, breezy conditions, perfect for the dissemination of mushroom spores.

Spores are analogous to the seeds in apples, except that spores are microscopic (most consist of a single cell) and are produced in mind-boggling numbers. Elio Schaechter, in his lively book *In the Company of Mushrooms: A Biologist's Tale*, writes: "A middle-sized mushroom with a four-inch cap may produce on the order of 20 billion spores over a period of four to six days, at a rate of some 100 million per hour." Depending on the shape and structure of the mushroom, its spores are ejected from between gills, trickle down through pores, waft away from branching structures, or come puffing out of bladders. Wind disperses the spores, sometimes carrying them for many miles. The spores land on the ground or on wood, where they form filaments that grow to become new fungi.

The color of a mushroom's spores is an important aid in identifying a fungus species. My father recommended placing a mushroom cap, minus its stem, on a combination of black and white paper, covering it with a jar or cup, and waiting an hour or so for a spore print to form: the print visible against either the white background or the black, depending on spore color. Other authorities suggest making spore prints on glass, then scraping the spores together with a knife blade to determine the color. Or one can make a spore print on transparent plastic, which can be held up against different-colored backgrounds to ascertain spore color.

Collecting mushrooms is a popular hobby. Although some fungi are edible, others are poisonous, and there are no hard and fast rules or tests by which a poisonous type can safely be discerned, other than by correctly identifying it. My father was fond of the saying "There are old mushroom hunters and bold mushroom hunters, but there are no old, bold mushroom hunters." Fortunately, most of the poisonous species are not fatal to people who ingest them: they bring on symptoms that resemble food poisoning, including nausea, cramps, vomiting, and diarrhea, lasting one or more days. Some mushrooms cause hallucinations. In general, the faster such symptoms show up, the less severe the ultimate outcome. Some mushrooms, however, deal death. On page 149, see "Destroying Angel," an essay I wrote some years ago, included here as a cautionary.

A friend of mine recently became enthusiastic about mushroom hunting. He equipped himself with several field guides and headed into the woods. Later he confided to me, "You really can't tell if something is a horse or an ass just from pictures in a book." He stressed the importance of collecting with a trustworthy tutor having close knowledge of the local fungi. I was lucky; my tutor was a professor of mycology. One can also get help from mycological societies and mushroom clubs (over a hundred in North America), and some schools and universities offer courses in mushroom identification.

To safely eat wild mushrooms, stick to easily identifiable ones that have no poisonous look-alikes. My father recommended what he called the "Foolproof Five": Shaggy Mane (*Coprinus comatus*), Morels or Sponge Mushrooms (*Morchella species*), Sulphur Shelf or Chicken of the Woods (*Laetiporus sulphureus*), Oyster Mushroom (*Pleurotus ostreatus*), and Giant Puffball (*Calvatia gigantea*).

The following precautions are in addition to those my father listed in his text:

- Thoroughly cook all mushrooms before eating.

- When trying a mushroom for the first time, eat only a small amount (remember, only eat one type of mushroom at a time). Save an uncooked specimen in the refrigerator for at least forty-eight hours; if symptoms develop, a mycologist can identify the mushroom, helpful to a doctor trying to treat any illness.

- Avoid feeding mushrooms to children, sick people, and the elderly, who are generally more susceptible to toxins than healthy adults.

- Do not pick mushrooms in contaminated places such as dumps, roadsides, industrial sites, and lawns and fields treated with pesticides. Some mushrooms concentrate environmental toxins.

You don't have to eat mushrooms to enjoy seeking and identifying them. Mushroom hunting is a great excuse to get out into the fields and forests, and learning about the lives of fungi opens up a new understanding of nature's cycles.

—Charles Fergus, Port Matilda, PA

Important Parts of Mushrooms

C. Leonard Fergus and Charles Fergus

This book is intended as a basic guide for persons untrained in mycology who wish to identify the common mushrooms that seem to appear from nowhere each year in lawns, fields, and woods. In order to separate harmless and edible species from poisonous kinds, the observer must be able to recognize certain important parts of mushrooms. These parts—some with their scientific as well as their common names—are presented with the drawing below and in the following list:

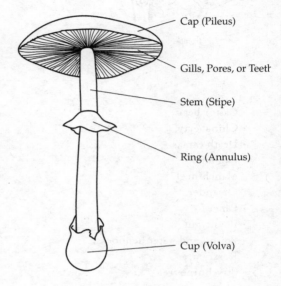

Guide to parts of mushrooms.

Annulus. The remnants of the partial veil, useful in the identification of certain mushrooms. See *ring*.

Bulb. A swelling at the base of the stem.

Cap. The expanded and often flattened part, usually at the top of a mushroom's stem. The underside of the cap bears the spore-dispensing gills, pores, or teeth. See *pileus*.

Convex. Rounded or regularly elevated toward the center; used in describing the caps of certain mushrooms.

Cup. The scales or sheath seen at the base of the stem in some mushrooms. The cup is the remnant of the universal veil that completely encloses the developing mushroom at first, but is ultimately broken and left at the base, usually partly underground. See *universal veil* and *volva*.

Flesh. The inner substance of the stem or cap, exclusive of the external layer and of gills, pores, or teeth.

Gills. Leaflike plates on the undersurface of the cap. See also *pores*, *teeth*, and *tubes*.

Lateral. Attached to one side of the cap; used in describing the stems of some mushrooms.

Partial veil. A membrane that extends from the unopened margin of a mushroom cap to the stalk, protecting the developing gills.

Pileus. The cap portion of a mushroom, which bears gills, pores, or teeth on the lower side. See *cap*.

Pores. The openings at the ends of the tubes of certain mushrooms, visible on the undersurface of the cap.

Continued ➡

Ring. The remnants of the partial veil on the stems of certain mushrooms. It usually encircles the stem and is therefore called a ring. See *annulus*.

Scale. A more or less raised portion of the outer, skinlike layer of the cap.

Spores. Tiny reproductive bodies of mushrooms, akin to the seeds of plants.

Stem. Stalk supporting the cap of a mushroom.

Stuffed. Said of the stem on some mushrooms, when the interior is filled with a material different from and usually softer than the outer part.

Teeth. Thornlike or spinelike structures on the undersurface of the caps or branches of certain mushrooms.

Tubes. Tubular or pipelike structures arranged vertically in the caps of certain mushrooms. Seen only when the cap is cut through.

Universal veil. A membrane surrounding the young developing mushroom in some species. See *cup* and *volva*.

Umbo. A raised knob in the middle of a mushroom's cap.

Volva. The cuplike structure surrounding the bases of some mushrooms, and a key identification mark for several poisonous species. See *cup*.

Some Common Edible and Poisonous Mushrooms of the Northeast

C. Leonard Fergus

Many species of fungi grow wild in eastern North America. With their sudden and bizarre appearance, rapid growth, striking colors, and possible use as food, mushrooms interest people of diverse ages and backgrounds. Mushrooms also are excellent objects for nature study and matchless photographic subjects.

As sources of food, wild mushrooms may be divided into those known to be dangerously poisonous, slightly poisonous, suspected, disagreeable in taste, edible but of mediocre quality, and of excellent flavor. The possibility of individual variable allergic reactions to mushrooms, just as to eggs and strawberries, must also be considered.

In this publication an attempt is made to describe, by means of text and photographs, some of the common edible mushrooms found in this region. Poisonous species are included so that collectors may know when and where to expect to find them and thus avoid them.

According to estimates, several thousand kinds of fungi appear in the Northeast. It is beyond the scope of this publication to consider them all. Obviously, the collector will encounter many mushrooms not included, since only forty-three are described. However, the ones included are quite common and will be found more frequently than the ratio would indicate.

The mushrooms described herein have been selected for various reasons. First, each possesses characteristics so distinctive that the average person may quickly learn to know them. Second, of the edible mushrooms listed, only those are included that have no suspicious history. Third, they are quite common, having been collected many times, in many places, year after year.

No rules are known by which an inexperienced person can distinguish poisonous from edible mushrooms. To be safe, a collector must be able to recognize edible species just as he or she recognizes a violet or a rose. The edibility of many of our wild mushrooms still is not known. One cannot tell by looking at any plant whether it is poisonous or not. Keep in mind that the only way to determine if a plant is poisonous is for someone to have been poisoned by it after eating it, and the same is true for mushrooms.

The following important precautions should be rigidly observed:

· Do not eat any mushroom that you cannot definitely identify and that has not been recorded as edible.

· Do not eat any mushroom just because it is not recognizable as of a poisonous species.

· Never eat a mushroom that is beginning to discolor or deteriorate, or that has been partially devoured or invaded by insects.

· Be sure to dig up the entire mushroom so that all underground parts will be collected. Never eat a mushroom that has both a cup (volva) at the base of the stem and a ring (annulus) around the upper part of the stem.

· Do not mix the mushrooms that you find. Sort them carefully, and keep each collection separate. Use coffee cans, paper bags, or waxed paper parcels; plastic bags trap moisture, leading to deterioration.

· Be extremely careful in the identification of any mushroom that has a white spore print or is in the early stage of development (button stage). At this time, certain important identifying characteristics will not yet be discernible. If in doubt about the identity of a specimen and the fruiting body is a gilled mushroom, a spore print should be made unless positive determination of the color of the expelled spores en masse is possible from the ground or debris at the time of collection. Spores are very small and are visible to the naked eye only when massed in large numbers. To make a spore print, always select a mature specimen. Cut the stem off flush with the gills and lay the cap, gills down, partly on white paper and partly on black paper. Cover this arrangement with a jar or cup so that air currents will not disrupt the spores and the mushroom will not dry out too rapidly. A spore print should become evident in one to two hours. You can determine the spore color as white, rosy or pink, yellow- to rusty-brown, dark brown or purple-brown, or black. Spore prints are beautiful. They may be used for decoration if sprayed with a fixative, such as a clear lacquer available at an arts and crafts store.

· If necessary, or if it is discovered that a poisonous fungus has been eaten, induce vomiting immediately and call your doctor or Poison Control Center.

Aids in Identification

A key in mycology is simply a specialized shortcut to positive identification. In the identification of mushrooms, one choice after another is eliminated until there is left but a single one to which the mushroom at hand can be assigned. The use of a key demands continual choosing: either the mushroom at hand does or does not exhibit a certain characteristic. When using a key, great care must be taken in making the various choices.

Let us select *Pleurotus ostreatus*, the Oyster Mushroom, as an example and attempt to key it down, using the key presented on page 148. Start with choice 1 in the key. The specimen is a mushroom with gills on the underside of the cap; hence, move to choice 2. Does it have a ring on the stem or not? It does not; move to choice 5. The gills or cap do not exude a milky juice when broken, so move to choice 6. Is the spore print white or black? Since it is white, go to choice 8. The gills are sharp-edged; therefore, move to choice 9. The stem is lateral: thus, the mushroom is classified in the genus *Pleurotus* or the very closely related genus *Hypsizygus*. Turn to the pages on which those mushrooms are described and compare your specimens with the text descriptions and photographs. If they agree, you know you have collected *Pleurotus ostreatus*. If the description of that species does not coincide closely with your specimen, or if you cannot find a name in the key of a mushroom that agrees with your find, you probably have collected a mushroom not included in this publication. You should discard such a collection unless you have available more complete and detailed mushroom books.

The mushrooms are described in the text in the same order as they are presented in the key.

Each description of a mushroom includes color, size, presence or absence of a ring (annulus) and a cup (volva), presence of gills or pores or teeth, locations or habitats where the species commonly occurs, substratum on which it usually grows (soil, rotting wood, etc.), season in which it usually appears, and other items of interest. Many mushrooms develop only in certain months, whereas others appear throughout the growing season. Weather influences the time when mushrooms fruit. In general, the broadest range of species and the greatest number of mushrooms emerge from late summer into early or mid-fall.

Joining a mushroom club is one of the best ways to learn how to identify wild mushrooms. Two particular organizations are of great help to amateur mushroom collectors and can offer information about local mushroom clubs. They are the North American Mycological Association (www.namyco.org), at 6615 Tudor Court, Gladstone, Oregon 97027-1032, and the Northeast Mycological Federation (www.nemf.org), at 141 River Road, Millington, New Jersey 07946-1303.

It's also a good idea to find the phone number of the local Poison Control Center and have it handy before you need it. The emergency phone number of the American Association of Poison Control Centers is 1-800-222-1222.

Continued →

1. Mushrooms with gills on underside of cap

  2. Mushrooms with ring on the stem

    3. Mushrooms with volva at base of stem

               . . . *Amanita*

    3. Mushrooms without volva

      4. Purple-brown spore print

        . . . *Agaricus, Psathyrella, Hypholoma*

      4. White or green spore print

. . . *Armillaria, Macrolepiota, Chlorophyllum, Lepiota*

  2. Mushrooms without ring

    5. Gills or cap exuding a milky juice if broken

               . . . *Lactarius*

    5. Without milky juice

      6. Spore print black

        7. Gills and cap dissolve at maturity
          into black ink

               . . . *Coprinus*

        7. Gills dark-spotted and do not
          dissolve into ink

               . . . *Panaeolus*

      6. Spore print white

        8. Gills blunt and thick on edge and
          usually united in a network

               . . . *Cantharellus*

        8. Gills sharp-edged

         9. Stem lateral

            . . . *Pleurotus, Hypsizygus*

         9. Stem central

          10. Gills running down the stem

             . . . *Omphalotus*

          10. Gills not running down
            the stem

           11. Edge of gills like saw-teeth

             . . . *Lentinus*

           11. Edge of gills not saw-
            toothed

            12. Stem tough-brittle,
             breaking with a snap

        . . . *Oudemansiella, Flammulina*

            12. Stem fleshy-fibrous,
             not breaking with a
             snap

               . . . *Lepista*

1. Mushrooms without gills

  13. Mushrooms with many small pores on
    the underside of the cap

    14. Stem central and unbranched

      . . . *Boletus, Leccinum, Suillus, Strobilomyces*

    14. Stem absent or lateral or branched
      multiple times

          . . . *Fistulina, Grifola, Laetiporus*

  13. Mushrooms without pores

    15. Fungi with teeth or spines on the
      pileus

          . . . *Hericium, Hydnum*

    15. Fungi without teeth or spines

      16. Mushroom coral-shaped or
      club-shaped or funnel-shaped

        17. Fungus looks like coral,
          consisting of many small,
          upright branches

             . . . *Clavaria, Ramaria*

        17. Fungus club-shaped or
          funnel-shaped

           . . . *Craterellus, Cantharellus*

      16. Mushroom looks like a sponge
      or saddle or ball

        18. Fungus looks like a sponge
        or saddle

         . . . *Morchella, Gyromitra*

        18. Fungus looks like a ball

             . . . *Calvatia*

The "Foolproof Five"

Coprinus comatus, the Shaggy Mane (Edible).
Sometimes emerges in spring but appears more
frequently in summer and fall. Easily distinguished from other fungi because the cap does
not open wide to a
horizontal position.
Cap 2 to 3 inches
long, expanding to
about 5 inches in
length, egg- to bell-
shaped, whitish
sometimes with
pinkish shades, with
many yellowish or
reddish brown scales;
stem 3 to 7 inches
long, white, pointed
at the base, hollow
and smooth to silky;
movable ring on
stem. Spore print
black. As the Shaggy
Mane ages, it quickly
breaks down into an
inky mass, with
dissolution, or deli-
quescence, starting
on the hanging rim
of the cap and
progressing upward;
this process
continues even if the
mushroom is refrig-
erated. *Coprinus comatus*
grows singly or in
clusters, rarely in
fairy rings, on bare
ground or in grass,
in rich earth along
roadsides, in
pastures, lawns,
gardens, and waste
dumping grounds.
Mushroom hunters
often cook this
flavorful mushroom with scrambled eggs; it is also
excellent in soups, sauces, and gravies. In Britain,
Coprinus comatus is dubbed the Lawyer's Wig.

Coprinus comatus,
the Shaggy Mane.

An aging Coprinus comatus.

Morchella species, the Morels or Sponge
Mushrooms (Edible). Spring. The several
species of Morels found in the Northeast are so
similar that they will be described here only in a
general way. All are edible. Height, 2 to 5
inches; cap bell-shaped, conic, or hemispherical, marked with very prominent ridges and
furrows or with prominent ridges connected by
cross ridges; cap looks like a sponge; caps vary in
color from white to gray to tan. Stem distinct,
thick, fleshy, and white, cream-colored, or buff.
Cap and stem both hollow. Spore color white to
creamy white. Usually occurs in woods on the
ground. Distribution is erratic: Morels grow
under tulip trees, oaks, and hickories in open
woods; under dead or dying elms; or far
removed from trees. They have been found with
regularity in uncultivated grassy apple orchards:
the older the orchard, the more likely that
Morels will emerge there. At times they grow
profusely in rich soil along streambanks where
overflows are common. Old fencerows in limestone areas may yield them in abundance.
Morels often are produced year after year in the
same place, and a wet spring promotes their best
development. One should look for them especially at the time that the first petals begin to fall
from the apple blossoms. The season lasts three
or four weeks.

    Soak Morels overnight in salt water to drive
out insects and slugs, and cut them lengthwise to
check for such creatures before cooking. The
Black Morel (*Morchella elata*; formerly *Morchella*

Morchella esculenta, *the Yellow Morel.*

Morchella esculenta.

Continued ➡

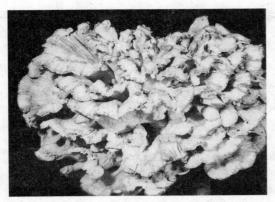

Laetiporus sulphureus, *the Sulphur Shelf.*

Calvatia gigantea, *the Giant Puffball.*

angusticeps) has been reported to cause gastrointestinal upset when eaten along with alcohol.

Laetiporus sulphureus (*Polyporus sulphureus*), the Sulphur Shelf or Chicken of the Woods (Edible). Late summer and fall. A large, conspicuous mush-room, 8 to 24 inches broad, fleshy and watery to rather firm when fresh, drying to a rigid, brittle consistency; clusters of the shelflike caps may overlap each other, or caps may be clustered together like a bouquet of flowers;

Laetiporus sulphureus *in the wild.*

upper surface of caps salmon, sulphur yellow, or bright orange, weathering to chalk white as time passes; margin smooth, at first thick and blunt, later thinner; inner tissue white, light yellow, or pale salmon, 1/4 to 3/4 inch thick; pores very small, tubes 1/4 to 1/2 inch long, pore surface bright sulphur yellow to cream or white. Spore print white. On stumps, trunks, and logs of deciduous and coniferous trees, especially oaks. Its color, shape, and growth on wood make it difficult to confuse this species with any other. Note where it is collected, for it may appear again in the same year and for several years thereafter. Large fruitings can weigh 20 or more pounds. For eating, select the fresh young fruiting bodies and the tender edges of older ones. In some locales, deer have learned to feed on *Laetiporus sulphureus*.

Puffballs

The fungi known as puffballs are almost all edible if eaten when young, when the interior flesh is pure white and has a firm consistency. Collectors should cut through the middle of smaller specimens to make sure they are not immature stages of stinkhorn fungi, which have a bad odor, or Amanita mushrooms, which can be deadly poisonous. The cut section will show a gelatinous inner layer if the specimen is the early stage of an inedible stinkhorn, or the developing cap and stem if it is an Amanita.

Puffballs are so named because the fruiting body is shaped like a ball, and at maturity the powdery spores come puffing out in a dusty cloud when the mushroom is stepped on or squeezed. Puffballs grow on the ground and on rotting wood.

Calvatia craniformis, the Skull-Shaped Puffball (Edible). Late summer and fall. Round, 3 to 6 inches across, whitish or pinkish brown, smooth, soon cracking into irregular areas, with a short, stemlike base. Mature spore tissue yellow-green. Usually occurs in groups of several to many individuals in grassy meadows and open woods. This species has a fine flavor; it should be peeled and eaten only when young.

Calvatia gigantea, the Giant Puffball (Edible). Summer and fall. Round or egg-shaped, 8 to 24

DESTROYING ANGEL: THE DEADLY MUSHROOM
Charles Fergus and C. Leonard Fergus

The Destroying Angel is *Amanita virosa*. It belongs to a large and widespread group of fungi, the amanitas, which have been affecting humans for millennia as food, religious symbols, hallucinogens, and poisons. No one really knows how many species of amanitas exist. A respected mycologist recognizes seventy-five worldwide, while the U.S. Department of Agriculture lists over six hundred species, subspecies, and varieties reported from places as various as Perth, Australia, and Blowing Rock, North Carolina.

Amanitas are large, showy mushrooms. Many measure 4 to 5 inches across the cap, and they come in a rainbow of colors—red, orange, brown, yellow, gray, green, white. Although only some of the amanitas are toxic, the group as a whole causes more than 90 percent of all fatal mushroom poisonings. The Destroying Angel is the most frequent killer in North America; in Europe, the major culprit is the Death Cap, *Amanita phalloides*. In the latter part of the twentieth century, the Death Cap immigrated to America, probably clinging to the roots of ornamental shrubs. Collectors have found this greenish-capped mushroom in Pennsylvania, Virginia, Delaware, New York, New Jersey, California, Oregon, and Washington. ...

An amanita has two distinguishing characteristics. The first is a cuplike structure, called a volva, at the base of the stem. The mushroom looks like it is growing out of this cup. The second characteristic is a white spore print, a pattern laid down by millions of microscopic spores—reproductive cells that can be thought of as tiny seeds—falling from the gills on the underside of the mushroom's cap. To make a spore print, separate the cap from the stem, place the cap gills-down on a piece of black paper, and wait a couple of hours. If the mushroom is an amanita, a white-on-black negative image of the gills will appear. Other mushrooms may make yellow, pink, brown, purple-brown, or black spore prints. (Note that a number of mushrooms yielding colored spore prints also are poisonous.) A few non-amanitas have volvas, and some make white spore prints, but only an amanita exhibits both. Another trait of

Three stages of Amanita virosa.

most, though not all, amanitas is a ring of tissue on the stem, a remainder of the partial veil that enclosed the growing mushroom.

Amanita toxins, called amanitins, are especially potent. A single bite of mushroom can bring on an agonizing, lingering death. The stem, gills, and cap are equally deadly. The toxins survive cooking, freezing, drying. And while most poisonous mushrooms cause symptoms an hour or two after they're eaten, an amanita doesn't tip its hand for six to twenty-four hours. A victim may enjoy another meal, perhaps finishing his collection of wild mushrooms, go to work, even sleep while the poison invades his body.

Finally, he is seized by stomach pains, violent vomiting, and diarrhea. But purging the system does no good, because the mushrooms have already been digested. If the victim is not hospitalized, and if he ate more than one average-size mushroom cap, the illness worsens and usually causes death.

In a hospital, doctors can relieve the vomiting and diarrhea and correct the dangerous dehydration they produce. The patient feels better and seems to recover. He may even be discharged if his illness has not been diagnosed. Then, three to six days later, the symptoms reappear. In many cases, the victim dies. An autopsy reveals massive liver and kidney damage.

—Excerpted from *Common & Edible Mushrooms of the Northeast*

Continued ➡

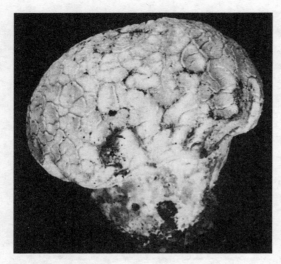

Calvatia craniformis, *the Skull-Shaped Puffball.*

inches across; practically no stem, attached to the ground by cordlike strands; outer surface smooth although sometimes slightly roughened, like chamois to the touch, white or whitish, later becoming yellow or brown; inner substance pure white at first, changing to yellowish, and finally becoming dingy olive. Occurs singly or in groups of a few, on lawns, in pastures, meadows, and open woods, sometimes on streambanks. This mushroom is so large and has such a unique form that it cannot be mistaken for any other. It is highly sought as food.

—From *Common Edible & Poisonous Mushrooms of the Northeast*

Edible Fungi

U.S. Army

About 16,000 varieties of edible fungi grow in different parts of the world. The mushrooms you eat on your steaks and the mold in the blue cheese that you spread on crackers are two forms of fungi.

Although fungi are not a good substitute for meat, they are comparable in food content to common leafy vegetables, and they often are available in areas where other edible plants are scarce.

Gilled fungi, or mushrooms, are the most common of edible fungi and are 98 percent safe to eat, but they have been subjected to many "old wives' tales" and, thus are considered untouchable foods by many people. The term "toadstools," for example, has been used so much to describe any inedible or poisonous variety of mushroom that people apply this name to most unfamiliar varieties. The distinguishing characteristics of "toadstools" such as odor, peeling of skin bruises, and livid colors may also be present in the edible forms. The best way to tell the difference is to study the general characteristics of both the edible and poisonous varieties. Supplement this information with the following list of hints for selecting edible mushrooms:

(a) Dig the gilled mushroom completely out of the ground. Eliminate those having a cup, or vulva, at the base.

(b) Avoid all gilled mushrooms in the young stage. This young mushroom will have a button-like appearance and may be distinguished from the young edible puffball because it will have a short stem, not a characteristic of the puffball.

(c) Avoid all ground-growing mushrooms with the underside of the cup full of minute reddish spores.

(d) Avoid gilled mushrooms with membrane-like cups or scaly bulbs at the base, especially if the gills are white.

(e) Avoid all gilled mushrooms with white or pale milky juice.

(f) Avoid all gilled woodland mushrooms with a smooth, flat, reddish top and white gills radiating out from the stem-like spokes.

(g) Avoid yellow or yellowish-orange mushrooms growing on old stumps. If they have crowded and solid stems, convex overlapping cups, broad gills extending irregularly down the stem, or surfaces that glow phosphorescently in the dark, they are probably poisonous.

(h) Avoid any mushroom which seems to be too ripe, water-soaked, spoiled, or maggoty.

(i) Become familiar with the following poisonous mushrooms of the Amanite family (the most deadly is the Death Angel). The Death Angel is widespread in Europe, Asia, and America but seems to be more common in north temperate regions. This plant produces one of the tox-albumin poisons, the poisons found in rattlesnakes and other venomous animals and the poisons that produce death in cholera and diphtheria. The amount of this fungus necessary to produce death is small.

(j) If you get sick after eating mushrooms, tickle the back of your throat to induce vomiting. Do not drink water until after you vomit; then drink lukewarm water and powdered charcoal.

All nongilled fungi are nonpoisonous when eaten fresh. A familiar example of a nongilled fungus is the puffball. Others include morels, coral fungi, coral hydnums, and cup fungi.

—From *Survival (Field Manual 21–76, 1970 Edition)*

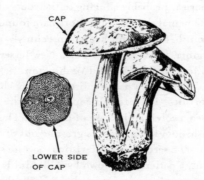

Boletus cap and the area in which to look for reddish spores.

CAP
LOWER SIDE OF CAP

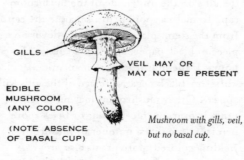

GILLS
VEIL MAY OR MAY NOT BE PRESENT
EDIBLE MUSHROOM (ANY COLOR)
(NOTE ABSENCE OF BASAL CUP)

Mushroom with gills, veil, but no basal cup.

(CHALK-WHITE INSIDE)
(1-12 IN. DIAMETER)

Puffball.

(ASHEN-GRAY)

Morel (Ashengray).

Identifying cups of Death Angel.

(WHITE, ORANGE, YELLOW, PALE VIOLET, BUFF) (2-6 IN. HIGH)

Coral fungus (2 to 6 inches high, white, orange, yellow, pale violet, or buff).

Identifying cups of fly agaric.

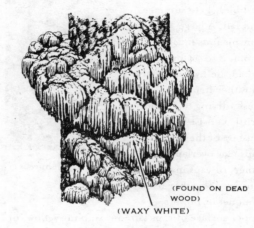

(FOUND ON DEAD WOOD)
(WAXY WHITE)

Coral Hydnum.

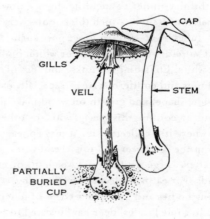

CAP
GILLS
VEIL
STEM
PARTIALLY BURIED CUP

Death Angel with gills, veil, stem, and cup.

REDISH-WHITE CAP WITH WHITE FLECKS

Fly agaric.

150

Food: Packing, Cooking, and Finding It

Ration Planning

Claudia Pearson

Each year, approximately 3,000 students spend between fourteen and ninety-four days in the backcountry on NOLS courses. How does NOLS plan meals for so many people over such a long period? Each course is divided into cook groups of two to four individuals, and each cook group is given a wide selection of bulk foods and spices. They decide what to cook with the help of *NOLS Cookery* and other knowledgeable peers or instructors. There are no set menus. Students learn how to cook in the field through experience.

We call this method NOLS bulk rationing and have found that it works well for our multi-week expeditions. Smaller groups going out for shorter lengths of time—five days or less—might want to consider menu planning instead. With menu planning, all meals are determined in advance, and the food is bought accordingly.

In this chapter from *NOLS Cookery*, we have provided the tools you need to plan rations on your own. Successful ration planning takes both effort and experience, and, as many of you already know, it can be challenging and time-consuming. Critical factors to consider when planning for an expedition are the availability, versatility, cost, and palatability of foods desired.

Happy campers must be well fed and hydrated. Plan on as much variety as possible, ask your trip members for their input, and organize most of the food ahead of time to ensure ease of preparation once in the field. Our goal has always been to please each student and instructor just once on any expedition. That leaves quite a safety margin!

If you have always used menu planning, bulk rationing may be a difficult concept to grasp at first, but the rewards can be great once you've mastered the basics. Planning and packing become easier. Complicated lists and menu schedules are eliminated. You'll have greater freedom in the field to prepare meals that suit your mood and the demands of the day. Cooking becomes more creative and flexible when you carry a "backcountry pantry" in your pack.

Factors to consider when ration planning:

- Group size
- Duration of trip
- Purpose of trip
- Exertion level
- Weather
- Altitude
- Individual appetites
- Food preferences within the group
- Nutritional balance

- Expense and availability
- Spoilage and ease of packaging
- Weight
- Possible dietary limitations of group members

The NOLS Rationing System

The first step in planning food for an expedition using the NOLS bulk rationing method is to calculate the total amount of food that will be needed during the trip. To do this, determine how many pounds (of food) per person per day (ppppd) you expect to use. This amount depends on everything from the intensity and duration of the trip to the ages and sizes of the participants. Charts and worksheets are included in this chapter to help you determine this figure.

Once you have figured out the total poundage, break it down into different food groups to get specific amounts. NOLS issues a combination of heavier "grocery store" foods and lighter dehydrated items.

Freeze-dried meals available at backpacking and sporting goods stores are lightweight and quick to cook, but they are often bland and expensive. If you decide to purchase freeze-dried foods, be forewarned that the suggested serving

Continued ➡

sizes should be doubled for most appetites. And beware, they tend to be high in salt. Freeze-dried food used in conjunction with staples can provide variety and save weight.

You can find many tasty, lightweight, nutritious, and inexpensive options at your local supermarket, natural foods store, or specialty market. Food dryers are a wonderful addition to any kitchen. They are available in most hardware, discount, or kitchen supply stores. A large variety of homegrown or store-bought fresh vegetables, fruits, and meats can be dried, providing tasty, affordable, and nutritious additions to a backpacker's menu. There are many books available on drying and dehydrating foods at the local library. You can even dry foods in your own oven.

Make note of the food preferences and allergies within your group, and avoid letting your personal likes and dislikes influence your choices. Variety is important and will help keep morale up. Balance expensive and less expensive items by using a predetermined budget.

Bulk Ration Planning Steps

Step 1: *Determine the amount of food per person per day (ppppd), using the following guidelines:*

- 1.5 ppppd is appropriate for hot days and warm nights. This amount works well when base camping (camping in one location for the duration of the trip) and is good for short trips (three to five days) when fresh veggies, canned goods, and/or fresh fish supplement the ration. An excellent amount for trips with children and for leisure days, 1.5 pounds equates to roughly 2,500 to 3,000 calories per person per day.

- 1.75 to 2 ppppd works well when you expect warm or cool days and nights or when hiking with full packs. If you are planning a long trip of more than seven to ten days, you might want to plan on 2 ppppd for later in the ration period, since appetites usually kick in after a few days in the mountains. For moderate to active workdays, 1.75 to 2 pounds is ideal and gives you roughly 3,000 to 3,500 calories per person.

- 2 to 2.25 ppppd is good for hiking or skiing with full packs during the cool days and cold nights of early spring, late fall, or winter. If you are planning a long trip of more than seven to ten days, you might want to plan on 2.25 ppppd for later in the ration period. Two to 2.25 pounds per day is ideal for heavy workdays and cold temperatures. It gives you roughly 3,500 to 4,500 calories per person per day.

- 2.5 ppppd is good for cold days and extremely cold nights, such as in midwinter, when you are skiing with full packs or sleds in mountain environments. Used for extremely strenuous workdays and very cold temperatures, 2.5 pounds gives you roughly 4,000 to 5,000 calories per person per day.

Step 2: *Figure the total amount of food needed for the trip.* The formula is: Number of people ? number of days ? ppppd. For example, for four people on an eight-day trip at 1.75 ppppd, the total amount of food needed would equal 56 pounds.

Step 3: *Break the total poundage into food groups.* The chart on the next page lists the breakdown of the poundage of different foods per person per day. Added together, these numbers (known as category multipliers) should equal the pounds per person per day selected in step 1. They have proved effective in planning NOLS rations for many years. (See chart 1)

Step 4: *Calculate the total pounds of each food category needed for the trip.* Using the example from step 2 of four people on an eight-day trip at 1.75 ppppd and the category multipliers from the table in step 3, the calculations would be as shown in chart 2.

Step 5: *Round the numbers up or down within categories (see the last column of the table in step 4) and make substitutions, depending on individual preferences.* For instance, if you don't want to bake, you can take that poundage (approximately 4 pounds in the example) and add it to another category such as breakfast or dinner. If you don't eat cheese, you can take some of that cheese weight (approximately 7 pounds in this example) and add it to the trail food category, where you can replace it

with nuts and/or nut butters (sesame, peanut, tahini, almond). The important thing to remember is to make exchanges with similar types of foods to maintain the balance among carbohydrates, proteins, and fats. If you make changes, the adjusted totals should still equal the amount determined in step 2.

The following worksheet can be used to plan your own ration.

Ration Planning Worksheet

If you have already chosen your pounds per person per day (ppppd), you are ready to fill in the worksheet.

Take the number of days × number of people × ppppd to find the total weight for the chosen ration period.

$$\frac{}{\text{(days)}} \times \frac{}{\text{(people)}} \times \frac{}{\text{(ppppd)}} = \frac{}{\text{(total weight)}}$$

At NOLS, we issue spice kits, tea bags, base packs, canned goods, fresh vegetables, toilet paper, matches, and soap (liquid or bar), in addition to the total weight planned for each ration. Make sure you include your choice of these items for your personal trips.

—From *NOLS Cookery*

CHART 1

Food Category	Category Multipliers for				
	1.5 ppppd	1.75 ppppd	2 ppppd	2.25 ppppd	2.5 ppppd
Breakfast	.24	.28	.33	.35	.38
Dinner	.27	.32	.35	.37	.40
Cheese	.19	.22	.24	.26	.28
Trail foods	.32	.35	.37	.45	.49
Flour and baking*	.11	.13	.16	.09	.10
Sugar and fruit drinks	.10	.12	.14	.15	.18
Soups, bases, desserts	.06	.09	.13	.15	.19
Milk, eggs, margarine, cocoa	.21	.24	.28	.31	.33
Meats and substitutes**	0	0	0	.12	.15

*The need for baking ingredients is lower in winter conditions, when only quick pan baking is feasible.
**High-fat and high-preservative meats are added in winter to meet higher fuel needs.

CHART 2

Food Category	Calculation	Rounded	
Trail foods	.35 x 4 x 8 = 11.2 lbs.	11	lbs.
Dinner	.32 x 4 x 8 = 10.24 lbs.	10.5	lbs.
Breakfast	.28 x 4 x 8 = 8.96 lbs.	9	lbs.
Milk, eggs, margarine, cocoa	.24 x 4 x 8 = 7.68 lbs.	7.5	lbs.
Cheese	.22 x 4 x 8 = 7.04 lbs.	7	lbs.
Flour and baking	.13 x 4 x 8 = 4.16 lbs.	4	lbs.
Sugar and fruit drinks	.12 x 4 x 8 = 3.84 lbs.	4	lbs.
Soups, bases, desserts	.09 x 4 x 8 = 2.88 lbs.	3	lbs.
Meats and substitutes	NOLS only uses in 2.25–2.5 lb. rations		
Total pounds		56	lbs.

Continued ➔

CHART 3

Break down total weight into food categories (see step 3 in text).

Category	No. of People	×	No of days	×	Category Multiplier	=	Total lbs. for Category
Breakfast	———	×	———	×	———	=	———
Dinner	———	×	———	×	———	=	———
Cheese	———	×	———	×	———	=	———
Trail foods	———	×	———	×	———	=	———
Flour and baking	———	×	———	×	———	=	———
Sugar and fruit drinks	———	×	———	×	———	=	———
Soups, bases, desserts	———	×	———	×	———	=	———
Milk, eggs, margarine, cocoa	———	×	———	×	———	=	———
Meats and substitutes	———	×	———	×	———	=	———
					Total weight =		———

Example (Trail foods, 1.75 ppppd): 4 people x 8 days x .35 ppppd = 11 total lbs.

CHART 4

List specific foods that you would like to take under each category listed below. You have generated these category totals in the formulas above.

Breakfast Item/lbs.	Dinner Item/lbs.	Cheese Item/lbs.	Trail Foods Item/lbs.	Flour and Baking Item/lbs.
———	———	———	———	———
———	———	———	———	———
———	———	———	———	———
———	———	———	———	———
———	———	———	———	———
———	———	———	———	———
Total lbs.———	Total lbs.———	Total lbs. ———	Total Lbs.———	Total lbs.———

Sugar and Fruit Drinks Item/lbs.	Soups, Bases, Desserts Item/lbs.	Milk, Eggs, Margarine, Cocoa Item/lbs.	Meats and and Substitutes Item/lbs.
———	———	———	———
———	———	———	———
———	———	———	———
———	———	———	———
———	———	———	———
———	———	———	———
Total lbs.———	Total lbs.———	Total lbs.———	Total lbs.———

Sample Shopping List
Claudia Pearson

Note: Items marked with an asterisk are available through mail-order from NOLS Rocky Mountain Rations Department, 502 Lincoln Street Lander, Wyoming 82520; 307-332-1419.

Breakfast

Cereals are a good source of carbohydrates and are high in protein when mixed with milk. Adding margarine or nuts to cereals provides fats and additional protein.

- **Cream of Wheat, Rice, or Rye; oatmeal; hominy grits.** Hot cereals are available in many forms: regular or instant, in bulk or individual packets. Some cereals come presweetened; others can be mixed with sugar, dried fruits, nuts, milk, and margarine for breakfast. Cereals such as oatmeal can be used in baked goods or in casseroles for dinner meals. Grits should be cooked and allowed to sit for a while before serving. They can then be refried and served with hot sauce or picante, lots of cheese, and pepper.

- **Couscous.** Couscous is available in two types: the whole wheat version, which is less processed and is a light brown color, or the more refined and traditional version, which is yellow. Both types cook fast and can be hydrated and eaten right out of your camp cup. Couscous can be mixed with sweetener, dried fruits, and nuts for a hot breakfast or combined with cheese and veggies for a tasty dinner.

- **Hash-brown potatoes—dried or shredded.*** Hash browns make an excellent breakfast or dinner. They are best served in fried form with cheese and seasonings, or with bacon or sausage for a hearty winter meal.

- **Granola or muesli.** Many varieties of granola and muesli are available commercially, or you can make your own. Granola and muesli make a good breakfast served hot or cold. They can also be used as a trail food or an ingredient in dessert crusts or can be added to baked goods or cookies.

- **Cold cereals.** Cold cereals can be used for breakfast, as a snack food, or as ingredients in desserts or baked goods. (The bulky nature of some cereals can be a problem for packing, however.)

- **Pancake mix/baking mix.** Make your own baking mix or use a quick add-water-only commercial brand.

- **Bagels, English muffins, muffins, coffee cake, quick breads.** Bread products are available commercially, or you can make your own. They are great for breakfast, trail foods, and dinner.

Continued ➡

Dinner

Pasta, grains, and potatoes are good sources of carbohydrates. The addition of beans or dairy products to these items makes complete proteins, and cheese and margarine provide added protein and fats.

- **Pasta.** Pastas are made from white and whole grain flours and come in a wide variety of shapes and colors. Pasta is a popular dinner food that can be used in many recipes from soups to casseroles.

- **Instant beans.** Pinto and black beans are available dried or refried in most big grocery stores or natural food shops. Beans are great with tortillas or rice or in combination with pasta. Leftovers make good dips or spreads with crackers or tortillas.

- **Instant lentils.** Lentils are good with rice, in soups, or to make vegetarian burgers. They are available in most natural food stores.

- **Falafel.** Instant falafel can be mixed with water, formed into patties, and fried as a veggie burger served with rice or bread. It is very spicy!

- **Barley.** Quick-cooking barley is a good ingredient in soups or mixed with various grains for a main meal.

- **Hummus.** Hummus makes an excellent dip or spread with crackers or pita bread.

- **Couscous.** Excellent as a main dish for breakfast or dinner. Couscous is very versatile.

- **Bulgur.** Bulgur is nice in soups or mixed with other grains. Bulgur is the main ingredient in tabouli, a popular cold Lebanese salad. It can be used in many ways, from baked goods to breakfast.

- **Instant potato pearls or flakes.*** Instant potatoes make a good thickener for soups and gravies. They are also excellent served alone or as an addition to a main meal. Cooked with cheese, margarine, and a cup-of-soup packet, instant potatoes make a quick mini-meal. They can also be used for a savory breakfast or mixed with flour to make potato pancakes.

- **Rice—white, brown, parboiled.** Rice is a versatile mainstay and is available in many varieties. Instant rice cooks the fastest and mixes well with lentils or beans.

- **Textured vegetable protein.** Textured vegetable protein is made from soybeans mixed with other ingredients to make a veggie burger or chili mix. It is a good source of protein for vegetarians.

- **Tortillas, pita breads, bagels, biscuits, flat breads.** These products are great additions to main meals or as ready-to-eat snacks for the trail. However, they can be bulky and are perishable.

Cheese

Cheese is a good source of protein and fats. Farmer, jack, cheddar, Swiss, mozzarella, and Parmesan are popular varieties. In winter, cube all cheeses for easy melting. Purchase cheese in vacuum-sealed blocks and open one at a time to ensure freshness. Also, individually wrapped cheese sticks are a great idea for quick trail snacks—kids love them!

Trail Foods

Trail food consists of high-calorie, tasty foods that are easy to eat while hiking on the trail. Nuts and seeds contain protein and fats, and dried fruits, crackers, and energy bars provide carbohydrates and fiber.

- **Nuts.** Nuts are available in most big grocery stores or natural food outlets. They are an expensive but concentrated form of calories. Roasted and salted nuts and seeds taste great but can go rancid quickly without refrigeration. Raw forms can be bland and chewy but perk up nicely when dry roasted and salted prior to eating. Nuts are a nice ingredient for main dishes or in baked goods. Choose from the many varieties available, use nut mixes, or try products such as gorp—a mix of nuts, fruits, and candy.

- **Seeds—roasted or raw.** Pumpkin, sunflower, sesame, and piñon seeds are popular and can be eaten plain or added to breakfasts, dinners, and baked goods.

- **Dried fruits.** Dried fruits are an expensive but concentrated form of calories easily found in grocery and natural food stores. For trips that require large quantities of trail food, try purchasing fresh fruit at a fraction of the cost and drying it on your own using a food dryer. This system also works well for vegetables such as tomatoes, zucchini, and mushrooms. Dried fruit options include individual fruits and berries, mixed fruit combinations, and fruit leathers.

- **Crackers.** Crackers come in countless varieties and are available everywhere. Pack them in plastic containers with peel-off lids for protection. Occasional crunchy foods are usually welcome on long trips. Crackers are great for dips and spreadables such as cheese and nut butters and hummus. Choose from flavored and shaped crackers, melba toasts, bagel chips, pretzels, and croutons.

- **Corn nuts and soy nuts.** Corn nuts and soy nuts are salty, crunchy, and cheap, with a strong flavor. But you need to be careful with them—they can break teeth. Soybeans are an excellent form of protein.

- **Cookies.** Cookies come in various types and flavors. Fig Newtons, fruit bars, animal crackers, granola bars, and Pop Tarts hold up well in a backpack.

- **Energy bars.** Numerous varieties of energy and high-protein bars such as Power, Luna, Clif, Pemmican, Balance, and Tiger's Milk—to name a few—are available for quick pick-me-ups or meal replacement. Make sure that they are edible in cold weather conditions—don't break a tooth!

- **Candy.** Backpacking favorites include candy bars, chocolate- or yogurt-covered nuts and fruits, and wrapped hard candies (remove wrappers as you bag them to prevent litter).

Baking Items

- **Powdered eggs.*** Whole powdered eggs are useful for baking or in quiches and omelets. They are less appealing for use as scrambled eggs. Powdered eggs lighten up many recipes.

- **Flours/meal.** Choose from white, whole wheat, and other flours; cornmeal and tortilla mixes such as masa harina (flour) or mast trego (corn); and various commercial baking, biscuit, muffin, and pancake mixes.

Sugar and Powdered Fruit Drinks

- Brown and white sugar (brown is less likely to be confused with other foods).

- Lemonade (pink or yellow).

- Mixes such as Tang, apple cider, and Gatorade.

- Jell-O gelatin (makes a great hot drink).

- Teas—bags or instant powder varieties.

- Presweetened Kool-Aid and Crystal Light are great weight savers, but watch the aspartame—it can cause headaches.

Soups, Bases, Dried Vegetables, and Desserts

- **Soups**
  —Cup-of-soups: Many varieties of cup-of-soup are available. They can be added to potato pearls and cheese cubes to make a quick hot meal.

  —Ramen soups: Ramen soups are tasty and nutritious when mixed with canned meats or cheeses to make a complete meal. They have a high fat content because the noodles are fried before being dried. Ramen is quick and easy to make.

  —Bulk or individual soup bases such as chicken, beef, veggie, and miso are good for seasoning. Adding broths to cooking water can help extend the life of your spice kit.

- **Bases / broth packets / broth cubes**
  —Tomato base*: Complete tomato product in powdered form.

  —Packaged sauce and seasoning mixes: Some choices are white, cheese, spaghetti, chili, pesto, and Alfredo sauces and gravies. Sauce packets are great to use with pasta.

Continued ➡

- **Dried vegetables.*** Dried veggies are an excellent way to add color and texture to colorless entrees. Mixed vegetables, green and red bell peppers, peas, and carrots are all used at NOLS. They are not included in the ration weights because they are issued in very small quantities and go a long way.

- **Desserts.** Desserts are high in carbohydrates, easy to digest, and, when milk products are added, good sources of protein. The easiest option is to buy premade dessert mixes that require only water.
  —Cheesecake mix: Grape Nuts, granola, or graham crackers make good crusts.
  —Brownie mix: Great scrambled for quick gratification or used as an ingredient for fudge and specialty cakes.
  —Gingerbread mix: Excellent added to flour for coffee cakes and pancakes.
  —Carrot cake mix: Many mixes come with cream cheese frosting.
  —Instant pudding or gelatin mixes.

Milk, Eggs, Margarine, and Cocoa

Milk and eggs are good sources of complete proteins. Cocoa has milk and sugar as ingredients. Margarine is a good source of fat.

- **Powdered milk.** Adding cold water works best.

- **Soy milk.** Soy milk is now available for vegetarians. At NOLS, we use Souvex Better than Milk brand. Many varieties are available, but taste test before your trip to make sure that you like it. You can combine chocolate and vanilla flavors to use as a cocoa replacement or use them separately. Carob flavor is also available.

- **Powdered eggs.** Whole powdered eggs.

- **Margarine.** Any kind of margarine works well. Beware of freeze or melt conditions and package accordingly. Squeeze tubes and containers with resealable peel-off lids work well but can open under pressure. Keep packaging easy, convenient, and tight.

- **Cocoa.** Instant bulk cocoa is a popular hot drink. You can stretch it by adding powdered milk.

- **Flavored coffee drinks.** These are popular with adults. They can be added to hot milk and cocoa for variety.

- **Coffee.** Many people like to carry grounds and use a coffee sock as a filter. Others use paper filters and cones or make Cowboy Coffee. Instant coffee works well in winter conditions, when convenience is so important. Whatever your morning ritual, choose the form that works best for your group. Coffee is not a standard ration item at NOLS because of its diuretic effect.

Meats and Meat Substitutes

Meat, soybean products, and nut butters are all excellent sources of fat and protein for the high energy demands of winter environments.

- **Sliced pepperoni, cooked bacon bits (real), and sausage crumbles.** These are all good for winter because they can withstand freeze-thaw conditions, are precooked, and are very flavorful.

- **Beef jerky.** Jerky is lightweight and tasty but does not have the high fat content that the meats listed above have.

- **Tempeh.** This is a soybean product that takes on the texture of meat and is used by many NOLS instructors as a meat or cheese replacement. It is perishable and must be watched for freshness. Tempeh is available in many flavors and can be used on short trips or as a meat replacement in the winter. It's best to cube the tempeh prior to using it on winter trips.

- **Nut butters.** These are commonly used to replace cheese and meat for vegetarians in the winter months. They are high in fat and protein and work well in winter conditions. Cashew, sesame, almond, and sunflower butters along with dried raisins and dates are a great alternative to meats and cheeses if you choose not to eat animal products and want to stay warm.

Spices

A spice kit is an important part of any cooking expedition. But remember that not everyone has the same tastes, so proceed with caution. Your spice kit might include the following:

- **Salt.** Used to add flavor to a flat-tasting meal.

- **Pepper.** Enhances most main dishes; tends to be a little hot.

- **Garlic powder.** Flavoring for breads, main dishes, soups, and sauces.

- **Chili powder.** Hot and spicy; good for Mexican dishes.

- **Curry.** Can be hot and spicy; used in Middle Eastern dishes.

- **Cinnamon.** Great for sweet breads, desserts, and hot drinks.

- **Spike.** Lemon-salt flavor appeals to many palates; great in cheesy casseroles or sprinkled on tortillas.

- **Oregano.** Good for Italian tomato sauces or casserole garnish.

- **Basil.** Used in tomato or white sauces.

- **Baking powder.** A quick leavening agent.

- **Baking yeast.** Great for breads, rolls, and pizza.

- **Cumin powder.** Used in rice or Mexican bean dishes.

- **Powdered mustard.** Good for white sauces or in grain and cheese casseroles.

- **Dill weed.** Excellent in soups, breads, muffins, or with fish.

- **Cayenne.** Very hot and spicy; used in sauces.

Liquids

- **Oil.** Good for sautéing or frying.

- **Vinegar.** Great for salad dressings, picante sauce, and other sauces.

- **Soy sauce.** Good over grains or in white sauces.

- **Vanilla.** Good for sweet baked goods, desserts, hot cereals, and drinks.

- **Tabasco/hot sauce.** A condiment for grains, pastas, and soups.

—From *NOLS Cookery*

Packaging Food

Claudia Pearson

The first thing to do once you have assembled all your food is to repackage it. Cardboard, paper, foil, and cans are all excess weight and potential litter.

At NOLS, we use two-ply clear plastic bags to package almost all our food. We purchase commercial bags that can be lightly tied in a knot. Plastic bags are lightweight and reusable and allow you to see what's inside. Use a permanent marker to identify contents if you're packing your own food.

We use small plastic bottles with screw-on lids for spices, and widemouthed Nalgene containers for honey, peanut butter, and margarine. Other possible food containers include Ziploc bags, freezer bags, Seal-a-Meal bags, Tupperware, and squeeze tubes.

If you are using a meal planning system, you may want to package each day's meals together or pack breakfasts, lunches, and dinners together by meal type. Label with a permanent marker and include recipe instructions.

Repackaged food in zippered carrying bag.

Always be careful when packaging food to avoid any chance of contamination by soap, stove fuel, or a leaking lighter. Try to keep the food above these items in your pack. Heavy items

Continued ➡

such as food should generally be high and close to your body, unless you'll be hiking through boulder fields or deadfall. In these conditions, carry most of the weight lower, for better balance when jumping or twisting.

—From *NOLS Cookery*

Equipment and Stoves
Claudia Pearson

At NOLS, we have learned to produce gourmet meals with a minimum of cooking utensils. Each student has a bowl, a mug (usually an insulated 12- or 20-ounce cup with a lid), and a spoon. Each cook group is issued one or two (2- or 4-quart) nesting stainless-steel pots, one nonstick or 12-inch fry pan with a flat lid and no plastic parts, one spatula, one large spoon, one collapsible 6-quart or 1 1/2- to 2 1/2- gallon water jug or water bag, and pliers/pot grips. Optional luxuries include a small cheese grater, a small whisk for blending sauces, and a 4-inch metal strainer.

There are a number of excellent backpacking stoves on the market today. The most practical ones use white gas. However, white gas (Coleman fuel) is not always available in foreign countries. If this is a concern, interchangeable parts are available for some stoves that allow you to use kerosene. At NOLS, we use mainly Mountain Safety Research (MSR) Whisper Lite Internationale 600 stoves. These stoves are lightweight, east to repair, relatively inexpensive, and reliable.

Have a clear understanding of how your stove works before you leave home. Carry the parts and tools necessary to repair it in an emergency. Keep it clean and dry, and clean the orifice after each use.

Locate your stove on a level surface protected from the wind and away from any vegetation. Watch out for sand and dirt that can clog the orifice or fuel line. If you are traveling in an area where it is impossible to get out of the sand or where you will be in snow, consider taking a stove pad or a piece of fire cloth to cook on. Position the stove with the on-off valve accessible. Keep the area clear of all burnable materials.

Because of the potential for flare-ups and carbon monoxide poisoning, we do not recommend using stoves inside a tent.

Store fuel in fuel bottles, and use funnels or pouring spouts to fill your stove. Fill stoves away from your cooking area and any open flames. Stoves should be filled after each use once they're cool. You never know when you'll have to start one in a hurry.

Figuring fuel amounts: During the summer with the Whisper Lites, we expect to use 1/3 liter of fuel per stove per day (based on a three-person cook group). Example: 1 stove x 8 days x 1/3 = 2 2/3 liters. During the winter, if you'll be melting snow for water (or if you'll be at altitudes over 10,000 feet), plan on 3/4 liter per stove per day, then round up the total to the next highest liter (based on a three-person cook group). If you round up your fuel amounts, you will have enough to run a small lantern—which is a definite plus during the long nights of winter.

Depressurizing a stove: The purpose of depressurizing your stove is to provide a low-output flame that is good for baking and simmering. This procedure must be done with utmost caution. First, follow the normal lighting process to heat up the stove. Then turn it off and blow out the flame—make sure that it is completely out. Carefully loosen the pump from the bottle (a 1/2 to 3/4 turn) to relieve pressure. It will hiss. Be careful to avoid gas spray on you or your food. Retighten the pump, pump twice, and light. You will need to pump occasionally to keep the stove going, but for the most part it will maintain a fairly consistent low flame.

—From *NOLS Cookery*

Cooking on Fires
Claudia Pearson

Campfires used to be a necessity in the backcountry; now they are usually a luxury. The growing number of backcountry travelers has resulted in the depletion of firewood in many areas, and the abuse of fire has caused everything from scarring to wildfires. Abuse is the key word here. Built properly, campfires can still be an enjoyable part of backcountry camping and cooking, but the decision to build one should never be made automatically or lightly. Regulations, ecological conditions, weather, skill, use level, and firewood availability should be considered when making the decision.

In a heavily used area, the best site for a fire is in an existing fire ring. In a pristine area, use Leave No Trace fire techniques. These techniques enable you to enjoy a fire without leaving any evidence. One quick, minimum-impact method in sandy areas is a shallow pit fire. Scrape a depression several inches deep in a dry

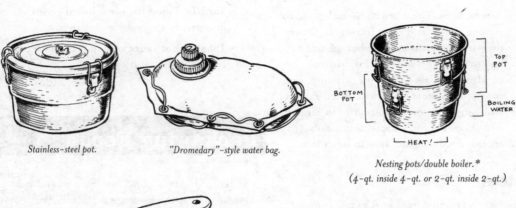

Stainless-steel pot.

"Dromedary"-style water bag.

Nesting pots/double boiler.*
(4-qt. inside 4-qt. or 2-qt. inside 2-qt.)

Spatula.

Pliers.

Stove.

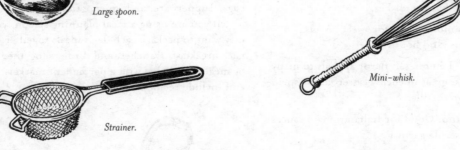

Large spoon.

Mini-whisk.

Strainer.

Grater.

NOLS cup, spoon, and bowl.

Continued →

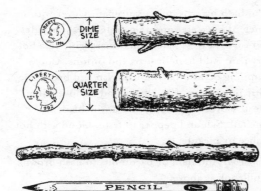

The best widths and lengths of wood to use for a cooking fire.

streambed, sandbar, or beach—any place with exposed soil that contains no decomposing organic material (mineral soil)—and build your fire in the depression. Never excavate a fire pit in vegetation. Research has shown that fire pits dug in sod are still evident years later. Avoid environmental damage by using stoves and existing fire rings.

A platform or mound of mineral soil can also be used for a Leave No Trace fire. Simply pile up mineral soil into a flat-topped platform 6 to 8 inches thick and about 2 feet across and build your fire on top. The platform insulates the ground and prevents scarring. Where do you find mineral soil? Uprooted trees, sandy areas near streambeds, or exposed soil near boulder areas are all excellent sources. A tarp or fire cloth laid under the soil facilitates cleanup. Finally, portable fire pans, such as metal oil-drain pans or backyard barbecue grills, allow you to enjoy small fires with virtually no impact. The pan should be lined with mineral soil or propped up on small rocks to protect the surface underneath from heat.

The best firewood is small in diameter (1 to 2 inches), lying loose on the ground, and not attached to downed or standing timer. Small-diameter wood is easier to burn to ash and is less critical to the ecosystem. Gather wood from a wide area; do not denude the immediate surroundings. Collect only enough for a small fire.

Be sure to allow yourself enough time for thorough cleanup and camouflaging of the site. Regardless of whether you used an established fire ring or constructed a fire in a pristine area, burn all the wood down to cold ash. Crush any remaining charcoal. If the ash is cool enough to sift your fingers through, your fire is out. Scatter the remains and any leftover firewood far from the site.

If you constructed a mound fire, after scattering the leftover ash and small bits of charcoal, return the soil to where you found it. If the mound was built on a rock, rinse the rock off. When using a shallow pit, disperse the ash and fill in the pit with the excavated soil. Finally, camouflage the area to match the surroundings.

This allows others to enjoy the same site later. Leaving no trace means leaving your cook site as clean as you found it (or cleaner) for the benefit of future campers.

Baking

You can use coals from your campfire to create a backcountry Dutch oven for baking. Set a baking pan on a flat bed of coals, and shovel coals onto the lid in an even layer for even cooking. The coals should feel very hot but not quite burn when you hold your hand 6 inches away for 8 seconds. They can be cooled by spreading them out or sprinkling them with sand. The coals on the top should be hotter than those on the bottom. Replenish coals as they go dead.

Be careful when you check the progress of your baked goods. It's safest to scrape all the coals off the lid before you peek. Don't peek too often (unless you smell burning), because the escaped heat cuts efficiency. Always wear an expendable pair of gloves—or better yet, a pair of oven mitts—when baking over an open fire.

It is also possible to bake on the stove. A great way to do this is to use a low flame (see page 006) under the baking pan and build a small fire with twigs on the lid. This is called a "twiggy" fire and demands a similar level of care as a larger fire (regulations, wind, wood replenishment, and so forth). For this method to work, you need a baking pan with a flat lid and no plastic parts. Bake slowly over a very low flame (offset the pan so that more than just the center gets heat), rotating the pan every few minutes to cook evenly. You can balance the pan on a flat rock to cook the outside edges. Another technique is to flip bake. This method works best with stiff breads and cakes and when you have a fairly heavy-gauge lid for the baking pan. Make sure you grease and flour the pan thoroughly, including the inside of the lid. When the dough is firm and cooked most of the way through, loosen the edges with a spatula and then flip the bread or cake onto the lid. Place the lid directly on the stove to finish cooking the top. You can also flip the entire baked good in the pan to cook both sides. This works especially

Use a rock to balance your pan in order to cook around the edges.

well with biscuits, bread, or brownies.

Other baking tips:

- Fill the pan only half full, since baked goods rise.

- The best backcountry baking pans are lightweight, have nonstick surfaces, and are of a relatively heavy gauge to distribute the often intense heat of fires and portable stoves.

- The pan should never be filled to the point that ingredients touch the lid, or they'll burn.

- Rotate the pan every few minutes to ensure even baking. This is called the "round the clock" method.

- You can use a frying pan turned upside down for rolling dough. Take a clean plastic bag, split it in half long-ways, and cover the pan with it, dusting with flour to prevent sticking. Improvise a rolling pin from a water bottle or a fishing rod case wrapped in clean plastic bags.

—From *NOLS Cookery*

Winter Food, Nutrition, and Cooking

Buck Tilton and John Gookin

Food and Nutrition

The value of food—as a source of power and warmth—is measured by its nutritional value. Nutrition is a somewhat imprecise science, but everyone agrees that a shortage of nutrients can cause energy slumps that bring early fatigue, lassitude, mind-numbness, and a predisposition for injury. Start every winter trip by planning to eat a nutritionally sound diet, balancing the best foods with what is practical to carry into the wild.

The most important element of good nutrition is water. Beyond this, there are three sources of energizing foods: carbohydrates, fats, and, to some extent, proteins. Although all foods must be digested into simple compounds before they can be burned for power, carbohydrate (sugars and starches) are digested most quickly and easily. Simple carbohydrates (simple sugars, such as granulated sugar, brown sugar honey, and molasses) are small molecular units that break down very fast, entering the bloodstream soon after you eat them. You get an energy boost right away, but most sugars are burned so quickly that energy levels can suddenly fall below your starting point if all you eat is simple carbohydrates. Therefore, complex carbohydrates (strings of simple sugars called starches, such as pasta, grains, fruits, and starchy vegetables) need to be a major portion of your winter diet. Being a more complex molecular unit, starches break down more slowly, providing power for the long haul. Simple sugars, in other words, are like kindling for a fire, and starches are the big, fat logs.

Fat is so important that your body will manufacture it from carbohydrates and proteins if you run short. Fats (cheese, nuts, butter, peanut butter, meat) break down very slowly in the digestive process, so more time is required for them to provide energy. That's a good thing when you need a steady source of energy over an extended period, such as long nights in the sleeping bag. But if you're used to eating a low-fat diet, add fats slowly to allow your digestive system to adjust.

Proteins are made up of amino acids, and amino acids are the basic substance of human tissue. Proteins (meat, milk products, eggs, cheese, seeds, nuts, whole grains) are not a

Continued →

primary energy source, but your body will use them if nothing else is available or if you exercise for a long time. But because tissue is continually lost and replaced (and new tissue is built after you exercise), proteins are essential. All the amino acids are synthesized by your body, except for eight, which have to be eaten. A "complete protein" has all eight of these amino acids.

If you eat a variety of foods from all three sources, and enough of it, you'll get not only the nutrition you need but also the vitamins and minerals necessary for health and performance in the cold. For more information, consult the *NOLS Nutrition Field Guide*.

Here are some more tips for planning your winter menu:

- Apart from basic nutrition, the single most important factor in cold-weather food consumption is eating food you enjoy.

- Your cold tolerance will improve if you eat a high-fat snack (about one-third of the calories from fat) every couple of hours. In fact, your blood sugar will stay sufficiently high if you eat a full breakfast and a full dinner and snack throughout the day's activities. Food and drink every hour helps to maintain warmth and strength. Another snack just before bedtime will help keep you warm while you sleep.

- Spoilage is not a problem on winter trips, because the cold temperature preserves the food. The biggest problem will be keeping food unfrozen. Wrap the food bag in your pack inside extra clothing for insulation. Keep snacks handy (and thawed) in a pocket near your body.

- Cut your cheese, meats, and butter into chunks before leaving home. Even if they freeze solid, you will still have manageable pieces.

- Think simple. You'll be cold and tired, so quick, one-pot meals will be more appealing. For recipes and abundant information on food and nutrition, consult *NOLS Cookery*.

Cooking in the Cold

Cooking in winter takes much more time and fuel than it does in summer—partly due to the colder air, and partly due to the fact that you might be melting snow for most of your water. Whether you construct an elaborate snow kitchen or simply fire up the stove in the lee of your tent, here are some guidelines:

- Cook in the open. Although you can, with adequate ventilation, cook in the vestibule of a tent or under a tarp, deadly carbon monoxide can build up quickly in an enclosed space, so cooking in the open is strongly recommended.

- Use a stove pad to keep the stove from melting into the snow underneath, and use pot pads (pieces of closed-cell foam work well) to avoid setting pots directly in the snow. (If you do set a pot in the snow, remember to brush the snow off the bottom before setting the pot back on the stove, or risk extinguishing your stove.)

NOLS Tip: Use Bulk Rationing

At NOLS, a bulk rationing method is used to calculate how much food will be needed for an expedition. Careful bulk rationing provides adequate nutrition while minimizing pack weight. With the NOLS system, you figure out how much food (in pounds) you'll need per person per day, then multiply that number by the number of people and the number of days. If you'll be skiing (or hiking) with a full pack, perhaps pulling a sled, and the temperature is expected to stay cold, you'll want 2 to 2.25 pounds of food per person per day. That provides approximately 3,500 to 4,500 calories per person per day. If you expect extremely cold air and strenuous exertion, you may choose to pack 2.5 pounds per person per day, with a value of 4,000 to 5,000 calories per person per day. As an example, three people headed out for ten days of extremely strenuous skiing in subfreezing temperatures would pack 75 pounds of food (3 x 10 x 2.5).

—From *NOLS Winter Camping*

- Warm, dry lighters work much better than cold, wet ones, so keep several spares in your clothes pockets, where they'll be warm, dry, and easy to find. Electric lighters are more reliable than flint lighters.

- Conserve as much fuel as possible by using wind-screens, windbreaks, and reflector shields for the stove; using lids for pots; and never letting a pot of water reach a full, rolling boil.

- Don't let the stove get icy overnight or between meals. Keep it well covered, preferably in a bag, when you're not using it.

- Be very careful when refilling the stove. Wear light gloves, because the evaporation of fuel from your skin can cause frostbite.

- Keep your kitchen well organized to prevent time-wasting searches for small items lost in the snow.

Favorite Outdoor Recipes from NOLS

Edited by Claudia Pearson

Hash Browns with Cheese
(serves 2)

1 1/2 cups hash browns
hot water
4 to 5 Tbs. margarine
1 Tbs. onion, rehydrated or
   fresh, finely chopped
   (optional)
1/2 cup cheese cubes or grated
   cheese
salt and pepper to taste

Hash Browns	
Servings	2
Calories	596
Carb (g)	53
Protein (g)	13
Fat (g)	38
Fiber (g)	5

Put hash browns into a saucepan. Cover with 1 inch of hot water and rehydrate for 15 minutes. Drain off excess water. Melt margarine in a hot fry pan. Add hash browns and onions. Cook, flipping occasionally, until crisp and browned. Stir in or cover with cheese and remove from heat. Cover and allow to sit until cheese is melted. Salt and pepper to taste. Good with hot sauce or picante.

Variation: Add ham or bacon bits to hash browns and cook as above.

Eggs McGulch
(serves 1)

2 heaping Tbs. powdered egg
1 Tbs. powdered milk
1 Tbs. flour
1/2 cup water
salt, pepper, and other spices
   to taste
margarine
1 bagel, sliced
cheese: cream, jack, or cheddar
salsa or ketchup

Eggs McGulch	
Servings	1
Calories	631
Carb (g)	77
Protein (g)	25
Fat (g)	24
Fiber (g)	3

In a bowl, mix egg, milk, and flour together and slowly add water, stirring constantly to avoid clumping. Pour mixture into a heated fry pan with a little bit of margarine, and stir constantly to avoid burning. Remove from heat when eggs reach a scrambled consistency. Add spices to taste. Spread margarine on bagel and toast in fry pan. Spread cream cheese, or place sliced cheese, on bagel; top with cooked eggs and salsa or ketchup. Makes one hearty breakfast sandwich.

Variations: Add fresh or rehydrated onions, green and red peppers, or cooked meat to eggs.

Our Famous Fried Macs
(serves 2 to 4)

handful of dried vegetables
1 lb. (4 cups) macaroni or any
   pasta
4 to 6 cups water
fresh or dried garlic
spices to taste, such as salt,
   pepper, soy sauce,
   oregano, basil
oil or margarine
cheese (any kind), cubed

Fried Macs	
Servings	4
Calories	595
Carb (g)	85
Protein (g)	23
Fat (g)	17
Fiber (g)	3

Add vegetables to cold water and bring to a boil. Add pasta, bring back to a boil, remove from heat, and cover. In another pan, sauté garlic and spices in oil or margarine and then add cooked, drained pasta. Stir and fry for 5 to 10 minutes. Add cubed cheese and fry until desired consistency. Top with Parmesan or salsa for added flavor.

Variations: Use other types of pasta, but be aware that spinach fettucine and egg noodles require constant heat while cooking to avoid mushiness. You can also add canned meats such as tuna or chicken or fresh meats such as pepperoni, cooked bacon, or sausage to this meal for added flavor and calories.

Hint: The smaller the cheese chunks, the faster the cheese will melt. Grated cheese works the best!

Continued ➡

Donna Orr's Gado-Gado Spaghetti
(serves 2 to 3)

Current NOLS employee and previous co-author of NOLS Cookery Donna Orr gets the award for the most popular recipe with this dish. A spicy peanut butter sauce makes it a treat either hot or cold.

1/2 lb. (2 cups) spaghetti or 2 packages ramen noodles
4 cups water
3 Tbs. + 1 tsp. oil
2 Tbs. sunflower seeds
1 Tbs. dried onion, rehydrated
1/2 Tbs. or one packet broth
3 Tbs. brown sugar
1 tsp. garlic
1/2 tsp. black pepper (optional)
1/2 tsp. hot sauce (optional)
1/2 tsp. spike (optional)
3/4 cup water, or more as needed
3 Tbs. vinegar
3 Tbs. soy sauce
3 Tbs. peanut butter
sliced green or wild onions, if available

Gado-Gado Spaghetti	
Servings	3
Calories	634
Carb (g)	81
Protein (g)	17
Fat (g)	28
Fiber (g)	8

Break pasta in half and put into boiling unsalted water to which 1 tsp. of oil has been added. Cook until done; drain immediately. In a fry pan, heat 3 Tbs. oil and add the sunflower seeds and rehydrated onions. Cook and stir over medium heat for 2 minutes. Add the broth with the brown sugar, garlic, other spices if desired, and 3/4 cup water. Add the vinegar and soy sauce. Add peanut butter and stir. *Do not burn!* To eat this hot, heat the sauce thoroughly and pour over hot spaghetti.

This dish can have a fairly salty taste. Cut back or eliminate the broth if you are concerned about saltiness. The recipe is best cold, and it loses some of its saltiness as it sits. Mix sauce and spaghetti, cool quickly, and serve chilled. If available, sliced green or wild onions as a garnish add to the flavor.

Variation: Fresh vegetables such as broccoli, onions, and cabbage, chopped and sautéed lightly and mixed into the sauce, make a tasty addition.

Mary Howley Ryan's Fantastic Bulgur Pilaf
(serves 4)

Contributed by our nutritionist. This vegetarian version is geared toward backcountry cuisine. It can be made as a main or side dish with many possibilities for variation.

1 cup bulgur wheat
1 cup boiled water
vegetarian soup base (bouillon cubes, powdered broth/stock, etc.; chicken-flavored varieties work well)
1 tsp. curry powder
1 tsp. soy sauce (or more to taste)
1/2 tsp. honey or other sweetener (e.g., brown sugar or maple syrup)
1/2 cup dried fruit, chopped
1/2 cup nuts and seeds

Bulgur Pilaf	
Servings	4
Calories	290
Carb (g)	46
Protein (g)	9
Fat (g)	9
Fiber (g)	9

Place bulgur in large pot or bowl. Boil water and mix in soup base. Pour over bulgur and add curry powder, soy sauce, honey, fruit, and nuts.

Mix well. Set aside in cool area for at least 1/2 hour (the longer it sits, the softer the pilaf).

Variations:

- Add canned chicken, fresh fish, cooked lentils, or sliced jerky for more protein.
- Season with hot sauce, Thai chili garlic sauce, fresh or powdered garlic, coconut, coconut milk, Garam Masala spice, or fresh herbs.

Meal-in-a-Mug
(serves 1)

This is popular when cold weather camping because there are no pots to clean!

12 to 16 oz. boiling water
2 packages of cup-of-soup
2 to 3 Tbs. potato pearls
2 Tbs. cubed cheese (cheddar or jack)
2 Tbs. cubed meat (e.g., summer sausage, ham, pepperoni, cooked bacon)
hot sauce to taste

Meal-in-a-Mug	
Servings	1
Calories	355
Carb (g)	47
Protein (g)	13
Fat (g)	13
Fiber (g)	4

Empty packages of cup-of-soup into a 20-oz. mug (any kind will do, but the favorites are cream of chicken and chicken noodle). Pour in boiling water and stir. Add potato pearls to thicken to desired consistency. Add cheese and meat and mix well. Stir well. For a little zing, top with hot sauce.

Hint: Potato pearls also make great thickeners in just about everything except cocoa.

Tarter's Tasty Taters
(serves 3 to 4)

1/2 lb. potato pearls
black pepper, salt, garlic powder, hot sauce, chili powder
3/4 lb. refried beans or instant black beans
3 Tbs. margarine
1/3 lb. Grape Nuts
3/4 lb. cheddar cheese

Tasty Taters	
Servings	4
Calories	917
Carb (g)	101
Protein (g)	37
Fat (g)	42
Fiber (g)	16

Boil 8 cups water. Use enough of it to hydrate potato pearls in a pot, spicing to taste with pepper, salt, garlic, hot sauce, and chili power. Then use leftover water to cook beans. In fry pan, melt margarine and add 2/3 of the Grape Nuts. Fry until coated with margarine and then pat into a crust on the bottom of the fry pan. Cover the crust with a layer of sliced cheddar. Scoop in potato pearls and flatten on top of crust. Pour beans on top of the layer of pearls. Cover beans with a layer of cheddar cheese. Sprinkle the remaining Grape Nuts on top of the cheese and sprinkle everything with a dash of chili powder for color. Bake the casserole until the cheese on top has started to melt and bubble (about 10 to 15 minutes).

Hint: It is safest to put the fry pan on top of the Whisper Lite windscreen so as not to burn the bottom layer of Grape Nuts.

Lisagna Whiznut Variation
(serves 3)

Named for current NOLS instructor Lisa Jaeger and John Whisnant, an instructor in the 1970s.

1/2 lb. pasta (shells, spirals, or macaroni works best)
2 broth packs
fresh onion slices and a couple cloves garlic, or 1 heaping Tbs. dried onion and 1 Tbs. garlic powder
1 can tomato paste or 1/2 cup dried tomato powder
spices: 1/2 tsp. salt, 2 heaping tsp. oregano, 2 heaping tsp. basil, 1/2 tsp. black pepper, 1 tsp. vinegar
4 rounded serving spoons flour
2 heaping tsp. baking power
1 rounded Tbs. powdered eggs
1 rounded Tbs. powdered milk
3/4 to 1 lb. cheese

Lisagna Whiznut	
Servings	3
Calories	1007
Carb (g)	91
Protein (g)	53
Fat (g)	48
Fiber (g)	8

Cook pasta in salt water or with two broth packs. Sauté onions and garlic in fry pan with oil or margarine. In a bowl, mix about 2 cups water and the tomato paste or powder. To this sauce, add the spices (*Hint:* Be sure to season tomato sauce to taste before layering it over pasta. A bit of sugar can reduce the pungent tomato flavor.) In a separate container, mix flour, baking powder, eggs, and milk with approximately 2 1/2 cups cold water. Mix to pancake batter consistency and pour over cooked, drained pasta. Stir and taste. Make sure that the pasta does not taste too bland. Layer thin slices of cheese on the bottom of the fry pan. Pour pasta mixture into fry pan over cheese slices. Spread tomato sauce over the pasta and cover with more thin slices of cheese. Sprinkle with oregano and cover. Bake over stove with twiggy fire for 20 minutes or until brown and bubbly on top. Be careful to rotate the pan over the bottom heat source so as not to burn the casserole.

Variations: Experiment with spices, add meat, or pour the flour batter over the pasta instead of mixing it in.

Mexican Grits and Cheese Casserole
(serves 4 to 6)

5 cups water
1 1/2 cups grits
2 tsp. salt
5 Tbs. powdered egg
1/2 cup water
2 tsp. chili powder
1 tsp. cumin (optional)
hot sauce to taste
4 to 6 Tbs. margarine or bacon grease
1 1/2 cups cheese, grated or diced small

Grits & Cheese Casserole	
Servings	4
Calories	573
Carb (g)	48
Protein (g)	19
Fat (g)	34
Fiber (g)	1

Bring 5 cups water to a boil. Stir in grits and salt. Cook, stirring, until thickened. Mix egg with 1/2 cup water. Add to grits with spices, hot sauce, margarine, and most of cheese. Pour into a greased frying pan. Cover with remaining cheese. Bake, covered, over low heat 30 to 45 minutes. Serve garnished with Grape Nuts for crunch and more hot sauce.

Hint: Grits need to sit covered for 15 minutes to solidify.

Continued ➡

NOLS Picante Sauce

(makes about 1 cup)

The test panel gave this a rave review.

1 Tbs. dried onion

1 Tbs. dried green and red
    peppers

1 cup water (¹/₂ hot and
    ¹/₂ cold)

2 Tbs. tomato base

dash garlic powder

¹/₄ tsp. hot sauce or cayenne
    (to taste)

1 tsp. each vinegar and brown
    sugar (optional, but adds
    good flavor)

dash black pepper

Picante Sauce	
Servings	4
Calories	24
Carb (g)	5
Protein (g)	1
Fat (g)	0
Fiber (g)	1

Rehydrate onions and peppers in ¹/₂ cup hot water. Add tomato base and stir until well mixed. Add remaining ingredients and ¹/₂ cup cold water. Mix well. You can thin this out more if you wish. Serve cold over nachos, main dishes, potato-cheese patties, or bean and lentil dishes.

Fry Bread

(serves 2)

2 tsp. yeast

1 tsp. salt

3/4 cup warm water

1 tsp. sugar

1 3/4 to 2 cups flour (a mix of
    white and whole wheat
    is good)

oil for frying

Fry Bread	
Servings	2
Calories	595
Carb (g)	98
Protein (g)	19
Fat (g)	16
Fiber (g)	12

Mix all ingredients except flour and oil. Let stand 5 minutes. Add flour and knead until smooth. Let rise. Heat oil in fry pan. Flatten dough into a fat tortilla 1/2 inch thick. Fry bread on both sides. Serve with a spread of honey or brown sugar, margarine, and cinnamon. How much oil you use for frying determines that crust and texture of this bread. Real fry bread uses a lot of oil, but it is not necessary. You can cut down on fat calories by just oiling the pan. If you double this recipe, cook half at a time.

Variation: For Indian fry bread, mix bread as above and use immediately without allowing it to rise.

Basic Biscuits

(makes 10 to 12)

2 cups baking mix (see page 69)

4 Tbs. margarine

¹/₂ to 3/4 cup water

Basic Biscuits	
Servings	4
Calories	325
Carb (g)	47
Protein (g)	7
Fat (g)	12
Fiber (g)	2

Cut margarine into baking mix using spoon edges. Add enough water to form a stiff dough. Knead in bowl about a dozen times. Pinch off enough dough for desired size biscuit; pat into shape. Bake in covered fry pan, using a twiggy fire, for about 15 to 20 minutes or until done. As an alternative to baking, fry in melted margarine until both sides are browned. Cover and cook on low heat about 8 to 10 minutes. Good served with margarine and a white sauce.

Variations:

- Cheesy biscuits:
Add ¹/₂ tsp. garlic powder and some rehydrated onions to dough. Form into balls and pull apart into halves. Insert a piece of cheese and pinch halves back together. Bake as above

Cheesy Biscuits	
Servings	4
Calories	381
Carb (g)	48
Protein (g)	10
Fat (g)	16
Fiber (g)	2

Fruit & Nut Biscuits	
Servings	4
Calories	403
Carb (g)	58
Protein (g)	8
Fat (g)	16
Fiber (g)	3

- Fruit and nut biscuits: Mix together 1 Tbs. margarine, 1 Tbs. brown sugar, and ¹/₃ cup chopped mixed fruits and nuts, and insert into biscuits using the method just described.

Crowns à La Sierra

(makes 8 to 10)

This recipe was an instant hit!

2 cups baking mix (see page 69)

¹/₂ cup brown sugar

1 tsp. nutmeg or cinnamon

3 heaping Tbs. margarine

¹/₂ to 3/4 cup water

filling (see below)

Crowns à La Sierra	
Servings	4
Calories	573
Carb (g)	93
Protein (g)	9
Fat (g)	19
Fiber (g)	3

Mix dry ingredients. Cut in margarine. Add water to make a stiff dough. Pinch off dough and roll into balls. Bake in fry pan, using a twiggy fire, for 5 minutes, then indent middle with a spoon and continue baking until brown, about 15 to 20 minutes more. Just before serving, fill depression in center with filling.

Filling:

¹/₂ cup nuts and chopped fruit (a good combination is raisins,
    chopped walnuts, and chopped apricots)

3 Tbs. honey or brown sugar (with sugar, add 1 Tbs. water)

1 heaping Tbs. margarine

dash of salt

¹/₂ tsp. cinnamon or nutmeg

Mix together and cook over low heat a few minutes until smooth.

Chappaties

(makes 4 5-inch flat breads)

¹/₂ cup flour (whole wheat is
    more authentic, but white
    is okay too)

¹/₂ cup cornmeal

pinch salt

¹/₂ cup water

margarine for frying

toppings: sliced cheese, bacon
    bits, chopped wild onions,
    cayenne to Tabasco

Chappaties	
Servings	4
Calories	157
Carb (g)	23
Protein (g)	3
Fat (g)	7
Fiber (g)	3

Mix all ingredients except margarine and toppings. Form in very thin patties and fry in lightly greased pan until golden brown. After they are turned, add desired toppings; cover pan to help cheese melt.

Variation: Combine 1 cup whole wheat flour, ¹/₄ tsp. salt, 1 Tbs. margarine, ¹/₄ cup water. Proceed as for making chappaties.

Scrambled Brownies or Gingerbread

This dessert earned its name because it never seems to make the "baked" stage.

2 cups brownie mix or
    gingerbread mix

6 Tbs. water (more if batter
    is dry)

Scrambled Brownies	
Servings	4
Calories	349
Carb (g)	56
Protein (g)	3
Fat (g)	13
Fiber (g)	2

Scrambled Gingerbread	
Servings	4
Calories	407
Carb (g)	59
Protein (g)	3
Fat (g)	18
Fiber (g)	1

Mix together. Spread in oiled fry pan. Cover and cook on low heat about 15 minutes until product is done on top. Scrape out of pan with a spatula. Let sit a few minutes before eating so it can stiffen. This is an alternative to baking with a twiggy fire. The end product is chewy and gooey.

Variation: Add chopped nuts, dried fruits, or chocolate chips to the mix before cooking.

No-Bake Eskimo Cookies

(makes about 16 cookies)

1 cup oatmeal (instant or regular)

6 Tbs. margarine

6 Tbs. brown sugar

3 Tbs. cocoa mix

¹/₂ tsp. vanilla

¹/₂ Tbs. water

Eskimo Cookies	
Servings	4
Calories	379
Carb (g)	50
Protein (g)	6
Fat (g)	19
Fiber (g)	2

Mix all ingredients together. Form into walnut-sized balls. Eat immediately or let sit in a cool place.

Variation: Roll in a combination of 1 Tbs. powdered milk and 1 Tbs. brown sugar, or in coconut.

No-Bake Powerhouse Cookies

(makes 20 to 24 cookies)

Our taste testers loved these!

1 cup brown sugar

¹/₄ cup margarine

3 Tbs. powdered milk

4 Tbs. water

1 cup oatmeal

1 cup peanut butter

¹/₂ cup nuts

¹/₄ cup chocolate or carob chips

¹/₂ tsp. vanilla

Powerhouse Cookies	
Servings	4
Calories	927
Carb (g)	91
Protein (g)	24
Fat (g)	57
Fiber (g)	8

Mix sugar, margarine, powdered milk, and water in a pan. Bring to a boil. Reduce heat and boil 3 minutes, stirring constantly to prevent scorching. Remove from heat and stir in remaining ingredients. Drop by spoonfuls onto a flat surface such as a pan lid. Let sit for about 10 minutes to set. In hot weather, they might not set as well.

—From *NOLS Cookery*

Home-Dried One-Pot Meals

Linda Frederick Yaffe

The ancient art of food dehydration is wonderfully basic. Heat and air circulation remove most of the water content from the food. This lack of water keeps microorganisms from living and growing. After many years of home-drying complete backpack meals, I have never lost food to spoilage. Follow the simple instructions . . . and you will enjoy the same success. Dehydration is especially suited to backpacking. Not only does drying forestall spoilage, it transforms bulky, heavy food into compact, featherweight meals.

Dehydration costs less than any other method of food preservation. It requires no chemicals. Complete meals can be dried year-round in any weather, at your convenience. Take advantage of each season's bounty, using the finest fresh ingredients available, or use good-quality canned or frozen meat, fish, fruit, or vegetables. Home-dried meals can be stored for several years. It's easy to keep a ready supply of home-dried dinners on hand for carefully planned extended treks, as well as last-minute weekend escapes.

Creating home-dried one-pot meals is this simple.

Creating home-dried one-pot meals is this simple: Cook your dinner at home, slicing, grating, or dicing the ingredients into small pieces. Spread the cooked meal on covered dehydrator trays and dry until the food looks and feels completely dry. In the field, cover the food with water, boil, stir, and serve with pleasure.

Food Choices

You don't have to settle for someone else's idea of a good hot dinner. When you make your own convenience meals, you are in control: more salt or less salt, high fat or low fat, meat or meat-less—the decision is yours. You can use your choice of diary, soy, or rice milk or cheese in any of these recipes. Like it hot? Add more jalapeños. Can't eat sugar? Use a substitute. Liberate yourself from one-size-fits-all commercial meals. You enjoy good meals at home; while backpacking, you need those same good-tasting, varied, nutritionally balanced meals more than ever. Some backpackers short-change themselves. They eat the same tired instant mashed potatoes or ramen noodles day after day. Varied, nutritionally balanced meals not only give you energy on the trail, but also keep your mind focused and make you happy and satisfied.

In the Home

Food Dehydrator

A high-quality electric food dehydrator with fan, heat source, and thermostat is the best food investment a backpacker can make. If you do not own a dehydrator, borrow one from a friend or relative. Try some of the recipes in this book. You will learn how simple it is to create your own one-pot meals. The dehydrator, not you, does the work.

A top-of-the-line dehydrator will pay for itself, compared to the price of commercially dried meals, during a one-week trip for a family of four. Air circulation is more important than heat when you are drying food, so be sure to choose a dehydrator with a fan as well as a heat source and a thermostat. Bargain dehydrators that lack a fan simply don't work. They will steam—not dry—your food. Either of the following brands of electric food dehydrators are recommended for decades of carefree home drying: Excalibur Products [6083 Power Inn Road, Sacramento, CA 95824, (800) 875-4254] or Nesco American Harvest [4064 Peavey Road, Chaska, MN 55318, (800) 288-4545].

Home Kitchen Basics

All of the one-pot dehydrated meals in this book serve four hungry backpackers—two cups or more per serving when rehydrated. The four large portions indicated in these recipes will fit comfortably in typical home food dehydrators without crowding. To cook these big, full-sized backpacking portions of food, you will need to use large cooking pots at home. Here are some suggested home kitchen basics:

- Dutch oven, at least three-quart capacity
- Large ovenproof skillet, at least 10 1/2-inch diameter
- Soup and pasta pot, at least five-quart capacity
- Colander to drain pasta, fruits, and vegetables
- Casserole dish, at least four-quart capacity, ten by thirteen inches
- Baking sheets, both flat and rimmed
- Blender or food processor to speed chopping
- Wire whisk for effortless lump-free sauces

Drying One-Pot Meals in a Dehydrator

Time-saving tip: Prepare extra food, enjoy some for dinner tonight, and dehydrate the rest.

Choose a one-pot complete meal recipe from this book. Cook your meal at home, just as though you are preparing tonight's dinner. If you choose a meal such as spaghetti, simply prepare a spaghetti sauce—your choice of beef, seafood, or vegetarian. Then boil the pasta al dente (cooked but still firm). Toss together the sauce and the drained pasta, and put the whole dish, freshly cooked and still warm, into the dehydrator. While preparing the food, chop, grate, dice, or slice the ingredients into small pieces. These will dehydrate much faster and more successfully than large pieces of food.

Virtually all cooked foods are safe and easy to dry at home. Two uncooked foods that should

never be dried at home are eggs and milk. When cooked, these foods dehydrate safely. Many of the recipes in this book contain cooked eggs and milk. To avoid the risk of salmonella contamination, buy commercially dried powdered eggs. They are readily available everywhere as whole eggs, egg whites, or egg substitutes for home cooking, baking, or emergencies. Dry milk is also readily available commercially as instant or regular, high or low fat, or buttermilk.

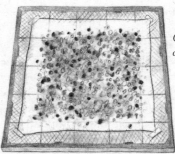

Cover mesh dehydrator trays.

While the food is cooking, cover your mesh dehydrator trays with plastic wrap or ovenproof parchment paper. If you use plastic wrap, buy a brand made from 100 percent polyethylene. Leave about an inch of space between the wrap or paper and the edge of the trays; this will allow more air circulation. To keep the covering from shifting, you can anchor the corners with tape. If your dehydrator has solid fruit leather trays or tray covers, you do not need to use any other covering. The wrap, paper, solid trays, or tray covers simply keep liquid foods such as soups, stews, or casseroles from leaking through the mesh of the dehydrator trays.

Preheat the dehydrator for ten minutes.

Spread the warm, cooked meal evenly in a thin layer on the dehydrator trays and put time in the dehydrator. Overloaded trays dry slowly. All of the one-pot recipes in this book—which make four serving them each—fit comfortably into a typical home dehydrator. For highest quality and food safety, speedy drying is best.

The meal will be completely dry in four to six hours. While your meal is drying, check it several times. To check the food and speed its drying, first wash your hands and dry them. Then pull out one tray at a time and turn and crumble the food on the tray, breaking up large pieces of food with your hands. This will ensure fast, even drying. If you are unable to check and turn the food during the drying process, a good dehydrator will successfully dry your meal anyway; drying will simply take a few hours longer. It is nearly impossible to overdry or otherwise ruin your home-dried meals using an electric dehydrator with a heat source and fan. If necessary, you can put the food in the dehydrator, leave the house, go to work for eight hours, and then turn off the dehydrator when you get home.

The recipes in this book contain some fat; backpackers need fat for fuel. However, too much fat will retard drying and could decrease the shelf life of your dried meal. While preparing your meals, carefully trim the fat from meats. Avoid excessive amounts of high-fat cheese, oil, or butter. Some especially fatty

Continued ➡

foods, such as bacon, can appear greasy during the drying process. If fat glistens on the food, simply blot it with paper towels, then return the trays to the dehydrator.

Drying times indicated in each recipe will vary due to your dehydrator and the fat and moisture content of your ingredients. The food is dry when it looks and feels dry. To test for dryness, choose a large piece of food from the dehydrator tray. Examine it and crumble it in your hand. If you notice any moisture, return the trays to the dehydrator and dry the food a bit longer. Don't worry about overdrying these meals; they are nearly foolproof.

When beans are fully dry, they feel hard and dry and can crumble into powder when crushed in your hand. Strands of spaghetti will feel dry but still slightly pliable. Meats should feel hard and leathery. Vegetables will feel hard and crisp. Fruit should be bendable and dry with no moist spots.

When the food looks and feels dry, turn off and unplug the dehydrator. Let the food rest in the dehydrator for several hours or overnight. This will let your food completely cool and release the last bits of moisture. The next day, your meal is ready to store.

Drying One-Pot Meals in an Oven

If you use an electric oven, remove the top heating element or place an empty baking sheet on the oven's top shelf. Whether your oven is electric or gas, use the coolest part of the oven.

To successfully dehydrate food in an oven, you need to keep the temperature low. Turn your oven to its lowest setting, usually 140 to 150 degrees Fahrenheit. Notoriously inaccurate home ovens often run 25 to 50 degrees hotter than the oven's temperature dial indicates. An oven thermometer is helpful; set it next to the drying food to keep the temperature within the 140 to 150 degree range. If the temperature rises above 150 degrees, turn off the oven for a while.

The accurate and stable Taylor Classic Oven Guide Thermometer, model 5921, can be obtained from KitchenEtc. [32 Industrial Drive, Exeter, NH 03833, (800) 232-4070, www.kitchenetc.com].

Air circulation is essential. Prop open the oven door a few inches while the food is drying. For increased air circulation, place an electric fan just outside the oven door; aim the airflow over the food.

Spread your one-pot meals in a thin layer on oiled, rimmed baking sheets. Check, shift, and crumble the food frequently while it is drying. The food around the edges of the baking sheets will dry much faster than the food in the center; protect it from scorching by checking it often.

As with an electric dehydrator, oven-dried food is dry when it looks and feels dry and crisp. Let the food cool completely for several hours or overnight before storing it.

Storing Home-Dried Meals

Bag each meal in small, sturdy plastic bags. Bag the meals according to your backpack needs. If you have dried four servings and will be backpacking in a party of two people, split the meals and store two servings per bag. If a dried meal remains high in volume after dehydration,

compact it. Crush the dried meal with your hands as you pour it into the storage bag. Squeeze as much air as possible from the bag, then seal it. Double-bag the meal in a second bag; in between the two bags, place a tiny label made from a small scrap of paper with the name of the recipe, the date it was dried, how many people it will serve, and directions for rehydrating the meal. This label will tell all members of your party what the bag contains and how to prepare the meal in the field.

For best quality, store your meals in individual meal-sized bags. Avoid packing many servings of food into a single large bag that must be opened repeatedly during a long trek. Each time you open the bag, you will expose the food to air and moisture, increasing the chance of spoilage.

Store the meals in a cool, dark, dry place. Protect them from exposure to air, light, and moisture by putting the individually bagged meals into a large black plastic bag. The black bag can then be stored in a cool, dark, dry room, but, for best quality, store the meals in your refrigerator for up to two years, or in your freezer for three years. They take up little space and will be fresh and handy to throw into your pack for an unexpected weekend trip.

When you're ready to backpack, store the meals bagged in black plastic in the cool, dark, dry interior of your pack. Home-dried one-pot meals make perfect cached food for long-distance treks, since their shelf life is long.

Recycling Dehydrating Materials

The plastic wrap, ovenproof parchment paper, and all plastic food bags can be washed, dried, and reused many times before you recycle them. After each use, wash them in warm, soapy water; then rinse and dry them well.

Menu Plan

If you have ever run out of food while backpacking, forgotten a crucial item (where's the coffee?), or conversely, grumbled as you packed out five pounds of unneeded food, a menu plan will make your trip smoother. Take a few minutes to write a menu plan before you leave home. A successful trip means walking out of the wilderness carrying no food except your small emergency supply.

While planning your trip at home, draw a grid menu plan, showing three meals plus two snacks per day, and an extra snack per day for very cold weather camping. Include all of your foods and beverages, plus one extra emergency dinner and snack for each member of the party. Writing a menu plan gives you an overview of your trip. You can plan for variety: beans one night, chicken the next. Plan a soothing cheese and noodle dish the night after a jazzy, spicy dish. Serve a hot breakfast in between days of cold cereal. At the bottom of your menu grid, list the total number of servings of multiple items, such as total servings of granola, coffee, tea, cocoa, cheese, crackers, dried fruit, energy bars, and lemonade mix.

Packing the Food

Measure all servings of food. Never guess how much you will need. Using your menu plan as a guide, sit down at a table with plenty of small plastic bags and measuring cups and spoons. Carefully measure each portion into the bags. If you are backpacking for ten days or fewer, you may want to label each meal—breakfast # 1, lunch # 1, and dinner # 1—with large-print, easy-to-read slips of paper. After you have labeled the individual meals in small bags, place them into four large plastic bags labeled breakfast, lunch, dinner, and snacks. If you are traveling in bear country and will need to hang (counterbalance) your food from a tree, take along fifty feet of nylon cord and two large nylon bags with drawstrings that can be counterbalanced from a tree limb.

To pack fragile foods, such as crackers or cookies, use waxed milk cartons or cardboard oatmeal boxes. Keep a supply of clean quart and half-gallon cartons on hand. Wash and dry the waxed cartons. Pack individual servings of fragile foods in plastic bags; then pack them tightly into the cartons. Label the cartons, and bag them in larger plastic bags. When the cartons are empty, they can be flattened and used as insulated seating during the rest of your trip while you are packing them out.

Rehydrating One-Pot Meals

These meals are ready to eat fast. Have your stove set up and ready to light. Keep a container of treated water handy. Have your pot and lid, spoons, serving cups, and home-dried meal ready. It's time for dinner.

Pour the home-dried meal into the pot. Cover the food with treated water. No measuring is necessary; simply cover soups or stews with plenty of water (one to two inches above the surface of the dried food in the pot), and more solid dishes such as pasta, quiches, or casseroles with barely enough water to cover (just above the surface of the dried food in the pot). Put the lid on the pot.

Cover pasta, quiches, or casseroles with water just above the level of food in pot.

Cover soups or stews with water one to two inches above level of food in pot.

Continued ➡

Light your stove. Place the pot of food on the stove. After a minute, check and stir the food. When it begins to bubble, stir until the food is fully boiling and the ingredients have softened. Turn off the stove and remove the pot. Serve and enjoy your meal.

If, while heating your meal, you find you have used too little water, simply add a bit more treated water and bring it to a full boil. If you have used a little too much water, enjoy the extra broth, or simply boil the meal a few minutes longer to reduce the extra water.

Meals and Snacks

BEEF JERKY
4 servings
Weight 1 dried serving = 1.5 ounces

This is easy and delicious.

1. Place in freezer until partially frozen:
   1 pound lean flank or round steak

2. Remove and discard fat.

3. Slice the meat into 1/4-inch-thick strips.

4. Mix together in a large, shallow glass casserole dish:
   3 tablespoons tamari soy sauce
   3 tablespoons Worcestershire sauce
   1 tablespoon liquid smoke
   1 tablespoon chili powder
   1 teaspoon hot sauce
   2 cloves garlic, minced

5. Marinate the strips in the sauce, stirring to coat, for 3 minutes.

6. Oil mesh dehydrator trays. Lay the strips directly on uncovered mesh trays.

7. Dehydrate for 6 hours at 145 degrees [F], turning the strips once while drying.

8. When completely cool, store in refrigerator or freezer in individual serving-sized bags prior to your trip.

Variation: Leftover *cooked* chicken or turkey makes tasty, slightly chewy jerky. Slice the cooked meat as thin as possible, trimming away every bit of fat, and follow the above recipe for Beef Jerky. Pork, cooked or not, is not suitable for jerky.

SPRING STRAWBERRY LEATHER
32 servings
Weight 1 dried serving = 0.5 ounce

This is the essence of strawberry flavor.

1. Wash, rubbing off seeds, then core and drain in a colander:
   3 pounds (10 cups) ripe fresh strawberries
   Purée the strawberries in a blender or food processor, along with:
   1/2 cup white corn syrup
   1/2 teaspoon ground ginger

2. Oil covered dehydrator trays with vegetable oil. Pour the purée onto the trays in even 8-inch-diameter circles.

3. Dehydrate at 135 degrees [F] for 7 to 10 hours, or until firm but leathery.

4. Roll up the leather while it is still warm; then cut each roll into 4 pieces. Let cool completely before storing in individual serving sized bags.

Fruit Leather Variations

Try the following fruits:
   Unpeeled apricots, peaches, pears, or plums
   peeled nectarines or pineapple

Use 10 cups of fresh fruit. Choose one fruit or a combination of several fruits. Purée the fruit along with a small amount of honey, sugar, or corn syrup, plus spice to taste.

For additional variety, sprinkle over the fruit leather before putting it into the dehydrator:
   any variety finely chopped nuts
   flaked coconut
   any variety hulled seeds
   granola cereal

BANANA CHIPS
Weight 1 dried serving (1 banana) = 1.5 ounces

1. Lightly oil uncovered mesh dehydrator trays with vegetable oil.

2. Peel, then cut into 1/8- to 1/4-inch-thick slices:
   ripe bananas

Place in a single layer directly on mesh dehydrator trays. Two bananas will fill three dehydrator trays.

3. Dehydrate at 145 degrees [F] for 5 hours, or until firm and leathery.

4. Let cool completely before storing in individual serving-sized bags.

HASH BROWNS WITH EGGS AND SAUSAGE
Serves 4
Weight 1 dried serving = 5 ounces

Enjoy this complete breakfast in only 3 minutes from pack to plate.

1. Grate, then drain in a colander, pressing out moisture:
   10 medium baking potatoes (about 4 1/2 pounds),
      scrubbed but not peeled
   2 large onions

2. Heat a Dutch oven over medium heat, then add:
   2 tablespoons olive oil

When the oil is hot, add the potatoes and onion, pressing them into the pan and stirring occasionally, for 10 minutes.

3. Stir in:
   10 ounces beef, pork, turkey, or soy sausage, minced
   1 teaspoon salt
   1 teaspoon freshly ground black pepper

Reduce heat to very low, cover, and cook for 10 minutes, stirring occasionally.

4. Preheat oven to 350 degrees [F]. Oil a 10-by-13-inch casserole dish.

5. Stir into the potato mixture:
   8 eggs, beaten
   1/2 cup finely grated Parmesan cheese

Spread the mixture in the casserole dish. Bake for 20 minutes, or until golden brown.

6. Spread on covered dehydrator trays and dehydrate for 4 1/2 hours at 145 degrees [F].

7. To rehydrate, cover with water 1/2 inch above level of food in pot, boil, stir, and serve.

BEAN AND PASTA SOUP
Serves 4
Weight 1 dried serving = 5.5 ounces

1. Cook, then drain in a colander:
   10 ounces vermicelli pasta, broken in thirds
   Return pasta to pot and set aside.

2. Heat a Dutch oven over medium-low heat. Add:
   1 tablespoon olive oil
   When the oil is hot, add:
   1 onion, minced
   1 large baking potato, scrubbed but not peeled, grated
   1 teaspoon minced fresh rosemary or 1/2 teaspoon
      dried rosemary
   Cook, stirring occasionally, for 7 minutes.

3. Add:
   14 ounces canned peeled Italian plum tomatoes, crushed
   15 ounces canned kidney beans, rinsed and drained
   3 cups any variety stock
   1 teaspoon salt
   1/2 teaspoon freshly ground black pepper
   Cook 5 minutes longer, then stir in the cooked pasta.

4. Spread on covered dehydrator trays and dehydrate for 6 hours at 145 degrees [F].

5. To rehydrate, cover with water 1 inch above level of food in pot, boil, stir, and serve.

QUICK CLAM CHOWDER
Serves 4

Weight 1 dried serving = 4.5 ounces

1. Heat a Dutch oven over medium-low heat. Add:
   2 tablespoons olive oil
   When the oil is hot, add and cook for 8 minutes:
   1 onion, minced
   2 cloves garlic, minced
   4 stalks celery, diced

2. Add, bring to a boil, then simmer, covered, 30 minutes longer, stirring occasionally:
   5 medium baking potatoes (about 2 1/2 pounds),
      scrubbed but not peeled, diced
   19 1/2 ounces canned minced clams
   3 cups chicken broth, clam juice, or vegetable stock
   1 Whole bay leaf

3. Remove bay leaf. Stir in:
   12 ounces canned evaporated milk
   1 teaspoon salt
   1/4 teaspoon freshly ground black pepper

4. Spread on covered dehydrator trays and dehydrate for 7 hours at 145 degrees [F].

5. To rehydrate, barely cover with water. Stir while bringing to a boil; then serve.

QUICK BEEF STEW
Serves 4
Weight 1 dried serving = 4.5 ounces

1. Heat a Dutch oven over medium heat. Add:
   1 tablespoon olive oil
   When the oil is hot, add and cook, stirring, for 4 minutes, or until light brown:
   1 pound lean ground round or ground turkey
   1 onion, minced
   1 carrot, grated

Continued →

2. Add and bring to a boil:

> 3 cups any variety stock
> 28 ounces canned crushed tomatoes
> 1 whole bay leaf
> 1 teaspoon minced fresh thyme or 1/2 teaspoon dried thyme
> 1 teaspoon salt
> 1 teaspoon chili powder
> 15 ounces canned small white beans, rinsed and drained
> 3/4 cup whole wheat couscous

Reduce heat and simmer, covered, for 12 minutes.

3. Spread on covered dehydrator trays and dehydrate for 5 1/2 hours at 145 degrees [F].

4. To rehydrate, cover with water 1 inch above level of food in pot, boil, stir, and serve.

Turkey Chili
Serves 4
Weight 1 dried serving = 4 ounces

1. Heat a Dutch oven over medium heat. Add:

> 1 tablespoon olive oil

When the oil is hot, add and cook, stirring, for 5 minutes:

> 1 onion, minced
> 1 bell pepper, minced
> 2 cloves garlic, minced

2. Add and stir 3 minutes longer:

> 1 pound uncooked ground turkey or diced roasted turkey
> 1 tablespoon chili powder
> 1 teaspoon ground cumin

3. Stir in and bring to a boil:

> 28 ounces canned crushed tomatoes
> 3 cups any variety stock or water
> 1/2 cups whole wheat couscous
> 1/2 teaspoon salt
> 1/4 teaspoon cayenne pepper

Reduce heat and simmer, covered, for 10 minutes.

4. Remove from heat and stir in:

> 1/2 cup finely grated Parmesan or Romano cheese

5. Spread on covered dehydrator trays and dehydrate for 6 hours at 145 degrees [F].

6. To rehydrate, cover with water 1 1/2 inches above level of food in pot, boil, stir, and serve.

Sierra Spaghetti
Serves 4
Weight 1 dried serving = 6 ounces

This is high in protein and full of flavor.

1. Heat a Dutch oven or large skillet over medium heat. Add:

> 2 tablespoons olive oil

When the oil is hot, add and sauté for 10 minutes:

> 1 onion, diced
> 10 fresh mushrooms, diced
> 4 cloves garlic, minced

2. Add and cook for 5 minutes, stirring occasionally:

> 3 1/2 cups spaghetti sauce
> 4 1/2 ounces canned chopped ripe (black) olives
> 15 ounces canned small white beans, rinsed and drained
> 1 teaspoon crushed red pepper flakes
> 1/2 teaspoon dried oregano

3. Cook, then drain in a colander:

> 12 ounces linguini pasta, broken in thirds

Place pasta back in pot. Add the sauce and stir well.

4. Spread on covered dehydrator trays and dehydrate for 6 hours at 145 degrees [F].

5. To rehydrate, cover with water 1/2 inch above level of food in pot, boil, stir, and serve.

Lazy Lasagna
Serves 4
Weight 1 dried serving = 5 ounces

Quick to assemble, this lasagna features your choice of beef, turkey, or tofu.

1. Heat a large skillet or Dutch oven over medium-low heat. Add:

> 1 tablespoon olive oil

When the oil is hot, add, stirring, for 3 minutes:

> 1 onion, minced
> 4 cloves garlic, minced

Add and cook, stirring, 5 minutes longer:

> 1 pound ground beef or turkey, or crumbled tofu

2. Reduce heat to low and add:

> 5 cups spaghetti sauce
> 1/2 teaspoon crushed red pepper flakes

Simmer for 5 minutes stirring occasionally

3. Preheat oven to 350 degrees [F]. Oil a 10-by-13-inch casserole dish.

4. Have ready:

> 9 sheets of uncooked oven-ready lasagna noodles

5. Finely grate:

> 8 ounces (1 cup) mozzarella cheese
> 8 ounces (1 cup) Parmesan cheese

6. Layer the ingredients in the casserole dish in the following order:

> 1/4 of the sauce, 3 of the sheets of noodles, 1/3 of the grated mozzarella, and 1/3 of the grated Parmesan.

Repeat, using all the ingredients and topping the casserole with the last 1/4 of the sauce.

7. Cover and bake for 30 minutes; then uncover and bake 10 minutes longer. Let stand outside the oven for 10 minutes.

8. Use a spatula to break up the noodles and spread on covered dehydrator trays.

9. Dehydrate for 5 1/2 hours at 145 degrees [F].

10. To rehydrate, cover with water just above level of food in pot, boil, stir, and serve.

Tortilla Chip Casserole
Serves 4
Weight 1 dried serving = 7 ounces

1. Bring to a boil in a large saucepan:

> 1 cup any variety stock
> 1/4 teaspoon salt

Add:

> 1 zucchini, diced
> 1 bell pepper, minced
> 1 onion, minced
> 3 cloves garlic, minced

Reduce heat and simmer for 5 minutes, or until just tender.

2. Preheat oven to 350 degrees [F]. Oil a 10-by-13-inch casserole dish.

3. Have ready:

> 18 ounces blue corn (or other variety) tortilla chips, slightly crushed
> 3 1/2 cups spaghetti sauce
> 1 1/4 cups grated Monterey Jack cheese

4. Layer the ingredients in the casserole dish in the following order:

> 1/3 of the spaghetti sauce, 1/2 of the chips placed in an even layer, 1/2 of the cheese, and 1/2 of the vegetables.

Repeat, using all of the ingredients and topping the casserole with the last 1/3 of the spaghetti sauce.

5. Spread over the casserole:

> 1/4 cup salsa, mild, medium, or hot

Pour over the casserole:

> 1/2 cup any variety stock

6. Bake, covered, for 25 minutes.

7. Spread on covered dehydrator trays and dehydrate for 5 1/2 hours at 145 degrees [F].

8. To rehydrate, cover with water just above level of food in pot, boil, stir, and serve.

Shrimp Jambalaya
Serves 4
Weight 1 dried serving = 4.5 ounces

1. Place in a saucepan:

> 1 1/2 cups quinoa, rinsed and drained
> 2 3/4 cups water

Bring to a boil; then reduce heat and simmer for 20 minutes or until tender and translucent. Set aside.

2. Heat a Dutch oven over medium-low heat. Add:

> 2 tablespoons olive oil

When the oil is hot, add and stir for 10 minutes:

> 1 onion, minced
> 1 bell pepper, minced
> 10 fresh mushrooms, minced

3. Stir in, bring to a boil, then simmer 5 minutes longer:

> 28 ounces canned crushed tomatoes
> 15 ounces canned small white beans, drained
> 8 ounces uncooked shelled, deveined shrimp, minced
> 2 teaspoons minced fresh thyme or 1 teaspoon dried thyme
> 1/2 teaspoon salt
> 1/4 teaspoon cayenne pepper

4. Add the quinoa to the shrimp mixture and blend.

5. Spread on covered dehydrator trays and dehydrate for 6 hours at 145 degrees [F].

6. To rehydrate, cover with water just above level of food in pot, boil, stir, and serve.

Saucy Tuna
Serves 4
Weight 1 dried serving = 6 ounces

This is very easy to make and very tasty.

1. Cook, then drain in a colander:

> 12 ounces vermicelli pasta, broken in thirds

Return the pasta to the pot and set aside.

2. Heat a large skillet over medium-low heat; then add:

Continued ➡

2 tablespoons olive oil

When the oil is hot, add and cook, stirring, for 5 minutes:

1 onion, minced

4 cloves garlic, minced

Add and cook 3 minutes longer:

28 ounces canned crushed tomatoes

4 ounces canned diced green chilies

12 ounces water-packed canned tuna, drained

1/2 teaspoon salt

3. Stir together the drained pasta and sauce. Stir in:

1/3 cup finely grated Parmesan cheese.

4. Spread on covered dehydrator trays and dehydrate for 5 1/2 hours at 145 degrees [F].

5. To rehydrate, cover with water 1/2 inch above level of food in pot, boil, stir, and serve.

Potato Soup Parmesan

Serves 4

Weight 1 dried serving = 3.5 ounces

1. Cut into quarters and place in a large saucepan:

4 medium baking potatoes (about 2 pounds), peeled

1 onion, peeled

Cover with:

6 cups any variety stock or water

Bring to a boil. Stir in:

1 cup TVP (textured vegetable protein)

Reduce heat and simmer, covered, for 20 minutes.

2. Mash the potato mixture along with the stock in the saucepan using a potato masher or fork. Stir in:

12 ounces canned evaporated milk

1 1/2 teaspoons salt

1 teaspoon freshly ground black pepper

3. Remove from heat and let cool for 1 minute. Stir in:

1/2 cup finely grated Parmesan cheese

4. Spread on covered dehydrator trays and dehydrate for 6 1/2 hours at 145 degrees [F].

5. To rehydrate, cover with water 1/2 inch above level of food in pot, boil, stir, and serve.

—From *Backpack Gourmet*

More Recipes from the Backpack Gourmet — No Dehydration Required

Linda Frederick Yaffe

Spiced Mixed Nuts

8 servings

Weight 1 serving (1/2 cup) = 4 ounces

These will keep for six weeks.

1. Toast in a large skillet over low heat for 3 minutes:

1/4 cup sesame seed

Add:

2 tablespoons sesame oil

1/2 cup packed brown sugar

1/2 teaspoon crushed red pepper flakes (hot) or 1/2 teaspoon paprika (mild)

Cook for 5 minutes, stirring occasionally.

2. Add and cook 3 minutes longer, or until brown and fragrant:

4 cups unsalted mixed nuts

1 tablespoon soy sauce

1/2 teaspoon liquid smoke

3. Turn out onto a large baking sheet to cool completely before storing.

Honey Nut Granola

18 servings

Weight 1 serving = 4 ounces

This is a satisfying, ready-to-eat breakfast.

1. Toast in a large skillet over medium heat, stirring frequently, until light brown:

2 cups whole wheat flour

1 cup wheat germ

1 cup flaked coconut

1 cup brewer's yeast (high-protein dried unleavened yeast)

2. Preheat oven to 350 degrees [F].

3. Heat gently in a saucepan until warm:

1/2 cup canola oil

1 cup honey

1 cup packed brown sugar

1/2 cup apple juice

4. Mix together in a 10-by-13-inch casserole dish:

7 cups rolled oats

1/2 cup hulled sunflower seeds

2 cups any variety chopped nuts

5. Pour the flour and honey mixtures over the oat mixture in the casserole dish. Mix well.

6. Bake for 15 minutes, stir; then bake 15 minutes longer. Turn off the oven. Stir the granola; then let it stand in the oven with the door closed for 2 hours.

7. Cool completely; then double-bag and store in the freezer until ready to use.

8. Before camping, package individual servings of granola in 6 1/2-inch-square plastic sandwich bags. Place in each bag:

3/4 cup granola

2 tablespoons instant dry milk

1 tablespoon any variety chopped dried fruit

To serve, pour one bag of granola mixture into a cup. Fill cup with cool treated water, stir, and enjoy.

Sweet Morning Granola

20 servings

Weight 1 serving = 4 ounces

1. Heat a large skillet over medium-low heat. Toast in the skillet, stirring frequently, for 8 minutes:

2 cups whole wheat flour

1 cup wheat germ

1 cup flaked coconut

1/2 cup sesame seeds

2. Preheat oven to 350 degrees.

3. Heat gently in a saucepan until warm:

1 cup peanut butter

1/2 cup canola oil

1/2 cup honey

3/4 cup brown sugar

1 tablespoon vanilla extract

4. Mix together in a 10-by-13-inch casserole dish:

8 cups rolled oats

1 cup any variety chopped nuts

5. Pour the browned flour and peanut butter mixtures over the oat mixture. Combine thoroughly.

6. Bake for 15 minutes, stir; then bake 10 minutes longer. Turn off the heat. Stir the granola; then let it stand in the oven with the door closed for 2 hours.

7. Cool completely; then double-bag and store in the freezer until ready to use.

8. Before camping, package individual servings of granola in 6 1/2-inch-square plastic sandwich bags. Place in each bag:

3/4 cup granola

2 tablespoons instant dry milk

1 tablespoon any variety chopped dried fruit

To serve, pour one bag of granola mixture into a cup. Fill cup with cool treated water, stir, and enjoy.

Granola Bars

8 servings

Weight 1 serving (1 bar) = 4.5 ounces

1. Toast in a skillet over low heat for 3 minutes, stirring frequently, until light brown:

1 cup any variety nuts, chopped

1 cup shredded coconut

Set aside.

2. Mix together in a large bowl:

2 cups rolled oats

1 cup whole wheat flour

1 cup graham cracker crumbs (5 whole crackers)

Cut in:

1/2 cup chilled butter or margarine

Stir in the toasted nuts and coconut and:

1/2 cup honey

1/2 cup packed brown sugar

3. Preheat oven to 275 degrees [F]. Oil a 10-by-6-inch pan.

4. Pat the mixture firmly into the pan. Bake for 50 minutes or until light brown.

5. Cut into 8 bars while still warm; then let them cool completely in the pan on a wire rack.

6. Store in individual serving-sized bags.

Indian Heaven Snacks

20 servings

Weight 1 serving (3 balls) = 3 ounces

No baking is needed to make these high-energy treats. They will keep fresh for more than a month.

1. Toast in a small skillet until lightly browned:

1/2 cup sesame seeds

Set aside.

2. Bring to a boil in a large skillet over medium heat:

1/2 cup packed brown sugar

1/2 cup honey

2 tablespoons canola oil

1/2 cup water

Reduce heat and simmer for 2 minutes.

3. Remove from heat. Stir in and mix thoroughly:

Continued ➡

1 cup peanut butter
1/2 cup whole wheat flour
2 1/2 cups rolled oats
1/2 cup wheat germ
1 1/2 cups any variety finely chopped nuts

4. Roll into balls the size of small walnuts; then roll them in the toasted sesame seeds.

5. Set on plates, cover, and chill in refrigerator for several hours, or until they are firm. Store in individual serving-sized bags at room temperature.

Puma Bars
8 servings
Weight 1 serving (1 bar) = 4 ounces

1. Preheat oven to 350 degrees [F]. Oil a 10-by-6-inch baking pan.

2. Heat in a large, heavy saucepan over medium heat:
    1/3 cup canola oil
    When the oil is hot, add:
    2/3 cup pecan pieces
    Cook, stirring, for 3 minutes, or until light brown. Remove from heat.

3. Add and beat well:
    1 1/4 cups packed brown sugar
    1 1/4 teaspoons vanilla extract
    2 eggs
    3/4 cup whole wheat flour
    1/4 cup unbleached white flour
    2 tablespoons wheat germ
    1 teaspoon baking powder
    1 cup butterscotch morsels

4. Pour into pan and bake for 18 minutes, or until just set. Cool completely on a wire rack before cutting into 8 bars. Store bars in individual serving-sized bags.

Karen's Oatmeal Breakfast Cake
16 servings
Weight 1 serving = 4 ounces

1. Stir together in a large, heatproof bowl:
    1 cup rolled oats
    1/2 cup canola oil
    1 cup honey
    1 1/3 cups boiling water
    Let cool for 20 minutes.

2. Preheat oven to 350 degrees [F]. Oil a 10-by-13-inch casserole dish.

3. Add to the oat mixture:
    2 eggs
    3/4 cup yogurt
    1/2 cup packed brown sugar
    1 1/2 cups whole wheat flour
    2 tablespoons toasted wheat germ
    2 tablespoons brewer's yeast
    2 tablespoons instant dry milk
    2 teaspoons ground cinnamon
    1 teaspoon baking powder
    1/2 teaspoon baking soda
    1 cup any variety nuts, finely chopped
    Beat well.

4. Pour the batter into the prepared dish.

5. Bake for 25 minutes, or until toothpick inserted in center comes out clean.

6. Let cool completely before cutting into 16 servings. Store servings in individual bags.

Multigrain Sunflower Rolls
8 servings
Weight 1 serving (2 rolls) = 4 ounces

These rolls will keep for a week.

1. Place in a heavy bowl:
    1 1/2 cups rolled oats
    2 tablespoons packed brown sugar
    1 tablespoon canola oil
    1 tablespoon dark molasses
    1/8 teaspoon salt

2. Add:
    1 1/2 cups boiling water
    Stir; then cool for 20 minutes.

3. Mix together in a cup:
    3/4 cup very warm water
    2 tablespoons (2 packages) active dry yeast
    Let stand for 20 minutes; then stir the yeast into the oat mixture.

4. Stir and knead in gradually:
    1 cup whole wheat flour
    1 cup unbleached white flour
    1/2 cup rye flour
    1/2 cup gluten flour
    1/4 cup hulled sunflower seeds

5. Cover and let rise in a warm place for 45 minutes, or until doubled in bulk.

6. Oil a baking sheet. Divide dough into 16 pieces. Shape into rolls and place them on the baking sheet. Let rise for 20 minutes.

7. Preheat oven to 350 degrees [F].

8. Bake rolls for 15 minutes. Let cool completely on wire racks before storing them in individual serving-sized bags.

Baked Potato Chips
2 servings
Weight 1 dried serving (1 potato) = 2 ounces

These are easy to make and delightfully not greasy.

1. Preheat oven to 350 degrees [F].

2. Lightly oil two large baking sheets.

3. Cut into 1/16-inch-thick slices:
    2 large baking potatoes, scrubbed but not peeled
    Place the slices in a single layer on the baking sheets. Sprinkle them with:
    1/2 teaspoon salt
    1/4 teaspoon ground white pepper

4. Bake for 20 to 30 minutes, or until golden brown, turning them once while baking.

5. Let cool completely before storing them in individual serving-sized bags.

Variation: Spicy Potato Chips

Along with the salt and pepper, sprinkle the potato slices with:
    1/8 teaspoon cayenne pepper
    1/4 teaspoon chili powder

—From *Backpack Gourmet*

Outdoor Kitchen Cleanup
Claudia Pearson

Leaving no trace in the kitchen starts before you leave town. Part of planning ahead and preparing involves repackaging your food to minimize potential litter as well as to lighten your load. With proper meal planning and careful cooking (no burning), you can eliminate most leftovers. But if you do end up with extra cooked food, use discretion and eat it at another meal or carry it out. Don't count on digging a hole or using a fire to dispose of kitchen waste or non-burnable trash such as Styrofoam or aluminum. Trash has no place in the backcountry. Pack out what you packed in.

Certain waste—including waste water from cooking and washing—cannot be packed out. This water should be scattered widely, at least 200 feet away from any water source and far away from campsites. Remove all food particles from the water before disposing of it (a small strainer is good for this), and pack them out with your trash. One exception to this is fish guts. In some parts of Wyoming, the recommended procedure for disposing of fish parts is to toss them back into the same water source from which they came. This helps to prevent the spread of whirling disease. Be sure to toss the viscera into deep (and, if possible, moving) water to help scatter the parts. For other parts of the country, check with local game and fish experts for recommendations. And remember, ask permission to hunt and fish on private property.

Natural scrubbers for cleaning can be pinecones, pine needles, sand, or snow.

At NOLS, we use soap only for washing hands before food preparation. We clean the dishes with nature's scrub brushes—sand, pinecones, snow, pine needles, and bunches of grass—and give them a good rinse with boiling water just prior to eating. With this method, no soapy dishwater is added to the environment, and it also avoids stomach upsets caused by soap residue on the dishes. However, if you want to use soap, carry a small bottle of biodegradable soap and use a few drops for cleaning. Do your dishes at least 200 feet away from any water source to prevent contaminating the water. Remember, even biodegradable soap is a foreign chemical in aquatic environments and should be used sparingly and far away from water sources.

—From *NOLS Cookery*

Continued ➡

Food Storage on the Trail

Linda Frederick Yaffe

When loading your backpack each morning of your trip, put that day's snacks in an easy-to-reach outside pack pocket. Store that day's lunch near the top of the pack for easy midday access. Stow all of the rest of your food deep in the cool, dark interior of your pack.

Arriving at a possible campsite, take a few minutes to examine the area before you unpack. Choose a sleeping area; then choose a safe, protected cooking area that is at least 100 feet from your sleeping area, preferably downwind. Pick a third area for dining that is 100 feet away from your cooking and sleeping areas. Find a fourth area well away from the other three for food storage. When you travel in bear country, you will be glad you are carrying home-dried one-pot meals; since they are not cooked in the field, but merely heated, they create little odor. Nothing attracts a bear more than odiferous fresh foods such as bacon cooking on an open fire. Eliminating cooking and open fires makes your campsite far less noticeable to wild creatures.

Keep your camp spotless. Never leave food or garbage unattended unless it is properly stored. The most secure method of storage is portable bearproof aluminum containers, available for sale or rent from camping stores and national parks. Some popular backcountry campsites are equipped with stationary bearproof lockers. Before you pack in, check with the rangers about the availability of lockers and ask about recent bear problems. Violation of food storage regulations can result in huge fines, injury to campers, and might cause a troublesome bear to be destroyed.

In bear country, you will find trees. These trees can be used to counterbalance your food. Find a lone tree limb that is seventeen to twenty feet off the ground. It must be healthy and strong enough to support your bags of food but not thick enough to hold a young bear. Divide all of your food and all other odiferous items (toothpaste, soap, scented lotions, garbage) into two sturdy nylon bags of roughly equal weight. Tie a rock to the end of a fifty-foot length of nylon cord. Throw the rock over your chosen tree limb, then remove the rock and tie the first food bag to the end of the cord. Pull the first bag all the way up to the limb. Tie the second bag to the cord, as high as you can reach. Tie a big loop or two of cord hanging from the second bag. Use the entire cord so no end is dangling. Using a long downed branch or your walking stick, push the second bag up so that the two bags are hanging

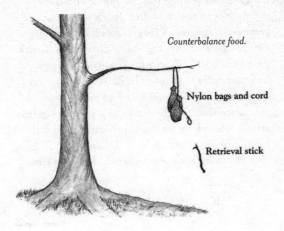

Counterbalance food.

Nylon bags and cord

Retrieval stick

If you don't have water, don't eat! It takes water to process food, and without water to replace what is lost, you'll accelerate the dehydration process.

Overcome food aversions. If you can't stomach eating a bug, cook it in a stew. In a survival setting bugs may be your only source of carbohydrates, protein, and fats.

Avoid mushrooms. Mushrooms have virtually no nutritional value, and since so many are poisonous, the risk is not worth the benefit.

—From *Wilderness Survival*

side by side. The bags should hang twelve to fifteen feet above the ground. When you are ready to retrieve the bags, hook the loop of cord with your stick and gently pull the bags down.

When camped at the edge of or above the treeline, where trees are stunted and signs of bears are nil, cache your food well away from your tent, cooking, and dining areas. Bag your backpack in a large plastic bag and cache it a few feet off the ground on a boulder. Weight the pack with rocks. This may keep bears from seeing or smelling the food. Whichever food storage method you choose, keep your food well away from your sleeping area.

—From *Backpack Gourmet*

Food for Survival: The Need for Food

Greg Davenport

One of the biggest problems with long-term survival is meeting your nutritional requirements. Many backcountry enthusiasts focus on meat as their main source of food and often overlook all the other supplies Mother Nature has to provide. The ideal diet has five basic food groups:

Carbohydrates: easily digested food that provides rapid energy; most often found in fruits, vegetables, and whole grains.

Fats: slowly digested food that provides long lasting energy that is normally utilized once the carbohydrates are gone; most often found in butter, cheese, oils, nuts, eggs, and animal fats. In cold environments it isn't uncommon for the natives to eat fats before bed, believing they will help keep them warm throughout the night.

Protein: helps with the building of body cells; most often found in fish, meat, poultry, and blood.

Vitamins: provide no calories but aid in the body's daily function and growth. Vitamins occur in most foods and when you maintain a well-balanced diet you will rarely become depleted.

Minerals: provide no calories but aid with building and repairing the skeletal system and regulating the body's normal growth. Like vitamins these needs are met when a well-balanced diet is followed. In addition to food, minerals are often present in our water.

The five major food groups and a sixth "use sparingly group" make up your basic dietary regimen:

- Fats, oils, and sweets—use sparingly.
- Milk and cheese group—two to three servings a day.
- Meat, poultry, fish, dry beans, eggs, and nuts group—two to three servings a day.
- Vegetable group—three to five servings a day.
- Fruit group—two to four servings a day.
- Bread, cereal, rice, and pasta group—six to eleven servings a day.

No one group is more important than the other—you need them all for good health. A healthy diet begins with plenty of grains, generous amounts of vegetables and fruits, and a smaller amount of meats and dairy products.

—From *Wilderness Living*

Animals as Potential Food Sources

U.S. Army

Unless you have the chance to take large game, concentrate your efforts on the smaller animals, due to their abundance. The smaller animal species are also easier to prepare. You must not know all the animal species that are suitable as food. Relatively few are poisonous, and they make a smaller list to remember. What is important is to learn the habits and behavioral patterns of classes of animals. For example, animals that are excellent choices for trapping, those that inhabit a particular range and occupy a den or nest, those that have somewhat fixed feeding areas, and those that have trails leading from one area to another. Larger, herding animals, such as elk or caribou, roam vast areas and are somewhat more difficult to trap. Also, you must understand the food choices of a particular species.

You can, with relatively few exceptions, eat anything that crawls, swims, walks, or flies. The first obstacle is overcoming your natural aversion to a particular food source. Historically, people in starvation situations have resorted to eating everything imaginable for nourishment. A person who ignores an otherwise healthy food source due to a personal bias, or because he feels it is unappetizing, is risking his own survival. Although it may prove difficult at first, a survivor must eat what is available to maintain his health.

Insects

The most abundant life-form on earth, insects are easily caught. Insects provide 65 to 80 percent protein compared to 20 percent for beef. This fact makes insects an important, if not overly appetizing, food source. Insects to avoid include all adults that sting or bite, hairy or brightly colored insects, and caterpillars and insects that have a pungent odor. Also avoid

Continued ➡

spiders and common disease carriers such as ticks, flies, and mosquitoes.

Rotting logs lying on the ground are excellent places to look for a variety of insects including ants, termites, beetles, and grubs, which are beetle larvae. Do not overlook insect nests on or in the ground. Grassy areas, such as fields, are good areas to search because the insects are easily seen. Stones, boards, or other materials lying on the ground provide the insects with good nesting sites. Check these sites. Insect larvae are also edible. Insects such as beetles and grasshoppers that have a hard outer shell will have parasites. Cook them before eating. Remove any wings and barbed legs also. You can eat most insects raw. The taste varies from one species to another. Wood grubs are bland, while some species of ants store honey in their bodies, giving them a sweet taste. You can grind a collection of insects into a paste. You can mix them with edible vegetation. You can cook them to improve their taste.

Worms

Worms (*Annelidea*) are an excellent protein source. Dig for them in damp humus soil or watch for them on the ground after a rain. After capturing them, drop them into clean, potable water for a few minutes. The worms will naturally purge or wash themselves out, after which you can eat them raw.

Crustaceans

Freshwater shrimp range in size from 0.25 centimeter up to 2.5 centimeters. They can form rather large colonies in mats of floating algae or in mud bottoms of ponds and lakes.

Crayfish are akin to marine lobsters and crabs. You can distinguish them by their hard exoskeleton and five pairs of legs, the front pair having oversized pincers. Crayfish are active at night, but you can locate them in the daytime by looking under and around stones in streams. You can also find them by looking in the soft mud near the chimneylike breathing holes of their nests. You can catch crayfish by tying bits of offal or internal organs to a string. When the crayfish grabs the bait, pull it to shore before it has a chance to release the bait.

You find saltwater lobsters, crabs, and shrimp from the surf's edge out to water 10 meters deep. Shrimp may come to a light at night where you can scoop them up with a net. You can catch lobsters and crabs with a baited trap or a baited hook. Crabs will come to bait placed at the edge of the surf, where you can trap or net them. Lobsters and crabs are nocturnal and caught best at night.

Mollusks

This class includes octopuses and freshwater and saltwater shellfish such as snails, clams, mussels, bivalves, barnacles, periwinkles, chitons, and sea urchins. You find bivalves similar to our freshwater mussel and terrestrial and aquatic snails worldwide under all water conditions.

EDIBLE MOLLUSKS

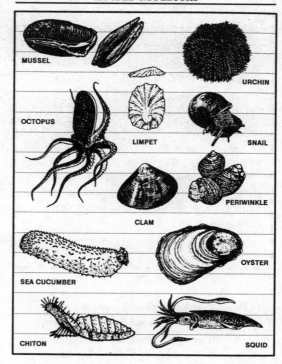

River snails or freshwater periwinkles are plentiful in rivers, streams, and lakes of northern coniferous forests. These snails may be pencil point or globular in shape.

In fresh water, look for mollusks in the shallows, especially in water with a sandy or muddy bottom. Look for the narrow trails they leave in the mud or for the dark elliptical slit of their open valves.

Near the sea, look in the tidal pools and the wet sand. Rocks along beaches or extending as reefs into deeper water often bear clinging shellfish. Snails and limpets cling to rocks and seaweed from the low water mark upward. Large snails, called chitons, adhere tightly to rocks above the surf line.

Mussels usually form dense colonies in rock pools, on logs, or at the base of boulders.

Steam, boil, or bake mollusks in the shell.

> **Caution**
> Mussels may be poisonous in tropical zones during the summer!

They make excellent stews in combination with greens and tubers.

> **Caution**
> Do not eat shellfish that are not covered by water at high tide!

Fish

Fish represent a good source of protein and fat. They offer some distinct advantages to the survivor or evader. They are usually more abundant than mammal wildlife, and the ways to get them are silent. To be successful at catching fish, you must know their habits. For instance, fish tend to feed heavily before a storm. Fish are not likely to feed after a storm when the water is muddy and swollen. Light often attracts fish at night. When there is a heavy current, fish will

rest in places where there is an eddy, such as near rocks. Fish will also gather where there are deep pools, under overhanging brush, and in and around submerged foliage, logs, or other objects that offer them shelter.

There are no poisonous freshwater fish. However, the catfish species has sharp, needle-like protrusions on its dorsal fins and barbels. These can inflict painful puncture wounds that quickly become infected.

Cook all freshwater fish to kill parasites. Also cook saltwater fish caught within a reef or within the influence of a freshwater source as a precaution. Any marine life obtained farther out in the sea will not contain parasites because of the saltwater environment. You can eat these raw.

Certain saltwater species of fish have poisonous flesh. In some species the poison occurs seasonally; in others, it is permanent. Examples of poisonous saltwater fish are the porcupine fish, triggerfish, cowfish, thorn fish, oilfish, red snapper, jack, and puffer. The barracuda, while not actually poisonous itself, may transmit ciguatera (fish poisoning) if eaten raw.

FISH WITH POISONOUS FLESH

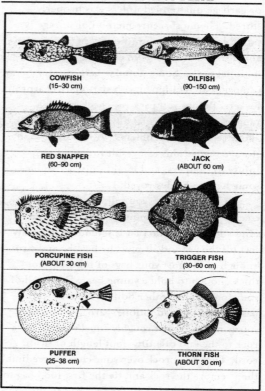

COWFISH (15–30 cm)
OILFISH (90–150 cm)
RED SNAPPER (60–90 cm)
JACK (ABOUT 60 cm)
PORCUPINE FISH (ABOUT 30 cm)
TRIGGER FISH (30–60 cm)
PUFFER (25–38 cm)
THORN FISH (ABOUT 30 cm)

Amphibians

Frogs and salamanders are easily found around bodies of fresh water. Frogs seldom move from the safety of the water's edge. At the first sign of danger, they plunge into the water and bury themselves in the mud and debris. There are few poisonous species of frogs. Avoid any brightly colored frog or one that has a distinct "X" mark on its back. Do not confuse toads with frogs. You normally find toads in drier environments. Several species of toads secrete a poisonous substance through their skin as a defense against attack. Therefore, to avoid poisoning, do not handle or eat toads.

Salamanders are nocturnal. The best time

Continued ➡

to catch them is at night using a light. They can range in size from a few centimeters to well over 60 centimeters in length. Look in water around rocks and mud banks for salamanders.

Reptiles

Reptiles are a good protein source and relatively easy to catch. You should cook them, but in an emergency, you can eat them raw. Their raw flesh may transmit parasites, but because reptiles are cold-blooded, they do not carry the blood diseases of the warm-blooded animals.

The box turtle is a commonly encountered turtle that you should not eat. It feeds on poisonous mushrooms and may build up a highly toxic poison in its flesh. Cooking does not destroy this toxin. Avoid the hawks-bill turtle, found in the Atlantic Ocean, because of its poisonous thorax gland. Poisonous snakes, alligators, crocodiles, and large sea turtles present obvious hazards to the survivor.

Birds

All species of birds are edible, although the flavor will vary considerably. You may skin fish-eating birds to improve their taste. As with any wild animal, you must understand birds' common habits to have a realistic chance of capturing them. You can take pigeons, as well as some other species, from their roost at night by hand. During the nesting season, some species will not leave the nest even when approached. Knowing where and when the birds nest makes catching them easier. Birds tend to have regular flyways going from the roost to a feeding area, to water, and so forth. Careful observation should reveal where these flyways are and indicate good areas for catching birds in nets stretched across the flyways. Roosting sites and waterholes are some of the most promising areas for trapping or snaring.

Nesting birds present another food source—eggs. Remove all but two or three eggs from the clutch, marking the ones that you leave. The bird will continue to lay more eggs to fill the clutch. Continue removing the fresh eggs, leaving the ones you marked.

Mammals

Mammals are excellent protein sources and, for Americans, the most tasty food source. There are some drawbacks to obtaining mammals. In a hostile environment, the enemy may detect any traps or snares placed on land. The amount of injury an animal can inflict is in direct proportion to its size. All mammals have teeth and

ANIMALS AND FISH POISONOUS TO EAT
U.S. Army

Survival manuals often mention that the livers of polar bears are toxic due to their high concentrations of vitamin A. For this reason, we mention the chance of death after eating this organ. Another toxic meat is the flesh of the hawksbill turtle. You recognize them by their down-turned bill and yellow polka dots on their neck and front flippers. They weigh more than 275 kilograms and are unlikely to be captured.

Many fish living in reefs near shore, or in lagoons and estuaries, are poisonous to eat, though some are only seasonally dangerous. The majority are tropical fish; however, be wary of eating any unidentifiable fish wherever you are. Some predatory fish, such as barracuda and snapper, may become toxic if the fish they feed on in shallow waters are poisonous. The most poisonous types appear to have parrotlike beaks and hard shell-like skins with spines and often can inflate their bodies like balloons. However, at certain times of the year, indigenous populations consider the puffer a delicacy.

Blowfish. Blowfish or puffer (Tetraodontidae species) are more tolerant of cold water. You find them along tropical and temperate coasts worldwide, even in some of the rivers of Southeast Asia and Africa. Stout-bodied and round, many of these fish have short spines and can inflate themselves into a ball when alarmed or agitated. Their blood, liver, and gonads are so toxic that as little as 28 milligrams (1 ounce) can be fatal. These fish vary in color and size, growing up to 75 centimeters in length.

Triggerfish. The triggerfish (Balistidae species) occur in great variety, mostly in tropical seas. They are deep-bodied and compressed, resembling a seagoing pancake up to 60 centimeters in length, with large and sharp dorsal spines. Avoid them all, as many have poisonous flesh.

Barracuda. Although most people avoid them because of their ferocity, they occasionally eat barracuda (*Sphyraena barracuda*). These predators of mostly tropical seas can reach almost 1.5 meters in length and have attacked humans without provocation. They occasionally carry the poison ciguatera in their flesh, making them deadly if consumed.

Fish with Toxic Flesh

There are no simple rules to tell edible fish from those with poisonous flesh. The most common toxic fish are shown on page 168.

All of these fish contain various types of poisonous substances or toxins in their flesh and are dangerous to eat. They have the following common characteristics:

- Most live in shallow water around reefs or lagoons.
- Many have boxy or round bodies with hard shell-like skins covered with bony plates or spines. They have small parrotlike mouths, small gills, and small or absent belly fins. Their names suggest their shape.

In addition to the above fish and their characteristics, barracuda and red snapper fish may carry ciguatera, a toxin that accumulates in the systems of fish that feed on tropical marine reefs.

Without specific local information, take the following precautions:

- Be very careful with fish taken from normally shallow lagoons with sandy or broken coral bottoms. Reef-feeding species predominate and some may be poisonous.
- Avoid poisonous fish on the leeward side of an island. This area of shallow water consists of patches of living corals mixed with open spaces and may extend seaward for some distance. Many different types of fish inhabit these shallow waters, some of which are poisonous.
- Do not eat fish caught in any area where the water is unnaturally discolored. This may be indicative of plankton that cause various types of toxicity in plankton-feeding fish.
- Try fishing on the windward side or in deep passages leading from the open sea to the lagoon, but be careful of currents and waves. Live coral reefs drop off sharply into deep water and form a dividing line between the suspected fish of the shallows and the desirable deep-water species. Deepwater fish are usually not poisonous. You can catch the various toxic fish even in deep water. Discard all suspected reef fish, whether caught on the ocean or the reef side.

—From *Survival (Field Manual 21-76)*

Types of Birds	Frequent Nesting Places	Nesting Periods
Inland birds	Trees, woods, or fields	Spring and early summer in temperate and arctic regions; year round in the tropics
Cranes and herons	Mangrove swamps or high trees near water	Spring and early summer
Some species of owls	High trees	Late December through March
Ducks, geese, and swans	Tundra areas near ponds, rivers, or lakes	Spring and early summer in arctic regions
Some sea birds	Sandbars or low sand islands	Spring and early summer in temperate and arctic regions
Gulls, auks, murres, and cormorants	Steep rocky coasts	Spring and early summer in temperate and arctic regions

Continued →

nearly all will bite in self-defense. Even a squirrel can inflict a serious wound and any bite presents a serious risk of infection. Also, a mother can be extremely aggressive in defense of her young. Any animal with no route of escape will fight when cornered.

All mammals are edible; however, the polar bear and bearded seal have toxic levels of vitamin A in their livers. The platypus, native to Australia and Tasmania, is an egg-laying, semi-aquatic mammal that has poisonous glands. Scavenging mammals, such as the opossum, may carry diseases.

—From *Survival* (*Field Manual 21-76*)

Animal Food Sources: Arctic and Subarctic Regions
U.S. Army

There are several sources of food in the arctic and subarctic regions. The type of food—fish, animal, fowl, or plant—and the ease in obtaining it depend on the time of the year and your location.

Fish

During the summer months, you can easily get fish and other water life from coastal waters, streams, rivers, and lakes.

The North Atlantic and North Pacific coastal waters are rich in seafood. You can easily find crawfish, snails, clams, oysters, and king crab. In areas where there is a great difference between the high and low tide water levels, you can easily find

shellfish at low tide. Dig in the sand on the tidal flats. Look in tidal pools and on offshore reefs. In areas where there is a small difference between the high- and low-tide water levels, storm waves often wash shellfish onto the beaches.

The eggs of the spiny sea urchin that lives in the waters around the Aleutian Islands and southern Alaska are excellent food. Look for the sea urchins in tidal pools. Break the shell by placing it between two stones. The eggs are bright yellow in color.

Most northern fish and fish eggs are edible. Exceptions are the meat of the arctic shark and the eggs of the sculpins.

The bivalves, such as clams and mussels, are usually more palatable than spiral-shelled seafood, such as snails.

Warning

The black mussel, a common mollusk of the far north, may be poisonous in any season. Toxins sometimes found in the mussel's tissue are as dangerous as strychnine.

NUTRITIONAL VALUE OF BUGS
Greg Davenport   Illustration by Steven Davenport

Many cultures around the world eat bugs as part of their routine diet. Pan-fried locusts are considered a delicacy in Algeria and several Mexican states. In Malaysia bee larvae are considered a special treat.

Bugs are a great source of food.

Our phobia about eating bugs is unfortunate, as they provide ample amounts of protein, fats, carbohydrates, calcium, and iron. Compared with cattle, sheep, pigs, and chickens, bugs are far more cost effective to raise and have far fewer harmful effects related to their rearing. Although bugs are not harvested for food in the United States, those of us who purchase our foods at the store are eating them every day. The FDA allows certain levels of bugs to be present in various foods. The accepted standards are for up to 60 aphids in 3 1/2 ounces of broccoli, two to three fruit fly maggots in 200 grams of tomato juice, 100 insect fragments in 25 grams of curry powder, 74 mites in 100 grams

of canned mushrooms, 13 insect heads in 100 grams of fig paste, and 34 fruit fly eggs in every cup of raisins.

A study done by Jared Ostrem and John VanDyk for the entomology department of Iowa State University comparing the nutritional value of various bugs to that of lean ground beef and fish showed the following results pre 100 grams (see chart below).

Bugs can be found throughout the world, and they are easy to procure. In addition, the larvae and grubs of many are edible and easily found in rotten logs, underground, or under the bark of dead trees. Although a fair number of bugs can be eaten raw, it is best to cook them in order to avoid ingesting unwanted parasites. As a general rule, avoid bugs that carry disease (flies, mosquitoes, and ticks), poisonous insects (centipedes and spiders), and bugs that have fine hair, bright colors, and eight or more legs.

—From *Wilderness Survival*

	protein (g)	fats (g)	carbohydrates (g)	calcium (mg)	Iron (mg)
crickets	12.9	5.5	5.1	75.8	9.5
small grasshoppers	20.6	6.1	3.9	35.2	5.0
giant water beetles	19.8	8.3	2.1	43.5	13.6
red ants	13.9	3.5	2.9	47.8	5.7
silkworm pupae	9.6	5.6	2.3	41.7	1.8
termites	14.2	n/a	n/a	0.050	35.5
weevils	6.7	n/a	n/a	0.186	13.1
lean ground beef (baked)	24.0	18.3	0	9.0	2.09
fish (broiled cod)	22.95	0.86	0	0.031	1.0

SNAKES AS FOOD
Greg Davenport
Illustration by Steven Davenport and Ken Davenport

All poisonous and nonpoisonous freshwater and land snakes are edible and can be located almost anywhere there is cover. For best results, hunt them in the early morning or evening hours. To catch or kill a snake, first stun it with a thrown rock or stick, and then use the forked end of a long stick to pin its head to the ground. Kill it with a rock, knife, or another stick. Be careful throughout this procedure, especially when dealing with poisonous snakes. Snakes can be cooked in any fashion, but all should be skinned and gutted. To skin a snake, severe its head (avoid accidental poisoning by burying the head), and peel back its skin until you can grab it and pull it down, inside out, the length of the snake. If you can't pull it free, make a cut down the length of the snake to help you free the skin. The entrails will usually come out during this process; if not, grab them at the top and pull them down to remove them.

—From *Wilderness Survival*

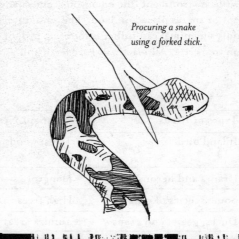
Procuring a snake using a forked stick.

Continued ➡

COOKING AND EATING IN COLD WEATHER: U.S. ARMY TIPS
U.S. Army

Importance of Balanced Meals

… The tendency to be lazy about preparing and eating satisfactory morning and evening meals before and after a hard day on the trail must be avoided, since it is exceedingly detrimental to continued good health. After having been without normal supplies for a period of time, it is essential that men be provided with a balanced meal containing the three basic food requirements (fats, protein, and carbohydrates). When possible and especially when troops are involved in rigorous activity, it may be desirable to feed four times daily. A desirable feeding plan would be the normal heavy breakfast meal, a light midmorning meal, a light afternoon meal, with the supper meal being the main meal of the day. The midmorning and midafternoon meal should consist of foods high in carbohydrates and include a hot liquid. Concentrated foods found in some special and survival rations are suitable for this purpose. Hot soup or tea are most desirable for the liquid. The evening meal should be heavily fortified with protein and eaten just before going to sleep. This heavy protein meal will increase body combustion above basal level, resulting in what is known as specific dynamic heat. This increase in the output of heat within the body also aids in keeping the individual warm while sleeping. If awakened by cold a small snack eaten inside the sleeping bag may increase heat production enough to permit further comfortable sleep.

Preparation

Meals must be prepared efficiently and as quickly as possible. Areas sheltered from the wind should be chosen for stoves or fires. A few blocks of snow or ice or a hole dug in the snow will serve as a windbreak and provide for more efficient use of fires. Heating tablets are not efficient in extremely cold weather accompanied by high winds. Individuals may have to prepare and eat one item at a time, but a hot meal will be worth the effort.

Canned foods are cooked and require little heat to make them edible. Overcooking will waste fuel. The juices in canned vegetables are tasty, and contain vitamins and minerals. Drinking them will conserve the water supply. Cans must be punctured or opened before heating by open fires or stoves. Failure to do this may result in an explosion. No puncturing is needed if the can is submerged in water during the heating process.

Canned rations, either frozen or thawed, can best be heated by immersion in boiling water. This water can then be used for making tea, coffee, or soups and for washing soiled utensils or personal hygiene.

—From *Basic Cold Weather Manual* (*Field Manual 31-70*)

Ptarmigans, owls, Canadian jays, grouse, and ravens are the only birds that remain in the arctic during the winter. They are scarce north of the tree line. Ptarmigans and owls are as good for food as any game bird. Ravens are too thin to be worth the effort it takes to catch them. Ptarmigans, which change color to blend with their surroundings, are hard to spot. Rock ptarmigans travel in pairs and you can easily approach them. Willow ptarmigans live among willow clumps in bottomlands. They gather in large flocks and you can easily snare them. During the summer months all arctic birds have a 2- to 3-week molting period during which they cannot fly and are easy to catch. Use one of the techniques described in Chapter 8 to catch them.

Skin and butcher game while it is still warm. If you do not have time to skin the game, at least remove its entrails, musk glands, and genitals before storing. If time allows, cut the meat into usable pieces and freeze each separately so that you can use the pieces as needed. Leave the fat on all animals except seals. During the winter, game freezes quickly if left in the open. During the summer, you can store it in underground ice holes.

—From *Survival* (*Field Manual 21-76*)

Animal Food Sources: the Seashore
U.S. Army

Obtaining food along a seashore should not present a problem.

There is a great variety of animal life that can supply your need for food in this type of survival situation.

Mollusks

Mussels, limpets, clams, sea snails, octopuses, squids, and sea slugs are all edible. Shellfish will usually supply most of the protein eaten by coastal survivors. Avoid the blue-ringed octopus and cone shells. Also beware of "red tides" that make mollusks poisonous. Apply the edibility test on each species before eating.

The sea cucumber is another edible sea animal. Inside its body are five long white muscles that taste much like clam meat.

In early summer, smelt spawn in the beach surf. Sometimes you can scoop them up with your hands.

You can often find herring eggs on the seaweed in midsummer. Kelp, the long ribbon-like seaweed, and other smaller seaweed that grow among offshore rocks are also edible.

Sea Ice Animals

You find polar bears in practically all arctic coastal regions, but rarely inland. Avoid them if possible. They are the most dangerous of all bears. They are tireless, clever hunters with good sight and an extraordinary sense of smell. If you must kill one for food, approach it cautiously. Aim for the brain; a bullet elsewhere will rarely kill one. Always cook polar bear meat before eating it.

Caution
Do not eat polar bear liver as it contains a toxic concentration of vitamin A.

Earless seal meat is some of the best meat available. You need considerable skill, however, to get close enough to an earless seal to kill it. In spring, seals often bask on the ice beside their breathing holes. They raise their heads about every 30 seconds, however, to look for their enemy, the polar bear.

To approach a seal, do as the Eskimos do—stay downwind from it, cautiously moving closer while it sleeps. If it moves, stop and imitate its movements by lying flat on the ice, raising your head up and down, and wriggling your body slightly. Approach the seal with your body sideways to it and your arms close to your body so that you look as much like another seal as possible. The ice at the edge of the breathing hole is usually smooth and at an incline, so the least movement of the seal may cause it to slide into the water. Therefore, try to get within 22 to 45 meters of the seal and kill it instantly (aim for the brain). Try to reach the seal before it slips into the water. In winter, a dead seal will usually float, but it is difficult to retrieve from the water.

Keep the seal blubber and skin from coming into contact with any scratch or broken skin you may have. You could get "spekk-finger," that is, a reaction that causes the hands to become badly swollen.

Keep in mind that where there are seals, there are usually polar bears, and polar bears have stalked and killed seal hunters.

You can find porcupines in southern subarctic regions where there are trees. Porcupines feed on bark; if you find tree limbs stripped bare, you are likely to find porcupines in the area.

SALTWATER CRAYFISH AND LOBSTER
Greg Davenport Illustration by Steven Davenport

Saltwater crayfish and lobster are found on the ocean bottom in 10 to 30 feet of water. These crustaceans behave similarly to the freshwater crabs and crayfish and

Crustaceans are a great source of food but in some instances may be poisonous.

can be procured using the same techniques. If you find yourself on land next to a tropical reef, avoid saltwater crabs. Many there are poisonous.

—From *Wilderness Survival*

Continued ➡

Worms

Coastal worms are generally edible, but it is better to use them for fish bait. Avoid bristle worms that look like fuzzy caterpillars. Also avoid tubeworms that have sharp-edged tubes. Arrowworms, alias amphioxus, are not true worms. You find them in the sand and are excellent either fresh or dried.

Crabs, Lobsters, and Barnacles

These animals are seldom dangerous to man and are an excellent food source. The pincers of larger crabs or lobsters can crush a man's finger. Many species have spines on their shells, making it preferable to wear gloves when catching them. Barnacles can cause scrapes or cuts and are difficult to detach from their anchor, but the larger species are an excellent food source.

Sea Urchins

These are common and can cause painful injuries when stepped on or touched. They are also a good source of food. Handle them with gloves, and remove all spines.

Sea Cucumbers

This animal is an important food source in the Indo-Pacific regions. Use them whole after evisceration or remove the five muscular strips that run the length of its body. Eat them smoked, pickled, or cooked.

—From *Survival (Field Manual 21-76)*

Food at Sea

Greg Davenport
Illustrations by Steven A. Davenport

You should be able to procure enough food while at sea to sustain your life for an extended period of time. As long as water is available, chow down.

Plants

Seaweed, which is easily found in all oceans, is a good source of protein, fiber, vitamins, and minerals. Although a small percentage of the slender-branching seaweeds can cause an upset stomach, most are edible. The broad-leaved seaweed, which looks like lettuce leaf, is not know to cause irritation and can often be found floating in the ocean. These floating islands of seaweed also provide a haven for small fish and crabs, which can be easily dislodged with a good shake. Seaweed should be rinsed, as long as you have enough freshwater, and may be eaten raw or dried until crisp.

Broad-leaved seaweed.

Plankton

Plankton is a term used for an assortment of marine and freshwater organisms that drift on or near the surface of the water. Since these organisms are too small to swim, their movement depends largely on tides, currents, and winds. Although plankton is more common near land, it can be found anywhere. There are three types of plankton:

- Phytoplankton—microscopic plants and bacteria
- Zooplankton—microscopic animals
- Macrozooplankton—larger fish eggs and larvae and pelagic invertebrates

All types of plankton are high in protein, carbohydrates, and fats and should not be overlooked as a food Source. Since they are located close to the water's surface, catching plankton is as simple as towing a net behind the raft. For beat results, the net should be moving faster than the current. Plankton has a grayish paste-like appearance and, depending on the source, can take on a multitude of flavors. It can be eaten fresh or dried and crushed. Crushing is a good option if a lot of spines are noted in the fresh plankton.

During warm seasons, various forms of phytoplankton produce toxins (secondary to their rapid reproduction and large numbers) that lead to a change in water color called "red tide." The toxins are harmful to both marine and human life, and many are quite potent and can be potentially fatal. In most instances, it is safe to eat fish, crabs, and shrimp during a red tide as long as you didn't find the fish sick or dead and you only eat the meat (fillet or muscle). Shellfish (oysters, clams, mussels, whelks, scallops, etc.) accumulate red tide toxins in their tissues. Do not eat these during or within a month of red tide. Ingesting these toxins can lead to paralytic shellfish poisoning, which can be a life-threatening illness. Better safe than sorry: Avoid eating fish or shellfish during red tide.

Barnacles

Given enough time, barnacles will appear on the bottom of your raft. Although they have a shell-like covering and look like mollusks, barnacles are crustaceans (related to lobsters, crabs, and shrimp). Newborn barnacles feed on plankton and in their larval stage look like tiny shrimp. As they grow, they let the currents carry them while they look for a place to build their shell-like home. If the life raft seems suitable, and it will, the barnacle secures itself to the surface using a self-made glue-like substance and then builds its home. Since they attach to the bottom of the raft, they are difficult to harvest and could actually result in raft damage. The best way to avoid this is to float sheet plastic around the raft. Barnacles will attach to the plastic, which makes them much easier to access. The plastic will also serve as a shark rub, reducing any potential problems related to sharks rubbing up against the side of the raft.

Turtles

Turtles are found in water throughout the temperate and tropic regions of the world. Of the more than 250 species of marine turtles, only about 5 are considered poisonous. Although the cause of their potentially fatal poison is unknown, many believe it is related to their ingestion of poisonous marine algae. Poisonous turtles are primarily found in the tropical and subtropical seas, especially in the warmer months. Almost 50 percent of those who eat this poison will die, and there is no way to tell if a turtle is poisonous or not. If you decide to throw caution to the wind and eat a turtle, never eat the liver since it has a high concentration of vitamin A, which poses a risk to you. The smaller turtles can be clubbed or perhaps caught with fishing line. To eat the turtle, you must remove the shell, which can be done from its belly side. Don't discard the shell as it will provide for many improvising needs.

Fish

Because fish are commonly found in almost all sources of water, you should put out lines to catch them. Be sure you have an assortment of fishing tackle in your survival kit.

Edibility of Fish

Most fish are edible, but not all are! As a general rule, deep-water fish are usually not poisonous. However, you can catch toxic fish in deep water, so you have no guarantee. To help decrease your chances of ingesting a poisonous fish, know these basic rules:

1. Fish with poisonous flesh commonly have bodies with a boxed or round appearance, hard shell-like skin, and bony plates or spines. They also often have small parrot-like mouths, small gills, and small or absent belly fins. (See illustration.)

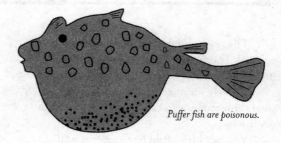
Puffer fish are poisonous.

2. Barracuda and red snapper have been known to carry ciguatera, which although poisonous to humans is usually not fatal. It is caused by eating fish that have accumulated these toxins through their diet. Fish that live around shallow waters or lagoons pose the greatest risk. The toxins originate from several dinoflagellate (algae) species, which are known to cause red tides.

3. Avoid fish that have slimy bodies, bad odor, suspicious color (gills should be pink and scales pronounced), and flesh that remains indented after being pressed on.

4. Do not eat fish organs as many are poisonous.

5. Avoid fish during or around red tide!

—From *Surviving Coastal and Open Water*

Continued ➡

Cooking and Preserving Wild Meat

Greg Davenport
Illustrations by Steven Davenport and Ken Davenport

Cooking Methods

In addition to killing parasites and bacteria, cooking your food can make it more palatable. There are many different ways to prepare game, and some are better than others from a nutritional standpoint. Boiling is best, but only if you drink the broth, which contains many of the nutrients that are cooked out of the food. Fried foods taste great, but frying is probably the worst way to cook something, as a lot of nutrients are lost during the process.

Boiling

Boiling is the best cooking method. If a container is not available, it may be necessary to improvise one. You might use a rock with a bowl-shaped center, but avoid rocks with high moisture content, as they may explode. A thick, hollowed-out piece of wood that can be suspended over the fire may also serve as a container. If your container cannot be suspended over the fire, stone boiling is another option. Use a hot bed of coals to heat up numerous stones. Get them really hot. Set your container of food and water close to your bed of hot stones, and add rocks to it until the water begins to boil. To keep the water boiling, cover the top with bark or another improvised lid, and keep it covered except when removing or adding stones. Don't expect a rolling rapid boil with this process, but a steady slow bubbling should occur.

Baking

Baking is the next preferred method of preparing meat to eat. There are several methods you can use to bake game.

Mud baking

When mud baking, you do not need to scale, skin, or pluck the fish or bird in advance since scales, skin, and feathers will come off the game when the dried mud is removed. Use mud that has a clay texture to it, and tightly seal the fish or bird in it. The tighter the seal, the better it will hold the juices and prevent the meat from drying out. A medium-size bird or trout will usually cook in about fifteen to twenty minutes, depending on the temperature of your coals.

Leaf baking

Wrapping your meat in a nonpoisonous green leaf and placing it on a hot bed of coals will protect, season, and cook the meat. When baking mussels and clams, seaweed is often used; when the shells open they're done. Avoid plants that have a bitter taste.

Underground baking

Underground baking is a good method of cooking larger meals since the dirt will hold the oven's heat. Dig a hole slightly larger than the meal you intend to cook; it needs to be big enough for your food, the base of rocks, and the covering. Line the bottom and sides with rocks, avoiding rocks with high moisture content, which may explode. Start a fire over them. To heat rocks that will be used on top of your food, place enough green branches over the hole to support another layer of rocks, leaving a space to add fuel to the fire. Once the green branches burn through and a hot bed of coals is present, remove the fallen rocks. Place green twigs onto the coals, followed by a layer of wetted green grass or nonpoisonous leaves. Add your meat and vegetables, and cover them with more wet grass or leaves, a thin layer of soil, and the extra hot rocks. The hole is then covered with dirt. Small meals will cook in one to two hours; large meals in five to six hours or perhaps days.

Frying

Place a flat rock on or next to the fire. Avoid rocks with high moisture content, as they may explode. Let it get hot, and cook on it as you would a frying pan.

Broiling

Broiling is ideal for cooking small game over hot coals. Before cooking the animal, sear its flesh with the flames from the fire. This will help keep the juices, containing vital nutrients, inside the animal. Next, run a nonpoisonous skewer—a branch that is small, straight, and strong—along the underside of the animal's backbone. Suspend the animal over the coals, using any means available.

Food Preservation

Keep It Alive

If possible, keep all animals alive until ready to consume. This ensures that the meat stays fresh. A small rodent or rabbit may attract big game, so be sure to protect it from becoming a coyote's meal instead of yours. This doesn't apply, of course, if your are using the rodent for bait.

Sun Drying

To sun-dry meat, you hang long, thin strips in the sun. To keep it out of other animals' reach, run snare wire or line between two trees. If using snare wire, skewer the line through the top of each piece of meat before attaching it to the second tree. If using other line, hang it first and then drape the strips of meat over it. For best results, the meat should not touch its other side or another piece. It may take one to multiple days to dry, depending on the humidity and temperature. You'll know it is done when the meat is dark and brittle.

Smoking

Smoke long, thin strips of meat in a smoker constructed using the following guidelines.

Build a 6-foot-tall tripod from three poles lashed together.

Attach snare wire or line around the three poles in a tiered fashion so that the lowest point is at least 2 feet above the ground.

If using snare wire, skewer it through the top of each slice of meat before extending it around the inside of the next pole. If using other line, hang it first and then drape the strips of meat over it. For best results, the meat should not touch its other side or another piece.

Cover the outer aspect of the tripod with any available material, such as a poncho. Avoid

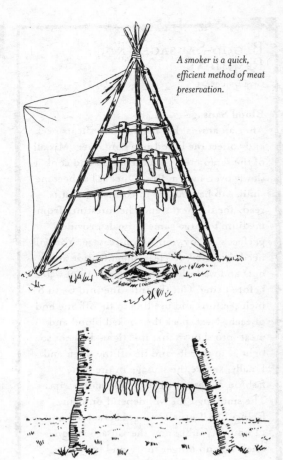

A smoker is a quick, efficient method of meat preservation.

Sun drying meat is an effective method of preserving it for later consumption.

contact between the outer covering and the meat. For proper ventilation, leave a small opening at the top of the tripod.

Gather an armload of green deciduous wood, such as alder, willow, or aspen. Prepare it by either breaking the branches into smaller pieces or cutting the bigger pieces into chips.

Build a fire next to the tripod. Once a good bed of coals develops, transfer them to the ground in the center of the smoker. Continue transferring coals as needed.

To smoke the meat, place small pieces or chips of green wood on the hot coals. Once the green wood begins to heat up, it should create a smoke. Since an actual fire will destroy the smoking process, monitor the wood to ensure that it doesn't flame up. If it does, put it out, but try to avoid disturbing the bed of coals too much. Keep adding chips until the meat is dark and brittle, about twenty-four to forty-eight hours. At this point it is done.

—From *Wilderness Survival*

Blood Sausage and Pemmican

Greg Davenport

Blood Sausage

After an animal has been killed, slit its neck and collect the blood in a container. Mix all of the scrap meat with the blood and cook it slowly over a warm fire. Once it has become similar to hamburger in consistency, it is ready for the next step. The intestines from medium to large game animals provide a perfect skin for your blood sausage. You will need, however, to clean them (inside and out) and wash them thoroughly in hot water before using. Cut the intestine into 6- to 8-inch sections and use line to tie off one end of each. Next, pack the cooked blood and meat into skin so that it is tight—but not so tight as to tear it—and tie off the open end. Finally, smoke the sausage in the same fashion as described above for meat strips. The smoking time will depend on many factors but it usually ranges between 6 and 12 hours. You'll know the sausage is done when it is no longer moist and has the consistency of store-bought sausage.

Pemmican

Making pemmican from dehydrated meat, dried berries, and suet tallow (animal fat most often taken from the loin and kidney area) creates an excellent meal for later use. Pound the berries into a paste, and dry, pounded jerky, and mix together with tallow. Roll the mixture into a ball and store in a sealed container out of animal and insect reach. In most cases, pemmican can be safely stored away for several months.

—From *Wilderness Living*

Cooking Fish

U.S. Army

Do not eat fish that appears spoiled. Cooking does not ensure that spoiled fish will be edible. Signs of spoilage are—

- Sunken eyes.
- Peculiar odor.
- Suspicious color. (Gills should be red to pink. Scales should be a pronounced shade of gray, not faded.)
- Dents stay in the fish's flesh after pressing it with your thumb.
- Slimy, rather than moist or wet body.
- Sharp or peppery taste.

Eating spoiled or rotten fish may cause diarrhea, nausea, cramps, vomiting, itching, paralysis, or a metallic taste in the mouth. These symptoms appear suddenly, one to six hours after eating. Induce vomiting if symptoms appear.

Fish spoils quickly after death, especially on a hot day. Prepare fish for eating as soon as possible after catching it. Cut out the gills and large blood vessels that lie near the spine. Gut fish that is more than 10 centimeters long. Scale or skin the fish.

You can impale a whole fish on a stick and cook it over an open fire. However, boiling the fish with the skin on is the best way to get the most food value. The fats and oil are under the skin and, by boiling, you can save the juices for broth. You can use any of the methods used to cook plant food to cook fish. Pack fish into a ball of clay and bury it in the coals of a fire until the clay hardens. Break open the clay ball to get to the cooked fish. Fish is done when the meat flakes off. If you plan to keep the fish for later, smoke or fry it. To prepare fish for smoking, cut off the head and remove the backbone.

—From *Survival (Field Manual 21-76)*

Improvised Cooking and Eating Utensils

U.S. Army

Many materials may be used to make equipment for the cooking, eating, and storing of food.

Bowls

Use wood, bone, horn, bark, or other similar material to make bowls. To make wooden bowls, use a hollowed out piece of wood that will hold your food and enough water to cook it in. Hang the wooden container over the fire and add hot rocks to the water and food. Remove the rocks as they cool and add more hot rocks until your food is cooked.

> **Caution**
> Do not use rocks with air pockets, such as limestone and sandstone. They may explode while heating in the fire.

You can also use this method with containers made of bark or leaves. However, these containers will burn above the waterline unless you keep them moist or keep the fire low.

A section of bamboo works very well, if you cut out a section between two sealed joints.

> **Caution**
> A sealed section of bamboo will explode if heated because of trapped air and water in the section.

Forks, Knives, and Spoons

Carve forks, knives, and spoons from nonresinous woods so that you do not get a wood resin aftertaste or do not taint the food. Nonresinous woods include oak, birch, and other hardwood trees.

Note: Do not use those trees that secrete a syrup or resinlike liquid on the bark or when cut.

Pots

You can make pots from turtle shells or wood. As described with bowls, using hot rocks in a hollowed out piece of wood is very effective. Bamboo is the best wood for making cooking containers.

To use turtle shells, first thoroughly boil the upper portion of the shell. Then use it to heat food and water over a flame.

Water Bottles

Make water bottles from the stomachs of larger animals. Thoroughly flush the stomach out with water, then tie off the bottom. Leave the top open, with some means of fastening it closed.

—From *Survival (Field Manual 21-76)*

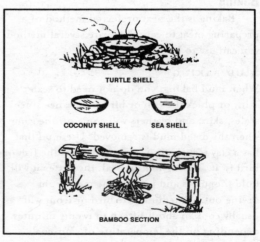

Containers for boiling food.

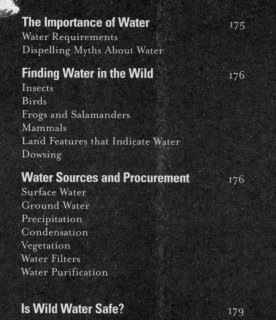

Drinking Water

The Importance of Water

Greg Davenport

Our bodies are composed of approximately 60 percent water, and it plays a vital role in our ability to get through a day. About 70 percent of our brains, 82 percent of our blood, and 90 percent of our lungs are composed of water. In our bloodstream, water helps to metabolize and transport vital elements, carbohydrates, and proteins that are necessary to fuel our bodies. Water also helps us dispose of our bodily waste.

Water Requirements

During a normal, nonstrenuous day, a healthy individual will need 2 to 3 quarts of water. When physically active or in extreme hot or cold environments, that same person would need at least 4 to 6 quarts of water a day. Being properly hydrated is one of the various necessities that wards off dehydration and environmental injuries. A person who's mildly dehydrated will develop excessive thirst and become irritable, weak, and nauseated. As the dehydration worsens, individuals will show a decrease in their mental capacity and coordination. At this point it will become difficult to accomplish even the simplest of tasks. The ideal situation would dictate that you don't ration your water. Instead you should ration sweat. If water is not available, don't eat.

Dispelling Myths About Water

Never Drink Urine!

By the time you think about drinking your urine, you are very dehydrated, and your urine would be full of salts and other waste products. For a hydrated person, urine is 95 percent water and 5 percent waste products like urea, uric acid, and salts. As you become dehydrated, the concentration of water decreases and the concentration of salts increases substantially. When you drink these salts, the body will draw upon its water reserves to help eliminate them, and you will actually lose more water than you might gain from your urine.

Never Drink Salt Water!

The concentrations of salts in salt water are often higher than those found in urine. When you drink these salts, the body will draw upon its water reserves to help eliminate them, and you will actually lose more water than you might gain from salt water.

Never Drink Blood!

Blood is composed of plasma, red blood cells, white blood cells, and platelets. Plasma, which composes about 55 percent of the blood's volume, is predominately water and salts, but it also carries a large number of important proteins (albumin, gamma globulin, and clotting factors) and small molecules (vitamins, minerals, nutrients, and waste products). Waste products produced during metabolism, such as urea and uric acid, are carried by the blood to the kidneys, where they are transferred from the blood into urine and eliminated from the body. The kidneys carefully maintain the salt concentration in plasma. When you drink blood, you are basically ingesting salts and proteins, and the body will draw upon its water reserves to help eliminate them. You will actually lose more water than you might gain from drinking blood.

—From *Wilderness Survival*

> ### SURVIVAL TIP
> Greg Davenport
>
> If you are thirsty, you are already dehydrated. Don't wait until it is too late. On average, you should drink at least 1/2 quart of water an hour when temperatures are below 100 degrees F and 1 quart an hour when the temperature is higher than that.
>
> —From *Surviving the Desert*

Finding Water in the Wild

Greg Davenport

Insects

If bees are present, water is usually within several miles of your location. Ants require water and will often place their nest close to a source. Swarms of mosquitoes and flies are a good indicator that water is close.

Birds

Birds frequently fly toward water at dawn and dusk in a direct, low flight path. This is especially true of birds that feed on grain, such as pigeons and finches. Flesh-eating birds can also be seen exhibiting this flight pattern, but their need for water isn't as great, and they don't require as many trips to the water source. Birds observed circling high in the air during the day are often doing it over water, as well.

Frogs and Salamanders

Most frogs and salamanders require water and if found are usually a good indicator that water is near.

Mammals

Like birds, mammals will frequently visit watering holes at dawn and dusk. This is especially true of mammals that eat a grain or grassy-type diet. Watching their travel patterns or evaluating mammal trails may help you find a water source. Trails that merge into one are usually a good pointer and following the merged trail often leads to water.

Land Features that Indicate Water

Drainages and valleys are a good water indicator, as are winding trails of deciduous trees. Green plush vegetation found at the base of a cliff or mountain may indicate a natural spring or underground source of water.

Dowsing

Dowsing, or witching, is a highly debated skill that some say helps them find water. Those who profess to have this skill use a forked stick (shaped like a Y) about 18 to 20 inches long and 1/8 to 1/4 inch in diameter. The most common branch used comes from a willow tree. The two ends of the Y are held in the hands, which are positioned palms up, while the dowser walks forward. The free end of the stick is supposed to react when it passes over water. This reaction may be toward or away from the body.

—From *Wilderness Living*

Water Sources and Procurement

Greg Davenport
Illustrations by Steven Davenport and Ken Davenport

Since your body needs a constant supply of water, you will eventually need to procure water from Mother Nature. Various sources include surface water, ground water, precipitation, condensation, plant sources, and man-made options that transform unusable sources.

Surface Water

Surface water may be obtained from rivers, ponds, lakes, or streams. It is usually easy to find and access, but because it is prone to contamination from protozoan, viruses, and bacteria, it should always be treated. If the water is difficult to access or has an unappealing flavor, consider using a seepage basin to filter the water. The filtering process is similar to what happens as ground water moves toward an aquifer. To create a seepage basin well, dig a 3-foot-wide hole

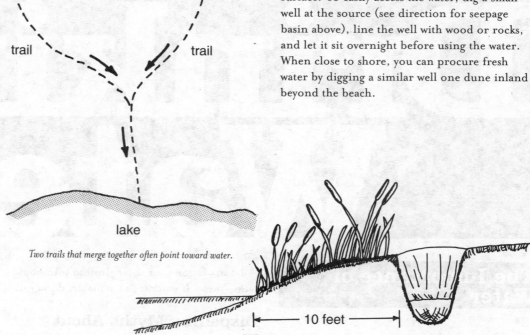

Two trails that merge together often point toward water.

Seepage basin well.

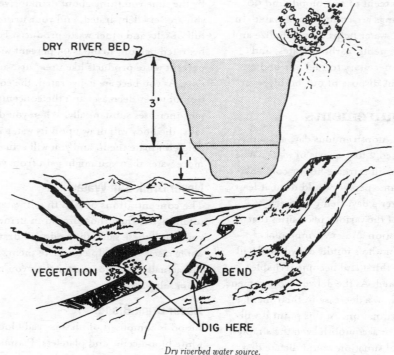

Dry riverbed water source.

about 10 feet from your water source. Dig it down until water begins to seep in, and then dig about another foot. Line the sides of your hole with wood or rocks so that no more mud will fall in, and let it sit overnight so the dirt and sand will settle.

Ground Water

Ground water is found under the earth's surface. This water is naturally filtered as it moves through the ground and into underground reservoirs called aquifers. Although treating this water may not be necessary, you should always err on the side of caution. Locating ground water is probably the most difficult part of accessing it. Look for things that seem out of place, such as a small area of green plush vegetation at the base of a hill or a bend in a dry riverbed that is surrounded by vegetation. A marshy area with a fair amount of cattail or hemlock growth may provide a clue that groundwater is available. Using these same clues, I have found natural springs in desert areas and running water less than 6 feet below the earth's surface. To easily access the water, dig a small well at the source (see direction for seepage basin above), line the well with wood or rocks, and let it sit overnight before using the water. When close to shore, you can procure fresh water by digging a similar well one dune inland beyond the beach.

Continued ➡

Precipitation

The four forms of precipitation are rain, snow, sea ice, and dew.

Rain

When it rains, you should sit out containers or dig a small hole and line it with plastic or any other nonporous material to catch the rainwater. After the rain has stopped, you may find water in crevasses, fissures, or low-lying areas.

Snow

Snow provides an excellent source of water, but it should not be eaten. The energy lost eating snow outweighs the benefit. Instead, melt it by suspending it over a fire or adding it to a partially full canteen and then shaking the container or placing it between the layers of your clothing and allowing your body's radiant heat to melt the snow. If you are with a large group, a snow-to-water generator can be created from a tripod and porous material. Create a large pouch by attaching the porous material to the tripod. Fill the pouch with snow, and place the tripod just close enough to the fire to start melting the snow. Use a container to collect the melted snow. Although the water will taste a little like smoke, this method provides an ongoing large and quick supply of water. If the sun is out, you could melt the snow by digging a cone-shaped hole, lining it with a tarp or similar nonporous material, and placing snow on the material at the top of the cone. As the snow melts, water will collect at the bottom of the cone.

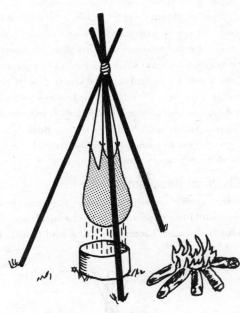

Snow water generators produce large volumes of water from snow.

Sea Ice

If using sea ice, you will want to make sure the ice is virtually free of any salts in the sea water. Sea ice that has rounded corners, shatters easily, and is bluish or black is usually safe to use. When in doubt, however, do a taste test. If it tastes salty, don't use it. As with snow, ice should be melted prior to consumption. Melt sea ice next to a fire or add it to a partially full container of water and either shake the container or place it between the layers of your clothing and allow your body's radiant heat to melt the snow.

Dew

Although dew does not provide a large volume of water, it should not be overlooked as a source of water. Dew accumulates on grass, leaves, rocks, and equipment at dawn and dusk and should be collected at those times before it freezes or evaporates. Any porous material will absorb the dew, and the moisture can be consumed by wringing it out of the cloth and into your mouth.

Condensation

Solar stills are a great water procurement option in hot climates. The vegetation bag and transpiration bag are great land options.

Vegetation Bag

To construct a vegetation bag, you will need a clear plastic bag and an ample supply of healthy, nonpoisonous vegetation. A 4- to 6-foot section of surgical tubing is also helpful. To use, open the plastic bag and fill it with air to make it easier to place vegetation inside. Next fill the bag one-half to three-quarters full of lush green vegetation. Be careful not to puncture the bag. Place a small rock or similar item into the bag, and if you have surgical tubing, slide one end inside and toward the bottom of the bag. Tie the other end in an overhand knot. Close the bag, and tie it off as close to the opening as possible. Place the bag on a sunny slope so that the opening is on the downhill side slightly higher than the bag's lowest point. Position the rock and surgical tubing at the lowest point in the bag. For best results, change the vegetation every two to three days. If using surgical tubing, simply untie the knot and drink the water that has condensed in the bag. If no tubing is used, loosen the tie and drain off the available liquid. Be sure to drain off all liquid prior to sunset each day, or it will be reabsorbed into the vegetation.

Vegetation bag.

Transpiration Bag

Because the same vegetation can be reused after allowing enough time for it to rejuvenate, a transpiration bag is better than a vegetation bag. To construct a transpiration bag, you will need a clear plastic bag and an accessible, nonpoisonous brush or tree. A 4- to 6-foot section of surgical tubing is also helpful. Open the plastic bag and fill it with air to make it easier to place the bag over the brush or tree. Next place the

bag over the lush leafy vegetation of a tree or brush, being careful not to puncture the bag. Be sure the bag is on the side of the tree or brush with the greatest exposure to the sun. Place a small rock or similar item into the bag's lowest point, and if you have surgical tubing, place one end at the bottom of the bag next to the rock. Tie the other end in an overhand knot. Close the bag, and tie it off as close to the opening as possible. Change the bag's location every two to three days to ensure optimal outcome and to allow the previous site to rejuvenate so it might be used again later. If using surgical tubing, simply untie the knot and drink the water that has condensed in the bag. If no tubing is used, loosen the tie, and drain off the available liquid. Be sure to drain off all liquid prior to sunset each day, or it will be reabsorbed into the tree or brush.

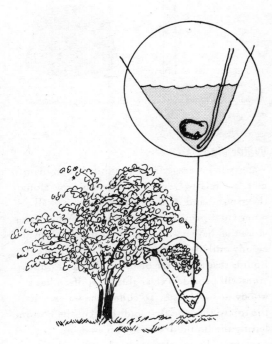

Transpiration bag.

Vegetation

Depending on your location, you may find an abundant source of water from vegetation. Plants and trees with hollow portions or leaves that overlap, such as air plants and bamboo, often collect rainwater in these natural receptacles. Other options include cacti, water vines, banana trees, and coconuts.

Cacti

Cacti are prominent in the deserts of the Southwest and can provide a limited supply of liquid. To procure it, cut off the top of a cactus (this will be difficult without a large knife because the cactus has a tough outer rind), remove the inner pulp, and place it inside a porous material, such as a cotton T-shirt. The pulp's moisture can now be easily wrung out directly into your mouth or an awaiting container. Since the amount of fluid obtained will be minimal, don't eat the pulp. It will require more energy and body fluids to digest the pulp than can be gained from it.

Banana Trees

Banana trees are common in the tropical rain forests and can be made into an almost unending water source by cutting them in half

Continued ➔

with a knife or machete, starting about 3 inches from the ground. Next, carve a bowl into the top surface of the trunk. Water will almost immediately fill the bowl, but do not drink it; the initial water will be bitter and upsetting to your stomach. Scoop the water completely out of the bowl three times before consuming.

The initial water from a banana tree will be very bitter and should be avoided.

Water Vines

Water vines average from 1 to 6 inches in diameter, are relatively long, and usually grow along the ground and up the sides of trees. Not all water vines provide drinkable water. Avoid water vines that have a white sap when nicked, provide cloudy milklike liquid when cut, or produce liquids that taste sour or bitter. Nonpoisonous vines will provide a clear fluid that often has a woody or sweet taste. To collect the water, cut the top of the vine first and then cut the bottom, letting the liquid drain into an awaiting container. If you plan to drink it directly from the vine, avoid direct contact between your lips and the outer vine as an irritation sometimes results.

Coconuts

Green unripe coconuts about the size of grapefruits provide an excellent source of water. Once coconuts mature, however, they contain an oil, which, if consumed in large quantities, can cause an upset stomach and diarrhea. If you do not have a knife, accessing the liquid in coconuts presents the greatest challenge.

Water Filters

Filtering water does not purify it. Filtering is done to reduce sediment and make the water taste better. There are several methods of filtering water.

Seepage basin

This system is used for stagnant or swamp water. For best results, dig a hole approximately 3 feet from the swamp to a depth that allows water to begin seeping in. Line the sides with rocks or wood to prevent dirt or sand from falling back into the hole. Allow the water to sit overnight so that all the sediment can settle to the bottom.

Three-Tiered Tripod Filter

This system should be used for filtering sediment from the water. To construct it, you'll need three 7- to 8-foot-long wrist-diameter poles, line, three 3-foot-square sections of porous cloth, grass, sand, and charcoal.

1. Build a tripod with the poles and line by laying the poles down, side by side, and lashing them together 6 inches to 1 foot from the top. For details on lashing see chapter 13.

2. With the lashed end up, spread the legs of the poles out to form a stable tripod.

3. Tie the three sections of cloth to the tripod in a tiered fashion with a 6-inch to 1-foot space between each section.

4. Place grass on the top cloth, sand on the middle cloth, and charcoal on the bottom cloth.

5. To use, simply pour the water into the top section of cloth and collect it as it filters through the bottom section.

Cloth Filter

Any porous material can be used to filter out sediment by simply pouring your liquid through it and into a container.

Water Purification

According to the Centers for Disease Control (CDC), water contaminated with microorganisms will cause over 1 million illnesses and 1,000 deaths in the United States each year. The primary pathogens (disease-causing organisms) fall into three categories: protozoan (including cysts), bacteria, and viruses. Other potential risks that can be found in water include disinfectants and their by-products, inorganic chemicals, organic chemicals, and radionuclides. There are three basic methods for treating your water: boiling, chemical treatments, and commercial filtration systems.

Boiling

To kill any disease-causing microorganisms that might be in your water, the Environmental Protection Agency's (EPA) Office of Water advocates using a vigorous boil for one minute. My rational mind tells me that this must be based on science and should work. After seeing a friend lose about 40 pounds from a severe case of giardiasis, however, I tend to over-boil my water. As a general rule, I almost always boil it longer. I'll let you decide what is right for you. Boiling is far superior to chemical treatments and should be done whenever possible.

Chemical Treatments

When unable to boil your water, you may elect to use chlorine or iodine. These chemicals are effective against bacteria, viruses, and *Giardia*, but

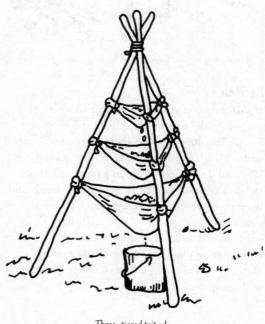

Three-tiered tripod.

Continued ➡

according to the EPA, there is some question about their ability to protect you against *Cryptosporidium*. In fact, the EPA advises against using chemicals to purify surface water. Once again, I'll let you decide. Chlorine is preferred over iodine since it seems to offer better protection against *Giardia*. Both chlorine and iodine tend to be less effective in cold water.

CHLORINE

The amount of chlorine to use for purifying water will depend upon the amount of available chlorine in the solution. This can usually be found on the label.

Available Chlorine	Drops per Quart of Clear Water
1%	10 drops
4–6%	2 drops
7–10%	1 drop
unknown	10 drops

WATER PURIFIER CARE
Greg Davenport

To increase the longevity of your system, use the following guidelines (in no way should they supersede the manufacturer's recommendations):

- **Cleaning.** Clean, scrub, and disinfect the filter after each use, following the manufacturer's guidelines. Note: Some filters should not be scrubbed, and some are self-cleaning.

- **Use clean water.** Whenever possible, procure clean water such as that found in a creek's pools or similar areas. To avoid sand, mud, and debris, keep the suction hose away from the water's bottom; this may require the use of a foam float.

- **Muddy water.** If muddy water is your only choice, fill a clean container with the muddy water and let it sit for several hours (overnight if time permits) or until the sediment has settled to the bottom of the container. Or you could first run the water through an improvised filter, as described above.

- **Backwash the filter.** Backwash the filter according to the manufacturer's recommended schedule. This process helps remove any accumulated debris from the system.

—From *Surviving the Desert*

If the water is cloudy or colored, double the normal amount of chlorine required for the percentage used. Once the chlorine is added, wait three minutes, and then vigorously shake the water with the cap slightly loose (allowing some water to seep out through the seams). Then seal the cap on the container, and wait another twenty-five to thirty minutes before loosening the cap and shaking it again. At this point consider the water safe to consume, provided there is no *Cryptosporidium* in the water.

IODINE

There are two types of iodine that are commonly used to treat water: tincture and tablets. The tincture is nothing more than the common household iodine that you may have in your medical kit. This product is usually a 2 percent iodine solution, and you'll need to add five drops to each quart of water. For cloudy water, double the amount. The treated water should be mixed and allowed to stand for thirty minutes before used. If using iodine tablets, you should place one tablet in each quart of water when it is warm and two tablets per quart when the water is cold or cloudy. Each bottle of iodine tablets should have instructions for how it should be mixed and how long you should wait before drinking the water. If no directions are available, wait three minutes, and then vigorously shake the water with the cap slightly loose (allowing some water to seep out through the seams). Then seal the cap on the container, and wait another twenty-five to thirty minutes before loosening the cap and shaking it again. At this point consider the water safe to consume, provided the water does not contain *Cryptosporidium*.

Commercial Purifying Systems

A filter is not a purifying system. In general, filters remove protozoan; microfilters remove protozoan and bacteria; and purifiers remove protozoan, bacteria, and viruses. Purifiers are simply a microfilter with an iodine and carbon element added. The iodine kills viruses, and the carbon element removes the iodine taste and reduces organic chemical contaminants like pesticides, herbicides, and chlorine, as well as heavy metals. Unlike filters, purifiers must be registered with the EPA to demonstrate effectiveness against waterborne pathogens, protozoan, bacteria, and viruses. A purifier costs more than a filter. You'll need to decide what level of risk you are willing to take, as waterborne viruses are becoming more and more prominent. One downside is that a purifier tends to clog more quickly than most filters. To increase the longevity of your system, you should carefully read and follow the manufacturer's guidelines on how to use and clean the system you have. Purifiers come in a pump style or a ready-to-drink bottle design.

PUMP PURIFIERS

There are many pump filters on the market, and new ones arrive each year. As a purifying system, they protect against protozoan, bacteria, and viruses. I advise choosing a system that is lightweight, easy to use, has a high output, and is self-cleaning.

BOTTLE PURIFIERS

Probably the best-known bottle filter is the 34-ounce Exstream Mackenzie, an ideal system for the wilderness traveler. As a purifying system, it protects against protozoan, bacteria, and viruses. The benefit of a bottle purifier is its ease of use—simply fill the bottle with water and start drinking (according to the manufacturer's directions). It requires no assembly or extra space in your pack. On the downside, it only filters about 26 gallons (100 liters) before you'll need to replace the cartridge, and unless you carry several, you will need to be in an area with multiple water sources throughout your travel.

—From *Wilderness Survival*

Is Wild Water Safe?
Linda Frederick Yaffe

The water rushing over rocks, shooting bubbly plumes into the air, forming blue pools, looks so clean, so inviting. Can you safely dip your cup into the clear blue pool and enjoy a refreshing drink?

Today, pollution from larger numbers of careless outdoorspeople and infected wildlife compel you to treat all of the water you drink, use to clean your teeth, and use to prepare your food. Never drink untreated water, no matter how "clean" it appears. Most of the surface water in the United States is contaminated with *Giardia lamblia* and *Cryptosporidium*. These disease-causing microorganisms are invisible to the naked eye. They can make you seriously ill, causing months of stomach cramps, diarrhea, nausea, dehydration, and fatigue. Cases of *Giardia*, the most common waterborne pathogen, have more than doubled in the United States during the past decade.

Giardia and *Cryptosporidium* are spread through fecal-oral transmission. They are passed from person to person and from domestic and wild animals to humans. You can avoid spreading these pathogens by using good field practices and common sense. Camp at least 200 feet from any water source. Properly bury your feces, pack out toilet paper, and always wash your hands thoroughly with soap and water after defecating or changing a diaper and before handling food. When scouting for a water source, use the best-looking one available. Avoid water that contains floating material or water with a dark color or an odor. Filter murky water through a clean cloth before treating it. ...

Carry plenty of treated water from home. Always carry five to ten gallons of treated water from home in your vehicle. Pack in as much as you can comfortably carry and have plenty available in your vehicle when you pack out of the wilderness.

—From *Backpack Gourmet*

Continued ➡

Treating Water: Comparing Methods

Linda Frederick Yaffe

Fortunately, you can choose from several effective drinking water treatment methods: boiling, filtering, purifying, ultraviolet purification, or chemical treatment (tablets). Choose the method or combination of methods that suit the locale of your trip, your style of camping for the trip, and your personal preference.

Boiling

This is the most effective, fail-safe field treatment method. Vigorously boil untreated water for one to two minutes to kill the microorganisms that can make you ill.

Advantages: This is a very effective and inexpensive method. Anyone with a cooking pot, a stove and fuel, or the resources to build an open fire, can treat as much water as they need, anywhere in the world.

Disadvantages: Boiling all of your drinking water is inconvenient unless you are staying in a base camp. It is time and fuel consuming to boil quantities of water, and then let it cool enough to drink. While you are base-camped, it is feasible to spend the evenings boiling and filling containers with purified water, but it is a big chore. Boiled water, having lost oxygen in the process, tastes unpleasantly flat. Aeration (pouring the boiled water back and forth from one clean container to another) can improve the flat taste. Try letting the boiled water stand for several hours or overnight, or add a small pinch of salt to each quart of boiled water to improve the flavor. Since the taste of good mountain water is one of the attractions of a wilderness adventure, boiled water makes the trip less special.

Water Filters

Choose a modern microporous water filter to pump water from a groundwater source into your water container. Look for a filter that has an absolute pore size of one micron or less for protection from *Cryptosporidium* as well as *Giardia*.

Advantages: Cool, good-tasting treated water is available immediately. In areas of frequent surface water availability, the filter weighs far less than extra containers filled with clean water.

Disadvantages: Filters weigh from eleven to twenty-three ounces. They are costly. You need to clean filters regularly and periodically replace the filtering cartridges. Filters do not protect against waterborne viruses such as polio and hepatitis. Waterborne viruses are rare in North America but prevalent in some other parts of the world.

Water Purifies

These are water filters with an added purifying device that forces the water through chlorine beads, killing most viruses as well as the *Giardia* and *Cryptosporidium* parasites.

Advantages: Worry-free water treatment.

Disadvantages: Purifiers are slightly heavier and more costly than regular water filters.

Water filter and bottle.

Ultraviolet Purification

A portable battery-powered wand uses ultraviolet light to neutralize bacteria, viruses, and protozoa.

Advantages: The wand is fast and easy to use: Just swish the device around in a container of water. No pumping is required, and there are no chemical flavors.

Disadvantages: This technology is new to the backcountry. It is costly.

Water Purification Tablets

Tiny, lightweight tablets kill viruses in groundwater, but they do not effectively eliminate *Giardia* or *Cryptosporidium*.

Advantages: Convenient and lightweight, the tablets effectively kill waterborne viruses. They can be used as emergency substitutes only when you are unable to boil or filter your water. Potable Aqua treatment tablets, used with P.A. Plus, which is added twenty minutes after the first tablets, erase the unpleasant iodine taste of the initial tablets. The flavor can be further improved by letting the water stand for several hours or by adding powdered drink mix.

Disadvantages: Not as effective as boiling, filtering, purifying, or ultraviolet purification, tablets are an excellent supplement to filtering your water in parts of the world where viruses are a threat.

—From *Backpack Gourmet*

Drinking Water at Sea

Greg Davenport

Packed Water

Packed water, which comes inside a pouch or a box, holds between 1/8 to 1 quart of water. USCG-approved packed water has a five-year shelf life. While emergency water is a great item to carry on your trip, you should also carry something that allows you to procure additional water once your emergency supply is gone. Be sure to protect the pouches and boxes of packed water so they aren't accidentally punctured. Storing them inside a hard plastic 1-quart water bottle (big-mouthed screw top) will not only protect them but will provide a container that will come in handy for storing other water that you procure. An option to the packed water

would be to bring along tap water inside the hard plastic 1-quart container. The shelf life for tap water is approximately six months.

Desalting Tablets

One desalting tablet will desalt 1 pint of water. Salt water treated this way tastes like water obtained from a water hose that has set out in the sun all day. Desalting tablets come alone or in a kit. Kits have a plastic bag that holds about 1 pint of water and has a filter that will keep the sludge by-product from being drunk. To use, place seawater in the bag with the tablet, and wait one hour—agitating the water periodically—before drinking the water through the valve attached to the bag. If you don't have a kit, follow the same process using an available container, and be sure not to drink the sludge left at the bottom.

Solar Stills

A solar still uses seawater and the sun to create drinkable water through a condensation process. Most stills are inflatable balls that allow you to pour seawater into a cup on top of the bottom. The balloon has a donut-shaped ballast ring that keeps it afloat and upright. It takes about a 1/2 gallon of seawater to fill the ballast. Note that the ballast ring has a fabric-covered center that must be wet before the balloon can be inflated. Additional seawater is required to fill the cup on top of the balloon, and this water provides a constant drip onto multiple cloth wicks located inside the balloon. As the outside air warms, condensation forms on the inner wall and runs down into a plastic container. The use of a solar still is limited to calm seas, and results will depend on temperatures. When seas are calm, stills should be put out as soon as possible even if clouds obscure the sun. For complete details on how to use these devices, read the manufacturers' directions.

Solar still.

Continued ➡

Reverse Osmosis Water Maker

Standard freshwater filters and purifiers will not desalt seawater and should not be used for this process. Instead, a reverse osmosis water maker that turns seawater into drinkable water should be part of your survival gear. These hand-powered devices range in weight from 2 to 7 pounds and can roughly produce 6 gallons of water a day, depending on the model you have. To use, simply place the hose of the device into seawater and pull the handle. To achieve the maximum amount of water output requires a pump rate of thirty to forty times a minute. Be sure to follow the manufacturer's maintenance and use instructions, and have the system serviced accordingly.

Collecting Precipitation

Most life rafts have canopies designed to catch rainwater. This catchment system uses gutters to funnel rainwater into a storage container inside the raft. Since salt spray has probably dried on top of the canopy, the initial water collected will probably be too contaminated to drink. Lining the gutters, when it starts to rain, with a space blanket or similar material can alleviate this problem. Contamination can also be an issue in rough seas where the wind and waves constantly splash seawater onto the canopy and raft. You can also procure rainwater by tying a piece of plastic (a space blanket or similar item) to two paddles and holding it out the raft's door in such a way as to funnel the rain into an awaiting container. Try to fill all available containers with rainwater, and drink this water before packaged water.

Water from Dew

Although dew does not provide a large amount of water, it should not be overlooked as a source of water. Dew accumulates on the raft and canopy (on land, it can be found on grass, leaves, rocks, and equipment) at dawn and dusk and should be collected at those times before it freezes or evaporates. Any porous material will absorb the dew, and the moisture can be consumed by wringing the water out of the cloth and into your mouth.

Ice

As with snow, ice should be melted prior to consumption. To melt ice, add it to a partially full container of water and either shake the container or place it between layers of your clothing and allow your body's radiant heat to melt the snow. On land, you can melt ice with a fire. If using sea ice, you will want to make sure the ice is virtually free of any salts in the seawater. Sea ice that has rounded corners, shatters easily, and is bluish or black in color is usually safe to use. When in doubt, however, do a taste test. If it tastes salty, don't use it.

—From *Surviving Coastal and Open Water*

Water Needs in High-Temperature Areas

U.S. Army

The subject of man and water in the desert has generated considerable interest and confusion since the early days of World War II when the U.S. Army was preparing to fight in North Africa. At one time the U.S. Army thought it could condition men to do with less water by progressively reducing their water supplies during training. They called it water discipline. It caused hundreds of heat casualties.

A key factor in desert survival is understanding the relationship between physical activity, air temperature, and water consumption. The body requires a certain amount of water for a certain level of activity at a certain temperature. For example, a person performing hard work in the sun at 43 degrees C requires 19 liters of water daily. Lack of the required amount of water causes a rapid decline in an individual's ability to make decisions and to perform tasks efficiently.

Your body's normal temperature is 36.9 degrees C (98.6 degrees F). Your body gets rid of excess heat (cools off) by sweating. The warmer your body becomes—whether caused by work, exercise, or air temperature—the more you sweat. The more you sweat, the more moisture you lose. Sweating is the principal cause of water loss. If a person stops sweating during periods of high air temperature and heavy work or exercise, he will quickly develop heat stroke. This is an emergency that requires immediate medical attention.

Understanding how the air temperature and your physical activity affect your water requirements allows you to take measures to get the most from your water supply. These measures are—

- Find shade! Get out of the sun!
- Place something between you and the hot ground.
- Limit your movements!
- Conserve your sweat. Wear your complete uniform to include T-shirt. Roll the sleeves down, cover your head, and protect your neck with a scarf or similar item. These steps will protect your body from hot-blowing winds and the direct rays of the sun. Your clothing will absorb your sweat, keeping it against your skin so that you gain its full cooling effect. By staying in the shade quietly, fully clothed, not talking, keeping your mouth closed, and breathing through your nose, your water requirement for survival drops dramatically.
- If water is scarce, do not eat. Food requires water for digestion; therefore, eating food will use water that you need for cooling.

Thirst is not a reliable guide for your need for water. A person who uses thirst as a guide will drink only two-thirds of his daily water requirement. To prevent this "voluntary" dehydration, use the following guide:

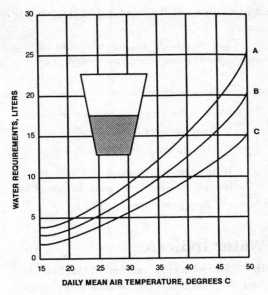

Daily water requirements for three levels of activity:
A: Hard work in sun (creeping and crawling with equipment on).
B: Moderate work in sun (cleaning weapons and equipment).
C: Rest in shade.
This graph shows water needs, in liters per day, for men at three activity levels in relation to the daily mean air temperature. For example, if one is doing 8 hours of hard work in the sun (curve A) when the average temperature for the day is 50 degrees C (horizontal scale), one's water requirement for the day will be approximately 25 liters (vertical scale).

From Technical Report E-P118. Southwest Asia: Environment and Its Relationship to Military Activities. July 1959.

- At temperatures below 38 degrees C, drink 0.5 liter of water every hour.
- At temperatures above 38 degrees C, drink 1 liter of water every hour.

Drinking water at regular intervals helps your body remain cool and decreases sweating. Even when your water supply is low, sipping water constantly will keep your body cooler and reduce water loss through sweating. Conserve your fluids by reducing activity during the heat of day. Do not ration your water! If you try to ration water, you stand a good chance of becoming a heat casualty.

—From *Survival (Field Manual 21-76)*

Desert Water Sources

Greg Davenport

In the desert, the lack of water plays a major role in survivability. It is an extremely valuable resource and is far more important than food. You can live anywhere from three weeks to two months without food, but only days without water. Thus you need to pack in enough water for at least one day, along with the necessary equipment to procure more. Check with the local authorities on accessible water related to your trip before departing. Don't rely on someone who hasn't been in the area recently or is giving you hearsay information. It's better to adjust or delay your trip than to run out of water . . .

The importance of water in a hot environment cannot be overemphasized, and its availability—carried on you or otherwise—must be

Continued ➔

continually assessed during any trip into the desert.

The best storage container for your water is your body. If water becomes scarce, do not ration it. Instead, follow these basic guidelines to limit water loss from sweat:

- Work in the evening and morning, when temperatures are lower.
- During the day, rest in a shaded area.
- Wear protective clothing in a loose and layered fashion, with a wide-brimmed hat and neck covering. ...

Water Indicators

In hot environments, water may be difficult to find. Map indicators may be misleading, since most desert water is intermittent. Map markings that represent intermittent streams and springs are often relevant only after it has rained, and the windmills, tanks, and troughs shown may be broken down or dry. Understanding water indicators created by plants and trees, insects, birds, mammals, and the terrain will be helpful when trying to find water.

Plants and Trees

Plush green vegetation found at the base of a cliff or mountain may indicate a natural spring or underground source of water. Most deciduous trees require large amounts of water to survive and often indicate the presence of surface water or groundwater.

Terrain

Drainages, valleys, and ground depressions are good water indicators and may hold surface water or groundwater, especially after a rain. Often springs can be found at the base of a plunge pool (dry waterfall) or the bend of a dry riverbed with lush green vegetation.

Natural Water Sources

Since your body needs a constant supply of water, you'll eventually need to procure water from Mother Nature. Various sources include surface water, groundwater, precipitation, and plants.

Surface Water

Surface water may be obtained from rivers, creeks, springs, basin lakes, and rock depressions. These sources may be found year-round, but in desert environments they typically are present only when there has been a recent rainfall. Most sources are stagnant or slow-moving and prone to contamination from protozoans, bacteria, and viruses. They should all be treated.

Rivers and creeks

Rivers often support deciduous trees and other vegetation not otherwise found in a desert. When you spot an area with vegetation, especially plants or trees that run in a line, you should investigate—surface water might be there, too. Creeks, on the other hand, are often dry, and finding water there may be a difficult task. Look for areas of lush green vegetation, which is often found downstream and at the bend of a pool. Water may be on the surface here, or you might find groundwater by digging down 2 or 3 feet.

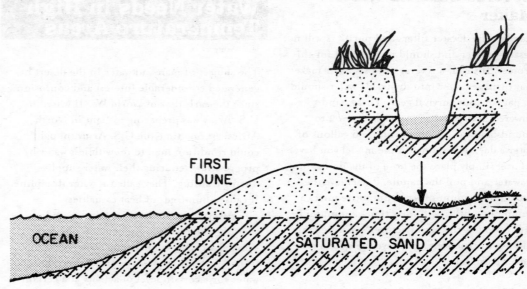

Beach well water source.

Springs

Springs occur when the water table crosses the ground's surface and are often dependent on rains. In other words, if it hasn't rained for some time, it is doubtful water will be present. It is hard to know where a spring will occur. However, they are often found in low-lying areas next to a hillside and support lush green vegetation.

Basin lakes

Basin lakes occur where water is trapped without any means of escape. They can appear in low-lying areas or when intermittent creeks or rivers flow into an area that provides no exit. Water may or may not be present, depending on when the last rainfall was.

Rock depressions

If there has been a recent rain, water is often trapped in rock depressions. This water is often stagnant, but it nevertheless is an option that should be considered in a desert climate. As with most water, it should be purified before consumed.

Groundwater

Groundwater is found under the earth's surface. This water is naturally filtered as it moves through the ground and into underground reservoirs known as aquifers. Although treatment may not be necessary, always err on the side of caution. Locating groundwater is probably the most difficult part of accessing it. Look for things that seem out of place, such as a small area of lush green vegetation at the base of a hill or a bend in a dry riverbed that is surrounded by sparser green or even brown vegetation. A marshy area with a fair amount of cattail or hemlock growth may provide a clue that groundwater is available. I have found natural springs in desert areas and running water less than 6 feet below the earth's surface using these clues. For ease of access, you can dig a small seepage basin well at the source, following the directions on page 176. If you are on a coastal desert, you can procure fresh water by digging such a well one dune inland from the beach.

Precipitation

The two forms of precipitation in a hot desert climate are occasional rain and dew. If it rains, set out containers or dig a small hole and line it with plastic or other nonporous material. After the rain has stopped, look for water in crevasses, fissures, and low-lying areas. If morning dew is present, use a porous cloth to absorb it, then wring out the moisture into your mouth.

Plants

Depending on the type of desert and time of year, you might be able to get some water from plants. Solar stills that collect moisture from plants in the form of condensation can provide some water in hot climates and should be considered. These include the vegetation bag and transpiration bag. Contrary to popular belief, most cacti (including the saguaro cacti) do not provide an unending water source when cut into. Often a moist pulp is present, and a small amount of water can be obtained by squeezing it inside a porous material.

Man-made Water Sources

Since water is often a scarce commodity in desert climates, mankind has derived multiple procurement, transport, and storage systems where it is found. These include windmills, storage tanks, pipelines, spring boxes, and man-made dams. Water from any source should be purified and, when appropriate, filtered.

Windmills

A water pump windmill, still common in many rural areas of the United States, uses the energy from wind to draw water from underground. These machines have several obliquely angled blades mounted on a descending horizontal shaft and a fantail rudder that steers the blades into the wind. When the windmill's blades turn, the energy is transmitted downward through a system of horizontal shafts and gears that operate a piston pump. These pumps use suction to transport water from underground to the earth's surface. Windmills are also used to help move water through pipes from the source to another location. When wind velocities become excessive, safety devices automatically turn the rotor out of the wind to prevent damage to the mechanism.

Continued ➡

If you come across a windmill, take the time to check it out. Although many have been abandoned, it may still provide a water source. However, don't get your hopes up. Most active sites have signs that maintenance has occurred, and there may be grease on the moving parts, newer paint, or a storage area with modern tools. Is the windmill over the water source, or is it part of a transport system? If it appears to be the original pump, look for a storage tank. In either situation, look for a smaller water container that might be kept full in case the pump needs to be primed during maintenance. The windmill will not work if the brake is on, so check to see if it is on or off. When on, the windmill's tail will be folded next to the fan, keeping it out of the wind. When off, the tail will be extended and cause the fan to turn into the wind. The brake lever is normally located at the base of the windmill. If a wind is present and you release the brake, an operational windmill should begin to work. If it doesn't, look for a hand pump or consider turning the blades by hand. If you decide to climb the tower to manually turn the blades, survey it well beforehand. If you fall and get hurt, your situation will be worse. If the fan is rusted or rotates but nothing happens, try hitting the windmill's shaft (not the casing) with a rock or similar object. Doing this might free it up from rust or dislodge a rock that is preventing it from working.

Storage Tanks and Pipelines

Storage tanks and pipelines can often be found next to windmills or other energy sources. These tanks and lines often have open and close valves, plugs, and spigots on the outlet pipe. If you can't access the water via a spigot, you may have trouble getting it from a valve or plug source without a wrench. If all else fails and your survival is in question, try to break the line by whatever means you can.

Spring Boxes and Man-made Dams

A spring box is a natural spring with a rock or concrete box built around it. Usually the source is covered, with pipelines carrying the water to a storage system. Man-made dams are often created in creek beds and drainages where rain runoff can be collected.

—From *Surviving the Desert*

Water pump windmills are still common in many rural areas.

Pipelines can often be found next to windmills and are a potential water source.

Water in the Jungle
U.S. Army

Vines

Vines with rough bark and shoots about 5 centimeters thick can be a useful source of water. You must learn by experience which are the water-bearing vines, because not all have drinkable water. Some may even have a poisonous sap. The poisonous ones yield a sticky, milky sap when cut. Nonpoisonous vines will give a clear fluid. Some vines cause a skin irritation on contact; therefore let the liquid drip into your mouth, rather than put your mouth to the vine. Preferably, use some type of container.

Roots

In Australia, the water tree, desert oak, and bloodwood have roots near the surface. Pry these roots out of the ground and cut them into 30-centimeter lengths. Remove the bark and suck out the moisture, or shave the root to a pulp and squeeze it over your mouth.

Palm Trees

The buri, coconut, and nipa palms all contain a sugary fluid that is very good to drink. To obtain the liquid, bend a flowering stalk of one of these palms downward, and cut off its tip. If you cut a thin slice off the stalk every 12 hours, the flow will renew, making it possible to collect up to a liter per day. Nipa palm shoots grow from the base, so that you can work at ground level. On grown trees of other species, you may have to climb them to reach a flowering stalk. Milk from coconuts has a large water content, but may contain a strong laxative in ripe nuts. Drinking too much of this milk may cause you to lose more fluid than you drink.

Often it requires too much effort to dig for roots containing water. It may be easier to let a plant produce water for you in the form of condensation. Tying a clear plastic bag around a green leafy branch will cause water in the leaves to evaporate and condense in the bag. Placing cut vegetation in a plastic bag will also produce condensation. This is a solar still.

—From *Surviving (Field Manual 21-76)*

Mountain Water Supply
U.S. Army

Mountain water should never be assumed safe for consumption. Training in water discipline should be emphasized to ensure soldiers drink water only from approved sources. Fluids lost through respiration, perspiration, and urination must be replaced if the soldier is to operate efficiently.

Maintaining fluid balance is a major problem in mountain operations. The sense of thirst may be dulled by high elevations despite the greater threat of dehydration. Hyperventilation and the cool, dry atmosphere bring about a three- to four-fold increase in water loss by

Continued ➔

evaporation through the lungs. Hard work and overheating increase the perspiration rate. The soldier must make an effort to drink liquids even when he does not feel thirsty. One quart of water, or the equivalent, should be drunk every four hours; more should be drunk if the unit is conducting rigorous physical activity.

Even though water is abundant in most tropical environments, you may, as a survivor, have trouble finding it. If you do find water, it may not be safe to drink. Some of the many sources are vines, roots, palm trees, and condensation. You can sometimes follow animals to water. Often you can get nearly clear water from muddy streams or lakes by digging a hole in sandy soil about 1 meter from the bank. Water will seep into the hole. You must purify any water obtained in this manner.

Animals as Signs of Water

Animals can often lead you to water. Most animals require water regularly. Grazing animals, such as deer, are usually never far from water and usually drink at dawn and dusk. Converging game trails often lead to water. Carnivores (meat eaters) are not reliable indicators of water. They get moisture from the animals they eat and can go without water for long periods.

Birds can sometimes also lead you to water. Grain eaters, such as finches and pigeons, are never far from water. They drink at dawn and dusk. When they fly straight and low, they are heading for water. When returning from water, they are full and will fly from tree to tree, resting frequently. Do not rely on water birds to lead you to water. They fly long distances without stopping. Hawks, eagles, and other birds of prey get liquids from their victims; you cannot use them as a water indicator.

Insects can be good indicators of water, especially bees. Bees seldom range more than 6 kilometers from their nests or hives. They usually will have a water source in this range. Ants need water. A column of ants marching up a tree is going to a small reservoir of trapped water. You find such reservoirs even in arid areas. Most flies stay within 100 meters of water, especially the European mason fly, easily recognized by its iridescent green body.

Human tracks will usually lead to a well, bore hole, or soak. Scrub or rocks may cover it to reduce evaporation. Replace the cover after use.

Water from Plants

Plants such as vines, roots, and palm trees are good sources of water.

Three to six quarts of water each day should be consumed. About 75 percent of the human body is liquid. All chemical activities in the body occur in water solution, which assists in removing toxic wastes and in maintaining an even body temperature. A loss of two quarts of body fluid (2.5 percent of body weight) decreases physical efficiency by 25 percent, and a loss of 12 quarts (15 percent of body weight) is usually fatal. Salt lost by sweating should be replaced in meals to avoid a deficiency and subsequent cramping.

Consuming the usual military rations (three meals a day) provides sufficient sodium replacement. Salt tablets are not necessary and may contribute to dehydration.

Even when water is plentiful, thirst should be satisfied in increments. Quickly drinking a large volume of water may actually slow the soldier. If he is hot and the water is cold, severe cramping may result. A basic rule is to drink small amounts often. Pure water should always be kept in reserve for first aid use. Emphasis must be place on the three rules of water discipline:

- Drink only treated water.
- Conserve water for drinking. Potable water in the mountains may be in short supply.
- Do not contaminate or pollute water sources.

Snow, mountain streams, springs, rain, and lakes provide good sources of water supply. Purification must be accomplished, however, no matter how clear the snow or water appears. Fruits, juices, and powdered beverages may supplement and encourage water intake (do not add these until the water has been treated since the purification tablets may not work). Soldiers cannot adjust permanently to a decreased water intake. If the water supply is insufficient, physical activity must be reduced. Any temporary deficiency should be replaced to maintain maximum performance.

All water that is to be consumed must be potable. Drinking water must be taken only from approved sources or purified to avoid disease or the possible use of polluted water. Melting snow into water requires an increased amount of fuel and should be planned accordingly. Nonpotable water must not be mistaken for drinking water. Water that is unfit to drink, but otherwise not dangerous, may be used for other purposes such as bathing. Soldiers must be trained to avoid wasting water. External cooling (pouring water over the head and chest) is a waste of water and inefficient means of cooling. Drinking water often is the best way to maintain a cool and functioning body.

Water is scarce above the timberline. After setting up a perimeter (patrol base, assembly area, defense), a watering party should be employed. After sundown, high mountain areas freeze, and snow and ice may be available for melting to provide water: In areas where water trickles off rocks, a shallow reservoir may be dug to collect water (after the sediment settles). Water should be treated with purification tablets (iodine tablets or calcium hypochlorite), or by boiling at least one to two minutes. Filtering with commercial water purification pumps can also be conducted. Solar stills may be erected if time and sunlight conditions permit. Water should be protected from freezing by storing it next to a soldier or by placing it in a sleeping bag at night. Water should be collected at midday when the sun thaw available.

—From *Military Mountaineering* (Field Manual 3–97.61)

U.S. Army

There are many sources of water in the arctic and subarctic. Your location and the season of the year will determine where and how you obtain water.

Water sources in arctic and subarctic regions are more sanitary than in other regions due to the climatic and environmental conditions. However, always purify the water before drinking it. During the summer months, the best natural sources of water are freshwater lakes, streams, ponds, rivers, and springs. Water from ponds or lakes may be slightly stagnant, but still usable. Running water in streams, rivers, and bubbling springs is usually fresh and suitable for drinking.

The brownish surface water found in a tundra during the summer is a good source of water. However, you may have to filter the water before purifying it.

You can melt freshwater ice and snow for water. Completely melt both before putting them in your mouth. Trying to melt ice or snow in your mouth takes away body heat and may cause internal cold injuries. If on or near pack ice in the sea, you can use old sea ice to melt for water. In time, sea ice loses its salinity. You can identify this ice by its rounded corners and bluish color.

You can use body heat to melt snow. Place the snow in a water bag and place the bag between your layers of clothing. This is a slow process, but you can use it on the move or when you have no fire.

Note: Do not waste fuel to melt ice or snow when drinkable water is available from other sources.

When ice is available, melt it, rather than snow. One cup of ice yields more water than one cup of snow. Ice also takes less time to melt. You can melt ice or snow in a water bag, MRE ration bag, tin can, or improvised container by placing the container near a fire. Begin with a small amount of ice or snow in the container and, as it turns to water, add more ice or snow.

Another way to melt ice or snow is by putting it in a bag made from porous material and suspending the bag near the fire. Place a container under the bag to catch the water.

During cold weather, avoid drinking a lot of liquid before going to bed. Crawling out of a warm sleeping bag at night to relieve yourself means less rest and more exposure to the cold.

Once you have water, keep it next to you to prevent refreezing. Also, do not fill your canteen completely. Allowing the water to slosh around will help keep it from freezing.

—From *Survival* (Field Manual 21–76)

Continued ➡

Water in Cold Weather and Cold Regions

U.S. Army

Importance of Liquids

In cold regions, as elsewhere, the body will not operate efficiently without adequate water. Dehydration, with its accompanying loss of efficiency, can be prevented by taking fluids with all meals, and between meals if possible. Hot drinks are preferable to cold drinks in low temperatures since they warm the body in addition to providing needed liquids. Alcoholic beverages should not be consumed during cold weather operations since they can actually produce a more rapid heat loss by the body.

Water

Water is plentiful in most cold regions in one form or another. Potential sources are streams, lakes and ponds, glaciers, freshwater ice, and last year's sea ice. Freshly frozen sea ice is salty, but year-old sea ice has had the salt leached out. It is well to test freshly frozen ice when looking for water. In some areas, where tidal action and currents are small, there is a layer of fresh water lying on top of the ice; the lower layers still contain salt. In some cases, this layer of fresh water may be 50 to 100 cm (20" to 40") in depth.

If possible, water should be obtained from running streams or lakes rather than by melting ice or snow. Melting ice or snow to obtain water is a slow process and consumes large quantities of fuel, 17 cubic inches of uncompacted snow, when melted, yields only 1 cubic inch of water. In winter a hole may be cut through the ice of a stream or lake to get water; the hole is then covered with snowblocks or a poncho, board, or a ration box placed over it. Loose snow is piled on top to provide insulation and prevent refreezing. In extremely cold weather, the waterhole should be broken open at frequent intervals. Waterholes should be marked with a stick or other marker which will not be covered by drifting snow. Water is abundant during the summer in lakes, ponds, or rivers. The milky water of a glacial stream is not harmful. It should stand in a container until the coarser sediment settles.

In winter or summer, water obtained from ponds, lakes and streams must be purified by chemical treatment, use of iodine tablets or in emergencies by boiling.

Types of Ice and Snow

When water is not available from other sources, it must be obtained by melting snow or ice. To conserve fuel, ice is preferable when available; if snow must be used, the most compact snow in the area should be obtained. Snow should be gathered only from areas that have not been contaminated by animals, humans, or toxic agents.

Ice sources are frozen lakes, rivers, ponds, glaciers, icebergs, or old sea ice. Old sea ice is rounded where broken and is likely to be pitted and to have pools on it. Its underwater part has a bluish appearance. Fresh sea ice has a milky appearance and is angular in shape when broken. Water obtained by melting snow or ice may be purified by use of water purification tablets, providing it has not been contaminated by toxic agents.

Procedures for Melting Snow and Ice

Burning the bottom of a pot used for melting snow can be avoided by "priming." Place a small quantity of water in the pot and add snow gradually. If water is not available, the pot should be held near the source of heat and a small quantity of snow melted in the bottom before filling it with snow.

The snow should be compacted in the melting pot and stirred occasionally to prevent burning the bottom of the pot.

Pots of snow or ice should be left on the stove when not being used for cooking so as to have water available when needed.

Snow or ice to be melted should be placed just outside the shelter and brought in as needed.

In an emergency, an inflated air mattress can be used to obtain water. The mattress is placed in the sun at a slight inclined angle. The mattress, because of its dark color, will be warmed by the sun. Light, fluffy snow thrown on this warm surface will melt and run down the creases of the mattress where it may be caught in a canteen cup or other suitable container.

—From *Basic Cold Weather Manual* (Field Manual 31–70)

Winter Water Sources

Buck Tilton and John Gookin

Subfreezing temperatures present an immediate problem for winter campers: natural water sources may become natural ice sources instead. Finding water in liquid form, either running or pooling, is a great reason to camp in a certain spot, or at least to stop and fill your water containers. It's easier and faster than melting snow, and it conserves petroleum products by saving you the burden of carrying extra fuel. Some streams are year-round sources of running water. Intermittent streams are usually dry or frozen in winter. Lakes are always liquid somewhere underneath the snow and ice. So, in the depths of winter, you'll need to carry a tool

> ## NOLS Tip
>
> ### Double Your Snow-Melting
> When melting snow, place a second pot, also full of snow, on the lid of the pot already on the stove. The heat from the bottom pot will begin to melt the snow in the top pot.

for breaking through ice to reach water. You can use an ice ax, but a good ice chisel is easier and faster. In early winter, you may find open water or thin ice at the inlets or outlets of lakes. In late winter, many frozen lakes have "overflow" on them—water on the surface that has seeped up from cracks in the old ice.

Taking water from a natural source in winter creates the potential for injury. You might slip, slide, or otherwise fall in. When streamside snowbanks are deep, dig into the snow to install a ramp to the water's edge. The ramp makes getting water safer and easier. Don't venture onto the surface of frozen lakes or rivers without a considerable amount of discriminating caution.

Melting Snow

Melting snow for water—always time-consuming and fuel-inefficient—is often your only option. There are bad ways and good ways to do it, however. Bad ways scorch the snow (actually the dust and other particulate matter in the snow), the pot, or both, and the taste of the water you make is startlingly unappealing. A good way is to start with a little water in the pot (using a large pot saves time). If you have no water at all, start with a little snow in the pot and stir it rapidly, over low heat, until it melts. Then add snow as it fits. Putting a lid on the pot speeds up the melting process. A small shovel makes your "water factory" more efficient, but you can also scoop snow with pots, your gloved hands, or whatever works. Soft, fluffy snow is beautiful but low in water content. Heavy, dense, icy snow has the most water. [NOLS Tip, see box at left]

It's a good idea to make sufficient water for the evening, plus enough to get started the next morning. In fact, it's wise to make all the water you can store before going to bed at night, filling your pots and water bottles. It's inefficient to make water in the morning. Besides, a winter evening is almost always warmer than a winter dawn.

You don't need to disinfect melted snow, if you choose your snow with care. Avoid any color but white, and pay attention—as you dig down into clean snow, you might hit a dirty layer.

Storing Water

A second challenge faced by winter campers is keeping water warm enough to stay a fluid. Some people sleep with their water bottles. This is fine, as long as the lids are screwed on tightly. If it's not screaming cold, a well-insulated bottle of water will not freeze in your tent at night.

Water can also be stored in camp by burying containers in snow. Use wide-mouthed containers, since those with narrow mouths freeze up faster and thaw more slowly. Snow is a wonderful insulator: under a foot of snow, a pot of water will remain mostly unfrozen, even if the temperature dips to minus 40. Take care to seal the hole well with snow to keep cold air out. Store water bottles with the top down, so that if a bit of ice forms on the top—which is now the bottom—the bottles will not be frozen shut. Mark the burial site, just in case it snows.

Continued ➡

Any insulation, even just a little, extends the time water will stay a fluid. Water placed near your body inside your pack usually gets enough heat from you to prevent freezing. Storing water in your pack wrapped in extra clothing, especially a good insulator such as fleece, gives you a lot more time before freezing starts—the exact amount of time depends on the ambient air temperature.

Thawing a Frozen Water Bottle

It takes about an hour to thaw a liter water bottle that has frozen solid. Therefore, the best advice is to do everything necessary to prevent your water bottle from freezing. If you fail, follow these directions:

1. Place the frozen water bottle upside down in a pot of boiling water until you can get the lid off.
2. Remove the lid and pour a little hot water into the bottle.
3. When a little ice has melted, pour that water into the pot to reheat.
4. Repeat the process until the ice is gone.
5. Use the hot water in the pot to make hot drinks.

—From *NOLS Winter Camping*

Water Storage and Conservation

Greg Davenport

Water Storage

An ideal water container will hold a minimum of 1 quart. It should have a wide mouth, which allows for easier filling. The best storage container, of course, is the survivor.

Improvised Water Containers

It sometimes becomes necessary to improvise containers in which to store water. You can use such things as plastic bags, cooking pots or pans, hollowed-out pieces of wood, ponchos (must use ingenuity to create a pouch), or nonlubricated and nonspermicidal condoms (these will work provided they are placed in a scarf or other forming structure). Don't limit yourself. Anything that doesn't leak can hold water.

Night Storage in Cold Environments

There is nothing worse than waking up with a frozen water bottle. Make sure you store your water in a way that keeps it liquid and allows you to remove the cap and continue using the container. If this can't be done and there is a replacement supply of water available, empty the container each night and leave the cap off. If water is scarce, store it in a sealed container between the layers of your bedding (make sure it doesn't leak), or place it in a snow refrigerator. A snow refrigerator can be made by digging a 2-

foot-square section 3 feet into the side of a snow bank, placing the water container inside, and then covering the outside opening with a foot-wide piece of snow. Make sure to loosen the water container caps, and place them inside the hole in an upright position.

Water Conservation

If water is in short supply, ration your sweat, not the water. In addition, don't eat unless you have water, limit your daytime physical activity, and try to work or travel at dawn and dusk.

—From *Wilderness Survival*

CamelBak

Greg Davenport

The CamelBak is a water carrier with drinking nozzle that provides easy access to drinking water. It not only ensures that you'll stay hydrated, but also gives you a way to carry more emergency gear in its cargo pockets. When in camp, I always have it on. On the trail, it is secured to the top of my large pack with the water bladder's hose draped over a shoulder strap. This gives me continual easy access to my water, and I can quickly get into my emergency gear when I stop. I have several sizes, all of which allow me to carry 100 ounces of water. The HAWG can carry 1,203 cubic inches (1,020 in the cargo pocket) and measures 9 by 7 by 19 inches. It weighs 1.9 pounds empty and approximately 8.2 pounds when its 100-ounce water reservoir is filled. The HAWG CamelBak costs about $100.

—From *Surviving the Desert*

The CamelBak is a great way to carry your water and emergency gear.

Finding Water and Making It Potable

U.S. Army

Water Sources

Almost any environment has water present to some degree. [The following chart] lists possible sources of water in various environments. It also provides information on how to make the water potable.

Note: If you do not have a canteen, a cup, a can, or other type of container, improvise one from plastic or water-resistant cloth. Shape the plastic or cloth into a bowl by pleating it. Use pins or other suitable items—even your hands—to hold the pleats.

If you do not have a reliable source to replenish your water supply, stay alert for ways in which your environment can help you.

Heavy dew can provide water. Tie rags or tufts of fine grass around your ankles and walk through dew-covered grass before sunrise. As the rags or grass tufts absorb the dew, wring the water into a container. Repeat the process until you have a supply of water or until the dew is gone. Australian natives sometimes mop up as much as a liter an hour this way.

Bees or ants going into a hole in a tree may point to a water-filled hole. Siphon the water with plastic tubing or scoop it up with an improvised dipper. You can also stuff cloth in the hole to absorb the water and then wring it from the cloth.

Water sometimes gathers in tree crotches or rock crevices. Use the above procedures to get the water. In arid areas, bird droppings around a crack in the rocks may indicate water in or near the crack.

Green bamboo thickets are an excellent source of fresh water. Water from green bamboo is clear and odorless. To get the water, bend a green bamboo stalk, tie it down, and cut off the top. The water will drip freely during the night. Old, cracked bamboo may contain water.

> **Caution**
> Purify the water before drinking it.

Wherever you find banana or plantain trees, you can get water. Cut down the tree, leaving about a 30-centimeter stump, and scoop out the center of the stump so that the hollow is bowl-shaped. Water from the roots will immediately start to fill the hollow. The first three fillings of water will be bitter, but succeeding fillings will be palatable. The stump will supply water for up to four days. Be sure to cover it to keep out insects.

Some tropical vines can give you water. Cut a notch in the vine as high as you can reach, then cut the vine off close to the ground. Catch the dropping liquid in a container or in your mouth.

> **Caution**:
> Do not drink the liquid if it is sticky, milky, or bitter tasting.

N/A

Continued ➡

Environment	Source of Water	Means of Obtaining and/or Making Potable	Remarks
Frigid areas	Snow and ice	Melt and purify.	Do not eat without melting! Eating snow and ice can reduce body temperature and will lead to more dehydration. Snow and ice are no purer than the water from which they come. Sea ice that is gray in color or opaque is salty. Do not use it without desalting it. Sea ice that is crystalline with a bluish cast has little salt in it.
At sea	Sea	Use desalter kit.	Do not drink seawater without desalting.
	Rain	Catch rain in tarps or in other water-holding material or containers.	If tarp or water-holding material has become encrusted with salt, wash it in the sea before using (very little salt will remain on it).
	Sea ice		See remarks above for frigid areas.
Beach	Ground	Dig hole deep enough to allow water to seep in; obtain rocks, build fire, and heat rocks; drop hot rocks in water; hold cloth over hole to absorb steam; wring water from cloth.	Alternate method if a container or bark pot is available: Fill container or pot with seawater; build fire and boil water to produce steam; hold cloth over container to absorb steam; wring water from cloth.
Desert	Ground · In valleys and low areas · at foot of concave banks of dry river beads · at foot of cliffs or rock outcrops · at first depression behind first sand dune of dry desert lakes · wherever you find damp surface sand · wherever you find green vegetation	Dig holes deep enough to allow water to seep in.	In a sand dune belt, any available water will be ound beneath the original valley floor at the edge of dunes.
	Cacti	Cut off the top of a barrel cactus and mash or squeeze the pulp. Caution: Do not eat pulp. Place pulp in mouth, suck out juice, and discard pulp.	Without a machete, cutting into a cactus is difficult and takes time since you must get past the long, strong spines and cut through the tough rind.
	Depressions or holes in rocks		Periodic rainfall may collect in pools, seep into fissures, or collect in holes in rocks.
	Fissures in rock	Insert flexible tubing and siphon water. If fissure is large enough, you can lower a container into it.	
	Porous rock	Insert flexible tubing and siphon water.	
	Condensation on metal	Use cloth to absorb water, then wring water from cloth.	Extreme temperature variations between night and day may cause condensation on metal surfaces. Following are signs to watch for in the desert to help you find water: · All trails lead to water. You should follow in the direction in which the trails converge. Signs of camps, campfire ashes, animal droppings, and trampled terrain may mark trails. · Flocks of birds will circle over water holes. Some birds fly to water holes at dawn and sunset. Their flight at these times is generally fast and close to the ground. Bird tracks or chirping sounds in the evening or early morning sometimes indicate that water is nearby.

Continued ➡

The milk from green (unripe) coconuts is a good thirst quencher. However, the milk from mature coconuts contains an oil that acts as a laxative. Drink in moderation only.

In the American tropics you may find large trees whose branches support air plants. These air plants may hold a considerable amount of rainwater in their overlapping, thickly growing leaves. Strain the water through a cloth to remove insects and debris.

You can get water from plants with moist pulpy centers. Cut off a section of the plant and squeeze or smash the pulp so that the moisture runs out. Catch the liquid in a container.

Plant roots may provide water. Dig or pry the roots out of the ground, cut them into short pieces, and smash the pulp so that the moisture runs out. Catch the liquid in a container.

Fleshy leaves, stems, or stalks, such as bamboo, contain water. Cut or notch the stalks at the base of a joint to drain out the liquid.

The following trees can also provide water:

- **Palms**. Palms, such as the buri, coconut, sugar, rattan, and nipa, contain liquid. Bruise a lower frond and pull it down so the tree will "bleed" at the injury.
- **Traveler's tree**. Found in Madagascar, this

CUT HERE

CUT OUT BOWL

Water will fill bowl from roots.

Water from plantain or banana tree stump.

Water from green bamboo.

tree has a cuplike sheath at the base of its leaves in which water collects.

- **Umbrella tree**. The leaf bases and roots of this tree of western tropical Africa can provide water.
- **Baobab tree**. This tree of the sandy plains of northern Australia and Africa collects water in its bottlelike trunk during the wet season. Frequently, you can find clear, fresh water in these trees after weeks of dry weather.

Caution
Do not keep the sap from plants longer than 24 hours. It begins fermenting, becoming dangerous as a water source.

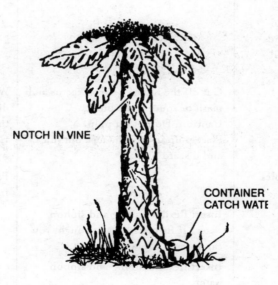

NOTCH IN VINE

CONTAINER CATCH WATE

Water from a vine.

Still Construction

You can use stills in various areas of the world. They draw moisture from the ground and from plant material. You need certain materials to build a still, and you need time to let it collect the water. It takes about 24 hours to get 0.5 to 1 liter of water.

Aboveground Still

To make the aboveground still, you need a sunny slope on which to place the still, a clear plastic bag, green leafy vegetation, and a small rock. To make the still—

- Fill the bag with air by turning the opening into the breeze or by "scooping" air into the bag.

- Fill the plastic bag half to three-fourths full of green leafy vegetation. Be sure to remove all hard sticks or sharp spines that might puncture the bag.
- Place a small rock or similar item in the bag.

Caution
Do not use poisonous vegetation. It will provide poisonous liquid.

- Close the bag and tie the mouth securely as close to the end of the bag as possible to keep the maximum amount of air space. If you have a piece of tubing, a small straw, or a hollow reed, insert one end in the mouth of the bag before you tie it securely. Then tie off or plug the tubing so that air will not escape. This tubing will allow you to drain out condensed water without untying the bag.
- Place the bag, mouth downhill, on a slope in full sunlight. Position the mouth of the bag slightly higher than the low point in the bag.
- Settle the bag in place so that the rock works itself into the low point in the bag.

To get the condensed water from the still, loosen the tie around the bag's mouth and tip the bag so that the water collected around the rock will drain out. Then retie the mouth securely and reposition the still to allow further condensation.

Change the vegetation in the bag after extracting most of the water from it. This will ensure maximum output of water.

Belowground Still

To make a belowground still, you need a digging tool, a container, a clear plastic sheet, a drinking tube, and a rock.

Select a site where you believe the soil will contain moisture (such as a dry stream bed or a low spot where rainwater has collected). The soil at this site should be easy to dig, and sunlight must hit the site most of the day.

To construct the still—

- Dig a bowl-shaped hole about 1 meter across and 60 centimeters deep.
- Dig a sump in the center of the hole. The sump's depth and perimeter will depend on the size of the container that you have to place in it. The bottom of the sump should allow the container to stand upright.
- Anchor the tubing to the container's bottom by forming a loose overhand knot in the tubing.
- Place the container upright in the sump.
- Extend the unanchored end of the tubing up, over, and beyond the lip of the hole.
- Place the plastic sheet over the hole, covering its edges with soil to hold it in place.
- Place a rock in the center of the plastic sheet.

Continued ➤

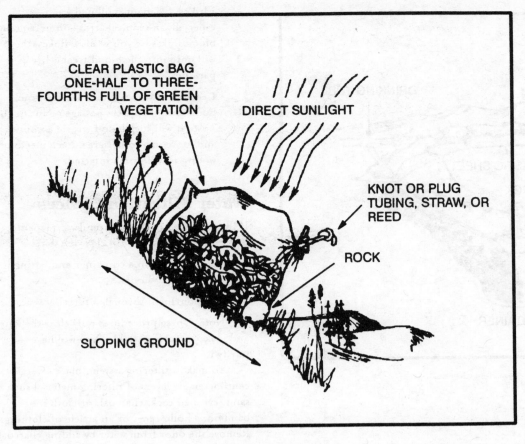

Aboveground solar water still.

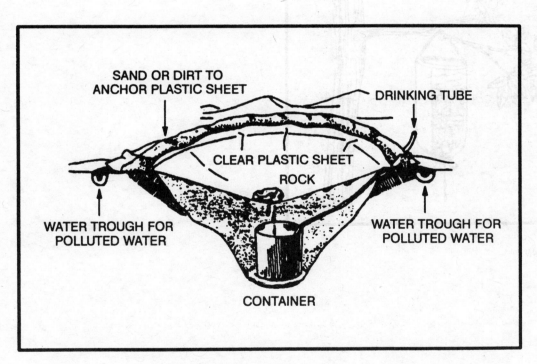

Belowground still to get potable water from polluted water.

- Lower the plastic sheet into the hole until it is about 40 centimeters below ground level. It now forms an inverted cone with the rock at its apex. Make sure that the cone's apex is directly over your container. Also make sure the plastic cone does not touch the sides of the hole because the earth will absorb the condensed water.

- Put more soil on the edges of the plastic to hold it securely in place and to prevent the loss of moisture.

- Plug the tube when not in use so that the moisture will not evaporate.

You can drink water without disturbing the still by using the tube as a straw.

You may want to use plants in the hole as moisture source. If so, dig out additional soil from the sides of the hole to form a slope on which to place the plants. Then proceed as above.

If polluted water is your only moisture source, dig a small trough outside the hole about 25 centimeters from the still's lip. Dig the trough about 25 centimeters deep and 8 centimeters wide. Pour the polluted water in the trough. Be sure you do not spill any polluted water around the rim of the hole where the plastic sheet touches the soil. The trough holds the polluted water and the soil filters it as the still draws it. The water then condenses on the plastic and drains into the container. This process works extremely well when your only water source is salt water.

You will need at least three stills to meet your individual daily water intake needs.

Water Purification

Rainwater collected in clean containers or in plants is usually safe for drinking. However, purify water from lakes, ponds, swamps, springs, or streams, especially the water near human settlements or in the tropics. When possible, purify all water you got from vegetation or from the ground by using iodine or chlorine, or by boiling.

Purify water by—

- Using water purification tablets. (Follow the directions provided.)

- Placing 5 drops of 2 percent tincture of iodine in a canteen full of clear water. If the canteen is full of cloudy or cold water, use 10 drops. (Let the canteen of water stand for 30 minutes before drinking.)

- Boiling water for 1 minute at sea level, adding 1 minute for each additional 300 meters above sea level, or boil for 10 minutes no matter where you are.

By drinking nonpotable water you may contract diseases or swallow organisms that can harm you. Examples of such diseases or organisms are—

- **Dysentery.** Severe, prolonged diarrhea with bloody stools, fever, and weakness.

- **Cholera and typhoid.** You may be susceptible to these diseases regardless of inoculations.

Continued →

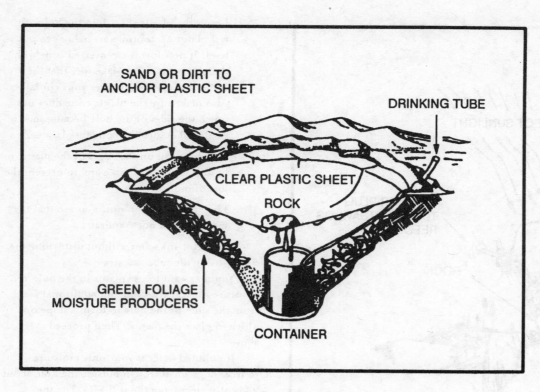

Belowground still.

SAND OR DIRT TO
ANCHOR PLASTIC SHEET

DRINKING TUBE

CLEAR PLASTIC SHEET

ROCK

GREEN FOLIAGE
MOISTURE PRODUCERS

CONTAINER

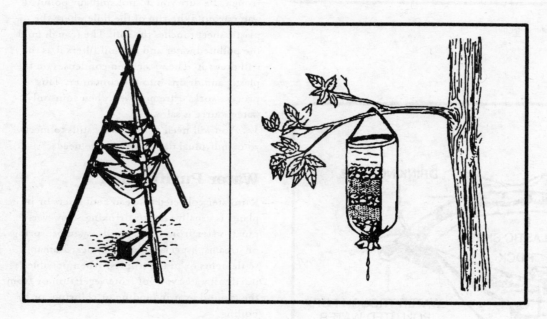

Water filtering systems.

- **Flukes**. Stagnant, polluted water—especially in tropical areas—often contains blood flukes. If you swallow flukes, they will bore into the bloodstream, live as parasites, and cause disease.

- **Leeches**. If you swallow a leech, it can hook onto the throat passage or inside the nose. It will suck blood, create a wound, and move to another area. Each bleeding wound may become infected.

Water Filtration Devices

If the water you find is also muddy, stagnant, and foul smelling, you can clear the water—

- By placing it in a container and letting it stand for 12 hours.

- By pouring it through a filtering system.

Note: These procedures only clear the water and make it more palatable. You will have to purify it.

To make a filtering system, place several centimeters or layers of filtering material such as sand, crushed rock, charcoal, or cloth in bamboo, a hollow log, or an article of clothing. Remove the odor from water by adding charcoal from your fire. Let the water stand for 45 minutes before drinking it.

—From *Survival (Field Manual 21–76)*

Hunting and Fishing for Survival

Trapping and Snaring Animals for Food

U.S. Army

For an unarmed survivor or evader, or when the sound of a rifle shot could be a problem, trapping or snaring wild game is a good alternative.

Several well-placed traps have the potential to catch much more game than a man with a rifle is likely to shoot. To be effective with any type of trap or snare, you must—

- Be familiar with the species of animal you intend to catch

- Be capable of constructing a proper trap

- Not alarm the prey by leaving signs of your presence

There are no catchall traps you can set for all animals. You must determine what species are in a given area and set your traps specifically with those animals in mind. Look for the following:

- Runs and trails
- Tracks
- Droppings
- Chewed or rubbed vegetation
- Nesting or roosting sites
- Feeding and watering areas

Position your traps and snares where there is proof that animals pass through. You must determine if it is a "run" or a "trail." A trail will show signs of use by several species and will be rather distinct. A run is usually smaller and less distinct and will only contain signs of one species. You may construct a perfect snare, but it will not catch anything if haphazardly placed in the woods. Animals have bedding areas, water-holes, and feeding areas with trails leading from one to another. You must place snares and traps around these areas to be effective.

For an evader in a hostile environment, trap and snare concealment is important. It is equally important, however, not to create a disturbance that will alarm the animal and cause it to avoid the trap. Therefore, if you must dig, remove all fresh dirt from the area. Most animals will instinctively avoid a pitfall-type trap. Prepare the various parts of a trap or snare away from the site, carry them in, and set them up. Such actions make it easier to avoid disturbing the local vegetation, thereby alerting the prey. Do not use freshly cut, live vegetation to construct a trap or snare. Freshly cut vegetation will "bleed" sap that has an odor the prey will be able to smell. It is an alarm signal to the animal.

You must remove or mask the human scent on and around the trap you set. Although birds do not have a developed sense of smell, nearly all mammals depend on smell even more than on sight. Even the slightest human scent on a trap will alarm the prey and cause it to avoid the area. Actually removing the scent from a trap is difficult but masking it is relatively easy. Use the

Continued ➡

fluid from the gall and urine bladders of previous kills. Do not use human urine. Mud, particularly from an area with plenty of rotting vegetation, is also good. Use it to coat your hands when handling the trap and to coat the trap when setting it. In nearly all parts of the world, animals know the smell of burned vegetation and smoke. It is only when a fire is actually burning that they become alarmed. Therefore, smoking the trap parts is an effective means to mask your scent. If one of the above techniques is not practical, and if time permits, allow a trap to weather for a few days and then set it. Do not handle a trap while it is weathering. When you position the trap, camouflage it as naturally as possible to prevent detection by the enemy and to avoid alarming the prey.

Traps or snares placed on a trail or run should use channelization. To build a channel, construct a funnel-shaped barrier extending from the sides of the trail toward the trap, with the narrowest part nearest the trap. Channelization should be inconspicuous to avoid alerting the prey. As the animal gets to the trap, it cannot turn left or right and continues into the trap. Few wild animals will back up, preferring to face the direction of travel. Channelization does not have to be an impassable barrier. You only have to make it inconvenient for the animal to go over or through the barrier. For best effect, the channelization should reduce the trail's width to just slightly wider than the targeted animal's body. Maintain this constriction at least as far back from the trap as the animal's body length, then begin the widening toward the mouth of the funnel.

Use of Bait

Baiting a trap or snare increases your chances of catching an animal. When catching fish, you must bait nearly all the devices. Success with an unbaited trap depends on its placement in a good location. A baited trap can actually draw animals to it. The bait should be something the animal knows. This bait, however, should not be so readily available in the immediate area that the animal can get it close by. For example, baiting a trap with corn in the middle of a corn field would not be likely to work. Likewise, if corn is not grown in the region, a corn-baited trap may arouse an animal's curiosity and keep it alerted while it ponders the strange food. Under such circumstances it may not go for the bait. One bait that works well on small mammals is the peanut butter from a meal, ready-to-eat (MRE) ration. Salt is also a good bait. When using such baits, scatter bits of it around the trap to give the prey a chance to sample it and develop a craving for it. The animal will then overcome some of its caution before it gets to the trap.

If you set and bait a trap for one species but another species takes the bait without being caught, try to determine what the animal was. Then set a proper trap for that animal, using the same bait.

Note: Once you have successfully trapped an animal, you will not only gain confidence in your ability, you also will have resupplied yourself with bait for several more traps.

—From *Survival* (Field Manual 21–76)

Basic Snares and Traps

Greg Davenport
Illustrations by Steven Davenport and Ken Davenport

You can also procure game with snares or traps. Once placed, they continue to work while you can tend to other needs. It shouldn't take much to find the indigenous animals' superhighways. These trails are located in heavy cover or undergrowth, or parallel to roads and open areas, and most animals routinely use the same pathways. Although several snares are covered in this section, for squirrel and rabbit-size game, a simple loop snare is the best method of procurement in all climates.

Simple Loop Snare

An animal caught in a simple loop snare will either strangle itself or be held secure until your arrival. To construct this type of snare, use either snare wire or improvised line that's strong enough to hold the mammal you intend to catch. If using snare wire, start by making a fixed loop at one end. To do this, bend the wire 2 inches from the end, fold it back on itself, and twist or wrap the end of the wire and its body together, leaving a small loop. Twist the fixed loop at its midpoint until it forms a figure eight. Fold the top half of the figure eight down onto the lower half. Run the free end of the wire through the fixed loop. The size of the snare will determine the resultant circle's diameter. It should be slightly larger than the head size of the animal you intend to catch.

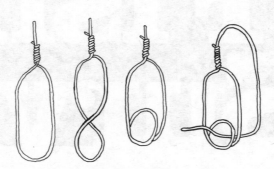

Four steps for constructing a simple loop snare

If using improvised line, make a slipknot that tightens down when the animal puts its head through it and lunges forward.

Avoid removing the bark from any natural material used in the snare's construction. If the bark is removed, camouflage the exposed wood by rubbing dirt on it. Since animals avoid humans, it's important to remove your scent from the snare. One method of hiding your scent is to hold the snaring material over smoke or underwater for several minutes prior to its final placement. Place multiple simple loop snares, at least fifteen for every animal you want to catch, at den openings or well-traveled trails so that the loop is at the same height as the animal's head. When placing a snare, avoid disturbing the area as much as possible. If establishing a snare on a well-traveled trail, try to use the natural funneling of any surrounding vegetation. If natural funneling isn't available, create

your own with strategically placed sticks. (Again, hide your scent.) Attach the free end of the snare to a branch, rock, or drag stick, a big stick that either is too heavy for the animal to drag or will get stuck in the surrounding debris when the animal tries to move. Check your snares at dawn and dusk. Always make sure any caught game is dead before getting too close.

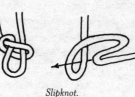

Slipknot.

Funneling.

Simple loop snare.

Squirrel Pole

A squirrel pole is an efficient means by which to catch multiple squirrels with minimal time, effort, or materials. Attach several simple loop snares to a 6-foot-long pole, then lean the pole onto an area with multiple squirrel feeding signs; look for mounds of pinecone scales, usually on a stump or a fallen tree. The squirrel will inevitably use the pole to try to get to his favorite feeding site.

Squirrel pole.

Twitch-up Strangle Snare

An animal caught in a twitch-up strangle snare will either strangle itself or be held securely until your arrival. The advantage of the twitch-up snare over the simple loop snare is that it will hold your catch beyond the reach of other predatory animals that might wander by. To construct this type of snare, begin by making a simple loop snare out of either snare wire or strong improvised line. Find a sapling that,

Continued →

when bent to 90 degrees, is directly over the snare site you have selected.

You'll need to construct a two-pin toggle trigger to attach the sapling to the snare while holding its tension. Procure two small forked or hooked branches that ideally fit together when the hooks are placed in opposing positions. If unable to find such branches, construct them by carving notches into two small pieces of wood until they fit together.

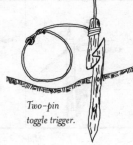

Two-pin toggle trigger.

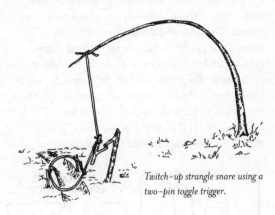

Twitch-up strangle snare using a two-pin toggle trigger.

To assemble the twitch-up snare, firmly secure one branch of the trigger into the ground so that the fork is pointing down. Attach the snare to the second forked branch, which is also tied to the sapling at the location that places it directly over the snare when bent 90 degrees. To arm the snare, bend the twig and attach the two-pin toggle together. The resultant tension will hold it in place. Adjust the snare height to the approximate position of the animal's head. When an animal places its head through the snare and trips the trigger, it will be snapped upward and strangled by the snare. If you're using improvised snare line, it may be necessary to place two small sticks into the ground to hold the snare open and in a proper place on the trail.

Figure-four Mangle Snare

A figure-four mangle snare is often used to procure small rodents such as mice, squirrels, and marmots. An animal caught in this snare will be mangled and killed. To construct this snare, procure two sticks that are 12 to 18 inches long and 3/4 to 1 inch in diameter (the upright and diagonal pieces) and one stick that is the same diameter but 3 to 6 inches longer (the trigger).

Upright Piece

Prepare the upright stick by cutting a 45-degree angle at its top end and creating a squared notch 3 to 4 inches up from the bottom. For best results, cut a diagonal taper from the bottom of the squared notch to the stick's bottom. This will aid in the trigger's release from the upright. In addition to being at opposite ends, the squared

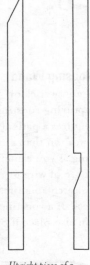

Upright piece of a figure-four mangle snare.

notch and the 45-degree angle must be perpendicular to one another.

Diagonal piece

To create the diagonal piece, cut a diagonal notch 2 inches from one end and a 45-degree angle on the opposite end. In addition to begin at opposite ends, the diagonal notch and the 45-degree angle must be on the same sides of the stick.

Trigger

The trigger piece needs to have a diagonal notch cut 1 to 2 inches from one end and a squared notch created at the spot where this piece crosses the upright when the three sticks are put together. To determine this location, place the upright perpendicular to the ground, and insert its diagonal cut into the notch of the diagonal piece. Put the angled cut of the diagonal stick into the trigger's notch and hold it so that the number four is created between the three sticks when the trigger passes the upright's square notch. Mark the trigger stick and make a squared notch that has a slight diagonal taper from its bottom toward its other notched end. If you intend to bait the trigger, sharpen its free end to a point.

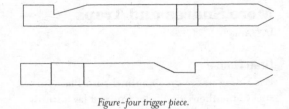

Figure-four trigger piece.

Using the Figure-Four

To use a figure-four, put the three pieces together, and lean a large rock or other weight against the diagonal, at an approximate 45-degree angle to the upright. The entire structure is held in place by the tension between the weight and the sticks. This object will fall and mangle an animal that trips the trigger.

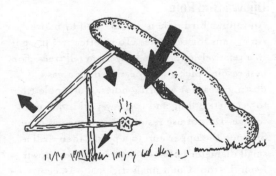

Figure-four mangle snare.

Paiute Deadfall Mangle Snare

Another option is the Paiute deadfall mangle snare. Its touchy trigger system is a unique part of its design. To construct a Paiute snare, gather four slender branches and a short piece of line. This trap has five parts: upright, diagonal, trigger, bait stick, and line.

Upright

The upright, the only piece in contact with the ground, needs to have a flat bottom and beveled top. It should be long enough to create a 45-degree angle between your mangle device (most often a rock) and the ground.

Diagonal

The diagonal piece is approximately two-thirds the length of the upright. Prepare this piece by cutting a notch on one end, about 1 inch from the tip, and a circular groove around the other end, 1/2 inch up.

Trigger

The trigger is a small branch long enough to extend 1 inch beyond both sides of the upright when placed perpendicular to it.

Bait Stick

The bait stick should be long enough to touch both the trigger stick (when in appropriate position) and the rock when it is held parallel to the ground.

Line

The line or cordage is attached to the diagonal piece's circular notch and needs to be long enough to wrap around the lower end of the upright while attached to the trigger. Attach the line to the trigger so that it's on the side that ends up opposite the line coming off the diagonal piece. It should be cut so that when the trap is set, it creates a 45-degree angle between the upper end of the diagonal and the upright piece.

Paiute deadfall mangle snare.

Using the Paiute Snare

Arm the Paiute snare as follows:

1. Tie the line to the circular groove of the diagonal stick.

2. Place the diagonal branch, with the notch side up, on the up side of the rock, forming a 45-degree angle between the rock and the ground.

3. Put the beveled side of the upright into the notch while maintaining the 45-degree angle. The upright should be placed so it is approximately perpendicular to the ground.

4. Attach the line to the trigger.

5. Run the line (off of the diagonal branch's groove) around the upright so that the trigger is perpendicular to the upright and on the side away from the rock.

6. Hold the trigger in place with the bait stick, which should be placed so that it is parallel to the ground, with one end touching the

Continued ➡

trigger (on the side opposite the line coming off the diagonal stick) and the other touching the lower end of the rock.

7. Place food on the bait stick prior to arming the trigger. When a rodent tries to eat the food, it trips the trigger, causing the rock to fall on it.

Box Trap

A box trap is ideal for small game and birds. It keeps the animal alive, thus avoiding the problem of having the meat spoil before it's needed for consumption. To construct a box trap, assemble a box from wood and lines, using whatever means are available. Be sure it's big enough to hold the game you intend to catch. Create a two-pin toggle trigger as described for the Twitch-up Strangle Snare, see page 192, by carving L-shaped notches in the center of each stick. For the two-pin toggle to work with this trap, it's necessary to whittle both ends until they're flat. Be sure the sticks you use are long enough to create the height necessary for the animal or bird to get into the box. Take time to make a trigger that fits well.

Set the box at the intended snare site. Secure two sticks at opposite ends on the outside of one of the box's sides. Tie a line to each stick, bring the lines under the box, and secure them to the middle of the lower section of your two-pin toggle. Connect the two-pin toggle together, and use it to raise the side of the box that's opposite the two stakes. Adjust the lines until they're tight and about 1 inch above the ground. Bait the trap. When an animal or bird trips the line, it'll be trapped in the snare.

Apache Foot Snare

The Apache foot snare is a trap that combines an improvised device that can't easily be removed when penetrated with a simple loop snare made from very strong line. This snare is most often used for deer or similar animals and is placed on one side of an animal trail obstacle, such as a log. The ideal placement is directly over the depression formed from the animal's front feet as it jumps over the obstacle.

A box trap created using an L-shaped two-pin toggle trigger.

To improvise the device that the animal's foot goes through, gather two saplings, one 20 inches and the other 14 inches long, and eight sturdy branches that are 1/2 inch in diameter and 10 inches long. Lash each sapling together to form two separate circles, and sharpen one end of each of the eight branches to a blunt point. Place the smaller circle inside the larger, and evenly space the branches over both so that the points approach the center of the inner circle. Lash the sharpened sticks to both of the saplings.

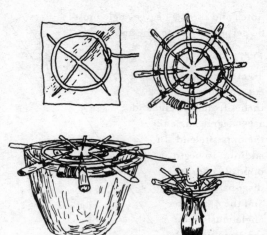
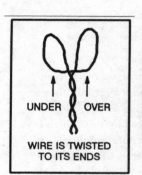

Apache foot snare.

To place the snare, dig a small hole at the depression site, lay the circular device over it, and place the snare line over it. When an animal's foot goes through the device, it will be unable to get it free. As it continues forward, the strong, simple loop snare will tighten down on its foot. When constructing a snare like this, I often use a three-strand braid made from parachute cord, but any strong braid will work. The free end of the snare line should be secured to a large tree or other stable structure. Camouflage the snare with leaves or similar material. Any large animal caught in this snare should be approached with caution.

—From *Surviving the Desert*

More Snares and Traps

U.S. Army

Drag Noose

Use a drag noose on an animal run. Place forked sticks on either side of the run and lay a sturdy crossmember across them. Tie the noose to the crossmember and hang it at a height above the animal's head. (Nooses designed to catch by the head should never be low enough for the prey to step into with a foot.) As the noose tightens around the animal's neck, the animal pulls the crossmember from the forked sticks and drags it along. The surrounding vegetation quickly catches the crossmember and the animal becomes entangled.

Ojibwa Bird Pole

An Ojibwa bird pole is a snare used by native Americans for centuries. To be effective, place it in a relatively open area away from tall trees. For best results, pick a spot near feeding areas, dusting areas, or watering holes. Cut a pole 1.8 to 2.1 meters long and trim away all limbs and foliage. Do not use resinous wood such as pine. Sharpen the upper end to a point, then drill a small diameter hole 5 to 7.5 centimeters down from the top. Cut a small stick 10 to 15 centimeters long and shape one end so that it will almost fit into the hole. This is the perch. Plant the long pole in the ground with the pointed end up. Tie a small weight, about equal to the weight of the targeted species, to a length of cordage. Pass the free end of the cordage through the hole, and tie a slip noose that covers the perch. Tie a single overhand knot in the cordage and place the perch against the hole. Allow the

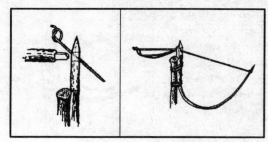

Ojibwa bird pole.

cordage to slip through the hole until the overhand knot rests against the pole and the top of the perch. The tension of the overhand knot against the pole and perch will hold the perch in position. Spread the noose over the perch, ensuring it covers the perch and drapes over on both sides. Most birds prefer to rest on something above ground and will land on the perch. As soon as the bird lands, the perch will fall, releasing the overhand knot and allowing the weight to drop. The noose will tighten around the bird's feet, capturing it. If the weight is too heavy, it will cut the bird's feet off, allowing it to escape.

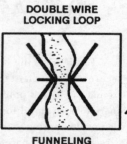

DOUBLE WIRE LOCKING LOOP

UNDER OVER

WIRE IS TWISTED TO ITS ENDS

FUNNELING

Drag noose.

Noosing Wand

A noose stick or "noosing wand" is useful for capturing roosting birds or small mammals. It requires a patient operator. This wand is more a weapon than a trap. It consists of a pole (as long as you can effectively handle) with a slip noose of wire or stiff cordage at the small end. To catch an animal, you slip the noose over the neck of a roosting bird and pull it tight. You can also place it over a den hole and hide in a

Noosing wand.

Continued ➡

Treadle Spring Snare.

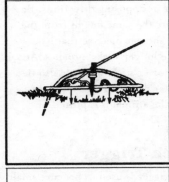
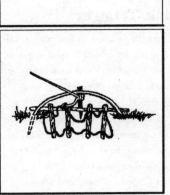
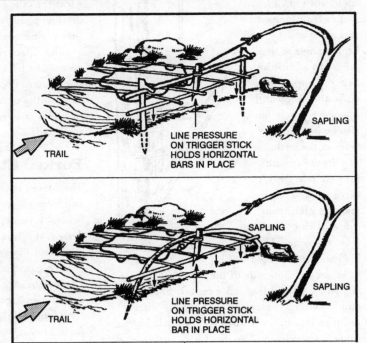

TRAIL

LINE PRESSURE
ON TRIGGER STICK
HOLDS HORIZONTAL
BARS IN PLACE

SAPLING

SAPLING

SAPLING

LINE PRESSURE
ON TRIGGER STICK
HOLDS HORIZONTAL
BAR IN PLACE

TRAIL

Bottle Trap

A bottle trap is a simple trap for mice and voles. Dig a hole 30 to 45 centimeters deep that is wider at the bottom than at the top. Make the top of the hole as small as possible. Place a piece of bark or wood over the hole with small stones under it to hold it up 2.5 to 5 centimeters off the ground. Mice or voles will hide under the cover to escape danger and fall into the hole. They cannot climb out because of the wall's backward slope. Use caution when checking this trap; it is an excellent hiding place for snakes.

—From *Survival (Field Manual 21-76)*

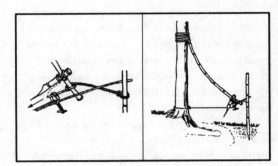

Pig spear shaft.

nearby blind. When the animal emerges from the den, you jerk the pole to tighten the noose and thus capture the animal. Carry a stout club to kill the prey.

Treadle Spring Snare

Use a treadle snare against small game on a trail. Dig a shallow hole in the trail. Then drive a forked stick (fork down) into the ground on each side of the hole on the same side of the trail. Select two fairly straight sticks that span the two forks. Position these two sticks so that their ends engage the forks. Place several sticks over the hole in the trail by positioning one end over the lower horizontal stick and the other on the ground on the other side of the hole. Cover the hole with enough sticks so that the prey must step on at least one of them to set off the snare. Tie one end of a piece of cordage to a twitch-up or to a weight suspended over a tree limb. Bend the twitch-up or raise the suspended weight to determine where you will tie a 5 centimeter or so long trigger. Form a noose with the other end of the cordage. Route and spread the noose over the top of the sticks over the hole. Place the trigger stick against the horizontal sticks and route the cordage behind the sticks so that the tension of the power source will hold it in place. Adjust the bottom horizontal stick so that it will barely hold against the trigger. As the animal places its foot on a stick across the hole, the bottom horizontal stick moves down, releasing the trigger and allowing the noose to catch the animal by the foot. Because of the disturbance on the trail, an animal will be wary. You must therefore use channelization.

Bow Trap

A bow trap is one of the deadliest traps. It is dangerous to man as well as animals. To construct this trap, build a bow and anchor it to the ground with pegs. Adjust the aiming point as you anchor the bow. Lash a toggle stick to the trigger stick. Two upright sticks driven into the ground hold the trigger stick in place at a point where the toggle stick will engage the pulled bow string. Place a catch stick between the toggle stick and a stake driven into the ground. Tie a trip

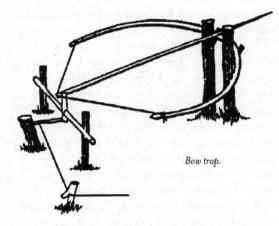

Bow trap.

wire or cordage to the catch stick and route it around stakes and across the game trail where you tie it off. When the prey trips the trip wire, the bow looses an arrow into it. A notch in the bow serves to help aim the arrow.

Warning
This is a lethal trap. Approach it with caution and from the rear only!

Pig Spear Shaft

To construct the pig spear shaft, select a stout pole about 2.5 meters long. At the smaller end, firmly lash several small stakes. Lash the large end tightly to a tree along the game trail. Tie a length of cordage to another tree across the trail. Tie a sturdy, smooth stick to the other end of the cord. From the first tree, tie a trip wire or cord low to the ground, stretch it across the trail, and tie it to a catch stick. Make a slip ring from vines or other suitable material. Encircle the trip wire and the smooth stick with the slip ring. Emplace one end of another smooth stick within the slip ring and its other end against the second tree. Pull the smaller end of the spear shaft across the trail and position it between the short cord and the smooth stick. As the animal trips the trip wire, the catch stick pulls the slip ring off the smooth sticks, releasing the spear shaft that springs across the trail and impales the prey against the tree.

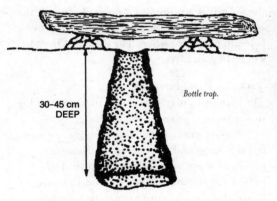

30–45 cm
DEEP

Bottle trap.

Snare Triggers

Greg Davenport
Illustrations by Steven A. Davenport

Toggle Triggers

One-Pin Toggle

The one-pin toggle trigger is primarily used to procure small game in a deadfall-mangling snare.

To construct a one-pin toggle, gather one straight 8- to 12-inch-long branch that can be easily cut in half. Cut across its diameter, creating two pieces that respectively measure one-third and two-thirds of its length. Create a small notch across the center of each branch (on the cut side) so that a small twig can sit between the pieces when they are placed back together. This twig will provide the trigger to the one-pin toggle.

To use the one-pin toggle, place the twig between the two pieces and place it perpendicular to the ground with the longer piece up. Laying a large rock against the upper end of the toggle provides enough weight to arm the trigger and hold it all together. The device is tripped when the twig is moved. This can be facilitated by having it placed in the direct travel pattern of an animal or putting food on the twig.

Two-Pin Toggle

The two-pin toggle trigger is primarily used to procure small game in a strangling snare.

Continued ➡

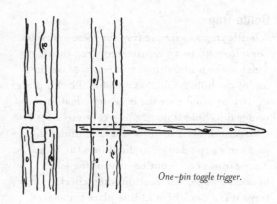

One-pin toggle trigger.

To construct a two-pin toggle, procure two small forked or hooked branches that ideally fit together when the hooks are placed in opposing positions. If unable to find two small forked or hooked branches, construct them by carving notches into two small pieces of wood until they fit together.

To use a two-pin toggle, firmly secure one branch into the ground so that the fork is pointing down. Attach the snare to the second forked branch, which is also tied to a sapling or other device so that when the trigger is tripped, the animal is captured or strangled. To arm the snare, simply bend the sapling and bring the two-pin toggle together. The resultant tension will hold it in place.

Three-Pin Toggle

The three-pin toggle is usually used to hold logs in a mangle-type snare or trap.

To construct a three-pin toggle, tie two 6-inch-long and 1- to 2-inch-diameter pieces of wood to a tree at about mid-leg height for the animal you intend to snare. Space these sticks approximately 2 inches apart. *Note:* Perhaps the tree can provide a similar design when two of its lower branches are cut 2 inches from the bark. A third stick (the trigger) needs to be about 4 inches long and 3/4 inches in diameter and should be placed under the two pins.

To use a three-pin toggle trigger, either attach meat to the trigger or run a trip line from it. To hold the trigger under the two other pieces (perpendicular), attach it to a line that will pull it upward when looped over a sturdy branch and secured to a suspended log or other heavy object. This object will fall and mangle an animal that trips the trigger.

Three-pin toggle trigger.

Upside Down Figure Four

This figure four design provides the perfect trigger for killing medium to large game with a mangle-type snare or trap.

To construct an upside down figure four, procure two sticks that are 12 inches long and approximately 3/4 to 1 inch in diameter (upright and trigger) and one stick that is 4 to 6 inches long and 3/4 to 1 inch in diameter (horizontal).

Notch the first long stick (upright) 2 inches from one end and cut it at a 45-degree angle at the other. In addition to being at opposite ends, the notch and 45-degree angle must also be on opposite sides of the stick.

In the second long stick (trigger), carve a notch approximately 1 inch from one end and 2 inches from the other. Here the two notches need to be on the same side of the stick and slightly angled away from the stick's center. Sharpen the end—where the notch is 2 inches away—into a point so that it can be used to hold bait when the snare is completed. The short stick (horizontal) should be carved so that both ends have a 45-degree angle, with the angles on the same side of the stick.

Upside down figure four trigger.

To use an upside down figure four, attach the upright to a tree so that the notch is up and the end with the 45-degree angle is down. Be sure the notch points out and the long end of the angled side is away from the tree. Place the trigger onto the upright so that the notch and pointed end are up. It is held in place when the horizontal piece is placed between the trigger and the upright, forming a figure four. The entire structure is held in place by the tension that occurs when the horizontal piece is attached to a line, which ideally loops over a sturdy branch and is secured to a suspended log or other heavy object. This object will fall and mangle an animal that trips the trigger.

Figure H Trigger

The figure H trigger is used to procure small game in a strangling-type snare. If this trigger is used properly, it will work regardless of which way the animal approaches the snare.

To construct a figure H, procure two sticks that are 18 inches long and 1 inch in diameter and one stick that is 8 to 10 inches long and 1 inch in diameter. Notch the two longer sticks approximately 1 inch from the top. Make the notch the same width as the diameter of the shorter stick. Notch the shorter stick, on opposing sides, 1/2 to 1 inch from its ends. These notches should be the same width as the diameter of the longer sticks.

Figure H trigger.

To use a figure H, pound the two longer sticks into the ground with their carved notches on the up side but in opposing directions. Be sure the notches are the same height from the ground. Place the shorter piece so that its grooves fit into the longer sticks' notches. Attach the snare to the shorter stick, which is also tied to a sapling or other device so that when the trigger is tripped the animal is captured or strangled.

Forked Stick Trigger

The forked stick trigger is used to procure small and large game. If used in a twitch up design, it is ideal for small game; when used in a mangle design, it can release a large rock or log on a medium to large animal.

To construct a forked stick trigger, procure a forked branch (one in which the forked ends are long enough to pound into the ground), a stick (trigger) that easily spans the width of the forked branch plus 6 to 8 inches, and a small third stick (release) that is approximately 2 to 3 inches long. Pound one or both ends of the forked branch into the ground (leaving enough height for the release to clear between it and the ground).

To use a forked stick trigger, place the trigger on one side of the forked branch and between it and the top of the fork, place the

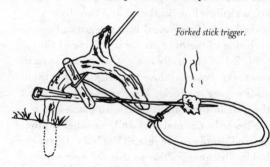

Forked stick trigger.

release. The entire structure is held in place by the tension that occurs when the release is attached to a line, which is then either tied to a sapling (twitch up design) or looped over a sturdy branch and secured to a suspended log or other heavy object (mangle design). Depending on your design, when the trigger is released, the device will either catch the animal in a snare or mangle it below a rock or log. If used as a twitch up device, be sure that the loop does not pass under the arch of the forked stick. Keep it on the same side as your sapling.

Spring Release Trigger

The spring release trigger is used to procure medium and large game. It can be used with both a twitch up and mangle design. Small game will usually fail to release the trigger.

To construct a spring release trigger, gather two sticks (with a forked branch at one end) that are 10 inches long and 3/4 to 1 inch in diameter, five 3/4-to-1-inch-diameter sticks that are about 2 feet long, two 3/4-to-1-inch-diameter branches (trigger) that are about 18 inches long, and one stick (release) that is 2 to 3 inches long with a diameter of 1/2 to 3/4 of an inch. Sharpen the far end of the forked branches and pound

Continued ➡

them securely into the ground (leave about 4 to 5 inches exposed) so that they are 12 to 15 inches apart. Place the two trigger sticks perpendicular to the forked branches and between the forks and the ground. Insert the five longer branches between and perpendicular to the two trigger pieces. These branches should be placed so that about 1 inch extends beyond the forked side of the trigger. The release should be sharpened on one end so that bait can be attached.

To use a spring release trigger, place the release between the two forked branches (from the forked side and at the center point) and perpendicular to the trigger sticks. The sharpened end should face up and can be used to hold bait. The entire structure is held in place by the tension that occurs when the release is attached to a line, which is then either tied to a sapling (twitch up design) or looped over a sturdy branch and secured to a suspended log or other heavy object (mangle design). This line pulls the release into the two trigger sticks by running between them and toward the sapling or log from the opposite side. The trigger is released when an animal steps on the five long branches (forcing the lower trigger branch down). The device will either catch the animal in a snare (placed over the five branches) or mangle it below a rock or log.

—From *Wilderness Living*

Bird Traps
Greg Davenport
Illustrations by Steven A. Davenport

Bird Tunnel Trap
Dig a funnel-shaped tunnel that narrows at its end. Using bait (bird seed, berries) create a trail that leads to the back of the tunnel. The bird will enter the tunnel while eating the seed and, once done, will be unable to back out since its feathers will become wedged into the tunnel's walls. This trap is most effective for birds that have guard feathers on their heads. (A quail is a good example of this.)

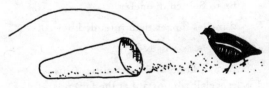

Bird tunnel trap.

Bird Hole Trap
In a piece of wood, cut a small circle that is barely big enough for a bird's head to get through. Like the tunnel trap, this design works best on birds with guard feathers. Securely place the wood over a small hole and use seed, fruit, or other bird bait to lead the fowl toward the

Bird hole trap.

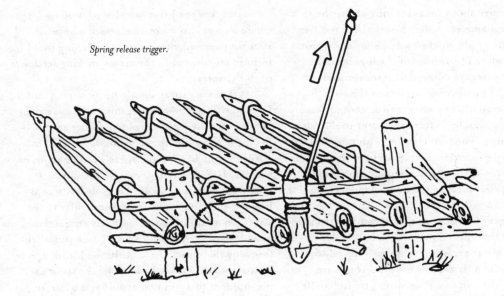

Spring release trigger.

trap. Be sure to place some on the board and at the bottom of the hole. When the bird puts its head through the wood, its feathers will become wedged when it tries to withdraw it head. *Note:* This can be used with a jar, but its slick sides make it less effective.

—From *Wilderness Living*

Traps for Snapping Turtles
Allan A. Macfarlan
Illustration by Paulette Macfarland

When food was scarce, Indians hunted and trapped snapping turtles. Today, many people relish snapper cutlets and snapper soup. The common snapper sometimes weighs as much as 50 pounds. The alligator snapping turtle of the South often weighs as much as 100, and 200-pounders have been recorded. Both turtles have strong jaws and their bites can sever fingers or even a wrist. The common snapping turtle can strike with the swiftness of a snake.

The Indians also hunted land tortoises and took them in various simple traps and by hand. These land tortoises were often caught in the early morning when they came out of their burrows to drink the cool dew.

Shown in the drawing is a snapping-turtle trap which the author developed from Indian designs. This trap is built from modern materials, and several Indian groups now use this modernized version of ancient traps with great success.

Small snapping-turtle trap.

An old but strong wooden box three or four feet square and ten or more inches high, depending on the size of the turtles to be taken, is the basis of the trap. The wood should be about three-quarters of an inch thick. Drill a number of one-inch holes through the sides and bottom of the box to allow it to sink quickly and to let the water out of it when it is lifted.

The trap may also be made by covering a strong wooden frame with 1 1/2-inch heavy wire mesh. That type is shown in the drawing. One end or side of the box or frame is hinged to form a door. The door should be made smaller than the frame so that the water will not swell the wood enough to jam it when closed. About one inch trimmed from one end and one side of a close-fitting door usually prevents jamming, but it is wise to soak the wood in water overnight before sawing the edges off to make sure that the door will not swell too much.

A block of hardwood nailed onto the frame of the floor of the trap at both corners or a narrow, thin strip of wood nailed across the bottom of the box, outside, prevents the door being pushed open from the inside by a trapped turtle. Once the doorstops are in place, hinge the door at the top with two strong, oiled-leather hinges, since metal hinges deteriorate too quickly. The door must be centered in the opening with the same clearance all around or it will not open smoothly. A screweye in each corner of the top of the box completes the trap. A short length of rope is tied to each screweye, and the ends of these lines are tied to a metal ring. The main handling line is also fastened to this ring. The trap can be weighted down with a few stones to keep it from floating, but it's convenient to nail on some heavy metal if it is available.

Raw meat, fishheads, or whole fish are placed inside the trap as bait. The trap is lowered to the bottom where snappers have been seen or where they have been caught on the hooks of trotliners or rod-and-reel fishermen. The free end of the main handling line is tied to a float or an overhanging branch. When the trap is left overnight, the catch is often surprising and may even include big fish.

Snappers should be grasped firmly about halfway down the shell, a hand on each side. The jaws cannot reach your hands that way, but you have to be careful to make sure that your hands are also out of reach of the sharp claws. A snapper cannot withdraw its head inside its shell; so some trappers like to slip a wire noose fastened to a stout pole around the snapper's neck and handle it that way. Keep your legs clear of the turtle's jaws and claws, too.

A big trap, often used to take snappers on a large scale, is also illustrated. The logs used in

Continued ➔

the frame are about four feet long and eight inches in diameter. A wire basket about two feet deep made of old chicken wire hangs down from all four sides. The insides of the logs bordering the wire basket are covered with sheet metal to prevent the turtles crawling out of the trap.

The trap is set in water and anchored there. A wooden ramp leads from the water to the edge of the frame. The trap is baited with raw meat or fish. It is a good idea to wrap some of the bait in wire mesh so that the first snapper caught will not eat it all. Smelling the bait, snappers climb the ramp and drop into the trap. They cannot get out again because their claws cannot grip the sheet metal on the frame.

Remove the trapped snappers carefully by hand or with a strongly made dip net or wire noose on the end of a pole. Don't try to handle any big alligator snapper alone. They are very strong.

This trap can take almost all turtles in the water where the trap is set. A sportsman keeps only the snappers. Most other freshwater turtles are poor table fare, and are not destructive to fish or waterfowl.

—From *Exploring the Outdoors with Indian Secrets*

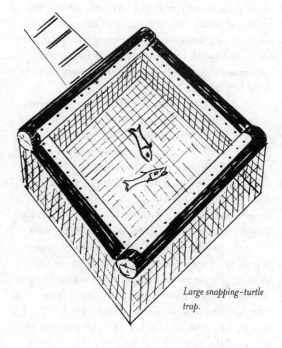

Large snapping-turtle trap.

Hand-Crafting Hunting Tools

Greg Davenport
Illustrations by Steven A. Davenport

Spear

To make a straight spear, procure a long, straight sapling and sharpen one end to a barbed point. If practical, fire harden the tip to make it more durable by holding it a few inches above a hot bed of coals until it's brown.

To make a forked spear, procure a long, straight sapling and fire harden the tip. Snuggly lash a line around the stick 6 to 8 inches down from one end. Using a knife, split the wood down the center to the lash. To keep the two halves apart, lash a small wedge between them. (For best results secure the wedge as far down the shaft as possible.) Sharpen the two prongs into inward pointing barbs.

Flint-knapped tips can also be used to create a spear. To make one, attach a bone or rock tip to the front of your spear, using the techniques covered in the arrow-making section of this chapter.

A throwing spear should be between 5 and 6 feet long. To throw a spear, hold it in your right hand, and raise it above your shoulder so that the spear is parallel to the ground. Be sure to position your hand at the spear's center point of balance. (If left-handed, reverse these instructions.) Place your body so that your left foot is forward and your trunk is perpendicular to the target. In addition, point your left arm and hand toward the animal to help guide you when throwing the spear. Once positioned, thrust your right arm forward, releasing the spear at the moment that will best enable you to strike the animal in the chest or heart.

Using a spear to procure fish is a time-consuming challenge but under the right circumstances can yield a tasty supper. When using a spear you'll need to compensate for difference in light refraction above and below the water's surface. In order to obtain proper alignment, you'll need to place the spear tip into the water before aiming. Moving the spear tip slowly will allow the fish to get accustomed to it until you are ready. Once the fish has been speared, hold it down against the bottom of the stream until you can get your hand between it and the tip of the spear.

A forked spear made from a long sapling can also be used as a rodent skewer. To use it, thrust the pointed end into an animal hole until you feel the animal. Twist the stick so that it gets tightly snagged in the animal's fur. At this point, pull the animal out of the hole. Realize the rodent will try to bite and scratch you, so keep it at a distance. Use a club or rock to kill it.

Wooden forked spear.

Bow and Arrow

A bow is an excellent method of increasing a projectile's speed and distance. Bows and arrows have been used for centuries by all cultures and many designs have been perfected over this time. Most bow construction follows simple guidelines. In fact, the biggest differences between most are whether they have a backing or not. A general rule of thumb is, the shorter the bow the greater its need for backing. Backing helps prevent it from breaking and decreases string follow, which in turn increases arrow speed. Backing will be discussed in more detail later. For our purposes I am going to describe how to make a self-bow (which doesn't have backing) from woods other than osage and yew. These woods include hickory, elm, ash, oak, birch, and walnut. They allow you to make the bow's back from the wood directly under the cambium layer and are far more forgiving to the first time bowyer. Building a bow begins with understanding the wood and how it should be prepared.

Bow: Wood Selection and Preparation

Tree Nomenclature

The vascular cambium, which lies between the bark and wood, is the main part of the tree that stays alive year-round. Although a tree's leaves, flowers, fruits, nuts, and seeds are alive they normally follow a cyclic process. The tree's outer bark and virtually all of its inner wood is dead. As the tree grows, its cambium creates new layers of dead inner wood and the most recently formed wood is called sapwood. Sapwood is relatively lighter (white to light tan) in color than the rest of the inner wood, called heartwood. As new layers are laid down by the cambium, each preceding layer moves inward converting into the darker heartwood. In most trees (osage orange is the exception) the sapwood is very strong and provides an excellent bow material.

In addition to the color changes created between sapwood and heartwood, annular rings can be seen. Two alternating rings, one dark and one light, usually represent a year of growth. The lighter ring is called earlywood, which is laid down as the tree comes out of hibernation. The dark ring represents latewood, which begins shortly after the tree rejuvenates and lasts until late fall when it goes back into hibernation. *Note*: Ash will have a dark earlywood and light latewood ring. Latewood is normally a wider ring that is far more dense and springy than earlywood is and as a general rule exposing earlywood on the back of a bow will compromise its strength. This is especially true with the harder woods. The ideal bow stave will have very thin earlywood rings and wide latewood rings.

Tree Selection and Preparation

It is best to collect your store (hickory, elm, ash, oak, birch, and walnut) during August when the bark is wet and sappy and a good solid layer of latewood has been laid down. (This differs from the normal process of collecting logs when the inner moisture is down—usually after the first thaw in mid-January). The ideal piece will meet the following criteria:

- 6- to 8-inch diameter.
- 2 inches longer than intended bow.
- Straight as possible.
- Free of knots and deformities (this is especially important at the far ends).
- Straight grained. A wood's grain runs from the center out like spokes of a tire or the cuts on a pie. To know if there is a twist in the tree grain, look at its bark. If it spirals up the trunk then the grain is twisted.

To decreases damage to the ends of your log, cut it with a saw and immediately seal the ends with varnish, paint, or Elmer's glue (at least 2 inches down the bark). Use a sledge-hammer, wedges, and ax to split the wood into staves. If able, identify a grain and make your split along its natural path. Finally, strip it of its bark and cambium layer (which should come off easily). Remember, the wood directly below your cambium will be the back of your bow so be gentle when removing it. If you need to cut the wood in the winter, you can follow the same

Continued ➡

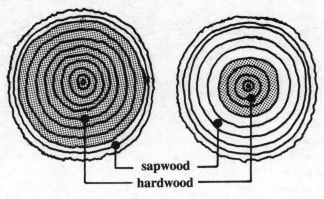

sapwood
hardwood

Sapwood is usually a lighter color than hardwood.

A latewood ring is normally darker and wider than an early-wood ring.

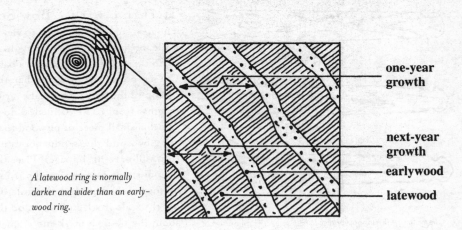
one-year growth

next-year growth
earlywood
latewood

steps but it may be harder to remove the inner bark (cambium) without damaging the sapwood (back of the future bow). To compensate, I have heard of people placing the wood in a hot steamy shower for 20 minutes until the cambium becomes swollen and easier to remove. As a general rule a 4-inch log yields two staves, 6-inch provides three, 8-inch four, and a 10-inch log produces five staves. Be sure to always split from the bark side.

There is much debate on how to properly dry the stave. Some advocate letting it air dry for a year or more while others use the highly debated kiln to speed up the process. I am too impatient to wait years for a stave and too scared to use a wood that is kiln dried. I normally place my wood inside for 2 weeks and then move it to an area that can provide a constant temperature between 90 and 120 degrees [F] until it's ready. In the summer, an attic or car work quite well as a hot box and can dry the wood in 1 to 3 months. The stave is considered ready when its moisture content is between 7 percent and 12 percent. Unless you have a moisture meter (a great tool to have), how will you know when this moisture content has been accomplished? Try weighing the wood every day and when it stops losing weight it has stopped losing moisture. As a general rule of thumb, wait another week and at this point the stave should have the proper moisture content and be ready to use.

Bow: Making a Bow

CUTTING THE WOOD

The exact style of bow you build will be of personal preference. If you use a wood other than osage but still use the designs created for osage it is advisable to increase the bow's width by approximately 30 percent to achieve a similar result in power. A bow that is 66 inches long with 2-inch wide limbs that taper into its distal notches is an ideal design for hickory, elm, ash, oak, birch, and walnut.

Identify the back (sapwood side) and belly of your bow before doing anything. Always work on the belly side of the wood. Using a dull 12-inch drawknife, thin the wood down (on the belly side) until the stave is approximately 2 inches thick from back to belly. Be sure to follow the contour of the wood's back maintaining a constant thickness from end to end. If the back side dips in, so should the belly side. If you have a knot in the wood be sure to work around it—don't cut through it. Once the 2-inch width is reached, identify the stave's flattest path and mark a line down its belly from one end to the

other. A chalk line works great for doing this. Decide where the bow's center will be on this line and mark it (this is commonly called the centerline). Make another mark 1 inch above and 3 inches below the centerline. This is where your handle will be. Next draw a line at the midpoint between the handles and the stave's ends.

Using a compass set at 1 1/2 inches, make a circle inside the handle margins by placing its pencil on the outer handle line and its point on the centerline that runs from end to end on the stave. Make this circle on both the upper and lower handle lines. Next, draw a 2-inch circle at the midway point of the limbs (between the handle lines and the ends) using the line-line intersection as the reference point on where to place your compass's point. Finally, draw a 3/4-inch circle at the far ends of the stave. Connecting the outsides of these circles provides the shape of the bow you will make.

Secure the board in a vise or similar item, with the edge of the wood facing up. If using a vise, be sure to pad the teeth so they won't damage the wood. With your drawknife, peel off the excess wood until just shy of your pencil markings. If doing this properly, the wood shaving should curl off the stave. Repeat on the other side. Using the outer edge of your handle circles draw a line from the back to the belly on each side of the wood. Using these four lines—two on each side—will provide a reference point for the handle while trimming is done on the belly side of the stave. Using your dull 12-inch drawknife, taper the bow's belly until the stave begins to resemble a bow (usually to around 1 1/4-inch thickness). To do this, start at the handle's reference points and draw the blade toward the end of each limb. What you do to

one side should be done to the other. Be sure to follow the contour of the wood's back maintaining a constant thickness from end to end. If the back side dips in, so should the belly side. If you have a knot in the wood be sure to work around it—don't cut through it. Cutting through the knot will compromise the wood's strength. Besides, a knot can add some character to the bow.

FLOOR TILLERING

At this point you can begin floor tillering your stave. With the back of the bow facing you, place the lower end against something solid (perhaps your foot or the corner of a wall and floor), and hold the upper end firmly in your hand. With your free hand, pull the handle toward you while observing the flex of the bow's limbs. At first there may not be much of a flex but by the time you're done the limbs should bend evenly from handle to tip. If the bow doesn't bend, place it back in the vise—belly side up—and use the flat side of a sharp 8- to 10-inch coarse rasp (the rasp should have one round and one sharp side) to thin the limbs. Do twelve strokes to each side and then try to floor tiller the stave again. Repeat this process until the stave bends when tillering. Be patient—don't get in a hurry and take off too much. Once it begins to bend, look for flat spots and use a pencil to mark the beginning and end of where they appear. Place the stave back into the vise and work the marked area. Watch the grain (on the belly side) as it can help you gauge your progress. It should be centered with its point directed toward the ends of each limb. (See illustration.) If it is off center, then the side they run to is too thick. Repeat the floor tillering process until you can easily and evenly bend the limbs and you feel you

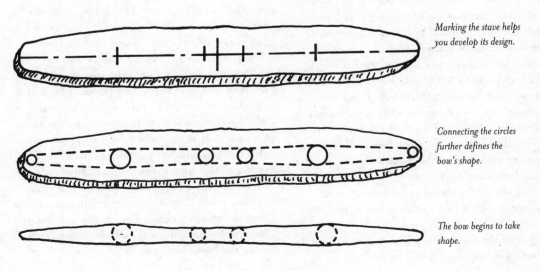

Marking the stave helps you develop its design.

Connecting the circles further defines the bow's shape.

The bow begins to take shape.

Continued ➔

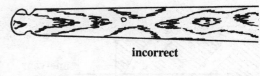

incorrect

incorrect

correct

Use the grain's feathering appearance to help you gauge your progress.

are getting close to the final product. At this point you're ready to begin using a tillering board, but first you'll need to nock the stave's ends so that a string can be attached.

To determine where the stave's nocks should be located, divide the bow's total length in half, measure this distance from the bow's exact center down both sides, and mark the final location with a pencil. Using a 5/32-inch chain saw file (a pocketknife will also work), file out a string groove on each end of the wood. Begin by placing the file on your mark and perpendicular to the bow's side. Work the file at this angle until you begin to feel the wood with your finger. Be careful not to damage the back of the bow. At this point, begin filing on the belly side at a 45-degree angle that is directed toward the handle. Work both sides evenly so that when the bow is strung the line runs down the center of the bow's belly. When done, use a strong line (bowstring) that can be loosely attached to the nocks without actually stringing the bow.

Self nocks.

Tillering Stick
A tillering stick is made from a strong 1- by 2-inch board that is approximately 4 to 5 feet long. It has a top groove for the bow's handle and multiple notches down one of its sides. The side notches allow you to increase the string's draw as you tiller the stave.

Set the bow's center on the top groove and pull the string downward, placing it in a notch that provides minimal pull on the bow's sides (usually 10 to 12 inches). Identify the stiffer limb and remove wood from its entire length (belly side) until both limbs look somewhat equal when drawn on the tillering stick. If a limb appears to have a hinge in it (an area that bends more then the rest of the limb) this will need to be fixed before moving on. Mark the hinge and remove wood on both sides of it until the entire limb bends evenly. Once the limbs pull evenly, string the bow so that there is a distance of approximately 3 to 4 inches between the belly side of the handle and the string (as the bow gets closer to the finished product this distance will most likely approach 5 to 6 inches).

Tillering with a Bow Scale
The next step in tillering is to view the limbs while weighing the bow's strength. The easiest way to do this is with a 2 by 2 and a bathroom scale. Cut a groove (slightly wider than the bow string) on top of the 2 by 2 and mark various draw lengths (from 10 to 30 inches) down its side. Attach a small piece of plywood to the bottom of the 2 by 2 and glue sandpaper to its underside (this will prevent slippage). Place the center of the bowstring into the wood's groove and the bottom of the board on the scale (be sure to zero out the scale first). Pull down on the handle to about the 15-inch mark and evaluate the bow's tiller. If unequal, remove wood from the stronger limb. Once the correct tiller is noted, then increase your pull in increments of 10 pounds (constantly adjusting the tiller with your rasp) until your final weight is reached (between 50 and 60 pounds for our bow's design). You will probably reach the desired weight with a very short pull. Don't forget to work the handle throughout the process so that a smooth transition occurs between it and each limb.

At this point exchange your coarse rasp for a fine cabinetmaker's rasp and use it to scrape a small amount off each limb until you reach full draw. Keep in mind that what you do to one side should be done to the other. The goal is to reach full draw while reducing the bow's mass but yet maintaining its draw weight. Don't get too overzealous and take off too much before checking the tiller. When you feel you're done, shoot the bow a dozen or so times and then check the tiller again. Do this for several days.

Bow: Sinew Backing
As a general rule, the shorter the bow the greater its need for a backing (in most cases a 66-inch bow does not need a backing). Backing helps prevent it from breaking and decreases string follow, which in turn increases arrow speed. Sinew takes a majority of the stress off the back of the bow, which allows you to pull the string to your desired draw length.

Before applying the sinew, be sure to clean the bow's back of any grease or oils that it obtained from your hands, etc. If you have lye, mix it with water (1 part lye to 4 parts water) and brush it onto the bow taking great care not to get it on your skin or in your eyes. Once cleaned, rinse it thoroughly with warm water (or vinegar) and let it dry. To protect yourself from the lye, wear gloves, goggles, and an apron.

Gather several bundles of sinew (various lengths), a crock-pot or double boiler filled with hide glue (discussed in chapter 13) and heated to 115 to 120 degrees, smoothing tool (bone, dowel, or other such item), and an insulated cup full of warm water to place the smoothing tool in between each use. Dip a long bundle of sinew in the glue, allowing it to become fully saturated. While removing it from the glue, draw the sinew between your thumb and palm letting the excess glue fall back into the container. Place the center of this strip at the center of the bow's back and press it in place from center to end. Use smoothing stick to help flatten the sinew onto the wood. Continue laying the bundles of sinew down until there is one continuous strip down the bow's center.

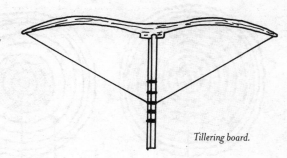

Tillering board.

Using the center strip as a guide, place the rest of the sinew one limb at a time. The next strips (placed on each side of the center strip) will begin at the exact middle of the bow and each new strip will be placed in alternating starting points as seen on a brick wall. Once again be sure to use a smoothing stick. As the limbs narrow, excess sinew can run down the sides and onto the belly. In fact, this will add strength to the bow.

As a general rule, you want the sinew to be no more than 25 percent of the bow's width when it is dry. For most bows, you'll need to apply three to four total layers to the back. Many factors such as humidity, number of layers, and the amount of glue used contribute to the time it takes for the sinew to dry. It will take approximately 2 to 6 months for it to dry. Make sure it is completely dry before even thinking about drawing on it. Once dry the bow may require some minor retillering. A bow backed with sinew is not well suited for wet climates since too much moisture will cause the glue to dissolve and the sinew to fall away. To help protect it, you should consider finishing it like you would any other bow.

Bow: Finishing the Bow
Before applying any finish, sand away all tool marks. The bow can be finished with oils that penetrate the pores or by applying a protective covering such as varathane.

Some common oils used are tung oil, linseed oil, cedar oil, and animal fats (avoid using animal fats on sinew-backed bows). The oils work by penetrating the pores of the wood and multiple applications are required to create a decent waterproof finish. In order to maintain the finish, additional treatments are required at least twice a year and even more often when used in wet conditions.

When using a protective covering like varathane, as many as five coats may need to be applied to achieve adequate protection. Once done, use a very fine grade sandpaper to remove all the shine created by the finish. Although varathane is a good product, you will still need to coat the bow with a layer of paste wax at least once a year and more often when used in wet conditions.

Bow: Bowstring
Bowstring can be made from such sources as sinew, artificial sinew, rawhide, nylon, and cambium. You may fantasize about using a bowstring made from sinew but realize it is not always the best choice. In areas of high humidity or moisture, sinew will stretch and may even break. Therefore in such climates you may be better off choosing another material. No matter

Continued ➔

Place down the sinew in a staggered pattern.

what you choose, make a two-strand braid from the material (covered in chapter 3).

To attach the bowstring, tie it to one of the bow's nocks and place that end down against the outside of your foot. Run the opposite knee slightly inside and against the bow's belly and let the handle rest against the leg. To tie the free end of the line to the upper nock, grab the high end of the bow and pull it down while pressing your knee outward on the belly. When done, the distance between the bow and string should be approximately the same distance as your fist plus the outstretched thumb.

Arrow
A bow is only as good as the arrow it shoots.

Arrow: Shaft Selection
The exact type of material used to construct an arrow often depends on what is available in the area. Bowyers have used everything from split timber or saplings to small shoots to create a shaft that is strong, lightweight, and straight. Here are just a few examples of different materials that can be used to make arrows (you are not limited by this list):

river reed	river cane
cattail	bamboo
sitka spruce	Douglas fir
Norway pine	Port Orford cedar
birch	dogwood
willow	serviceberry
osage orange	hickory
maple	black locust
oak	ramon
ash	hazel

Arrow: How to Make an Arrow Shaft
The exact length of your arrow depends upon your draw (usually 25 to 30 inches). It is best to procure arrow blanks that are 4 to 6 inches longer than your draw length.

ARROW SHAFTS MADE FROM SHOOTS
River reed, river cane, cattail, and bamboo can all provide an excellent and lightweight shaft for arrow making. Since they have a hollow or pithy center, however, you'll need to make a hardwood foreshaft that is inserted and secured to the front end. To decrease the amount of work you'll have to do, try to select shafts that are straight with a 3/8-inch diameter at the base. Make the lower cut 1/2 inch below a joint and the upper cut 3 to 4 inches beyond one. Cutting the lower end close to the joint provides stability and strength for the nock; cutting the upper end 3 to 4 inches beyond a joint provides an area for the foreshaft to be inserted. If green when cut, create a bundle of around a dozen or so and let them season in a cool dry place for several months. The exact length of your shaft will depend upon your draw (usually 25 to 35 inches).

When the shafts are ready, they will need to be straightened. To do this, heat them over a bed of hot coals until warm and then lightly bend and hold them into position until cool. To prevent the shaft from breaking it is best to bend

it only at its joints. An arrow wrench (usually an antler with a hole drilled in it) will make this task even easier. Simply insert the heated shaft through the hole and use the antler to pry it straight. As with hand straightening, be sure to bend at the joints.

ARROW SHAFTS MADE FROM SAPLINGS
The perfect sapling will have a straight grain, be 3 to 4 feet long, and have a base about 1/2 inch in diameter. If you can, cut saplings in the winter when the sap is down, tie them together in bundles of twelve, and let them season for 2 to 3 months in a cool dry room. After several weeks, go ahead and scrape off the bark using a 90-degree angle between your knife blade and the wood. Once seasoned, use a coarse rock, grooved sanding block, or sandpaper to smooth the shaft down to a diameter of 1/4 to 3/8 inches. The lighter the wood, the bigger the diameter should be. Your goal is to create something similar to a dowel you might find at the hardware store. At this point, prepare the shaft for straightening by heating it over hot coals and using the same techniques as discussed under arrows made from shoots.

ARROW SHAFTS MADE FROM SPLIT TIMBER
Sitka spruce, Douglas fir, cedar, and hickory are just a few examples of the many woods that can be used to make a split-timber arrow. Collect your wood using the same technique as you did when making a bow (there is no need to seal the ends). Try to select wood that has a good straight grain and is free of knots. Split the material into 1- to 2-inch wide shakes and store them in a warm, dry room for 1 to 2 months. For best results store them on top of each other using an alternating pattern (each successive row angled 90 degrees to the previous one) with scrap wood spacers between each row. This will allow air to circulate around the wood. In addition, turn the shafts over once a week to aid in the drying process. Once dry, use your knife to split the wood into 1-inch square sections. Next, with a hand plane create a square dowel that is about 3/8 of an inch. The exact size will depend on the wood you are using. The lighter the wood, the bigger the shaft's diameter needs to be. To do this, you'll first need to create a flat surface on one side. Once done, place the flat side down and do the same on the other side so that the distance between the two is 3/8 of an inch. Repeat this process on the other two remaining sides. The final product should be a perfectly squared 3/8-inch dowel.

To transform the square dowel into a round one, plane off the four corners, which will create eight. Next, plane down the newly created eight corners, which creates sixteen corners and a nearly round shaft. Sanding is the last step. When done your goal is to have a perfectly straight and round dowel that is 1/4 to 3/8 inch around.

Arrow: Finishing the Arrow

NOCK THE ARROW
The easiest way to nock an arrow is to tape two to three hacksaw blades together and saw a 1/2-inch-deep slot into the exact center of the shaft's end. For optimal arrow strength, make the cut at a 90-degree angle to the wood's grain. Use a rat-tail file to enlarge the nock until your bowstring almost fits (but still doesn't) and then finish with sandpaper. When done the string should snap into the nock with the application of only a slight amount of pressure. Wrap sinew around the arrow from the bottom of the nock to about 1 inch up the shaft. Glue is optional. If you don't have hacksaw blades, use your knife (man-made or improvised) to create the nock.

CUT AND SEAL THE SHAFT
You need to cut your arrow shaft to the appropriate length, which is a personal preference and usually ranges between 25 and 30 inches. Don't forget to adjust for the type of arrowhead you intend to use. To seal the arrow shaft, apply paint, lacquer, or oil. Regardless of what you use, avoid products that create an unnatural, shiny finish.

ATTACH AN ARROWHEAD
If hunting small game, simply sharpen and fire harden the tip of your arrow shaft (this should be done before the shaft is sealed). If hunting big game, you'll need to attach an arrowhead to the arrow's shaft. Once again use the hacksaw blades to cut into the end of the shaft (where you'll be attaching the arrowhead) and create a perfectly centered split that is in line (parallel) with the arrow's nock. Work both sides of the split until its width and depth allow a snug fit for your arrowhead. If you don't have hacksaw blades, use your knife to create a split that extends 1 inch down the middle of the shaft's end. Next, use your knife to work both sides until the depth and width provide a snug fit for your arrowhead.

Another method of using your knife to do this is to cut a small notch on each side of the shaft at the point where it should end. These cuts should be perpendicular to the nock at the other end. About 1/4 inch above (toward the close end of the shaft) cut another notch on each side of the shaft (perpendicular to the first two). Finally, use a gentle up and down pressure on the excess shaft until it breaks free, leaving a deep notch. Regardless of how the notch is prepared, insert the arrowhead and secure it in place with hide glue and sinew.

For a shoot (a lightweight and somewhat fragile material), it is advisable to use a hardwood foreshaft that is inserted into its forward end. The 3- to 4-inch-long plug should be carved on one end and have a flint-knapped spear tip hafted to the other (as just described). To create a snug fit, bevel the shaft so that when it is fully inserted it slightly cracks the end of the shoot. To help hold the foreshaft in place, use hide glue and tightly wrap sinew around the end.

FLETCHING THE ARROW
Fletching stabilizes the arrow's flight. Gather three feathers from the same side of a bird's wing or tail. Using a knife, cut down the center of the quill and split each of the feathers in half. Note: To make the splitting process easier, you

Continued ➡

How to attach an arrowhead to a shaft.

may want to gently pound on the quills first. Separate the halved quills so that those from similar sides of the feather are used on the same arrow. Cut the feathers to preferred length (usually 3 to 6 inches) and trim 1/2 inch up on both ends of each feather's quill. This area will be used to tie the feather to the arrow's shaft. Next, trim the feather so that it has an even height from one end to the other (usually about 3/8 of an inch). Finally, smooth the inside of the quill so that it will conform to the arrow's natural curve when it is attached.

Apply hide glue to the quill side of the feathers and secure them, 120 degrees apart, with sinew. The hide-glue-soaked sinew should be tied at the top and bottom of the feathers. Place the feathers on the arrow (nock end) so the side that was attached to the bird is closest to the arrowhead side of the shaft. Let dry.

Atlatl and Dart

The word *atlatl* is derived from the Aztecs who used this throwing device when fighting the Spanish. A spear thrower, it is believed to be the predecessor of the bow and arrow. The atlatl, simply put, is a stick that is used to throw a light spear or dart. The stick increases the arm's extension, which in turn greatly increases the distance and velocity of the spear being thrown.

Making an Atlatl

Most atlatls are 15 to 24 inches long, approximately 2 inches wide, and 1/2 inch thick. The handgrip is usually the heaviest end and most designs taper back toward a prong that fits into the notch located at the back end of the dart.

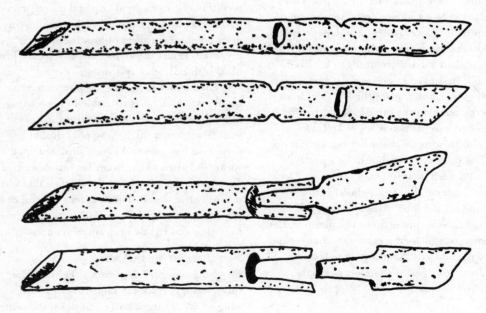

Creating a notch using your knife.

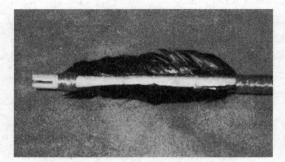

Fletching stabilizes the arrow's flight.

This arrow is ready to use.

Many different woods have been used to construct an atlatl. The lighter woods, however, will allow a better and faster throw. Juniper, cedar, and yew are three good options. To aid in throwing the dart, two loops are tied to the handle so that the thumb and index finger can slide through them when holding the atlatl. This allows you to throw the dart using a motion that is similar to throwing a baseball. Another option is to place the index and middle fingers through the loops and to adjust your throw appropriately. Some atlatl designs have a weight attached to their underside. These weights work as a counterbalance to the dart and they allow a

hunter to hold the dart in a ready position for long periods of time. The exact position and weight of the counterbalance will depend on your atlatl design and the size and length of your spear. You will probably need to adjust it until it feels balanced when holding the atlatl and dart in the ready position. To protect the atlatl from the elements, I'd advise finishing it in a fashion similar to the bow (using either an oil or protective covering).

Although I have heard of people using atlatl darts that are only 18 inches long, most are 4 to 7 feet long. The ideal material for the shaft is reeds, canes, or shoots. If you are lucky enough to find a straight sapling (or branch), however, it will also work well. Cattail, which can be found around the world in wet marshy areas, provides an excellent lightweight shaft for your dart. Attaching an arrowhead to the atlatl dart is done in the same fashion as described for making an arrow. The back of the dart needs a small grove (hole) that allows it to sit into the atlatl's notch.

—From *Wilderness Living*

Hand-Crafting Handheld Weapons

Greg Davenport
Illustrations by Steven Davenport and Ken Davenport

Handheld weapons include rocks, throwing sticks, spears, bolas, weighted clubs, slingshots, and rodent skewers. Skill and precise aim are the keys to success when using these devices, and acquiring them requires practice.

Rocks

Hand-size stones can be used to stun an animal long enough for you to approach and kill it. Aiming toward the animal's head and shoulders, throw the rock as you would a baseball.

Throwing Stick

The ideal throwing stick is 2 to 3 feet long and thicker or weighted on one end. Holding the thin or lighter end of the stick, throw it in either an overhand or sidearm fashion. For best results, aim for the animal's head and shoulder.

Bola

A bola is a throwing device that immobilizes small game long enough for you to approach and kill it. To construct a bola, use an overhand knot to tie three 2-foot-long lines together about 3 to 6 inches from one end. Securely attach a 1/2-pound rock to the other end of each of the three lines. To use the bola, hold the knot in your hand, and twirl the lines and rocks above your head or out to your side until you have attained adequate control and speed. Once this is accomplished, release your grip when the bola is directed toward the intended target.

Weighted Club

A weighted club can not only be used to kill an

Continued ➡

Atlatl.

animal at close range, but it's also a valuable tool for meeting other survival needs. To construct one, find a rock that is 6 to 8 inches long, 3 to 4 inches wide, and about 1 inch thick. Cut a 2- to 3-foot branch of straight-grained wood that is 1 to 2 inches in diameter. Hardwood is best, but softwood also works. Snugly lash a line around the stick 6 to 8 inches down from one end. Split the wood down the center and to the lash with a knife. Insert the stone between the wood and as close to the lashing as possible, and secure the rock to the stick with a tight lashing above, below, and across the rock. You can also use a strong forked branch and secure the rock between the two forked branches. Use the weighted club in the same fashion as a throwing stick.

Slingshot

A slingshot is a fairly effective tool for killing small animals. To construct one, you'll need elastic cord, bungee cord, or surgical tubing, as well as webbing or leather to make a pouch. Cut a strong forked branch with a base 6 to 8 inches long and 3- to 5-inch forked sides. Carve a notch around the top of each forked side, 1/2 inch down from the top. Cut two 10- to 12-inch pieces of elastic cord or line, and secure them to the branches by wrapping one end of each cord around the carved notches, and then tightly lashing them in place. Cut a piece of webbing or leather 3 inches long and 1 to 2 inches wide. Make a small hole that is centered and 1/2 inch in from each side. Using the free end of the two elastic cords, run 1/2 inch through the hole in the webbing or leather. Secure each cord to the webbing or leather by lashing it in place. To use the slingshot, hold a marble-size rock in the slingshot's pouch between the thumb and pointer finger of your right hand. Place your body so that your left foot is forward and your trunk is perpendicular to the target. Holding the slingshot with a

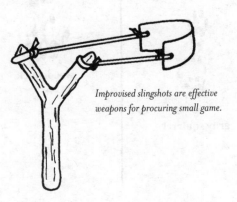
Improvised slingshots are effective weapons for procuring small game.

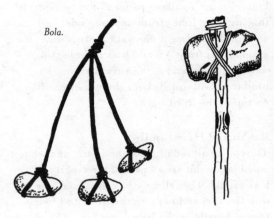
Bola.

Weighted club.

straightened left arm, draw the pouch back toward your right eye. Position the animal between the forked branches, and aim for the head and shoulder region. Release the rock.

Rodent Skewer

A forked spear made from a long sapling can be used as a rodent skewer. To use it, thrust the

Rodent skewer.

pointed end into an animal hole until you feel the animal. Twist the stick so that it gets tightly snagged in the animal's fur, then pull the animal out of the hole. The rodent will try to bite and scratch you if it can, so keep it at a distance. Use a club or rock to kill it.

—From *Surviving the Desert*

Hunting Basics

Greg Davenport
Illustrations by Steven A. Davenport

Snares are excellent tools since they work for you while you attend to other things. At times, however, it may be necessary for you to actually hunt down your game. If this should be the case, take the time to prepare before going out. Wear dark clothes, camouflage your skin with dirt or charcoal, cover your scent with smoke or pungent plants from the local area, and try to stay downwind from the animal. In addition, try to hunt at dawn or dusk, as this is the most active time for many animals. Any of the following techniques can be used to hunt wild game.

Tracking and Stalking Game

Tracking an Animal
To stalk an animal, you must first see it. If there is none in sight, you'll need to find it using the tracks and sign it leaves behind. You don't need to be an expert tracker to do this. You simply need a few basic skills that will allow you to determine where the best hunting and trapping are a might be.

ANIMAL TRACKS AND PATTERN OF MOVEMENT
An animal's track is simply the impression its foot leaves on the ground. As time passes, this impression is changed by the sun, rain, and wind along with insect and other animal overlay. All tracks begin to deteriorate soon after they are made. In addition, the type of ground in which the track is made will directly impact its longevity. As a general guideline, use the following to help you determine the approximate age of an animal's track.

Continued ➡

- **Crispness.** Once an impression is made the effects of the sun and wind will begin to deteriorate its borders. The crisper its defined borders are, the fresher it is.

- **Weather.** If there has been a recent rain or snowfall, you can determine if the track occurred before or after it happened. The same can be said for dew and frost. If there is crisp dew on the ground but the track is absent of it, this is a good indication that the track is fresh.

- **Evaporation.** If you are in an area where the ground is dry but an imprint creates moisture, you can estimate how old the impression is based on the amount of moisture it still contains.

- **Vegetation.** If a track has new undisturbed growth within it, then it is old. If an animal's track contains compressed and broken young vegetation, it is usually a good indication of recent passage.

- **Dislodged materials.** Snow, dirt, sand, water, and so on will normally be sprayed forward in the direction of travel. As time passes, the displaced material will dry and harden and bond with its underlying surface, or it will evaporate.

For the purpose of this book, I am going to focus on three types of animal's tracks. These include rodents, rabbit and hares, and hoofed mammals. All three can provide an abundance of food for someone who is living in the wild.

Rodent Family
The white-footed mouse, gray squirrel, and woodchuck are all part of the rodent family. They all have a front foot with four toes with nails, three palm pads, two heel pads, and a vestigial thumb near the inner heel pad. Although these rodents have bigger hind feet, with five toes and nails, there are a few small differences between them. The white-footed mouse usually has three palm pads with two heel pads; the gray squirrel normally supports four palm pads with two heel pads; and the woodchuck is known to have three palm pads and two heel pads (one of which is hard to notice). *Note*: The heel pads on the hind feet of these rodents are rarely seen in their tracks.

Most rodents have a similar galloping pattern of movement. The woodchuck, however, tends to alternate between a galloping and a walking pattern. In the galloping pattern, the animal's front feet will hit the ground first and—as it continues its forward momentum—its hind legs will land in front of this position, allowing it to push off and continue its movement. Thus, when looking at these tracks, the imprints will normally show the hind feet ahead of the tracks created by the two front feet. In addition, the front feet tracks are usually side-by-side and closer together then the imprints made by the back feet. As mentioned, woodchucks are also known to use a walking pattern of movement. In this instance, limbs from opposite sides and ends of the body will move at the same time (for example, its front left and back right leg will move together) and as the animal moves, its hind track will usually land close to or partially on top of the front track.

Rabbit and Hare Family
The cottontail rabbit, snowshoe hare, and white-tailed jackrabbit are all part of the rabbit and hare family. They all have heavily furred feet with five toes and nails on the front and four toes with nails on the larger rear feet. The white-tailed jackrabbit is bigger then the cottontail and hare and thus, its tracks tend to be bigger and more deeply imprinted. (This doesn't account for the size variance seen with young or female jackrabbit.) However, the snowshoe hare can spread its toes out as much as 4 inches when traveling on snow. Thus, its tracks can be quite impressive in size but not necessarily in depth. *Note*: The dense hair on a rabbit's or hare's foot makes it hard to see the animal's toe and toe pad marks (the toe pad marks are fairly small to begin with) when its tracks are made in snow.

Like rodents, rabbits use a galloping pattern of movement (covered under rodents). Unlike the rodent, however, its front feet will land with

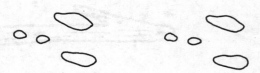

Rabbits and hares use a triangular galloping pattern of movement.

Hoofed mammals use a walking pattern of movement.

one in front of the other. When looking at these tracks, the imprints will normally show a triangular pattern created when the hind feet land ahead of the two front feet, which are one in front of the other.

Hoofed Mammals
The white-tailed deer, elk, and moose are all hoofed mammals. They all have feet that consist of two crescent-shaped halves and two dewclaws (located behind and just up from the hoof). They all leave heart-shaped prints with the sharp end pointing in the direction of the animal's travel. Adult male tracks made by moose, elk, and deer decrease in size in that order respectively. Elk tracks have a less drastic heart-shaped appearance, looking larger and wider then a deer's and smaller and rounder then a moose's.

Hoofed mammals use a walking pattern of movement similar to that described for a woodchuck (see preceding). With this type of movement, the animal's hind track will usually land close to or partially on top of the front track.

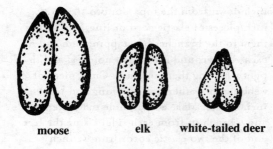

moose   **elk**   **white-tailed deer**

Tracks of various hoofed mammals.

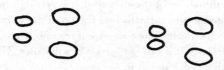

Most rodents use a galloping pattern when walking.

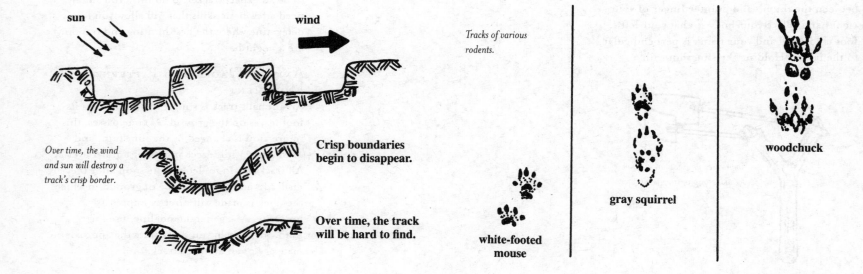

sun

wind

Over time, the wind and sun will destroy a track's crisp border.

Crisp boundaries begin to disappear.

Over time, the track will be hard to find.

Tracks of various rodents.

white-footed mouse

gray squirrel

woodchuck

Continued ➔

Understanding and Identifying an Animal's Sign

The term sign simply refers to any vegetation or landscape changes that indicate the animal has been there. This can include scat, food remains, bedding areas, trail corridors through the woods, stunted vegetation, and damage to trees and shrubs. When tracking an animal, learning to identify its sign is probably more important than finding a track. The sun, rain, and wind along with insect and other animal overlay will all affect the crispness of a track. The animal's sign, however, has a greater impact on the landscape and deteriorates at a far slower rate and thus may be the only indicator that an animal has been in the area. Here are a few basic ideas that may help.

- **Scat (droppings)**. Every animal has droppings that are unique to it. Not only is scat useful in identifying that an animal is in the area, it can also help us determine how long ago it was there and what it has been eating. By taking the time to check the droppings for moisture, warmth, and content, you can provide yourself with a multitude of useful information.

- **Food remains**. Squirrels will often leave mounds of pinecone scales on stumps or fallen logs. The abundance and freshness of these mounds will help you determine if squirrels are active in the area. Hoofed mammals and rabbits browse on saplings and leaves. A deer will often leave a frayed top, whereas rabbits leave it looking like it was cut at a 45-degree angle with a knife. A good indicator of recent deer or rabbit activity would be a branch that has a fresh and white inner surface versus one that is brown and weathered.

- **Bedding areas**. Rodents tend to live in underground dens or tree nests. If a nest is seen, watch for activity and look for other sign in the area. If an opening to an underground den is spotted, look for other sign in the area. Don't forget to evaluate the opening for spider webs or dead pine needles covering the entrance, as this usually indicates a lack of activity. Hoofed animals tend to disturb an area when they bed down. Bent-over grass, scraped dirt, and scraped snow are good indicators of a bedding area. If grassy, then look at how far it is displaced toward the ground. If it is well worn, it may have been just a napping spot. If the snow has been scraped, does it look fresh or has there been a frost or new snowfall since the bed was created.

- **Trail signs**. Often an animal's trail can be easily identified, especially when looking for rabbits or hoofed animals. Animals, like humans, tend to take the path of least resistance whenever they can. After time, trails that lead from a bedding area to a water source can become very pronounced. A less traveled trail should be evaluated for recent activity by looking for vegetation displacement (vegetation that is bent, broken, flopped over, or

pressed in), trees with displaced bark, pine needle movement, and recently broken twigs on the ground. Note: Broken twigs will usually lay in a V position with the point indicating the direction of the animal's travel and any other displaced vegetation will usually do the same.

Stalking an Animal

Once you have located your food source, if you intend to hunt it, you will need to use good stalking techniques. Staying downwind, move when the animal's head is down. I once heard that an animal (deer) will keep its head down for approximately 20 seconds while feeding and then lift it up to look around for movement. As a general rule, move for 10 seconds and then stop, staying perfectly still. Wait for the animal to pick up its head, look around and start grazing again, before moving for another 10 seconds. If the animal looks up while you are moving, freeze. As long as you don't move, it will think you are a tree stump and will not comprehend that you're getting closer. If the creature is close to a creek, you may be able to move quicker without it hearing you. In addition, realize that noise is bound to happen. The key is to freeze (if you make noise) until you are sure the animal is comfortable. Getting close enough to use your weapon will take practice and skill.

Driving

Often done with a team of hunters, driving is a process of moving an animal into an awaiting ambush. Several members of the hunting party actually make themselves known to the animal and walk toward it, constantly adjusting to ensure that the animal follows a certain path. This method works best when the creature can be funneled into a valley or similar location.

Calling

Understanding that animals communicate with each other is the first step in learning how to call them in. I have often kissed the back of my hand (making a short smacking sound) or scrapped two mussel shells together to attract a curious squirrel. Changing how I kiss my hand by making a long drawn out squalling sound can draw predators who think I am a hurt rabbit. This sound has also been known to catch the attention of a moose if it is done just right. Banging antlers together often attracts deer during their rutting season. Some hunters have perfected the art of attracting elk or duck by blowing on a blade of grass. Take the time to listen to the creatures in your area and practice different techniques of imitating their sounds. If perfected, you can draw the animal to your location—making the hunt a lot easier.

Stand (Ambush) Hunting

Observe an animal's behavior, look for its sign, and select an ambush location that is downwind from the animal's approach.

—From *Wilderness Living*

Reading Tracks and Foreseeing Animal Moves

After a boy or a man has taken a fair share of squirrels and rabbits and has scored on a few deer as a lone stillhunter, he begins to develop something akin to the skill of an Indian hunter or frontiersman. He starts doing the right thing at the right time without thinking about it much. That type of skill can't be learned from any book, but there are some useful things that a book can point out.

The tracks in this book appear on the page as they would in soft snow, damp sand, or mud, though clear prints are rare on the leaf-strewn forest floor or on hard, dry ground. The experienced tracker going into a new region seeks out likely areas where he can find clear prints in order to take his own census of the animals in the area. Good trappers are expert at it, and Indian hunters were good too. The trapper doesn't think in terms of exact numbers, but somehow, the tracks that he finds tell him whether or not there are enough pelts in the area to make running a trapline there worthwhile.

Tips on Hard-To-Follow Tracks

Tracks are often distorted, and you may see only disturbed leaves, clots of thrown-up earth, bent grass, broken twigs, and other clues running in a line. You often can't tell what animal made them unless you follow them for a while. The animal will probably cross a soft spot, and then you may find just one clear print of one foot.

The Problem of Dead-End Tracks

After identifying the tracks and deciding to follow them, don't step right on the tracks. Sometimes a fox or coyote will suddenly reverse himself and step in his own tracks to get back to a piece of cover where he can jump aside. That leaves a baffling dead end for the tracker, especially if he has obliterated the animal's tracks by walking on them so that he can't backtrack and find the jumping-off place. Sometimes, the track cannot be followed to the animal, but backtracking may lead to the animal's den or lie-up and a shot or a photograph. If the hunter or the photographer suddenly comes to a dead end in the tracks, the animal has backtracked in its own prints (or close to them), or its has jumped to a leaning tree, log, stone wall, or other object well off the ground. Coons and foxes are experts at this. Do as the Indian hunters did. Look around at the dead end for such a means of escape, and if you don't find one, try backtracking. Sometimes you'll see one or two prints that missed the original ones, and they may point in the opposite direction.

Some animals are very clever about entering water to throw a tracker off. If the tracks you're following enter a stream and do not come out again on the opposite side, the animal has probably walked along in the water for a while to throw the pursuer off. Many animals are quick to sense when a predator or a

Continued ➡

hunter is on their trail. Foxes, bears, and some other animals often circle back to identify their pursuer or get the scent.

CHANGING THE ANGLE OF VISION
The light is very important because of the shadows it throws. From one angle, the tracks may be almost invisible unless you look closely. From another angle with favorable light, the line of slight depressions or disturbed earth or leaves is clear because of the shadows that they cast. If tracks fade or disappear, try the Indian trick of moving from side to side to get the light right.

INTERPRETING AN ANIMAL'S LINE OF ADVANCE
In order to keep your eyes off the ground so that you can spot the animal ahead, it helps if you can deduce the line of advance and move from point to point. Deer, for instance, especially those with large antlers, will almost always take the easiest way unless pushed hard and trying to conceal themselves. They find it difficult to force their racks through thick cover. An otter on dry land will almost always be moving toward the nearest water. Foxes usually move from thick cover to thick cover, but sometimes pause on high ground to sun themselves and look around. During late fall, most bears are making beelines to nut groves, bee tress, berry patches, and other sources of food in their haste to fatten up before hibernation.

Move fairly fast from point to point, checking now and then to make sure that the line of prints is still there. Some Indian trackers were so good at this that they seldom looked at the tracks. They almost read the animal's mind, knowing what it was looking for or traveling toward, and they could follow the route more by knowing what the animal wanted than by doggedly following the prints that it had made.

If you lose the tracks, circling ahead will often cut them again. Go back to the last prints, pause a while, and try to figure out the route. See if you can locate any terrain feature that would have caused a sudden change of direction. If so, it may be profitable to make a circle in that direction. Remember, though, that it is difficult to pick up a line of faint tracks or sign when you cut it from the side. The tracks are under your eyes only for a few seconds as you move along, and you may have to make several circles.

When to Freeze
A good trail-watcher stays as quiet as possible while waiting for game, but sooner or later has to move camera or weapon to take a shot. Stillhunters and trackers must move along even if they do so slowly. At the first sight of the game, is it best to make an instant shot or freeze in your tracks and raise your weapon or camera in a deliberate manner? There is no exact answer in each situation, but there are a few things to bear in mind.

Moose, bear, mule deer, and most forest game have rather poor eyesight. Mountain and plains game—goats, sheep, and antelope—have excellent eyesight at all ranges. But all game is very sensitive to movement. If you remain still, the animal will probably not bolt if it doesn't get your scent. So you freeze in order to keep the animal where it is or in the hope that it will

come closer. But now you must move your weapon or camera to take the shot.

Surprising as it may seem, you can often move so that the animal seems unaware of the motion. It is nerve-racking to bring rifle or camera into position in slow motion while a game animal is staring right at you, but it can be done. One old-timer tells how: "If the buck or moose is looking right at me, I wait a while, hoping he'll put his head down to feed or that he'll turn his head away. If he doesn't, and it looks like he'll stay put, I bring my rifle up so slowly that I can't see my arms moving." Practice that sometime for an exercise in control.

This slow movement is especially important to archers and photographers. A rifleman or a shotgunner can hope to get off a going-away shot even if the animal does come unstuck. The archer finds it very difficult to shoot accurately that fast, and the photographer is seldom interested in an animal's departing rump. Deer are so very fast, for instance, that they often "jump the string." That is, they get out of the way in the slight time interval from the twang of the bowstring to the instant when the arrow arrives where the buck was; so many archers use string silencers—rubber buttons slipped on the bowstring that deaden the twang of the string. Many Indians used tufts of feathers for the same purpose.

The Secrets of Successful Calling

Hunters must spend a lot of time listening carefully to the sounds of game if they want to be successful callers, as one experienced guide on the shore of Chesapeake Bay well knew. One day the guide and a partner were sitting in a duck blind. It was a calm, quiet day, and ducks were going over at an elevation appropriate to transatlantic jets. The hunters had a good decoy rig out, but it seemed hopeless to expect a shot. Finally, one pair of black ducks came down out of the north. They were low enough, but they seemed to be about a mile away. The guide's partner whipped his wooden duck call out of his pocket and sucked in air in preparation for a mighty series of quacks.

The old-timer grabbed his companion's arm before the latter could blow and shook his head. Then he made a most astonishing noise with his mouth—*heek-heek, heek-heek*, he called, high-pitched and slightly plaintive like a split clarinet reed. The pair of blacks wavered and swung around into the hunters' rig. Two shotgun shells later, the two sportsmen had the makings of a fine meal.

"Fred," said the guide's partner, "that didn't sound any more like a black duck than a fog horn. What were you trying to imitate?"

The old-timer only glanced at his fellow-hunter oddly for an instant while the Labrador retrieved the birds. Then he revealed the secret of his success. "Son," he said, "I was imitating a drake black duck—which you likely never listened to before. The hen blacks sound off and quack, quack just like most ducks on a farm pond, but the drake, he makes the sound I made. I saw you puffing up to blow those loud highball quacks, and I don't think the ducks would have come to that. The season's been open for a while now,

and everybody's been quacking at those blacks from here to Hudson Bay. Most people think the black goes quack because that's all they ever really hear. Now you *really* listen to a flock some time when you get the chance, and then you'll hear the drakes going *heek-heek*, just like me. The birds don't hear hunters calling like that so often; so they'll come to it."

This wily guide could recognize ducks at a great distance from the blind and then make the appropriate calls in time to bring them in. His big spread of mixed geese and duck decoys helped too, of course.

Good Indian callers had similar skills, and many northern Indians still show astonishing ability to get birds when less-experienced white guides fail. The northern Crees of Canada take a big toll of Canada geese by calling them to crude brush blinds built on shore. These Crees are so expert that they call high-flying flocks of wily Canada geese to their shotguns by barking out *ee-ronk, ee-ronk, ee-ronk* with mouth and throat. When you hear Canadas "barking," you'll wonder how a human throat and mouth can produce the same noise.

Calling waterfowl was an art among the Indians long before the white man arrived in North America. Until about thirty years ago, few white men tried to call birds or animals, except, of course, those moose callers who learned from the Indians to use the birchbark horn and those few hunters who lived in areas where the turkey was still abundant. Nowadays, calling has become very popular, and a wide variety of manufactured calls is available.

This book includes information on calling each kind of animal or bird (covered later) provided that the animal or bird does respond to calls, but there are certain more general principles behind good calling that will be discussed here.

Learning Animal Communication Systems
To call well, you must have some idea of the means of communication used by birds and animals. From the chickadee to the moose, birds and animals communicate with each other in one way or another. As hunters who have listened to them carefully know, some wild creatures carry on conversations, accented for emotion as well as meaning.

Squirrels that chatter and chase up and down tree trunks and scamper madly over the rustling leaves, pausing from time to time with menace or "follow me" on their expressive faces, are not just romping. They are communicating. Male squirrels confront each other for a moment and communicate by definite signs. One animal retreats. The pursuer is then recognized as the master of the other and has first choice of available food and females.

Foxes, wolves, and some other animals mark their regular runways by urinating on stones, trees, and boulders to attract or warn off others of their kind by means of scent. The beaver perfumes clay and mud patties with his glandular castor scent to attract females. Mink use their musk glands to communicate, and male cottontail rabbits leave signs of their presence by rubbing their chins on a stump or tree. Few woodsmen can ignore the devastating scent left

Continued ➡

206
Chapter 5
Hunting and Fishing for Survival

by a wolverine that forces its way into a cabin. Even snakes leave scent trails and follow others that interest them.

Sometimes a hunter calls perfectly, knowing that the quarry is nearby, but gets no response. It is often his scent that disturbs the animal, or it may be an alarming scent from another animal. Indians have long known that the sounds made by animals and birds are only one part of the entire communication pattern, and that a hunter's call must fit in with it. Indians would never attempt, for instance, to call in a wild turkey if a red-tailed hawk or other large predatory bird were circling overhead.

Hoofed animals paw the ground, stamp their feet, and snort to signal impatience or anger and to warn off an intruder. The bellow of a moose or the belling of an elk conveys two meanings—the search for a mate and a challenge to fight other males. These animals also communicate with each other by rattling their antlers against trees, branches, or bushes. Whitetail deer and antelope communicate with their flashing flags and rumps. When a deer's flag goes up or a pronghorn's rump hairs stand erect and flash white, the animal is warning that danger is present. When you see those signals, it's almost always useless to try a stalk. Beaver and muskrats communicate by diving into the water with a warning splash. The beaver also slaps the water with his flat tail to signal danger.

Calling Birds

Any novice hunter learning to communicate with crows soon discovers that the birds have several distinct calls with definite variations in rhythm and loudness. Each one has a definite meaning. This is evident when a novice crow caller sounds the alarm call instead of the rally call. Grackles communicate through their calls and chatter, but they also signal with eyes, beak, head, wings, and tail.

When calling most birds, one is always right to give the signature call of the species in order to arouse interest and inform the bird that others of its kind are within hearing. During the breeding season, male songbirds perch and sing. The male bird does not sing out of sheer joy. The songs are territorial signals, warning off other male birds of its own kind and notifying other intruders that the singer has established his boundaries. The calls also attract the female. If you imitate the territorial song or call of a songbird, the male bird often comes quickly to investigate or even to attack the intruder, and you may attract a female. That's the time when you may get an interesting photograph, and it's a good way to draw small birds out of thick cover where photography is difficult.

A low, unspecific warbling or whistling sometimes has a similar effect, and it may attract females as well as males during the breeding season and afterward. One mechanical call consists of two disks that rub against each other when they are rotated. The resulting squeaks and warbles sound like no particular bird, but they arouse curiosity. Many birds respond either by singing or coming to investigate. If you can recognize the various responses, you can locate the various species. Indians often whistled and

warbled in this way to call in predatory birds and animals that hoped to prey on nestlings.

Many birds are known by names based on their calls; for instance, the kildeer, a big plover, calls *kill-dee, kill-dee,* usually when in flight, and the bob-white's name is based on its signature call. Going through a standard bird guide and checking the names of the birds against the notations on the sounds they make will give you a large vocabulary of calls. You may already know the names and appearance of many birds. If you find that the name is based on the sound the bird makes, you are adding greatly to your knowledge.

Types of Calling

There are three general types of calling. In one of them, the caller imitates the sounds made by the bird or animal that he wishes to attract. In calling predators, the caller most often imitates the calls of the prey. For instance, the most popular call for foxes, coyotes, and birds of prey is the sound of a dying rabbit. A third type of calling depends on making noises that simply arouse curiosity. The Indians depended on these curiosity calls, and by experience, learned that low tapping, scratching, quiet and indistinct whistling, or blowing on a wide blade of grass or a leaf held between the base and tip of the thumbs, as shown in the drawing, often works. This

Holding leaf in position for calling.

type of quiet calling is often effective when the caller really does not know what kind of bird or animal to except. The sounds are not human, but they represent no specific animal or bird.

The sounds made by the predators themselves can sometimes be used to advantage. The Indians often imitated the call of a hunting hawk to freeze quail, squirrels, rabbits, and other small game so that they would stay still long enough for an easy shot with a bow.

Indian and Eskimo callers were often more successful than white men because the natives had an astonishing range of vocal sounds in their languages that the white caller found it very difficult to imitate. These sounds were often used to decoy animals and birds.

The Salish hunters of the Northwest Coast could place a stiff leaf between the teeth and blow on it to imitate the bleat of a fawn—a sure call for wolves, wildcats, and other predators as well as does and even bucks. The Salish hunters also made effective calling devices for moose and elk from the hollow stalks of sunflowers and hollow bones.

Good Indian callers could keep up a regular conversation with the quarry. They often called from blinds or thick cover, but if the game would not come to the blind, the hunter would leave it and stalk the animal, meanwhile keeping up the animal's interest with intermittent calling. Of course, the volume of the call had to be reduced as the hunter and the game came closer and closer together.

Manufactured Calls

Modern manufactured calls are available for almost every purpose, and their complexity and prices vary greatly too. For a beginner, a hard-rubber, mouth-operated call is satisfactory since he doesn't have the necessary skills to use the finely made hardwood calls. With mouth-operated calling devices, the instrument should incorporate some means of varying the pitch. If the call is capable of only one pitch, there's no possibility of adjusting it higher or lower if you find that the single pitch is off.

When mouth-operated calls are used in cold weather, saliva often enters them and freezes, silencing the call or altering the pitch. Moisture from the breath may also accumulate and freeze. Most good calling devices can be taken apart and wiped free of moisture. Calling devices that operate with vibrating reeds should be easy to take apart so that the reed can be cleaned and dried or replaced. If the call is a one-piece device, blow into it backwards from time to time to clear out moisture. It's best to carry two calls on a hunting trip. If one freezes or clogs, the other is ready.

Some calling devices depend on friction to make the sounds. Typical of this type are the cedar-box calls used for turkeys. These devices require the use of two hands, and make it difficult to hold a camera or a gun. Some calling devices are operated by squeezing a rubber bulb to force air through a reed. A few hunters do not squeeze these calls with their fingers. Instead, they place them under a foot or a knee and gently squeeze the bulb that way, leaving both hands free.

Mouth-operated calls should be light enough so that they can be held in the mouth without the use of the hands. A lanyard loop around the neck helps when you drop the call out of your mouth to use binoculars, camera, or weapon. Some calling devices can be inserted entirely inside the mouth. One turkey call consists of a vibrating diaphragm that is pushed up against the roof of the mouth and blown. It's very popular with archers, who usually like to have both hands free to keep an arrow on the string.

Scent

How to Eliminate Human Odors

Many Indian tribesmen took ritual baths in order to cleanse themselves before hunting. Some of them even spent long periods in steam baths made by plunging red-hot stones into water in dugouts. The Indians believed that this cleansing of the flesh made them more acceptable to the gods and that hunting success would be granted. The elimination of the sour human odor that is easily detected by game was probably more important, however. Indian hunters did not smoke or eat while on stand or stillhunting because the odor of tobacco and food is alarming to most game animals, though they may not connect it with man.

Some modern hunters who must come close to the game imitate the Indians in this and will not bring their deer-hunting clothes into the house. They believe that the clothes would pick up the thick indoor odors inside. The Indian's

Continued ➡

rule still stands; it's not wise to smoke a cigar, pipe, or cigarette on deer stand or break out a salami sandwich if you're waiting for a fox or coyote.

Scent Clues that Animals Leave Behind

The human nose is not a precise instrument, and few hunters claim that they use it to find game, but sometimes it does work. In heavy cover, you may catch a whiff of the very distinctive smell given off by elk. The odor of rotting meat after a bear, a mountain lion, or some other predator has made a kill sometimes leads a hunter to a productive area. The urine of most game animals has a very powerful, acrid smell, and Indians could sometimes locate a big moose by first catching the odor of its urine and then seeing the tracks.

Fresh-spilled blood has a distinct, sweetish, almost overwhelming smell. You may smell blood after a shot at a big-game animal before you actually see it. A fleeing wounded animal often lies down to try to regain its strength, and in its terror, it usually urinates freely. If you are tracking a wounded animal and catch the combined odor of fresh blood and acrid urine, you may be close to your quarry.

Men who live a great deal of their lives outdoors are much more adept at using the sense of smell to hunt than the average city dweller. In the city, the smells of gasoline, motor exhaust, millions of people, cooking, and all sorts of manufacturing processes blunt a human being's sense of smell. In clean air, it is possible to smell many animal odors, and some big-game kills have been made because the hunter smelled the animal even before he saw it or its tracks.

Scent Lures for Game

Indian hunters sometimes used female deer scent made from the glands to attract buck deer, and concentrated deer scent is available in bottled from today. Trappers also use artificial and natural concentrates to attract animals to their sets. For instance, professional predator trappers working for the government often keep coyotes captive to collect urine for use on their traps.

How game scents attract animals is something of a mystery. Sometimes they work, and sometimes they don't. Female deer scent of the animal in heat sometimes attracts buck deer during the rut. If the buck is not breeding any longer, he may lose his caution when he smells the scent on the hunter's clothes because he believes that he is dealing only with a harmless doe. And that may be the secret of animal scents. When the hunter sprinkles his clothes, particularly his boots, with them, it masks the human smell and the smell of cooked foods and tobacco. One western hunter used to douse himself with buck lure before going after Columbia blacktail deer. He once was sitting in a clump of brush when he was amazed to see a coyote coming in from downwind. Normally, a coyote would never approach a man from that direction, but this one did, and the hunter shot him. Presumably, the coyote was investigating the enticing scent of doe deer in hopes of picking up an injured animal and never caught the masked human scent.

Varmint hunters may be missing a good bet by not masking their own odors when calling. However, only a few men have tried it, and their results were not conclusive.

The Art of Becoming Invisible

Techniques of Concealment

An elaborate blind isn't always needed. Instead, the hunter may take advantage of natural cover such as reeds or brush. "Hides"—a term used in England—are used by many hunters who must move around because they cannot expect the game they await to show up near a permanent structure. Outdoorsmen who live where game is so abundant that an elaborate blind is not needed use similar temporary, often portable, hides. In Alaska and the Canadian North, few Indians and Eskimos build complicated, permanent blinds. These hunters more often pile up a rough semicircle of ice and snow or force evergreen boughs into the ground when hunting waterfowl. Elaborate waterfowl blinds are used farther south where the migrating birds follow specific flyways and are more wary after encountering many hunters on the flight south.

The Importance of Hiding Hands and Face

Indian hunters relied more on hides and clever concealment than they did on any form of blind or camouflage. You often see a white man afield at a distance as three white dots when he is wearing dull clothing. Face and hands stand out vividly. A good outdoorsman knows that his chief problem in a blind or when using camouflage is to conceal his human form. The white of hands and face and, at close range, the contrast between the white of the eye and the dark pupil are the chief giveaways. Waterfowl hunters almost always keep their faces hidden until the last moment before shooting, and turkey hunters favor face nets of dark makeup.

Breaking up the Human Outline

Indians often decorated their bows with colorful designs and often painted their faces and bodies with decorative patterns. At close range, these patterns showed up clearly, especially when very bright paint was used, but at longer range these bright patterns were difficult to pick out. Bright colors break up the human outline, and since the Indian did not show white hands and face, he was well concealed in his paint.

There is a lesson here for the modern hunter. Unless you are hunting or photographing color-sensitive game such as wild turkeys and waterfowl, your outline is more important than the colors you use. Bulky, loose clothing is better than well-fitting, tighter clothing.

How Movement Alarms Game

To most game animals and birds, movement is much more noticeable than color. A careless gesture or a nervous shifting of the leg on deer stand will often spook an oncoming buck. Indians seldom used branches or leaves tied to the headdress or body, since leafy branches sway and accentuate movement. A nod of the head that would go unnoticed by the game is exagger-

ated when the branches move. The branches or twigs also increase the height of the hunter. It's difficult to keep low with several inches of foliage sticking up over your head and shoulders. Good hunters know that they should look around a boulder, a hummock, or a log—not over them—and that is harder to do with leafy camouflage on head and shoulders.

Camouflage is of little concern to those who hunt big game with firearms. In most states and provinces, the law requires the firearms hunter to wear bright clothing during the big-game season. The water-fowler, varmint hunter, bowhunter, and photographer, on the other hand, use camouflage a great deal.

Outwitting Small Game

Rabbits, hares, and squirrels provide good hunting throughout the United States. Probably more hunters learn their craft by going after these animals than any other, and this was true of the young Indian, who learned a great deal about deer and elk hunting by using his first bow on the elusive squirrel and the erratic rabbit and hare.

The cottontail rabbit is small, fourteen to sixteen inches long, and weighs no more than two or three pounds. The white puffy tail, distinguishing the cottontail from the larger hares, is clearly visible even at a distance when the animal is going away fast. Local variations of the cottontail include the New England variety, the desert cottontail, the swamp rabbit, and the marsh rabbit. The ranges of these animals often overlap. For the hunter, the animals are much the same and inhabit similar territories, except for the swamp rabbit and the marsh rabbit, both of which favor freshwater swales in the South.

In Europe, rabbits live by the thousands in large warrens and dig their own burrows. They dig so many holes in a confined area that they often undermine roads, railroad right-of-ways, and even airfields. In the United States, "rabbits" and hares do not live crowded together, and they rarely dig their own burrows. Instead, they establish forms—nests in depressions in the ground often lined with soft grasses and the fur of the doe. Sometimes, however, cottontails take refuge in burrows dug by other animals, the woodchuck in particular. If this happens when you are hunting, it's almost useless to try to dig the rabbit out since it will use the escape hole made by the chuck. Digging out rabbits or almost any form of game is illegal in most states.

In the United States and Canada, the term "hare" includes the arctic hare, the snowshoe hare (sometimes called the snowshoe rabbit), and the various jackrabbits of the West. Among the latter are the black-tailed jack, the white-

Cottontail rabbit.

Continued ➡

sided jack, and the white-tailed jack. All species of hare are larger and heavier than the various forms of cottontail. The white-tailed jack may be as long as twenty-eight inches, and weigh as much as ten pounds. The meat of the jacks is stringy, tough, and almost without flavor. The Indians and most white men prefer the flesh of the cottontail. Arctic hares and the snowshoe rabbit (varying hare) are good eating.

In upper New York State and the area around the Great Lakes in the United States and Canada, the hunter may be confused when he brings down a big hare resembling the black-tailed jackrabbit but with no black on its rump. This is the European hare, long escaped from the hutches of early settlers and gone wild. Eastern Indians soon discovered that this hare is flavorful and big enough to be meaty.

Hunting Cottontails

Walking Them Up

Walking them up assures a well-filled bag if the hunter knows the terrain and where rabbits are likely to be found. After a slight snow, look for tracks to locate concentrations of them. Even when there is no snow, you can often locate the well-worn runways that the cottontail establishes in thick cover such as brier patches, thick clumps of berry bushes, and other dense vegetation. Overgrown pastures and fields near woods and other fringe areas are always a good bet.

Cottontails prefer thorny bushes or vines for cover because they can run below the thorns, though dogs, foxes, coyotes, and larger birds of prey find it difficult to negotiate that kind of cover. Some Woodland Indians wore full-length rawhide leggings that resembled the chaps worn by cowmen for this kind of hunting. Nowadays, cottontail hunters often wear heavy leather-faced trousers.

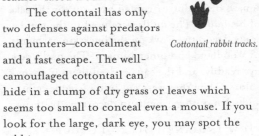

The cottontail has only two defenses against predators and hunters—concealment and a fast escape. The well-camouflaged cottontail can

Cottontail rabbit tracks.

hide in a clump of dry grass or leaves which seems too small to conceal even a mouse. If you look for the large, dark eye, you may spot the rabbit.

Bolting the Cottontail

To bolt the cottontail from its hide, try the Indian trick of taking a few steps and then standing stock still for a minute or two. The rabbit may panic and break cover. If two or three hunters work together, walking a stretch of cover abreast, it's best for all of them to pause and wait at frequent intervals. Good hunters, who know how to walk and stop, can often get their limits out of a single abandoned pasture, while the man who insists on walking miles may pass through the same territory without getting a single shot.

Locating the Runways

In heavy cover, it may be possible to trail-watch for cottontails. Go through the cover slowly some time when you are not hunting or when the season is closed and look for the runways. The best place to stand is where two or more

Gray squirrel.

runways cross, and when you go out with your gun or bow, try to stay downwind. You'll often find tufts of rabbit hair caught on thorns and branches if the runway is used often. Sitting on a good runway early in the morning or late in the afternoon when cottontails are on the move will often put a few of them in the bag.

Squirrels

There are five kinds of tree squirrels in the United States, and the range of some of them extends into Canada.

The most common is the familiar gray squirrel of the East, which becomes almost tame where hunting is not permitted. It can be a nuisance as well. In the wild, the gray squirrel is a clever, wary game animal. These animals weigh about one pound.

Many squirrel hunters have never seen a fox squirrel because they have grown scarce in some areas, although the overall range of the fox squirrel is about the same as that of the gray. These animals have much more red in their fur and are sometimes called big red squirrels or red-tailed squirrels. They weigh from about 2 1/4 to 2 3/4 pounds. The fox squirrel is so large that he looks as big as a marten to the man who is used to hunting grays. The fox squirrel is much clumsier in trees than the gray or any other tree squirrel, and that may be the reason why this animal is almost extinct in some parts of his range. A hunter usually has little difficulty in hitting a fox squirrel, and predators find it an easy prey.

The tiny red squirrel is edible, too, but is so small that few men hunt him. It is only about ten inches long and the tail makes up four to six inches of this length. The average weight is less than half a pound.

The reddish-pelted animal, often called chickaree, is a woods sentinel. The red squirrel seems unafraid of hunters, perhaps because he is seldom hunted, and scolds intruders noisily. Often a deer stalk is spoiled by a nervous chickaree scolding the silent stillhunter, who should try to get away from red as quickly as possible. Even then, red may follow, scolding the hunter and alerting every deer for hundreds of yards. Indian hunters often avoided his scolding by moving silently and staying away from nut trees and den trees where he was likely to be found or by screaming like a hunting hawk. This scares a chickaree and makes him freeze until the hunter passes by. The hawk scream must be a perfect imitation in order to avoid frightening off the deer or other game you are hunting.

The red squirrel is regarded as vermin in many states and no limit or closed season is imposed, though a few states do classify him as a game animal. He is destructive and eats nestlings

and eggs. Reds also seem to be able to kill off the larger gray squirrel in certain areas and take over that more valuable animal's range. They do this by raiding the nests of gray squirrels and killing the kits to eat, but sometimes a tiny red squirrel pursues the larger gray adult and bites at his rear. Sometimes the red manages to do an effective castration job.

Hunting the red squirrel is good conservation. Where there is no limit, a dozen or more in the stew pot make an excellent meal. Woodland Indians often used them for food when other game was scarce.

There is a California gray squirrel, and there are two forms of tassel-eared squirrels that inhabit the area along the Colorado River, but few westerners hunt squirrels for food. The few who do are almost always from back East. Western hunters are missing a good bet when they disdain tree squirrels as game.

Most tree squirrels are subject to melanism, and albinos are to be found. In some areas, you may run across glossy-black gray squirrels. These are melanistic, though some southern hunters insist that they are a separate species.

Squirrels' Favorite Foods

All tree squirrels eat nuts, fruits, berries, seeds, some soft twigs and bark, a few kinds of fungus, and some farm crops, especially corn. The primary food of the fox squirrel and the gray is nuts, and you'll almost always find these animals among oaks, beech trees, hickories, and other nut trees. Since the Indians gathered many different kinds of nuts for their own food, an Indian squirrel hunter had an advantage over most modern urban hunters. While gathering nuts, he kept an eye open for a flaunting tail. If you want to hunt squirrels successfully, one good way to prepare yourself is to study trees so that you can recognize nut-bearers at a distance. When you can pick out a black walnut among the other trees in a grove, you'll probably find squirrels in it if it is nut-bearing at the time.

Squirrels can bite deeply enough to make a nasty wound. If you stun or wound a squirrel, don't pick it up too soon. The Indians often finished off squirrels by pressing a foot firmly on the animal's shoulders below the neck so that the squirrel could not bite the moccasined foot. The pressure stopped the heart and lungs. This method works well with other small game.

Stillhunting

Stillhunting for squirrels is primarily a matter of recognizing good country in which to hunt them and stalking in silence. Some stillhunters use squirrel calls to imitate the contented sounds that the animals make when they have found abundant food. Indian hunters often tapped and rubbed two round, smooth pebbles together to imitate a squirrel chewing on a nut shell to get at the meat inside. Most of the time, those two sounds will bring squirrels to the feast through the treetops. Since the squirrels usually travel fairly high in the treetops, the hunter seldom has

Gray squirrel tracks.

Continued ➜

to worry about his scent reaching the animals. A good stillhunter moves silently through the woods, but should pause often to conceal himself and call. Sometimes the squirrels will not come but they will answer, and then the hunter stalks them.

Hunting in Pairs

The gray squirrel is an expert at keeping a tree trunk between himself and the hunter. If you're on one side of the tree, the squirrel almost always seems to be on the opposite side. He often climbs the tree on that side until he reaches the crown and then jumps to another tree without being seen. Indians often hunted squirrels in pairs, and modern hunters often do the same. When two hunters approach a nut tree and a squirrel whisks around to the other side, one man remains where he is, weapon ready, and the other quickly moves around the tree. One or the other will usually get a shot. If there is a third man in the party, he backs off a few yards so that he can see the topmost branches. Often he is able to pick off the squirrel if it is out of sight of the two other men.

Indian Ruses for Fooling Squirrels

If you're hunting alone, it sometimes helps to prop up your coat and perhaps your hat on a bush near the tree. When you go around the trunk, the squirrel will usually circle around, too. When he sees your coat and hat, he may become alarmed and freeze for an instant, so that you may get a shot.

Some Indian hunters carried a long fiber cord or thong. When the squirrel dodged around the trunk, the Indian hitched the line to a sapling or bush before he went around the trunk. When the squirrel came around to his original position, the Indian pulled on the line to shake the bush or sapling violently. This often held the squirrel's attention so that the hunter could fire. Modern squirrel hunters who use this trick often tie a short stick to the end of the line. It's quicker to hitch the stick behind a low fork in a bush than it is to tie the line.

Sitting for Squirrels

Some hunters find it pays off to sit for squirrels. Take up a favorable position near or in a grove of hardwoods and remain quiet. If you can conceal yourself, so much the better. Some Indians lie prone on the ground on their backs and shoot from that position, and many shotgunners and riflemen do the same. Putting leaves over yourself to break up your outline helps, and some men carry a camouflage ground cloth that they throw over themselves, but that's dangerous in heavily hunted squirrel groves. If you know of a den tree, try sitting for squirrels there. As a rule, a den tree has large hollows where branches have broken off and the stub has rotted out, or the trunk may be hollow. Some hunters sit near a den tree and then use their calls to make the alarmed sounds that squirrels make when they spot a predator or a hunter. That often brings the squirrels running to the shelter of the den tree, and the hunter may be able to take as many as three or four of them as they come.

Squirrels sometimes ignore the discharge of a rifle of a shotgun. After a shot, remain still, and the animals will begin to move again in fifteen minutes or so. If you are sitting for squirrels, it's wise to let cleanly killed animals lie until you are finished hunting in that area. Mark where they fall by noting bushes, branches, or stones near the animal and wait until you are finished before picking up the kill. The less you move, the better.

Squirrel hunters sometimes concentrate so much on watching tree trunks and high branches that they miss squirrels on the ground. If berries and fruits are available on low bushes or have fallen to the ground, or if the nuts are falling, you may find squirrels almost underfoot if you walk quietly enough.

Some squirrel hunters have the unsportsmanlike habit of firing a charge of shot into every squirrel nest they see in hopes of knocking a squirrel out of them. These leafy breeding nests are almost always empty by the time the hunting season starts.

Best Hunting Weather

On windy, cold days or when rain or snow is falling, squirrels remain at home and wait the weather out; so it's wiser to hunt on calm, rather warm days, and the best time is early in the morning or late in the afternoon. Squirrel hunting, as the Indians knew, is usually good just after a cold snap or a storm has ended because the denned-up animals come out to make up for time in their feeding.

If you hunt during bad weather, the middle of the day is sometimes productive. The squirrel stays at home until hunger drives him to feed, and that's usually later in the day than usual. If the weather is bad during the forenoon, but improves later in the day, that's the time to be out with gun or bow.

Porcupines

These big, blundering rodents with their many quills grow to nearly a yard in length and may weigh over forty pounds. The barbed quills—about 32,000 of them—give an adult porcupine the look of a black, elongated pincushion with white streaks. Porcupines like to sit in the high branches of a tree and sway back and forth in the wind. They are so large that it's quite possible to mistake one high in a tree for a bear cub.

To defend himself, porky pokes his unarmed face into shelter such as the space under a log or between ground and a boulder and lashes out with his quill-armed tail. If he's unusually aggressive, he'll "charge" suddenly backwards toward the enemy, but will likely lumber back to his improvised shelter.

Porcupine.

The fisher (pekan), a big tree-climbing weasel, is about the only woods animal that manages to dine regularly on porcupines. The lightning-fast fisher turns the porcupine over onto his back and bites at the unprotected underside. Coyotes can do it, too. One coyote engages porky's attention, and the other rushes in from the side and flips him over; then one or both may get in a killing bite.

Porcupine tracks.

The quills are hollow and enable the porcupine to float with ease, but he spends most of his time aloft eating tree bark and tender twigs, which makes him hated by tree farmers and timber companies. The porcupine will often work his way right around a trunk, eating bark as he goes. That girdles the tree and kills it. He also likes to eat canoe paddles, axes, and tool handles for the salty sweat on them.

The laws in some places prohibit the killing of porcupines except by a man who is lost in the woods and starving. The porcupine is so slow that a man can easily kill one with a club. If the bark and twig supply holds up, a porcupine will stay in a small clump of trees for an entire year, and he may stay in one small area for his entire life. If Indians saw a porcupine and had no immediate need for meat, they would note its location. When other game grew scarce, they often had several porcupines pinpointed and could kill them as needed. Since the porcupine does not hibernate, he is accessible all year round.

Porky lives in a stub hole in a tree, a cleft in the rocks, a cave, a hollow under tree roots or boulders—any shelter that doesn't require too much work to make it comfortable. Indian squaws often dug or rooted him out for the sake of his quills. The quills were used in the handsome decorative work on the buckskin garments of Woodland and other Indians. The quills take dye readily, and the squaws dyed them in many colors. Then they were cut into varied lengths and sewn onto garments in decorative patterns.

How Indians Pulled Porcupines from Their Dens

At times, squaws dug porky out, but usually it was enough to pull him out of his den with a stick. The squaw took a supple length of sapling about an inch thick and split one end of it to form four or more long, flexible "fingers." The porcupine stick was shoved into the den until contact was made, and then the stick was pushed and twisted until the ends caught in the animal's quills. The porcupine was then dragged out of the hole and killed with a club. If you try the same procedure, be sure about the identity of the animal in the hole. It may be a skunk. Tracks and sign near the den will usually identify the animal inside.

Woodchucks

The common chuck that burrows under boulders and stumps in almost every pasture in the eastern states and southern Canada is a surprisingly big and bold animal. A large adult weighs

Continued →

ten pounds or a little more, and he is well armed with strong rodent teeth and earthmoving claws.

The woodchuck feeds early and late on tender green vegetation including timothy, hay, alfalfa, and garden crops. His burrows are a constant hazard to horses and cattle.

Where Chucks Dig Their Burrows

The woodchuck's burrow is usually dug on rather high, dry ground, and it must be close to green ground vegetation, for the chuck does not climb trees and does not range far from home to feed.

Indian youngsters used to stalk woodchucks to demonstrate their stalking skill and courage. While the chuck was feeding outside his burrow, the would-be brave tried to place himself between the chuck and the entrance to the hole and then kill him with club or bow. The chuck is a brave animal, and the Indian youngster often found it difficult to stand up to the animal's angry growls and menacing jaws and meet its headlong charge.

Woodchuck tracks.

Bowhunters often try this trick today, and find that the chuck hasn't changed. He is still one of the few animals in North America that will charge boy, man, or dog and bite when he attacks.

The Crees, Ojibways, and Algonquins all hunted the chuck for practice in stalking and shooting and for food when other game was scarce. A young chuck, carefully cleaned and cooked, is a tasty dish, and some modern hunters eat them. Today, the chuck is a valued animal in many areas because he provides a living target for long-range riflemen who go after him with the latest in flat-shooting firearms equipped with rifle scopes. Almost everywhere, farmers welcome the chuck hunter because he thins out these crop-eating rodents and helps to cut down on the number of dangerous chuck holes in the pastures.

The Right Ranges for Archers and Riflemen

The bowhunter who goes after chucks is taking on a tough challenge. The rifleman shoots from 100 yards or more for the sake of long-range practice, and will often hold his fire at short range. The bowhunter must get within fifteen or twenty yards of the small, wary target, and that's difficult in areas where the chucks have become hunter-shy. A chuck vanishes into long grass or down a hole so fast that he seems to disappear into thin air, but if you remain quiet, he often pops up again and sits up on his haunches to peer around. Walking heavily sends vibrations through the ground and warns the chuck to stay below.

The chuck remains in his burrow all winter and emerges in February or March. He goes below ground again with the first frost. Chucks seldom come above ground during bad weather.

Woodchuck.

In almost every state, the chuck is regarded as vermin by farmers and cattlemen, and he is a legal target whenever he can be found above ground. But in some areas where he is heavily hunted, sportsmen voluntarily refrain from killing young (small) chucks and nursing females with young following them. Thinning them out a bit helps the farmer; killing too many young ones and nursing females may cut down on the sport.

Other Small Game

On occasion, the Indians hunted several other small animals with bow and arrow or firearms. Muskrats and beaver were sometimes hunted, and the Indian trapper would do almost anything to rid himself of a raiding wolverine. Most often, though, the beaver, muskrat, wolverine, lynx, mink, marten, sable, river otter, the various weasels, and other small fur-bearers were and still are taken with traps and snares rather than firearms. The Aleuts of Alaska did hunt the sea otter from kayaks with harpoons, and after the Russian fur traders arrived, they sometimes used firearms too. The sea-otter trade led to the exploration of Alaska and Russian colonization there. It is interesting to know that the pursuit of this valuable fur-bearer by Indian hunters working for the Russians led to the early exploration of the western coast just as the lust for beaver pelts led to the exploration of much of the American and Canadian West.

Weapons and Ruses for taking Birds

The Indians often trapped and hunted birds such as eagles, turkeys, hawks, and the large woodpeckers to obtain feathers for decoration and for fletching arrows. The feathers of the turkey, turkey buzzard, and the various geese were used a great deal for fletching.

Small birds were seldom taken with bow and arrow, though some young hunters took them with very light, pronged spears or with arrows with blunt points that killed or stunned by impact. Boys of the Plains tribes were taught to snare birds with nooses made of horsehair. The small nooses were tied about six inches apart on a stick that was placed on the ground. Seeds or grain were scattered as bait. Some birds nearly always got their legs entangled in these snares, and the watching boys ran from cover to kill them before they could escape. The stick to which the nooses were tied acted as a drag.

Quail

By studying the habits of quail, California Indians learned that the western forms of this game bird like to follow a low fence, natural hedge, or line of brush rather than fly over it. To trap the quail, they attached nooses made of fine thongs to bushes or branches at openings in the runways and also placed the nooses where the runways ended. Sometimes the Indians baited the ground near the nooses. From time to time, boys or women removed the birds caught in the snares, which were then reset.

Turkeys

An odd, simple trap was used to catch the wary wild turkey. Two poles were driven into the ground about ten feet apart. A much lighter pole was tied between the two uprights about fourteen inches above the ground. The trap was then baited with grains of maize. Knowing the habits of the birds, the Indians knew the direction of their approach and scattered corn under the length of the pole and six to twelve inches beyond it. A few women and boys then hid nearby and stayed quiet. When the turkeys reached the trap and began feeding on the grain, they soon had to stretch their necks beneath the crossbar to reach the grain. A wild turkey does not seem to be able to withdraw its head from under a low horizontal pole. The hidden trappers rushed from their blind and snatched the self-trapped birds.

Geese

Canada geese, snow geese, and blue geese were trapped in an equally simple way. A trench about eighteen feet long, eighteen inches deep, and fourteen inches wide was dug in the ground. Kernels of maize were sparingly scattered along the length of the trench, and the trench trap was ready. The trappers took cover close to the trap. When the geese flew in, they began to eat the grain at the ends of the trench, then continued into the trench itself in search of more corn. When several geese were in the trench, the trappers rushed from cover and seized the birds. The geese could not fly away because they did not have enough room to spread their wings in the narrow trench.

Aiming for the Vital Areas of Game

Most novice hunters have very little idea of the anatomy of animals and therefore they do not place their shots properly. The best possible training, of course, is to skin and cut up game animals or help someone do it as Indian young-sters did.

Four-footed Animals

The placement of the heart and lungs of four-footed animals is quiet low in the chest. Not knowing this, many hunters place their shots too high. From the side, the total lung-heart area of a deer is only about 10 inches high and about 14 inches long—a small target at 200 or more yards, and a very small target for the archer at almost any range.

As shown in the drawing, the line formed by the rear of the upper leg cuts the heart-lung area in half when viewed from the side. Placing a bullet or an arrow on that line at just the right

Continued ➡

height may pierce the lung on your side, the upper part of the heart, and the lung on the other side. Most hunters describe this shot as hitting just "behind the shoulder." The use of the word "shoulder" is deceptive. It gives the impression that the vital area is high in the chest because most people think in terms of human anatomy. Almost all four-footed animals have the vital organs in the lower two-thirds of the body. If you are a little high with a rifle, you may smash the spine above the lungs, but that's hard to hit and it's easy to shoot high over the animal's back.

Going-away Shots

It is rare to find a wary game animal standing still broadside to the hunter. Most often, game animals are going away from the hunter, and that fact-poses something of a problem, particularly for archers. If a deer, elk, antelope, or other nondangerous game runs straight away from the hunter, he has only two possible targets. He can aim at the neck (including the back of the head), intending to kill by cutting or smashing the spinal column or the brain, or he can aim directly between the hams, fairly high, to drive the bullet right through the intestinal tract and into the heart-lung area. Both are difficult shots even for a skilled hunter firing an accurate, high-powered rifle.

Limitations of Archery Tackle

Chiefly because of the small target area, both of these shots from the rear are almost impossible for the archer. Most experienced archers who know the limitations of bow and arrow and who are good sportsman pass up every shot that must be taken directly from the rear, because it results in so much wounded game.

The archer does have a good shot if the animal's rump is presented at a slight angle. In fact, many archers prefer to angle the arrow into the animal just behind the ribs so that it ranges forward into the heart-lung area from the rear, inside the ribs. A precisely placed shaft touches no bone from that angle. If the animal is facing away at a fairly acute angle, and the archer holds just in front of the swell of the haunch, his target is comparatively large, and hemorrhage caused by the broadhead may involve both lungs and heart. Piercing one of these organs will kill fairly rapidly.

There is little or no shocking power to an arrow even when shot from a hunting bow with a 60- or 70-pound pull. An arrow kills by causing bleeding, especially when the broadhead happens to cut a vital organ. By contrast, a .30/06 rifle bullet at 100 yards hits with about 2,400 foot-pounds of energy. A rifleman who switches to archery tackle sometimes has difficulty in realizing its limitations—something that the Indian knew from childhood.

The vast majority of big game killed with arrow dies by bleeding alone. For this reason, the archer has a heavy obligation to place his shots very carefully. Rifleman and those who hunt deer with shotguns have the same obligation.

Shots from in Front

When hunting nondangerous game from directly in front, the best target is the lower chest. If you're a little high, but centered, an arrow will go into the lower throat and will probably kill fairly quickly. If you're dead on, the animal will be hit in the heart; if you're slightly to one side, one lung will be affected. The same aiming points work well with a rifle.

An archer who faces big game from the front or at a slight quartering angle is in a dangerous position. It can be difficult to down a charging bear or an angry moose even with a rifle. This is why many responsible big-game hunters who use bows recommend a back-up-gun—another hunter or a guide armed with a heavy rifle who intervenes if the situations becomes too dangerous. Foolish bravado with archery tackle may result in a mauling or death. This is why Indian archers either left big bears alone or only took sure shots.

Indian archers were experts at placing their arrows correctly because there was enough game to provide them with almost unlimited practice. Lately, modern archers are turning to three-dimensional, animal-shaped targets made of foam plastic. Try hitting vital areas on these targets from every angle expect directly from the rear, and you'll learn how accurate affective bow-and-arrow work must be.

Shooting from Elevated Stands

When shooting from an elevated stand in a tree or on a steep hillside, the best target is usually the middle of the back when using firearms. Try to angle your shot downward toward the heart-lung area. If you are slightly forward of the animal, aim right at the top of the shoulders. From the side, angle in just to the near side of the spine. All these shots make a humane kill if you are using an adequate rifle, and if the shot can be centered, you may smash the backbone before the bullet even reaches heart or lung.

Good archers aim slightly to the side of the spine when shooting from above because an arrow from a powerful bow can be depended on

to drive between or through the upper ribs and penetrate the heart-lung area. The spine itself is too tough.

The archer should always have another shaft ready after the first shot. If at all possible, get off a second shaft before the animal can run. A quiver mounted on the bow helps, but holding the second arrow in the bow hand parallel to the bow works well, too, provided you practice using it enough so that it doesn't throw your shooting style off. Many archers stick their second broad-headed arrow into soft ground when they are shooting from a stand at ground level. It can be picked up quickly by the nock. Broadheads should be very sharp, and an arrow that has been stuck into rocky or sandy ground has lost its sharp edges even before it is nocked. Carry a file and a small honing stone on bowhunting trips and go over the edges of every arrow you recover after a shot. If a broadhead is shot into brush and recovered, one or more of the edges are usually dulled.

No sporting firearms hunter or archer ever aims for a game animal's paunch. A hit there does not kill, and it usually does not cause much bleeding. Instead, the intestines or the stomach are pierced, and the animal may die in agony miles away.

—From *Exploring the Outdoors with Indian Secrets*

Trailing Wounded Animals

Dwight Schuh

Even a well-hit animal can travel some distance. And, of course, you can't always guarantee a perfect hit. Eventually, if you hunt enough, you'll trail some game, which is part of bowhunting. Trailing must be perfected right along with shooting ability and hunting technique.

Follow up every shot. If you're in open country, run to the nearest vantage point and keep the animal in sight as long as possible. The easiest way to recover animals is to watch them go down, but, of course, that's not always possible. In some cases, you may not even know whether you hit an animal. If you aren't sure, go immediately to the point where the deer was standing and mark that place so you can find it again. Then look for your arrow. If you find it clean, you know you missed. If not, the arrow could tell you a lot about the hit. If you don't find the arrow, begin searching carefully for blood sign. If you don't find any blood, track the animal as far as possible. He could travel some distance, 100 yards or more, before any blood hits the ground.

If you find signs of a hit, you must decide whether to wait or follow the animal immediately. If you're sure of a solid chest hit, or if you see foamy blood sprayed onto the ground, you know the deer was hit in the lungs and is already down. If you know you hit him in the chest, but aren't sure where, wait an hour or so. Even if he dies immediately, the meat won't spoil in that time, and you've lost nothing but a little time. If the animal doesn't die quickly, the longer you wait, the better your chances of recovery. A

Vital area of the whitetail deer.

BRAIN
SPINE
LARGE ARTERY
LUNGS
VITAL AREA
HEART

Continued ➡

liver-hit animal, for example, will bleed to death in an hour, and you'll find him in his first bed. But if you push him, he could travel far enough to make recovery difficult.

If you know the animal was hit in the gut—either you saw the hit or find greenish juices on the arrow or on the ground—then back off. He will lie down soon, and that's where you must find him. If you startle him, he could travel several miles, leaving little or no blood trail, and your chances of finding him are zip. If you shot him in late afternoon, wait until the next morning to start trailing.

My friend Larry D. Jones taught me a cardinal rule of trailing: stick with the trail. That might seem obvious, and it's not hard to do when you find blood sprayed out by the pint, but sometimes the blood trial gets sparse, a drop or two of blood every ten feet. You may convince yourself the animal has quit bleeding, so you quit the trail to course ahead like a bird dog, hoping to find the animal or luck onto obvious sign.

Stick with the trail. On several occasions while hunting with Larry, I've gone on ahead, trying to anticipate an animal's route. While I did that, Larry patiently snooped around, looking for the trail. Time after time, he picked it up heading the opposite direction. I no longer put much credence in the theories that wounded animals head downhill or seek water or hole up in the nearest cover. Those are good last-resort guidelines, but before you try them, out the trail instead.

Following a major blood trail is easy. But even mortally wounded animals may leave a sparse trail, especially with a high chest hit that bleeds inside the body. That's when you learn trailing skills. If you just walk along, you'll miss hidden sign and swear the animal has quit bleeding, but if you get on your hands and knees, the trial will be obvious. Late one evening I shot an elk that covered a lot of ground quickly. Before long, darkness set in, and I had to trial with a flashlight. I couldn't see well in the dim beam, so I crawled and was amazed at how easily I detected pinhead spots of blood with my face close to the ground. You can trail very well in the beam of a flashlight (a gas lantern works even better), so don't give up just because of darkness. That's one reason your hunting pack should include a flashlight along with spare batteries and an extra bulb.

Crawling not only gives you a close-up view, but a better angle. Often, blood running down an animal's side or leg won't drip to the ground, but it will smear onto bushes and grass. You may never see this sign looking downward. But from a low angle looking up, you'll see blood smears on the underside of vegetation.

On a skimpy blood trial, you must rely on other signs, too. Overturned rocks, broken twigs, and mud smeared on rocks all indicate an animal's passing. Once, while trailing an elk, I lost the blood trail. Noticing several places where pine needles had been distributed, I crawled along for half an hour and finally found a speck of blood, confirming that these were indeed the elk's tracks. I eventually recovered the elk.

Tracks, of course, are the surest sign next to blood. At the very start of a trail, study the

AVOIDING INJURY FROM WOUNDED ANIMALS
Allan A. Macfarlan

Approach all "dead" game with caution. The stories of careless deer hunters mutilated on the antlers of seemingly dead deer are legion, and many other animals are dangerous when wounded. Even the inoffensive pronghorn antelope can injure a man severely with his sharp hoofs if he kicks convulsively just as the hunter bends over the motionless animal or kneels down beside it. The safest approach is from the animal's back as it lies on the ground. In some cases, the nature of the wound is quite conclusive. A solid hit in a vital area or a dislocated or shattered spine is usually apparent to the eye, but take no chances. Gently touch the animal's eye with the muzzle of your gun or the tip of an arrow. Even an unconscious animal will blink if it is still alive. If the animal does blink, put another bullet into it or use another broadhead.

If you are anxious to save meat, the neck just below the skull is a good place for a finishing shot with firearm or bow, but that mars the animal's cape for purposes of taxidermy. Some hunters cut the throat of every big game animal that they put down in order to make sure that it is dead and bleed it, but that mars the cape, too. If you want a head-and-neck mount, it's probably best to put another bullet or arrow into the heart-lung area.

Following up a wounded game animal is a difficult and sometimes dangerous task, especially if you have shot the animal in rough country just before sunset. Good sportsmanship demands a quick, merciful kill. In addition, you'll avoid a lot of troublesome tracking if you shoot well enough to anchor the animal.

Every time a humane hunter fires a shot, he investigates the results even if he believes that he has missed. Game is too scarce today to be wasted, and even in frontier times, Indians and white men valued wild meat and hides too much to waste an animal.

Before making any move to follow a wounded animal, take a few minutes to look at the lay of the land and think about the nature of the hit. You may save yourself hours of difficult, perhaps dangerous tracking by figuring out where the animal is likely to go.

Look for blood on the ground, grass, or leaves, and don't give up until you have followed the animal's tracks or general line of flight for a considerable distance. If the animal has gotten into thick cover, and you can't see a clear blood trail or tracks, it often pays to zigzag back and forth as you follow its general direction.

—From *Exploring the Outdoors with Indian Secrets*

animal's tracks for distinctive marks. Then they'll stand out surprisingly well as you follow the trail, even when they're mixed with other animal's tracks. Every animal has a distinctive stride length. When you find two clearly visible tracks made by your animal, use an arrow or a stick to measure the distance from one track to the next (a big buck might have a stride of twenty-four inches, a bull elk twenty-eight). Then use the arrow or stick as a tracking gauge on the visible track and inspect the ground at the other end of the gauge. If you find one track but can't clearly see the next, lay one end of the gauge. That's where the next track will be. I've tracked elk and deer several hundred yards across hard ground using this method.

If you simply can't follow the trail any longer, your last resort is to visually search for the animal. Try to anticipate where he might have gone and search systematically. Don't wander haphazardly. Mentally map out the area in quadrants, and then search back and forth to make sure you're not overlooking any possible cover. Keep looking until you've covered every base. If you've spent a full day, ten to twelve hours, searching for an animal and still can't find him or any fresh clues, then you've probably done all you can. But until that point, keep looking.

—From *Fundamentals of Bowhunting*

Methods for Preparing Game

Preparing Game

Greg Davenport
Illustrations by Steven Davenport and Ken Davenport

In order to eat your catch, you'll first need to skin, gut, and butcher most game. Always do this well away from your camp and your food cache. Before skinning an animal, be sure it is dead. Once you're sure, cut the animal's throat, and collect the blood in a container for later use in a stew. If time is not an issue, wait thirty minutes before starting to skin. This allows the body to cool, which makes it easier to skin and also provides enough time for most parasites to leave the animal's hide.

Glove skinning is the method most often used for skinning small game. Hang the animal from its hind legs, and make a circular cut just above the leg joints. Don't cut through the tendon. To avoid dulling your knife by cutting from the fur side, slide a finger between the hide and muscle, and place your knife next to the muscle so that you cut the hide from the inside. Cut down the inside of each leg, ending close to the genital area, and peel the skin off the legs until you reach the animal's tail. Firmly slide a finger under the hide between the tail and spine until you have a space that allows you to cut the tail free. Follow the same procedure on the front side. At this point, the hide can be pulled down and free from the animal's membrane with little effort. Avoid squeezing the belly, as this may cause urine to spill onto the

Continued ➜

meat. Pull the front feet through the hide (inside out) by sliding a finger between the elbow and the membrane and pulling the leg up and free from the rest of the hide. Cut off the feet. The head can either be severed or skinned, depending on your talents.

A larger animal can be hung from a tree by its hind legs or skinned while lying on the ground. To hang it by its hind legs, find the tendon that connects the upper and lower leg, and poke a hole between it and the bone. If musk glands are present, remove them. These are usually found at the bend between the upper and lower parts of the hind legs. Free the hide from the animal's genitals by cutting a circular area around them, and then make an incision that runs just under the hide and all the way up to the neck. To avoid cutting the entrails, slide your index and middle fingers between the hide and the thin membrane enclosing the entrails. Use the V between the fingers to guide the cut and push the entrails down and away from the knife. The knife should be held with its backside next to the membrane and the sharp side facing out, so that when used, it cuts the hide from the non-hair side. Next, cut around the joint of each extremity. From there, extend the cut down the inside of each leg until it reaches the midline incision. You should attempt to pull off the hide using the same method as for small game. If you need to use your knife, cut toward the meat so as not to damage the hide. Avoid cutting through the entrails or hide. If skinning on the ground, use the hide to protect the meat, and don't remove it until after you gut and butcher the animal. Once the hide has been removed, it can be tanned and used for clothing, shelter cover, and containers.

To gut an animal, place the carcass, belly up, on a slope or hang it from a tree by its hind legs. Make a small incision just in front of the anus, and insert your index and middle fingers into the cut, spreading them apart to from a V. Slide the knife into the incision between the V formed by your two fingers. Use your fingers to push the internal organs down, away from the knife, and as a guide for the knife as you cut up the abdominal cavity to the breastbone. Avoid cutting the bladder or other internal organs. If they are punctured, wash the meat as soon as possible. Cut around the anus and sex organs so that they will be easily removed with the entrails.

Remove the intact bladder by pinching it off close to the opening and cutting it free. Remove the entrails, pulling the down and away from the carcass. To do this, you will need to sever the intestines at the anus. Save the liver and kidneys for later consumption. If the liver is spotted, a sign of disease, discard all internal organs and thoroughly cook the meat. Cut through the diaphragm and reach inside the chest cavity until you can touch the windpipe. Cut or pull the windpipe free and remove the chest cavity contents. Save the lungs and heart for later consumption. All internal organs can be cooked in any fashion but are best when used in a stew.

If you intend to eat the liver, you'll need to remove the small black sac, the gallbladder, as it's not edible. If it breaks, wash the liver immediately to avoid tainting the meat. Since fat spoils quickly, it should be cut away from the meat and promptly used. The fat is best in soups.

To butcher an animal, cut the legs, back, and breast sections free of one another. When butchering large game, cut it into meal-size roasts and steaks that can be stored for later use. Cut the rest of the meat along the grain into long, thin strips about ⅛ inch thick, to be preserved by smoking or sun drying. The head meat, tongue, eyes, and brain are all edible, as is the marrow inside bones.

—From *Surviving the Desert*

Skinning and Butchering Game

U.S. Army

Bleed the animal by cutting its throat. If possible, clean the carcass near a stream. Place the carcass belly up and split the hide from throat to tail, cutting around all sexual organs. Remove the musk glands at points A and B to avoid tainting the meat. For smaller mammals, cut the hide around the body and insert two fingers under the hide on both sides of the cut and pull both pieces off.

Note: When cutting the hide, insert the knife blade under the skin and turn the blade up so that only the hide gets cut. This will also prevent cutting hair and getting it on the meat.

Remove the entrails from smaller game by splitting the body open and pulling them out with the fingers. Do not forget the chest cavity. For larger game, cut the gullet away from the diaphragm. Roll the entrails out of the body. Cut around the anus, then reach into the lower abdominal cavity, grasp the lower intestine, and pull to remove. Remove the urine bladder by pinching it off and cutting it below the fingers. If you spill urine on the meat, wash it to avoid tainting the meat. Save the heart and liver. Cut these open and inspect for signs of worms or other parasites. Also inspect the liver's color; it could indicate a diseased animal. The liver's surface should be smooth and wet and its color deep red or purple. If the liver appears diseased, discord it. However, a diseased liver does not indicate you cannot eat the muscle tissue.

Cut along each leg from above the foot to the previously made body cut. Remove the hide by pulling it away from the carcass, cutting the connective tissue where necessary. Cut off the head and feet.

Cut larger game into manageable pieces. First, slice the muscle tissue connecting the front legs to the body. There are no bones or joints connecting the front legs to the body on four-legged animals. Cut the hindquarters off where they join the body. You must cut around a large bone at the top of the leg and cut to the ball and socket hip joint. Cut the ligaments around the joint and bend it back to separate it. Remove the large muscles (the tenderloin) that lie on either side of the spine.

Separate the ribs from the backbone. There is less work and less wear on your knife if you break the ribs first, then cut through the breaks.

Cook large meat pieces over a spit or boil them. You can stew boil smaller pieces, particularly those that remain attached to bone after the initial butchering, as soup or broth. You can cook body organs such as the heart, liver, pancreas, spleen, and kidneys using the same methods as for muscle meat. You can also cook and eat the brain. Cut the tongue out, skin it, boil it under tender, and eat it.

—From *Survival (Field Manual 21-76)*

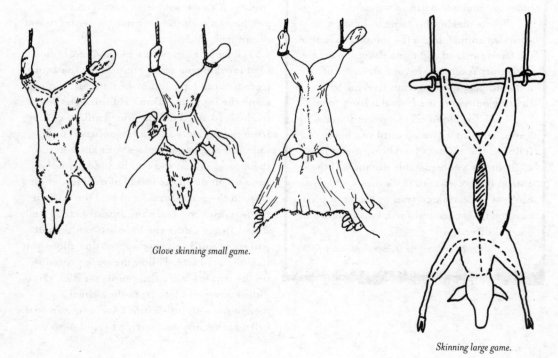

Glove skinning small game.

Skinning large game.

1) Cut the hide around the body.
2) Insert two fingers under the hide on both sides of the cut and pull both pieces off.

Continued ➡

Meat Care: Big Game

Dwight Schuh

Allowing meat to spoil through neglect or ignorance is worse than losing a wounded animal.

From mid-October on, meat care isn't a major problem in northern latitudes, because fall weather will cool meat quickly. If you're hunting close to home, you can drag a deer out to your car and take it home for processing. But in the West, many bow seasons open in August, when the weather is too hot for quick meat cooling. Under these conditions, you can find yourself in the backcountry, where you can't get meat to a cooler for several days. In those situations, you must know how to handle an animal.

The key is to get body heat out of a carcass. It's not air temperature that spoils meat, but internal body heat. Hot weather keeps body heat from dissipating rapidly enough to prevent spoilage. Field-dressing (gutting) the animal is the first step.

To field-dressing a deer, lay the animal on its back and slit the hide along the belly from chin to anus, being careful not to cut into the stomach or intestines. (If you plan to cape the deer for mounting, cut only from the brisket to the anus.) Cut the windpipe and esophagus at the chin and loosen them from the neck so they can be pulled into the body cavity. Next, cut around the anus to loosen it so the intestines can be pulled out through the body cavity. Reach into the body cavity and cut the diaphragm loose from the inside of the rib cage. Roll the deer onto its side and pull the viscera onto the ground. You may have to cut additional connective tissue loose inside to get everything out. Wipe the inside of the body cavity with a clean rag. If any internal organs have been punctured, contaminating the inside of the deer, wash the body cavity thoroughly with clean water and then wipe it dry.

Skinning

In cold weather, when temperatures drop to freezing or lower at night, skinning isn't really necessary. Besides, leaving the hide on prevents drying and helps keep the meat clean, which can be especially helpful in horse-packing and other backcountry situations where you can't handle the meat as carefully as you'd like. Leave the hide on until you take the animal to cold storage or to camp. There you can skin and bag it under clean conditions.

In hot weather—say with daytime temperatures higher than sixty degrees and nighttime temperatures no lower than forty—skinning promotes the needed cooling and could save the meat. During hot, late-summer bow seasons, I suggest skinning an animal immediately in the field. While doing that, you need to bag the meat to keep it clean and to keep flies off. I recommend that you always carry lightweight cheesecloth game bags for that purpose when early-season hunting.

To promote cooling, hang the carcass in the shade or drape it over a log so air can circulate on all sides. Smaller animals such as deer and antelope will cool well this way, although it's good idea to open up the hip and shoulder joints for quicker cooling. Big animals such as

elk should be quartered; they cool very slowly otherwise. Bone sour, the result of slow cooling, is particularly common in the hip joints and shoulders. To prevent that, slice down the insides of the back legs to open up the hip joints and cut under the front legs to open up a space between the legs and the chest.

Boning

If you have to pack animals a long way on your back, boning the meat (that is, removing all the bones) can reduce the weight you have to carry. Boning also enhances cooling. When boning an animal in the field, you must have game bags available to keep the meat clean.

Boning helps to reduce weight and speeds cooling. With the animal lying on its side, start by skinning the upper half of the animal from head to tail. Then cut off the front leg. (This is easy to do because it's held in place only by muscle.) Bag the leg to keep it clean.

Remove the back leg next. Start on the inside of the pelvis and work toward the back, slicing the meat cleanly from the pelvic bone. Soon you'll come to the hip joint. Push hard on the leg to break this joint open, and then continue to cut along the pelvis until the entire back leg comes loose. Bag the leg. To reduce weight further, you can later remove the bones from the front and back legs.

Finally, slice the meat off the ribs. Start at the brisket and work around the body to the backbone, much as you'd fillet a fish. Rib meat, flanks, backstrap, and neck come off in one big piece. You can cut this into two or three pieces to keep weight down.

When you've finished the top side, flip the carcass over and do the same on the other side. In hot weather, you must bag meat to keep off flies. Hang the meat in the shade, or if daytime temperatures are too hot, hang the meat at night and wrap it in sleeping bags during the day to keep it cool.

Preserving Meat

Meat processors say life begins at forty (forty degrees, that is), so if nighttime temperatures are dropping to forty degrees or lower, you can keep meat in the field for several days. The best way, especially if daytime temperatures are getting too warm, is to hang the meat at night without the game bags to cool it thoroughly. Then in the morning re-bag the meat, stack it on a clean tarp, and cover it with sleeping bags. With a good layer of bags, the meat temperature will rise no more than three to four degrees during the day. After sundown, hang it again for re-cooling. You can keep meat in the field for a week or more this way, even if daytime temperatures rise to sixty degrees or higher. This is also a good way to transport meat in your vehicle on a long drive home.

If you can't cool meat to forty degrees or lower at night, then you need to get it into cold storage within three days. If you're going into the backcountry, always line up packing services ahead of time, so you know you can get the meat out. If you follow these steps, you end up with great table fare, the sign of a successful hunter.

—From *Fundamentals of Bowhunting*

Preparing Birds

Greg Davenport

Pluck all birds unless they are scavengers or seabirds, which should be skinned. Leaving the skin on other kinds of birds will retain more of their nutrients when cooked. Cut the neck off close to the body. Cut open the chest and abdominal cavity, and remove the insides. Save the neck, liver, heart, and gizzard, which are all edible. Before eating the gizzard, split it open and remove the stones and partially digested food. Cook in any desired fashion. Cook scavenger birds a minimum of twenty minutes to kill parasites.

—From *Surviving the Desert*

Cleaning a Snake

U.S. Army

To skin a snake, first cut off its head and burry it. Then cut the skin down the body 15 to 20 centimeters. Peel the skin back, then grasp the skin in one hand the body in the other and pull apart. On large, bulky snakes it may be necessary to slit the belly skin. Cook snakes in the same manner as small game. Remove the entrails and discards. Cut the snake into small sections and boil or roast it.

—From *Survival (Field Manual 21-76)*

First, kill the snake, then—

1 Grip the dead snake firmly behind the head.

2 Cut off at least 15 cm behind the head.

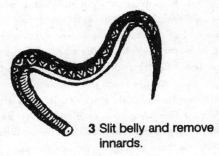

3 Slit belly and remove innards.

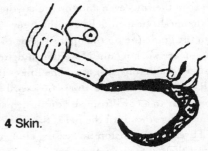

4 Skin.

Continued ➡

Improvised Fishing Devices

U.S. Army

You can make your own fishhooks, nets and traps and use several methods to obtain fish in a survival situation.

Improvised Fishhooks

You can make field expedient fishhooks from pins, needles, wire, small nails, or any piece of metal. You can also wood, bone, coconut shell, thorns, flint, seashell, or tortoise shell. You can also make fishhooks from any combination of these items.

To make a wooden hook, cut a piece of hardwood about 2.5 centimeters long and about 6 millimeters in diameter to form the shank. Cut a notch in one end in which to place the point. Place the point (piece of bone, wire, nail) in the notch. Hold the point in the notch and tie securely so that it does not move out of position. This is a fairly large hook. To make smaller hooks, use smaller material.

A gorge is a small shaft of wood, bone, metal, or other material. It is sharp on both ends and notched in the middle where you tie cordage. Bait the gorge by placing a piece of bait on it lengthwise. When the fish swallows the bait, it also swallows the gorge.

Stakeout

A stakeout is a fishing device you can use in a hostile environment. To construct a stakeout, drive two supple saplings into the bottom of the lake, pond, or steam with their tops just below the water surface. Tie a cord between them and slightly below the surface. Tie two short cords with hooks or gorges to this cord, ensuring that they cannot wrap around the poles or each other. They should also not slip along the long cord. Bait the hooks or gorges.

Gill Net

If a gill net is not available, you can make one using parachute suspension line or similar material. Remove the core lines from the suspension line and tie the casing between two trees. Attach several core lines to the casing by doubling them over and tying them with prusik knots or girth hitches. The length of the desired net and the size of the mesh determine the number of core lines used and the space between them. Starting at one end of the casing, tie the second and the third core lines together using an overhand knot. Then tie the fourth and fifth, sixth and seventh, and so on, until you reach the last core line. You should now have all core lines tied in pairs with a single core line hanging at each end. Start the second row with the first core line, tie it to the second, the third to the fourth, and so on.

To keep the rows even and to regulate the size of the mesh, tie a guideline to the trees. Position the guideline on the opposite side of the net you are working on. Move the guideline down after completing each row. The lines will always hang in pairs and you always tie a cord from one pair to a cord from an adjoining pair. Continue tying rows until the net is the desired width. Thread a suspension line casing along the bottom of the net to strengthen it.

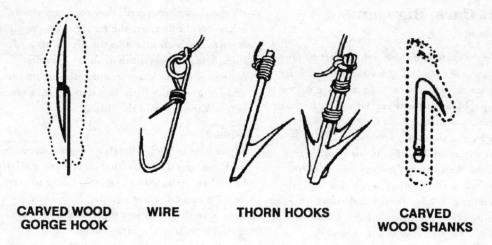

CARVED WOOD GORGE HOOK   WIRE   THORN HOOKS   CARVED WOOD SHANKS

Improvised fishhooks.

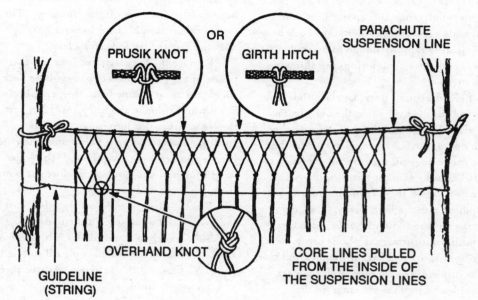

PRUSIK KNOT   OR   GIRTH HITCH   PARACHUTE SUSPENSION LINE

GUIDELINE (STRING)   OVERHAND KNOT   CORE LINES PULLED FROM THE INSIDE OF THE SUSPENSION LINES

Making a gill net.

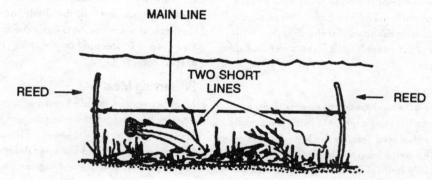

MAIN LINE

REED   TWO SHORT LINES   REED

Stakeout.

Setting a gill net in the stream.

Fish Traps

You may trap fish using several methods. Fish baskets are one method. You construct them by lashing several sticks together with vines into a funnel shape. You close the top, leaving a hole large enough for the fish to swim through.

You can also use traps to catch saltwater fish, as schools regularly approach the shore with the incoming tide and often move parallel to the shore. Pick a location at high tide and build the trap at low tide. On rocky shores, use natural rock pools. On coral islands, use natural pools on the surface of reefs by blocking the openings as the tide recedes. On sandy shores, use sandbars and the ditches they enclose. Build the trap as a low stone wall extending outward into the water and forming an angle with the shore.

Continued ➡

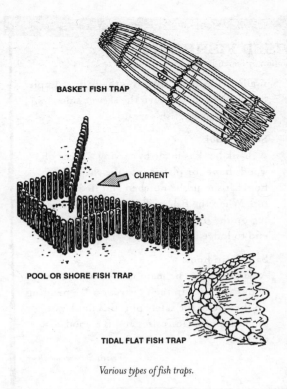

BASKET FISH TRAP

CURRENT

POOL OR SHORE FISH TRAP

TIDAL FLAT FISH TRAP

Various types of fish traps.

Spearfishing

If you are near shallow water (about waist deep) where the fish are large and plentiful, you can spear them. To make a spear, cut a long, straight sapling. Sharpen the end to a point or attach a knife, jagged piece of bone, or sharpened metal. You can also make a spear by splitting the shaft a few inches down from the end and inserting a piece of wood to act as a spreader. You then sharpen the two separated halves to points. To spear fish, find an area where fish either gather or where there is a fish run. Place the spear point into the water and slowly move it toward the fish. Then, with a sudden push, impale the fish on the stream bottom. Do not try to lift the fish with the spear, as it will probably slip off and you will lose it; hold the spear with one hand and grab and hold the fish with the other. Do not throw the spear, especially if the point is a knife. You cannot afford to lose a knife in a survival situation. Be alert to the problems caused by light refraction when looking at objects in the water.

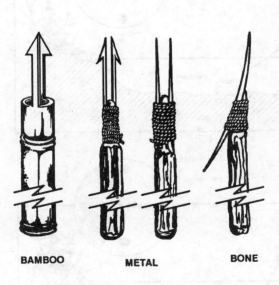

BAMBOO   **METAL**   **BONE**

Types of spear points.

Chop Fishing

At night, in an area with a good fish density, you can use a light to attract fish. Then, armed with a machete or similar weapon, you can gather fish using the back side of the blade to strike them. Do not use the sharp side as you will cut them in two pieces and end up losing some of the fish.

Fish Poison

Another way to catch fish is by using poison. Poison works quickly. It allows you to remain concealed while it takes effect. It also enables you to catch several fish at one time. When using fish poison, be sure to gather all of the affected fish, because many dead fish floating downstream could arouse suspicion. Some plants that grow in warm regions of the world contain rotenone, a substance that stuns or kills cold-blooded animals but does not harm persons who eat the animals. The best place to use rotenone, or rotenone-producing plants, is in ponds or the headwaters of small streams containing fish. Rotenone works quickly on fish in water 21 degrees C (70 degrees F) or above. The fish rise helplessly to the surface. It works slowly in water 10 to 21 degrees C (50 to 70 degrees F) and is ineffective in water below 10 degrees C (50 degrees F).

The following plants, used as indicated, will stun or kill fish:

Anamirta cocculus. This woody vine grows in southern Asia and on islands of the South Pacific. Crush the bean-shaped seeds and throw them in the water.

Croton tiglium. This shrub or small tree grows in waste areas on islands of the South Pacific. It bears seeds in three angled capsules. Crush the seeds and throw them into the water.

Barringtonia. These large trees grow near the sea in Malaya and parts of Polynesia. They bear a fleshly one-seeded fruit. Crush the seeds and bark and throw into the water.

Derris eliptica. This large genus of tropical shrubs and woody vines is the main source of commercially produced rotenone. Grind the roots into a powder and mix with water. Throw a large quantity of the mixture into the water.

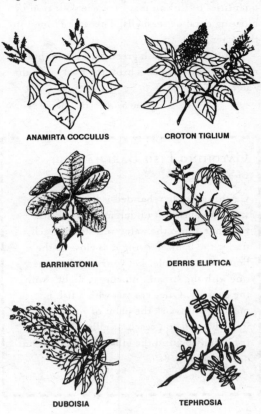

ANAMIRTA COCCULUS   **CROTON TIGLIUM**

BARRINGTONIA   **DERRIS ELIPTICA**

DUBOISIA   **TEPHROSIA**

Fish-poisoning plants.

IMPROVISED FISHING LINES
Greg Davenport   Illustrations by Steven Davenport and Ken Davenport

If you don't have fishing line, use a 10-foot section of improvised cordage. Although you could attach your line to a single pole, I'd advise setting out multiple lines tied to the end of one or several long, straight branches. Sticking these poles into the ground allows you to catch fish while attending to other chores. The goal is to return and find a fish attached to the end of each line.

To attach a standard hook, safety pin, or fixed loop to your line, use an improved clinch knot. All other improvised hooks can be attached to line using any knot. Following are the steps to attach a hook with a clinch knot.

1. Run the free end of the through the hook's eye and fold it back onto itself.

2. Wrap the free end up and around the line six or seven times.

3. Run the line's free end down and through the newly formed loop that is just above the hook's eye.

4. Finally, run the line through the loop formed between the two lines twisted together and the free end that just went though the loop next to the hook's eye.

5. Moisten the knot and pull it tight. Cut the excess line.

—From *Surviving the Desert*

Multiple fishing lines set out

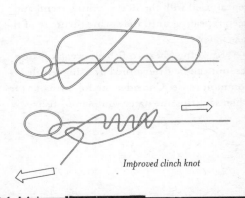

Improved clinch knot

Continued ➡

Duboisia. This shrub grows in Australia and bears white clusters of flowers and berrylike fruit. Crush the plants and throw them into the water.

Tephrosia. This species of small shrubs, which bears beanlike pods, grows throughout the tropics. Crush or bruise bundles of leaves and stems and throw them into the water.

Lime. You can get lime from commercial sources and in agricultural areas that use large quantities of it. You may produce your own by burning coral or seashells. Throw the lime into the water.

Nut husks. Crush green husks from butternuts or black walnuts. Throw the husks into the water.

—From *Survival (Field Manual 21–76)*

Catching Fish Barehanded
Greg Davenport

Catching fish barehanded is best done in small streams with undercut banks. Place your hand into the water and slowly reach under the bank, moving it as close to the bottom as possible. Let your arm become one with the stream, moving it slightly with the current. Once contact with a fish is made, gently work the palm of your hand up its belly until you reach its gills. Grasp the fish firmly behind the gills, and scoop it out of the water.

—From *Wilderness Survival*

When to Fish
Gene Kugach

Early Season Fishing

After the first warming trends of spring, just after ice-out (in March or April), try some of the following tips.

When to Fish

The time of day for early season fishing is critical for the best results. The following illustrations can be used as a general rule.

Cold Fronts

During the early season, cold fronts are one of the key factors that will affect fishing. After a warming trend has set in for a few days and a cold front approaches, the effects of the front are usually as follows:

After the cold front hits, fishing will drop off or come to a complete stop. The cycle will repeat itself with the next warming trend and keep repeating until the spring turnover of the lake water.

Knowing where to fish after early season ice-out can be determined by using a little common sense. Consider the following factors when selecting the water you plan to fish.

THREE IMPROVISED FISHHOOKS
Greg Davenport Illustration by Steven Davenport

Some commonly used improvised hooks are skewer and shank hooks, made from bone, wood, or plastic, and safety pin hooks.

Skewer hook

A skewer hook is a sliver of wood, bone, or plastic that is notched and tied at the middle. When baited, this hook is turned parallel to the line, making it easier for the fish to

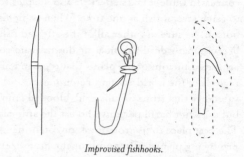

Improvised fishhooks.

swallow. Once the fish takes the bait, a simple tug on the line will turn the skewer sideways, lodging it in the fish's mouth.

Shank hook

A shank hook is made by carving a piece of wood, bone, or plastic into the shape of a hook. It should be notched and tied at the top. When the fish swallows the hook, a gentle tug on the line will set it by causing the hook end to lodge in the throat.

Safety pin hook

A safety pin can be manipulated to create a hook, as shown in the illustration. Depending on the size of the safety pin, this hook can catch fish of various sizes and is a good option.

—From *Survival the Desert*

EARLY MORNING: 6:00 TO 9:00 A.M.
Cool water temperature and low angle of the sun's rays, which bounce off the water, provide little action.

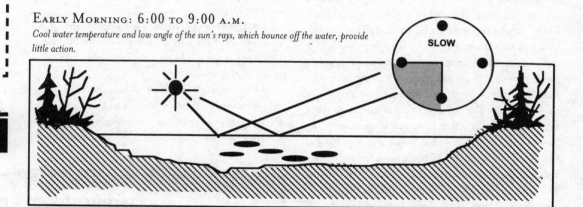

LATE MORNING TO EARLY AFTERNOON: 9:00 A.M. TO 1:00 P.M.
Sun starts to penetrate water, surface starts to warm up. Often produces, but could be irregular.

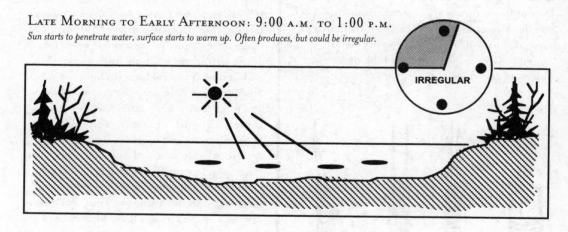

AFTERNOON TO EARLY DUSK: 1:00 TO 5:00 P.M.
Sun's rays at maximum penetration. Best time to fish, when air and water temperatures are warmest.

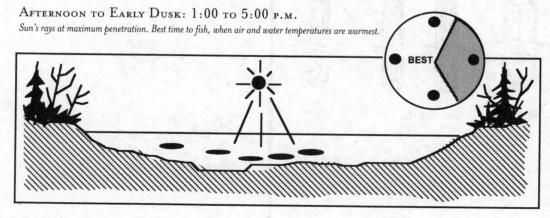

Continued ➡

First day of warming trend

Excellent fishing for a couple of hours during the warmest part of the day.

1:00 to 3:00 P.M.

Second day of warming trend

Excellent fishing same as first day except for a longer period of time.

12:00 to 4:00 P.M.

Third day of warming trend

Good fishing in the late morning as well as in the afternoon.

9:00 A.M. to 4:00 P.M.

Fourth day of warming trend—Cold front to hit mid-day

Excellent fishing during the period before the cold front hits.

8:00 A.M. to mid-day

Best Places

- **SMALL LAKES**
- **PONDS**
- **QUARRIES**

Best Water

Remember, darker bottom areas such as mud flats and shallow, silt-covered areas absorb heat and warm up quicker than light-bottomed areas such as sand or gravel. Most early season fish will seek out the warmest water.

Mid-Season Fishing

Here are just a few tips to try during the summer months (mid-June through mid-September) when the fishing slows down.

When to Fish

During the summer, as a general rule, early morning and late evening are the best times to fish.

EARLY MORNING: 4:30 TO 9:00 A.M.
Fish are active just before daybreak (4:30 a.m.) up to about 9:00 a.m. Fishing will be excellent.

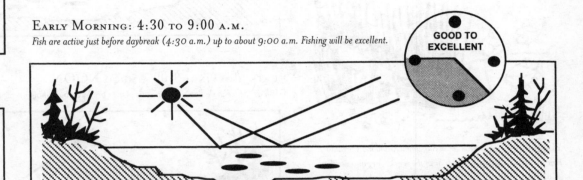

GOOD TO EXCELLENT

Scoop Nets

Greg Davenport

A scoop net can help secure a line-caught fish or can be used alone to scoop a fish out of the water. To make a scoop net, bend the two ends of a 6-foot sapling or similar material together to form a circle, allowing some extra length for a handle. You can also form a circle with the ends of a forked branch. Lash the ends together. The net's mesh can be made using the same method described for building a gill net, tying the initial girth hitch to the sapling. Once the net is the appropriate size, tie all the lines together with an overhand knot, and trim off any excess. A scoop net should be used in shallow water or other area where fish are visible. Because you'll need to compensate for light refraction below the water, first place the net into the water to obtain the proper alignment. Next, slowly move the net as close to the fish as possible, and allow them to become accustomed to it. When ready, scoop the fish up and out of the water.

—From *Surviving the Desert*

MID-MORNING TO LATE AFTERNOON: 9:00 A.M. TO 5:00 P.M.
Fish are inactive during most of the day (9:00 a.m. to 5:00 p.m.). Most species will be in deep water.

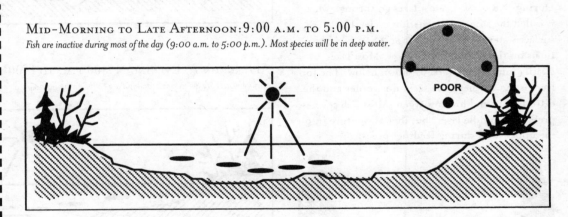

POOR

SUNSET TO EARLY EVENING: 6:00 P.M. TO 9:00 P.M.
Fish are again active when the sun starts to set (6:00 p.m. to 9:00 p.m.). Excellent fishing.

BEST

Continued ➔

During the summer months, fish are harder to catch for two main reasons.

1. THE FOOD CHAIN IS AT ITS PEAK.

Fish become very selective. They feed less often, but gorge themselves when they do start feeding.

2. FISH ARE HARDER TO FIND DUE TO ABUNDANT COVER.

Weed growth is at its maximum in the summer, and most predators hide in ambush in the weed beds or at the edges. They also use them as resting places between feeding sprees

Summer Stagnation

During mid-season, most lakes go through what is called the summer stagnation cycle. The surface water warms to well over 39.2° F. and floats on the heavier water below. Most lakes stratify into three layers, as shown below. The top layer is the warmest, the second is cooler and the third is cold and low in oxygen. Most fish species prefer the middle layer, but they all venture into the upper layer during feeding sprees.

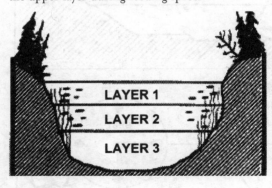

Wind Effect

Wind can matter during the hot days of mid-season fishing. Strong winds can push cooler offshore water close in to shore, bringing in bait fish and predators to feed. The bait fish will be attracted to insects blown into the water by the wind, which in turn will attract the larger predators.

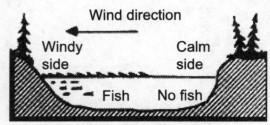

The next time you're tempted to fish the calm side of the lake where you may be more comfortable, remember that you may have better luck on the windy side.

Late Season Fishing

The following are just a few tips to try during the fall months (late September through ice-up), when the fall turnover is in process.

EARLY MORNING: DAYBREAK TO 9:00 A.M.
Cool water temperature and little sun penetration into water results in poor action.

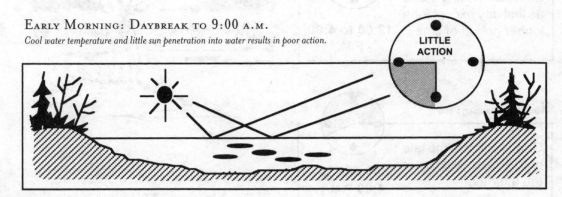

LATE MORNING: 9:00 A.M. TO NOON
Fish are active in shallow warmer water. Often produces, but fishing is irregular.

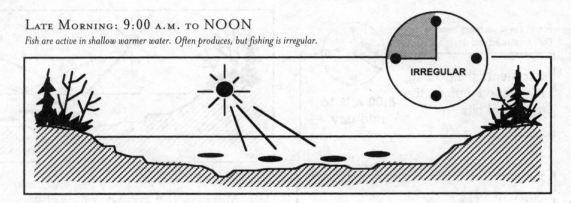

AFTERNOON TO EVENING: 12:00 P.M. TO 6:00 P.M.
Surface waters are the warmest, and fish are active, including deep water species. Best fishing.

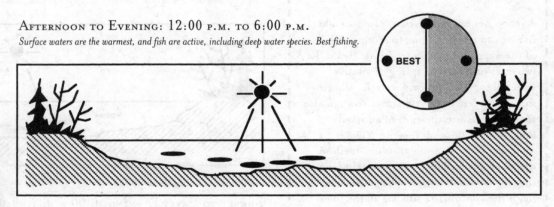

During the fall season, fish become more active. They feed more often and migrate away from their summer haunts.

CONCENTRATIONS OF BAIT FISH

To find active fish consistently in the fall, fish areas having concentrations of bait fish.

When to Fish

Water temperature is the most important factor to consider during this period. Daylight hours are shorter, limiting the warming effects of the sun. Conditions will be similar to early spring fishing. As a general rule, most fish will be scattered throughout the lake, feeding near the surface.

WARMEST WATER

Heat from the sun will be the single most important factor that governs fish activity on most lakes in the fall. Fish will seek the warmer surface waters or the shallows.

Continued ➡

Fall Turnover

During the fall season, the surface water cools until it becomes heavier than the water beneath it. It sinks and mixes with the deeper water until all the water has the same temperature. This process will continue until ice-up and most fish will be scattered through-out the lake, feeding near the surface.

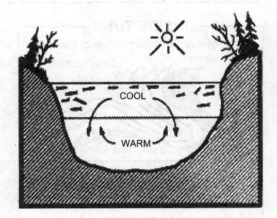

Best Waters

As is true in the spring, darker bottom areas such as mud flats or slit-covered areas will attract more fish because they absorb heat and warm the water around them.

During the late fall season, fish continue to feed much better in very clear water.

When fishing around the time of fall turnover, be willing to change lakes. Some lakes have longer turnover periods than others.

Seasonal Lake Turnovers

A body of water goes through an annual cycle of temperature changes paralleling the seasons. Knowing what the water conditions are and how they affect the fish during each season change can improve your chances of a better catch. The following illustrations depict each season change and the effects on the fish.

Spring Turnover

After ice-out, surface water warms from 32° F to its maximum density at 39° F. The heavier surface waters then sink and mix with the deeper, lighter waters. As the stagnant deep water reaches the surface, it is charged with oxygen by the spring winds and warmed by the sun, repeating the cycle until the water temperature is uniform throughout the lake.

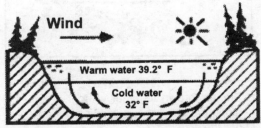

Most fish will be found in the shallower areas of the lake where the waters warm more quickly.

Summer Stagnation

During the summer, surface water warms and rapidly becomes less dense than the water below it. It floats on top of the colder water throughout the entire summer without mixing with the deeper waters. The upper layer of water will vary between 2 and 10 feet in depth, depending on the size of the lake.

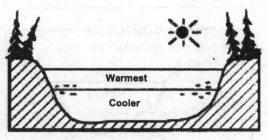

Most fish will be found just below the warm surface band of water.

Fall Turnover

In the fall season, the surface water cools until it approaches the temperature of the lower water beneath it. When it cools and becomes heavier, it sinks and mixes with the deeper waters until all the water has the same temperature. This process continues until the water reaches 32°F or freezes up.

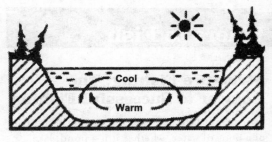

During this cooling period, most fish will be scattered throughout the lake.

Water Temperature

In most cases, fish activity is governed by water temperature. It affects their movements and spawning and is an important factor to consider during the various seasons. Most fish prefer a particular water temperature and seek out the depths that suit them best. Learn those depths and you'll catch more fish.

Fishing by Degrees

The following chart shows the temperature that specific species of fish prefer. Although you may not find the exact water temperature, most fish will be found in the water closest to the temperature listed on the chart below.

—From *Fishing Basics*

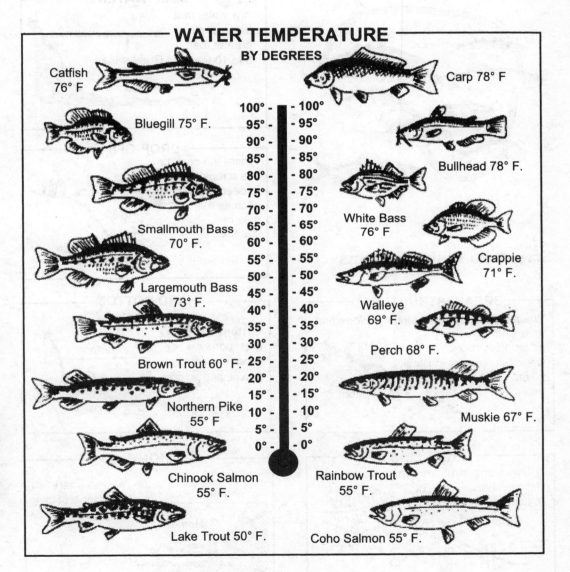

WATER TEMPERATURE
BY DEGREES

Catfish 76° F
Carp 78° F
Bluegill 75° F.
Bullhead 78° F.
Smallmouth Bass 70° F.
White Bass 76° F
Largemouth Bass 73° F.
Crappie 71° F.
Walleye 69° F.
Perch 68° F.
Brown Trout 60° F.
Northern Pike 55° F
Muskie 67° F.
Chinook Salmon 55° F.
Rainbow Trout 55° F.
Lake Trout 50° F.
Coho Salmon 55° F.

Continued ➡

Where to Fish

Gene Kugach

Structure Fishing: The Answer to Successful Fishing

Structure fishing refers to the bottom contour of a body of water, whether it is a pond, lake, stream, or river. Structure can be defined as anything unusual on the bottom of a body of water that will attract fish.

Structure can be a variety of things, such as reefs, bars, drop-offs, holes, weed beds, sunken islands, old road beds, sunken logs, or piers, but they all have one thing in common: They provide the fish with cover. Because structure provides cover, it becomes an important factor when fishing.

Most waters that are void of structure are also void of fish. If you can identify structure and fish it properly, you will improve your chances of catching more fish.

Basic Rules for Success

- Always fish structure
- Learn to read rtructure
- Fish where the fish live

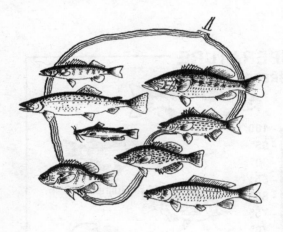

Structure Fishing Terms

BRUSHLINE
A line along the edge (deep or shallow side) of a large area of sunken brush.

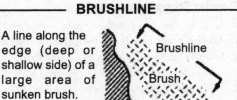

CONTOUR
The outline of the bottom's surface elevations, drop-offs, ridges, holes, and so on.

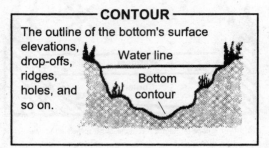

CONTOUR LINE
A line on a map connecting the points on the bottom's surface that have the same elevations.

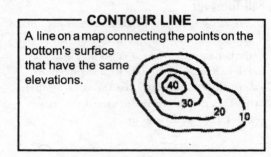

DEEP WATER
Any water that has a depth greater than 8 to 10 feet.

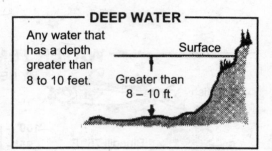

DROP-OFF
Where the contour has a rapid drop to deeper water such as a hole or channel.

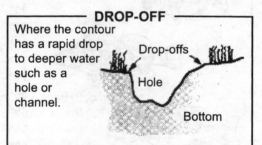

BREAK (STRUCTURE)
When the contour is no longer uniform due to a change such as drop-off, rocks, weed beds, and so on.

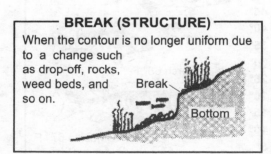

BREAKLINE
A line along structure where there is a definite change in depth.

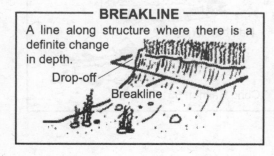

HARD BOTTOM
Bottom surface that consists of sand, clay, rocks, gravel, and so on.

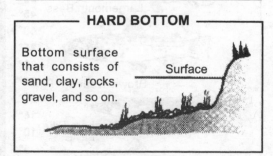

HOME
The area where fish spend most of their time; deep water or heavy cover.

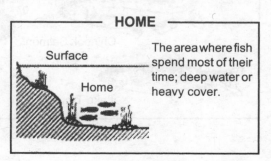

INSIDE EDGE
The shallow water edge of structure, weed beds, brush; where the cover ends toward the shoreline.

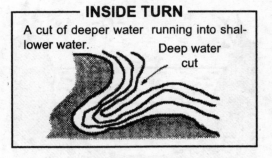

INSIDE TURN
A cut of deeper water running into shallower water.

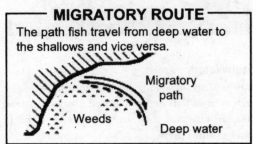

MIGRATORY ROUTE
The path fish travel from deep water to the shallows and vice versa.

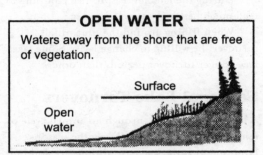

OPEN WATER
Waters away from the shore that are free of vegetation.

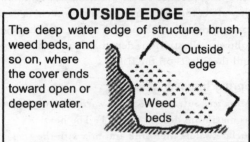

OUTSIDE EDGE
The deep water edge of structure, brush, weed beds, and so on, where the cover ends toward open or deeper water.

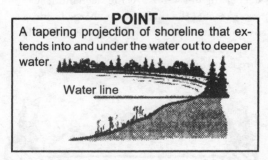

POINT
A tapering projection of shoreline that extends into and under the water out to deeper water.

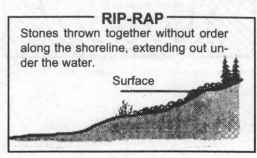

RIP-RAP
Stones thrown together without order along the shoreline, extending out under the water.

Continued ➡

SHALLOW WATER

Any water that has a depth less than 8 feet.

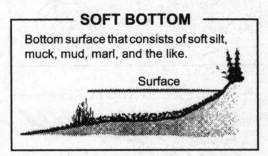

SOFT BOTTOM

Bottom surface that consists of soft silt, muck, mud, marl, and the like.

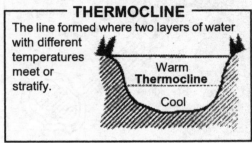

THERMOCLINE

The line formed where two layers of water with different temperatures meet or stratify.

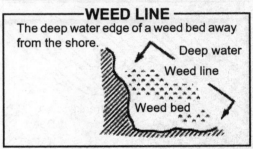

WEED LINE

The deep water edge of a weed bed away from the shore.

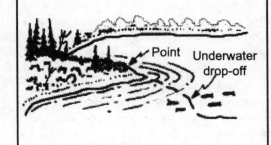

Basic Locations

No one can predict just where the fish will be, but certain areas can be identified as preferable locations to try. Look for some of the basic locations shown in the following illustrations.

Finding Structure

The following examples provide a general guideline of what to look for along a shoreline if you want some clues about the structure of a pond, lake, river, or stream. Although not always true, they are a good starting point for finding fish.

LILY PADS

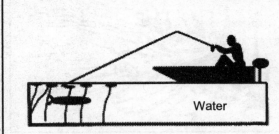

Lily pad patches provide excellent cover for a variety of fish. Work the edges and openings.

WEED BEDS

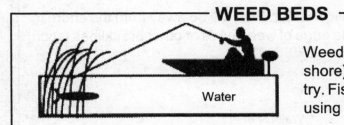

Weed beds (submerged or near shore) are also good areas to try. Fish the edges or in the beds using weedless lures.

SUBMERGED OBJECTS

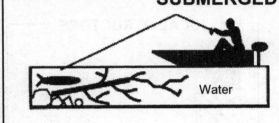

Sunken trees, logs, rocks, and so on are all excellent areas to try. Cover the area from different angles.

PIERS AND DOCKS

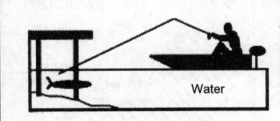

Piers and docks provide fish with shelter from the sun. Many lunkers hang around or near piers or docks. Don't pass them up.

STEEP SHORES

Steep shorelines indicate deep water. Fish will be found at any breakline along the walls.

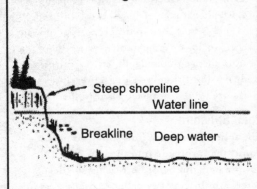

POINTS

Points along a shoreline extend under water and indicate drop-offs where fish will be located.

Continued ➡

CREEK MOUTHS

Creek mouths indicate possible holes or drop-offs where fish will be located.

Drop-offs

Hole

FLAT SHORES

Flat shorelines indicate shallow water. Fish will be away from the shore in deep water along the outside edge of weed beds or other breaklines (such as rocks, humps, and dips).

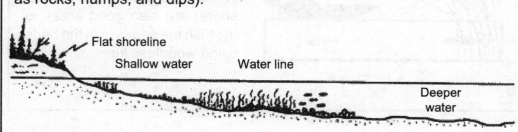

Flat shoreline

Shallow water   Water line

Deeper water

UNPRODUCTIVE STRUCTURE

Water line

NO STRUCTURE
No fish

Deep water

IDEAL STRUCTURE

Water line

STRUCTURE

Breakline

Deeper water

UNPRODUCTIVE STRUCTURE

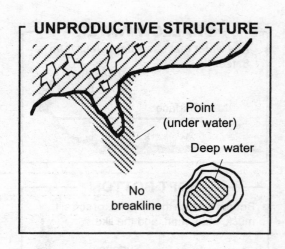

Point (under water)

Deep water

No breakline

IDEAL STRUCTURE

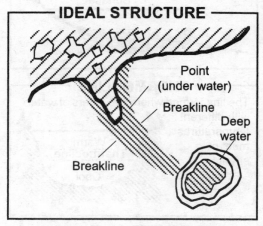

Point (under water)

Breakline

Deep water

Breakline

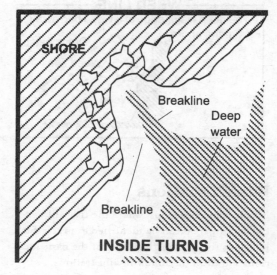

SHORE

Breakline

Deep water

Breakline

INSIDE TURNS

Reading Structure

One thing to remember about structure fishing is that not all so-called structure found in a pond, lake, river, or stream will hold fish.

The most ideal form of structure is any irregularity on the bottom that provides fish with cover from deep water to the shallows and vice versa. Most fish will use these breaklines as their migratory routes when they leave their home (deep water) in search of food. Also remember that most fish spend most of their time in deep water (home) and move or migrate to shallower water along the breaklines provided by some form of structure, whether it is a drop-off, weed bed, sunken brush, or logs.

Important: Ideal structure will provide cover from deep water to shallow water. It must in some way tie in to the deep or deepest water in the area being fished.

A few examples of ideal and unproductive structure are shown below.

Steep Shore Structure

The illustrations below show two types of steep shorelines and the effect they have on attracting fish.

The first picture shows a shoreline without any type of structure, which for the most part will also be void of fish.

The second picture shows how fish relate to structure such as a rocky ledge or a breakline, which provides cover and access to deeper water.

What Are Breaklines?

Breaklines can be defined as lines along any structure, whether it is a weed bed, brush pile, edge of a channel, a hole, or two different types of water meeting (color or temperature) where there is a definite change in the depth, either sudden or gradual. Most fish move along a breakline as a migratory route from deep water to the shallows.

Point Structure

The following illustrations show two possible points that protrude into the water. The first point peters out before it reaches the deep water, eliminating any path or cover access for the fish from the deeper water. The second point reaches the deep water, giving the fish easy access to the shallows from the deep water along the breakline. Of the two points, the second is the best to fish and the most productive.

Inside Turns

An inside turn is the opposite of a point. It's a cut of deep water running into shallow water along the shoreline, forming a small inlet. The sharp edges of the deep water form the breakline which will hold the fish.

> **Important**
> Always remember, the most productive structure will provide the fish with cover from deep water (home) to shallow water. They will use the breakline as their migratory route in search of food.

Inlet or Feeder Creek Mouth Structure

The illustration to the right shows a typical inlet into a lake, river, or stream. Most inlets or feeder creeks will create a channel (structure) or what is known as a "cut" in the bottom to deeper water. Areas along the cut will hold debris (structure) washed into the main body of water from rain storms, which will attract both bait fish and predators.

The edges of the cut will be the breakline which fish will follow as their migratory route

Continued ➡

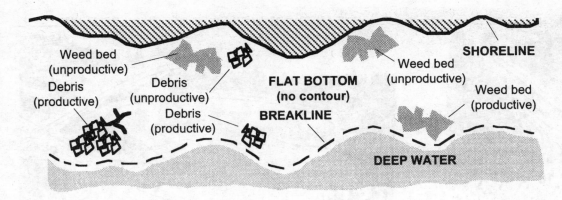

Weed bed (unproductive)
Debris (productive)
Debris (unproductive)
Debris (productive)
FLAT BOTTOM (no contour)
BREAKLINE
Weed bed (unproductive)
SHORELINE
Weed bed (productive)
DEEP WATER

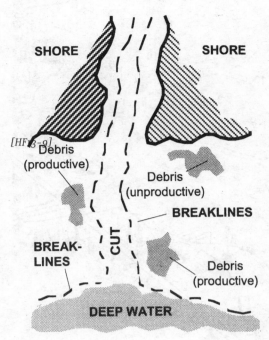

SHORE **SHORE**

[HF13-9]
Debris (productive)
Debris (unproductive)
BREAKLINES
BREAK-LINES
CUT
Debris (productive)
DEEP WATER

from deep water (home) to the shallows in search of food. Fish move along the channel edges and the areas where debris is concentrated, with easy access to the deeper water.

Flat Shore Structure

The illustration below shows a top view of a typical flat shoreline common in most lakes or reservoirs. Many locations along this type of bottom will have various forms of structure. The breakline in this type situation will be the line formed where the depth of the water has a sudden drop.

The ideal structure, and the most productive, is the closest structure to the breakline, which provides the fish with cover from the deep water.

Pond, Lake, and Reservoir Fishing

Pond Fishing

Ponds are usually excellent fishing waters. They have abundant growth, which provides cover for bait fish as well as a variety of game fish. The game fish population in a pond can include bass, pike, pickerel, perch, panfish, and in some areas, members of the trout family. Most ponds are either creek- or spring-fed, both of which provide excellent water quality.

Lake Fishing

Lakes vary in size, shape, and depth. They provide the same sort of food and cover for the fish population as do most ponds. They can also be fished in the same areas as a pond, and can

include bass, pike, pickerel, perch, panfish, and, in some areas, trout as the principal species. Most lakes are creek-, spring-, or river-fed.

Reservoir Fishing

Reservoirs or impoundments also vary in size, shape, and depth. They provide the same sort of food and cover for the fish population as most lakes and ponds. They can also be fished in the same areas as a pond or lake, and can include most game fish species, depending on their location in the various parts of the country. Most reservoirs or impoundments are creek-, stream-, or river-fed.

Most ponds, lakes, and reservoirs can be fished from shore or from a boat using a variety of equipment such as spinning gear, cane poles, bait casting gear, or a fly fishing outfit.

Pond, Lake, and Reservoir Locations

Various areas to try in a typical pond, lake, or reservoir are described below and keyed to the illustrations on the following pages.

POND FISHING LOCATIONS

1. Stream or River Mouths

Excellent areas to try, as incoming water brings in a variety of food that attracts both bait fish and game fish.

2. Stream or River Channels

In most ponds, lakes, or reservoirs formed by the damming of a stream or river, the original stream or river bed will have the deepest water. The deep water will be home for most fish, which will use the channel as a migratory route to and from the shallows as they search for food. The edges of the channel's breaklines formed by the original stream or river are excellent areas to try.

3. Submerged Rock Piles

In shallow water they attract spawning fish. In deep water they provide cover and are excellent areas if there is access to deeper water.

4. Points

Look for the point that has easy access to deep water. Fish the tip as well as corners.

5. Humps or Ridges

The edge of a hump of ridge provides excellent breaklines to fish. Shallow humps attract spawning fish in the spring. Deep humps are most productive in the summer and fall.

6. Spillway or Dam

Both above and below the spillway or dam are excellent areas to try. Some of the largest fish in a lake, pond, or reservoir lurk around the spillway.

7. Deep Holes or Springs

Most any of the game fish may hold along the edges of the breakline, or some species may suspend at mid-depth over the hole.

8. Submerged Tree Stumps or Fallen Trees

These are excellent areas depending on the amount of shade provided and access to deeper water or a breakline.

9. Weed Beds or Lily Pads

These areas are also excellent, depending on access to deeper water. Inside edges (shallow) are most productive in the spring or fall. Outside edges are used as a breakline or migratory route.

10. Reeds

Reeds are excellent areas in early spring for bass or pike, particularly if they connect to marshy areas or they are located at the mouth of a feeder creek.

11. Old Road Beds

Old road beds are good areas to try that provide breaklines as migratory routes to and from shallow water when fish are in search of food.

Continued →

Stream and River Fishing

Streams and rivers can provide excellent fishing waters if fished properly. The game fish population in a river or stream can include most any species, depending on where it's located. The most important factor to consider when fishing a river or stream is the current and the structure that affect it.

Most fish holding locations will be areas where the fast-moving water passes some form of structure, which will slow the water down and also provide cover for the fish. A few places to try are described below and illustrated on the following page.

1. Dams or Spillways

Both above and below the dam or spillway are excellent areas to try. Fish the rip-rap areas above the dam or spillway along the shoreline, and the first bank eddies at the base or below the dam or spillway.

2. Humps

Humps provide excellent staging areas for spawning walleyes and saugers during early spring. They also provide holding areas for both catfish and walleyes. Upstream humps, closest to the dam or spillway, provide the best results.

3. Eddies

Eddies provide cover and the best potential to produce a mixed stringer of most species found in the river or stream. They can be fished from either the shore or from a boat.

4. Points of Bars

Points or bars along the shoreline can be holding areas for a variety of species. They cause the current to form eddies or holes on the downstream side, which are excellent areas to try.

5. Bays or Backwaters

These are excellent areas to try during early spring. Bays and backwaters provide spawning areas for walleye, bass, and northern pike.

6. Main Channel Edges

Main channel edges downstream for a mile below a dam or spillway are excellent areas to try. They will hold large catfish most any time and female walleyes prior to spring spawning.

7. Outside Bends

Outside bends along the shoreline are excellent holding areas for bass and crappies.

Continued ➡

8. Stream or Creek Mouths

Excellent areas to try during early spring for northern pike. They also will hold the same pike throughout the summer season.

9. Boulders or Rock Piles

Downstream sides will provide cover for a variety of species which will lie in ambush waiting for food to be washed down by the river or stream current. Fishing above the boulders or rocks and allowing the current to take your bait past the holding areas will provide the best results.

10. Islands

Excellent areas to try along the sides away from the main channel. Favorite spawning areas for crappies during early spring. Also good for northern pike along the down stream points.

Summary

By applying everyday common sense to your fishing, you should be able to catch fish or at least improve your chances of finding them. Like anything you do, you can do it well only if you spend some time evaluating the conditions or circumstances surrounding the situation and making sound judgments to accomplish the results

you're after. To succeed, you must have the facts or knowledge necessary to make your decision.

To catch fish, you must apply the same kind of thinking. You first have to find them, and to find them you need to know something about them. You need to know what affects them and you must learn to recognize their habits. Once you learn a few of these facts, you can make some judgments necessary to find and catch them.

The following list gives a few important facts that you'll need when you're trying to locate fish, regardless of the type of waters you will be fishing.

- Ninety percent of all waters contain no fish.
- Fish are creatures of habit; once you learn their habits, you can find them.
- Fish require some form of cover (structure) in which to live.
- Fish require some form of cover (structure) in which to move about (migration routes) when they search for food.
- Fish concentrate in areas where cover (structure) is available.
- Most game fish are in deep water most of the time (greater than 8 or 10 feet deep).

—From *Fishing Basics*

Ice Fishing: Picking the Right Spot

Gene Kugach

Unless your familiar with the water you are planning to fish or you have a depth sounder, picking the right spot to make your hole(s) in the ice can present a problem. Here's a trick to try when your fishing some of those smaller lakes or ponds.

Get down on your knees and look through the ice to see what type of bottom structure will be below you. In most cases, if the lake or pond is free of snow cover, you will be able to see the bottom. Look for some form of structure or cover, (weed-beds, dropoffs, rocks, or sunken logs) before making your hole.

—From Fishing Basics

How to Rig Live Bait

Gene Kugach

The following drawings illustrate how to attach live bait to a hook. These methods have proven to be very successful over the years.

Minnows

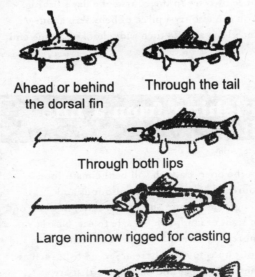

Ahead or behind the dorsal fin

Through the tail

Through both lips

Large minnow rigged for casting

Large minnow rigged with double hooks.

Insects

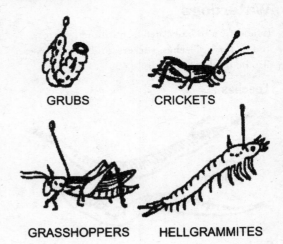

GRUBS

CRICKETS

GRASSHOPPERS

HELLGRAMMITES

Worms

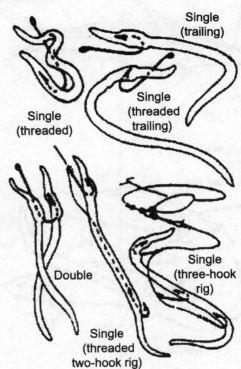

Single (threaded)

Single (trailing)

Single (threaded trailing)

Double

Single (three-hook rig)

Single (threaded two-hook rig)

Frogs

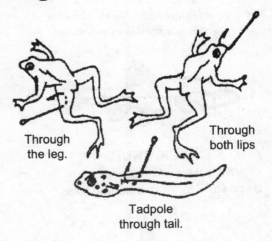

Through the leg.

Through both lips

Tadpole through tail.

Crayfish

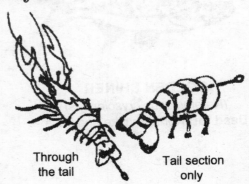

Through the tail

Tail section only

Continued ➡

Leeches, Suckers, and Waterdogs

In addition to baits such as minnows, worms, and so forth, leeches, suckers, and waterdogs can also be used as bait.

Leeches

Through the head

Suckers

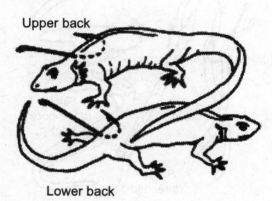

Through the nose

Waterdogs

Upper back

Lower back

Minnow Selection

The following illustration shows just a few of the more common minnows used as live bait.

CREEK CHUB
(Semotilus atromaculatus)
Used for: Northern pike and bass

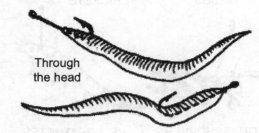

GOLDEN SHINER
(Notemigonus crysoleucas)
Used for: Northern pike and bass

FATHEAD MINNOW
(Pimephales promelas)
Used for: Crappie, walleye, bass and panfish

BLUNTNOSE MINNOW
(Pimephales notatus)
Used for: Crappie, walleye and bass

Emergency Bait

Try the following if you run out of bait or if the fishing slows down.

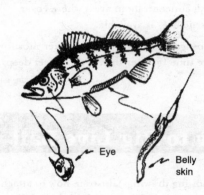

Eye

Belly skin

Use the eyes from the fish you already caught. Eyes make exceptional bait, and it is seldom necessary to rebait the hook more than once or twice in the course of a day's fishing. You can also try a piece of belly skin about 1/2 inch long and 1/8 inch wide, hooked at one end.

—From *Fishing Basics*

Fishing from a Life Raft

U.S. Army

In the open sea, fish will be the main food source. There are some poisonous and dangerous ocean fish, but, in general, when out of sight of land, fish are safe to eat. Nearer the shore there are fish that are both dangerous and poisonous to eat. There are some fish, such as the red snapper and barracuda, that are normally edible but poisonous when taken from the waters of atolls and reefs. Flying fish will even jump into your raft!

Fish

When fishing, do not handle the fishing line with bare hands and never wrap it around your hands or tie it to a life raft. The salt that adheres to it can make it a sharp cutting edge, an edge dangerous both to the raft and your hands. Wear gloves, if they are available, or use a cloth to handle fish and to avoid injury from sharp fins and gill covers.

In warm regions, gut and bleed fish immediately after catching them. Cut fish that you do not eat immediately into thin, narrow strips and hang them to dry. A well-dried fish stays edible for several days. Fish not cleaned and dried may spoil in half a day. Fish with dark meat are very prone to decomposition. If you do not eat them all immediately, do not eat any of the leftovers. Use the leftovers for bait.

Never eat fish that have pale, shiny gills, sunken eyes, flabby skin and flesh, or an unpleasant odor. Good fish show the opposite characteristics. Sea fish have a saltwater or clean fishy odor. Do not confuse eels with sea snakes that have an obviously scaly body and strongly compressed, paddle-shaped tail. Both eels and sea snakes are edible, but you must handle the latter with care because of their poisonous bites. The heart, blood, intestinal wall, and liver of most fish are edible. Cook the intestines. Also edible are the partly digested smaller fish that you may find in the stomachs of large fish. In addition, sea turtles are edible.

Shark meat is a good source of food whether raw, dried, or cooked. Shark meat spoils very rapidly due to the high concentration of urea in the blood, therefore, bleed it immediately and soak it in several changes of water. People prefer some shark species over others. Consider them all edible except the Greenland shark whose flesh contains high quantities of vitamin A. Do not eat the livers, due to high vitamin A content.

Fishing Aids

You can use different materials to make fishing aids as described in the following paragraphs:

- **Fishing line**. Use pieces of tarpaulin or canvas. Unravel the threads and tie them together in short lengths in groups of three or more threads. Shoelaces and parachute suspension line also work well.

- **Fish hooks**. No survivor at sea should be without fishing equipment but if you are, improvise hooks.

- **Fish lures**. You can fashion lures by attaching a double hook to any shiny piece of metal.

- **Grapple**. Use grapples to hook seaweed. You may shake crabs, shrimp, or small fish out of the seaweed. These you may eat or use for bait. You may eat seaweed itself, but only when you have plenty of drinking water. Improvise grapples from wood. Use a heavy piece of wood as the main shaft, and lash three smaller pieces to the shaft as grapples.

- **Bait**. You can use small fish as bait for larger ones. Scoop the small fish up with a net. If you don't have a net, make one from cloth of some type. Hold the net under the water and scoop upward. Use all the guts from birds and fish for bait. When using bait, try to keep it moving in the water to give it the appearance of being alive.

Helpful Fishing Hints

Your fishing should be successful if you remember the following important hints:

Continued ➡

- Be extremely careful with fish that have teeth and spines.

- Cut a large fish loose rather than risk capsizing the raft. Try to catch small rather than large fish.

- Do not puncture your raft with hooks or other sharp instruments.

- Do not fish when large sharks are in the area.

- Watch for schools of fish; try to move close to these schools.

- Fish at night using a light. The light attracts fish.

- In the daytime, shade attracts some fish. You may find them under your raft.

- Improvise a spear by tying a knife to an oar blade. This spear can help you catch larger fish, but you must get them into the raft quickly or they will slip off the blade. Also, tie the knife very securely or you may lose it.

- Always take care of your fishing equipment. Dry your fishing lines, clean and sharpen the hooks, and do not allow the hooks to stick into the fishing lines.

—From *Survival (Field Manual 21-76)*

Landing Your Catch

Gene Kugach

Here are a few tips on how to handle your catch after you've played it out. Don't try to land a fish until it's ready. Wait until all the flight is gone and the fish is wobbly and on its side.

Eye Pick-up

You can lift pike, muskie, and pickerel out of the water by putting your hane over the head and grasping the fish by the eye sockets.

Mouth Pick-up

Bass or fish with small teeth can be picked up by the lower lip. This hold will paralyze the fish as long as you hang on to it. When placing your thumb in the fish's mouth, make certain that you avoid the hooks on your lure or bait.

Gaffing

When using a gaff, put it in the water under the fish and come up either under the jaw or the belly.

Net Landing

Never scoop at the fish with the net. Hold the net in the water and lead the fish (headfirst) into it. If you miss on the first try, wait until the fish tires more or calms down, and try again.

—From *Fishing Basics*

Cleaning Fish: Step by Step

Gene Kugach

The following steps are just a few tips on various ways to clean your catch.

Panfish

Most panfish are less than 12" long and are difficult to fillet. Unless you are experienced at filleting fish, use the following method for panfish.

STEP 1
Hold the fish by the tail and scrape from tail to head to loosen and remove the scales, using a dull knife or a fish scraper.

Scraper

STEP 2
Cut off the head behind the pectoral fin and cut open the belly cavity.

Cut

Cut

Cut

STEP 3
Remove fins by cutting into flesh on both sides and then pulling them out.

Clean out belly cavity → Pull

Filleting

STEP 1
Cut deep on each side of dorsal fin.

STEP 2
Cut deep around head, gills, and fins.

STEP 3
Separate flesh from the rib cage.

STEP 4
Cut fillet loose.

STEP 5
Repeat steps 1 through 5 on opposite side.

STEP 6
Skin fillets by starting at tail end and inserting blade between skin and meat.

Cleaning Pike

Many people don't like to keep pike because they consider them too bony to eat and too difficult to clean. The following illustrations show a simple method to fillet a pike and remove those pesky "Y" bones.

STEP 1
Starting with the top of the fish, cut down behind the head to the backbone. Follow the backbone back to the top rear fin and cut up and remove the piece from the fish as shown in the illustration.

Continued →

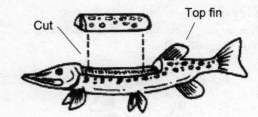

Step 2

Next, lay the piece on its side and cut it lengthwise along the cartilage, which runs down the center of the piece (both sides).

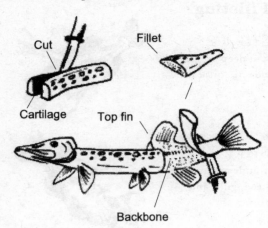

Step 3

Next, place the rest of the fish on its side, as shown in the illustration at right, and from the top fin (tail section), cut down through the side to the backbone and along the backbone to the tail. Repeat this step on the opposite side.

Step 4

After removing the two tail fillets, take the remaining fish and, with the exposed backbone up, feel for the "Y" bones with your fingers (they feel like sharp needles). Slip your knife under the "Y" bones and cut carefully down to the backbone and to the back. Do the same on the opposite side.

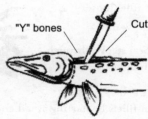

Step 5

Next, cut down behind the gill cover to the belly and, with the tip of the knife just below the "Y" bones, cut back along the rib cage. Repeat the same on the opposite side, and also remove the two bottom fins.

Step 6

Take all the fillets and remove the skin by inserting the blade between the skin and meat and pulling on the skin while holding the knife in a stationary position.

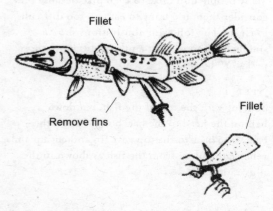

Cleaning Tips

Filet Mignon

The cheeks are the filet mignon of the fish. When cleaning large fish, don't forget to remove these choice tidbits before you discard the head.

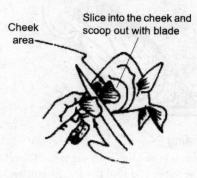

Fish Steaks

Large fish like salmon can be cut into steaks rather than fillets after you gut them and remove the fins.

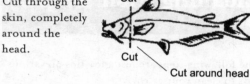

Skinning Catfish/Bullheads

Step 1

Cut through the skin, completely around the head.

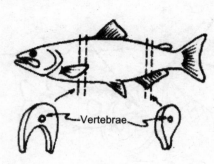

Step 2

Nail head to board and peel skin back with pliers.

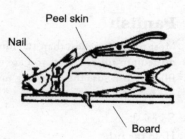

Step 3

After skin is peeled back, cut through the backbone behind the dorsal fin at an angle toward the head.

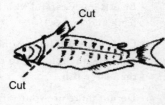

Step 4

Break the head downwards from the body, removing the head and entrails at the same time.

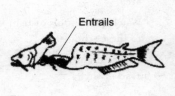

Cleaning Tools

If you can't find your scraper or you forget to bring it with you, try using a teaspoon or a tablespoon as a scraper. The spoon will do an excellent job, and the dull edges won't cut the fish.

Spoon Scrapper

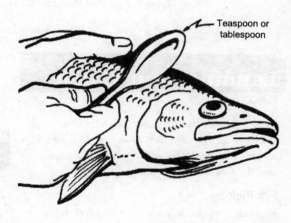

Homemade Fish Scaler

All you need to make a dandy scaler are two bottle caps from a soft drink or beer bottle, a couple of screws, and a piece of wood 1" wide x ¹/₂" thick and 6" long.

—From *Fishing Basics*

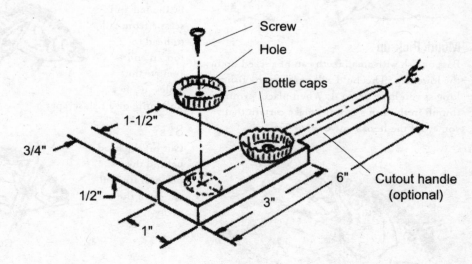

Fire

The Essentials of Fire

Greg Davenport
Illustrations by Steven Davenport and Ken Davenport

Fire is the third line of personal protection and in most cases will not be necessary if you've adequately met your clothing and shelter needs. In extreme conditions, however, fire is very beneficial for warding off hypothermia and other exposure injuries. Fire serves many other functions as well: providing light, warmth, and comfort; a source of heat for cooking, purifying water, and drying clothes; and a means of signaling. In addition, a fire is relaxing and helps reduce stress. For some of these purposes, building a fire is not always necessary. You might instead use a backpacking stove, Sterno stove, or solid compressed fuel tablets.

Man-made Heat Sources

A man-made heat source can be used in any shelter, provided there is proper ventilation. If you are in a tent, however, limit its use to the vestibule area to avoid fuel spills or burning the tent.

Backpacking Stove

The two basic styles of backpacking stoves are canister and liquid fuel. Canister designs use butane, propane, or isobutane cartridges as their fuel source. The most common types of liquid fuels used are white gas and kerosene. (For more details on the various styles of backpacking stoves, see page xxx).

Sterno

Sterno has been around for a long time and still has a place for many backcountry explorers. The fuel is a jellied alcohol that comes in a 7-ounce can. Under normal conditions, it has a two-hour burn time. Although far inferior to a good

backpacking stove for cooking, it is very effective at warming water and a shelter in an emergency. An inexpensive folding stove is made for use with Sterno, but with a little imagination, you can create the same thing.

Solid Compressed Fuel Tablets

Esbit, Trioxane, and Hexamine are the three basic compressed fuel tablets on the market. Esbit is the newest of the three, and unlike its predecessors, it is nontoxic. This nonexplosive, virtually odorless and smokeless tablet can generate up to 1,400 degrees F of intense heat, providing twelve to fifteen minutes of usable burn time per cube. When combined with a commercial or improvised stove, it can sometimes boil a pint of water in less than eight minutes. These tablets easily light from a spark and can also be used as a tinder to start your fire.

Building a Fire

When man-made heat sources are not available or don't meet your needs, you may elect to build a fire. Always use a safe site, and put the fire completely out, so that it is cold to the touch, before you leave. Locate the fire in close proximity to fire materials and your shelter. It should be built on flat, level ground and have adequate protection from the elements. Before starting the fire, prepare the site by clearing a 3-foot fire circle, scraping away all leaves, brush, and debris down to bare ground, if possible. To successfully build a fire, you need to have all three elements of the fire triad present—oxygen, fuel, and heat.

Oxygen

Oxygen is necessary for the fuel to burn, and it needs to be present at all stages of a fire. To ensure this, you'll need a platform and brace.

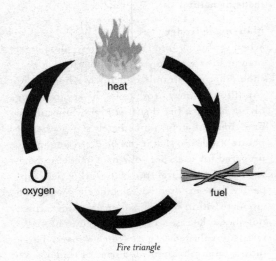

Fire triangle

Gather or create a platform and brace before you start breaking your fuel down, and use it to keep the smaller stages off the wet moist ground.

PLATFORM

A platform can be any dry material that protects your fuel from the ground, such as dry tree bark or dry nonporous rock. Waterlogged rocks may explode when wet; don't use them. In snow-covered areas, a snow platform may be necessary. To build this platform, use green wrist-size logs, and break or cut them into workable lengths (approximately 3 feet long). Construct a 3-foot-square platform by using two rows of the green logs. Place the top row perpendicular to the bottom row.

BRACE

A brace is vital. It ensures that the fire will get the oxygen it needs to exist. A 6-foot-long wrist-thick branch or a dry, nonporous rock 2 to 3 inches high will suffice. (Caution: Waterlogged rocks may explode when heated. Don't use them.) Lay the brace on or next to the platform. Leaning the kindling against the brace, and over the tinder, allows oxygen to circulate within the fire.

Continued →

A platform and brace keep tinder dry and help ensure adequate oxygen flow to your fuel.

Fuel

Fuel can be separated into three categories: tinder, kindling, and fuel. Each builds upon the previous one. Before gathering the fuel, make sure to prepare your site and position the platform and brace in the center. Next, gather enough fuel to build three fires. This allows you to step back to a smaller fuel if your fire has problems igniting a larger stage. When breaking the fuel down, lay the smaller stages of kindling against the brace, keeping it off the ground, and within reach of the fire you intend to build. The exact type of fuel used will vary depending on your location.

TINDER

Tinder is any material that will light from a spark. It's extremely valuable in getting the larger stages of fuel lit. Tinder can be man-made or natural.

Man-made tinder

When venturing into the wilderness, always carry man-made tinder in your survival kit. If you should become stranded during harsh weather conditions, it may prove to be the key in having or not having a fire that first night. Since it is a one-time-use item, immediately start gathering natural tinder so that it can be dried out and prepared for use once your man-made tinder is used up. For natural tinder to work it needs to be dry, have exposed edges, and allow oxygen to circulate within it. For man-made tinder, this is not always the case; it may just need to be scraped or fluffed so it can catch a spark. The most common man-made forms of tinder are petroleum-based, compressed tinder tabs, and solid compressed fuel tablets.

Petroleum-based tinder: This is very effective, even under harsh, wet, windy conditions. Many kinds are available, but perhaps the most common is the Tinder-Quik tab. It is waterproof, odorless, and made from a light compressible fiber that is impregnated with beeswax, petroleum, and silicones. To use it, simply fluff the fiber so that it has edges exposed to catch a spark. The tinder will burn for approximately two minutes. Although Tinder-Quik was designed for use with the spark-lite flint system (see heat sources) it can be used with any heat source. Less expensive petroleum-based tinder can be made by saturating 100 percent cotton balls with petroleum jelly and carrying them in a 35-millimeter film canister.

Compressed tinder tabs: WetFire tinder tablets are perhaps the most common compressed tinder tablets. Each tablet is waterproof, nontoxic, odorless, smokeless, and burns around 1,300 degrees F for two to three minutes. Unlike the Tinder-Quik Fire Tabs, they are not compressible. To use, prepare the tinder by making a few small shavings to catch the sparks from your metal match (see heat sources).

Solid compressed fuel tablets: Besides serving as a heat source, these tablets easily light from a spark and can also be used as tinder to start a fire. More details can be found under man-made heat sources.

Natural tinder

For natural tinder to work, it generally needs to be dry, have exposed edges, and allow oxygen to circulate within it. Gather natural materials for tinder before you need it so that you have time to dry it in the sun, between your clothing, or by a fire. Remove any wet bark or pith before breaking the tinder down, and keep it off the damp ground during and after preparation. Some tinder will collect moisture from the air, so prepare it last and keep it dry until you're ready to use it. Natural tinder falls into three basic categories: bark; scrapings; and grass, ferns, and lichen. If you are uncertain if something will work for tinder, try it.

Bark: Prepare layered forms of tinder by working pieces of bark between your hands and fingers until they're light and airy. To do this, start by holding a long section of the bark with both hands, thumb to thumb. Use a back-and-forth twisting action, working the bark until it becomes fibrous. Next, place the fibrous bark between the palms of your hands and role your hands back and forth until the bark becomes thin, light, and airy. At this point, you should be able to light it from a spark. Prepare this tinder until you have enough to form a small bird's nest. Place any loose dust created from the process in the center of the nest. Many barks will work as tinder, but birch is best as it will light even when wet due to a highly flammable resin it contains.

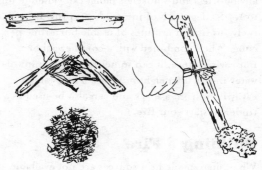

Breaking down bark*.   Making wood shavings*.

Wood scrapings: Wood scrapings are created by repeatedly running your knife blade, at a 90-degree angle, across a flat section of pitch wood or heartwood. To be effective, you'll need enough scrapings to fill the palm of your hand. Like birch bark, pitch wood will light even when wet. The high concentration of pitch in the wood's fibers makes it highly flammable.

Grass, ferns, leaves, and lichen: As with bark, fashion a bird's nest with these materials. You may need to break them down further, depending on the materials at hand. This form of tinder needs to be completely dry to work successfully.

illustrations from Surviving Cold Weather

KINDLING

Kindling is usually comprised of twigs or wood shavings that range in diameter from pencil lead to pencil thickness. It should easily light when placed on a small flame. Sources include small dead twigs found on the dead branches at the bottom of many trees; shavings from larger pieces of dry dead wood; small bundles of grass; dry sagebrush or cactus; heavy cardboard; and gasoline- or oil-soaked wood.

Wood shavings.

FUEL

Fuel is any material that is thumb-size or bigger that will burn slowly and steadily once it is lit. Kinds of fuel include dry dead branches at the bottom of trees; heartwood (the dry inside portion of a dead standing tree, fallen tree, tree trunk, or large branch); green wood that is finely split; dry grasses twisted into bunches; dry cacti or sagebrush; and dry animal dung.

Dry, dead branches at the bottom of trees

This material is great during dry or very cold weather. It provides all of the various stages of fuel when broken down properly. To decrease injury, wear gloves to protect your hands, and protect your eyes by looking away when snapping the branch off the tree. If the branches are wet, you'll need to prepare them by scraping off all of the wet bark and lichen. Run your knife across the wood's surface at a 90-degree angle. If it is still too wet, split the wood to expose its inner dry material.

Heartwood

Heartwood requires a lot more energy and time when used to build a fire. However, it is ideal during wet conditions when you need a dry surface that will easily ignite. The best source is a stump that has a sharp pointed top—in other words, a stump that wasn't created with a chainsaw. Stumps that have a flat surface can absorb massive amounts of moisture, especially when capped with snow. In addition, certain coniferous trees that die from natural causes will contain large amounts of pitch. This wood is commonly called pitch wood and is a great find when you are cold and in need of a quick fire, since it easily lights even under the worst conditions. To gather heartwood, pull, kick, or rip the pieces off of the stump. If unable to separate the wood from the stump, wedge a sturdy pole between the stump and a loose piece of wood, or use your ax or large fixed blade knife to help it along. A small-diameter standing dead tree can be knocked over and broken into workable sections by running it between two trees (a foot or so apart) and pulling one end back until the pole snaps in half. Once gathered, break the wood down from large to small. If using an ax or knife, follow basic safety rules.

Green wood

If you have a hot fire, green wood that is finely split will burn. However, it should not be used

Continued ➡

in the early stages of your fire. To increase your odds of success, remove the outer bark and cambium layer.

Dry grass twisted into bunches
Dry grass is not only great tinder, but also provides an excellent fuel when tied into bundles. If this is your only source of fuel, tie the grass into bundles that are 12 to 24 inches long with varying diameters, so you can stage your fire up from small to big.

Dead cacti and sagebrush
Once cacti are devoid of moisture, the material provides an excellent fuel source, and can quickly be broken down into the various stages of fuel. Cacti may be standing or lying on the desert floor. Sagebrush often has dead lower portions similar to the dead lower branches found on many trees. Breaking these branches away and then preparing them into the various stages of fuel is an easy process.

Dead sagebrush and shrubs provide an excellent fuel source for building fires.

Animal dung
Because herbivores eat grass and other plants, their dried dung makes excellent fuel. Break the dung into various sizes to create tinder, kindling, and fuel. I consider them Mother Nature's Pres-to-Logs.

Heat

Heat is required to start a fire. Before applying heat to your fuel, however, make sure you have enough of each stage to light three fires. This allows you to step back to a smaller fuel when your fire has problems igniting a larger stage. Since matches and lighters often fail and will eventually run out, you must consider alternative sources of heat to start your fire. Options include both man-made (often spark-based) and primitive (friction-based) heat sources, and several are covered here.

MAN-MADE AND SPARKED-BASED HEAT SOURCES
Man-made heat sources include matches, lighters, artificial flint, flint and steel, pyrotechnics, battery and steel wool, and convex glass. Most man-made heat sources are easy to use, and at least one should be part of your emergency survival kit.

Matches
Matches run out, get wet, and seem to never work in a time of crisis. However, if you are dead set on using matches, I'd recommend NATO-issue survival matches, which have hand-dipped and varnished heads that are supposed to light even when wet and exposed to strong wind or rain. These matches will burn around twelve seconds—enough time to light most fires. In order to protect the match from going out, light it between cupped hands while positioning your body to block the flame from the wind and rain. Regardless of the type you carry, store them in a waterproof container until ready for use.

Lighters
Lighters are a form of flint and steel with an added fuel source that keeps the flame going. Like matches, they have a tendency to fail when used during inclement weather, and once the fuel runs out, they become dead weight. If you understand a lighter's shortcoming and still elect to use one, I recommend a Colibri Quantum. These high-end lighters are water resistant, shockproof, ignite at high altitudes, and are marketed as windresistant. To use, simply place the flame directly onto the tinder.

Metal match (artificial flint)
A metal match is similar to the flints used in a cigarette lighter but much bigger. When stroked with an object, the friction creates a long spark that can be used to light tinder. Most metal matches are made from a mixture of metals and rare earth elements. The mixture is alloyed at high temperature and then shaped into rods of various diameters.

To use a metal match, place it in the center of your tinder, and while holding it firmly in place with one hand, use the opposite hand to strike it with your knife blade, using a firm yet controlled downward stroke, at 45 to 90 degrees. The resulting spark should provide enough heat to ignite the tinder. This may take several attempts. If after five tries it has not lit, the tinder should be reworked to ensure that adequate edges are exposed and oxygen is able to flow within it. The S.O.S Strike Force is the most popular commercial metal match available. There also are two one-hand-use metal matches on the market: the Spark-Lite and the BlastMatch.

S.O.S. Strike Force: The S.O.S. Strike Force has a half-inch round alloy flint attached to a hollow, hard plastic handle that houses emergency tinder. It also has a flint cover with a hardened steel striker attached, making this system completely self-sufficient. Although the system is a little bulky, it weighs slightly less than 4 ounces.

Spark-Lite: The Spark-Lite is small and light, measuring approximately 2 1/4 by 9/32 by 9/32 inches. Its spark is also smaller than that of the larger metal matches. It has a serrated wheel, similar to that of a cigarette lighter, that strikes a

Unlike matches and lighters, an artificial flint virtually never runs out.

small flint when stroked. In order to make this a one-hand-use item, the flint is spring-loaded, maintaining contact with the wheel at all times. The small flint is supposed to allow for approximately 1,000 strokes before it runs out. To use, stroke the sparking wheel with your thumb while holding the Spark-Lite's body with your fingers from the same hand.

BlastMatch: The BlastMatch is larger and weighs more than the Spark-Lite, measuring 4 by 1 3/8 by 7/8 inches. It has a much larger molded plastic body that holds a 2 1/2-inch-long by 1/2-inch-diameter rod of flint. The flint is spring-loaded, and when the cap is released the flint is propelled out. To use it, place the flint tip in the center of your tinder, apply pressure to the side catch with your thumb, and push the body downward. This action will force the scraper, located inside the catch, down the flint, creating a large spark.

Flint and steel and charred cloth.

Flint and steel
Flint and steel are effective for starting fires, but the necessary materials may be hard to find. Some flint options are quartzite, iron pyrite, agate, or jasper. Any steel can be used with the flint, but most people use an old file. By striking the iron particles, heart is created when they are crushed and torn away. To use the flint and steel, hold the flint in one hand as close to the tinder as possible. With the steel in your other hand, strike downward onto the flint. Direct the resulting spark into the center of the tinder. The best tinder to use is charred cloth, which can be created in advance by placing several 2-inch squares of cotton cloth inside a tin can with ventilation holes in its top. Place this in a fire's coals for fifteen to thirty minutes. Turn the can every couple of minutes, and remove from the fire when smoke stops coming out of the holes.

Pyrotechnics
Flares should be used only as a last resort to start fires. It's best to save these signaling devices for their intended use. However, if you are unable to start a fire and the risk of hypothermia is present, a flare is a very effective heat source. Using it is simple: After preparing the tinder, safely ignite it by lighting the flare and directing its flames onto the tinder. Time will be of the essence, so prepare your firelay in advance, leaving an opening large enough to direct the flare's flame onto the underlying tinder.

Battery and steel wool
Stretching a fine grade 0000 steel wool between the positive and negative posts of a battery will ignite the steel wool. Lit steel wool can be used

Continued ➔

to ignite tinder, using the same technique discussed under friction-based heat sources. This method works best with a 9-volt battery.

Burning glass

A convex-shape piece of glass, such as that from binoculars, a broken bottle, or a telescope, can be used to ignite tinder by focusing the sun's rays into a concentrated source of heat.

Natural Friction-Based Heat Sources

Friction-based heat works through a process of pulverizing and heating appropriate woods until an ember is created. This ember can be used to ignite awaiting tinder. The biggest problems associated with these techniques are muscle fatigue, poor wood selection, and moisture that prevents the material from reaching a hot enough temperature. Once you have an ember, relax and take your time. Don't blow on it; the moisture from your mouth may put it out. If you feel it needs more oxygen, gently fan it with your hand. In most cases, however, simply waiting a few seconds will allow the ember to achieve its pleasant glow. Two circular methods covered here are the bow and drill and hand drill.

Bow and Drill

The bow and drill is often used when the spindle and baseboard materials are not good enough to create a char using a hand drill technique. The bow helps establish the friction that is needed in order to use materials that would otherwise be inferior or when bad weather adversely affects your ability to create an ember with the hand drill. The bow and drill is composed of four separate parts.

Bow: The bow is a 3- to 4-foot branch of hardwood that is seasoned, stout, slightly curved, about 3/4 inch in diameter, and with a small fork at one end. If the bow doesn't have a fork, create one by carving a notch at the appropriate place. Add a strong line, attached to the bow to create enough tension to turn the spindle once it is inserted. You can use a strip of leather, parachute line, shoelace, or improvised cordage (details on how to make cordage are covered in chapter 13). Securely attach the line to one end of the bow by carefully drilling a hole through the bow with a pump drill or knife, tying a knot in the line, and then running the line through the hole. The knot ensures that the line will not slip or slide forward, and since the line's tension will inevitably loosen, it allows you to make quick adjustments. Use a fixed loop to attach the line's free end to the fork on the other side.

Cup: Made from hardwoods, antlers, rocks, or pitch wood, the cup has a socket for the top of the spindle. The cup's purpose is to hold the spindle in place while it is turned by the bow. When using deadwood, you must lubricate the cup's socket to decrease the friction between the cup and the spindle. You can use body oils, animal fat, or soap shavings to accomplish this.

Spindle: The spindle is a smooth, straight cylinder made from a dry, soft wood or other plant material that is approximately 3/4 inch in diameter and 8 to 12 inches long. The ideal spindle is made from yucca, sotol (a variation of yucca), cottonwood, aspen, willow, sage, or cactus. Dead smaller branches of cedar, locust, and ash may also be used for a spindle. The best

way to evaluate the material is to press on it with a fingernail; if it makes an indention, the material should work. To prepare the spindle for use, carve both ends so that one is cone-shaped and smooth and the other is round with rough edges.

Fireboard: Fireboard should be made from a material similar in hardness to the spindle. The ideal fireboard is 15 to 18 inches long, 3/4 inch thick, and 2 to 3 inches wide. The fireboard needs to be prepared for use using the following steps.

1. Carve a circular socket three-quarters the diameter of the spindle, at least 4 inches from one end, close to the long side (but not right on the side), and about one-quarter the thickness of the board. If the socket is too close to the side, there will not be enough material to prevent the spindle from kicking out of the hole.

2. Prime the hole by twisting the bowline around the spindle so that the coned end is up and the rounded blunt end is down. If it doesn't feel like it wants to twist out, then the bow's line needs to be tightened. While holding the bow and spindle together, kneel on your right knee and place your left foot on the fireboard. Insert the cone end of the spindle inside the cup, and place the round, blunt end into the fireboard socket that you created with your knife. Holding the bow in the right hand (at the closest end) and the cup in the left, apply gentle downward pressure on the spindle, keeping the spindle perpendicular to the ground. For added support and stability, rest the left arm and elbow around and on the left knee and shin. (If left-handed, do the reverse.) With a straightened arm, begin moving the bow back and forth with a slow, even, steady stroke. Once the friction between the spindle and the fireboard begins to create smoke, gradually increase the downward pressure and continue until a smooth, round indentation is made in the fireboard.

The various parts of the bow and drill.

3. Using your knife or saw, cut a pie-shape notch through the entire thickness of the fireboard so that its point stops slightly short of the hole's center. Place a piece of bark, leather, or other appropriate material under your fireboard for the ember to sit on. This will protect it from the moist ground and help you move it to your tinder.

Once the separate parts of the bow and drill are prepared, it is then ready. Simply apply the same technique used for priming the hole when preparing the fireboard. Once the smoke is bellowing out and you can't go any longer, check within or below the fireboard's notch for an ember created by the friction.

The bow and drill in use.

Hand drill

The hand drill is similar to the bow and drill, except you use your hands to turn the spindle. This method is used when conditions are ideal; no moisture is in the air, and you have excellent materials. The hand drill is composed of two parts:

Spindle: The spindle is a smooth, straight cylinder made from a dry, soft wood or other plant material that is approximately 1/2 to 3/4 inch in diameter and 2 to 3 feet long. The ideal spindle is made from yucca or sotol. I have heard reports of people using cattail and mullein, but these materials can be finicky. To prepare the spindle for use, carve the fatter end so that it is round with rough edges. If you can find a straight spindle, you might use a piece of cattail, bamboo, or other available reed as the shaft. Create a plug from a short piece of sotol or other material to fit inside the end, leaving 2 to 3 inches of the plug extending out of the shaft. To help protect the end of the shaft from splitting, wrap it with a thin strand of cord. You could also use this technique to drill holes by replacing the friction plug with a stone bit.

Fireboard: The fireboard is created from a soft wood or plant material of similar but not quite the same hardness as the spindle. Yucca and sagebrush are my favorites. The optimal size is 15 to 18 inches long, 2 to 3 inches wide, and 1/2 to 3/4 inch thick. Prepare a notch as described above for the bow and drill.

When using a hand drill, some people sit and others kneel. The key is to be comfortable while still being able to turn the spindle and apply appropriate downward pressure. To use, while sitting or kneeling, rub the spindle between your hands. In order to optimize the number of revolutions the spindle makes, start at the top and use as much of the hands, from heel to fingertip, as you can. Apply downward pressure, as your hands move down the spindle, until you reach bottom, and then quickly move both hands up while ensuring that the spindle and fireboard maintain contact at all times. Since the spindle will cool rapidly, this step is very crucial to your success. When you begin to see smoke, increase your speed and downward pressure until you can't do it anymore. Just before you finish, push the top of the spindle slightly

Continued

away from the fire-board's notch to help push the coal out. At times, it may be necessary to create additional downward pressure on your spindle. Two methods that are commonly used are:

Creating a coal using a hand drill.

Mouthpiece: A mouthpiece is created similarly to the cup of a bow and drill, but instead of using your hands to hold it on the spindle you use your teeth. When using this technique, shorten the spindle to 18 to 24 inches in length.

Thumb thong: To make a thumb thong, tie a thumb loop at each end of a thong, and attach its center to the top of the spindle. By sliding your thumbs into the loops you are able to provide a nonstop spin with increased downward pressure. As with the mouthpiece, this technique will require you to use a shorter spindle.

Bark and grass are the most common tinder used with a friction heat source such as the bow and drill and hand drill. Form a bird's nest, and put it in a dry place where it is protected from the elements. Once you have created an ember, gently move it into the center of the bird's nest, and loosely fold the outer nest around it. Holding it all above your head, lightly blow on

---

---

the ember, increasing in intensity until the tinder ignites. To avoid burning your fingers, it may be necessary to hold the tinder between two sticks. Once the tinder ignites, place it on your platform next to the brace, and begin building your fire.

Steps to Building a Fire

When building a fire, it is important to gather enough fuel to build three knee-high fires. This allows you to go back to a previous stage if the fire starts to die and to keep the fire going while you get more material. Once the wood or other fuel is gathered, break it down from big to small, always preparing the smallest stages last. This will help decrease the amount of moisture your tinder and kindling collect during the preparation process. If conditions are wet, you'll need to strip off all lichen and bark, and for best results, split the branches in half to expose the inner dry wood. Construct a platform and brace (described under oxygen on page 231), and use the brace to keep the various stages of fuel off the ground while breaking it down.

Once all the stages are prepared, either light or place the lit tinder on the platform next to the brace. Use the brace to place your smaller kindling directly over the flame. Spread a handful of kindling over the flame all at once, instead of one stick at a time. Once the flames lick up through the kindling, place another handful perpendicularly across the first. When this stage is burning well, advance to the next size. Continue crisscrossing your fuel until the largest size is burning and the fire is self-supporting. If you have leftover material, set it aside in a dry place so that it can be used to start another fire later. If you have a problem building your fire, reevaluate your heat, oxygen, and fuel to determine which one is not present or is inadequate for success.

Fire Reflector

Consider building a firewall to reflect the fire's heat in the direction you want. Secure two 3-foot-long poles into the ground 1 foot behind the fire circle. In order to pound the poles into the ground, you'll need to sharpen the ends and use a rock or another sturdy pole to safely drive them in.
Next, place two poles of similar size 4 to 6 inches in front of the first ones. Gather green logs of wrist diameter, and place them between the poles to form a 3-foot-high wall.

Fire reflector.

You can angle the wall slightly to reflect the heat down or up.

Maintaining a Heat Source

Several methods are commonly used to maintain a heat source for ongoing or later use.

Keeping a Flame

The best way to keep a flame is to provide an ongoing fuel source. The type of wood you use will directly impact this process. Soft woods such

---

SNOW PLATFORM AND BRACE
Greg Davenport
Illustration by Steven A. Davenport

Oxygen is necessary for the fuel to burn, and it needs to be present at all stages of a fire. To ensure this, you'll need a platform and brace. A platform is any dry material that protects your fuel from the ground or snow. During extremely wet conditions or when there is a heavy snow covering, a platform can be made by laying multiple green logs next to one another. Building the fire on the green logs will protect it from the snow or moist ground. A brace is usually a wrist-diameter branch that allows oxygen to circulate through the fuel when the fuel is leaned against it. This will prevent the snow from putting the fire out.

—From *Surviving Cold Weather*

Snow platform and brace.

---

as cedar, pine, or fir provide an excellent light and heat source, but they burn up rather fast. Hardwoods, such as maple, ash, oak, or hickory, will burn longer and produce less smoke. These woods are ideal for use at night.

Keeping a Coal

Either banking the fire or storing it inside a fire bundle can maintain a coal.

BANKING THE FIRE

If you are staying in one place, bank the fire to preserve its embers for use at a later time. Once you have a good bed of coals, cover them with ashes and/or dry dirt. If done properly, the fire's embers will still be smoldering in the morning. To rekindle the fire, remove the dry dirt, lay tinder on the coals, and gently fan it until the tinder ignites.

FIRE BUNDLE

If you plan on traveling, use a fire bundle to transport the coal. A fire bundle can keep a coal for six to twelve hours. To construct it, surround the live coal with dry punk wood or fibrous bark, such as cedar or juniper, and wrap this with damp grass, leaves, or humus. Around this, wrap a heavy bark such as birch. The key to success is to ensure that there is enough oxygen to keep the ember burning but not enough to promote its ignition. If the bundle begins to burn through, it may be necessary to stop and build another fire from which to create another coal for transport.

Fire bundle.

Continued ➔

PUMP DRILLS

Greg Davenport   Illustrations by Steven Davenport and Ken Davenport

In addition to drilling holes, a pump drill can also be adapted into a friction heat source that works similarly to the bow and drill. It consists of a spindle, crosspiece, flywheel, and fireboard.

• **Spindle**. The spindle is made from a piece of straight, debarked hardwood that measures about 30 inches long with a diameter of 1 1/8 inch on one end tapering to 7/8 inch on the other. On the wider end, drill a 1- to 2-inch-deep hole, slightly bigger than 1/2 inch diameter, into its exact center. This can be started with a hand drill with a 1/2-inch stone bit (described in the Hand Drill section above), and then finished by replacing the bit with a 1/2-inch wood plug of medium hardness. This technique should create a nicely rounded, burned hole that has an equal diameter throughout its depth. If the hole ends up not being centered, cut it off and start over.

Create a plug from a dry, soft wood or other plant material such as yucca, sotol, cottonwood, aspen, willow, sage, cacti, cedar, locust, or ash. This plug should fit snugly into the spindle's tip, with 2 to 3 inches extending out of the shaft. Wrap sinew around the end of the spindle for about 3 inches up its shaft to secure the plug and also help prevent the end of the spindle from splitting. On the other end of the spindle, cut a 1/4-inch notch into the center of the shaft. The string from the pump drill's crosspiece will ride there. To help protect the area, wrap the end with sinew from the bottom of the notch to about 1 inch down.

• **Crosspiece**. The crosspiece is made from a piece of straight-grained, knotfree hardwood that measures 22 to 24 inches in length and about 1 1/2 to 2 inches wide. Create a hole in the exact center of the crosspiece that is 1/8 inch bigger around than the spindle. This can be done with your hand drill or perhaps by

using a hot coal. Tie a line to the far ends of the crosspiece so that the line measures 31 to 35 inches from one end to the other. When done, the crosspiece should easily slide up and down the spindle, and the line should fit within the spindle's notch.

• **Flywheel**. The flywheel sits on the lower end of the spindle, providing balance and weight. The ideal flywheel weight for creating an ember is 2 1/2 to 3 pounds. To make one, gather two pieces of hardwood that are about 8 inches long by 2 inches wide, and burn or drill a hole into the exact center of each piece of wood. The size of the hole depends on the spindle's diameter. A proper fit allows the lower piece to wedge 4 inches up from the bottom of the spindle and the upper piece 2 1/2 inches above that. Next, find two rocks that weigh about 1 1/4 to 1 1/2 pounds each, and tie them between the two pieces of wood, one on each side of the hole, making sure that the holes are exposed and are in line with each other when done. Since it is doubtful that the rocks will weigh exactly the same, you may need to add twigs or line to one side of the flywheel to balance it out.

• **Fireboard**. The fireboard should be made from a material similar in hardness to the spindle plug. The ideal fireboard is 15 to 18 inches long, 3/4 inch thick, and 2 to 3 inches wide. Prepare the fireboard by carving a circular socket three-quarters the diameter of the spindle, at least 4 inches from one end, close to the long side (but not right on the side), and about one-quarter the thickness of the board.

Pump-drill Technique

Place the plug inside the spindle and the flywheel over the top and into position. Advance the crosspiece down the spindle, letting the center of its line come to rest inside the upper notch. Place the spindle into the socket, and

turn it by hand until the line is wrapped around it and the crosspiece has moved up the shaft. At this point, you are ready to begin. This system is not much different from the bow and drill or hand drill. The spindle turns one way and then another while inside the fireboard's socket. The constant rotation creates friction, which in turn creates heat and eventually an ember. As with both of the other systems, your technique of execution will play a major role in success or failure.

Place one hand on each end of the crosspiece, kneel on your right knee, and place your left foot on the fireboard. Apply a smooth yet forceful downward stroke that has a rapid acceleration early on. As the crosspiece gets close to the bottom, don't relax. Continue to apply downward pressure while the line is rewrapping itself around the spindle in the opposite direction. By doing this, you maintain a friction force (contact) between the spindle and the fireboard. Try to time it so that as the crosspiece reaches the top, you can quickly accelerate back downward. Stop when a smooth, round indentation is made in the fireboard, and cut your notch in the same manner as described for the bow and drill. Once the notch is prepared, put bark, leather, or other dry material under your fireboard to catch the coal. Place the spindle back in the notch, and repeat the steps as just outlined until you have a solid wall of smoke and an ember is present.

Fine Tuning the Pump Drill

• **Revolutions**. The ideal number of revolutions per complete cycle, top to bottom to top, is four—two down and two up. If you have more than that, the spindle loses its momentum when going up and, in turn, friction heat. Adjusting your string length will correct this problem.

• **Flywheel weight**. Although 2 1/2 to 3 pounds is considered the ideal weight, this is not always true. To determine the best weight, use the following guidelines: If your spindle plug produces a dark brown dust and ember, it is just right. If it produces a light brown dust or no dust at all, it is too light. If the spindle is destroyed during use or it goes through the fireboard, the flywheel is too heavy.

• **Torque**. In order to obtain a fluid motion during operation, the torque applied during the downward motion of the crosspiece needs to approximate the torque created during its upswing. Adjusting the string's position on the crosspiece—equally on both sides—will correct this problem. You also may need to readjust the string's length to get the desired number of revolutions.

—From *Surviving the Desert*

Using the pump drill.

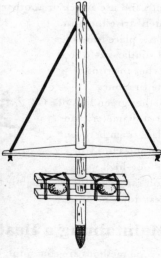

The various parts of a pump drill.

Continued ➡

Fire Bed

In extremely cold temperate or desert environments, a fire bed will help keep you warm during the night. It takes about two hours to prepare. Used in large shelters or when none is available, the heat generated from these beds has been known to last as long as two days.

Dig a 4- to 6-inch-deep rectangle that is big enough for you to lie in. Since the heat will radiate outward, you may make the area smaller if digging is hard. If available, line the bottom with flat rocks (avoid rocks that contain moisture). Build a long fire inside the large rectangular hole. As the fire grows, spread out the wood until it evenly covers the whole area and let it burn for one to two hours before you stop feeding it new fuel. Once only coals remain, spread them out so they cover the bottom of the hole evenly. Next, place dirt over the coals, stamping it down as you go, until there is approximately 4 inches of it covering the bed. To make sure the dirt covering is enough, push your whole index finger into the dirt that is over the coals. If your fingertip can't handle the heat, add more dirt. Finally, cover the fire bed with an insulating material like duff, boughs, or leaves. Make sure there aren't any loose embers that may ignite your insulation bed. Sleeping on this soft, warm fire bed will take the bite out of most cold nights. Once a bed has been created, this process can be repeated as needed. Subsequent fire beds will be easier to make since the dirt will require less energy to remove.

—From *Wilderness Survival*

Firecraft
U.S. Army

In many survival situations, the ability to start a fire can make the difference between living and dying. Fire can fulfill many needs. It can provide warmth and comfort. It not only cooks and preserves food, it also provides warmth in the form of heated food that saves calories our body normally uses to produce body heat. You can use fire to purify water, sterilize bandages, signal for rescue, and provide protection from animals. It can be a psychological boost by providing peace of mind and companionship. You can also use fire to produce tools and weapons.

Fire can cause problems, as well. … It can cause forest fires or destroy essential equipment. Fire can also cause burns and carbon monoxide poisoning when used in shelters.

Basic Fire Principles

To build a fire, it helps to understand the basic principles of a fire. Fuel (in a nongaseous state) does not burn directly. When you apply heat to a fuel, it produces a gas. This gas, combined with oxygen in the air, burns.

Understanding the concept of the fire triangle is very important in correctly constructing and maintaining a fire. The three sides of the triangle represent air, heat, and fuel. If you remove any of these, the fire will go out. The correct ratio of these components is very important for a fire to burn at its greatest capability. The only way to learn this ratio is to practice.

Site Selection and Preparation

You will have to decide what site and arrangement to use. Before building a fire consider—

- The area (terrain and climate) in which you are operating.
- The materials and tools available.
- Time: how much time you have?
- Need: why you need a fire?
- Security: how close is the enemy?

Look for a dry spot that—

- Is protected from the wind.
- Is suitably placed in relation to your shelter (if any).
- Will concentrate the heat in the direction you desire.
- Has a supply of wood or other fuel available.

If you are in a wooded or brush-covered area, clear the brush and scrape the surface soil from the spot you have selected. Clear a circle at least 1 meter in diameter so there is little chance of the fire spreading.

If time allows, construct a fire wall using logs or rocks. This wall will help to reflect or direct the heat where you want it. It will also reduce flying sparks and cut down on the amount of wind blowing into the fire. However, you will need enough wind to keep the fire burning.

In some situations, you may find that an underground fireplace will best meet your needs. It conceals the fire and serves well for cooking food. To make an underground fireplace or Dakota fire hole—

- Dig a hole in the ground.
- On the upwind side of this hole, poke or dig a large connecting hole for ventilation.
- Build your fire in the hole as illustrated.

> **Caution**
> Do not use wet of porous rocks as they may explode when heated.

If you are in a snow-covered area, use green logs to make a dry base for your fire. Trees with wrist-sized trunks are easily broken in extreme cold. Cut or break several green logs and lay them side by side on top of the snow. Add one or two more layers. Lay the top layer of logs opposite those below it.

FIRE THONG AND BAMBOO FIRE SAW
Greg Davenport Illustrations by Steven A. Davenport

Bamboo Fire Saw

The fire saw is a technique most often used with hollow materials such as bamboo. It is composed of two pieces:

- **Saw:** cut a straight piece of the hollow material and sharpen the edge on one of its long sides.
- **Baseboard:** cut the hollow material in half (long ways) and then cut a notch across the width of its convex side. It is usually 12 inches in length.

Fire Saw Technique

The baseboard is the moving piece of the fire saw. Place well-prepared tinder in the concave side of the baseboard (in line with the notch you created) and hold it in place with a small twig or piece of the bamboo. Next, place the groove of the baseboard so that a cross is created between it and the sharp end of the saw (which needs to be stationary). Begin moving the baseboard back and forth on the saw, increasing your speed as it begins to smoke and continue until you can't go any longer. The coal will form on the concave side of the baseboard within the awaiting tinder.

Bamboo fire saw.

Fire Thong

The fire thong is a friction system that is often used in the tropics where rattan is abundant. It consists of two parts:

- **Thong:** made of twisted rattan that is 4 to 6 feet long and less than 1 inch in diameter.
- **Baseboard:** usually a deciduous material that is softer than the rattan and measures about 4 feet in length.

Fire Thong Technique

To use this method, a cross beam is needed to keep the baseboard off the ground and allow the thong to move freely across it. (See the following illustration.) It's the friction between the thong and the baseboard that creates the heat needed to produce a coal from this method. Be sure to place a piece of bark,

Fire thong.

leather, or other appropriate material under your baseboard for the coal to sit on. This will protect it from the moist ground and help you move it to your tinder.

—From *Wilderness living*

Continued ➔

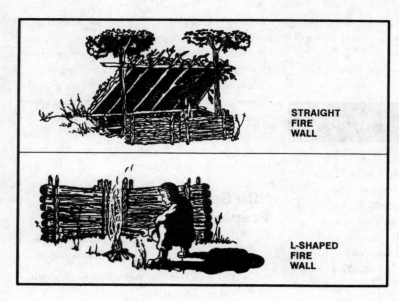

STRAIGHT FIRE WALL

L-SHAPED FIRE WALL

Types of fire walls.

TREE TO DISPERSE SMOKE

AIRFLOW

15–35 cm OPENING

25–30 cm

15–20 cm OPENING

20–25 cm

Dakota fire hole.

Fire Material Selection

You need three types of materials to build a fire—tinder, kindling, and fuel.

Tinder is dry material that ignites with little heat—a spark starts a fire. The tinder must be absolutely dry to be sure just a spark will ignite it. If you only have a device that generates sparks, charred cloth will be almost essential. It holds a spark for long periods, allowing you to put tinder on the hot area to generate a small flame. You can make charred cloth by heating cotton cloth until it turns black, but does not burn. Once it is black, you must keep it in an airtight container to keep it dry. Prepare this cloth well in advance of any survival situation. Add it to your individual survival kit.

Kindling is readily combustible material that you add to the burning tinder. Again, this material should be absolutely dry to ensure rapid burning. Kindling increases the fire's temperatures so that it will ignite less combustible material.

Fuel is less combustible material that burns slowly and steadily once ignited.

How to Build a Fire

There are several methods for laying a fire, each of which has advantages. The situation you find yourself in will determine which fire to use.

Tepee

To make this fire, arrange the tinder and a few sticks of kindling in the shape of a tepee or cone. Light the center. As the tepee burns, the outside logs will fall inward, feeding the fire. This type of fire burns well even with wet wood.

Lean-to

To lay this fire, push a green stick into the ground at a 30-degree angle. Point the end of the stick in the direction of the wind. Place some tinder deep under this lean-to stick. Lean pieces of kindling against the lean-to stick. Light the tinder. As the kindling catches fire from the tinder, add more kindling.

Cross-ditch

To use this method, scratch a cross about 30 centimeters in size in the ground. Dig the cross 7.5 centimeters deep. Put a large wad of tinder in

the middle of the cross. Build a kindling pyramid above the tinder. The shallow ditch allows air to sweep under the tinder to provide a draft.

Pyramid

To lay this fire, place two small logs or branches parallel on the ground. Place a solid layer of small logs across the parallel logs. Add three or four

Base for fire in snow-covered area.

Tinder	Kindling	Fuel
• Birch bark	• Small twigs	• Dry, standing wood and dry, dead branches
• Shredded inner bark from cedar, chestnut, red elm trees	• Small strips of wood	• Dry inside (heart) of fallen tree trunks and large branches
• Fine wood shavings	• Split wood	
• Dead grass, ferns, moss, fungi	• Heavy cardboard	• Green wood that is finely split
• Straw	• Pieces of wood removed from the inside of larger pieces	• Dry grasses twisted into bunches
• Sawdust	• Wood that has been doused with highly flammable materials, such as gasoline, oil, or wax	• Peat dry enough to burn (this may be found at the top of undercut banks)
• Very fine pitchwood scrapings		• Dried animal dung
• Dead evergreen needles		• Animal fats
• Punk (the completely rotted portions of dead logs or trees)		• Coal, oil shale, or oil lying on the surface
• Evergreen tree knots		
• Bird down (fine feathers)		
• Down seed heads (milkweed, dry cattails, bulrush, or thistle)		
• Fine, dried vegetable fibers		
• Spongy threads of dead puffball		
• Dead palm leaves		
• Skinlike membrane lining bamboo		
• Lint from pocket and seams		
• Charred cloth		
• Waxed paper		
• Outer bamboo shavings		
• Gunpowder		
• Cotton		
• Lint		

Continued ➡

more layers of logs or branches, each layer smaller than and at a right angle to the layer below it. Make a starter fire on top of the pyramid. As the starter fire burns, it will ignite the logs below it. This gives you a fire that burns downward, requiring no attention during the night.

There are several other ways to lay a fire that are quite effective. Your situation and the material available in the area may make another method more suitable.

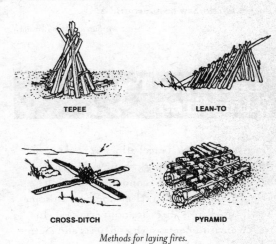

Methods for laying fires.

How to Light a Fire

Always light your fire from the upwind side. Make sure to lay your tinder, kindling, and fuel so that your fire will burn as long as you need it. Igniters provide the initial heat required to start the tinder burning. They fall into two categories: modern methods and primitive methods.

Modern Methods

Modern igniters use modern devices—items we normally think of to start a fire.

MATCHES

Make sure these matches are waterproof. Also, store them in a waterproof container along with a dependable striker pad.

CONVEX LENS

Use this method only on bright, sunny days. The lens can come from binoculars, camera, telescopic sights, or magnifying glasses. Angle the lens to concentrate the sun's rays on the tinder. Hold the lens over the same spot until the tinder begins to smolder. Gently blow or fan the tinder into flame, and apply it to the fire lay.

Lens method.

METAL MATCH

Place a flat, dry leaf under your tinder with a portion exposed. Place the tip of the metal match on the dry leaf, holding the metal match in one hand and a knife in the other. Scrape your knife against the metal match to produce sparks. The sparks will hit the tinder. When the tinder starts to smolder, proceed as above.

BATTERY

Use a battery to generate a spark. Use of this method depends on the type of battery available. Attach a wire to each terminal. Touch the ends of the bare wires together next to the tinder so the sparks will ignite it.

GUNPOWDER

Often, you will have ammunition with your equipment. If so, carefully extract the bullet from the shell casing, and use the gunpowder as tinder. A spark will ignite the powder. Be extremely careful when extracting the bullet from the case.

Primitive Methods

Primitive igniters are those attributed to our early ancestors.

FLINT AND STEEL

The direct spark method is the easiest of the primitive methods to use. The flint and steel method is the most reliable of the direct spark methods. Strike a flint or other hard, sharp-edged rock edge with a piece of carbon steel (stainless steel will not produce a good spark). This method requires a loose-jointed wrist and practice. When a spark has caught in the tinder, blow on it. The spark will spread and burst into flames.

FIRE-PLOW

The fire-plow is a friction method of ignition. You rub a hardwood shaft against a softer wood base. To use this method, cut a straight groove in the base and plow the blunt tip of the shaft up and down the groove. The plowing action of the shaft pushes out small particles of wood fibers. Then, as you apply more pressure on each stroke, the friction ignites the wood particles.

Fire-plow.

BOW AND DRILL

The technique of starting a fire with a bow and drill is simple, but you must exert much effort and be persistent to produce a fire. You need the following items to use this method:

- **Socket.** The socket is an easily grasped stone or piece of hardwood or bone with a slight depression in one side. Use it to hold the drill in place and to apply downward pressure.
- **Drill.** The drill should be a straight, seasoned hardwood stick about 2 centimeters in diameter and 25 centimeters long. The top end is round and the low end blunt (to produce more friction).
- **Fire board.** Its size is up to you. A seasoned softwood board about 2.5 centimeters thick and 10 centimeters wide is preferable. Cut a depression about 2 centimeters from the edge on one side of the board. On the underside, make a V-shaped cut from the edge of the board to the depression.

- **Bow.** The bow is a resilient, green stick about 2.5 centimeters in diameter and a string. The type of wood is not important. The bow-string can be any type of cordage. You tie the bowstring from one end of the bow to the other, without any slack.

To use the bow and drill, first prepare the fire lay. Then place a bundle of tinder under the V-shaped cut in the fire board. Place one foot on the fire board. Loop the bowstring over the drill and place the drill in the precut depression on the fire board. Place the socket, held in one hand, on the top of the drill to hold it in position. Press down on the drill and saw the bow back and forth to twirl the drill [see illustration below]. Once you have established a smooth motion, apply more downward pressure and work the bow faster. This action will grind hot black powder into the tinder, causing a spark to catch. Blow on the tinder until it ignites.

Note: Primitive fire-building methods are exhaustive and require practice to ensure success.

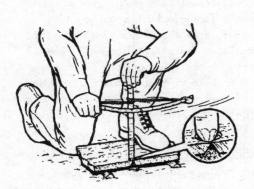

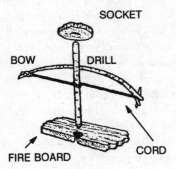

Bow and drill.

Helpful Hints

- Use nonaromatic seasoned hardwood for fuel, if possible.
- Collect kindling and tinder along the trail.
- Add insect repellent to the tinder.
- Keep the firewood dry.
- Dry damp firewood near the fire.
- Bank the fire to keep the coals alive overnight.
- Carry lighted punk, when possible.
- Be sure the fire is out before leaving camp.
- Do not select wood lying on the ground. It may appear to be dry but generally doesn't provide enough friction.

—From *Survival (Field Manual 21–76)*

Cutting Firewood

Greg Davenport
Illustrations by Steven A. Davenport

Ax

An ax is a must when traveling into cold-weather environments. It can be used to fell a tree, cut poles, or split wood. Should a large fire be required, the ax enables you to obtain the larger dead wood necessary to sustain a fire. Rhythm, rather than brute force, is the key to properly using an ax. The last thing you want is a broken handle caused by a misguided forceful swing. The weight of a properly aimed ax is all that is required to get the job done.

Felling Trees

If possible, always fell the tree in the direction of its naturally occurring lean. For safety, make sure to clear all debris and obstacles from the area within the scope of your swing. Make the first cut—a wedge—on the tree's downward-leaning side and as close to the ground as safely possible. The second cut should be on the opposite side, and just slightly higher than the first. *Caution:* Since trees often kick back at the last minute, make sure you have a clear escape route established. When cutting the tree's limbs, start at the bottom, and always stand on the side of the tree that is opposite of the side you are working on.

Cutting Poles

When cutting poles hold the wood in your left hand and let it rest on top of and perpendicular to a downed log. With the ax in your right hand, strike the pole in a controlled downward motion, as illustrated. *Note:* Reverse this if you are left-handed. Not only does this technique help prevent physical injury, it also decreases the chances of damaging your ax. If you need to cut a pole in half and don't have an ax or a large knife, you can either burn it in half or use a small knife to cut notches around it until it easily snaps into separate pieces.

Splitting Poles

When splitting a pole, hold it firmly in your left hand while, at the same time, holding the ax in your right hand. The pole and ax should be parallel to one another and the sharp side of the ax head should be on top and at the far end of the pole. Swing both the pole and the ax together, striking them on top of a downed log that is perpendicular to the pole and ax. If you are using a knife to split a pole, do not swing the knife down onto the pole. Instead, place the sharp side of the blade on top of the pole's cut end, and use a pounding stick to drive the knife into the wood, eventually splitting it.

A sharp ax is easier to use, thus decreasing the chances of injury. A file is often used to sharpen an ax. To do this, work the file from one end of the cutting edge to the other, using a controlled motion. Do this an equal number of times on each side. To help prevent accidental injury, file away from—not toward—the cutting edge. Once the edge is sharp, use a honing stone to smooth out any roughness.

Saws

The Sven Saw and Pocket Chain Saw are two great items to consider taking into cold climates. Although I wouldn't consider them a replacement for the ax, both will help break down bigger sections of wood into a more workable size.

Sven Saw

The lightweight Sven Saw is made from an aluminum handle and 21-inch steel blade that folds inside the handle for easy storage. When open, the saw forms a triangle measuring 24 x 20 x 14 inches; when closed, it measures 24 x 1 1/2 x 1/2 inches. The saw weighs 16 ounces and costs around $22.

Pocket Chain Saw

The 31-inch heat-treated steel Pocket Chain Saw weighs only 6.2 ounces when stored inside a small 2 3/4 x 7/8 inch tin can. The saw has 140 bidirectional cutting teeth that will cut wood just like a chain saw; the manufacturer claims it can cut a 3-inch tree limb in less than 10 seconds. The kit comes with two small metal rings and plastic handles. The rings attach to the ends of the saw blade, and the handles slide into the rings, providing a grip that makes cutting easier. In order to save space, however, I don't carry the handles and simply insert two sturdy branches, about 6 x 1 inch, into the metal rings. The Pocket Chain Saw costs around $20.

—From *Surviving Cold Weather*

"Leave No Trace" Campfires

U.S. Forest Service

Practice **Leave No Trace!** ethics by cooking on a stove and avoid building campfires. Today's backpacking stoves are economical and light-weight and provide fast, clean cooking. In some heavily used areas, fires are not permitted. In fragile environments, such as deserts and alpine meadows, fire leaves scars for many years and depletes wood supplies. Ask at the local Ranger Station or District Office about fire restrictions or closures and whether a campfire permit is required in the area you plan to visit.

Heavy-Use Areas: If you are camping in a heavy-use area, there are probably some existing campfire rings nearby that are maintained for this use. Use them to concentrate the use to one area and lessen the overall impact.

Remote Areas: When camping in remote areas, you may choose to build a campfire, making sure the site is away from trees and shrubs. Campfires are best built on a sandy spot or hard ground since the scar can easily be hidden there. Never build a fire next to a rock because smoke will blacken it. Wildfire can easily start from campfires built on forest duff or peat.

With your trowel, dig up the organic layer of soil and set it aside for later use. Avoid encircling the fire with rocks. There is a misconcep-

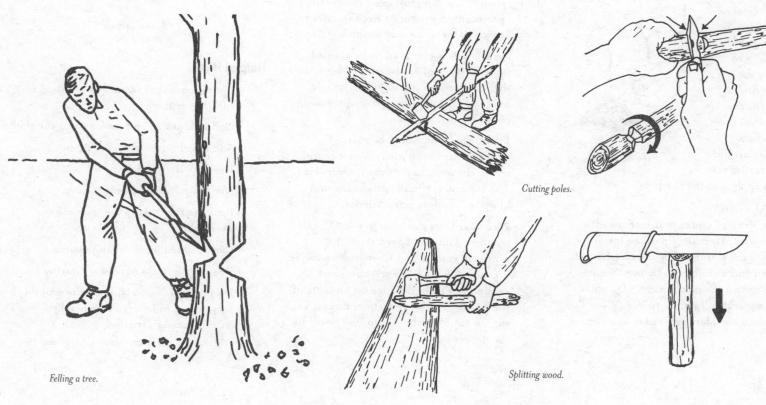

Felling a tree.

Cutting poles.

Splitting wood.

Continued ➡

tion that the rocks will keep a fire from spreading. Actually, the rocks may explode from intense heat, and the blackened rocks are hard to conceal.

Wood: Burning small sticks gathered from the ground is the best source of wood. Use only down, dead wood. Never cut green trees or branches; they won't burn. Standing dead trees will burn but are valuable for cavity-nesting birds and aesthetics, so don't cut them. Small wood will burn completely, providing good coals for cooking. The remaining white ash is easier to dispose of than partially burned logs. Remember, never leave a fire unattended.

Leave No Trace: In heavily used camping areas, some fire rings are maintained and should be used. Make sure your fire is dead out before you pick out trash that did not burn. To verify that the fire is out, sprinkle it with water and stir the coals. If the coals are cold to the touch, the fire is out. The remaining ash and coals should be carried several hundred feet from the campsite and widely scattered. After you pick up the trash to carry home, your campsite area is ready for the next visitor. A last-minute check of your site for cigarette butts or gum wrappers, etc., will help ensure that you **Leave No Trace!**

In remote areas, follow the same procedures and then replace the organic material you set aside earlier. Be sure to completely naturalize the area. If you think all this is a bother, difficult, and dirty—it is! Cooking on a stove eliminates these problems.

Remember:

- Use a lightweight stove rather than building a fire.
- Check local Ranger Station for fire regulations.
- Use existing fire circles in heavy-use areas.
- Save sod for naturalizing fire rings.
- Build fires away from trees, shrubs, rocks, and meadows.
- Burn only small sticks.
- Make sure the fire is dead out.
- Scatter the ashes and naturalize the area.

—From *Leave No Trace! An Outdoor Ethic*

The Campfire

Cecil Kuhne
Illustrations by Cherie Kuhne

Starting into the flames of a campfire is for many canoers the ideal way to end a day of paddling in the wild. But in some areas, fires have left scars that will take decades or more to heal, and trees have been stripped of their branches (and even cut down) to provide firewood. Even collecting deadwood can damage the environment if not enough is left to replenish the soil with nutrients and to provide shelter for birds and animals.

One alternative to the problem is to ban campfires and to use only stoves for cooking. Doing so would certainly eliminate fires, but it would also take some of the pleasure out of wilderness travel. Most ecology experts agree that a complete ban isn't necessary. It is important, however, to treat fires as a luxury and ensure that they have the smallest impact possible.

Fires may have to be banned, for example, when dry conditions render the fire risk high. Such regulations seem restrictive, but they prevent further destruction. Fires, officially permitted or not, are inappropriate in some areas anyway. In particular, fires should not be lit near and above the timberline, because of the slow growth of trees and the soil's need to be replenished by nutrients from deadwood.

In other areas, fires can be lit even on pristine sites without much harm to the environment, as long as you take certain precautions. You should leave no sign of your fire, and if possible, use a firepan (discussed in detail at right). Do not leave behind partially burnt wood. If you don't use a firepan, refill the shallow pit you've created with sod or dirt removed when it was dug; spreading dirt and loose vegetation over the site will help conceal it. The ideal place for fires is below the flood level along rivers, since any traces will eventually be washed away.

Do not build a ring of rocks around a fire— the campsite soon becomes littered with blackened rocks. Although the idea is to contain a fire, the best way to do that is to clear the area of flammable materials; a couple of feet is usually large enough. You should also make sure there are no low branches or tree roots above or below the fire. Pitch your tent and other gear well away, preferably upwind, so sparks can't harm them.

If you camp at a well-used site with many rock-ringed fireplaces, use an existing one rather than make a new one. Take time to dismantle the other fire rings, removing any ashes and charcoal as garbage. Some designated backcountry sites provide metal fireboxes, and when present, they should be used.

If you collect wood, do so with care. First and foremost, do not remove wood—even deadwood—from living trees; deadwood is needed by wildlife and it adds to the site's attractiveness. Nothing is worse than a campsite surrounded by trees stripped of their lower branches and a ground bare of any fallen wood. In high-use

areas, search for wood farther afield. Collect only what you need, and use small sticks that can be broken by hand—and easily burned to ash.

Firepans

If you build fires, seriously consider bringing a firepan—a metal container with three- or four-inch sides to contain fire and ashes. They're often required by the government agency managing the area, and they're the best way to contain ashes and prevent fire scars. If the firepan doesn't have legs, set it on rocks so it doesn't scorch the ground.

On large-volume or silty rivers, the ashes

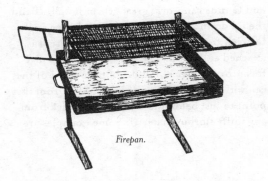

Firepan.

can be disposed of by dumping them into the main current of the river. If you deposit them in an eddy by the camp, the ashes eventually wash back to shore, soiling the beaches. Some campsites have become so littered that the soil has turned black. To prevent this, boaters should dump ashes where the current is strong and will quickly disperse any trace. Better yet, you can store the ashes as garbage and carry them out. To prepare ashes for storage, moisten them until they're cool and then shovel them into a container (an old surplus ammo can is ideal). At the next camp, dump the ashes out of the container and into the firepan before starting the fire. As the ashes are burned again at each camp, they are gradually reduced to a fine dust.

If possible, locate the firepan near the river, so high water can clean away any small coals that are accidentally dropped. An additional safety tip for removing firepans: Throw a little water on the ground as soon as the pan is removed, because the ground below can burn bare feet.

Continued ➡

Fires without Firepans

If you must build a fire without a firepan, build it where it will have less impact; either below the high-water mark on a rocky shoreline, or in a bare spot where it's easy to remove all remains.

Build as small a fire as you can. An entire meal can be cooked with amazingly little wood. When you're finished with the fire, thoroughly douse it with water and restore the site to its former condition. Throw any blackened rocks into the river.

—From *Padding Basics: Canoeing*

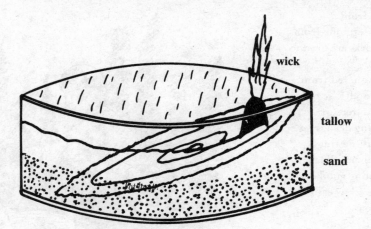

wick

tallow

sand

Birch bark torch.

Lamps, Stoves, and Torches

Greg Davenport
Illustrations by Steven A. Davenport

Fat Lamp

To create a fat lamp you will first need to render your animal fat into tallow. To do this, cook it over a low temperature until it is completely melted. It is common to have a few small particles left in the soup. To remove these particles, strain the liquid fat through a porous cloth. If you do not intend to use it immediately, store it in clean jars (fill close to the top), cover, and put in a cool dark place. The tallow can be used to meet many of your needs. It can be used as a lubricant, to make soap, or perhaps as a fuel for a fat lamp.

To create an oil lamp from tallow, use a small can that has its lid slightly attached at one end (a tuna can works great—clean it well). Bend the lid down so that it forms a 45-degree angle between the bottom of the can and where it is attached at the top. The lid will provide a platform for your wick. Fill the bottom third of the can with sand and fill it with liquid fat from that point to just below the top. Create a wick from any fluffy fibrous material. Some examples are

milkweed seedpods, cattail seed heads, or perhaps even cotton. Fluff the wick up and set it on the lid platform so that its bottom is touching the fat. Fat lamps are a great outdoor heat source but should not be used indoors for extended periods of time. *Note:* This same design can be used with gasoline instead of tallow by simply pouring a small amount of fuel over the sand and allowing the bottom side of the wick to slightly penetrate it.

Paraffin Stove

A paraffin stove can be created from corrugated cardboard, paraffin, and an empty tuna can. To make it, cut corrugated cardboard in strips that are approximately 1-inch wide, roll them together, and set them inside the tuna can. Try to pack them inside the can as tightly as possible. Using a double boiler technique melt the paraffin. *Caution:* Paraffin is extremely flammable and should never be melted over direct heat. Slowly pour the liquid over the cardboard and into the tuna can (a little goes a long way). Let it cool. If the lid is still attached, it can be used as a cover. Although placing a cotton wick in the center of the cardboard makes lighting easier, it

isn't necessary. To use, simply light the cardboard. A paraffin stove can be used for warmth and to cook. If used to prepare food, simply place it under an improvised cooking platform.

Torches

BIRCH BARK TORCH

Birch bark is excellent tinder that lights when wet. To make a birch torch, gather up long 2-inch-wide strips of birch and a green sapling that is about 3 feet long. Fold the bark strips in half—lengthwise. Split and trim the end of the sapling so that the bark can slide through it but not so much that it won't be held in place. To use, light the bark and as it burns down feed the fresh bark forward. Another method of using birch as a torch is to simply wrap and tie it around the end of a sapling. This method is wasteful and I don't prefer it.

CATTAIL TORCH

A cattail can provide an excellent torch with its built-in handle and medium for holding fuel. To make, cut the stalk 3 feet from the cattail's head and dip the head into tallow or another fuel source. To use, simply light the head.

—From *Wilderness Living*

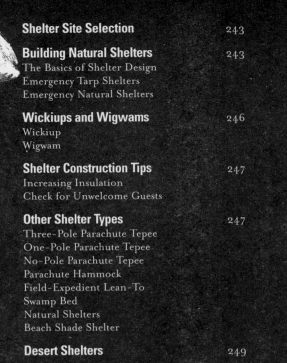
Shelter: From Tents and Tarps to Wigwams and Igloos

Shelter Site Selection

U.S. Army

When you are in a survival situation and realize that shelter is a high priority, start looking for shelter as soon as possible. As you do so, remember what you will need at the site. Two requisites are—

- It must contain material to make the type of shelter you need.
- It must be large enough and level enough for you to lie down comfortably.

When you consider these requisites, however, you cannot ignore your tactical situation or your safety. You must also consider whether the site—

- Provides concealment from enemy observation.
- Has camouflaged escape routes.
- Is suitable for signaling, if necessary.
- Provides protection against wild animals and rocks and dead trees that might fall.

- Is free from insects, reptiles, and poisonous plants.

You must also remember the problems that could arise in your environment. For instance—

- Avoid flash flood areas in foothills.
- Avoid avalanche or rockslide areas in mountainous terrain.
- Avoid sites near bodies of water that are below the high water mark.

In some areas, the season of the year has a strong bearing on the site you select. Ideal sites for a shelter differ in winter and summer. During cold winter months you will want a site that will protect you from the cold and wind, but will have a source of fuel and water. During summer months in the same area you will want a source of water, but you will want the site to be almost insect free.

When considering shelter site selection, use the word BLISS as a guide.

B — Blend in with the surroundings.

L — Low silhouette.

I — Irregular shape.

S — Small.

S — Secluded location.

—From *Survival (Field Manual 21-76)*

Building Natural Shelters

Greg Davenport
Illustrations by Steven Davenport and Ken Davenport

The Basics of Shelter Design

The environment, materials on hand, and the amount of time available will determine the type of shelter you choose. Regardless of type, you should construct your shelter so that it is safe and durable.

Framework

Ridge and other supporting poles need to be sturdy, wrist diameter, destubbed (surface made smooth), and long enough to create the desired shelter size. The ridgepole is the main beam—it supports all other structures. Supporting poles often rest on the ridgepole (at a 90-degree

Continued ➜

angle). Support poles need to be cut so they don't extend beyond the ridgepole. In addition, these poles should be capped using tarp, bark, or other roofing material. Poles that extend beyond the ridgepole allow moisture to track down into the shelter. If using a tarp, support poles may or may not be needed. For nontarp shelters, you can increase the strength of the overall structure by weaving sapling-sized branches between the supporting poles (at 90 degrees).

Roof

In order to withstand the elements (wind, rain, heat, and cold) make sure shelter's roof and walls have a 45- to 60-degree pitch. Tarps, boughs, bark, sod, or ground covering is used to create the roof.

Lashings

When building your shelter, various lashings may be needed to hold the structure together. Two are listed below.

SHEAR LASH

This lash is best used when making a bipod or tripod structure. Lay the poles side by side, attach the line to one of the poles (a clove hitch will work), run the line around all the poles three times (called a wrap). Next, run the line two times between each of the parallel poles (called a frap). It should go around and over the wrap. Make sure to pull it snug each time. Finish by tying another clove hitch.

SQUARE LASH

The square lash is used to join poles at right angles. As with the shear lash, start with a clove hitch. Wrap the line, in a box pattern, over and under the poles, alternating between each pole. After you have done this three times, tightly run several fraps between the two poles and over the preceding wrap. Pull it snug, and finish with a clove hitch.

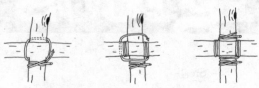

The square lash secures two perpendicular poles together.

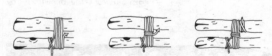

The shear lash attaches several parallel poles together.

Drainage

The ideal solution to drainage problems is to build your shelter so that it sits slightly higher than the surrounding ground. However, if this is not possible, it will only take you a few minutes to dig a trench around your shelter and the benefit will make it a worthwhile process. The small trench should fall directly below the roof's ends and follow the ground's natural pitch until the water is directed far away from your home. This design works similar to the gutters on a modern home. The trench collects the water, and via a small slope that extends from one end to another, it directs the water away from the house.

Bedding

A bed is necessary to protect you from the cold, hard ground. If a commercial sleeping pad is unavailable, bedding may be prepared using natural materials such as dry leaves, grasses, ferns, boughs, dry moss, or cattail down. For optimal insulation from the ground, the bed should have a loft of at least 18 inches.

Emergency Tarp Shelters

An emergency shelter can be made using a tarp, poncho, blanket, or other similar item. The exact type of shelter you build will depend on the environment, available materials, and time. Whatever you choose, it must meet basic camp and design criteria already outlined. Tarp layers, line attachments, and how to safely pound an improvised stake into the ground are a few items unique to building a tarp shelter.

Tarp Layers

If you have two tarps, adding a rain fly (second tarp) over the first increases insulation and decreases potential misting during hard rains.

Attaching Line

If you use line, attach it to the tarp's grommet or a makeshift button created from rock, grass, or other malleable substance that will not tear or cut the tarp. To create a makeshift button, ball up the material inside a corner of the tarp and secure it with a slipknot. You can fasten the shelter piece to the ground by tying the free end of the line to vegetation, rocks, big logs, or an improvised stake.

Improvised Stake

If using an improvised stake, make sure to pound it into the ground so it is learning away from the tarp at a 90-degree angle to the wrinkles in the material. To avoid breaking your hand when pounding the stake into the ground, hold the stake so that your palm is facing up. Holding it this way allows a missed strike to hit the forgiving palm verses the unforgiving back of the hand.

Various options for building an emergency tarp shelter are outlined here. Don't limit yourself to these options. Each situation is different. There might be a time when combining a tarp and natural material is the best choice. As long as you meet the basics of shelter design, you should be okay.

A-Tent

The A-tent is most often used in the warm temperate and snow environments. To construct, tightly secure a ridgeline or ridgepole 3 to 4 feet above the ground and between two trees approximately 7 feet apart. When using a

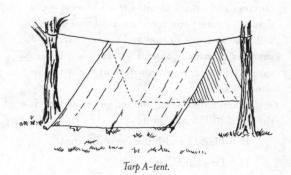

Tarp A-tent.

ridgepole, secure it in place using a square lash so that it spans at least 6 inches beyond each tree. Drape the tarp over the stretched line (or pole) and use trees, boulders, tent poles, twigs, or stakes to tightly secure its sides at a 45- to 60-degree angle to the ground.

A-Frame

An A-frame is most often used in the warm temperate and snow environments. Find a tree with a forked branch about 3 to 4 feet high on the trunk of a tree. Break away any other branches that pose a safety threat or interfere with the construction of your A-frame. Place your ridgepole into the forked branch, forming a 30-degree angle between the pole and the ground. The ridgepole should be 12 to 15 feet long and the diameter of your wrist. If you are unable to find a tree with a forked branch, lash the ridgepole to the tree. Other options include finding a fallen tree that forms an appropriate 30-degree angle between the tree and ground or laying a strong ridgepole against a 3- to 4-foot-high stump. Drape the tarp over the pole and using trees, boulders, tent poles, or twigs tightly secure both sides of the tarp at a 45- to 60-degree angle to the ground. For best results you'll most likely need to use line and attach it to the tarp with a makeshift button.

Tarp A-frame.

Lean-To

Like the A-tent and A-frame, a lean-to is most often used in the warm, temperate and snow environments. To construct, find two trees about 7 feet apart with forked branches 4 to 5 feet high on the trunk. Break away any other branches that pose a safety threat or interfere with the construction of your lean-to. Place a ridgepole (a fallen tree that is approximately 10 feet long and the diameter of your wrist) into the forked branches. If unable to find two trees with forked branches, lash the ridgepole to the trees. Another option is to tie a line tightly between the two trees and use it in the same fashion as you would the pole. Lay three or more support poles across the ridgepole at a 45- to 60-degree angle to the ground. Support poles need to be about 10 feet long and placed 1 to 2 feet apart. (If using a line instead of the ridgepole, you may elect not to use support poles.) Drape the tarp over the support poles, and attach the top to the ridgepole. Tightly secure the tarp over the support poles and to the ground using lines, rocks, logs, or another stabilizing method. You may elect to draw the excess tarp underneath the shelter, providing a ground cloth in which to sleep on.

If you have a life raft and a tarp, you can make a quick and easy to lean-to on a sandy shore beyond the reach of high tide. To

Continued ➡

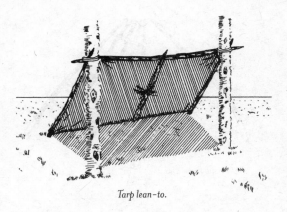

Tarp lean-to.

construct, bury approximately one-fifth of the raft while it is perpendicular to the ground, attach a tarp to the top of the raft, and secure the tarp to the ground forming a 45- to 60-degree angle between the tarp and the ground.

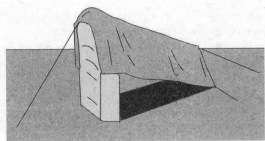

Improvised lean-to using a life raft and tarp.

Emergency Natural Shelters

A natural shelter is composed of materials that are procured from the wilderness. The exact type of shelter you build will depend on the environment, available materials, and time. Whatever you choose, it must meet basic camp and design criteria already outlined. A natural shelter must have a well-designed and well-crafted roof and walls.

Framework

The framework must be strong enough to support the roof and wall weight (which is often substantial). Without a tarp, the wall angle is one of the keys to a shelter that repels moisture. Make sure it has a 45- to 60-degree pitch. Make sure to cut the support poles so they don't extend beyond the ridgepole, and cap them using bark or other roofing material. Uncut and uncapped poles allow moisture to track down into the shelter. For nontarp shelters, you can increase the strength of the overall structure by weaving sapling-sized branches between the supporting poles (at 90 degrees).

Roofs and Walls

Roofs created using boughs, bark, or sodlike material need to be layered, from bottom to top, so that the upper piece overlaps the bottom. Overlapping the material creates a shingle-type roof that prevents moisture from entering the shelter. If you have enough ground covering or snow is available, throw about 18 inches on top of the existing roof. This added material greatly increases the insulating quality of your shelter. Using snow, however, should only be done in a climate with temperatures below freezing. Make sure to ventilate any shelter that is completely enclosed.

Various options for building an emergency natural shelter are outlined here. As with a tarp shelter, don't limit yourself to these options. Each situation is different. There might be a time when combining a tarp and natural material is the best choice. As long as you meet the basics of shelter design, you should be okay.

Tree Pit

A tree pit shelter is a quick immediate-action shelter used in most forested environments. The optimal tree will have multiple lower branches—like a Douglas or grand fir—that protect its base from the snow, rain, and sun. Pine and deciduous trees provide little protection and are not a good choice. In snow environments, the snow level rises around the tree, creating an excellent source of insulation for your shelter. To make a tree pit, remove any lower dead branches and snow from the tree's base, making an area big enough for you and your equipment. If snow is present, dig until you reach bare ground, and remove obstructive branches, which can be used for added overhead cover to protect you from the elements.

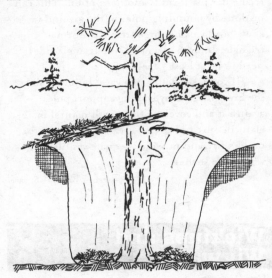

Tree pit.

A-Frame

An A-frame is most often used in the warm temperate and snow environments. The A-frame's basic design is covered under tarp shelters. Unlike the tarp shelter, however, the A-frame built using only natural materials requires support poles and roofing material. Lay support poles across the ridgepole, on both sides, at a 60-degree angle to the ground. Support poles need to be long enough to extend above the ridgepole slightly, and they should be placed approximately 1 to 1½ feet apart. Crisscross small branches into the support poles. Cover the framework with any available grass, moss, boughs, and so forth. The material is placed in a layered fashion, starting at the bottom. If snow is available, throw at least 8 inches (you may add

Natural A-frame.

more but this is the minimum) over the top of the shelter. Cover the door opening with your pack or similar item. When using snow, don't allow the temperature inside your shelter to rise above 32 degrees or the snow will stat to melt.

Lean-To

A lean-to is most often used in the warm temperate and snow environments. The lean-to's basic design is covered under tarp shelters. Unlike the tarp shelter, however, the lean-to built using only natural materials requires additional support poles and roofing material. Lay several support poles across the ridgepole at a 45- to 60-degree angle to the ground. Support poles need to be long enough to provide this angle and yet barely extend beyond the top of the ridgepole. Weave small saplings into and perpendicular to the support poles. Cover the entire shelter with 12 to 18 inches of boughs, bark, duff, and snow in that order (depending on availability of resources). The material should be placed in a layered fashion starting at the bottom. If snow is available, throw a minimum of 8 inches on top of the shelter. The lean-to allows you to build a fire in front of the shelter as long as the fire is safely spaced away from you and your gear. To help heat your shelter, build a fire reflector behind the fire. In cold climates create an opposing lean-to by making a front wall in the same fashion as the back wall. Be sure to incorporate the sides into the framework and leave enough room for a small doorway on either side. The doorway can be covered with your pack or a snow block when needed. For an opposing lean-to make a vent hole in top if you plan to have a small fire inside. As always, when using snow, don't let the temperature inside your shelter go above 32 degrees Fahrenheit or the snow will start to melt.

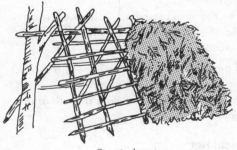

Opposing lean-to.

Hobo Shelter

A hobo shelter is used in the temperate oceanic environments, where a more stable long-term shelter is necessary. To construct one, you will need to find several pieces of driftwood or boards that have washed ashore. Next locate a sand dune beyond the reach of high tide, and on the land side of the dune, dig a rectangular space big enough for you and your equipment. Place the removed sand close by so that you can use it later. Gather as much driftwood and boards as you can find, and using any available line, build a strong frame inside the rectangular dugout. Create a roof and walls by attaching driftwood and boards to the frame, leaving a doorway. If your wood supply is limited, don't place support walls at the back or on the two sides of the structure. Some sand may fall into the shelter, but the design will still meet your needs. If you have

Continued ➡

Hobo shelter.

a poncho or tarp that's not necessary for meeting your other needs, consider placing it over the roof. Insulate the shelter by covering the roof with 6 to 8 inches of sand.

Cave

A cave is the ultimate natural shelter. With very little effort it can provide protection from the various elements. However, caves are not without risk. Some of these risks include, but are not limited to, animals, rodents, reptiles, and insects; bad air; slippery slopes, rocks, and crevasses; floods or high-water issues; and combustible gases (most common in caves with excessive bat droppings). When using a cave as a shelter, follow some basic rules:

1. Never light a fire inside a small cave. It may use up oxygen or cause an explosion if there are enough bat droppings present. Fires should be lit near the entrance to the cave, where adequate ventilation is available.

2. To avoid slipping into crevasses, getting lost, or breathing bad gases, never venture too far into the cave.

3. Make sure the entrance is above high tide.

4. Be constantly aware of water movement within a cave. If the cave appears to be prone to flooding, look for another shelter.

5. Never enter or use old mines as a shelter. The risk is not worth it. Collapsing passages and vertical mine shafts are just a few of the potential dangers.

6. If possible, use a cave where the entrance is facing the sun (a south entrance if north of the equator; north entrance if south of the equator).

Tropical Hut

These huts are used in tropical regions, swamps, or areas that have excessive amounts of rain. The elevated bed and floor provide protection from the moist or water-covered ground while the overhead roof keeps you dry. To construct a small tropical hut, pound four poles (8 to 12 feet long) 8 to 12 inches into the ground at each of the shelter's four corners. Tap dirt around

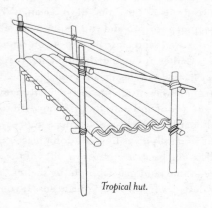

Tropical hut.

them to make them more secure. Create the floor by lashing a strong pole 2 feet off the ground on each side of the shelter so that the poles connect to form a square or rectangle. Next, create a solid platform by laying additional poles on top of and perpendicular to the side poles. Make sure that all the poles are strong enough to support your weight. Finish the floor by using moss, grass, leaves, or branches.

The create the roof, use the same support poles that you used to build the floor. A lean-to roof is quick and easy. Attach two support poles to the front and back of the shelter so that they are horizontal to the ground and perpendicular to the shelter's sides. The front support pole should be higher than the back support pole so that a 45- to 60-degree downward angle forms when the roof poles are placed. Lay roof poles on top of and perpendicular to the roof's support poles and lash them in place. Cover the roof with tarp, large overlapping leaves (placed shingle-style), or other appropriate shingling material.

If time or materials are an issue, building a triangular platform is another option. This can be done by pounding poles in the ground (as above) or by using three trees that form a triangle. In both scenarios, the triangle sides need to be at least 7 feet long.

If you take shelter in a cave, build a wall at the cave entrance by leaning support poles against it and covering them with natural materials. Be sure to leave an area large enough to build a fire and provide adequate ventilation within the shelter.

—From *Wilderness Survival*

Wickiups and Wigwams

Greg Davenport
Illustrations by Steven Davenport and Ken Davenport

Wickiup

The wickiup shelter can be used anywhere that poles, brush, leaves, and grass can be found. The wickiup is not an ideal shelter during prolonged rains, but if the insulation material is heaped on thick, it will provide adequate protection from most elements.

Gather three strong 10- to 15-foot poles, and connect them together at the top with a shear lash. If any of the poles has a fork at the top, it may not be necessary to lash them together. Spread the poles out to form a tripod; a 60-degree angle is optimal. They will be able to stand without support. Fill in the sides with additional poles by leaning them against the top of the tripod. Don't discard shorter poles; they can be used in the final stages of this process. Leave a small entrance that can later be covered with man-made or improvised materials. For immediate use, cover the shelter with brush, leaves, reeds, bark, or similar materials.

For additional protection, layer on roofing materials in the following manner: Working from bottom to top, cover the framework with grass and/or plant stalks. Next, cover it, from bottom to top, with mulch and/or dirt. To hold

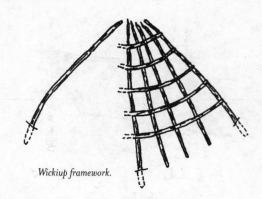

Wickiup framework.

this material in place, lay poles around and on top of the wickiup. Leave a vent hole at the top if you plan to have fires inside the shelter. The roofing options described for the wigwam may also be used to roof a wickiup.

Wigwam

The wigwam may be a viable option in some desert regions, depending on availability of materials. The wigwam's greatest asset is the space and headroom provided by its vertical walls. This dome-type shelter provides protection from all directions and has a low wind profile. The following instructions are for a wigwam with a 10-foot floor space, providing enough room for several people and their equipment.

Wigwam framework.

Cut twenty-four saplings that are 10 to 15 feet long and 2 inches in diameter. Willow and maple work best, but any sapling will do. If unable to use the saplings the day you cut them, store them so they are bent into a U shape. With a stick or your foot, mark a 10-foot circle where you intend to place the shelter. Using the circle as your guide, evenly place the saplings around it. Make holes for the saplings by pounding a solid wooden stake into the ground and the removing it. Then bury the large end of each sapling 6 to 10 inches into the ground, and tap dirt around it to help hold it in place. Next, create the basic framework by bending opposing saplings together, overlapping by at least 2 feet, and using a shear lash to secure them together. Once completed, the twenty-four poles should create a domelike structure with a center at least 7 feet high. Wrap additional saplings horizontally around the framework. Leave a 3- to 4-foot-high doorway that can later be covered with a hide or other appropriate material. For optimal roofing support, place the horizontal poles 12 to 18 inches apart.

Finally, you need to construct a roof from available natural materials. The ones most

Continued ➡

commonly used are grass (most common in deserts), mats made from various stalks, birch and elm bark, and wood shingles. Regardless of the material, a wigwam roof is constructed using a shingle design, placing the material from bottom to top, and so that the higher rows overlap those below by about one-third. Leave a vent hole at the top if you plan to have fires inside the shelter.

Grass Roofing

Although grass can be used as a roofing material, its biggest drawback is the amount of time required to harvest enough to cover a shelter. Ideally, you should collect tall grass that is dry and grew the previous year. Older grass is usually brittle and rotted, and new grass must be dried before used. Separate the grass into small bundles, 1 to 2 inches in diameter, with the root ends together. Place the bundles close to one another. Fold a long piece of cordage in half, and place it about 4 inches down from the top of the first bundle (details on how to make cordage appear on page 469). Tie an overhand knot, slide in another bundle, and repeat. If you run out of line before you reach the end, simply tie another piece to the first and continue the process. At the same time, tie a second line about 3 or 4 inches below the first. This pattern should effectively weave the bundles together, holding them securely in place. Once you have made enough of these grass skirts to cover the shelter, lash them to the framework using proper shingling techniques as you go up the shelter.

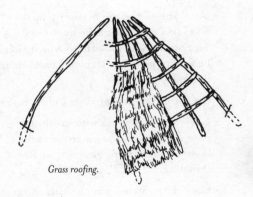
Grass roofing.

Mat Roofing

A mat made by weaving reeds or the leaves and stalks of cattails, sotol, or yucca together provides a strong covering for most shelters. Like the grass skirts, these mats are made and then attached to the shelter. Begin by laying your material down on the ground side by side. To create a tighter fit, alternate the stalks' thick and skinny ends. Fold a long piece of cordage in half, and place it about 4 inches down from the top of the first stalk. Tie an overhand knot, slide in another stalk, and repeat. If you run out of line before you reach the end of the mat, simply tie another piece to the first and continue the process. Once the first row is done, perform the same process every 4 inches down the mat until you reach the bottom. This pattern should effectively weave the bundles together, holding them securely in place.

Birch and Elm Bark Shingles

Birch and elm are the most common types of bark used for covering a shelter. Large pieces of bark can easily be cut and stripped from a tree or log. Use a knife to make a rectangular cut from top to bottom, and peel the bark off along the vertical cut. If you experience difficulty removing the bark, beating the area with a log will help release it from the tree. Once the bark is removed, lay it flat on the ground, weight it down with a heavy material such as rocks or wood, and allow it to dry. When dry, the bark can be lashed to the horizontal beams and shingled up the shelter's framework. For best results, the shingles that are side by side should have a slight overlap. You can sew bark together if the size is not adequate for its intended use. If you don't have sewing material, you might make a needle from bone or wood or perhaps use cordage and run it through holes created with your knife.

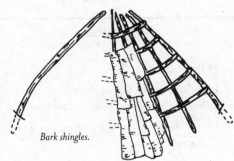
Bark shingles.

Wood Shingles

Straight-grained woods like cedar are the most commonly used wood roofing material. Where live cedar trees can be found, you will easily find old fallen, dead, and seasoned cedar. Without much difficulty, large half-inch-thick shingles can be removed with a knife, ax, or in some instances, your bare hands. The soft wood can be lashed or nailed to the horizontal beams and shingled up the shelter's framework. If lashed, you'll need to make holes in the top of each shingle; use an awl-like tool to perform this easy task.

—From *Surviving the Desert*

Shelter Construction Tips

Greg Davenport

Increasing Insulation

Creating a second wall inside or out around your shelter will increase its ability to keep you warm or cool. Doing something as easy as tying mats or grass skirts to the interior walls and roof can create the second wall. To make an elaborate insulation wall, drive a row of tall stakes, about 1 foot apart, 6 to 8 inches into the ground and 12 to 18 inches from the shelter wall. Then weave willow branches or similar material between and perpendicular to the stakes. Fill in the space between walls with grass, duff, or leaves.

Check for Unwelcome Guests

Before getting into a shelter or sleeping bag, check it for small creatures. They find these areas just as comfortable and inviting as you do, and they do not like to share. Odds are they will let you know this if you crawl in without letting them exit first.

—From *Surviving the Desert*

Other Shelter Types

U.S. Army

When looking for a shelter site, keep in mind the type of shelter (protection) you need. However, you must also consider—

- How much time and effort you need to build the shelter.
- If the shelter will adequately protect you from the elements (sun, wind, rain, snow).
- If you have the tools to build it. If not, can you make improvised tools?
- If you have the type and amount of materials needed to build it.

To answer these questions, you need to know how to make various types of shelters and what materials you need to make them.

Three-Pole Parachute Tepee

If you have a parachute and three poles and the tactical situation allows, make a parachute tepee. It is easy and takes very little time to make this tepee. It provides protection from the elements and can act as a signaling device by enhancing a small amount of light from a fire or candle. It is large enough to hold several people and their equipment and to allow sleeping, cooking, and storing firewood.

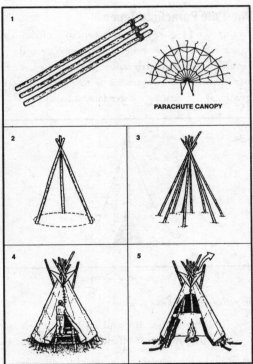
Three-pole parachute tepee.

You can make this tepee using parts of or a whole personnel main or reserve parachute canopy. If using a standard personnel parachute, you need three poles 3.5 to 4.5 meters long and about 5 centimeters in diameter.
To make this tepee—

- Lay the poles on the ground and lash them together at one end.
- Stand the framework up and spread the poles to form a tripod.
- For more support, place additional poles against the tripod. Five or six additional poles work best, but do not lash them to the tripod.

Continued →

- Determine the wind direction and locate the entrance 90 degrees or more from the mean wind direction.

- Lay out the parachute on the "backside" or the tripod and locate the bridle loop (nylon web loop) at the top (apex) of the canopy.

- Place the bridle loop over the top of a free-standing pole. Then place the pole back up against the tripod so that the canopy's apex is at the same height as the lasing on the three poles.

- Wrap the canopy around one side of the tripod. The canopy should be of double thickness, as you are wrapping an entire parachute. You need only wrap half of the tripod, as the remainder of the canopy will encircle the tripod in the opposite direction.

- Construct the entrance by wrapping the folded edges of the canopy around two free-standing poles. You can then place the poles side by side to close the tepee's entrance.

- Place all extra canopy underneath the tepee poles and inside to create a floor for the shelter.

- Leave a 30- to 50-centimeter opening at the top for ventilation if you intend to have a fire inside the tepee.

One-Pole Parachute Tepee

You need a 14-gore section (normally) of canopy, stakes, a stout center pole, and inner core and needle to construct this tepee. You cut the suspension lines except for 40- to 45-centimeter lengths at the canopy's lower lateral band.

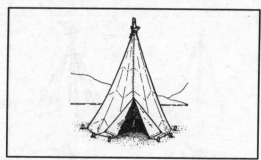

One-pole parachute tepee.

To make this tepee—

- Select a shelter site and scribe a circle about 4 meters in diameter on the ground.

- Stake the parachute material to the ground using the lines remaining at the lower lateral band.

- After deciding where to place the shelter door, emplace a stake and tie the first line (from the lower lateral band) securely to it.

- Stretch the parachute material taut to the next line, emplace a stake on the scribed line, and tie the line to it.

- Continue the staking process until you have tied all the lines.

- Loosely attach the top of the parachute material to the center pole with a suspension line you previously cut and, through trail and error, determine the point at which the parachute material will be pulled tight once the center pole is upright.

- Then securely attach the material to the pole.

- Using a suspension line (or inner core), sew the end gores together leaving 1 or 1.2 meters for a door.

No-Pole Parachute Tepee

You use the same materials, except for the center pole, as for the one-pole parachute tepee.

No-pole parachute tepee.

To make this tepee—

- Tie a line to the top of parachute material with a previously cut suspension line.

- Throw the line over a tree limb, and tie it to the tree trunk.

- Starting at the opposite side from the door, emplace a stake on the scribed 3.5- to 4.3-meter circle.

- Tie the first line on the lower lateral band.

- Continue emplacing the stakes and tying the lines to them.

- After staking down the material, unfasten the line tied to the tree trunk, tighten the tepee material by pulling on this line, and tie it securely to the tree trunk.

Parachute Hammock

You can make a hammock using 6 to 8 gores of parachute canopy and two trees about 4.5 meters apart.

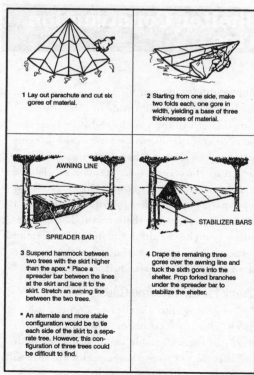

1 Lay out parachute and cut six gores of material.

2 Starting from one side, make two folds each, one gore in width, yielding a base of three thicknesses of material.

AWNING LINE

SPREADER BAR

3 Suspend hammock between two trees with the skirt higher than the apex.* Place a spreader bar between the lines at the skirt and lace it to the skirt. Stretch an awning line between the two trees.

* An alternate and more stable configuration would be to tie each side of the skirt to a separate tree. However, this configuration of three trees could be difficult to find.

STABILIZER BARS

4 Drape the remaining three gores over the awning line and tuck the sixth gore into the shelter. Prop forked branches under the spreader bar to stabilize the shelter.

Parachute hammock.

Field-Expedient Lean-To

If you are in a wooded area and have enough natural materials, you can make a field-expedient lean-to without the aid of tools or with only a knife. It takes longer to make this type of shelter than it does to make other types, but it will protect you from the elements.

You will need two trees (or upright poles) about 2 meters apart; one pole about 2 meters long and 2.5 centimeters in diameter; five to eight poles about 3 meters long and 2.5 centimeters in diameter for beams; cord or vines for securing the horizontal support to the trees; and other poles, saplings, or vines to crisscross the beams.

Field-expedient lean-to and fire reflector.

To make this lean-to—

- Tie the 2-meter pole to the two trees at waist to chest height. This is the horizontal support. If a standing tree is not available, construct a bipod using Y-shaped sticks or two tripods.

- Place one end of the beams (3-meter poles) on one side of the horizontal support. As with all lean-to type shelters, be sure to place the lean-to's backside into the wind.

- Crisscross saplings or vines on the beams.

- Cover the framework with brush, leaves, pine needles, or grass, starting at the bottom and working your way up like shingling.

- Place straw, leaves, pine needles, or grass inside the shelter for bedding.

In cold weather, add to your lean-to's comfort by building a fire reflector wall. Drive four 1.5-meter-long stakes into the ground to support the wall. Stack green logs on top of one another between the support stakes. Form two rows of stacked logs to create an inner space within the wall that you can fill with dirt. This action not only strengthens the wall but makes it more heat reflective. Bind the top of the support stakes so that the green logs and dirt will stay in place.

With just a little more effort you can have a drying rack. Cut a few 2-centimeter-diameter poles (length depends on the distance between the lean-to's horizontal support and the top of the fire reflector wall). Lay one end of the poles on the lean-to support and the other end on top of the reflector wall. Place and tie into place smaller sticks across these poles. You now have a place to dry clothes, meat, or fish.

Continued ➜

Swamp Bed

In a marsh or swamp, or any area with standing water or continually wet ground, the swamp bed keeps you out of the water. When selecting such a site, consider the weather, wind, tides, and available materials.

Swamp bed.

To make a swamp bed—

- Look for four trees clustered in a rectangle, or cut four poles (bam-boo is ideal) and drive them firmly into the ground so they form a rectangle. They should be far enough apart and strong enough to support your height and weight, to include equipment.
- Cut two poles that span the width of the rectangle. They, too, must be strong enough to support your weight.
- Secure these two poles to the trees (or poles). Be sure they are high enough above the ground or water to allow for tides and high water.
- Cut additional poles that span the rectangle's length. Lay them across the two side poles, and secure them.
- Cover the top of the bed frame with board leaves or grass to form a soft sleeping surface.
- Build a fire pad by laying clay, silt, or mud on one corner of the swamp bed and allow it to dry.

Another shelter designed to get you above and out of the water or wet ground uses the same rectangular configuration as the swamp bed. You very simply lay sticks and branches lengthwise on the inside of the trees (or poles) until there is enough material to raise the sleeping surface above the water level.

Natural Shelters

Do not overlook natural formations that provide shelter. Examples are caves, rocky crevices, clumps of bushes, small depressions, large rocks on leeward sides of hills, large trees with low-hanging limbs, and fallen trees with thick branches. However, when selecting a natural formation—

- Stay away from low ground such as ravines, narrow valleys, or creek beds. Low areas collect the heavy cold air at night and are therefore colder than the surrounding high ground. Thick, brushy, low ground also harbors more insects.
- Check for poisonous snakes, ticks, mites, scorpions, and stinging ants.
- Look for loose rocks, dead limbs, coconuts, or other natural growth than could fall on your shelter.

Beach Shade Shelter

This shelter protects you from the sun, wind, rain, and heat. It is easy to make using natural materials.

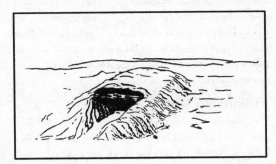

Beach shade shelter.

To make this shelter—

- Find and collect driftwood or other natural material to use as support beams and as a digging tool.
- Select a site that is above the high water mark.
- Scrape or dig out a trench running north to south so that it receives the least amount of sunlight. Make the trench long and wide enough for you to lie down comfortably.
- Mound soil on three sides of the trench. The higher the mound, the more space inside the shelter.
- Lay support beams (driftwood or other natural material) that span the trench on top of the mound to form the framework for a roof.
- Enlarge the shelter's entrance by digging out more sand in front of it.
- Use natural materials such as grass or leaves to form a bed inside the shelter.

—From *Survival (Field Manual 21-76)*

Desert Shelters

U.S. Army

In an arid environment, consider the time, effort, and material needed to make a shelter. If you have material such as poncho, canvas, or a parachute, use it along with such terrain features as rock outcroppings, mounds of sand, or a depression between dunes or rocks to make your shelter.

Using rock outcroppings—

- Anchor one end of your poncho (canvas, parachute, or other material) on the edge of the outcrop using rocks or other weights.
- Extend and anchor the other end of the poncho so it provides the best possible shade.

In a sandy area—

- Build a mound of sand or use the side of a sand dune for one side of the shelter.
- Anchor one end of the material on top of the mound using sand or other weights.
- Extend and anchor the other end of the material so it provides the best possible shade.

Note: If you have enough material, fold it in half and form a 30-centimeter to 45-centimeter airspace between the two halves. This airspace will reduce the temperature under the shelter.

A belowground shelter can reduce the midday heat as much as 16 to 22 degrees C (30 to 40 degrees F). Building it, however, requires more time and effort than for other shelters. Since your physical effort will make you sweat more and increase dehydration, construct it before the heat of the day.

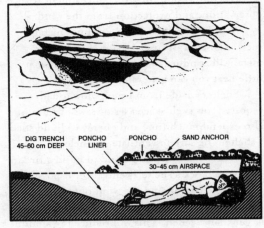

Belowground desert shelter.

To make this shelter—

- Find a low spot or depression between dunes or rocks. If necessary, dig a trench 45 to 60 centimeters deep and long and wide enough for you to lie in comfortably.
- Pile and sand you take from the trench to form a mound around three sides
- On the open end of the trench, dig out more sand so you can get in and out of your shelter easily.
- Cover the trench with your material.
- Secure the material in place using sand, rocks, or other weights.

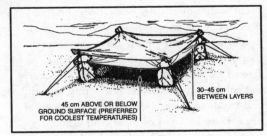

Open desert shelter.

If you have extra material, you can further decrease the midday temperature in the trench by securing the material 30 to 45 centimeters above the other cover. This layering of the material will reduce the inside temperature 11 to 22 degrees C (20 to 40 degrees F).

Another type of belowground shade shelter is of similar construction, except all sides are open to air currents and circulation. For maximum protection, you need a minimum of two layers of parachute material. White is the best color to reflect heat; the innermost layer should be of darker material.

—From *Survival (Field Manual 21-76)*

Continued

Expedient Cold-Weather Shelters

U.S. Army

Your environment and the equipment you carry with you will determine the type of shelter you can build. You can build shelters in wooded areas, open country, and barren areas. Wooded areas usually provide the best location, while barren areas have only snow as building material. Wooded areas provide timber for shelter construction, wood for fire, concealment from observation, and protection from the wind.

Note: In extreme cold, do not use metal, such as an aircraft fuselage, for shelter. The metal will conduct away from the shelter what little heat you can generate.

Shelters made from ice or snow usually require tools such as ice axes or saws. You must also expend much time and energy to build such a shelter. Be sure to ventilate an enclosed shelter, especially if you intend to build a fire in it. Always block a shelter's entrance, if possible, to keep the heat in and the wind out. Use a rucksack or snow block. Construct a shelter no larger than needed. This will reduce the amount of space to heat. A fatal error in cold weather shelter construction is making the shelter so large that it steals body heat rather than saving it. Keep shelter space small.

Never sleep directly on the ground. Lay down some pine boughs, grass, or other insulating material to keep the ground from absorbing your body heat.

Never fall asleep without turning out your stove or lamp. Carbon monoxide poisoning can result from a fire burning in an unventilated shelter. Carbon monoxide is a great danger. It is colorless and odorless. Any time you have an open flame, it may generate carbon monoxide. Always check your ventilation. Even in a ventilated shelter, incomplete combustion can cause carbon monoxide poisoning. Usually, there are no symptoms. Unconsciousness and death can occur without warning. Sometimes, however, pressure at the temples, burning of the eyes, headache, pounding pulse, drowsiness, or nausea may occur. The one characteristic, visible sign of carbon monoxide poisoning is a cherry red coloring in the tissues of the lips, mouth, and inside of the eyelids. Get into fresh air at once if you have any of these symptoms.

There are several types of field-expedient shelters you can quickly build or employ. Many use snow for insulation.

Snow Cave Shelter

The snow cave shelter is a most effective shelter because of the insulating qualities of snow. Remember that is takes time and energy to build and that you will get wet while building it. First, you need to find a drift about 3 meters deep into which you can dig. While building this shelter, keep the roof arched for strength and to allow melted snow to drain down the sides. Build the sleeping platform higher than the entrance. Separate the sleeping platform from the snow cave's walls or dig a small trench between the platform and the wall. This platform will prevent the melting snow from wetting you and your equipment. This construction is especially important if you have a good source of heat in the snow

cave. Ensure the roof is high enough so that you can sit up on the sleeping platform. Block the entrance with a snow block or other material and use the lower entrance area for cooking. The walls and ceiling should be at least 30 centimeters thick. Install a ventilation shaft. If you do not have a drift large enough to build a snow cave, you can make a variation of it by piling snow into a mound large enough to dig out.

Snow Trench Shelter

The idea behind this shelter is to get you below the snow and wind level and use the snow's insulating qualities. If you are in an area of compacted snow, cut snow blocks and use them as overhead cover. If not, you can use a poncho or other material. Build only one entrance and use a snow block or rucksack as a door.

Snow Block and Parachute Shelter

Use snow blocks for the sides and parachute material for overhead cover. If snowfall is heavy,

you will have to clear snow from the top at regular intervals to prevent the collapse of the parachute material.

Snow House or Igloo

In certain areas, the natives frequently use this type of shelter as hunting and fishing shelters. They are efficient shelters but require some practice to make them properly. Also, you must be in an area that is suitable for cutting snow blocks and have the equipment to cut them (snow saw or knife).

Lean-To Shelter

Construct this shelter in the same manner as for other environments; however, pile snow around the sides for insulation.

Fallen Tree Shelter

To build this shelter, find a fallen tree and dig out the snow underneath it. The snow will not

SNOW HOUSES

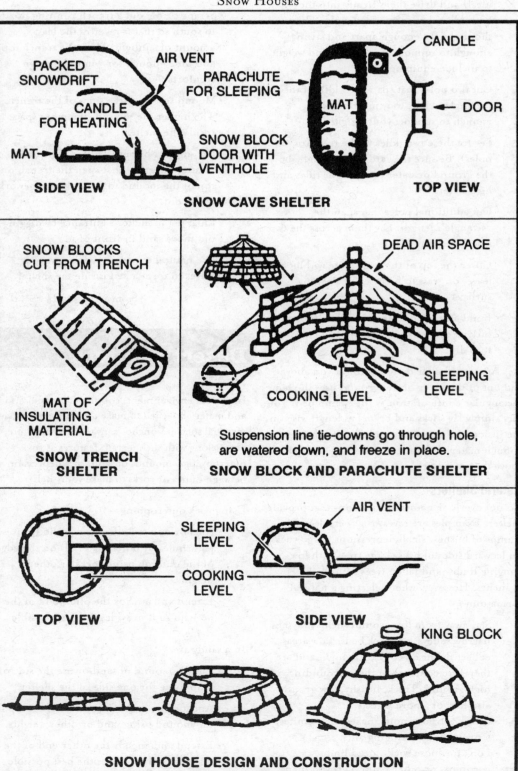

SNOW CAVE SHELTER

SNOW TRENCH SHELTER

SNOW BLOCK AND PARACHUTE SHELTER

Suspension line tie-downs go through hole, are watered down, and freeze in place.

SNOW HOUSE DESIGN AND CONSTRUCTION

Continued ➡

Fallen tree as shelter.

be deep under the tree. If you must remove branches from the inside, use them to line the floor.

—From *Survival (Field Manual 21-76)*

Snow walls and Snow Holes

U.S. Army

Snow Wall

In open terrain with snow and ice, a snow wall may be constructed for protection form strong winds. Blocks of compact snow or ice are used to form a windbreak.

Sleeping behind snow wall.

Snow Hole

A snow hole provides shelter quickly. It is constructed by burrowing into a snowdrift or by digging a trench in the snow and making a roof of ponchos and ice or snow-blocks supported by skis, ski poles or snow-shoes. A sled provides excellent insulation for the sleeping bag. Boughs, if available, can be used for covering the roof and for the bed.

—From *Basic Cold Weather Manual (Field Manual 31-70)*

Emergency Winter Shelters

Greg Davenport
Illustrations by Steven A. Davenport

Thermal A-Frame

A thermal A-frame is most often used in the warm temperate and snow environments, where there is an abundance of trees and snow. Find a tree with a forked branch that's 3 to 4 feet above the base of its trunk after you have dug down to bare ground. Break away any other branches that pose a threat or interfere with the construction of your A-frame. Place a ridgepole (a fallen tree 12 to 15 feet long and the diameter of your wrist) into the forked branch, forming a 30-degree angle between the pole and the ground. If you're

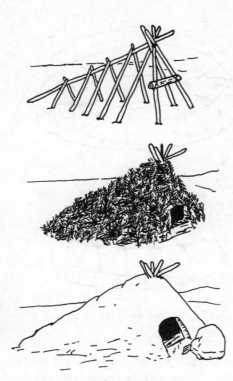

Thermal A-frame.

unable to find a tree with a forked branch, lash the ridgepole to the tree. Other options are to locate a fallen tree that's at an appropriate 30-degree angle to the ground, or to lay a strong ridgepole against a 3- to 4-foot-high stump. Lay support poles across the ridgepole, on both sides, at a 60-degree angle to the ground. Support poles need to be long enough to extend above the ridgepole *slightly*, and they should be placed approximately 1 to 1½ feet apart. If the support poles end up above the roof material moisture will run down them and into your shelter. Crisscross small branches into the support poles. Cover the framework with any available grass, moss, boughs, and so forth. Place the materials in a layered fashion, starting at the bottom. Finally, throw at least 8 inches (you may add more, but this is the minimum) of snow over the top of the shelter. Cover the door opening with your pack or similar item.

Snow Cave

A snow cave is most often used in warm temperate (winter) and snow environments and is a quick and easily constructed one- or two-man shelter. When using these shelters, the outside temperature must be well below freezing to ensure that the walls of the cave will stay firm and the snow will not melt. Never get the inside temperature above freezing, or the shelter will lose its insulating quality, and you'll get wet from the subsequent moisture. With this in mind, these shelters are not designed for large groups, since the radiant heat will raise the temperature above freezing, making it a dangerous environment. As a general rule of thumb, if you cannot see your breath, the shelter is too warm. When constructing the cave, use the COLDER principle [see page 287] and take care not to overheat or get wet.

To construct a snow cave, find an area with firm snow at a depth of at least 6 feet (a steep slope such as a snowdrift will suffice, provided there is no risk of an avalanche). Dig an entryway into the slope deep enough to start a

tunnel (approximately 3 feet) and wide enough for you to fit into. Since cold air sinks, construct a snow platform 2 to 3 feet above the entryway. It should be flat, level, and large enough for you to comfortably lie down on. Using the entryway as a starting point, hollow out a domed area that is large enough for you and your equipment. To prevent the ceiling from settling or falling in, create a high domed roof. To prevent asphyxiation, make a ventilation hole in the roof. For best results, the hole should be at a 45-degree angle to your sleeping platform (creating an imaginary triangle between the platform, the door, and the hole). If available, insert a stick or pole through the hole so that it can be cleared periodically. To form an A-frame above the trench. For best results, cut one of the first opposing blocks in half lengthwise. This will make it easier to place the additional blocks on—one at a time versus trying to continually lay two against one another. Fill in any gaps with surrounding snow, and cover the doorway.

A quick and easy variation of the snow A-frame shelter can be made when the snow is not wind-packed and a snow cave is not an option. Simply dig a trench as described above, but make one side higher than the other; cover it with a lean-to type framework of branches or similar material; and then add a thick layer of snow as roofing.

SNOW CAVE SAFETY
U.S. Army

Heating and Safety Measures

The cave can be heated with the one-burner gasoline stove or with candles. The fires should be extinguished when individuals are sleeping, thus reducing the danger of fire and asphyxiation. If the weather is severe and it becomes necessary to keep a fire going while the individuals are asleep, an alert fire guard must be posted in each cave. The ventilation holes must be inspected every 2 or 3 hours to insure that they have not become clogged by snow or by icing.

Insulation

To insure that the cave is warm, the entrance should be blocked with a rucksack, piece of canvas, or snowblock when not in use. All available material, such as ponchos, cardboard, brush, boughs, etc., should be used for ground insulation.

Other Precautions

Walking on the roof may cause it to collapse. At least two ventilators, one in the door and one in the roof, are used. A ski pole can be stuck through the roof ventilator to clear it from the inside. Extra care must be exercised to keep air in the cave fresh when heating or cooking. The entrance should be marked by placing a pair of skis or other equipment upright on each side of the entry way.

—From *Basic Cold Weather Manual*
(Field Manual 31-76)

Continued ➡

Igloo

An igloo can provide a long-term winter shelter for a small family. This shelter is normally used in areas where the snow is windblown and firmly packed. An igloo that has a diameter of 8 feet is adequate for one person; a diameter of 12 feet can easily house four people. Its construction requires a snow saw or large knife.

Find a windblown snowdrift or field, 2 feet deep, firm enough that it will support your weight with only a slight indent. Draw a circle in the snow that represents the desired igloo size. The marked outline will become the inside diameter of the igloo. Establish a door location, which should be at a 90-degree angle to the wind. Make two parallel lines in the snow that are 30 inches apart and perpendicular to the door entrance. These lines should extend one-third of the way toward the center of the circle and an equal distance away. This area will eventually become your entrance, cooking, and storage area. Since cold air sinks, it also serves as a cold sump for the shelter. Using the two lines as your guide, cut blocks that measure 30 inches long, 15 inches deep, and 8 to 12 inches thick. Start at the outside of the circle and continue until the two parallel lines end (one-third of the way to the center of the circle). Set the blocks aside. In order to finish the shelter, you will need to acquire additional blocks from another location. Once all the blocks are cut, you can begin building the igloo.

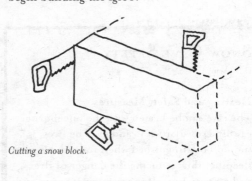

Cutting a snow block.

Start by placing four full-size blocks, side by side, on the outside of the circle. Next, make a diagonal cut that runs from the ground of the second block to the top of the fourth. The fifth and following blocks will be the standard 15-inch height. The slope will provide a spiral effect that makes the construction easier and provides stability to the igloo. Continue adding blocks until the first layer is complete. You may need to add support pillars under the blocks that go over the entrance. As your dome begins to take form, trim the blocks (see illustration) and tilt them slightly inward to increase the contact and stability. In addition, greater stability is obtained if each block placed doesn't end on the same seam as the one below it (you may need to trim one or two blocks to avoid this).

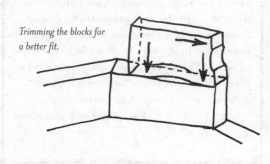

Trimming the blocks for a better fit.

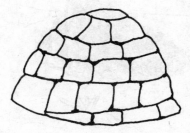
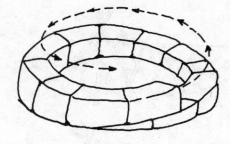

Construction an igloo.

As the dome wall gets higher, you'll need to work from inside the igloo, exiting through the doorway created when the blocks were cut. The last layers of blocks need to be trimmed at an angle so the key block can be positioned on top. The key, or final, block is the centerpiece. It is round and tapered in from the top toward the shelter.

To finish the igloo, use snow as the mortar to close all weak areas. If you want to increase the insulation quality of the shelter, simply pile more snow around it. Create a roof over the entryway similar to that described for the snow A-frame variation, page 251. If you intend to have a small fire, don't forget a vent hole, and don't allow the temperature inside the igloo to get too warm. You should be able to see your breath.

Molded Dome

A variation of the snow cave and igloo is a molded dome, used in conditions where the snow is not wind-packed and a snow cave is not an option. Use your gear, boughs, or other material to create a cone that will serve as the foundation to your shelter. Pile snow on top of the cone until you have a dome that is approximately 5 feet high and has at least 3 feet of snow covering the inner core. Smooth the outer surface, and let the snow sit for one to two hours so that it can settle (the time frame depends on your weather conditions). Since 18 inches is an ideal insulating depth for a molded dome, gather multiple 2-foot-long branches and insert them into the dome, pointing toward its center, leaving approximately 6 inches exposed. Decide where you'd like your entryway,

Molded dome.

and dig a 3-foot-deep entry tunnel. Dig approximately one-third of the way toward the center of the molded dome, or until you reach the core material. Remove the gear, boughs, or other material, and hollow out the inside, using the 2-foot branches you inserted as your guide for inner-wall thickness.

Molded dome.

Survival Tips

Heat inside Snow Shelters

If the temperature in a shelter made partially or completely of snow exceeds 32 degrees F, it will begin to melt and will get you and your equipment wet. As a general rule of thumb, as long as you can see your breath, the temperature is probably not too high.

Avoiding Carbon Dioxide (CO_2) Poisoning

If you intend to use any heating device inside an enclosed shelter, make sure to create a vent hole that will allow the CO_2 to escape. This is usually placed at a 45-degree angle between the top of the shelter and the shelter's opening.

Increasing the Insulation Value of a Cold-Weather Shelter

Once your shelter is complete, you may elect to add a snow wall on the windward side to decrease the wind's effects on your site.

Staking Out a Tent or Poncho Shelter

In deep snow, you may have to use dead-men to secure your shelter sides in place. Tie one end of a piece of line to the shelter material, and secure its other end to a 1-inch-diameter branch that is about 6 inches long. Pull the attached line at a 90-degree angle to the wrinkles in the shelter's material and secure the branch in place. To do this, kick a small hole in the snow, jam the line and branch into it, and while holding the branch in place, cover it with snow. These dead-men work great when temperatures are below freezing, but when the sun is out, if the temperature gets above freezing, these anchors may pop free, and your shelter will fail down.

Creating a Cooking Pit or Community Area

Digging a 6-foot-deep round hole, along with a sitting platform 2 feet up from the bottom, creates a wonderful, wind-blocked area for cooking and community gatherings.

—From *Surviving Cold Weather*

Continued ➡

Digloos and Quinzhees

Buck Tilton and John Gookin
Illustrations by Joan M. Safford

Digloos

A digloo is a snow cave that can be dug from the top and the side at the same time. The final result is the same: a dome-shaped room accessible via a tunnel. A digloo requires the same depth of snow as a snow cave—a minimum of five to six feet, with ten feet or more being better. The disadvantage of a digloo is the need for snow blocks to cap the hole in the roof. The process of making and setting snow blocks is more complex than the simple digging of a snow cave. The primary advantages of a digloo over a snow cave are that two people can dig at the same time, so the work tends to go faster, and snow doesn't have to be burrowed into and ferried down a tunnel.

After probing to find an appropriate depth, ski-pack the snow above the building site. An area about six feet square is sufficient for two people. The sleeping chamber will be located below this work-hardened area, and the packed snow provides a foundation for the cap blocks. If the snowpack is relatively shallow, shovel some extra snow on top of the packed platform to raise it. The shoveled snow doesn't need to be boot-packed, but it should be tamped with a shovel to firm it. This initial packing is best done as soon as you've chosen a site. Other parts of construction must wait, since you need to allow time for the packed snow to sinter, making it possible to dig a stable hole.

Unless you're very far north or south, in the Arctic or Antarctic, you'll probably need to make a quarry from which to cut blocks. Boot-packing an area about eight feet square will provide ample blocks for a digloo. Just smash the snow up with your boots for a while, and then ski-pack the top smooth. It is easier to cut good blocks out of a quarry with a smooth top. Don't walk on the quarry after it has been smoothed, or you will crack the snow. This is

another job that should be done early, so it can strengthen by sintering. For instance, if you break trail to a snow shelter site the day before you move camp to that site, you can make a quarry that will yield industrial-strength blocks.

Once it has firmed up—a process that takes at least an hour or two—dig a round hole in the center of the packed area above the future digloo. Make the hole just big enough to sneak the shovel in and out of with the digger standing in it. The smaller the hole, the easier it will be to cap with blocks. Carefully avoid stepping on the hard snow immediately around the hole. If you do plunge into the snow, fill the accidental hole with packed snow, and try not to set a block corner on that weak spot later. (If the snow is too dry to pack into your mistake, you can make a quick-setting "epoxy" with water and snow.) Dig down a couple of feet, and then start digging to the sides, carving an inverted funnel shape in the snow. This will be the sleeping chamber. As the chamber grows, it will become easier to stand in the hole while you dig. Dig to the ground as you widen the bottom of the hole or, in deeper snow, until you have a room the size you want. Basic snow shelter construction principles are important here—the dome shape of the room, the smooth ceiling, and cutting the snow rather than prying out large chunks.

As you pitch snow from the hole, try to create a rough snow wall to remind others to stay off the roof of the digloo. Shape a floor that slopes very slightly toward the intended door. Leave some "debris" inside—snow you've dug out for the room—to fill holes that tend to show up in the floor and for finishing touches. When the room is relatively complete, begin to dig toward the tunnel, and the second digger.

The second digger begins about ten feet downhill from the packed area, digging straight down, following the directions for a snow cave. The goal here is a clean face on the uphill side. Then a tunnel is dug uphill, toward where the room is being constructed. The tunnel digger may move faster than the room digger, and a lot of unnecessary energy can be wasted digging the tunnel too far. Estimate the length needed for the tunnel, dig it out, and back off until the room is complete.

When the digger in the room starts to dig toward the tunnel, the tunnel digger can resume digging until both ends of the tunnel are joined. From this point on, the snow can be removed via the tunnel.

On a steep slope, leave enough of the snowpack on the bottom of the tunnel to build large steps. Steps are difficult, if not impossible, to add later.

With the tunnel and room complete, it's time to cut blocks from the quarry. Blocks can be cut with a snow saw, a wood saw, or, if you're careful and skillful, a wide shovel. A good block size is about eighteen to twenty inches wide, two feet long, and six inches thick. Square the blocks as much as possible, leaving the corners intact. The work goes faster with bigger blocks, but smaller blocks are easier to handle. If the blocks are too heavy, consider making them thinner rather than narrower and shorter. If one long side of a block is obviously fatter, and thus heavier, than the other side, place the heavier side down for better balance.

Carry the blocks to the edge of the roof of the digloo, and pass them to someone standing inside the hole. Lean the blocks against each other at about a forty-five-degree angle, with their "feet" on top of the packed circle at the edge of the opening. Each block should rest on its corners, not the middle, or it will rock and be unstable. A bit of mitering may help, but don't try to shape the blocks too much—this often leaves you needing more blocks. The force of the blocks leaning against each other increases their strength over time. If the hole is no more than three feet across, three blocks should be enough. A smaller, lighter block is needed to cap the pyramid. Ideally, this final cap block should fit snugly, with no rocking. You can accomplish this best by setting the cap in place and sawing gently from the inside, mitering the block until it fits snugly. Chink the large holes left in the triangle of blocks by shoveling softer snow from the outside until the cap is sealed. Now you can vent the room and add finishing touches, such as storage shelves and sleeping platforms, as desired.

Quinzhees

Many areas do not commonly have adequate snow depth or appropriate snow type to build caves or igloos. In these circumstances, you can build a quinzhee, which is a hollowed-out pile of snow—a pile that you make. This type of snow shelter was traditionally used by the Athabascans on the taiga and is appropriate in the dry snows of the Rockies. You can build a quinzhee with less than two feet of snow on the ground.

Follow the directions given earlier to choose a site for the pile of snow. Determine the quinzhee's size by drawing a rough circle big enough to house all the intended occupants without touching the walls. For a group of four, you can create a workable circle by rotating a 170 cm ski around a pole placed upright in the center. A large group may choose to build several quinzhees, since smaller snow structures generally have stronger walls. Walk around the

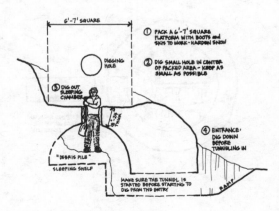

DIGLOO: A DOME-SHAPED ROOM ACCESSIBLE BY TUNNEL. BASICALLY, A SNOW CAVE THAT CAN BE DUG FROM THE TOP AND THE SIDE AT THE SAME TIME.

① PACK A 6'-7' SQUARE PLATFORM WITH BOOTS and SKIS TO WORK-HARDEN SNOW

② DIG SMALL HOLE IN CENTER OF PACKED AREA - KEEP AS SMALL AS POSSIBLE

③ DIG OUT SLEEPING CHAMBER

④ ENTRANCE: DIG DOWN BEFORE TUNNELING IN

MAKE SURE THE TUNNEL IS STARTED BEFORE STARTING TO DIG FROM THIS ENTRY

⑤ CUT BLOCKS FROM PLATFORM and CAP THE DIGLOO

FIRST TWO BLOCKS / ADD A THIRD BLOCK / CAP BLOCK

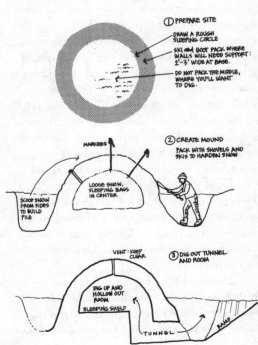

QUINZHEE: A PILE OF SNOW YOU MAKE and THEN HOLLOW OUT INTO A SHELTER.

① PREPARE SITE

② CREATE MOUND

③ DIG OUT TUNNEL AND ROOM

rim of the circle to break up the soft snow so that it will harden. This is important, because the walls will be two to three feet thick at the base, and you'll need firm footing for these walls. Be sure that some of your steps punch all the way to the ground. Not doing this can lead to collapse of the structure while hollowing it out. Be careful not to pack the middle of the circle. That's the part you're going to dig out, so you want to leave the snow there as easy to move as possible. You can even throw tightly closed packs and well-protected sleeping bags in the middle as filler, before you start shoveling. If you have a long, slim pole, place it upright in the middle of the area to serve as a guide, telling the digger when the middle of the pile has been reached.

When you start shoveling snow into a pile—the not-so-fun part of construction—throw softer snow where the wall will be, since it will sinter into a stronger uniform density. Toss any chunks of snow into the middle. Chunks have air spaces around them, making them easy to dig out, and using chunks in the wall would leave holes. You can also throw crumbling snow into the middle. It, too, will be easy to dig out later. Keep piling up snow until the mound is large and dome shaped. It should have no points or horizontal flat spots on it, characteristics that create weakness in the walls.

When the pile is large enough, pack the snow on the outside with a ski or the flat of a shovel. This increases the density of the outer wall, and it also shortens the time for sintering to occur. The pile of snow must firm up substantially before you can hollow it out. Sintering happens slowly when the snowpack is cold and quickly when the snow is warm. You can speed up the sintering process by double-packing the walls and roof: pack, add snow, and pack it again. In bitterly cold conditions, it's best to wait a couple of hours before hollowing. When it's warm, you can dig almost immediately, although too much rushing increases the risk of collapse. If the snowpack is so warm that it feels wet, don't build a quinzhee.

After the pile of snow has firmed up adequately, start to tunnel in from the lowest side of the mound. But first, discuss rescue procedures in case the snow collapses on the "mole" digging out the inside. Keep the tunnel as low and as small as possible. You can easily enlarge an entrance, but you can rarely make one smaller. As soon as you're in a couple of feet, start hollowing out the quinzhee. Once you can kneel and then stand, you'll get less wet while digging. Many people like to work quickly to the center of the room for a better frame of reference for digging. Be careful to cut the snow and not pry it with the shovel—prying puts unnecessary stress on the still-sintering walls.

From the middle of the mound, dig up, keeping the interior in a dome shape (no flat spots or points). Leave a layer of snow for the floor. And once again, for the most efficient heat-trapping, make the floor higher than the top of the door.

Hollow out the room until you can see a little blue light showing through the snow. If there's too much bright light coming in the door, have someone block the entrance. Once you see light in an area of the ceiling, dig elsewhere. Once you see light all over the interior of the dome, smooth out the ceiling. Instead of using light to estimate wall thickness, you can use markers, such as ski poles, stuck into the mound before the hollowing-out process. Stick them in about two feet, the approximate wall thickness you want. When you reach the markers from the inside, you can stop digging. Pack the floor by crawling around on it, and then smooth it out as flat as possible. Put a vent in the roof to draw off moisture (as for snow caves), and leave for a while to allow the floor to sinter.

During the hollowing-out process, the snow pile may occasionally settle with a disturbing "whoomp." The lighter and colder the snow, the more likely this is to happen. Don't worry—this seldom signals a collapse. However, you may want to dig a bit less aggressively or stop and double-pack the walls before continuing to hollow out the interior.

The larger the quinzhee, the trickier the construction. Larger quinzhee require thicker walls. If you want to house an especially large group, make the snow pile longer instead of wider, sort of a Quonset hut shape. This ovate shape gives full strength to conventional snow walls but allows for virtually infinite expansion lengthwise. With a really long quinzhee, you can tunnel in from both ends and seal one entrance later.

Maintaining Your Snow Shelter

· Keep the vent clear to preserve air flow.

· Do not burn stoves and lanterns that consume oxygen unless they have special hooded ventilation systems.

· Lay out ground cloths and sleeping pads so they overlap and cover cold spots.

· Keep warm items like sleeping bags away from the snow walls.

· Burn a candle for light and a pleasant atmosphere.

· Watch for sagging or other shelter damage, and repair as necessary.

—From *NOLS Winter Camping*

DESERT CAMPSITE TIP
Greg Davenport

Decrease the Sun's Impact
Position the shelter so that it has a northern exposure if you're north of the equator and a southern exposure if south of it; this allows for optimal shade and decreases the sun's impact throughout the day. In addition, try to position the door so that it faces east, since an east-side opening will decrease mid- to late-day sun exposure.

—From *Surviving the Desert*

Buck Tilton and John Gookin
Illustration by Joan M. Safford

Site and Shelter Selection: General Guidelines

Any site for a snow shelter needs to have, in addition to snow, subfreezing temperatures. Avoid building a snow shelter when the temperature allows melting, because the snow will be too weak and too heavy. The conditions that make a site safe and comfortable for a snow shelter are generally the same as those described in the beginning of this chapter. Wind, however, is not as big of a problem with a snow shelter, so a more open spot can be chosen. Specific conditions required for each type of snow shelter are discussed on pages 251 to 252.

Whatever type of shelter you choose, start small and simple. Smaller shelters take less work and, more importantly, tend to be stronger. With the same wall thickness, for instance, a small sphere is stronger than a large sphere, not only because the walls are fatter in relation to the space they enclose, but also because smaller spheres have sharper angles, which makes for stronger structures. The type of shelter you choose also depends on the type of snow:

Drifted snow—snow cave or digloo
Wind slab—igloo
Deep, soft snow—quinzhee
Shallow, soft snow—quinzhee
Wet snow—tent or tarp

—From *NOLS Winter Camping*

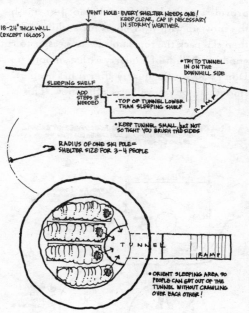

BASIC PRINCIPLES OF SNOW SHELTER CONSTRUCTION

Continued ➡

Choosing a Campsite
Greg Davenport

When selecting a campsite, make sure its location allows you to easily meet your other survival needs. The environment, materials on hand, and the amount of time available will determine the type of shelter you choose. The ideal site will meet the following conditions.

Location and Size
Your site should be level and big enough for both you and your equipment. If close to shore, make sure it is above the high-tide mark and at least one dune shoreward beyond the sea.

Optimize the Sun's Warmth
Position the shelter for a southern exposure if it's north of the equator or a northern exposure if south of it. This allows for optimal light and heat from the sun throughout the day. Try to position the door so that it faces east, since an east-side opening will allow for the best early-morning sun exposure.

Avoid Wind Problems
Since wind can wrap over the top of a tent and through its opening, do not place the door in the path of or on the opposite side of the wind's travel. Instead, position the door 90 degrees to the prevailing wind. Avoid shelter on ridgetops and open areas. When setting up your tent, secure it in place by staking it down. It doesn't take much of a wind to move or destroy your shelter.

Use the Snow's Insulation
If you are in snow, dig down to bare ground whenever possible. The ground's radiant heat will help keep you warmer at night.

Water Source
To avoid having to melt snow or traveling for water, build your shelter 100 feet or so from a stream or lake, if you can find one.

Safety First
Avoid sites with potential environmental hazards that can wipe out all your hard work in just a matter of seconds. Examples include avalanche slopes; drainage and dry riverbeds with a potential for flash floods; rock formations that might collapse; dead trees that might blow down; overhanging dead limbs; and large animal trails. If you are near bodies of water, stay above the high-tide mark.

Survival
During an emergency, make sure your camp is located next to a signal and recovery site.

—From *Surviving Coastal and Open Water*

Tents and Bivouvac Bags
Greg Davenport

Tent
The majority of tents are made of nylon and held up with aluminum poles. Tents need to be waterproof and breathable—waterproof to prevent moisture from entering from the outside, and breathable to avoid condensation formation on the inside. Nylon is not waterproof, so some manufacturers use a breathable waterproof coating or a breathable laminated waterproof membrane for the tent's inner wall. Both of these options allow moisture to escape but prevent outside moisture from entering. If an outer wall is used, this is not necessary. To make the outer wall water repellent, a polyurethane coating is often added. Some tents come with UV protection and even have a fire-retardant finish. The tent's seams will either have a tape weld or require that you apply a seam sealant before its first use. Follow the manufacturer's recommendations on how to seal the tent's seams. A tent's poles need to be durable enough to handle the wind and snow without bending or breaking. For general use, get poles that have a diameter of 8.5 millimeters. For extreme conditions, use a 9-millimeter or greater pole to add more durability to the tent's frame.

A tent's size, strength, and weight will all factor into your decision on which one to use. A tradeoff between weight and strength is often foremost in people's minds. When choosing a tent, you'll have to decide which is more important: less weight on your back or more durability and comfort in camp. I'd advise against a single-walled tent, unless it has multiple vents that can be opened to prevent inner condensation moisture. A double-walled tent provides a breathable inner wall and an outer waterproof rain fly. Since moisture from inside the tent will escape through the breathable wall and collect on the inside of the rain fly, the two walls should not touch, or the moisture will not escape and condensation will form inside the tent. The ideal rain fly will allow for a small area of

protection—between the door and outside—commonly called a vestibule. This area allows for extra storage, boot removal, and cooking. For information on zippers, see page 288.

Most tents are classified as three-season or four-season tents. There are also combo tents that can be used as either.

Three-Season Tents
Three-season tents are normally lighter and often have see-through mesh panels, which provide ventilation.

Four-Season Tents
Four-season tents are made from solid panels and in general are heavier and stronger. Typically, they have stronger poles and reinforced seams.

Combo Tents
Some tents are marketed to be used in either three or four seasons by providing a solid panel that can be zipped shut over the ventilating mesh.

Bivouac Bag
The original concept of bivouac bags was to allow the backpacker or mountaineer an emergency lightweight shelter. However, even though these shelters are made for just one person, many travelers now carry them as their primary three-season shelter. A good bag will be made from a breathable waterproof fabric such as Gore-Tex or Tetra-Tex, with a coated nylon floor. A hoop or flexible wire sewn across the head area, along with nonremovable mosquito netting, is advised for comfort and venting when needed.

—From *Surviving Cold Weather*

A bivouac.

Commercial tent.

Greg Davenport
Illustrations by Steven Davenport and Ken Davenport

Poncho or Tarp

A poncho or tarp is a multiuse item that can meet shelter, clothing, signaling, and water procurement needs. Its uses are unlimited, and you should take one along on most outdoor activities. The military ripstop nylon poncho measures 54 1/2 by 60 inches and features a drawstring hood, snap sides, and corner grommets.

Emergency All-Weather Blanket

Don't waste your money or risk your life carrying one of those flimsy foil emergency blankets. Instead, carry a durable, waterproof, 10-ounce, 5 by 6-foot all-weather blanket. These blankets are made from a four-ply laminate of clear polyethylene film, a precise vacuum deposition of pure aluminum, a special reinforcing fabric (Astrolar), and a layer of colored polyethylene film. The blanket will reflect and help retain more than 80 percent of the body's radiant heat. In addition to covering the body, these blankets have a hood and inside hand pockets that aid in maintaining your body heat. When compressed, these blankets take up about twice as much space as the smaller foil design, but the benefits far outweigh the size issue. The all-weather blanket is a multiuse item that can double as an emergency sleeping bag, signal, poncho, or shelter.

Emergency all-weather blanket.

Anchors

In desert regions, it may be difficult to drive a stake into the ground or find underbrush necessary to put up a shelter or improvise items to use in your camp. To compensate for these problems, carry along several pieces of 2-foot-square ripstop material and para cord. To make an anchor, attach three or four pieces of 2-foot line to a piece of the material in various loca-

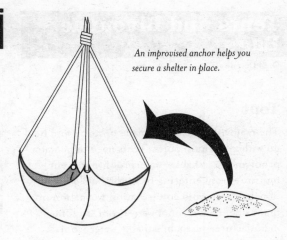

An improvised anchor helps you secure a shelter in place.

tions, and tie the lines' free ends together with an overhand knot. Attach another line to the overhand knot, and run it to your shelter. Fill the material with sand, and place it so that it holds the shelter in place at the desired location. Use as many anchors as needed to hold the shelter securely.

Sleeping Bag

Many types of sleeping bags are available, and the type used varies greatly among individuals. There are several basic guidelines you should use when selecting a bag. The ideal bag should be compressible, have an insulated hood, and be lightweight but still keep you warm. Most manufacturers rate their bags as summer, three-season, or winter expedition use and provide a minimum temperature at which the bag will keep you warm. This gross rating is used as a guide and should help you select the bag that best meets your needs. Sleeping bag covers are useful for keeping your bag clean and add an extra layer of insulating air. How well the bag keeps you warm depends on the design, amount and type of insulation and loft, and method of construction. When selecting a bag, don't forget that deserts can get very cold at night. I'd advise against bags that have a minimum temperature rating higher than 20 degrees F.

Design

Without question, the hooded, tapered mummy style is the bag of choice for all conditions. In cold conditions, the hood can be tightened around your face, leaving a hole big enough for you to breathe through. In warmer conditions, you may elect to leave your head out and use the hooded area as a pillow. The foot of the bag should be somewhat circular and well insulated. Side zippers need good, insulated baffles behind them.

Insulation

Sleeping bags will use either a down or synthetic insulation material.

Down

Down is lightweight, effective, and compressible. A down bag is rated by its fill power in cubic inches per ounce. A rating of 550 is standard, with values increasing over 800. The higher ratings provide greater loft, meaning a warmer bag. The greatest downfall to this insulation is its inability to maintain its loft and insulating value when wet. In a desert climate, this may not be an

issue, so down bags are an excellent, albeit expensive, option.

Synthetic Insulation

Synthetic materials provide a good alternative to down. Their greatest strength is the ability to maintain most of their loft and insulation when wet along with the ability to dry relatively quickly. On the flip side, they are heavier and don't compress as well as down. Although cheaper than down, they tend to lose loft more quickly over long-term use. Lite loft and Polarguard are two great examples of synthetic insulation. If you are traveling in a desert area during its rain season, it is best to carry this type of bag.

Method of Construction

Insulation material is normally contained in baffles, tubes created within the bag. There are three basic construction designs for sleeping bags: slant tube, offset quilt, and square box. Each design has its benefits, and the type you choose depends on many factors, including weight, temperature, and compressibility. However, the slant tube and offset quilt are more comfortable and provide better from the ground.

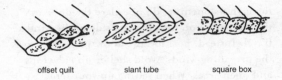

offset quilt   slant tube   square box

Sleeping bag construction designs.

Improvising a Bag

Understanding the basic bag design is the key to improvising a bag in a time of crisis. I once made a bag using ripstop parachute material, dry leaves, and moss.

Fleece or Quilted Blanket

A blanket can be used to increase the insulating ability of your lightweight sleeping bag or carried as emergency gear when taking day hikes in the desert.

Fleece Blanket

A fleece blanket is soft, comfortable, and durable, and some say it provides more warmth for its weight than wool. The biggest drawbacks are its inability to repel wind and its lack of compressibility.

Enhanced Infantry Thinsulate Poncho Liner

This lightweight quilted blanket measures 91 by 60 inches and can be used in emergencies and for general survival needs. The newer lightweight Thinsulate blanket provides superior warmth and can be compressed down 25 percent smaller than its predecessor, which was made from polyester.

Continued

Sleeping Pad

A sleeping pad is essential for insulating you from the ground. Most commercial pads are closed-cell or open-cell foam or a combination of the two. Each style has its pros and cons.

Closed-Cell Foam

These pads provide excellent insulation and durability but are bulky to carry. They may or may not have an outer nylon shell covering.

Open-Cell Foam

These pads are often self-inflating, using a high-flow inflation valve. Their ability to compress and rebound makes them ideal when space is a concern. Open-cell foam pads are usually covered with a durable, low-slip polyester fabric.

Improvising a Pad

If you don't have a pad, you can improvise one using boughs, moss, leaves, or similar dry materials. Made an 18-inch-high mound that is large enough to protect your whole body from the ground.

—From *Surviving the Desert*

Winter Tent Camping

Buck Tilton and John Gookin
Illustrations by Joan M. Safford

Campsite Selection

One of the most rewarding parts of winter camping is getting to bed down at night in a well-made winter camp. If you're a camper—winter-wise or not—you already appreciate the value of choosing the perfect spot to set up camp. Beyond a great view in a peaceful place, "perfect" here means safe and comfortable. And in winter, fewer daylight hours mean longer nights, so you'll be spending more time in camp than you do in other seasons—and thus enjoying your choice of sites longer.

Safety considerations require a careful look around and up. If your campsite is anywhere beneath an avalanche slope, measure the alpha angle—the angle from your site to the highest avalanche starting zone above you. An alpha angle of twenty degrees or higher is too close for comfort. For hard glacial ice, use fifteen degrees. Also look out for "widowmakers," large dead limbs or whole dead trees that could fall from old age, a load of snow, a high wind, or some combination of factors. Camp away from cliff edges that someone might stumble off of, and avoid cliff bottoms, where sliding rocks or snow could come to rest.

Unless you're very confident of the weather forecast, you should also evaluate your campsite with respect to a storm. If a blizzard drops a load of snow, will you be able to leave your camp in safety? If nearby slopes, now lightly dusted with snow, become heavily laden, could they become avalanche-prone?

With deep snow cover, the choice of sites becomes, in some respects, easier. You don't need a flat spot, because you can make one. You don't need to avoid logs, roots, and rocks, because they're buried. You don't need a water source (although a source of liquid water is a major score), because you can melt snow.

Whether the landscape is frozen or not, avoiding human pollution of natural water sources must be a high priority. Winter camps must not leave trash, gear, food, or spilled fuel behind. The snow will eventually go away, but your garbage will remain. Set your camp at least 200 feet (about 70 adult paces) from springs, streams, rivers, ponds, and lakes. In some areas, out of a desperate need to preserve water quality and the overall quality of the wilderness experience, land managers have established regulations that require camps to be located an acceptable distance from water sources.

Wind, often a blessing on a bug-ridden summer day, tends to be a curse in winter. Gusty winds can rattle ice-stiffened tent walls throughout the night, keeping you awake. Windblown snow can bury the door of the tent, and it may find its way through the tiniest opening to drift across your bedroom. If the view from an open ridge is irresistible, hope for a calm night. Better yet, choose a site out of the wind or the possibility of wind. The lee side of a broad ridge may be a good choice, as long as you stay off slopes that could avalanche. A site behind natural windbreaks—a thick stand of trees, a large rock, a rise in the ground—is another possibility, but remember that windbreaks create natural snowdrifts roughly five times longer than the breaks are high. In the open, you can build a windbreak around your shelter.

Choose higher or lower campsites based on the weather and temperature. Calm, cold air sinks, keeping the upper end of a valley slightly warmer than the lower end. On blustery nights, however, higher ground may catch the wind and be colder than lower, protected sites. Always avoid the lowest ground in the area, such as a valley bottom, where the frosty air will settle overnight. If possible, select a site that will catch the early-morning sun, adding many degrees of joy to your own rising. Atop a knoll protected by trees is often an excellent spot.

Tents

Unless the snowpack is unusually dense—dense enough to support your weight—you'll need to ski-pack a platform for your tent. Wearing your skis, walk back and forth over an area about twice the size of the "footprint" of the tent until the snow is firmly packed. The extra space compressed around the tent will come in handy: you can set up the tent more easily, since you won't have to wear your skis, and you'll have room to move around outside the tent without putting on your skis.

It's going to be an hour—more or less—before the snow platform sinters enough to walk on it without skis. Use this time to ski-pack a route to the latrine areas and a water source, and a platform for your snow kitchen.

Consider building a snow wall on the windward side of the tent as a windbreak, or all around the tent if the wind doesn't come steadily from one direction. For maximum effectiveness, the windbreak must be close to the tent. When the winds are severe and a sheltered spot is unobtainable, dig down into the snow a couple of feet before stomping out the tent platform. This will provide some protection from the wind while you're building the platform and more protection for the tent.

Pitch your tent with a low end toward the wind and the door at a ninety-degree angle to the wind, if possible. High wind or a snow load can put tremendous pressure on the nylon, so pitch the tent as tightly as possible. A tightly pitched tent is at its strongest. Stake the tent out snugly at all possible points. Stretch it tight via the reinforced points that allow taut lines.

Setting stakes in winter requires a particular technique. The stakes need to be pushed deep,

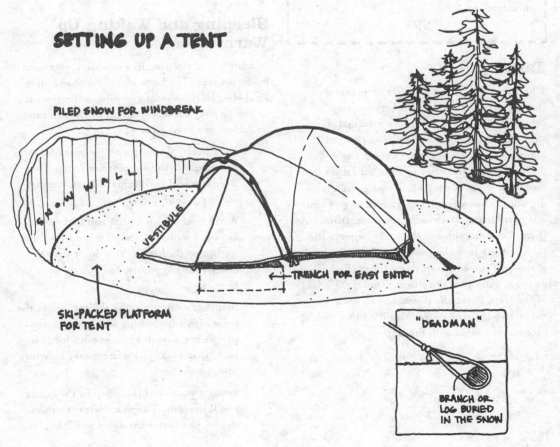

SETTING UP A TENT

PILED SNOW FOR WINDBREAK

SNOW WALL

VESTIBULE

TRENCH FOR EASY ENTRY

SKI-PACKED PLATFORM FOR TENT

"DEADMAN"

BRANCH OR LOG BURIED IN THE SNOW

Continued ➡

and the snow should be allowed to sinter around them. Even then, stakes might melt out over time, and the tent will lose its tautness. You can use skis, poles, and ice axes, if you don't need them for their intended purposes, as stakes to provide greater stability.

Snow also allows the possibility of staking out the tent with a few deadmen. If possible, use a stick one to two feet long as a deadman. Buried gear—like a stuff sack filled with snow—also works, but it can be hard to dig back out after a night or two of sintering. To set a deadman, tie it with at least a couple of feet of cord to a stake-out point on the tent. The cord should be looped around the deadman, with the knot—a taut-line hitch, ideally—far enough from the deadman that it will be above the snow when placed; this will allow for tightening later on. Stomp aggressively into the snow with your booted foot at the appropriate distance. Set the deadman in the bottom of the stomped hole and fill the hole with snow. Then stomp on the surface to help it set. You should place all of your deadmen and let them sinter before tightening any of them.

If a strong wind whips through camp before the tent is set, the procedure is more problematic. Securely stake out the upwind side of the tent before placing any of the tent poles. If the tent has a fly, it is less likely to become a kite if someone holds on to it while someone else attaches it to the tent. Holding the fly down during a strong wind also helps minimize the tangle of knots in the lines attached to the fly.

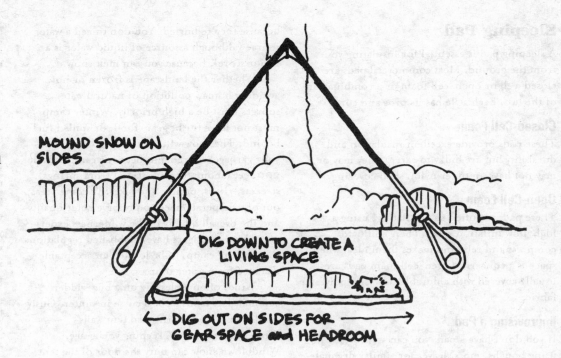

MOUND SNOW ON SIDES

DIG DOWN TO CREATE A LIVING SPACE

← DIG OUT ON SIDES FOR → GEAR SPACE and HEADROOM

SETTING UP A TARP

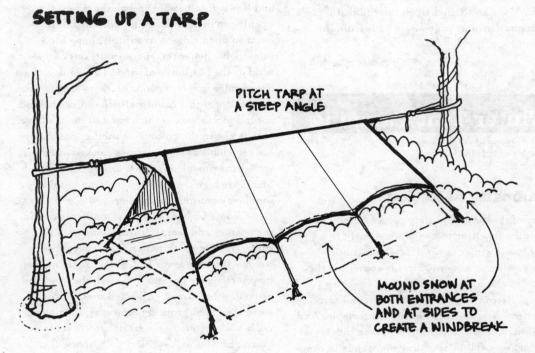

PITCH TARP AT A STEEP ANGLE

MOUND SNOW AT BOTH ENTRANCES AND AT SIDES TO CREATE A WINDBREAK

NOLS Tip
Set Up Early
Begin setting up camp early, while you still have light. Trying to pitch a tent in the dark increases the risk not only of fatigue and short tempers but also of accidents and damage to both relationships and the environment.

Tarps

Whether you're using a simple or pyramid-shaped tarp, the differences between tarp camping and tent camping are minimal. First, stomp out a platform and let it work-harden. Hang and secure the tarp at a steep angle—you definitely want the snow to slide off rather than build up. Once the tarp is hung between trees, dig out the snow from underneath to give yourself more living space and protection from wind. If you bevel the sides of the space beneath the tarp, cutting into the snow away from the living space, you can add even more room. Pack the dug-out snow into the spaces around the edges of the trap, especially if it has open ends, to enclose your living space. You'll end up with a nice room roofed with the tarp.

Sleeping and Waking Up Warm

In addition to sleeping in a safe spot, you need to sleep warm. The basic idea, says Shannon Rochelle, NOLS winter camping instructor, is to "enter your bag as warm and dry as you can be." Here are some tips:

· Eat a hearty dinner, with plenty of fat, and drink lots of fluids before retiring. You need the fuel and fluids to burn during the long, cold night.

· Warm yourself up before you bed down. Go for a walk, ski, shovel some snow, do sit-ups or push-ups. You don't want to enter your bag sweaty, but you do want to be toasty.

· Before crawling into the shelter, brush the snow off your clothing and boots (some people use a small whisk broom for this job). Don't take any unnecessary moisture into the shelter.

· Remove your clothing down to the layers you'll sleep in. The more layers you wear to bed, the better insulated you'll be. You

Tidying up
Falling or windblown snow may bury anything left lying around. Before hitting the sack, tidy up the camp. Some nights, tidying up won't make a major difference, but wise winter campers are storm-proof every night. Better to be safe than sorry. Pick up litter, and store all items in packs or in the kitchen. Stick your skis and poles upright in the snow (but don't let the baskets of your ski poles stick into the snow and get frozen, requiring digging and possible damage to remove them). Then tether lightweight sleds to the skis or poles. Move all your clothing into the tent or under the tarp, and store your pack in the shelter or secured to your sled. Also, fill the stoves and get things ready for morning so you can minimize chores for the following day.

Continued ➡

are seeking a balance, however. Too much clothing compresses the dead air space, reducing your insulation. Too little clothing may let the chill in. And be sure to sleep in loose-fitting clothing: tight clothing reduces circulation.

- Replace any damp layers of clothing with dry layers. Take special care to sleep in dry socks. If your feet tend to get cold, wear down or synthetic booties, or shove your feet into a pile jacket or sweater.

- Sleep in a comfortable cap or a balaclava. The brain will sacrifice the rest of the body to save itself, so don't give it a reason.

- Place slightly damp clothing in your sleeping bag, near the trunk of your body, to dry overnight.

- Place extra dry layers of clothing inside your sleeping bag, if there's adequate room. They can also be shaped into a comfy pillow. Put outer layers that you aren't wearing between you and the ground for insulation. If the outer layers are relatively dry, put them between your sleeping bag and your top sleeping pad. If they're damp, put them between your sleeping pads.

- To prevent freezing, place leather boots and boot liners in your sleeping bag's stuff sack (turned inside out), and place the stuff sack between your legs.

- Put a full water bottle and a snack in your sleeping bag in case you need to fire up the internal furnace during the night. Or keep an insulated container of hot, sweet tea or chocolate in your tent. Be sure to distinguish the water bottle from the pee bottle.

- Sleep with your face out to prevent the moisture of respiration from building up in your bag. Wear a scarf around your neck or a neck gaiter rather than cinching up the drawcord of a mummy bag around your head.

- You'll probably wake up several times during the night, to urinate or just to change position. This is normal in cold weather. Don't waste energy trying to fight the urge to urinate. Moving around gets your circulation stirred up, generating a bit of heat.

Maintaining Warmth in the Morning

- Do a few sit-ups or stretches while still in your bag. This generates a little body heat before you expose yourself to the cold.

- Dress quickly to prevent loss of body heat. Put on your boots while they and your feet are still warm from the bag. It's much more efficient to maintain body heat than to generate it.

- Get the stove going, and stoke the internal furnace. There's nothing like a hot drink and a hot breakfast to ease the stress of the cold. Try to drink at least a quart of

liquid. Consider cooking extra food and packing it for a quick lunch.

- Move your stuff outside. Hang clothing that still feels damp on tree limbs or ski poles. Hang your sleeping bag inside out between your skis stuck in the snow. The outside air is generally drier than the air inside the shelter, and the drier the air, the faster your things will dry out.

- If you have a tent, pull the stakes (unless the wind is whipping through camp) and turn the tent on its side to allow the bottom to dry before packing it. Don't pack or haul any more weight than you need to.

- Use teamwork to help speed up the morning chores: have some people cook while others pack.

—From *NOLS Winter Camping*

"Leave No Trace" Campsite Selection

U.S. Department of Agriculture, Forest Service

Choose a campsite away from popular places for more solitude and privacy. Try to camp 200 feet or more from lakes, streams, meadows, and trails when you have a choice. There will be less chance of damage to fragile areas.

Select campsites in your local area that are designated or already well established. This will concentrate impacts in already disturbed places. Try to confine most activities to areas of the site that are already bare.

When camping in pristine places, disperse your activities and use extra care. Space the tents, kitchen, and latrine, and try to avoid repeated traffic over any area. Before leaving camp, naturalize the area by replacing rocks and scattering leaves and twigs around the site.

The best campsites are generally found on ridges, hills, or near canyon walls. These areas provide natural drainage so your camp will not flood. To hide it from view, arrange your camp-

site around trees, rocks, and shrubs. Beware of hazard trees, avalanche areas, potential hazards from falling rocks, or flash-flood sites.

Never ditch or build trenches around your tent because they can start soil erosion and create lasting scars. Limit your stay to as few nights as possible to avoid waste accumulation and injury to plants. One night in each campsite is best and will make it easier to **Leave No Trace!** of your visit when you depart.

Remember:

- Select a campsite 200 feet or more from trails, lakes, streams, and wet meadows.

- Hide your campsite from view.

- Don't dig ditches around the tents.

- Stay as few nights as possible in one place.

- Use designated or already impacted campsites when appropriate.

—From *Leave No Trace!: An Outdoor Ethic*

Log Cabins and Sod Shelters

Greg Davenport
Illustrations by Steven A. Davenport

Log Cabin (without Notches)

A log cabin is a long-term shelter that is most often used in cold and temperate climates. The logs provide a safe, stable, and insulated structure that delivers excellent protection from the elements. These structures can be built with an A-frame or lean-to-style roof. If you are alone and/or resources are limited, however, I recommend a lean-to roof design. When selecting logs to use, make sure the weight is not unmanageable. If alone, a log with a diameter of 6 inches or less is advised. The length of each log depends on your shelter size and on which wall it is going to be used.

Since the logs are not notched you will need to provide a framework that will hold them in

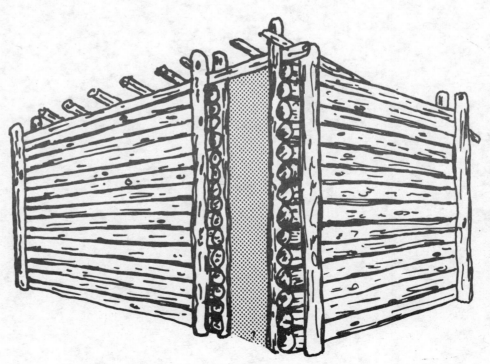

Log cabin shelter.

Continued ➜

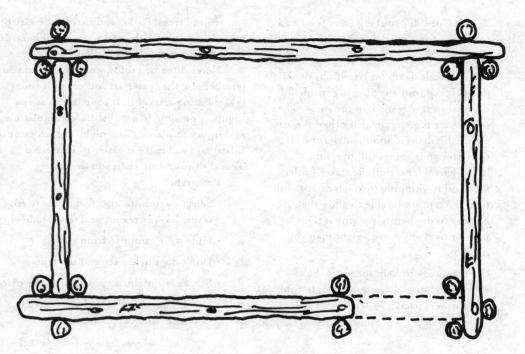

Building a log cabin that doesn't use notching requires the use of vertical poles to support the walls.

place. Gather fourteen strong 8- to 10-foot poles. At each of the four corners bury three of the poles (twelve total poles used) 8 to 12 inches into the ground and tap dirt around them to help hold them in place. Two feet to the left of the front right corner place two more poles. The 2-foot area will become your doorway. *Note*: All support poles are placed so they can hold the horizontal logs that create the shelter's wall.

Once all the support poles are in place, stack the logs between them. Use a moderate amount of straw-and-mud mortar to help hold them in place and seal up any openings.

A straw-and-mud mortar can be made by thoroughly mixing an equal amount of mud with a fibrous material like dry grass, straw, or ferns. Once dry, the mixture acts like extremely strong glue.

The back wall should be about 5 to 6 feet high and the front wall about 7 to 8 feet high. Run a log over the front wall and doorway so the sidewalls support it. Finish the walls by applying generous amounts of mortar inside and out.

Roof the shelter by placing logs side by side

Sod shelter.

(perpendicular to the doorway) until it is covered. Fill in all openings with your mud mortar and cover it with boughs, sod, brush, or duff. If you intend to build a fire inside, make sure you provide an adequate ventilation hole that can be opened and closed. The door can be covered with any appropriate material or you may choose to build a wooden one out of your available resources.

Sod Shelter

The sod shelter is most common in areas where there is a lack of trees. Sod is soil that has a strong root structure of grass or various vegetation holding it together. Sod can be used to build any number of shelter types—from a sod igloo to a small rectangular house. In most instances the sod is cut into 6- by 18-inch pieces of turf and laid in place like one might use a brick or block of packed snow. The roof will need a support structure stronger than the existing sod walls. Gather four poles that are approximately 10 feet long and vertically bury them 8–12 inches—one at each of the shelter's four corners. Tap dirt around them to make them more secure. Next, lash a pole to the top of the front two poles and another to the top of the back poles. Use the horizontal poles as the basic support structure for the roof. The roof may consist of poles laid side by side and lashed together, mats, thatching, or sod.

The Fire Pit

Since the shelter you build will become your home, creating an area for fire is important. The fire provides light, heat, cooking, and entertainment. If not used wisely, fire can cause burns and may even kill you. Before lighting any fire in your shelter, ensure there is enough ventilation to allow the smoke to escape and help prevent asphyxiation. A good fire pit is normally placed between the door and the center of the shelter. This location allows the back of the shelter to be used. For best results, dig a 2- to 3-foot circular fire pit that is approximately 8 inches deep and line the bottom and sides with stones. Caution: Be sure not to use stones from riverbeds or those that appear to retain moisture. The stones will hold the fire's heat, help prevent sparks from flying across the shelter and onto your sleeping mat, and ensure adequate oxygen circulates under the fire. To decrease the smoke within your house, use wood that is less apt to smoke—dry, without bark or lichen, and pitch free.

—From *Wilderness Living*

Travel on Land

Desert Climates

Greg Davenport
Illustrations by Steven Davenport and Ken Davenport

Deserts present a survivor with a myriad of problems, including water shortages, intense heat, wide temperature ranges, sparse vegetation, sandstorms, and surface soil that is potentially irritating to the skin. There are some twenty deserts around the world, covering about 15 percent of the total land surface. Understanding the various types of deserts will help you overcome the multitude of problems each can present.

Most deserts get less than 10 inches (25 centimeters) of rainfall a year and/or have a very high rate of evaporation. What little rain there is does not come throughout the year, but usually occurs in big bursts and at irregular intervals. In some instances, dry intervals extend over several years. The desert surface is often so dry that, even during hard downpours, the water runs off and evaporates before soaking into the ground.

Continued ➤

Most deserts lie in high-pressure zones where limited cloud cover makes the earth's surface vulnerable to the sun's radiation. As a result of constant sun exposure, the area heats up quickly, creating high temperatures. These high temperatures cause surface water to evaporate quickly. In areas with strong winds, the rate of evaporation is greatly increased.

Types of Deserts and How They Form

Deserts are classified by their location and weather pattern. There are high-pressure deserts, rain-shadow deserts, continental deserts, and cool coastal deserts.

High-Pressure Deserts

High-pressure deserts occur at the polar regions and between 20 and 30 degrees latitude on both sides of the equator. These deserts are located in areas of high atmospheric pressure where ongoing weather patterns cause dry air to descend. As the dry air descends, it warms up and absorbs much of the moisture in the area.

HIGH-PRESSURE DESERTS IN THE POLAR REGIONS

People often don't think of the polar regions as having deserts because of the cold temperatures. But there are polar areas with an annual precipitation of less than 10 inches a year that qualify as deserts. A polar desert rarely has temperatures over 50 degrees F and often has day and night temperature changes that cross over the freezing point of water.

HIGH-PRESSURE DESERTS BETWEEN 20 AND 30 DEGREES LATITUDE

High-pressure deserts located between 20 and 30 degrees latitude north or south of the equator are hot as a result of the wind's weather pattern and their proximity to the equator. These deserts have been known to reach temperatures as high as 130 degrees F. Most of the world's deserts, including the Arabian Desert and the Sahara Desert, are located in this area.

Rain-Shadow Deserts

Rain-shadow deserts occur as a result of a mountain range's effects on the prevailing winds. As wind travels over a mountain range, it cools and dumps its moisture in the form of rain or snow. As it descends to lower elevations on the other side of the mountain range, the wind becomes very dry and warm. Unless moisture is provided in some other form, a rain-shadow desert will form on the protected side of the mountain range as a result. Rain-shadow deserts include the Patagonian Desert, created by the Andes, and the Great Basin Desert, created by the Cascade Range.

Continental Deserts

Continental deserts occur in the centers of large continents. As inland winds travel from the sea over land, they lose moisture in the form of rain, and by the time they reach the center of a large continent, they are very dry. Continental deserts include portions of the Australian Desert and the Gobi Desert.

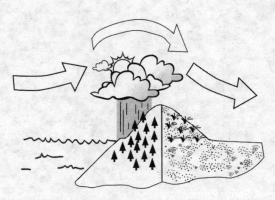

A rain-shadow desert forms when air loses its moisture as it travels over a mountain range.

Cool Coastal Deserts

Cool coastal deserts are the result of the cold ocean currents that parallel the western coastline near the Tropics of Cancer and Capricorn. At these locations, the cold ocean current touches a warm landmass, and as a result, almost no moisture is transferred from the ocean's cold water to the air that flows over the adjoining coastline. The descending air mass, which is already dry, becomes even drier. These deserts are some of the driest in the world. Cool coastal deserts include the Atacama Desert of South America and Mexico's Baja Desert.

Desert Characteristics

Terrain

Approximately 20 percent of the world's deserts are covered in sand that often resembles unmoving ocean waves. Half of all deserts are gravel plains—extensive areas of level or rolling, treeless country created by the wind's removal of ground soil, leaving only loose pebbles and cobbles. The remaining desert terrains include scattered barren mountain ranges; rocky plateaus, often seen as steep-walled canyons; and salt marshes, flat desolate areas with large salt deposits.

Climate

Deserts may be both hot and cold and may or may not have seasonal rainfall. However, most deserts have large temperature swings between day and night as a result of low humidity and clear skies. In addition, desert winds increase the already prevalent dryness in the atmosphere.

Vegetation

Little plant life is found in deserts due to the hostile environment created by the lack of water and temperature extremes. Plants that survive do so through drought escaping, rapidly reproducing when rain arrives; drought resistance, storing water in their stems and leaves; drought enduring, efficiently absorbing what little water they receive; or obtaining water from sources other than precipitation. As an adaption to the sun's unrelenting heat, many desert plants have small leaves oriented in a near vertical position. To avoid being consumed by herbivores, most desert plants have thorns, spines, and chemical compounds such as tannins and resins.

Animals

A wide assortment of wildlife can be found in deserts. In order to survive, most creatures avoid the temperature extremes. Most small game

Rain-shadow desert.

Gobi Desert.

Continued ➡

animals live in burrows during the day and come out at night, and some remain dormant during the rainless seasons. Larger game animals are often active during the day but routinely seek shade during the hottest hours. Most desert creatures have learned to compensate for the lack of water by developing the ability to meet this need from the food they metabolize.

—From *Surviving the Desert*

Desert Terrains, Environment, and Hazards

U.S. Army

Terrain

Most arid areas have several types of terrain. The five basic desert terrain types are—

- Mountainous (High Altitude).
- Rocky plateau.
- Sand dunes.
- Salt marshes.
- Broken, dissected terrain ("gebel" or "wadi").

Desert terrain makes movement difficult and demanding. Land navigation will be extremely difficult as there may be very few landmarks. Cover and concealment may be very limited; therefore, the threat of exposure to the enemy remains constant.

Mountain Deserts

Scattered ranges or areas of barren hills or mountains separated by dry, flat basins characterize mountain deserts. High ground may rise gradually or abruptly from flat areas to several thousand meters above sea level. Most of the infrequent rainfall occurs on high ground and runs off rapidly in the form of flash floods. These floodwaters erode deep gullies and ravines and deposit sand and gravel around the edges of the basins. Water rapidly evaporates, leaving the land as barren as before, although there may be short-lived vegetation. If enough water enters the basin to compensate for the rate of evaporation, shallow lakes may develop, such as the Great Salt Lake in Utah, or the Dead Sea. Most of these lakes have a high salt content.

Rocky Plateau Deserts

Rocky plateau deserts have relatively slight relief interspersed with extensive flat areas with quantities of solid or broken rock at or near the surface. There may be steep-walled, eroded valleys, known as wadis in the Middle East and arroyos or canyons in the United States and Mexico. Although their flat bottoms may be superficially attractive as assembly areas, the narrower valleys can be extremely dangerous to men and material due to flash flooding after rains. The Golan Heights is an example of a rocky plateau desert.

Sandy or Dune Deserts

Sandy or dune deserts are extensive flat areas covered with sand or gravel. "Flat" is a relative term, as some areas may contain sand dunes that are over 300 meters high and 16 to 24 kilometers long. Trafficability in such terrain will

depend on the windward or leeward slope of the dunes and the texture of the sand. Other areas, however, may be flat for 3,000 meters and more. Plant life may vary from none to scrub over 2 meters high. Examples of this type of desert include the edges of the Sahara, the empty quarter of the Arabian Desert, areas of California and New Mexico, and the Kalahari in South Africa.

Salt Marshes

Salt marshes are flat, desolate areas, sometimes studded with clumps of grass but devoid of other vegetation. They occur in arid areas where rainwater has collected, evaporated, and left large deposits of alkali salts and water with a high salt concentration. The water is so salty it is undrinkable. A crust that may be 2.5 to 30 centimeters thick forms over the saltwater.

In arid areas there are salt marshes hundreds of kilometers square. These areas usually support many insects, most of which bite. Avoid salt marshes. This type of terrain is highly corrosive to boots, clothing, and skin. A good example is the Shat-el-Arab waterway along the Iran-Iraq border.

Broken Terrain

All arid areas contain broken or highly dissected terrain. Rainstorms that erode soft sand and carve out canyons form this terrain. A wadi may range from 3 meters wide and 2 meters deep to several hundred meters wide and deep. The direction is takes varies as much as its width and

depth. It twists and turns and forms a mazelike pattern. A wadi will give you good cover and concealment, but do not try to move through it because it is very difficult terrain to negotiate.

Environmental Factors

Surviving and evading the enemy in an arid area depends on what you know and how prepared you are for the environmental conditions you will face. Determine what equipment you will need, the tactics you will use, and the environment's impact on them and you.

In a desert area there are seven environmental factors that you must consider—

- Low rainfall.
- Intense sunlight and heat.
- Wide temperature range.
- Sparse vegetation.
- High mineral content near ground surface.
- Sandstorms.
- Mirages.

Low Rainfall

Low rainfall is the most obvious environmental factor in an arid area. Some desert areas receive less than 10 centimeters of rain annually, and this rain comes in brief torrents that quickly run off the ground surface. You cannot survive long without water in high desert temperatures. In a desert survival situation, you must first consider "How much water do I have?" and "Where are other water sources?"

TYPES OF HEAT GAIN

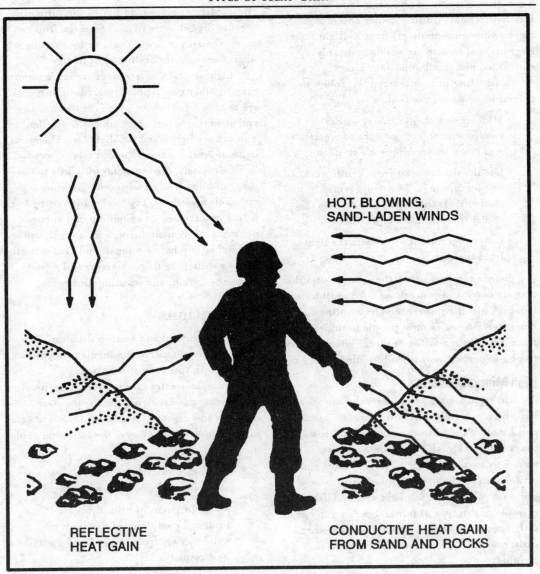

HOT, BLOWING, SAND-LADEN WINDS

REFLECTIVE HEAT GAIN

CONDUCTIVE HEAT GAIN FROM SAND AND ROCKS

Continued →

Intense Sunlight and Heat

Intense sunlight and heat are present in all arid areas. Air temperature can rise as high as 60 degrees C (140 degrees F) during the day. Heat gain results from direct sunlight, hot blowing winds, reflective heat (the sun's rays bouncing off the sand), and conductive heat from direct contact with the desert sand and rock.

The temperature of desert sand and rock averages 16 to 22 degrees C (30 to 40 degrees F) more than that of the air. For instance, when the air temperature is 43 degrees C (110 degrees F), the sand temperature may be 60 degrees C (140 degrees F).

Intense sunlight and heat increase the body's need for water. To conserve your body fluids and energy, you will need a shelter to reduce your exposure to the heat of the day. Travel at night to lessen your use of water.

Radios and sensitive items of equipment exposed to direct intense sunlight will malfunction.

Wide Temperature Range

Temperatures in arid areas may get as high as 55 degrees C (131 degrees F) during the day and as low as 10 degrees C (50 degrees F) during the night. The drop in temperature at night occurs rapidly and will chill a person who lacks warm clothing and is unable to move about. The cool evenings and nights are the best times to work or travel. If your plan is to rest at night, you will find a wool sweater, long underwear, and a wool stocking cap extremely helpful.

Sparse Vegetation

Vegetation is sparse in arid areas. You will therefore have trouble finding shelter and camouflaging your movements. During daylight hours large areas of terrain are visible and easily controlled by a small opposing force.

If traveling in hostile territory, follow the principles of desert camouflage—

- Hide or seek shelter in dry washes (wadis) with thicker growths of vegetation and cover from oblique observation.

- Use the shadows cast from brush, rocks, or outcroppings. The temperature in shaded areas will be 11 to 17 degrees C cooler than the air temperature.

- Cover objects that will reflect the light from the sun.

Before moving, survey the area for sites that provide cover and concealment. You will have trouble estimating distance. The emptiness of desert terrain causes most people to underestimate distance by a factor of three: What appears to be 1 kilometer away is really 3 kilometers away.

High Mineral Content

All arid regions have areas where the surface soil has a high mineral content (borax, salt, alkali, and lime). Material in contact with this soil wears out quickly, and water in these areas is extremely hard and undrinkable. Wetting your uniform in such water to cool off may cause a skin rash. The Great Salt Lake area in Utah is an example of this type of mineral-laden water and soil. There is little or no plant life; therefore, shelter is hard to find. Avoid these areas if possible.

Sandstorms

Sandstorms (sand-laden winds) occur frequently in most deserts. The "Seistan" desert wind in Iran and Afghanistan blows constantly for up to 120 days. Within Saudi Arabia, winds average 3.2 to 4.8 kilometers per hour (kph) and can reach 112 to 128 kph in early afternoon. Expect major sandstorms and dust storms at least once a week.

The greatest danger is getting lost in a swirling wall of sand. Wear goggles and cover your mouth and nose with cloth. If natural shelter is unavailable, mark your direction of travel, lie down, and sit out the storm.

Dust and wind-blown sand interfere with radio transmissions. Therefore, be ready to use other means for signaling, such as pyrotechnics, signal mirrors, or marker panels, if available.

Mirages

Mirages are optical phenomena caused by the refraction of light through heated air rising from a sandy or stony surface. They occur in the interior of the desert about 10 kilometers from the coast. They make objects that are 1.5 kilometers or more away appear to move.

This mirage effect makes it difficult for you to identify an object from a distance. It also blurs distant range contours so much that you feel surrounded by a sheet of water from which elevations stand out as "islands."

The mirage effect makes it hard for a person to identify targets, estimate range, and see objects clearly. However, if you can get to high ground (3 meters or more above the desert floor), you can get above the superheated air close to the ground and overcome the mirage effect. Mirages make land navigation difficult because they obscure natural features. You can survey the area at dawn, dusk, or by moonlight when there is little likelihood of mirage.

Light levels in desert areas are more intense than in other geographic areas. Moonlit nights are usually crystal clear, winds die down, haze and glare disappear, and visibility is excellent. You can see lights, red flashlights, and blackout lights at great distances. Sound carries very far.

Conversely, during nights with little moonlight, visibility is extremely poor. Traveling is extremely hazardous. You must avoid getting lost, falling into ravines, or stumbling into enemy positions. Movement during such a night is practical only if you have a compass and have spent the day in a shelter, resting, observing and memorizing the terrain, and selecting your route.

Precautions

In a desert survival and evasion situation, it is unlikely that you will have a medic or medical supplies with you to treat heat injuries. Therefore, take extra care to avoid heat injuries. Rest during the day. Work during the cool evenings and nights. Use a buddy system to watch for heat injury, and observe the following guidelines:

- Make sure you tell someone where you are going and when you will return.

- Watch for signs of heat injury. If someone complains of tiredness or wanders away from the group, he may be a heat casualty.

- Drink water at least once an hour.

- Get in the shade when resting; do not lie directly on the ground.

- Do not take off your shirt and work during the day.

- Check the color of your urine. A light color means you are drinking enough water, a dark color means you need to drink more.

Desert Hazards

There are several hazards unique to desert survival. These include insects, snakes, thorned plants and cacti, contaminated water, sunburn, eye irritation, and climatic stress.

Insects of almost every type abound in the desert. Man, as a source of water and food, attracts lice, mites, wasps, and flies. They are extremely unpleasant and may carry diseases. Old buildings, ruins, and caves are favorite habitats of spiders, scorpions, centipedes, lice, and mites. These areas provide protection from the elements and also attract other wildlife. Therefore, take extra care when staying in these areas. Wear gloves at all times in the desert. Do not place your hands anywhere without first looking to see what is there. Visually inspect an area before sitting or lying down. When you get up, shake out and inspect your boots and clothing.

All desert areas have snakes. They inhabit ruins, native villages, garbage dumps, caves, and natural rock outcroppings that offer shade. Never go barefoot or walk through these areas without carefully inspecting them for snakes. Pay attention to where you place your feet and hands. Most snakebites result from stepping on or handling snakes. Avoid them. Once you see a snake, give it a wide berth.

—From *Survival (Field Manual 21–76)*

Desert Travel

Greg Davenport
Illustrations by Steven Davenport and Ken Davenport

Before heading into the desert, leave an itinerary with someone you can trust. Set up check-in times when you will let him or her know you are OK. This insurance is key to a short survival stay versus a lone one. If you don't check in, this person can let rescuers know your intended route of travel and initiate a search long before you'd otherwise be missed.

In a desert, limit the amount of travel you do in a survival situation. Leave an area only when it no longer meets your needs, rescue doesn't appear imminent, and you know where you are and have navigational skills. Travel in the desert increases your exposure to aridity and heat, and thus your need for water. To minimize the effects of the desert climate, follow these simple rules:

1. **Travel during the cooler hours**. Rest during the day in a shaded area, and travel in the early morning and late afternoon. Avoid travel in temperatures over 100 degrees F.

2. **Decrease exposure**. Wear proper desert clothing. Cover your body, including your arms and legs, and wear a hat that shades

Continued ➡

your head and neck. Use sunscreen on exposed areas to prevent sunburn.

3. **Ensure adequate water.** Before departing, drink enough water to ensure that you are well hydrated. So that you stay hydrated during travel in hot desert conditions, carry enough water to drink 1 quart per hour. Also make sure water sources are on your intended route of travel. If not, adjust your course so that they are.

How to Carry a Pack

The type of pack you carry will depend on personal preference, buy in a hot desert climate, an external frame pack is usually preferable because the frame allows air to flow between the pack and your back. To carry a pack on trail, organize your gear so that the heavier items are on top and close to your back. This method places most of the pack's weight on your hips, making it easier to carry. For off-trail travel, organize the pack so that the heavy items are close to the back, from the pack's top to its bottom. With this method, most of the pack's weight is carried by your shoulders and back, allowing you better balance. Pack your larger survival items in the pack so that they can be easily accessed, and carry a smaller survival kit on your person.

Basic Travel Techniques

Breaking Trail and Setting the Pace

If traveling in a team, the person breaking trail is working harder than anyone else, and this job needs to be traded off at regular intervals among the members of a team. The leader should set a pace distance and speed that are comfortable for all team members.

Kick-Stepping

When in scree (small rocks or sand), kick-stepping will make your ascent much easier. Using the weight of your leg, swing the toe of your boot into the rocks, creating a step that supports at least the ball of your foot if going straight up, or at least half of your foot if traversing. When going uphill, lean forward until your body is perpendicular to the earth's natural surface—not that of the hill.

Plunge-stepping.

Plunge-Stepping (Down-Climbing)

Plunge-stepping is similar to kick-steeping, except that you are going downhill and kicking your heels rather than your toes into the slope. Slightly bend the knees, and lean backward until your body is perpendicular to the ground at the base of the hill—not the hill's slope.

Traversing

Traversing, or diagonal climbing, is a quick and easy method for getting up or down a hill. When traversing a hill, it may be necessary to slightly shorten your strides as the grade changes. The same technique can be used to descend a hill.

Rest Step

When walking uphill, use a rest step, which is done by locking the knee with each step. This process takes the weight off the muscle, allowing it to rest, and places it on the skeletal system. For best results, you'll need to take a short pause with each step.

Using a Ridgeline to Your Advantage

When traveling in mountainous terrain, try to stay high on the ridgeline as much as you can. It's better to travel a little farther than to deal with the constant up-and-down travel associated with frequent elevation changes.

Terrain Issues

Loose Rock Surface

Some deserts have a rock floor that is either extremely firm or on occasion soft and brittle. The biggest problem with a firm, rocky desert surface is that it can be hard on your feet and ankles. Constant awareness is necessary to avoid a twist or break that can turn a nice hike into a survival situation.

Rocky Peaks

Although it might be tempting to climb a rocky desert peak, be careful. Often people start to climb up a rock only to discover that it is too difficult to reach the top. At this point, most people try to downclimb, and many are surprised to find that the route down is much more difficult than it was going up. If the downclimb becomes too hard, you may slip and get hurt or become stranded on the rock.

Canyons and Similar Structures

A canyon can be like a maze, and unless you have good navigational skills, it's easy to get lost. Before entering a canyon, make sure you can get back out. Do your research. Avoid canyons during peak flash flood seasons. A flash flood in a canyon has the same potential as an avalanche for sweeping you away and taking your life.

Creeks

If you need to cross a small creek, loosen your pack's shoulder straps and undo your waistband so you can quickly remove the pack if you fall in. Cross the stream in a shallow area by way of a diagonal downstream route. For added stability, use a long walking staff for support. You can also decrease the current's impact on your legs by placing the stick on the upstream side of your position to form a V with you in its center.

Lava Beds

Lava beds create unending areas of uneven, hard-to-negotiate terrain. These areas are often filled with obstacles that you cannot go around and that require you to move from one elevated rock to another. Make sure of your footing with each move before you transfer your weight, and always be ready to move on to another location should the one you're on become unstable.

Dunes

Sand dunes form as a result of the wind's movement off the sand. It is far easier to hike on the windward side of a slope, where the sand is packed and more stable. On the leeward side, the sand is soft, and it requires far greater work to get from one point to another.

Dry Lakes

Dry lakebeds are often hard, crusty surfaces that are devoid of visible landmarks. Navigation through these areas should be avoided unless other options are not available. If you do travel through a dry lake, keep an adequate pace count—it may be the only way you'll be able to identify your current location.

Kick-stepping.

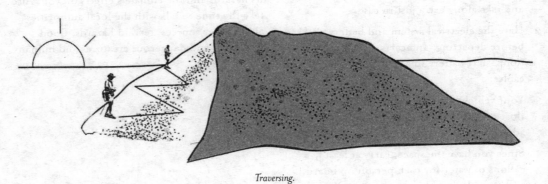

Traversing.

Continued ➡

Hazards

Extreme Temperatures

Deserts are known to have temperature extremes, with hot days and cold nights. Travel during midday is not advised; limit your travel to the morning and evening hours.

Sandstorms

Sandstorms are a common occurrence in most deserts, and it will be impossible to travel during these times. The potential for eye injury and skin irritation make it important to find or establish a shelter until the storm subsides. In addition, when a storm is present, it doesn't take much for the sand to ruin exposed electronic devices. Take the time to protect them from exposure.

Flash Floods

Avoid dry riverbeds, canyons, and other depressions during the flash flood season. A flash flood has the same life-threatening potential as an avalanche and can easily sweep you up and carry you away. In fact, these floods have been known to originate from up to 100 miles upriver, catching travelers unaware in an area where the sun is shining.

Mirages

A mirage is an optical illusion that is often seen in the desert or on a hot road. It occurs when alternate layers of hot and cool air distort light, creating the appearance of a sheet of water where none exists. Mirages make it difficult to identify land features during the day. If mirages are occurring, it may be best to triangulate and plan your routes of travel at dawn or dusk or during moonlight hours.

Car Travel

You can travel great distances in a vehicle. The opportunity to do this allows you to see a vast array of desert beauty, but it also takes you farther away from civilization. If you break down, you may be so far from town that your survival odds will greatly depend on what you brought with you and how well you understand the area you are in. Because desert climates are not user-friendly, it's best to leave the driving to someone experienced in such regions. If, however, you decide to do it yourself, leave an itinerary with a friend with specific check-in times and directions on what to do if you don't check in, and observe the following guidelines:

1. Use a vehicle you know has had proper maintenance and is capable of handling the terrain you intend to travel into. Personally check all the fluid levels before you depart, and take along extra just in case.

2. Have the electrical system and battery checked before departing, and carry a spare battery or jump-start battery in addition to jumper cables.

3. Your vehicle's tires should be wide enough to float on sand and have an aggressive tread for adequate traction.

4. Since you have the space, carry at least 5 gallons of water for each person on board, and an additional large survival kit beyond what you might have in your backpack.

5. Before traveling on a rocky desert, make sure your vehicle has enough clearance to handle the terrain.

6. It's best not to drive on a sandy desert, as it's easy to bog down and get stuck. If you must, put your vehicle in four-wheel-drive and let some air out of the tires to increase surface contact. Avoid speed fluctuations and hard turns.

7. Avoid driving on silt and dry lakes unless you have no other option. Silt often has a false floor that won't be able to handle the weight of your vehicle. Dry lakes often have areas with false floors or that are too damp to support your vehicle. In either instance, the vehicle is likely to break through or bog down and get stuck. If you have to cross, take the time to get out of the vehicle and survey the situation. Look for an area where the ground appears solid and is more apt to handle your vehicle's weight.

8. Water crossings should be surveyed before you begin. Make sure the ground is hard enough to support your vehicle and the water is not too deep. In addition, look the selected route over carefully to ensure that your vehicle has enough clearance.

9. If your vehicle breaks down, stay with it. It's the best signal you have and provides a multitude of items that you can use to improvise to meet your various needs.

Survival Tips

Travel Only in Morning and Evening

Limit your travel to morning and evening hours. During the day, it's too hot and you increase your odds of developing a heat injury. During the night, your vision becomes impaired and it may be hard to avoid the creatures that are out looking for a tasty meal.

Traveling in Survival Situations

If you're in a survival situation and rescue doesn't appear imminent, the area you're in doesn't meet your needs, and you have solid navigational skills, you may elect to travel out to safety. If you do, leave a note for potential rescuers giving your time of departure, route, and intended destination. In addition, mark your trail by tying flags to branches or other landmarks and/or breaking branches.

Familiarize Yourself with the Area

Before planning a weeklong trip into the desert, become familiar with the area by taking short trips that pose little risk. Become accustomed to its hazards and the climate's effects on you. Also take the time to talk with the local authorities about water sources, terrain hazards, flood potential, and dangerous creatures and humans.

—From *Surviving the Desert*

Dressing for the Desert

Greg Davenport
Illustrations by Steven Davenport and Ken Davenport

It is estimated that over one million Americans will develop skin cancer each year. Considering these statistics, it is hard to imagine why an individual would travel into a desert without protection from the sun. Desert hikers can receive direct sun exposure to their heads, necks, arms, and legs. Some believe their clothing will protect them and dress in long-sleeved shirts and full pants and wear broad-rimmed hats. However, unless this clothing is able to block at least 93 percent of the sun's ultraviolet (UV) rays, damage will still occur. Your clothing's ability to block out UV radiation is based on its construction (knit or woven), color, and fiber count, and whether it is wet or dry. Knit fabrics tend to provide better protection than woven; dark colors are thought to provide five times more protection than white; clothes with high fiber count have better protection; and wet clothes tend to lose their ability to block UV penetration. A tightly woven cotton shirt blocks out approximately 86 percent of the sun's harmful UV rays and even less when wet. Polyester, on the other hand, has been shown to provide two to three times more UV protection than other fabrics of equal quality.

In recent years, the clothing industry has recognized the need for UV protective fabrics and has designed clothes that protect wearers from harmful solar radiation. These clothes will become as commonplace as Gore-Tex has for wet environments. Most of these clothes are variations of nylon and work by reflecting or absorbing the UV rays. When absorbed, the UV is transmitted across the fiber and released externally as heat. Solar Weave is an example of this type of fabric and provides 97 to 99 percent UV protection.

Understanding UV, SPF, and UPF

Since many fabrics will list their sun protection factor (SPF) or ultraviolet protection factor (UPF) instead of their UV protection, you will need to understand how they relate to one another. SPF relates to the degree to which a sun cream or lotion provides protection for the skin against the sun. The rating describes how much longer you can stay in the sun before your skin starts to burn. In other words, a rating of SPF 10 means you can stay in the sun 10 times longer with the sunscreen on than without it. SPF rating was developed for lotion and accounts for its evaporation, but this rating shouldn't be used to establish clothing's protection value. However, it often is. For optimal results, clothes need 93 percent UV protection, which equates to an SPF rating of approximately 15. A UV rating of 95 is equivalent to an SPF of 20; a UV rating of 97 is equivalent to an SPF of 33; and a UV rating of 99 is equivalent to an SPF of 100.

Ultraviolet protection factor (UPF) details how much UV radiation passes through a garment. A fabric with a UPF rating of 30 allows

Continued ➡

1/30 of the sun's UV radiation to pass through. There are three categories of UPF protection:

Good	UPF rating between 15 and 24
Very good	UPF rating between 25 and 39
Excellent	UPF rating between 40 and 50

Shirts and Pants

When selecting shirts and pants for hot climates, you must consider the sun's effects. In addition to heat injuries, long-term sun exposure increases your chance of skin cancer. Wearing sun-protective clothing is one way to reduce these risks. Garments made with sun-protective fabrics have an ultraviolet protection factor (UPF) rating that designates how much ultraviolet (UV) radiation the fabric absorbs.

These ratings are based on a new garment that is dry and not worn too tight. Over time, older garments will lose some protective qualities due to repeated washings and basic wear and tear. Although darker colors provide better UV protection, a balance between this factor and how much heat is absorbed into the fabric must be considered. Clothes that are light-colored, such as off-white, tan, or khaki, tend to absorb less heat and are probably better for this environment.

Shirt

In hot climates, I often wear a lightweight, long-sleeved, well-ventilated nylon shirt with a UPF of 30 or more. Button tabs secure the sleeves when they're rolled up. In addition, shirts with a vented back help keep you extra cool. Nylon shirts dry quickly and provide better wind protection than polyester shirts. They are excel-

Dressing for the desert.

lent option for desert travel. These shirts can be worn alone or over a lightweight loose-fitting polyester shirt.

Pants

Look for the same qualities in pants as in a shirt. The ideal design is made from lightweight nylon, provides UV protection, has good ventilation, and can easily convert to shorts. Cargo pockets add the ability to store emergency survival gear; any pants you buy should include this option. Pants with a drawcord at the cuff help keep critters and dirt away from your skin. Nylon pants are fast drying and provide better wind protection than most alternatives. They are an excellent option for desert travel.

Parka and Rain Pants

Although rain probably won't be a problem in the desert, wind will, so a lightweight parka and rain pants are essential. They are available in nylon with a polyurethane coating, breathable waterproof coating, or breathable laminated waterproof membrane (Gore-Tex). Some parkas come with an insulating liner that can be zipped inside. In hot climates choose a parka shell that is lightweight yet durable. Look for the following criteria when choosing a parka and rain pants:

Appropriate Size

These garments should be big enough that you can comfortably add wicking and insulating layers underneath without compromising your movement. The parka's lower end should extend beyond your hips to keep wind and moisture away from the top of your pants.

Dual Separating Zippers

Zippers should separate at both ends.

Ventilation Adjustment

Parkas should have openings for ventilation in front, at your waist, under your arms, and at your wrist. For rain pants, the openings should be located in the front and along the outside of the lower legs, extending to about mid-calf, making it easier to put on or remove your boots. For females, pants are available with a zipper that extends down and around the crotch. The added benefit is obvious. These openings can be adjusted with zippers, Velcro, or drawstrings.

Sealed Seams

Seams should be taped or well bonded so that moisture will not penetrate through the clothing.

Accessible Pockets

What good is a pocket if you can't get to it? In addition, the openings should have protective rain baffles. Rain baffles will help keep blowing sand from damaging zippers or entering pockets.

Brimmed Hood

The brim will help protect you from the sun and, if it does rain, will channel moisture away from your eyes and face.

Boots

Sandals are not appropriate footwear for desert hikes. You need a pair of sturdy boots to provide support and protect your feet. For hot climates, lightweight leather/fabric boots are best. These are popular fair-weather boots, as they are

lighter and dry faster than all-leather boots. The Danner Desert Acadia is a great boot for desert wear. It has an 8-inch upper made from leather and 1,000-denier Cordura that provides good ankle support and circulation, a liner that promotes rapid drying, and a Vibram outsole and rubber/polyurethane midsole that provide enough stability for any desert terrain. If you buy new boots, break them in before your trip.

Your boots will protect you better if you keep them clean. Wash off dirt and debris using a mild soap that won't damage leather.

Socks

Socks need to provide adequate insulation, reduce friction, and wick and absorb moisture away from the skin. Socks most often are made of wool, polyester, nylon, or an acrylic material. Wool tends to dry more slowly than the other materials but is still a great option. Cotton should be avoided, as it loses its insulating qualities when wet. For best results, wear two pairs of socks. The inner sock (often made of polyester or silk) wicks the moisture away from the foot; the outer sock (often a wool or synthetic blend material) provides the insulation that protects your feet. Keep your feet dry, and change your socks at least once a day. If any hot spots develop on your feet, immediately apply moleskin to prevent blisters from forming.

Gloves

Gloves provide hand protection and decrease radiant heat loss from the hands. The type you need depends on your activity. I often take a pair of lightweight fingerless fleece gloves, which protect me during most activities and keep my hands warm during cold desert nights.

Headgear

When traveling in the hot desert sun, it's essential to protect your head, face, and neck from harmful UV rays and sunburn. Headgear should be worn at all times during the day. A hat or headdress also will reduce radiant heat loss on cold desert nights. If you are working during cold nights and begin to overheat, remove your headgear only when other options, such as slowing down and adjusting your clothing layers, have not cooled you down enough. Neck-draping Sahara hats, wide-brimmed bush hats, and Arab head cloths are three great options.

Sahara Hat

The Sahara hat has a wide forward bill that provides UPF sun protection and shades the eyes and face, as well as a rear cape that shields the neck and creates a dead air space that helps keep you cooler. The ideal Sahara hat has a moisture-wicking headband that keeps sweat out of your eyes and a nylon strap that allows you to adjust the hat to a proper fit. This hat style is ideal for use in a desert climate.

Wide-Brimmed Bush Hat

A bush hat for the desert should be lightweight and durable while providing high UPF sun protection from the sun's harmful rays. It should repel moisture, dry quickly, and have a wide brim that shades the face and neck. A moisture-wicking headband will keep sweat out of your eyes, crown grommets will help increase air circulation, and a chinstrap will keep you

Continued →

Wide-brimmed bush hat.

from losing your hat to a sudden gust of wind. These hats are often made of nylon or a similar material.

ARAB-STYLE HEADDRESS

A turban headdress usually consists of a long scarf of linen or silk wound around the head and neck. The kaffiyeh is similar but is draped over the head. To make a kaffiyeh, take a rectangular piece of cloth, fold it diagonally, and then drape it over your head. The cloth is fastened to the head by an exterior headband.

Eye Protection

Goggles or sunglasses with side shields that filter out UV wavelengths from the sunlight and reflections off bright sand are a must for travel in desert environments. It doesn't take long for the sun's reflection off the ground to burn the eyes, and once this occurs, you will have several days of eye pain along with light sensitivity, tearing, and a foreign body sensation. Since the symptoms of the burn usually don't show up for four to six hours after exposure, your eyes can get burned without your even realizing it's happening. Once a burn occurs, you need to get out of the light, remove contacts if wearing them, and cover both eyes with a sterile dressing until the light sensitivity subsides. If pain medication is available, you'll probably need to use it. Once healed, protect your eyes to prevent another burn. If no goggles or sunglasses are available, improvise by covering the eyes with either a man-made or natural material with a narrow horizontal slit cut for each eye.

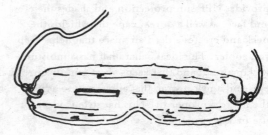
Improvised eye protection.

Skin Protection

In a hot desert environment, ultraviolet radiation from above and reflected off the ground can be very intense and can cause painful and potentially debilitating sunburn. The best way to avoid this problem is to wear loose-fitting clothes that provide adequate UV protection.

For skin that cannot be covered, use sunscreen or sunblock. Sunscreens work by absorbing the UV radiation and are available with various sun protection factor (SPF) ratings, which indicate how much longer than normal you can be exposed to UV radiation before burning. Sunblock reflects the UV radiation and is most often used for sensitive areas where intense exposure might occur, like the ears and nose. You need to constantly reapply these products throughout the day, as their effectiveness is lost over time and due to sweating.

Survival Tips

Avoid midday sun. In hot deserts, the harmful effects of the midday sun far outweigh any benefits of working during that time. Most survival essentials can be met during dawn and dusk. At these times the temperature are cooler and you're less apt to develop a heat-related injury. During the heat of the day, find a cool place to rest.

—From *Surviving the Desert*

Rain Forest Climate

Greg Davenport

Location

Most tropical rain forests are between 23.5 degrees north latitude and 23.5 degrees south latitude in South and Central America, Asia, Africa, and Australia. The largest rain forest is located in the Amazon River basin in Brazil and neighboring countries of South America. Other rain forests can be found in Asia (examples include Borneo, Republic of the Philippines, New Guinea, and Northern Australia) and Africa (along the Atlantic coast and the Congo River Basin). Small temperate rain forests exist in the northern and southern hemispheres. An example of this type of rain forest can be found in the Olympic Peninsula of Washington state, where rainfall and humidity are high and the winters are mild.

Distinguishing Characteristics

Rain forests typically have an abundance of lush vegetation, high temperatures, and excessive rainfall. Although only 7 percent of the earth is covered by rain forests, 50 percent or more of the earth's animal and plant life exist there. The vegetation can be from three to five stories with an upper canopy of trees ranging from 150 to 180 feet high. The density of the underlying layers depends upon how much sun penetrates the upper canopy. The more sun that gets through, the greater the density.

Average Temperature

Temperatures are greater than 64.5 degrees F with a monthly average of close to 80 degrees F. The actual temperature in a rain forest depends on its distance from the equator and its altitude (rain forests are rarely seen above 3,000 feet).

Average Precipitation

Rainfall is greater than 80 inches per year and exceeds annual evaporation. As a general rule, at least four inches of rain falls each month. There are no true dry seasons.

Life Forms

Rain forests have more plants and animals than any of the other world habitats. The rain forest's understory and midstory plants often have large leaves, allowing them to catch as much sunlight as possible. The upper-story plants have smaller leaves that spread out so that they touch plants around them, creating a canopy. Plants on the forest floor feed themselves by collecting falling debris or trapping animals and insects in their leaves. Almost 90 percent of the rain forest animal species are insects, and of these, most are beetles. In fact, one rain forest tree can host up to 150 species of beetles. The rain forest has an abundance of various mammals that can be found on the ground and in the trees. Most are nocturnal, choosing to sleep during the hot days. Almost half the rain forest mammals are bats. Ground dwellers of the rain forest include gorillas, elephants, tapirs, rodents, and wild pigs.

Problems for the Survivor

Insects, steep terrain, extreme moisture, and difficulty finding an appropriate signaling site.

—From *Wilderness Survival*

Travel in Tropical and Jungle Areas

U.S. Army

Tropical Weather

High temperatures, heavy rainfall, and oppressive humidity characterize equatorial and subtropical regions, except at high altitudes. At low altitude, temperature variation is seldom less than 10 degrees C and is often more than 35 degrees C. At altitudes over 1,500 meters, ice often forms at night. The rain has a cooling effect, but when it stops, the temperatures soars.

Rainfall is heavy, often with thunder and lightning. Sudden rain beats on the tree canopy, turning trickles into raging torrents and causing rivers to rise. Just as suddenly, the rain stops. Violent storms may occur, usually toward the end of the summer months.

Hurricanes, cyclones, and typhoons develop over the sea and rush inland, causing tidal waves and devastation ashore. In choosing campsites, make sure you are above any potential flooding. Prevailing winds vary between winter and summer. The dry season has rain once a day and the monsoon has continuous rain. In Southeast Asia, winds from the Indian Ocean bring the monsoon, but it is dry when the wind blows from the landmass of China.

Tropical day and night are of equal length. Darkness falls quickly and daybreak is just as sudden.

Jungle Types

There is no standard jungle. The tropical area may be any of the following:

- Rain forests.
- Secondary jungles.
- Semievergreen seasonal and monsoon forests.

Continued →

- Scrub and thorn forests.
- Savannas.
- Saltwater swamps.
- Freshwater swamps.

Tropical Rain Forests

The climate varies little in rain forests. You find these forests across the equator in the Amazon and Congo basins, parts of Indonesia, and several Pacific islands. Up to 3.5 meters of rain fall evenly throughout the year. Temperatures range from about 32 degrees C in the day to 21 degrees C at night.

There are five layers of vegetation in this jungle. Where untouched by man, jungle trees rise from buttress roots to heights of 60 meters. Below them, smaller trees produce a canopy so thick that little light reaches the jungle floor. Seedlings struggle beneath them to reach light, and masses of vines and lianas twine up to the sun. Ferns, mosses, and herbaceous plants push through a thick carpet of leaves, and a great variety of fungi grow on leaves and fallen tree trunks.

Because of the lack of light on the jungle floor, there is little under-growth to hamper movement, but dense growth limits visibility to about 50 meters. You can easily lose your sense of direction in this jungle, and it is extremely hard for aircraft to see you.

Secondary Jungles

Secondary jungle is very similar to rain forest. Prolific growth, where sunlight penetrates to the jungle floor, typifies this type of forest. Such growth happens mainly along river banks, on jungle fringes, and where man has cleared rain forest. When abandoned, tangled masses of vegetation quickly reclaim these cultivated areas. You can often find cultivated food plants among this vegetation.

Semievergreen Seasonal and Monsoon Forests

The characteristics of the American and African semievergreen seasonal forests correspond with those of the Asian monsoon forests. These characteristics are—

- Their trees fall into two stories of tree strata. Those in the upper story average 18 to 24 meters; those in the lower story average 7 to 13 meters.
- The diameter of the trees averages 0.5 meter.
- Their leaves fall during a seasonal drought.

Except for the sago, nipa, and coconut palms, the same edible plants grow in these areas as in the tropical rain forests.

You find these forests in portions of Columbia and Venezuela and the Amazon basin in South America; in portions of southeast coastal Kenya, Tanzania, and Mozambique in Africa; in Northeastern India, much of Burma, Thailand, Indochina, Java, and parts of other Indonesian islands in Asia.

Tropical Scrub and Thorn Forests

The chief characteristics of tropical scrub and thorn forests are—

- There is a definite dry season.
- Trees are leafless during the dry season.
- The ground is bare except for a few tufted plants in bunches; grasses are uncommon.
- Plants with thorns predominate.
- Fires occur frequently.

You find tropical scrub and thorn forests on the west coast of Mexico, Yucatan peninsula, Venezuela, Brazil; on the northwest coast and central parts of Africa; and in Asia, in Turkestan and India.

Within the tropical scrub and thorn forest areas, you will find it hard to obtain food plants during the dry season. During the rainy season, plants are considerably more abundant.

Tropical Savannas

General characteristics of the savanna are—

- It is found within the tropical zones in South America and Africa.

- It looks like a broad, grassy meadow, with trees spaced at wide intervals.
- It frequently has red soil.
- It grows scattered trees that usually appear stunted and gnarled like apple trees. Palms also occur on savannas.

You find savannas in parts of Venezuela, Brazil, and the Guianas in South America. In Africa, you find them in the southern Sahara (north-central Cameroon and Gabon and southern Sudan), Benin, Togo, most of Nigeria, northeastern Zaire, northern Uganda, western Kenya, part of Malawi, part of Tanzania, southern Zimbabwe, Mozambique, and western Madagascar.

Saltwater Swamps

Saltwater swamps are common in coastal areas subject to tidal flooding. Mangrove trees thrive in these swamps. Mangrove trees can reach heights of 12 meters, and their tangled roots are an obstacle to movement. Visibility in this type of swamp is poor, and movement is extremely difficult. Sometimes, streams that you can raft form channels, but you usually must travel on foot through this swamp.

You find saltwater swamps in West Africa, Madagascar, Malaysia, the Pacific islands, Central and South America, and at the mouth of the Ganges River in India. The swamps at the mouths of the Orinoco and Amazon rivers and rivers of Guyana consist of mud and trees that offer little shade. Tides in saltwater swamps can vary as much as 12 meters.

Everything in a saltwater swamp may appear hostile to you, from leeches and insects to crocodiles and caimans. Avoid the dangerous animals in this swamp.

Avoid this swamp altogether if you can. If there are water channels through it, you may be able to use a raft to escape.

Freshwater Swamps

You find freshwater swamps in low-lying inland areas. Their characteristics are masses of thorny undergrowth, reeds, grasses, and occasional short palms that reduce visibility and make travel difficult. There are often islands that dot these swamps, allowing you to get out of the water. Wildlife is abundant in these swamps.

Travel through Jungle Areas

With practice, movement through thick undergrowth and jungle can be done efficiently. Always wear long sleeves to avoid cuts and scratches.

To move easily, you must develop "jungle eye," that is, you should not concentrate on the pattern of bushes and trees to your immediate front. You must focus on the jungle further out and find natural breaks in the foliage. Look through the jungle, not at it. Stop and stoop down occasionally to look along the jungle floor. This action may reveal game trails that you can follow.

Stay alert and move slowly and steadily through dense forest or jungle. Stop periodically to listen and take your bearings. Use a machete to cut through dense vegetation, but do not cut unnecessarily or you will quickly wear yourself out. If using a machete, stroke upward when

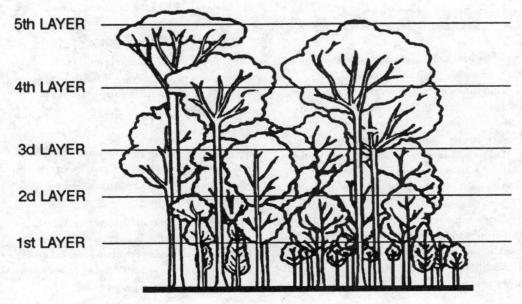

5th LAYER

4th LAYER

3d LAYER

2d LAYER

1st LAYER

Five layers of tropical rain forest vegetation.

Continued ➡

cutting vines to reduce noise because sound carries long distances in the jungle. Use a stick to part the vegetation. Using a stick will also help dislodge biting ants, spiders, or snakes. Do not grasp at brush or vines when climbing slopes; they may have irritating spines or sharp thorns.

Many jungle and forest animals follow game trails. These trails wind and cross, but frequently lead to water or clearings. Use these trails if they lead in your desired direction of travel.

In many countries, electric and telephone lines run for miles through sparsely inhabited areas. Usually, the right-of-way is clear enough to allow easy travel. When traveling along these lines, be careful as you approach transformer and relay stations. In enemy territory, they may be guarded.

Travel Tips

- Pinpoint your initial location as accurately as possible to determine a general line of travel to safety. If you do not have a compass, use a field-expedient direction finding method.

- Take stock of water supplies and equipment.

- Move in one direction, but not necessarily in a straight line. Avoid obstacles. In enemy territory, take advantage of natural cover and concealment.

- Move smoothly through the jungle. Do not blunder through it since you will get many cuts and scratches. Turn your shoulders, shift your hips, bend your body, and shorten or lengthen your stride as necessary to slide between the undergrowth.

Immediate Considerations

There is less likelihood of your rescue from beneath a dense jungle canopy than in other survival situations. You will probably have to travel to reach safety.

If you are the victim of an aircraft crash, the most important items to take with you from the crash site are a machete, a compass, a first aid kit, and a parachute or other material for use as mosquito netting and shelter.

Take shelter from tropical rain, sun, and insects. Malaria-carrying mosquitoes and other insects are immediate dangers, so protect yourself against bites.

Do not leave the crash area without carefully blazing or marking your route. Use you compass. Know what direction you are taking.

In the tropics, even the smallest scratch can quickly become dangerously infected. Promptly treat any wound, no matter how minor.

—From *Survival (Field Manual 21-76)*

Mountain Terrain and Hazards

U.S. Army

Mountain Terrain

Definition

Mountains are land forms that rise more than 500 meters above the surrounding plain and are characterized by steep slopes. Slopes commonly range from 4 to 45 degrees. Cliffs and precipices may be vertical or overhanging. Mountains may consist of an isolated peak, single ridges, glaciers, snowfields, compartments, or complex ranges extending for long distances and obstructing movement. Mountains usually favor the defense; however, attacks can succeed by using detailed planning, rehearsals, surprise, and well-led troops.

Composition

All mountains are made up of rocks and all rocks of minerals (compounds that cannot be broken down except by chemical action). Of the approximately 2,000 known minerals, seven rock-forming minerals make up most of the earth's crust: quartz and feldspar make up granite and sandstone; olivene and pyroxene give basalt its dark color; and amphibole and biotite (mica) are the black crystalline specks in granitic rocks. Except for calcite, found in limestone, they all contain silicon and are often referred to as silicates.

Rock and Slope Types

Different types of rock and different slopes present different hazards. The following paragraphs discuss the characteristics and hazards of the different rocks and slopes.

Granite. Granite produces fewer rockfalls, but jagged edges make pulling rope and raising equipment more difficult. Granite is abrasive and increases the danger of ropes or accessory cords being cut. Climbers must beware of large loose boulders. After a rain, granite dries quickly. Most climbing holds are found in cracks. Face climbing can be found, however, it cannot be protected.

Chalk and Limestone. Chalk and limestone are slippery when wet. Limestone is usually solid; however, conglomerate type stones may be loose. Limestone has pockets, face climbing, and cracks.

Slate and Gneiss. Slate and gneiss can be firm and or brittle in the same area (red coloring indicates brittle areas). Rockfall danger is high, and small rocks may break off when pulled or when pitons are emplaced.

Sandstone. Sandstone is usually soft causing handholds and footholds to break away under pressure. Chocks placed in sandstone may or may not hold. Sandstone should be allowed to dry for a couple of days after a rain before climbing on it—wet sandstone is extremely soft. Most climbs follow a crack. Face climbing is possible, but any outward pull will break off handholds and footholds, and it is usually difficult to protect.

Grassy Slopes. Penetrating roots and increased frost cracking cause a continuous loosening process. Grassy slopes are slippery after rain, new snow, and dew. After long, dry spells clumps of the slope tend to break away. Weight should be distributed evenly; for example, use flat hand push holds instead of finger pull holds.

Firm Spring Snow (Firn Snow). Stopping a slide on small, leftover snow patches in late spring can be difficult. Routes should be planned to avoid these dangers. Self-arrest should be practiced before encountering this situation. Beginning climbers should be secured with rope when climbing on this type surface. Climbers can glissade down firn snow if necessary. Firn snow is easier to ascend than walking up scree or talus.

Talus. Talus is rocks that are larger than a dinner plate, but smaller than boulders. They can be used as stepping-stones to ascend or descend a slope. However, if a talus rock slips away it can produce more injury than scree because of its size.

Scree. Scree is small rocks that are from pebble size to dinner plate size. Running down scree is an effective method of descending in a hurry. One can run at full stride without worry—the whole scree field is moving with you. Climbers must beware of larger rocks that may be solidly planted under the scree. Ascending scree is a tedious task. The scree does not provide a solid platform and will only slide under foot. If possible, avoid scree when ascending.

In North America the Yosemite Decimal System (YDS) is used to rate the difficulty of routes in mountainous terrain. The YDS classes are:

- Class 1—Hiking trail.

- Class 2—Off-trail scramble.

- Class 3—Climbing, use of ropes for beginners (moderate scrambling).

- Class 4—Belayed climbing. (This is moderate to difficult scrambling, which may have some exposure.)

- Class 5—Free climbing. (This class requires climbers to be roped up, belay and emplace intermediate protection.)

Class 5 is further subdivided into the following classifications:

Class 5.0–5.4—Little difficulty. This is the simplest form of free climbing. Hands are necessary to support balance. This is sometimes referred to as advanced rock scrambling.

Class 5.5—Moderate difficulty. Three points of contact are necessary.

Class 5.6—Medium difficulty. The climber can experience vertical position or overhangs where good grips can require moderate levels of energy expenditure.

Class 5.7—Great difficulty. Considerable climbing experience is necessary. Longer stretches of climbing requiring several points of intermediate protection. Higher levels of energy expenditure will be experienced.

Continued ➡

Class 5.8—Very great difficulty. Increasing amount of intermediate protection is the rule. High physical conditioning, climbing technique, and experience required.

Class 5.9—Extremely great difficulty. Requires well above average ability and excellent condition. Exposed positions, often combined with small belay points. Passages of the difficult sections can often be accomplished under good conditions. Often combined with aid climbing (A0-A4).

Class 5.10—Extraordinary difficulty. Climb only with improved equipment and intense training. Besides acrobatic climbing technique, mastery of refined security technique is indispensable. Often combined with aid climbing (A0-A4).

Class 5.11–5.14—Greater increases of difficulty, requiring more climbing ability, experience, and energy expenditure. Only talented and dedicated climbers reach this level.

Additional classifications include the following.

1. Classes are further divided into a, b, c, and d categories starting from 5.10 to 5.14 (for example, 5.10d).

2. Classes are also further divided from 5.9 and below with +/= categories (for example, 5.8+).

3. All class 5 climbs can also be designated with "R" or "X", which indicates a run-out on a climb. This means that placement of inter mediate protection is not possible on portions of the route. (For example, in a classification of 5.8R, the "R" indicates periods of run-out where, if a fall was expe rienced, ground fall would occur.) Always check the local guidebook to find specific designation for your area.

4. All class 5 climbs can also be designated with "stars." These refer to the popularity of the climb to the local area. Climbs are repre sented by a single "star" up to five "stars;" a five-star climb is a classic climb and is usually aesthetically pleasing.

Aid climb difficulty classification includes:

A0—"French-free." This technique involves using a piece of gear to make progress; for example, clipping a sling into a bolt or piece of protection and then pulling up on it or stepping up in the sling. Usually only needed to get past one or two more difficult moves on advanced free climbs.

A1—Easy aid. The placement of protection is straight forward and reliable. There is usually no high risk of any piece of protection pulling out. This technique requires etriers and is fast and simple.

A2—Moderate aid. The placement of protection is generally straight forward, but placement can be awkward and strenuous. Usually A2 involves one or two moves that are difficult with good protection placement below and above the difficult moves. No serious fall danger.

A3—Hard aid. This technique requires testing your protection. It involves several awkward and strenuous moves in a row. Generally solid placements which will hold a fall and are found within a full rope length. However, long fall potential does exist, with falls of 40 to 60 feet and intermediate protection on the awkward placements failing. These falls, however, are usually clean and with no serious bodily harm.

A4—Serious aid. This technique requires lots of training and practice. More like walking on eggs so none of them break. Leads will usually take extended amounts of time which cause the lead climber to doubt and worry about each placement. Protection placed will usually only hold a climber's weight and falls can be as long as two-thirds the rope length.

A5—Extreme aid. All protection is sketchy at best. Usually no protection placed on the entire route can be trusted to stop a fall.

A6—Extremely severe aid. Continuous A5 climbing with A5 belay stations. If the leader falls, the whole rope team will probably experi ence ground fall.

Aid climbing classes are also further divided into +/− categories, such as A3+ or A3-, which would simply refer to easy or hard.

Grade ratings (commitment grades) inform the climber of the approximate time a climber trained to the level of the climb will take to complete the route.

- I—Several hours.
- II—Half of a day.
- III—About three-fourths of a day.
- IV—Long hard day (usually not less than 5.7).
- V—1½ to 2 ½ days (usually not less than 5.8).
- VI—Greater than 2 days.

Mountain Hazards

Hazards can be termed natural (caused by natural occurrence), man-made (caused by an individual, such as lack of preparation, carelessness, improper diet, equipment misuse), or as a combination (human trigger). There are two kinds of hazards while in the mountains—subjective and objective. Combinations of objective and subjective hazards are referred to as cumulative hazards.

Subjective Hazards

Subjective hazards are created by humans; for example, choice of route, companions, overexertion, dehydration, climbing above one's ability, and poor judgment.

Falling. Falling can be caused by carelessness, over-fatigue, heavy equipment, bad weather, overestimating ability, a hold breaking away, or other reasons.

Equipment. Ropes are not total security; they can be cut on a sharp edge or break due to poor maintenance, age, or excessive use. You should always pack emergency and bivouac equipment even if the weather situation, tour, or a short climb is seemingly low of dangers.

Objective Hazards

Objective hazards are caused by the mountain and weather and cannot be influenced by man; for example, storms, rockfalls, icefalls, lightning, and so on.

Altitude. At high altitudes (especially over 6,500 feet), endurance and concentration is reduced. Cut down on smoking and alcohol. Sleep well, acclimatize slowly, stay hydrated, and be aware of signs and symptoms of high-altitude illnesses. Storms can form quickly and lightning can be severe.

Visibility. Fog, rain, darkness, and or blowing snow can lead to disorientation. Take note of your exact position and plan your route to safety before visibility decreases. Cold combined with fog can cause a thin sheet of ice to form on rocks (verglas). Whiteout conditions can be extremely dangerous. If you must move under these conditions, it is best to rope up. Have the point man move to the end of the rope. The second man will use the first man as an aiming point with the compass. Use a route sketch and march table. If the tactical situation does not require it, plan route so as not to get caught by darkness.

Gullies. Rock, snow, and debris are channeled down gullies. If ice is in the gully, climbing at night may be better because the warming of the sun will loosen stones and cause rockfalls.

Rockfall. Blocks and scree at the base of a climb can indicate recurring rockfall. Light colored spots on the wall may indicate impact chips of falling rock. Spring melt or warming by the sun of the rock/ice/snow causes rockfall.

Avalanches. Avalanches are caused by the weight of the snow overloading the slope. (Refer to page 306 for more detailed information on avalanches.)

Hanging Glaciers and Seracs. Avoid, if at all possible, hanging glaciers and seracs. They will fall without warning regardless of the time of day or time of year. One cubic meter of glacier ice weighs 910 kilograms (about 2,000 pounds). If you must cross these danger areas, do so quickly and keep an interval between each person.

Crevasses. Crevasses are formed when a glacier flows over a slope and makes a bend, or when a glacier separates from the rock walls that enclose it. A slope of only two to three degrees is enough to form a crevasse. As this slope increases from 25 to 30 degrees, hazardous icefalls can be formed. Likewise, as a glacier makes a bend, it is likely that crevasses will form at the outside of the bend. Therefore, the safest route on a glacier would be to the inside of bends, and away from steep slopes and icefalls. Extreme care must be taken when moving off of or onto the glacier because of the moat that is most likely to be present.

—From *Military Mountaineering (Field Manual 3–97.61)*

Continued ➡

Mountain Walking Techniques

U.S. Army

Basic Principles

Up scree or talus, through boulder fields or steep wooded mountainsides, over snow or grass-covered slopes, the basic principles of mountain walking remain the same.

The soldier's weight is centered directly over the feet at all times. He places his foot flat on the ground to obtain as much (boot) sole-ground contact as possible. Then, he places his foot on the uphill side of grass tussocks, small talus and other level spots to avoid twisting the ankle and straining the Achilles tendon. He straightens the knee after each step to allow for rest between steps, and takes moderate steps at a steady pace. An angle of ascent or descent that is too steep is avoided, and any indentations in the slope are used to advantage. …

Downhill walking uses less energy than uphill but is much harder on the body. Stepping down can hammer the full bodyweight onto the feet and legs. Blisters and blackened toenails, knee damage, and back pain may follow. To avoid these problems the soldier should start by tightening bootlaces to ensure a snug fit (also keep toenails trimmed). A ski pole, ice ax, or walking stick will help take some of the load and give additional stability. Keep a moderate pace and walk with knees flexed to absorb shock.

Side hill travel on any surface should be avoided whenever possible. Weighted down with a rucksack, the soldier is vulnerable to twisted ankles, back injury, and loss of balance. If side hill travel is necessary, try to switchback periodically, and use any lower angle flat areas such as rocks, animal trails, and the ground above grass or brush clumps to level off the route.

Techniques

Mountain walking techniques can be divided according to the general formation, surface, and ground cover such as walking on hard ground, on snow slopes and grassy slopes, through thick brush, and on scree and talus slopes.

Hard Ground. Hard ground is firmly compacted, rocky soil that does not give way under the weight of a soldier's step. It is most commonly found under mature forest canopy, in low brush or heather, and areas where animals have beaten out multiple trails.

When ascending, employ the rest step to rest the leg muscles. Steep slopes can be traversed rather than climbed straight up. To turn at the end of each traverse, the soldier should step off in the new direction with the uphill foot. This prevents crossing the feet and possible loss of balance. While traversing, the full sole-to-ground principle is accomplished by rolling the ankle downhill on each step. For small stretches the herringbone step may be used—ascending straight up a slope with toes pointed out. A normal progression, as the slope steepens, would be from walking straight up, to a herringbone step, and then to a traverse on the steeper areas.

Descending is best done by walking straight down the slope without traversing. The soldier keeps his back straight and bends at the knees to absorb the shock of each step. Body weight is kept directly over the feet and the full boot sole is placed on the ground with each step. Walking with a slight forward lean and with the feet in a normal position make the descent easier.

Snow Slopes. Snow-covered terrain can be encountered throughout the year above 1,500 meters in many mountainous areas. Talus and brush may be covered by hardened snowfields, streams make crossable with snowbridges. The techniques for ascending and descending moderate snow slopes are similar to walking on hard ground with some exceptions.

Diagonal Traverse Technique. The diagonal traverse is the most efficient means to ascend snow. In conjunction with the ice ax it provides balance and safety for the soldier. This technique is a two-step sequence. The soldier performs a basic rest step, placing the leading (uphill) foot above and in front of the trailing (downhill) food, and weighting the trail leg. This is the in-balance position. The ice ax, held in the uphill hand, is placed in the snow above and to the front. The soldier shifts his weight to the leading (uphill) leg and brings the unweighted trail (downhill) foot ahead of the uphill foot. He shifts weight to the forward (downhill) leg and then moves the uphill foot up and places it out ahead of the trail foot, returning to the in-balance position. At this point the ax is moved forward in preparation for the next step.

Step Kicking. Step kicking is a basic technique used when crampons are not worn. It is best used on moderate slopes when the snow is soft enough to leave clear footprints. On softer snow the soldier swings his foot into the snow, allowing the leg's weight and momentum to carve the step. Fully laden soldiers will need to kick steps, which take half of the boot. The steps should be angled slightly into the slope for added security. Succeeding climbers will follow directly in the steps of the trailbreaker, each one improving the step as he ascends. Harder snow requires more effort to kick steps, and they will not be as secure. The soldier may need to slice the step with the side of his boot and use the diagonal technique to ascend.

Descending Snow. If the snow is soft and the slope gentle, simply walk straight down. Harder snow or steeper slopes call for the plunge step, which must be done in a positive, aggressive manner. The soldier faces out, steps off, and plants his foot solidly, driving the heel into the snow while keeping his leg straight. He shifts his weight to the new foot plant and continues down with the other foot. On steeper terrain it may be necessary to squat on the weighted leg when setting the plunge step. The upper body should be kept erect or canted slightly forward.

Tips on Snow Travel. The following are tips for traveling on snow.

Often the best descent is on a different route than the ascent. When looking for a firmer travel surface, watch for dirty snow—this absorbs more heat and thus hardens faster than clean snow.

In the Northern Hemisphere, slopes with southern and western exposures set up earlier in the season and quicker after storms, but are more prone to avalanches in the spring. These slopes generally provide firm surfaces while northern and eastern exposures remain unconsolidated.

Travel late at night or early in the morning is best if daytime temperatures are above freezing and the sun heats the slopes. The night's cold hardens the snow surface.

Avoid walking on snow next to logs, trees, and rocks as the subsurface snow has melted away creating hidden traps.

Grassy Slopes. Grassy slopes are usually composed of small tussocks of growth rather than one continuous field.

When ascending, step on the upper side of each hummock or tussock, where the ground is more level.

When descending a grassy slope, the traverse technique should be used because of the uneven nature of the ground. A climber can easily build up too much speed and fall if a direct descent is tried. The hop-skip step can be useful on this type of slope. In this technique, the lower leg takes all of the weight, and the upper leg is used only for balance. When traversing, the climber's uphill foot points in the direction of travel. The downhill foot points about 45 degrees off the direction of travel (downhill). This maintains maximum sole contact and prevents possible downhill ankle roll-out.

Note: Wet grass can be extremely slippery; the soldier must be aware of ground cover conditions.

Thick Brush. For the military mountaineer, brush is both a help and a hindrance. Brush-filled gullies can provide routes and rally points concealed from observation; on the other hand steep brushy terrain is hazardous to negotiate. Cliffs and steep ravines are hidden traps, and blow downs and thickets can obstruct travel as much as manmade obstacles. When brush must be negotiated take the most direct route across the obstacle; look for downed timber to use as raised paths through the obstacle; or create a tunnel through the obstacle by prying the brush apart, standing on lower branches and using upper limbs for support.

Scree Slopes. Slopes composed of the smallest rocks are called scree slopes. Scree varies in size from the smallest gravel to about the size of a man's fist.

Ascending scree slopes is difficult and tiring and should be avoided, if possible. All principles of ascending hard ground and snow apply, but each step is carefully chosen so that the foot does not slide down when weighted. This is done by kicking in with the toe of the upper foot (similar to step-kicking in snow) so that a step is formed in the loose scree. After determining that the step is stable, weight is transferred to the upper leg, the soldier then steps up and repeats the process with the lower foot.

The best method for descending scree slopes is to come straight down the slope using a short shuffling step with the knees bent, back straight, feet pointed downhill, and heels dug in. When several climbers descend a scree slope together, they should be as close together as

Continued ➡

possible (one behind the other at single arm interval) to prevent injury from dislodged rocks. Avoid running down scree as this can cause a loss of control. When the bottom of the slope (or run out zone) cannot be seen, use caution because drop-offs may be encountered.

Scree slopes can be traversed using the ice ax as a third point of contact. Always keep the ax on the uphill side. When the herringbone or diagonal method is used to ascend scree, the ax can be used placing both hands on the top and driving the spike into the scree slope above the climber. The climber uses the ax for balance as he moves up to it, and then repeats the process.

Talus Slopes. Talus slopes are composed of rocks larger than a man's fist. When walking in talus, ascending or descending, climbers should always step on the uphill side of rocks and stay alert for movement underfoot. Disturbing unstable talus can cause rockslides. Climbers must stay in close columns while walking through talus so that dislodged rocks do not reach dangerous speeds before reaching lower soldiers. To prevent rock fall injuries, avoid traversing below other climbers. All other basics of mountain walking apply.

Safety Considerations

The mountain walking techniques presented here are designed to reduce the hazards of rock fall and loss of control leading to a fall. Carelessness can cause the failure of the best-planned missions.

Whenever a rock is kicked loose, the warning, "Rock!" is shouted immediately. Personnel near the bottom of the cliff immediately lean into the cliff to reduce their exposure, and do not look up. Personnel more than 3 meters away from the bottom of the cliff may look up to determine where the rock is heading and seek cover behind an obstacle. Lacking cover, personnel should anticipate which way the rock is falling and move out of its path to the left or right.

If a soldier slips or stumbles on sloping terrain (hard ground, grass, snow, or scree) he must immediately self-arrest, digging into the slope with hands, elbows, knees and toes. If he falls backwards and rolls over he must immediately try to turn over onto his stomach with his legs downhill and self-arrest with hands and toes.

When traveling through steep terrain, soldiers should be trained in the use of the ice ax for self-arrest. The ax can be used to arrest a fall on solid ground, grass and scree as well as snow. It may also be used a third point of contact on difficult terrain. If not in use the ice ax is carried in or on the rucksack with its head down and secured.

—From *Military Mountaineering (Field Manual 3-97.61)*

Climbing
U.S. Army

A steep rock face is a terrain feature that can be avoided most of the time through prior planning and good route selection.

Sometimes steep rock cannot be avoided. Climbing relatively short sections of steep rock (one or two pitches) may prove quicker and safer than using alternate routes.

Climbing Fundamentals

A variety of refined techniques are used to climb different types of rock formations. The foundation for all of these styles is the art of climbing. Climbing technique stresses climbing with the weight centered over the feet, using the hands primarily for balance. It can be thought of as a combination of the balanced movement required to walk a tightrope and the technique used to ascend a ladder. No mountaineering equipment is required; however, the climbing technique is also used in roped climbing.

Route Selection
The experienced climber has learned to climb with the "eyes." Even before getting on the rock, the climber studies all possible routes, or "lines," to the top looking for cracks, ledges, nubbins, and other irregularities in the rock that will be used for footholds and handholds, taking note of any larger ledges or benches for resting places. When picking the line, he mentally climbs the route, rehearsing the step-by-step sequence of movements that will be required to do the climb, ensuring himself that the route has an adequate number of holds and the difficulty of the climb will be well within the limit of his ability.

Spotting
Spotting is a technique used to add a level of safety to climbing without a rope. A second man stands below and just outside of the climbers fall path and helps (spots) the climber to land safely if he should fall. Spotting is only applicable if the climber is not going above the spotters head on the rock. Beyond that height a roped climbing should be conducted. If an individual climbs beyond the effective range of the spotter(s), he has climbed TOO HIGH for his own safety. The duties of the spotter are to help prevent the falling climber from impacting the head and or spine, help the climber land feet first, and reduce the impact of a fall.

Caution

The spotter should not catch the climber against the rock because additional injuries could result. If the spotter pushes the falling climber into the rock, deep abrasions of the skin or knee may occur. Ankle joints could be twisted by the fall if the climber's foot remained high on the rock. The spotter might be required to fully support the weight of the climber causing injury to the spotter.

Climbing Technique
Climbing involves linking together a series of movements based on foot and hand placement, weight shift, and movement. When this series of movements is combined correctly, a smooth climbing technique results. This technique reduces excess force on the limbs, helping to minimize fatigue. The basic principle is based on the five body parts described here.

Five Body Parts. The five body parts used for climbing are the right hand, left hand, right foot, left foot, and body (trunk). The basic principle to achieve smooth climbing is to move only one of the five body parts at a time. The trunk is not moved in conjunction with a foot or in conjunction with a hand, a hand is not moved in conjunction with a foot, and so on. Following this simple technique forces both legs to do all the lifting simultaneously.

Stance or Body Position. Body position is probably the single most important element to good technique. A relaxed, comfortable stance is essential. The body should be in a near vertical or erect stance with the weight centered over the feet. Leaning in towards the rock will cause the feet to push outward, away from the rock, resulting in a loss of friction between the boot sole and rock surface. The legs are straight and the heels are kept low to reduce fatigue. Bent legs and tense muscles tire quickly. If strained for too long, tense muscles may vibrate uncontrollably. This vibration, known as "Elvis-ing" or "sewing-machine leg" can be cured by straightening the leg, lowering the heel, or moving on to a more restful position. The hands are used to maintain balance. Keeping the hands between waist and shoulder level will reduce arm fatigue.

Whenever possible, three points of contact are maintained with the rock. Proper positioning of the hips and shoulders is critical. When using two footholds and one handhold, the hips and shoulders should be centered over both feet. In most cases, as the climbing progresses, the body is resting on one foot with two handholds for balance. The hips and shoulders must be centered over the support foot to maintain balance, allowing the "free" foot to maneuver.

The angle or steepness of the rock also determines how far away from the rock the hips and shoulders should be. On low-angle slopes, the hips are moved out away from the rock to keep the body in balance with the weight over the feet. The shoulders can be moved closer to the rock to reach handholds. On steep rock, the hips are pushed closer to the rock. The shoulders are moved away from the rock by arching the back. The body is still in balance over the feet and the eyes can see where the hands need to go. Sometimes, when footholds are small, the hips are moved back to increase friction between the foot and the rock. This is normally done on quick, intermediate holds. It should be avoided in the rest position as it places more weight on the arms and hands. When weight must be placed on handholds, the arms should be kept straight to reduce fatigue. Again, flexed muscles tire quickly.

Climbing Sequence. The steps defined below provide a complete sequence of events to move the entire body on the rock. These are the

Continued ➜

basic steps to follow for a smooth climbing technique. Performing these steps in this exact order will not always be necessary because the nature of the route will dictate the availability of hand and foot placements. The basic steps are weight, shift, and movement (movement being either the foot, hand, or body).

STEP ONE: Shift the weight from both feet to one foot. This will allow lifting of one foot with no effect on the stance.

STEP TWO: Lift the unweighted foot and place it in a new location, within one to two feet of the starting position, with no effect on body position or balance (higher placement will result in a potentially higher lift for the legs to make, creating more stress, and is called a high step) The trunk does not move during foot movement.

STEP THREE: Shift the weight onto both feet. (Repeat steps 1 through 3 for remaining foot.)

STEP FOUR: Lift the body into a new stance with both legs.

STEP FIVE: Move one hand to a new position between waist and head height.

During this movement, the trunk should be completely balanced in position and the removed hand should have no effect no stability.

STEP SIX: Move the remaining hand as in Step 5.

Now the entire body is in a new position and ready to start the process again. Following these steps will prevent lifting with the hands and arms, which are used to maintain stance and balance. If both legs are bent, leg extension can be performed as soon as one foot has been moved. Hand movements can be delayed until numerous foot movements have been made, which not only creates shorter lifts with the legs, but may allow a better choice for the next hand movements because the reach will have increased.

Many climbers will move more than one body part at a time, usually resulting in lifting the body with one leg or one leg and both arms. This type of lifting is inefficient, requiring one leg to perform the work of two or using the arms to lift the body. Proper climbing technique is lifting the body with the legs, not the arms, because the legs are much stronger.

When the angle of the rock increases, these movements become more critical. Holding or pulling the body into the rock with the arms and hands may be necessary as the angle increases (this is still not lifting with the arms). Many climbing routes have angles greater than ninety degrees (overhanging) and the arms are used to support partial body weight. The same technique applies even at those angles.

The climber should avoid moving on the knees and elbows. Other than being uncomfortable, even painful, to rest on, these bony portions of the limbs offer little friction and "feel" on the rock.

Safety Precautions

The following safety precautions should be observed when rock climbing.

When ascending a seldom or never traveled route, you may encounter precariously perched rocks. If the rock will endanger your second, it may be possible to remove it from the route and trundle it, tossing it down. This is extremely dangerous to climbers below and should not be attempted unless you are absolutely sure no men are below. If you are not sure that the flight path is clear, do not do it. Never dislodge loose rocks carelessly. Should a rock become loose accidentally, immediately shout the warning "ROCK" to alert climbers below. Upon hearing the warning, personnel should seek immediate cover behind any rock bulges or overhangs available, or flatten themselves against the rock to minimize exposure.

Should a climber fall, he should do his utmost to maintain control and not panic. If on a low-angle climb, he may be able to arrest his own fall by staying in contact with the rock, grasping for any possible hold available. He should shout the warning "FALLING" to alert personnel below.

Caution

Grasping at the rock in a fall can result in serious injuries to the upper body. If conducting a roped climb, let the rope provide protection.

When climbing close to the ground and without a rope, a spotter can be used to safety. The duties of the spotter are to ensure the falling climber does not impact the head or spine, and to reduce the impact of a fall.

Avoid climbing directly above or below other climbers (with the exception of spotters). When personnel must climb at the same time, following the same line, a fixed rope should be installed.

Avoid climbing with gloves on because of the decreased "feel" for the rock. The use of gloves in the training environment is especially discouraged, while their use in the mountains is often mandatory when it is cold. A thin polypropylene or wool glove is best for rock climbing, although heavier cotton or leather work gloves are often used for belaying.

Be extremely careful when climbing on wet or moss-covered rock; friction on holds is greatly reduced.

Avoid grasping small vegetation for handholds; the root systems can be shallow and will usually not support much weight.

Margin of Safety

Besides observing the standard safety precautions, the climber can avoid catastrophe by climbing with a wide margin of safety. The margin of safety is a protective buffer the climber places between himself and potential climbing hazards. Both subjective (personnel-related) and objective (environmental) hazards must be considered when applying the margin of safety....

When climbing, the climber increases his margin of safety by selecting routes that are well within the limit of his ability. When leading a group of climbers, he selects a route well within the ability of the weakest member.

When the rock is wet, or when climbing in other adverse weather conditions, the climber's ability is reduced and routes are selected accordingly. When the climbing becomes difficult or exposed, the climber knows to use the protection of the climbing rope and belays. A lead climber increases his margin of safety by placing protection along the route to limit the length of a potential fall.

Use of Holds

The climber should check each hold before use. This may simply be a quick, visual inspection if he knows the rock to be solid. When in doubt, he should grab and tug on the hold to test it for soundness BEFORE depending on it. Sometimes, a hold that appears weak can actually be solid as long as minimal force is applied to it, or the force is applied in a direction that strengthens it. A loose nubbin might not be strong enough to support the climber's weight, but it may serve as an adequate handhold. Be especially careful when climbing on weathered, sedimentary-type rock.

Climbing with the Feet

"Climb with the feet and use the hands for balance" is extremely important to remember. In the early learning stages of climbing, most individuals will rely heavily on the arms, forgetting to use the feet properly. It is true that solid handholds and a firm grip are needed in some combination techniques; however, even the most strenuous techniques require good footwork and a quick return to a balanced position over one or both feet. Failure to climb any route, easy or difficult, is usually the result of poor footwork.

The beginning climber will have a natural tendency to look up for handholds. Try to keep the hands low and train your eyes to look down for footholds. Even the smallest irregularity in the rock can support the climber once the foot is positioned properly and weight is committed to it.

The foot remains on the rock as a result of friction. Maximum friction is obtained from a correct stance over a properly positioned foot. The following describes a few ways the foot can be positioned on the rock to maximize friction.

Maximum Sole Contact. The principle of using full sole contact, as in mountain walking, also applies in climbing. Maximum friction is obtained by placing as much of the boot sole on the rock as possible. Also, the leg muscles can relax the most when the entire foot is placed on the rock.

Smooth, low-angled rock (slab) and rock containing large "bucket" holds and ledges are typical formations where the entire boot sole should be used.

On some large holds, like bucket holds that extend deep into the rock, the entire foot cannot be used. The climber may not be able to achieve a balanced position if the foot is stuck too far underneath a bulge in the rock. In this case, placing only part of the foot on the hold may allow the climber to achieve a balanced stance. The key is to use as much of the boot sole as possible. Remember to keep the heels low to reduce strain on the lower leg muscles.

Edging. The edging technique is used where horizontal crack systems and other irregularities

Continued →

in the rock form small, well-defined ledges. The edge of the boot sole is placed on the ledge for the foothold. Usually, the inside edge of the boot or the edge area around the toes is used. Whenever possible, turn the foot sideways and use the entire inside edge of the boot. Again, more sole contact equals more friction and the legs can rest more when the heel is on the rock.

On smaller holds, edging with the front of the boot, or toe, may be used. Use of the toe is most tiring because the heel is off the rock and the toes support the climber's weight. Remember to keep the heel low to reduce fatigue. Curling and stiffening the toes in the boot increases support on the hold. A stronger position is usually obtained on small ledges by turning the foot at about a 45-degree angle, using the strength of the big toe and the ball of the foot.

Effective edging on small ledges requires stiff-soled footwear. The stiffer the sole, the better the edging capability....

Smearing. When footholds are too small to use a good edging technique, the ball of the foot can be "smeared" over the hold. The smearing technique requires the boot to adhere to the rock by deformation of the sole and by friction. Rock climbing shoes are specifically designed to maximize friction for smearing; some athletic shoes also work well. ... Rounded, down-sloping ledges and low-angled slab rock often require good smearing technique.

Effective smearing requires maximum friction between the foot and the rock. Cover as much of the hold as possible with the ball of the foot. Keeping the heel low will not only reduce muscle strain, but will increase the amount of surface contact between the foot and the rock.

Sometimes flexing the ankles and knees slightly will place the climber's weight more directly over the ball of the foot and increase friction; however, this is more tiring and should only be used for quick, intermediate holds. The leg should be kept straight whenever possible.

Jamming. The jamming technique works on the same principal as chock placement. The foot is set into a crack in such a way that it "jams" into place, resisting a downward pull. The jamming technique is a specialized skill used to climb vertical or near vertical cracks when no other holds are available on the rock face. The technique is not limited to just wedging the feet; fingers, hands, arms, even the entire leg or body are all used in the jamming technique, depending on the size of the crack. Jam holds are described in this text to broaden the range of climbing skills. Jamming holds can be used in a crack while other hand/foot holds are used on the face of the rock. Many cracks will have facial features, such as edges, pockets, and so on, inside and within reach. Always look or feel for easier to use features.

The foot can be jammed in a crack in different ways. It can be inserted above a constriction and set into the narrow portion, or it can be placed in the crack and turned, like a camming device, until it locks in place tight enough to support the climber's weight. Aside from these two basic ideas, the possibilities are endless. The toes, ball of the foot, or the entire foot can be used. Try to use as much of the foot as possible for maximum surface contact. Some

positions are more tiring, and even more painful on the foot, than others. Practice jamming the foot in various ways to see what offers the most secure, restful position.

Some foot jams may be difficult to remove once weight has been committed to them, especially if a stiffer sole boot is used. The foot is less likely to get stuck when it is twisted or "cammed" into position. When removing the boot from a crack, reverse the way it was placed to prevent further constriction.

Using the Hands

The hands can be placed on the rock in many ways. Exactly how and where to position the hands and arms depends on what holds are available, and what configuration will best support the current stance as well as the movement to the next stance. Selecting handholds between waist and shoulder level helps in different ways. Circulation in the arms and hands is best when the arms are kept low. Secondly, the climber has less tendency to "hang" on his arms when the handholds are at shoulder level and below. Both of these contribute to a relaxed stance and reduce fatigue in the hands and arms.

As the individual climbs, he continually repositions his hands and arms to keep the body in balance, with the weight centered over the feet. On lower-angled rock, he may simply need to place the hands up against the rock and extend the arm to maintain balance; just like using an ice ax as a third point of contact in mountain walking. Sometimes, he will be able to push directly down on a large hold with the palm of the hand. More often through, he will need to "grip" the rock in some fashion and then push or pull against the hold to maintain balance.

As stated earlier, the beginner will undoubtedly place too much weight on the hands and arms. If we think of ourselves climbing a ladder, our body weight is on our legs. Our hands grip, and our arms pull on each rung only enough to maintain our balance and footing on the ladder. Ideally, this is the amount of grip and pull that should be used in climbing. Of course, as the size and availability of holds decreases, and the steepness of the rock approaches the vertical, the grip must be stronger and more weight might be placed on the arms and handholds for brief moments. The key is to move quickly from the smaller, intermediate holds to the larger holds where the weight can be placed back on the feet allowing the hands and arms to relax. The following describes some of the basic handholds and how the hand can be positioned to maximize grip on smaller holds.

Push Holds. Push holds rely on the friction created when the hand is pushed against the rock. Most often a climber will use a push hold by applying "downward pressure" on a ledge or nubbin. This is fine, and works well; however, the climber should not limit his use of push holds to the application of down pressure. Pushing sideways, and on occasion, even upward on less obvious holds can prove quite secure. Push holds often work best when used in combination with other holds. Pushing in opposite directions and "push-pull" combinations are excellent techniques.

An effective push hold does not necessarily require the use of the entire hand. On smaller holds, the side of the palm, the fingers, or the thumb may be all that is needed to support the stance. Some holds may not feel secure when the hand is initially placed on them. The hold may improve or weaken during the movement. The key is to try and select a hold that will improve as the climber moves past it.

Most push holds do not require much grip; however, friction might be increased by taking advantage of any rough surfaces or irregularities in the rock. Sometimes the strength of the hold can be increased by squeezing, or "pinching," the rock between the thumb and fingers (see paragraph on pinch holds).

Pull Holds. Pull holds, also called "cling holds," which are grasped and pulled upon, are probably the most widely used holds in climbing. Grip plays more of a role in a pull hold, and, therefore, it normally feels more secure to the climber than a push hold. Because of this increased feeling of security, pull holds are often overworked. These are the holds the climber has a tendency to hang from. Most pull holds do not require great strength, just good technique. Avoid the "death grip" syndrome by climbing with the feet.

Like push holds, pressure on a pull hold can be applied straight down, sideways, or upward. Again, these are the holds the climber tends to stretch and reach for, creating an unbalanced stance. Remember to try and keep the hands between waist and shoulder level, making use of intermediate holds instead of reaching for those above the head.

Pulling sideways on vertical cracks can be very secure. There is less tendency to hang from "side-clings" and the hands naturally remain lower. The thumb can often push against one side of the crack, in opposition to the pull by the fingers, creating a stronger hold. Both hands can also be placed in the same crack, with the hands pulling in opposite directions. The number of possible combinations is limited only by the imagination and experience of the climber.

Friction and strength of a pull hold can be increased by the way the hand grips the rock. Normally, the grip is stronger when the fingers are closed together; however, sometimes more friction is obtained by spreading the fingers apart and placing them between irregularities on the rock surface. On small holds, grip can often be improved by bending the fingers upward, forcing the palm of the hand to push against the rock. This helps to hold the finger tips in place and reduces muscle strain in the hand. Keeping the forearm up against the rock also allows the arm and hand muscles to relax more.

Another technique that helps to strengthen a cling hold for a downward pull is to press the thumb against the side of the index finger, or place it on top of the index finger and press down. This hand configuration, known as a "ring grip," works well on smaller holds.

Pinch Holds. Sometimes a small nubbin or protrusion in the rock can be "squeezed" between the thumb and fingers. This technique is called a pinch hold. Friction is applied by increasing the grip on the rock. Pinch holds are often overlooked by the novice climber because

Continued ➡

they feel insecure at first and cannot be relied upon to support much body weight. If the climber has his weight over his feet properly, the pinch hold will work well in providing balance. The pinch hold can also be used as a gripping technique for push holds and pull holds.

Jam Holds. Like foot jams, the fingers and hands can be wedged or cammed into a crack so they resist a downward or outward pull. Jamming with the fingers and hands can be painful and may cause minor cuts and abrasions to tender skin. Cotton tape can be used to protect the fingertips, knuckles, and the back of the hand; however, prolonged jamming technique requiring hand taping should be avoided. Tape also adds friction to the hand in jammed position.

The hand can be placed in a crack a number of ways. Sometimes an open hand can be inserted and wedged into a narrower portion of the crack. Other times a clenched fist will provide the necessary grip. Friction can be created by applying cross pressure between the fingers and the back of the hand. Another technique for vertical cracks is to place the hand in the crack with the thumb pointed either up or down. The hand is then clenched as much as possible. When the arm is straightened, it will twist the hand and tend to cam it into place. This combination of clenching and camming usually produces the most friction, and the most secure hand jam in vertical cracks.

In smaller cracks, only the fingers will fit. Use as many fingers as the crack will allow. The fingers can sometimes be stacked in some configuration to increase friction. The thumb is usually kept outside the crack in finger jams and pressed against the rock to increase friction or create cross pressure. In vertical cracks it is best to insert the fingers with the thumb pointing down to make use of the natural camming action of the fingers that occurs when the arm is twisted towards a normal position.

Jamming technique for large cracks, or "off widths," requiring the use of arm, leg, and body jams, is another technique. To jam or cam an arm, leg, or body into an off width, the principle is the same as for fingers, hands, or feet—you are making the jammed appendage "fatter" by folding or twisting it inside the crack. For off widths, you may place your entire arm inside the crack with the arm folded and the palm pointing outward. The leg can be used, from the calf to the thigh, and flexed to fit the crack. Routes requiring this type of climbing should be avoided as the equipment normally used for protection might not be large enough to protect larger cracks and openings. However, sometimes a narrower section may be deeper in the crack allowing the use of "normal" size protection.

Combination Techniques

The positions and holds previously discussed are the basics and the ones most common to climbing. From these fundamentals, numerous combination techniques are possible. As the climber gains experience, he will learn more ways to position the hands, feet, and body in relation to the holds available; however, he should always strive to climb with his weight on his feet from a balanced stance.

Sometimes, even on an easy route, the climber may come upon a section of the rock that defies the basic principles of climbing. Short of turning back, the only alternative is to figure out some combination technique that will work. Many of these type problems require the hands and feet to work in opposition to one another. Most will place more weight on the hands and arms than is desirable, and some will put the climber in an "out of balance" position. To make the move, the climber may have to "break the rules" momentarily. This is not a problem and is done quite frequently by experienced climbers. The key to using these type of combination techniques is to plan and execute them deliberately, without lunging or groping for holds, yet quickly, before the hands, arms, or other body parts tire. Still, most of these maneuvers require good technique more than great strength, though a certain degree of hand and arm strength certainly helps.

Combination possibilities are endless. The following is a brief description of some of the more common techniques.

Change Step. The change step, or hop step, can be used when the climber needs to change position of the feet. It is commonly used when traversing to avoid crossing the feet, which might put the climber in an awkward position. To prevent an off balance situation, two solid handholds should be used. The climber simply places his weight on his handholds while he repositions the feet. He often does this with a quick "hop," replacing the lead foot with the trail foot on the same hold. Keeping the forearms against the rock during the maneuver takes some of the strain off the hands, while at the same time strengthening the grip on the holds.

Mantling. Mantling is a technique that can be used when the distance between the holds increases and there are no immediate places to move the hands or feet. It does require a ledge (mantle) or projection in the rock that the climber can press straight down upon.

When the ledge is above head height, mantling begins with pull holds, usually "hooking" both hands over the ledge. The climber pulls himself up until his head is above the hands, where the pull holds become push holds. He elevates himself until the arms are straight and he can lock the elbows to relax the muscles. Rotating the hands inward during the transition to push holds helps to place the palms more securely on the ledge. Once the arms are locked, a foot can be raised and placed on the ledge. The climber may have to remove one hand to make room for the foot. Mantling can be fairly strenuous; however, most individuals should be able to support their weight, momentarily, on one arm if they keep it straight and locked. With the foot on the ledge, weight can be taken off the arms and the climber can grasp the holds that were previously out of reach. Once balanced over the foot, he can stand up on the ledge and plan his next move.

Pure mantling uses arm strength to raise the body; however, the climber can often smear the balls of the feet against the rock and "walk" the feet up during the maneuver to take some of the weight off the arms. Sometimes edges will be available for short steps in the process.

Undercling. An "undercling" is a classic example of handholds and footholds working in opposition. It is commonly used in places where the rock projects outward, forming a bulge or small overhang. Underclings can be used in the tops of buckets, also. The hands are placed "palms-up" underneath the bulge, applying an upward pull. Increasing this upward pull creates a counterforce, or body tension, which applies more weight and friction to the footholds. The arms and legs should be kept as straight as possible to reduce fatigue. The climber can often lean back slightly in the undercling position, enabling him to see above the overhang better and search for the next hold.

Lieback. The "lieback" is another good example of the hands working in opposition to the feet. The technique is often used in a vertical or diagonal crack separating two rock faces that come together at, more or less, a right angle (commonly referred to as a dihedral). The crack edge closest to the body is used for handholds while the feet are pressed against the other edge. The climber bends at the waist, putting the body into an L-shaped position. Leaning away from the crack on two pull holds, body tension creates friction between the feet and the hands. The feet must be kept relatively high to maintain weight, creating maximum friction between the sole and the rock surface. Either full sole contact or the smearing technique can be used, whichever seems to produce the most friction.

The climber ascends a dihedral by alternately shuffling the hands and feet upward. The lieback technique can be extremely tiring, especially when the dihedral is near vertical. If the hands and arms tire out before completing the sequence, the climber will likely fall. The arms should be kept straight throughout the entire maneuver so the climber's weight is pulling against bones and ligaments, rather than muscle. The legs should be straightened whenever possible.

Placing protection in a lieback is especially tiring. Look for edges or pockets for the feet in the crack or on the face for a better position to place protection from, or for a rest position. Often, a lieback can be avoided with closer examination of the available face features. The lieback can be used alternately with the jamming technique, or vice versa, for variation or to get past a section of crack with difficult or nonexistent jam possibilities. The lieback can sometimes be used as a face maneuver.

Stemming. When the feet work in opposition from a relatively wide stance, the maneuver is known as stemming. The stemming technique can sometimes be used on faces, as well as in a dihedral in the absence of solid handholds for the lieback.

The classic example of stemming is when used in combination with two opposing push holds in wide, parallel cracks, known as chimneys. Chimneys are cracks in which the walls are at least 1 foot apart and just big enough to squeeze the body into. Friction is created by pushing outward with the hands and feet on each side of the crack. The climber ascends the chimney by alternately moving the hands and feet up the crack. Applying pressure with the back and bottom is usually necessary in wider chimneys. Usually, full sole contact of the shoes will provide the most friction, although

Continued ➡

smearing may work best in some instances. Chimneys that do not allow a full stemming position can be negotiated using the arms, legs, or body as an integral contact point. This technique will often feel more secure since there is more body to rock contact.

The climber can sometimes rest by placing both feet on the same side of the crack, forcing the body against the opposing wall. The feet must be kept relatively high up under the body so the force is directed sideways against the walls of the crack. The arms should be straightened with the elbows locked whenever possible to reduce muscle strain. The climber must ensure that the crack does not widen beyond the climbable width before committing to the maneuver. Remember to look for face features inside chimneys for more security in the climb.

Routes requiring this type of climbing should be avoided as the equipment normally used for protection might not be large enough to protect chimneys. However, face features, or a much narrower crack in one or both corners, may sometimes be found deeper in the chimney allowing the use of normal size protection.

Slab Technique. A slab is a relatively smooth, low-angled rock formation that requires a slightly modified climbing technique. Since slab rock normally contains few, if any, holds, the technique requires maximum friction and perfect balance over the feet.

On lower-angled slab, the climber can often stand erect and climb using full sole contact and other mountain walking techniques. On steeper slab, the climber will need to apply good smearing technique. Often, maximum friction cannot be attained on steeper slab from an erect stance. The climber will have to flex the ankles and knees so his weight is placed more directly over the balls of the feet. He may then have to bend at the waist to place the hands on the rock, while keeping the hips over his feet.

The climber must pay attention to any changes in slope angle and adjust his body accordingly. Even the slightest change in the position of the hips over the feet can mean the difference between a good grip or a quick slip. The climber should also take advantage of any rough surfaces, or other irregularities in the rock he can place his hands or feet on, to increase friction.

Down Climbing. Descending steep rock is normally performed using a roped method; however, the climber may at some point be required to down climb a route. Even if climbing ropes and related equipment are on hand, down climbing easier terrain is often quicker than taking the time to rig a rappel point. Also, a climber might find himself confronted with difficulties part way up a route that exceed his climbing ability, or the abilities of others to follow. Whatever the case may be, climbing is a skill well worth practicing.

Caution

1. Down climbing can inadvertently lead into an unforeseen dangerous position on a descent. When in doubt, use a roped descent.
2. Down climbing is accomplished at a difficulty level well below the ability of the climber. When in doubt, use a roped descent.

On easier terrain, the climber can face outward, away from the rock, enabling him to see the route better and descend quickly. As the steepness and difficulty increase, he can often turn sideways, still having a good view of the descent route, but being better able to use the hands and feet on the holds available. On the steepest terrain, the climber will have to face the rock and down climb using good climbing techniques.

Down climbing is usually more difficult than ascending a given route. Some holds will be less visible when down climbing, and slips are more likely to occur. The climber must often lean well away from the rock to look for holds and plan his movements. More weight is placed on the arms and handholds at times to accomplish this, as well as to help lower the climber to the next foothold. Hands should be moved to holds as low as waist level to give the climber more range of movement with each step. If the handholds are too high, he may have trouble reaching the next foothold. The climber must be careful not to overextend himself, forcing a release of his handholds before reaching the next foothold.

Caution

Do not drop from good handholds to a standing position. A bad landing could lead to injured ankles or a fall beyond the planned landing area.

Descending slab formations can be especially tricky. The generally lower angle of slab rock may give the climber a false sense of security, and a tendency to move too quickly. Down climbing must be slow and deliberate, as in ascending, to maintain perfect balance and weight distribution over the feet. On lower-angle slab the climber may be able to stand more or less erect, facing outward or sideways, and descend using good flat foot technique. The climber should avoid the tendency to move faster, which can lead to uncontrollable speed.

On steeper slab, the climber will normally face the rock and down climb, using the same smearing technique as for ascending. An alternate method for descending slab is to face away from the rock in a "crab" position. Weight is still concentrated over the feet, but may be shifted partly onto the hands to increase overall friction. The climber is able to maintain full sole contact with the rock and see the entire descent route. Allowing the buttocks to "drag behind" on the rock will decrease the actual weight on the footholds, reducing friction, and leading to the likelihood of a slip. Facing the rock, and down-climbing with good smearing technique, is usually best on steeper slab.

—From *Military Mountaineering* (Field Manual 3-97.61)

Basic Bouldering Moves

Bobbi Bensman
Photographs by Jim Surette

[Editor's note: Bouldering is the sport of rock climbing on large boulders or low cliffs.]

Holds and Grips

Crimping. This is the basic way boulderers grab the rock. To crimp, take a hold with your fingers close together and bent at the first knuckle. It's a simple but effective technique that will let you hang on to some of the worst holds on the planet—incut flakes, microthin edges, even near slopers. Sometimes you can even find a groove or a little nubbin on a sloper that you hold onto by crimping.

You'll hold on better if you can get as many of your fingers on the hold as possible. Wrap your thumb over your index finger for a firmer grip. This also distributes the weight more evenly and places less stress on the other finger joints. The pinky will want to come off the rock when you crimp; at least it always does for me. It's important to keep as many fingers as you can on that crimp.

The crimp is an essential grip, but it requires a lot of arm and hand strength to use it effectively. Crimping also stresses the tiny

Crimping.

Open-handed grip.

Continued ➡

Pinch grip.

tendons in the hand, putting them at great risk of injury. Crimping properly reduces your chances of getting hurt.

Pinch Grip. The pinch grip is a favorite of mine; I use it all the time. It's used when the only way to grip a hold is to pinch or squeeze it with your fingers or hands. To pinch properly, place four fingers on one side of the hold and the thumb on the other side—then squeeze as hard as you can. Like crimping, pinching requires strength that takes time to develop. Pinching sounds simple, but it does require practice to master and use effectively. Once you can do it right, you'll use pinching all the time. Pinch-gripping is a good way to protect an injured tendon; it's easier on the tendons than crimping and pocket pulling are.

Open-handed Grip. The open-handed grip is less stressful than the pinch grip, since it spreads the weight over more of the skeletal system of the hand. Open-handed grips can be completely open—with the fingers held straight, the fingertips not gripping anything at all—to near pinch grips. Open grips work great when the holds are giant, rounded, and slopey. Using a completely open grip is known as palming; the hand is flat and the entire palm is placed directly on the rock. Palming works because of the friction between the rock and the skin of the palm. Moving the hand even a little breaks the friction, and the hand starts to slide—so don't move it.

A side note: When you're concentrating on your grip, don't become so focused that you forget to keep your torso strong and tucked in. The grip will be more effective if you keep up your energy from the sternum to just below the hips. When I climb, I think of that part of my body as a steel cable and try to keep it tight, especially when I take open-handed grips and pinches. Even with your feet on big, comfortable jugs, you need body tension to hold you in. The more powerful your abdominal area is, the easier it will be to keep yourself on the rock . . . Good grips and tension in the torso will bring you much bouldering success. I promise.

Static Motion and Dynamic Motion

There are two basic ways the boulderer can move over vertical space: static motion and dynamic motion. Beginning boulderers tend to move statically almost all the time. The body freezes, a hand or foot moves to another hold, the body moves, locks off, then the hand or foot reaches again, and so on. Beginners usually concentrate on maintaining three points of contact with the rock while moving the fourth point, which is very deliberate and controlled and feels relatively safe. Experienced boulderers, too, fall back on using three-point contact climbing—especially when they are gripped out of their gourds—because it enables them to down-climb from a perilous position to safety, which is almost impossible to do using dynamic moves.

After beginners start to feel comfortable, they'll appreciate how dramatically dynamic movement can extend their range. "Dynos" are a way to reach holds that seem to be just beyond the climber's grasp. To do a dyno, the climber sinks slightly, then pushes off with the legs and whichever hand has the current hold, before reaching for the new hold with the other hand. The dyno's energy comes from the strength of the leg muscles.

You simply have to master dynamic movement to be a good boulderer (I admit it: dynos are one of my longtime weaknesses). Dynos are the only way to reach handholds that are far apart—beyond the reach of the climber who's trying to maintain three points of contact. They also can get you out of sticky situations: Let's say you just can't hold a locked-off position and at the same time reach up and feel for the next hold. And to make things worse, your present hold is shaky and you're starting to lose it. You spot a killer jug a few feet above you. It's definitely farther than you can reach, so you use momentum, jump up, and snag it! That's a dyno—an all-or-nothing move, a belief move. If you miss it, you hit the crash pad (but hey, life goes on).

Women sometimes shy away from doing dynamic moves. I've heard many say they're afraid because they feel they are too short. But it's shorter climbers—men and women—who can benefit the most from dynamic movement. It definitely should be a part of every climber's repertoire.

Dynos are also the key to making a big move from a solid hold. Say you have one supersolid hold and the next one is four feet above you and there's nothing but smooth rock in between. The only way to reach the hold is to do a gigantic jump: You need to make a dyno. A big part of doing dynos properly is sensing the best time to throw your hand up and snag the hold. You'll get the most height gain if you grab the hold at the absolute peak of the jump, the instant before you change direction, which is known as the "dead point." Just before gravity starts to pull you back down, latch the hold. It takes lots of practice to be able to sense the dead point. Believe in yourself; you can do it.

There are different types of dynos. The one described above is a single-handed dyno. A double dyno is when you lunge upward and

reach with both hands—all four of your limbs come off the wall at once. A well-done double dyno is an unbelievable move. You are airborne, moving upward, and at the very top of the flight, just before you start to drop down to the earth, you snag the hold with both hands.

The key to a good dyno is to get your feet in the proper position before you start your lunge. You want a firm, predictable push from the rock, so you need a solid base. It's important to experiment with foot placement. Sometimes you'll want your feet placed on lower holds, sometimes on higher ones. Don't fall prey to tunnel vision and look for the same type of foothold every time you set up for a dyno. Be creative and try everything. Every dynamic situation is different, and your footholds will need to be, too.

Indoor climbing gyms are great places to practice dynos. You can make up your own lunges and try them again and again until they're perfect. Start slow and build up your confidence and skills with smaller moves until you feel ready to try bigger lunges. I kid you not, once you get hooked on bouldering, you'll find that many of the world's greatest problems require lunges.

A dyno is a dramatic move that will improve your climbing skills enormously once you master it. But doing a dyno isn't always the best choice. You must carefully assess the risks involved to help you decide whether to dyno or not. If the only consequence of failure is a short drop on to a crash pad, you'll probably conclude that you have nothing to lose and go for it. On the other hand, if you are bouldering high above sharp, hard rocks, you might decide that the best choice is to not dyno and statically down-climb your way to safety.

The dead point (not the same dead point mentioned before) is a mini-dyno. In a true dyno, one or both feet come off the wall or rock. Usually in a dead point, the holds you are moving off of are poor and the hold you are moving to is just within reach, but you have to thrutch a bit in a dynamic manner to get there. When you dead point, your feet stay on the rock, but you're really using a dynamic motion to get to the next hold.

Good boulderers can dyno to and from a variety of grips—pinch grips, crimps, open-handed grips—and from laybacks and under-clings (described on pages 275 and 276). Versatility is an important part of the sport.

Cross-Through Move

The cross-through move is the basic way boulderers move across the rock. Boulderers traverse—move vertically across the face of the rock—a lot more than conventional rock climbers do. In fact, sideways movement dominates some boulder problems. To cross-through, you grab a handhold with the hand farthest away from the hold—if you're moving to the right, you reach with your left hand, which puts your body in the correct position for the next move; it's really a set-up for the next sequence.

To imagine a climber moving across the rock using cross-through moves, picture six handholds between points A and B, going from left to right. One way the climber could tackle the sequence is to start with both hands matched on the first hold, move the right hand to hold

Continued ➡

#2, then the left to hold #2, then move the right hand to hold #3, then the left to hold #3, and so on all the way to hold #6. This adds up to ten hand movements—not the most efficient path.

But if the climber starts with both hands matched on hold #1, moves the right hand to #2, then crosses the left hand over to #3, the right hand over to #4, crosses the left hand over to hold #5, and ends with the right hand on #6, she's completed the sequence in only five hand movements. This efficient movement makes a big difference: five hand movements are way less fatiguing than ten.

Crossing through is a "hip" thing—each time you cross through you must keep your hip as close to the wall as possible. For example, reach far with your left arm across your body, keeping your left hip close to the wall, left foot in a backstep position. As soon as you gain the left hold, pivot your body to the exact opposite position. You don't want to "barn door" away from the wall, so once the hold is gained, be ready to find a hold for the back-stepping right foot and then roll the shoulders through. Voila! To me, a well-done cross-through move feels very much like telemark skiing: pretty and precise, with no wasted energy.

One-Arm Lock-off
The one-arm lock-off stabilizes one handhold while freeing the other hand to make a static movement. Say you have a hold with each hand. With the hand you want to lock off, pull down hard and far. Keep your body as close to the rock as possible, so your locked-off hand is close to and at the same height as your shoulder. You're now in a better position to move than if you were half bent. Also, keeping the locked-off hand close to the shoulder takes advantage of your upper back muscles, which are stronger than your arm muscles.

Sometimes doing a lock-off and moving statically is more energy-efficient than throwing a dyno. Climbers who shy away from dynos are usually lock-off masters, and vice versa, but it's best to be great at both, so work to master the technique that's weaker.

Second Generation or "Bumping"
You have a solid right handhold and a good potential handhold (#1) in the distance. You decide it's best to reach for #1 with your left hand so you'll be in the proper position for the next sequence. Then you notice an intermediate handhold (#2) a teeny bit lower than the first one you saw. You see that #2 can help you gain #1, so in one smooth, quick, continuous motion you snag #2 with your left hand and then use your momentum to gain #1 with the same hand. That's the quick double-hand move called bumping, which seems like a real '90s fad, but is actually something boulderers have done for a long time.

Gaston
The Gaston is a move that helps you make use of even the tiniest holds the rock might offer, especially vertical handholds, or flakes. To picture how you do a Gaston, imagine you have a five-inch-long vertical handhold. To make use of it you must place all of your fingers on it and push it away from your body in the direction of the next hold. Sometimes, if the hold is tiny, you can only get bits of your fingers on it. I use the Gaston a lot, even though it's a strenuous move that really puts my arm and shoulder muscles to work.

(Why's it called a Gaston? It's named after Frenchman Gaston Rebuffat, a climber, author, and film maker who was a pioneer of many modern climbing techniques.)

Laybacking
All boulderers depend on laybacking, especially when they're faced with sloping or vertical holds. It's tiring but energy efficient—a fundamental move all good boulderers have to master. I think of laybacking as kind of like climbing a palm tree, if you can imagine that. To layback properly, grab the lip of a crack, then bring your feet up and push straight into the rock. Pull with your arms and push with your feet to create opposing pressure against opposite sides of a crack. You need to find a comfortable middle position for your feet: too high and your arms won't be able to hold, too low and your feet will slip out. Move one limb at a time. Don't try big moves during a layback. Shuffle.

Underclinging
Underclinging is how you take an upside-down hold, one that faces the earth. Grab it with your palms facing skyward, fingers on one side, thumb on the other. You can undercling an edge, crimp, or sloper, but to do it effectively you'll need strong arm muscles. You'll know instantly if a climber does a lot of underclinging: they'll have bulging biceps.

Like in laybacking, the feet play an important role in underclinging. You want good footholds that offer a firm foundation. When you undercling, the less there is to stand on, the higher your feet need to be—this enables you to get more weight on your feet. To practice moving sideways on an undercling, shuffle one hand and one foot at a time.

More Moves

MANTELING
Boulderers seem to forget that the fundamental move of manteling can often come in handy, especially when they find themselves on a severely sloping ramp or shelf—no edge, no grip, no nothing in sight—just below the top of a problem. You're up high, you've come far, you've got one more move to make; how do you finish?

You gotta mantel. Place both hands flat on the rock, wrists out, fingers pointing in. Pull yourself up so your chest is even with the top of the boulder, then lock off with one arm and place the heel of the other hand on the ledge, fingertips pointing inward toward the other hand. Cock the elbow of the arm not locked off up into a vertical position, as though you were going to support your weight with that arm. Do the same with the other arm—both elbows are now pointing to the sky. Push down until both arms are straight, then bring one foot up to support your weight. Press up to a standing position—staying balanced—and you've done it.

You can mantel nice edges, too, and you don't have to mantel with both arms. If one hand is on a solid crimp and the other is on a nice edge that's a little too low to help you reach the next hold, turn your fingers inward and mantel the hold.

One-arm lock-off.

Continued ➡

Laybacking.

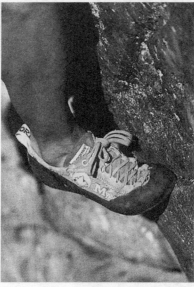

Edging.

Smearing.

strength and allow climbers to do some amazing things on the rock. You don't have to be a superstar or a honed mama to be a great boulderer. Of course, it does help to have it all. But—for crying out loud—who *does* have it all?

Good footwork takes time to develop. Too often boulderers just slap their feet on the rock and then shuffle around looking for a solid hold. When they do this, they usually find the worst one. To learn good footwork, boulderers have to improve what I call their "eye-to-foot coordination." Here's how: Make sure you always place your feet on the best part of every foothold. Watch yourself do it. Take your time. Consciously look for and use the best part of each and every foothold. On real and artificial holds, look for tiny pits or slopes.

It's important to think "feet first." Establishing solid foot placements *before* making a move helps take pressure off the upper body. Flow up the rock like a stream of water, moving along the path of least resistance. Take advantage of everything you can. Let your lower body carry the weight whenever possible; leg muscles, especially the quads, are always stronger than biceps or pecs, no matter how many push-ups you do.

Smearing. Smearing is the footwork technique beginners are most familiar with. To smear, you put as much footsole rubber on the rock as possible to create friction that allows you to grip. Smooth slopes without edges require you to smear like crazy. To do it properly, place your foot on the part of the rock that slopes the least. Spread your weight solidly and evenly over the entire sole of your foot. If you push hard enough and keep your torso tense, you can get a good hold even on overhangs and vertical rock.

Smearing is a belief move—you have to trust your technique. Sometimes your feet will sketch right off the rock and you'll be outta there. Experiment to build confidence. Also, try different kinds of boots with sticky rubber. Boots with soft or no mid-soles work best—slip last boots instead of *board* last boots.

Edging. Another basic foot technique is edging—butting the edge of your boot onto a mini rock ledge. Although you'll usually edge with the inside part of your foot, an inch or two from the toe, you can use all of the edges of your sticky rubber sole or rand. Carefully place the inside edge of your boot on even the smallest of features—you'll be surprised at how easily you can stand on them.

You'll use smearing and edging on steep rock, but you'll also need to use some fancier footwork.

Backstepping. Backstepping, long popular in France, is an effective way to extend your vertical reach. It involves butting the outside edge of your boot into nubbins or vertical edges while keeping your hip as close to the wall as possible. If you're reaching up with your hip against the wall, you'll get a lot more extension than if you face the wall straight on. Try it, you'll see.

So often climbers focus on using only the inside edges of their boots, which always puts their body in a straight-on position. Backstepping adds variety to the climber's repertoire, but, to be honest, it's not always efficient, especially if the next handhold is far away.

FIGURE-FOUR REACH

The figure-four reach is not real common, but it can be effective in certain situations. It's a wild, long static move that can get you up as high as a dyno can. Say you have both hands on a jug and you want to get your left hand on a hold that's fairly far away. Lift the left foot and thread it between your hands, putting the foot then the leg over your right wrist; turn and twist until your crotch is resting on your right wrist. Now pull yourself into an upright position—the handhold that seemed so distant is now reachable.

The figure-four requires you to pull hard, so you definitely need to start with as friendly a hold as you can find. Even so, sharp edges cutting into your skin is a price you might have to pay to make the move. If you do it, beware of any sudden wrist pain; the figure-four puts tons of stress there.

FOOTWORK

Footwork is often overlooked, but it's absolutely critical in bouldering. Some people think bouldering is strictly an upper-body sport. They're wrong. Masterful footwork and smart body positioning can make up for a lack of upper-body

Continued ➡

Heel-hooking.

In a straight-arm position, the climber will have to do one heck of a lock-off to gain that hold, which uses up a lot of energy. Try back-stepping and using straight arms and rolling your hips to gain that hold instead.

Drop-Knee. A more intense version of the backstep—to do a drop-knee, put your foot on a vertical edge and then pivot, moving the inside part of your knee away from the rock, far enough so that your hip is against the wall and your knee is facing earthward. The drop-knee is especially useful on overhanging rock to hold your body into the wall and give you height.

Foot Dynos. When you're struggling with one strong foothold and two precarious hand-holds, maybe a pinch grip and a two-finger thin pocket undercling, your next best move might be to throw a foot up into the next hold: a foot dyno.

Step-Throughs. Crossing through with your feet (a step-through) just like you cross through with your hands is a great technique for traverses. I know its' tempting to match on every hold of a traverse, but step-throughs allow you

to eliminate moves and save your energy. Efficiency is the name of the game. (You'll also look good doing it.)

Heel-Hooking. Heel-hooking—using your foot as a kind of third hand or claw—is another great technique for traverses. To heel-hook, raise your foot over your head and hook the heel of your boot over or behind any feature that looks like it will hold your weight. (Your hamstrings have to be well stretched to try this move.) Heel-hooking takes weight off your upper body, letting you cop a quick rest on the rock.

Remember that if you heel-hook in slip-pers, they tend to pull off; boots offer more support. Remember, too, that heel-hooking can be dangerous to your health. Don't forget to turn your heel-hook into a "toe-on" foot place-ment as you stand up to avoid damaging your inner knee, and to gain more height.

A similar technique, toe-hooking, is espe-cially useful on overhanging rock. To toe-hook, use the toe of your boot the same way you would use your fingers in an upward pull. If you can hold this position and find something to push

against, you are "push-pulling" or bicycling—one foot is pulling toward your body while the other pushes away. This technique, too, takes weight off your upper body, saving energy you may need later.

High Stepping. High stepping offers a good way to get some quick vertical height gain. Step up high and plant the inside edge of your boot or your toe, then put all your weight on that foot. Flagging the opposite foot out as you make a high step can help you stay balanced.

Warning: this move can be hazardous to your health! Many climbers, including me, have torn the medial meniscus, the soft cartilage surrounding the knee joint, while high stepping. Pain is the unmistakable warning sign that proceeding is a bad idea. If you feel even a slight twinge while high stepping, retreat and use another technique, a back-step or a drop-knee.

Knee-Barring. A knee bar is a jam that works well if the spacing of the rock is just right. To knee-bar, put your toe or foot on one hold and your knee up against an opposing corner, roof, or bulge. Flexing the calf muscle or pushing against the knee takes weight off your upper body; if the knee bar is good enough, it can provide a no-hands rest. Even if the knee bar is a little shaky, it can still be useful for taking some weight off (a knee scum), which can let you make a quick shake out or a move forward.

Remember, knee bars can be extremely painful, especially if the rock is sharp. Wear long pants or kneepads to help protect your legs. Pull the pad up above the kneecap and use it as a thigh pad. I sometimes sew sticky La Sportiva rubber on my kneepad, which not only adds cushioning, but also makes me feel as if I stick better in the jam. I've seen Chris Knuth climb while wearing cut-off Levis for this effect. Whatever works.

Flagging. Your body will tend to want to flag a leg out as a natural way to stay balanced during a move. Say you are rocking onto one foot in a high step. Flagging the opposite leg out behind creates proper balance by forcing your center of gravity downward. Flagging your leg inside does likewise.

There are quite a few footwork techniques and body positions that will help you tackle just about any bouldering problem you'll face. Learn and master them all and you'll have a full bag of tricks to take to the rock.

Crack Technique

Boulderers often encounter all kinds of cracks they can grip with the hands or the feet. They must know how to climb them. *Free Climbing with John Bachar*, another book in this series, offers a detailed look at crack-climbing techniques, including finger locks, finger stacking, and all types of jams.

Completing Boulder Problems

Onsight flashing is, to me, the purest form of climbing. The *onsight flash* is when you approach a boulder problem knowing absolutely nothing about how to solve it except what you can learn from studying the holds you can see, then, with no other knowledge of the hand- or foothold

Continued ➔

sequences, you do the route, start to finish, without falling. To me, the onsight flash is the ultimate—a beautiful thing, pure and free, just you and the rock.

In most cases, boulder problems are short enough and close enough to the ground that you can see every hold, especially if you follow the trail of chalk left by other climbers. While you're standing on the ground, you might be able to picture yourself moving from hold to hold, positioning your feet and body to solve the sequence in its entirety. If you can do this, you'll know exactly what you want to do before you jump on the boulder. As you climb, take note if what you planned to do really worked, or how you had to change the plan once you were on the rock. Learn from your mistakes.

If you do a boulder problem knowing the right moves in advance—if another climber has told you that the fourth move is a dyno with the left hand, for example, or if you've watched another climber send the problem—then that would be a *flash*. Not an onsight, but definitely a good effort.

Red-pointing a route is when you link all the moves from start to finish without falling. You might have already tried to onsight the problem, or maybe even flash it, and failed. So you went back to the drawing board, rehearsed all the necessary moves, and got to know the rock. Then you solved it—a red point.

I love red-pointing because it gives me an ongoing project to work on. I can wake up in the morning and have a mission, a problem I can focus on, confident that I'll succeed. That's the versatility of bouldering: it offers an in-the-moment workout or a work in progress.

Sometimes it takes a couple of tries to send a boulder problem; it might take years, or you might never get it right. I've flashed, onsighted, and red-pointed boulder problems all over the world, but there are plenty of problems still waiting for me to solve—in the Fontainebleau, Hueco Tanks, the Buttermilks. Some days you can't climb a thing, and you might have to wait weeks, months, or even years until you return to a particularly nagging problem. *Stick with it.* Believe me, it'll be worth the wait.

More and more climbers are into *beta-flashing*, which I must admit kind of bugs me. Beta-flashing is when a climber completes a problem by following the instructions of people on the ground who tell you the moves: right hand to sloper, left to dime edge, and so on. The problem with this for me is that not all climbers are alike. What works for one climber might not work for another. There's usually more than one way to send a problem. You have to do what works best for you.

Falling and Spotting

Bouldering by yourself can be a blast, but it's safer, more productive, and usually more fun to go with other people, especially if you're just starting out. Bouldering with others offers a more relaxed atmosphere in which you'll probably feel more comfortable pushing yourself and testing your limits. I think climbers should use as many spotters as it takes to ensure safety. Those who don't want to use a spotter because they think it shows weakness might be hurting

Flagging outside.

their chances of success; they might not push themselves as hard as they would if they had a spotter. Spotters allow you to relax, concentrate on the climb, and push yourself harder without worrying about falling and getting hurt.

How to Fall. Falling is a part of bouldering, so falling properly is something every boulderer needs to know. Even if you have a dozen spotters, you must take responsibility for your own safety. You must always know how high off the ground you are and exactly where the safe landings are. When you are on lead or top rope, you can fall without much consequence, but when you're bouldering, you must be able to jump off the rock and know how to land correctly. Try to land on both feet, keeping your balance. Bend your knees and sag into the landing so your knees aren't jolted on impact. Stay in control. Don't flail your arms; you might smack your spotter in the face.

Falling properly demands that you know where your body parts are in space, which takes

practice. Learn to fall slowly, just as you would any other climbing skill. Do a single move and take a fall close to the ground. Add another move, and another, and before you know it you're up high enough that a poor landing could do some damage. After your next move, you're up even higher, which can be intimidating. Learning to fall under control will give you the confidence to go on.

How to Spot. The spotter should always have both arms up and both feet solidly on the ground. He should always be moving to where he thinks the climber will land if he comes off the rock. Spotters don't necessarily have to camp out directly below the climber; if the climber is leaning left while doing a hard move, the spotter must move left of the climber's body while keeping an eye on his head. When the climber is close to the ground, the spotter should keep his hands close to the climber's head, preventing it from hitting the rock or the ground if a fall occurs. The spotter should shift his focus to the climber's waist as the climber goes higher; if the climber falls, the waist is where the spotter

Continued ➜

should try to catch—it's the climber's center of gravity. Even if the spotter misses, he should be able to cushion the fall and help the climber land on his feet.

If you can't catch a falling climber by the waist, try latching under the armpits. This can be a bit disgusting if the climber is wearing a tank top, but a brief, unpleasant experience is a small price to pay for saving a life or preventing an injury.

The number-one rule of spotting: Spotters must absolutely stay one hundred percent focused, even if some hottie walks by. Remember: a good spotter focuses exclusively on the climber—catching them if they fall, but otherwise not touching them.

—From *Bouldering with Bobbi Bensman*

Snow and Ice Climates
Greg Davenport

Snow Climates

The interior continental areas of the two great landmasses of North America and Eurasia that lie between 35 and 70 degrees north latitude constitute the snow climates. The pole side usually meets with the tundra climate, and the southern side with a temperate forest. Vegetation is similar to that found in the temperate climates. The inland animals are migratory yet obtainable. Most shorelines are scraped free of vegetation and animals by winter ice. The larger game animals, such as caribou, reindeer, goats, and musk oxen migrate in these climates. Small animals, such as snowshoe hares, mice, lemmings, and ground squirrels, are prominent. Many birds breed in snow climates. There are two basic kinds of snow climates: continental subarctic and humid continental.

Continental Subarctic Climates
These are regions of vast extremes. Temperatures can have large swings, from −100 degrees F to 110 degrees F, and may fluctuate up to 50 degrees in several hours. These climates are most often seen in Alaska to Labrador and Scandinavia to Siberia. They are cold, snowy forest climates most of the year, with short summers. Winter is the dominant season.

Humid Continental Climates
These regions are generally located between 35 and 60 degrees north latitude, in the central and eastern parts of continents of the middle latitudes. Seasonal contrasts are strong, and the weather is highly variable. In North America, this climate extends from New England westward beyond the Great Lakes region, into the Great Plains and the prairie provinces of Canada. Summers are cooler and shorter than in other temperate zones. A high percentage of precipitation is snow.

In both of these types of snow climates, there are seasonal extremes of daylight and darkness. Long nights and minimal sun exposure are common and present a problem for a survivor.

Ice Climates

The terrain of an ice climate varies greatly. Most of the landmass is composed of tundra. In its true form, the tundra is treeless. Vast, rugged mountain ranges are found in the area and rise several thousand feet above the surrounding areas. Steep terrain, snow and ice fields, glaciers, and very high wind conditions make this a very desolate place. Continental glaciers, such as the ice caps covering Greenland and the Antarctic continent, are large expanses of wind-swept ice moving slowly toward the sea. Animal life is poor in species but rich in numbers. Commonly, large animals, birds, and fish can be found. In the Antarctic, however, animals are virtually nonexistent. Most common are seals and penguins, along with seabirds. There are three kinds of ice climates: marine subarctic, tundra, and ice cap.

Marine Subarctic Climate
This climate is found between 50 and 60 degrees north latitude and 45 and 60 degrees south latitude on the windward coasts, on islands, and over wide expanses of ocean in the Bering Sea and North Atlantic, touching points of Greenland, Iceland, and Norway. In the Southern Hemisphere, the climate is found on small land-masses. These regions typically have persistent cloudy skies, strong winds, and high rainfall.

Tundra Climate
This climate is found north of 55 degrees north latitude and south of 50 degrees south latitude. The average temperature is below 50 degrees F. Proximity to the ocean and persistent cloud cover keep summer air temperatures down, despite abundant solar energy at this latitude near the summer solstice. There are several types of tundra.

Shrub tundra. Shrubs, herbs, and mosses occur in this zone.

Wooded tundra. Subarctic wooded areas include a variety of tree species.

Bogs. Bogs are characterized by large peat moss mounds.

Ice Cap Climate
There are three vast regions of ice on the earth: Greenland, the Antarctic continental ice caps, and the larger area of floating sea ice in the Arctic Ocean.

—From *Surviving Cold Weather*

A Snow Primer
Buck Tilton and John Gookin

Familiarity with snow is essential for safe and disciplined winter camping. When the temperature drops below freezing and water vapor condenses into crystals, snow falls. What we call snowflakes are more accurately described as crystals that form around tiny, solid particles in the air, such as dust or salt. As condensed water vapor falls, it encounters a variety of air temperatures, air currents, and humidity levels, and these factors determine what kind of crystals form. Cold, still air usually produces feathery plates or "stellars" the lightest and driest snow,

falling with infinite grace and beauty. As the mercury rises, the snow becomes harder, forming needles, columns, dendrites, and, irregular clumps. When the air warms to near freezing, the snow crystals may form into sleet (balls of snow with a hard shell and a soggy center) or hail (solid ice balls that can strike the earth—and winter campers—with ruinous force).

Rime
Technically, rime is not snow at all but rather ice that forms from the freezing of supercooled liquid when it contacts a subfreezing surface. When wind and humidity are particularly high, rime ice may appear as little "flags" that point into the direction of the prevailing wind. At other times, rime ice takes on a wispy look, resembling "snow feathers."

Snow Metamorphosis

One way to think about snow is to distinguish between snow crystals falling or recently fallen from the sky and those on or in the ground that have been altered by a variety of forces and conditions. In winter, each storm lays down a layer of snow. The accumulated layers, known collectively as the snowpack, meet the atmosphere at a boundary called the snow surface, and they meet the earth at the ground surface.

Snowpacks are prone to constant structural change over time, a process called metamorphosis. Metamorphosis alters the form and structure of snow crystals from the moment they land on earth until they are completely melted. Snow metamorphosis is controlled primarily by temperature, happening quickly near freezing and stopping almost altogether below minus 40 degrees F. Pressure and proximity to the warm ground also participate in metamorphosis, causing snow deep in the snowpack to change faster than snow near the surface. Snow on the surface may change rapidly in response to wind, sun, and other factors. These changes in the snow surface—from powder to ice to slush—make backcountry endeavors both fun and challenging.

Layers within the snowpack may be relatively weak (not well-bonded) or strong (well-bonded). When there is a consistent temperature gradient throughout the snowpack (1 degree C [33.8 degrees F] per 10 cm), the crystals, whatever their original forms, consolidate into a well-bonded mass. This is called rounded or equilibrium snow, and the crystals are often just called rounds. A strongly cohesive layer of snow can be cut neatly into blocks for an igloo or shaped creatively into a snow cave or kitchen countertop.

When the temperature gradient within the snow cover is greater, water vapor tends to migrate from the warmer snow close to the ground toward the colder snow at the surface. Under these conditions, entirely new snow crystals, called facets, are formed. Facets tend to crumble in your hand, and are often found by protruding bushes or near the ground in early-season snowpacks. They are common at high altitude, where the snow surface grows colder and a greater gradient is created between surface and ground. Higher elevations also tend to be windier and to avalanche more often, both of

Continued ➡

which keep the snow thinner and the gradient greater.

Depth hoar (a type of facet) is created early in the season after the first winter storm, usually when temperatures are cold the sky is clear. It is fragile, collapses easily, and is very noncohesive, constituting a weak layer that is prone to avalanche. You're dealing with depth hoar if you dig into the snowpack and, right before you reach the ground, hit a layer of snow that crumbles at your touch. Depth hoar is most dangerous in the early months of the season; as the snowpack deepens and the pressure on it increases, the danger lessens.

Surface hoar is created on top of the snowpack on nights that are humid, cold, and clear. It is recognizable by its feathery appearance. When buried in a snowpack, it becomes a dangerously thin middle layer that is susceptible to avalanche.

Just as there may be strong or weak bonds within a given layer, entire layers may bond well or poorly to adjoining layers. If two layers are poorly bonded, or if a strongly bonded layer sits atop a weakly bonded one, there is the potential for a slab avalanche.

When snow melts and then refreezes, it forms and icy layer that may become a slippery, sliding surface for snow deposited in later storms. This is referred to as melt-freeze metamorphosis. If the melt phase is long enough for water to percolate down through the snow to the ground, a lubricating layer can cover an entire mountainside—a potentially dangerous condition for mountain travelers.

Wind, the greatest mechanical mover of snow, is a powerful change agent. When snow is moved by wind—or by human shoveling or stomping—and is then allowed to set, it hardens through a process called sintering, in which the snow crystals bond firmly together. Old, wind-hammered snow may be thousands of times harder than fresh, powder snow. Sintered snow forms an extraordinarily cohesive layer, one you can walk on without sinking in, and it cuts very nicely into blocks for snow shelters.

Snowpacks developing on slopes undergo another type of mechanical deformation. This deformation occurs because of snow's elasticity (the ability to stretch and return to its original shape) and viscosity (the resistance to free flow) and the force of gravity. Snow tends to flow, or "bend," downhill, a movement called creep. Snow also tends to slide downhill along a slope, a movement called glide. As with metamorphosis, creep and glide are affected by temperature. Snow has minimum viscosity near the freezing point, but as the temperature drops, viscosity increases, and creep and glide slow down. Creep and glide explain some of the marvelous shapes snow can assume.

Dry Snow Versus Wet Snow

The water content of snow is closely related to temperature, and both will impact how easily you can travel through snow-covered terrain. Very dry snow may hold as little as 5% liquid, while wet snow may contain up to 25%. Snow falling at temperatures near the freezing point can weigh three times as much as snow falling at colder temperatures, because it has a much higher water content.

Dry snow (powder) is generally better for traveling, until its depth reaches the point where you are struggling to make headway. After a heavy snowfall of light powder, it may take a day or two for the snow to consolidate enough to keep you on top with skis. It may be spring before it is firm enough to support your weight without skis.

Wet snow not only gets you wet but also adds considerably to your traveling difficulty. Wet snow sticks to skis, crampons, and sometimes boots. Since wet snow falls when the air is relatively warm, it is also difficult to keep from overheating when you are huffing along under a pack. Maritime areas typically receive wet snow, and inland (or "continental") areas receive much drier snow, but early-winter snowfalls in any region can be wet.

One advantage of wet snow is that its frozen surface can often easily be crossed if you travel at night, after the temperature drops, or early in the morning, before the sun softens the surface. When the snow softens, however, you may end up postholing—breaking through the surface up to you knees or higher. If the sunny surface won't support you, try staying in the shade, where the cold lingers longer. If you must posthole, keep your weight on your back leg, step halfway into your next footfall, and wait for the snow to firm up. If postholing overwhelms you, try crawling.

—From *NOLS Winter Camping*

Snow and Terrain
U.S. Army

Snow Composition

Snowflakes are formed from water vapor, at or below 32°F., without passing through the liquid water state. Newly fallen snow undergoes many alternations on the ground. As the snowmass on the ground packs and becomes denser, the snowflakes consolidate and the entrapped air is expelled. These changes are caused by effects of temperature, humidity, sunlight and wind.

Temperature. In general, the lower the temperature, the drier the snow and the less consolidation. As the temperature rises, the snow tends to compact more readily. Temperatures above freezing cause wet snow conditions. Lowered night temperatures may refreeze wet snow and form an icy crust on the surface.

Sunlight. In the springtime, sunlight may melt the surface of the snow even though the air temperature is below freezing. When this occurs, dry powder snow is generally found in shaded areas and wet snow in sunlight areas. Movement from sunlit areas into shaded areas is difficult because the wet snow will freeze to skis and snowshoes. After sunset, however, wet snow usually refreezes and the ease of movement improves.

Wind. Wind packs snow solidly. Wind-packed snow may become so hard that skiing or even walking on it makes no appreciable impression on its surface. Warm wind followed by freezing temperatures may create an icy, unbreakable crust on the snow. Under such conditions, skiing and snowshoeing are very difficult. Another effect of wind is that of drifting the snow. The higher the wind velocity and the lighter the snow, the greater the tendency to drift. All troop movement is greatly affected by drifting snow and wind, the effect depending on the relative direction and velocity. In addition, as the wind, increases, the effect of extreme cold (windchill effect) on the body may slow down or temporarily stop movement, possibly requiring troops to take shelter. The snowdrifts created by wind usually make the snow surface wavy, slowing down movement, especially in darkness.

Snow Characteristics

The characteristics of snow which are of greatest interest to the soldier are—

a. **Carrying Capacity.** Generally, when the snow is packed hard, carrying capacity is greater and movement is easier. Although the carrying capacity of ice crust may be excellent, movement generally is difficult because of its slippery surface.

b. **Sliding Characteristics.** All-important to the skier are the sliding characteristics of snow. They vary greatly in different types of snow and temperature variations and materially increase or decrease the movement of the skier, according to the conditions that exist.

c. **Holding Capacity.** The holding capacity of snow is its ability to act upon ski wax in such a way that backslapping of the skis is prevented without impairing the forward sliding capability. Holding capacity changes greatly with different types of snow, making it necessary to have a variety of ski waxes available.

Effects of Snow and Terrain on Individual Movement

...Snow cover, together with the freezing of waterways and swampy areas, changes the terrain noticeably. Generally, the snow covers minor irregularities of the ground. Many obstacles such as rocks, ditches, and fences are eliminated or reduced. Lakes, streams, and muskeg, impassable during the summer, often afford the best routes of travel in the winter when they are frozen and snow-covered. During breakup periods this advantage is reduced, since the snow becomes slushy and the carrying capacity is poor. Even so, skiing or snowshoeing, although slow, is often the only practical way to move during this period. The drop in temperature at night will still freeze the snow surface, creating a good route for a skier or snowshoer during the night and early morning.

The effects of snow and terrain on individual movement vary in different areas.

(1) The arctic tundra and vast subarctic plateaus are similar. They are characterized by large plains and gently rolling terrain with scant vegetation where rocky ridges, scattered rock outcroppings, riverbanks, and scrubby brush still create obstacles to individual movement, when encountered. The shallow snow cover normally found in these areas, as a rule, is firmly packed by wind action and will usually support a man on foot. When the snow has not been wind packed and is still soft, mobility will be increased by the use of skis or snowshoes.

Continued ➔

(2) Forested areas include vast coniferous forests, dense brush, swamps, and numerous lakes and rivers. Skiing and snowshoeing are relatively easy on frozen, snow-covered rivers, lakes, and swamps. In wooded areas concealment is best, but movement is hampered by vegetation and soft snow, therefore, greater skill is required in skiing to avoid trees and other obstacles. These disadvantages are reduced by careful selection of the best routes and following proper trailbreaking procedures. Woods retard the melting of snow in spring often allowing skiing after the open fields are clear of snow. In autumn, the situation is reversed; the deeper snow is generally found in the open fields allowing skiing earlier than in wooded areas.

(3) Mountains present special problems. Their varied and steep terrain place additional demands upon the skill of a skier and make movement on snowshoes or skis very difficult. Slopes which are easy to negotiate in summer often become difficult and dangerous to cross in winter because of deep snow cover which is prone to avalanche. Large drifts and snow cornices present other obstacles and dangers. Snow cover on glaciers obscures crevasses and makes their crossing hazardous.

—From *Basic Cold Weather Manual* (Field Manual 31-76)

Cold-Weather Gear

Greg Davenport
Illustrations by Steven A. Davenport

When traveling into a cold-weather environment, the type of gear you carry can either help or hamper your efforts. Take the time to choose tools that will make your travel and stay more comfortable.

Ice Ax

An ice ax can be used as an anchor for climbing, as a self-belay, to help you self-arrest when sliding down a snow slope (glissading), and to help steady you while climbing by providing a third point of contact. The proper size of an ice ax depends on your body size and the ax's intended use. To size an ice ax, hold its head in one hand, with your fingers draped down the side of the shaft. While standing up straight, let your arm hang free so that the ice ax shaft is pointing toward the ground. From this position, use the following guidelines:

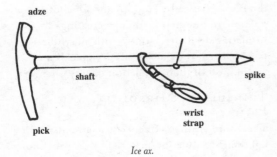

Ice ax.

For basic climbing (general use)
The ax tip should be just shy of touching the ground.

For intermediate climbing (high-angle use)
The ax tip should be 2 to 4 inches (5 to 10 centimeters) shy of the ground.

For snowshoeing
The ax tip should extend 2 to 4 inches (5 to 10 centimeters) beyond the ground.

Snow Shovel

A snow shovel can be used to evaluate avalanche hazards, dig out an avalanche victim, or help build a snow shelter. The ideal snow shovel is small and light enough to carry, yet big and strong enough to perform the needed task. A 20- to 24-inch-long aluminum shovel that has a removable D-shaped handle and one-foot-square blade is a good all-purpose design. A snow or ice saw is often used with a snow shovel, especially when snow blocks are needed for shelter walls. In a pinch, I have used my snowshoes to shovel snow. Should you do this, however, be careful not to break a snowshoe!

Mountaineering Poles

Mountaineering poles help you maintain your balance when carrying a heavy pack and assist you in getting up should you fall. Unlike ski poles, most mountaineering poles have adjustable telescoping features that allow them to do multiple tasks, adjusting for uphill, downhill, and traversing pole lengths. In addition, when not in use, they can collapse down for easy storage. When using a pole, adjust its length so that when your elbow is bent, your forearm is slightly less than perpendicular to your body, with the hand higher than the elbow. If you are evaluating this length in a store, place the handle side down and grasp the pole below its basket, since the length is based on the pointed tip being inserted into the snow up to the basket.

Probe

A probe is an essential item when traveling into terrain where the chance for avalanche conditions is present. Probes should be lightweight, strong, and quickly assembled. Most probes run from 8 to 10 feet and can be broken down into 16- to 18-inch lengths for ease of carrying. Aluminum is the most common material, as it is lightweight and inexpensive. In a pinch, a mountaineering pole can be used.

Avalanche Transceiver

An avalanche transceiver is an electronic device that, when used properly, helps searchers find a victim who has been buried in an avalanche. When traveling in avalanche hazard areas, each member of the team should carry a transceiver, or beacon. The newer transceivers are digital with dual antennas, digital and analog, which has made them far more efficient. The Barryvox digital transceiver (RED 457) has an integrated microprocessor, digital technology, a simple pushbutton menu, and an easy-to-follow digital display that displays the direction and distance to your subject.

PIEPS avalanche transceiver.

Avalung

The AvaLung is an innovative idea that should become standard gear for anyone traveling into avalanche country. It is a filtration system designed to help an avalanche victim breathe by drawing air directly from the snow-pack through a mouthpiece attached to the apparatus. Exhaled carbon dioxide is directed out an exhaust tube, ensuring that you receive a fresh air supply and preventing the formation of an oxygen-depriving ice layer in front of your face. To be effective, the mouthpiece must be quickly inserted into your mouth before debris restricts your movement.

Clinometer

A clinometer helps you determine avalanche hazards by measuring the slope of a hillside. Avalanches most often occur on slopes of 30 to 45 degrees, but they sometimes start on slopes as gentle as 25 degrees or as steep as 60 degrees. Recognizing a slope angle is key to identifying a slope's avalanche potential. The clinometer is simply a protractor with a plumb bob attached. While the plumb bob is hanging free, you hold the base parallel to the hillside. The number where the plumb bob line crosses the protractor is your slope angle.

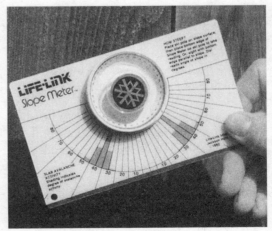

Clinometer.

Continued →

Altimeter

A digital altimeter can provide information about your elevation that, when used along with a map and the terrain, can help you pinpoint your location. Since an altimeter reading is based on air pressure, like a barometer, it is affected by changes in weather. With this in mind, you'll need to set its elevation from a known point when you start, and again on a regular basis as you reach new known points.

—From *Surviving Cold Weather*

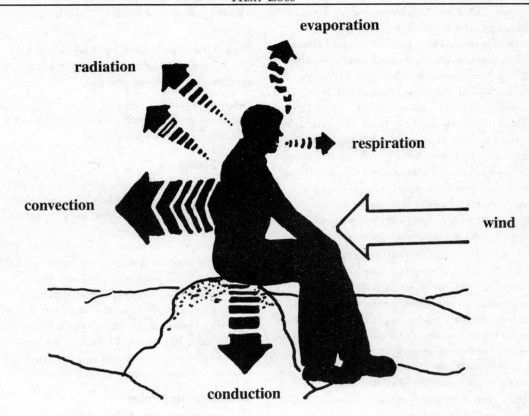

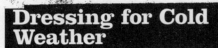

Dressing for Cold Weather

Greg Davenport
Illustrations by Steven A. Davenport

Clothing is your first line of defense against the environment. In cold weather, your clothing insulates you, keeping you warm; in hot weather, proper clothing helps keep you cool.

Heat Loss

The body is constantly regulating itself in an attempt to keep its thermostat approximately between 97 and 99 degrees F. As heat is lost through radiation, conduction, convection, evaporation, and respiration, you'll need to adjust your clothing to help maintain your body's core temperature.

Radiation

Heat transfers from your body into the environment through the process of radiation. The head, neck, and hands pose the greatest threat for heat loss due to radiation. Increased clothing will slow the process but doesn't stop it from occurring.

Conduction

Heat is lost from the body through conduction when it comes in contact with any cold item. This poses a significant problem when clothing is soaking wet, and in such circumstances, you should remove and change the clothes or wring out as much moisture as possible.

Convection

Similarly to radiation, convection is a process of heat loss form the body to the surrounding cold air. But unlike radiation, convection would be absent if you were standing completely still and there was absolutely no wind. The wind and your movements cause you to lose heat from convection. Wearing clothes in a loose and layered fashion will help trap the warm air next to your body, which in turn decreases the heat lost from convection and also insulates you from the environment.

Evaporation

Heat is lost through the evaporation process that occurs with perspiration. Monitoring your activity to ensure that you avoid sweating helps. If you are inactive, layered clothing will trap dead air; this will decrease the amount of heat lost through evaporation and actually keep you warmer.

Respiration

Heat is lost through the normal process of breathing. To decrease the heat lost by breathing in cold air, cover or encircle your mouth with a loose cloth. By doing this, you will trap dead air and allow it to warm up slightly prior to breathing it in.

Materials

How well you adjust to heat loss depends on how well your clothes insulate you. Most clothing materials are made of intertwined fibers, which create spaces that trap dead air. Clothes made of down trap air between the feather fibers. As the body loses heat, it is trapped inside the dead air space, and that's how clothes keep you warm. The clothing you select to take on a trip should not only protect you from cold and wet conditions but also provide the breathability needed to avoid overheating. Winter clothes are made from many materials, both natural and synthetic. When choosing clothing for cold climates, it's helpful to understand the characteristics of these materials.

Natural Fabrics

Cotton

Cotton has been nicknamed "death cloth," since it loses almost all of its insulating quality when wet. Wet cotton will absorb many times its weight, has extremely poor wicking qualities, and takes forever to dry.

Down

Down is a very good lightweight, natural insulating material. Like cotton, however, down becomes virtually worthless when wet, the feathers clumping together and no longer trapping dead air. The material is best used in dry climates or when you can guarantee it won't get wet.

Wool

Wool retains most of its insulating quality when wet. Wool also retains a lot of the moisture, however, making it extremely heavy when wet. Wool is also fairly effective at protecting you from wind, allowing it to be worn as an outer layer. Its main drawbacks are its weight and bulkiness.

Synthetic Fabrics

Polyester and polypropylene

As a wicking layer polyester and polypropylene wick well, maintain their insulating quality when wet, and dry quickly. As an insulating layer, these fabrics are lightweight and compressible. They are not very effective at protecting you from the wind, however, and are best accompanied by an outer shell. Common examples of polyester used for the insulating layer are polyester pile and fleece.

Polarguard, Hollofil, and Quallofil

Although these synthetic fibers are most often used in sleeping bags, they can also be found in heavy parkas. Polarguard is composed of sheets, Hollofil of hollow sheets, and Quallofil of hollow sheets that have holes running through the fibers. Basically, Hollofil and Quallofil took Polarguard one step further by creating more insulating dead air space. As with all synthetic fabrics listed, these materials dry quickly and retain most of their insulation quality when wet.

Thinsulate, Microloft, and Primaloft

These thin synthetic fibers create an outstanding lightweight insulation material by allowing more layers. Thinsulate is the heaviest of the three and is most often used in clothing. Microloft and Primaloft are extremely lightweight and are an outstanding alternative to the lightweight down sleeping bag, since they retain their insulation quality when wet.

Continued ➔

NYLON

Nylon is a common shell material often used in parkas, rain and wind garments, and mittens. Since nylon is not waterproof, most manufacturers use either special fabrication techniques or treatments to add the feature.

Polyurethane coatings

These inexpensive lightweight coatings protect from outside moisture, but since they are nonbreathable, they don't allow inside moisture to escape. Only use this type of outer garment when physical exertion is at a minimum.

Breathable waterproof coatings

When applied to the inside of a nylon shell, this coating leaves billions of microscopic pores that are large enough for inside vapors to escape yet small enough to keep raindrops out. These coats cost more than those with polyurethane, but less than those with a breathable laminated waterproof membrane.

Breathable laminated waterproof membrane

Instead of an inner coating, a separate waterproof and breathable membrane is laminated to the inside of the nylon. The membrane is perforated with millions of microscopic pores that work under the same principle as the waterproof coating. Gore-Tex is the most common example.

In order for the breathable fabrics to be effective, you'll need to keep the pores free of dirt and sweat. In addition, only wash and dry them in accordance with the tag instructions, as some will be ruined if cleaned wrong. Finally, don't expect these breathable coats to be perfect. If your heat output is high and you begin to sweat, this moisture cannot escape any more than the rain can get in. To prevent this, you'll need to wear your clothing in a loose and layered fashion.

COLDER Acronym

An acronym that can help you remember how to care for and wear your clothing is COLDER.

CLEAN

Clothes are made of intertwined fibers that, when clean, trap dead air that works as insulation to keep you warm. If clothes are dirty, they lose their ability to insulate you.

AVOID OVERHEATING

Clothes either absorb or repel sweat, causing them to lose their insulating quality or make you wet. In addition, when you become overheated, you lose valuable body heat through evaporation.

LOOSE AND LAYERED

Clothing that is too tight will constrict circulation and predispose you to frostbite. Wearing multiple layers increases the amount of dead air space surrounding the body. It also allows you to add or remove individual layers of clothing as necessary for the given weather conditions. The ability to take a layer off or add it back when needed allows you to avoid getting too cold or overheating by adapting to the climate and the amount of work you are doing. I normally wear three layers: one that wicks moisture away, an insulating layer, and an outer shell.

Wicking layer

Perspiration and moisture wick through this layer, keeping you dry. This is a very important layer, since having wet clothes next to the skin causes twenty-five times greater heat loss than dry ones. Polyester and polypropylene are best for this layer. Cotton is not recommended.

Insulating layer

This layer traps warm air next to the body. Multiple insulating layers may work better than one, as additional air is trapped between them. The best fabrics for this layer are wool, polyester pile, compressed polyester fleece, Hollofil, Quallofil, Polarguard, Thinsulate, Microloft, and Primaloft. Down can be used in dry climates or when you're sure it won't get wet. Sometimes I wear two middle layers, creating another dead air space and providing a finer ability to adjust my layers.

Outer shell

This layer protects you from wind and precipitation. The ideal shell will protect you from getting wet when exposed to rain or snow but has enough ventilation for body moisture to escape. Best for this layer are waterproof coatings that breathe or laminated waterproof membranes that breathe (Gore-Tex). Headgear and gloves are a must, as one-third to one-half of body heat loss occurs from the head and hands.

DRY

Wet clothes lose their insulating quality. To keep the inner layer dry, avoid sweating. Protect your outer layer from moisture by either avoiding exposure to rain or snow or by wearing proper clothing as described above. If your clothes do become wet, dry them by a fire or in the sun. If it's below 32 degrees F and you can't build a fire, let the clothes freeze; once frozen, break the ice out of the clothing. If snow is on your clothes, shake it off; don't brush it off; as this will force the moisture into the fibers.

EXAMINE

Examine your clothing daily for tears and dirt.

REPAIR

Repair any tears as soon as they occur. This may require a needle and thread, so make sure you pack them.

Parka and Rain Pants

A parka and rain pants are needed for protection from moisture and wind. They will normally be made from nylon with a polyurethane coating, a waterproof coating that breathes, or a laminated waterproof membrane that breathes (Gore-Tex). In some cases, a parka will come with an insulating garment that can be zipped inside. Besides the material, there are other criteria to consider when choosing these garments:

APPROPRIATE SIZE

These garments should be big enough that you can comfortably add wicking and insulating layers underneath without compromising your movement. In addition, the parka's lower end should extend beyond your hips to keep moisture away from the top of your pants.

DUAL SEPARATING ZIPPERS

Look for zippers that separate at both ends.

VENTILATION ADJUSTMENT

Parkas should have openings for ventilation in front, at your waist, under your arms, and at your wrist. For rain pants, the openings should be located in the front and along the outside of the lower legs, extending to about mid-calf, making it easier to put on or remove your boots. For females, there are pants available with a zipper

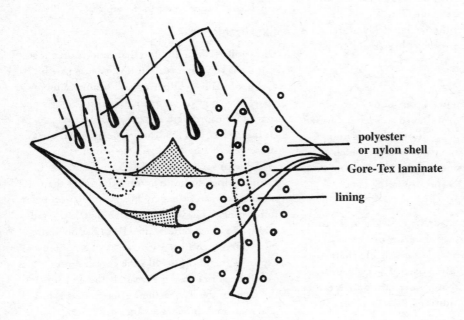

Waterproof breathable nylon.

polyester
or nylon shell
Gore-Tex laminate
lining

Layers of clothing.

Continued ➡

that extends down and around the crotch. The added benefit is obvious. These openings can be adjusted with zippers, Velcro, or drawstrings.

Sealed Seams
Seams should be taped or well bonded, or they will allow moisture to penetrate through the clothing.

Accessible Pockets
What good is a pocket if you can't get to it? In addition, make sure the openings have protective rain baffles.

Brimmed Hood and Neck Flap
A brimmed hood will help channel moisture away from the eyes and face. In addition, a neck flap will help prevent radiant body heat loss from the neck area.

Boots
Boots are a very important part of your clothing. Always choose the right type for your needs, and break the boots in before your trip. When selecting boots, consider the type of travel you intend to do. I have four styles that I use, and each serves a different purpose. They are leather, lightweight leather/fabric, plastic, and rubber.

Leather Boots
Leather boots are ideal all-purpose boots. A stiff upper provides protection for the ankle, and a hard sole will help when kick-stepping and technical climbing. For extreme conditions, you'll need to treat them with a waterproofing material (read the manufacturer's directions on how this should be done) and wear a comfortable, protective wool-blend sock. Another popular option in leather boots is an added Thinsulate and Gore-Tex liner, which helps protect your feet from the cold and moist conditions. If you elect to use Thinsulate or Gore-Tex, be sure you follow the manufacturer's directions explicitly on how to care for and treat the boots. If oils soak through the leather and into the lining, they will nullify their insulating qualities.

Lightweight Leather/Fabric Boots
The lightweight leather/fabric boot is a popular fair-weather boot, since it is lighter and dries faster than the leather boot. On the downside, moisture easily soaks through the fabric, these boots provide less stability for your ankle, and on difficult terrain, they are not rigid enough for a good kick-step and not generally hard enough to be worn with crampons or snowshoes.

Plastic Boots
Plastic waterproof boots are ideal when traveling on hard snow and when conditions require kick-stepping or crampon use for long periods of time. This extremely stiff boot has a removable inner insulating boot that can be quickly dried. Although your feet will get hot and sometimes the liner will get wet from perspiration, the heat will be trapped by the plastic, keeping your feet warm.

Rubber Boots
Rubber boots are most often used for nontechnical extreme cold-weather conditions. They normally have nylon uppers with molded rubber bottoms and removable felt inner boots. As with the plastic boots, the inner boots can be easily removed and dry quickly.

Keeping your boots clean will help them protect you better. For leather and lightweight leather/fabric boots, wash off dirt and debris using a mild soap that doesn't damage leather. For plastic and rubber boots, wash and dry the liners, and clean all dirt and debris from the outer boots.

Socks
Socks need to provide adequate insulation, reduce friction, and wick away and absorb moisture from the skin. Socks most often are made of wool, polyester, nylon, or an acrylic material. Wool tends to dry more slowly than the other materials but is still a great option. Cotton should be avoided, as it loses its insulating qualities when wet. For best results, wear two pairs of socks. The inner sock (often made of polyester) wicks the moisture away from the foot; the outer sock (often a wool blend) provides the insulation that keeps your feet warm. Gore-Tex socks are often worn over the outer pair during extremely wet conditions. Keep your feet dry, and change your socks at least once a day. If any hot spots develop on your feet, immediately apply moleskin before they become blisters.

Gaiters
When traveling in snow or wet conditions, you don't want moisture to enter your boots over the top cuffs. Full-length gaiters will help prevent this from occurring by covering your lower legs from the boots' lower laces to just above the calf muscles. Most gaiters are made of Gore-Tex or a similar breathable material that is waterproof yet allows perspiration to escape. Gaiters are often held together with Velcro, snaps, or zippers. If the gaiters have zippers, make sure they are strong and have protective covering flaps.

Hand Coverings
Since a fair amount of heat is lost from the hands, it is best to keep them covered with gloves or mittens. Gloves encase each individual finger and allow you the dexterity to perform many of your daily tasks. Mittens encase the second through fifth fingers, decreasing your dexterity, but increasing hand warmth from the captured radiant heat. Which you should wear depends on your activity. To get the best of both worlds, I insert my gloved hands inside mittens. I remove just the mittens when I need to work with my hands. My gloves are made from a polyester fleece or a wool-synthetic blend. My mittens are made from a waterproof yet breathable fabric, like Gore-Tex.

Headgear
Since over 50 percent of your body heat is lost through the head, you'll need to keep it covered. There are many types of headgear, and your activity and the elements will dictate which one you choose. As a general rule, there are two basic categories: rain hats and insulating hats.

Rain Hat
A rain hat is often made from nylon or an insulation material with an outer nylon covering. For added waterproof and breathable characteristics, Gore-Tex is often used. For extra protection, choose a hat that has earflaps, which can be used in extreme conditions.

Insulating Hat
An insulating hat is made from wool, polypropylene, or polyester fleece. The most common styles of these are the watch cap and the balaclava. The balaclava is a great option, since it can cover the head, ears, and neck (front and back side), yet leaves an opening for your face.

Because so much heat is lost through the head, headgear *should not* be the first thing you take off when you are overheating. Mild adjustments—such as opening the zipper to your coat—will allow for the gradual changes needed to avoid sweating. In cold conditions, headgear should be removed only when other options have not cooled you down enough.

Eye Protection
Goggles or sunglasses with side shields that filter out UV wavelengths are a must for travel in snow environments. It doesn't take long to burn the eyes, and once this occurs, you will have several days of eye pain, along with light sensitivity, tearing, and a foreign body sensation. Since the symptoms of the burn usually don't show up for four to six hours after the exposure, you can get burned and not even realize it is happening. Once a burn occurs, you'll need to get out of the light, remove contacts if wearing them, and cover the eyes with a sterile dressing until the light sensitivity subsides. If pain medication is available, you'll probably need to use it. Once healed, make sure to protect the eyes to prevent another burn. If no goggles or sunglasses are available, improvise by using either a man-made or natural material that covers the eyes, with a narrow horizontal slit for each eye.

Zippers
Zippers on garments and sleeping bags often break or get stuck. Under mild conditions, this may not present a great problem. In a cold-weather environment, however, you can lose a lot of body heat when you are unable to close a zipper properly. To decrease the odds of zipper problems, your gear should have zippers with a dual separating system (separates at both ends) and teeth made from a material that won't rust or freeze, such as polyester. Your zippers should also be waterproof. If they don't have a baffle covering, apply a waterproof coating to the zipper's backing. The latter option has the advantages of lighter weight and easier access to the zipper.

Skin Protection
Ultraviolet (UV) radiation that reflects off snow and ice is very intense, and it can cause painful and potentially debilitating and sunburn during travel in a snow or ice environment. The best way to avoid this problem is to wear protective clothing. For skin that cannot be covered, use a sunscreen or sun-block. These products are available in various sun protection factor (SPF) ratings, which indicate how much longer than normal you can be exposed to UV radiation prior to burning. They work by absorbing the UV radiation. Sunblock reflects the UV radiation and is most often used in sensitive areas where intense exposure might occur, like the ears and nose. You'll need to constantly reapply these products throughout the day, as their effectiveness is lost over time and due to sweating.

—From *Surviving Cold Weather*

Basic Snow and Ice Travel

Greg Davenport
Illustrations by Steven A. Davenport

How to Load Your Pack

When carrying an internal frame pack on a trail, organize your gear so that the heavier items are on top and close to your back. This method places most of the pack's weight on your hips, making it easier to carry. If you'll be traveling off-trail, organize the pack so that the heavy items are close to the back, from the pack's top to its bottom. With this method, most of the pack's weight is carried by your shoulders and your back, allowing you better balance.

Basic Travel Techniques

Breaking Trail and Setting The Pace

The person breaking trail is working harder than anyone else, and this job needs to be switched at regular intervals between the members of a team. If in a team, set your pace distance so that it is comfortable for all members. Remember the COLDER acronym. If you have dropped layers of clothing and are still sweating, you're going too fast.

Kick-Stepping

When traveling in snow, kick-stepping will not only make your ascent easier, but it will also make it easier for those who are following you. Using the weight of your leg, swing the toe of your boot into the snow, creating a step that

Kick-stepping.

Plunge-stepping.

supports at least the ball of your foot if going straight up, or at least half of your foot if traversing. If you're in a group and are leading an ascent using this technique, consider the strides of those who are following you. When going uphill, lean forward until your body is perpendicular to the earth's natural surface—not that of the hill.

Plunge-Steeping (Down-Climbing)

Plunge-stepping is similar to kick-stepping, except that you are going downhill and kicking your heels into the slope rather than your toes. Slightly bend the knees, and lean backward until your body is perpendicular to the ground at the base of the hill—not the hill's slope.

Traversing

Traversing, or diagonal climbing, is a quick and easy method for getting up or down a hill. When traversing a hill, it may be necessary to slightly shorten your strides as the grade changes. It's times like this that an adjustable pole would be nice. This same technique can be used to descend a hill.

Traversing uphill.

Using a Ridgeline to Your Advantage

When traveling in mountainous terrain, try to stay high on the ridgeline as much as you can. It is better to travel a little farther than to deal with the constant up-and-down travel associated with frequent elevation changes.

Rest Step

When walking uphill, use a rest step, which is done by locking the knee with each step. This process takes the weight off the muscle, allowing it to rest, and places it on the skeletal system. For best results, you'll need to take a short pause with each step.

Terrain Issues

Cornices

Cornices are usually formed on the downwind, or leeward, side of a ridge. This happens as a result of the wind blowing snow off and over the windward side of a cliff, depositing it on the downwind side. If you are approaching a peak from the windward side, you may not be aware that a cornice exists. Since wind patterns are similar throughout an area, take the time to look at the downwind side of other peaks in your location. Try to identify a cornice in advance,

and stay well below its potential fracture line. If you're unsure whether a cornice exists, keep your elevation well below the peak, going no higher than two-thirds of the way up the ridge. If approaching from the leeward side, look for wavelike formations that extend from the peak, and avoid these areas.

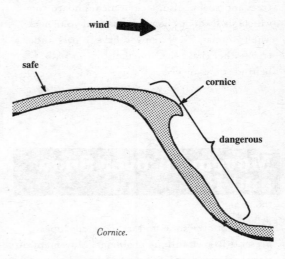

Cornice.

Glaciers and Crevasses

A glacier is basically a snow and ice river that forms over many years. It is created when snow is in a location that doesn't allow it to melt before the next year's snowfall. Each year, new layers are added to the top of the glacier, and it loses some of its lower portion as it melts away. The point at which it melts occurs where the glacier is low enough that no new snow can accumulate and the temperatures are high enough to cause melting. Crevasses are cracks in a glacier that result when a glacier stretches or bends too fast. They often run about 100 feet deep. On occasion, low-elevation glaciers will completely fracture at a crevasse, causing an ice avalanche, which can be deadly. These usually occur during late summer and early fall. Unless you have achieved specific training in glacier travel, you should avoid these areas. If no other travel option exists, cross close to the top, where the glacier is more stable.

Creeks

Crossing a creek is often a problem during the winter. If it's a small creek, loosen your pack's shoulder straps, and undo your waistband so you can quickly remove the pack if you fall in. Try to cross at a shaded area where there is a large amount of snow and no water can be seen. Take off your skis or snowshoes, and use a pole to evaluate the snow's depth and stability before taking each step. Cross one person at a time. For larger creeks where no bridge or road crossing is available, try to find a narrow area where passage is possible (you may need to travel upstream closer to the creek's origin to find such a place).

Frozen Bodies of Water

Avoid crossing large bodies of ice—the risk associated with breaking through is too high. Always go around a lake. If approaching a river and you have no other choice but to cross, however, cross on the outside of a bend or at a straight stretch where the water is apt to be shallow. Avoid areas that have anything sticking up out of the ice, such as a log, stump, or rock, since radiant heat from the object will have weakened the ice directly next to it.

Continued →

Trees and Rocks

In snowy conditions, trees and rocks can present problems for the backcountry traveler. Steep-sided wells form around rocks and tree trunks, due to wind and the radiant heat that these objects produce. To avoid falling into these deep air pockets, avoid walking too close to exposed trees and rocks. Also, tree branches hoard snow, which gladly drops down the back of your neck when you pass by. When you have to pass under a tree, either shake the branches first or walk behind someone else.

—From Surviving Cold Weather

Movement over Snow and Ice

U.S. Army

Movement over snow and ice-covered slopes presents its own unique problems. Movement on steeper slopes requires an ice ax, crampons, and the necessary training for this equipment. Personnel will also have to learn how to place solid anchors in snow and ice to protect themselves during these movements if roped. Snow-covered glaciers present crevasse fall hazards even when the slope is relatively flat, requiring personnel to learn unique glacier travel and crevasse rescue techniques.

All the principles of rock climbing, anchor placement, belays, and rope usage...apply to snow and ice climbing as well. This chapter will focus on the additional skills and techniques required to move safely through snow-covered mountains and over glaciated terrain.

Movement over Snow

...on steep slopes in deep snow, the climber may climb straight up facing the slope. The ice ax shaft, driven directly into the snow, provides a quick and effective self-belay in case of a slip—the deeper the shaft penetrates the snow, the better the anchor. It is usually best, however, to climb snow-covered slopes in a traversing fashion in order to conserve energy, unless there is significant avalanche danger.

The progression from walking on flat terrain to moving on steep terrain is the same as for moving over snow-free terrain. If the snow is packed the sole of the boot will generally hold by kicking steps, even on steep slopes. Where it is difficult to make an effective step will the boot, a cut made with the adze of the ice ax creates an effective step. In these situations crampons should be used for faster and easier movement.

When descending on snow, one can usually come straight downhill, even on steep terrain. Movement downhill should be slow and deliberate with the climber using an even pace. The heels should be kicked vigorously into the snow. The body may be kept erect with the aid of an ice ax, which may be jammed into the snow at each step for additional safety. Here again, crampons or step cutting may be necessary. A technique known as glissading may also be used as an easy method of descent and is covered in detail later in this chapter.

Movement over Ice

Ice is found in many areas of mountains when snow is present, and during the summer months also where perennial snowpack exists. Many times an ice area will be downslope of a snow-field and sometimes the ice pack itself will be lightly covered with snow. Even if using an ice ax and or crampons, movement will still be difficult without proper training.

—From Military Mountaineering (Field Manual 3-97.61)

Using an Ice Ax

Greg Davenport
Illustrations by Steven A. Davenport

When traveling in mountainous regions where snow or ice is present, always take along an ice ax. When not in use, the ice ax should be snugly secured on your pack or carried in one hand—at the balance point—so that it is parallel to the ground, with the pick toward the ground and the spike facing forward. The ice ax should have a long lanyard, the length of your reach plus 6 inches, attached to your wrist.

Using an Ice Ax to Self-Belay

When self-belaying with an ice ax, the ax is used as an anchor that supports and stops your descent down the hill should you fall. When using the ice ax as a self-belay device, hold it so that the palm is on top of the adze and the thumb and index finger hang—on opposite sides—over the pick. A self-belay hold is employed when the ice ax is used for an anchor and to help with balance.

While Going Diagonally up a Slope

When going diagonally up a hill, hold the ax perpendicular to the slope's angle, one hand grasping the head while the other holds the shaft, which is jammed into the snow on the uphill side. Since the ice ax will cross in front of you, make sure the pick doesn't point toward your body. While the ax is planted in the snow,

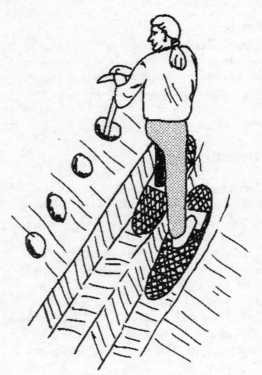

Using an ice ax to go diagonally uphill.

Using an ice ax to go directly uphill.

Using an ice ax to go downhill.

take one step with each foot, secure and balance yourself, and then pull the ax free. Move it forward on the uphill side, and replant it into the snow.

While Going Directly up a Slope

When going straight up a hill, always keep the ax on your uphill side, jam its spike deep into the snow's surface, and take one step with each foot, using a kick step. Once you are secure in your new position, pull the ice ax free and move it uphill, replanting it deep into the snow's surface, and repeat your two steps. Continue doing this until a belay is no longer needed.

While Going Down a Slope

When going straight down a hill, hold the ice ax in one hand on the downhill side with its spike pointing toward the snow's surface, and use a plunge step. This method keeps the ax ready to be jammed into the snow should you lose your balance. On steep slopes, the ax should be planted firmly into the snow on the downhill side every two steps (one with each foot) and used to help with balance and protection. On a very steep slope, you should face into the slope and, using a kick step, climb down the hill backward. When using this technique, the ax should be kept on the uphill side and continually planted and replanted after every two steps.

—From Surviving Cold Weather

Continued ➡

Use of Ice Ax and Crampons

U.S. Army

Movement over snow and ice is almost impossible without an ice ax and or crampons.

Ice Ax. When walking on snow or ice, the ice ax can be used as a third point of contact. When the terrain steepens, there are a number of ways to use the ice ax for snow or ice climbing. Some positions are more effective than others, depending on the intended result. You may find other ways to hold and use the ax, as long the security remains in effect.

Cane Position. The ice ax can be used on gentle slopes as a walking stick or cane. The ax is held by the head with the spike down and the pick facing to the rear in preparation for self-arrest. When moving up or down gentle slopes the ice ax is placed in front as the third point of contact, and the climber moves toward it. When traversing, the ax is held on the uphill side, in preparation for a self-arrest.

Cross Body Position or Port Arms Position. On steeper slopes the ax can be used in the port arms position, or cross body position. It is carried across the chest, upslope hand on the shaft, spike towards the slope. The head of the ax is held away from the slope with the pick to the rear in preparation for self-arrest. Ensure the leash is connected to the upslope hand, which allows the ax to be used in the hammer position on the upslope side of the climber. The spike, in this case, is used as an aid for maintaining balance.

Anchor Position. As the slope continues to steepen, the ax may be used in the anchor position. The head is held in the upslope hand and the pick is driven into the slope. The spike is held in the downhill hand and pulled slightly away from the slope to increase the "bite" of the pick into the ice. If the climber is wearing a harness, the pick can be deeply inserted in the ice or hard snow and the ax leash could be connected to the tie-in point on the harness for an anchor (ensure the ax is placed for the intended direction of pull).

Push-Hold Position. Another variation on steep slopes is the push-hold position. The hand is placed on the shaft of the ax just below the head with the pick forward. The pick is driven into the slope at shoulder height. The hand is placed on top of the ax for use as a handhold.

Dagger Position. The dagger position is used on steep slopes to place a handhold above shoulder height. The hand grasps the head of the ax with the pick forward and the shaft hanging down. The ax is driven into the surface in a stabbing action. The hand is then placed on the ax head for use as a handhold.

Hammer Position. The hammer position will set the pick deepest in any snow or ice condition. The ax is used like a hammer with the pick being driven into the slope. On vertical or near-vertical sections, two axes used in the hammer position will often be required.

Crampons. Walking in crampons is not complicated but it does present difficulties. When walking in crampons, the same principles are used as in mountain walking, except that

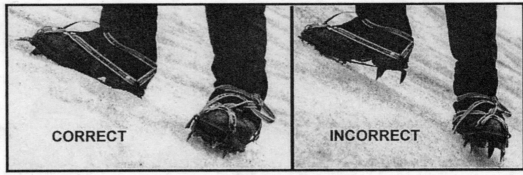

Correct and incorrect crampon technique.

when a leg is advanced it is swung in a slight are around the fixed foot to avoid locking the crampons or catching them in clothing or flesh. The trousers should be bloused to prevent catching on crampons. All straps should be secured to prevent stepping on them and, potentially, causing a fall. The buckles should be located on the outside of each foot when the crampons are secured to prevent snagging. Remember, when the crampon snags on the pants or boots, a tear or cut usually results, and sometimes involves the skin on your leg and or a serious fall.

Two methods of ascent are used on slopes: traversing and straight up.

A traverse on ice or snow looks much like any mountain walking traverse, except that the ankles are rolled so that the crampons are placed flat on the surface. On snow the points penetrate easily; on ice the foot must be pressed or stamped firmly to obtain maximum penetration. At the turning points of a traverse, direction is changed with the uphill foot as in mountain walking.

A straight up method is for relatively short pitches, since it is more tiring than a traverse. The climber faces directly up the slope and walks straight uphill. As the slope steepens, the herringbone step is used to maintain the flatfoot technique. For short steep pitches, the climber may also face downslope, squatting so the legs almost form a 90-degree angle at the knees, driving the spike of the ice ax into the slope at hip level, and then moving the feet up to the ax. By repeating these steps, the ax and crampon combination can be used to climb short, steep pitches without resorting to step cutting. This method can be tiring. The technique is similar to the crab position used for climbing on slab rock and can also be used for short descents.

A technique known as "front-pointing" may be used for moving straight uphill. It is especially useful on steep terrain, in combination with the ice ax in the push-hold, dagger, or hammer position. Front-pointing is easiest with the use of more rigid mountain boots and rigid crampons. The technique is similar to doing calf raises on the tips of the toes and is much more tiring than flat-footing.

The technique starts with the feet approximately shoulder width apart. When a step is taken the climber places the front points of the crampons into the ice with the toe of the boot pointing straight into the slope.

When the front points have bitten into the ice the heel of the boot is lowered slightly so that the first set of vertical points can also bite. The body is kept erect, with the weight centered over the feet as in climbing on rock.

Vertical Ice. When a climb on ice reaches the 60- to 70-degree angle, two ice axes may be helpful, and will become necessary as the angle approaches 90 degrees. The same basic climbing techniques described on page xxx should be applied. If leashes of the correct length and fit are attached to both axes, it may be possible to hang completely from the axes while moving the feet.

Descending with Crampons and Ice Ax. Whenever possible, descend straight down the fall line. As the slope steepens, gradually turn sideways; on steeper slopes, bend at the waist and knees as if sitting, keeping the feet flat to engage all vertical crampon points and keep the weight over the feet as in descending rock slab. On steep terrain, assume a cross body or port arms position with the ax, and traverse. The crab position or front-pointing may also be used for descending. Regardless of the technique used, always ensure the points of the crampons are inserted in the snow or ice and take short, deliberate steps to minimize the chance of tripping and falling down the slope.

Normal Progression. The use of the ice ax and crampons follows a simple, logical progression. The techniques can be used in any combination, dictated by the terrain and skill of the individual. A typical progression could be as follows:

Crampons. Use crampons in the following situations:

· Walking as on flat ground.

· Herringbone step straight up the slope.

· Traverse with feet flat.

· Backing up the slope (crab position).

· Front-pointing.

Ice Ax. Use the ice ax in these situations:

· Cane position on flat ground.

· Cane position on uphill side as slope steepens.

Front-pointing with crampons.

Continued ➡

- Port arms position with spike on uphill side.

- Anchor position with pick on uphill side.

- Push-hold position using front-pointing technique.

- Dagger position using front-pointing technique.

- Hammer position using front-pointing technique.

Climbing Sequence. Using most of these positions, a single ax can be "climbed" in steps to move upslope on low-angle to near vertical terrain. Begin by positioning the feet in a secure stance and placing the ax in the hammer position as high as possible. Slowly and carefully move the feet to higher positions alternately, and move the hand up the ax shaft. Repeat this until the hand is on top of the head of the ax. Remove the ax and place it at a higher position and begin again.

Step Cutting. Step cutting is an extremely valuable technique that is a required skill for any military mountaineer. Using cut steps can save valuable time that would be spend in donning crampons for short stretches of ice and can, in some cases, save the weight of the crampons altogether. Steps may also have to be cut by the lead team to enable a unit without proper equipment to negotiate snow- or ice-covered terrain. As units continue to move up areas where steps have been cut they should continue to improve each step. In ascending, steps may be cut straight up the slope, although a traverse will normally be adopted. In descending, a traverse is also the preferred method. When changing direction, a step large enough for both feet and crampons must be made. Once the step is formed, the adze is best used to further shape and clean the step.

Snow. On slopes of firm snow and soft ice, steps may be cut by swinging the ax in a near-vertical plane, using the inside corner of the adze for cutting. The step should be fashioned so that it slopes slightly inward and is big enough to admit the entire foot. Steps used for resting or for turning must be larger.

Ice. Hard ice requires that the pick of the ax be used. Begin by directing a line of blows at right angles to the slope to make a fracture line along the base of the intended step. This technique will reduce the chance of an unwanted fracture in the ice breaking out the entire step. Next, chop above the fracture line to fashion the step. When using the pick it should be given an outward jerk as it is placed to prevent it from sticking in the ice.

Step Cutting in a Traverse. When cutting steps in a traverse, the preferred cutting sequence is to cut one step at an arm's length from the highest step already cut, then cut one between those two. Cutting ahead one step then cutting an intermediate step keeps all of the steps relatively close to one another and maintains a suitable interval that all personnel can use.

Handholds. If handholds are cut, they should be smaller than footholds, and angled more.

Self-Arrest. The large number of climbers injured or killed while climbing on snow and ice can be attributed to two major failings on the part of the climber: climbing unroped, and a lack of knowledge and experience in the tech-

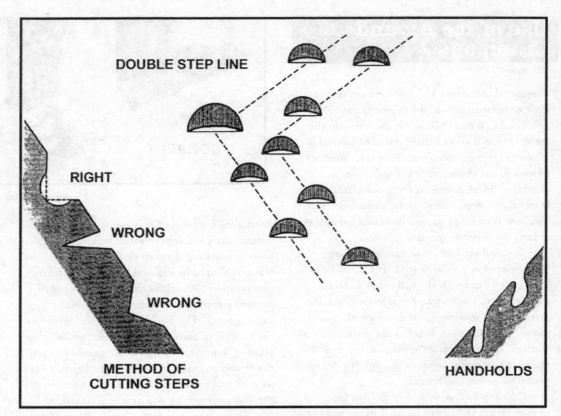

Step cutting and handhold cutting.

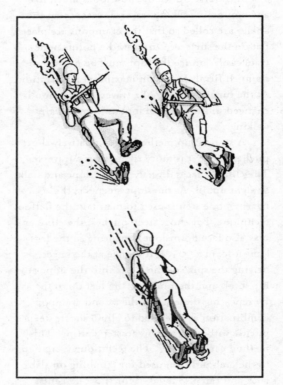

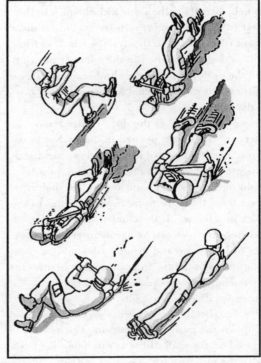

Self-arrest technique.

niques necessary to stop, or arrest, a fall. A climber should always carry an ice ax when climbing on steep snow or ice; if a fall occurs, he must retain possession and control of his ice ax if he is to successfully arrest the fall. During movement on steep ice, the ax pick will be in the ice solidly before the body is moved, which should prevent a fall of any significance (this is a self-belay not a self-arrest).

The toe of the boots may be dug into the slope to help arrest the fall. The ax is held diagonally across the chest, with the head of the ax by one shoulder and the spike near the opposite hip. One hand grasps the head of the ax, with the pick pointed into the slope, while the other hand is on the shaft near the spike, lifting up on it to prevent the spike from digging into the slope.

Caution
Self-arrest requires the ax pick to gradually dig in to slow the descent. Self-arrest is difficult on steep ice because the ice ax pick instantly "bites" into the ice, possibly resulting in either arm or shoulder injury, or the ax is deflected immediately upon contact.

Note: If crampons are worn, the feet must be raised to prevent the crampons from digging into the snow or ice too quickly. This could cause the climber to tumble and also could severely injure his ankles and legs.

When a fall occurs, the climber should immediately grasp the ax with both hands and hold it firmly as described above. Once sufficient control of the body is attained, the climber

Continued

drives the pick of the ice ax into the slope, increasing the pressure until the fall is arrested. Raising the spike end of the shaft increases the biting action of the pick. It is critical that control of the ice ax be maintained at all times.

Glissading

Glissading is the intentional, controlled, rapid descent, or slide of a mountaineer down a steep slope covered with snow. Glissading is similar to skiing, except skis are not used. The same balance and control are necessary, but instead of skis the soles of the feet or the buttocks are used. The only piece of equipment required is the standard ice ax, which serves as the rudder, brake, and guide for the glissade. The two basic methods of glissading are:

Squatting Glissade. The squatting glissade is accomplished by placing the body in a semi-crouched position with both knees bent and the body weight directly over the feet. The ice ax is grasped with one hand on the head, pick, and adze outboard (away from the body), and the other hand on the shaft. The hand on the shaft grips it firmly in a position that allows control as well as the application of downward pressure on the spike of the ax.

Sitting Glissade. Using this method the glissader sits on the snow with the legs flat, and the heels and feet raised and pointed downslope. The ice ax is firmly grasped in the same manner as the squatting glissade, with the exception that the hand on the shaft must be locked against the hip for control. The sitting glissade is slower but easier to control than the squatting glissade.

Safety. A glissade should never be attempted on a slope where the bottom cannot be seen, since drop-offs may exist out of view. Also, a sitting glissade should not be used if the snow cover is thin, as painful injury could result.

—From *Military Mountaineering (Field Manual 3-97.61)*

Glissading techniques.

U.S. Army

Ice climbing ratings can have commitment ratings and technical ratings. The numerical ratings are often prefaced with WI (waterfall ice), AI (alpine ice), or M (mixed rock and ice).

Commitment Ratings. Commitment ratings are expressed in Roman numerals.

I—A short, easy climb near the road, with no avalanche hazard and a straightforward descent.

II—A route of one or two pitches within a short distance of rescue assistance, with little objective hazard.

III—A multipitch route at low elevation, or a one-pitch climb with an approach that takes about an hour. The route requires anywhere from a few hours to a long day to complete. The descent may require building rappel anchors, and the route might be prone to avalanche.

IV—A multipitch route at higher elevations; may require several hours of approach on skis or foot. This route is subject to objective hazards, possibly with a hazardous descent.

V—A long climb in a remote setting, requiring all day to complete the climb itself. Requires many rappels off anchors for the descent. This route has sustained exposure to avalanche or other objective hazards.

VI—A long ice climb in an alpine setting, with sustained technical climbing. Only elite climbers will complete it in a day. A difficult and involved approach and descent, with objective hazards ever-present, all in a remote area.

VII—Everything a grade VI has, and more of it. Possibly days to approach the climb, and objective hazards rendering survival as questionable. Difficult physically and mentally.

Technical Ratings. Technical ratings are expressed as Arabic numerals.

1—A frozen lake or stream bed.

2—A pitch with short sections of ice up to 80 degrees; lots of opportunity for protection and good anchors.

3—Sustained ice up to 80 degrees; the ice is usually good, with places to rest, but it requires skill at placing protection and setting anchors.

4—A sustained pitch that is vertical or slightly less than vertical; may have special features such as chandeliers and run-outs between protection.

5—A long, strenuous pitch, possibly 50 meters of 85- to 90-degree ice with few if any rests between anchors. The pitch may be shorter, but on featureless ice. Good skills at placing protection are required.

6—A full 50-meter pitch of dead vertical ice, possibly of poor quality; requires efficiency of movement and ability to place protection while in awkward stances.

7—A full rope length of thin vertical or overhanging ice of dubious adhesion. An extremely tough pitch, physically and mentally, requiring agility and creativity.

8—Simply the hardest ice climbing ever done; extremely bold and gymnastic.

—From *Military Mountaineering (Field Manual 3-97.61)*

Movement on Glaciers
U.S. Army

Movement in mountainous terrain may require travel on glaciers. An understanding of glacier formation and characteristics is necessary to plan safe routes. A glacier is formed by the perennial accumulation of snow and other precipitation in a valley or draw. The accumulated snow eventually turns to ice due to metamorphosis. The "flow" or movement of glaciers is caused by gravity. There are a few different types of glaciers identifiable primarily by their location or activity.

- Valley glacier—resides and flows in a valley.
- Cirque glacier—forms and resides in a bowl.
- Hanging glacier—these are a result of valley or cirque glaciers flowing and or deteriorating. As the movement continues, portions separate and are sometimes left hanging on mountains, ridgelines, or cliffs.
- Piedmont glacier—formed by one or more valley glaciers; spreads out into a large area.
- Retreation glacier—a deteriorating glacier; annual melt of entire glacier exceeds the flow of the ice.
- Surging glacier—annual flow of the ice exceeds the melt; the movement is measurable over a period of time.

Characteristics and Definitions
This paragraph describes the common characteristics of glaciers, and defines common terminology used in reference to glaciers.

Firn is compacted granular snow that has been on the glacier at least one year. Firn is the building blocks of the ice that makes the glacier.

The accumulation zone is the area that remains snow-covered throughout the year because of year-round snowfall. The snowfall exceeds melt.

The ablation zone is the area where the snow melts off the ice in summer. Melt equals or exceeds snowfall.

The firn line separates the accumulation and ablation zones. As you approach this area, you may see "strips" of snow in the ice. Be cautious, as these could be snow bridges remaining over crevasses. Remember that snow bridges will be weakest lower on the glacier as you enter the accumulation zone. The firn line can change annually.

A bergschrund is a large crevasse at the head of a glacier caused by separation of active (flowing) and inactive (stationary) ice. These will usually be seen at the base of a major incline and can make an ascent on that area difficult.

Continued ➡

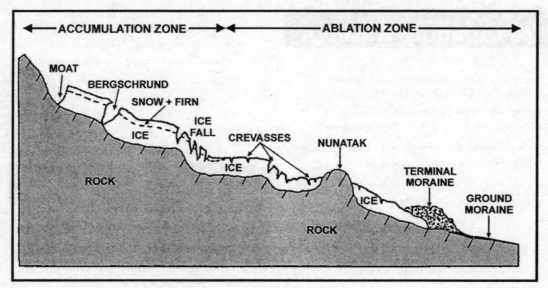

Glacier cross section.

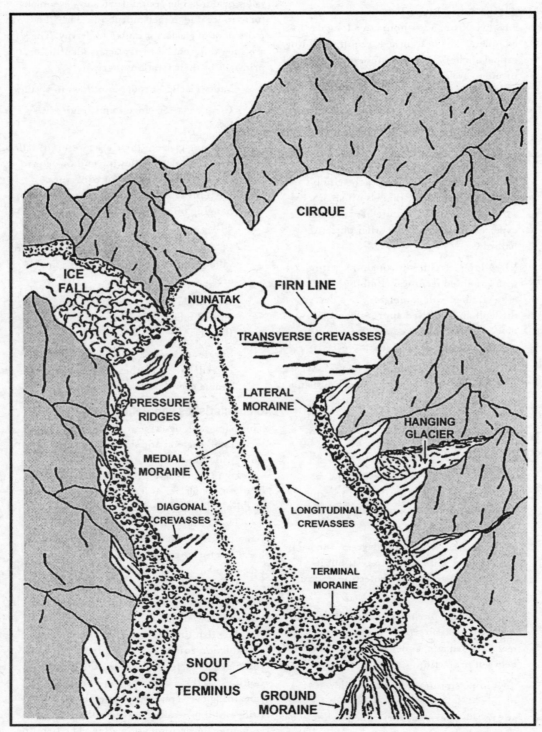

Glacier features.

A moat is a wall formed at the head (start) of the glacier. These are formed by heat reflected from valley wall.

A crevasse is a split or crack in the glacier surface. These are formed when the glacier moves over an irregularity in the bed surface.

A transverse crevasse forms perpendicular to the flow of a glacier. These are normally found where a glacier flows over a slope with a gradient change of 30 degrees or more.

Longitudinal crevasses form parallel to the flow of a glacier. These are normally found where a glacier widens.

Diagonal crevasses form at an angle to the flow of a glacier. These are normally found along the edges where a glacier makes a bend.

A snow bridge is a somewhat supportive structure of snow that covers a crevasse. Most of these are formed by the wind. The strength of a snow bridge depends on the snow itself.

Icefalls are a jumble of crisscross crevasses and large ice towers that are normally found where a glacier flows over a slope with a gradient change of 25 degrees or more.

Seracs are large pinnacles or columns of ice that are normally found in icefalls or hanging glaciers.

Ice avalanches are falling chunks of ice normally occurring near icefalls or hanging glaciers.

The moraine is an accumulation of rock or debris on a glacier caused by rockfall or avalanche of valley walls.

The lateral moraine is formed on sides of glacier.

The medical moraine is in the middle of the glacier. This is also formed as two glaciers come together or as a glacier moves around a central peak.

The terminal moraine is at the base of a glacier and is formed as moraines meet at the snout or terminus of a glacier.

The ground moraine is the rocky debris extending out from the terminus of a glacier. This is formed by the scraping of earth as the glacier grew or surged and exposed as the glacier retreats.

A Nunatak is a rock projection protruding through the glacier as the glacier flows around it.

An ice mill is a hole in the glacier formed by swirling water on the surface. These can be large enough for a human to slip into.

Pressure ridges are wavelike ridges that form on glacier normally after a glacier has flowed over icefalls.

A glacier window is an opening at the snout of the glacier where water runs out of the glacier.

Dangers and Obstacles

The principle dangers and obstacles to movement in glacial areas are crevasses, icefalls, and ice avalanches. Snow-covered crevasses make movement on a glacier extremely treacherous. In winter, when visibility is poor, the difficulty of recognizing them is increased. Toward the end of the summer, crevasses are widest and covered by the least snow. Crossing snow bridges constitutes the greatest potential danger in movement over glaciers in the summer. On the steep pitch of a glacier, ice flowing over irregularities and cliffs in the underlying valley floor cause the ice

Continued →

to break up into ice blocks and towers, criss-crossed with crevasses. This jumbled cliff of ice is known as an icefall. Icefalls present a major obstacle to safe movement of troops on glaciers.

Moving on glaciers brings about the hazard of falling into a crevasse. Although the crevasses are visible in the ablation zone in the summer, the accumulation zone will still have hidden crevasses. The risk of traveling in the accumulation zone can be managed to an acceptable level when ropes are used for connecting the team members. Crampons and an ice ax are all that is required to safely travel in the ablation zone in the summer.

When conditions warrant, three to four people will tie in to one rope at equal distances from each other. To locate the positions, if three people are on a team, double the rope and one ties into the middle and the other two at the ends. If four people are on a team, form a "z" with the rope and expand the "z" fully, keeping the end and the bight on each "side" of the "z" even. Tie in to the bights and the ends.

Connect to the rope with the appropriate method and attach the Prusik as required. The rope should be kept relatively tight either by Prusik belay or positioning of each person. If the team members need to assemble in one area, use the Prusik to belay each other in.

If a team member falls into a crevasse, the remaining members go into team arrest, assess the situation, and use the necessary technique to remove the person from the crevasse. The simplest and most common method for getting someone out of a crevasse is for the person to climb out while being belayed.

All items should be secured to either the climber or the rope/harness to prevent inadvertent release and loss of necessary items or equipment. Packs should be secured to the rope/harness with webbing or rope. If traveling with a sled in two, secure it not only to a climber to pull it, but connect it to the rope with webbing or rope also.

If marking the route on the glacier is necessary for backtracking or to prevent disorientation in storms or flat-light conditions, use markers that will be noticeable against the white conditions. The first team member can place a new marker when the last team member reaches the previous marker.

Roped Movement

The first rule for movement on glaciers is to rope up. A roped team of two, while ideal for rock climbing, is at a disadvantage on a snow-covered glacier. The best combination is a three-man rope team. Generally, the rope team members will move at the same time with the rope fully extended and reasonably tight between individuals, their security being the team arrest. If an individual should break through a snow bridge and fall into a crevasse, the other members immediately perform self-arrest, halting the fall. At points of obvious weakness in the snow bridges, the members decide to belay each other across the crevasse using one of the established belay techniques.

Even with proper training in crevasse rescue techniques, the probability exists that an individual may remain suspended in a crevasse for a fairly lengthy amount of time while trying to get himself out or while awaiting help from his rope team members. Because of this, it is strongly recommended that all personnel wear a seat/chest combination harness, whether improvised or premanufactured.

Rope team members must be able to quickly remove the climbing rope from the harness(es) during a crevasse rescue. The standard practice for connecting to the rope for glacier travel is with a locking carabiner on a figure-eight loop to the harness. This allows quick detachment of the rope for rescue purposes. The appropriate standing part of the rope is then clipped to the chest harness carabiner.

If a rope team consists of only two people, the rope should be divided into thirds, as for a four-person team. The team members tie into the middle positions on the rope, leaving a third of the rope between each team member and a third on each end of the rope. The remaining "thirds" of the rope should be coiled and either carried in the rucksack, attached to the rucksack, or carried over the head and shoulder. This gives each climber an additional length of rope that can be used for crevasse rescue, should one of the men fall through and require another rope. If necessary, this excess end rope can be used to connect to another rope team for safer travel.

Note: The self-arrest technique used by one individual will work to halt the fall of his partner on a two-man rope team; however, the chance of it failing is much greater. Crevasse rescue procedures performed by a two-man rope team, by itself, may be extremely difficult. For safety reasons, movement over a snow-covered glacier by a single two-man team should be avoided wherever possible.

Use of Prusik Knots

Prusik knots are attached to the climbing rope for all glacier travel. The Prusiks are used as a self-belay technique to maintain a tight rope between individuals, to anchor the climbing rope for crevasse rescue, and for self-rescue in a crevasse fall. The Prusik slings are made from the 7-millimeter by 6-foot and 7-millimeter by 12-foot ropes. The ends of the ropes are tied together, forming endless loops or slings, with double fisherman's knots. Form the Prusik knot on the rope in front of the climber. An overhand knot can be tied into the sling just below the Prusik to keep equal tension on all the Prusik wraps. Attach this sling to the locking carabiner at the tie in point on the harness.

Note: An ascender can replace a Prusik sling in most situations. However, the weight of an ascender hanging on the rope during movement will become annoying, and it could be stepped on during movement and or climbing.

Securing the Backpack/Rucksack

If an individual should fall into a crevasse, it is essential that he be able to rid himself of his backpack. The weight of the average pack will be enough to hinder the climber during crevasse rescue, or possibly force him into an upside down position while suspended in the crevasse. Before movement, the pack should be attached to the climbing rope with a sling rope or webbing and a carabiner. A fallen climber can immediately drop the pack without losing it. The drop cord length should be minimal to allow the fallen individual to reach the pack after releasing it, if warm clothing is needed. When hanging from the drop cord, the pack should be oriented just as when wearing it (ensure the cord pulls from the top of the pack).

Routes

An individual operating in the mountains must appreciate certain limitations in glacier movement imposed by nature.

Additional obstacles in getting onto a glacier may be swift glacier streams, steep terminal or lateral moraines, and difficult mountain terrain bordering the glacier ice. The same obstacles may also have to be overcome in getting on and off a valley glacier at any place along its course.

Further considerations to movement on a glacier are steep sections, heavily crevassed portions, and icefalls, which may be major obstacles to progress. The use of current aerial photographs in conjunction with aerial reconnaissance is a valuable means of gathering advance information about a particular glacier. However, they only supplement, and do not take the place of, on-the-ground reconnaissance conducted from available vantage points.

Crossing Crevasses

Open crevasses are obvious, and their presence is an inconvenience rather than a danger to movement. Narrow cracks can be jumped, provided the take off and landing spots are firm and offer good footing. Wider cracks will have to be circumvented unless a solid piece of ice joins into an ice bridge strong enough to support at least the weight of one member of the team. Such ice bridges are often formed in the lower portion of a crevasse, connecting both sides of it.

In the area of the firn line, the zone that divides seasonal melting from permanent falls of snow, large crevasses remain open, though their depths may be clogged with masses of snow. Narrow cracks may be covered. In this zone, the snow, which covers glacier ice, melts more rapidly than that which covers crevasses. The difference between glacier ice and narrow snow-covered cracks is immediately apparent; the covering snow is white, whereas the glacier ice is gray.

Usually the upper part of a glacier is permanently snow covered. The snow surface here will vary in consistency from dry power to consolidated snow. Below this surface cover are found other snow layers that become more crystalline in texture with depth, and gradually turn into glacier ice. It is in this snow-covered upper part of a glacier that crevasses are most difficult to detect, for even wide crevasses may be completely concealed by snow bridges.

Snow Bridges

now bridges are formed by windblown snow that builds a cornice over the empty interior of the crevasse. As the cornice grows from the windward side, a counter drift is formed on the leeward side. The growth of the leeward portion will be slower than that to the windward so that the juncture of the cornices occurs over the middle of the crevasse only when the contributing winds blow equally from each side.

Continued ➡

Bridges can also be formed without wind, especially during heavy falls of dry snow. Since cohesion of dry snow depends only on an interlocking of the branches of delicate crystals, such bridges are particularly dangerous during the winter. When warmer weather prevails the snow becomes settled and more compacted, and may form firmer bridges.

Once a crevasse had been completely bridged, its detection is difficult. Bridges are generally slightly concave because of the settling of the snow. This concavity is perceptible in sunshine, but difficult to detect in flat light. If the presence of hidden crevasses is suspected, the leader of a roped team must probe the snow in front of him with the shaft of his ice ax. As long as a firm foundation is encountered, the team may proceed, but should the shaft meet no opposition from an underlying layer of snow, a crevasse is probably present. In such a situation, the prober should probe closer to his position to make sure that he is not standing on the bridge itself. If he is, he should retreat gently from the bridge and determine the width and direction of the crevasse. He should then follow and probe the margin until a more resistant portion of the bridge is reached. When moving parallel to a crevasse, all members of the team should keep well back from the edge and follow parallel but offset courses.

A crevasse should be crossed at right angles to its length. When crossing a bridge that seems sufficiently strong enough to hold a member of the team, the team will generally move at the same time on a tight rope, with each individual prepared to go into self-arrest. If the stability of the snow bridge is under question, they should proceed as follows for a team of three glacier travelers:

The leader and second take up a position at least 10 feet back from the edge. The third goes into a self-belay behind the second and remains on a tight rope.

The second belays the leader across using one of the established belay techniques. The boot-ax belay should be used only if the snow is deep enough for the ax to be inserted up to the head and firm enough to support the possible load. A quick ice ax anchor should be placed for the other belays. Deadman or equalizing anchors should be used when necessary. The leader should move forward, carefully probing the snow and evaluating the strength of the bridge, until he reaches firm snow on the far side of the crevasse. He then continues as far across as possible so number two will have room to get across without number one having to move.

The third assumes the middle person's belay position. The middle can be belayed across by both the first and last. Once the second is across, he assumes the belay position. Number one moves out on a tight rope and anchors in to a self-belay. Number two belays number three across.

In crossing crevasses, distribute the weight over as wide an area as possible. Do not stamp the snow. Many fragile bridges can be crossed by lying down and crawling to the other side. Skis or snowshoes help distribute the weight nicely.

Arresting and Securing a Fallen Climber

The simplest and most common method for getting someone out of a crevasse is for the person to climb out while being belayed. Most crevasse falls will be no more than body height into the opening if the rope is kept snug between each person.

To provide a quick means of holding an unexpected breakthrough, the rope is always kept taut. When the leader unexpectedly breaks through, the second and third immediately go into a self-arrest position to arrest the fall. A fall through a snow bridge results either in the person becoming jammed in the surface hole, or in being suspended in the crevasse by the rope. If the leader has fallen only partially through the snow bridge, he is supported by the snow forming the bridge and should not thrash about as this will only enlarge the hole and result in deeper suspension. All movements should be slow and aimed at rolling out of the hole and distributing the weight over the remainder of the bridge. The rope should remain tight at all times and the team arrest positions adjusted to do so. It generally is safer to retain the rucksack, as its bulk often prevents a deeper fall. Should a team member other than the leader experience a partial fall, the rescue procedure will be same as for the leader, only complicated slightly by the position on the rope.

When the person falls into a crevasse, the length of the fall depends upon how quickly the fall is arrested and where in the bridge the break takes place. If the fall occurs close to the near edge of the crevasse, it usually can be checked before the climber has fallen more than 6 feet. However, if the person was almost across, the fall will cause the rope to cut through the bridge, and then even an instantaneous check by the other members will not prevent a deeper fall. The following scenario is an example of the sequence of events that take place after a fall by the leader in a three-person team. (This scenario is for a team of three, each person referred to by position; the leader is number 1.)

Once the fall has been halted by the team arrest, the entire load must be placed on number 2 to allow number 3 to move forward and anchor the rope. Number 3 slowly releases his portion of the load onto number 2, always being prepared to go back into self-arrest should number 2's position begin to fail.

Once number 2 is confident that he can hold the load, number 3 will proceed to number 2's position, using the Prusik as a self belay, to anchor the rope. In this way the rope remains reasonably tight between number 2 and number 3. Number 3 must always be prepared to go back into self-arrest should number 2's position begin to fail.

When number 3 reaches number 2's position he will establish a bombproof anchor 3 to 10 feet in front of number 2 (on the load side), depending on how close number 2 is to the lip of the crevasse. This could be either a deadman or a two-point equalized anchor, as a minimum.

Number 3 connects the rope to the anchor by tying a Prusik with his long Prusik sling onto the rope leading to number 1. An overhand knot should be tied into the long Prusik sling to shorten the distance to the anchor, and attached

to the anchor with a carabiner. The Prusik knot is adjusted towards the load.

Number 2 can then release the load of number 1 onto the anchor. Number 2 remains connected to the anchor and monitors the anchor.

A fixed loop can be tied into the slack part of the rope, close to number 2, and attached to the anchor (to back up the Prusik knot).

Number 3 remains tied in, but continues forward using a short Prusik as a self-belay. He must now quickly check on the condition of number 1 and decide which rescue technique will be required to retrieve him.

These preliminary procedures must be performed before retrieving the fallen climber. If number 3 should fall through a crevasse, the procedure is the same except that number 1 assumes the role of number 3. Normally, if the middle person should fall through, number 1 would anchor the rope by himself. Number 3 would place the load on number 1's anchor, then anchor his rope and move forward with a Prusik self-belay to determine the condition of number 2.

Crevasse Rescue Techniques

Snow bridges are usually strongest at the edge of the crevasse, and a fall is most likely to occur some distance away from the edge. In some situations, a crevasse fall will occur at the edge of the snow bridge, on the edge of the ice. If a fall occurs away from the edge, the rope usually cuts deeply into the snow, thus greatly increasing friction for those pulling from above. In order to reduce friction, place padding, such as an ice ax, ski, ski pole, or backpack/rucksack, under the rope and at right angles to the stress. Push the padding forward as far as possible toward the edge of the crevasse, thus relieving the strain on the snow. Ensure the padding is anchored from falling into the crevasse for safety of the fallen climber.

Use of Additional Rope Teams. Another rope team can move forward and assist in pulling the victim out of a crevasse. The assisting rope team should move to a point between the fallen climber and the remaining rope team members. The assisting team can attach to the arresting team's rope with a Prusik or ascender and both rope teams' members can all pull simultaneously. If necessary, a belay can be initiated by the fallen climber's team while the assisting team pulls. The arresting team member closest to the fallen climber should attach the long Prusik to themselves and the rope leading to the fallen climber, and the assisting team can attach their Prusik or ascender between this long Prusik and the arresting them member. As the assisting team pulls, the Prusik belay will be managed by the arresting team member at the long Prusik.

Note: Safety in numbers is obvious for efficient crevasse rescue techniques. Additional rope teams have the necessary equipment to improve the main anchor or establish new ones and the strength to pull a person out even if he is deep in the crevasse. Strength of other rope teams should always be used before establishing more time-consuming and elaborate rescue techniques.

Fixed Rope. If the fallen climber is not injured, he may be able to climb out on a fixed rope. Number 1 clips number 3's rope to himself.

Continued ➡

He then climbs out using number 3's rope as a simple fixed line while number 2 takes up the slack in number 1's rope through the anchor Prusik for a belay.

Prusik Ascending Technique. There may be times when the remaining members of a rope team can render little assistance to the person in the crevasse. If poor snow conditions make it impossible to construct a strong anchor, the rope team members on top may have to remain in self-arrest. Other times, it may just be easier for the fallen climber to perform a self-rescue. The technique is performed as follows:

The fallen climber removes his pack and lets it hang below from the drop cord.

The individual slides their short Prusik up the climbing rope as far as possible.

The long Prusik is attached to the rope just below the short Prusik. The double fisherman's knot is spread apart to create a loop large enough for one or both feet. The fallen climber inserts his foot/feet into the loop formed allowing the knot to cinch itself down.

The individual stands in the foot loop, or "stirrup," of the long sling.

With his weight removed from the short Prusik, it is slid up the rope as far as it will go. The individual then hangs from the short Prusik while he moves the long Prusik up underneath the short Prusik again.

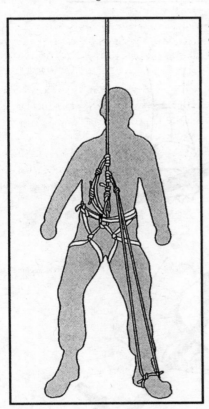

Prusik ascending technique.

The procedure is repeated, alternately moving the Prusiks up the rope, to ascend the rope. Once the crevasse lip is reached, the individual can simply grasp the rope and pull himself over the edge and out of the hole.

Besides being one of the simplest rope ascending techniques, the short Prusik acts as a self-belay and allows the climber to take as long a rest as he wants when sitting in the harness. The rope should be detached from the chest harness carabiner to make the movements less cumbersome. However, it is sometimes desirable to keep the chest harness connected to the rope for additional support. In this case the Prusik knots must be "on top" of the chest harness carabiner so they can be easily slid up the rope without

interference from the carabiner. The long Prusik sling can be routed through the chest harness carabiner for additional support when standing up in the stirrup.

Z-Pulley Hauling System. If a fallen climber is injured or unconscious, he will not be able to offer any assistance in the rescue. If additional rope teams are not immediately available, a simple raising system can be rigged to haul the victim out of the crevasse. The Z-pulley hauling system is one of the simplest methods and the one most commonly used in crevasse rescue. The basic Z rig is a "3-to-1" system, providing mechanical advantage to reduce the workload on the individuals operating the haul line. In theory, it would only take about 33 pounds of pull on the haul rope to raise a 100-pound load with this system. In actual field use, some of this mechanical advantage is lost to friction as the rope bends sharply around carabiners and over the crevasse lip. The use of mechanical rescue pulleys can help reduce this friction in the system. The following describes rigging of the system. (This scenario is for a team of three, each person referred to by position; the leader is number 1.)

After the rope team members have arrested and secured number 1 to the anchor, and they have decided to install the Z rig, number 2 will attach himself to the anchor without using the rope and clear the connecting knot used. Number 3 remains connected to the rope.

The slack rope exiting the anchor Prusik is clipped into a separate carabiner attached to the anchor. A pulley can be used here if available.

Number 3 will use number 2's short Prusik to rig the haul Prusik. He moves toward the crevasse lip (still on his own self-belay) and ties number 2's short Prusik onto number 1's rope (load rope) as close to the edge as possible.

Another carabiner (and pulley if available) is clipped into the loop of the haul Prusik and the rope between number 3's belay Prusik and the anchor is clipped (or attached through the pulley). Number 3's rope becomes the haul rope.

Number 3 then moves towards the anchor and number 2. Number 2 could help pull if necessary but first would connect to the haul rope with a Prusik just as number 3. If the haul Prusik reaches the anchor before the victim reaches the top, the load is simply placed back on the anchor Prusik and number 3 moves the haul Prusik back toward the edge. The system is now ready for another haul.

Caution

The force applied to the fallen climber through use of the Z-pulley system can be enough to destroy the harness-to-rope connection or injure the fallen climber if excess force is applied to the pulling rope.

NOTES:

1. The Z-pulley adds more load on the anchor due to the mechanical advantage.

The anchor should be monitored for the duration of the rescue.

2. With the "3-to-1" system, the load (fallen climber) will be raised 1 foot for every 3 feet of rope taken up during the haul.

—From *Military Mountaineering (Field Manual 3-97.61)*

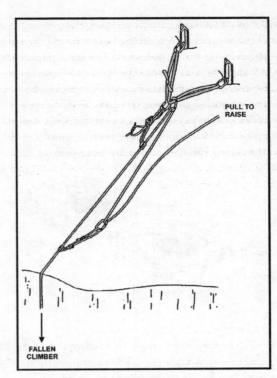

Z-pulley hauling system.

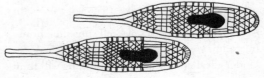

Snowshoe Travel

Greg Davenport
Illustrations by Steven A. Davenport

Snowshoes are an outstanding aid when traveling on snow and are especially helpful when carrying a pack. They make travel easier by dispersing your weight over a greater surface area, which in turn eliminates the post-hole effect caused by snowshoeless feet. Snowshoes are superior to cross-country skis in snow-covered areas that also have brush or rock obstacles, and they are easier to use than skis for those who are inexperienced. Modern snowshoes are made of an oval-shaped, lightweight, tubular frame that supports a durable decking material. Most bindings are easy to attach to your boots and come with cramponlike metal plates at the toes and heels to aid in traction. The type of snowshoes you'll need depends on their intended use and your weight. Smaller-style snowshoes allow greater maneuverability, whereas larger ones provide greater flotation.

Snowshoe Designs

There are four basic snowshoe designs: Yukon, Beavertail, Bearpaw, and Western.

YUKON

Yukon, or trail, snowshoes are large, measuring on average 40 to 60 inches long and 10 inches wide, with a 6- to 8-inch toe turnup. They are good shoes for open terrain where deep powder is present. Although you can travel up and down steep slopes, you will have to traverse them. These shoes are often made from wood and have neoprene laced decking.

Yukon snowshoes.

Continued ➡

Beavertail

The Beavertail design ranges in size from 9 by 40 inches to 20 by 44 inches. The most popular size appears to be the 12-by-34-inch. These shoes are generally flat, with a large, oval body that supports a long tail. They are decent shoes for kick-stepping but do not perform well when traversing a hill. These shoes are often made from wood and have neoprene laced decking.

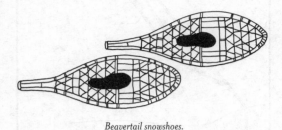

Beavertail snowshoes.

Bearpaw

The Bearpaw design ranges in size from 12 by 24 inches to 19 by 26 inches. The most popular size appears to be the 12-by-28-inch. These flat-toed, short, and wide snowshoes support no tail and are good shoes for kick-stepping but not for open terrain. These shoes are often made from wood and have neoprene laced decking.

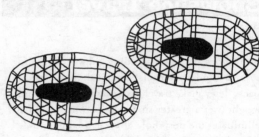

Bearpaw snaowshoes.

Western

The Western design ranges in size from 8 by 22 inches to 9 by 38 inches. These shoes have an aluminum frame and most often use a plastic decking. The tubular aluminum is very strong and light, and the solid plastic decking provides superior flotation compared with lace decking. The Western-style mountaineering snowshoe is a great all-purpose design, which allows travel in all terrains and performs well when ascending or descending slopes.

Choosing Snowshoes

Atlas Snow-Shoe Company provides the FACT (Flotation, Articulation, Comfort, and Traction) acronym for selecting Western-style snowshoes. These are the basic factors you should consider when purchasing snowshoes.

Flotation

A snowshoe's surface area provides flotation that keeps you from sinking through the snow's surface. Pick the smallest snowshoes that will support your weight plus the weight of your backpack and gear. As a general rule, however, choose larger snowshoes for dry snow and smaller ones for snow that is wet and dense.

Articulation

Articulation refers to how well snowshoe bindings allow your foot to move once attached. Under ideal circumstances, a binding will limit stepping rotation, allow the ankle freedom of rotation, and minimize heel twist.

Stepping rotation

Snowshoes should allow your feet to bend—from front to back—in a motion similar to walking. At the same time, the snowshoes' tips should not hit your shins and the shoes should not drag.

Ankle rotation

A snowshoe binding should support the foot while still allowing the ankle to naturally rotate from side to side. To accomplish this, bindings need to flex enough to allow the ankle to freely rotate from side to side, keeping it in a neutral position regardless of the terrain.

Heel support

A snowshoe's binding should allow for stepping rotation and ankle rotation, while keeping your foot centered—from side to side—regardless of the terrain.

Comfort

A comfortable binding, like a comfortable boot, should be made for the specific foot, not have any pressure points when snugly attached to the arch and ball of the foot, and be easy to put on and take off.

Traction

Unless you intend to snowshoe on perfectly level ground, you'll need snowshoes that can provide traction when ascending, descending, or traversing a slope. To provide this traction, your snowshoes should have cleats, or crampons, located at the toes, heels, and along the sides.

Improvising Snowshoes

In a crisis, snowshoes can be improvised from boughs. Use boughs from a tree on which the smaller branches and needles are thick and abundant, such as fir. Cut five to ten boughs that are 4 to 5 feet long each, lash the bases of all the branches together, and loosely tie them around their midpoint. Secure the bough snowshoes to your feet by tying a line around the toe of your boot and the forward third of the boughs.

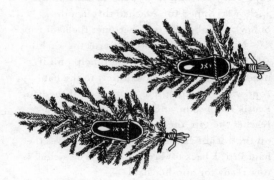

Snoshoes made from boughs.

Traveling on Snowshoes

In general, it won't take long to learn the art of snowshoeing. Once they are strapped on, just start walking. When on a slope, you should carry an ice ax, on the uphill side, and use it as an anchor and support. An ice ax used for snowshoeing should extend 2 to 4 inches beyond the ground. This measurement is determined by standing erect while holding the ice ax in one hand (with fingers extended down its shaft) and pointing it straight down toward the ground. An ice ax can be used to help steady you while climbing by providing a third point of contact.

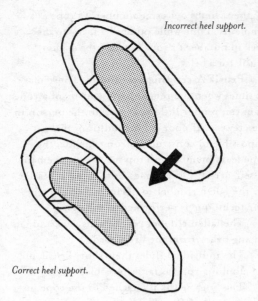

Incorrect heel support.

Correct heel support.

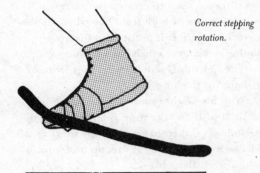

Correct stepping rotation.

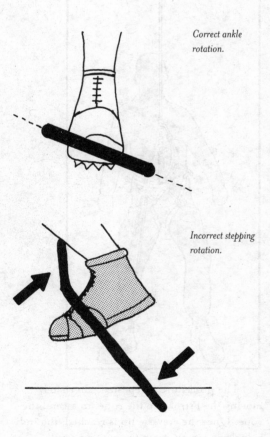

Correct ankle rotation.

Incorrect stepping rotation.

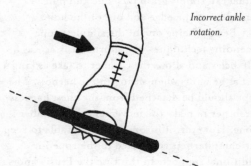

Incorrect ankle rotation.

Continued ➡

Kick-stepping

Kick-stepping on an ascent can be done with the Western, Bearpaw, and Beavertail style snowshoes. Use an ice ax as a self-belay to help anchor and balance your movement. To do this, keep it on the uphill side and plant its spike in the snow every two steps.

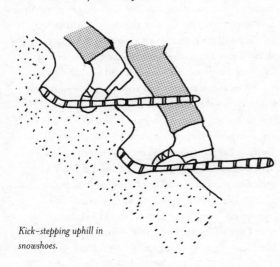

Kick-stepping uphill in snowshoes.

Downhill Travel

When going down a gradual grade, slightly bend your knees, lean back, and point your toes down so that the snowshoes' crampons make full contact with the snow's surface. If the hill is too steep for this technique, either traverse down it or take off your snowshoes and descend by plunge-stepping.

Traversing

To traverse with snowshoes, create a platform in the side of the hill by edging in, forcing the uphill side of the snowshoe into the slope, at least half of your foot width. As always, if in a group, consider the strides of those following you. It's times like this that an adjustable pole would be nice. This same technique can be used to come down a hill. All shoe types can be used for this technique. Use an ice ax as a self-belay to help anchor and balance your movement. To do this, keep it on the uphill side and plant its spike in the snow every two steps.

Repairing Broken Snowshoe

Most snowshoe breaks occur when the shoe is bridged between the ground and a log or similar object. When this happens, the pressure at the middle of the frame is too great, and the shoe breaks. Once the shoe has broken, it will be difficult to travel on until it's repaired. The best quick and simple fix is to tie a sturdy branch to the broken section so that it extends 3 to 4 inches beyond the break on both sides.

—From *Surviving Cold Weather*

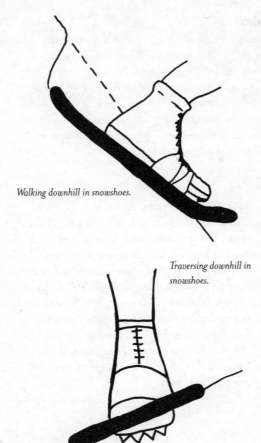

Walking downhill in snowshoes.

Traversing downhill in snowshoes.

Choosing Cross-Country Skis

Greg Davenport
Illustration by Steven A. Davenport

Nordic and mountaineering skis are good tools for snow travel but may not be the best option when carrying heavy backpacks or in a densely forested area. These skis use boot bindings that attach to your toes but leave the heels free. Mountaineering skis are slightly wider and heavier than the Nordic style and use bindings that leave the heels free for uphill travel but allow you to secure them when going downhill. If you intend to use your skis to travel uphill, you'll need climbing skins. These skins are attached to the bottom of the skis, providing the traction needed for uphill travel. An advanced cross-country skier can go almost anywhere, using skins to conquer uphill challenges and telemarking to descend steeper slopes.

Selecting Cross-Country Skis, Boots, Bindings, and Poles

If you intend to travel off-trail, purchase gear that is rated for touring to backcountry use. Cross-country skis allow you to move forward through a kicking and gliding process. While one foot is gliding, with only the toe and heel of the ski making firm contact with the snow, the other ski is kicking; the ski's center has traction

IMPROVISED SNOWSHOES

Greg Davenport   Illustrations by Steven Davenport and Ken Davenport

In the odd circumstance you may find yourself in a snow-laden terrain where your shoes aren't enough to keep you on top of the snow. If you have snowshoes, this isn't a problem. Snowshoes (even improvised ones) help distribute your body weight over a greater surface area, making snow travel much easier. In a crisis, snowshoes can be improvised from boughs. Use boughs from a tree where the smaller branches and needles are thick and abundant, such as fir. Cut five to ten boughs that are each four to five feet long, lash the base of all the branches together, and loosely tie them around their midpoint. Secure the bough snowshoe to your foot by tying a line around the toe of your boot and the forward third of the boughs. If you have more time on your hands, an elaborate trail snowshoe can be improvised using saplings and cords.

Gather two saplings 5 feet long (1 inch in diameter), lay them side by side, and lash them together at each end.

Spread the saplings 18 inches back from the front of the snowshoe, and lash a 12-inch stick perpendicular to them. Lash another stick, of similar size, 8 inches beyond the first. (For best results, notch the ends of each stick before lashing.)

Lash two more sticks between and perpendicular to the 12-inch ones. Place them approximately 2 inches from each sapling, and don't forget to notch the ends. (The middle space provides an opening for the toe of your boot.)

Lash two 10-inch-long sticks to the snowshoe where the heel of your boot rests when the toe is centered in the forward opening. (Once again, notch the sticks for better results.)

Incorporate parachute line, nylon line, or other durable material in all other spaces between the two saplings. This will increase the amount of surface area contacting the snow.

Using one piece of line, attach the boot to the snowshoe so that it can pivot while you walk. This is done by securing a line to the second stick (from the front) and then wrapping it over the top of the boot and around the heel. Finish by tying the two free ends together.

—From *Wilderness Survival*

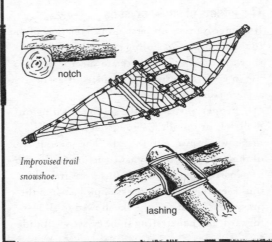

notch

Improvised trail snowshoe.

lashing

Continued ➡

and is making firm contact with the snow while moving backward and propelling you forward. If a ski is too firm in the center, you will have a great glide, but it will also require more work to propel you forward. These skis are best left to the pros. If a ski is too soft in the center, you will have less glide, but it will be easier to propel you forward. Some skis require wax, and others are waxless. Both styles, however, work on the same principle: They are slick at the ends and sticky at the center. On waxless skis, the front and back have little or no pattern, and the center has a tread pattern. If the skis require wax, the ends are waxed with a glide wax and the center with a sticky kick wax. Unless you are an advanced skier, I'd advise using waxless skis. They are easy to use and require little maintenance. You'll never have to worry about whether you have applied the right wax. A waxless ski, however, is slower than one that uses wax. Nevertheless, it is very versatile, allowing you to use it for a multitude of conditions, excluding ice travel. For backcountry skiing, use skis that are heavier and wider; when on groomed trails, use skis that are light and narrow. To select a ski that will optimize your abilities, you should consider your weight, height, and cross-country skiing ability.

Weight and ability
To determine the appropriate ski for your weight, hold the skis upright so that their bases are touching. There will be a gap in the center, caused by the skis' camber, or slight arching. As a basic rule of thumb, while holding these skis in this position, you should be able to squeeze the camber completely together using both hands. If you can't, the skis are probably too stiff and should be left for the advanced skier; if you can do it with one hand, they are probably too soft.

Height and ski length
For general use, when you hold the ski perpendicular to the ground and raise an arm over your head, it should reach your wrist. For backcountry use, however, select a ski that reaches to about the top of your head. The shorter ski will provide greater ease of turning and maneuverability between obstacles.

Boots and Bindings
Be sure to buy boots designed for skiing and not skating. The boots need to have toe bars for binding attachment. Buy the boots first, and then select the bindings that will work with them. Most bindings are either step-in or manual styles. To use a step-in binding, you simply insert the toe of your boot into the binding's forward bar, and press down until it snaps into place. A manual binding requires you to secure a latch over the top of the boot's toe bar. Bindings should be mounted by a professional.

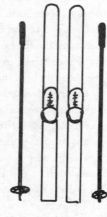

Cross-country skis, boots, and poles.

Poles
Your poles should have round baskets at the bottom. For general use, they should be somewhere between armpit and shoulder height. If touring, longer poles are better, but when in treed, mountainous terrain, shorter poles will serve you better. Expandable poles are ideal, since they allow you to change their length as needed for ascents and descents.

Sled
A sled allows you to carry more gear than just what fits into your pack and is a great option for long trips. Most commercial sleds come with a cover, waist harness, and support poles that connect the sled to your harness. You can make a similar item by attaching a child's sled to your pack or waist harness with rope. The benefit of the commercial sled is its rigid poles, which help you control it when traversing or going downhill. You might fashion such support poles by attaching lengths of thick PVC pipe to the sled and your pack or belt.

—From *Surviving Cold Weather*

Waxing and Caring for Skis
U.S. Army

General
The purpose of ski wax is to provide the ski with necessary climbing and sliding qualities to prevent backslip in various snow conditions. When snow conditions and temperature change, the type and method of application of ski wax will also differ. Before wax can be properly selected and applied, the individual must learn to recognize the different types of snow conditions. It is also valuable to have some knowledge of how ski wax performs in relation to snow.

After snow has fallen on the ground, its crystalline structure is continuously altered by the effects of temperature, wind, and humidity. In very cold weather these changes occur much more slowly than when temperature is near 32°F. Therefore, the most important factor of waxing is the effect that temperature has on the character of the snow and its sliding qualities.

Snow and Its Effects on Wax

The effects of snow crystals
It is important to understand the relation of wax to the holding and sliding capabilities of the snow. For this reason there are specific waxes to use in cross-country skiing under different snow surface conditions.

Proper wax. When the soldier is skiing on the level, or uphill, his body weight gives maximum pressure to the skis. The soft quality of the wax allows the crystal structure of the snow to penetrate the wax under this pressure and thus keep the ski from backslapping. When the pressure is lifted and the ski allowed to slide forward, the penetrating snow crystals will slide free from the surface of the wax reducing friction. Continuous forward motion, as in sliding, keeps the crystals from penetrating the wax.

Wax too soft. When the skis slide poorly, the following condition generally exists: the snow crystals have penetrated into the wax but will not slide free. This causes clogging of the snow on the running surface and may eventually cause ice to form. Under these conditions the soldier will find that even vigorous sliding of the ski will not break the snow loose from the wax surface. Little or no forward slide can be gained.

Wax too hard. When the skis slide well, but backslip on the level and when moving uphill, the following condition exists: the snow crystals are not penetrating the wax. The soldier will find he has excellent sliding when going downhill, but climbing uphill or skiing on level ground is very exhausting because of backslip. This is the primary deterrent to the use of "downhill" waxes for cross-country skiing.

Classification of snow. Snow is classified here into four general types. This classification is intended to assist the soldier in snow identification, choice of wax, and its proper application under these different conditions.

(a) *Wet snow.* This type of snow is mostly found during the spring, but it may also occur in the fall or late winter, particularly in regions of moderate climate. This type of snow can be readily made into a heavy, solid snowball. In extreme conditions, wet snow will become slushy and contain a maximum amount of water.

(b) *Moist snow.* This type of snow is generally associated with early winter, but may also occur in midwinter during a sudden warmup period. This type of snow can be made into a snowball, but will not compress as readily or be as heavy as a wet snowball. It will have a tendency to fall apart.

(c) *Dry snow.* This type of snow is generally associated with winter at its height, but it can occur in late fall as well as in spring, when abnormally low temperatures occur. This snow is light and fluffy. It cannot be compressed into a snowball unless the snow is made moist by holding it in the hand. At extremely low temperatures, such as those found in the far northern regions, this snow is like sand, and has very poor sliding qualities.

(d) *New snow.* This is snow which is still falling or has recently fallen on the ground, but has not been subject to changes due to the sun or temperature variation. It can be wet, moist, or dry in nature.

Proper Selection and Application of Waxes
Cross-country ski waxes are formulated to provide optimum sliding and climbing characteristics for various types of snow conditions. Each type is labeled with appropriate instructions on its intended use, i.e., wet, moist or dry snow conditions. Since the types of wax vary between manufacturers, no particular types of wax can be prescribed for each classification of snow; however, the instructions on each container specifies the weather conditions and type of snow where performance of the wax is best. Proper application of all waxes is important to achieve desired results whether they be trac-

Continued ➡

tion or sliding action. As a general rule, the wax that gives the best sliding surface for all types of snow provides an excellent base for application of other waxes. To provide traction, varying amounts, combinations, and methods of application of other waxes are used. When pulling a sled or carrying a heavy load, thicker coats of wax may be required to insure traction.

Waxing Procedure

Whenever possible, the waxing of skis should be done. ... when shelter and heat are available, as the running surface of the ski should be warm and dry to obtain best results. ... [S]ki wax should be carried in the pockets, if possible, so that body heat will keep the wax soft and easy to use. If the skis need waxing during the march, the running surfaces are dried as much as possible by the use of paper or dry mittens. Whenever possible, old wax should be removed before rewaxing skis particularly when a different type of wax is being used. ...

To apply, cover the running surface with wax. Next, smooth the wax by rubbing it with the hand, using the heel of the palm or the fingers, a waxing cork, or a heated iron. When heat is available, this process can be made easier by warming the wax that has been applied. It is normally best to work progressively on a section at a time, from the ski tip towards the heel. If the waxing is done in a shelter, or heat is used, the skis should be allowed to cool to outside air temperature before being used. Do not place the running surfaces of skis on snow immediately after waxing if heat is used or if waxing is done in a heated room or shelter as the snow may stick and freeze to the running surface. For the same reason protect the running surfaces against wind driven snow. To insure that wax is properly chosen and applied, the skis should be tested before being used. ...

Care of Ski Equipment

General

...Skins must be checked for...evidence of possible warping and splitting, loss of camber, defective edges, and broken steel edge sections or screws. At the same time bindings must be checked for worn straps, missing rivets and screws, and proper adjustment. Ski poles should be checked to insure that wrist straps, handgrips, baskets, and points are firmly fastened and that no breakage has occurred.

Daily Care

After each day's use, the skis and the skiing equipment should be checked and necessary repairs made by the individual as follows:

Skis. Remove any snow or ice that has frozen to the ski. This may be done with heat. If heat is not available, this can be done with a mitten, wooden stick, or piece of metal. Check the heels and tips of the skis for cracks. Badly cracked skis must be replaced, as they are weakened and break easily. At the same time, check for and replace defective or missing edges and screws. The condition of ski bottoms is then checked and, if needed, additional pine tar or base wax is applied. The surface waxing for the next day's march is deferred until snow condi-

tions are determined in the morning or shortly prior to departure. After maintenance of skis is completed, they should be placed indoors, preferably in a ski rack. Under field conditions, skis are placed in an improvised ski rack, planted upright in the snow or stacked.

Bindings. Insure that all straps, buckles, screws and rivets are present and in good condition. Replace parts which are unserviceable. If necessary, readjust the fit of the bindings.

Poles. Check wrist straps, handgrips, shafts, baskets, and points to insure that they are in good condition. Broken parts should be replaced at the first opportunity. Temporary repairs can be made with wire, cord, or tape.

When snow cover is comparatively thin, be careful not to damage the skis while skiing in rocky or stumpy terrain. Sometimes there is water under the snow cover on frozen rivers or lakes. Try to cross them at a dry place; make an improvised hasty bridge from trees or boughs, if time permits. If the skis become wet during a crossing of water, the ice which forms on the skis must be removed after reaching the bank. A long march or sudden change in temperature may require rewaxing of skis during the march. When skis are removed, do not leave them on the snow. It may stick and freeze on the running surface. Remove the snow from the skis and stack them beside the ski tracks or lean the skis against a tree.

—Excerpted from *Basic Cold Weather Manual (Field Manual 31-70)*

Cross-Country Ski Travel

Buck Tilton and John Gookin
Illustrations by Joan M. Safford

With skis on feet, pack on back, and sled in tow, you're ready to head out on an adventure in the world of the cold and the white. An untracked vastness awaits, silent but alive, and spectacular in ways that only the winter traveler will experience. There are challenges ahead, especially if you lack experience in making those boards strapped to your boots move the way you want them to. What follows here is basic information that should be helpful, but as always, you will learn by doing (again, if at all possible, under the guidance of a good teacher).

The most important thing to remember about backcountry skiing is that you can have a great trip even if you are a poor skier. Beyond basic safety, the critical element, at all levels of ability, is fun. The basic idea of backcountry skiing is to move across the snow with as little effort as possible. Forget those pictures of Olympic cross-country skiers gracefully speeding across the finish line, though. You're a winter camper, carrying everything you will need for your adventure, crossing many kinds of "wild" snow, and facing a variety of exciting challenges.

Flat and Rolling Terrain

Skiing on flat or relatively gentle, rolling terrain is a skill that comes quickly with just a little practice. As you're moving along, sliding your feet

instead of lifting them, you will soon realize that a push or "kick" off of the back ski sends you gliding forward on the front ski. You've discovered the simplest technique for ski travel: the kick-and-glide.

To improve your kick-and-glide, stay relaxed, and keep your knees slightly flexed and shoulder-width apart. When you "kick" forward, shift all your weight onto the ski you're gliding on and then swing your arm and reach forward with the ski pole on the opposite side from the forward ski. You'll gain a little momentum by pushing with your ski pole, but you should rely primarily on your legs. When the snow is firm, or you're on a track or trail, you can gain speed by double-poling—reaching forward with both poles to get an extra "umph" out of each push. Bend at the waist, and use the mass of your upper body to add momentum. Keep in mind that this technique requires more energy to maintain.

When it's time to change direction on flat terrain, just about anything works if it involves picking up a ski and turning it in the new direction. To do an about-face, use a common method known as the kick turn: (1) Stop, and plant your poles slightly behind you, with the pole on the side you're turning toward between your skis. (2) Lift the ski you'll turn first, kick it out, and swing it entirely around so that it's facing in the opposite direction. (3) Bring the offside pole across and plant it farther away from you than usual. (4) Lift the second ski, bring it around, and shift your ski poles into a more normal position. You end up with both skis pointing in the same new direction. The kick turn can be used on just about any terrain (even steep side hills)—as long as you can stop first.

Uphill Terrain

When the terrain gets steeper, you need to shorten your stride and maintain proper balance. The most common mistake made by newcomers is leaning forward on uphill terrain. The center for traction is the center of the ski, under your foot. Leaning forward weights the front of the ski, and you lose traction. Stand up straighter, push down firmly with your heels, keep your stride short (think baby steps), and use your legs as your primary power source (poles are secondary).

```
NOLS TIP

Practice Star Turns
Star turns are an excellent way for your body
to learn important muscle movements for
skiing. On flat terrain, stick a pole in the snow
to serve as a reference point. Face the pole and
walk sideways around it, keeping your ski tips
pointed toward the pole. Go 360 degrees
around the pole, then reverse and walk side-
ways back around the pole to your starting
point. Now face away from the pole and repeat
the exercise. Repetition of this fundamental
drill will improve your skiing ability.
```

Continued →

At a certain level of steepness, you need to change your technique, or you'll end up downhill skiing—backward. On firmly packed snow of moderate steepness, you may find the herringbone technique useful. Spread your tips wide, but keep the tails close together, forming a letter V. Roll your knees inward as you climb, digging the inside edges of the skis into the snow. Keep making the letter V again and again as you ascend. Once mastered, the herringbone can get you up short climbs quickly.

THE 'HERRINGBONE' TECHNIQUE:

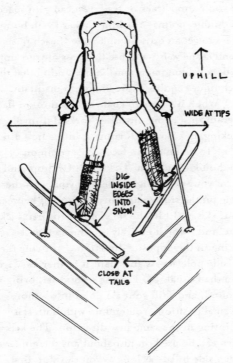

UPHILL

WIDE AT TIPS

DIG INSIDE EDGES INTO SNOW!

CLOSE AT TAILS

Side-stepping is an easier but slower way to ascend short, steep distances, especially when the snow is soft. Stand side-ways on the slope, keeping your skis perpendicular to the fall line (the route you would take if you were falling down the slope). Dig your edges into the snow by rolling your knees uphill. Step up with the uphill ski, then bring the downhill ski up beside the uphill ski. For better balance and a little push, hold the downhill ski pole at the top of the grip and shorten your grip on the uphill pole.

Another uphill method, particularly useful on long ascents, involves traversing the hillside—skiing back and forth, gaining a little elevation with each pass, and then doing a kick turn and traversing back, until you reach the top. Performing the kick turns while facing downhill (i.e., turning away from the hillside) is much easier than while facing uphill, and the chance of falling is reduced. With skins, you may be able to negotiate the direction changes of a traverse without a kick turn.

If you anticipate skiing uphill in the backcountry for more than relatively short distances, skins are a necessary piece of gear . . . You can climb up amazingly steep slopes with skins (far steeper than wax would allow), and you use a lot less energy. Skins that use glue generally require removal of the kick wax. Otherwise, they may "gum up" and come unglued. Glueless skins can be used directly over your kick wax, but they don't usually glide as well. Because skins in general glide less efficiently than either waxed or waxless skis, most people take them off on flat or downhill terrain.

① PLANT POLES BEHIND YOU

② KICK UP, and TURN ONE SKI INTO THE NEW DIRECTION

UPHILL

SKIS POINT IN OPPOSITE DIRECTIONS

The KICK TURN

③ BRING POLE ACROSS

④ BRING SECOND SKI INTO NEW DIRECTION

⑤ READY TO GO!

UPHILL TECHNIQUES

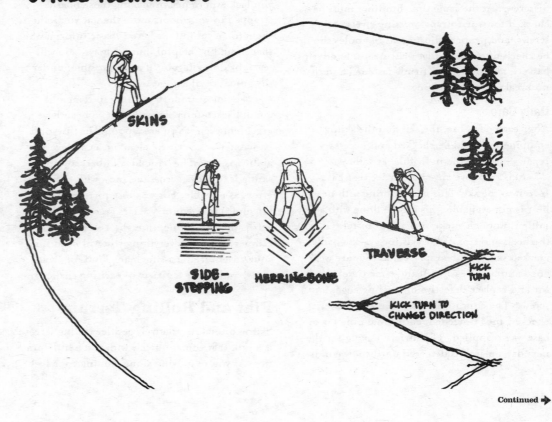

SKINS

SIDE-STEPPING

HERRINGBONE

TRAVERSE

KICK TURN

KICK TURN TO CHANGE DIRECTION

Continued ➡

Downhill Terrain

When a downhill run is not too steep, you can just point your skis toward the bottom and go for it. If you feel out of control on the descent, you can always fall—a method of stopping that seldom fails.

With just a bit of practice, you can gain control of a descent on relatively well-packed snow by using the basic snowplow. In the snowplow, you turn your skis into an inverted V, with the point at the tips and the wide part at the tails. By rolling your knees slightly inward, you slide on the inside edges of the skis, while the outsides of the skis "plow" the snow. By shifting your weight to one ski, you slowly turn in the opposite direction. Weighting the right ski, for instance, turns you to the left. Practice the snowplow without a pack before attempting it with a pack.

For many, the best method of controlling a downhill run is by traversing back and forth across the fall line of the slope, losing a little elevation with each traverse. This is the reverse of the uphill method mentioned earlier.

If it's just too steep and icy and otherwise scary, you can take off your skis and hike down the hill. The best way to go down a steep snowfield is to plunge your heels hard into the snow with your knees slightly bent, a technique known as plunge-stepping. Bend forward at the waist for more stability. Hike off to the side of the slope to prevent gouging holes in the hillside, leaving a clean field for those who might be more daring or accomplished.

For many, the ultimate backcountry, free-heel skiing experience is mastering the telemark turn. Telemark turns are initiated with the body in a low position on the skis. The downhill ski is pushed forward, the leg on that side is flexed so that the knee is over the toes, and the uphill leg is bent so that the heel comes off the ski far enough to point up at the skier's hindquarters. Ideally, the skier's weight remains equally distributed on both legs. When the hips are turned toward the fall line, the skis turn. As the uphill ski becomes the downhill ski, it is turned slightly inward to form a "V" with the other ski, which sharpens the turn. As the turn is completed, reversing the leg positions prepares the skier for the next turn.

When done correctly, the telemark turn is a ferociously lovely maneuver. Learning it involves a lot of practice. You can read about it, but to master the telemark turn, you'll need a teacher and lot of time on skis. In the words of author and master tele-skier Allen O'Bannon, "All it takes to be able to ski well in the different conditions possible in the backcountry is time skiing the different conditions in the backcountry."

Falling on Skis

There are bad ways and good ways to fall. Bad ways include planting your face in the snow and tumbling out of control down a steep incline. The best way to fall is simply to sit down, off to the side, on your buttocks if possible. It hurts less to sit down, and it's easier to get back up from a sitting position. On steep terrain, try to fall to the uphill side. To get up, shift your body around to the front of your skis, slide one foot back, and stand. On an incline, if your skis are

uphill, roll over so they're on your downhill side. In deep, soft snow, take your poles off and cross them in the snow, forming the letter X. By holding the poles at the cross of the X, you can support your weight while you regain a standing position. If you're burdened with a heavy pack, you'll probably have to take it off.

Breaking Trail

When there is no trail through the snow, someone has to break one, an ambitious and tiring task, especially in the deep stuff. After each step, you have to free your ski from the snow for the next step. This involves kicking and pulling up until the ski breaks free of the snow, then stepping forward. Leaning back a bit while kicking and pulling usually lends power to the attempt to free the ski.

A group will move faster, and stay happier, if the person breaking trail is relieved periodically. As soon as the trailbreaker tires or feels overheated, she or he steps off the trail and rejoins the group as the last person in line. This type of relay keeps a fresh skier in front, full of energy and psychologically supported by the fact that in fifteen to twenty minutes she or he will be replaced.

When the breaking is really tough—such as in deep snow with a thin crust that supports a skier's weight for a second or two—a group may choose to take turns breaking trail without a pack or sled. One or two skiers move ahead, breaking the trail, then ski back for their packs or sleds, hauling them along a well-groomed track. In some conditions, groups may even choose to break trail one day and move camp down the track the next day.

Skiing with a Pack

It's more difficult skiing with a pack than without one, and only practice can refine your skill. The big difference is that your center of gravity shifts farther back. You have to compensate by developing a good packing system. The

load should be balanced so that it rides evenly on your center of gravity. The heavier items ride best close to your body, especially when you're skiing. Otherwise, you tend to be pulled backward or thrown sideways. Whether you pack the heavy gear high or low depends on personal preference and terrain. Packing the weight high requires less effort to haul but makes you a little more wobbly—not a problem when the terrain is relatively flat and the skiing is easy. Packing the load low makes your job a bit more strenuous but gives you better balance when the going gets rough or steep.

In a well-organized pack, the load is fitted snugly so that it doesn't shift, throwing you off balance when you least expect it. Everything that you might want on short notice should be readily accessible. You don't want to have to conduct an extended search for your lunch, camera, parka, or asthma medication. Place small items together in a stuff sack to avoid losing them in the depths of your pack. Items such as your sleeping bag can be buried deep. Nothing with hard edges should be placed where it can jab into your back.

Skiing with a Sled

A sled helps to manage the weight and bulk of an extended winter expedition. When skiing with one an important consideration is how you will attach yourself to it. Sometimes, skiers attach their sleds to their packs. This works, but it's better if the sled is attached separately to your hips, in which case you just point the sled in the direction of travel, hook yourself to it, and put on your pack. This way, the pull is more from the core of your body, and therefore easier. This also allows you to throw off the pack, haul the sled up a steep incline, and return for the pack. Finally, a sled attached directly to your hips is easier to turn.

In open, relatively flat areas, a simple harness system consisting of a couple of towropes tied—or, even better, clipped with carabiners—to the hip belt of your pack will

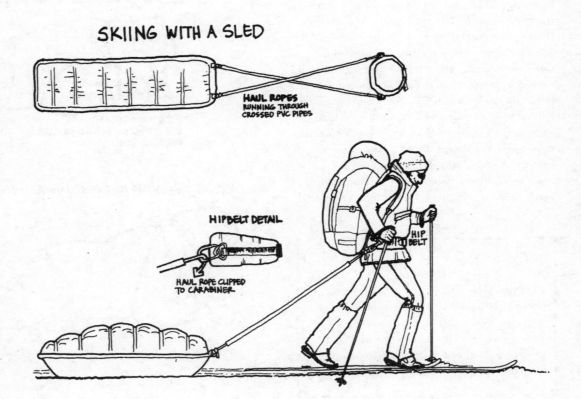

SKIING WITH A SLED

HAUL ROPES
RUNNING THROUGH
CROSSED PVC PIPES

HIPBELT DETAIL

HAUL ROPE CLIPPED
TO CARABINER

HIP
BELT

Continued ➡

suffice. But the more you need to turn and the steeper the terrain, the more rigid the harness system needs to be to keep the sled from veering back and forth. Rigidity can be supplied by poles, six feet long or so, between you and the sled. You can also create rigid poles for a plastic sled by running two towropes, one from each side of the forward end of the sled, through two lengths of PVC pipe or conduit. (Be careful with PVC in extreme cold, or it will break.) The poles work best in terms of control if they are crossed in the middle, then attached to a well-padded hip belt. The crossover allows you to use natural hip movements to steer the sled into your ski track when you make turns. The crossed poles tend to keep the sled in your track as long as you ski normally.

Loading the sled also requires some ingenuity. First, knock off any ice that might be stuck to the bottom (doing this after loading is unnecessarily difficult). Place a duffel bag in the bottom of the sled, and load the heavy items in the middle with the weight spread out evenly on either side. Pack lighter, bulkier items in the front and back. Your shovel can be lashed to the top of the duffel bag, for quick access. Nylon webbing works great for lashing the bag to the sled, and it should hold the load down tightly so that it won't shift; this also reduces the chance of snagging trees. Keep the lash lines as short and simple as possible, for easy adjustment. Six short straps, for instance, are much easier to handle than one long strap. Rather than threading them around the load and tying knots, use lash straps that are clipped together with quick-release buckles.

On flats and rolling terrain, sled hauling is basically a process of overcoming inertia and keeping it overcome. It usually takes a little jolting pull to start the sled sliding. Once you get going, you can adjust it, if, for instance, you feel it pulling to one side.

Uphills require only a change in effort, primarily in creating long traverses and switchbacks. A well-broken track on the side of a hill may have a small retaining wall that holds the sled in the track. You can also create such a track by slowly and laboriously stomping out a wider-than-usual track. Be sure to have a competent skier up front breaking trail. Despite careful attempts at control, sometimes the sled slips down the slope, so stay attentive and be prepared to stop it. On nasty sidehills, you can put a tether on the back of the sled, so that the person behind you can hold the back up if it starts to slide. If it's a very steep and unavoidable sidehill, try crossing the slope without your sled to "groom" a track for it, When you make a traverse, turning back to cross the same sidehill again, find an area that is free of trees and not

too deep; aim to make more of a U-turn than a kick turn. Seasoned skiers may choose to do an uphill-facing kick turn and then muscle the sled up into a track that now heads off in the opposite direction.

When it comes to downhill runs with a sled, your style is largely determined by your ability to ski. You can race the sled to the bottom and see who wins, or you can let the sled pass you and follow it down. On a wide open slope, some skiers can negotiate slow, gradual turns, keeping the sled somewhat under control. With a long, safe run-out, you may choose to abandon the sled to its own fate and ski down without it. There's one method that never fails: carrying your skis and walking down with your sled.

Crossing Frozen Water

Traveling on the flat, frozen surface of a lake can be a lot easier than struggling through nearby snow, but it is not without hazards, even in northern climes, where the ice may be several feet thick. Springs and swirling currents sometimes create thin ice that is difficult to detect until you plunge through. And snow-covered lakes may be covered with surprisingly thin ice because the snow insulates the surface of the water, preventing it from freezing solid enough

to support you. When possible, avoid any lakes that you are unsure of. If you are going to cross a frozen lake, keep these tips in mind:

- Keep your skis on. This disperses your weight over a larger area, reducing the chance that you will break through.

- Spots where streams enter and leave lakes are notorious for thin ice.

- Dark areas are sometimes indicators of thin ice.

- Objects sticking out of the ice, such as logs and rocks, sometimes trap and radiate solar energy, creating weak spots.

- Tap the ice ahead of you with your ski pole. A solid "thunk" means thick ice, and a hollow "bonk" indicates thin ice.

- Areas shadowed by trees or cliffs usually provide the thickest ice, because the sun has less time to warm them.

- If you fall through, don't panic. Spread your arms wide over the edge of the hole, kick your feet vigorously to get them to the surface, and swim up onto the ice, pulling with your arms as you kick.

- If you anticipate crossing frozen lakes often, carry a pair of ice picks on a string

SELF RESCUE FROM ICE

EXTEND ARMS PAST THE EDGE OF THE HOLE

PULL YOUR LOWER BODY TO THE SURFACE

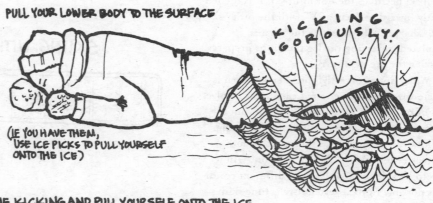

KICKING VIGOROUSLY!

(IF YOU HAVE THEM, USE ICE PICKS TO PULL YOURSELF ONTO THE ICE)

CONTINUE KICKING AND PULL YOURSELF ONTO THE ICE

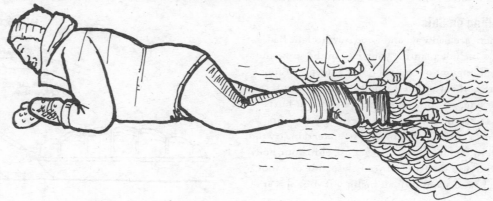

Continued ➡

NOLS Tip

Pace yourself
When hauling a sled (and even when you're not), use a pace that you can maintain all day. If you can't talk to someone while you're moving, you're breathing too hard and should probably slow down.

MINIMUM DEPTHS FOR CROSSING ICE SAFELY

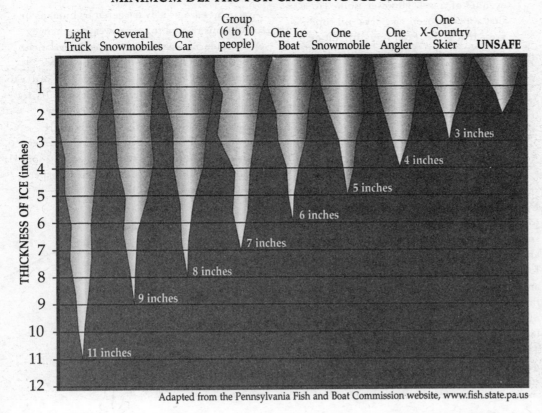

Adapted from the Pennsylvania Fish and Boat Commission website, www.fish.state.pa.us

around your neck to facilitate climbing back onto the slippery surface if you fall through.

Fast-moving rivers typically fail to freeze solid enough to support your weight, but slow-moving water may provide excellent pathways in the dead of winter. The tips for crossing frozen lakes apply here as well, plus the following:

- Avoid ice over the fastest current, which is easier said than done. The strongest current—and the weakest ice—tends to lie on the outside of bends and where the river drops.

- Wind-scoured ice tends to be weaker than ice in sheltered areas.

- If you think the water is deep enough to submerse you, don't cross. A break-through may cause you to be sucked under the ice.

- Look for braids in the river where the flow separates into two or more narrow channels. These generally offer a few narrow, shallow crossings.

Additionally, if you're able to determine the depth of the ice, keep in mind the minimum safe depths above.

—From *NOLS Winter Camping*

Basic Principles of Cold-Weather Survival

U.S. Army

It is more difficult for you to satisfy your basic water, food, and shelter needs in a cold environment than in a warm environment. Even if you have the basic requirements, you must also have adequate protective clothing and the will to survive. The will to survive is as important as the basic needs. There have been incidents when trained and well-equipped individuals have not survived cold weather situations because they lacked the will to live. Conversely, this will has sustained individuals less will-trained and equipped.

There are many different items of cold weather equipment and clothing issued by the U.S. Army today. Specialized units may have access to newer, lightweight gear such as polypropylene underwear, Gore-Tex outerwear and boots, and other special equipment. Remember, however, the older gear will keep you warm as long as you apply a few cold weather principles. If the newer types of clothing are available, use them. If not, then your clothing should be entirely wool, with the possible exception of a windbreaker.

You must not only have enough clothing to protect you from the cold, you must also know how to maximize the warmth you get from it. For example, always keep your head covered. You can lose 40 to 45 percent of body heat from an unprotected head and even more from the unprotected neck, wrist, and ankles. These areas of the body are good radiators of heat and have very little insulating fat. The brain is very susceptible to cold and can stand the least amount of cooling. Because there is much blood circulation in the head, most of which is on the surface, you can lose heat quickly if you do not cover your head.

There are four basic principles to follow to keep warm. An easy way to remember these basic principles is to use the word COLD—

C — Keep clothing *clean*.

O — Avoid *overheating*.

L — Wear clothes *loose* and in *layers*.

D — Keep clothing *dry*.

C—Keep clothing clean. This principle is always important for sanitation and comfort. In winter, it is also important from the standpoint of warmth. Clothes matted with dirt and grease lose much of their insulation value. Heat can escape more easily from the body through the clothing's crushed or filled up air pockets.

O—Avoid overheating. When you get too hot, you sweat and your clothing absorbs the moisture. This affects your warmth in two ways: dampness decreases the insulation quality of clothing, and as sweat evaporates, your body cools. Adjust your clothing so that you do not sweat. Do this by partially opening your parka or jacket, by removing an inner layer of clothing, by removing heavy outer mittens, or by throwing back your parka hood or changing to lighter headgear. The head and hands act as efficient heat dissipaters when overheated.

L—Wear your clothing loose and in layers. Wearing tight clothing and footgear restricts blood circulation and invites cold injury.It also decreases the volume of air trapped between the layers, reducing its insulating value. Several layers of light-weight clothing are better than one equally thick layer of clothing, because the layers have dead-air space between them. The dead-air space provides extra insula tion. Also, layers ofclothing allow you to take off or add clothing layers to prevent excessive sweating or to increase warmth.

D—Keep clothing dry. In cold tempera tures, your inner layers of clothing can become wet from sweat and your outer layer, if not water repellent, can become wet from snow and frost melted by body heat. Wear water repellent outer clothing, if available. It will shed most of the water collected from melting snow and frost. Before entering a heated shelter, brush off the snow and frost. Despite the precautions you take, there will be times when you cannot keep from getting wet. At such times, drying your clothing may become a major problem. On the march, hang your damp mittens and socks on your rucksack. Sometimes in freezing temperatures, the wind and sun will dry this clothing. You can also place damp socks or mittens, unfolded, near your body so that your body heat can dry them. In a campsite, hang damp clothing inside the shelter near the top, using drying lines or improvised racks. You may even be able to dry each item by holding it

Continued ➡

before an open fire. Dry leather items slowly. If no other means are available for drying your boots, put them between your sleeping bag shell and liner. Your body heat will help to dry the leather.

A heavy, down-lined sleeping bag is a valuable piece of survival gear in cold weather. Ensure the down remains dry. If wet, it loses a lot of its insulation value. If you do not have a sleeping bag, you can make one out of parachute cloth or similar material and natural dry material, such as leaves, pine needles, or moss. Place the dry material between two layers of the material.

Other important survival items are a knife; waterproof matches in a waterproof container, preferably one with a flint attached; a durable compass; map; watch; waterproof ground cloth and cover; flashlight; binoculars; dark glasses; fatty emergency foods; food gathering gear; and signaling items.

Remember, a cold weather environment can be very harsh. Give a good deal of thought to selecting the right equipment for survival in the cold. If unsure of an item you have never used, test it in an "overnight backyard" environment before venturing further. Once you have selected items that are essential for your survival, do not lose them after you enter a cold weather environment.

Travel

As a survivor ... in an arctic or subarctic region, you will face many obstacles. Your location and the time of the year will determine the types of obstacles and the inherent dangers. You should—

- Avoid traveling during a blizzard.

- Take care when crossing thin ice. Distribute your weight by lying flat and crawling.

- Cross streams when the water level is lowest. Normal freezing and thawing action may cause a stream level to vary as much as 2 to 2.5 meters per day. This variance may occur any time during the day, depending on the distance from a glacier, the temperature, and the terrain. Consider this variation in water level when selecting a campsite near a stream.

- Consider the clear arctic air. It makes estimating distance difficult. You more frequently underestimate than overestimate distances.

- Do not travel in "whiteout" conditions. The lack of contrasting colors makes it impossible to judge the nature of the terrain.

- Always cross a snow bridge at right angles to the obstacle it crosses. Find the strongest part of the bridge by poking ahead of you with a pole or ice axe. Distribute your weight by crawling or by wearing snowshoes or skis.

- Make camp early so that you have plenty of time to build a shelter.

- Consider frozen or unfrozen rivers as avenues of travel. However, some rivers that appear frozen may have soft, open areas that make travel very difficult or may not allow walking, skiing, or sledding.

- Use snowshoes if you are traveling over snow-covered terrain. Snow 30 or more centimeters deep makes traveling difficult. If you do not have snowshoes, make a pair using willow, strips of cloth, leather, or other suitable material.

It is almost impossible to travel in deep snow without snowshoes or skis. Traveling by foot leaves a well-marked trail for any pursuers to follow. If you must travel in deep snow, avoid snow-covered streams. The snow, which acts as an insulator, may have prevented ice from forming over the water. In hilly terrain, avoid areas where avalanches appear possible. Travel in the early morning in areas where there is danger of avalanches. On ridges, snow gathers on the lee side in overhanging piles called cornices. These often extend far out from the ridge and may break loose if stepped on.

—From *Survival (Field Manual (21-76)*

Avalanches
Greg Davenport
Illustrations by Steven A. Davenport

Statistics have shown that 90 percent of all avalanche victims rescued within five minutes survive, but less than 50 percent are still alive after thirty minutes. These statistics, however, are proving to be far more favorable for individuals who use the AvaLung breathing device. Proper preparation and avalanche rescue knowhow are key to survival, since time is of the utmost importance. Educate yourself through reading and taking avalanche training classes. Learn about conditions, both past and present, where you intend to go: any hazards located in the area, such as slide paths, cornices, or crevasses, and the current weather report and avalanche dangers associated with it. Make sure all members of the group have compatible beacons. Most accidents could have been avoided through proper preparation. Take the time to do it, and if conditions seem questionable, go another day.

Avalanche Types

Point Release Avalanche
This type of avalanche begins at a single point and collects snow as it heads downhill, growing bigger and bigger. A point release avalanche occurs most often in the spring, when new snow falls on a smooth snow surface that was created by repeated thawing, freezing, or rain. The risk is high after heavy snowfall (10 to 12 inches total, or when it has fallen at more than 1 inch per hour).

Slab Avalanches
A slab avalanche is a solid, cohesive layer of snow that slides all at once after breaking free from its bond to an underlying surface. Most avalanche victims are caught in this type of avalanche. These usually occur during or after a winter storm and are often triggered by someone.

Avalanche Triggers

Avalanches are usually triggered by humans or conditions related to recent weather changes. Most wilderness areas stay abreast of avalanche conditions and closely monitor the snow's condition for the potential of slides. In order to pass this information onto the backcountry traveler, the United States Avalanche Danger Descriptors guide was created. This guide provides a color reference to describe current avalanche conditions. This information should be used in addition to your judgment, experience, and knowledge of the area.

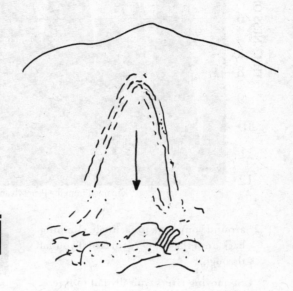

Point release avalanche.

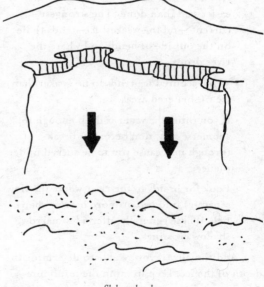

Slab avalanche.

Identifying Avalanche Hazards

Four factors should be considered when evaluating the potential risk of an avalanche: terrain, snowpack, weather, and the human factor.

Terrain
A terrain's potential for an avalanche is based on the angle, aspect, and configuration of the slope.

SLOPE ANGLE
A slope angle between 25 and 60 degrees has the potential to be an avalanche hazard. Most avalanches occur between 30 and 45 degrees.

Continued ➡

Steeper slopes rarely hold on to snow, and shallow slopes rarely produce enough momentum for the snow to slide. Unless you are highly experienced at measuring these angles, use a clinometer (see page 285).

Slope Aspect

A slope's aspect describes its position in relation to the sun and wind. In winter, your odds are better when using slopes that have sun exposure, since the snow will normally settle and stabilize faster. In spring and summer, however, the sun-exposed slopes tend to be less stable, and odds favor slopes that had limited sun during the winter. Slopes that directly face the wind tend to be safer than those that don't since the wind either rids them of new snow or packs it down. Leeward slopes, those sheltered from the wind, collect the snow blown off the windward side, resulting in cornices, deep unconsolidated snow, and wind slabs.

Slope Configuration

Does the slope have a convex or concave appearance? Snow on a convex slope is under a great deal of tension and is more prone to release than snow covering a concave slope. A straight, open, and steep slope is an obvious hazard. Trees that are bent down and away from the upward slope and are missing limbs on the uphill side are signs that a major avalanche has traveled through that area.

Snowpack

A snowpack is created by episodes of intermittent storms, changes in weather, and temperature fluctuations. Through this process, multiple layers of consolidated snow are formed, one on top of the other. New layers may or may not adhere to the underlying layer. Slabs are formed when an upper cohesive layer does not bond with a thin, weak layer that sits underneath it. The stability of a snowpack can be evaluated by doing the Rutschblock test and paying close attention to Mother Nature's clues. However, it's important to consider all factors related to potential avalanche hazards.

Rutschblock Test

The Rutschblock test can be used to evaluate the stability of a slope and its potential to slide. In this test, the skier or snowshoer actually stands on a large block of snow to see if it can support his or her weight. The test should be performed on a slope that has similar conditions to the one you intend to approach. Using a shovel or snow saw (improvise if neither is available), cut three sides of a square block—the front and two sides—each about 6 feet long and 3 feet deep, or until the lower weaker layer is exposed. Using a saw, ski, or other improvised device, cut the back wall free of the slope and to the same depth as the other sides. Wearing your skis or snowshoes, step onto the center of the block, from the uphill side. Does the block support your weight? If it does, then safely do a series of jumps to see if the block slides free of the weaker surface. A slope is considered *extremely unstable* if the test slab breaks free while you are approaching the site, creating it, or simply standing on the block; a slope is considered *unstable* if the slab breaks free when you're flexing in preparation for the first jump or during the first jump itself; a slope is considered *relatively stable* when it takes repeated hard jumps to break the slab free; and a slope is considered *stable* when the slab doesn't fail after repeated jumps. Other tests may be used to evaluate a slope's stability, but they are not as reliable as the Rutschblock test, and it's difficult to interpret the value of the information they provide. If you are concerned about a slope's stability, take the time to do the Rutschblock test.

Nature's Clues

Mother Nature provides clues about the snowpack's stability. Paying close attention to them will provide additional information about the relative risk associated with your present location.

Recent avalanches on similar slopes

This is probably the best clue you'll ever get, and it's advisable to avoid similar slopes.

Shooting cracks

A shooting crack could be a precursor to a slab avalanche. If snow conditions create this effect, avoid avalanche terrain.

Whumping noises

When a snowpack's weak layer collapses, it makes a whump sound. If you hear this sound, avoid avalanche terrain.

Hollow sounds

A hollow, drumlike sound radiating up from the snowpack may indicate that a weak layer is underneath an upper cohesive layer (slab) of snow. If you hear this sound, avoid avalanche terrain.

Weather

Snowfall, rain, wind, and temperatures all affect the bond between layers of snow.

Recent Snowfall or Rain

The risk of avalanche is extremely high after a heavy snowfall (10 to 12 inches total, or when it has fallen at more than 1 inch per hour). Rain penetrates the snow and weakens the bond between layers, making it easier for a slab to break free.

Wind

Wind-loaded snow forms slabs on the leeward side of a hill, making it a potential avalanche hazard. Avoid areas where wind loading is a concern. (Also see Slope Aspect, above.)

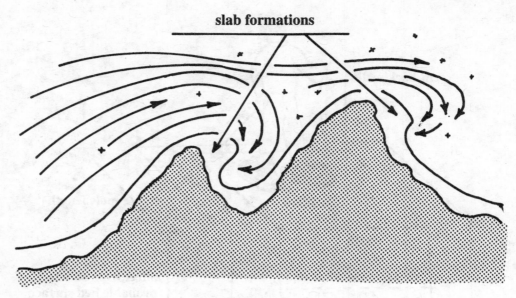

slab formations

Slope aspect.

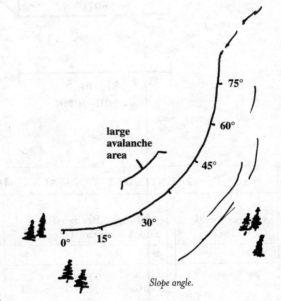

75°
60°
45°
large avalanche area
30°
0° 15°
Slope angle.

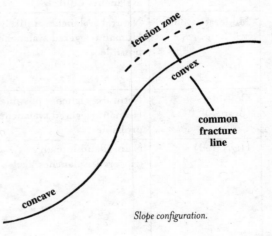

tension zone
convex
common fracture line
concave
Slope configuration.

Temperatures

Warm or cool temperatures can create various conditions that may cause a greater potential for avalanche.

Warm temperatures

If warm temperatures do not occur rapidly, they will increase the density and bond of the snowpack, making it less prone to avalanche. A rapid warming trend, on the other hand, will weaken the snow, making the bond between layers less stable and more prone to human-triggered slab avalanches.

Depth hoar

Depth hoar is a layer of snow, close to the ground's surface, created when there is a signifi-

Continued ➡

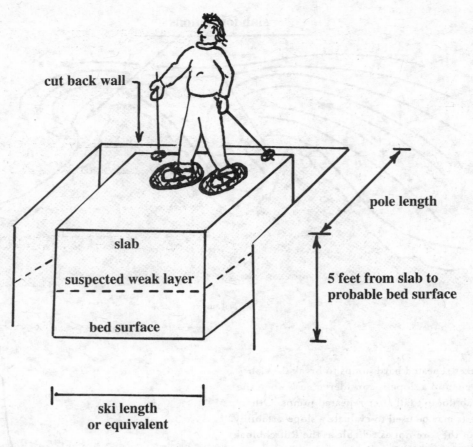

cut back wall

pole length

slab

suspected weak layer

5 feet from slab to probable bed surface

bed surface

ski length or equivalent

Rutschblock test.

UNITED STATES AVALANCHE DANGER DESCRIPTORS			
Danger Level (& Color)	Avalanche Probability and Avalanche Trigger	Degree and Distribution of Avalanche Danger	Recommended Action in the Backcountry
What	Why	Where	What to Do
Low (green)	Natural avalanches very unlikely. Human triggered avalanches unlikely	Generally stable snow. Isolated areas of instability.	Travel is generally safe. Normal caution is advised.
Moderate (yellow)	Natural avalanches unlikely. Human triggered avalanches possible.	Unstable slabs possible on steep terrain.	Use caution in steeper terrain on certain aspects (defined in accompanying statement).
Considerable (orange)	Natural avalanches possible. Human triggered avalanches probable.	Unstable slabs probable on steep terrain.	Be increasingly cautious in steeper terrain.
High (red)	Natural and human triggered avalanches likely.	Unstable slabs likely on a variety of aspects and slope angles.	Travel in avalanche terrain is not recommended. Safest travel on windward ridges of lower angle slopes without steeper terrain above.
Extreme (black)	Widespread natural or human triggered avalanches certain.	Extremely unstable slabs certain on most aspects and slope angles. Large, destructive avalanches possible.	Travel in avalanche terrain should be avoided and travel confined to low angle terrain well away from avalanche path run-outs.

AVALANCHE SAFETY BASICS

Avalanches don't happen by accident, and most human involvement is a matter of choice, not chance. Most avalanche accidents are caused by slab avalanches which are triggered by the victim or a member of the victim's party. However, any avalanche may cause injury or death and even small slides may be dangerous. Hence, always practice safe route finding skills, be aware of changing conditions, and carry avalanche rescue gear. Learn and apply avalanche terrain analysis and snow stability evaluation techniques to help minimize your risk. Remember that avalanche danger rating levels are only general guidelines. Distinctions between geographic areas, elevations, slope aspects, and slope angles are approximate and transition zones between dangers exist. No matter what the current avalanche danger there are avalanche-safe areas in the mountains.

cant difference in temperature between the snow's surface and the ground. It is composed of highly faceted snow crystals and cannot support much weight, making it a dangerous underlying layer that rarely bonds to the subsequent layers of snow that cover it. The risk of depth hoar formation is highest during the early season. If present, the potential for an avalanche is extremely high.

Surface hoar

Surface hoar is similar to dew and is created on the snow's surface when cool, cloudless, and calm nights are present. Like depth hoar, it doesn't bond well with subsequent snow cover, and its weak layer creates a potential avalanche hazard.

The Human Factor

All too often, individuals believe that no disaster will ever happen to them. They don't realize how often people have perished when decisions were based on similar attitudes. Travel decisions should be made on a multitude of factors, including everything discussed to this point. The group's attitude about the conditions, their goals, and the risks involved should all be considered, along with each member's technical skills, physical strength, and available equipment. Take the time to think things through. After all, traveling into the backcountry is supposed to be time spent having fun, not fighting for your life.

Route Selection

Sometimes it may be necessary to cross an area that presents an avalanche risk. If this should be the case, try to avoid large, steep, leeward bowls, gullies, and cornices. Choose safer routes, such as ridgetops, valley floors, dense timber, and low-angle slopes. Before starting, remove ski pole straps; undo pack buckles for quick doffing; secure all zippers and openings on your clothing and gear; make sure your avalanche beacon is on and in the transmit mode; identify any safe islands that might be located in your route of travel, such as rocks or trees; and establish an escape route. Once ready, cross one person at a time, with all other members of the group watching. Try to cross at either the top or bottom of the slope; avoid the center, where escape may be impossible.

Avalanche Necessities

Avalanche Transceivers

All members in your group should carry avalanche transceivers with fresh batteries. Before departing the trailhead, check your beacons by doing a walk-by. This is done by having one member's beacon turned to receive and having each other member walk by with his or her beacon on in the transmit mode. The receiving beacon should have an increased sound and visual signal as each member approaches. Don't forget to check the receiving beacon also. Once you've assured that all transceivers are working properly, turn them all to the transmit mode. If someone becomes buried, all other members of the party then switch to the receive mode to locate the victim.

Continued ➤

Other Avalanche Gear

Each member traveling into avalanche country should also carry a probe, a snow shovel, and an Avalung (described in detail on page xxx).

Surviving an Avalanche

Always try to avoid avalanche areas and risk. If you decide to enter an avalanche-prone area, however, make sure you have your avalanche gear with you, and that it is operational. Beacons should have been checked in advance, have new batteries, and turned on to transmit. The AvaLung mouthpiece should be located within inches of your mouth, so that you can quickly insert it if needed. If an avalanche occurs, immediately shout to let everyone else know. Insert the AvaLung mouthpiece, and dry to discard gear such as your skis and poles. The exception to discarding gear would be if you can ski to the side and out of danger, or you are wearing items like snowshoes that cannot be quickly taken off. If a safe area is accessible, try to get to it. If you are knocked down, try to stay on top of the surface, using a swimming motion, while heading toward the side of the avalanche. If unable to escape, once the slide begins to slow down, try to get a hand to the surface so it can be seen, and make an air space in front of your face with your other arm. The AvaLung will greatly increase your potential of rescue, and at this point, if you are using one, it's best to relax and conserve your energy.

Avalanche Rescue

Once an avalanche has occurred, the most experienced member of the team should immediately take charge and organize the search. Before doing anything, however, the risk of another avalanche needs to be ruled out, escape routes established, and a lookout assigned. Have all members of the rescue party turn their beacons to the receive mode. If anyone leaves his or her beacon in the transmit mode, you'll waste time tracking this signal. Mark the last position where the victim was seen, and use this as your starting

point. Time is crucial. At this point, no one should be sent for help. Every member of the team should stay and search.

Searching with an Avalanche Rescue Beacon

An avalanche rescue has three phases: coarse, fine, and pinpoint. Each phase builds upon the preceding one.

COARSE SEARCH

The coarse search begins by quickly evaluating the snow's surface for partially covered subjects, discarded gear, or terrain features that may predict the person's travel route or resting point. Mark the subject's last known site, along with any other clues, such as found equipment. Trees and rocks are common areas where an individual may become trapped during an avalanche, so probe any that are located in the avalanche's path. This should be a quick, methodical process. Next, starting just above the subject's last known location, line up your team members, spacing them approximately 50 feet apart and facing downhill. Have all members turn their beacon volume all the way up and begin a parallel (to one another) downhill search pattern. Rescuers should rotate the beacons left and right and forward and back as they move. This is necessary due to the wire wrap antenna. A signal can be stronger or weaker based on the rescue beacon's position relative to the subject's beacon. If only one person was caught in the avalanche, once a signal is obtained, two rescuers should begin the fine search process, and all others should get their digging gear ready. If more than one person was involved, one rescuer should begin a fine search and the other members of the rescue team should continue the coarse search; in this situation, turn off the transmitting beacon once a subject is found.

A beacon signal has a cone of silence.

cone of silence

curved path of beacon transmission

cone of silence

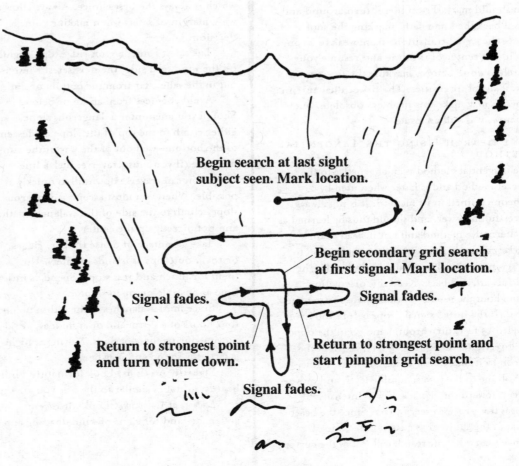

Begin search at last sight subject seen. Mark location.

Begin secondary grid search at first signal. Mark location.

Signal fades.   **Signal fades.**

Return to strongest point and turn volume down.   **Return to strongest point and start pinpoint grid search.**

Signal fades.

Coarse and fine search for avalanche subject.

Continued ➡

Fine Search Using the Bracket Method

When a signal is picked up, orient the beacon to the strongest signal by rotating it left and right and forward and back. Once the strongest signal is obtained, keep that orientation throughout the search. Walk in a straight line toward the increasing signal, continually reducing the beacon's volume to the lowest audible level. Keeping the beacon oriented, continue your straight line of travel until the signal fades. Mark this spot. Without changing the beacon's orientation, turn around and head back the same way you came. When the signal fades, mark the spot. Move to the center of the bracketed line, turn 90 degrees, and walk in a straight line, reducing the volume as you go. As before, once the signal begins to fade, mark the spot, turn around, and retrace your steps, marking where the signal fades. Keep the beacon oriented throughout this process. You now have four fade-out points. Move to the center of this second line, turn 90 degrees, and repeat the process. Continue this process of returning to the center of a line, turning 90 degrees, and marking fade-out points until the distance between these fade-out points is less than 6 feet. You can now move to the pinpoint search.

The cone of silence

A beacon puts out an oval signal that runs up and away on both sides of the antenna, wrapping around the beacon in an oval shape and returning to its base. These centrally connected oval signals create an area called the cone of silence, which is located directly above and below the antenna. If you move through this area, your signal will drop in intensity while in it but become strong again when you reach the other side. For this reason, when doing the bracket search, you should always go a few feet beyond the signal's weakest point to make sure it doesn't increase again. If it does, then that is the area you should mark. From there, turn around and travel back the same path, marking the spot where the signal transitions from weak to strong. Go to the center of this line and resume your search as done before, marking the line's two lowest signal intensities. The newer dual antenna beacons may make this problem obsolete, but for now, it is still an issue.

Fine Search Using the Tangential Method

The tangential method is an alternative to the bracket method and is faster when used by someone trained in its method. It is not always successful, however, and should thus be learned as an alternative method and not instead of the bracket method. To use it, orient the beacon to the strongest signal by rotating it left and right and forward and back. Keep this orientation throughout the rescue. Travel toward the strongest signal. If the initial signal drops before you have traveled 15 feet, turn around and go in the opposite direction. After going 15 feet, reorient the beacon to its maximum signal intensity, reduce the volume to the lowest audible level, and move 15 feet, toward the signal's *strongest* intensity. Repeat this process every 15 feet. Since the beacon signal of the subject has a curve (the cone of silence's curve), your search will follow the curve.

Pinpoint Search

With your beacon oriented and close to the snow's surface, begin moving from side to side and front to back, trying to pinpoint the subject's location. During this process, identify the area where the beacon's signal produces its highest intensity while the volume is turned to its lowest level. A lot of beacons actually change tone sound when directly over another one. At this point, begin a quick but gentle probe of the area, taking care not to hurt the subject.

Digging Out and Treating the Subject

Once the subject has been located with the probe, leave it in place as a guide and begin digging. While digging, be careful not to injure the subject. Remove snow from the subject's mouth and assess his or her status. If rescue breathing or CPR is indicated, begin it immediately. Treat for hypothermia and shock, and evaluate for a head or spinal injury.

Probe Searches

If a rescue beacon is not available, begin a probe search. Taking care not to hurt the subject, gently probe at locations where he or she was last seen, at areas where equipment was found (especially the lowest location), and at likely resting spots. If you don't have a probe, use ski poles or tree branches. After probing likely locations, establish a probe line that starts at the base of the debris and extends up the most likely trajectory.

AVALANCHE SURVIVAL
U.S. Army

Protective Measures. Avoiding known or suspected avalanche areas is the easiest method of protection. Other measures include:

Personal Safety. Remove your hands from ski pole wrist straps. Detach ski runaway cords. Prepare to discard equipment. Put your hood on. Close up your clothing to prepare for hypothermia. Deploy avalanche cord. Make avalanche probes and shovels accessible. Keep your pack on at all times—do not discard. Your pack can act as a flotation device, as well as protect your spine.

Group Safety. Send one person across the suspect slope at a time with the rest of the group watching. All members of the group should move in the same track from safe zone to safe zone.

Route Selection. Selecting the correct route will help avoid avalanche prone areas, which is always the best choice. Always allow a wide margin of safety when making your decision.

The safest routes are on ridge tops, slightly on the windward side; the next safest route is out in the valley, far from the bottom of slopes.

Avoid cornices from above or below. Should you encounter a dangerous slope, either climb to the top of the slope or descend to the bottom—well out of the way of the run-out zone. If you must traverse, pick a line where you can traverse downhill as quickly as possible. When you must ascend a dangerous slope, climb to the side of the avalanche path, and not directly up the center.

Take advantage of dense timber, ridges, or rocky outcrops as islands of safety. Use them for lunch and rest stops. Spend as little time as possible on open slopes.

Since most avalanches occur within twenty-four hours of a storm and or at midday, avoid moving during these periods. Moving at night is tactically sound and may be safer.

Stability Analysis. Look for nature's billboards on slopes similar to the one you are on.

Evidence of Avalanching. Look for recent avalanches and for signs of wind-loading and wind-slabs.

Fracture Lines. Avoid any slopes showing cracks.

Sounds. Beware of hollow sounds—a "whumping" noise. They may suggest a radical settling of the snowpack.

Survival. People trigger avalanches that bury people. If these people recognized the hazard and chose a different route, they would avoid the avalanche. The following steps should be followed if caught in an avalanche.

1. Discard equipment. Equipment can injure or burden you; discarded equipment will indicate your position to rescuers.

2. Swim or roll to stay on top of the snow. FIGHT FOR YOUR LIFE. Work toward the edge of the avalanche. If you feel your feet touch the ground, give a hard push and try to "pop out" onto the surface.

3. If your head goes under the snow, shut your mouth, hold your breath, and position your hands and arms to form an air pocket in front of your face. Many avalanche victims suffocate by having their mouths and noses plugged with snow.

4. When you sense the slowing of the avalanche, you must try your hardest to reach the surface. Several victims have been found quickly because a hand or foot was sticking above the surface.

5. When the snow comes to rest it sets up like cement and even if you are only partially buried, it may be impossible to dig yourself out. Don't shout unless you hear rescuers immediately above you; in snow, no one can hear you scream. Don't struggle to free yourself—you will only waste energy and oxygen.

6. Try to relax. If you feel yourself about to pass out, do not fight it. The respiration of an unconscious person is more shallow, their pulse rate declines, and the body temperature is lowered, all of which reduce the amount of oxygen needed.

—From *Military Mountaineering*
(*Field Manual 3-97.61*)

Continued ➡

Survival Tips

Don't Take Risks

Don't be macho and dead! Take the time to evaluate avalanche conditions, and heed the warnings when they are present.

Avoid Avalanche Areas Whenever You Can

If you must travel into these areas, learn avalanche safety in advance and practice beacon rescue before you begin each trip.

Make Sure Your Beacons Work

Beacons operate on batteries and are prone to failure from cold soaking and life expectancy. To avoid cold soaking make sure to keep the beacons between your clothing layers. To avoid life expectancy issues, replace batteries before each trip.

—From *Surviving Cold Weather*

Water Crossings

U.S. Army

In a survival situation, you may have to cross a water obstacle. It may be in the form of a river, a stream, a lake, a bog, quicksand, quagmire, or muskeg. Even in the desert, flash floods occur, making streams an obstacle. Whatever it is, you need to know how to cross it safely.

Rivers and Streams

You can apply almost every description to rivers and streams. They may be shallow or deep, slow or fast moving, narrow or wide. Before you try to cross a river or stream, develop a good plan.

Your first step is to look for a high place from which you can get a good view of the river or stream. From this place, you can look for a place to cross. If there is no high place, climb a tree. Good crossing locations include—

- A level stretch where it breaks into several channels. Two or three narrow channels are usually easier to cross than a wide river.
- A shallow bank or sandbar. If possible, select a point upstream from the bank or sandbar so that the current will carry you to it if you lose your footing.
- A course across the river that leads downstream so that you will cross the current at about a 45-degree angle.

The following areas possess potential hazards; avoid them, if possible:

- *Obstacles on the opposite side of the river that might hinder your travel.* Try to select the spot from which travel will be the safest and easiest.
- *A ledge of rocks that crosses the river.* This often indicates dangerous rapids or canyons.
- *A deep or rapid waterfall or a deep channel.* Never try to ford a stream directly above or even close to such hazards.
- *Rocky places.* You may sustain serious injuries from slipping or falling on rocks. Usually, submerged rocks are very slick, making balance extremely difficult. An occasional rock that breaks the current, however, may help you.

- *An estuary of a river.* An estuary is normally wide, has strong currents, and is subject to tides. These tides can influence some rivers many kilometers from their mouths. Go back upstream to an easier crossing site.
- *Eddies.* An eddy can produce a powerful backward pull downstream of the obstruction causing the eddy and pull you under the surface.

The depth of a fordable river or stream is no deterrent if you can keep your footing. In fact, deep water sometimes runs more slowly and is therefore safer than fast-moving shallow water. You can always dry your clothes later, or if necessary, you can make a raft to carry your clothing and equipment across the river.

You must not try to swim or wade across a stream or river when the water is at very low temperatures. This swim could be fatal. Try to make a raft of some type. Wade across if you can get only your feet wet. Dry them vigorously as soon as your reach the other bank.

Rapids

If necessary, you can safely cross a deep, swift river or rapids. To swim across a deep, swift river, swim with the current, never fight it. Try to keep your body horizontal to the water. This will reduce the danger of being pulled under.

In fast, shallow rapids, lie on your back, feet pointing downstream, finning your hands alongside your hips. This action will increase buoyancy and help your steer away from obstacles. Keep your feet up to avoid getting them bruised or caught by rocks.

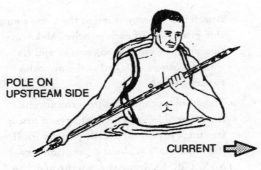

POLE ON
UPSTREAM SIDE

CURRENT ➡

One man crossing swift stream.

In deep rapids, lie on your stomach, head downstream, angling toward the shore whenever you can. Watch for obstacles and be careful of backwater eddies and converging currents, as they often contain dangerous swirls. Converging currents occur where new watercourses enter the river or where water has been diverted around large obstacles such as small islands.

To ford a swift, treacherous stream, apply the following steps:

- Remove your pants and shirt to lessen the water's pull on you. Keep your footgear on to protect your feet and ankles from rocks. It will also provide you with firmer footing.
- Tie your pants and other articles to the top of your rucksack or in a bundle, if you have no pack. This way, if you have to release your equipment, all your articles will be together. It is easier to find one large pack than to find several small items.
- Carry your pack well up on your shoulders and be sure you can easily remove it, if necessary. Not being able to get a pack off quickly enough can drag even the strongest swimmers under.
- Find a strong pole about 7.5 centimeters in diameter and 2.1 to 2.4 meters long to help you ford the stream. Grasp the pole and plant it firmly on your upstream side to break the current. Plant your feet firmly with each step, and move the pole forward a little downstream from its previous position, but still upstream from you. With your next step, place your foot below the pole. Keep the pole well slanted so that the force of the current keeps the pole against your shoulder.
- Cross the stream so that you will cross the downstream current at a 45-degree angle.

Using this method, you can safely cross currents usually too strong for one person to stand against. Do not concern yourself about your pack's weight, as the weight will help rather than hinder you in fording the stream.

If there are other people with you, cross the stream together. Ensure that everyone has prepared their pack and clothing as outlined

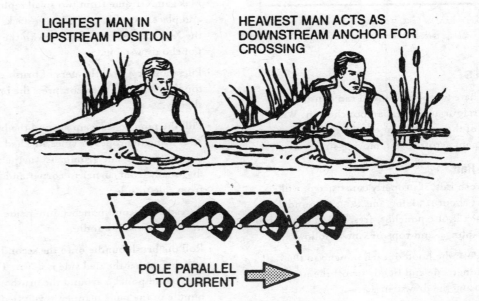

LIGHTEST MAN IN
UPSTREAM POSITION

HEAVIEST MAN ACTS AS
DOWNSTREAM ANCHOR FOR
CROSSING

POLE PARALLEL
TO CURRENT ➡

Several men crossing swift stream.

Continued ➡

above. Position the heaviest person on the downstream end of the pole and the lightest on the upstream end. In using this method, the upstream person breaks the current, and those below can move with relative ease in the eddy formed by the upstream person. If the upstream person gets temporarily swept off his feet, the others can hold steady while he regains his footing.

If you have three or more people and a rope available, you can use the technique shown [top right] to across the stream. The length of the rope must be three times the width of the stream.

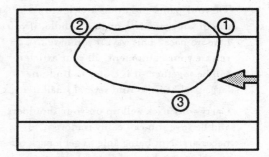

The person crossing is secured to the loop around the chest. The strongest person crosses first. The other two are not tied on — they pay out the rope as it is needed and can stop the person crossing from being washed away.

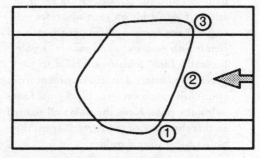

When he reaches the bank, 1unties himself and 2 ties on. No. 2 crosses, controlled by the others. Any number of people can be sent across this way.

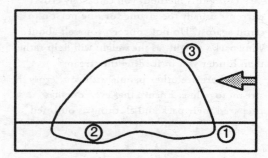

When 2 has reached the bank, 3 ties on and crosses. No.1 takes most of the strain, but 2 is ready in case anything goes wrong.

Rafts

If you have two ponchos, you can construct a brush raft or an Australian poncho raft. With either of these rafts, you can safely float your equipment across a slow-moving stream or river.

Brush Raft

The brush raft, if properly constructed, will support about 115 kilograms (253.5 pounds). To construct it, use ponchos, fresh green brush, two small saplings, and rope or vine as follows.

- Push the hood of each poncho to the inner side and tightly tie off the necks using the drawstrings.

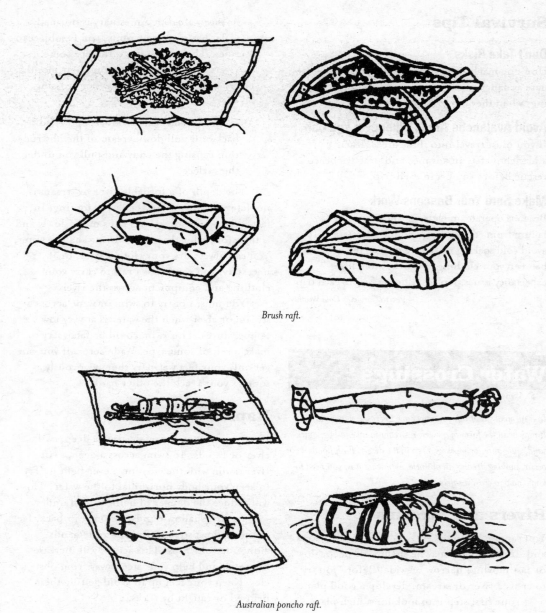

Brush raft.

Australian poncho raft.

- Attach the ropes or vines at the corner and side grommets of each poncho. Make sure they are long enough to cross to and tie with the others attached at the opposite corner or side.

- Spread one poncho on the ground with the inner side up. Pile fresh, green brush (no thick branches) on the poncho until the brush stack is about 45 centimeters high. Pull the drawstring up through the center of the brush stack.

- Make an X-frame from two small saplings and place it on top of the brush stack. Tie the X-frame securely in place with the poncho drawstring.

- Pile another 45 centimeters of brush on top the X-frame, then compress the brush slightly.

- Pull the poncho sides up around the brush and, using the ropes or vines attached to the coroner or side grommets, tie them diagonally from corner to corner and from side to side.

- Spread the second poncho, inner side up, next to the brush bundle.

- Roll the brush bundle onto the second poncho so that the tied side is down. Tie the second poncho around the brush bundle in the same manner as you tied the first poncho around the brush.

- Place it in the water with the tied side of the second poncho facing up.

Australian Poncho Raft

If you do not have time to gather brush for a brush raft, you can make an Australian poncho raft. This raft, although more waterproof than the poncho brush raft, will only float about 35 kilograms (6.6 pounds) of equipment. To construct this raft, use two ponchos, two rucksacks, two 1.2-meter poles or branches, and ropes, vines, bootlaces, or comparable material as follows:

- Push the hood of each poncho to the inner side and tightly tie off the necks using the drawstrings.

- Spread one poncho on the ground with the inner side up. Place and center the two 1.2-meter poles on the poncho about 45 centimeters apart.

- Place your rucksacks or packs or other equipment between the poles. Also place other items that you want to keep dry between the poles. Snap the poncho sides together.

- Use your buddy's help to complete the raft. Hold the snapped portion of the poncho in the air and roll it tightly down to the equipment. Make sure you roll the

Continued ➡

full width of the poncho.

- Twist the ends of the roll to form pigtails in opposite directions. Fold the pigtails over the bundle and tie them securely in place using ropes, bootlaces, or vines.

- Spread the second poncho on the ground, inner side up. If you need more buoyancy, place some fresh green brush on this poncho.

- Place the equipment bundle, tied side down, on the center of the second poncho. Wrap the second poncho around the equipment bundle following the same procedure you used for wrapping the equipment in the first poncho.

- Tie ropes, bootlaces, vines, or other binding material around the raft about 30 centimeters from the end of each pigtail. Place and secure weapons on top of the raft.

- Tie one end of a rope to an empty canteen and the other end to the raft. This will help you to tow the raft.

Poncho Donut Raft

Another type of raft is the poncho donut raft. It takes more time to construct than the brush raft or Australian poncho raft, but it is effective. To construct it, use one poncho, small saplings, willow or vines, and rope, bootlaces, or other binding material as follows:

- Make a framework circle by placing several stakes in the ground that roughly outline an inner and outer circle.

- Using young saplings, willow, or vines, construct a donut ring within the circles of stakes.

- Wrap several pieces of cordage around the donut ring about 30 to 60 centimeters apart and tie them securely.

- Push the poncho's hood to the inner side and tightly tie off the neck using the drawstring. Place the poncho on the ground, inner side up.

- Place the donut ring on the center of the poncho. Wrap the poncho up and over the donut ring and tie off each grommet on the poncho to the ring.

Poncho donut raft.

- Tie one end of a rope to an empty canteen and the other end to the raft. This rope will help you to tow the raft.

When launching any of the above rafts, take care not to puncture or tear it by dragging it on the ground. Before you start to cross the river or stream, let the raft lay on the water a few minutes to ensure that it floats.

If the river is too deep to ford, push the raft in front of you while you are swimming. The design of the above rafts does not allow them to carry a person's full body weight. Use them as a float to get you and your equipment safely across the river or stream.

Be sure to check the water temperature before trying to cross a river or water obstacle. If the water is extremely cold and you are unable to find a shallow fording place in the river, do not try to ford it. Devise other means for crossing. For instance, you might improvise a bridge by felling a tree over the river. Or you might build a raft large enough to carry you and your equipment. For this, however, you will need an axe, a knife, a rope or vines, and time.

Log Raft

You can make a raft using any dry, dead, standing trees for logs. However, spruce trees found in polar and subpolar regions make the best rafts. A simple method for making a raft is to use pressure bars lashed securely at each end of the raft to hold the logs together. [See page below.]

Flotation Devices

If the water is warm enough for swimming and you do not have the time or materials to construct one of the poncho-type rafts, you can use various flotation devices to negotiate the water obstacle. Some items you can use for flotation devices are—

- **Trousers**. Knot each trouser leg at the bottom and close the fly. With both hands, grasp the waistband at the sides and swing the trousers in the air to trap air in each leg. Quickly press the sides of the waistband together and hold it underwater so that the air will not escape. You now have water wings to keep you afloat as you cross the body of water.

   Note: Wet the trousers before inflating to trap the air better. You may have to reinflate the trousers several times when crossing a large body of water.

- **Empty containers**. Lash together empty gas cans, water jugs, ammo cans, boxes, or other items that will trap or hold air. Use them as water wings. Use this type of flotation device only in a slow-moving river or stream.

- **Plastic bags and ponchos**. Fill two or more plastic bags with air and secure them together at the opening. Use your poncho and roll green vegetation tightly inside it so that you have a roll at least 20 centimeters in diameter. Tie the ends of the roll securely. You can wear it around your waist or across one shoulder and under the opposite arm.

- **Logs**. Use a stranded drift log if one is available, or find a log near the water to use as a float. Be sure to test the log before starting to cross. Some tree logs, palm for example, will sink even when the wood is dead. Another method is to tie two logs about 60 centimeters apart. Sit between

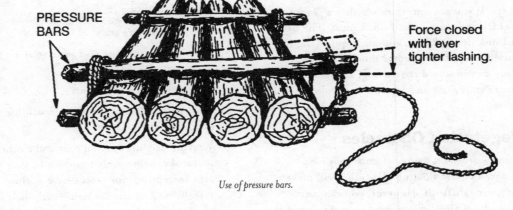

PRESSURE BARS

Force closed with ever tighter lashing.

Use of pressure bars.

Log flotation.

Continued →

the logs with your back against one and your legs over the other. [See page 313.]

- **Cattails.** Gather stalks of cattails and tie them in a bundle 25 centimeters or more in diameter. The many air cells in each stalk cause a stalk to float until it rots. Test the cattail bundle to be sure it will support your weight before trying to cross a body of water.

There are many other flotation devices that you can devise by using some imagination. Just make sure to test the device before trying to use it.

Other Water Obstacles

Other water obstacles that you may face are bogs, quagmire, muskeg, or quicksand. Do not try to walk across these. Trying to lift your feet while standing upright will make you sink deeper. Try to bypass these obstacles. If you are unable to bypass them, you may be able to bridge them using logs, branches, or foliage.

A way to cross a bog is to lie face down, with your arms and legs spread. Use a flotation device or form pockets of air in your clothing. Swim or pull your way across moving slowly and trying to keep your body horizontal.

In swamps, the areas that have vegetation are usually firm enough to support your weight. However, vegetation will usually not be present in open mud or water areas. If you are an average swimmer, however, you should have no problem swimming, crawling, or pulling your way through miles of bog or swamp.

Quicksand is a mixture of sand and water that forms a shifting mass. It yields easily to pressure and sucks down and engulfs objects resting on its surface. It varies in depth and is usually localized. Quicksand commonly occurs on flat shores, in silt-choked rivers with shifting watercourses, and near the mouths of large rivers. If you are uncertain whether a sandy area is quicksand, toss a small stone on it. The stone will sink in quicksand. Although quicksand has more suction than mud or muck, you can cross it just as you would cross a bog. Lie face down, spread your arms and legs and move slowly across.

Vegetation Obstacles

Some water areas you must cross may have underwater and floating plants that will make swimming difficult. However, you can swim through relatively dense vegetation if you remain calm and do not thrash about. Stay as near the surface as possible and use the breaststroke with shallow leg and arm motion. Remove the plants around you as you would clothing. When you get tired, float or swim on your back until you have rested enough to continue with the breaststroke.

The mangrove swamp is another type of obstacle that occurs along tropical coastlines. Mangrove trees or shrubs throw out many prop roots that form dense masses. To get through a mangrove swamp, wait for low tide. If you are on the inland side, look for a narrow grove of trees and work your way seaward through these. You can also try to find the bed of a waterway or creek through the trees and follow it to the sea. If you are on the seaward side, work inland along streams or channels. Be on the lookout for croc-

odiles that you find along channels and in shallow water. If there are any near you, leave the water and scramble over the mangrove roots. While crossing a mangrove swamp, it is possible to gather food from tidal pools or tree roots.

To cross a large swamp area, construct some type of raft.

—From *Survival (Field Manual 21-76)*

"Leave No Trace" Back-country Travel

U.S. Forest Service

Guidelines

Leave No Trace! guidelines help protect the land and lessen the sights and sounds of your visit.

Because most visitors do not live outdoors, they unknowingly violate the **Leave No Trace!** ethic by:

- Traveling and camping in large groups.
- Traveling off trails or roads, thereby causing scars and soil erosion, and trampling vegetation.
- Leaving campfire scars.
- Leaving human waste and garbage at a campsite.
- Polluting lakes and streams.
- Making loud noises that disturb wildlife and other visitors.
- Wearing brightly colored gear and clothes that make them visible to others in the area (exception: for rescue have a "fluorescent" vest or similar item—include it in your pack).

Planning

Lots of planning must go into a back-country trip if it is to be safe and fun. Gathering information from Forest Service, Bureau of Land Management, and National Park Service offices can help. They can provide current maps, firsthand information on trails and campsites, and anything else pertinent to the anticipated trip. Consider the group size, when and where to go, equipment, and food selection when planning a trip.

Group Size: Small groups are ideal in open areas such as deserts, meadows, and above timberline. Plan to travel and camp with fewer than 8-10 people, who can be divided into

hiking groups of 2–4 during the day. It also is easier to plan for small groups and to keep them together. Campsites for smaller groups are easier to find and they harmonize better with the environment. Check ahead to see if there is a group size limitation in the area you plan to visit.

When and Where to Go: To find maximum solitude, avoid back-country trips on holidays and even some weekends. Since many popular trails and wildernesses always seem to be crowded, visit less popular areas. Plan such trips for the spring or fall, or even the winter.

What's Needed and What's Not: Brightly colored clothing, packs, and tents should be avoided because they can be seen for long distances and contribute to a crowded feeling. Consider choosing earth-tone colors to lessen the visual impact. Lighten your pack by repacking the food and removing glass and aluminum packing. They do not burn and add extra weight. Check for local restrictions prohibiting cans and bottles. IF YOU PACK IT IN, YOU SHOULD PACK IT OUT. Carry extra trash bags for litter pickup in and around your campsite. They also make great emergency rain gear.

Other suggested equipment is a small trowel or plastic garden shovel for burying human waste and for digging **Leave No Trace!** firepits. Leave the axe and saw at home, unless you are traveling by horse and need them to cut a trail. Firewood that cannot be broken by hand should be left as part of the natural system.

Be Prepared: Obtain a good map, plan your route, and leave your itinerary with someone at home, in case someone has to search for you. Know what weather conditions to expect in that area at that time of year and come prepared for the extreme temperature, wind, snow, and rain you might be exposed to. A day hike requires minimal survival gear: extra food, a signal mirror, whistle, and warm clothing. A highly visible vest ("fluorescent" orange or red) should be included in your pack for rescue in the event you become lost. Carry extra water in desert areas (a minimum of 2 quarts per day per person).

Remember:

- Plan for small groups.
- Obtain information about the trip ahead of time and plan your route.
- Visit a less popular area.
- Plan an off-season trip if you wish to avoid crowds.
- Select earth-tone colors (clothing and tents) to blend with the environment.
- Repackage food.

Continued ➡

- Check on local rules and regulations.
- Filter or boil water.

Travel

Trails are an important part of back-country travel. They are designed to get people from one place to another with varying degrees of difficulty. Trails are also designed to drain off water with a minimum amount of soil erosion. Make an effort to stay on the trails no matter how you are traveling.

Switchbacks are the most abused portion of the trail system. A switchback is a reversal in trail

direction. Many people shortcut switchbacks and create new trails trying to save time and energy. Cutting switchbacks creates a new scar on the hillside that will cause soil erosion and scarring.

Cross-country: Hiking or riding horses cross-country, off established trails is ok, but remember to stay spread out and off "social trails" that other users have begun. Avoid traveling through meadows and wet areas. They are fragile and will show the effect of footprints or hoofprints and group travel much longer than forested and rocky areas.

Bicycles and motorized vehicles are allowed in some back-country areas but not in wildernesses. To ride them cross-country will create social trails and cause erosion.

The feeling of solitude or adventure is broken when you see ribbons, signs, or even blazed trees that visitors have left to mark a path. Always discuss the planned route with your group members to avoid leaving these markers. If you must mark a route, remove markers before departing.

Remember:

- Stay on designated trails.
- Do not cut switchbacks.
- Plan your route so everyone knows where you plan to be.
- Select rocky or forested areas when traveling cross-country.
- Don't mark or blaze your cross-country route.

Back-country Courtesy

One of the most important components of back-country ethics is to maintain courtesy toward others. It helps everyone enjoy their outdoor experience. Incompatible or competing

activities must share limited facilities and areas. Excessive noise, unleashed pets, and damaged surroundings distract from a quality experience in the back country.

Keep the noise level down while traveling on trails. Radios and tape players do not belong in the back country. If your group meets another group, give uphill hikers the right-of-way. When you encounter groups leading or riding livestock, you should step off the trail on the lower side and let them pass. Stand quietly since some horses are spooked easily.

Keeps pets under control at all times. No one wants someone's pets running through the area and frightening people and wildlife. Some wildernesses prohibit dogs or require them to be on a leash at all times.

Wildflowers, picturesque trees, and unusual rock formations all contribute to the back-country beauty we enjoy. Picking flowers, hacking trees, and chipping rocks disturb the natural ecosystem. Please leave them alone and protect them for others to enjoy. Take nothing but pictures...leave with only fond memories.

—From *Leave No Trace! An Outdoor Ethic*

Knives, Packs, and Other Back-country Travel Gear

Greg Davenport
Illustrations by Steven Davenport and Ken Davenport

Backpack

Two basic pack designs are used backcountry travelers: internal- and external-frame packs.

External-Frame Backpack

The external-frame pack uses a frame that holds the pack away from your back. This is an advantage when traveling in hot weather, but it also makes the pack prone to sudden shifts that can occur without warning and disrupt your balance. An external-frame pack is best when used in extremely hot weather (during nontechnical travel) and when hiking on a trail.

Internal-Frame Backpack

When hiking off-trail, an internal-frame pack is preferable. This pack rides low on the body and close to the back, which allows you better balance as you travel. In hot climates, look for a frame that provides some degree of ventilation between your back and the pack. To do this, some manufacturers use a synthetic open mesh or ridges on the back of the pack that help wick moisture away from the body and allow for better air circulation.

The size of the pack you'll need depends on its use. For overnight trips, 3,000 to 5,000 cubic inches are sufficient. For long trips, you'll need 5,000 or more cubic inches. The pack should fit your back's length and contour, have strong webbing, provide thick shoulder and waist padding, and have external pouches to carry extra water bottles.

An external-frame pack allows better circulation between the pack and your back.

Knives

You'll need a folding pocketknife for the majority of your cutting work and a larger, fixed-blade knife or saw for the bigger projects. I consider the pocketknife one of my most important tools and use it in virtually all of my improvised tasks, including cutting line, improvising shelter, preparing fire, and skinning game. The weakest part of a folding-blade knife is its lock—the part that keeps the blade open and prevents it from closing on your fingers. A good lock will secure the blade tightly to the handle when it is open. I prefer a blade length of 3 inches.

For most big projects, such as cutting dead sage branches or prepping the larger stages of firewood, a large, fixed-blade knife is all you need. Avoid knives that have multiple modifications to the blade that supposedly allow you to do the unimaginable; it's just a bunch of marketing hype. I prefer a 7- to 9-inch knife blade, with the total length measuring around 15 to 17 inches.

A knife has many uses and is probably one of the most versatile tools you can carry. The potential for injury is high, however, so take every precaution to reduce this risk. Always cut away from yourself and maintain a sharp blade.

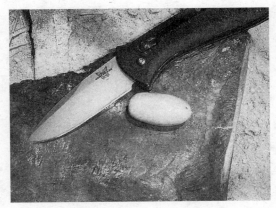

The Benchmade knife has a patented axis lock that sets the standard for the folding-blade knife.

Continued ➡

The SCOLD acronym—Sharp, Clean, Oiled, Lanyard, and Dry—can help you remember the proper care and use of your knives.

Sharp

A sharp knife is easier to control and use, decreasing the chances of injury. Two methods of sharpening a knife are outlined below. To establish the best sharpening angle, lay the knife blade flat onto the sharpening stone, then raise the back of the blade up until the distance between it and the stone is equal to the thickness of the blade's back side. To obtain an even angle, repeat the sharpening procedure on both sides of the blade. Each side should be done the same number of times.

Bill Seigle makes solid performing fixed-blade knives.

Push-and-Pull Technique

In a slicing fashion, repeatedly push and pull the knife's blade across a flat sharpening stone. If a commercial sharpening stone isn't available, use a flat, gray sandstone (often found in dry riverbeds.) For best results, start with the base of the blade on the long edge of the stone, and pull it across the length of the stone so that when you're done, its tip has reached the center of the stone.

Circular Technique

In a circular fashion, repeatedly move the knife blade across a circular sharpening stone or gray sandstone. Starting with the base of the blade at the edge of the stone, move the knife in a circular pattern across the stone.

Clean

Dirt and sand that get into the folding joint can destroy it and cause it to freeze closed or open, or even break. Dirt and sand can also be harmful to the blade's steel and can lead to its deterioration. To clean a knife blade, use a rag and wipe it from the backside to avoid cutting yourself. Never run it across your pants or shirt, which would transfer the dirt into the pores of your clothing and risk a cut. Use a twig to help get the cleaning rag into hard-to-reach spots.

Oiled

Keeping the knife's blade and joint oiled will help protect them and decrease the chances of rust.

Lanyard

Before using your knife, attach it to your body with a lanyard. To determine the lanyard's proper length, hole the knife in your hand and fully extend your arm over your head, then add 6 inches. This length allows you full use of the knife and decreases the risk of cuts due to a lanyard that is too short.

Dry

Keeping your knife dry is an important part of preventing rust, which can ruin the blade and the joint.

Backpacking Stove

When selecting a stove, consider its weight; the altitude and temperatures of where you are going; the stove's ease of operation, even in cold or windy conditions; and fuel availability. The two basic styles are canister and liquid fuel. Canister designs use butane, propane, or isobutene cartridges as their fuel source. The most common types of liquid fuels used are white gas and kerosene.

Butane or Propane

A canister allows for a no-spill fuel that is ready for immediate maximum output. Butane and propane canisters are available throughout the United States and most of the world. I like these types of stoves due to their ease of use and unmatched performance. Some versions do not perform well in temperatures below freezing, however, and disposal of the used canisters and availability of fuel may sometimes be problems.

White Gas

White gas has a high heat output and is readily available in the United States. Although the fuel quickly evaporates, it is highly flammable if spilled. The stove often does not require priming in order to start.

Kerosene

Kerosene has a high heat output and is available throughout the world. Unlike white gas, when spilled this fuel evaporates slowly and will not easily ignite. The stove requires priming in order to start.

Using a Stove

The exact use of the stove depends upon the manufacturer's recommendations and the type of fuel you use. As a general rule, a windshield is a must, preheating the stove helps it work better, and a stove that has a pump performs better when pumped up. For safety purposes, don't use a stove in a tent or enclosed area, except when considered absolutely necessary. If you do, make sure the area is vented and do everything in your power to avoid fuel leaks. Always change canisters and lines, fill the fuel tank, and prime the stove outside of the shelter.

Headlamp

A headlamp has become a great alternative to the old hand-held flashlight. The greatest benefit of a headlamp is that it frees up your hands so that you can use them to meet your other needs. When selecting a headlamp, consider its comfort, battery life, durability, weight, water resistance, and whether it will have a tendency to turn on while in a pack. I prefer the newer style headlamps, which provide a compact profile with the battery pack directly behind the bulb.

Cooking Pots

Cooking pots are luxury items that can be used to cook food and boil water. Many types are available; the kind you should use depends on your needs. I recommend a cookware set that includes a frying pan that doubles as a lid, several pots, and a pot gripper or handle. Pots are available in four basic materials:

Aluminum: Aluminum is cheap and the most common material used by backpackers. Unless the pan has a nonstick coating on the inside, however, plan on eating scorched food.

Stainless steel: Stainless steel is far more rugged than aluminum but weighs considerably more.

Titanium: Titanium is lighter than aluminum, but the cost may be prohibitive. It has a tendency to blacken your food unless you constantly stir it.

Composite: Composite cooking pots are durable yet lightweight. The inside is made from steel to reduce scorching, and aluminum is used on the outside to decrease weight.

—From *Surviving the Desert*

Travel on the Water

Entering, Exiting, and Carrying Kayaks

Cecil Kuhne

Entering the Kayak

To enter the kayak without capsizing, avoid putting all of your weight on one side. Keep your center of gravity low, using your paddle as a steadying outrigger against the bank.

With the kayak in ankle-deep water, place the end of the paddle shaft across the rear of the coaming, and hold it in place with your fingers inside the coaming and your thumb around the

Entering the Kayak

shaft. With the opposite hand behind you, grip the shaft on the side you are entering. Now place one foot in the cockpit and sit on the back deck, being careful not to put too much strain on the paddle. Place your other leg in the cockpit and slide yourself down inside the boat.

Securing the Spray Skirt

The best way to secure the spray skirt is to begin by fitting the hem of the skirt around the rear of the coaming. Next, put the front of the skirt in place. Finish up with the sides. The spray skirt should fit tightly enough to keep water out, but not so tightly that it's difficult to release if necessary.

Continued →

Securing the Spray Skirt.

Exiting the Kayak

To exit the boat, you need to first remove the spray skirt. Then draw both knees toward your chest. Place the paddle behind you and, while holding it, grip the rear of the coaming with one hand. Grip the paddle shaft with your other hand to provide stability as the paddle blade rests on the shore. Carefully lift your foot out of the boat and place it onshore. Then do the same with your other foot. Now you can stand up.

Exiting the Kayak.

Carrying the Kayak

The kayak is best carried on your shoulder. To get it there, try this: Lift the boat by the front of the cockpit, and then place your shoulder into the cockpit, with the stern of the boat still resting on the ground. Lean slightly forward to balance the kayak evenly on your shoulder. To pick up your paddle without bending over, try a quick flick of the foot to bring it into your hand.

—From *Paddling Basics: Kayaking*

Carrying the Kayak.

Kayak River Launch

Wayne Dickert and Jon Rounds
Photographs by Skip Brown and Pat McDonnell

Shore Launch

A shore launch is done by simply getting into the boat on land and pushing yourself into the water. Roto-molded polyethylene hulls are virtually indestructible, so you can do a shore launch over most surfaces—even tree roots—without damaging the boat. (Avoid banks with sharp rocks, however.)

1. Set the boat down on the bank, get into the cockpit, and attach the spray skirt.

2. Push yourself into the water.

3. Launched!

Water Launch

If the bank is not suited to a shore launch—if it's steep or rocky—or you don't want to put surface scratches on your pristine hull, use a water launch.

1. Place the paddle across the deck, right behind the cockpit, with the far blade over the water and the near blade resting on shore. If you're facing the boat with the bow pointing to your left, reach down with your right hand and grasp the paddle shaft, wrapping your fingers over the shaft and around the lip of the cockpit rim.

2. With your left hand, grab the other end of the shaft on the near side of the boat. Thus braced, sit down on the back deck of the kayak.

3. Then put one leg at a time into the cockpit, straighten your legs, and push yourself forward into the seated position, with your feet on the pegs.

—From *Basic Kayaking*

Sea Kayak Travel

Greg Davenport

Before departing on any kayak adventure, carefully consider the difficulty of the trip, your skills, what gear to take, and how it should be packed. Do you have the skills necessary for the trip? As you inventory your gear, make sure it meets your daily and survival needs, is protected from moisture, and is packed to allow for vessel buoyancy. For proper balance, heavy items should be securely located close to the center and centerline of the vessel. As disposable items are used up, fill the empty space with air-filled dry bags. Filling the space helps to keep all items secure. Once the kayak is packed, you are ready to enter the water.

The following pages summarize basic kayaking use. To fully understand these skills, I encourage you to attend classes from a qualified kayaking instructor.

Continued →

Getting in and out of the Kayak

Getting in and out of your kayak will often leave you wet and frustrated. A balance or support is the key to staying dry when entering the vessel. Try entering from a dock or in shallow water using a paddle....

High-dock Entry

A high-dock entry refers to docks that are above the kayak's coaming but not higher than 3 or 4 feet. To perform a high-dock entry, set the kayak in the water parallel to the dock, and lay the paddle parallel and close to the dock's edge. While facing the front of the kayak, place your feet in the vessel, bend at your waist, lift your buttocks, and roll onto your belly. This position should place you so that your buttocks is directly above the cockpit. From this position, slide your weight down into the cockpit, and extend your legs into the vessel while supporting yourself with your hands on the deck. To get out, reverse the steps.

Low-dock Entry

A low-dock entry refers to docks that are at or below the kayak's coaming. To perform a low-dock entry, set the kayak in the water parallel to the dock, and lay the paddle perpendicular and behind the kayak's coaming to the rear. Extend the paddle so that approximately two-thirds of it is in contact with the dock and the blade is flat with its surface. With your hands opening toward the back of the vessel, use your hand over the cockpit to hold the paddle and coaming together while your other hand is placed on the dock. Avoid placing excessive weight on the paddle. While facing the front of the vessel, squat down and sit on the edge of the cockpit. Insert one foot at a time into the cockpit, and slide in while using the dock and kayak to maintain balance. To get out, reverse the process.

Shallow-water Entry

To enter a kayak in shallow water, use a paddle to balance the vessel. Place the paddle perpendicular to the vessel and behind the cockpit coaming. Extend the blade so that the paddle on your side can rest on the water's bottom. With your hands opening toward the back of the vessel, use your hand over the cockpit to hold the paddle and coaming together while your other hand holds the paddle's shaft. Avoid placing excessive weight on the paddle. While facing the front of the vessel, squat down and sit on the edge of the cockpit. Insert one foot at a time into the cockpit, and slide in while using the paddle and kayak to maintain balance. To get out, reverse the process.

Launching a Kayak through Surf

Try to avoid launching your kayak through surf! If you can, plan your trips so that they begin and end in protected areas. If you have no choice, take the time to evaluate the waves and surrounding underwater structures. The two basic types of beach breakers (waves) are often referred to as "spilling" and "curling." Spilling breakers have foam that falls over the front of the wave as it breaks; curling breakers curl over the front and extend to the bottom of a breaking wave. Because spilling breakers are the calmer of the two, seek them out. Take the time to evaluate the timing and sequence of the waves, and plan your launch accordingly. Before launching your vessel, make sure everything is secured and that the vessel has adequate buoyancy. To launch, decrease the impact of the wave's force by attacking the surf straight on so that your vessel is perpendicular to the waves. Time your entry with the beginning of a wave, and paddle aggressively through a surf, making sure you're out of the wave before it begins to break. Waves greater than 6 feet should not be attempted. To know when a wave is reaching this height, stand on the shore and watch the horizon and the waves as they break. If the top of a breaking wave extends above the horizon, the wave is too high.

Landing a Kayak through Surf

Landing a kayak through surf presents a great problem: You will not be able to evaluate the type of wave you will be tackling since you'll be looking at the back side of the wave and will not be able to see it break. Before attempting a surf landing, be sure you have exhausted all other options. If no other option is available and you have a chart of the area, take a look at the various shoreline options. What type of bottom contours and makeups (sand, rock, etc.) do you see? Are there any obstacles (man-made or natural) that you should avoid? Take time to evaluate the waves' patterns. Waves usually come in sets, and not all sets are the same. Pick the least threatening approach you can, and begin your approach with the start of a set of gentler waves. To keep control of your vessel, don't surf the waves.

With your kayak facing 90 degrees to the waves, paddle backward when contact is made with the first wave. Doing this allows you to maintain control and prevent the vessel from taking off when its front is lifted by the wave. Begin a forward hard paddle as soon as you feel the front of the vessel dropping. This drop indicates that the wave has passed. As another wave overtakes you, repeat this process.

If the kayak capsizes in the surf, grab hold of it and try to ride it in. If you lose the kayak and have to swim ashore, use the side or breast stroke. If you're in moderate surf, swim with the wave and dive just below the water before the wave breaks. In high surf, swim toward the shore in the wave's trough, and submerge just before the next wave starts to overtake you. If an undertow pulls you down, push off the bottom and swim to the surface. As you get closer to the shore, select a landing spot where the waves run up on to shore rather than violently crash upon the beach. Once you enter the breakers, move into a sitting position with your feet forward and about 2 to 3 feet lower than your head. You are better off absorbing the shock of an unexpected reef or rock with your feet than your head.

—From *Surviving Coastal and Open Water*

Posture and Body Movement in Kayaks

Wayne Dickert and Jon Rounds
Photographs by Skip Brown
Illustrations by Roberto Sabas

Posture and Torso Rotation

The three cardinal rules of kayak posture and body movement are:

1. Sit up straight, without leaning forward or backward. A straight-up posture is especially important in river running, because leaning back increases the water pressure on the stern of the boat and increases the likelihood of a flip. Remember, though, that sitting up straight does not mean sitting rigid. Don't tense your muscles.

2. Keep your head over the center of the boat.

3. Perform strokes by rotating your torso rather than by reaching with your arms.

Correct posture, with torso erect and head centered.

Incorrect posture. Don't lean back.

These principles are interconnected: a straight-up, balanced posture lets the body rotate more freely.

Why torso rotation? Power. Your abdominal and back muscles are much stronger than your arms, and if you learn proper technique—if you execute strokes by rotating your torso rather than by reaching with your arms—you'll go faster and farther with less strain. This is the same principle that a boxer uses to deliver a powerful punch or a slugger uses to hit a homerun: each athlete generates power by rotating his waist and hips.

To illustrate the concept for yourself, stand in front of a wall with your shoulders square to it. Position yourself so that with your arm extended straight out in front of you, your fist is six inches from the wall. There are two ways you can reach the wall. You can lean forward at the waist till your fist touches it, or you can remain upright and touch it by rotating your torso. Assuming you wanted to hit the wall hard, which technique do you think would deliver the most powerful punch?

Continued →

When you're out on the water, remember the rules of posture and torso rotation, and think of your back and abdominal muscles as the engine that drives the boat and your arms simply as the link between the engine and paddle blade.

Leaning the Boat

Leaning or "edging" the boat is an essential skill in kayaking. You do it by shifting your lower body, not by leaning your upper body out over the deck. Your upper body should remain vertical, which will keep your center of gravity directly over the centerline of the boat. Your mantra should be lean the boat, not your body.

To lean the boat, keep your hips loose and lift one knee while pushing down with your opposite buttock. As the boat leans, your body should stay perpendicular to the waterline, not to the deck of the boat, so you must be flexible at the waist. (This is sometimes called the "J-Lean," after the shape made by your torso and the boat.) The farther over the boat leans, the more flexible you must be at the waist to keep your torso perpendicular to the water.

For effective leaning, keep your knees spread and slightly bent. Place the balls of your feet on the footbraces with your heels together and toes pointed outward. You use your lower body to lean and balance the boat, and this wide stance maximizes side-to-side control.

To lean the boat to your left side, press down with your left buttock while lifting your right knee (and vice versa).

Keep your torso upright and your head over the center of the boat.

Leaning your body over the side of the boat...

...will cause you to capsize.

The Hip Snap

The hip snap is simply a quicker, more forceful version of the basic movement used to lean a boat. It is the most powerful force you can apply to bring a boat level again, and is thus an essential skill for whitewater kayaking—the key component in braces, rolls, and Eskimo rescues.

Once you get the hang of leaning the boat, as described at left, you can practice the hip snap by rocking the boat from side to side, edging it over as far as you can without capsizing, then snapping it back into place with hip action: lifting your on-side knee (i.e., the knee on the side toward which the boat is leaning) while lowering your off-side buttock. Remember to keep your torso vertical and let your lower body do the tilting.

The next step is to practice righting an overturned boat with the hip snap in a controlled situation, where you can hold onto the edge of a pool or the deck of a friend's boat. The key difference between righting a leaned boat and a capsized boat is that in the latter case, you must keep your head down until your hips have righted the boat. This is counterintuitive, because when a boat overturns and your head is underwater, your instinct is to raise your head immediately to grab a breath. The problem is that this motion counteracts the momentum of the hip snap and makes it much harder for you to right the boat. Instead, keep your head down until the boat and your torso are upright. Your head should be the last thing to come up.

Practice the hip snap first by leaning the boat from side to side...

...and snapping it upright with your hips...

...keeping your upper body perpendicular to the water's surface.

Practicing the Hip Snap

1. While hanging onto the bow of a partner's boat (or the edge of a pool), lean the boat over until your body is in the water.

2. Keeping your head down, use your hips to snap the boat upright.

3. Keep your head down throughout the righting phase. Don't bring it up until your boat is completely level.

—From *Basic Kayaking*

Basic Kayak Strokes and Maneuvers

Greg Davenport
Illustrations by Steven A. Davenport

How to Hold a Paddle

The position of your hands on the paddle may change, depending on your activity. When you need a slow powerful stroke to overcome wind or other forces, hands are often extended out on the paddle. Determining how far to extend this grasp is personal, but as a general rule you will want to extend your hands equal to the distance created when your upper arms are perpendicular (90 degrees) to your body and your forearms are parallel to it.

For a cruising stroke, which expends less energy, place your hands closer together at a distance equal to your shoulder width. Regardless of the type of stroke you use, a nonfeathered paddle allows for two control hands, whereas a feathered paddle allows for only one control hand. A control hand is placed on the paddle (palm back) with your knuckles closest to the wrist in line with the top edge of the blade so that its working side is facing the back of the kayak. To maintain a proper blade angle, the handgrip should be firm and unchanging. Both hands are used this way for a nonfeathered paddle; only one hand is used for a feathered paddle. When the blade-to-water angles change, adjust the paddle angle using your wrists and forearms, but do not change your grip.

Maneuvering a Kayak

Basic forward stroke

For a basic stroke, extend your forward hand and bend the other one close to the body. The forward hand, which is on the side with the paddle in the water, pulls its end of the paddle back and through the water while the other hand pushes its end forward and away. Adding a torso twist to the stroke makes it more powerful and less tiring. Good paddlers will use the torso and

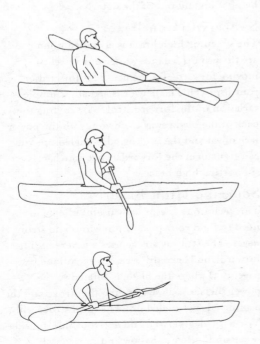

Forward stroke.

not their arms to drive the stroke. A torso twist stars with the upper body parallel to the paddle with the shoulder on the extended arm side forward, and as the stroke proceeds, the powerful torso rotates from the waist, augmenting the pushing and pulling movements of the arms. Developing a smooth cadence and keeping your upper arm below chin height, thus ensuring a low paddle angle, will produce the best results while expending the least amount of energy.

Basic forward stroke.

Turning the Kayak

To turn a kayak, simply make strokes on one side of the vessel. For better results, use log sweeping strokes, which start similar to the basic stroke except the forward arm and shoulder are extended as far outward as they will go. Keep the paddle close and as near level as possible. Completely immerse the blade into the water, and using a torso twist, swing the blade through the water in a low, broad sweeping motion. A reverse sweep has the same effect, except the stroke begins at the rear of the vessel and the back side of the blade leads the stroke. In addition to turning the kayak, sweeping strokes can be used to stop the vessel.

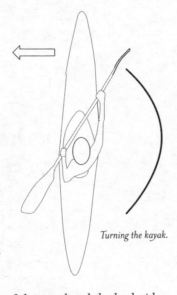

Turning the kayak.

Stopping and Backing Up

Stopping a kayak is an important skill to master, as the ability to stop allows you to plan a route of attack or avoid upcoming obstacles. To stop, keep the blade slightly behind your hips with its angle vertical or slightly forward. Without changing your handgrip, immerse the blade in the water and give a slight forward push to the back of the blade. The process should last one to two seconds and be repeated from side to side. To back up the kayak, extend the forward hand while the other hand is kept bent and close to the body. The back hand on the side with the paddle in the water pushes its end of the paddle

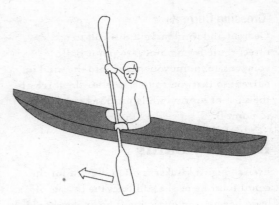

Backing up the kayak.

forward and through the water while the forward hand pulls its end back. Adding a torso twist to the stroke makes it more powerful and less tiring. Good paddlers will use the torso rather than their arms to drive the stroke. A torso twist starts with the upper body parallel to the paddle, with the shoulder on the extended arm side forward, and as the stroke proceeds, the powerful torso rotates from the waist, augmenting the pushing and pulling movements of the arms. Developing a smooth cadence and keeping your upper arm below chin height, thus ensuring a low paddle angle, will produce the best results while expending the least amount of energy. To maintain paddle orientation, use the back of the paddle and do not move your hand placement with this stroke.

Moving Sideways

A draw stroke is often used to move a kayak sideways. To perform, rotate your torso in the direction of the movement, insert the blade 2 to 3 feet into the water (keep the paddle perpendicular to the kayak with the blade parallel to it), and using the power surface of the blade, draw the blade toward the kayak. At the start of the stroke, the lower arm should be straight and the upper arm bent. The lower arm pulls the paddle as the upper arm pushes it away. The stroke's power comes from the pulling lower arm. Just before the paddle reaches the kayak, rotate the blade so it is perpendicular to the vessel and remove it from the water. Avoid letting the blade move under the kayak.

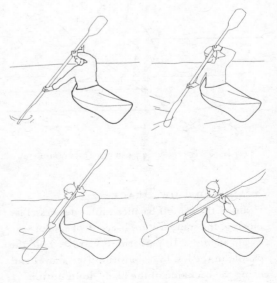

Draw stroke.

Continued →

Crossing Currents

Current and wind make it difficult to take a direct route from point A to point B. To compensate, point your vessel into the wind or current so that you compensate for the force of the current or wind while paddling from point A to point B.

Recovery Skills

Even though a kayaker is often dressed for the conditions, he or she still faces the threats of hypothermia and drowning if he or she should capsize. The keys to surviving are knowledge, skill, and remaining calm, all of which came from practice. Take lessons and learn how to correct your kayak before, during, and after it capsizes. Bracing strokes can be broken down into two categories: support and recovery. A support stroke helps you maintain stability; a recovery stroke brings you upright if an unstable posture has occurred. For details on capsized recovery, refer to page 323. These strokes can be classified as either low or high brace, which best describes how the paddle is held when they are performed.

Low Bracing Strokes

With low bracing strokes, you must hold the paddle perpendicular to the boat's plane and at your side or slightly behind your hips. The paddle's shaft should be shifted to the bracing side and held in a low horizontal position with the back side of the blade down. All low brace strokes use the back side (nonpower surface) of the blade. Hands should be placed on the shaft with palms down, which allows for optimal control and force when performing the maneuver. The bracing arm should be out and away from the vessel, often almost straight, and the hand on the nonbracing arm should be held close to the stomach, where it provides a pivot point for the low bracing strokes. Low bracing strokes position you right over the paddle and allow you to push down with all your weight. Once the maneuver stops the capsizing process, the kayak can be flicked back into the upright position.

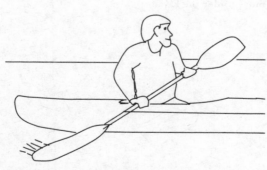

A standard low brace helps you quickly regain balance in a kayak.

STANDARD LOW BRACE

If you're thrown off balance while your vessel is moving, the standard low brace stroke helps you regain stability. To perform this stroke, hold the paddle in the low brace position (see above) and bring the back side of the blade down until it skims the water's surface. For optimal lift, the leading edge of the blade should be tilted up. (The angle will vary.) Once a lift is felt, place your weight down and forward over the blade as

much as is necessary to push you back up. If you need additional leverage, pull up with your nonbracing arm while you continue to push down with the bracing arm. This stroke can also help when you are bracing against surf that is pushing you sideways. To be effective against a wave, you must get your vessel perpendicular to the force of the wave, place the back side of the paddle on top of the breaker, and lean on the paddle. Note that this maneuver is not effective in boats that are not moving.

SWEEPING LOW BRACE

When the vessel is at a stop or just barely moving, you can use a sweeping low brace stroke in place of the standard low brace to help regain vessel stability. To perform this stroke, hold the paddle in the low brace position (see above) and twist your body—opening up on the bracing side—until the back side of the paddle can be placed in the water near the rear of the boat. Use the heel of the palm on your bracing hand to create a broad arched stroke that ends when your blade is perpendicular to the craft. Just before the stroke is to end, place your weight down and forward over the blade as much as is necessary to push you back up, although this may not be required. For optimal results, the leading edge of the blade should be tilted up (angles will vary) during the core of the stroke.

A sweeping low brace helps regain kayak stability.

SLAP BRACE (LOW BRACE MANEUVER)

A slap brace is a reflex stroke that you can use when rapid recovery is necessary. To perform this stroke, hold the paddle in the low brace position (see above right) and strike the water on the bracing side with the back side of the blade. The movement should allow you enough momentary stability to quickly regain control of your vessel.

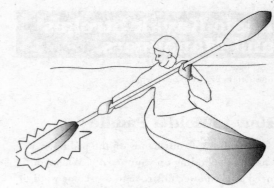

A slap brace is used when rapid recovery is needed.

High Bracing Strokes

High bracing strokes are helpful for stability and recovery when your paddle is located within the front half of your kayak. This technique requires you to shift the paddle's shaft to the bracing side and to place the blade's power surface down. All high brace strokes use the front side (power surface) of the blade. Place your hands on the shaft with your palms facing up and away from your body and your elbows pointing down close to your body. To use this technique, keep the paddle shaft as level as you can and never let your hands go above your head. The nonbracing hand provides a pivot point for the high bracing strokes. Recovery occurs when you pull down on the paddle's shaft. Once the maneuver stops the capsizing process, the kayak can be flicked back into the upright position.

DOWNWARD HIGH BRACE

Use the downward high brace stroke when you are thrown off balance while your vessel is moving forward and the paddle is forward of your hips. To perform this stroke, hold your paddle in the high brace position (see page 323) and reach out approximately 3 feet to strike the water with the flat surface on the power side of the blade. Let your nonbracing arm act as a pivot, while your bracing arm is pulling the blade down and toward you. As the blade approaches your position, it will likely increase its water depth and blade steepness, which in turn will cause a decrease in the amount of support provided. To retrieve the blade, turn it until it is perpendicular to the water surface and bring it up and out of the water.

SWEEPING HIGH BRACE

The sweeping high brace is also used when you are thrown off balance while your vessel is moving forward and the paddle is forward of your hips. This maneuver is actually a simple variation of the forward stroke. By angling the back of the blade away from you, with the power face down and the leading edge angled up, you can transform the forward stroke into a supporting high brace.

SCULLING HIGH BRACE

This technique is especially useful when you need to hold your position in winds and strong waves. The sculling stroke uses a never-ending forward and backward sweeping technique (see page 323) where the blade is rotated so the power surface is always leading the stroke and the leading edge is angled up. The ideal stroke will have a 45-degree arch and a 3-foot side-to-side sweep and follow a shallow and horizontal figure-eight pattern. To use this stroke to main-

Continued ➡

tain your position in strong winds or surf, lean into the wind or wave and use the sculling stroke on the opposite windward side.

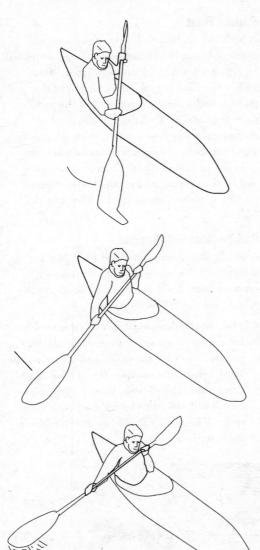

The sweeping high brace is a simple variation of the forward stroke.

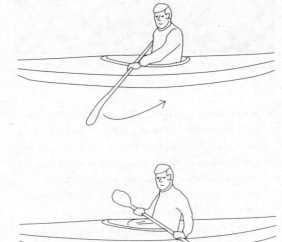

The sculling high brace helps you hold your position in winds and strong waves.

—From *Surviving Coastal and Open Water*

The Veering Problem
Cecil Kuhne

When you execute the forward stroke, you would expect the kayak to move straight ahead. Unfortunately, this usually is not the case. Most kayaks tend to veer somewhat whenever you make a stroke, and the more rocker the kayak has, the worse the veering problem will be.

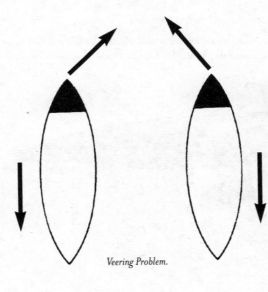

Veering Problem.

A forward stroke on the right side usually causes the kayak to veer left. A forward stroke on the left side causes the kayak to veer right. This unbalanced situation requires the paddler to both propel and steer the boat at the same time. A common cause of veering is that the kayaker inadvertently takes a more powerful stroke on the side with the stronger arm. Veering also may be caused by unintentional movement of the noncontrol hand toward the middle of the shaft, leading to an imbalance of power.

Proper tracking of the boat in a straight line requires a subtlety of paddling style and delicate pressure that comes only from experience. In order to keep the boat going straight, tiny corrections should be taken with each paddle stroke rather than more forceful corrections on one side after the boat has begun to turn substantially.

It's best to correct the boat's veering before you're too far off course. At that point, it becomes nearly impossible to correct the veering without coming to a stop. The most abrupt correction stroke is a stern rudder, where the paddle is held in a fixed position alongside the

Stern Rudder.

back of the boat in a straight line. This very effective, but it creates excessive drag and therefore slows the boat's forward speed.

Try to attune yourself to subtle shifts in the boat's momentum. If the boat starts to veer, lean to the same side to diminish the veer and make a small correction stroke. Make your correction strokes as early as possible and as small as you can to avoid overcompensating. Paddling smoothly, which will come with practice, will also prevent much of this unintentional turning.

—From *Paddling Basics: Kayaking*

When the Kayak Capsizes

Tuck Position and Wet Exit
Wayne Dickert and Jon Rounds
Photographs by Skip Brown
Illustrations by Roberto Sabas

Before you do any whitewater paddling in a kayak, you've got to know what to do when the boat flips. Note the wording: not "if" the boat flips, but "when." Whitewater kayaks tend to turn upside down, sometimes because you intend them to, other times not. Though this is a potentially dangerous position, it's one you can easily get yourself out of. In fact, righting a capsized boat or just rolling for the sheer fun of it will soon become routine. However, there will be situations where you can't roll an overturned boat, either because you haven't yet mastered the technique or for some other reason beyond your control. In these situations, you must know how to extract yourself from the cockpit.

First, sitting in your boat on shore or in calm water, practice what is known as the tuck position. Simply lean forward at the waist as far as you can, as if trying to touch the deck with your nose. On the river, you should get into this position the instant you roll over. For one thing, it protects your head from rocks and other underwater hazards as you're swept along.

The tuck position.

After you've flipped, the next step is to perform a wet exit, which is the process of pushing yourself out of the cockpit. You can practice the first part—the spray skirt release and the basic movements of your hands and legs—on land.

The final part of the maneuver—which is like doing a straight-legged somersault out of

Continued ➡

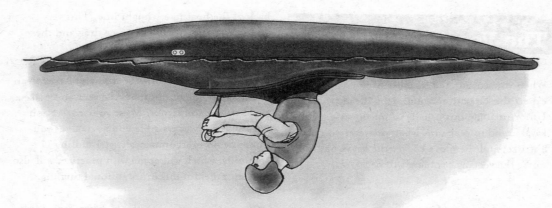

1. First, you must free the spray skirt from the kayak. You may need to lean back to access the skirt; nonetheless, try to remain as close to the boat as you can. Release the spray skirt by grasping the grab loop. Pull it up and away from the cockpit rim and then back toward you to release the sides and back.

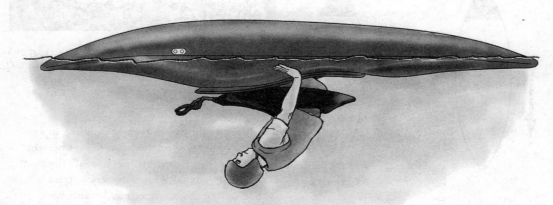

2. Still leaning forward, place your palms on the deck on either side of the cockpit, outside the spray skirt. Relax your legs and feet so they no longer press against the inside of the boat, and, keeping your legs straight, push yourself out of the boat.

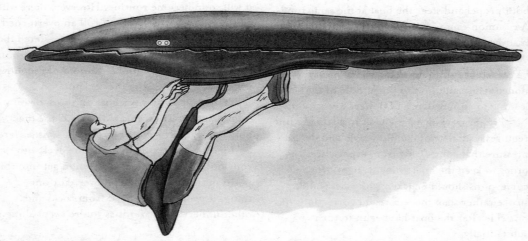

3. Then, push the boat away from you with your legs. Once you're free of the boat, your PFD will pop you to the surface. The most common beginner mistake in a wet exit is trying to get out of the boat by leaning back in the cockpit and swimming to the surface. This strategy just tangles your legs. Somersault out of the cockpit and push the boat away from you with your legs before heading for the surface.

the boat—is a lot easier underwater, and you should practice it there before you go paddling. With a friend by your side, paddle into waist-high water that has a smooth, hazard-free bottom (no rocks or snags). Take a deep breath, lean your upper body to the side until the boat flips, and complete the first two steps of the exit.

You may be wondering what to do with the paddle during all this. You can hold onto it after you flip, grasping it in the middle with one hand while releasing the grab loop with the other.

Then, still holding the paddle with one hand, you can place it lengthwise against the hull as you push off the sides of the cockpit with both hands. Alternatively, you can let go of the paddle when you flip and try to recover it at the surface.

Mastering the wet exit before you go out on the river is not only a necessary safety precaution. Knowing you can extract yourself from the boat also gives you the confidence to paddle in water that might otherwise be intimidating.

—From *Basic Kayaking*

Reentry

Greg Davenport
Illustrations by Steven A. Davenport

Paddle Float

A paddle float helps a kayaker to reenter a capsized boat. To use the paddle float, which will be either a foam block or an inflatable float, inflate the float, slip it over one end of the paddle, and slide the other end of the paddle onto the kayak behind the cockpit. Before entering the water, you might consider rigging some line behind the cockpit since it can help hold the paddle in place. Once in place, the paddle float helps stabilize the kayak, thereby making it easier for you to climb back in the boat.

Paddle-float Self-Rescue

A paddle float, either made of foam block or an inflatable material, helps a kayaker reenter a capsized boat. To perform a paddle-float self-rescue, use the following steps:

1. Move to the downwind side of your vessel.
2. Inflate the float, slip it over one end of the paddle, and slide the other end on top of the kayak behind the cockpit. If you have rigged line behind the cockpit, inserting the blade into it will make this technique much easier to do. The paddle should be at a 90 degree angle to the kayak.

The paddle float helps a kayaker reenter a capsized boat.

3. While keeping a low and flat center of gravity, pull your torso up and onto the back deck—turn your head so it is facing the back side of the kayak—and lift your upside knee to rest it on the paddle. Try to keep as much body contact with the raft as you can. Do not get up on your knees or elbows.
4. While keeping your center of gravity on the kayak's paddle side, rotate your body and place the forward leg into the cockpit. Once it is inside, your other leg on the paddle should follow. At this point, you should be lying on top of and parallel to the kayak with your head and torso on the back deck in a facedown position.
5. Rotate your body and torso until you are sitting up and facing forward. For this maneuver to be done successfully, you need to keep your weight toward the side of the kayak with the paddle.

Continued ➡

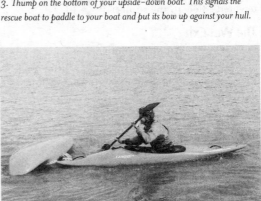

2. Roll the boat over.

3. Thump on the bottom of your upside-down boat. This signals the rescue boat to paddle to your boat and put its bow up against your hull.

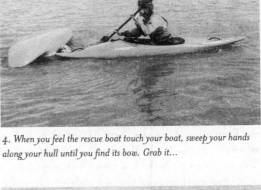

4. When you feel the rescue boat touch your boat, sweep your hands along your hull until you find its bow. Grab it...

...and use a hip snap to right your boat.

Paddle-float rescue.

6. Bail and pump out any remaining water and replace the kayak's skirt.

7. Remove the paddle float and reattach it to the kayak.

The paddle-float rescue is a good way to reenter a capsized boat when the shore is not close by. While it can be used in most circumstances, it will probably not be successful if used inside the surf line. If you capsize inside the surf line, swim to shore for reentry into the vessel.

Assisted Rescue

If you are traveling in a group and become separated from your kayak or it sank or is damaged beyond repair, then an assisted rescue can keep you afloat and, if applicable, help to reunite you with your vessel. Drowning and hypothermia are your biggest threats once you are in the water. The sooner you get out of the water, the better your chance of survival. Often, the wisest decision is to climb aboard another kayak. To do this, the rescuing kayaker should get close to you and hold this position while you climb aboard the back deck of the vessel with your head toward the kayaker. For stability, keep a low and flat center of gravity with your head down, grab the kayaker's waist, and spread your legs so that your feet hang off the sides. Try to keep as much body contact with the raft as you can. Do not get up on your knees or elbows. If your kayak is still afloat, it is most likely drifting broadside to the wind and can be approached from the windward side. Once there, an assisted reentry can easily reunite the kayaker with his or her kayak. If the vessel is disabled, it may need to be towed to shore. If you must tow a boat, use a system that allows for a quick release of the boat and always tow the boat so that it is a safe distance, usually two to three boats, away.

Assisted Reentry

An assisted reentry is easier and faster than a paddle-float rescue and often occurs after an assisted rescue has taken place. The following steps detail an assisted reentry:

Ideally, the rescuing kayaker should approach the vacant vessel from the windward side so that the two boats are parallel and bow to stern. Use common sense as this may not always be practical.

The person in the water should right the capsized kayak.

The rescuer should place both paddles behind his or her kayak's cockpit, perpendicular to the vessel, and position the middle of the paddles under his or her armpits so that each paddle runs between the rescuer's forearm at the bicep and his or her body. With the paddles in this position, the rescuer can lean over and grab the free kayak's coaming. The weight of the rescuer on the paddles helps to stabilize the two kayaks.

While keeping a low and flat center of gravity, the person in the water should pull his or her torso up and onto the back deck, turning his or her head so it is facing the back side of the kayak. This person should try to keep as much body contact with the raft as he or she can and should not get up on his or her knees or elbows.

The person being rescued should try to keep his or her center of gravity toward the rescuing kayak and rotate his or her body until able to place a forward leg into the cockpit. Once that leg is inside, the outside leg can follow. At this point, he or she should be lying on top of and parallel to the vessel with his or her head and torso on the back deck in a facedown position.

The rescued person should then rotate his or her body and torso until he or she is sitting up and facing forward. For the assisted entry to be performed successfully, he or she must keep his or her weight shifted forward toward the rescuing vessel, and the rescuer must provide a constant counterbalance.

—From *Surviving Coastal and Open Water*

The Eskimo Rescue

Wayne Dickert and Jon Rounds
Photographs by Skip Brown

The Eskimo rescue is a technique for righting a capsized boat using a hip snap and the bow of a nearby boat as support. If you've not yet mastered rolling, this is the handiest way to right your boat, and it's a lot quicker and more convenient than doing a wet exit and swimming to shore. However, it does require that another boat be nearby and that the paddler in that boat knows you need his or her assistance.

1. With a partner's boat nearby, get into tuck position.

Remember to keep your head down until your boat is completely level.

—From *Basic Kayaking*

Rolls

The Eskimo Roll

Cecil Kuhne
Illustrations by Cherie Kuhne

The Eskimo roll is one of the most dramatic maneuvers in kayaking. It involves the complete overturning of the kayak, followed by a self-recovery full circle to an upright position. The Eskimo roll was once considered an advanced technique performed only by the expert, but it's actually a skill that anyone can learn with practice. It is now regarded as essential to safety on a whitewater river or a large body of water. Mastery of the roll also promotes confidence. You know that if you capsize, you can right yourself immediately with a reliable roll.

Learning the Eskimo roll does take some patience, however. It's best to learn the skill from an experienced kayaking instructor. There are also a number of helpful books and videos devoted solely to the subject.

The Wet Exit

Even if you're paddling gentle waters, it's good to be prepared for the possibility of turning over. Beginning paddlers are often afraid they'll be trapped in the kayak if it overturns. Those fears are groundless. Getting out of an overturned kayak is easy—you simply fall out of the boat.

To practice this, place your hands on the sides of the boat, take a deep breath, and then slowly turn the boat over by leaning to one side. When you're upside down, remove your knees from the knee braces and draw your feet up. As you do this, pull the spray skirt off the cockpit by the loop attached to the front of it. Relax, and you will automatically slip out of the cockpit. You can then push the boat away with your feet.

Practice the wet exit with a paddle. Try to hold on to the paddle. With your paddle and the boat's grab loop in one hand, use the other hand to propel yourself to shore.

Whenever you exit your boat, remember these safety concerns:

- Always maintain contact with your kayak. The easiest way to do this is to keep one hand on the cockpit's coaming as you come to the surface of the water. Then swim quickly down to the bow or stern grab loop and begin to tow your boat to the nearest shore.

- Keep the boat upside down when you're towing it to shore after a wet exit. It will ride higher in the water because of the air trapped inside.

- Always stay upstream of your boat when you're swimming with it in moving current so that you won't become pinned between the boat and a rock or other obstruction.

Performing the Eskimo Roll

There is more than one way to do the Eskimo roll, but most rolls are basically the same. The key to any roll is the hip snap. Although it takes the entire body to accomplish the roll, it is really the action of the hips that rotates the boat upright.

The roll is really nothing more than a sweeping brace done underwater. In brief, the roll works like this: When you're upside down in the water, you crouch your body close to the surface of the water while at the same time placing the paddle in position on the surface of the water for the sweep stroke that will follow. You then sweep the paddle out from the boat in a wide arc. The angle of the blade as it moves through the water is critical; a climbing angle will keep the blade high in the water and near the surface. Then you execute the hip snap, which is a combined motion of the hips and knees to flip the boat upright. Your body, however, remains in the water. The last step in the roll is a high brace that lifts your body out of the water after the boat has been flipped upright. Another common mistake made by beginners is to raise the body above the water before doing the hip snap.

The Eskimo roll can be broken down into four basic steps:

- Place the paddle in the correct position on the surface of the water.
- Sweep the paddle out from the boat.
- Perform the hip snap.
- Do a high brace to lift your body out of the water.

To learn the Eskimo roll, it's far better to watch someone perform it than to just read about it. Doing so in person is the best way, and watching a videotape is the next best. Diagrams can also be helpful; the accompanying illustrations present a sequential view of the Eskimo roll as seen from the front, back, and side. Study the movements of these kayakers as they roll the kayak, and then visualize yourself doing the same.

If possible, seek the assistance of an instructor or experienced paddler to help you learn the skill. He or she will be able to spot anything you are doing wrong and provide helpful suggestions. In the process, you'll learn the roll much more quickly.

Using a pair of goggles to watch someone else perform the roll from underwater can be extremely helpful. A pair of nose clips will make the experience more comfortable when it's your turn. A helmet and life jacket will only get in the way at this point, so don't worry about them until you've learned the roll.

1

2

3

4
Front View.

5

6

7
Front View.

Continued ➔

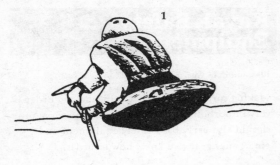

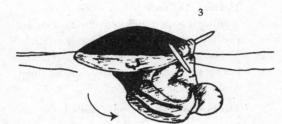

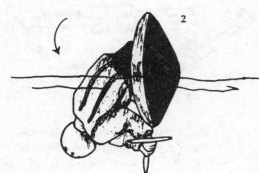

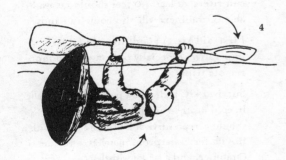

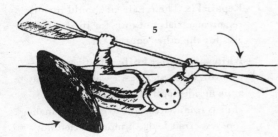

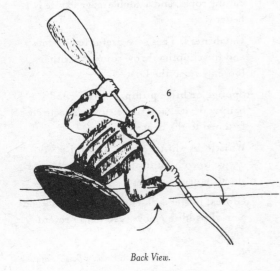

Back View.

Side View.

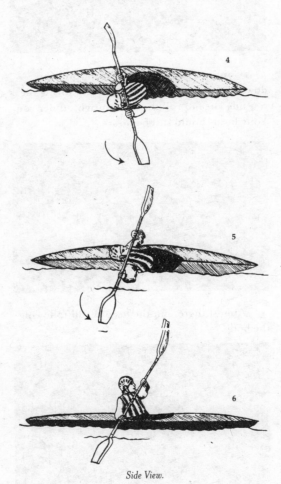

Side View.

Back View.

Starting Position.

the power blade at this angle planes across the top of the water instead of slicing through it and then diving. Now you're ready to sweep the paddle. Make sure you get as wide an arc as possible and that you sweep the front blade across the surface of the water and away from the bow.

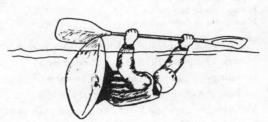

Blade Angle.

THE HIP SNAP
The snap of the hips is really the key to the Eskimo roll, as it is this movement that brings the boat upright. The sweep of the paddle and the movement of the body help, but it's really the hip snap that causes the boat to flip back over, and in fact, many experienced kayakers can do a roll without a paddle at all.

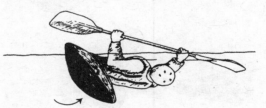

The Hip Snap.

THE HIGH BRACE
As you complete the sweep, the brace naturally pulls you upright. To get some support from the water, you may need to push down on the paddle. You may also want to lean back on the deck to make the return to the upright position easier.

POSITIONING THE PADDLE
To start the roll, you need to place the paddle in the proper position. The paddle should be parallel to the water's surface, with the blade slightly tilted so that its outside edge is closer to the water. You need to maintain the blade in this position as you overturn the kayak.

SWEEPING THE PADDLE
You've tipped over and you're upside down. The power face of the blade should be at a 30- to 45-degree angle to the water. As with the brace,

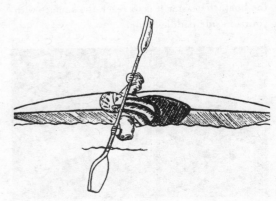

The High Brace.

Continued ➡

The Pawlata Roll

If you're having trouble doing the Eskimo roll, you might try the extended-paddle roll, or Pawlata roll (named after Hans Pawlata, the first European to do an Eskimo roll). To do this roll, you slide the paddle forward in your hands in order to get more leverage in the sweep action.

Pawlata Roll.

C-to-C Roll

Wayne Dickert and Jon Rounds
Photographs by Skip Brown
Illustrations by Roberto Sabas

The C-to-C rights the boat primarily through a sudden and powerful hip snap, aided by a sweeping high brace. This roll is so-named because the change in the curve of the spine provides the righting force. You begin with your spine in a C-shaped curve toward the water, and as you right the boat it shifts to a curve in the opposite direction. In essence, this is a continuation of the hip snap and Eskimo rescue techniques—you're just using your paddle to right yourself rather than another boat.

The C-to-C roll is powered by the shift that occurs in a hip snap.

Executing the C-to-C Roll

After tipping the boat upside-down, place your paddle parallel to the hull, above the surface of the water, with the powerface of the front blade facing down. At this point, your torso should be bent forward in tuck position. The farther you can extend your off-side arm across the hull of the boat, the easier it is to reach the surface with your on-side paddle blade.

Begin sweeping the blade out, keeping it at or near the surface. Note that the off-side arm is bent at the elbow and close to the hull.

As the sweeping paddle comes perpendicular to the boat, begin a strong hip snap by first leaning your torso toward the surface and relaxing your off-side knee (here, the left). Note the off-side arm is still bent and tight against the hull and the shaft is angled to prevent the sweeping blade from diving. Also note that the paddler's head is still in the water; you must resist the impulse at this stage to raise your head and gasp for air.

Continue the strong hip snap, pressing down with your off-side buttock and lifting the on-side knee to roll the boat upright under you. Your head should still be down.

Almost there, but the head is still following the body.

The righted boat at the end of the roll.

—From *Basic Kayaking*

Kayak Safety Equipment

Cecil Kuhne
Illustrations by Cherie Kuhne

Making sure that your boat is in working order is very important, especially on remote rivers. You should also carry basic safety equipment and emergency gear and know how to use it.

River Knife.　　　　*Bilge Pump.*

- **PFD**. The most indispensable piece of safety equipment is your personal flotation device (PFD). Be sure it will provide sufficient flotation for the water you'll be tackling.

- **Helmet**. On rocky rivers where overturning is even a slight possibility, helmets provide an important measure of safety. On easier waters, helmets aren't necessary, but on more difficult whitewater, a helmet could save your life.

- **Throw rope**. Throw ropes made for rescuing boaters are excellent because they float and can be easily tossed. Each kayak should carry one.

- **Rescue lines**. In the case of rescue, plenty of rope is the key. For boat rescue on difficult rivers, at least 50 feet should be available. Carabiners will also come in handy.

- **First-aid kit**. A good first-aid kit is imperative, especially on longer and more remote trips.

- **Survival kit**. Individual paddlers, especially in cold weather or wilderness situations, should carry a survival kit on the PFD, with a fire starter, waterproof matches, a rescue carabiner, and a signal whistle.

- **Repair kit**. The repair kit should include repair materials not only for the boats but also for the other equipment.

- **Whitewater safety knife**. Most kayakers who run whitewater wear a whitewater safety knife upside down on the PFD so that the knife is readily accessible to cut an entangling rope. A serrated edge is more efficient for cutting ropes, and a double-edged knife is better yet.

- **Catabiners**. These are useful for rescues and for clipping throw ropes and other loose items in the boat.

- **Sponge or bilge pump**. Carry a good bailing device, and make sure it's securely fastened to the boat.

- **Whistle**. A whistle can be a useful safety device to communicate with other boaters at a distance.

- **Gloves**. Blisters will ruin a trip, and a good pair of paddling gloves can help prevent them.

—From *Paddling Basics: Kayaking*

Launching, Landing, and Trimming a Canoe

Jon Rounds and Wayne Dickert
Illustrations by Tania Litwak

Launching and Landing

There's nothing difficult about launching a canoe, but an unloaded craft is tippy, and a misstep can put you in the drink. The American Canoe Association recommends maintaining three points of contact on the canoe while boarding: two hands and one foot, or vice versa. Always place your steps along the centerline, not the edges, of the hull.

To save wear on the hull and to improve launching stability, the canoe should be fully afloat before being loaded or entered. Don't load a canoe on shore and shove it into the water or load it in water so shallow that the hull scrapes bottom. If the water's not deep enough right at the shore, walk the canoe out a little ways before getting in or loading.

A note on tandem boarding: Because the ends of a symmetrical canoe are identical externally, it may not be apparent to beginning paddlers which is the bow and which the stern. The clue is the positioning of the seats: the bow seat has more room in front of it for your legs.

Broadside Launch

This is a handy position for entering and loading because the full length of the canoe is alongside the shore or dock. To do a broadside launch without wading, however, the water must be deep enough right at the shoreline to float the boat.

With the stern paddler steadying the boat from shore or dock, the bow paddler steps in, placing the paddle across the gunwales as a brace, and gets down into his paddling position. The bow paddler then steadies the boat by holding the dock or shore while the stern paddler gets in.

For a solo launch, stand beside the boat at the point you will kneel or sit, and board using the same paddle-bracing technique. Get right down into your paddling position.

In a broadside launch, the stern paddler steadies the boat from dock or shore while the bow paddler gets in, placing the paddle across the gunwales as a brace.

Bow-First Launch

Along a wooded or rocky shore there may not be enough room to position the canoe for a broadside launch. Also, when waves are crashing parallel to shore, a broadside launch risks swamping the boat. In such cases, use a bow-first launch.

In a bow-first launch, the stern paddler steadies the boat while the bow paddler steps in and walks forward down the center to his seat, holding the gunwales.

With the bow of the canoe pointing out from shore and the stern paddler steadying the boat from the rear, the bow paddler steps in and walks forward down the center, leaning over and holding onto the gunwales, until he reaches his seat. The stern paddler then gets in.

Launching in Moving Water

When boarding a canoe in a river, steady the boat by holding the upstream end. If you hold the downstream end, the boat will swing out into the current.

Landing and Exiting the Canoe

In a broadside landing, one paddler gets out and steadies the canoe against the shore or dock while the other gets out.

In a bow-first landing, don't push the canoe too far onto shore. Walking on the bottom of a grounded canoe, or one in which the bow is resting on land, can damage the hull. Also, a canoe with any curvature to the bottom is very unstable on land. Nose the bow onto shore just enough to keep it from drifting away, leaving as much of the hull in the water as possible. Then walk forward in the same posture as in a bow-first launch, leaning over with hands on gunwales.

Trim and Pivot Point

Trim refers to how level a boat sits in the water, both fore and aft and side to side. A trim boat is completely level—neither bow nor stern sticks up higher than the other and the boat isn't tilted to either side. An easy way to check trim once paddlers and gear are in place is to pour a little water in the canoe and watch where it collects. In practice, canoes are seldom perfectly trim. A solo paddler, simply because of his position, tilts the boat toward his paddle side. Likewise, a canoe is often leaned into a turn. In fast water, many paddlers prefer a slightly bow-light canoe, for maneuverability. However, a boat that is significantly out of trim fore or aft is unwieldy and even dangerous. A bow-heavy boat tends to plow into the water, and a stern-heavy boat is difficult to steer.

Trim is directly related to a boat's pivot point, the point around which the boat turns. Several variables affect the pivot point: the position of the paddler or paddlers, the weight distribution of the gear, and the design of the hull.

A lone paddler in the stern of a tandem canoe—a common beginner mistake—is a classic example of how trim and pivot point affect boat handling. This paddling position creates a rearward pivot point and a severely out-of-trim boat that is impossible to control in wind or current. The paddler's weight sinks the stern and lifts the bow, and when wind (or current) catches the canoe broadside, it spins the hull with too much leverage for the paddler to counteract. The solution is simple: move the pivot point forward. For a solo paddler in a tandem boat, this means kneeling in front of the bow seat and facing the stern, creating a more central pivot point and a trim boat that is much easier to control. This also has the advantage of putting the paddler where the hull is wider and more stable.

Similarly, tandem paddlers may need to make adjustments to get their boat in trim. If the bow paddler is significantly lighter than the stern paddler, some gear can be moved forward to bring the bow down. If there is no gear to shift, the paddlers can move the bow seat back and/or the stern seat forward. If the seats are fixed, the paddlers will have to use the kneeling position and move slightly fore or aft.

This tandem canoe is trim, fore and aft. Neither bow nor stern sits higher than the other. Paddlers can adjust trim by moving slightly forward or back or by shifting gear fore or aft inside the canoe.

A paddler in a solo canoe kneels near the center of the canoe to keep it trim.

A solo paddler in the stern seat of a tandem canoe lifts the bow out of the water, putting the boat severely out of trim.

Kneeling vs. Sitting

Experts are unanimous that for boat control, stroke efficiency, and safety, kneeling is better than sitting. Kneeling lowers your center of gravity, allows greater rotation of your torso, and puts more of your body in contact with the hull. Always use this position when paddling in rapids or in rough water on lakes. Spread your knees as far apart as comfortable and rest your butt against the seat or thwart behind you. Kneeling pads or a kneeling saddle make this position much more comfortable and also give you more control by keeping your knees from sliding around on the bottom of the canoe.

Continued →

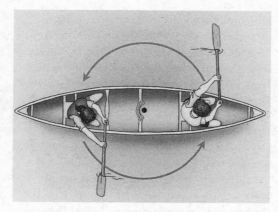

The pivot point is the axis around which the boat turns. Tandem paddlers should position themselves so this point is in the middle of the boat.

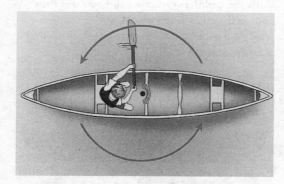

A solo paddler in a tandem canoe should sit in or kneel in front of the bow seat and face the rear. This puts the pivot point nearer the center of the canoe.

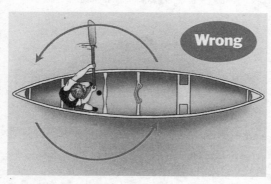

Wrong

A solo paddler sitting in the stern seat of a tandem canoe creates a pivot point too far to the rear. Because of the length of hull in front of him, he lacks the leverage to turn the boat into even a moderate wind, which will spin the boat like a weather vane.

But there are times when sitting is just fine. Most people find it more comfortable than kneeling, and if you're just out for a relaxing trip across calm water, sit and paddle to your heart's content. You can also sit periodically as a break from kneeling on a long haul across open water.

—From *Basic Canoeing*

Basic Canoe Strokes

Cecil Kuhne
Illustrations by Cherie Kuhne

Paddling Strokes

Paddling strokes can be divided into three major groups: power strokes, turning strokes, and bracing strokes.

- Power strokes propel the canoe forward or backward.
- Turning (or corrective) strokes move the canoe in a new direction or bring the canoe back on course.

- Bracing strokes provide stability, though they can be used to turn the boat. They are most often used in whitewater.

Strokes are also described as dynamic, when the paddler pulls on the blade, and static, when the paddler plants the blade and holds it, letting the momentum of the boat or the pull of the current complete the stroke.

It's best to learn and practice the strokes in their pure form. With experience, you can combine power and turning strokes into one smooth motion. This chapter discusses the basic power strokes: the forward stroke (along with the corrective J-stroke and C-stroke) and the back stroke. The next chapter discusses the turning strokes—the sweep, the draw, and the pry—and the bracing strokes, the low brace and the high brace.

Gripping the Paddle

To determine where you should grip the paddle, hold the paddle just over your head. Your grip on the shaft is correct when your elbows form right angles. This is the basic grip, though it will be varied slightly to meet circumstances we'll discuss below.

Holding the Paddle.

A Little Terminology

Canoeing isn't about technicalities, of course, but a little terminology is helpful to explain the paddling stroke.

Phases of the Stroke

The phases of the stroke are described by the following:

- The catch, or plant, phase is the starting point of a stroke.
- The power, or propulsion, phase is the application of force with the paddle against the water, which causes the canoe to move.
- The recovery phase involves the return of the paddle blade back to the original catch position, which involves feathering the blade above the water or slicing it through the water.

Faces of the Paddle

The sides of the paddle blade used in strokes are described as follows:

- The power face is the side of the paddle that pushes against the water during the forward stroke.
- The backface (or nonpower face) is the opposite side, i.e., the back of the blade. During the back stroke, the backface pushes the water.

POWER FACE ⟶ ⟵ NONPOWER FACE

Faces of the Paddle.

Pivot Point

The point around which the boat turns is called the pivot point. It is usually near the center of the boat, but the pivot point can change.

One important factor affecting the pivot point is the distribution of weight in the boat. Another factor is the accumulation of external forces. For example, when the boat initially accelerates, the pivot point moves.

Solo vs. Tandem

In a tandem canoe, the bow paddler provides most of the power and only a small part of the steering. The stern paddler provides less power because he will be putting more effort into steering. Therefore, the more skilled paddler typically takes the stern.

Both solo and tandem strokes will be covered in this book, but we'll start with solo paddling and concentrate on each stroke in its pure form. Tandem strokes are mostly a combination of solo strokes, and those combinations will be covered on page 332.

Forward Stroke

The forward stroke is the standard power stroke. Because it's so instinctive, many paddlers think it requires little discussion: Just place the paddle in the water and pull. However, there is much more to this stroke than meets the eye, and proper form can make a huge difference in its effect. The key is using the heavier muscles of the torso rather than the arms alone. The forward stroke is made close to the side of the boat, with the paddle shaft moving on a nearly vertical plane to the water.

Catch

- To begin the stroke, extend the lower arm full length and bend the upper arm at the elbow. If you're on the right side of the canoe, thrust your right shoulder forward by rotating your body at the waist. Do not extend the paddle by leaning forward.
- Place the blade close to the boat and dip it almost completely into the water.

Power

- Most of the power of a forward stroke is delivered in the first five to seven inches of the paddle's travel, as the torso unwinds. It makes sense, then, to explode on the stroke; that is, to put everything you have into the first part of the stroke, rather than keeping the pull even. Several short, powerful strokes are better than one long one.

Continued ➡

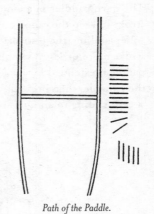

- Keep your right arm straight but not stiff. The left arm stays slightly bent at about eye level.
- Keep the paddle vertical, and keep the power flowing parallel to the boat's centerline.
- The right arm pulls backward until the hand is near the hip. Bringing the paddle back any farther wastes time and power. At this point, both arms are relaxed, with the upper arm dropping down.

Recovery

- This action causes the blade to rise to the surface of the water and the stroke can now begin again.

In executing the forward stroke, only a slight rotation of the body and shoulders should accompany the arm motion. Eliminating unnecessary body motion allows greater smoothness and efficiency. Use the stronger and larger muscles of your back, abdomen, and upper body. Uncoil your body, keep your arms straight, and make your shoulder and stomach muscles do the work.

We'll now take a look at both the side view and the front view of the forward stroke.

Forward Stroke—Side View.

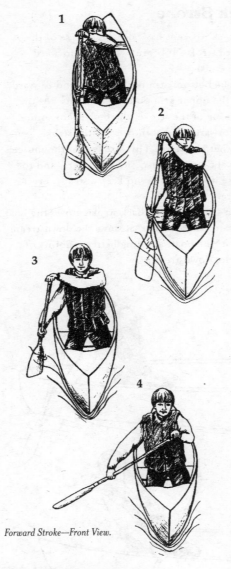

Forward Stroke—Front View.

Movement of the Canoe

When you execute the forward stroke, you might expect the canoe to move straight ahead. Unfortunately, this is not the case. A canoe tends to turn whenever you make a stroke. A forward stroke on the right side causes the canoe to veer left. A forward stroke on the left side causes the canoe to veer right. This unbalanced situation requires the paddler to propel and steer the boat at the same time.

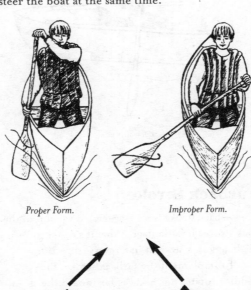

Proper Form.   *Improper Form.*

Canoe Movement.

The J-Stroke: A Corrective for Tandem Canoers

As we've seen, even if you have a good forward stroke, there's still the problem of unintentional turning of the boat. To keep the boat going in a straight line, the paddler must use some sort of correction stroke.

Solo paddlers have to put in a corrective stroke with almost every power stroke. Tandem paddlers fare better, since the bow and stern paddlers balance each other to some extent. Even so, the stern paddler must frequently make corrective strokes.

Path of the Paddle.

The most elementary corrective stroke used to compensate for this slight deviation is a stern rudder. The rudder, however, creates excessive drag and makes paddling in unison difficult. Using a J-stroke as a corrective stroke will keep the canoe tracking straight without affecting forward speed. The J-stroke allows a quick and subtle correction at the end of the stroke. The J-stroke is basically a forward stroke with a turning stroke added at the end. At the end of each forward stroke, twist your top hand to turn your blade perpendicular to the water. Give a quick outward hook to provide the correcting push-away force.

Proper Grip.

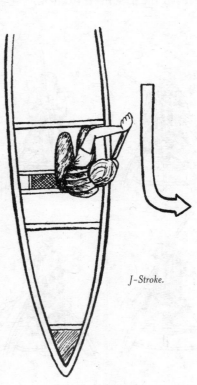

J-Stroke.

Continued ➤

The C-Stroke: A Corrective for Solo Canoers

The stern paddler in a tandem canoe uses a J-stroke to keep the canoe on a straight course. In solo paddling, the J-stroke is modified into a stroke more or less resembling the letter C. The paddle is extended forward and slightly out from the gunwale, then brought back in an inward sweep, ending in an outward sweep.

C-Stroke.

Paddle Switch

When paddling long, skinny touring boats in the flatwater, there is another technique for keeping the boat straight: It's called the paddle switch, the sit 'n' switch, or the Minnesota switch. In consists of using forward strokes taken alternately on either side of the boat, using them to balance the boat's tendency to turn.

The solo paddler takes several forward strokes on one side of the boat, then switches hands and puts in several more strokes on the other side, keeping the boat straight under power. Any time lost by switching sides is more than compensated for by not having to use the less efficient corrective strokes. It is often done with a bent-shaft paddle while sitting rather than kneeling (hence the name sit 'n' switch).

Tandem boats use a similar system. Even if the paddlers are stroking on opposite sides, the canoe will drift slightly to one side. Switching sides at the same time, they can correct for this movement. When switching sides, the bow paddler sets the pace for the switch.

Paddle Switch Technique.

Back Stroke

The back stroke is basically the reverse of the forward stroke. It begins where the forward stroke ends.

The bottom arm pushes down and forward, while the upper arm pulls up and back. At the beginning of the stroke, the body leans somewhat forward, and at the end of the stroke, somewhat backward. This stroke uses the muscles of the abdomen, arms, and shoulders, and to execute it it's necessary to keep a steady, erect posture.

In still water, the back stroke moves the boat upstream. In fast water, it slows the downstream speed of the boat, allowing better visibility of obstacles downstream.

Back Stroke.

Farback Stroke

The farback stroke is an exaggerated version of the back stroke. Its advantage is that it's easier to keep the boat going straight in a reverse direction.

To implement the farback stroke, the paddler rotates her body as far toward the stern as she can. She then reverses her paddle and plants the power face almost vertical behind her. When the stroke is taken, it extends no farther than the paddler's body. The paddler then feathers the blade and begins another stroke.

—From *Paddling Basics: Canoeing*

Farback Stroke.

Tandem Canoe Maneuvering

Jon Rounds and Wayne Dickert
Illustrations by Taina Litwak

Roles of Bow and Stern Paddler

Bow and stern paddlers have slightly different roles, and though you may gravitate to one end or the other, depending on your skills and inclinations, learn both positions. This will make you a better paddling partner, because you'll understand the difference between bow and stern strokes and how to complement your partner's moves. It will also make you more flexible for those times you're paired with someone who prefers the end you're used to. So it's a good idea to switch positions every few hours when you're learning.

Bow Paddler

The bow paddler is the navigator. He or she is generally responsible for power strokes and immediate turning decisions. Turning strokes themselves have more effect on the boat from the stern, but the bow paddler has a better vantage point from which to see the route ahead and spot hazards, so it is he or she who decides where the boat should go and communicates this to the stern. With experienced pairs, this communication becomes nonverbal; the bow paddler does a certain stroke and the stern automatically responds with a complementary stroke.

Stern Paddler

Steering strokes have more effect from the stern because the stern paddler has more hull in front of him and therefore more leverage. While the bow paddler does power strokes, it is the stern paddler who performs corrective strokes to adjust the boat's course over the long term.

Continued ➡

However, the stern paddler must be attentive to the bow paddler's moves or verbal directions—especially in rapids or passages with underwater hazards—and respond with complementary strokes.

Tandem Sweeps

A tandem sweep travels half the arc of a solo sweep because its purpose is to turn just one end of the boat. Extending a sweep through its full swing exerts turning force on the other end and counteracts what your partner is doing. The general rule, then, is that the arc of a tandem sweep stays between a point across from your knees and your end of the boat. Thus, a *bow forward sweep* begins exactly where a solo sweep does, but ends when the paddle is directly across from your knees, rather than continuing behind. Conversely, a *bow reverse sweep* begins alongside your knees, rather than as far back as you can reach, but ends where the solo version does. (Because this stroke slows the boat's forward momentum, it doesn't have as many applications as other tandem strokes, but it can be used in combination with a stern forward sweep to spin the boat to the on-side.)

The *stern forward sweep* begins across from your knees, rather than farther forward, and a *stern reverse sweep* ends alongside your knees, rather than continuing forward to the bow.

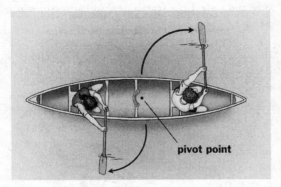

The arc of a tandem sweep is about 90 degrees.

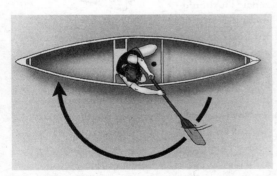

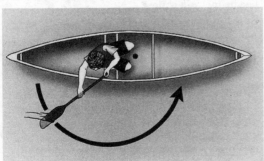

The arcs of both forward and reverse solo sweeps are about 180 degrees.

Tandem Combinations

Bow and stern paddlers in a tandem canoe use complementary strokes to turn the boat, and the basic repertoire of solo strokes covered in this chapter provide a myriad of combinations. The four combinations shown here are a good set to begin with: two turn the boat to the right, and two to the left. Practice them with a partner on flatwater to get the feel for how the boat responds.

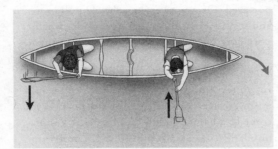

Cross Bow Draw + Stern Pry. Turns the boat sharply to the right. A good combination for punching across an eddy line.

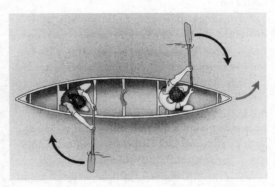

Bow Reverse Sweep + Stern Forward Sweep. Spins the boat to the left (counterclockwise).

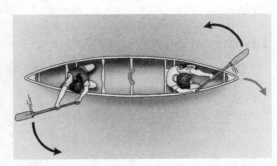

Bow Forward Sweep + Stern Reverse Sweep. Spins the boat to the right (clockwise). Complementary sweeps are the fastest way for tandem paddlers to turn a boat around. Remember that a tandem sweep travels through half the arc of a solo sweep.

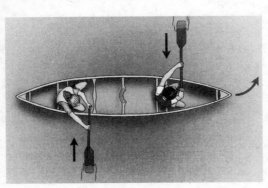

Stern Draw + Bow Draw. Spins the boat to the left in a right circle.

Tandem paddlers should use complementary forward and reverse sweeps to spin the boat on its pivot point. In fact, a combination of sweeps is the most efficient way to point a boat in a new direction.

The need for quick, powerful turns arises most often on rivers, where you have to steer the boat away from obstacles toward which the current is propelling it, get in and out of eddies, and make upstream maneuvers. In a fast current, you may get just one shot to make the right move, so a tandem pair with practiced complementary strokes is at a big advantage. The bow paddler may call for a turn or simply initiate one; the tandem paddler, seeing the stroke his partner has done, reacts with a complementary one.

—From *Basic Canoeing*

Brace Strokes: Keep Your Canoe Upright

Basic Low and High Brace

Cecil Kuhne
Illustrations by Cherie Kuhne

Bracing Strokes

Experienced canoers make good use of bracing strokes, which utilize the paddle as a lever to provide stability by using the force of the water to keep the boat right side up. On a river you must always lean and brace downstream. Leaning upstream will cause you to capsize. There are two forms of brace: a low brace and a high brace.

Low Brace
The low brace is used when the canoe suddenly leans toward the side on which you are paddling. To execute a low brace, you reach out of the canoe with a nearly horizontal paddle. The key to the low brace is a stern thrust of the paddle on the water, which helps push you back to the upright position.

Low Brace.

High Brace
The high brace is used when the canoe leans away from the side on which you are padding. It's as if you are grasping onto the water with your paddle to pull yourself into the upright position.

—From *Paddling Basics : Canoeing*

High Brace.

Continued ➡

Canadian Low Brace

Jon Rounds and Wayne Dickert
Photographs by Skip Brown

Prevents a capsize to the on-side; better for whitewater than the standard low brace.

—From *Basic Canoeing*

As the boat leans toward the water, rotate your shoulders toward your on-side and bring the paddle blade down against the water. Unlike the standard low brace, don't extend your grip hand out over the gun-wale.

Lean forward and lower your head as you brace with the paddle, keeping your grip hand inside the boat.

Sweep the blade across the surface toward the bow, rotating your torso forward and shifting your weight to your off-side knee.

Don't bring your head up until your body is centered over the upright boat. Your paddle is now in position for a forward stroke.

Portaging and Lining

Jon Rounds and Wayne Dickert

The most sensible and sometimes the only way to get around a river hazard is to pull ashore upstream of it, get out of the boat, and either portage around it or lead the boat through it on a line.

Portaging

Portages are common in longer canoe trips because of the greater chance of encountering unrunnable rapids or dams or the need to go overland between bodies of water. For a long wilderness trip, you will have studied the route enough to know the stretches that must be portaged. On any river, you should pull over and scout a difficult stretch to consider whether portaging around it is smarter than running it.

The two-person, right-side-up carry is fine for short distances, and especially over rough terrain, where an overhead carry would mean greater risk of dropping the boat. If you come to a hazard—a low-head dam or a short but dangerous rapid—pull to shore upstream, leave the gear in the canoe, and simply carry it down-river along the bank with one person at each end.

For longer portages, under the boat and divide the duties: one person carries the canoe in a solo overhead carry, while the other leads the way down the trail, packing the gear.

For solo overhead carries, most boats have a carrying yoke in the center that is shaped to fit the shoulders. You can use a PFD or towel on your shoulders for padding. If there is no yoke, or if you want more comfort for a long portage, lash paddles between the fore and aft thwarts (or between the bow thwart and portage yoke) about shoulder-width apart, and put padding on your shoulders. This setup allows you to adjust your balance point fore or aft and gives you a little more freedom in shifting weight over a long carry.

Lining

Lining is a strategy for getting around a hazard when you can't portage or don't really need to. One such situation is if you come upon a dangerous-looking rapid where the bank is too steep to pull the boat out for a portage. Another is a short rapid or hazard with relatively shallow water alongside it or a path along the river. In these cases, you can pull to shore, tie a line to the bow and stern, and, walking on shore or wading at the edge, lead the canoe through the bad stretch.

The person in front leads the canoe while the person behind keeps the stern from swinging broadside to the current. Always wear your PFD. Wading can be treacherous.

—From *Basic Canoeing*

Canoe Safety Equipment

Cecil Kuhne
Illustrations by Cherie Kuhne

Making sure that your boat is in good working order is very important, especially on remote rivers. In the case of unfamiliar rivers, you should also make certain that your safety equipment is adequate.

PFD. The most indispensable piece of safety equipment, of course, is the life jacket. It must provide sufficient flotation for the water you will be tackling.

Rigging. Rigging the boat properly is critical to safety. You must eliminate any sharp projections that could possibly cause injury. Check to insure that nothing will cause entanglement if the boat should overturn.

Bailer. Carry a good bailing device, and make sure it's securely fastened to the boat.

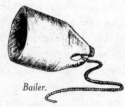

Bailer.

Spare paddle. Always carry a spare paddle.

Rescue lines. In the case of rescue, plenty of rope is the key. For lining or boat rescue on difficult rivers, there should be at least fifty feet available in addition to that ordinarily used for bow and stern lines (carabiners will also come in handy).

Throw rope. For rescue of boaters, the throw ropes made for that purpose are excellent because they float and can be easily tossed. (See the discussion on throw ropes later in this chapter.)

First-aid kit. A good first-aid kit is imperative, especially on longer and more remote trips.

First-Aid Kit.

Repair kit. The repair kit should include repair materials for boats and other equipment such as paddles and stoves.

Helmets. These days whitewater canoers are beginning to wear helmets, just like hardshell kayakers. This is mostly because canoers are challenging tougher, rockier rivers where helmets provide an important measure of safety. On easier waters, helmets aren't necessary, but on more difficult whitewater, a helmet could save your life. The helmet you choose should be snug, but not so tight that it causes discomfort. The protective internal suspension is usually foam, but cheaper versions have plastic strapping. Whitewater helmets are designed with ear openings so you can hear upcoming rapids and warnings from fellow canoers.

Helmet.

River knives. Also helpful are whitewater safety knives. Most canoers wear these knives upside down on their PFDs so the knives are readily accessible. A serrated edge is more efficient for cutting ropes, and a double-edged knife is better yet.

—From *Paddling Basics: Canoeing*

Reading a River

Jon Rounds and Wayne Dickert
Illustrations by Roberto Sabas

What happens when fast water hits a submerged obstacle? What causes a wave to form in a river? How do changes in the volume of water affect the river?

One way to gain this knowledge is by spending a lot of time on the water and making a lot of mistakes. A better way to begin is by studying some basic principles of the physics of moving water.

Force of the Current

Three factors affect the force of the current: the gradient of the riverbed, the width of the riverbed, and the volume of flowing water.

Gradient

Gradient is the slope of the riverbed, expressed in the number of feet it drops per mile. A steeper riverbed creates a faster current. A very rough rule of thumb is that gradients of less than 30 feet per mile produce mild whitewater, up to Class II (see International Scale of River Difficulty [page 337]), and that gradients between 30 and 60 feet per mile produce Class III and IV rapids. However, since gradient is an average over the length of a mile, you can't tell the character of a particular stretch by this number alone. A river with a moderate gradient may be flat for a long way and then plummet fifty feet. On the other hand, a river with a relatively high gradient may have a constant rate of drop over its entire length and produce fast water but no major hazards.

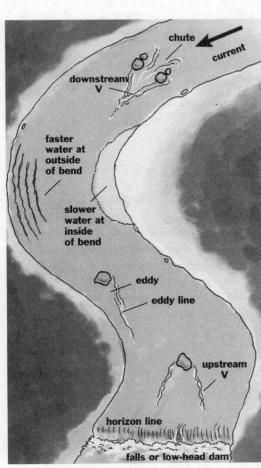

Common river features.

Another significant point about gradient is that the force of the water increases at a greater rate than gradient: if the gradient doubles, the force quadruples. Thus, even a slightly steeper stretch of river will be many times more powerful than a flatter stretch.

Flow

Flow is the volume of water carried past a point in a fixed amount of time, expressed in cubic feet per second (CFS). Unlike gradient, flow is variable: it changes in response to rainfall and dam releases. A river's CFS is crucial because, like gradient change, a change in volume has a profound effect on the force of the water: if the flow doubles, the force triples. Thus, a creek that's an easy float in June may have dangerous rapids in May. And at any time, torrential rain or a dam release can transform a placid river into a drowning machine.

Many of the most popular whitewater rivers in the United States are dam-controlled, including the Ocoee and Nantahala in North Carolina, the New and the Gauley in West Virginia, the Upper Youghiogheny in Maryland and Pennsylvania, the Kern and American in California, and the Colorado through the Grand Canyon. Local boaters become well-acquainted with dam-release timetables, and anyone who runs such rivers should seek this information.

Another point to consider about flow is that a significant increase in volume changes the character of river features important to paddlers. At high volume, rocks that are normally exposed become buried under the surface, and where once there were eddies, now there are holes. Eddy lines (see page 337), the key feature in the paddler's waterscape, vanish. So before running a river, check river levels in local newspapers, paddling club websites, or boat shops.

Gradient and flow are related and must be considered together when evaluating the risk of a river. A river with a relatively low gradient—one that drops 20 feet per mile, say—may still be very powerful if it has a high-volume flow. Conversely, there are relatively low-volume streams with very steep gradients—several hundred feet per mile—that make them impossible to run.

Width

Current speed is also affected by the width of the river. As the river narrows, the current speeds up, because the same volume of water is being squeezed through a tighter channel. A narrows or canyon may also have turbulent water where the currents from the wider stretch slam together.

Current Lanes

The current is faster in the middle of a straight stretch of river because there is less friction there than against the banks. The water in the middle also tends to be deeper, with fewer obstructions. However, when a river goes around a bend, most of the water is thrown to the outside, creating much faster current there and slower current on the inside. The fast

current erodes the outsides of bends, undercutting banks and dredging deep channels, whereas the slow current on the inside of the bend drops sediment and debris there, forming bars and shallower water.

Because of this current differential in river bends, the most fun is to be had on the outside, but that's also where the hazards are—the downed trees and undercut banks. So keep your head up when approaching a bend. If you want to get to the inside, you've got to take action early; unless you do something, your boat will be swept to the outside.

Rocks and Other Hazards

Rocks, the most common obstacle in whitewater, are responsible for creating the holes, waves, and eddies that experienced kayakers seek. The size, shape, and depth of rocks in the current determine how water behaves as it flows around and over them, and the froth, waves, or current lines around a rock will tell you how to approach it. You should learn to recognize a few basic patterns.

A large, rounded rock with its top above the surface has a buildup of water called a pillow on its upstream side where the oncoming water hits. The pillow is a benefit to the paddler because it pushes a boat away from the rock. On the downstream side there may be a pocket of lower water and an eddy—an upstream flow circulating water back into the pocket.

A large rounded rock with its top above the surface has a "pillow" of water on its upstream side where the water hits it.

A rock with an undercut face has no pillow because the water flow is drawn beneath the surface around the rock.

A rock with an undercut face has no pillow: the water flows around the rock beneath the surface. Any obstacle with an undercut face is extremely dangerous in fast water because it can suck a boat against it and trap it there. If you see a large rock in a swift current with no pillow above it, steer clear.

If you're being swept into a rock or other obstacle, lean into it. Although your instinct may be to lean away, doing so lowers the upstream deck of the boat to the onrushing current, a position that may cause the boat to flip or to be pinned against the rock with such force that you won't be able to free yourself. But if you lean downstream, into the rock, the current will be pushing against the rounded bottom of the boat and won't have as much pinning force. Also, by leaning this way you'll be able to fend off the rock with your paddle or arms and continue downstream.

Continued ➡

Downstream and Upstream Vs

The water pointing downstream in a smooth, V-shaped tongue is the path to follow: it points to a channel between rocks, also known as a chute. Conversely, upstream Vs point to obstacles. Learn to recognize this pattern as you look downstream from your vantage point in the boat and plot a course following the downstream Vs.

Holes and Hydraulics

A hole is the paddler's term for the depression just downstream of a submerged rock into which water is recirculating. A rock below the surface of a fast river is marked by a pillow of water just upstream of it and some degree of turbulence right behind it, from froth to waves. Holes can be entertaining rides or hazardous traps, depending on the size and position of the rock and the volume of water pouring over it. It's very easy to get into them—the current just sucks you in—but it can be difficult or impossible to get out. In checking out a hole, you must evaluate its size, shape, and the amount of water involved.

A large volume of fast water flowing over a large submerged rock or ledge can create a hole: a depression with a strong recirculating current. Depending on their size and shape, holes can be places to play or dangerous traps.

Smaller holes are marked by short lengths of backwash behind them and perhaps a standing wave just downstream. These holes are relatively safe to run. More challenging and potentially dangerous holes form when a significant volume of water pours over a large rock or ledge, creating a recirculating current called a hydraulic. The most severe hydraulics are called "keepers" because they literally keep boats in them. One way to gauge the power of a hydraulic is to note the length of the eddy behind the rock or ledge. If the water behind a large submerged rock is moving back upstream from more than three feet away, you're headed into a powerful hole.

Another element to consider in assessing a hole is its shape, because this determines how you'll get out. If the sides of the hole are farther downstream than the middle, then the hole is said to be "smiling." It will be easy to exit because you can paddle out either side into the main current. If, however, the hole's sides are farther upstream than the middle, it is said to be "frowning." A frowning hole is dangerous because you must fight an upstream current to paddle out of it.

Particularly deadly hydraulics form below low-head dams. These dams may not appear dangerous; they're just low concrete walls with a smooth flow of water going over. But the volume of water is actually huge, and the force of the hydraulic this creates, as well as the fact that it stretches all the way across the river, creates an inescapable trough. Stay away from low-head dams or any holes so wide that they offer no routes of escape.

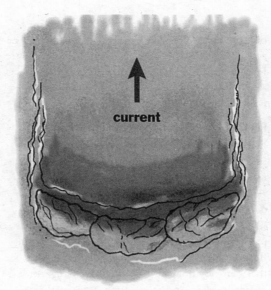

A smiling hole is relatively easy to escape by paddling to either side of the main flow.

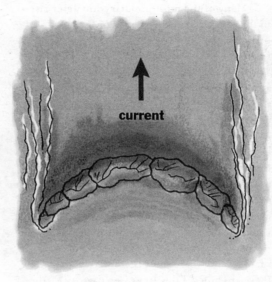

A frowning hole is more dangerous because the boater must fight the current to get out.

Horizon Lines

A level, unbroken line of water across the river downstream of you may mean danger. It can signal a precipitous drop—a ledge, falls, or low-head dam—over which a large volume of water is flowing. Either the drop or the hydraulic behind a horizon line is a potential killer, and if you get too close, the strong current just above the ledge can pull you over. Learn to recognize horizon lines visually from upstream, and listen for the sound of a large volume of water going over a ledge. Paddle to shore and portage around or scout a safe route.

Strainers

A strainer is an underwater object, commonly a downed tree, that allows water to flow through it. Strainers are extremely dangerous because they "strain" the water while trapping objects—including people and boats—too large to pass through them.

Along wooded rivers, strainers are most often found on the outside of bends, where the fast water undercuts banks and uproots trees. Other submerged objects, including fences, cables, grates, or debris deposited by floods, can act as strainers and may be found anywhere in the river. Ask local paddlers about such hazards.

Rising water is another factor that can create strainers by covering brush and trees along the bank. Keep an eye on the river ahead, and stay away from strainers.

Downed trees are the most common form of strainer—any obstacle through which water flows but which can trap a boat or a person. Downed trees are commonly found in the swift water on the outside of river bends.

Waves

Unlike waves on lakes or seas, which travel across the water, waves in a river are stationary. They're created when fast-moving water hits the slower-moving water below it. This happens in a few different situations. A standing wave forms where a sheet of water plunging over a submerged rock or through a chute between rocks hits the slower water just below.

If the wave is tall enough to break back on itself, it's called a stopper, because it can literally stop a boat. Holes often have stoppers below them, but such holes aren't as dangerous as hydraulics because enough water is flowing through the hole to push your boat downstream after it's momentarily stopped by the wave.

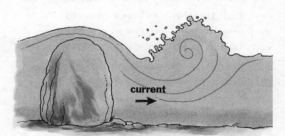

Stopper waves are those that are steep enough to crash back on themselves. So-named because they can literally stop a boat, stoppers are favorites of advanced whitewater kayakers, who seek them out for surfing and other play moves.

A wave trains is a regularly spaced series of waves that occurs where deep, swift water is squeezed into a channel and piles up on the slower-moving water downstream. Wave trains are relatively safe to run because there are no rocks beneath them. In fact, they mark the channel and, hence, the best route to follow. The key to recognizing a wave train is the even spacing of the waves. A wave off by itself or out of alignment with the series marks a rock.

A wave train is a regularly-spaced series of waves that occur where deep, swift water is squeezed into a channel and hits slower-moving water. Wave trains normally mark the channel and are a safe route to follow downstream.

Continued ➡

Eddies

An eddy is a teardrop-shaped area of water behind a rock or other obstacle. The significant feature for boaters is that an eddy has an upstream flow, a phenomenon created when water rushing downstream around a rock sucks the water from directly behind the rock, creating a depression that the downstream water rushes back to fill. An eddy line marks the boundary between these upstream and downstream currents.

Recognizing eddies and getting in and out of them are the most basic skills in paddling rivers. In most cases, eddies are safe havens. Boaters use them as resting places and as stations from which to scout the river below. As we have seen, the lengths of eddy lines can also signal the power of the hydraulics that created them—another important reason to learn to recognize them.

An eddy forms behind an obstacle, with the tip pointing downstream. An eddy's upstream current is strongest at the top, right behind the obstacle. The farther from the obstacle, the weaker the upstream current becomes, until eventually it dissipates altogether and joins the downstream flow. Of particular significance to boaters is the fact that the downstream current is strongest right next to the eddy line. Some instructors call this the "rejector line," because if you don't cross it with enough speed or at the right angle, it will push your boat into the main current.

Recognizing eddies and getting in and out of them are the most basic skills in paddling rivers. In most cases, eddies are safe havens. Boaters use them as resting places and as stations from which to scout the river below. As we have seen, the lengths of eddy lines can also signal the power of the hydraulics that created them—another important reason to learn to recognize them.

—From *Basic Canoeing*

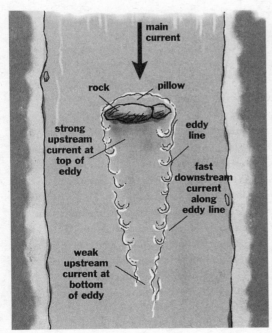

Parts of an eddy.

The International Scale of Whitewater Difficulty

Cecil Kuhne

CLASS I—Easy. Waves small; passages clear; obstacles easy to spot well in advance and avoid.

CLASS II—Novice. Rapids of moderate difficulty; passages mostly clear, some maneuvering required.

CLASS III—Intermediate. Waves numerous, high, and irregular. Rocks and eddies present. Rapids with clear passages, but may be through narrow spots, requiring expertise in maneuvering. Scouting may be necessary.

CLASS IV—Advanced. Long rapids; waves powerful and irregular. Dangerous rocks and boiling eddies. Passages difficult to scout; powerful and precise maneuvering required. Scouting mandatory first time. Risk of overturning or wrapping boat, and long swims for paddlers. For very skilled boaters.

CLASS V—Expert. Extremely difficult, long, and very violent rapids, following each other almost without interruption; riverbed extremely obstructed. Big drops; violent current; very

RIVER BENDS

Cecil Kuhne
Illustrations by Cherie Kuhne

A river's tendency to meander causes erosion of its banks. As this erosion continues, the current gradually carves out a new bend, and the current then begins to pile up on the outside of the bend. The inside of the bend becomes increasingly shallow. On the outside of the bend, there are often large boulders, overhanging trees, undercut cliffs, and other hazards.

[CHANNEL]
SLOWEST — FASTEST

Cross Section of Currents in a Bend.

Hazards in River Bends.

—From *Paddling Basics: Kayaking*

steep gradient. Scouting mandatory but often difficult. Risk of boat damage and serious injury to paddlers. For teams of experts with excellent equipment.

CLASS VI—Extreme. Extraordinarily difficult. Extremes of navigability. Nearly impossible and very dangerous. For teams of experts only, at favorable water levels and after close study with all precautions.

—From *Paddling Basics: Kayaking*

Eddy Turns, Peel-Outs, and Ferries for Kayaks

Wayne Dickert and Jon Rounds
Illustrations by Roberto Sabas

Eddy Turns

Cutting out of the main current into an eddy—the eddy turn—is the most fundamental skill in river running. It requires a basic understanding of eddy anatomy (see the illustration at far left), along with the ability to paddle decisively and to lean your boat effectively. The formula for eddy turns (as well as peel-outs and ferries) is: Angle, Speed, and Lean. If you've positioned your boat correctly as you approach the eddy, and if you hit the eddy line at the right place with some momentum and the correct lean, the turn works like gravity—rather than frantically fighting against the current, you harness the river's force. The boat just falls into the eddy.

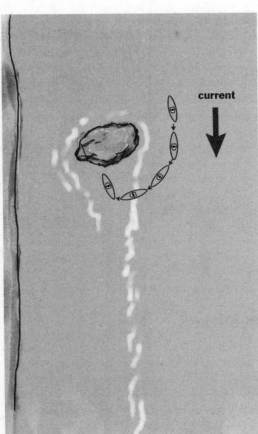

Enter eddy at its upstream end, just beyond the rock or obstacle that creates it, and punch across the eddy line with at least a 45-degree angle.

Continued ➡

Angle

Aim to hit the eddy line just downstream of the rock, at an angle between 45 and 90 degrees, depending on the type of boat you're in. Setting this angle involves the vision principle mentioned previously: before the river carries you past the rock, you must have positioned the boat far enough out from the eddy line that you can turn into it at the right angle, yet not so far away that you'll be swept past the eddy entirely. You want to hit the eddy where its upstream current is strongest, right behind the rock. If the angle is too great—more than 90 degrees—the main current may sweep your stern downstream. If your angle is too little—if you're nearly parallel to the eddy line—you won't be able to punch through it.

Speed

Paddle hard across the eddy line. You've chosen your entry point behind the rock because the upstream current is strongest there and will pull your bow into the eddy. But the downstream current is also strongest right outside the eddy line, just before you cross it, so you'll need some hull speed to punch across.

Lean

Remember the mantra: lean into turns. For eddy turns, this means leaning upstream. At the moment your bow hits the eddy line—just when you feel the eddy current start turning your bow upstream—lift your downstream knee and sink the opposite buttock to carve the boat into the eddy. The mechanics of turning are key here. If you lean your body instead of the boat, or lean the wrong way—away from the turn, downstream—you may flip the boat.

Strokes for Eddy Turns

Strokes are most important in the set-up phase of eddy turns, when you're still in the middle of the river trying to fix the point and the angle at which you'll hit the eddy line. Once you hit that line, hull speed and boat lean will take care of the turn itself. But as you approach the eddy line, you may have to adjust the boat's angle with a quick, powerful stroke. For example, if you find your approach angle is too little you'll need to do a sweep stroke on the downstream side of the boat to turn the bow upstream and achieve a better angle for punching across the eddy line. Conversely, if your angle is too great—if you're more than perpendicular to the eddy line as you approach it—you'll need to decrease that angle with a sweep or forward stroke on the upstream side of the boat.

Peel-Outs

A peel-out is the maneuver for leaving an eddy and getting back into the main current. It is simpler than the eddy turn because you don't have to set up an angle while you're moving. But peel-outs do require more powerful initial strokes than eddy turns, because you're starting from a standstill and don't have the main current pushing you as you do when approaching an eddy. However, the same angle-speed-lean formula applies.

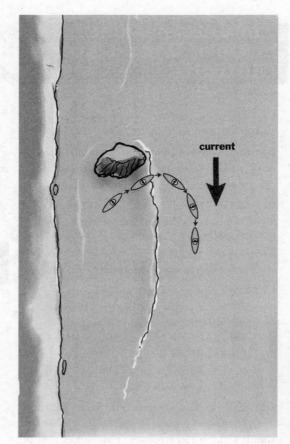

Start well within the eddy, and with the boat angled upstream, head towards the spot at the head of the eddy where you first entered. Lean into the turn and let the current swing the boat downstream.

Angle

Exit the eddy at about the same place and angle—45 degrees or more—that you entered it. Your staring point is key. Position the boat as far back in the eddy as you can without getting out of its upstream current. Being far back gives you distance to build up momentum for breaking across the line, and gives you enough room to prepare a proper angle for exiting.

Speed

Breaking across an eddy line, whether leaving or entering the eddy, takes forward momentum, but in a peel-out you don't have the current pushing you. Starting from a standstill within the eddy, you need powerful forward strokes to gain speed. So solid form—strong torso rotation, using your body and not your arms to generate power—is essential.

Lean

Just before you hit the eddy line, lift your upstream knee and shift your weight to your downstream side to lean the boat into the turn. If your boat is flat when it hits the eddy line, the main current can catch its edge and flip you. In fact, the failure to lean downstream soon enough is the most common cause of capsizing in peel-outs. Once you break across the eddy line, the main current will catch the bow, turning it downstream. Keep leaning downstream until the boat straightens out and its up to speed in the main current.

Strokes for Peel-Outs

Just like eddy turns, peel-outs require strong forward strokes to break through the eddy line. Just before you reach the main current, you'll need to switch strokes. Your choices will depend on the kind of boat you're using. A displacement-hull kayak often calls for strokes or sweeps

on the upstream side to help with turning. A planning hull, on the other hand, will be turned more easily by the current, and you should maintain a forward stroke on the downstream side in order to keep the boat moving past the eddy line.

Ferries

A ferry is a maneuver for crossing a river from one eddy to another without moving downstream. It's an important skill, for you'll often find yourself in situations where you need to go directly across the river to set up for a run through a rapid or to get a better approach to a play spot. The ferry begins with a move similar to a peel-out and ends with an eddy turn, but in between requires you to set the correct angle to arrive at your target.

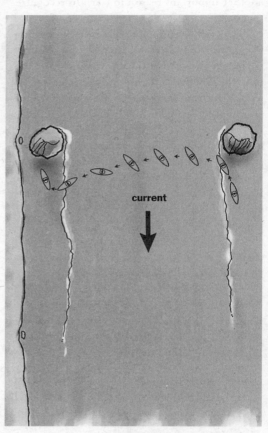

Exit the eddy much like you would for a peel-out, but keep the boat angled upstream as you move across the river. Use a properly angled eddy turn to enter the destination eddy.

Angle

Setting and maintaining the right angle as you cross the river is crucial in ferries. You must be pointed upstream, because if you try to paddle directly across the river, the current will take you far downstream of your target. The swifter the current, the more upstream your angle must be. It is always better to set an angle too far upstream that too far down, because it's easy to let the current swing your bow downstream but very hard to push it back upstream.

Once again, your starting point is crucial. Position the boat as far back in the eddy as you can without getting out of its upstream current, and stay no more than a foot or so inside the eddy line. This rule is especially true for beginners. Err on the side of too little angle. If the current is really ripping, point the boat almost directly upstream at the beginning of the ferry, and let the bow swing down as you cross. For most ferries, the right exit angle is about 20

Continued ➡

degrees for displacement hulls, up to 45 degrees for planning hulls. However, the particular angle varies with current speed, river width, and the paddler's strength.

Although a ferry begins with a move like a peel-out—paddling out the side of an eddy into the main current—here you don't want your bow to swing downstream as it crosses the eddy line, but to head across the river at an upstream angle. Therefore, you'll need to plant a strong forward stroke on your downstream side just as you cross the eddy line to counteract the force of the main current.

Once you're headed upstream in the main current, you start paddling with forward strokes, letting the bow swing to between 45 to 60 degrees upstream.

Speed

Since you're beginning with what is essentially a peel-out, be sure to build up enough speed to break past the eddy line.

Lean

Lean the boat downstream during the ferry so the current doesn't catch the edge of your boat and flip it. When you get to the eddy on the far side of the river, shift your weight to your upstream knee, as in an eddy turn, as you cross the eddy line.

Back Ferry

The back ferry is a maneuver for moving across a river or avoiding an obstacle. Unlike the standard ferry, where you angle the boat upstream and use forward strokes, the back ferry uses reverse strokes with the boat facing downstream.

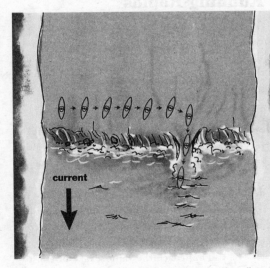

Use reverse strokes and careful leaning to move your boat laterally across the river toward an eddy, chute, or other target.

S-Turn

The S-turn is a maneuver for crossing a chute or narrow current lane, or for traveling through a mid-river eddy, going in one side and out the other. It is actually a quick, truncated ferry—it begins with a peel-out and ends with an eddy turn, and it requires you to lean the boat first one way and then the other in quick succession.

—From *Basic Kayaking*

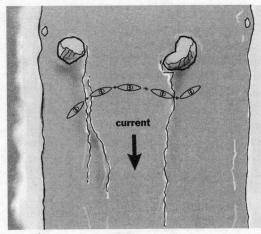

Think of the S-turn as a ferry for traveling short distances. It begins with a standard peel-out and ends with an eddy turn.

Ferries and Eddies for Canoes

Cecil Kuhne
Illustrations by Cherie Kuhne

The Ferry

The technique for crossing a river is commonly known as the ferry, and there are several types.

Upstream Ferry

In the forward, or upstream, ferry, you point your canoe upstream and, with forward strokes, paddle against the current. Set your canoe at a thirty- to forty-five-degree angle to the current, with the bow pointing toward the shore you wish to travel to. In a tandem canoe, the stern paddler is responsible for setting and maintaining the proper angle to the current.

When you set an angle to the current and paddle forward, the forces applied against your canoe move you across the river. Varying your paddling force and/or the angle to the current will determine your final direction of travel.

The disadvantage to this method is that you have to look over your shoulder to see obstacles downstream.

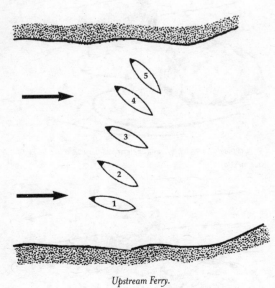

Upstream Ferry.

Downstream Ferry

The downstream ferry, with the bow of the boat headed downstream, uses the power of the river's current and a forward stroke to move your boat

across the river as you angle the bow toward the opposite bank. The angle is set and maintained by the bow paddler. With the back ferry, the bow is turned downstream as in the downstream ferry, only the paddle stroke is reversed. With the back ferry, you face the obstacle you want to avoid and backpaddle away from it. This technique allows you to see hazards downstream and to slow your speed in the current while moving laterally across the river. Unfortunately, the back ferry uses the much weaker back stroke.

Ferry Angle

You must adjust the ferry angle to account for the speed of the current and for how quickly you want to get across the river. To move across the river quickly, you should increase the angle of the canoe so that it is more perpendicular to the current. This increased angle, however, will increase the boat's speed downstream because there is more surface area to moved by the current.

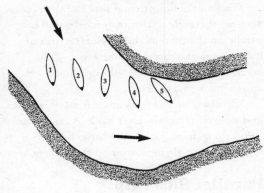

Downstream Ferry.

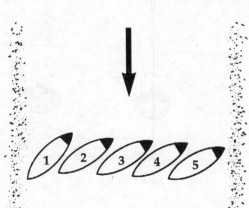

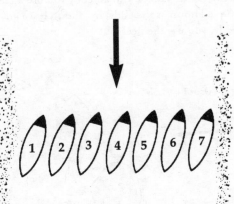

Ferry Angle.

Continued →

To slow the downstream speed of the canoe, decrease the angle so that the canoe is more parallel to the current and the surface area of the canoe in the current is decreased. This decreased angle, however, will not allow quick movement across the river.

Remember: The ferry angle is always relative to the current, not the river bank. A canoe may appear to be broadside to the bank, but have a proper ferry angle in relation to the current.

Parallel Side Slip

An easy maneuver that can be used to avoid rocks in a slow-moving current is the parallel side slip.

The bow paddler picks the route through the rocks by moving the front of the canoe to the left or right. The stern paddler quickly moves the back of the canoe in the left or right. The stern paddler quickly moves the back of the canoe in the canoe in the same direction, keeping the canoe parallel to the current.

The strokes used for this maneuver are the draw and the pry. The stern paddler counters with strokes opposite to those of the bow paddler. For example, the bow paddler, with a quick pry, points the front of the canoe in the desired direction until the middle of the canoe is past the obstacle. The stern paddler, with a quick draw, then straightens out the canoe so it is parallel to the current again.

The parallel side slip is effective only in a slow-moving current. As the current's speed increases, you must use a different maneuver. A canoe moving sideways, even slightly, makes a larger target for a rock.

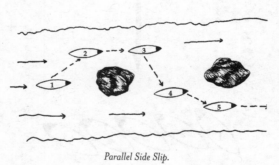

Parallel Side Slip.

Eddy Turns

Eddies often offer superb resting places in the river, and for this reason they are very useful to canoers. To paddle into an eddy you use a technique known as the eddy-in, and to leave an eddy, you use the peel-out.

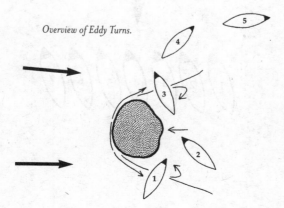

Overview of Eddy Turns.

Entering an Eddy

To eddy-in, point your canoe toward the top (upstream end) of the eddy, starting well upstream of the eddy so that the current will not carry you past it. Paddle forward and enter the eddy with good forward momentum.

The moment the bow crosses the eddy line and enters the calm water in the eddy, your canoe will start to spin because of the current differentials. As the canoe spins, you must lean into the turn, (i.e., upstream) to avoid overturning.

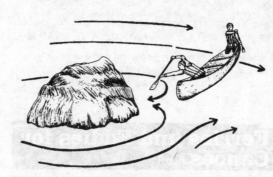

The bow paddler uses a high brace, and the stern paddler uses a forward sweep to enter an eddy.

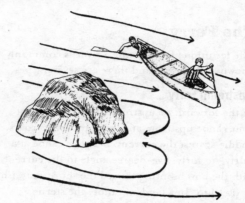

The bow paddler uses a pry, and the stern paddler uses a low brace to enter an eddy.

Leaving an Eddy

The peel-out is the method used to leave an eddy. A similar maneuver to the eddy-in, it uses the same techniques of turning on the eddy line.

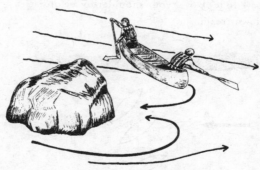

The bow paddler uses a pry, and the stern paddler uses a low brace to leave an eddy.

The bow paddler uses a high brace, and the stern paddler uses a forward sweep to leave an eddy.

Paddle upstream in the eddy, and point the canoe so that it will cross the eddy line at a ninety-degree angle. It is important to have enough forward speed to carry you across the eddy line and into the current. Then, you must lean into the turn (i.e., downstream).

—From *Paddling Basics: Canoeing*

Tackling Other River Hazards: Kayaks and Canoes

Cecil Kuhne
Illustrations by Cherie Kuhne

Avoiding Rocks

Some rivers have rapids strewn with rocks and boulders. These are called boulder gardens or rock gardens. Scout such rapids and plan a careful route through them. Use eddies that form behind rocks to assist your turns and to slow your boat down.

It is best to anticipate upcoming rocks well in advance. If you're about to broach on a rock and you can't avoid the collision, lean toward the rock, allowing the current to flow underneath your boat. If you follow your instincts and lean away from the rock, the kayak or canoe could flip, fill with water, and become pinned against the rock. Fortunately, many boulders have a pillow on the upstream side, which tends to push you away from the rock.

Running Rapids

After you've taken a long, close look at the rapids ahead, either from the boat or from shore, and have decided on your route through the whitewater maze, it's time for the run—and some fun!

The Entry

Selecting the proper entry into a set of rapids is very important, because it often determines the rest of the run. The V-shaped tongue at the head of most rapids typically points to the deepest and least obstructed channel. When there's more than one tongue, the best one will usually be the longest one or the one that drops most quickly.

As you approach the rapids, take one last look at where you're going. Once you've decided on the route, don't change your mind midstream unless you see something significant that you didn't spot earlier.

The basic rule is to keep the boat headed directly into the waves of the rapids. This is the most stable position; a boat that's sideways to the current is much more prone to overturning.

Avoiding Holes

Knowing which holes to avoid is the essence of the art. Slowing your speed downstream is essential, and this is typically accomplished through a series of ferry maneuvers across the river, moving the boat along the deepest and least obstructed channels.

If there are holes you can't avoid, try to punch through them as hard and fast as you can. This maneuver takes advantage of the current

Continued ➡

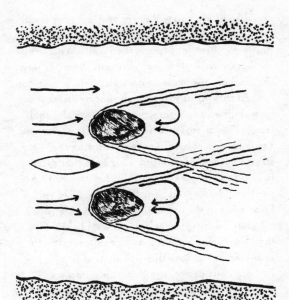

Proper Entry into the Tongue.

flowing downstream of the hole. Throwing your weight downstream may also help you push through.

Negotiating Bends

The ferry maneuver is especially important on a bend in the river. Currents don't curve with the river's bends. Instead, they flow in a straight line from the inside of the bend to the outside. The river's tendency, as a result, is to move a boat to the outside of the bend, where the deepest and fastest current is usually found. The swift currents tend to sweep boaters into cliff walls, large boulders, and downed trees. You need to anticipate this well in advance and begin correcting your course immediately. The back ferry is often the most effective stroke in this situation, since it allows you to see downstream and to slow your course downriver.

It's best to approach rapids on the inside of a bend, so that you can avoid any obstacles along the outside. Once you've determined that the outside is clear, you can move to the deeper and faster current there.

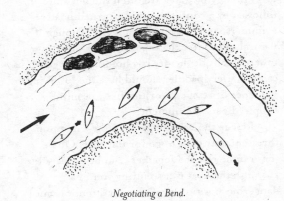

Negotiating a Bend.

Low-Water Technique

A river is generally less intimidating at lower water levels. There may be more obstacles to avoid, but the river is moving more slowly, allowing more time to scout rapids and make decisions. Less volume means reduced power as well, so the river may be more forgiving.

Constant rock dodging can be tiring, however. Load the kayak or canoe lightly so it

will be more maneuverable and easier to float over shallows.

To avoid the frustration of coming to a halt in shallow spots, watch ahead for signs of shoals. If the river is clear, a color change may alert you to shallows. Watch the surface of the river and follow the waves. River current favors the high bank and the outside bend.

High-Water Technique

Large rapids demand special skills. Don't attempt large-volume rivers until you're ready for them. The main problem is the incredible force of the current. Scout big-water rapids carefully from shore. Keep a lookout for eddies, which will offer a temporary haven from the rapids around you. If the water's cold, wear protective clothing.

Once on the river, you have to paddle hard into big waves so that the kayak or canoe doesn't slide backward. If you get knocked sideways by a powerful wave, correct your position immediately so that the kayak or canoe doesn't flip.

The greatest danger in high water comes from reversals, which can swell to enormous proportions. If you find yourself in a large hole, head in bow-first and paddle furiously. You'll need to generate enough speed to push through the wave and power your boat out of the hole. Should you lose momentum, you'll feel the kayak or canoe sliding backward. Brace hard downstream to keep it upright. You may be able to catch the current below the surface with your paddle, and then propel the beat free. The danger of reversals is that strong back currents can easily trap a swimmer, who is then recirculated until flushed out.

If you're caught in such a predicament, don't panic. The recirculating effect ends at the sides of the reversal; try to work your way out toward the sides. If this fails, thrust your paddle below the surface to reach the forward-flowing current.

You may have seen photographs of kayakers jumping waterfalls. This is definitely not recommended. Even experts have suffered neck injuries, leaving them quadriplegics for life. It's simply not worth the risk.

Surfing Waves

The art of surfing a river wave is much like riding an ocean swell, except that on a river the waves are stationary and the water moves through them.

Look for waves that are regular in shape and form. Turn your boat to face upstream as you enter the waves, then paddle as hard as you can, straight upstream. When the boat stalls on a wave, you're surfing. A rudder stroke will keep your boat from slipping sideways.

Wind

Wind can be just as much a hazard on a lake as rocks and rapids are on a river. There are a few techniques that will help you deal with windy conditions.

Headwinds

It's important to know the techniques for paddling into headwinds to keep the kayak or canoe from capsizing. Before crossing open waters, study your map or the horizon for the route that offers the best wind protection and the most possibilities for getting off the water should the wind increase.

To hold a kayak on course while heading into the wind, you need to paddle hard with quick and effective correction strokes. As waves increase in size and speed, the top of the wave curls over in a dangerous condition known as a breaking wave. As a breaking wave approaches, try to turn the bow straight into it. You'll lose some forward speed, but pushing straight into the waves reduces your chance of capsizing. When whitecaps occur, it is time to get off the lake.

Crosswinds

Paddling in crosswinds requires yet another set of tactics. Even in a light crosswind, you may be blown sideways and, as a result, you will arrive downwind of your desired destination. As crosswinds increase, the risk of being rolled over by the waves also increases. To avoid these problems, you need to angle into the waves, known as quartering the waves. Turn the bow into large breaking waves to avoid capsizing.

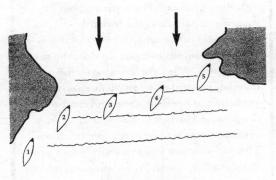

Negotiating Crosswinds.

Tailwinds

Paddling in tailwinds may sound simple because the wind is behind you. This may be true in light winds, but as wind and waves increase, tailwinds can become challenging. When a wave comes from behind you, it pushes the stern up. The kayak starts to pick up speed as it surfs down the face of the wave and buries its bow in the wave ahead. As the wave passes under the kayak it may pivot the boat sideways into the trough created between the two waves. If this happens, the kayak can easily capsize. To keep the kayak from turning into the trough, use a strong rudder or draw stroke.

—From *Paddling Basics: Kayaking*

Continued ➔

Wind and Canoes
Cecil Kuhne

Headwinds

The techniques for paddling into headwinds are important to keep the canoe from capsizing.

Before battling headwinds, study your map for possible windbreaks and resting spots. These might include the leeward shoreline, islands, or points of land. Plot a route that offers you the best wind protection and the most options for getting off the water if the wind should increase.

When you paddle into headwinds through large waves, you may need to lighten the bow so that it rises over the waves and takes in less water. This can be done by shifting gear toward the stern or putting the lighter paddler in the bow. Too light a bow can also be a problem, as it may catch the wind and be blown off course.

A little skill is required to hold a canoe on course while heading into the wind. To ensure forward progress, both paddlers need to paddle hard, with the stern paddler executing quick and effective correction strokes. If the stern paddler rudders, not only does he miss forward strokes, but the dragging paddle slows the forward momentum of the canoe.

As headwinds increase, so does the size of the waves. When the waves reach the point that they recirculate upon themselves, they are known as breaking waves and can be dangerous. The best tactic for dealing with breaking waves is to head directly into them. This will slow you down but will reduce your chances of capsizing. When whitecaps start to occur, it is time to get off the lake.

Crosswinds

Paddling crosswinds requires you to use another set of techniques. Even in a light crosswind, you can be blown sideways, and as the winds increase, so does the risk of capsizing. To avoid this possibility, you need to quarter the waves, which involves negotiating the waves at an angle. This angle is typically forty or fifty degrees, but in a strong wind, you will need to use a smaller angle to avoid your exposure to the wind. Remember to turn the bow into large breaking waves to avoid taking in water.

Tailwinds

You would think that paddling in a tailwind is helpful because the wind is behind you. This is true in light winds, but tailwinds can become a problem as they increase in strength. A large tailwind tends not only to lift the stern of the boat, but to push its bow into the wave ahead. As the wave picks up speed, it can pivot the canoe sideways. When this happens, you can easily turn over. To keep the canoe from turning sideways, use a strong rudder or draw stroke.

—From *Paddling Basics: Canoeing*

River Safety and Rescue
Wayne Dickert and Jon Rounds
Illustrations by Roberto Sabas

Staying Safe

The Paddling Group

Beginners, especially, should paddle in a group that includes at least one experienced paddler.

In a downriver group, the lead boater should be a strong paddler who, ideally, knows the particular river. But even on unfamiliar water, a skilled boater can run a rapid, then get out and direct the trailing members of the group to the best route through....The last boat in the group, the "sweep boat," should also have an experienced paddler, and this person must carry rescue gear and a first-aid kit and know how to use them. The least experienced or skilled paddlers should stay between the lead and sweep boats.

Five Factors Associated with Boating Fatalities

Statistics show five factors recur in boating fatalities.

1. Lack of PFD
At the scene of fatal boating accidents, PFDs are often found inside a swamped boat or floating beside it. Failure to have a PFD, or to wear it, is a common ingredient in drownings.

2. Cold Water or Air
Hypothermia caused by immersion in cold water is a leading cause of death in boating accidents. Such accidents often occur in the spring, when the air temperature is warm but the water is still cold, and boaters are not dressed warmly enough. Layered clothing of the right fabrics is essential in cold weather, especially when water is involved.

3. Inexperience
Inexperienced paddlers with no formal training are more likely to be victims of fatal accidents than trained, experienced paddlers.

4. Alcohol
Alcohol is a leading contributor to boating fatalities, as it inhibits both coordination and judgment.

5. Inability to Swim
Nonswimmers are more frequent drowning victims than swimmers.

Adapted from The American Canoe Association's Canoe and Kayaking Instruction Manual *by Laurie Gullion. Used with permission of Menasha Ridge Press.*

Scouting the River

When you're headed downriver and you approach a difficult-looking stretch, remember that you always have two choices: you can run it or carry around it. How can you possibly make this decision without seeing what's ahead? You can't. If you come to a blind corner, paddle to shore and get out of the boat to scout ahead. In a straight run, you can rarely see a whole stretch of river from down there at river level in your boat. If no one in your group has run the stretch, paddle to shore and walk downstream along the bank to scout it.

From a vantage point above the river, look at the whole rapid, from top to bottom, and visualize where you will enter and where you will exit. Can you locate the eddies and holes and plot a good route through the rapid? What are the hazards? Is there a way around them? If not, do you have the skills to navigate them?

At this point you have to soberly assess your own skills and how they match up with the challenges. Then answer this basic question: Are you ready for the consequences of running the stretch? If you can't avoid a big hole that's likely to flip you, do you have a solid Eskimo roll? Are you confident about doing a wet exit? Do you know what to do if someone throws you a rope?

Such decisions are complicated by the fact that whitewater kayakers, as a group, tend to be risk-takers, a personality profile that may include confidence, optimism, or simply a thrill-seeking defiance of danger. It's also true that most decisions about whitewater involve uncertainty. But in making such decisions, a veteran boater factors in the worst-case scenario and what he needs to do to survive it.

The very best way to orient yourself to the water is to bring someone who has paddled the route. Otherwise, talk to someone who has or consult guidebooks, maps, local paddling clubs, or paddling shops for river information. In using guidebooks, remember that river ratings are general guidelines that should be supported with more current and local information. You cannot assess the nature of a stretch solely on its difficulty rating. Fifty feet of Class III water is much less challenging than a full mile of it. Also, check the river level on the day of the run. Levels very dramatically with rainfall, drought, or dam releases, and there is no way to know the state of a river on a particular day without checking.

Finally, if you'll be paddling several miles, check a map to see where roads are in relation to the river, in case you have to pull out and go for help in an emergency.

River Rescue

Rescue Priorities

Flips in moving water are often sudden and followed by a confusion of overturned boats, swimmers, and floating equipment. Though it's natural to go after the expensive kayak floating toward a falls or the dry bag holding your good camera, every paddler should have the following sequence of rescue priorities fixed in mind: People, Boats, Equipment.

Rescue the swimmer first. If he's in a non-threatening situation, go for the boat. Often they can be rescued together. But be prepared to abandon the boat if it's putting you in a dangerous position or if all your attention must be focused on the swimmer. Lastly, retrieve equipment.

Safe Swimming Position

As a general rule, if you are thrown from a boat in fast water, immediately roll onto your back and float with your legs downstream, knees slightly bent and feet out of the water. This position lets you fend off rocks with your feet, rather than your head. Never stand up in fast water that is more than ankle-deep. The force of rushing water can shove a lifted foot between

Continued ➔

rocks so tightly that you can be knocked over and held under. Standing up in fast water is one of the most common causes of ankle and leg injuries—and worse, of drowning—among boaters.

There are three exceptions to the safe swimming position. (1) If you see a route to shore through navigable water, turn over on your stomach and swim aggressively toward it. In some situations, you can stay on your back and backstroke upstream into an eddy (just like backferrying in a boat). In any case, there are times when taking action is better than floating into a worse situation. (2) If you're being swept into a strainer—a downed tree or other obstruction with water flowing through it—turn around and approach it head-first. This position will let you pull yourself up onto the strainer with your arms. If you approach feet-first, the force of the current may drive you into the strainer below the surface and entrap you. (3) If you are about to be swept over a steep vertical drop, ball up: tuck your knees against your chest and wrap your arms around your legs.

If you are ejected from your boat in fast water, it's usually best to enter the safe swimming position. Float through the rapids on your back with your knees bent and your feet facing downstream. The rule is: "Toes and nose on the surface."

It's sometimes advisable to abandon the safe swimming position and swim for shore if there's a route through relatively safe water, especially if you're about to be swept into a more dangerous situation downstream. In these instances, roll over on your stomach and swim aggressively for safety.

Staying with the Boat

If you're ejected from your boat and it is within reach, hand onto it—if you can do so without endangering yourself. Grab the upstream grab loop, and always stay upstream of the boat. If you're downstream of the boat in a strong current, the boat can push you against an obstruction and pin you there. Don't get caught between your boat and a rock, and always be ready to let go of the boat if it's dragging you into a dangerous situation—it can be replaced.

Rope Rescue

A basic rule of river ethics is that every paddler should be prepared to rescue himself or others. Rope throwing is an essential rescue technique for whitewater paddlers. Every kayak in a group should carry a throw bag and every paddler should be practiced in throwing one. Putting a throw bag where you want it takes a little practice. Before a whitewater trip, each member should spend some time tossing a throw bag at a target. You may get only one shot in a critical situation. If there is only one rope in your group, it should be in the most experienced paddler's boat.

SWIMMING RAPIDS
Cecil Kuhne   Illustrations by Cherie Kuhne

Every paddler should know the basic safety rules for swimming through whitewater.

Posture
Hold on to your paddle, if you can, and get to the boat's upstream end. A boat full of water can otherwise pin you against an obstruction.

Float on your back with your feet held high and pointed downstream. That way, your feet, not your head, will meet the obstruction first. Backpaddle with your arms for control.

Breathing
Take a breath as you are carried into the trough of the wave. When the current lifts you to the crest of the wave, hold your breath. Depending on how large it is, the wave will probably come crashing over your head, inhibiting breathing for a few seconds.

Position
Stay with the boat until you get your strength and can see a safe place to land.

Swim to shore as quickly as possible.

Don't try to stand until the water is very shallow. If your feet get caught under a ledge or between two rocks, the current can knock you over and keep your head underwater.

Hazards
If you're about to be swept into a fallen tree, face forward and try to climb up onto it so you aren't swept underneath and trapped.

If you're headed for a big drop, tuck into a ball. This will protect your body if you hit the riverbottom.

Let go of your boat and any other gear if it drags you into a dangerous situation.

Most holes are too small to be keepers. If you aren't flushed out of a hole immediately, try to swim sideways out of the hole. Large holes can recirculate a swimmer almost indefinitely; the best way to escape the force is to reach the powerful downcurrent. You can do this by tucking yourself into a cannonball position (to avoid injury when you hit the riverbed) and then swimming hard after hitting the bottom to reach the deep currents moving downstream.

Currents that flow through sweepers and strainers pose some of the worst river hazards. If a collision with a downed tree is inevitable, approach it headfirst, and the moment before you hit it, kick with your legs and try to pull your body over it. Do anything you can to avoid entrapment.

Avoiding Entrapment
Stay alert for possible entrapment situations, such as sweepers and strainers, undercut rocks, and loose ropes. Never tie yourself into a boat on moving water. When being rescued by a throw line or when swimming in whitewater, never wrap or tie a rope around any part of your body. Secure all loose lines, and have cargo tied down with straps that are just long enough to do the job, without any extra length hanging loose. Carry a whitewater safety knife.

—From *Paddling Basics: Kayaking*

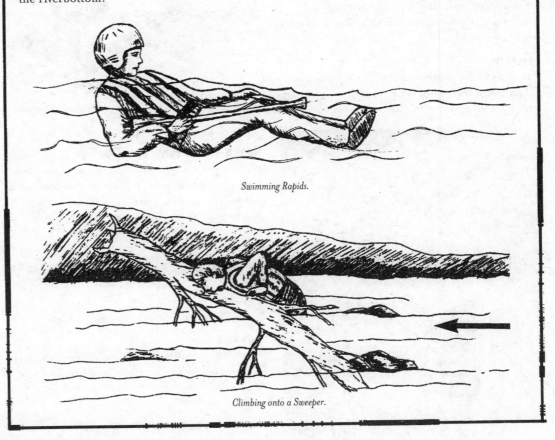

Swimming Rapids.

Climbing onto a Sweeper.

Continued ➡

Two general rules of rope rescue: (1) Never tie a rope to yourself, whether you're the thrower or the swimmer. You must be able to release the rope if it's pulling you under. (2) Carry a knife. Cutting a rope may save a life in the case of entanglement.

The rope thrower should be downstream of the swimmer and should throw the rope when the swimmer is still upstream of him.

ROPE-THROWER'S POSITION

When your group approaches a difficult stretch where capsizing is likely, a rope-thrower should be positioned on shore at a spot just downstream of the stretch, one that has solid footing and from which the swimmer can be pulled into calm water or an eddy.

THROW

First yell to the swimmer to get his attention. Then pull a few feet of rope from the throw bag and hold it in your non-throwing hand. When

Throw the rope underhand, aimed over the swimmer or just downstream of him—never short or upstream. You can always pull in some rope if the throw is too long.

you're ready to throw, yell "Rope!" and fling the bag toward the swimmer with an underhand or sidearm toss, holding the tag end of the rope with your non-throwing hand. The rope should land a little downstream of the swimmer, so he's floating toward, not away, from it. In other words, throw long, not short. The swimmer can always grab a rope that goes over him, but a short throw may be out of his reach.

BRINGING THE SWIMMER IN

Once the swimmer grabs the rope, brace yourself for his weight by leaning back or sitting down and digging your heels into the ground. Hold on and let the current swing him into shore. Don't pull the rope out of his hands trying to yank him in.

SWIMMER'S GRIP AND POSITION

If you're being rescued, hold the thrown rope to your chest once you catch it—never tie or wrap it around any part of your body. Roll over on your back with the rope over your shoulder while being pulled in. If you face forward on your stomach, your face will get the full force of the water your head could be towed under.

Lie on your back with the rope over your shoulder when being towed to shore.

If you are face-down when being towed, your head can be dragged underwater.

Reach-Throw-Row-Tow-Go

When a paddler goes overboard and you're faced with a rescue decision, remember this lifesaver's adage. The sequence proceeds from shore-based, to boat-based, to water-based rescue.

Reach.
First try to reach the swimmer while standing on shore.

Throw.
If you can't reach him, throw him a rope.

Row and Tow.
If you have no rope or he's too far away to reach with a rope, paddle or row out to him and tow him in.

Go.
The last resort is going into the water after a swimmer, which is the most dangerous option, especially for someone untrained in lifesaving.

—From *Basic Kayaking*

SELF-RESCUE: KAYAKERS

Cecil Kuhne
Illustration by Cherie Kuhne

The most important rescue technique to know is the self-rescue. If you should go overboard, there may be no one else around, and even with other paddlers around you, it's easier and faster for you to rescue yourself than to depend on someone else.

First and most important, don't panic. Remember to hold on to your paddle, because you're going to need it once you're back in the boat. Next, look for your boat; in most cases, it will be right next to you.

Grab onto the kayak. The bottom of the kayak will be smooth and slippery, and therefore difficult to hold. The grab loops at the bow and stern offer good handholds, as does the cockpit.

Once you grab the kayak, keep it upside down while you tow it to shore. Air is trapped inside, causing it to ride higher on the water. Always stay upstream from the boat to avoid being pinned between it and a rock or other obstruction.

Don't try to stand up in a moving current, even if the water is shallow, because it can easily knock you over. Your feet could then become pinned under a rock, and if the current pushes your head underwater, you could drown in a few feet of water.

—From *Paddling Basics: Kayaking*

Pulling the Swamped Boat to Shore.

Continued →

HAND/PADDLE SIGNALS
Cecil Kuhne Illustrations by Cherie Kuhne

A set of hand or paddle signals, agreed upon at the beginning of the trip, can be helpful in communicating from boat to boat. This is especially the case where there is some distance between boats and the roar of rapids makes communication impossible. Signals should be simple: hands or paddle outstretched horizontally for stop, a waved hand or paddle for help, and a hand or paddle outstretched vertically for all clear.

—From *Paddling Basics: Kayaking*

"Stop!"

"Help! Emergency!"

"All Clear—Proceed Down Center."

"All Clear—Proceed This Way."

SELF-RESCUE: CANOERS
Cecil Kuhne Illustrations by Cherie Kuhne

If you should go overboard, the most important rescue technique to know is self-rescue. First of all, there may be no one else around. And even with other paddlers around you, it's easier and faster for you to rescue yourself than to depend on someone else.

Most important, don't panic. Hold onto your paddle, because you're going to need it once you're back in the boat. Next, look for your boat. In most cases, it will be right next to you.

Now is when handholds attached to the boat come into play. The bottom of the canoe will be smooth and slippery, and therefore difficult to hold onto. But the painters at the bow and stern will offer good handholds.

Once you grab the canoe, you will need to turn it upright. If the boat is empty, you may be able to turn it over in the middle of the river or lake. If the boat is loaded, you will probably have to swim the boat to shore.

Getting back into an upright boat is a matter of pulling yourself over the side. Put the paddle inside first. If you're on a river, approach the boat from the upstream side, to avoid being pinned between it and a rock. If you can't get back into the canoe, you will still want to keep the boat downstream so there's no chance of being wedged between it and a rock. If you can't reenter the boat in the river, pull it to shore or into an eddy.

Don't try to stand up in a moving current, even if the water is shallow, because it can easily knock you over. Your feet could then become pinned under a rock, and if the current pushed your head under water, you could drown in a few feet of water.

—From *Paddling Basics: Canoeing*

Pulling the Swamped Boat to Shore.

Getting Back into the Boat.

Life Jackets/PFDs

Personal Flotation Devices (PFDs)
Greg Davenport

All recreational vessels are required to carry one wearable PFD (Type I, II, III, or V PFD) for each person aboard. Boats 16 feet and longer, except canoes and kayaks, must also carry one throwable PFD (Type IV). All PFD devices must be in good serviceable condition, meet coast guard approval, and fit the intended user. For best results, a PFD should be worn at all times, but if you are not wearing the device, it should be easily accessible and you should know how to put it on quickly in case of an emergency. The throwable device also should be visible and ready for immediate use. Although federal law does not require PFDs on racing shells, rowing sculls, racing canoes, and racing kayaks, state laws vary greatly and may mandate otherwise.

Three basic designs for personal flotation devices

INHERENTLY BUOYANT
Mostly made of foam, this very reliable wearable and throwable PFD comes in all sizes and is made for both swimmers and nonswimmers.

INFLATABLE
This wearable PFD is made for the adult swimmer at least sixteen years old. Its compact design makes it easy to wear and perform routine tasks without getting in the way. To meet coast guard requirements, this PFD must have a full cylinder, and all status indicators on the inflator must be green.

HYBRID
Foam and inflatable combined, this reliable wearable PFD comes in all sizes and is made for both swimmers and nonswimmers.

Types of personal flotation devices

TYPE I
Type I is created for offshore use and is effective in all waters, including rough seas, or where rescue may be delayed. This extremely buoyant PFD is designed to turn an unconscious wearer face up in the water.

TYPE II
Type II is created for near-shore use and is effective in calm inland waters or where a quick rescue can be expected. This PFD will also turn an unconscious wearer face up in the water, but not as often or with the same ease as type I.

TYPE III
Type III is created for use in calm, inland water where a quick rescue can be expected. The wearer must actively maintain a face-up position and must therefore be conscious for the PFD to work.

TYPE IV
This throwable PFD is for use in calm, inland waters where help is always available. Not intended as a wearable PFD, this device is thrown into the water so that the person overboard can grasp it and be pulled to the vessel.

Continued ➡

TYPE V

This special-use PFD comes in many formats depending on the type of activity it was made to be used with. It can be carried instead of another PFD, but only if it is used in accordance with its labeling. Because some of these devices provide hypothermia protection, they make excellent multiuse items.

Purchasing a PFD

When purchasing a personal floatation device, be sure it is Coast Guard approved. Try it on. The PFD should fit snuggly to your body yet allow you to freely move your arms. To make sure it fits right, zip it up, tighten down the straps, and raise your arms over your head. Are you able to move them freely while the device is tightened down? Next, have someone raise the PFD straight up your shoulders. If the zipper reaches your nose or higher, get a smaller PFD. If you are able, test the PFD in water to make sure that it keeps your mouth and nose above the waterline when your head is tilted back. The optimal PFD includes pockets and clips capable of storing emergency gear like whistles, mirrors, strobes, and flares.

—From *Surviving Coastal and Open Water*

Life Jackets for Kayaks and Canoes

Cecil Kuhne
Illustration by Cherie Kuhne

Few pieces of boating gear have progressed more in comfort and safety than the life jacket. The "personal flotation device," or PFD, as they are called by the Coast Guard, can generally be described by their type.

For safety, you'll need a Type III or Type V PFD. Type III PFDs, usually shorter and with flotation "ribs" rather than "slabs," are designed for canoers and kayakers who require more freedom of motion than Type V PFDs allow. The Type V category covers special designs for whitewater, generally with commercial raft passengers in mind. These jackets offer greater flotation and safety than the Type III, but tend to be bulkier and more restrictive. (Incidentally, Type I is the bulky, orange "Mae West" jacket filled with kapok; Type II is the horse-collar version, which is inadequate for river use; and Type IV is a buoyant seat cushion, unsuitable for just about everything.)

When choosing a PFD, favor safety over comfort. PFDs designed for hard-shell kayakers often have extra flotation in the area below the waist, and these can be flipped up for comfort. The amount of flotation you require in a life jacket depends primarily on your body's own flotation, your experience, and the kind of whitewater you'll be tackling.

Life Jacket

For easy rivers, a "shortie" Type III offers a good measure of safety and unrestricted motion. In whitewater, a Type V or a high-flotation version of a Type III is better. There should be sufficient buckles and straps to secure the jacket firmly around your body. You'll want to wear the PFD snugly to keep it from riding up over your head, so make certain your jacket fits well.

Always fasten all buckles, zippers, and waist-ties when you put the life jacket on. Never wear the PFD loose or open in the front, and pull the side straps down snug. This is also important to avoid entangling yourself should the boat overturn. Make a habit, too, of securing your life jacket when you take it off, so the wind doesn't blow it away.

A good PFD will give you years of protection if treated properly. Don't use your life jacket as a seat cushion. After each trip, hang the jacket to maintain its shape and prevent it from getting mildew. Clean it often, using a mild soap so as not to harm the interior foam.

—From *Paddling Basics: Canoeing*

Clothing at Sea

Greg Davenport

Parka and Rain Pants

A parka and rain pants will protect you from moisture and wind. They are normally made from nylon with a polyurethane coating, a waterproof coating that breathes, or a laminated waterproof membrane that breathes (Gore-Tex). Sometimes, a parka will come with an insulating garment that can be zipped inside. Regardless of which material you choose, your parka and rain pants should meet the following criteria.

Size

These garments should be big enough for you to comfortably add wicking and insulating layers underneath without compromising your movement. The parka's lower end also should extend beyond your hips to keep moisture away from the top of your pants.

Dual Separating Zippers

Look for zippers that separate at both ends.

Ventilation Adjustment

The openings for parkas should be located in front, at your waist, under your arms, and at your wrist. The openings for rain pants should be located in the front and along the outside of the lower legs to about midcalf to make it easier to add or remove boots. Pants for women are available with a zipper that extends down and around the crotch. These openings can be adjusted with zippers, Velcro, or drawstrings.

Sealed Seams

Seams must be taped or well bonded to prevent moisture from penetrating through the clothing.

Accessible Pockets

What good is a pocket if you can't access it? Make sure the pocket opening has a protective rain baffle.

Brimmed Hood

A brimmed hood will help channel moisture away from the eyes and face. In addition, a neck flap will help prevent loss of radiant body heat from the neck area.

Dry and Wet Suits

When deciding whether to wear a wet or dry suit, consider the insulation and protective qualities of the suits. How cold is the water, and how long will you be submersed? Are you in an area where you need to protect your skin? Without an appropriate suit, long submersions in water with temperatures below 98 degrees F will decrease your body's core temperature, which could lead to hypothermia. The two types of suits available are wet and dry. When deciding which suit to buy, select one that provides the best protection from exposure and skin scrapings. A bright-colored suit is a better signal and preferred to the black versions. Consider a full body suit that has a snug fit without any compromise in arm or leg movement. Make sure the suit fits well and has good seam placement and that its wrist and ankle seals are tight but not too tight as to cut off circulation. Next, consider the thickness of the material. Use the following guide as a general rule of thumb when deciding how thick your suit should be. Recognize that thicker is probably better, and you should always err on the conservative side.

Water Temperature	Recommended Thickness
75°–85° F	1/16-inch (1.6 mm) neoprene, Lycra, Polartec
70°–85° F	1/8-inch (3 mm) neoprene
65°–75° F	3/16-inch (5 mm) neoprene
50°–70° F	1/4-inch (6.5 mm) neoprene
35°–65° F	3/8-inch (9.5 mm) neoprene, dry suit

Wet Suits

Although some wet suits are used in cold water, most are created for use in cool to warm waters. Mostly made of closed-cell foam called neoprene, the suits come in a variety of thicknesses and are made to fit snuggly to the body. Wet suits keep you warm by decreasing the amount of heat lost from conduction (direct contact) and convection (current movement around the body). Trapped air bubbles in the neoprene help to insulate you from heat loss due to conduction, and a well-fitting suit with minimal inside water flow helps to protect you from heat loss due to convection. A polyester layer next to the skin and an outer jacket that is coated rubber or Gore-Tex will increase the insulation value of your wet suit. Because a full-body wet suit is too restrictive in the arms for some, they use a farmer john's suit (a full wet suit with no arms) instead. These suits are mostly appropriate in places with mild to moderate weather conditions most of the time.

Dry Suits

Dry suits were originally created for use in cold water, but they may also be worn in places with mild to moderate temperatures. These watertight suits are made of foam neoprene, coated rubber, or Gore-Tex. Because neoprene and coated rubber don't allow body heat and moisture to escape, you will get wet from the inside.

Continued ➡

Gore-Tex, on the other hand, allows body moisture (radiant heat), not droplets of sweat, to escape while it still protects you from outside moisture. All of the options provide little to no insulation value, so to keep warm, you will need to wear an inner wicking layer and a middle insulation layer under the dry suit. The seals at the wrist, ankles, and neck of the suit must be extremely tight but not too tight to cut off your circulation. Some dry suits come with boots and hoods as part of the garment. Once you have the suit on, you will need to burp the suit to expel all of its excess inner air.

Immersion Suits

Most immersion suits are full-body type V flotation devices designed to handle prolonged exposure to cold water and provide face-up flotation. These brightly colored suits often have built-in buoyancy support, adjustable spray shields, reflective tape, hoods, booties, gloves, and inflatable head rests. Adult suits are sold as one size fits all and can be worn by a person weighing anywhere from 110 to 330 pounds. Suits should be inspected at least once a year and placed in an area that you can quickly access should an emergency occur. Because time is of the essence in an emergency when you need to put on an immersion suit, the USCG recommends that you practice until you can get the suit on in sixty seconds or less.

Headgear and Neoprene Hoods

Since more than 50 percent of your body heat is lost through your head, you must keep it covered. There are many styles of headgear, and your activity and the elements will dictate which style you choose. As a general rule, there are two basic types of headgear: rain hat and insulating hat.

Rain Hat

A rain hat is often made from nylon or an insulation material with an outer nylon covering. For added waterproof and breathable characteristics, Gore-Tex is often used. For added protection in extreme conditions, choose a hat with earflaps. These hats perform best when worn while in the vessel or on shore.

Insulating Hat

An insulating hat is made from wool, polypropylene, polyester fleece, or neoprene. The most common styles are the watch cap, the balaclava, and the neoprene hood or hooded vest. The balaclava is a great option in the vessel or on shore since it covers the head, ears, and neck yet leaves an opening for your face. Neoprene hoods and hooded vests are good choices for water wear.

Since so much heat is lost through the head, headgear should not be the first thing you take off when you are overheating. Mild adjustments, such as opening the zipper to your coat, will allow for the gradual changes you need to avoid sweating. In cold conditions, headgear should only be removed when other options have not cooled you down enough.

Gloves and Mittens

Since a fair amount of heat is lost from the hands, you should keep them covered. Gloves encase each individual finger and allow you the dexterity to perform many of your daily tasks. Mittens, which encase the fingers together, decrease your dexterity but increase hand warmth from the captured radiant heat. Which type you decide to wear will depend on your activity. I often will wear gloves when working with my hands, and then when not working, I will insert the gloved hand inside a mitten. My gloves are made from a polyester fleece or a wool/synthetic blend. My mittens are made from a waterproof yet breathable fabric, such as Gore-Tex. When in the water, I often will wear neoprene gloves.

Shoes/Boots

Boots, a very important part of your clothing, should fit your needs and be broken in before your trip. When selecting boots, consider the type of travel you intend to do. I have four styles of boots, each of which serves a different purpose. They are made of leather, lightweight leather/fabric, rubber, and neoprene.

Leather Boots

Leather boots are the ideal all-purpose boot. Under extreme conditions, you will need to treat them with a waterproofing material (read the manufacturer's directions on how this should be done) and wear a comfortable, protective wool-blend sock. Another popular option in leather boots is the added Thinsulate and Gore-Tex liner, which help to protect your feet from cold and moist conditions. If you decide to use Thinsulate or Gore-Tex, be sure to follow the manufacturer's directions explicitly on how to care for and treat the boots. If oils soak through the leather and into the lining, the insulating qualities of the boots will be nullified. Although leather makes a good boot for on shore, it might not be the best option for on a deck or in a kayak.

Lightweight Leather/Fabric Boots

The lightweight boot is a popular fair-weather boot because it is lighter and dries faster than the leather boot. On the downside, moisture easily soaks through the fabric and creates less stability for your ankle. Depending on the style of boot sole, it may or may not be a good option for deck or kayak use.

Rubber Boots

Rubber boots are most often used for extreme cold-weather conditions. They normally have nylon uppers with molded rubber bottoms. The felt inner boot can be easily removed and dries quickly. These boots perform well on a deck but tend to be too bulky for kayak use.

Neoprene Bootie

Neoprene booties that are made for kayaking are a good option to wear both in the kayak and on the deck. They have the insulation qualities of neoprene, boast a rigid sole, and provide good support when walking.

Keeping your boots clean will help them protect you better. For leather and lightweight leather/fabric boots, wash off dirt and debris using a mild soap that doesn't damage leather. For rubber and neoprene boots, wash and dry the liners and clean all dirt and debris from the outer boots. If you decide to waterproof the leather boot, check with the manufacturer on its recommendations for what to use.

Socks

Socks need to provide adequate insulation, reduce friction, and wick away and absorb moisture from the skin. Most socks are made of wool, polyester, nylon, or an acrylic material. Wool tends to dry slower than the other materials but its still a great option. Cotton should be avoided because it collapses when wet and loses its insulation qualities. For best results, wear two pairs of socks. The inner sock (often made of polyester) wicks moisture away from the foot; the outer sock (often a wool-blend material) provides insulation to keep your feet warm. During extremely wet conditions, Gore-Tex socks are often worn over the outer pair of socks. Regardless of which sock you decide to wear, be sure to keep your feet dry and change your socks at least once a day. Immediately apply moleskin to any hot spots that develop on your feet before they become blisters.

Eye Protection

Goggles or sunglasses with side shields that filter out UV wavelengths are a must while traveling in open water. It doesn't take long to burn the eyes, and once this happens, you will have several days of eye pain along with light sensitivity, tearing, and a foreign body sensation. Since the symptoms of the burn usually don't show up until four to six hours after the exposure, you will get burned and not even realize it is happening. Once a burn occurs, you must get out of the light, remove contacts if you are wearing them, and cover the eyes with a sterile dressing until the light sensitivity subsides. If pain medication is available, you will probably need to use it. Once healed, be sure to protect the eyes to prevent another burn. If you do not have goggles or sunglasses, improvise some by using either a manmade a natural material to cover the eyes and provide a narrow horizontal slit for each eye.

Zippers

Zippers often break or get stuck on garments and sleeping bags. While this may not present a great problem under mild conditions, you can lose a lot of body heat when you are unable to use a zipper properly in a wet and cold-weather environment. To decrease the odds of this occurring, make sure your gear has a zipper with a dual separating system (separates at both ends) and teeth made from a material, such as polyester, which won't rust or freeze. To waterproof your zippers, either use a baffle covering or apply a waterproof coating to the zipper's backing. The waterproof coating allows for lighter weight and easier access to the zipper.

Continued →

Skin Protection

Ultraviolet (UV) radiation that reflects off of the water is very intense. The best way to avoid debilitating and painful sunburn during travel into a hot or cold, wet environment is to wear protective clothing. For skin that cannot be covered, use a sunscreen or sunblock. Sunscreens are available in various sun protection factor (SPF) ratings, which indicate how much longer than normal you can be exposed to UV radiation before burning. Sunscreens work by absorbing the UV radiation. Sunblock reflects the UV radiation and is most often used in sensitive areas such as the ears and nose, where intense exposure might occur. Regardless of what you use, you will need to constantly reapply it throughout the day as its effectiveness is lost over time and due to sweating.

—From *Surviving Coastal and Open Water*

Sea Gear

Greg Davenport
Illustrations by Steven A. Davenport

The coast guard has established minimum standards for recreational vessels and associated safety equipment. These standards require most equipment to meet coast guard-approval guidelines for performance and construction.

Survival Crafts

If you are a recreational boater, you should have a buoyant apparatus, an inflatable buoyant apparatus, or a life raft.

Buoyant apparatus

A buoyant apparatus is a quick-response lifesaving device that comes in a variety of shapes, sizes, and styles. Its rigid double-sided reversible design allows for rapid manual launching—with minimal preparation—during a crisis. A buoyant apparatus can be used as a lifeline during a rescue or to keep you afloat in case your vessel is sinking. Often rectangular in shape, the apparatus has either a solid platform or a solid outer ring with a central compartment that can be used to keep gear afloat. Lifelines attached to the

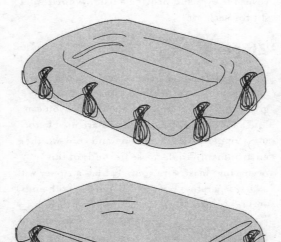

Buoyant apparatus.

outside of the apparatus are designed so that someone immersed in the water can hold on to them to stay afloat.

Inflatable buoyant apparatus

Although better than a buoyant apparatus, an inflatable buoyant apparatus falls short of a life raft. The inflatable buoyant apparatus is intended for use aboard vessels operating close to shore. This device comes in various shapes and sizes, and unlike a buoyancy apparatus, it will support you and a varying number of occupants out of the water. Normally these devices have only one buoyancy tube and do not have an inflatable floor or canopy. Like a life raft, they can be stored in a valise or hard deck-mount type of container.

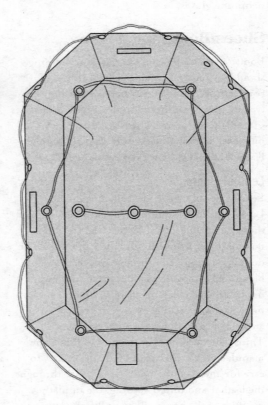

Inflatable buoyant apparatus.

Life Raft

The inflatable life raft is an extremely important lifesaving device that all boats should have. Life rafts vary greatly from manufacturer to manufacturer and from one style to another. Take the time to become familiar with the raft you carry before it is time to use it. Since your raft is packed, ask your vendor or servicing representative to demonstrate how to inflate your particular raft. You should also make sure to have the raft serviced in accordance with the manufacturer's recommendations. When purchasing a life raft, consider the following.

SIZE AND SHAPE

Inflatable life rafts, which must be coast guard approved, come in round, oval, octagonal, or boat shapes. Raft capacities normally range from four to twenty-six people. The type and size of raft you choose for your vessel will depend on many factors: Are you staying close to the coastline? Are you heading into international waters? How many people will be on board the vessel, and what is their experience?

INFLATION TUBES

The ideal raft will have two separate inflation tubes (buoyancy tubes) located on its outer edge. For increased stability and decreased tube bending, tubes need to be at least 12 inches in diameter when inflated. A cylinder of carbon dioxide (CO_2) alone or in combination with nitrogen is used to inflate the raft. The cylinder is normally attached to the bottom of the raft and can be activated by sharply pulling the line, usually a 100-foot-long operating cord, attached to it.

PRESSURE RELIEF VALVES

Most rafts have a pressure relief valve located in the inflation tubes that allows excess gas to escape. The valves will also allow air to escape during warm days when the gas in the tube expands. On the flip side, in the evening when cooler temperatures cause the air to contract, you may have to manually pump more air into the chambers. While it is normal for pressure relief valves to hiss while gas escapes right after the raft is inflated, this process should last only a few minutes. On occasion, pressure relief valves will fail and continue to leak gas. If that happens, you will have to plug the valve using one of the plugs in your life raft repair kit.

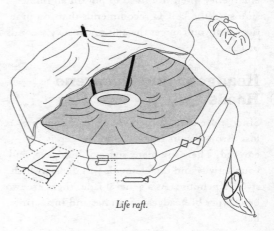

Life raft.

RAFT FLOOR

Most life rafts have a double floor that can be inflated with a hand pump. In cold weather, inflating the floor will keep you warmer by creating an insulating dead air space between you and the cold water. In hot weather, however, keeping the floor deflated allows the cooler seawater to keep you cool.

ARCHES

Most rafts have an inflatable arch, and some have two or three. The arches support a canopy that can be used to protect you from rain, wind, and sun.

STABILIZERS

A life raft is stabilized by its ballasts and sea anchor. Ballasts are water pockets located under the life raft that allow seawater inside when the raft is launched. In addition to stabilizing the raft by making it less likely to capsize, the ballasts also help slow the raft's drift. The number and size of ballasts on a raft vary from one manufacturer to another. Like the ballasts, a sea anchor is used to help stabilize the raft, especially in rough seas when waves are coming from the same direction as the wind. Make sure the anchor is made of a strong durable material and is big enough to make a difference in rough water.

Continued ➡

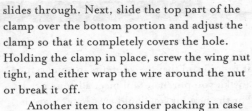

Refer to chapter 12 for further details on how to use a sea anchor.

SURVIVAL KIT

USCG-approved life rafts provide a survival kit. Be sure to check its contents and talk to your vendor about adding any other materials when the raft is packed or serviced. For more details on life raft survival kits, refer to page 350.

LIFE RAFT STORAGE

If your life raft is kept in a canister, it will probably sit on a cradle that is secured on top of the open deck. The greatest benefit of this storage method is easy access. Another benefit to this system is that the canister will float free of the vessel in case it would sink before you can manually launch the raft. The canister is made of two compartments that create a watertight seal when combined. The two compartments are held together by bands that break when the raft is inflated. Holes on the bottom of the canister allow condensation drainage and air circulation, and the words "this side up" on the top of the container will help you make sure the holes are down. Tie-down straps, which often are used to secure a container to the cradle, support a hydrostatic release that can be kicked to free the canister from the cradle. Other releases are used, so be sure to familiarize yourself with your system. Often, a cleat is located near the cradle and can be used to tie a retaining line when manually launching the raft. Since most inflation lanyards separate from the raft when activated, don't mistake them for a retaining line. Life rafts that are stored in a valise are often stowed below deck and out of the way. During an emergency, these rafts must be brought to the surface for launching.

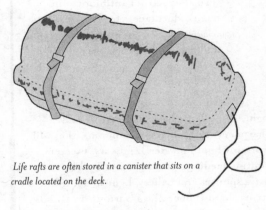

Life rafts are often stored in a canister that sits on a cradle located on the deck.

LIFE RAFT PADDLES

Life raft paddles come in many designs, and the exact type of paddle you have will depend on your life raft. While these paddles are helpful near land, when trying to make landfall, and when moving away from a sinking vessel, they are seldom used otherwise. This is because paddling a raft uses up precious energy that should be conserved during a life-threatening situation. If you decide to move the raft by paddling, pull in the sea anchors, empty the ballast pockets, and place one paddler at each side of the raft.

A smaller life raft without the canopy.

The same raft with the canopy up.

Life Raft Repair Kits

If your life raft would develop a hole, you would be glad you packed a repair kit. Don't be fooled into thinking that a kit containing rubber tube patches and cement will fix your problem. Not only do these patches require a dry work area and are only useful for extremely small holes, but you cannot completely inflate the raft until the patch has had twenty-four hours to dry. If you do decide to use these patches, be sure to cut the patch at least 1 inch larger than the hole it is covering. Next, apply cement to both the patch and the area around the hole, and allow both to completely dry before applying a second coat to both. Once the second coating reaches a tacky texture, press the patch on the hole. Do not completely inflate the raft until the patch has had twenty-four hours to dry.

A better way to seal raft holes is to carry raft repair clamps. Unlike the patches, clamps provide an immediate fix to your problem. Repair clamps come in small, medium, and large sizes (3, 5, and 8 inches), allowing you to choose the size that best fits the needed repair. The clamp is made of two pieces of convex metal, with outer rubber edges, that are connected by a post and wing nut that run through the center of each. When using a clamp, loop its cord around your wrist to prevent the accidental loss of the clamp overboard. Next, get the clamp wet so that it will be easier to insert inside the hole. Push the clamp's bottom plate through the hole, and pull it up against the inner surface of the tube. If the hole is too small, enlarge it enough so that the clamp barely

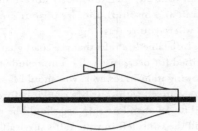

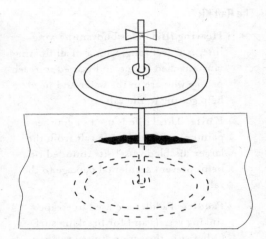

Raft repair clamps are ideal for sealing a hole in your raft.

slides through. Next, slide the top part of the clamp over the bottom portion and adjust the clamp so that it completely covers the hole. Holding the clamp in place, screw the wing nut tight, and either wrap the wire around the nut or break it off.

Another item to consider packing in case

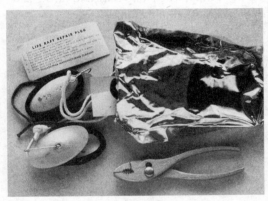

Life raft repair clamps.

you need to repair raft leaks is a roll of sail-mending tape or duct tape. Sail-mending and duct tape are effective for sealing small leaks that occur above the waterline. Not all sail-mending and duct tape brands are the same, so make sure the one you select sticks when wet. Leaks can also occur at pressure release and topping valves. Be sure to know whether your raft has a plug for these devices and to carry several spares of each in case one is lost.

Abandon-Ship Bags

An abandon-ship bag is simply a survival and first-aid kit that floats. The contents of each kit will depend upon many variables, including your sport, the length of your outing, and the time of year. These bags are great for storing emergency gear and should be placed in an easily accessible location. You should also tie a lanyard line to the bag's D-ring with a carabiner at the other

Continued ➡

ABANDON-SHIP BAGS
Greg Davenport

It is doubtful that the contents in your raft or any kit you purchase will meet all your needs. For the best kit you could ever have, make it yourself! Many factors will influence what you put in your kit, including cost, storage space (in raft and on ship), the size of your crew, and where you're traveling.

Inflatable life rafts that are coast guard certified for ocean use will often include the following items. However, you should familiarize yourself with your life raft kit before you need it. An abandon-ship bag should be used to fill the voids left in your raft's survival kit.

The Raft Kit

- **Heaving line**: This buoyant heaving line, 100 feet long, with a small floating ring attached at one end is used to reach people who are in the water and need help getting to the raft.

- **Knife**: This knife is used to cut the painter and free the life raft from the larger disabled vessel. Its rounded tip helps prevent accidental damage to the raft.

- **Paddles**: Paddles are used to escape sinking vessels and for breaking surf. Otherwise, they are not used at open sea except as a shark club.

- **Pump**: The pump is used to inflate and adjust cell inflation as needed.

- **Sea anchors**: Often two sea anchors, which are attached to 50 feet of nylon, are provided. Usually one deploys when the raft inflates, and the other is a spare.

- **Bailers**: Bailers are used to ride the raft of water.

- **Sponges**: Used to dry the bottom of the raft, sponges play an important role in preventing saltwater sores and heat loss.

- **First-aid kit**: Most rafts include a first-aid kit. Take time to look it over and augment it as appropriate.

- **Flashlight**: A coast guard–approved flashlight with several spare batteries and bulbs should be provided. These flash-lights are waterproof and have a blinker button for signaling.

- **Signal mirror**: A signal mirror is perhaps the most effective signal you'll have.

- **Whistle**: A whistle may be helpful up close, but wave and boat noises may make it ineffective.

- **Parachute flares**: Most kits contain two red rocket parachute flares, which keep the flare in the air longer and make it more likely to be seen by rescue.

- **Handheld red flares**: Many kits contain up to six handheld red flares, which can be used to attract rescue to your position.

- **Provisions**: Most kits have 1 pound of hard bread, packed in sealed containers, or an approved nutritional equivalent for the raft's size (number of people).

- **Water**: The kit will have water in quantities that range from 1 pint per person and up. The water is normally held in 4-ounce plastic pouches. (Four pouches make a pint.)

- **Can openers**: Sometimes, water and food rations will be in cans, and thus a can opener might be included.

- **Drinking cup**: A flexible drinking cup marked in ounces is provided.

- **Fishing tackle kit**: A small amount of fishing tackle is provided. Don't count on this being enough—augment it.

- **Seasickness tablets**: You will be happy to have these. Use them before it is too late.

- **Repair kit**: This kit is used to repair buoyancy tubes. Take the time to see if it includes patches, plugs, or clamps. If it doesn't have enough or any plugs and clamps, augment it.

Abandon-Ship Bag

When making an abandon-ship bag, take the time to review what your raft kit contains and build your bag based on this information and the five survival essentials.

1. **Personal protection**
   Clothing: Dry clothes, survival suits, etc.
   Shelter: Tarps, blankets, space blankets, etc.
   Fire: Only an issue on shore. Consider carrying a metal match, lighter, and tinder.

2. **Signaling**: EPIRB, VHF radio, signal mirror, flares and smoke devices, sea marker dye, etc. Be sure to carry fresh batteries as needed.

3. **Sustenance**
   Water: Four-ounce plastic water bottles, hand-powered reverse-osmosis water maker, solar stills, desalting kits, plastic sheets and tubing, water purification tablets, water storage containers, etc.
   Food: Freeze-dried foods, vitamins, fishing tackle and snare line, plankton net, etc.

4. **Travel**: Magnetic compass, watch, charts, tables related to navigation along with detailed instructions on use, calculator, paper, pencils, protractor, etc.

5. **Health**
   Psychological stress: Family photo, religious material, something to read, etc.
   Traumatic injuries: A large yet varied dressing and bandage kit (adhesive and nonadhesive), medical tape, bee sting kit, broad-spectrum antibiotics, aspirin, narcotic pain pills, tincture of benzoin, Bactroban ointment (broad-spectrum antibiotic ointment), duct tape, etc.
   Environmental injuries: Sunglasses, sunscreen, multivitamins, seasickness pills (transderm scop patch, acupressure, and relief bands), etc.

Other items to consider include flashlight, cup, plastic bags, pocketknife and sharpener, nonlubricated condoms (they will work for holding water!), scissors, tweezers, routine medications, moleskin, lip balm, extra sponges and bailers, light sticks, nylon string, hard rubber plugs (various sizes), hose clamps (various sizes), long needle-nose pliers, sewing kit, and aluminum foil.

—From *Surviving Coastal and Open Water*

Continued ➡

end that could easily be attached to your raft or PFD harness. While most commercial abandonship bags will float, only the more expensive dry bags are waterproof. The Landfall Navigation Abandon Ship Dri-Bag, the leader in this arena, can keep approximately 100 pounds of gear afloat and dry. The bag is 21 inches wide and 13.5 inches tall with 3/16-inch-thick closed-cell foam padding covering its bottom and sides. Its exterior is made from heavily reinforced 1,000-denier Antron nylon cloth, and its interior is welded polyurethane-coated 420-denier nylon. Its zipper provides a positive seal and extends 4.5 inches down the sides. The bag's handles are made of heavy-duty webbing and come with two stainless steel D-rings for attaching such items as a float-free automatic strobe.

Reliefband Medical Device

The ReliefBand Device has been approved by the Food and Drug Administration as a treatment for nausea and vomiting related to motion sickness. Worn like a wristwatch, the device emits an electrical signal on the underside of the wrist that somehow interferes with the nerves that cause nausea. The band has five settings that allow you to adjust it to the amount of relief you need for your nausea. The best part about using the ReliefBand is avoiding the drowsiness caused by oral antiseasickness medications.

Bilge Pump

The bilge is that part of a vessel that sits below the waterline. Given time, most vessels will get water in this area, and the bilge pump allows you to easily remove the water from your boat. These pumps come in manual and electric options. Before deciding on a pump, consider your vessel and how it might be used. Be sure the pump you choose will meet your needs. If you decide to get an electric pump, carry a manual backup just in case it stops working.

—From *Surviving Coastal and Open Water*

Tides

Elizabeth P. Lawlor
Illustrations by Pat Archer

The Ocean's Pulse

Will the moon be out tonight? Will it be a full moon, a half moon, or just a thin sliver of a moon? What time will the moon rise? Will there be a high tide this morning or this afternoon? Will the high tide be a regular high tide or a spring tide? These may seem like strange and unimportant questions in an age when our attention is more likely to be riveted on Monday night football, the ever present "impending world crisis" on the evening news, elections, the Olympics, and TV specials. Except for a few evening strollers or coastal fishermen, hardly anyone notices the moon or the tide.

Our grandfathers could probably answer questions about the moon and the tides, and so could their grandfathers back a hundred generations. Until very recently, the phases of the moon and the ebb and flow of the tide were an important part of daily life for mankind. For farming and hunting peoples, the passage of the moon through its phases marked off the year like a monthly calendar in the sky. The moon signaled the time to plant and to hunt, the time to fish and to harvest. The moon was a source of myth and legend. The moon marked important religious events like Easter, Passover, and Ramadan.

The question "What time is high tide?" is as important today as it was in days past for those who live near the sea and draw their living from it and for those who enjoy catching an occasional seafood meal. Certain species of fish and crabs can be caught on the turn of the tide, while others are best caught at high tide. Before the advent of rail transport, highway systems, trucks, cars, buses, and planes, when the sea was the highway for all kinds of transport, the tides regulated the arrival and departure of people and goods.

Our ancestors not only routinely knew the current phase of the moon and the times of the local tides, they also understood that the questions we started with about the moon and the tides were related. They knew that when there was a full moon, the high tide was extra high and

PHASES OF THE MOON: POSITIONS AND APPEARANCES

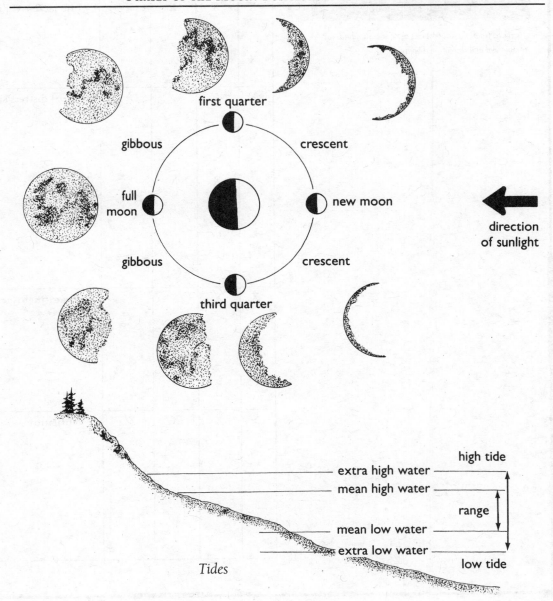

Tides

Continued →

FEDERAL REQUIREMENTS FOR BOATING SAFETY

Greg Davenport

The minimal federal requirements for recreational boaters area conservative guideline and do not guarantee the safety of a vessel or its passengers. In most cases, additional gear is advised. A number of states have additional regulations beyond these federal requirements that must be met. To see if you are in compliance with state laws, check with the boating authority for the area you plan to boat in. The following USCG quick reference chart shows the minimal requirements for recreational boats.

The U.S. Coast Guard provides minimum standards for commercial and recreational boats.

USCG Reference Chart
Federal Requirements and Safety Tips for Recreational Boats

Vessel Length (in feet)				Equipment	Requirement
<16	16–26	26–40	40–65		
X	X	X	X	Certificate of number (state registration)	All undocumented vessels equipped with propulsion machinery must be registered with the state where they are located. Certificate of number must be on board when the vessel is in use. Note that some states require all vessels to be registered.
X	X	X	X	State numbering	a) Plain block letters/numbers at least 3 inches in height must be affixed on each side of the forward half of the vessel in a color that contrasts with the boat's exterior. b) State validation sticker must be affixed within 6 inches of the registration number.
	X	X	X	Certificate of documentation	Applies only to "documented" vessels: a) Original and current certificates must be on board. b) Vessel name/hailing port is marked on exterior part of hull in letters at least 4 inches in height. Official number is permanently affixed on interior structure in numbers at least 3 inches in height.
X	X	X	X	Life jackets (PFDs)	(a) One Type I, II, III, or V wearable USCG-approved PFD for each person on board.
X	X	X			(b) Must carry one Type IV (throwable) PFD.
X				Visual distress signal (VDS)	(a) One electric distress light or three combination (day/night) red flares. Note: These are only required to be carried on board when operating between sunset and sunrise.
	X	X	X		(b) One orange distress flag and one electric distress light or three handheld or floating orange smoke signals and one electric distress light or three combination (day/night) red flares: handheld, meteor, or parachute-type.
X	X			Fire extinguishers	a) One B-I (when enclosed compartment).
		X			b) One B-II or two B-I. (Note: A fixed system equals one B-I.)
			X		c) One B-II and one B-I or three B-I. (Note: A fixed system equals one B-I or two B-II.)
X	X	X	X	Ventilation	a) All vessels built after April 25, 1940, that use gasoline for fuel with an enclosed engine and/or fuel tank compartments must have natural ventilation (at least two ducts fitted with cowls). b) In addition to paragraph (a), a vessel built after July 31, 1980, must have rated power exhaust blower.

Continued ➡

Vessel Length (in feet)				Equipment	Requirement
<16	16–26	26–40	40–65		
X	X	X		Sound-producing devices	a) A vessel 39.4 feet in length must, at a minimum, have some means of making an "efficient" sound signal (i.e., a handheld air horn or athletic whistle. Human voice/sound is not acceptable).
	X	X			b) A vessel 39.4 feet (12 meters) or greater in length must have a sound-signaling appliance capable of producing an efficient sound signal, audible for a half-mile with a four- to six-second duration. In addition, the vessel must carry on board a bell with a chapter (bell size not less than 7.9 inches, based on the diameter of the mouth).
X	X	X	X	Backfire flame arrestor	Required on gasoline engines installed after April 25, 1940, except for out-board motors.
X	X	X	X	Navigational lights	Required to be displayed from sunset to sunrise and in or near areas of reduced visibility.
		X	X	Oil pollution placard	a) Placard must be at least 5 × 8 inches in size and made of durable material. b) Placard must be posted in the machinery space or at the bilge station.
		X	X	Garbage placard	a) Placard must be at least 4 × 9 inches in size and made of durable material. b) Displayed in a conspicuous place notifying all on board about the discharge restrictions.
X	X	X	X	Marine sanitation device	If installed, the vessel must have an operable marine sanitation device Type I, II, or III toilet.
		X	X	Navigation rules (inland only)	The operator of a vessel 39.4 feet (12 meters) or greater in length must have on board a copy of these rules.

These USCG recommendations are the minimum requirements and by no means should be considered adequate. Additional items you should consider include the following:

· Communication equipment

· Emergency Position Indicating Radio Beacon (EPIRB)

· Navigation gear (including a GPS)

· Inflatable life raft

· Survival kit that accounts for your five survival essentials (reviewed earlier in this chapter)

· First aid kit created with consideration given to circumstances that might arise in open and coastal waters

· Immersion suit for everyone on board, if you will be in cold water.

—From *Surviving Coastal and Open Water*

the low tide was extra low. They knew that the tides followed the lunar calendar, so that by knowing the phase of the moon, they could predict the time and height of tomorrow's tides. Many of the old clocks displayed the phase of the moon as well as the time of day. For many people today, this knowledge is lost. Did you know that the moon rises about fifty minutes later each day according to our twenty-four-hour solar clocks? Did you know that if there is a high tide this morning, the high tide tomorrow morning will be about fifty minutes later than it was today?

Ancient peoples had difficulty making sense of the connections between the moon and the tides. Three hundred years ago, Sir Isaac Newton gave us our modern understanding of tides by explaining that gravity is a force, a pull, exerted by every object on every other object. Huge objects exert huge pulling forces on each other. These forces keep the speeding planets in orbit around the sun and keep the moving moon in orbit around the earth. There is a balanced between the attractive forces and the outward forces produced by the forward motion of the orbiting bodies. According to these ideas of Newton, the tides in the oceans of the earth result from the pull exerted on the earth's oceans by the moon and the sun. On the side of the earth facing the moon, this gravitational attraction pulls up a mound of water about half a yard high. This mound points toward the moon. As the earth spins one turn every twenty-four hours, this mound, or high tide, also circles the earth. This should give every point on the oceans one high tide each day. However, we know that many places have two high tides every day. This happens because our moon is so large that its pull on earth causes both moon and earth to whip around a point that is not at the center of the earth but offset about three thousand miles toward the moon. This whipping action causes a second tidal bulge in the oceans on exactly the opposite side of the earth from the gravitational tidal bulge. Presto, two high tides occur every day. The second high tide, caused by this whipping action, is lower than the high tide caused by the moon's gravitational attraction.

This explanation is based only on the fact that the earth rotates, or spins, and the explanation makes it seem that the high tides should arrive at the same time every day. However, we must also remember that the moon is not standing still in space. The moon is moving rapidly at about two thousand miles per hour, orbiting the spinning earth once every twenty-seven and one-half days. This fact causes the high tides to operate on the moon's schedule, which is about fifty minutes later every day for a given point on the earth. For example, if on some clear evening you see the moon rising like an enormous yellow orb on the eastern horizon, mark down the time. Then look in the same spot the following evening for Old Man Moon. You will find that moonrise is about fifty minutes later than it was the first evening. Since we have two high tides each day, there must be about twelve hours and twenty-five minutes between them.

Continued ➡

There is another interesting thing about the tides that needs an explanation. During the lunar month of about twenty-nine and one-half days, there are two higher-than-usual high tides called spring tides, which occur at full moon and at new moon. There are also two lower-than-usual high tides called neap tides, which occur at the first and third quarters of the lunar cycle. The spring tides are called this because the extrahigh water level at that time looks as though the water is "springing" from the earth. Spring tides have nothing to do with the spring season of the year. They are caused by the relative positions of the earth, sun, and moon, when they are lined up. The word *neap*, which comes from the German word for napping, is used to describe those tides in which there is very little movement of water. The water is "taking a snooze" at neap high tide.

Newton comes to the rescue here also. This spring-neap cycle is due to the gravitational attraction of the sun on the earth and its waters. The sun also exerts a gravitational pull on earth, causing a 46 percent smaller tidal bulge in the oceans. This does not result in another set of high tides; instead, it causes a tide that adds to, or reinforces, the moon tide when moon, earth, and sun are lined up. This additive tide is spring tide. When earth, moon, and sun are at right angles in space, then the smaller sun tide partially cancels the moon tide, resulting in neap tide.

That might seem to be whole story of the tides, a complete explanation; however, the story is complicated by the weird shapes of the solid parts of the earth's surface. In New York City there is approximately a five-foot difference between low and high tides, while Rockport,

Maine, has a ten-foot tidal range, and the Bay of Fundy boasts a more-than-thirty-foot tide. The very uneven coastline causes these variations. Almost anywhere you travel, you will find strange things about local tides if you ask a fisherman or someone who lives on the shore. Most places have two high tides per day, but some communities, like Pensacola, Florida, on the Gulf of Mexico, have only one high tide per day, and San Francisco has one big high tide and one little high tide every day. These strange effects are also due to the way the land masses interact with tidal movements.

It may seem odd, but far out at sea, the effects of the tide cause a bulge in the surface of the ocean, which people on ships cannot notice. For a few hours each day, the ship is half a yard closer to the moon, and then six hours later, half a yard farther from the moon. When the tidal bulge reaches shallow water, there may be a great rush of water into the bays, sounds, and estuaries. These tidal currents can be very powerful, and they move gigantic quantities of water in a daily rhythm. Man has dreamed of using this movement of water to produce useful power. This is done now on a small scale, but the harmful ecological effects of using this power on a large scale may outweigh the potential savings in oil and coal.

Since every aspect of planet earth is intimately associated with living things, the tides have an important life-related role. With each rise of the tide, nutrients generated in the oceans are brought into bays, into estuaries, and even into the smallest of tidal creeks. Similarly, the falling tide carries with it food matter originating in marshlands, mud flats, and rivers. The churning associated with tidal shifts moves this food material vertically as well as horizontally. The beat of life in the intertidal zone is directed by tidal motion.

When you think of it, there is no aspect of planet earth that is not intimately bound up with the teeming miracle of life. Even the ancient partnership between the earth and the moon provides a kind of life pulse that goes on and on. We are all part of this pulsating rhythm, part of this eternal beat.

Notes

1. The Uneven Coming and Going of the Tide.
The amount of horizontal rise in tidal water follows a fairly regular pattern. In the first hour, the tide will rise only very slightly; during the second hour, it will move quite noticeably; and during the third hour (at half tide), the rate is at its maximum. Then the amount of rise each hour decreases until the sixth hour, when its rise is again hardly noticeable. The falling tide shows the same pattern: the tide falls slowly at first, then more rapidly, and then slowly again.

2. Sources for Tide Charts.
Tide charts are published by the National Oceanographic and Atmospheric Administration of the United States Department of Commerce (NOAA). You can request these tables from the United States Government Printing Office, North Capitol and H Streets,

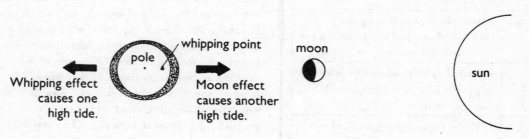

Two high tides daily.

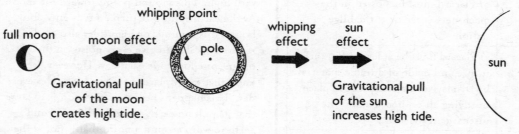

Spring tide: earth between sun and moon.

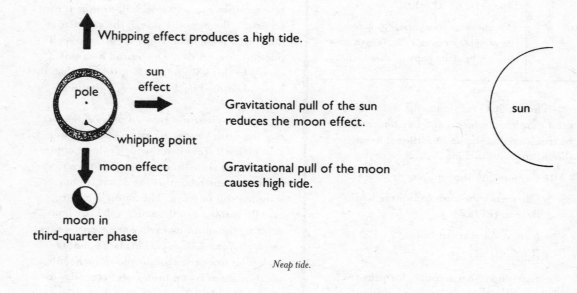

Neap tide.

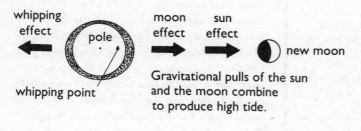

Spring tide: moon between earth and sun.

Continued ➡

N.W., Washington, D.C. 20401 (202-275-2051). These same charts and brief excerpts from them are often available in marine supply stores, bait shops, coastal book stores, hardware stores, banks, marine insurance offices, and other unexpected places. Some of these tables have more information than others, so check them out carefully.

3. High and Low Water.

There are two high tides and two low tides in a twenty-four-hour period. This tidal pattern is called semidiurnal, and it occurs on the Atlantic and Pacific coasts of the United States.

—From Discover Nature at the Seashore

Sea Safety Markers

Greg Davenport
Illustrations by Steven A. Davenport

Charts provide several navigational aids that help mariners avoid hazards and identify their position. These aids consist of lighthouses, buoys, and markers.

Lighthouses

Since the visibility of light increases with height, lighthouses provide an exceptional marker that can be seen from a great distance. They help mariners with navigation and to avoid dangerous areas. In addition to light, lighthouses often have fog-signaling and radio-beacon equipment.

A lighthouse helps mariners avoid obstacles.

Buoys

Buoys are anchored floating markers that help vessels avoid dangers and navigate in and out of channels. Buoys come in several shapes and colors, which help identify their purpose.

Right-sided Buoys

Buoys located on the right side of a channel—leading in from seaward—will be painted red and support even numbers that decrease as you move seaward. If a light is used, it will be red. Nun-shaped buoys (buoys with a cone-shaped top) are used when the buoys aren't lit.

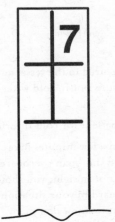

Cans and buoys located on the left side of a channel leading in from seaward.

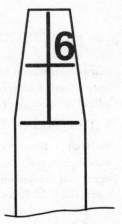

Nuns are buoys located on the right side of a channel leading in from seaward.

Left-sided Buoys

Buoys located on the left side of a channel—leading in from seaward—will be painted green and support odd numbers that decrease as you move seaward. If a light is used, it will be green. Can-shaped buoys (buoys with a cylinder shape) are used when the buoys aren't lit.

Channel Junction and Safe Approach Buoys

Buoys located at a junction or midchannel can be either nuns or cans and may or may not have numbers on them. Junction buoys are painted with horizontal red and green stripes, and midchannel buoys are painted with horizontal red and white strips. If a light is used, it will be white.

Day Markers

Day markers are small signs held in place by poles. During daylight hours, these markers help vessels avoid dangers and navigate in and out of channels. Markers come in several shapes and colors, which help identify their purpose.

Right-sided Day Markers

Markers located on the right side of a channel—leading in from seaward—will be triangular-shaped, painted red, and support even numbers that decrease as you move seaward.

Triangular day markers are located on the right side of a channel leading in from seaward.

Left-sided Day Markers

Markers located on the left side of a channel—leading in from seaward—will be square-shaped, painted green, and support odd numbers that decrease as you move seaward.

Square day markers are located on the left side of a channel leading in from seaward.

Midchannel markers

Markers located midchannel will be in the shape of an octagon.

Midchannel markers have an octagonal shape.

—From Surviving Coastal and Open Water

Man Overboard Procedures

Greg Davenport
Illustrations by Steven A. Davenport

When someone goes overboard, hypothermia and drowning are his or her biggest threats, and a rapid recovery from the water is often the key to the person's survival. How quickly and successfully a person is recovered hinges on the training and experience of the crew and the person in the water. While training is important to a successful outcome, time is also critical, especially in cold water where hypothermia will quickly set in. The following guidelines can be used as a general rule to determine the average survivable time in cold water. It should be noted, however, that this guideline was established using young, healthy individuals and is probably overly optimistic.

Water Temperature		Average Survival Time
Less than 34° F	Less than 2° C	Less than 45 minutes
34° to 40°F	2° to 4° C	Less than 90 minutes
40° to 50° F	4° to 10° C	Less than 3 hours
50° to 59° F	10° to 15° C	Less than 6 hours
59° to 69° F	15° to 20° C	Less than 12 hours
Greater than 70° F	Greater than 20° C	Indefinite (depends on physical condition)

Hypothermia, the result of an abnormally low body temperature, occurs when body heat is lost due to radiation, conduction, evaporation, convection, and respiration. While in cold water, the body loses heat twenty-five times faster than it would while in a similar air temperature. Signs and symptoms of hypothermia include uncontrollable shivering, slurred speech, abnormal behavior, fatigue and drowsiness, decreased hand and body coordination, and a weakened respiration and pulse.

Subject Behavior

If you find yourself in the water, most likely the seas will be cold and rough. Not only is it doubtful that you can swim to your vessel, but the heat you would lose trying to could hasten a hypothermic state. Your best bet is to signal the vessel, use the techniques outlined here, and wait for the vessel to pick you up. Hopefully you will be dressed appropriately for the conditions and will be wearing a life jacket. As quickly as you can, try to get out of the water by getting back aboard your vessel, in a life raft, or on top of debris. Since approximately 50 percent of your body heat is lost from the head, make every effort to keep your head dry and above the waterline. If you are unable get out of the water, use the following method to increase your chances of survival.

Continued ➡

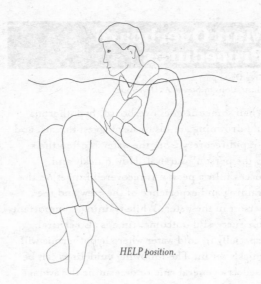

HELP position.

Group huddle to retain body heat.

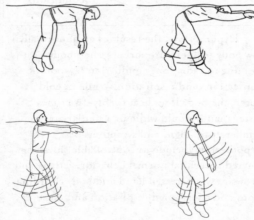

In warm water, drownproofing is an excellent option for staying afloat.

Wearing a Life Jacket

In cold water, try to insulate your head, neck, sides, and groin, which are areas of high heat loss, by assuming the Heat-Escape-Lessening Position (HELP). To do this, hold your upper arms against your sides and cross your lower arms across your chest. At the same time, keep your legs close together with ankles crossed and pull your knees to your chest. Be sure to keep your head above the waterline. If there are other persons in the water, face each other in a huddle, making as much body contact as possible. Exercising while surviving in cold water is not recommended as this actually hastens the loss of body heat due to convection.

Without a Life Jacket

If for some unforeseen reason you should end up in the water without a life jacket, your biggest concern will be to prevent drowning. In cold water, this can create a dilemma as moving hastens heat loss, but if you do not move, you will drown. As best you can, keep your head dry and tread water to stay afloat. You will actually expend less energy doing this than if you perform the popular floating technique called drownproofing.

In warm water, however, drownproofing decreases the amount of energy lost when compared to treading water or swimming. The maneuver, which uses the lungs for buoyancy, can increase you chances of survival in warm water significantly. Practice the following steps of drownproofing before you need to use it in an emergency:

Resting position: Take a deep breath and go limp with your face in the water. The back of your head and back should be parallel with the surface of the water.

Preparing to exhale: When it is time to take another breath, slowly lift your arms to shoulder height and separate your legs into a scissors-type position.

Exhale: This step is done immediately once the arms are up and the legs are separated. Raise your head just high enough to get your mouth out of the water and exhale.

Inhale: Once you have exhaled, slowly press your arms down and bring your legs together while inhaling.

Return to rest position: Resume the resting position by relaxing your arms, allowing your legs to dangle, and placing your face back down into the water.

Crew Behavior

Within 20 seconds, a vessel moving at 5 knots will be 168 feet away from the person who fell overboard. At 10 knots, the vessel will be 336 feet away. When someone goes overboard, immediate action by the remaining crew is vital to a successful rescue. The crew should take the following steps immediately upon seeing someone fall overboard:

1. **Sound an alarm.** Immediately begin yelling "man overboard" along with his or her position in relation to the vessel. For example, if on the right side of the vessel, yell "man overboard, starboard side!" On the left side, yell "man overboard, port side!" In front of the vessel, yell "man overboard at the bow!" and at the rear of the vessel, yell "man overboard at the stern!"

2. **Mark the spot.** During daylight hours, immediately throw a ring buoy or similar item toward the person, and if possible, drop a smoke float that will mark the spot where the person fell overboard. During darkness, immediately throw a life preserver or buoy ring with water lights and keep the vessel's searchlight fixed on the subject. If you have a GPS, mark your position.

3. **Position the vessel.** The pilot of the vessel should immediately begin maneuvering the stern side away from the subject.

4. **Post a lookout.** Post a lookout whose only job is to keep the subject in sight and provide a direction guide to the crew by extending an arm and pointing toward the subject. This job is crucial since even small waves will make it hard to see a bobbing head. The person who witnessed the fall is usually the best suited for this task.

Steps 2 through 4 require teamwork and should occur simultaneously. Try to practice before an actual emergency occurs.

5. **Remove obstacles.** Retrieve or cut free any outlying gear that interferes with how the vessel moves.

6. **Vessel approach.** As long as the person is still in sight, circle your vessel so that it points into the wind, which allows you to better control boat speed and position. Keep the propeller away from the person in the water. Note that this approach may not be practical for all conditions, and your situation may dictate otherwise.

7. **Retrieval.** Retrieving someone who has fallen overboard may be the most difficult part of this process. How successful a recovery is depends on the subject's physical condition, the number and experience of the crew members, and the type of vessel and its recovery gear. Once the vessel is alongside the subject, disengage the propeller by placing the engine in neutral. Use whatever line and equipment are available to reach the person in the water and have him or her secure the line around his or her body. Lifting the person out of the water will take exceptional skill and strength since his or her water weight will make the person extremely heavy. However, no one should enter the water unless all other options fail or don't appear to be safe. If someone must enter the water to help retrieve the subject, then

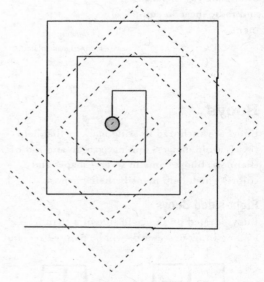

Expanding square search pattern.

that person should be secured to the vessel and wear either an antiexposure suit in cold water or a PFD in warm water.

8. **First aid.** Treat the patient for cold injuries.

9. **What if.** If more than a few minutes have passed since you sounded the "man overboard" signal and the person is not in sight, you should notify the U.S. Coast Guard of your situation. The coast guard will want to know how many people are on board, your location, any identifying features of the vessel, and what the crisis is (see page 357 on contacting the Coast Guard).

Continued ➜

MAN OVERBOARD: BEING PREPARED
U.S. Coast Guard

If you are a man overboard, you've probably caught all those who can help you by surprise—including yourself. Some useful advice to follow for preventing this situation and being better prepared is:

1. Always wear a lifevest when safety regulations require it or when you have to go on deck for any reason in poor weather.

2. Use extreme care when walking along decks, up and down ladders, and across gangplanks.

3. Use your hands to grip rails and other support devices. Do not lean on rails or lifelines.

4. Be alert when moving around the outside of the ship and especially around cable and rope. Keep hands out of pockets, free to grab for support in the event you fall.

5. Be particularly careful at night or in fog. Poor visibility increases both the chances of accident and the difficulties in locating you in the water.

6. If possible, avoid walking on an open deck in poor weather or rough water conditions.

7. Inform someone of your plan to go on deck, especially if the weather conditions are poor.

8. Walk or work in pairs, if possible. Try not to be alone.

9. Common sense says dress appropriate to the weather, but some care in selection of clothes can make a difference in survival. If possible, wear many layers of clothing, including a waterproof outer layer. Make certain that the neck, wrist and ankle portions of the clothing are snugfitting. This will reduce the exchange of water within your clothing should you go into or under water. Also, woolen clothes are better insulators than cotton, especially when wet.

10. Carry at least one reliable distress signal with you at all times. Preferably, this should be in the form of a good quality battery powered light or chemical light stick and a Coast Guard approved whistle.

11. Wear an outer garment that is bright in color. As an alternative sew strips of reflective tape on upper portions of your outer garment. Reflective tape is available at drug, sporting goods, or auto supply stores.

—From A Pocket Guide to Cold Water Survival

10. **Search pattern.** If you cannot see the subject, begin a search pattern. The search pattern starts at the last known position of the person who is overboard and follows an ever-expanding square shape. Continue this search process until the subject is rescued or until the USCG arrives.

11. **Use the alert call Pan-Pan** to notify other vessels that you have a man overboard. The Pan-Pan call will alert others and allow you to notify them on how you intend to maneuver in the area.

Prevention

Most overboard falls occur when someone is moving, standing, or leaning over the edge of a vessel. Other potential causes include poor visibility, rapid accelerations or sharp turns, large waves, and slippery surfaces. To avoid an overboard incident, use handrails, always be aware of ground obstacles, wear a lifeline when working near the edge of the vessel, and never horse around when on the deck.

—From Surviving Coastal and Open Water

Abandon Ship Procedures
Greg Davenport
Illustrations by Steven A. Davenport

At the first sign of a potential problem, establish communication with the U.S. Coast Guard. Don't wait until it is too late. The coast guard can provide valuable advice on improvising methods that can delay or stop a vessel from sinking. In addition, they often deliver fuel, dewater pumps, and other necessary survival items.

The key to successfully abandoning ship is proper preparation and practice. Become familiar with the abandon-ship process and your gear before a crisis occurs. Such preparation helps to control anxiety in this stressful situation. Also make sure that those on board know the abandon-ship procedure and can step in should you be unable to take charge. Leadership both on board the vessel and in the life raft plays an important role in ensuring the survival of a crew. Once the decision has been made to abandon ship and the alarm has been sounded, follow the steps below.

Step 1: Mayday
Broadcast a Mayday on channel 16 VHF or 2182-kHz SSB using MAYDAY, MAYDAY, MAYDAY. Repeat your vessel name and call sign three times. State your present location three times (give latitude and longitude if you can, along with a distance and direction from a known point), the nature of the distress, and the number of people on board. Repeat this process until you either get a response or are forced to leave your vessel.

Step 2: Dress Up
If you have time and your wardrobe allows, dress in layers that will wick moisture away from your body, insulate you even when wet, and provide a degree of waterproofing. (See page 346 on clothing.) If you have a hat and gloves, put them on.

Step 3: Life Jacket
A life jacket is a must. If you have to tread water without a life jacket, your body will lose 35 percent more heat than it would if you were wearing a life jacket. While a life jacket is important, in cold climates you are better off with a buoyant survival suit (immersion suit). If you have one, put it on.

Step 4: Survival Kit
Grab the abandon-ship bag, survival and first-aid kits (if separate), portable radio, EPIRB, and cell phone, if you have one. If you have extra time, take along navigation gear, food and water, medicines, blankets, line, and anything else you think you might need. However, do not delay launching the life raft to gather these extra items.

Step 5: Launch the Raft
If a canister raft, release the tie-down straps by pressing on the hydrostatic release or pelican hook. Holing the canister or valise pack in the upright position, carry it to the lee (downwind) side of the vessel. Don't roll the canister. Depending on your system—be sure to know it in advance—you will need to tie the operating cord (painter/lanyard) to the vessel *above* the weak link. Be sure to do this before launching the raft. To do this, pull several feet of the painter line from the canister, and attach it to the vessel so that the weak link is beyond the knot. The weak link needs to be between the knot and the free end. Bypassing the weak link ensures a strong connection between the vessel and the life raft. The weak link is only useful during a float-free launch (see below). Leaving the bands in place, two members of the crew should throw the canister overboard. Once the life raft and canister are in the water, pull on the painter (operating cord). You may need to pull out the line until you feel resistance and then give it a

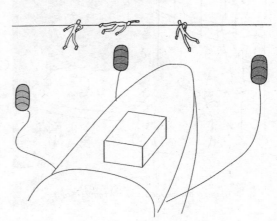

Free-floating container will rise to the surface.

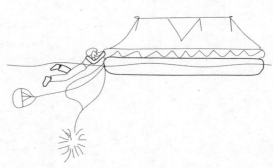

As the raft inflates and the vessel sinks, the painter cord will break, freeing the raft.

Continued ➔

sharp tug. Keep the line free of tangles. The bands will release the two halves of the container, and the life raft will inflate. Never inflate the raft on the vessel since the container halves could fly off and cause harm or the raft could become jammed between separate areas of the vessel. For now, leave the operating cord attached to the vessel.

If you are unable to deploy the raft before your vessel sinks, you may still be in luck as long as your raft is in a canister stored on the vessel's cradle and the painter has been attached to the vessel. The hydrostatic release on the raft is set to automatically release when it reaches a depth of 10 to 15 feet. The freed container will rise to the surface, and the ship will pull on the canister's bands, causing them to part and triggering the inflation of the raft. Within approximately thirty seconds, the life raft should be fully inflated and ready to board. In time, the raft's buoyancy and the sinking ship will reach a point where the weak link (located where the painter is attached to the cradle) will break, thus freeing the raft from the vessel.

Step 6: Board the Raft

When boarding the raft, try to keep dry. You may be able to board directly from a ladder, line, or net. If the distance is short, you might want to jump into the canopy entrance. Some rafts allow this and some don't, so check with your vendor. If you do jump, land on the balls of your feet so that you don't fall backward into the water. Also stretch out your arms so that you land with your chest against the inflated canopy arch to decrease the chance of injuring others already on board the raft.

If you must enter the water to board the raft, do so as close to the raft as you can. Also,

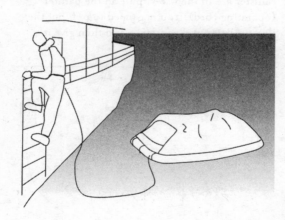

Whenever possible use a ladder to board the raft.

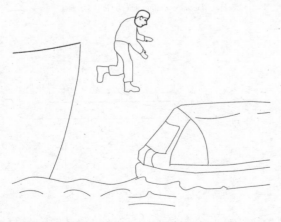

Jump into the canopy opening only when other options are not available.

jump from the lowest point and hold on to the painter (line) so that you are not swept away. The line can also guide you over to the raft. To board the raft from the water, place your feet on the boarding ladder, grab the handholds or internal lifelines, and pull yourself into the raft headfirst. Life boat canopies are known to tear, so you should not use them to pull yourself into the raft. If someone is injured or needs help getting into the raft, two people can pull that person on board using the following technique:

1. Place your knee that is away from the center of the door on the top of the buoyancy tube.

2. Turn the person in the water so that his or her back is toward the life raft door.

3. Grab the subject's life jacket with your hand that is closest to the center of the door.

4. With your other hand, grab the subject's upper arm (each rescuer should take an arm) and then push the individual slightly down before pulling him or her up and over the buoyancy tubes and into the life raft.

5. While pulling the person up, fall to one side on the raft's floor and allow the subject to fall between you and the other rescuer.

Pulling someone aboard the life raft.

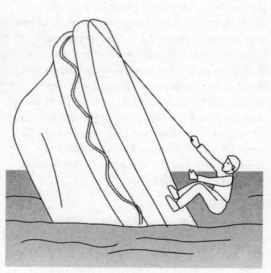

Flipping an overturned life raft.

If the life raft deploys upside down, one person can right the raft as long as it is done before the canopy fills with seawater. Find the raft's CO_2 cylinder, which is typically marked with the words "RIGHT HERE." Flipping the raft over from this position ensures that the CO_2 cylinder does not hit you and possibly knock you out. If there are strong winds, try to get the canister side of the raft on the downwind side, which will make the raft easier to turn. The bottom of the raft will have righting straps. Grab the straps and pull

yourself—kicking your feet may help—up and onto the raft. Next, stand on the edge next to the cylinder, and pull on the righting straps while leaning back. If the raft lands on top of you, swim face up until you clear its edge. If you need to catch your breath during this time, simply create an air pocket by pushing your arms and head upwards against the floor of the raft. If the canopy of the capsized raft has filled with seawater, it may take two people to right the raft.

Step 7: Cut free of Sinking Vessel

Remove the knife that should be included in your raft, and cut the operating cord to free the life raft from the sinking ship. Keep the knife sheathed until needed, and immediately sheath it after each use. If the vessel is on fire, paddle away from it. If the vessel remains afloat, however, stay as close to the boat as long as you can. Rescue will start at that location.

Step 8: Deploy the Sea Anchor

Once you are away from the sinking vessel, let out the sea anchor, which will help stabilize the life raft and make it less prone to tipping over in rough seas.

Step 9: Attend to Medical Needs

Any life-threatening injuries, such as airway, bleeding, circulation, and shock, should be treated immediately. In cold water, treat and prevent hypothermia. Other injuries should be attended to once all life-threatening problems are treated. Avoid dehydration by taking seasickness pills.

Step 10: Inventory Your Materials

Review the contents of your abandon-ship bag, survival kit, and medical kit, and take the time to tie everything, including the paddles, to the raft.

Step 11: Use Your Signals

Make sure you know how to use the signals before you need them. If the EPIRB has not been activated, do so now. If you were able to take the VHF radio on board the raft, transmit another Mayday. If you have a cell phone, try to reach someone. Post a lookout, sweep the horizon with your signal mirror, and familiarize yourself and your crew with the signals and how they should be used. For signaling information, refer to chapter 11.

Step 12: Personal Protection

Bail out any water in the raft, inflate the floor, and put up the canopy if you have one. Wring out wet clothes, and try to empty water out of immersion suits.

Step 13: Read the Survival Manuals

Life rafts normally come equipped with a survival manual. Read it. You may find some helpful information.

Continued ➡

Abandoning Ship in Cold Water

U.S. Coast Guard

If you are involved in a ship casualty and are forced to abandon, your survival procedure should be preplanned, thereby increasing your chances for a successful rescue. Records show that ship sinkings, even in the worst cases, usually require at least 15 to 30 minutes for the vessel to fully submerge. This affords valuable time for preparation. Here are some sound pointers for you to remember in a situation of this type:

Put on as much warm clothing as possible, making sure to cover head, neck, hands and feet.

If an immersion (exposure) suit is available put it on over the warm clothing.

If the immersion (exposure) suit does not have inherent flotation, put on a lifejacket and be sure to secure it correctly.

All persons who know that are likely to be affected by seasickness should, before or immediately after boarding the survival craft, take some recommended preventive tablets or medicine in a dose recommended by the manufacturer. The incapacitation caused by seasickness interferes with your survival chances; the vomiting removes precious body fluid while seasickness in general makes you more prone to hypothermia.

Avoid entering the water if possible. Board davit-launched survival craft on the embarkation deck. If davit-launched survival craft are not available, use overside ladders, or if necessary lower yourself by means or a rope or fire hose.

Unless it is unavoidable do not jump from higher than 5 meters (16.4 feet) into the water. Try to minimize the shock of sudden cold immersion. Rather than jumping into the cold water, try to lower yourself gradually. A sudden plunge into the cold water can cause rapid death or an uncontrollable rise in breathing rate may result in an intake of water into the lungs. On occasions it may be necessary to jump into the water; if so, you should keep your elbow at your sides, cover your nose and mouth with one hand while holding the wrist or elbow firmly with the other hand. One should not jump into the water astern of the liferaft lest there is any remaining headway on the ship.

Once in the water, whether accidentally or by ship abandonment, orientate yourself and try to locate the ship, lifeboats, liferafts, other survivors or other floating objects. If you were unable to prepare yourself before entering the water, button up clothing now. In cold water you may experience violent shivering and great pain. These are natural body reflexes that are not dangerous. You do, however, need to take action as quickly as possible before you lose full use of your hands; button up clothing, turn on signal lights, locate whistle, etc.

While afloat in the water, do not attempt to swim unless it is to reach a nearby craft, a fellow survivor, or a floating object on which you can lean or climb. Unnecessary swimming will "pump" out any warm water between your body and the layers of clothing, thereby increasing the rate of the body-heat loss. In addition, unnecessary movements of your arms and legs send warm blood from the inner core to the outer layer of the body. This results in a very rapid heat loss. Hence it is most important to remain as still as possible in the water, however painful it may be. Remember, pain will not kill you, but heat loss will!

The body position you assume in the water is also very important in conserving heat. Float as still as possible with your legs together, elbows close to your side and arms folded across the front across the front of your lifejacket. This position minimizes the exposure of the body surface to the cold water. Try to keep your head and neck out of the water. Another heat conserving position is to huddle closely to one or more persons afloat, making as much body contact as possible. You must be wearing a lifevest to be able to hold these positions in the water.

Try to board a lifeboat, raft, or other floating platform or object as soon as possible in order to shorten your immersion time. It is always better to get out of the water than it is to stay in.

Remember, you lose body heat many times faster in water than in air. Since the effectiveness of your insulation is seriously reduced by water soaking, you must now try to shield yourself from wind to avoid a wind-chill effect (convective cooling). If you manage to climb aboard a lifeboat, shielding can be accomplished with the aid of a canvas cover or tarpaulin, or an unused garment. Huddling close to the other occupants of the lifeboat or raft will also conserve body heat.

Do not use "drownproofing" in cold water. "Drownproofing" is a technique whereby you relax in the water and allow your head to submerge between breaths. It is an energy saving procedure to use in warm water when you are not wearing a life vest. However, the head and neck are high heat loss areas and must be kept above the water. That is why it is even more important to wear a lifevest in cold water. If you are not wearing a vest, tread the water only as much as necessary to keep your head out of the water.

Keep a positive attitude about your survival and rescue. This will improve your chance of extending your survival time until rescue comes. Your will to live does make a difference!

—From *A Pocket Guide to Cold Water Survival*

Sea Survival

U.S. Army

Perhaps the most difficult survival situation to be in is sea survival. Short- or long-term survival depends upon rations and equipment available and your ingenuity. You must be resourceful to survive.

Water covers about 75 percent of the earth's surface, with about 70 percent being oceans and seas. You can assume that you will sometime cross vast expanses of water. There is always the chance that the plane or ship you are on will become crippled by such hazards as storms, collision, fire, or war.

The Open Sea

As a survivor on the open sea, you will face waves and wind. You may also face extreme heat or cold. To keep these environmental hazards from becoming serious problems, take precautionary measures as soon as possible. Use the available resources to protect yourself from the elements and from heat or extreme cold and humidity.

Protecting yourself from the elements meets only one of your basic needs. You must also be able to obtain water and food. Satisfying these three basic needs will help prevent serious physical and psychological problems. However, you must know how to treat health problems that may result from your situation.

Precautionary Measures

Your survival at sea depends upon—

- Your knowledge of and ability to use the available survival equipment.

- Your special skills and ability to apply them to cope with the hazards you face.

- Your will to live.

When you board a ship or aircraft, find out what survival equipment is on board, where it is stowed, and what it contains. For instance, how many life preservers and lifeboats or rafts are on board? Where are they located? What type of survival equipment do they have? How much food, water, and medicine do they contain? How many people are they designed to support?

If you are responsible for other personnel on board, make sure you know where they are and they know where you arr.

Down at Sea

If you are in an aircraft that goes down at sea, take the following actions once you clear the aircraft. Whether you are in the water or in a raft—

- Get clear and upwind of the aircraft as soon as possible, but stay in the vicinity until the aircraft sinks.

- Get clear of fuel-covered water in case the fuel ignites.

- Try to find other survivors.

A search for survivors usually takes place around the entire area of and near the crash site. Missing personal may be unconscious and floating low in the water

The best technique for rescuing personnel from the water is to throw them a life preserver attached to a line. Another is to send a swimmer (rescuer) from the raft with a line attached to a flotation device that will support the rescuer's weight. This device will help conserve a rescuer's energy while recovering the survivor. The least acceptable technique is to send an attached swimmer without flotation devices to retrieve a survivor. In all cases, the rescuer wears a life preserver. A rescuer should not underestimate the strength of a panic-stricken person in the water. A careful approach can prevent injury to the rescuer.

When the rescuer approaches a survivor in trouble from behind, there is little danger the survivor will kick, scratch, or grab him. The rescuer swims to a point directly behind the survivor and grasps the life preserver's backstrap. The rescuer uses the sidestroke to drag the survivor to the raft.

Continued ➜

- **Dog paddle**. This stroke is excellent when clothed or wearing a life jacket. Although slow in speed, it requires very little energy.

- **Breaststroke**. Use this stroke to swim underwater, through oil or debris, or in rough seas. It is probably the best stroke for long-range swimming; it allows you to conserve your energy and maintain a reasonable speed.

- **Sidestroke**. It is a good relief stroke because you use only one arm to maintain momentum and buoyancy.

- **Backstroke**. This stroke is also an excel lent relief stroke. It relieves the muscles that you use for other strokes. Use it if an underwater explosion is likely.

If you are in an area where surface oil is burning—

- Discard your shoes and buoyant life preserver.

Note: If you have an uninflated life preserver, keep it.

- Cover your nose, mouth, and eyes and quickly go underwater.

- Swim underwater as far as possible before surfacing to breathe.

- Before surfacing to breathe and while still underwater, use your hands to push burning fluid away from the area where you wish to surface. Once an area is clear of burning liquid, you can surface and take a few breathes. Try to face downwind before inhaling.

- Submerge feet first and continue as above until clear of the flames.

If you are in oil-covered water that is free of fire, hold your head high to keep the oil out of your eyes. Attach your life preserver to your wrist and then use it as a raft.

1. Float upright in the water and take a deep breath.

2. Lower your face into the water (keeping your mouth closed) and bring your arms forward to rest at water level.

If you are in the water, make you way to a raft. If no rafts are available, try to find a large piece of floating debris to cling to. Relax; a person who know how to relax in ocean water is in very little danger of drowning. The body's natural buoyancy will keep at least the top of the head above water, but some movement is needed to keep the face above water.

Floating on your back takes the least energy. Lie on your back in the water, spread your arms and legs, and arch your back. By controlling your breathing in and out, your face will always be out of the water and you may even sleep in this position for short periods. Your head will be partially submerged, but you face will be above water. If you cannot float on your back or if the sea it too rough, float facedown in the water.

The following are the best swimming strokes during a survival situation:

FLOATING POSITIONS

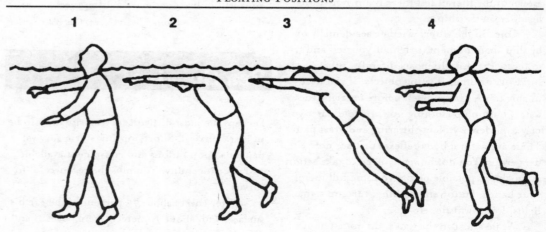

1 Float upright in the water and take a deep breath.

2 Lower your face into the water (keeping your mouth closed) and bring your arms forward to rest at water level.

3 Relax in this position until you need to take in more air.

4 Raise your head above the surface, treading water, and exhale. Take another breath and return to the relaxed position.

Continued ➡

3. Relax in this position until you need to take in more air.

4. Raise your head above the surface, treading water, and exhale. Take another breath and return to the relaxed position.

If you have a life preserver, you can stay afloat for an indefinite period. In this case, use the "HELP" body position: Heat Escaping Lessening Posture (HELP). Remain still and assume the fetal position to help you retain body heat. You lose about 50 percent of your body heat through your head. Therefore, keep your head out of the water. Other areas of high heat loss are the neck, the sides, and the groin.

If you are in a raft—

- Check the physical condition of all on board. Give first aid if necessary. Take seasickness pills if available. The best way to take these pills is to place them under the tongue and let them dissolve. There are also suppositories or injections against seasickness. Vomiting, whether from seasickness or other causes, increases the danger of dehydration.

- Try to salvage all floating equipment— rations; canteens, thermos jugs, and other containers; clothing; seat cushions; parachutes; and anything else that will be useful to you. Secure the salvaged items in or to your raft. Make sure the items have no sharp edges that can puncture the raft.

- If there are other rafts, lash the rafts together so they are about 7.5 meters apart. Be ready to draw them closer together if you see or hear an aircraft. It is easier for an aircrew to spot rafts that are close together rather than scattered.

- Remember, rescue at sea is a cooperative effort. Use all available visual or electronic signaling devices to signal and make contact with rescuers. For example, raise a flag or reflecting material on an oar as high as possible to attract attention.

- Locate the emergency radio and get it into operation. Operating instructions are on it. Use the emergency transceiver only when friendly aircraft are likely to be in the area.

- Have other signaling devices ready for instant use. If you are in enemy territory, avoid using a signaling device that will alert the enemy. However, if your situation is desperate, you may have to signal the enemy for rescue if you are to survive.

- Check the raft for inflation, leaks, and points of possible chafing. Make sure the main buoyancy chambers are firm (well rounded) but not overly tight. Check inflation regularly. Air expands with heat; therefore, on hot day, release some air and add air when the weather cools.

- Decontaminate the raft of all fuel. Petroleum will weaken its surfaces and break down its glued joints.

- Throw out the sea anchor, or improvise a drag from the raft's case, bailing bucket, or a roll of clothing. A sea anchor helps

you stay close to your ditching site, making it easier for searchers to find you if you have relayed your location. Without a sea anchor, your raft may drift over 160 kilometers (99.4 miles) in a day, making it much harder to find you. You can adjust the sea anchor to act as a drag to slow down the rate of travel with the current, or as a means to travel with the current. You make this adjustment by opening or closing the sea anchor's apex. When open, the sea anchor acts as a drag that keeps you in the general area. When closed, it forms a pocket for the current to strike and propels that raft in the current's direction. Additionally, adjust the sea anchor so that when the raft is on the wave's crest, the sea anchor is in the wave's trough.

- Wrap the sea anchor rope with cloth to prevent its chafing the raft. The anchor also helps to keep the raft headed into the wind and waves.

- In stormy water, rig the spray and windshield at once. In a 20-man raft, keep the canopy erected at all times. Keep your raft as dry as possible. Keep it properly balanced. All personnel should stay seated, the heaviest one in the center.

- Calmly consider all aspects of you situation and determine what you and your companions must do to survive. Inventory all equipment, food, and water. Waterproof items that salt water may affect. These include compasses, watches, sextant, matches, and lighters. Ration food and water.

- Assign a duty position to each person: for example, water collector, food collector, lookout, radio operator, signaler, and water bailers.

Note: Lookout duty should not exceed 2 hours. Keep in mind and remind others that cooperation is one of the keys to survival.

- Keep a log. Record the navigator's last fix, the time of ditching, the names and physical condition of personnel, and the ration schedule. Also record the winds, weather, direction of swells, times of sunrise and sunset, and other navigational data….

- Decide whether to stay in position or to travel. Ask yourself, "How much information was signaled before the accident? Is your position known to rescuers? Do you know it yourself? Is the weather favorable for a search? Are other ships or aircraft likely to pass your present position? How many days supply of food and water do you have?"

Cold Weather Considerations

If you are in a cold climate—

- Put on an antiexposure suit. If unavailable, put on any extra clothing available. Keep clothes loose and comfortable.

- Take care not to snag the raft with shoes or sharp objects. Keep the repair kit where you can readily reach it.

- Rig a windbreak, spray shield, and canopy.

- Try to keep the floor of the raft dry. Cover it with canvas or cloth for insulation.

- Huddle with others to keep warm, moving enough to keep the blood circulating. Spread an extra tarpaulin, sail, or parachute over the group.

- Give extra rations, if available, to men suffering from exposure to cold.

The greatest problem you face when submerged in cold water is death due to hypothermia. When you are immersed in cold water, hypothermia occurs rapidly due to the decreased insulating quality of wet clothing and the result of water displacing the layer of still air that normally surrounds the body. The rate of heat exchange in water is about 25 times greater than it is in air of the same temperature.

Your best protection against the effects of cold water is to get into the life raft, stay dry, and insulate your body from the cold surface of the bottom of the raft. If these actions are not possible, wearing an antiexposure suit will extend your life expectancy considerably. Remember, keep your head and neck out of the water and well insulated from the cold water's effects when the temperature is below 19 degrees C. Wearing life preservers increases the predicted survival time as body position in the water increases the chance of survival.

Hot Weather Considerations

If you are in a hot climate—

- Rig a sunshade or canopy. Leave enough space for ventilation.

- Cover your skin, where possible, to protect it from sunburn. Use sunburn cream, if available, on all exposed skin. Your eyelids, the back of your ears, and the skin under your chin sunburn easily.

—From *Survival (Field Manual 21-76)*

Travel in a Life Raft

Greg Davenport
Illustrations by Steven A. Davenport

Once you have identified your position and planned a route, you will want to use a few travel techniques to get from point A to point B. Remember, if you are at sea, you are better off staying close to your distressed vessel… If traveling on open water, head for shipping lanes, land, or rain. Your movement at sea will be influenced by paddles, wind, and current.

Travel at Sea

Life Raft

Movement in a life raft is influenced by wind and currents, and to some extent you can influence this movement by using paddles, sails, and a sea anchor.

PADDLES

Trying to move a life raft with a paddle is often futile and a waste of energy. Paddles should only be used for steering when approaching shore.

Continued ➔

Sailing

Some rafts come with sails, and for those that don't, you can improvise one, although a sail is not advisable for a bigger twenty- to twenty-five-man life raft. You cannot sail a raft into the wind, so you should sail about 10 degrees off from the wind's direction. Sailing a raft does have its risks and thus should not be done unless land is near and the direction of the wind will move you toward land. If these criteria are met, fully inflate the raft, take in the sea anchor, improvise a sail, and use the paddle as a rudder. Stow the sea anchor so that it will deploy in case the raft would capsize. To avoid falling out of the raft, don't make any sudden movements, stand up, or sit on the raft's sides. If seas are rough, don't use a sail, leave the sea anchor out (but keep it away from the bow), and sit low in the raft with everyone's weight toward the upwind side.

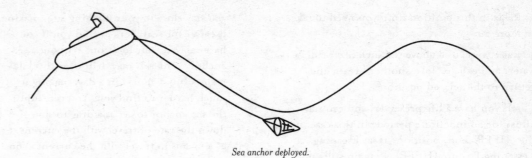

Sea anchor deployed.

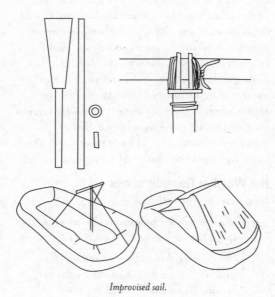

Improvised sail.

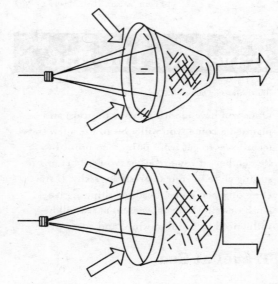

Sea anchor.

Improvised square sails can be made using paddles and any other solid panel of material, such as a tarp or blanket. Tie the paddles together using a square lash to form a T, and then secure the paddles upright to the raft with line. If the raft doesn't have a mast socket, pad the bottom to prevent damage to the raft. You could try using a shoe on top of a protective cloth and insert the mast into the shoe's heel. If you can, slip the toe of the shoe under the seat to hold it in place. Attach the top of your square sail to the mast, but hold the lower lines in your hand so that you can adjust tension or let go when winds gusts.

Sea Anchor

A sea anchor, which will help you control the raft's movement, may automatically deploy with the raft, or you may need to deploy it once aboard. If you don't have a sea anchor, improvise one from a duffle bag or bucket. Most sea anchors have an apex that opens and closes and allows you to adjust for the impact of the current on your movement. When the apex is open, the sea anchor acts like a drag and keeps your movement to a minimum. You may decide to do this when you want to stay close to your vessel or within a shipping lane. When the apex is closed, the sea anchor allows the current to push the raft in its direction of movement. Do this when you want to move faster to reach your destination. Some sea anchors come with a trip line that allows you to collapse the sea anchor and makes it easier to vary your speed or pull in the anchor. If you sea anchor does not have a trip line, you can improvise one by attaching a floating line to the outside edge of the sea anchor. The line will need to be long enough to allow the sea anchor to fully open. If you don't have any floating line, improvise a float and tie the line so that it runs from the sea anchor to the float and then the raft. Make sure that the improvised trip line is rigged in such a way that you avoid getting it tangled in the sea anchor or its line. For best performance, adjust the sea anchor so it is in the wave's trough when the raft is at the wave's crest. To prevent damage to the raft, wrap the line of the sea anchor with a cloth or similar material.

Reaching Shore

Beaching a raft is perhaps the most dangerous part of your journey. Before attempting a surf landing, exhaust all other options first. If no other option is available and you have a chart of the area, take a look at the various shoreline options. What type of bottom contours and makeups (sand, rock, etc.) do you see? Are there any obstacles (man-made or natural) that should be avoided? Avoid coral reefs and rocky cliffs, and try to land on the lee side of the island or at the junction of a stream and the sea. Take time to evaluate the wave's patterns. Waves usually come in sets, and not all sets are the same. Pick the least threatening approach you can, and begin your approach with the start of a set of gentler waves. To keep control of your vessel, don't surf the waves.

Before starting your approach to shore, let the sea anchor out, remove the sail, and use your oar to paddle and steer toward the shore. If you are in a large raft with a group, disperse the weight equally on both sides of the raft. When contact is made with the first wave, paddle backward on both sides of the raft to maintain control and prevent the raft from taking off when its front is lifted by the wave. Begin a forward hard paddle as soon as you feel the front of the vessel dropping. This drop Indicates that the wave has passed. As another wave overtakes you, repeat this process.

If the raft capsizes in the surf, grab hold of it and try to ride it in. if you lose the raft and have to swim ashore, use the side- or breaststroke. If you're in moderate surf, swim with the wave and dive just below the water before the wave breaks. In high surf, swim toward the shore in the wave's trough, and submerge just before the next wave starts to overtake you. If an undertow pulls you down, push off the bottom and swim to the surface. As you get closer to the shore, select a landing spot where the waves run up onto shore rather than violently crash upon the beach. Once you enter the breakers, move into a sitting position with your feet forward and about 2 to 3 feet lower than your head. You are better off absorbing the shock of an unexpected reef or rock with your feet than your head.

—From *Surviving Coastal and Open Water*

Finding Land and Coming Ashore

U.S. Army

Detecting Land

You should watch carefully for any signs of land. There are many indicators that land is near.

A fixed cumulus cloud in a clear sky or in a sky where all other clouds are moving often hovers over or slightly downwind from an island.

In the tropics, the reflection of sunlight from shallow lagoons or shelves of coral reefs often causes a greenish tint in the sky.

In the arctic, light-colored reflections on clouds often indicate ice fields or snow-covered land. These reflections are quite different from the dark gray ones caused by open water.

Deep water is dark green or dark blue. Lighter color indicates shallow water, which may mean land is near.

At night, or in fog, mist, or rain, you may detect land by odors and sounds. The musty odor of mangrove swamps and mud flats carry a long way. You hear the roar of surf long before you see the surf. The continued cries of seabirds coming from one direction indicate their roosting place on nearby land.

There usually are more birds near land than over the open sea. The direction from which flocks fly at dawn and to which they fly at dusk may indicate the direction of land. During the day, birds are searching for food and the direction of flight has no significance.

Mirages occur at any latitude, but they are more likely in the tropics, especially during the middle of the day. Be careful not to mistake a mirage for nearby land. A mirage disappears or its appearance and elevation change when viewed from slightly different heights.

You can be able to detect land by the pattern of the waves (refracted) as they approach land. By traveling with the waves and parallel to the slightly turbulent area marked "X" on the illustration, you should reach land.

Rafting or Beaching Techniques

Once you have found land, you must get ashore safely. To raft ashore, you can usually use the one-man raft without danger. However, going ashore in a strong surf is dangerous. Take your time. Select your landing point carefully. Try not to land when the sun is low and straight in front of you. Try to land on the lee side of an island or on a point of land jutting out into the water. Keep your eyes open for gaps in the surf line, and head for them. Avoid coral reefs and rocky cliffs. There are no coral reefs near the mouths of freshwater streams. Avoid rip currents or strong tidal currents that may carry you far out to sea. Either signal ashore for help or sail around and look for a sloping beach where the surf is gentle.

If you have to go through the surf to reach shore, take down the mast. Keep your clothes and shoes on to avoid severe cuts. Adjust and inflate your life vest. Trail the sea anchor over the stern using as much line as you have. Use the oars or paddles and constantly adjust the sea anchor to keep a strain on the anchor line. These actions will keep the raft pointed toward shore and prevent the sea from throwing the stern around and capsizing you. Use the oars or paddles to help ride in on the seaward side of a large wave.

The surf may be irregular and velocity may vary, so modify your procedure as conditions demand. A good method of getting through the surf is to have half the men sit on one side of the raft, half on the other, facing away from each other. When a heavy sea bears down, half should row (pull) toward the sea until the crest passes; then the other half should row (pull) toward the shore until the next heavy sea comes along.

Against a strong wind and heavy surf, the raft must have all possible speed to pass rapidly through the oncoming crest to avoid being turned broadside or thrown end over end. If possible, avoid meeting a large wave at the moment it breaks.

If in a medium surf with no wind or offshore wind, keep the raft from passing over a wave so rapidly that it drops suddenly after topping the crest. If the raft turns over in the surf, try to grab hold of it and ride it in.

As the raft nears the beach, ride in on the crest of a large wave. Paddle or row hard and ride in to the beach as far as you can. Do not jump out of the raft until it has grounded, then quickly get out and beach it.

If you have a choice, do not land at night. If you have reason to believe that people live on the shore, lay away from the beach, signal, and wait for the inhabitants to come out and bring you in.

If you encounter sea ice, land only on large, stable floes. Avoid icebergs that may capsize and small floes or those obviously disintegrating. Use oars and hands to keep the raft from rubbing on the edge of the ice. Take the raft out of the water and store it well back from the floe's edge. You may be able to use it for shelter. Keep the raft inflated and ready for use. Any floe may break up without warning.

Swimming Ashore

If rafting ashore is not possible and you have to swim, wear your shoes and at least one thickness of clothing. Use the sidestroke or breaststroke to conserve strength.

If the surf is moderate, ride in on the back of a small wave by swimming forward with it. Dive to a shallow depth to end the ride just before the wave breaks.

In high surf, swim toward shore in the trough between the between waves. When the seaward wave approaches, face it and submerge. After it passes, work toward shore in the next trough. If caught in the undertow of a large wave, push off the bottom or swim to the surface and proceed toward shore as above.

If must land on a rocky shore, look for a place where the waves rush up onto the rocks. Avoid places where the waves explode with a high, white spray. Swim slowly when making your approach. You will need your strength to hold onto the rocks. You should be fully clothed and where shoes to reduce injury.

After selecting your landing point, advance behind a large wave into the breakers. Face toward shore and take a sitting position with your feet in front, 60 to 90 centimeters (2 or 3 feet) lower than your head. This position will let your feet absorb the shock when you land or strike submerged boulders or reefs. If you do not reach shore behind the wave you picked, swim with your hands only. As the next wave approaches, take a sitting position with your feet forward. Repeat the procedure until you land.

Water is quieter in the lee of a heavy growth of seaweed. Take advantage of such growth. Do not swim through the seaweed; crawl over the top by grasping the vegetation with overhand movements.

Cross a rocky or coral reef as you would land on a rocky shore. Keep your feet close together and your knees slightly bent in a relaxed sitting posture to cushion the blows against the coral.

—From *Survival (Field Manual 21-76)*

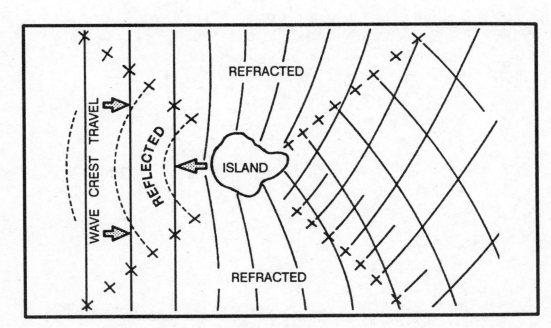

Wave patterns about an island.

Rescue at Sea

Greg Davenport
Illustration by Steven A. Davenport

A rescue by a surface rescue is often a simple process. In most cases, the rescue craft will direct its approach so that you are on the lee side. The rescue vessel will then drift toward you. To avoid contact with the boat's propeller, be sure to pull in your sea anchor. Once contact with a rescue vessel is made, follow the guidance of the rescue crew.

A helicopter rescue may not be as simple. Movement caused by waves, wind, and the helicopter itself will make it difficult to stay balanced in the life raft. To avoid losing gear and potential damage to the helicopter's roto system, secure all gear to the raft. A rescue basket, rescue sling, or stokes litter might be used to hoist you aboard the helicopter, and in most cases a rescue swimmer will be dropped down to help you put on the rescue device.

To avoid potential injury, there are several things you should know. First, the cable coming from the helicopter can have a static charge. Do not touch the cable until it has made contact with your vessel or the water, thus allowing the static electricity to discharge. Second, if a litter or basket is dropped, it normally has a trail line that, once grounded, you can use to stabilize the

basket as it gets closer to your vessel. Once the rescue swimmer has secured you to the rescue device, he or she will give vigorous thumbs up to the helicopter crew so it will know to begin the hoist process.

Rescue Basket

For survivors who are not injured, the U.S. Coast Guard usually uses a rescue basket, which is simple to use. Once the basket has landed in the water, the rescue swimmer will disconnect the cable, help you climb in, and direct you to sit down with your hands and arms inside. Once the cable is reattached you will be hoisted up to the helicopter door.

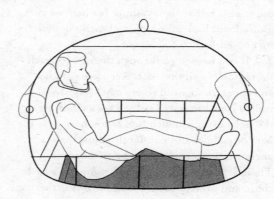

Rescue basket.

Rescue Sling

A rescue sling (padded loop) is used in other countries and in some isolated rescues by the USCG. Once the sling has been lowered into the water, slip it over your body and under your armpits so that the loop goes around your back. For added security fasten the chest strap that is often affixed to the outside of the sling.

Stokes Litter

A stokes litter is often used for survivors who have serious injuries or illnesses. This device requires that help be available. Once the litter has been lowered to the water, the rescue swimmer will disconnect the cable and straps, remove the blankets, place the survivor inside, cover him or her with the blankets, and refasten the straps and cable. Since the litter is hoisted at a head-up (feet down) angle, it's important that chest straps are secured under the victims' arms. Otherwise, he or she could slip out.

—From *Surviving Coastal and Open Water*

Helicopter rescue.

Rescue sling.

Weather

Clouds

Tim Herd
Illustrations by Patrice Kelly

The most visible manifestation of the weather is the endlessly mutating variety of clouds. Riding the winds and delivering the juice of the sky, clouds also portend the future. In their formation and development, their shapes and patterns, and their travel and distribution, we can find a more thorough understanding of the nature of the weather and its far-reaching influences.

Clouds come in an infinite variety of shapes, but a limited number of forms. Recognizing this, a basic cloud classification system was developed by the English pharmacist Luke Howard in 1803 even before the atmosphere processes involved were clearly understood. Using Latin names to describe what he saw, his work remains the basis of today's system, with minor improvements: *cumulus* (a heap, pile, or mound) for convective clouds; *stratus* (spread or strewn) for layered clouds; *cirrus* (filament) for fibrous clouds; and *nimbus* (rain cloud) for storm clouds.

Today we recognize two basic atmospheric processes that develop three basic types of clouds: local convection (upward heat flow) producing scattered individual heaped *cumuliform clouds*; large-scale lifting producing the widespread sheet formation known as *stratiform clouds*; and a combination of these forces producing clouds showing elements of both mechanisms, the *duo-process clouds*. Clouds are also categorized according to the range of heights at which they frequently form.

Clouds range from sea level and the earth's surface up to the tropopause—as high as 60,000 feet (about 11 miles) in the tropics. Altostratus and nimbo-stratus often extend upward into the high level; nimbostratus often lowers to the surface as well. Cumulus and cumulonimbus have their bases in the lowest group, but their vertical extent may push their tops into the middle and high levels. The table on the following page gives the ranges of approximate elevations at which each type of cloud occurs most frequently in the polar, temperate, and tropical regions of the atmosphere.

Cumuliform Clouds: Popcorn Heaps

The *cumuliform* family of heap clouds are convective in nature, as warmed air rises and expands and condensation forms cauliflower-shaped domes with flat bottoms. The flattened bottoms mark the level where rising air reaches saturation and condensation begins. The degree of instability and lifting and moisture content determine how high the cloud may continue to grow above that level.

The smallest cumulus clouds pop up with dimensions of just a few yards wide and high. These little white clouds show settled weather and usually appear in late mornings and early afternoons, after the day's sunshine warms the surface air a bit. The warmed air becomes an invisible rising bubble, called a *thermal*, seeking a level of temperature equilibrium as it rises and cools and its relative humidity increases. If the thermal reaches saturation, condensation occurs and the cumulus forms. The latent heat of condensation is released inside the thermal, raising its temperature and increasing its buoyancy. Eventually the thermal cools to the point where its temperature is no longer warmer than that of the surrounding air, and it stops rising.

The stability in the atmosphere generally limits growth of these *fair-weather cumulus* (also known as *cumulus humilis*) to about 3,000 feet. These clouds never produce precipitation.

At the boundaries of the fair-weather cumulus, there is always mixing between moist and dry air, with simultaneous condensation and evaporation. Sharply defined edges of the cloud show expansion and growth, where condensation is strong. But when the rate of evaporation into the drier air exceeds the rate of condensation, the air cools and sinks, and the cloud edges fray and tear.

The evaporation and sinking motion on the outside of the cloud keep its width nearly constant and prohibit any other clouds from forming near its own boundaries, which is why small cumulus are always separated by clear air. When all the air inside the thermal becomes mixed or diluted with dry air, the cloud begins to sink and deteriorate into *fractocumulus* (from the Latin *fractus*, meaning "broken"). The constant mixing and evaporation limit life spans to mere minutes, but the continual resurgence of new thermals and new cumulus humilis give the effect of little change over time.

Middle-level cumulus show more energy and instability in the atmosphere, as the same process that developed the fair-weather cumulus is allowed to continue vertical growth. Individual *towering cumulus* (also known as *cumulus mediocris*) clouds show many rising cells that are in turn composed of still smaller cells, all at different stages of development in which the overall condensation outstrips the overall evaporation. The general air motion is upward within the cloud, with localized sinking motions, and the

Continued ➡

cauliflower appearance takes on a distinct domed tower shape. The base remains generally flat, but cloud tops may reach as high as 19,000 feet.

In unstable air, the towering cumulus may sprout very quickly and generate much greater height than width. These turret-like formations have inspired their name of *cumulus castellanus*. If the turrets evaporate rather quickly, appearing like flocks or tufts of wool, they are descriptively called *cumulus floccus*.

In a more unstable environment, a towering cumulus will swell with hundreds of thousands of individual convective cells, as a huge amount of energy is released into the air through latent heat of condensation, making the rising air more buoyant. This cycle feeds on itself, building bulging *cumulus congestus* clouds as high as 45,000 feet.

At such high altitudes, water droplets develop into ice crystals, marking the defining transition to *cumulonimbus clouds*. High winds at this upper level where convection is capped may draw out a flattened, wispy *anvil* top to the cloud. The anvil is a separate ice cloud produced by the lifting of a layer of air above the cumulonimbus, and is actually a type of cirrus cloud. The cumu-

lonimbus is often very dark and may have low ragged clouds sweeping along; a large base may stretch a few dozen miles wide. Heavy precipitation is usual. An especially intense cumulonimbus may develop downward protuberances on its anvil called *mamma*, indicating very strong downdrafts that mix moist, cloudy air with drier surrounding air.

Stratiform Clouds

Layered clouds have no convective warming and rising involved in their formation, are much shorter than they are wide, and last much longer than cumulus clouds. Appearing as featureless sheets of clouds, they may extend in width from 5 to 500 miles or more, yet their thickness may be no more than 1,500 to 3,000 feet. One altostratus cloud may spread over more than 350,000 square miles—about the size of Texas, Oklahoma, and Kansas combined.

Layered, or stratiform, clouds are formed by forced lifting of stable air on a large scale; they can form at any altitude. Air that gradually ascends over a denser layer of air, or over a gentle incline of land, will expand and cool,

allowing condensation to permeate the entire layer. Air convergence and its associated uplift does the same. Other processes produce the various types of fogs, which are simply stratus clouds on the ground.

Most stratiform clouds form in the ascent of air associated with cyclones in the boundary zone between cold and warm air masses. As the large horizontal mass of warm air is lifted over the cold and denser air, the layer expands, cools, and condenses. The earliest signal of an approaching warm front are the very highest clouds. Found at heights over 40,000 feet near the top of the troposphere are the wispy *cirrus* clouds, composed entirely of very small, sparse ice crystals, which accounts for their transparency. Unlike most stratiform clouds, layers of cirrus clouds are not continuous. White and delicate in appearance, they average about 5,000 feet thick.

In addition to the wispy, filament form, cirrus clouds may take on a tufted or bent whisk-broom shape, when ice crystals grow large enough to fall out of the cloud as dark, vertical streaks. These streaks are usually curved or slanted, shaped by changes in the horizontal wind. Popularly known as *mare's tails*, this form has also been tagged with Latin: *cirrus uncinus*.

The cirrus of the warm front are followed by a very thin, transparent layer of *cirrostratus* some 5 miles high. Also made of ice crystals, the cirrostratus is so thin at times that it may be invisible, yet sunlight shining through it may reveal its presence by the appearance of halos as it refracts through the six-sided crystals. It is never thick enough to prevent objects on the ground from casting a shadow, certainly when the sun is at least 30 degrees above the horizon.

Cirrostratus is followed by lower and thicker *altostratus*, 3 to 4 miles (16,000 to 21,000 feet) high and about 1 to 2 miles thick. Altostratus is generally not a precipitation producer, although it may happen when ice crystals at the top of the cloud fall through supercooled droplets in the lower portion of the cloud to create snow or drizzle. These clouds appear gray or bluish, fibrous, striated, or lightly striped. *Coronas*— brightly colored rings about the sun or moon— may be created by light diffracted through the small water droplets of the altostratus.

An altostratus cloud thickens and darkens as its base lowers close to the ground with the approach of a weather-front boundary. As it becomes thick enough to mask the sun and begins to produce rain or snow, it becomes the

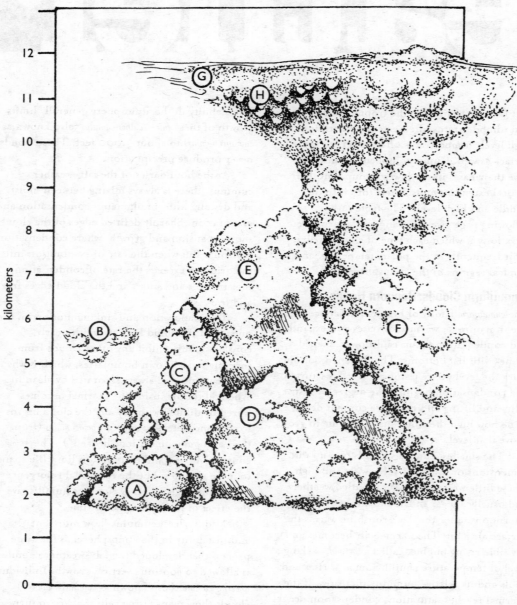

Cumuliform Clouds.
The vertical scale shows approximate and typical heights.

a. cumulus humilis (fair-weather cumulus)   b. cumulus floccus   c. cumulus castellanus
d. cumulus mediocris   e. cumulus congestus   f. cumulonimbus
g. anvil   h. mamma (towering cumulus)

Continued ➡

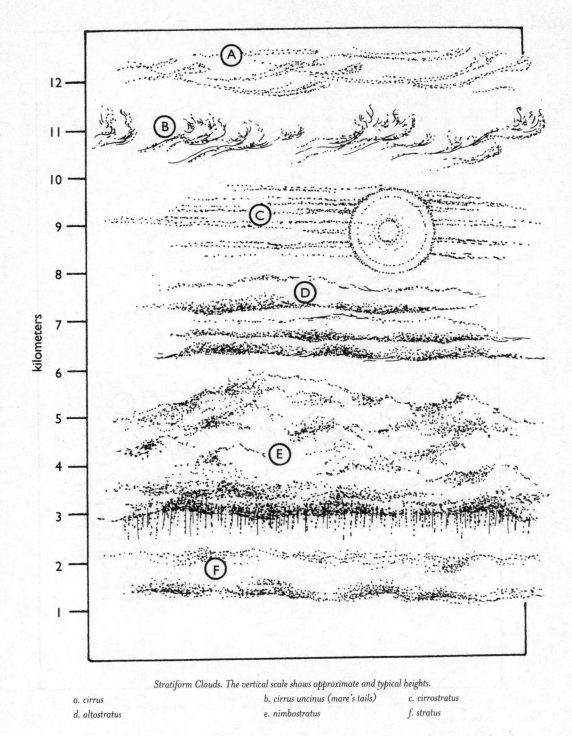

12
11
10
9
8
7
6
5
4
3
2
1

kilometers

Ⓐ Ⓑ Ⓒ Ⓓ Ⓔ Ⓕ

Stratiform Clouds. The vertical scale shows approximate and typical heights.

a. cirrus	b. cirrus uncinus (mare's tails)	c. cirrostratus
d. altostratus	e. nimbostratus	f. stratus

Duo-Process Clouds: Layered Popcorn Combo

The third type of cloud formation combines aspects of both cumuliform and stratiform.

As a sheet of stratus, contained under a temperature inversion, begins to radiate heat to the air above it, the top of the cloud cools. Rising moist air creates a downward motion of cooler, drier air that sinks into the cloud and begins the breakup of the stratus into *stratocumulus*. Small convective cells, with their associated rising and sinking air parcels, produce characteristic thick and thin regions of a lumpy-looking cloud 5,000 to 10,000 feet up. When stratocumulus fill the sky, they often appear in long, heavy ridges, looking like sheets of corrugated roofing.

Turbulence and Mountain-generated Clouds

Being warm clouds, stratocumulus produce little precipitation. What does coalesce and fall as drizzle usually evaporates below the cloud and does not reach the ground. This action cools the air below the cloud, establishing stability there, cutting off any upward transport of air and moisture, and ensuring its dissipation.

Should a layer of stratocumulus divide into smaller units, *altocumulus* may develop. Frequently formed between 12,000 and 20,000 feet, altocumulus clouds appear as white or gray sheets or patches with shaded, rolled masses that look like puffy cotton balls, which may or may not be connected.

The altocumulus pattern appears in a higher, thinner form in the subfreezing temperatures over 20,000 feet as *cirrocumulus*, composed of super-cooled water and ice crystals. Small convection currents produce the characteristic ripples that reminded old-time mariners of fish scales. Their old proverb "Mackerel sky and mare's tails/Make lofty ships carry low sails" is perceptive in that cirrocumulus are associated with the approach of warm fronts and may precede thunderstorms.

Holding your fist at arm's length can help you identify the duo-process clouds. Stratocumulus lumps will be the size of your fist or larger. Altocumulus puffs will appear the size of your thumb. Cirrocumulus scales will match your thumbnail in apparent size.

true rain cloud, the primary precipitation producer of the atmosphere: *nimbostratus.*

With a base at about 6,500 feet, nimbostratus can extend several miles vertically, often consisting of supercooled droplets and ice particles at the cold top and water droplets in the lower, warmer bottom. This is an ideal setup for precipitation through the growth of ice crystals. With the air supersaturated with respect to ice, droplets evaporate and ice crystals eventually grow large enough to fall as snow.

Whether the crystals reach the ground as snow depends on the temperature of the air through which they fall. If the melting level occurs inside the cloud, it is visible as a change in the cloud's color: The area above the melting line is a darker color than that below it. Most nimbostratus precipitation that reaches the ground as rain originated as snow. Rain-moistened air beneath the nimbostratus often develops small, ragged and dark clouds known as scud. At times these may merge into a continuous layer extending up to the base of the nimbostratus.

Stratus is the term reserved for the lowest stratiform clouds, those widespread and uniformly gray layers below 5,000 feet. Stratus clouds are often the result of fog lifting off the surface, although they also commonly develop under the precipitating influences of altostratus, nimbostratus, or cumulonimbus. Consisting of small water droplets, and too warm to initiate ice crystals, the stratus cloud is unable to produce much rain or snow; drizzle is its more likely output. The stratus is usually capped by a temperature inversion that inhibits vertical growth. When the stratus breaks up, it forms a new category of cloud, which combines the processes of both layers and heaps.

lenticular wave clouds

rotor clouds

a. Wave clouds *appear in the crests of a stable air flow that undulates after having been forced over a mountaintop or rolling terrain. They are often polished into smooth lens-shaped billows that are then called lenticularis. A* rotor cloud *shaped like a long cylinder sometimes forms in a turbulent eddy on the lee side.*

Continued ➡

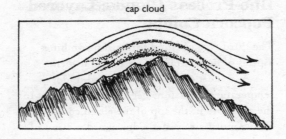

cap cloud

b. A cap cloud may form in cool, dry air that has been lifted to its dew point over a mountain or by a rising thermal. The cloud appears to be stationary, although it continues to grow on the windward side and dissipate on the leeward side. The same result may occur when the strong growth of a towering cumulus obstructs moist upper-level winds. As the winds are forced over the rising thermal, the cap cloud formed is called pileus, *and may feature several stacked together.*

banner cloud

c. Turbulent lift created on the lee side may force moist air to condense in a banner cloud appearing like a pennant waving from the crest.

Kelvin-Helmholz waves

d. Strong wind shear in the upper levels may produce a special kind of cirrus that appear much like breaking ocean waves. Vertical eddies produce a distinctive undulating pattern known as Kelvin-Helmholtz waves. *Without sufficient moisture to form the visible clouds, the eddies create dangerous clear air turbulence.*

Duo-Process Clouds. The vertical scale shows approximate and typical heights.

a. cirrocumulus
b. altocumulus
c. altocumulus castellanus
d. stratocumulus
e. stratocumulus undulatis

Fog: Mist Soup

The lowest clouds are grounded. Composed of tiny droplets like most other clouds, fog is simply a cloud that forms on or sinks to the surface of the earth. In temperatures less than −22°F, ice crystals may form an ice fog. The thickness of fog depends on the size and density of the water droplets. Fog thickness is, of course, a prime consideration because it limits visibility and can result in traffic accidents, airport closures, and other serious problems.

Fogs are categorized according to the processes that produce them. They are further classified as cooling or warming fogs.

Fogs affect both the weather and the climate. On clear days, a fog will reflect sunlight and retard warming and the tendency for convection. Thunderstorms rarely grow over areas that had morning fog. Extensive fogs found off the west coasts of continents cool the climate by reflecting significant amounts of solar radiation.

Fog can be both intensified and dissipated through human intervention. The famous London "pea soup" fogs were exacerbated by widespread burning of coal and its resulting airborne particulates. Now that coal-burning has been greatly restricted, London gets 50 percent more sunshine during the winter months.

Radiation Fog. *The most common fog over land is radiation fog, a cooling fog, which usually forms in still, moist air overnight as the earth radiates heat away and the air cools to its dew point. Radiation fog occurs most frequently in valley bottoms where cool air accumulates after draining down hillsides.*

Fog dissipation can be attempted if the fog is shallow and the wind is gentle. This is sometimes feasible at airports, where helicopters hover over the fog layer, stirring the warmer air above with that at the surface to evaporate it. Another procedure is to seed the fog with salt particles or ice crystals to make the fog droplets

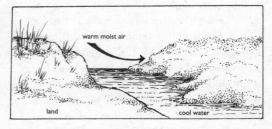

warm moist air

land / cool water

Advection Fog. *Advection fog, another cooling fog, forms when moist air flows over a cold surface; most sea fogs are advection fogs. Advection-radiation fog, called ground fog, arises due to both influences and is generally only a few feet thick. At times, ground fog may sink into valleys and is then called valley fog. Aerial and satellite photos have often shown the soft and branching beauty of fog settled in the drainage pattern of a watershed.*

Continued ➡

Upslope Fog. *A third type of cooling fog is formed as air is forced upward along a surface and expands and cools, and its vapor condenses to form an* upslope fog. *Mount Washington in New Hampshire, which forces both easterly and westerly winds to rise over its summit, experiences upslope fog more than 300 days each year.*

Steam Fog. *Warming fogs may form as air warms. Cold air passing over a warm water surface produces* steam fog, *also known as sea smoke. Water vapor rising from the comparatively warmer water rises into the cooler air and rapidly condenses into fog droplets.*

Frontal Fog. *Frontal fog is produced in the passage of a warm front as warm rain falls into colder air below, and the evaporating raindrops saturate the colder layer. This warming fog occurs more frequently after a prolonged period of precipitation from winter storms.*

grow large enough to fall out. To be successful, these expensive approaches must be done continually while conditions persist; otherwise, fog from the surrounding area quickly closes in as a reminder of nature's obvious advantage in size and might.

—From *Discover Nature in the Weather*

Stormy Weather: Disturbances

Tim Herd
Illustrations by Patrice Kelly

Fair skies, despite their provision of beautiful sunsets and enjoyable weather, do not command the same amount of fascination as does stormy weather. Storms, being the squeaky wheels of the atmosphere, always generate the engaged attention of the innocent and interested victims of their fury: scientists and forecasters, farmers and outdoor workers, business owners and merchants, aviators and mariners, and nearly everyone else. Yet a storm's delivery of its products doesn't affect only humans and their immediate concerns, but the greater biosphere as a whole. All living inhabitants and natural resources are both unsettled and refreshed by the change in weather and the redistribution of air, water, heat, and pressure. This is the stuff of storms: the dynamic energy pitched about in association with low pressure areas, the results of the atmosphere being disturbed by solar radiation and forced over the rotating topography of the earth's crust.

Millions of small-scale circulations and turbulent motions throughout the world form and dissipate each minute. Though small, these weather events are not insignificant, because they are both caused by and influence larger-scale patterns. On the order of a few feet to a few dozen yards, and lasting mere seconds to several minutes, are the *microscale* phenomena. In this category are harmless small eddies and whirlwinds a few feet across that twirl dust and debris for a few seconds, but it also includes dangerous clear-air turbulence and thunderstorm microbursts that can slam an airplane to the ground and severe and highly damaging tornadoes and waterspouts that can last nearly an hour.

Medium-size *mesoscale* patterns on the order of 1.25 to 1,250 miles (roughly 2 to 2,000 kilometers) in size include towering cumulus and thunderstorms, the squall lines and gust fronts they spawn, circulations of land/sea and mountain/valley breezes, weather fronts, air pollution episodes, and severe weather outbreaks. This is the scale in which the Coriolis force becomes an important factor in their movements.

At a size over 1,250 miles (2,000 kilometers) are the longer-lasting *macroscale* events of midlatitude cyclones and anticyclones, jet streams, and large-scale troughs and ridges in the prevailing westerlies.

The weather at any particular location may be influenced by many interacting scales of motion, from the rogue dust devil to globe-girdling planetary waves. At any one time, a site may experience small-scale turbulence, convection, and a sea breeze, as well as the influence of the larger systems of weather fronts, a cyclone, and accompanying jet stream. It can be overwhelming at best, and confounding at worst, to try to understand all the forces and dynamics involved as a whole. Therefore we'll isolate certain disturbances and examine them individually to become better acquainted with the diversity, intensity, and peculiarities of weather's stormy portfolio.

Turbulence

Chaotic motions that fluctuate wildly in seemingly random and unpredictable ways are called *turbulence*. *Thermal turbulence* is the sort caused by the rising air columns of convection. When these thermals contain enough moisture, cumulus clouds form. *Mechanical turbulence* is formed in airstreams roughed up by rugged terrain. Both types are involved in everyday observations: the random shape of clouds as they evolve; smoke dispersed by the wind; steam billowing from a cooling tower; the unpredictability of weather patterns themselves—all exhibit the influence of turbulence in the environment.

Turbulence may be large or small, occur at any altitude, and be with or without clouds. Frequent small-scale eddies only a few inches in diameter form as chaotic swirls in the air, caused by a meeting of breezes from different directions. Such a little *dust whirl* can often be observed on city corners where winds along the streets meet at the intersections. Over a dry and dusty or sandy area, a rapidly rotating column of air may develop from strong convection during hot, sunny, and calm days. The *dust devil* picks up dust, leaves, dried cornstalks, and other light debris, may grow to several yards in diameter at the base, and rotate in either a clockwise or counterclockwise direction. The rotating column is not funnel-shaped like a tornado—nor is it attached to any cloud—but is wider at its base and top, and skinnier in the middle, rather like two cones with their apexes joined. The height is generally between 100 and 300 feet, but in a hot desert may even reach upwards of 2,000 feet. Its movement is slowly erratic during its life span of only a few minutes, as it makes its way to other patches of heated air.

Higher altitudes, with their low humidities and more frequent dramatic changes in wind shear, tend to produce clear-air turbulence. This is especially true near the wind-speed maximums that center along the jet streams. Encountered in flight, clear-air turbulence may make one feel like laundry applied to a washboard. On average, significant turbulence is encountered every other day on a commercial flight over the United States, sometimes severe enough to suddenly drop the plane as much as 200 feet, hurling flight attendants and food carts—and anything else not fastened down—to the ceiling. In December 1997, a jumbo jet over Japan plummeted several hundred feet in a matter of seconds in clear-air turbulence, killing one woman and injuring 102 other passengers.

Recent research has found that turbulence is composed not only of random movements, but also of an ordered, predictable form of eddying. This discovery may lead to a greater understanding of this hazardous marvel.

Continued ➡

Weather

Thunderstorms and Their Progeny

During the lifetime of a large cumulonimbus cloud and its kin, several different microscale storm events may be spawned by one severe mesoscale thunderstorm. To fully understand the relationships, causes, and effects, we'll take a look at the types of thunderstorms and how they grow, as well as their troublesome offspring.

> **Fact:**
> To be classified as severe by the National Weather Service, a thunderstorm must produce at least one of the following: hail of three-quarter-inch diameter or greater; wind gusts 58 mph or greater; any size or duration of tornado.

It is helpful to speak of a cell as one set of updrafts and downdrafts in a storm. Thunderstorms are categorized by the size and strength of their cells as single-cells, multicell cluster, multicell line, and supercell.

Single-cell thunderstorm development begins with convective instability forming a cumulus cloud with its base at the lifting condensation level. If at that point, the air in the updraft remains sufficiently moist and warmer than its surroundings, the new cloud continues to grow upward, eventually becoming a towering cumulus. Ultimately, however, the rising air reaches a level at which its temperature is cooler than its surroundings, it is no longer buoyant, and it begins to sink. In larger storms, this does not happen until it reaches the warmer stratosphere, where temperature increases with height or remains constant.

The altitude at which the rising air's temperature matches that of its environment is appropriately called the equilibrium level. While the air at the top of the rising column is no longer buoyant, the updraft continues to pump air up to that level. As more and more arrives, it begins to spread horizontally, and further condensation forms the ice-filled anvil cloud, capping the towering cumulus and marking its transition to cumulonimbus.

Because this rising air can develop considerable momentum, it can also overshoot the equilibrium level and pierce the anvil with a "boiling-over" dome on the cloud. The amount of this overshoot, as measured by infrared satellite imagery, is used as an indicator of the degree of severity.

The mature stage of the thunderstorm begins when ice crystals and water droplets grow large enough to overcome the updraft and begin falling. The falling precipitation drags cooler air from the higher parts of the cloud into the lower, warmer section, producing downdrafts. The differences in temperature between the falling air and the rising air create stronger upward and downward motions, creating the strom's most violent stage.

> **Fact:**
> In severe weather, many birds will not leave their shelters to find food, because doing so would use more energy than what could be replaced by the food.

Lightning

During the explosive growth stage of the thunderstorm and start of the precipitation, a static charge builds up within the cloud as ice crystals and water droplets grow, interact, and collide. It is believed that the smaller particles tend to accumulate a positive charge near the top of the cloud, while larger ones that fall acquire a more negative charge. Thus the upper part of the cumulonimbus takes on a strong positive charge; the lower part assumes a negative charge, which in turn induces a positive charge on the ground for several miles around the storm.

The voltage difference between areas of opposite charges can reach up to 7,500 volts over the distance of just one inch, and millions of volts over the entire cloud! Once the voltage difference exceeds the insulating capacity of the air, a lightning stroke occurs to complete the electrical circuit and discharge the buildup of static electricity, making the official transformation from rain cloud to thunderstorm.

The first lightning flash of a thunderstorm is generally contained entirely within the cloud. A *luminous leader* traveling between charge centers initiates the discharge, and a lightning strike illuminates the interior of the storm for just two-tenths of a second. The charge is estimated to be a few thousand amperes.

Cloud-to-ground lightning flashes carry greater currents and each year kill as many as one hundred people, damage more than $40 million in property, and set over ten thousand fires consuming $50 million worth of marketable timber in the United States alone.

a. **Growth Stage**. *Thermals rise and vapor condenses, forming a towering cumulus, with its base at the lifting condensation level.*

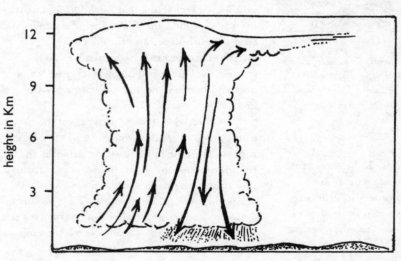

b. **Mature Stage**. *The top of the towering cumulus reaches the equilibrium level and spreads out. Ice particles form the anvil top. Falling precipitation creates downdrafts and more forceful vertical motions. Electrical charges build and separate; lightning is discharged.*

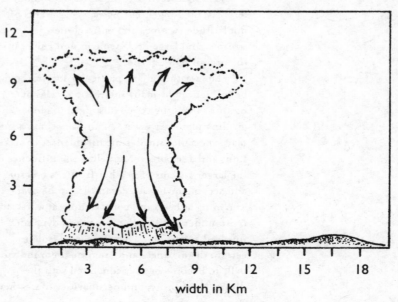

c. **Dissipating Stage**. *Downdrafts eventually bring enough cool dry air to the surface that the supply of warm moist air is diminished, updrafts cease, precipitation tapers off, and the storm dissipates.*

Single-cell Thunderstorm Life Cycle

Continued ➡

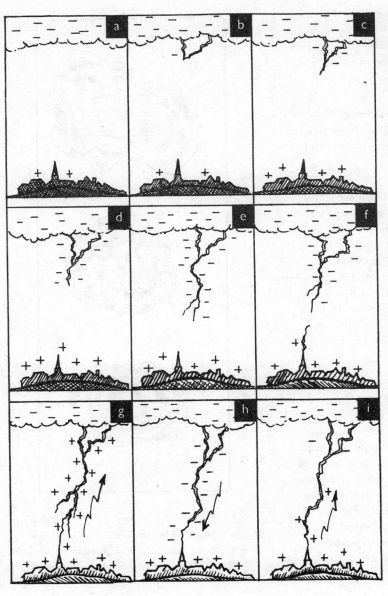

a. Positive charges accumulate near the top of the cloud; negative charges gather near the cloud's base, inducing a positive charge on the ground.

b. c. d. e. A stepped leader emerges from the cloud, carrying negative charges earthward, too fast for the eye to see.

f. A positively charged streamer from a tree or tall structure may form and meet the stepped leader, creating an ionized channel.

g. A brilliant ground-to-cloud return stroke flashes upward carrying positive charges; a shock wave is created from the extreme heating of the air in the channel.

h. A dart leader forms a cloud-to-ground strike following the same track downward without branching.

i. A second return stroke occurs upward. Dart leaders and return stroke exchanges may be repeated several times to constitute one lightning flash. Typical total stroke time elapsed: 30-300 microseconds. Typical total flash time elapsed: less than half a second.

What our eyes see as a single stroke of cloud-to-ground lightning is usually several strokes in rapid succession, in both directions. The series begins as a *stepped leader* emerges from the thundercloud. Composed of luminous electrons, it moves in discrete steps of about 150 feet at a time, for just one-millionth of a second, pausing about fifty microseconds between steps, depositing a charge along a branching channel toward the ground. As it nears the ground, the stepped leader may draw a positively charged streamer upward, to intercept it and complete an ionized path to the ground. The cloud is then short-circuited and a brilliant return stroke flashes upward at about 60,000 miles per second, carrying 30,000 to 200,000 amps, peaking in just a few millionths of a second.

Such an instantaneous rise in current instantaneously heats the air in the lightning channel to temperatures exceeding 50,000°F. The heated air explosively expands, compressing the surrounding clear air, generating a shock wave that becomes an acoustic wave as it propagates away from the channel.

LIGHTNING STROKE SEQUENCE

The noise is thunder. Because sound travels relatively slowly, thunder heard as a sudden "crack" has been generated close by. Rumbling reverberations that follow may have actually been generated first, several miles away, at the start of the lightning stroke.

Upon completion of the first return stroke, small streamers occur in the cloud as precursors to the next stroke, followed by a luminous *dart leader* that emerges and follows the same track to the ground without branching, and a second stroke occurs. This is followed by another return stroke upward. Cloud-to-ground lightning flashes typically consist of three to four individual strokes, and at times as many as twenty or more, all in less than a second.

With the arrival of lightning, the thunderstorm has arrived, statistically speaking. A single-cell thunderstorm typically lasts twenty to thirty minutes and is capable of producing dangerous lightning and heavy rainfall. When convective conditions are favorable, a group of single-cell thunderstorms may merge and move as a unit, with each cell in a different stage of its life cycle. These *multicell cluster storms* are tempests ripe for even more violence, as they strengthen and assault the environs for an hour or longer.

FLASH-TO-BANG COUNTDOWN

Since light travels at 186,000 miles per second, the flash is seen the instant it occurs. Sound travels much more slowly—at about one-fifth of a mile per second. To estimate how far away the lightning stroke occurred, in miles, count the number of seconds between seeing the lightning flash and hearing the thunder, and divide by five.

If the count is 10 to 15 seconds, meaning the flash was 2 to 3 miles away, seek shelter. Successive lightning strokes can be 2 to 3 miles apart, and you could be the next target. Don't be lulled into complacency that the storm is still a ways off. Lightning has been known to leap through clear air to strike several miles away from the storm, in what is the proverbial "bolt from the blue." Remember the 30-30 Rule: When you see lightning, count the seconds until you hear thunder. If that is 30 seconds or less, you're in the danger zone; seek shelter. Wait for 30 minutes since the last lightning strike before going back out.

THE MANY FACES OF LIGHTNING

Forked. Typical cloud-to-ground lightning, also called streak lightning.

Sheet. Intracloud flash in which no branches of the stroke are visible.

Heat. Cloud-to-ground flash seen from a distance; no thunder is heard; appears red or orange.

Ribbon. Rare form of cloud-to-ground lightning that occurs in strong wind blowing perpendicular to the line of sight, spreading the channel sideways as successive strokes follow in it, widening the observed flash.

Bead. Cloud-to-ground lightning in which some sections of the channel remain luminous longer than others; also called pearl or chain lightning.

Ball. Extremely rare, luminous ball of light 1 to 3 feet in diameter that may move rapidly among objects or float through the air. It is usually preceded by a lightning flash, and lasts a few seconds to a few minutes. Accompanied by hissing noise, it may explode or disappear noiselessly. Although observed and reported, it has not been proven scientifically.

St. Elmo's fire. A luminous greenish or bluish glow above pointy objects at the surface. First observed on ship masts, and named for the patron saint of sailors, it is caused by the soft glow of an electrical field as positive charges stream skyward toward negative charges in the cloud. Technically called a *corona discharge*.

Red sprites, blue jets, green elves. Recently discovered, distinctively shaped colored flashes, discharging from the tops of thunderstorms into high altitudes above; occur at the same time as discharges within the cloud.

SYMBOLS FOR STORMY WEATHER

≺ lightning	T thunder	↯ St. Elmo's fire
polar aurora	℞ thunderstorm	℞ severe thunderstorm
℞ thunderstorm with rain and/or snow	℞ severe thunderstorm with hail	∀ squall
	)(funnel cloud	

"May Lightning Strike Me If. . . "

The top six most common activities associated with lightning strikes:

6. Using or repairing electrical appliances.

5. Using the telephone.

4. Playing golf.

3. Working on heavy farm or construction equipment.

2. Boating, fishing, swimming.

1. Being out in an open field.

Lightning Safety

The following lifesaving tips are from the National Weather Service disaster preparedness program.

Don't seek shelter under a lone tree. Isolated trees, especially tall ones, make very effective lightning rods and attract lightning. Standing under trees is probably the deadliest thing you can do in a thunderstorm.

Do go indoors, if at all possible. Most lightning deaths and injuries occur outdoors. Indoor casualties are rare and come mostly from being in contact with electrical appliances and plumbing fixtures, or from lightning-caused fires.

Don't be the highest object around. If you're unable to go indoors, don't stand on a hilltop, in an open field, or on a boat.

Do plan ahead. Get the latest weather information on NOAA weather radio. Listen for static on your AM radio. Keep a sharp weather eye. Give yourself time to get to safety.

Don't stay in the water. Get out, regardless of whether it's a swimming pool, lake, or ocean. Get off the beaches.

Do get off of and away from farm and construction equipment, unless it has an enclosed metal cab. Get off of and away from motorcycles and bicycles, too.

Don't be near wire fences, metal plumbing, railings, and other metallic paths that might conduct electricity to you from a distance.

Don't use golf clubs, aluminum tennis rackets, or other metal objects when thunderstorms threaten. Get to safety.

Do spread out. Groups caught in a thunderstorm should split up. That way, if lightning strikes the group, the least possible number will be affected.

As a last resort. Suppose you're unable to go indoors or seek other appropriate shelter. You find yourself hopelessly isolated in a level field. Suddenly you feel your hair standing on end—indicating your body is taking on a strong electrical charge. It means you're about to become a lightning target. *Immediately drop to your knees and bend forward, with your hands on your knees.* This will not necessarily prevent your being struck, but it's the best compromise between keeping a low profile and minimizing the flow of current between you and the ground. You can survive lightning. About two-thirds of lightning victims fully recover.

The Deadly Myths of Lightning

Deadly Myth #1

Lightning never strikes the same place twice. Wrong! If a spot is exposed and vulnerable, it is very likely to be struck frequently. "Taking the path of least resistance" also means that lightning is actually more likely to strike in the same place more than once, since the channel is already warmed and conducive to a lightning stroke.

Deadly Myth #2

Rubber-soled shoes protect you from lightning. Think of it: a giant spark travels miles through the air, carrying several thousand amps, to be stopped by a half-inch of rubber? Wrong!

(Possibly) Deadly Myth #3

The car is the safest place to be in a thunderstorm. Not necessarily. Assuming we're not talking about a convertible, a car is relatively safe because the metal body of the car would conduct the electrical current of a strike around you to the ground, provided you're not touching anything metal inside the car. The rubber tires do not insulate the car. A safer place to be during a thunderstorm is in a strongly constructed building installed with lightning rods.

Hail

At the cloud top where individual ice crystals may remain for a time in an area of supercooled water droplets, an ice pellet will grow as water droplets strike the ice and freeze on contact. This hailstone, in order to survive melting as it falls through the cloud and to the ground, must remain for at least a few minutes in the presence of supercooled water. This in turn requires updrafts strong enough to counteract the terminal fall velocity of the hailstone, typically 10 to 40 mph. Most thunderstorms do not develop such strong updrafts, and that is why hail that reaches the ground is relatively uncommon.

In more severe storms, updrafts can easily suspend the hailstone above the melting level for long periods. When this happens, hail will grow

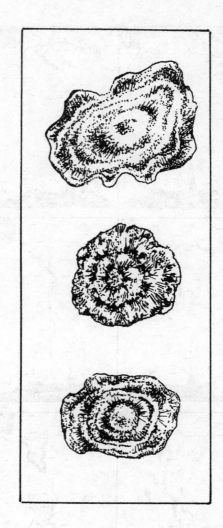

Cross Sections of Hailstones. *The concentric pattern is formed by alternating layers of rime and glaze as the hailstone revisits both sides of the freezing/melting level in its ride through the thunderstorm.*

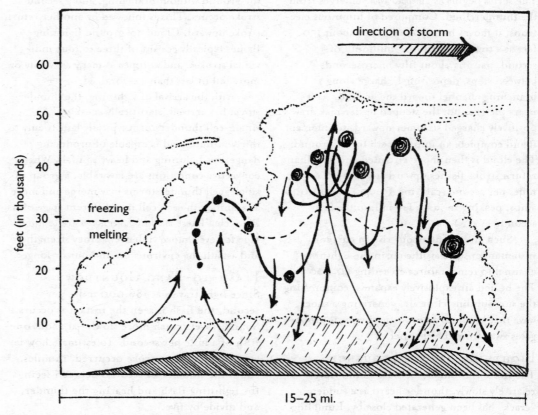

Multicell Cluster Thunderstorm Showing Hail Formation.
Multicells are the most common variety of thunderstorms, in which individual cells, clustered and moving as one cloud, exist at varying stages of growth, maturity, and dissipation. Varying strengths of updrafts and downdrafts, which also progress forward as the storm advances, provide the means for hailstone growth, and account for the varying intensities and amounts of rainfall measured at points along the surface track.

Continued ➡

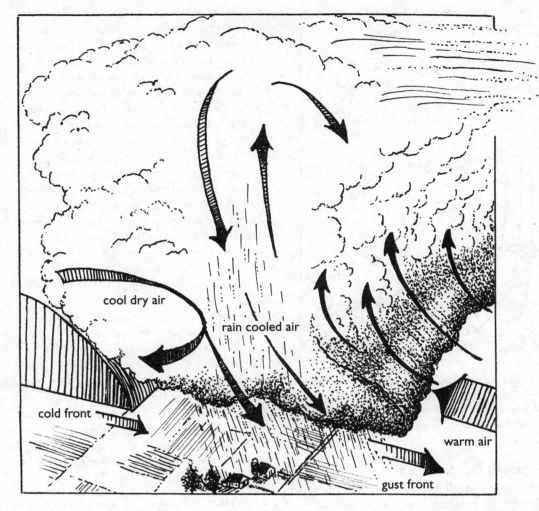

cool dry air

rain cooled air

cold front

warm air

gust front

Squall Line and Gust Front. *The squall line consists of several multicell storms organized into a row and moving as one unit. A coordinated series of downdrafts along its leading edge may develop a gust front of high winds and sharp difference in temperature.*

the cold and warm air, the depth of the cold air, and the speed of the warm air, but typically ranges from 20 to 45 mph. In some cases the gust front can exceed 50 mph and sustain damaging winds. Should the speed of the gust front outrace the thundercloud itself, the convection machine of the storm suddenly finds itself cut off from its source of buoyant air, with only rain-cooled, dense air beneath it, and sees the start of the dissipating stage: the beginning of the end of the storm.

If the warm air at the ground moves so rapidly toward and into the thunderstorm that the gust front can make no headway against it, a different danger arises. Such strong convection stalls the forward momentum of the storm, and it may simply "camp out" for a while in one location, bringing a steady downpour and causing flash flooding.

In a Flash

Flash floods can move with incredible speed, tearing out trees, washing away roads, destroying buildings and bridges, and scouring new channels. Advance warnings are not always possible; take precautions when a watch is issued. When a flash flood warning is issued, act immediately; there may only be seconds to save your life.

Get to higher ground immediately.

Get out of areas subject to flooding: dips, low spots, canyons, swales and so forth.

Avoid already flooded areas. Do not attempt to cross a flowing stream where the water is above your knee.

Do not drive through flooded areas. Shallow, swiftly flowing water can wash a car from the roadway, which may not even be intact under the water.

Abandon a stalled vehicle immediately and seek higher ground. Rapidly rising water may engulf the vehicle and sweep it and its passengers away.

until it is too heavy, or is heaved into a part of the cloud where the updrafts are weak, and it makes a hasty exit to the ground. Because the thunderstorm is usually on the move, hail is typically deposited in a swath 10 to 15 miles wide and up to 100 miles long.

In the varying stages of a multicell cluster storm, stronger, wetter updrafts of the more mature cells coexist next to younger, dryer, and weaker updrafts. As the storm advances and a hail embryo grows, it rides a looping roller-coaster trip through varying-strength updrafts and downdrafts, rising and falling several times past the freezing/melting level and through varying concentrations and sizes of cloud droplets.

Partial melting occurs in the warm parts of the cluster, and freezing in the cold parts, producing a multilayered hailstone of varying textures and appearances, formed by alternate layers of glaze and rime. As it grows in size, a roughly spherical shape may give way to a conical or irregular cluster of smaller stones clumped together. Eventually, the stone's weight can no longer be supported, and the cloud starts spitting ice.

Squall Lines and Gust Fronts

Cumulo-nimbus, like smaller clouds, have a tendency to align themselves into lines, which reduce their overall surface area vulnerable to evaporation. *A multicell line storm*, or *squall line*, consists of a continuous row of thunderstorms that may extend hundreds of miles. Unlike isolated storms, these menaces are frequently associated with larger-scale motions and are

often harbingers of a rapidly advancing cold front. Squall lines are usually in a hurry to move eastward, and they persist for several hours.

A characteristic feature of a squall line is a well-developed *gust front* at its leading edge, formed from a series of downdrafts. This cold, dry air originated some 1.5 to 4 miles up, where frozen and liquid precipitation fell through it, melting and evaporating as it went, thereby cooling it and making it denser and heavier than the surrounding air. Falling to the ground and spreading laterally, it forcibly displaces the warmer air at the surface.

If the motion of the warmer air is contrary to the direction of the newly arrived cold air, a gust front forms. Its passage is marked by strong, gusty winds and a sharp temperature drop—as much as 15°F in a few seconds.

The gust front displays a distinctive shelf cloud along its leading edge. When viewed front-on, it appears as an ominous, smooth black shelf sloping up and back toward the storm, almost like a huge, old-time locomotive cow-catcher, extending from horizon to horizon at a low altitude. When viewed from behind, its fierce internal turbulence is on display, eerily backlit and sinister.

The shelf cloud forms within the warm layer being force-fed into the updrafts of the convection cells by the cold downdrafts. As the warm air is lifted, it all becomes saturated at the same altitude, forming the uniform base of the cloud, and propelling the storm's growth and advance.

The forward speed of the gust front depends on the temperature difference between

Downbursts and Microbursts

The downdrafts in a thunderstorm sometimes gain such momentum and force that they plummet right out of the bottom of the storm and smash on the ground. This downward vigor can be so strong that when it hits the ground and spreads horizontally, it is capable of tornado-force winds, but is no tornado. Called a *downburst*, it is generally directed toward the front of the storm, where it contributes to the storm's forward momentum.

At times a downburst may concentrate damaging winds in excess of 150 mph to an area no larger than 2.5 miles across. Such *microbursts* are the more probable culprits in many storm damages blamed on tornadoes, especially in cases where victims have not seen or heard a funnel cloud. Unlike tornadoes, which scour circular or semicircular swaths, microbursts leave a tell-tale starburst pattern of radiating damage away from ground zero. Not identified until the mid-1970s, microbursts have since been linked to several aircraft crashes. Most microbursts last only a few minutes, but some have lasted as long as half an hour.

Continued →

Microbursts. *Because microbursts are very small, and may or may not be marked by rainfall, they are difficult for a pilot to spot, and even harder to respond to quickly enough if caught in one. As a low-flying plane enters a microburst, the plane suddenly has a strong headwind, which is fine for flying. But as the plane proceeds through it, the head wind rapidly shifts to a tailwind, which suddenly and dramatically cuts the amount of lift generated by the wings. The plane may crash before it is able to regain enough speed to create the necessary lift.*

Such large and long-lasting thunderstorms are known as *supercells*, in which updrafts can approach an unbelievable 170 mph! In the presence and right combination of strong wind shear, updrafts 2 to 6 miles in diameter twist in the wind as they rise, forming a column of air called a *mesocyclone*, rotating at a speed of 50 mph or more. This becomes the difference between "the men and the boys" of thunderstorm activity.

Unlike the up and down pulses of other thunderstorms, supercells organize just one or two cells, each with its own steadily maintained updraft and coexiting—but noninterfering—downdraft, fueling and intensifying the storm. The mesocyclone core, tilted toward the northeast by the wind shear, prevents hail and rain from falling back down into the rising air. Instead, precipitation falling out of the tilted updraft evaporates in the dry, midlevel air on the northeast side of the supercell, causing this air to cool and fall to the earth.

In lesser thunderclouds, precipitation falling into the rising air dampens the upward momentum, and the storm slits its own throat, so to speak, cutting off its lifeblood of buoyant air and dissipating in thirty minutes or so. But the supercell, with its unique internal circulation system, can sustain an intense terrorizing spree for several hours over hundreds of miles.

DERECHO

An especially large and windy squall line that creates a series of downbursts as it races along is called a *derecho* (pronounced day-RAY-cho; from the Spanish, meaning "straight ahead" or "direct"). Derechos produce damaging straight-line winds (not associated with any rotation) in excess of 58 mph, over areas hundreds of miles long and more than 100 miles across. They are especially common to the Midwest in late spring and into summer.

FIRESTORM

Microbursts, with their tremendous surges of oxygen, can transform small wildfires into major conflagrations. Large wildfires, in turn, can create their own circulations of rotating rising air, as the extreme heating leads to highly unstable conditions. If the convective column generates its own inflow, a firestorm is born, and the resultant cloud even gets its own name: *pyrocumulus*. With winds fierce enough to uproot trees and break limbs, the storm multiplies the peril by scattering burning embers for miles around, setting new fires.

SEVERE WEATHER WORDS

These advisories are issued exclusively by the National Weather Service, and are coupled with an announcement of what type of hazard exists (severe thunderstorm warning, tornado watch, etc.).

Watch. The hazard is possible. Conditions are move favorable for its occurrence than usual. The watch recommends planning, preparation, and increasing awareness.

Warning. The hazard exists. It is either imminent or has been reported. The warning indicates the need for action to protect life and property.

Supercell Thunderstorms

As nasty as a squall line can be with its arsenal of downpours, lightning, hail, gust front, and microbursts, it can get worse. The granddaddy thunderstorm of all is one in which everything is more intense: heavier precipitation, more dangerous lightning, larger hail, higher wind gusts, greater potential for greater numbers of microbursts, and, lest we forget, greater outbreaks of tornadoes.

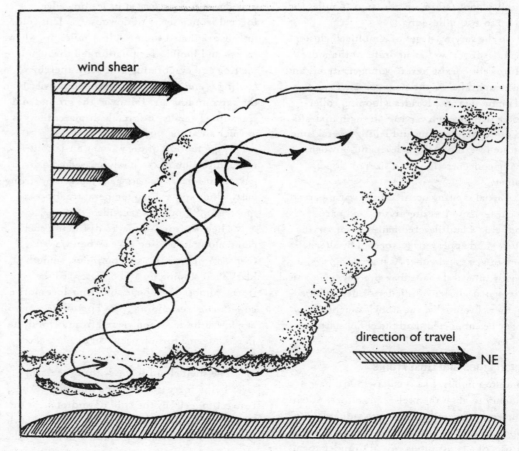

Supercell Thunderstorm. *Unlike the varying-stage cells of multicell storms, supercells organize just one or two that create a rotating mesocyclone core. A vertical wind shear tilts the cloud and its spiraling center toward the northeast, which prohibits precipitation and downdrafts from interfering with the rising air racing to the top of the troposphere. A rotating wall cloud may drop out of the rear flank minutes before a tornado appears.*

Tornado!

I don't think it's possible to say that word without an exclamation point! No man-made structure is able to take a direct hit by a strong tornado. A twisting vortex of winds that can exceed 300 mph, the tornado in action is one of nature's most awesome—and humbling—displays of power.

All categories of thunderstorms can generate tornadoes. In smaller, non-supercell thunderstorms, a weak tornado can form in the

Continued ➡

gust front of the storm, without the characteristics condensation of a funnel cloud attached to a parent cloud, and is sometimes called a *gustnado*. Its formation is similar to that of a small eddy that swirls in a fast-flowing stream as it pours around an object. With a shallow vortex, gustnadoes generally last less than five minutes and rarely exceed 150 mph.

The potential for tornadoes is greatest in the supercell thunderstorm, which is more likely to develop during springtime in the Midwest, although they can and do form at all times of the year. Prime supercell habitat is found where a mile-deep layer of warm, moist air at the surface is overlaid with cool, dry air. A vertical wind shear penetrates both air masses. Separating them is a thin, stable temperature inversion, which serves as a lid to the inherent stability.

If the low-level air can be forced upward to break through the inversion layer, runaway convection results in the highly unstable environment. This may occur through one or more common means: The sun heats the surface, generating thermals; jet streams and upper-level disturbances cause low-level convergence; or the frontal systems of an invading cyclone force-lifts it.

Such mixing produces perfect conditions for the development of surface low pressure and growth of supercells along the frontal boundaries. The formation of a rotating mesocyclone further intensifies the low at the surface, and rapid, fierce convergence of low-level air streams toward the center of the updraft.

Just as the spin of an ice-skater increases as his arms pull inward—due to conversation of angular momentum—a 40 mph wind flowing around the low pressure area at a distance of 5 miles from its center can escalate considerably when reined in to a radius of 1 mile. As the low pressure dramatically deepens, the air at the center expands and cools below its dew point, producing the ominous funnel cloud of the tornado.

The exact process by which tornadoes form is still not clearly understood. Doppler radar shows that the funnel cloud first forms in the midlevels of the cloud, then expends both upward into the storm's higher levels and downward to the ground. But the tornado can exist on the ground without a visible cloud and still inflict calamity.

Sometimes its presence is first noted by a column of swirling debris before the funnel cloud condenses. Sometimes the vortex itself is hidden by surrounding clouds, precipitation, flying dust and debris, hills, trees, or buildings.

The funnel may appear black from the load of debris it carries, white from the condensed water vapor, or take on the color of the dust it sucks up. It may look like a vast rotating cloud on the ground, or as a narrow rope extending 1,000 feet into the sky. As it dissipates, it may contort and become nearly horizontal in its stretched connection to the ground.

About 98 percent of all tornadoes have winds of less than 200 mph and last for just a few minutes, with typical damage paths about 150 feet wide and 9 miles long. The fraction that exceed that level, however, account for about 70 percent of all tornado deaths, and may cut up to a mile wide and 200 miles long.

Damage on the ground often exhibits a capricious and malefic nature: utter devastation sprinkled with fully unscathed swatches. The destruction is primarily caused by the high winds, not by the extreme low pressure, as was once thought. Roofs are commonly lifted by gusts of under 100 mph, and ceilings and walls are forced upward and outward by wind entering broken windows and blown-in doors. Trees are pulled out of the ground by their roots; railroad cars and mobile homes may be tossed about like empty soda cans. The landscape can be swept completely clean, and houses pared to their slab foundations. Pieces of debris, large and small, become missiles in the fantastic wind, to impale themselves in anything not yet moving. An unmistakable, earsplitting clamor, likened to that of a thousand freight trains, narrates the maelstrom.

Most tornadoes consist of a single column rotating cyclonically, but some are accompanied by a pair or more of smaller condensation funnels or debris clouds called *suction vortices* revolving around a common center, scouring

---

TORNADO SAFETY

When in a vehicle:
    Never try to outdrive a tornado. Tornadoes often change direction quickly and can toss cars and trucks through the air.
    Abandon the car immediately and take shelter in a nearby building.

When outdoors:
    Get inside a building if at all possible.
    Lie in a ditch or low-lying area, or crouch near a strong building, if shelter is not available. Be aware of the potential for flooding.
    Always use your arms to protect your head and neck, no matter where you are.

---

their own swirls of damage about the main swath. Such an arrangement is called a *multi-vortex tornado*.

The largest, longest-lasting, and most damaging tornadoes are spawned in the rain-free area of a supercell, under a low, cyclonically rotating *wall cloud*.

Formed by an abrupt lowering of the storm's base, wall clouds are persistently localized at the rear (south–southwest) edge of the storm, where humid, rain-cooled air is ingested into the updraft. With a diameter of a few thousand feet up to 5 miles, wall clouds usually develop a few minutes to an hour before spinning off a violent tornado. The lifespan of these tornadoes may be twenty to thirty minutes or longer as they touch down, disappear, and reappear sporadically and erratically along the travel path of the thunderstorm.

Waterspout

Should a tornado move over open water, it becomes known as a *waterspout*, and can do just as much damage to properties on and near the water. But most true waterspouts that form entirely over water are not as big or as intense as their land-based kin: maybe 150 feet wide, with wind speeds of 50 mph.

Like a tornado, the visible cloud of a waterspout is composed of water droplets, not water that's been sucked up from the surface. Unlike a tornado, however, a waterspout often forms in relatively fair weather, attached to towering cumulus that may have reached only 8,000 feet—not even high enough to freeze at its top. By comparison, the supercells of land-based tornadoes may extend to greater than 50,000 feet high, and well into the freezing zone.

Waterspouts are more common than tornadoes, especially over warm, shallow water; the Florida Keys sees nearly one hundred waterspouts per month during the summer, and up to

Multi-vortex Tornado. *An especially violent tornado may have accomplices revolving about it. These suction vortices can create even stronger winds at the ground, but generally do not last as long as the main twister.*

Continued ➜

five hundred a year. The high water surface temperatures and high humidities in the lowest 2,000 feet of the air favors such frequent development. This unstable condition is very similar to that produced in strongly heated deserts, making waterspouts more closely related to dust devils than to true tornadoes.

—From *Discover Nature in the Weather*

Understanding and Predicting the Weather

Greg Davenport
Illustrations by Steven A. Davenport

How Weather Forms

Weather is a result of the sun's variable heat along with the differences in the thermal properties of the land and ocean surfaces. When temperatures of two bordering areas become unequal, the warmer air tends to climb and flow over the colder, heavier air. Wind currents are the product of the vertical (or near-vertical) process that occurs during the natural horizontal movement of the atmosphere. For example, this process occurs at the equator where the sun's rays heat up the surrounding air. The heated air is lighter and thus rises high into the atmosphere, where it travels toward the poles, cools, becomes denser, and sinks, before it circles back toward the warmer air located at the equator. The returning cool air slides under the lighter warm air, displacing it upward, and the whole process starts over.

Wind and precipitation are often created when the cool dense air rushes back and displaces the warmer air. The earth's rotation deflects the wind from taking a direct north or south route, an effect called the Coriolis force. In the Northern Hemisphere, this force causes the air to spin clockwise around a high-pressure systems and counterclockwise around a low-pressure system. The Coriolis force has the same impact on high- and low-pressure system in the Southern Hemisphere, only in the opposite direction. The Coriolis Effects also will cause the prevailing winds (see below) in the Northern Hemisphere to deflect to the right and those in the Southern Hemisphere to deflect to the left.

Wind

Basic wind patterns consist of prevailing winds, seasonal winds, and local winds.

Prevailing Winds

The prevailing winds are characterized as winds that blow more frequently from one direction than any other. Four pressure systems contribute to this process:

Doldrums: A belt of low pressure around the equator that is created when heated air expands and rises. Shifting slightly north or south depending on the season, the doldrums often produce light winds, depressing humidity, and afternoon thunderstorms and showers.

Horse latitudes: A belt of high pressure located at 30 degrees north and south latitude that is characterized by its regions of descending air.

Polar front: A belt of low pressure located at the polar fronts at 60 degrees north and south latitude.

Polar caps: A belt of high pressure located at the North and South Poles.

Prevailing winds are created when air is moved from a high-pressure region toward an adjacent low-pressure belt. Because the earth rotates, prevailing winds in the Northern Hemisphere are deflected to the right and those in the Southern Hemisphere are deflected to the left. The following are the general prevailing winds.

Trade Winds

Northeast Trades: Located between the equator and 30 degrees north of the equator (wind blows in a northeast direction).

Southeast Trades: Located between the equator and 30 degrees south of the equator (wind blows in a southeast direction).

Prevailing Westerlies

Southwest Antitrades: Located between 30 and 60 degrees north of the equator (wind blows in a southwest direction).

Roaring Forties: Located between 30 and 60 degrees south of the equator (wind blows in a northwest direction).

Polar Easterlies

Polar Easterlies: Located between 60 and 90 degrees north of the equator (wind blows in a northeast direction).

Polar Easterlies: Located between 60 and 90 degrees south of the equator (wind blows in a southeast direction).

Seasonal Winds

The air located above land is warmer during the summer and colder during the winter than the air located above the ocean. Since cold air produces a higher-pressure system, wind, as a general rule, will blow inland during the summer and toward the ocean during the winter.

Local Winds

Local winds are created as a result of temperature changes that occur between day and night, especially during summer months. When compared to adjoining ocean air, the air above land is warmer during the day and colder at night. Since cold air produces a higher-pressure system, wind usually will blow inland during the day and toward the ocean during the night. Mountain and valley breezes are created from a similar process. During the day when the air along the sides of mountains and at valley heads is warmer than the air below it, wind will blow up the valleys. At night, the opposite is true.

Pressure Systems

Atmospheric pressure at the earth's surface directly affects weather. Air located in an area of high pressure will compress and warm as it descends, thus inhibiting cloud formation. So even though a slight haze or fog might occur in a high-pressure area, most days are sunny. Just the opposite happens within an area of low atmospheric pressure.

High Pressure

A high-pressure center is where the pressure has been measured to be the highest in relation to its surroundings. Air moving away from that location will result in a decrease in pressure. On a weather map, the center of a high-pressure area is shown as a blue "H". In the Northern Hemisphere, the winds will flow clockwise around these high-pressure areas, while in the Southern Hemisphere, the winds will travel in a counterclockwise direction. Air in high-pressure areas will compress and warm as it descends. This warming process inhibits the formation of clouds and often results in bright, sunny days with calm weather.

Low Pressure

A low-pressure center is where the pressure has been measured to be the lowest in relation to its surroundings. Air moving away from that location will result in an increase in pressure. On a weather map, the center of a low-pressure area is shown as a red "L". In the Northern Hemisphere, winds will flow counterclockwise around these low-pressure areas, and in the Southern Hemisphere, the winds will travel in a clockwise direction. In low-pressure areas, the light warm air tends to rise, cool, condensate, and form clouds, which often leads to precipitation.

Fronts

When two air masses of different density meet, they seldom mix. Instead, the lighter, warmer air mass is pushed up and over the more dense, cooler air. The resulting boundary between the two is called a front. The four basic fronts are warm, cold, stationary, and occluded.

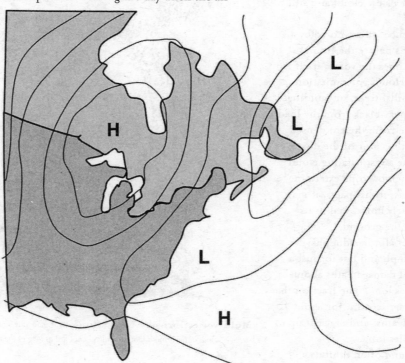

High- and low-pressure centers on a weather map

Continued ➡

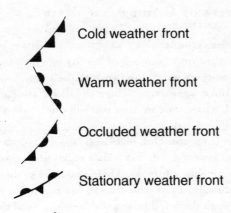

Cold weather front

Warm weather front

Occluded weather front

Stationary weather front

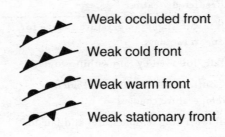

Weak occluded front

Weak cold front

Weak warm front

Weak stationary front

How various fronts appear on a weather map.

Beaufort Wind Scale

Force	Wind (Knots)	*WMO Classification	Appearance of Wind Effects	
			On the Water	On Land
0	Less than 1	Calm	Sea surface smooth and mirror-like	Calm; smoke rises vertically
1	1–3	Light air	Scaly ripples; no foam crests	Still wind vanes; smoke drift indicates wind direction
2	4–6	Light breeze	Small wavelets; crests glassy; no breaking	Wind felt on face; leaves rustle; vanes begin to move
3	7–10	Gentle breeze	Large wavelets; crests begin to break; scattered whitecaps	Leaves and small twigs constantly moving; light flags extended
4	11–16	Moderate breeze	Small waves 1–4 feet, becoming longer; numerous whitecaps	Dust, leaves, and loose paper lifted; small tree branches move
5	17–21	Fresh breeze	Moderate waves 4–8 feet, taking longer form; many whitecaps; some spray	Small trees in leaf begin to sway
6	22–27	Strong breeze	Larger waves 8–13 feet; whitecaps common; more spray	Larger tree branches moving; whistling in wires
7	28–33	Near gale	Sea heaps up; waves 13–20 feet; white foam streaks off breakers	Whole trees moving; resistance felt walking against wind
8	34–40	Gale	Moderately high (13–20 feet) waves of greater length; edges of crests begin to break into spindrift; foam blown in streaks	Whole trees in motion; resistance felt walking against wind
9	41–47	Strong gale	High waves 20 feet; sea begins to roll; dense streaks of foam; spray may reduce visibility	Slight structural damage occurs; slate blows off roofs
10	48–55	Storm	Very high waves 20–30 feet with overhanging crests; sea white with densely blown foam; heavy rolling; lowered visibility	Seldom experienced on land; trees broken or uprooted; considerable structural damage
11	56–63	Violent storm	Exceptionally high (30–45 feet) waves; foam patches cover sea; visibility more reduced	
12	64+	Hurricane	Air filled with foam; waves over 45 feet; sea completely white with driving spray, visibility greatly reduced	

*World Meteorological Organization

Warm Front

A warm front is the boundary between warm and cold air where the warm air is advancing and replacing cold air. Most warm fronts form on the east side of a low-pressure center as a result of the southerly winds that push the warm air northward. The advancing warm air rides above the colder, heavier air where its water vapor commonly condenses into clouds that can produce rain, snow, sleet, or freezing rain. The weather map symbol for a warm front is a red line with half-circles pointing in the direction the cold air is moving.

Cold Front

A cold front is the boundary between warm and cool air where the cool air is arriving and replacing warm air. Winds preceding a cold front typically approach from a southerly direction, while cool winds behind the front tend to be northerly. The advancing dense cold air rides below the warm light air it is replacing. The warm air cools while rising, often resulting in precipitation, depending on humidity. The weather map symbol for a cold front is a blue line with triangles pointing in the same direction that the cold air is moving.

Stationary Fronts

A stationary front occurs when the meeting between cool and warm air results in a standoff. Often several days of cloudy, wet weather occur. Stationary fronts are breeding grounds for new low-pressure areas to form, some of which have been known to grow into storms. The weather map symbol for a stationary front combines the cold and warm front symbols by alternating blue triangles that point away from the cold air and red half-circles that point away from the warm air.

Occluded Fronts

Often seen when a storm advances, a frontal occlusion results from warm air being lifted off of the ground. Both cold and warm occluded fronts can occur. A cold occlusion develops when the air behind the front is colder than the air ahead of it. The colder dense air undercuts the cool air and produces results similar to a cold front. A warm occlusion develops when the air behind the front is warmer than the air ahead of it. The lighter, less cold air rises up and over the colder air and produces results similar to a warm front. Both occluded fronts have well-defined boundaries between the coldest air, the cool air, and the warm air.

Predicting the Weather

Beaufort Wind Scale

The Beaufort wind scale has been used to predict wind velocity since Francis Beaufort created it in 1805. Although slightly modified since its invention, it remains a great tool to help you understand the present wind conditions for your area.

Using Barometric Pressure to Forecast Weather

Before the technical revolution, a barometer was used to predict weather patterns. Atmospheric pressure is affected by high- and low-pressure systems and the elevation where you are (air pressure decreases as you gain altitude). An aneroid (without fluid) barometer measures

Continued ➡

Wind Direction	Barometric Reading	Predicted Weather
SW to NW	30.10 to 30.20 and steady	Fair with slight temperature change for one to two days
SW to NW	30.10 to 30.20 and rising rapidly	Fair, followed by rain within two days
SW to NW	30.20 and above and stationary	Continued fair, with no decided temperature changes
SW to NW	30.20 and above and falling slowly	Slowly rising temperatures and fair for two days
S to SE	30.10 to 30.20 and falling slowly	Rain within twenty-four hours
S to SE	30.10 to 30.20 and falling rapidly	Wind increasing in force, with rain within twelve to twenty-four hours
SE to NE	30.10 to 30.20 and falling slowly	Rain in twelve to eighteen hours
SE to NE	30.10 to 30.20 and falling rapidly	Increasing wind and rain within twelve hours
E to NE	30.10 and above and falling slowly	During summer and times of light winds, rain may not fall for several days; in winter, rain within twenty-four hours
E to NE	30.10 and above and falling rapidly	During summer, rain is probable within twelve to twenty-four hours; in winter, rain or snow with increasing winds
SE to NE	30.00 or below and falling slowly	Rain will continue for one to two days
SE to NE	30.00 or below and falling rapidly	Rain with high wind, followed (usually within thirty-six hours) by clearing (and colder conditions in winter)
S to SW	30.00 or below and rising slowly	Clearing within a few hours, followed by several days of fair weather
S to E	29.80 or below and falling rapidly	Severe storm imminent, followed within twenty-four hours by clearing (and colder conditions in winter)
E to N	29.80 or below and falling rapidly	Severe northeast gale and heavy precipitation; in winter, often heavy snow followed by a cold wave
West wind	29.80 or below and rising rapidly	Clearing and colder

atmospheric pressure. The instrument's pointer will rise or fall as the pressure of the atmosphere increases or decreases. Air pressure at sea level is normally 29.92 inches of mercury, and as a general rule, when the air pressure drops, bad weather is imminent.

Using Barometric Pressure and Wind Direction to Forecast Weather

The National Weather Service provides a guideline for predicting weather in the United States based on wind direction and barometric readings (sea-level pressure). To use this guideline to predict the weather for your area, you will need to convert the barometric pressure so that it is based on sea level at your present location. A simple way to calculate this difference is to subtract about 1 inch of mercury for every 1,000 feet of altitude over sea level.

For example, a barometric pressure of 30 at sea is roughly equal to a barometric pressure of 32 at a 2,000-foot elevation. In order to use the following guide, you must convert the barometric pressure to its sea-level reading. Subtracting 1 inch for every 1,000 feet above sea level gives you 30 inches of mercury and a reading relevant to the National Weather Service Guidelines.

Using Clouds to Forecast Weather

Clouds have a direct role in our weather and can provide valuable clues about what type of weather to expect. In addition to bringing precipitation, clouds warm the earth by preventing its radiant heat from escaping and cool the earth by blocking it from the sun. Clouds are usually classified by height and type.

CLOUD TERMINOLOGY

Prefix "cirro"
Clouds above 20,000 feet (high-level) have the prefix "cirro" assigned to their name. Cirrus clouds usually contain ice crystals and are typically very thin and translucent.

Prefix "alto"
Clouds at 6,500 to 23,000 feet (mid-level) have the prefix "alto" assigned to their name. These clouds usually contain liquid water droplets in summer and a liquid droplet—ice crystal mix during the winter.

Prefix "nimbo"
Clouds that produce precipitation often have the prefix "nimbo" assigned to their name. Nimbus clouds will typically be big and black with ragged dark edges.

TYPES OF CLOUDS AND THEIR MEANING

Stratus clouds

Stratus clouds, which look similar to a high fog, often cover most of the sky with their gray uniform appearance. These clouds are associated with warm, mild weather that will often have a mist or drizzle.

Cirrostratus: Thin high-level (above 20,000 feet) stratus clouds that form a milky, white sheet covering the entire sky. These clouds are so thin that the light rays from the sun and moon pass through them and form a visible halo around the sun and moon. Cirrostratus clouds often indicate the arrival of rain or snowfall within twenty-four hours of an approaching warm or occluded front.

Altostratus: Thin mid-level (between 6,500 and 23,000 feet) stratus clouds that form a gray sheet covering the sky. The sun can be seen under thin sections of altostratus clouds as a dim round disc often referred to as a watery sun. Although the sun might be seen, the clouds will not allow enough rays to pass through to produce a visible shadow on the ground. Altostratus clouds often indicate an impending storm with heavy precipitation.

Nimbostratus: Low-level (below 6,500 feet) stratus clouds are dark gray and usually associated with continuous light to moderate precipitation. This cloud formation provides no information about impending weather since it has already arrived. The sun and moon will not be visible through these clouds.

Stratocumulus: Low-level (below 6,500 feet) stratus clouds are white to dark gray and can be seen in rows or patches or as rounded masses with blue sky in between individual cloud formations. Although these clouds can be associated with strong winds, precipitation is rarely seen.

Cumulus clouds

Cumulus clouds are an isolated group of clouds that look similar to a cotton ball with a flat base and a fluffy top. These clouds typically have large areas of blue sky between each cloud and are normally, but not always, associated with fair weather.

Altocumulus: Mid-level (between 6,000 and 20,000 feet) isolated groups of cumulus clouds with the typical flat-based cotton ball appearance, often found in parallel waves of bands. These clouds typically have a darkened area (often at their flat base) that sets them apart from the higher cirrocumulus clouds. Although these clouds usually indicate good weather, when they appear as "little castles" in the sky, especially on a warm humid summer morning, afternoon thunderstorms have been known to follow.

Cirrocumulus: High-level (above 18,000 feet) isolated groups of cumulus clouds that look like rippled sand or globular masses of cotton (without shadows). As with most cumulus clouds, fair weather is often present or expected when these clouds are prominent in the sky, although a storm may be approaching.

Cumulonimbus: These high mountainous clouds are more commonly known as thunderstorms. The towering clouds will often look like the top of an anvil, which is a classic appearance for thunderstorms, and when present, bad weather can be expected in the immediate area.

—From *Surviving Coastal and Open Water*

Weather Forecasting

U.S. Army

The use of a portable aneroid barometer, thermometer, wind meter, and hygrometer help in making local weather forecasts. Reports from other localities and from any weather service, including USAF [U.S. Air Force], USN [U.S. Navy], or the National Weather Bureau, are also helpful. Weather reports should be used in conjunction with the locally observed current weather situation to forecast future weather patterns.

Weather at various elevations may be quite different because cloud height, temperature, and barometric pressure will be different. There may be overcast and rain in a lower area, with mountains rising above the low overcast into warmer clear weather.

To be effective, a forecast must reach the small-unit leaders who are expected to utilize weather conditions for assigned missions. Several different methods can be used to create a forecast. The method a forecaster chooses depends upon the forecaster's experience, the amount of data available, the level of difficulty that the forecast situation presents, and the degree of accuracy needed to make the forecast. The five ways to forecast weather are:

Persistence Method. "Today equals tomorrow" is the simplest way of producing a forecast. This method assumes that the conditions at the time of the forecast will not change; for example, if today was hot and dry, the persistence method predicts that tomorrow will be the same.

Trends Method. "Nowcasting" involves determining the speed and direction of fronts, high- and low-pressure centers, and clouds and precipitation. For example, if a cold front moves 300 miles during a 24-hour period, we can predict that it will travel 300 miles in another 24-hours.

Climatology Method. This method averages weather statistics accumulated over many years. This only works well when the pattern is similar to the following years.

Analog Method. This method examines a day's forecast and recalls a day in the past when the weather looked similar (an analogy). This method is difficult to use because finding a perfect analogy is difficult.

Numerical Weather Prediction. This method uses computers to analyze all weather conditions and is the most accurate of the five methods.

Recording Data

An accurate observation is essential in noting trends in weather patterns. Ideally, under changing conditions, trends will be noted in some weather parameters. However, this may not always be the case. A minor shift in the winds may signal an approaching storm.

Wind Direction. Assess wind direction as a magnetic direction from which the wind is blowing.

Wind Speed. Assess wind speed in knots.

If an anemometer is available, assess speed to the nearest knot.

If no anemometer is available, estimate the speed in knots. Judge the wind speed by the way objects, such as trees, bushes, tents, and so forth, are blowing.

Visibility in Meters. Observe the farthest visible major terrain or man-made feature and determine the distance using any available map.

Present Weather. Include any precipitation or obscuring weather. The following are examples of present weather:

- Rain—continuous and steady liquid precipitation that will last at least one hour.

- Rain showers—short-term and potentially heavy downpours that rarely last more than one hour.

- Snow—continuous and steady frozen precipitation that will last at least one hour.

- Snow showers—short-term and potentially heavy frozen downpours that rarely last more than one hour.

- Fog, haze—obstructs visibility of ground objects.

- Thunderstorms—a potentially dangerous storm. Thunderstorms will produce lightning, heavy downpours, colder temperatures, tornadoes (not too frequently), hail, and strong gusty winds at the surface and aloft. Winds commonly exceed 35 knots.

Total Cloud Cover. Assess total cloud cover in eighths. Divide the sky into eight different sections measuring from horizon to horizon. Count the sections with cloud cover, which gives the total cloud cover in eighths. (For example, if half of the sections are covered with clouds, total cloud cover is 4/8.)

Ceiling Height. Estimate where the cloud base intersects elevated terrain. Note if bases are above all terrain. If clouds are not touching terrain, then estimate to the best of your ability.

Temperature. Assess temperature with or without a thermometer.

With a thermometer, assess temperature in degrees Celsius (use Fahrenheit only if Celsius conversion is not available). To convert Fahrenheit to Celsius: C = F minus 32 times .55. To convert Celsius to Fahrenheit: F = 1.8 times C plus 32.

Example: 41 degrees F − 32 x .55 = 5 degrees C.
5 degrees C x 1.8 + 32 = 41 degrees F.

Without a thermometer, estimate temperature as above or below freezing (0°C), as well as an estimated temperature.

Pressure Trend. With a barometer or altimeter, assess the pressure trend.

A high pressure moving in will cause altimeters to indicate lower elevation.

A low pressure moving in will cause altimeters to indicate higher elevation.

Observed Weather. Note changes or trends in observed weather conditions.

Deteriorating trends include:

- Marked wind direction shifts. A high pressure system wind flows clockwise. A low pressure system wind flows counterclockwise. The closer the isometric lines

are, the greater the differential of pressure (greater wind speeds).

- Marked wind speed increases.

- Changes in obstructions to visibility.

- Increasing cloud coverage.

- Increase in precipitation. A steady drizzle is usually a long-lasting rain.

- Lowering cloud ceilings.

- Marked cooler temperature changes, which could indicate that a cold front is passing through.

- Marked increase in humidity.

- Decreasing barometric pressure, which indicates a lower pressure system is moving through the area.

Improving trends include:

- Steady wind direction, which indicates no change in weather systems in the area.

- Decreasing wind speeds.

- Clearing of obstructions to visibility.

- Decreasing or ending precipitation.

- Decreasing cloud coverage.

- Increasing height of cloud ceilings.

- Temperature changes slowly warmer.

- Humidity decreases.

- Increasing barometric pressure, which indicates that a higher pressure system is moving through the area.

Update. Continue to evaluate observed conditions and update the forecast.

—From Military Mountaineering (Field Manual 3-97.61)

Nature's Weather Forecasters

Tim Herd
Illustrations by Patrice Kelly

By taking cues from the sky, trees, flowers, insects, and animals, from aching bunions and bones, and a thousand and one other indicators, the art of weatherlore can lead to accurate short-range forecasts. Observational forecasting requires a certain sensitivity to all of nature in all its forms—its sights, sounds, smells, textures, and even tastes. A simple, practical, and accurate assessment of what the weather is up to can be made by interpreting subtle causes and effects.

Scarlet Pimpernel. *The scarlet pimpernel has been called the "poor man's weatherglass," for its tiny red flowers that open for sunny days and close for rainy days. A member of the primrose family that grows in sandy soil, its starlike blossoms bloom from June through August.*

Signs of Changes in Temperature
The pretty shrub of the wetland woods with the

Continued ➡

long evergreen leaves is rhododendron. To the early Americans, it was known as the wild azalea, and they had a saying about it:

When the wild azalea shuts its doors,
That's when the winter's tempest roars.

Though the rhododendron's leaves don't fall in autumn, they do drop as the temperature does, as an adaptation to conserve warmth and moisture. It is a true thermometer of the forest, reacting to the cold. At 60°F, the leathery leaves branch out horizontally, broad and dark green. At 40°, they droop. At 30°, they begin to curl, and at 20°, they hang straight down, tightly curled and black.

Crickets and katydids trill and chirp by the means of a stridulating organ on the base of their wings, whose pitch is higher in warmer temperatures. An array of formulas has been developed to correlate the chirping frequency with the temperature, in degrees Fahrenheit. The males' chirps are fairly reliable, but their rate is also influenced by age, success in finding a mate, and other factors. See if you can verify any of the following, or develop your own correlations.

The katydid not only changes its frequency, but its song as well with declining temperatures. At 78°F and above it insists *katy-did-it*, changing its mind at 74°F to *katy-didn't*. By 70°F, it's back to *katy-did*, switching to just katy at 65°F, and the monosyllabic *kate* at 58°F, before falling silent below 55°F.

Signs of Changes in Humidity

The moisture content of the air increases as stormy wet weather approaches. In the clearing after a storm's passage, the humidity decreases. This pattern is also associated with advancing and retreating cloud formations.

Here are some sayings to test out:

If clouds be bright,
Twill clear tonight;
If clouds be dark,
Twill rain, do you hark?

If wooly fleeces spread the heavenly way,
No rain, be sure, will mar the summer's day.

A rain-topped cloud with flattened base
Carries rain drops on its face.

When hill or mountain has a cap
Within six hours we'll have a drap.

When clouds appear like rocks and towers,
Earth's refreshed by frequent showers.

When halos appear, this rhyme is accurate nearly 80 percent of the time:

When sun or moon is in its house
Likely there will be rain without

Wildlife particularly sensitive to moisture, such as amphibians, tend to be more overtly active in humid conditions, while animals who tend to avoid it, like insects, decrease or alter their normal activities.

Tree frogs piping during rain indicate that it will continue.
If toads come out of their holes in great number, it will rain soon.

When frogs warble, they forecast rain.

Ants that move their eggs and climb
Rain is coming anytime.

When bees to distance wing their flight,
Days are warm and skies are bright;
But when their flight ends near their home,
Stormy weather is sure to come.

Materials that absorb water will do so in humid conditions, and release it in drier conditions. Notice of such things usually precedes the noticeable changes in the weather.

Doors and windows are harder to open and shut in damp weather.

Salt becomes damp before rain.

Ropes are more difficult to untwist before bad weather.

Seaweed dry, sunny sky;
Seaweed wet, rain you'll get.

As the humidity rises, the dew point generally does too, and the more likely it is for dew or condensation to form on cool surfaces, like a concrete garage floor.

When stones sweat in the afternoon, it indicates rain.

Barn Swallows. *Swallows are a family of fast-flying, streamlined birds with long, pointed wings and a graceful ease in the air. Their skillful maneuverability and wide mouths enable them to feed almost exclusively on flying insects. With lower pressure and higher humidity, the insects they feed on stay closer to the ground.*

Signs of Changes in Pressure

Falling pressure is a sure sign of an approaching cyclone, and its associated frontal systems, higher winds, and wet weather. Lower pressure, with its less dense air, makes flying more difficult for birds. Sudden changes in pressure affect joints and old injuries, as the greater difference in internal and external pressures cannot be equalized as quickly. Rising pressure is a sign of clearing and the fair weather of anticyclones.

Swallows fly high: clear blue sky;
Swallows fly low: rain we shall know.

Expect fine weather if larks fly high and sing long.

A coming storm your shooting corns presage,
And aches will throb, your hollow tooth will rage.

Martins fly low before and during rain.

Seagull, seagull, sit on the sand,
It's never good weather while you're on the land.

When water rises in wells and springs, rain is approaching.

If kites fly high, fair weather is coming.

Signs of Changes in the Wind

Because of the wind's direct association with the weather—stormy or fair—even the phrase "changes in the wind" has come to mean the inevitability of future events. West and north winds are known for bringing cooler and drier air; south and east winds bring warmer air and rain. Backing winds (shifting counterclockwise) are a sign of an approaching low pressure center. Veering winds (shifting clockwise) foretell of the calmer and fairer, clockwise-rotating winds about a high. Greater wind speeds and higher gusts travel with faster-moving storms and in the steep pressure gradients they create, although the advance warning they give may be very short.

Test these sayings about wind:

Wind in the west,

Weather at its best.

A wind in the south,

Has rain in her mouth.

A southerly wind with showers of rain,

Will bring the wind from the west again.

When the wind is from the east,

Neither good for man nor beast.

Winds that swing against the sun,

And winds that bring the rain are one.

Winds that swing round with the sun,

Keep the rainstorm on the run.

When the wind backs and the pressure falls,

Be on your guard against gales and squalls.

The sharper the blast,

The sooner it's past.

A veering wind will clear the sky,

A backing wind says storms are nigh.

Complementary and Contradictory Signs

Because nature is so diverse, some weather proverbs can be proven factual for more than just one scientific reason. We may even make a case for the truth of some statements that are obviously contradictory. But this can be expected, for everything is interrelated, and contrariness has a part in nature—as well as in the practice of the weatherlore art. Here are a few sprigs of weather wisdom, based on human sensory detection, and their multiple roots.

Higher humidity increases the sense of smell for some people. (You may test yourself by smelling vanilla or some other spice, then

Species	Count the Number of Chirps in	Temperature
Katydid	60 seconds − 40 Π 4 + 60 =	
Field cricket	15 seconds + 37 =	
Snowy tree cricket	60 seconds − 40 Π 4 + 50 =	
Black field cricket	14 seconds + 40 =	
Others	60 seconds + 100 Π 4 =	
	14 seconds + 32 =	

Continued ➜

wetting the tip of your nose and your upper lip and taking another whiff.) Hence:

When the perfume of flowers is unusually strong, expect rain.

Moreover, areas of lower pressure, being less dense, may allow odors to travel more freely with the currents, as well as release bubbles of gas from the fermenting muck of a swamp, to wit:

When the ditch and pond affect the nose,
Then look out for rain and stormy blows.

Folks with sensitive hearing may detect changes in familiar sounds. Sound vibrations are carried farther in calm, humid, less dense air.

When stringed instruments give forth clear, ringing sounds, there will be fair weather.

On the other hand, a temperature inversion may distort sounds by reflecting and refracting acoustic waves back toward the earth (as well as create acoustical mirages!). For example, if an inversion occurs over a river with steep sides, vertically moving sound may be reflected within and constrained to the shallow inversion layer; horizontally moving sound may be reflected from the banks; and sound nearest the river may move at a different speed than that just several meters higher, with the result of an amazing, partially inverted, partially repeated, incomprehensible, long-distance call propagating along the river in calm conditions.

On yet another hand, if there is substantial wind, as there often is with approaching storms, vibrating sound waves may be easily carried along as a portion of the moving air for a great distance. Too, an approaching storm's dense cloud cover may reflect a portion of the sound waves back toward the earth, and help make the case for just the opposite atmospheric conditions:

Sound traveling far and wide
A stormy day will betide.

Drier air is also clearer air, affording greater visibility of distant objects. With a great amount of water in the air, visibility decreases; as it reaches saturation and mist forms, sight distance is greatly diminished.

When day is dry, the mountain view
cross valley stream and sky of blue.
When day is wet, the mountain sleeps
neath foggy mist and sky that weeps.

On the other hand, dry air that has become stagnant often becomes hazy, containing dust and aerosols, while the movement of a coming low pressure area clears the air before the storm. This is especially true with the haze of airborne salts over the ocean's surface. Hence the following proverb, also true, from the old-time mariners:

The farther the sight,
The nearer the rain.

—From *Discover Nature in the Weather*

Marine Weather Terminology

Greg Davenport
Illustrations by Steven A. Davenport

The following list of terms relate to severe weather conditions, which include unusual water, waves, currents, or wind.

Advisory: Provides information related to impending or present tropical cyclones. Details include the location, intensity, and movement of the storm as well as precautions that should be taken.

Coastal flood watch/warning: A coastal flood watch reflects the possibility of a flood. A coastal flood warning means a flood is expected or occurring.

Heavy surf advisory: Warns of heavy (high) surf conditions that may threaten life and property.

Small-craft advisory: Issued when winds of 18 to 33 knots (21 to 38 mph) are predicted or occurring.

Gale warning: Issued when winds of 34 to 47 knots (39 to 54 mph) are predicted or occurring.

Storm warning: Issued when sustained surface winds of 48 knots (55 mph) or higher are anticipated or occurring.

Tropical storm watch: Issued, usually within thirty-six hours, of when a tropical storm poses a threat in a specific location.

Tropical storm warning: Issued when sustained winds of 34 to 63 knots (39 to 73 mph) are expected to occur within twenty-four hours or less in a specific coastal area.

Hurricane watch: Issued usually within thirty-six hours of when a hurricane poses a threat to a specific location.

Hurricane warning: Issued when sustained surface winds of 64 knots (74 mph) or higher are expected to occur within twenty-four hours or less in a specific coastal area.

Abbreviations Often Used

SCT	Scattered
ISOLD	Isolated
NMRS	Numerous
STNRY	Stationary
DVLPG	Developing
WKNG	Weakening
LTL	Little
FCST	Forecast
OTLK	Outlook
KT	Knots
VSBY	Visibility
CHG	Change

—From *Surviving Coastal and Open Water*

 5-knot wind from NW

 10-knot wind from NW

 15-knot wind from NW

 50-knot wind from NW

 65-knot wind from NW

Wind and wind direction symbols.

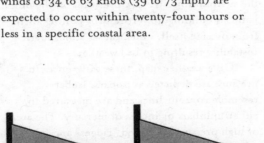

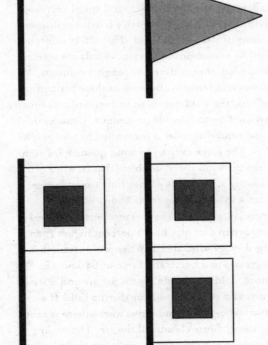

Wind advisory flags.

Continued ➡

Most people subconsciously "forecast" the weather. If they look outside and see dark clouds they may decide to take rain gear. If an unexpected wind strikes, people glance to the sky for other bad signs. A conscious effort to follow weather changes will ultimately lead to a more accurate forecast. An analysis of mountain weather and how it is affected by mountain terrain shows that such weather is prone to patterns and is usually severe, but patterns are less obvious in mountainous terrain than in other areas. Conditions greatly change with altitude, latitude, and exposure to atmospheric winds and air masses. Mountain weather can be extremely erratic. It varies from stormy winds to calm, and from extreme cold to warmth within a short time or with a minor shift in locality.

Mountain Air

High mountain air is dry and may be drier in the winter. Cold air has a reduced capacity to hold water vapor. Because of this increased dryness, equipment does not rust as quickly and organic material decomposes slowly. The dry air also requires soldiers to increase consumption of water. The reduced water vapor in the air causes an increase in evaporation of moisture from the skin and in loss of water through transpiration in the respiratory system. Due to the cold, most soldiers do not naturally consume the quantity of fluids they would at higher temperatures and must be encouraged to consciously increase their fluid intake.

Pressure is low in mountainous areas due to the altitude. The barometer usually drops 2.5 centimeters for every 300 meters gained in elevation (3 percent).

The air at higher altitudes is thinner as atmospheric pressure drops with the increasing altitude. The altitude has a natural filtering effect on the sun's rays. Rays are absorbed of reflected in part by the molecular content of the atmosphere. This effect is greater at lower altitudes. At higher altitudes, the thinner, drier air has a reduced molecular content and, consequently, a reduced filtering effect on the sun's rays. The intensity of both visible and ultraviolet rays is greater with increased altitude. These conditions increase the chance of sunburn, especially when combined with a snow cover that reflects the rays upward.

Weather Characteristics

The earth is surrounded by an atmosphere that is divided into several layers. The world's weather systems are in the lower of these layers known as the "troposphere." This layer reaches as high as 40,000 feet. Weather is a result of an atmosphere, oceans, land masses, unequal heating and cooling from the sun, and the earth's rotation. The weather found in any one place depends on many things such as the air temperature, humidity (moisture content), air pressure (barometric pressure), how it is being moved, and if it is being lifted or not.

Air pressure is the "weight" of the atmosphere at any given place. The higher the pressure, the better the weather will be. With lower air pressure, the weather will more than likely be worse. In order to understand this, imagine that the air in the atmosphere acts like a liquid. Areas with a high level of this "liquid" exert more pressure on an area and are called high-pressure areas. Areas with a lower level are called low-pressure areas. The average air pressure at sea level is 29.92 inches of mercury (hg) or 1,013 millibars (mb). The higher in altitude, the lower the pressure.

High Pressure. The characteristics of a high-pressure area are as follows:

- The airflow is clockwise and out.
- Otherwise known as an "anticyclone."
- Associated with clear skies.
- Generally the winds will be mild.
- Depicted as a blue "H" on weather maps.

Low Pressure. The characteristics of a low-pressure area are as follows:

- The airflow is counterclockwise and in.
- Otherwise known as a "cyclone."
- Associated with bad weather.
- Depicted as a red "L" on weather maps.

Air from a high-pressure area is basically trying to flow out and equalize its pressure with the surrounding air. Low pressure, on the other hand, is building up vertically by pulling air in from outside itself, which causes atmospheric instability resulting in bad weather.

On a weather map, these differences in pressure are depicted as isobars. Isobars resemble contour lines and are measured in either millibars or inches of mercury. The areas of high pressure are called "ridges" and lows are called "troughs."

Wind

In high mountains, the ridges and passes are seldom calm; however, strong winds in protected valleys are rare. Normally, wind speed increases with altitude since the earth's frictional drag is strongest near the ground. This effect is intensified by mountainous terrain. Winds are accelerated when they converge through mountain passes and canyons. Because of these funneling effects, the wind may blast with great force on an exposed mountainside or summit. Usually, the local wind direction is controlled by topography.

The force exerted by wind quadruples each time the wind speed doubles; that is, wind blowing at 40 knots pushes four times harder than a wind blowing at 20 knots. With increasing wind strength, gusts become more important and may be 50 percent higher than the average wind speed. When wind strength increases to a hurricane force of 64 knots or more, soldiers should lay on the ground during gusts and continue moving during lulls. If a hurricane-force wind blows where there is sand or snow, dense clouds fill the air. The rocky debris or chunks of snow crust are hurled near the surface. During the winter season, or at high altitudes, commanders must be constantly aware of the wind-chill factor and associated cold-weather injuries.

Winds are formed due to the uneven heating of the air by the sun and rotation of the earth. Much of the world's weather depends on a system of winds that blow in a set direction.

Above hot surfaces, air expands and moves to colder areas where it cools and becomes denser, and sinks to the earth's surface. The results are a circulation of air from the poles along the surface of the earth to the equator, where it rises and moves to the poles again.

Heating and cooling together with the rotation of the earth causes surface winds. In the Northern Hemisphere, there are three prevailing winds:

Polar Easterlies. These are winds from the polar region moving from the east. This is air that has cooled and settled at the poles.

Prevailing Westerlies. These winds originate from approximately 30 degrees north latitude from the west. This is an area where prematurely cooled air, due to the earth's rotation, has settled to the surface.

Northeast Tradewinds. These are winds that originate from approximately 30° north from the northeast.

The jet stream is a long meandering current of high-speed winds often exceeding 250 miles per hour near the transition zone between the troposphere and the stratosphere known as the tropopause. These winds blow from a generally westerly direction dipping down and picking up air masses from the tropical regions and going north and bringing down air masses from the polar regions.

The patterns of wind mentioned above move air. This air comes in parcels called "air masses." These air masses can vary from the size of a small town to as large as a country. These air masses are named from where they originate:

- Maritime—over water.
- Continental—over land
- Polar—north of 60° north latitude.
- Tropical—south of 60° north latitude.

Combining these parcels of air provides the names and description of the four types of air masses:

- Continental Polar—cold, dry air mass.
- Maritime Polar—cold, wet air mass.
- Maritime Tropical—warm, wet air mass.
- Continental Tropical—warm, dry air mass.

Two types of winds are peculiar to mountain environments, but do not necessarily affect the weather.

Anabatic Wind (Valley Winds). These winds blow up mountain valleys to replace warm rising air and are usually light winds.

Katabatic Wind (Mountain Wind). These winds blow down mountain valley slopes caused by the cooling of air and are occasionally strong winds.

Continued →

Humidity

Humidity is the amount of moisture in the air. All air holds water vapor even if it cannot be seen. Air can hold only so much water vapor; however, the warmer the air, the more moisture it can hold. When air can hold all that it can the air is "saturated" or has 100 percent relative humidity.

If air is cooled beyond its saturation point, the air will release its moisture in one form or another (clouds, fog, dew, rain, snow, and so on). The temperature at which this happens is called the "condensation point." The condensation point varies depending on the amount of water vapor contained in the air and the temperature of the air. If the air contains a great deal of water, condensation can occur at a temperature of 68 degrees Fahrenheit, but if the air is dry and does not hold much moisture, condensation may not form until the temperature drops to 32 degrees Fahrenheit or even below freezing.

The adiabatic lapse rate is the rate at which air cools as it rises or warms as it descends. This rate varies depending on the moisture content of the air. Saturated (moist) air will warm and cool approximately 3.2 degrees Fahrenheit per 1,000 feet of elevation gained or lost. Dry air will warm and cool approximately 5.5 degrees Fahrenheit per 1,000 feet of elevation gained or lost.

Cloud Formation

Clouds are indicators of weather conditions. By reading cloud shapes and patterns, observers can forecast weather with little need for additional equipment such as a barometer, wind meter, and thermometer. Any time air is lifted or cooled beyond its saturation point (100 percent relative humidity), clouds are formed. The four ways air gets lifted and cooled beyond its saturation point are as follows.

Convective Lifting. This effect happens due to the sun's heat radiating off the Earth's surface causing air currents (thermals) to rise straight up and lift air to a point of saturation.

Frontal Lifting. A front is formed when two air masses of different moisture content and temperature collide. Since air masses will not mix, warmer air is forced aloft over the colder air mass. From there it is cooled and then reaches its saturation point. Frontal lifting creates the majority of precipitation.

Cyclonic Lifting. An area of low pressure pulls air into its center from all over in a counterclockwise direction. Once this air reaches the center of the low pressure, it has nowhere to go but up. Air continues to lift until it reaches the saturation point.

Orographic Lifting. This happens when an air mass is pushed up and over a mass of higher ground such as a mountain. Air is cooled due to the adiabatic lapse rate until the air's saturation point is reached.

Cloud Interpretation. Serious errors can occur in interpreting the extent of cloud cover, especially when cloud cover must be reported to another location. Cloud cover always appears greater on or near the horizon, especially if the sky is covered with cumulus clouds, since the observer is looking more at the sides of the clouds rather than between them. Cloud cover estimates should be restricted to sky areas more than 40 degrees above the horizon—that is, to the local sky. Assess the sky by dividing the 360 degrees of sky around you into eighths. Record the coverage in eighths and the types of clouds observed.

Fronts

Fronts occur when two air masses of different moisture and temperature contents meet. One of the indicators that a front is approaching is the progression of the clouds. The four types of fronts are warm, cold, occluded, and stationary.

Warm Front. A warm front occurs when warm air moves into and over a slower or stationary cold air mass. Because warm air is less dense, it will rise up and over the cooler air. The cloud types seen when a warm front approaches are cirrus, cirrostratus, nimbostratus (producing rain), and fog. Occasionally, cumulonimbus clouds will be seen during the summer months.

Cold Front. A cold front occurs when a cold air mass overtakes a slower or stationary warm air mass. Cold air, being more dense than warm air, will force the warm air up. Clouds observed will be cirrus, cumulus, and then cumulonimbus producing a short period of showers.

Occluded Front. Cold fronts generally move faster than warm fronts. The cold fronts eventually overtake warm fronts and the warm air becomes progressively lifted from the surface. The zone of division between cold air ahead and cold air behind is called a "cold occlusion." If the air behind the front is warmer than the air ahead, it is a warm occlusion. Most land areas experience more occlusions than other types of fronts. The cloud progression observed will be cirrus, cirrostratus, altostratus, and nimbostratus. Precipitation can be from light to heavy.

Stationary Front. A stationary front is a zone with no significant air movement. When a warm or cold front stops moving, it becomes a stationary front. Once this boundary begins forward motion, it once again becomes a warm or cold front. When crossing from one side of a stationary front to another, there is typically a noticeable temperature change and shift in wind direction. The weather is usually clear to partly cloudy along the stationary front.

Temperature

Normally, a temperature drop of 3 to 5 degrees Fahrenheit for every 1,000 feet gain in altitude is encountered in motionless air. For air moving up a mountain with condensation occurring (clouds, fog, and precipitation), the temperature of the air drops 3.2 degrees Fahrenheit with every 1,000 feet of elevation gain. For air moving up a mountain with no clouds forming, the temperature of the air drops 5.5 degrees Fahrenheit for every 1,000 feet of elevation gain.

An expedient to this often occurs on cold, clear, calm mornings. During a troop movement or climb started in a valley, higher temperatures may often be encountered as altitude is gained.

This reversal of the normal cooling with elevation is called temperature inversion. Temperature inversions are caused when mountain air is cooled by ice, snow, and heat loss through thermal radiation. This cooler, denser air settles into the valleys and low areas. The inversion continues until the sun warms the surface of the earth or a moderate wind causes a mixing of the warm and cold layers. Temperature inversions are common in the mountainous regions of the arctic, subarctic, and mid-latitudes.

At high altitudes, solar heating is responsible for the greatest temperature contrasts. More sunshine and solar heat are received above the clouds than below. The important effect of altitude is that the sun's rays pass through less of the atmosphere and more direct heat is received than at lower levels, where solar radiation is absorbed and reflected by dust and water vapor. Differences of 40 to 50 degrees Fahrenheit may occur between surface temperatures in the shade and surface temperatures in the sun. This is particularly true for dark metallic objects. The difference in temperature felt on the skin between the sun and shade is normally 7 degrees Fahrenheit. Special care must be taken to avoid sunburn and snow blindness. Besides permitting rapid heating, the clear air at high altitudes also favors rapid cooling at night. Consequently, the temperature rises fast after sunrise and drops quickly after sunset. Much of the chilled air drains downward, due to convection currents, so that the differences between day and night temperatures are greater in valleys than on slopes.

Local weather patterns force air currents up and over mountaintops. Air is cooled on the windward side of the mountain as it gains altitude, but more slowly (3.2 degrees Fahrenheit per 1,000 feet) if clouds are forming due to heat release when water vapor becomes liquid. On the leeward side of the mountain, this heat gained from the condensation on the windward side is added to the normal heating that occurs as the air descends and air pressure increases. Therefore, air and winds on the leeward slope are considerably warmer than on the windward slope, which is referred to as Chinook winds.

Weather Hazards

Weather conditions in the mountains may vary from one location to another as little as 10 kilometers (6.2 miles) apart. Approaching storms may be hard to spot if masked by local peaks. A clear, sunny day in July could turn into a snowstorm in less than an hour. Always pack some sort of emergency gear.

Winds are stronger and more variable in the mountains; as wind doubles in speed, the force quadruples.

Precipitation occurs more on the windward side than the leeward side of ranges. This causes more frequent and denser fog on the windward slope.

Above approximately 8,000 feet, snow can be expected any time of year in the temperate climates.

Lightning is frequent, violent, and normally attracted to high points and prominent features in mountain storms. Signs indicative of thun-

Continued ➡

derstorms are tingling of the skin, hair standing on end, humming of metal objects, crackling, and a bluish light (St. Elmo's fire) on especially prominent metal objects (summit crosses and radio towers).

Avoid peaks, ridges, rock walls, isolated trees, fixed wire installations, cracks that guide water, cracks filled with earth, shallow depressions, shallow overhangs, and rock needles. Seek shelter around dry, clean rock without cracks; in scree fields; or in deep indentations (depressions, caves). Keep at least half a body's length away from a cave wall and opening.

Assume a one-point-of-contact body position. Squat on your haunches or sit on a rucksack or rope. Pull your knees to your chest and keep both feet together. If half way up the rock face, secure yourself with more than one point—lightning can burn through rope. If already rappelling, touch the wall with both feet together and hurry to the next anchor.

During and after rain, expect slippery rock and terrain in general and adjust movement accordingly. Expect flash floods in gullies or chimneys. A climber can be washed away or even drowned if caught in a gully during a rainstorm. Be especially alert for falling objects that the rain has loosened.

Dangers from impending high winds include frostbite (from increased wind-chill factor), windburn, being blown about (especially while rappelling), and debris being blown about. Wear protective clothing and plan the route to be finished before bad weather arrives.

For each 100-meter rise in altitude, the temperature drops approximately one degree Fahrenheit. This can cause hypothermia and frostbite even in summer, especially when combined with wind, rain, and snow. Always wear or pack appropriate clothing.

If it is snowing, gullies may contain avalanches or snow sloughs, which may bury the trail. Snowshoes or skis may be needed in autumn or even late spring. Unexpected snowstorms may occur in the summer with accumulations of 12 to 18 inches; however, the snow quickly melts.

Higher altitudes provide less filtering effects, which leads to greater ultraviolet (UV) radiation intensity. Cool winds at higher altitudes may mislead one into underestimating the sun's intensity, which can lead to sunburns and other heat injuries. Use sunscreen and wear hat and sunglasses, even if overcast. Drink plenty of fluids.

—From *Military Mountaineering*
(*Field Manual 3-97.61*)

Signs of Weather Changes in Cold Climates

U.S. Army

Wind

You can determine wind direction by dropping a few leaves or grass or by watching the treetops. Once you determine the wind direction, you can predict the type of weather that is imminent. Rapidly shifting winds indicate an unsettled atmosphere and a likely change in the weather.

Clouds

Clouds come in a variety of shapes and patterns. A general knowledge of clouds and the atmospheric conditions they indicate can help you predict the weather.

Smoke

Smoke rising in a thin vertical column indicates fair weather. Low rising or "flattened out" smoke indicates stormy weather.

Birds and Insects

Birds and insects fly lower to the ground than normal in heavy, moisture-laden air. Such flight indicates that rain is likely. Most insect activity increases before a storm, but bee activity increases before fair weather.

Low-Pressure Front

Slow-moving or imperceptible winds and heavy, humid air often indicate a low-pressure front. Such a front promises bad weather that will probably linger for several days. You can "smell" and "hear" this front. The sluggish, humid air makes wilderness odors more pronounced than during high-pressure conditions. In addition, sounds are sharper and carry farther in low-pressure than high-pressure conditions.

—From *Survival* (*Field Manual 21-76*)

Windchill

U.S. Army

Windchill increases the hazards in cold regions. Windchill is the effect of moving air on exposed flesh. For instance, with a 27.8-kph (15-knot) wind and a temperature of -10 degrees C, the equivalent windchill temperature is −23 degrees C. ...

Remember, even when there is no wind, you will create the equivalent wind by skiing, running, being towed on skis behind a vehicle, working around aircraft that produce wind blasts.

—From *Survival* (*Field Manual 21-76*)

COOLING POWER OF WIND EXPRESSED AS "EQUIVALENT CHILL TEMPERATURE"																					
WIND SPEED		TEMPERATURE (DEGREES C)																			
CALM	CALM	4	2	-1	-4	-7	-9	-12	-15	-18	-21	-23	-26	-29	-32	-34	-37	-40	-43	-46	-48	-51
KNOTS	KPH	EQUIVALENT CHILL TEMPERATURE																			
4	8	2	-1	-4	-7	-9	-12	-15	-18	-21	-23	-26	-29	-32	-34	-37	-40	-43	-46	-48	-54	-57
9	16	-1	-7	-9	-12	-15	-18	-23	-26	-29	-32	-37	-40	-43	-46	-51	-54	-57	-59	-62	-68	-71
13	24	-4	-9	-12	-18	-21	-23	-29	-32	-34	-40	-43	-46	-51	-54	-57	-62	-65	-68	-73	-76	-79
17	32	-7	-12	-15	-18	-23	-26	-32	-34	-37	-43	-46	-51	-54	-59	-62	-65	-71	-73	-79	-82	-84
22	40	-9	-12	-18	-21	-26	-29	-34	-37	-43	-46	-51	-54	-59	-62	-68	-71	-76	-79	-84	-87	-93
26	48	-12	-15	-18	-23	-29	-32	-34	-40	-46	-48	-54	-57	-62	-65	-71	-73	-79	-82	-87	-90	-96
30	56	-12	-15	-21	-23	-29	-34	-37	-40	-46	-51	-54	-59	-62	-68	-73	-76	-82	-84	-90	-93	-98
35	64	-12	-18	-21	-26	-29	-34	-37	-43	-48	-51	-57	-59	-65	-71	-73	-79	-82	-87	-90	-96	-101
(Higher winds have little additional effects)	LITTLE DANGER			INCREASING DANGER (Flesh may freeze within 1 minute)				GREAT DANGER (Flesh may freeze within 30 seconds)													
DANGER OF FREEZING EXPOSED FLESH FOR PROPERLY CLOTHED PERSONS																					

Windchill table.

Continued ➡

Weather Effects on Human Health

Tim Herd
Illustrations by Patrice Kelly

Weather affects us in ways both large and small, but knowing these effects permits us to prepare for them. Over the climate average of a few decades, we may delineate floodplains, adjust energy distribution networks, or prepare for natural disasters. We may prepare our gardens based on the average date of the last killing frost, or purchase flood insurance based on probabilities for just such an event.

Over a season's length, we can approximate the amount of heating oil required, or the needed capacity of an air conditioner. We may vaccinate against a new strain of influenza, or vacation in a warmer and dryer locale. We may predict market prices of fruit and vegetable crops, and adjust transportation and distribution networks of the produce.

Over the matter of a few hours, we may decide to carry an umbrella or cancel an outdoor concert based on a probability-of-precipitation forecast. We may dress to avoid the wind and possible frostbite, or drink more water and avoid hyperthermia.

Health Effects. Weather has a direct and profound effect on human health. Mortality rates increase during heat and cold waves; conception rates are higher in winter than in summer; illnesses are transmitted by airborne viruses; even work performance, learning, and emotional well-being are tied to specific weather events and patterns. Indirectly, weather impacts human health by affecting crop yields, food supplies, and disease-carrying pest populations. The major known effects of broad weather conditions are summarized in the preceding table.

Exposure to Wind and Cold. Whenever the mercury drops below 58°F or so, our internal temperature also starts to drop. To compensate, we have several responses. Increasing our metabolic rate by eating food or by increasing muscular activity are two voluntary things we can do.

But the body itself (with no help from the thinking part of us) keeps its own thermostat; even if we wanted to be cold, signals are sent in spite of us to the muscles to increase tensing, resulting in shivering. Involuntary shivering increases body metabolism to help maintain a higher body temperature.

Vasoconstriction also kicks into gear when the temperature drops. Vasoconstriction is the narrowing of peripheral blood vessels in the body to reduce blood flow to the outer layers of skin, thereby reducing heat loss.

Add a breeze to the cooler temps and the body loses heat much more quickly. It's a familiar experience that windy days are much colder than calm days of the same temperature. Air is such a poor conductor of heat that if no wind is blowing and we are not moving, a thin layer of warm air forms next to the skin and we may feel quite comfortable. But with air in motion, the wind specializes in heat loss by convection.

Temp. °F	Relative Humidity (%)									
	10	20	30	40	50	60	70	80	90	100
70	65	66	67	68	69	70	70	71	71	72
75	70	72	73	74	75	76	77	78	79	80
80	75	77	78	79	81	82	85	86	88	91
85	80	82	84	86	88	90	93	97	102	108
90	85	87	90	93	96	100	106	113	122	
95	90	93	96	101	107	114	124	136		
100	95	99	104	110	120	132	144			
105	100	105	113	123	135	149				

HEAT INDEX

HOW HOT IT FEELS

UV INDEX

Value	Exposure	Time to Burn	Precautions
0–2	Minimal	60 min.	Hat
3–4	Low	45 min.	Hat, sunscreen
5–6	Moderate	30 min.	Hat, sunscreen SPF 15
7–9	High	15–24 min.	Hat, sunscreen SPF 15 to 30, sunglasses; limit midday exposure
10+	Very high	10 min or less	Hat, sunscreen SPF 30, sunglasses, protective clothing, avoid sun exposure 10 A.M.–3 P.M.

The wind chill index relates how cold it really is (the actual temperature) to how cold it feels (the apparent temperature due to the cooling power of the wind). Its calculated values, displayed in the following chart, are approximations because of variations of individual body sizes, shapes, and metabolic rates. But it is also an approximation because it is based on the cooling rate of a nude body in the shade—not a practical daily application for most of us. Nonetheless, many of us do not dress warmly enough to compensate for the wind chill: Heed it and prepare properly.

Exposure to Heat and Humidity. A one-time *Nancy* comic strip starts off with Sluggo saying that he can't believe how hot the day is.

"Yeah, but it's not the heat that bothers me," Nancy responds as she dives into the air and swims through it, "it's the humidity."

At times it seems that just might be possible. Summertime in the east could definitely be more tolerable without the excessive humidity.

Because our bodies cool by evaporation, the relative humidity affects how cool we feel. If the relative humidity is low (say 10 to 25 percent), perspiration on the skin absorbs heat from the body and evaporates into the air, carrying away body heat. However, as humidity (the vapor pressure) increases, the rate of evaporation decreases. Hence the perspiration does not readily evaporate but stays on the skin, creating that warm, sticky feeling. Body heat does not dissipate through evaporational cooling but

builds up instead, making us feel even hotter than what we would expect to feel at that temperature.

The heat index, the counterpart to the wind chill index, relates how warm it feels with high humidity compared to a dry environment. Various other indices have been developed to address this discomfort we all feel; they include the apparent temperature, the heat stress index, the "humiture," the "humidex," even a "summer simmer index." Some account for effects of solar radiation, wind speed, and barometric pressure on the human condition.

A temperature of 90°F at 30 percent relative humidity is bad enough, you would think, but couple that heat with 90 percent relative humidity, and it feels like 122 degrees! For most people, no discomfort is felt until an apparent temperature of 85°F is reached. Increased discomfort is felt at an apparent 90–93°F. At an apparent temperature of 100–105°F the possibility of heat stroke surfaces, and a prolonged exposure at apparent temperatures over 120, the danger of heat stroke is very real.

Maybe you'd rather not be reminded of how hot it feels. Albert Schweitzer, who did not keep a thermometer with him in equatorial Africa, declared that if he knew how hot it was, he couldn't stand it. So you may or may not want to use this chart. But if you do, remember, it's not the heat—it's the humidity.

Exposure to Sunlight. The ultraviolet (UV) portion of insolation is largely absorbed by the

Continued ➡

ozone layer in the stratosphere. The little bit that reaches the earth's surface, however, is known as biologically active UV (UVB) and is what causes sunburns and other skin problems. Heavy UV exposure releases chemical substances in the body causing local inflammations and suppresses certain immune responses. Chronic sunburn and long-term exposure to the sun can lead to cataracts and result in premature aging of the skin. UV-induced damage to DNA has been linked to cancer and genetic mutations.

The exposure to UV radiation varies with the time of day, season of the year, latitude, altitude, amount of clouds, as well as the length of time spent outdoors, the surface environment, and skin pigmentation. While clouds cut the exposure, they do not screen all the UV, and even cloudy days present some risk. Water, sand, and snow all reflect UV rays, increasing exposure. People with fairer skin are more at risk than those with darker skin.

The following precautions can help minimize exposure and the long-term risks:

Minimize sun exposure between 10 A.M. and 4 P.M.

Wear clothing that covers your body and a wide-brimmed hat that shades your face and neck.

Avoid unnecessary exposure from sunlamps and tanning devices.

Apply a sunscreen with SPF 15 or higher to all exposed areas sufficiently for protection, especially after swimming, perspiring, or sunbathing, even on cloudy days. Apply liberally and frequently to children older than six months.

Wear sunglasses that absorb that full UV spectrum in bright sunlight.

The UV index (see page 385), developed by the National Weather Service and the Environmental Protection Agency, provides a way to help plan outdoor activities and prevent overexposure to the sun. the index values are developed using a computer model that relates forecasted ozone levels in the stratosphere to the amount and specific frequencies of UV reaching the ground. This is then correlated with the forecasted cloud coverage over 58 forecast cities, along with their elevations, to prepare forecasts of the likely levels of ultraviolet radiation at solar noon time the next day.

—From *Discover Nature in the Weather*

Navigation

Before Entering the Wilderness

Darren Wells

People generally get truly lost in the wild because they become separated from their party, have inadequate navigation skills, or leave the map and compass behind. People who get into real trouble are those who get truly lost and don't have the right skills, food, or gear to stay alive until they get found.

Before the Trip

A few simple trip-planning steps will make a world of difference. If you've taken the following precautions before leaving, you will be less likely to get lost, and much more at ease if you do.

- Know your navigation techniques. Don't wait until you are five miles into the backcountry before learning to read a map and compass. Make sure your navigation skills are always a few notches above where they need to be for the terrain you are in. Practice in city parks or near trailheads before setting out on a multi-day trip.

- Carry essential gear and extra food so that you can spent an unplanned night or two out if an emergency arises.

- For overnight trips, write a travel plan and leave it with a responsible adult. Be sure to include a detailed description of your route and return time.

- Take some time to study your route before the trip. Brief your entire group, so that everyone knows what to expect.

- Have more than one navigator in your group. What happens if the only person who knows how to read a map gets sick or injured?

—From *NOLS Wilderness Navigation*

Survival Tips: Navigation

Greg Davenport

Don't Try to Navigate Unless You Know How
Navigation is a skill that requires years of practice to become proficient. If you haven't learned to navigate, you have a greater chance of survival if you stay put and wait for rescuers to find you.

Traveling at Night
If you travel at night, use a sturdy, 7-foot-long walking stick. When walking, keep the stick in front of you to protect your face from branches and to feel for irregularities on the ground.

Learning to Navigate Takes Time
Practice is the key, and you should get lots of it. Knowing how to navigate may even allow you to rescue yourself by walking out.

Never Go into the Wilderness without a Map and Compass, Along with a General Idea of Where you're Going and Where You Are
Before departing, always establish an emergency heading, to the nearest well-traveled road, that will remain constant no matter where you are.

Never Leave Your Camp or Shelter without a Heading, and Pace Count Back
Otherwise you may not be able to find it when trying to return.

When on a Gross Heading, You Can Use Your Shadow to Maintain a General Direction of Travel
To do this, orient your shadow to the heading

Continued ➔

you're taking and keep it there while hiking. Since the sun moves approximately 15 degrees an hour you'll need to adjust your shadow's position, related to your heading, every 15 minutes or so.

—From *Surviving the Desert* and *Surviving Cold Weather*

Seeing Stars

Tom Van Holt
Illustrations by Greg Hardin

Look Where the Sun Has Set

The east-west arc that the sun travels through the sky each day migrates with the seasons: south in the winter, north in the summer, just like the birds. After the summer solstice (around June 21), the arc moves southward. If you note the place where the sun rises or sets each day, you will see this point slowly creep along the objects on the horizon as the days go by. This is why the shadows in winter become so long, the days so short, and sunset seems forever imminent. It's worth noting, because this change in our angle to the sun is why we have the four seasons. It's so easy to observe that it can be seen while commuting or simply stepping outside and observing where the sun is peaking over the roof. In ten days, the motion will become quite apparent.

After the winter solstice (around December 21), the pathway migrates northward to a position higher in the sky. The sun's rays are striking us more directly and making the temperature increasingly warmer. The sun is the only star you can see move independently in the sky, and this apparent motion doesn't affect the motion or position of anything else.

Look Opposite the Sun, to the East

This is where every star makes its nightly debut. You may find it easier to use your peripheral vision to pick out fainter stars or bits of color, such as the red of the planet Mars or the yellow of the star Sirius. Why? The optic nerve linking the eyes to the brain connects directly behind the pupil. In doing so, it displaces the light-sensitive cells that line the inside of the eyeball. By looking at objects not quite so directly, you take full advantage of your eyes' strength.

A useful way to locate objects in the night sky is to use your hand as a ruler. This method has been used for at least three thousand years—it likely will work for you, too. Hold your fist at arm's length, and sight over the back of your hand. This spans an arc of roughly 10 degrees (one finger is about 2 degrees). With a little practice, you will know exactly the width of your hand. This method is used a great deal in this book, and you will find yourself naturally using it to point things out to others.

You can use the fist method to find the one part of the sky that never appears to move; it is around this point that the entire heavens seem to turn. It hovers above the axis that the Earth spins on, and you can find it with your compass. Face directly north, then sight four fist widths above the horizon (roughly 40 degrees). The star sitting on top of your finger is Polaris, the North Star (see Telling Direction). This is true north. The best compass in the world gives a less honest north than this star. Though not very bright, it

has guided people for hundreds of years.

The North Star barely moves and never sets, just as the axle of a wheel can be seen to spin but not change place. There are many more stars that circle tightly around it, and they never set either. These stars, along with Polaris, are known as the circumpolar stars. You will learn to cherish them and the constellations they form as your loyal guides to the sky. They are easy to see and always visible, pointing the way to other stars.

When the stars appear to set, it's because the Earth is spinning us away from them, eventually taking us back into the blinding rays of the sun. …

As the Earth revolves around the sun, we are able to peek into a new little slice of the universe each night—and another little slice passes from view. We see more and more as we journey along our circular path around the sun, until ultimately we have made a full tour of our arm of the Milky Way galaxy each year, at a speed of 70,000 miles per hour! Our stargazing would be much simpler if there were no sun, for it's always blinding us to half the view. If we could just shut it off for a day, we could see all the galaxy in just one twenty-four-hour turn of the Earth (by which time, however, we would have frozen to death).

What this revolving around the sun means to the stargazer is that the stars rise four minutes earlier each night. But they never change where they rise, nor do they change in relation to each other. They will advance deeper and earlier into the night, so that a star that had just been rising at 9:00 P.M. is well clear of the horizon at the same time a week later. It then becomes necessary to stay up later and to keep the same ones in view. Eventually they'll be absent for a few months from our night sky. This is why stars visible at 11:00 P.M. in March can be seen in the same position at 9:00 P.M. in April, 7:00 P.M. in May, and not at all by June. The stars are always there; it's just that we may not be turned away from the sun so that we can see them at a particular time.

This movement of the Earth—spinning on its axis while moving in a great circle around the sun—is entirely what accounts for the apparent motion of the stars. …

The Useful Universe

It was the unfailing dependability of the stars in the sky that allowed mankind to emerge from dark caves and build empires. This dependability is just as valuable to us today in discovering the most essential of knowledges: time, location, and direction. …

Telling Direction

By night, the simplest way to tell direction is to look at the stars just barely above the horizon. You may have to search a few moments to find a prominent star. To the east, they will be rising. In the west, they will be setting. In the south, they can be seen to move in a flattened, downward-facing arc. This can be observed in only a few minutes. It's just the opposite in the north, but it's harder to observe the increasing lack of motion, that characterizes the stars as you look northward (a clue that you're looking north), and the North Star will not move at all.

The best method for learning direction is the one made popular by the Arabs five hundred years ago: finding the North Star, which resides extremely close to true north. This is only by happy coincidence, not because of any special affinity between it and the Earth. (It deeply impressed our ancestors to see a magnetized object point toward it—no wonder they believed in the influence of the stars.) There is no corresponding star in the Southern Hemisphere, and we are extremely lucky to have this one. This star-marked point is directly above the Earth's axis and is more accurate than your compass. It's so dead-on, as a matter of fact, that it can be used to make sure your compass hasn't become demagnetized.

To locate the North Star, first find the "pointer stars" in the constellation the Big Dipper. It's shaped like a squarish soup ladle (it really looks like its name) and may be found in any position—upside down, level, on end—in the north. It's roughly 25 degrees long, and all of its stars are about the same brightness, which is why it's so easy to find. Using the two stars on the outer edge of the bowl, draw a line out of the bowl. This line will shoot through the North Star, roughly four fist widths above the horizon.

If the Big Dipper and North Star still elude you, you can cheat and use a compass your first time out—but just this once. Follow the red half of the arrow to the horizon, then count up roughly four fist widths. The farther south in the United States you are, the closer it will be to the three fists; the farther north, the closer to five fists. This may give you some indication how the North Star has been used to determine latitude, or your position between the equator and the North Pole. Since the North Star never moves, if you move up or down on the face of the Earth, its position in the sky will appear to go up or down. This is how it's been used by travelers for thousands of years.

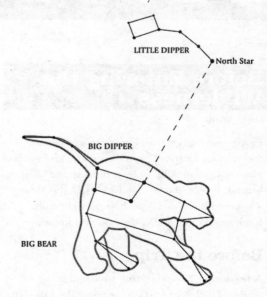

Approximate north can also be found by using the stars in the bold winter constellation Orion the Hunter. A line drawn from the star Saiph (pronounced sife), in the hunter's left foot, through shimmering red Betelgeuse (bee´-tel-jooz), in his left shoulder, will point approximately north. This particular piece of information is not very useful by itself and may be distracting for the beginner. But together with

Continued ➡

other direction-finding tools, it will help you develop an instinct for finding your way in the outdoors.

Here in North America, we are well above the equator and are effectively looking down on the plane of the solar system. This is why the path of the sun (the plane of the ecliptic), moon, and all of the planets is always in the south. Their positions on this pathway may range from extreme southeast to extreme southwest, but they're in the south nonetheless. This gives us several direction finders.

The morning shadows of the sun will point to the northwest. They will then incline to the northeast through the afternoon. These shadows change so slowly that once their angle to your direction of travel has been established, your course need not be checked again for over an hour. Using the sun to find your way is surprisingly useful, especially to a city dweller. The moon can be used in a similar fashion at night. It is helpful to remember that the sun and the moon always move to the right as you face them, from east to west. Because of the southerly position of the plane of the ecliptic, we also know the following:

- The sun is at true south at high noon, and its shadow points toward true north.

- The full moon at its highest point (about midnight) is at true south.

- The quarter moon (what appears as a semicircle) around sunrise or sunset is in the south.

The sun appears to move east to west, so it follows that if you could somehow plot its course, you'd have an east-west line. Drive a stick into the ground or find a shadow of a branch. Mark the tip of the shadow. Half an hour later, mark it again. A line drawn from the first shadow tip through the new one will run approximately east-west. Since the sun always moves to the right, or west, the motion of the sun will tell you which end is which. A perpendicular line through this one will run north-south.

If it's cloudy day, open a knife and hold it horizontally over a light, even surface, such as a book or a flat rock, with the blade turned vertically as though you were slicing. Turn it until the shadow cast by its edge is narrowest, or the shadow is the same width on either side of the blade. This indicates the direction of the sun. Just because it's a cloudy day doesn't change the fact that Earth's source of light radiates from a single point. Mark each end of the knife on a flat surface. An hour later, place the butt of the knife where it was before, and pivot the knife until once again the shadow of the blade is narrowest. A line draw from tip to tip will go east-west.

Generally speaking, approximate directions are good enough to get you home. Still, it is a fair question: Who can afford to spend an hour waiting for a shadow to move or the sun to peak, only to get your direction once? It'll just have to be found all over again in a little while, won't it?

The fact is, your travel direction only needs to be found one time. No matter how hopelessly lost you may be, once you've found your line of travel, it's easy to keep track of it. Simply sight on a distant object along the line of travel and note a landmark where you are now. When you get to the distant object, sight back to your original starting point. A line through this and the onetime distant object (your new location) will allow you to continue along your original bearing.

Telling Time

By themselves, any one of these time-telling techniques might be helpful for telling the time only once, at a moment that is unlikely to serve your needs. Working together, they overlap and reinforce each other so that it is possible to have a reasonably good idea of the time throughout the day and into the night. How nice it would be to live in a world where a reasonably good idea of the time is the biggest hurry we'd ever be in.

Believe it or not, the verdigris sundial that stands so proudly in Aunt Tillie's flower plot works just as well on a rainy day as on a sunny one. This is because unless you have access to complicated schedules and positional information, it doesn't work at all. It's useful only in determining the position of the sun, which can be gauged rather more accurately by looking at the sun itself.

Even high noon on the dial is unlikely to match 12:00 on your watch, owing to daylight saving time and your distance from your time zone's boundary. Suppose one location is 300 miles west of another, but both are within the Mountain Standard Time Zone. Though both have the same official time, the sun will be overhead at each place at different times. Just because people divide the Earth into full-hour designations doesn't mean nature does so.

Man's artificial (but useful) manipulations of the time make it impossible to look at the sky and say, "It's 6:17, Bob, turn the steaks." Using solely natural means is most useful in judging how much time has passed, not exactly what time it is. On the other hand, if you know what the local time is when you start using astronomical signs, the sky is a reliable chronometer for both local and natural time.

Because the Earth revolves around the sun, we see each individual star rising and setting four minutes earlier every night. Thus, if you know the time that a given star rose above the horizon, you may dependably subtract four minutes for each day afterward and know the time. Say you saw the star Arcturus rise at 7:44 on Tuesday evening. Then suddenly your watch batteries died! A week later you would know it was 7:16 when you saw it rise again (seven days times four minutes subtracted from 7:44). This is an excellent method for checking the dependability of your watch.

Unfortunately, the sun is so close to the Earth that it cannot reliably be used for so exacting a purpose. Early men initially used the passage of the sun to establish the length of the day and year. In just a few years, however, this would always lead to inconsistencies that had devastating results.

It's precisely because the stars are so distant that they are so dependable. We cannot see their actual motion, so it is only the motion of the Earth that makes them appear to move, and this we can allow for. For this reason, we've come to adopt the sidereal (star) year over the solar (sun) year. It is our position relative to the stars, not the sun, that is now used to measure the year—just as you should set your watch.

But knowing the time only at sunrise and sunset is almost as useful as a broken watch, which is also accurate only twice a day. There are several method that, used together, can keep you on time throughout the day, without a man-made timepiece.

If the moon is present, we may count on its chronic tardiness to tell the time. As well as turning with the stars, it revolves around the Earth. So every night—and day—it delays its appearance onstage by about fifty minutes. To tell where the moon is today compared with yesterday, sight it over a feature such as a tree, saddle, or mountain. When it crosses that same point the next day, it's roughly fifty minutes later than the day before.

This is the same motion that causes the moon to move across the background of stars at the speed of one moon width every hour, or half a degree. But it's difficult to judge this, if only because the surrounding stars are overwhelmed by its brightness. It's best, then, to find two stars that are endpoints for a line running next to the moon, and judge its passage compared to that.

What if there's a new moon—that is to say, no moon at all? This occurs when the moon is directly between the sun and Earth, and all we can see as its shadow, or nothing. Never fear, for the night sky is the very model for our clocks and watches. Remember how a line drawn through the bowl of the Big Dipper points toward the North? The Big Dipper circles the North Star just as the hour hand circles a clock, and so does this stellar line sweep out the passage of time. The only difference is that the celestial timepiece is on a twenty-four-hour dial, not a mere twelve, and it moves counterclockwise. The same turning of the Earth that inspired man to mark time with round-faced clock is the same motion that makes the starry sky appear to turn as well.

It's too much to expect, of course, that when our clocks point to 3:00 P.M., the stellar clock would too. But the motion is the same. Suppose you went to bed and saw that the pointer stars pointed straight down, at a watch's 6:00. When you woke up they had moved counterclockwise, to 2:00. The four "regular" hours are doubled—eight hours have passed since you went to bed, and the sun will be up shortly.

If you have an idea what time the sun has been rising and setting (check the weather section of the newspaper or observe yourself), you know how many hours of daylight there are. So if the sun is a quarter of the way across the sky, simply add a quarter of the hours in the day to the time you know that the sun rose. This will give you a useful, if approximate, time.

Continued ➡

The Constellations

People often have a lot of trouble finding the constellations. It's so difficult to take connect-the-dot pictures of stars on paper and see them in the sky that most can never find anything more than Orion the Hunter and the Big Dipper at best. But the most spectacular constellations really do look exactly like their names: Leo the lion, Scorpio the scorpion, Cygnus the swan, Pegasus the winged horse. And better still, most of them can be found by using simple, ever-present skymarks. ...

The Hunters and the Hunted

Winter nights are the best for stargazing. This is the season of the most brilliant constellations, the clearest air, the longest nights, and the most expansive views. But it's cold! So make yourself comfortable. Take along blankets and hot chocolate. Don't feel guilty about temporarily retreating to the house or car. If you must turn on a light, mask it in red using tape, tissue paper, or marking pen, so that you can return to stargazing with your night vision intact. Swinging your arms in circles gets the heart pumping and whips blood into the fingertips, an excellent method for retaining the warmth in your hands.

The best time for viewing the Hunters and the Hunted is from the middle of January through April. The Big and Little Bears, since they are among the never-setting circumpolar stars, can be seen year-round. ...

... The Big and Little Bears are confined to the very center of the sky, around which everything else revolves, and are never permitted to dip below the horizon and into the seas.

These and all the other stars that are forever above the horizon are known as the circumpolar stars. The Big Dipper forms the tail and hindquarters of the Big Bear. It is easier to find if you first locate the North Star by following the red arrow on your compass to north and going up roughly four fist widths.

Now look for the Big Dipper circling around it. It's about three fist widths away from the North Star and is two and a half fist widths across. At the time of year that the Hunters and the Hunted are best seen, the Big Dipper either will appear to be pouring from the left to right or will be about level. The stars that make up the rest of the Big Bear are not as bright as those in its dipper part, but they clearly outline a large constellation in the shape of a bear.

The Little Bear is one and the same as the Little Dipper, the North Star being the tip of its tail (or handle). It takes some imagination to see a young cub here, but there's no problem identifying it as the Little Dipper. It's important that you are able to find the Big and Little Bears (Dippers), because they are used to find many of the other constellations.

Now take the two stars that complete the far edge of the bowl in the Big Dipper, the ones that point directly to the North Star. Shoot them four fist widths in the opposite direction. This will take you straight to the heart of Leo the lion.

Parallel to and facing the same direction as the Big Bear, Leo is angled to pounce on some unsuspecting varmint. He's about two and a half fists across and just over a fist from the bright star Regulus in his chest to the top of his head, an area that resembles a backward question mark. ...

Now look to the south. See the three bright stars in a row, the width of two outstretched fingers? These form the belt of Orion the Hunter, the most brilliant of all constellations. Now, imagine where a man's shoulder and legs would be (about two fists from shoulder to thigh), and you'll find a brighter star at each point. You may notice that the star in his left shoulder, Betelgeuse (bee´-tel-jooz), is red in color. You can even see a faint sword of stars swinging from his belt. ...

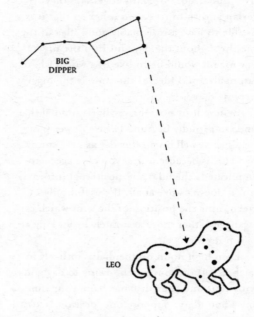

His two hunting dogs—the Big and Little Dogs—follow him. It is often difficult to see anything but one bright star in each, but those are hard to miss. Sirius (seer´-ee-su), the Dog Star, is the brightest star in the sky and is just over two fists to Orion's left, on a straight line drawn through his belt. Procyon (pro´-see-on) is the same distance on a line drawn through Orion's shoulders (drop down a bit toward Sirius). The three stars Betelgeuse, Procyon, and Sirius form what is known as the Winter Triangle.

Orion and his dogs are chasing after the Seven Sisters, or Pleiades (plee´-uh-deez), a beautiful but faint cluster of stars also on the line through Orion's belt, but to the right by four and a half fists. ...

... Taurus (tor´-us) the bull is between Orion and the Seven Sisters. This V-shaped constellation appears as only the head and horns of a bull. The bull's eye can be found midway along the line running from Orion's belt to the Seven Sisters—you can see its angry red glare.

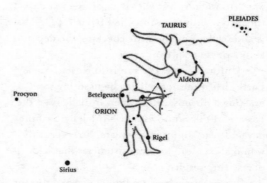

The key to the winter stars is finding the three bright stars in Orion's belt, in the southern sky. They're in a straight row the width of one outstretched finger.

(The tips of the horns are a fist and a half above, as though Taurus is crashing down on Orion.)...

The Summer Triangle

There is another prominent triangle in the sky, the Summer Triangle. You might guess that that's the best time to look for it, but you're wrong. (Hah!) The Summer Triangle is best seen in the fall, directly overhead, although it's visible from midsummer to early winter. There are a few simple clues to finding it. One is to simply look for a large triangle, roughly three fist widths on each side, that is formed by the three brightest stars directly overhead and a little to the west. If you're in the country, you can see the Milky Way galaxy streaming through the triangle as well.

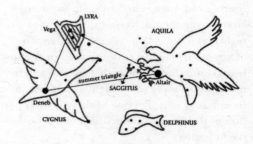

The Summer Triangle. In the fall, three bright stars can be seen directly overhead: Deneb, Altair, and Vega, roughly three fist widths apart from each other.

These three stars are the brightest in their constellations, two of which are the beautiful outlines of birds. The third is a lyre, a type of harp. Accompanying this triangle are two other constellations, an arrow and a dolphin....

Altair (al-tare´) is the bright star in Aquila's head, and of the stars in the Summer Triangle, it is the one farthest from the Big Dipper. Aquila is two fists long from head to tail and just over two fists from wingtip to wingtip....

... Vega (vay´-guh) is the brightest star in Lyra; actually, it's a double star. It's the closest of the three Summer Triangle stars to the line coming from the bowl of the Big Dipper or, if you're facing north, the leftmost of the two triangle stars that are closest to north. The rest of the constellation is comparatively dim, forming a pretty diamond of four stars under one fist across, pointing toward Altair in Aquila....

If you continue the line of the Big Dipper's pointer stars through the North Star, about five fists and a little to the right, you will arrive at Cassiopeia (six fists from the pointer stars) and then Pegasus. Cassiopeia appears as a W of stars one and a half fists wide, opening toward the Big and Little Dippers (Bears). It's easiest to picture this W as a throne with Cassiopeia seated on it.

Extending the pointer star line another three fists beneath the throne, you will arrive at the Great Square of Pegasus, roughly one fist on each side. This forms his body, and it is possible to see hindlegs, forelegs, neck, and head, all in proportion. The line you have extended strikes him in the belly, and he appears to be galloping to the left if you're seeing him right side up (facing the south).

Andromeda is one and the same with the hindlegs of Pegasus, and this is the location of the only other galaxy besides our own that we can see with the naked eye, the Andromeda galaxy. If

Continued →

you draw a line from the shoulders of Pegasus through his rear thigh (from one corner of the square to another) and continue it just under five fist widths, you will arrive at the bottom of Perseus. This is a diffuse stream of stars with no clear shape. Though neither Perseus nor Andromeda look much like their names, they are easy to find. Both Cassiopeia and Perseus lie in the trail of the Milky Way.

The Herdsman, the Northern Crown, and the Zodiac

The constellations of summer are not especially bright, but the warm weather encourages one to lie down on a blanket and comfortably pick them out....

These summer constellations are best seen from mid-June through late September. ...

Boötes may easily be found by extending the arch of the Big Dipper's handle three fists until you find the bright star Arcturus (ark-tur´-us). This is where his legs join his body, which forms an elongated diamond (his torso) two and a half fists long, stretching toward the north.

Coming off Boötes' right shoulder is a constellation of beautiful simplicity. This is the Corona Borealis (kor-oh´-nuh boar-ee-al´-is), or northern crown. ...

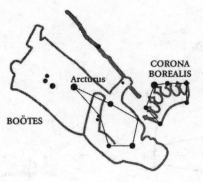

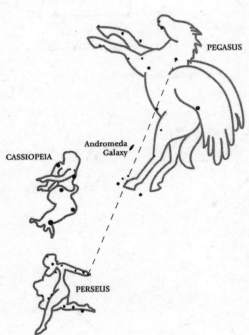

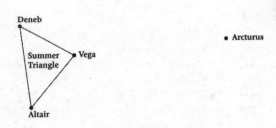

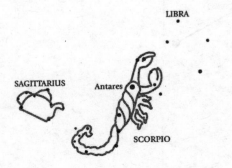

In the south on summer nights, look for the huge scorpion standing on his tail, three fist widths in height.

There is a constellation that bears no resemblance to its name whatsoever, but looks exactly like a teapot. Its stars are those of Sagittarius (sa-ji-tare´-ee-us)....

Scorpio the scorpion looks just like his name. As Orion, his foe, rules the southern skies of winter, so Scorpio rules the summer. Between his two claws is another constellation of the zodiac, Libra (lee´-bruh), visible only as a box of four fainter stars. All three of these zodiacal constellations appear in a row, Sagittarius-Scorpio-Libra, just above the southern horizon. It may not be possible for people in more northerly latitudes to see them. Sagittarius is one and half fists across, and Scorpio sprawls three fist widths. Libra is only two to three fingers on a side, barely visible as a box within the arc of Scorpio's claws.

—Excerpted from *Stargazing*

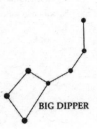

Winter Constellations

Elizabeth P. Lawlor
Illustrations by Pat Archer

Star Movement. Every twenty-four hours, the earth rotates counterclockwise on its axis, from west to east. This rotation causes the stars, sun, and moon to appear as though they move in a great arc across the sky from east to west. For observers in the United States, stars and other heavenly bodies that pass near the zenith seem to move in half-circles as they rise, cross the sky, and set. Stars to the south seem to scribe smaller arcs rather than half-circles. Stars to the north, especially those close to the North Star, make circles overhead. The closer the stars are to the poles, the tighter the circles they make (see illustration).

Only those constellations that pass overhead at night are visible to us. In the winter months, these include Gemini, Taurus, Orion, the Great Bear (Ursa Major), the Little Bear (Ursa Minor), Leo, Boötes, and Virgo.

Star Rise. Stars do not rise and cross the sky and set at exactly the same time every night; they rise and set four minutes earlier each night. In fifteen days, they will rise and set an hour earlier, and in thirty days, two hours earlier. As the months go on, those stars that you saw initially in the western sky at about 9 P.M. will not be visible at all; they will cross the sky after sunrise. This is why different constellations are overhead at night at different times throughout the year.

Circumpolar Stars. The circumpolar stars and constellations are those that revolve around Polaris, also known as the North Star or polestar, like spots on a record spinning on a turntable. The illustration represents a time-lapse photo of the path these stars follow when viewed directly overhead. These stars neither rise nor set. They are constantly turning overhead, even when they are hidden from our view by sunlight. In the Southern Hemisphere, there is no visible star located so conveniently. A time-lapse photo in the Southern Hemisphere would also show circular star paths, with a piece of empty sky at the center.

You can see the circumpolar stars from anywhere in North America on a cloudless night. Your location on the earth will determine where in the sky you will see these stars. If you live in Alaska or northern Canada, the circumpolar stars will appear almost directly overhead; if you live in the southern states, these stars will appear close to the horizon. Use the instructions below to find the North Star. Put a camera on a flat spot outdoors on a dark, clear night to make your own star-track photos. The shutter must remain open for at least ten or fifteen minutes. An hour or more is better.

Winter Constellations. Each season of the year has its own set of constellations. With a little practice you will be able to identify these star patterns. You can use the constellations to locate additional stars in the winder sky.

The Big Dipper. Almost everyone recognizes the seven stars conspicuously arranged in the shape of a very large scoop or dipper in the northern sky. This well-known landmark, the Big Dipper, is a good place for you to begin your study of the stars. Although often referred to as a constellation, astronomers call this group of stars an asterism that is within the Great Bear constellation.

Seven major stars form the Big Dipper. Look for the curved handle of the dipper and the four stars that make its bowl. The "pointer stars," Merak and Dubhe (pronounced "Dubby"), are the two bright stars that form the outer side of the dipper's bowl. If you draw an imaginary line up (away from the horizon) from them to the nearest star that is moderately bright, you will have reached the North Star. Don't be surprised that it is not very bright. Polaris is a magnitude 2 star, important but not glamorous.

The North Star has guided navigators throughout the millennia. This is an important star, because the northern end of the earth's axis is pointed toward it. This places it almost directly above our geographical North Pole. It is an important navigational star, even with today's high-tech navigational equipment. The other

Continued ➡

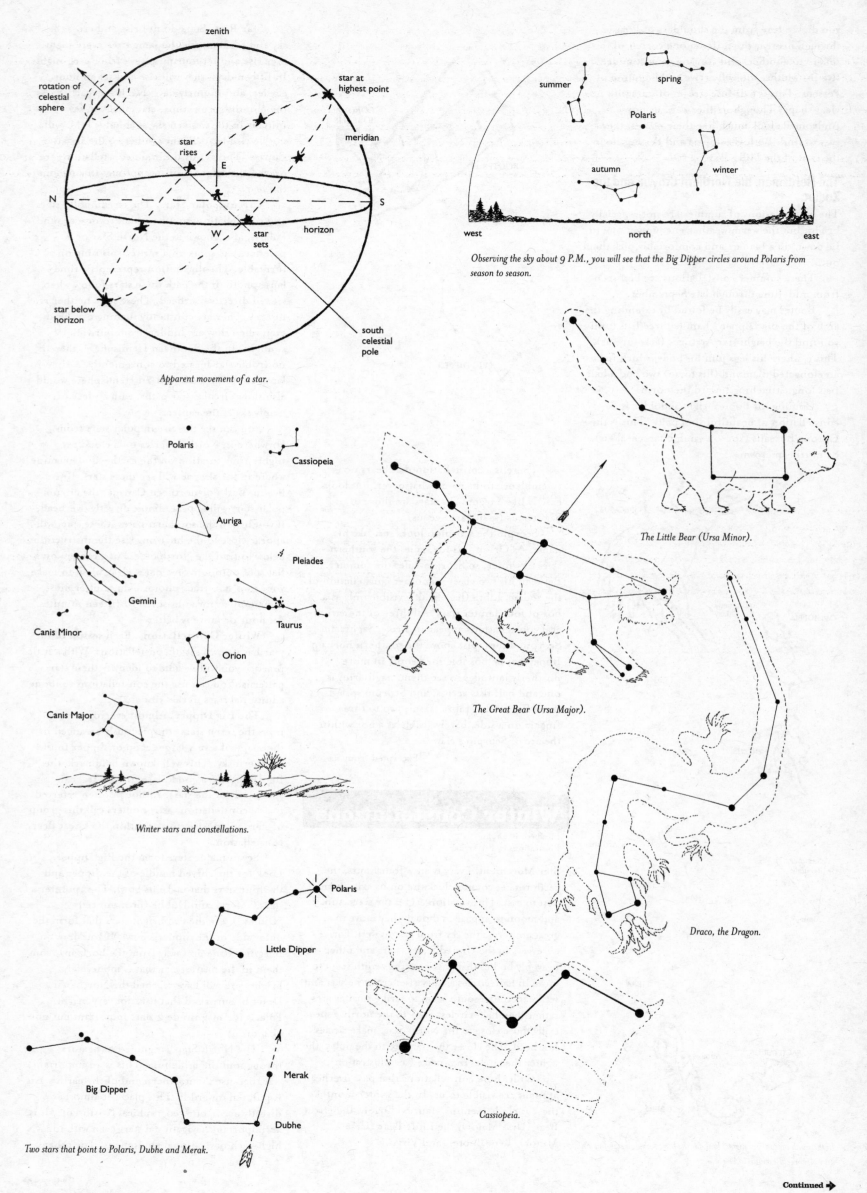

zenith

rotation of
celestial
sphere

star at
highest point

star
rises

meridian

E

N

S

W

star
sets

horizon

star below
horizon

south
celestial
pole

Apparent movement of a star.

summer

spring

Polaris

autumn

winter

west

north

east

Observing the sky about 9 P.M., you will see that the Big Dipper circles around Polaris from season to season.

Polaris

Cassiopeia

Auriga

Pleiades

Gemini

Taurus

Canis Minor

Orion

Canis Major

Winter stars and constellations.

Polaris

Little Dipper

Big Dipper

Merak

Dubhe

Two stars that point to Polaris, Dubhe and Merak.

The Little Bear (Ursa Minor).

The Great Bear (Ursa Major).

Draco, the Dragon.

Cassiopeia.

Continued ➔

polar constellations turn in a great circle around Polaris, as though it were the hub of a wheel. What do you think the Big Dipper would look like when viewed from the North Pole?

The Pleiades. This cluster of stars, frequently called The Seven Sisters, is part of the constellation Taurus. You can find the cluster if you draw an imaginary line from the star that marks Orion's left shoulder and pass it through Aldebaran, which is also located in Taurus. Continue the line to the cluster of stars beyond Aldebaran and you will reach the Pleiades. For a special treat, look at them with a pair of binoculars.

The Great Bear (Ursa Major). This circumpolar constellation is made up of the Big Dipper and other stars. After you have located the Big Dipper, look for the stars that form the Great Bear. The handle of the dipper is the bear's tail, and the bowl of the dipper contributes to the bear's back. Can you find the bear's head and front legs? Use the accompanying illustration as a guide, but make your own drawing in your notebook. Don't forget to identify compass directions in your notes.

The Little Dipper. The stars that form this group are part of a larger constellation called the Little Bear (Ursa Minor). As in the Big Dipper, there are seven stars. Four stars make the bowl, and three form the curved handle. If you follow the line of the handle stars, you will find a small and lonely star. This is the North Star.

Because all the stars of the Little Dipper are small and faint, it is not as easy to find as the Big Dipper. If you remember that the Little Dipper appears as though it were pouring something into the Big Dipper, it is easier to find. Again,

don't confuse this with the Pleiades. In your notebook, make a drawing of this star group. Compare the positions of the dippers with each other at 8 P.M. in January, February, and March. What did you notice?

Draco, the Dragon. This is a long, sprawling line of stars that begins with an irregular diamond that forms the dragon's head. Look for the last two tail stars, which are about ten degrees (one fist width) from the pointers of the Big Dipper. They are of equal brightness and lie between the cups of the Big and Little Dippers. Draw an imaginary line from the tail stars in the direction of the handle of the Big Dipper, making an arc below the Little Dipper, until the line of stars ends at the dragon's head.

Cassiopeia. The queen's chair is found on the other side of Polaris from the Big Dipper. Find Alioth, the third star in from the handle of the Big Dipper. Draw a line from Alioth to Polaris. Draw another line of equal length from Polaris to a group of stars of equal brightness that are in the shape of a relaxed upside-down W or an M. You have found Cassiopeia, or Cassiopeia's Chair, as the constellation is sometimes called.

Cepheus. Look between Draco's head and Cassiopeia, and you will find Cepheus. It looks like a rectangle wearing a dunce cap. Don't be discouraged if you have trouble finding Cepheus, because it is not as easy to locate as the other circumpolar constellations.

Orion. Orion, the hunter, seems to consume the southern region of the sky. This constellation is so dominant that we often describe the location of other stars relative to it.

Look for the mighty hunter early in the evening. The three bright stars in his belt (magnitude 2) are easy to find. Two widely separated stars above the belt mark his shoulders, and two similarly separated stars below the belt mark his arms and legs. A curving line of stars hanging obliquely from the belt form Orion's sword. Orion's sword contains a hazy region called the Orion Nebula. In this area of gas and dust clouds, new stars are forming. You can see the nebula with a pair of binoculars.

Betelgeuse is the only bright, orange star in the constellation. To find it, look above and to the left of the belt. It marks Orion's right shoulder. If you look an equal distance below the belt, you will find another bright star, called Rigel, forming the left foot. These two stars illustrate star evolution. Betelgeuse is an old star burning red like the embers in a tired campfire, and Rigel burns in the blue-white heat of youth.

The stars in the constellation of Orion can help you find your way around the winter sky. Use the map on the next page as a guide to the landmarks.

Canis Major. You can find this constellation by tracing a line southeast from Orion's belt to Sirius, the Dog Star. Sirius is the brightest star in the constellation, and astronomers say it is the brightest star in the heavens (magnitude -1.6).

Canis Minor. A line drawn west from Betelgeuse to the next bright star will bring you to Procyon. This is usually the only visible star in the constellation Canis Minor. Canis Major and Canis Minor are Orion's two faithful dogs that follow the hunter across the winter sky.

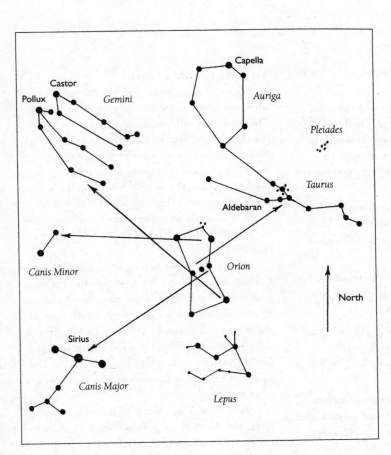

Orion as a guide to the winter sky.

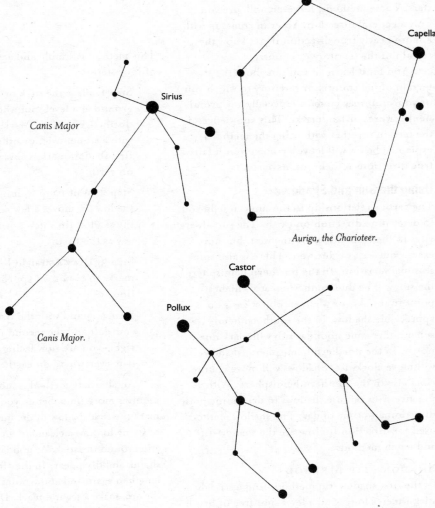

Canis Major.

Auriga, the Charioteer.

Gemini, the Twins.

Continued ➡

Taurus, the Bull. Draw a line northwest of Orion's belt the same length as the line to Sirius, and you will find a V-shaped group of stars. These are in the constellation Taurus, the bull. Aldebaran is the brightest star in the constellation and burns bright red.

Gemini. A line from Rigel through Betelgeuse will bring you to Castor and Pollux. Look for these matched stars directly overhead. (With the help of larger, more powerful telescopes, astronomers have learned that Castor is really a stellar system made up of seven stars.) Although they appear to be close to each other, they are separated by eleven light-years. Castor is about fourteen light-years farther away from us than Pollux. Pollux is brighter and is the more southerly.

Auriga, the Charioteer. To locate this five-sided constellation, draw a line northward between Betelgeuse and Aldebaran. The brightest star in this group is Capella. It glows a bright yellow.

—From *Discover Nature in Winter*

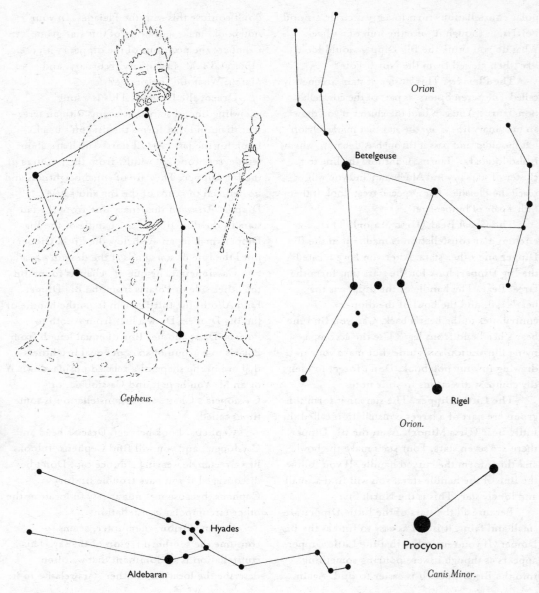

Cepheus.

Orion.

Taurus, the Bull.

Canis Minor.

Navigating without a Map and Compass

U.S. Army

In a survival situation, you will be extremely fortunate if you happen to have a map and compass. If you do have these two pieces of equipment, you will most likely be able to move toward help. If you are not proficient in using a map and compass, you must take the steps to gain this skill.

There are several methods by which you can determine direction by using the sun and the stars. These methods, however, will give you only a general direction. You can come up with a more nearly true direction if you know the terrain of the territory or country.

You must learn all you can about the terrain of the country or territory to which you or your unit may be sent, especially any prominent features or landmarks. This knowledge of the terrain together with using the methods explained below will let you come up with fairly true directions to help you navigate.

Using the Sun and Shadows

The earth's relationship to the sun can help you to determine direction on earth. The sun always rises in the east and sets in the west, but not exactly due east or due west. There is also some seasonal variation. In the northern hemisphere, the sun will be due south when at its highest point in the sky, or when an object casts no appreciable shadow. In the southern hemisphere, this same noonday sun will mark due north. In the northern hemisphere, shadows will move clockwise. Shadows will move counterclockwise in the southern hemisphere. With practice, you can use shadows to determine both direction and time of day. The shadow methods used for direction finding are the shadow-tip and watch methods.

SHADOW-TIP METHODS

In the first shadow-tip method, find a straight stick 1 meter long, and a level spot free of brush on which the stick will cast a definite shadow.

This method is simple and accurate and consists of four steps:

Step 1. Place the stick or branch into the ground at a level spot where it will cast a distinctive shadow. Mark the shadow's tip with a stone, twig, or other means. This first shadow mark is always west—everywhere on earth.

Step 2. Wait 10 to 15 minutes until the shadow tip moves a few centimeters. Mark the shadow tip's new position in the same way as the first.

Step 3. Draw a straight line through the two marks to obtain an approximate east-west line.

Step 4. Stand with the first mark (west) to your left and the second mark to your right—you are now facing north. This fact is true everywhere on earth.

An alternate method is more accurate but requires more time. Set up your shadow stick and mark the first shadow in the morning. Use a piece of string to draw a clean arc through this mark and around the stick. At midday, the shadow will shrink and disappear. In the afternoon, it will lengthen again and at the point where it touches the arc, make a second mark. Draw a line through the two marks to get an accurate east-west line.

THE WATCH METHOD

You can also determine direction using a common or analog watch—one that has hands. The direction will be accurate if you are using true local time, without any changes for daylight savings time. Remember, the further you are from the equator, the more accurate this method will be. If you only have a digital watch, you can overcome this obstacle. Quickly draw a watch on a circle of paper with the correct time on it and use it to determine your direction at that time.

In the northern hemisphere, hold the watch horizontal and point the hour hand at the sun. Bisect the angle between the hour hand and the 12 o'clock mark to get the north-south line. If there is any doubt as to which end of the line is north, remember that the sun rises in the east, sets in the west, and is due south at noon. The sun is in the east before noon and in the west after noon.

Note: If your watch is set on daylight savings time, use the midway point between the hour hand and 1 o'clock to determine the north-south line.

In the southern hemisphere, point the watch's 12 o'clock mark toward the sun and a midpoint halfway between 12 and the hour hand will give you the north-south line.

Continued ➡

1 Mark the shadow's tip.

2 Mark the new position and draw a line through the two marks.

3 Stand with the first mark to your left and the second mark to your right—you are now facing north.

Shadow-tip method.

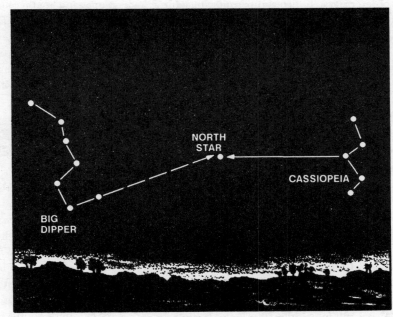

NORTH STAR

CASSIOPEIA

BIG DIPPER

The Big Dipper and Cassiopeia.

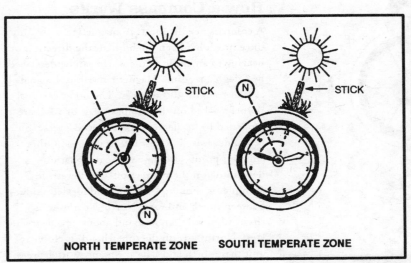

STICK

STICK

N

N

NORTH TEMPERATE ZONE   **SOUTH TEMPERATE ZONE**

Watch method.

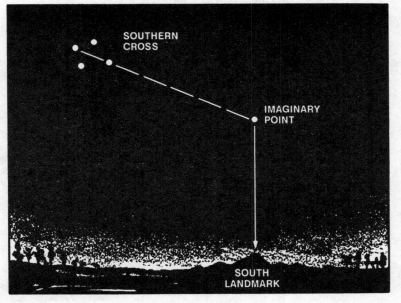

SOUTHERN CROSS

IMAGINARY POINT

SOUTH LANDMARK

Southern Cross.

Using the Moon

Because the moon has no light of its own, we can only see it when it reflects the sun's light. As it orbits the earth on its 28-day circuit, the shape of the reflected light varies according to its position. We say there is a new moon or no moon when it is on the opposite side of the earth from the sun. Then, as it moves away from the earth's shadow, it begins to reflect light from its right side and waxes to become a full moon before waning, or losing shape, to appear as a sliver on the left side. You can use this information to identify direction.

If the moon rises before the sun has set, the illuminated side will be the west. If the moon rises after midnight, the illuminated side will be the east. This obvious discovery provides us with a rough east-west reference during the night.

Using the Stars

Your location in the Northern or Southern Hemisphere determines which constellation you use to determine your north or south direction.

The Northern Sky

The main constellations to learn are the Ursa Major, also known as the Big Dipper or the Plow, and Cassiopeia. Neither of these constellations ever sets. They are always visible on a clear night. Use them to locate Polaris, also known as the polestar or the North Star. The North Star forms part of the Little Dipper handle and can be confused with the Big Dipper. Prevent confusion by using both the Big Dipper and Cassiopeia together. The Big Dipper and Cassiopeia are always directly opposite each other and rotate counterclockwise around Polaris, with Polaris in the center. The Big Dipper is a seven star constellation in the shape of a dipper. The two stars forming the outer lip of this dipper are the "pointer stars" because they point to the North Star. Mentally draw a line from the outer bottom star to the outer top star of the Big Dipper's bucket. Extend this line about five times the distance between the pointer stars. You will find the North Star along this line.

Cassiopeia has five stars that form a shape like a "W" on its side. The North Star is straight out from Cassiopeia's center star.

After locating the North Star, locate the North Pole or true north by drawing and imaginary line directly to the earth.

The Southern Sky

Because there is no star bright enough to be easily recognized near the south celestial pole, a constellation known as the Southern Cross is

Continued ➡

used as a signpost to the South. The Southern Cross or Crux has five stars. Its four brightest stars form a cross that tilts to one side. The two stars that make up the cross's long axis are the pointer stars. To determine south, imagine a distance five times the distance between these stars and the point where this imaginary line ends is in the general direction of south. Look down to the horizon from this imaginary point and select a landmark to steer by. In a static survival situation, you can fix this location in daylight if you drive stakes in the ground at night to point the way.

Making Improvised Compasses

You can construct improvised compasses using a piece of ferrous metal that can be needle shaped or a flat double-edged razor blade and a piece of nonmetallic string or long hair from which to suspend it. You can magnetize or polarize the metal by slowly stroking it in one direction on a piece of silk or carefully through your hair using deliberate strokes. You can also polarize metal by stroking it repeatedly at one end with a magnet. Always rub in one direction only. If you have a battery and some electric wire, you can polarize the metal electrically. The wire should be insulated. If not insulated, wrap the metal object in a single, thin strip of paper to prevent contact. The battery must be a minimum of 2 volts. Form a coil with the electric wire and touch its end to the battery's terminals. Repeatedly insert one end of the metal object in and out of the coil. The needle will become an electromagnet. When suspended from a piece of nonmetallic string, or floated on a small piece of wood in water, it will align itself with a north-south line.

You can construct a more elaborate improvised compass using a sewing needle or thin metallic object, a nonmetallic container (for example, a plastic dip container), its lid with the center cut out and waterproofed, and the silver tip from a pen. To construct this compass, take an ordinary sewing needle and break in half. One half will form your direction pointer and the other will act as the pivot point. Push the portion used as the pivot point through the bottom center of your container; this portion should be flush on the bottom and not interfere with the lid. Attach the center of the other portion (the pointer) of the needle on the pen's silver tip using glue, tree sap, or melted plastic. Magnetize one end of the pointer and rest it on the pivot point.

Other Means of Determining Direction

The old saying about using moss on a tree to indicate north is not accurate because moss grows completely around some trees. Actually, growth is more lush on the side of the tree facing the south in the Northern Hemisphere and vice versa in the Southern Hemisphere. If there are several felled trees around for comparison, look at the stumps. Growth is more vigorous on the side toward the equator and the tree growth rings will be more widely spaced. On the other hand, the tree growth rings will be closer together on the side toward the poles.

Wind direction may be helpful in some instances where there are prevailing directions and you know what they are.

Recognizing the differences between vegeta-tion and moisture patterns on north- and south-facing slopes can aid in determining direction. In the northern hemisphere, north-facing slopes receive less sun than south-facing slopes and are therefore cooler and damper. In the summer, north-facing slopes retain patches of snow. In the winter, the trees and open areas on south-facing slopes are the first to lose their snow, and ground snowpack is shallower.

—From *Survival* (Field Manual 21-76)

Basic Directions
Darran Wells

You probably know that the four main cardinal directions are north, south, east, and west. As you can see on the compass rose below, they can be divided into northwest (NW), northeast (NE), southwest (SW), and southeast (SE). And those directions can be further broken down into north-northeast (NNE), east-northeast (ENE), east-southeast (ESE), south-southeast (SSE), south-southwest (SSW), west-southwest (WSW), west-northwest (WNW), and north-northwest (NNW).

—From *NOLS Wilderness Navigation*

The Compass
Don Geary

A compass is the basic tool of navigation, and you need to learn to use it before you can expect to travel with any kind of confidence. A compass is not a toy, but a reasonably precise instrument that is invaluable for navigating over land, on the water, or in the air. Learning to use one will enable you not only to navigate, but also to reach predetermined objectives with the confidence that is the true mark of an experienced outdoorsman.

Mastering the compass is not difficult if you understand the basic fundamentals. To begin with, magnetism is the force that makes a compass work. The earth's surface is covered by an invisible magnetic field, which affects, and is affected by, all other magnetic materials on, above, and below it. Picture the earth's axis as a very long bar magnet with north and south poles. All magnetic objects on the earth, if allowed to swing freely, will align themselves with this north-south line. A compass needle will align itself along this line no matter where in the world it is placed.

… The compass has a magnetized needle or card that is allowed to swing freely on some type of pivot. A compass card shows, at the very least, the four compass points of north, south, east, and west. Such things as a damping feature, luminous dial, sights, and a magnetic declination adjusting mechanism may be added for various purposes.

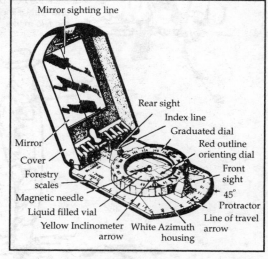

Exploded view of a compass.

How a Compass Works

A compass needle points to magnetic north, and once north has been established, the direction or bearing to anything in the world can be described by a degree reading. Magnetic north is designated as 0 degrees or 360 degrees. The other cardinal points marked on the compass dial, or rose, are separated by 90 degrees. East is 90 degrees, south is 180 degrees, and west is 270 degrees. Other compass points also have name designations depending on their direction. Northwest, for example, is about 315 degrees and located midway between north and west. North-Northwest is closer to north than west and about 340 degrees. West-Northwest, on the other hand, is closer to west than north and falls at roughly 290 degrees. Other compass points are described in a similar manner—Southwest, for example, is located midway between south and west and is roughly 225 degrees.

The dial on any good compass will be marked in degrees, usually indicated by short lines, called tick marks, every 2, 5, or 10 degrees. A compass without degree readings, or only showing the cardinal compass points, is really useless for navigating.

The degree reading or bearing for an objective changes with the point of view. For example, the corner of a house might have a value of 200 degrees when viewed from the center of a room but a different value when viewed from another room or a point outside the house. Readings of specific objects will change whenever the location of the compass has changed.

When using a topographical map and compass, you need to make some adjustments, because all compasses point to magnetic north but all topo maps are oriented to geographical north. The difference between these two points (about 1,300 miles!) is called magnetic declination. …

Continued ➡

Almost any metal object can affect how your compass operates. A belt buckle, handgun, sheath knife or pocketknife, rifle, camera, and binoculars are probably the most common offenders. Natural and unavoidable influences include iron deposits in the earth, lightning storms, high-voltage power lines, and periods of high static electricity in the atmosphere. Even a lit flashlight bulb is a powerful electromagnet that may influence a compass needle or dial. Keep this in mind when traveling in the dark with the aid of a compass and flashlight.

Check for compass interference regularly by watching the action of the compass needle. If your compass needle swings erratically it is being influenced by something other than magnetic north. Even if the compass is equipped with a dampening mechanism or fluid, the action of the needle should not be abrupt. It should swing left and right a few moments before coming to rest.

Probably the best way to determine if your compass is being influenced by other forces is to set it down on a log, the ground, or a rock. It is important that the compass lie flat and that there are no deposits in the area, in a rock for example. (A metal deposit will cause a compass needle to stop abruptly.) Now back a few steps away from the compass and let the needle come to a rest. After a minute or so, slowly move back to the compass, at the same time watching the action of the compass needle. If the needle moves as you approach, something on your person is causing the compass needle to deviate. Remove any metal, such as a metal belt buckle or pocketknife, and try this test again. The things that can affect a compass needle are surprising; even the metal in a ballpoint pen can cause some needle deviation.

Choosing a Compass

There are four basic types of compasses in use today by outdoor travelers: floating dial, fixed dial, cruiser, and orienteering. All of them indicate direction, but their special features are designed for specific uses. Before buying a compass, examine your needs and choose the kind that will do the best job for you.

Floating dial compass.

Floating Dial Compasses

Any compass that has a joined compass card and needle that work as a single unit is a floating dial compass. Floating dial compasses include automobile, aircraft, and boat compasses, as well as military surplus and lensatic compasses.

On a ship, the floating dial compass is set in the center of the cockpit or wheelhouse so that the line on the compass housing runs in the same direction as the keel of the ship. This line, called the lubber line, indicates the direction of travel, as if the ship were an arrow. The compass dial or card is allowed to swing freely, and the direction of travel is read off the card where the lubber line points.

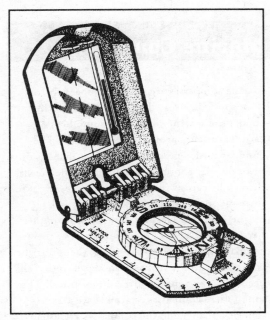

Lensatic compass.

On a lensatic compass, the principle is the same except that a sight is commonly used to pick up an object in the distance. A wire is set into the compass cover, and a V sight is on the other side of the compass housing. An object is sighted in the distance, and the degree reading is noted through a lens below the V sight.

A lensatic compass is not the easiest or quickest to use, because you must hold the compass so that you can see both your objective and the degree reading. This necessitates holding the compass close to your eye, and it leaves a lot of room for error. For this reason, a lensatic compass may not be your best choice for wilderness travel.

Fixed Dial Compasses

Fixed dial compasses are the ones most commonly carried and used by outdoorsmen. They are a poor choice, however, because they are not as accurate or easy to operate as other types of compasses. The popularity of the fixed dial compass undoubtedly lies in its low price. Many outdoorsmen reason that they should carry a compass but do not see why they should pay very much money for one.

A fixed dial compass resembles a pocketwatch with a pop-up cover. Inside are a needle and compass card. Few show more than the major compass points, and even fewer are damped to slow needle travel. There is rarely any

Fixed dial compass.

sighting device or direction-of-travel arrow, so they are suitable only for showing general direction. Fixed dial compasses are one step above a magnetized needle stuck in a cork and floated in a bowl of water. Their operation is very slow and their accuracy never better than questionable. They make nice prizes in caramel-covered popcorn, but there are infinitely better choices for wilderness route finding.

Cruiser Compasses

Cruiser compasses are the most accurate you can buy and are also the most expensive of the handheld compasses. Cruiser compasses are designed for professionals such as timber cruisers, geologists, and survey crews. Prices start at over $100. If you want a quality instrument and are not concerned with price or weight, then a cruiser compass is your best choice. If, however, you are interested only in direction, expressed in degree readings, the lower-priced light-weight orienteering compass would be more suitable. Probably the best cruiser compasses available today are Brunton's Pocket Transits. Brunton has been making very high-quality compasses for professionals since 1894.

The standard cruiser compass is easy to identify because the compass card is numbered counterclockwise. Other standard features include an adjustment for magnetic declinations (a screw mechanism that moves the compass card left or right as required) and tick marks for each of the 360 degrees on the compass card. On most models, the needle locks in position when the cover is closed; this cuts down on needle wear over the life of the instrument. Several other features commonly built into cruiser compasses are really of interest only to professionals—for example, scales and bubble levels that determine slope incline and elevation and measure both horizontal and vertical angles. Most cruiser compasses are a little too heavy (8 ounces and up) for people concerned about excess weight, such as backpackers. Brunton has recently introduced a lightweight cruiser compass (about 5 ounces), however, with all of the features of heavier units.

Continued →

Orienteering Compasses

The orienteering compass has a needle that operates independently of the card. The compass housing, which has 0- to 360-degree readings stamped in a clockwise direction around the dial, can be turned so that any degree reading is indicated by the direction-of-travel arrow. The direction-of-travel arrow itself is permanently stamped into the base.

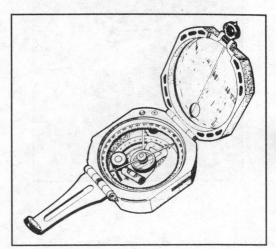

Cruiser compass (Brunton Pocket Transit).

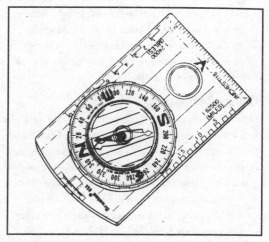

Orienteering compass.

An orienteering compass is the best type for almost any kind of travel in the great outdoors. These familiar-looking compasses are inexpensive, lightweight (less than an ounce), rugged, and dependable. They have a clear plastic base and a rotating degree ring, and are commonly filled with a damping liquid. Orienteering compasses are widely sold in sporting-goods, backpacking-equipment, and even department stores throughout the country. At one time all units were made by the Silva Company, but now several other companies (including Brunton) offer high-quality units as well.

For around $10, you can purchase a good orienteering compass that has all of the features necessary to navigate in the wilds. Usually, however, an adjustment for magnetic declination is not one of the features on an orienteering compass.

An orienteering compass is the simplest to use for following a compass bearing. Point the direction-of-travel arrow at your objective, then turn the compass dial or housing until the needle points to the N symbol (or 0- or 360-degree mark). This is known as orienting the compass to north. The degree reading just above the direction-of-travel arrow is the bearing of the objective. While walking toward the objective, you need only to hold the compass flat and steady, keeping the needle oriented to north, the direction-of-travel arrow will point the way. When you reach this objective, check the compass again and sight to a new objective, with the compass needle oriented to north on the compass housing. Anyone can learn to use an orienteering compass in about twenty minutes. Using this type of compass, you will be surprised at the speed and ease with which you are able to follow a course.

—From *Using a Map and Compass*

Marine Compasses

Greg Davenport

Marine compasses are designed especially for vessels in rough seas. Unlike an orienteering compass, a marine compass has numbers on a card that rotates around a fixed needle. The compass card is mounted on a float that sits on a pivot directly above the magnetic needle mechanism. The card is finely balanced, allowing it to float and move constantly as it aligns with magnetic north. Headings are taken from the fixed lubber line located on the body of the compass. If attached to the vessel, the lubber line is aligned with the front of the vessel so that all headings represent the direction of travel. The top of these compasses typically have a hemispherical shape, and the compasses are usually mounted close to the steering apparatus but away from metals that may interfere with their heading. When mounted, compass bowls are kept horizontal by the use of gimbals, which allow the compass to compensate for sea roll.

While an orienteering compass has its scale (0 to 360 degrees) located on the circular housing, which rotates around the arrow seeking magnetic north, a marine compass uses a circular scale located on the compass card. With an orienteering compass, a heading is only established when the circular housing is turned and the north-seeking arrow is boxed (see page 407). With a marine compass, the numbers are simply read below the lubber line (stationary index line).

—From *Surviving Coastal and Open Water*

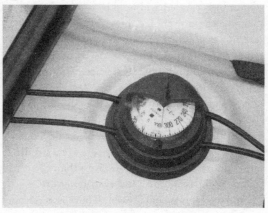

A marine compass mounted on a kayak.

Parts of a Compass

Darran Wells
Illustrations by Jon Cox

A compass is simply a device that responds to the Earth's magnetic fields by pointing to magnetic north, which is near Baffin Island, Canada (page 407 for more details). All the plastic, rulers, numbers, and arrows are there to make a compass easier to use, but its essence is its north-pointing magnet. When used properly, it can help you to determine cardinal directions from almost any location on the planet.

The illustrations here and … show compasses with various basic and advanced features. At the very least, your compass must have a needle, bezel, and base plate. If you plan on traveling in the backcountry regularly or if you need a high level of precision (to compete at orienteering, for example), it is well worth investing in a more advanced compass. If you already own a compass, pull it out now and take a look the following parts:

Needle or Magnetic Disc

The needle, which is made of magnetized iron, balances on a pivot so that it can swing easily in any direction. The north-seeking end of the needle is red; some have a convenient glow-in-the-dark stripe. Brunton Eclipse compasses use a magnetized disc rather than a standard needle. The disc works precisely the same, but is less likely to snag or stick on the housing. The housing for both needle and disc compasses is filled with a non-freezing damping liquid so that it doesn't move erratically or freeze in sub-zero temperatures.

Housing and Bezel

The housing is the liquid-dampened case that surrounds the needle. The bezel is the numbered plastic dial around the housing; also called the azimuth ring, it is marked with 360 degrees, usually in 2-degree increments. Engraved into the bottom of the bezel are meridian lines and an orienting arrow. The meridian lines will help you determine declination. On most compasses, the orienting arrow looks like a tiny shed that outlines the needle; it is used to box the needle when determining your bearing or direction of travel. Eclipse compasses feature a blue circle instead of an orienting arrow.

Base Plate

The base plate is the transparent rectangle of plastic that the bezel rests on. It is often marked with rulers or UTM grid readers. There is also usually a "direction-of-travel" arrow that, along with the bezel's orienting arrow, helps you take and follow bearings. The end of this arrow that is closest to the bezel is called the index line; this is where bearings are read. Eclipse-style compasses feature a magnetized index line to make reading bearings easier and more precise.

Continued ➔

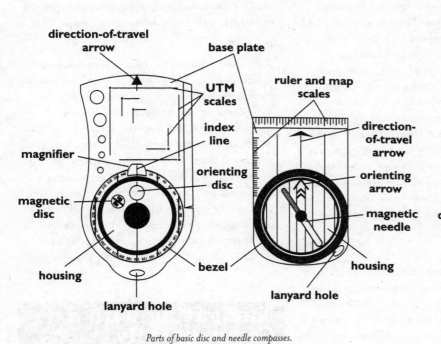

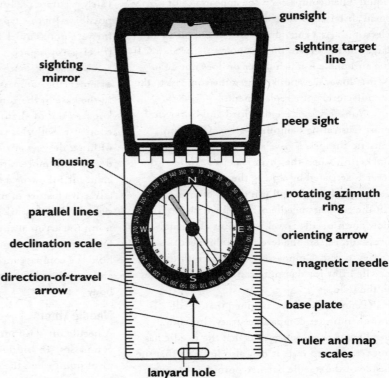

Parts of basic disc and needle compasses.

Parts of an advanced compass.

Sighting Mirror

Sighting mirrors are small mirrors that fold over the top of the bezel to close the compass. Compasses with sighting mirrors are sometimes called prismatic compasses. When open they are used to more precisely align the compass with distant objects when taking or following a bearing. The advantage of the mirror is that it allows you to adjust the bezel while sighting a distant object. Tilting the mirror toward you enables you to view the orienting arrow while holding the compass at eye level and an arm's length away.

This adds a significantly higher level of accuracy when using bearings. When fully opened, sighting mirrors are also handy as a longer straightedge for drawing bearing lines on your map.

Lanyard

This is a fancy name for a cord attached to the base plate. Many lanyards have an adjustable plastic toggle of some sort that can be used to measure distance on a map. While most folks use the toggle and lanyard to wear the compass around their necks when it's not in use, beware that the lanyard can occasionally catch on very thick brush or climbing gear.

Declination Adjustment

Many compasses feature an adjustable orienting arrow. This allows you to set the declination on your compass so that you do not have to add or subtract in the field while switching between magnetic and true bearings—a welcome convenience after an exhausting day in the mountains. Most compasses with a declination adjustment also have a tiny screwdriver attached to the lanyard for adjusting the declination screw on the back of the bezel.

Global Pivot

Ignore this feature unless you are planning to use your compass outside North America. A global pivot allows the needle to tilt vertically in such a way that it is not affected by the Earth's different magnetic dip zones.

Clinometer

Some compasses have a second free-moving needle attached to the pivot inside the bezel. This non-magnetic arrow is usually black and is used to measure the angle of a slope in the field when the compass is tilted on its side. This is a critical tool for those needing to assess avalanche potential.

Magnifying Glass

Even if your vision is good, it is nice to have a small magnifying glass built in to the base plate for reading tiny names and map features.

—From *NOLS Wilderness Navigation*

Compass Features

Don Geary

Some features make a compass easier to use or more accurate; others increase the versatility of the instrument. When shopping for a compass, consider only those features that will be an aid to

Tilt the mirror to see the face of the compass

Sight the object while looking over the tips of the front and rear sights

V or rifle sights are used for determining a bearing.

you. For example, a surveyor could use a clinometer, for measuring angles of inclination, on a cruiser compass, but a backpacker or hunter really has no use for this feature. Here are brief descriptions of the most popular—and most useful—features.

Damping

Damping slows down movement of the needle so that it will come to rest more quickly. This saves time when you are taking many readings, such as when following a route. There are three systems for damping a compass needle: induction damping, liquid damping, and needle lock levers.

Induction damping works by magnetic force, dependent on the velocity of the needle. The more the needle swings, the greater the force to dampen the swing. When the needle stops, the magnetic force of the induction damping system also stops, so the damping effect on the compass needle at rest is nil.

The Brunton Company builds induction damping into its line of Pocket Transits. On models with induction damping, there is a magnet mounted on each side of the compass needle, just above the pivot point. Surrounding the center of the pivot point is a tiny copper cup. As the compass needle swings, the magnets set up their own magnetic field inside the cup and help to quickly bring the needle to rest. When the swing of the compass needle stops, the induction damping magnets no longer affect it.

Liquid damping is probably the most common method of slowing down compass needle movement, and nearly all orienteering compasses are liquid damped. Liquid damping is fast and reliable. The liquid commonly has a freezing point of around −40 degrees F, so for most of us, liquid damping will work well. The case of a liquid-damped compass must be well made to prevent damage that could cause the liquid to drain out of the unit. One problem often encountered with

Continued ➡

liquid-filled compasses is the appearance of a small air bubble inside the case, especially at high elevations. As a rule, unless the air bubble is larger than 1/4 inch, there is no cause for alarm. If the air bubble is much larger or does not disappear at lower elevations, return the compass to the manufacturer for a replacement.

Needle lock levers are the third and by far the most frustrating damping system. Old army lensatic compasses have a needle lift lever that works only when the cover is closed. In fact, the lever is activated by closing the cover. Other compasses have a small pin that is depressed to lift the compass needle off the pivot point. To slow down needle travel, you must alternately press and release the lever until the needle comes to rest. Compasses equipped with only a needle lifter for damping can be a chore to use in the field.

People often have assumed that needle quiver indicates compass accuracy. In truth, needle quiver merely means that the needle has not yet come to rest. It may also indicate that the inside of the needle balance point has been worn by the jeweled needle pivot and therefore cannot come to rest. If a compass needle quivers excessively—and it will if not damped in some way—consider buying another compass, as this one will prove quite annoying and will offer questionable accuracy at best.

Sights

Sights are built into many compasses for ease in pinpointing an objective. Any compass that does not have some means of sighting an objective will leave a lot to be desired during use in the field. The main types of sights currently in use are lensatic sights, prismatic sights, V or rifle-type sights, and direction-of-travel-arrow sights.

Lensatic sights are found on old military compasses. A lens, which is part of the rear sight, has a twofold purpose: to magnify the compass dial, so that you can determine a degree reading, and to sight the objective. To use a lensatic sight, you line up the notch on top of the lens housing with a wire on the cover of the compass (the front sight) and the objective. A lensatic compass must be held close to the face for sighting and for reading the compass bearing, which can lead to error, especially if the sights are not perfectly aligned.

Prismatic sights are slow to operate. The objective must be lined up between rear and front sights, and then a degree bearing read through the prism part of the rear sight. Prismatic sights can be very accurate when the alignment of the prism is true. Unfortunately, there is little you can do to determine if these sights are, in fact, true. As with lensatic sights, these work best when held relatively close to your eye. Another drawback is that a prismatic sight is difficult to read in low-light conditions.

V or rifle-type sights are offered on several compasses, often in conjunction with a mirrored cover. To use this type, you simply hold the compass at eye level about 12 inches from your face and sight the objective with a V-shaped trough or slot on the compass housing. Once you've lined up the objective in the sight, you read the bearing from the mirror cover, where a line crosses the compass card degree readings.

Fairly accurate readings, within 2 degrees, are possible with this type of sighting system, but they are not as quick to use as direction-of-travel-arrow sights.

Direction-of-travel-arrow sights are found on orienteering compasses. The arrow is inscribed in the base of the compass, so it cannot be knocked out of alignment. Orienteering compasses with this type of sight are accurate within 2 degrees at a quick glance (within 1 degree with more care), which is generally sufficient for following a compass bearing. The most attractive feature of direction-of-travel-arrow sights is that they are very fast to use—you simply point the arrow at your objective, orient the housing to north, and read the bearing. You can hold the compass anywhere between your chin and your hip, out about 6 inches from your body.

Needle Lifters

A needle lifter is found on most cruiser compasses. To lift the compass needle off the pivot point when the compass is not in use, a lever is activated when the cover of the compass is closed. Precision surveying instruments should have some means of lifting the compass needle when not in use to prevent wear. On lightweight orienteering compasses, however, a needle lifter is rare. A needle lifter, as mentioned earlier, can also be used to dampen needle movement.

Luminous Dials

A luminous dial is a handy feature when you are traveling in the dark or in low-light conditions. As a rule, you can charge up a luminous dial by shining a flashlight on it for a few moments, and then it will glow for several hours.

Level Indicators

Level indicators use a tiny, round bubble to indicate that the compass is being held flat. Because precise accuracy is dependent, at least in part, on holding a compass level, this feature is important on professional navigating and surveying instruments. Less expensive orienteering compasses will rarely have a level indicator; most users have no problem holding the compass level enough to obtain reasonably accurate readings.

Adjustment Features. A magnetic declination adjustment feature is found on all cruiser compasses and most of the expensive orienteering compasses. This feature adds to the cost of the unit, but is well worth the price if you plan to use the compass with a topographical map. In the extreme eastern and western parts of the United States, magnetic declination can be as great as 22 degrees. Travel is much easier if this deviation is taken care of by an adjustment to the compass rather than by a mental calculation at each reading. Although adding or subtracting the magnetic deviation for a particular part of the country is not difficult, there is always a chance that you might forget to perform the necessary calculation. Failing to take a 20-degree magnetic declination into consideration on a 3-mile hike will steer you more than a mile from your objective. Many people feel that a magnetic declination adjustment feature is well worth the added cost.

Magnifying Glasses

A magnifying glass is a common addition to orienteering compasses. It is usually mounted in the flat, clear plastic base and is handy for reading detail on topographical maps, especially the larger-scale (15-minute series) maps.

Cases

A compass is useless to you if it is crammed somewhere inside your pack. If your compass is handy, you will use it frequently and become more familiar with its operation. Many compasses come with a special carrying case that can be attached to your belt. If you are backpacking and are using a hip belt, attach the case to your hip belt. An even better way to carry a compass is on a lanyard around your neck. You can tuck the compass into a shirt pocket or allow it to hang when not in use. A compass carried in this manner is always accessible and tough to lose.

—From *Using a Map and Compass*

Navigating with a Compass Only

Don Geary

In many cases, a compass can be of tremendous value alone—for example, if you are camping and plan a day hike for exploring, fishing, hunting, photographing, or just plain wandering. Before leaving camp, pick out some objective in the distance, say a mountain peak, and note the compass bearing to it. Later, when you want to return to camp, simply reverse the process and calculate your back bearing—a compass heading in reverse. Determine a back bearing as follows: If the bearing is more than 180 degrees, subtract 180 degrees to determine your back bearing; if the bearing is less than 180 degrees, add 180 degrees. If you headed out at 300 degrees, your back bearing is 120 degrees (300 minutes 180).

Whenever you are heading out on a compass bearing and returning on a back bearing, it is imperative that you keep checking your compass to make certain you're on course. This is not always easy to do, because of detours around fallen trees, boulders, swamps, and other natural obstacles. One way to build a safety cushion into your readings is to deliberately follow a course that will put you left or right of your objective.

For example, let's assume that you are camped on a river that flows south, and you plan a day hike to a nearby lake for some fishing. You've been told that this lake lies about 1 mile due east of the camp, so your bearing will be east (90 degrees) to find the lake and west (270 degrees) to return to camp. You easily find the lake after an hour's walk, catch some nice trout, and now are ready to return to camp. Following a back bearing of 270 degrees (90 plus 180) should lead directly back to camp. On the hike in, however, you encountered several natural detours that really prevented a straight route. While it would be easy to find the river on which you are camped, you might not know if you should go upstream or down to find camp. By following a compass bearing of about 290 degrees, you can be sure that when you do finally reach the river, camp will be downstream. Thus,

Continued ➜

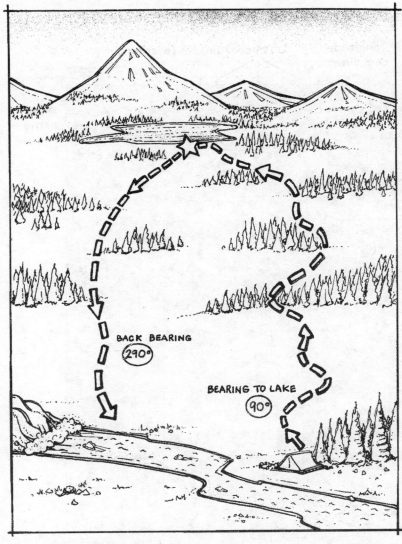

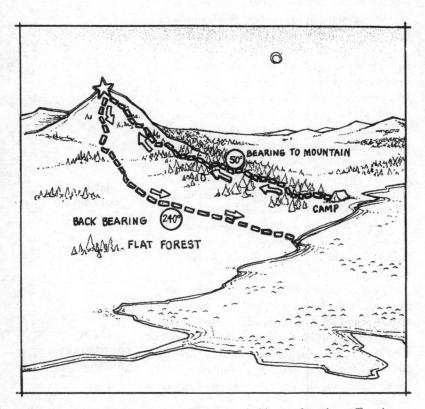

Deliberate error can be used to your advantage when you are trying to reach a distant line (such as a river, trail, or road) and the terrain does not lend itself to a straight line of travel.

Return by a back bearing of 240 degrees, rather than a true back bearing of 230 degrees. Then when you reach the lake, you know to simply turn left and follow the shoreline back to camp. Traveling in this manner builds some margin for error into your plan, and you can be certain of reaching your objective.

deliberate error can help you find the way back if the objective lies on a river, road, or trail.

Using the back bearing also works well when objectives can be seen for the rips both to and from a given point. This time you are camping on the end of a small lake surrounded by relatively flat forest terrain. In the distance, clearly visible from camp, is a mountain peak on a bearing of 50 degrees. You decide to climb to its summit to see the view from up there. Compass secured around your neck, you head out from camp on a 50-degree compass bearing. Soon the forest is deep, and neither camp nor mountain peak can be seen. Nevertheless, you proceed on a 50-degree bearing and eventually reach the base of the mountain. The view from the top is spectacular—you can see for miles. In fact, you can see the lake.

When it's time to go back to camp, the formula for determining the back bearing yields 230 degrees (50 plus 180). Trying to hit the camp, however, which is on one end of the lake, may result in missing both the lake and the camp. The lake is large enough that you can use it as an objective instead of the camp. Before descending, you take a bearing on the center of the lake: 240 degrees. Armed with this information, you should be able to make it back to camp quite easily; once you reach the lakeshore, you simply walk to the left until you hit camp.

A compass can also help you set up a more comfortable camp. If your camp faces east, the first warming rays of sun will take the chill off the camp while various morning chores are

done. This is especially handy when snow-camping in the winter or at high elevations in the summer, where nights tend to be cold. If you plan to sleep late, as on a rest day, or are camping in hot weather, locate camp on the west side of a hill or facing west to avoid the early warming rays of the sun.

—from *Using a Map & Compass*

Finding the Right Map

Darran Wells

Most of the maps you have probably seen are called planimetric maps. They show everything in one plane, as if the world is flat. Gas station road maps and atlases are planimetric. Two kinds of planimetric maps suited for planning trips to wilderness areas are recreation and guidebook maps. Recreation maps are printed by government agencies like the Bureau of Land Management and National Park Service for a specific use, such as mountain biking or horse-packing. Guidebook maps are intended to get you to a specific trail or land feature; some feature trail profile maps telling you how long and steep a trail will be. You can use these maps or a roadmap to plan where you will enter the wilderness. And for shorter trips on clearly marked trails, one of these may be all you need.

For trips into the wilderness, however, you will want a topographic map. Topographic maps depict the shape of the land (its topography)

with what are known as contour lines. Each contour represents a specific elevation. By developing your ability to read contour lines and match them to features on the land, you can locate yourself in almost any place on earth.

You may not be surprised to learn that there are different kinds of topo maps. The most important distinguishing feature of a topo is its scale. You can find topos in scales from 1:10,000 to 1:100,000 and up. Don't let the numbers scare you—they simply tell how much the map has been reduced. On a 1:24,000-scale map, one inch on the map represents 24,000 inches (0.4 mile) on land, and one foot equals 24,000 feet (4.5 miles). A large-scale map has a smaller number in its ratio (e.g., 1:24,000). It represents a smaller area and has more details. Large-scale maps are best for hiking, canoeing, or skiing. The smaller the map's scale, the larger the area it represents, and the more difficult it becomes to use for wilderness travel. (If you were hiking along in the woods for several days, your location wouldn't change much on a map of the entire United States, for instance.) Topo maps start to become difficult to use for land navigation when the scale gets below 1:100,000 (e.g. 1:250,000). The best scale for learning wilderness navigation is 1:24,000 or 1:25,000. In Alaska, you may be using a 1:63,360 map, where 1 inch equals 1 mile. In Europe and Canada, you will commonly find 1:50,000-scale maps, where 20 millimeters equals a kilometer.

In the U.S., most backcountry travelers use

Continued ➤

United States Geological Survey quadrangle maps, known as quads. USGS quads are developed from aerial photographs, which are used to determine where the contour lines should appear. The National Geographic Society, among others, produces a series of topo maps that feature shaded areas to give a three-dimensional view. While these "relief" maps help in identifying topography, they are rarely found in large scales.

If you travel in the backcountry often enough, there will come a time when you will need to read your map in the rain. Weatherproofing maps can be as simple or as complicated as you wish to make it. One easy method is to carry your maps in plastic bags with zip tops. Ideally, they will be large enough to allow you to keep two to four folded maps together, for when you are traveling on the margins or corners of the maps. Disposable plastic bags are the lightest, and they are cheap and easy to replace when they get damaged. Use one bag for the map or maps you are traveling on, and another to store the rest of your maps in an accessible place.

There are also several waterproofing laminates and specially designed map cases on the market. The laminates work well, but they make it difficult to write on the map in pencil. Some hikers prefer to use map cases that hang from their neck for easy access. If you're in a hurry, however, hanging cases can flop around and snag on heavy brush.

—from *NOLS Wilderness Navigation*

Reading and Using a Topographic Map

Darran Wells
Illustrations by Jon Cox, except where noted

Open a topo map and lay it out in front of you so that you can see the entire surface. The top of the map always faces north; in fact, on a USGS quad, the lines that make up the side margins are the only ones guaranteed to point

In the Margins

There are various useful tools and pieces of information located along the edges of USGS maps. Look for the following elements on your map:

The name of the quadrangle appears in both the upper and lower corners on the right side. The quad gets its name from a prominent land feature or population center located on the map. If you fold your map as shown in the illustration, you'll be able to read the name from either side; this makes searching through a pile of maps much easier.

The date the map was created or last revised is located below the name in the bottom right corner. While government agencies work to regularly update these quadrangles, they often cannot keep up with new trails and other features for every inch of North America. In some places, especially developing countries, a map made in the 1940s may be the most recent one available. Pay careful attention to the date of your map. The older the map, the more likely it is that glaciers have receded, ponds have dried

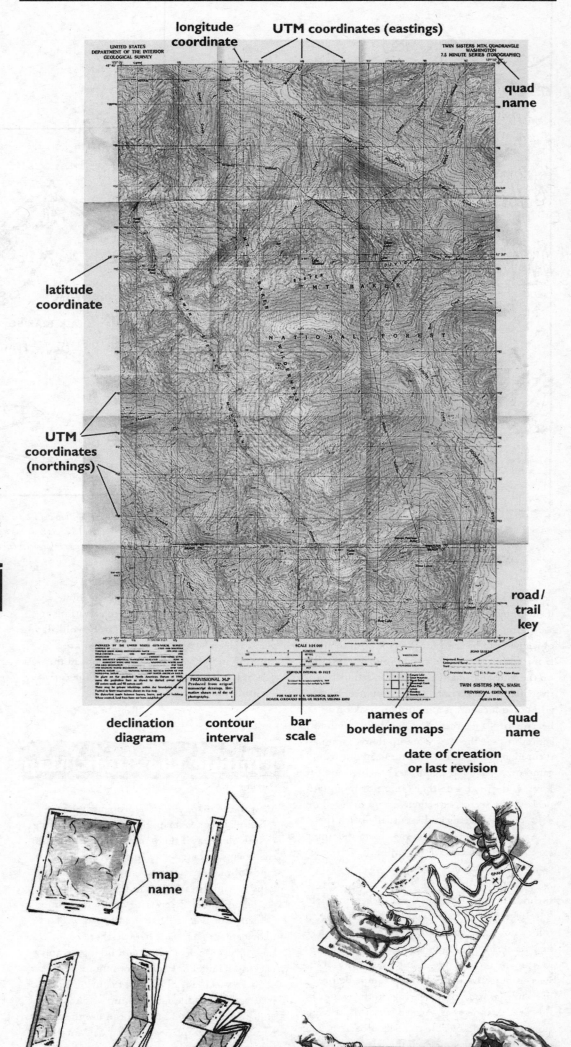

Fold your maps so that the map name can be read from either side.

By using a piece of string, you can determine the mileage for even the most winding trails.

Continued ➡

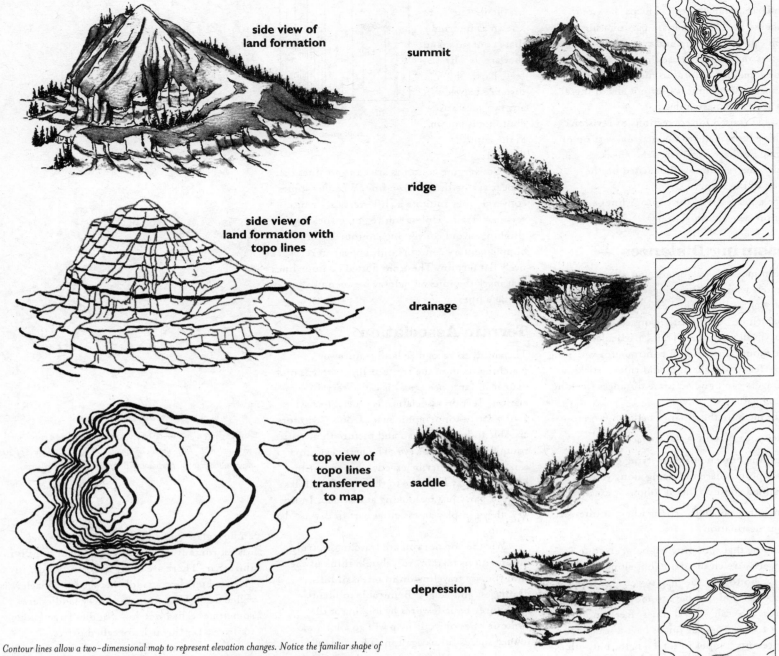

side view of land formation

side view of land formation with topo lines

top view of topo lines transferred to map

summit

ridge

drainage

saddle

depression

Contour lines allow a two-dimensional map to represent elevation changes. Notice the familiar shape of this particular land formation? You can achieve a similar effect by making a fist and drawing concentric circles around your knuckles—the view from above is like looking at a topo map.

Contour patterns of common topographical features.

up, trails and roads have moved, or things have otherwise changed.

The bar scale is located along the bottom center of the map. It consists of rulers that give distances in miles, feet, and kilometers.

Below the scale is the contour interval. This is the elevation difference between contour lines. On 1:24,000-scale USGS quads, the contour interval is usually 40 feet (12.19 meters). A contour interval of 50 feet (15.24 meters) or less will make it easier for you to learn to read contour lines. Contour intervals greater than 100 feet (30.48 meters) are rarely useful for foot travel outside very large mountain ranges like the Himalayas.

The declination diagram is located in the lower left. It consists of two vectors that indicate the differences between magnetic north (MN), true north (TN), and grid north (GN). These distinctions are explained in the sections on declination and GPS.

The numbers running along the edges of the map are coordinates. These are useful in giving your precise location over a radio or cell phone (e.g., for a helicopter evacuation) or when you are using GPS. Newer maps will have Universal Transverse Mercator (UTM) grid lines printed across the face of the map to assist in determining your coordinates.

Most quads will also feature a key titled "Highways and Roads" or "Road Classification" in the bottom right. This shows how roads and trails will be represented on the map.

The names of bordering maps appear in parentheses on every side and in the corners of older maps. Newer maps feature a diagram in the lower right showing the names of all the adjoining quads.

Map Colors

USGS maps all use the same color system. Look for examples of the following colors on the map you are using:

White indicates an area that is not forested. There may be snow, sand, boulders, tundra, sagebrush, or the occasional tree—anything other than forest or water. White doesn't automatically mean easy travel!

Green indicates a forested area, defined by the USGS as having trees dense enough to conceal a platoon (around 40 soldiers) in one acre. The border areas between green and white are often patchy and feature spotty tree coverage.

Blue means water. Solid blue shapes indicate lakes or ponds, while thick, continuous blue lines represent rivers. On older maps, dashed blue lines indicate seasonal streams, which run during the snowmelt in spring and early summer; newer maps use thin, solid lines. White areas covered with tiny blue shrubs and dashes mark seasonal marshes in a clearing. Marshes that are underwater year-round appear on a blue background. Springs show up as tiny blue squiggles and are often labeled "spring." Glaciers and permanent snowfields are enclosed by a dashed blue line. Blue is also used for contour lines on glaciers.

Black is used for names and human-made features—trails, dirt roads, boundaries, buildings, bridges, and mines. Black is also used for elevations that have been field-checked.

Red markings are reserved for US land

Continued ➡

survey lines, trail numbers, and major roads and boundaries. Many older US maps show red, numbered grid lines that are part of a survey system called "township and range." Today, only foresters and surveyors use this grid system. It can be somewhat helpful in measuring linear distance, however: most (but not all) of these grids are one square mile.

Purple is used for corrections or revisions that have been made to the original version of the map but have not been field-checked. Usually, the revisions will be dated on the bottom of the map.

Brown is reserved for contour lines and their elevations (except on glaciers).

Measuring Distances

You can measure any distance on a map very accurately using only a string. Strings that do not stretch will work the best. A shoelace, piece of "parachute" cord, or the lanyard on your compass will work fine. Trails, particularly those in the mountains, seldom continue for very long in a perfectly straight line, and rulers, sticks, and fingers can't give accurate distances for long, winding paths.

To measure the distance between two points:

1. Place your map on a flat surface.

2. Keeping one end of your string on the start point, place the string along your planned route so that it follows it exactly.

3. Pinch the spot in the string where it intersects your destination.

4. Keeping that spot pinched between your fingers, stretch the string out along the scale at the bottom of the map to get your linear distance. You may have to move the string across the scale several times. Keep in mind that 1:24,000-scale quads have a scale that represents 2 miles in total length, but with a "0" in the middle and "1"s on either end.

Reading Contour Lines

Reading and understanding contour lines is the essence of map reading. While they may seem like a jumbled mess now, they will soon tell you volumes about the land you are traveling through. Contour lines are imaginary lines that run through areas of equal elevation. If you were to follow the path of one on land, you would be walking at a constant elevation above sea level. The quintessential natural contour line is the shoreline of a lake.

The elevation difference between each line remains the same throughout a given map. This means that you can easily tell how steep an area is by how close together the contour lines are. Where the lines are spread far apart, the land is fairly flat. Where the lines are close together, it is steep. In a very flat area, like a desert, there may be only a few contour lines on the whole map. In a very steep, cliff-filled area, like Washington's North Cascades, there will be many contour lines crowded together.

Index contours are the heavier brown lines that include elevation numbers. On 1:24,000-scale quads, index lines are 200 feet apart in elevation. Between each pair of index contours are four light-brown lines that do not have

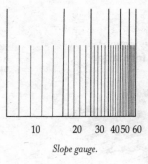

elevations marked on them. These are known as intermediate contours, and they are usually 40 feet apart. The distance between any two successive contours is known as the contour interval.

Slope gauge.

Converging contours are contour lines that appear as one thick brown line. When contours converge, they indicate a cliff—vertical or near-vertical terrain. Unless you're going rock or ice climbing, avoid converging contour lines. Supplementary contours only appear in relatively flat terrain. These are dotted contour lines that mark the interval halfway between two intermediate lines.

Terrain Association

The ability to recognize land features by matching them to the contour line patterns on your map (and vice versa) is called terrain association. Terrain association is crucial to navigating with a topographic map. Good navigators are able to look at a map and picture their entire route in their mind's eye. The best navigators can accurately describe exactly what an entire hiking day may look like to the rest of the folks in their party just by looking at the map. In this way, they can play an essential part in day-to-day planning....

Whether or not you are traveling in truly mountainous terrain, you should think of the land you are traveling on in terms of hills, drainages, and ridges. Being able to identify these three basic features by looking at the contour lines on your map will go a long way toward successful navigation. Try to identify examples of each of them on your map.

A summit or peak is the highest point on any hill or mountain. A small circle surrounded by increasingly larger shapes usually indicates a summit—as they grow larger, elevation drops. Significant summits with verified elevations are often indicated on maps by a benchmark (marked "BM"), triangle, X, or elevation.

A ridge or spur is a relatively narrow area of elevation descending from a summit. It is the topographic opposite of a drainage. A ridge is indicated in contour lines by U shapes with the curve of the U pointing downhill.

A drainage or reentrant is any linear area where water would flow if it were poured on to the surface. There are countless names for the different kinds of drainages depending on their size and location. Gullies, couloirs, valleys, arroyos, crevasses, and canyons are all drainages. Drainages are indicated in contour lines by V shapes, where the apex of the V points uphill.

While mountains do have a general cone shape, their sides are textured by ridges and drainages. If you look at a large aerial photograph of virtually any mountain, you will probably see instances of both descending from the summit. They tend to alternate—ridge, drainage, ridge, drainage, and so on.

A saddle is a low point on a ridge between two summits. The contour lines of a saddle form

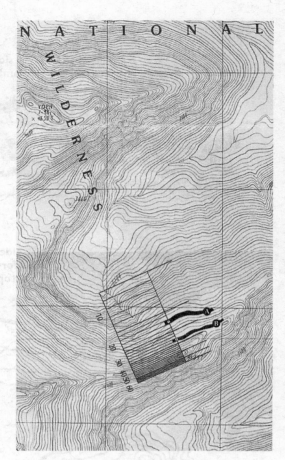

A slope gauge allows you to measure the slope angle at a given point on a topo map. The point along contour "A" has a slope angle of 20 degrees; the point along contour "B" has an angle of 30 degrees.

an hourglass shape. Saddles are usually the easiest route from one side of a chain of hills to the other. There are many different kinds. In glaciated terrain, a saddle between two glaciers is called a col. Very steep and rocky saddles are sometimes called notches. Saddles large enough to drive a car through are called passes.

Once you develop an eye for land features, you will be able to look at a route and easily determine whether it ascends or descends the features it crosses. Until then, you can read the elevations on the index lines. Are the numbers going up or down?

Estimating Steepness

The measurement of a hill's steepness is called the slope angle. If you are traveling in the mountains, you may need to determine the slope angle to decide whether or not to follow a particular route. An angle from 0 to 5 degrees is fairly easy; you may not even notice that it is slightly inclined. From 5 to 25 degrees, you will certainly know you're going uphill. Slopes above 15 degrees will take more time to travel upon than flat terrain, which you should factor into your route planning. A 30-degree slope can be a significant challenge, particularly if you are traveling off-trail with a back-pack. In most cases, you do not want to be on a slope above 45 degrees unless you are using a climbing rope. A 90-degree slope, of course, is a vertical wall or cliff.

A warning: On slopes over 30 degrees, you should start to be concerned with falling rocks. The safest way to deal with steep, rocky slopes is to avoid them. If you must ascend one, keep your group close together and follow a zigzag pattern on the way up to minimize the chance of

Continued →

someone knocking rocks down on to those below. And before you even think about climbing a snowy slope of more than 25 degrees, you should learn how to use an ice axe and assess avalanche danger from a trained professional. If in doubt, avoid steep terrain all together.

As you travel in mountainous terrain with your map, you will develop an eye for how steep a hill is by looking at contour lines. The closer the contours are to each other, the steeper the hill. There are several ways to get a more precise idea of how steep a slope may be. The easiest is by using a slope gauge. This navigational tool is designed for a given scale (e.g., 1:24,000) and provides the slope angle for a series of contour lines. Using a slope gauge when you're starting out will also help develop your eye for contours. You can find one at an outdoor retailer or through the NOLS website, www.nols.edu.

To determine the slope angle using a slope gauge:

1. Make sure the scale of the gauge matches the map scale.

2. Draw a straight line along the route you plan to take up the hill.

3. Move the gauge along the line until a section of the gauge aligns with the contours at the steepest part of your route. The index lines should overlap precisely.

The number indicated on the gauge is the slope angle for that part of the hill.

If you are a math geek or just prefer to have more factors to consider when planning routes, you may be interested in the grade of the slope. If you've driven in the mountains, you've seen road signs warning of a steep grade. The grade is the change in height of a slope divided by its distance (as the crow flies, not the distance on the ground), rendered as a percentage. For a slope that covers a distance of 400 feet and drops 100 feet, the grade is 25%. A slope 400 feet long and 400 feet high has a grade of 100% (45 degrees). As a general rule, you should avoid slopes where the height is equal to or greater than the distance.

Total Elevation Gain

Measuring the elevation you will gain on a particular route before starting out allows you to estimate how much time and energy you will expend. Measuring elevation is as simple as counting contour lines. Be careful, however, not to count the lines where you are losing elevation. While you are learning to identify map features, it may help to double-check by looking at the elevation of each contour line. Are the numbers increasing or decreasing as you travel along your route?

At first, it may be tempting to simply add or subtract the elevation change between your origin and final destination. However, this will not give you an accurate idea of what your travel time may be. It is all those ups and downs you encounter during your hiking day that will slow you down. For example, if you start on the North Rim of the Grand Canyon and want to travel to the South Rim (ending the day at nearly the same elevation), you cannot neglect the close to 1 mile of elevation you will have to regain as you climb back out of the canyon. If you ignored the elevation gain, your travel time would be off by at least six hours—try explaining that mistake to your exhausted hiking partners as you crawl up to camp in the dark! A hike such as this might actually need to be broken into two or three days.

The following guidelines are estimates based on typical speeds for an average party:

- 1,000 feet of elevation gain = 1 mile on flat trail; 200 meters of elevation gain = 1 kilometer on flat trail.

- 2 miles (about 3 kilometers) on flat trail with heavy packs takes approximately 1 hour.

- 1 mile (about 1.5 kilometers) of off-trail travel with heavy packs takes approximately 1 hour.

—From *NOLS Wilderness Navigation*

Navigating with Map Only

Don Geary

On many occasions, a topographical map will be the only navigational tool needed. The most accurate means for the wilderness traveler—and the only way to truly bushwhack—is with both map and compass, but that method is not necessary if your route follows blazed trails. With just the topo, you are left free to observe wildlife, plants, scenery, and just generally enjoy the trip.

Following a marked trail through a wilderness area is quite simple, and its advantages should not be overlooked. In some parts of the country—along the Appalachian Trail in the East, for example—all main trails are marked with metal disks nailed to trees along the route at about eye level. These metal disks are painted a solid color that indicates the particular trail you are following. The trial name or designation is often printed on each marker; in this case, it is very easy to identify the trail if you can find a marker. Trail markers are nailed to both sides of a tree so that they can be seen coming and going, and are spaced about fifty yards apart.

In the West, trails are generally marked in a different manner. More often than not, these trails are marked with an ax blaze cut into the bark of trees along the route. It's common to find a splash of white paint in some national forest trail systems as well. On heavily used western trails—national forest trails, for example—you'll usually find signs at trailheads and junctions that give distances to various objectives, such as a large lake or mountain summit.

On many marked trail systems, you almost don't have to look for trail markers; just follow the well-beaten path. This is especially true when pack animals are commonly used on the trails. The farther you get into the backcountry, however, the less trodden the path and the more valuable the trail markers or ax blazes.

In desert areas, where trees are not available, piles of rocks, called cairns or ducks, are the most common means of marking trails. These markers are usually easy to follow because the piles of stone look unnatural and are easy to spot.

On the trail, a quick glance at the topo will reveal how much distance you've traveled: the name of that lake, or pond, or mountain off in the distance; and the best place for your next rest stop. Where trails intersect, the map shows where the new trail came from and where it goes. When I stop for a rest, the first thing I do is to pull out the topo map-not because I'm afraid of getting lost, but because I'm naturally curious. How far is it to Spruce Lake, and how difficult will the trail ahead be compared with the terrain I've covered so far? How high is that peak in the distance? What elevation have I reached?

Working with a map in a marked trail will familiarize you with how the actual terrain looks in relation to a topographical map. This skill can be developed only through actual practice, and it can be developed surprisingly fast by traveling with map close at hand. On later trips that lead through true wilderness on unmarked trails, you'll be better equipped to plan and follow your own route if you have a firm grasp of map-reading skills.

—From *Using a Map and Compass*

Reading Nautical Charts

Greg Davenport

Chart Features

Most nautical charts are published by the National Ocean Service (NOS) and use the following standard features.

CHART COLORS

Land areas on charts often have a yellowish or gray tint.

Shallow or shoal waters are often shown in blue, and deep-water areas are shown in white.

Shoal areas are often circled or shaded to give them greater visibility.

Areas that may be submerged at high tide, such as sandbars, mud flats, and marshes, are often shown in green.

Magenta is used for a lot of chart information because it is easier to read under a boat's red night-lights.

LETTERS AND NUMBERS

Bottom soundings (depth), which are marked in feet, fathoms, or meters throughout the chart, relate to depths at mean low water.

Slanting or italic lettering identifies submerged or floating features with their height at mean high tide.

Upright or Roman lettering is used to identify features that are dry at high water.

LINES TO SHOW CHANNEL LIMITS

The shoreline is represented as a solid line with the land portions shaded.

Land features on charts are often limited to major landmarks that help you with navigation. These include peaks, buildings, radio towers, and other prominent man-made and natural features.

Continued →

The location of man-made safety markers are labeled with a symbol and brief description. Lighthouses, buoys, and markers help you to avoid shallow water and other dangerous areas (covered on page 355 of Ch. 9).

Charts have a multitude of symbols that help you navigate the waterways. An inexpensive booklet called *Chart No. 1*, published by the National Oceanic and Atmospheric Administration (NOAA), and National Image and Mapping Agency (NIMA), provides the most comprehensive review of chart symbols and is well worth the purchase. Take the time to review these symbols in advance of your trip, and learn to recognize their meaning. Knowledge is power.

Scale and Series

Exactly how much surface area (water or land) a map represents can be found within its margins and will be shown as either a scale or series relationship.

Scale

A scaled map or chart represents the ratio of the map to real life. Here are some common examples of a scale. (An inch is used in this example, but any unit of measurement can be done using the same process.)

- 1:10,000 to 1:50,000: Extremely detailed maps covering small areas, these charts are often used by backpackers and kayakers who travel in harbors, anchorage areas, and smaller inland waterways.

- 1:50,000 to 1:150,000: These charts are used by vessels that navigate large bays and harbors and navigate large inland waterways.

- 1:150,000 to 1:600,000: These charts are used by vessels that navigate beyond the reefs yet within sight of land or navigational aids.

- 1:600,000 and up: Often called a sailing chart and used by vessels covering large areas of water, these charts cover large surface areas, and their details are limited to larger features.

Series

A series map represents the relationship of the map to the amount of latitude and longitude that is displayed. Here are some common examples:

- 15-minute series: This map covers 15 minutes of latitude and 15 minutes of longitude.

- 7.5-minute series: This map covers 7.5 minutes of latitude and 7.5 minutes of longitude. It would take four of these maps to cover the same surface area as one 15-minute series map.

—From *Surviving Coastal and Open Water*

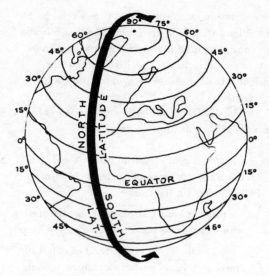

Latitude lines run east/west and are numbered from 0 to 90 degrees north and south of the equator.

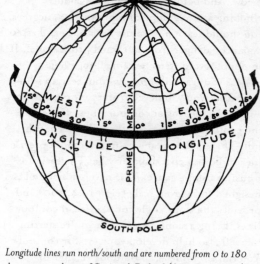

Longitude lines run north/south and are numbered from 0 to 180 degrees east and west of Greenwich England (the prime meridian).

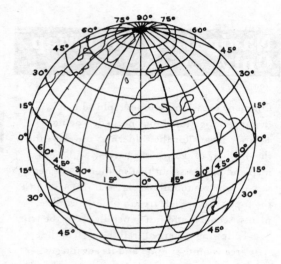

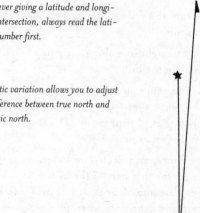

Whenever giving a latitude and longitude intersection, always read the latitude number first.

Magnetic variation allows you to adjust the difference between true north and magnetic north.

Magnetic Variation, Longitude, and Latitude

Greg Davenport
Illustrations by Steven A. Davenport

Magnetic Variation

The magnetic variation is usually listed at the bottom of a topographic map. An arrow labeled "MN" indicates magnetic north; a second line, with a star at the end, is true north. Maps are set up for true north. This variation, commonly called declination, is valuable in compensating for the difference between true north and magnetic north, which will be your compass heading.

Latitude and Longitude Lines

Latitude and longitude lines are imaginary lines that encircle the globe, creating a crisscross grid system. These lines help you identify your location.

LATITUDE LINES

These are east-west-running lines numbered from 0 to 90 degrees north and south of the equator. The 0-degree latitude line runs around the globe at the equator, and from there the numbers rise to north 90 degrees and south 90 degrees. In other words, the equator is 0 degrees latitude, the North Pole is 90 degrees north latitude, and the South Pole is 90 degrees south latitude. Latitude is often noted at the extreme ends of the horizontal map edges.

LONGITUDE LINES

These are north-south-running lines numbered from 0 to 180 degrees east and west of Greenwich, England, the line commonly referred to as the prime meridian. Longitude lines begin at 0 at Greenwich, England, traveling east and west until they meet at the 180th meridian, which is often referred to as the international dateline. The 0 meridian becomes the 180th meridian once it intersects the extreme north and south sections of the globe. Longitude is often noted at the extreme ends of the vertical map edges.

RULES FOR READING LATITUDE AND LONGITUDE

Both latitude and longitude lines are measured in degrees (°), minutes ('), and seconds ("). There are 60 minutes between each degree and 60 seconds between each minute. It's also important to distinguish north from south when defining your latitude, and east from west for longitude. Whenever giving latitude and longitude coordinates, always read the latitude first.

Latitude: A latitude might read, for example, 45° 30' 30". If north of the equator, your latitude would be 45 degrees, 30 minutes, and 30 seconds north latitude; if south of the equator, 45 degrees, 30 minutes, and 30 seconds south latitude. A latitude line will never be over 90 degrees north or south.

Longitude: A longitude might read, for example, 120° 30' 30". If east of the prime meridian, your longitude would be 120 degrees,

Continued ▶

30 minutes, and 30 seconds east longitude; if west of the prime meridian, 120 degrees, 30 minutes, and 30 seconds west longitude. A longitude line will never be over 180 degrees east or west.

—From *Surviving Cold Weather*

Declination

Darran Wells
Illustrations by Jon Cox

Unless disrupted by magnets nearby, a magnetic compass needle will only ever point to the Earth's northern magnetic pole. Contrary to popular belief, however, this is not the North Pole. If you're in North America, magnetic north is currently located in northern Canada, northwest of Baffin Island. To further complicate things, magnetic north moves over time due to changes in the Earth's molten core. The good news is that it is currently moving only about 5 miles per year, to the northwest. In the United States and Canada, declination may move several degrees east or west over many years before it swings back like a pendulum.

For ease of discussion, let's just say that your compass needle points to Baffin Island. The only thing you need to know to understand declination is that your compass needle points to Baffin Island instead of the North Pole. Declination is just the angular difference between the two. If you imagine a triangle with you, the North Pole, and Baffin Island as its three corners, the angle at your corner of the triangle would be the declination.

Your declination changes depending on where in North America you happen to be. If you are in Wisconsin, Illinois, or Mississippi, your declination is close to zero, and you may not need to set your declination at all. If you are in Seattle, your declination is about 19 degrees east, while in New York the declination is about 15 degrees west.

To adjust precisely for declination, you must use the declination diagram in the bottom left on your topo map. Ignore the magnetic needle during this process; you are only concerned with adjusting the bezel correctly.

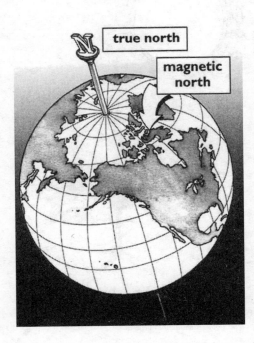

The needle of a compass does not point to the North Pole but to a point near Baffin Island, Canada.

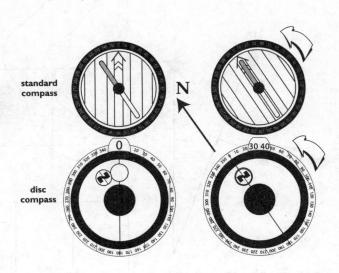

Boxing the needle.

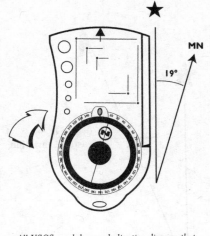

All USGS quads have a declination diagram that will allow you to reconcile magnetic north with true north. Simply place your compass over the diagram, matching the direction-of-travel arrow to true north and the orienting arrow to magnetic north.

Start with the bezel set to north, so that it reads 0 degrees at the index line. Lay the compass over the declination diagram so that the star (representing the North Pole) is under the N on the bezel. Then, holding the base-plate still, rotate the bezel until the orienting arrow is pointing to the "MN" on the diagram.

As a rule, if you are east of the 0 degree declination line, you will turn your bezel counter-clockwise; if you are to the west, you will turn it clockwise. Declination is given in degrees east or west. Thus, although your index line will read 341 degrees in Seattle, the declination will be 19 degrees east. Folks with basic compasses may choose to mark their declination with a small, triangular piece of colored tape on the base plate. This is well worth doing if you will be traveling in one general area for an extended period of time, as it will help you to turn the bezel in the right direction. If you are confused about which way to turn the dial, simply place your compass over the declination diagram again.

If you have a compass with a declination adjustment feature, you will probably adjust it by turning the screw on the back of the bezel, perhaps with a tiny screwdriver on your lanyard. Brunton compasses are adjusted by holding the bezel's azimuth ring while pinching and rotating the needle housing. In either case, the N on the azimuth ring should still be at the index line, while the orienting arrow arrow should point to the correct declination. If your compass features a dial for adjusting declination on the back of the bezel, remember when you turn it over that in the West you are dealing with east declination and vice versa.

Also remember that magnetic north is constantly changing. If your map is more than five years old, the declination may be off a little. For areas in the United States, call the USGS at 1-888-ASK-USGS or visit them on the Web at www.USGS.gov to get the most current declination in the area in which you will be traveling.

Boxing the Needle

After setting your declination, you can use your compass to face true north. You accomplish this by boxing the needle—moving the compass until the magnetic end (the red end) of the needle is

outlined by the orienting arrow. There are two ways to box the needle: by holding the base plate still while turning the bezel, and by rotating the entire compass without touching the bezel. Give them both a try.

The second method is the one you want for finding true north. Set your compass declination to your present location and box the needle by rotating the entire compass. The direction-of-travel arrow on the base plate is now pointing to true north. Pick the compass up and hold it in front of you, perpendicular to your chest, while the needle is boxed and the declination is set. You are now facing true north.

—From *NOLS Wilderness Navigation*

Orienting Your Map

Greg Davenport
Illustrations by Steven A. Davenport

Orienting the map aligns its features to those of the surrounding terrain. This process is extremely helpful in determining your specific location.

1. Get to high ground. This will help you to evaluate the terrain once the map is oriented.

2. Open the map and place it on a flat, level surface. If possible, protect it from the dirt and moisture with something such as a poncho.

3. Rotate the circular housing on the compass, until the bottom of the direction-of-travel arrow is touching the true north heading. When doing this, you must account for the area's given declination. Declination is the difference between magnetic north (MN) and true north (★). True north is north as represented on a map, and magnetic north is the compass heading. In other words, a 360-degree map heading—true north—is not necessarily a 360-degree compass heading. This variation is usually depicted on the bottom of most topographic maps. If magnetic north is located west of true north, which is the case for most of the eastern United States, you would add your declina-

Continued ➡

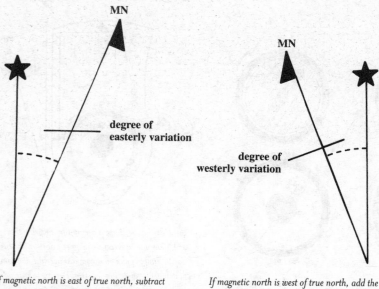

If magnetic north is east of true north, subtract the variation from 360 degrees.

degree of easterly variation

degree of westerly variation

If magnetic north is west of true north, add the variation to 0 degrees.

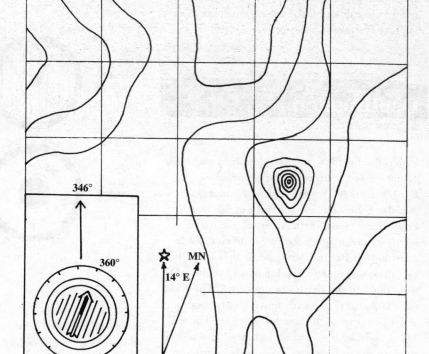

Be sure to account for the magnetic variation when orienting the map with a compass.

tion to 360 degrees. The resultant bearing would be the compass heading equivalent to true north at that location. If magnetic north is located east of true north, which is the case for most of the western United States, you would subtract your declination from 360 degrees. The resultant bearing would be the compass heading equivalent to true north at that location.

4. Set the compass on the map, with the edge of the long side resting next to, and parallel to, the left north-south margins (on USGS maps the map's left edge is a longitude line). Be sure that the direction-of-travel arrow is pointing toward the north end of the map.

5. Holding the compass in place on the map, rotate the map and compass until the floating magnetic needle is inside the etched orienting arrow of the base plate, with the red portion of the needle forward. This is called boxing the needle.

6. Double-check to ensure that the compass is still set for the variation adjustment, and if correct, weigh down the map edges to keep it in place.

7. At this point, the map is oriented to the lay of the land, and the map features should reflect those of the surrounding terrain.

—From *Surviving Cold Weather*

Orienting Your Map without a Compass

Darran Wells
Illustrations by Jon Cox

To orient your map, you must turn it so that the cardinal directions on the map match those on land. An oriented map helps you determine your exact location and shows what lies between you and your destination. There are two ways to do this without a compass—using the sun and the stars or using terrain association. It's recommended that you practice both methods and learn to use them together whenever possible.

Using the Sun and Stars to Orient Your Map

You probably learned in grade school that the sun rises in the east and sets in the west. This is in essence true, though as the seasons change, the points where the sun crosses the horizon gradually shift. Nonetheless, you should be able to roughly orient your map using the sun alone, particularly at dawn and dusk.

In the middle of the day, you can use a different technique to determine north. In the northern hemisphere, the sun does not cross directly overhead as it does at the equator. It actually passes just to the south. (This is the reason you find more snow and shade on the north faces of North American mountains.) Because of this, the shadow of a perfectly straight tree points north at mid-day, i.e., the moment exactly halfway between sunrise and sunset for that time of the year—it's usually between noon and 2:00 P.M. The length of this shadow will vary depending on your location. The farther north of the equator you are, the longer the shadow. At the equator, there is no shadow at all, and in the southern hemisphere, of course, the shadow points south.

You can also find north at night if you can see the stars. In the northern hemisphere, it's as simple as finding the Big Dipper. Look for the two stars at the end of this familiar constellation, the ones that lie farthest from the handle. They form a straight line that points directly toward Polaris, which is known as the North Star because it always lies directly to the north. On a clear night in the northern hemisphere, you can hardly miss Polaris: it is a bright star that stands alone, and as the night progresses, the other stars will appear to revolve around it. The farther north you are, the higher it will appear in the sky, and the more difficult it will be to tell in which direction it is pointing.

In the northern hemisphere at midday, the shadows of vertical objects will point north.

Continued ➡

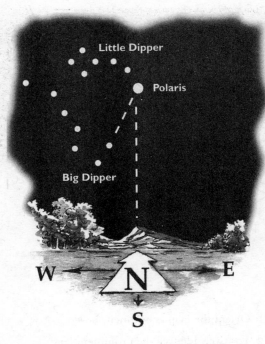

You can use the Big Dipper to locate Polaris, the North Star.

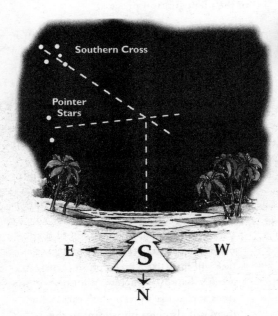

In the southern hemisphere, navigators can use the Southern Cross for guidance.

In the southern hemisphere, Polaris may be too low on the horizon to be seen, and there is no "South Star" over the South Pole. In places such as southern Chile or New Zealand, the Southern Cross is often used for direction. It is a smaller constellation (it is less than half the size of the Big Dipper) and actually looks more like a kite than a cross, because it lacks a bright star in the middle. If you draw an imaginary line along the long beam of the cross and another one from the two "Pointer Stars" near the Cross, the intersection marks true south.

Note: Traveling at night can be a magnificent experience, but it is considerably more difficult and dangerous than traveling during the day. It is the domain of expert navigators. Don't consider it unless you are in a very safe environment or are with experienced people.

Using Terrain Association to Orient Your Map

Unfortunately, the sun and stars are not always visible when we need them. While you are learning navigation, you should think of them the way you will come to think of your compass—as a tool to verify that you have oriented your map correctly using terrain association. The first step in terrain association is to locate a nearby terrain feature that is easy to find on your map. Linear features such as trails, ridges, and drainages are best. If you can't find a land feature that you can match to contour lines, you can't orient your map with terrain association alone. Next, rotate your map until the shape on the map is aligned with the terrain feature you can see. Then verify that the map is oriented correctly. Take a look around to make sure that the positions of what you see on land match those on the map, and that the cardinal directions correspond to those given by the sun.

—From *NOLS Wilderness Navigation*

Determining General Direction

Greg Davenport

Anytime you're traveling in the wilderness, you should maintain a constant awareness of your general location, focusing on the surrounding terrain and how it relates to the map you are carrying. If you do this throughout your trip, you shouldn't ever need to use other means of establishing where you are. One way to keep a constant awareness is with dead reckoning. Dead reckoning uses a simple mathematical formula to help you determine you present location:

$$time \times rate = distance$$

Time refers to the amount of time that has passed since you left the last known location, so keep track of your location throughout the day.

The rate of speed you travel is usually measured in miles per hour on land or knots per hour at sea. In a vehicle, keep aware of your speed. The average backpacker travels at a speed of 1 to 3 miles per hour, depending on the weight carried and terrain covered. Take the time to evaluate your speed using known variables. Consider purchasing an electronic pedometer to measure the distance traveled, and use it to determine your average rate of speed by applying it to the following formula, where time and distance are known:

$$distance \div time = rate$$

Once you've determined the distance you've traveled, apply this to your line of travel (heading) from your starting point to figure out your approximate location.

Adjusting your location (latitude and longitude) can be done based on your direction of travel and the distance traveled. There are several other methods you might use to determine your location and direction of travel.

—From *Surviving the Desert*

Triangulating to Determine Your Position

Greg Davenport
Illustrations by Steven A. Davenport

Triangulating is a process of identifying your specific location. For best results, get to high ground with 360 degrees of visibility.

1. Orient the map as outlined above.

2. Positively identify three of the surrounding landmarks, ideally 120 degrees apart, on your map by using the following guidelines:

- Contour: Evaluate the landmark's contour, translating it into a two-dimensional appearance, and search for a matching contour outline on your map.

- Distance: Determine the distance from your present position to the landmark to be identified. This may be estimated as follows:

   From 1 to 3 kilometers (0.62 to 1.86 miles), you should be able to see the individual branches of a tree.

   From 3 to 5 kilometers (1.86 to 3.1 miles), you should be able to see individual trees.

   From 5 to 8 kilometers 3.1 to 4.97 miles, a group of trees will look like a green plush carpet.

   At greater than 8 kilometers (4.97 miles), not only will the trees appear like a green plush carpet, but there will also be a bluish tint to the horizon.

- Elevation: Determine your landmark's height as compared with that of your location.

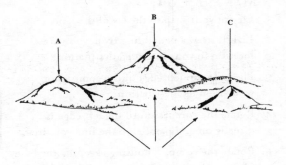

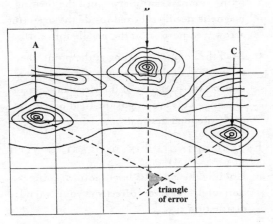

Continued ➡

3. Using your compass, point the direction-of-travel arrow at one of the identified landmarks, and then turn the compass housing until the etched orienting arrow boxes the magnetic needle (red end forward). At the point where the direction-of-travel arrow intersects the compass housing, read and record the magnetic bearing. Repeat this process for the other two landmarks.

4. Before working further with the map, ensure that it's still oriented.

5. Place the front left tip of the long edge of the compass on the identified map landmark, and while keeping the tip in place, rotate the compass until the magnetic needle is boxed (red end forward). Double-check that your compass heading is correct for the landmark being used.

6. Lightly pencil a line from the landmark down, following the left edge of the compass base plate. You may need to extend the line. Repeat this process for the other two landmarks. Each time, double-check the map to ensure that it's still oriented.

7. Ultimately, a triangle will form where the three lines intersect. Your position should be located within or around the triangle.

8. For final position determination, evaluate the surrounding terrain and how it relates to the triangle displayed on the man.

—From *Surviving Cold Weather*

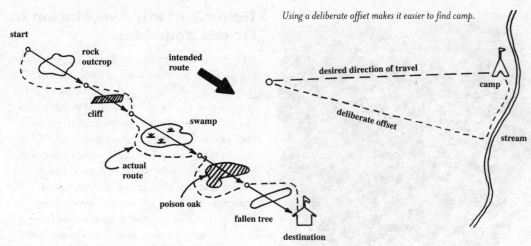

Using a deliberate offset makes it easier to find camp.

Point-to-point navigation allows you to steer clear of obstacles.

Establishing a Field Bearing

Greg Davenport
Illustrations by Steven A. Davenport

Never travel unless you know both your present position and where you intend to go.

Establishing a Field Bearing with a Map and Compass:

1. Orient your map to the lay of the land.

2. Lightly draw a pencil line from your present location to your intended destination.

3. Place the top left edge of the compass on your intended destination.

4. Rotate the compass until the left edge is directly on and parallel to the line you drew.

5. Rotate the compass housing—keeping the base of the compass stationary—until the floating magnetic needle is boxed inside the orienting arrow (red portion of the needle forward).

6. Read the compass heading at the point where the bottom of the direction-of-travel arrow touches the numbers of the circular compass housing. This heading is the field bearing to your intended destination.

Establishing a Field Bearing with Only a Compass:

1. Holding the compass level, point the direction-of-travel arrow directly at your intended destination site.

2. Holding the compass in place, turn its housing until the magnetic needle is boxed directly over and inside the orienting arrow (red portion of the needle forward).

3. Read the heading at the point where the bottom of the direction-of-travel arrow touches the numbers of the circular housing. This heading is the field bearing to your intended destination.

Deliberate Offset
If your destination is a road or waterway, consider a heading with a deliberate offset, using a field heading several degrees to one side of your final location. Since it is very difficult to be precise in wilderness travel, this offset will help you in deciding whether to turn left or right once you intersect the road.

Maintaining a Field Bearing

Point-to-Point Navigation
Pick objects in line with your field bearing. Once one point is reached, recheck your bearing and pick another. This method allows you to steer clear of obstacles.

Following the Compass
Holding the compass level, and while keeping the magnetic needle boxed, walk forward in line with the direction-of-travel arrow.

Using Line of Position to Determine Your Location

Greg Davenport

A single line of position can be used when at least one prominent land feature can be seen. A prominent land feature includes any easily identified man-made or natural feature. For best results, get to high ground with 360 degrees of visibility.

1. Orient the map as outlined above.

2. Positively identify the prominent land feature. The following guidelines related to contour, distance, and elevation can help in the identification process.

   · *Contour*. Evaluate the landmark's contour translating it into a two-dimensional appearance, and search for a matching contour outline on your map.

   · *Distance*. Determine the distance from your present position to the landmark to be identified.

   · *In treed terrain*. From 1 to 3 kilometers (approximately 1 to 2 miles), you should be able to see the individual branches of each tree. From 3 to 5 kilometers (approximately 2 to 3 miles), you should be able to see each individual tree. From 5 to 8 kilometers (approximately 3 to 4 miles), the tree will look like a green plush carpet. At greater than 8 kilometers, not only will the trees appear like a green plush carpet, but there will also be a bluish tint to the horizon.

   · *In flat, open terrain*. In flat, open terrain, you can calculate a gross distance once a prominent landmark becomes visible on the horizon. To apply this formula, you must first calculate how far you are from the viewed horizon. To do this, take the square root of your eye's height above the ground and multiply it times 1.23 [equation (a)].

   Next, apply the same formula to the object's height above the ground, and add that to the already calculated horizon distance [equation (b)]. The result is a rough estimation of the object's distance from your present location.

   · *Elevation*. Determine your landmark's height as compared with that of your location.

(a) $\sqrt{\text{your eye's height above ground}} \times 1.23$ = distance to the horizon in miles

(b) $(\sqrt{\text{height of the object above ground}}) \times 1.23$ + distance to the horizon in miles = distance to the object in miles

Continued ➜

3. Using your orienteering compass, point the direction-of-travel arrow at the identified landmark, and then turn the compass housing until the etched orienting arrow boxes the magnetic needle (red end forward). At the point where the direction-of-travel arrow intersects the compass housing, read and record the magnetic bearing.

4. Before working further with a topographic map, ensure that it's still oriented.

5. Place the front left tip of the long edge of the compass (or a straight edge) on the identified map landmark, and while keeping the tip in place, rotate the compass until the magnetic needle is boxed (red end forward). Double-check that your compass heading is correct for the landmark being used.

6. Lightly pencil a line from the landmark down, following the left edge of the compass base plate or straight edge. You may need to extend the line. If you have a protective plastic cover on your map, you can draw on it with grease pencils to avoid exposing the map to moisture and dirt.

7. Your position should be located on or close to the line. For final position determination, evaluate the surrounding terrain and how it relates to your line, along with believed distances to land or light features.

—From *Surviving the Desert*

Determining Your Position by Resection

Don Geary

If two landmarks can be clearly seen and located on the map, your exact position can be determined by resection. Using the compass alone, determine the bearing to each landmark. Then calculate the back bearings by subtracting 180 degrees if the bearing is more than 180 degrees, or adding 180 degrees if the bearing is less than 180 degrees. For example, you can see several mountain peaks in the distance. On your map, you identify the two highest peaks, A and B (see image on this page). The bearing to peak A is 280 degrees, so the back bearing from that peak to your position is 100 degrees (280 minus 180). The bearing to peak B is 340 degrees, so the back bearing is 160 degrees (340 minus 180). To use resection successfully, you have to read the compass very carefully. Double- or triple-check your calculations just to be on the safe side.

The next step is to draw on your map back-bearing lines from the landmarks. Place the compass on one of the landmarks, and orient it so that the needle points to north and the direction-of-travel arrow points to the back bearing to your position. Draw a line following the back bearing. A clear plastic ruler is handy for drawing resection lines. In an emergency, fold one edge of the map over and use it as a straightedge. Repeat the procedure for the other landmark. The point where the two lines intersect is your approximate position. For the above example, you would place the compass on peak

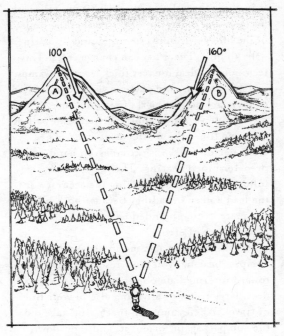

Use resection to determine your position with a map and compass. First locate two prominent landmarks in the distance, and find them on the map. Next, shoot a bearing to these two landmarks. Then calculate a back bearing for each by adding or subtracting 180 degrees. Your position on the map is where the two back-bearing lines intersect.

A, with the direction-of-travel arrow set at 100 degrees, and rotate the entire compass until the needle lines up with north. Now draw a straight line from the peak at 100 degrees; the direction-of-travel arrow will indicate this direction. Repeat this procedure for peak B, drawing a straight line on a bearing of 160 degrees.

Resection can be used only when distinguishing landmarks can be clearly seen and located on the topographical map. Choosing prominent or unique landmarks will greatly reduce your chances of error.

—From *Using a Map and Compass*

Checking Your Position

Don Geary

Checking Your Position with an Altimeter

You can also check your position by comparing altimeter readings with elevation marks or lines on a topographical map. To do this, however, you must understand how an altimeter operates, have a general idea of your present position, and be able to locate this position on your map. In effect, you're checking your altimeter with the aid of your topographical map.

An altimeter indicates a given altitude by measuring air pressure. At sea level, air pressure is much higher than at 10,000 feet. The barometric cell inside an altimeter expands in low air pressure and contracts in high air pressure. The expansion or contraction of the barometric cell operates the dial of the instrument.

Altimeters have a tendency to give inaccurate readings when the weather is about to change. For example, if you're certain that you're on a mountaintop at 8,000 feet, but your altimeter reads 7,000 feet, it could be

because the barometric pressure is rising. Even if you reset your altimeter, the advancing change in weather will affect future readings. Even expensive altimeters tend to give inaccurate readings when the weather is changing. As a result, you have to adjust your altimeter whenever you reach a known elevation. I don't feel that an altimeter is a worthwhile investment (good ones can easily cost several hundred dollars) for the average outdoorsman. You cannot simply look at your altimeter for an elevation reading, find a corresponding elevation on your topographical map, and assume that that's where you are.

Using Secondary Objectives to Determine Position

Accurately determining your position becomes much more difficult when no landmarks can be distinguished. On relatively flat terrain with no high points visible in the distance, in dense forest, or on a cloudy day, resection or line position simply will not be of any value to you. The best you can do is to check your progress against several secondary objectives, and keep track of your direction of travel after you reach each identifiable place. Features such as small streams, cliffs, lakes, and man-made structures serve as good checkpoints. For example, a lake may have a stream entering it at 50 degrees. Provided that there are no other lakes in the vicinity with a stream running in at 50 degrees, this fact can establish your position.

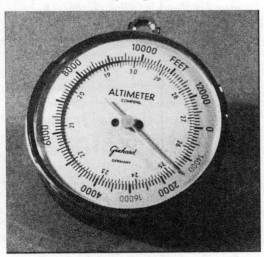

A pocket altimeter.

An entire trip can easily be navigated in this way. A fisherman may be looking for a certain lake in a forest area where the terrain is flat, such as the Adirondack Forest Preserve in upper New York State. He hikes in for one day on a marked trail system and camps at the junction of two marked trails and a stream. He can locate this junction on the map because the Conservation Department has erected a footbridge here. The next morning, he heads off on a compass bearing of 210 degrees for about a half mile and easily finds a small pond. He follows the stream, reaching another small pond and finally a large pond, which was his objective. Using secondary objectives is one trick you can use to check your progress.

—From *Using a Map and Compass*

Continued ➜

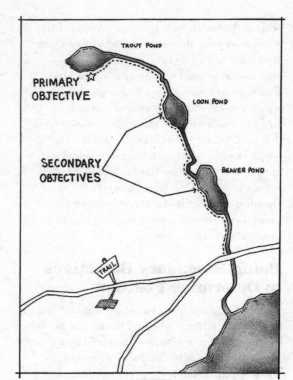

When traveling cross-country, use easily identifiable landmarks—in this case, small ponds connected by a stream—as checks on your progress.

Staying on Course

Don Geary

Once you know your present position and the location of your objective, it's a simple matter to calculate your bearing to that objective. Begin by orienting your map to magnetic north. Locate your position, lay your compass on the map over your position, and note the compass bearing to your objective.

The best type of compass for cross-country travel is the orienteering compass. Simply line up the direction-of-travel arrow with your bearing. When the compass is oriented to magnetic north, the direction-of-travel arrow will point out your heading. If you are inexperienced at cross-country travel, keep your compass handy and check it often. Although checks can be less frequent after you develop some course-following skills, it's a small task to verify your line of travel with a quick check of the compass.

There would be little joy in traveling with one eye on the compass and another on the route. The trick is to pick out landmarks in the distance and on the same heading as your destination. Then you merely have to walk toward it, while taking the terrain into consideration. Let's say you want to take a shortcut to a jeep trail shown on the map to be about 2 miles away on a compass bearing of 250 degrees. First, set the direction-of-travel arrow at 250 degrees. When the compass is oriented to north, you see that a mountain peak also lies at 250 degrees. As long as you can see that peak, you need not check your compass. Simply walk as straight as the terrain will allow toward the mountain peak, and you should cross the jeep trail in less than an hour.

When walking cross-country with a companion, it's much easier to stay on a compass bearing. One partner can serve as the landmark. One hiker stands in one spot, and the other walks in the direction of the bearing, compass in hand. The stationary person should

help guide the walker and check his progress with his compass. When the walker reaches the limit of the other's visibility, he stops, and his partner walks to him. Then they can change roles. This technique is ideal for very thick terrain, swamps, marshes, deserts, and anytime visibility is limited or there are no landmarks in the distance.

In open country, both partners can walk at the same time, about 100 yards apart. The front person walks with compass in hand on a predetermined bearing. The rear person follows, periodically checking the accuracy of the lead walker's heading. Because both hikers are aware of the intended bearing, there is little chance of error.

If there's no magic mountain on your compass bearing, you must resort to navigating toward intermediate objectives such as boulders, large trees, or anything else in your line of travel. When you reach that point, take out the compass again, orient it, and sight down the direction-of-travel arrow to find another prominent land feature. Because these check-points are nearby, there's the possibility of slight error, but trying to navigate without them can result in having a search party out looking for you.

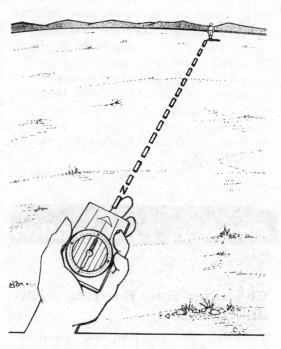

When you are traveling in relatively flat, featureless terrain, use a hiking companion as a compass-bearing aid.

Natural obstacles can often make straight-line travel to a given destination impossible. If your bearing leads you to the edge of a pond, for example, simply sight across it to a prominent land feature that's in your line of travel, such as a clump of boulders or a large tree; walk around the pond until you reach that point; then head out again on your original course.

Actually, small obstacles are very good checks on your progress. When you plan your route, you should keep an eye out for such obstacles and use them to your advantage. Obviously, large obstacles such as a lake, steep canyon, or cliff should be avoided, but stream

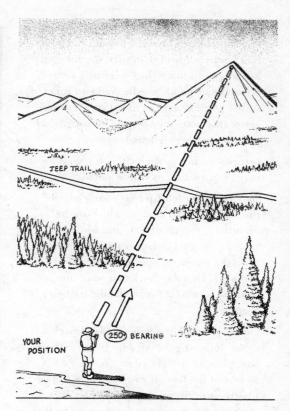

If a prominent and feature such as a mountain lies on a bearing that's the same as (or close to) the bearing you wish to travel, you can use it as a guide. This will make travel easier, as you can stay on course simply by walking toward the land feature rather than having to check your compass often.

junctions, small ponds, or other obstacles that are easy to walk around are good choices. Your route should not be an exercise in detours, but rather as direct a course as possible with built-in, fail-safe checkpoints.

Besides checking the topo, another way to determine the best course of travel is to survey the terrain from a vantage point such as a mountain peak, high ridge line, or other over-look. Even the best eyesight cannot see details in terrain at distances greater than a few hundred yards, so binoculars are a piece of extra equipment worth carrying. Binoculars have many uses on an outdoor trip, and you should consider carrying a pair on every hike. Because they're an important navigational tool, let's take a brief look at the basics.

All binoculars have two numbers separated by an x stamped on the lens housing, such as 8x5. The first number is the magnification of the binoculars. If this number is 8, for example, this means that the magnification of these binoculars is eight power, and an object 120 feet away will appear to be only 15 feet away (120 divided by 8).

The second number indicates the diameter in millimeters of the objective lens. Generally, a larger objective lens diameter lets in more light, gives a brighter image, and allows you to see more clearly in low-light conditions, such as at dusk or dawn, or in a dark forest. If the second number is low, as in 8x15, the glasses will be adequate for normal daylight viewing but will be difficult to see through in low light. If the second number is high, as in 8x60, the glasses can almost be considered night binoculars. A good rule of thumb is that a pair of binoculars will be adequate for daylight use if the objective lens diameter is 2½ times its magnification— 8x20, for example.

Continued ➡

Estimating Distance and Travel Time

Before starting toward any objective, estimate how long it will take you to get there. If you don't reach your objective in a reasonable amount of time, look for a landmark or land feature against which your progress can be measured. The amount of time that is "reasonable" depends, of course, on terrain, weather, detours, rest stops, stops to cast a fly or photograph scenery, and many other factors. Experienced wilderness travelers develop an ability to estimate this with a fair degree of accuracy.

As a rule, the average hiker carrying a moderate load and in reasonably sound condition can cover about three miles an hour on a marked and cleared trail. Traveling cross-country through forest and brush will reduce this pace by about half. Here your pace will be slower because you will have to pick your way through, around, under, and over obstacles such as fallen trees, boulders, swamps, and under-brush. Dense cover and difficult terrain require not only more time, but they also make estimating difficult. Sometimes the ground will be relatively clear and your pace good, and other times heavy growth will slow your progress. In true wilderness, you also tend to be slowed more by your observations of animals, birds, plants, and the landscape.

Some outdoorsmen use a pedometer to measure distance covered. Worn on the belt, a pedometer records the number of steps taken and indicates distance based on how many of the user's steps equal a quarter mile. All pedometers must be preadjusted to the length of the user's stride. Most record distances up to 25 miles.

In theory, a pedometer is a handy gadget, but on a wilderness trek, it may not be accurate, as your steps will vary in length over any ground that is not flat. Steep grades shorten your step; downhill slopes lengthen it. Over broken terrain, such as deadfalls or talus slopes, the length of any one step will be different from all others. A pedometer that could automatically adjust for variations in stride length would be very worthwhile, but to my knowledge no such instrument exists. Instead, I measure and estimate distance on a topographical map.

When traveling cross-country with the aid of a map and compass, the important things to keep track of are your general direction of travel and approximately how long you've been traveling. Estimating distance covered becomes easier as you develop a feel for how long it takes you to cover a given type of terrain. The more you use a topographical map and compass, the more proficient you'll become at determining the best route to follow and estimating the time necessary to cover the distance. As you develop navigational skills, you'll be able to discover true wilderness while always knowing how to find your way back to civilization.

—From *Using a Map and Compass*

Finding Your Position with a Marine Chart and Compass

Greg Davenport

If you stay constantly aware, you should be able to determine your general and specific location at all times.

Determining General Location

Anytime you're traveling in the wilderness or at sea, you should maintain a constant awareness of your general location. This awareness keeps you focused on the surrounding terrain and how it relates to the map you are carrying. If you have done this throughout your trip, you will never have to use any other means of establishing where you are. One way to keep a constant awareness is with dead reckoning. Dead reckoning uses a simple math formula to help you find your present location:

$$\text{Rate} \times \text{Time} = \text{Distance}$$

Rate

The rate of speed you have been traveling is usually measured in knots per hour at sea and miles per hour (kilometers per hour) on land. One knot equals a traveling speed that covers one nautical mile per hour. A nautical mile is equal to one minute of latitude—1.852 kilometers or 1.1508 miles or 6,076 feet—and is used as the distance reference in most charts. Note that a nautical mile is not equal to a statute mile, which is used for measurement on land. If your vessel is propelled in a direction by paddling or motor, then you must consider the impact of the current and wind on your rate and adjust the formula accordingly. For our scenario, however, we are using the current and the wind as a means of moving our vessel.

The best way to determine your vessel's rate of speed is with a chip log, which consists of a heaving line and a heavy object that floats. This object could be improvised from something as simple as a container filled with seawater. Make sure the container weighs enough to prevent the wind from affecting its movement in the water. To build a chip log, attach a line to the container and tie two knots in the line. The first knot should be positioned far enough away from the container so that it meets the water after the container has settled. The second knot should be placed at a premeasured distance from the first. To use, place the container in the water and allow the line to pass through your hands. As the line advances, calculate the time that passes between hand contact with the first knot and second knot. Using this time along with the distance between the two knots, you can calculate your speed with the following formula:

$$\text{Speed in knots} = \frac{0.6 \times \text{feet between marks}}{\text{Seconds of time between knots}} = \text{feet/second}$$

Measurements (speed, heading, etc.) should be taken every hour to ensure accuracy and constant awareness. Applying the result to your dead-reckoning formula helps you determine how far you have traveled. Note that one nautical mile per hour equals $1\,2/3$ feet per second.

Time

If you have kept track of your location throughout the day, time will be related to the amount of time that has passed since leaving the last known location.

Distance

For this formula to work, you will need to know your starting point and the heading you took. Apply the answer (distance) to your line of travel (heading) to give you an approximate location. Direction of travel can be calculated by shooting an azimuth off your chip line (once extended and straight) and adding or subtracting 180 degrees.

Adjusting your location (latitude and longitude) can be done based on your direction of travel and the distance traveled. There are several other methods you might use to determine your location and direction of travel.

Line of Position to Determine Your Location

A line of position is used when either land features can provide an optimal fix or no other features are available. Optimal land features include a road that runs east to west or north to south or two land features that can be visualized in a straight line. For best results on land, go to high ground with 360 degrees of visibility. At sea, try to shoot your headings on features during the height of a wave.

1. Orient the map as outlined above. Note that charts with a compass rose do not need to be oriented; however, all headings must be used with the middle ring of the compass rose in order to skip this step. It is a major error to use the outer ring of the compass rose without orienting the chart.

2. Positively identify the prominent land feature, buoy, or light used to aid with sea navigation.

On charts, land features, buoys, or lights may be shown as symbols, making it relatively easy to identify them.

Lights are described on charts by their behavior, height (at mean high-water tide level), and projected visible range. For example, a chart that lists a light as Fl 4sec 20ft 10M is telling you that the light flashes every four seconds, is 20 feet above mean high-water tide level, and has a predicted range of ten nautical miles.

LIGHT BEHAVIOR CHART SYMBOLS

Symbol	Meaning
F	Fixed light; a continuous steady light.
Fl	Flashing lights; a single flash at regular intervals where the duration of the flash is always less than the duration of darkness.

Continued →

F Fl	Fixed light varied by bright flashes at regular intervals.
F Gp Fl	Fixed light varied by two or more bright flashes at regular intervals.
Gp Fl	Two or more bright flashes shown at regular intervals.
Gp Fl (1 + 2)	Bright flashes are shown in an alternating sequence of numbers.
E Int	Flashing lights; a single flash at regular intervals where the duration of the flash is equal to the duration of darkness.
Occ	Flashing lights; a single flash at regular intervals where the duration of the flash is always longer than the duration of darkness.
Gp Occ	Two or more bright flashes shown at regular intervals (flash longer than darkness).
Gp Occ	Bright flashes shown in an alternating sequence of numbers (flash longer than darkness).

When floating at sea level, the height of the light is probably the single most impor tant factor at how well and far away it can be seen. Charts that list a light's projected visibility do so based on the brightness of the light. This normal range is calculated using a direct line of sight and doesn't account for the earth's curvature. If sitting on the floor of a life raft or deck of a sea kayak, the earth's curvature will reduce the light's visible distance.

3. Using your orienteering compass, point the direction-of-travel arrow at one of the identified landmarks, and then turn the compass's housing until the etched orienting arrow boxes the magnetic needle (red end forward). At the point where the direction-of-travel arrow intersects the compass housing, read and record the magnetic bearing. When using a handheld marine compass, point the front of the compass at the landmark and read the heading under the fixed lubber line; when using a deck-mounted marine compass, point the front of the vessel at the landmark.

4. Before working further with a topographic map, be sure it's still oriented.

5. For topographical maps, place the front left tip of the long edge of the compass on the identified map landmark, and while keeping the tip in place, rotate the compass until the magnetic needle is boxed (red end forward). For a chart, position your compass so that the desired heading (to the landmark) is under the lubber line, and while holding this posi tion, rotate the chart until an imaginary line (from the left side of the compass's long edge) crosses the identical heading on the inner circle of the compass rose (magnetic heading). Be sure the imaginary line is drawn

backwards and crosses the closest compass rose to your general location. In both instances, double-check that your compass heading is correct for the landmark being used (see step 3).

6. Using a pencil, lightly draw a line from the landmark down, following the left edge of the compass base plate or straightedge. You may need to extend the line. If you have a protec tive plastic cover, grease pencils are an ideal way to avoid exposing the map or chart to moisture and dirt.

7. Your position should be located on or close to the line.

8. For final position determination, evaluate the surrounding terrain and how it relates to your line along with believed distances to land or light features.

Establishing a Magnetic Bearing Using a Chart and Compass Rose

Determining a bearing with a chart's compass rose is a fairly simple process. Draw a line from your present position to your desired destina tion. Find your heading by identifying where the line crosses or runs parallel to the middle circle on the compass rose. Make sure you read the heading on the side closest to your destination.

Establishing a Magnetic Bearing with a Marine Compass

For a handheld marine compass, hold your compass so that the lubber line is pointing toward your destination and read the heading beneath it. For deck-mounted marine compasses, simply turn your vessel toward your intended target and read the heading.

Deliberate Offset

If your destination is a road or shore structure, consider a heading with a deliberate offset. In other words, use a heading several degrees to one side of your final location. Since it is very difficult to be precise in wilderness travel, this offset will help you in deciding to turn left or right once you intersect the road.

—From *Surviving Coastal and Open Water*

Using GPS Receivers
Darran Wells
Illustration by Jon Cox

Today, it is foolish to head days-deep into the backcountry without a map and compass—GPS or no GPS. Electronic things, just like motor ized things, can and do break. GPS is not a replacement for good map skills or a shortcut to the backcountry. Learn to read a topographic map and use a compass before relying on elec tronics to tell you where to go. The search-and-rescue stories of GPS users who didn't have adequate navigation skills or were not even carrying a topo map when they were finally found are adding up. Please, please, please, don't become one of them. If you really want to become a competent land navigator, use your map and compass to navigate and only use the GPS to track, confirm a tricky location, or mark a waypoint. Whether you have a GPS receiver or not, learn to read the terrain and always bring along your map and compass.

What Is GPS?

The Global Positioning System is a network of satellites orbiting the earth broadcasting radio signals. A GPS receiver is a small gadget that can read the radio signals from the satellites and determine your location anywhere on earth— truly an amazing bit of technology. While the letters "G-P-S" actually refer to the whole system of satellites, radio towers, and receivers, users commonly refer to the GPS receiver they hold in their hand as "a GPS."

Because GPS can keep track of time and your location, receivers can use that data to provide you with some important information:

· Your exact coordinates in UTM or lati tude/longitude

· Your altitude (though not as accurately as a properly used barometric altimeter)

· Your speed—average, maximum, and current

· Your distance traveled

· Your estimated time of arrival at a known destination

· Your current heading or direction of travel (only while you are moving)

· The bearing to your destination (only while you are moving)

· The bearing to any previous destination —you should be able to retrace your steps at any time using the tracking feature.

Depending on the features of the model you have and how it may integrate with map software, there are a number of other things GPS can do for you, including giving you a real-time display of your location on a digital map.

There is a growing number of handheld and wristtop GPS units available today. This chapter focuses on commonalities between most recre ational GPS units and gives non-owners an idea how GPS receivers work. Think of the sugges tions here as a supplement to your user's manual. Yes...you still have to read the manual.

Continued ➔

Who Needs GPS?

. . . Not every backcountry traveler needs GPS! Whether you should consider getting a GPS depends on where you will be traveling and for what purpose. GPS receivers really come into use during navigation in featureless terrain like oceans, deserts, and polar regions. They also work wonders in low-visibility conditions like traveling at night or in nasty storms.

Here are a few questions to aid your decision: Will you be traveling for extended periods of time in areas where the terrain is difficult to read? What are the consequences of being disoriented in the areas you are planning to visit? Will you be sticking to shorter trips into the mountains or canyons? Do new toys excite you or do they seem like one more thing to lug along or lose? Will you be spending most of your time in the jungle under a dense canopy, or in another environment where GPS may not work very well? Is it important to know your exact speed and distance traveled?

Operating a GPS

Getting the Right Settings

Before getting started, you have to make sure you, your map, and your GPS are speaking the same language. If not, you are headed for some miscommunication and probably some bad directions. Take some time to get your settings correct each time you are heading to a new area.

The Earth is not a perfectly round ball. It actually has an irregular ellipsoid shape, which makes creating an accurate two-dimensional map a fairly complicated event. The map datum is the mathematical model that corresponds to the shape of the Earth. There are more than one hundred sets of map datum made from different mathematical measurements around the Earth, and each map series has its own datum. What all of this means for you is you must always make sure the datum setting in your GPS matches the datum on your map. If you are using the wrong datum for the map you are on, your location may be hundreds of meters off. On a USGS quad, the datum is in the margin at the bottom left hand corner, near the UTM zone. Luckily, most quads use either the World Grid System of 1984 Datum (WGS 84) or the North American Datum of 1927 (NAD 27). By default, GPS receivers use the WGS 84 Datum. A common mistake is to use NAD 27 map data without setting your GPS to that datum, which can direct you up to 800 feet in the wrong direction. Many people also forget to change the datum setting when they travel internationally.

Another setting to check is your position format. Position format is the coordinate system in which you would like the GPS to display your location. You can choose UTM, latitude/longitude, or one of many other options. Unless you are traveling in one of the polar regions, UTM or latitude/longitude will suit your needs. On the position format screen, there may be several options for how to view your latitude and longitude. You can choose degrees, minutes, and seconds (D,M,S); degrees and decimal minutes (D.M.M); or decimal degrees (D.DD). Which option you choose is not nearly as important as

knowing how to measure it on your map. Pick the display to which your map ruler is calibrated.

Yet another setting to consider is metric/statute distances. This choice should be based simply on which system you are most comfortable with and what is on your map. Statute distances are given in miles, yards, and feet; metric distances are in kilometers and meters. Generally, it's best to have your GPS set according to whatever units are displayed on your map.

If all this seems a bit complex, relax—you won't need to change your settings every time you go out. Unless you're a jet setter, you'll probably even be using the same map datum most of the time.

Acquiring Signals

When you turn your GPS on for the first time in a new area, it will take a few minutes to acquire satellite signals. Most units will acquire signals within a minute or so after being turned on, though this process can take up to five minutes if the GPS is in a completely new area or does not have a clear view of the sky. While it will work in most tree cover, it generally won't work well inside a building or under a very dense tree canopy, like that of a tropical jungle.

Your GPS will give you an estimated degree of accuracy as it acquires and loses satellite signals. With current technology and NAVSTAR satellites, recreational GPS receivers will only be accurate to within about 50 feet. Your GPS may claim to be more accurate, but don't bet your life on it. When you add in the human error factor, getting within 50 feet of your target is actually quite remarkable. And unless you are literally looking for a needle in a haystack, 50 feet should be as close as you need to get to see your objective. A tent, a pond, a trail junction, a car, a bicycle, and even a baseball are visible from 50 feet in most terrain. If you are navigating with your GPS, it is smart to start to slow down and look for your objective once the GPS says you are within 100 feet.

Once the GPS has acquired signals, it can give you your current position. This is called getting a position fix.

Waypoints

A waypoint (or "landmark," for some users) is GPS lingo for a specific location that is stored in your GPS. You can have your GPS mark a waypoint at any time, anywhere you have a signal. You can use waypoints to mark your current location, in case you want to return later or track where you've been on a map.

There may also be times when you would like to enter the coordinates for a location you have never visited and ask the GPS to direct you to that location. This is how the military sends precision "smart bombs" to their targets and how geocachers locate caches . . . You must first determine the coordinates you would like to enter, which probably means plotting them on your topo map, . . . though if you have digital map software, getting the coordinates may be as simple as moving the mouse to the location on your screen. If you are using UTM, be sure you've entered the correct zone.

The GPS will automatically remember the waypoint and assign it numerical name (001,

002, etc.) unless you rename it. It is wise to give each waypoint a name that will not be confusing later: Car, Camp 1, Fishing Spot 3, Waterfall, and so on. The best names combine something unique about the location with the date.

The Goto Function

Once you have waypoints recorded in the GPS, you can ask it to point you directly to any waypoint at any time by using the "Goto" function. The unit will display an arrow that points directly at the waypoint and tell you your current distance from the waypoint.

Remember, however, that you may still have some routefinding to do. The GPS may be telling you that your waypoint is only two miles south of your current location, but it will not tell you that you need to cross a 3,000-foot canyon and swim two massive rivers to get there. As always, the direct route may or may not be the best way to go.

The display arrow does not work like the magnetic needle on your compass. The GPS cannot determine which way it is oriented when it is sitting still. *You must be moving for the arrow to be accurate.* That means that any time you are routefinding with your GPS, you must be walking and looking at the display screen at the same time.

The advantage of routefinding with a GPS it that it is easy to go around obstacles (like a lake or a big boulder) and get right back on your bearing: the display arrow will always adjust to point directly at your target. Gone is the need to make 90-degree turns and count steps off your bearing.

You can save batteries by using the GPS to get your direction, sighting a landmark with your compass, turning the GPS off, following the bearing with your compass. Stay on the compass bearing until you have another big obstacle to go around and need to change your heading. Remember not to set a bearing with the compass right next to the GPS—the metallic parts and batteries in the GPS will throw off the compass needle! Keep the compass and GPS in separate hands and at least six inches apart.

Tracking

Most handheld GPS units today feature automatic tracking. This means you can set the GPS to automatically mark points at intervals according to distance or time. All you have to do is leave the GPS on and let it mark points for you. You can then use the "pan track" feature to scroll back in time to any location you have visited. Many units also have a "track-back" feature that enables the GPS to direct you back along your tracks. This means that if you are following a difficult route in low visibility or in an emergency you can ask the GPS to guide you in retracing your steps—think of needing to return to a scarce water source in canyon country, or to base camp when a blizzard hits in the mountains. If you are using digital software, you can even download your tracks on to a topographic map and see exactly where you've been.

While using the tracking feature has a number of advantages, if you pass through dense brush while your GPS is tracking, it may drop a few of the tracks due to a weak satellite signal. Tracking also requires a lot more batteries than

Continued ➡

turning the unit on occasionally to check your current location. If you use tracking, have plenty of extras on hand.

Choosing the Right GPS

For land navigation alone, the number of GPS units hitting the market is growing rapidly. Like other outdoor toys, they are getting smaller, lighter, more specialized, and easier to use. Which one you buy should depend largely on how you answer these questions:

What is the main activity you will be doing with GPS?

Some models offer specialized features for cycling, running, hunting, fishing, climbing, or geocaching. For athletes, special software is available for monitoring your training. If you plan to use special software, make sure the GPS unit you buy will be compatible with it. As more units hit the market, consumers will need to be careful not to buy one that is so specialized that it can't meet all their needs.

How much can you spend?

Recreational GPS units range in price from around $80 to $800, depending on features. If you need to save some coin, come up with a list of "must have" features and resist the temptation to buy more than you can afford.

Accuracy is fairly standard for all recreational models without WAAS compatibility; if you do want better-than-average accuracy, you'll need to pay more for WAAS. Unless you are buying a professional-grade GPS unit (for surveying or GIS integration), more money does not necessarily mean more accuracy.

Do you own a PDA?

If you own a personal digital assistant or PDA (e.g., a Pocket PC or Palm Pilot), you may prefer to add hardware or software that will turn it into a GPS. In fact, some PDAs are already sold with GPS receivers built right in.

Handheld or wristtop?

Where you once wore your watch, you may soon be wearing a wristtop computer. By the time you read this, there will be loads of GPS watches available. The year 2004 saw the Casio "Pathfinder," the Suunto "X9," the bulkier Garmin "Forerunner 201," and GPS watches from Timex bursting onto the market.

If your "watch" tells you your heart rate, altitude, air temperature, speed, and location along with the time, it's clearly more than a watch. There are several considerations in deciding whether to choose a wristtop or hand-held model. If you're planning to do any long-distance running, adventure racing, or fast-packing, then size and weight are important, and a wristtop may be the way to go. If you don't see yourself ever racing along, consider a handheld unit instead of a wristtop—they are generally more user-friendly, with more features and a slightly larger size that makes it easier to manually enter data. If you want to be able to see a digital topo map on your GPS, you will need a handheld unit or a GPS-enabled PDA. Also, if you will be entering waypoints in the field, the tiny buttons on wristtops can be tedious, though you may still be able to enter routes and waypoints into some wristtops by uploading them from your computer. Overall, it's important to balance ease of use with the need to save weight. Some of the newer handheld units are surprisingly small but still very functional. In 2003 and 2004, NOLS Rocky Mountain used hundreds of Garmin's handheld "Geko 201" models.

Do you need computer compatibility?

If you're not a computer person, you might save a few bucks and buy an older GPS that isn't computer-friendly. If you are, you want to make sure the software and GPS you buy will work with your computer and operating system. Most of the receivers being sold today are designed to interface with a computer—Mac, PC, or both.

Do you need a map display?

While all GPS receivers have some sort of digital screen to display information, not all of them can display maps. All of the wristtop GPS "watches" and the cheaper handhelds with smaller screens will not display maps. As far as digital map displays go, there are three kinds of handheld GPS units suitable for land navigation:

- Those the display digital maps right on the unit

- Those that don't display digital maps on the unit, but may still link up to your computer

- Those that are actually enhanced PDAs with GPS capabilities.

A map display on your GPS may not be worth the extra size, weight, and cost. Being able to see maps on your GPS screen is pretty cool, but whether you really need it depends in part on what kind of traveling you will be doing. Do you need to go fast and light, or are you setting up a three-week base camp somewhere?

Batteries

Whatever else you do, make sure you have enough battery power for your entire trip. For most units, that means always carrying at least one spare set. Make sure you know exactly how long a set of batteries will last in your GPS, before heading into the backcountry.

When your GPS is on and operating normally, it is processing satellite signals about every second. Some models will burn through a set of batteries in just three to six hours if the unit is continuously on. But there are several things you can do to make the battery issue less painful:

- Get a GPS unit with a battery saver mode, and learn how to use it with the model you have.

- Don't actually navigate with the GPS unless you have to. Turn the unit off and travel with your map and compass most of the time. Save the GPS for emergencies or for verifying a difficult-to-read location. Make sure, however, that you practice with it and know how to navigate with it when the time comes.

- Use rechargeable batteries when you can. It is the environmentally smart thing to do, and it will save you some major dough in the long run. While no rechargeables can hold a single charge as long as a regular disposable alkaline, nickel metal hydrides ("NiMH") stay charged the longest and can be used up to one thousand times. Nickel cadmium ("NiCad") batteries don't hold a charge for long and are not worth your money. Rechargeable alkalines are cheaper than NiMH, but won't stay charged or last as long. For extended trips, buy a lightweight solar recharger panel and attach it to the top of your pack or your tent; Brunton makes excellent rechargers for that purpose.

- If recharging is not an option or you will be in extreme cold, take disposable lithium batteries. While they are considerably more expensive, lithiums are lighter and have the longest single charge of any battery. Some newer models are using non-replaceable lithium-ion batteries similar to those found in cell phones and laptops. Lithium-ions are very convenient around town and are great for short trips. However, if you will be in the backcountry for an extended period of time, be sure that know how long your unit will stay charged and whether you can recharge in the field or not. Remember, without battery power, you'll be carrying around an expensive, colored rock for the rest of your trip.

—From *NOLS Wilderness Navigation*

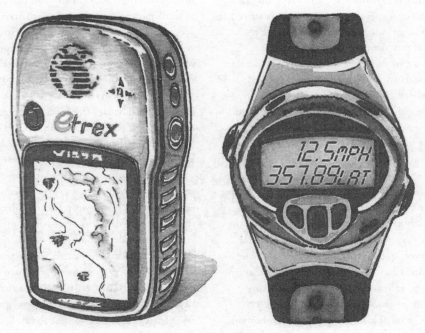

Typical handheld mapping GPS unit and wristwatch GPS (not to scale).

What to Do If You Get Lost

Don Geary

Occasionally, even outdoorsmen who have mastered the basics of map and compass get turned around a bit. If you ever find yourself in such a position, probably the most important thing to remember is to remain clam. Stop walking, sit down, and break out your map and compass. Use resection, line position, or both to determine your position.

Once you've determined your position, you can decide on your next course of action. Pick an objective, determine a bearing, and then proceed toward it. Choose clear secondary objectives—prominent land features such as springs, valleys, or ponds—along the route so that you can be positive of your progress.

Occasionally, poor visibility will make this impossible. If the condition seems temporary, it is probably best to wait until you can see distant land features clearly, then walk out on a predetermined course. If poor visibility seems like it will last for more than about eight hours, you must decide if your want to wait that long or move on now and use your map and compass to help you navigate.

With a map and compass, the chances are small that you'll ever become truly lost in any wilderness area in the continental United States. The more you know about an area before you go into it, the better able you will be to find your way out. Here again, thorough planning can pay off. Before your trip, commit to memory certain facts about the area, such as the approximate location of large rivers, mountain ranges, or other prominent natural features. Also note their relationship to roads and other marks of civilization, as well as the direction of flow of any rivers or streams.

In the event that you feel you are totally lost—which is just about impossible if you've been using your map and compass correctly—your best bet is to stay put. This may also be necessary if you become injured. If you've left word with responsible folks back in civilization as to where you'll be wandering and the expected time of your return, it's fair assumption that they will notify the proper authorities and a search will be initiated. You must have faith that in time you'll be discovered by a rescue party.

In the meantime, explore the general vicinity. Without wandering very far from your position, try to find a field, meadow, or large body of water. If you can find such a place relocate to this spot so that you will be more visible to an air search party.

Your chances of being spotted are much greater if you can create an unnatural-looking symbol on the ground that can be easily seen from the air. This is also an excellent approach if a member of a hiking party is injured and requires medical attention. One or more members of the party should stay with the injured hiker while one or more of the others go for help. Help most often arrives in a helicopter, so by marking the location, you help

the rescue aircraft spot the area much more easily. Know in advance that many federal and state search-and-rescue teams now charge for their time spend locating lost or injured hikers. Even if you never find yourself in a situation where you require some type of assistance from above, someday you may discover another hiker in need of some help. This is reason enough to know some ground-to-air symbols.

A long panel means that you need medical assistance. Two long parallel panels indicate that you require medical supplies. A large X means that you are unable to proceed. An arrow pointing in one direction indicates the route you have headed on. A large triangle means that it is probably safe to land an aircraft in the area. If you need food or water, a large F is the symbol. A large square means that you need a map and compass (shame on you!). VV means that you need firearms and ammunition. N means no, Y means yes, and LL means all is well.

Another way to signal for help is a flare-type distress signal. Several backpacking-equipment companies now sell various signals that are similar to pistols or flares used by seamen except that they are much smaller, less expensive, lighter in weight, and safer. Distress signals are usually self-contained flares with some type of firing mechanism that shoots the flare (commonly brilliant red or international orange) 100 to 150 feet up into the sky. If you're in trouble and an air search is looking for you, some type of emergency flare might help the searchers locate your position much more quickly.

A strobe light is another means of attracting attention from the air. MPI Outdoor Safety sells a lightweight strobe light that can be seen from up to three miles away. It is powered by one D-cell battery and flashes a 300,000 candlepower strobe for up to sixty hours. This strobe is safe to use and can be quite effective in an emergency situation.

Still another way to attract the attention of aircraft from the ground is with a smoky fire. Pour water on a fire at a time when you think the smoke would be seen from the air.

The universal firearm signal for help is three shots fired at close and equal intervals. Whether or not you decide to carry a firearm, you should know this signal. Although the likelihood of attracting the attention of aircraft with three shots is slim, you may someday hear a series of shots that means someone close to you is in need of help.

If you use the tools of navigation wisely, however, your chances of ever becoming lost are slim.

—From *Using a Map and Compass*

INTERNATIONAL GROUND-TO-AIR SIGNALS

UNABLE TO PROCEED.

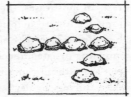
TRAVELING IN THIS DIRECTION.

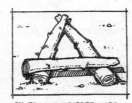
OK TO LAND AIRCRAFT HERE.

REQUIRE FOOD & WATER.

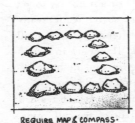
NO

YES

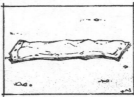
REQUIRE MAP & COMPASS.   REQUIRE FIREARMS & AMMUNITION.

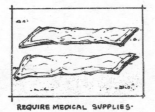
ALL IS WELL.   REQUIRE MEDICAL ASSISTANCE.

REQUIRE MEDICAL SUPPLIES.

Staying Found

Darren Wells

Here are some additional tips for staying found:

- Keep everyone in your group involved in the navigation, even if they are not all "experts." Relying on a single person to do all the navigating for a group is usually a mistake.

- Stop and do map checks when visibility is good. Try to take breaks in areas where you have a good view so you can confirm your location.

- Look for handrails and backstops to ensure you are following your route.

- Keep the group together. If you have to split up, do it according to a plan, and have a contingency plan if one party doesn't make it back.

- Don't commit to a route unless you know you will be able to retrace your footsteps or complete the route safely. Keep asking yourself if you could really retrace your steps if you needed to. Never descend something you can't climb back up or climb something you can't descend unless you are absolutely sure you want to commit to that route.

- If you'll be following the same path on the return trip, look over your shoulder on the way out to see what it will look like on the way back.

- Have a designated "sweep" person whose job it is to follow along and make sure there are no stragglers drifting too far behind the rest of the hiking group.

But What If I Really Do Get Lost?

Stop! Do not continue! Cease and desist! Every step in the wrong direction is a step in the wrong direction. Stand still, pull out your maps, take off your pack, and think. The worst thing you can possibly do is speed ahead.

Most lost people have a mental map of where they think they are. But that map is usually wrong. This is why lost people who keep moving tend to move quite far in the wrong direction. You initial efforts toward getting found need to be about finding landmarks to get your head back onto the right map, not moving quickly using your incorrect mental map.

Try not to panic, or you will waste valuable energy that could be used to determine your location. Relax—merely being lost is not an emergency. Even if you are injured, out of food, and alone in a blinding snowstorm, giving up or losing your cool will not do you or anyone else any good. What you do now that you realize you are lost is what is critical to whether this goes from a valuable learning experience to a crisis.

Once you have calmed down, consider retracing your steps. What is the last point at which you knew exactly where you were? How long has it been since you were there? What direction have you been traveling to get to where you are? Can you safely reverse your course?

If there is a clearing or high point nearby where you can get your bearings, consider going there to check the maps. If you have just become separated from your group, there is no shame in yelling. Smart people carry whistles for just such an occasion.

If you can retrace your steps with certainty to the last place where you knew your location (or, if you have become separated, the last place you saw the group), then do so. Use sticks or rocks to make arrows on the trail showing the direction you are traveling. Otherwise, sit tight until you have a plan or until a third party is able to locate you.

If your entire party gets caught near dark while you are lost, stop, set camp, and get some rest. In most cases, the morning sun will go a long way toward helping you get reoriented. In hot climates, travel only during the early morning or late afternoon. In cold climates, if you are without camping gear, you may have to sleep during the day because it will be too cold at night. Stay hydrated. Although it may be unpleasant, most people can go at least a week without food, so make water your first priority.

In a situation where your party is lost for an extended period of time, you may need to search away from your camp for short distances to see if you can get your bearings. Send parties of two or more people if possible. Be sure to mark trees, use flagging tape, or build rock cairns as you go so that you can easily retrace your steps back to your camp. Leave No Trace concerns should always come second to safety concerns.

If you happen to have a satellite phone or cell phone with reception, calling out for search and rescue should be used only as a last resort. Unless someone in your party is in danger of losing their life or a limb, try to get yourselves out. Involving a search team means not just cost and inconvenience but potentially putting other lives at risk. If you are in a situation that warrants calling for outside help, be aware that it can take twenty-four hours or longer to mobilize a significant search team. If you think you do have a true crisis, call immediately.

—From *NOLS Wilderness Navigation*

Searching for a Lost Person

Darran Wells
Illustration by Jon Cox

You can avoid having to search for a lost person by having the group agree that you will all stay within sight while you are moving. Also, clear camp boundaries and a designated general area for bathroom use make it less likely that someone will wander too far from camp and get lost. If, however, someone from your group gets separated, there are steps you can take to make locating them easier.

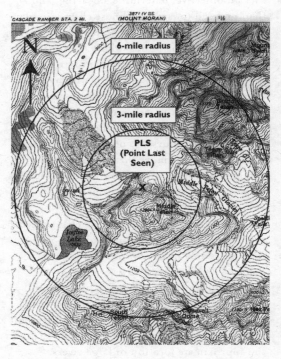

"Point Last Seen" circles help to focus the search for a lost person.

Immediately give a few quick shouts and pause to listen for a response. Often, that's all it takes to locate someone nearby. If you get no response, mark the spot on the map where the person(s) was last seen—the Point Last Seen (PLS). If the PLS is close (less than a quarter mile) head back right away to that spot, yelling or whistling every minute or so. Otherwise, draw two circles, one with a 3-mile radius around the PLS, another with a 6-mile radius. Half of all lost people are found within the first circle; a full ninety percent are found within the second. Focus your effort within the first circle, then the second one, keeping in mind the following suggestions:

- Set up an area of confinement that "boxes in" the lost person by leaving notes, sleeping bags, or other signals in likely traffic areas like trail intersections, trailheads, etc. Confine quickly and farther than you suspect the lost person may have gone.

- Determine the urgency of the situation by considering the lost person's age, mental state, wilderness skill level, clothing, food, gear, special medical concerns, weather, and terrain, as well as your own intuition.

Continued

- Identify likely areas the separated person might be and mark those on the map as well. Could they be looking for water? Trying to photograph something? Fishing? Did they just make a wrong turn at a recent trail intersection?

- In an area where an accident is possible (steep rocks, river crossings, etc.) search potential accident sites first.

- Look downhill. Rarely do lost people stray uphill. Often, they simply keep descending when they are unsure where to go.

- If you have a large group, break into search teams and set specific meeting times and locations for reuniting. Send one team to the PLS and the rest to other likely areas.

- Have teams travel light and look for clues as well as the missing person.

- Don't search at night unless there is a true emergency. It is very strenuous and much less efficient.

You may use the method of drawing a circle to help you locate yourself if you become lost. Instead of the PLS, draw a circle around your last known point. How long have you traveled since you were there? The distance you can travel in that time should be the radius of your circle. Have you been going uphill or downhill? In one continuous direction or meandering a bit? What land features can you see that match those in the circle?

In North America, if you are long enough overdue, a search-and-rescue team will eventually be activated to locate your group. Often searches are conducted by both ground and air. An air search is likely if the weather permits—planes and helicopters will not fly in bad weather, and they generally will not fly at night either.

If you are resigned to sitting still and waiting to be rescued, here are some things you should know:

- Big searches in wilderness areas can take days. You will need food, water, and shelter if you are sitting and waiting. Stay organized and plan how you will conserve resources and stay safe and alive during this period.

- You should camp in a visible area—the more open, the better. Try to get to a spot that is easily seen from above. Large, smoky fires are visible from great distances. Build one and keep it going. But don't make a bad problem worse by letting it get out of control. Make it visible, but keep it safe and controlled by building it out in the open and away from trees.

- Carry signal mirrors and know how to use them before you need them in an emergency. Have them ready to use before you hear air traffic.

- Geometric patterns are often visible from the air. Triangles, squares, or circles made with rocks, branches, dirt, or extra gear may help. Using brightly colored clothing and gear will also help to get you noticed—blues and reds are the most likely to get a pilot's attention.

—From *NOLS Wilderness Navigation*

Lost at Sea
Greg Davenport

Whether you are stranded at sea or on land, rescue attempts are far more successful when rescuers search for someone who is at their last known location. At sea, you're better off staying close to your distressed vessel. On land, as long as you are able to meet your survival needs, stay put. When on land, only consider traveling from your present location to another in three situations:

1. Your present location doesn't have adequate resources to meet such needs as personal protection, sustenance, and signaling.

2. Rescue doesn't appear to be imminent.

3. You know your location and have the navigational skills to travel to safety.

At sea, stay put unless your vessel is burning or sinking and poses a threat. In that case, cut free of the boat and move away from it as soon as possible. Since resources will be limited, you should travel toward shipping lanes, land, or rain.

1. Shipping lanes. These lanes run from continent to continent and tend to have an east-west pattern.

2. Land. Most large land masses are oriented north and south.

3. Rain. Since rain forms from accumulated vapor and wind picks up vapors when traveling over water, following the winds is perhaps the best way to find rain.

Hopefully, you will have an idea of your general location. Knowing how to identify your location to determine a direction of travel and to avoid obstacles requires a good understanding of a compass and map or nautical chart's nomenclature.

Looking for Nearby Land While at Sea

When you are searching for land while stranded at sea, look for the following indicators.

- Cumulus clouds often hover over or slightly downwind from an island.

- The sky will often have a greenish tint close to shallow lagoons or shelves of coral reefs. Look for this tint on the bottoms of clouds.

- The sky will often show a reflection of light on the bottoms of clouds when close to snow or ice-covered land.

- Deep water is often dark, whereas shallow water close to land tends to be a lighter shade.

- You will probably hear the sounds of birds and surf long before seeing the shore.

- Likewise, you will probably smell wood smoke, fruits, and other shore scents long before seeing the shore.

- An increase in the bird population may indicate land, but don't count on it. But note that birds often fly toward land and their nesting areas at dusk. During day hours, the flight pattern of birds is not reliable since they tend to search for food during this time.

- Winds often blow toward land during the day and out to sea at night. However, unless land is close, the pattern of the wind is not a factor you can rely on.

—From *Surviving Coastal and Open Water*

Rules for Signaling
Greg Davenport

A properly used signal increases a survivor's chances of being rescued. A signal has two purposes: to attract rescuers to your whereabouts, and then to help them pinpoint your exact location. When preparing a signal, use the following rules:

- **Stay put.** Once you realize you're lost, stay put. Depart only if the area you are in doesn't meet your survival needs, rescue is not imminent, and you know where you are and have the navigational skills to get to where you want to go. If you are lost or stranded in a car, plane, or ATV, stay with it; the vehicle will serve as a ground-to-air signal. When a search is activated, rescuers will begin looking for you in your last known location. If for some reason you need to move, leave a ground-to-air signal pointing in your direction of travel, along with a note telling rescuers of your plans. If you do move, go to high ground and find a large clearing from which to signal.

- **Properly locate your signal site.** Your signal site should be close to your camp or shelter, located in a large clearing that has 360-degree visibility, and free of shadows.

- **Use one-time-use signals at the appropriate time.** Many signals are one-time-use items and thus should be ignited only when you see or hear a potential rescuer and are sure he or she is headed in your direction.

- **Know and prepare your signal in advance.** Since seconds can mean the difference between life and death; don't delay in preparing or establishing a signal.

—From *Surviving the Desert*

Types of Signals

Greg Davenport
Illustrations by Steven A. Davenport

During an average year, the U.S. National Park System has around four thousand search-and-rescue operations. Of these, approximately half of the missions involve a seriously injured or ill subject, and in 5 percent of the cases the victim dies. A properly utilized signal increases a survivor's chances of being rescued. A signal has two purposes: First, it attracts rescuers to your whereabouts; and second, it helps them hone in on your exact location.

Signals that Attract Rescue

The most effective distress signals for attracting attention are aerial flares and parachute flares, because they are moving, spectacular, and cover a large sighting area.

Aerial Flare

This signal is a one-time-use item and should be used only if a rescue team, aircraft, or a vessel is sighted. As with all pyrotechnic devices, it is flammable and should be handled with caution. Most aerial flares are fired by pulling a chain. In general, you'll hold the launcher so that the firing end—where the flare comes out—is pointed overhead and skyward, allowing the chain to drop straight down. Make sure the hand holding the launcher is located within the safe area, as detailed on the device you are using. Then, while the flare is pointed skyward, use your free hand to grasp and pull the chain sharply downward. For safe use and best results, hold the flare away from your body and perpendicular to the ground. The average aerial flares will have a 500-foot launch altitude, six-second burn time, and 12,000 candlepower. Under optimal conditions, these flares have been sighted up to 30 miles away. Many aerial flares float and are waterproof, and most have an average size of 1 inch in diameter and about 4 1/2 inches long, when collapsed. Some flares are disposable; others allow replacement cartridges. The Orion Star-Tracer and the Sky Blazer XLT aerial flares are two good examples and can be found in most sporting-goods or marine stores.

Parachute Flare

A parachute flare is simply an aerial flare attached to a parachute. The parachute allows for a longer burn time while the flare floats down to earth. Like the aerial flare, this signal is a one-time-use item and should be used only if a rescue team, aircraft, or a vessel is sighted. It, too, is flammable and should be handled with caution. The Pains Wessex SOLAS Mark 3 parachute flare can reach a height of 1,000 feet and produce a brilliant 30,000 candlepower. The flare's red light drifts down to earth under a parachute and has a burn time of about forty seconds.

When using an aerial or parachute flare, you need to adjust for any drift from the wind. Since you want the flare to ignite directly overhead, you'll need to point the flare slightly into the wind. Exactly how much you'll need to

point it into the wind is hard to determine, but usually 5 to 10 degrees will suffice.

Signals that Pinpoint Your Location

Once help is on the way, handheld red signal flares, orange smoke signals, signal mirrors, kites, strobe lights, whistles, and ground-to-air signals serve as beacons to help rescuers pinpoint your position and keep them on course.

Handheld Red Signal Flare

This signal is a one-time-use item and should be used only if a rescue team, aircraft, or a vessel is sighted. It is flammable and should be handled with caution. To light one, stand with your back to the wind, and point the flare away from your face and body during and after lighting. Most red signal flares are ignited by removing the cap and striking the ignition button with the cap's abrasive side. To avoid burns, hold the flare in its safe area, and never hold it overhead. Most devices will burn for two minutes, have a candlepower of 500, and are about 1 inch in diameter by 9 inches long. For increased burn time and candlepower, you might consider getting a handheld marine red signal flare, which average a burn time of three minutes and a 700 candlepower.

Orange Smoke Signal

This signal also is a one-time-use item and should be used only if a rescue team, aircraft, or a vessel is sighted. It, too, is flammable and should be handled with caution. To light one, stand with your back to the wind, and point the device away from your face and body during and after its lighting. Other than wind, snow, or rain, the biggest problem associated with a smoke signal is that cold air keeps the smoke close to the ground, sometimes dissipating it before it reaches the heights needed to be seen.

SkyBlazer Smoke Signal

The SkyBlazer smoke signal is about the size of a 35-millimeter film container and thus is easy to carry. It's easy to use, and the directions are on the container. Simply remove its seal, pull the chain, and then place it on the ground. The signal lasts for only forty-five seconds under optimal conditions and produces only a small volume of orange smoke. In order to increase the smoke to a more appropriate level, I have used two at once. Note: The SkyBlazer smoke signal is not a handheld device and should be set on the ground once ignited.

Orion Handheld Orange Smoke Signal

The Orion signal is bigger than the SkyBlazer. It comes in two sizes: marine and wilderness. The marine signal is about the size of a road flare, and the wilderness signal is half that. The Orion, too, has easy-to-read directions right on the signal. Simply remove the cap, and strike the ignition button with the abrasive part of the cap. To avoid burns, hold the flare in its safe area, and never hold it overhead. These signals put out a lot of smoke and last over sixty seconds. If space permits, this is a far more

effective signal than the SkyBlazer. *Note*: Orion also makes a floating orange smoke signal that lasts for four minutes.

Signal Mirror (with Sighting Hole)

On clear, sunny days, signal mirrors have been seen from as far away as 70 to 100 miles. Although the signal mirror is a great signaling device, it requires practice to become proficient in its use. Most signal mirrors have directions on the back, but the following are general guidelines on how they should be used. Holding the signal mirror between the index finger and thumb of one hand, reflect the sunlight from the mirror onto your other hand. While maintaining the sun's reflection on your free hand, bring the mirror up to eye level and look through the sighting hole. If done properly, you should see a bright white or orange spot of light in the sighting hole. This is commonly called the aim indicator, or fireball. Holding the mirror close to your eye, slowly turn it until the aim indicator is on your intended target. If you lose sight of the aim indicator, start over. *Note*: If signaling an aircraft, stop flashing the pilot after you're certain he's spotted you, as the flash may impede his vision. On land, slightly wiggle the mirror to add movement to the signal. At sea, hold the mirror steady to contrast the sparkles created by the natural movement of the water. Since the mirror can be seen from great distances, sweep the horizon periodically throughout the day, even if no rescue vehicles are in sight. To avoid obstructive shade, be sure to remove your hat when using a signal mirror.

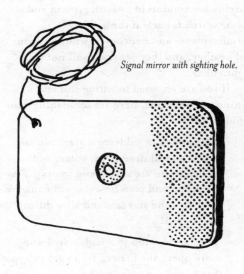

Signal mirror with sighting hole.

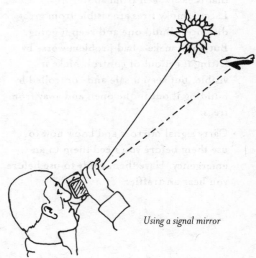

Using a signal mirror

Continued ➡

Kite

A kite is a highly visible signal that not only attracts attention to your location, but also helps rescuers pinpoint where you are. David Instrument's Sky-Alert Parafoil Rescue Kite is a good example. The 28-by-38-inch kite files in 5 to 25 knots of wind and requires only about 8 to 10 knots to lift another signaling device such as a strobe or handheld flare. A benefit of this signal is that it can be working for you while you attend to other needs. In addition to providing a great signal, flying the kite can also help alleviate stress.

Strobe Light

A strobe light is a device that fits in the palm of your hand and provides an ongoing intermittent flash. ACR Electronics Personal Rescue Strobe is a good example of this. It delivers a bright flash (250,000 peak lumens) at one-second intervals and can run up to eight hours on AA batteries. It is visible for up to 1 nautical mile on a clear night. As with all battery-operated devices, strobe lights are vulnerable to cold, moisture, sand, and heat; protect the strobe from these hazards by any means available.

Whistle

A whistle will never wear out, and its sound travels father than the screams of the most desperate survivor. Always carry a whistle on your person. If you become lost or separated, immediately begin blowing your whistle in multiple short bursts. Repeat every three to five minutes. If rescue doesn't appear imminent, go about meeting your other survival needs, stopping periodically throughout the day to blow the whistle. It may alert rescuers to your location, even if you're unaware of their presence. Strom Whistle's Storm Safety Whistle is a good example. Its unique design makes it the loudest whistle you can buy, even when soaking wet. It is made from plastic and has easy-to-grip ridges.

Ground-to-Air Pattern Signal

A ground-to-air signal is an extremely effective device that allows you to attend to your other needs while continuing to alert potential rescuers of your location. Although you can buy signal panels, I'd suggest purchasing a 3-foot-wide by 18-foot-long piece of lightweight nylon—orange for winter, white for summer. There are three basic signal designs you can construct using the nylon.

    V=Need assistance
    X=Need medical assistance
    ↑=Proceed this way

Once you've made the appropriate signal design, stake it out so that it holds its form and doesn't blow away. For optimal effect, follow these guidelines:

Size: The ideal signal will have a ratio of 6:1, with its overall size at least 18 feet long by 3 feet wide.

Contrast: The signal should contrast the surrounding ground cover: orange on snow, white on brown or green.

Angularity: Because nature has no perfect lines, a signal with sharp angles will be more effective.

Shadow: In summer, elevate the signal. In winter, stomp or dig an area around the signal that is approximately 3 feet wide. If the sun is shining, either of these methods will create a shadow, which ultimately increases the signal's size.

Movement: Setting up a flag next to your signal may create enough movement to catch the attention of a rescue party. It is also advisable to suspend a flag high above your shelter so that it can be seen from all directions by potential rescuers.

Cellular Phones

Although a cellular phone is a great thing to have, it's not without limitations and often doesn't work in remote areas. Do not rely on one as your sole signaling and rescue device. Not only are cell phones limited by their service area, but they are also vulnerable to cold, moisture, sand, and heat. You'll need to protect the phone from these hazards by any means available.

Improvised Signals

Many manufactured signals are one-time-use items or are limited by their battery life, and it may be necessary to augment them with an improvised signal. A fire can be as effective as a red flare; an improvised smoke generator works better and lasts longer than an orange smoke signal; an improvised signal mirror can be as useful as a manufactured one; and a ground-to-air signal can be made from materials provided by Mother Nature.

Fire as a Signal

During the night, fire is probably the most effective means of signaling available. One large fire will suffice to alert rescuers to your location; don't waste time, energy, and wood building three fires in a distress triangle unless rescue is uncertain. If the ground is covered with snow, build the fire on a snow platform to prevent the snow's moisture from putting out the fire. Prepare the wood or other fuel for ignition prior to use, as described in chapter 6.

Smoke Generator

Smoke is an effective signal if used on a clear, calm day. If the weather is bad, however, chances are that the smoke will dissipate too quickly to be seen. The rules for a smoke signal are the same as those for a fire signal: You only need one; use a platform in snow environments; and prepare the materials for the signal in advance. To make the smoke contrast against its surroundings, add any of the following materials to your fire:

To contrast snow: Use tires, oil, or fuel to create black smoke.

To contrast darker backgrounds: Use boughs, grass, green leaves, moss, ferns, or even a small amount of water to create white smoke.

In heavy snow or rain, you'll need to set up your smoke generator in advance and protect it form the moisture. To accomplish this, build an elevated platform by driving two 6-foot-long wrist-diameter branches 3 feet into the snow, at a 10- to 20-degree angle to the ground. For best results, insert the branches in a location where the ground has a 10- to 20-degree slope, creating a level foundation for smoke generator. Next, place multiple wrist-diameter branches on top of and perpendicular to the first two, so that they are touching one another. In the center of

foundation

wood shavings, kindling, twigs, etc.

small opening to light the fire

Elevated smoke generator.

this newly created surface, build, but don't light, a tepee firelay, using a lot of tinder and kindling in the process. Then construct a log-cabin-style firelay around the tepee, using fuel that is thumb-size and larger. Leave a small, quick-access opening that will allow you to reach the tinder when it comes time to light it. Finally, place a heavy bough covering over the top of the whole thing. The bough covering should be thick enough to protect the underlying structure from the snow and rain. When done, the generator should look like a haystack of boughs. Once rescuers have been spotted or appear to be headed in your direction, light the smoke generator, gently picking up and reaching under one side of the boughs. If you should have trouble getting it lit, this is one of the rare circumstances where I'd advise using your red smoke flare as a heat source.

Improvised Signal Mirror

A signal mirror can be created from anything shiny, such as a metal container, coin, credit card, watch, jewelry, or belt buckle. Although an improvised signal mirror is a great signaling device, it requires practice to become proficient in its use. To use one, follow these steps. Holding the device between the index finger and

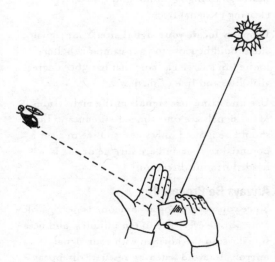

Any shiny reflective material can be used as an improvised signal mirror.

Continued ➡

thumb of one hand, reflect the sunlight from the mirror onto the palm of your other hand. While keeping the reflection on that hand, create a V between your thumb and index finger. Move the light reflection and your until the rescue aircraft or other rescuer is in the V. At this point, move the reflected light into the V and onto your intended target. (Also see the note under Signal Mirror, page 421.)

Improvised Ground-to-Air Pattern Signal

If you haven't brought along a signal panel, you can improvise one from whatever Mother Nature provides—boughs, bark, snow, logs, or any other material that contrasts with the ground color. See the guidelines under Ground-to-Air Pattern Signal, page 420, for basic guidelines of design and construction.

Helicopter Rescue

Helicopter rescues are becoming more frequent as more and more people head into the wilderness. Rescue crews may be civilians, but more often than not, they are either military or Coast Guard. If the helicopter can land, it will. If not, a member of the rescue team will be lowered to your position. At this point, you'll either be hoisted to the helicopter or moved to a better location while in a harness or basket and dangling from the helicopter. Secure all loose items before the helicopter lands, or they may be blown away or sucked up into the rotors. Once the helicopter has landed, do not approach it until signaled to do so, and only approach from the front side. This will ensure that the pilot can see you and decrease your chances of being injured or killed by the rotor blades.

Survival Tips

If you become lost or a member of your team is hurt and unable to be moved, stay put: Only depart if the area you are in doesn't meet your needs, rescue is not imminent, and you know how to navigate. If you are lost or stranded in a car, plane, or ATV, stay with it. The vehicle will serve as a ground-to-air signal. When a search is activated, rescuers will begin looking for you in your last known location. If for some reason you need to move, leave a ground-to-air signal pointing in your direction of travel, along with a note telling rescuers of your plans. If you do move, go to high ground, and find a large clearing to signal from.

Property locate your signal site: Your signal site should be close to your camp or shelter; located in a large clearing that has 360-degree visibility; and free of shadows.

Use one-time-use signals at the right time: Many signals are one-time-use items and thus should be ignited only when you see or hear a potential rescuer and are sure he or she is headed in your direction.

Always Be Prepared

Since you never know if someone is nearby, blow your whistle every five to ten minutes, and occasionally scan the horizon with your signal mirror. To avoid watching rescuers disappear while still fumbling with your signal, learn how

to use them in advance, and make sure they are ready to use before rescue is near. Since seconds can mean the difference between life and death, don't delay in preparing or establishing a signal.

Using a Space Blanket as a Signal

A strong, silver-and-orange space blanket can serve as an improvised signal. Silver will contrast with the brown or green color of bare ground, and orange will do the same in a snowy environment. To use as a signal, place the space blanket in a clearing, with the appropriate contrasting side up, and weigh down the edges so it won't blow away. As you meet your other needs, a well-positioned space blanket will alert any potential rescuers to your location. The space blanket should be used as a signal only when not needed to meet other survival needs.

—From *Surviving Cold Weather*

Sea-Specific Signals
Greg Davenport

The Need for a Signal

During an average year, the U.S. Coast Guard performs thousands of search-and-rescue missions. Some are successful, while others end without ever finding the lost vessel or passengers. Many factors contribute to a successful search. Leaving a float plan will help give rescuers an idea of where to look. Having signals and knowing how to use them will aid in the process. Although filing a float plan is optional (do it!), carrying visual distress signals is not. Coast guard regulations require visual distress signals (VDSs) on all boats that operate on the high seas, coastal waters (including the Great Lakes), territorial seas, and all waters directly connected to the Great Lakes or the territorial seas up to a point where the waters are less than two miles wide. For boats less than 16 feet, the USCG requires one electric distress light or three combination (day/night) red flares, which are only required to be carried on board when operating between sunset and sunrise. For boats between 16 and 65 feet, the USCG requires one orange distress flag and one electric distress light *or* three handheld or floating orange smoke signals and one electric distress light combination (day/night) red flares, whether handheld, meteor, or parachute-type. All signals, except for the distress flag and light, must show the words "Coast Guard Approved" and be marked with the service life of the signal. The distress flag and light must carry the manufacturer's certification that they meet coast guard requirements. I strongly suggest carrying additional signaling devices! You can never have too many.

Although you should always carry a VDS, the USCG does allow exceptions for certain vessels during day operations. (Night signals are required for all vessels from sunset to sunrise.) These vessels include recreational boats less than 16 feet in length, boats participating in organized events, open sailboats less than 26 feet in length not equipped with propulsion machinery, and manually propelled boats.

Rules of Signaling

Correctly using a signal increases a survivor's chances of being rescued. A signal has two purposes: to alert rescuers to your whereabouts, and to help them hone in on your exact location. The most effective electronic distress signals are your VHF handheld radio and the 406-MHz Emergency Position Indicating Radio Beacon. Aerial flares and parachute flares are the most effective nonelectronic signals because they move, are spectacular, and cover a large sighting area. Once help is on the way, signal mirrors, handheld signal flares, smoke signals, sea/rescue signal streamers, kites, sea marker dye, strobe lights, whistles, and ground-to-air signals serve as beacons to help rescuers pinpoint your position and keep them on course. When preparing a signal, use the following rules.

Stay Put

Once lost, stay put. Only leave if the area you are in doesn't meet your needs, rescue is not imminent, and you know how to navigate (know where you are and have the skills to get to where you want to go). If you are lost or stranded in a car, plane, or ATV, stay with it. If your distressed vessel doesn't present a hazard, stay close to it. The vessel or vehicle will serve as a ground-to-air signal, and when a search is activated, rescuers will begin looking for you in your last known location. If you are on land and for some reason you need to move, be sure to leave a ground-to-air signal pointing in your direction of travel along with a note telling rescuers of your plans. If you do move, go to high ground and find a large clearing to signal from.

Signal Site

At sea, your signal site is not often something you can control. On land, however, your signal site should be close to your camp or shelter, located in a large clearing with 360-degree visibility, and be free of shadows.

One-Time-Use Signals

Many signals may be used just one time and thus should only be ignited when you see or hear a potential rescuer headed in your direction.

Know and Prepare Your Signal in Advance

Since seconds can make the difference between life and death, don't delay in preparing or establishing a signal.

Be Safe

Read the instructions for your flare in advance so you will know how to use it when a ship or aircraft is seen. Always fire the signal on the downwind side on your vessel while holding it slightly down and over the water. Never fire it above or inside the raft since burning particles might fall and burn you or damage your raft.

Signals that Attract Rescue

The most effective distress signals for attracting attention are electronic devices. Other options include parachute and aerial flares, both of which cover a large area and attract rescuers with spectacular visual effects and movement.

Continued ➡

VHF Radio

The VHF radio is a quick and easy way to make a distress call. Because it does not use satellites, it has limits to how far away it can be picked up. Its normal range varies greatly but is estimated to average between 20 and 60 miles. If a repeater is within that 20- to 60-mile range, however, the signal range can increase significantly. Channel 16 is the recognized emergency channel.

Protect your VHF radio from moisture and wind, and consider having a radio that runs on alkaline or lithium batteries rather than rechargeable batteries. However, be sure you have packed multiple replacement batteries in the abandon-ship bag. There are three internationally recognized marine radio signals: Mayday, Pan-Pan, and Security. Mayday, which is used when there is an immediate threat to the loss of your vessel or someone's life, takes priority over all other calls.

A Mayday call should follow this basic design: Call MAYDAY, MAYDAY, MAYDAY. Repeat your vessel name and call sign three times. State your present location (give latitude and longitude if you can along with a distance and direction from a known point), the nature of the distress, and the number of people on board three times. Repeat this process until you either get a response or are forced to leave your vessel.

A Pan-Pan call is used when a potential threat exists, but at that moment there is no immediate danger to persons or vessel. Security calls are low priority and usually alert vessels to monitor another station for a safety message.

Satellite Epirbs

Emergency Position Indicating Radio Beacons (EPIRBs) are well worth the cost, and every vessel should carry one. When activated, these beacons quickly and with great accuracy alert rescuers to your location. The 406-MHz EPIRB is the gold standard and by far outperforms the older rescue beacons, which, if you have them, should be replaced. Once activated, they automatically transmit a signal on two international distress frequencies that will be picked up by military and civilian aircraft. Most of these devices float, but make sure you have a good strong lanyard attached to your EPIRB before you even contemplate putting it in the water. Be sure to register the EPIRB according to the beacon manufacturer's instructions.

Sea Marker Dye

These signals, which may be used just once, should only be used during daylight when an aircraft or a vessel is sighted, close by, and headed in your direction. The sea marker's yellow/green fluorescent dye comes in various sizes and words by making you appear larger in contrast to the water's natural color. The dye will last about twenty to thirty minutes in calm seas and less than what when seas are rough. From the air, the dye can be seen from as far as 10 miles away. To use, simply add the powder to the surrounding water. Avoid skin contact with the powder as it is caustic and can burn your skin. On land, the sea marker dye provides excellent contrast to snow, which makes it a great ground-to-air signal.

Sea Rescue Signal Streamer

An option to the marker dye is a sea rescue signal streamer. Unlike the dye, it never runs out and can provide a constant ongoing signal that is easily seen from the air. The orange plastic floating streamer is 40 feet long and comes in various widths.

—From *Surviving Coastal and Open Water*

Codes and Signals

U.S. Army

Now that you know how to let people know where you are, you need to know how to give them more information. It is easier to form one symbol than to spell out an entire message. Therefore, learn the codes and symbols that all aircraft pilots understand.

SOS

You can use lights or flags to send an SOS—three dots, three dashes, three dots. The SOS is the internationally recognized distress signal in radio Morse code. A dot is a short, sharp pulse; a dash is a longer pulse. Keep repeating the signal. When using flags, hold flags on the left side for dashes and on the right side for dots.

Ground-to-Air Emergency Code

This code is actually five definite, meaningful symbols. Made these symbols a minimum of 1 meter wide and 6 meters long. If you make them larger, keep the same 1:6 ratio. Ensure the signal contrasts greatly with the ground it is on. Place it in an open area easily spotted from the air.

Body Signals

When an aircraft is close enough for the pilot to see you clearly, use body movements or positions to convey a message.

Panel Signals

If you have a life raft cover or sail, or a suitable substitute, use the symbols shown to convey a message.

Aircraft Acknowledgments

Once the pilot of a fixed-wing aircraft has sighted you, he will normally indicate he has seen you by flying low, moving the plane, and flashing lights as shown. Be ready to relay other messages to the pilot once he acknowledges that he received and understood your first message. Use a radio, if possible, to relay further messages. If no radio is available, use the codes covered in the previous paragraphs.

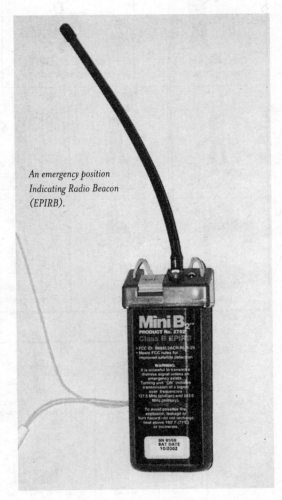

An emergency position Indicating Radio Beacon (EPIRB).

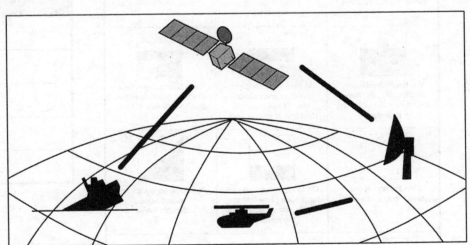

EPIRB transmission.

Continued ➡

Aircraft Vectoring Procedures

If you can contact a friendly aircraft with a radio, guide the pilot to your location. Use the following general format to guide the pilot:

- Mayday, Mayday.
- Call sign (if any).
- Name.
- Location.

- Number of survivors.
- Available landing sites.
- Any remarks such as medical aid or other specific types of help needed immediately.

Simply because you have made contact with rescuers does not mean you are safe. Follow instructions and continue to use sound survival and evasion techniques until you are actually rescued.

—From *Survival (Field Manual 21-76)*

Body Signals

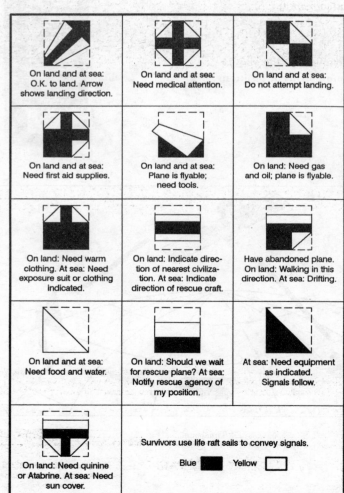

Panel signals.

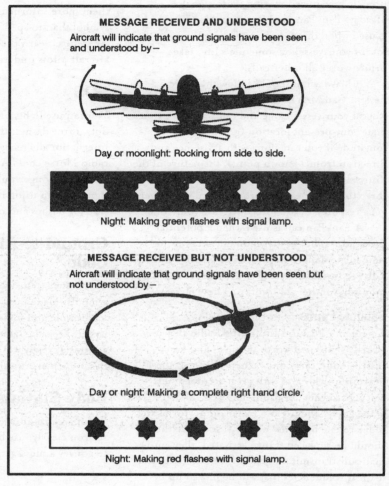

Aircraft acknowledgments.

Number	Message	Code symbol
1	Require assistance.	V
2	Require medical assistance.	X
3	No or negative.	N
4	Yes or affirmative.	Y
5	Proceed in this direction.	↑

Ground-to-air emergency code (pattern signal).

First Aid and the Psychology of Survival

Chapter 12

Immediate First Aid Steps for Survival Situations

U.S. Army

> **Warning**
> These emergency medical procedures are for survival situations. Obtain professional medical treatment as soon as possible.

> **Remember the ABCs of Emergency Care**
> **A**irway **B**reathing **C**irculation

Immediate First Aid Actions

Determine Responsiveness as Follows:

(1) If unconscious, arouse by shaking gently and shouting.

(2) If no response—

    (a) Keep head and neck aligned with body.

    (b) Roll victims onto their backs.

(c) Open the airway by lifting the chin (figure V-1).

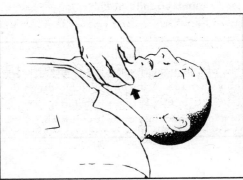

Figure V-1. Chin Lift

Continued →

(d) Look, listen, and feel for air exchange.

(3) If victim is not breathing—

   (a) Check for a clear airway; remove any blockage.

   (b) Cover victim's mouth with your own.

   (c) Pinch victim's nostrils closed.

   (d) Fill victim's lungs with 2 slow breaths.

   (e) If breaths are blocked, reposition airway; try again.

   (f) If breaths still blocked, give 5 abdominal thrusts:

      · Straddle the victim.

      · Place a fist between breastbone and belly button.

      · Thrust upward to expel air from stomach.

   (g) Sweep with finger to clear mouth.

   (h) Try 2 slow breaths again.

   (i) If the airway is still blocked, continue (c) through (f) until successful or exhausted.

   (j) With open airway, start mouth to mouth breathing:

      · Give 1 breath every 5 seconds.

      · Check for chest rise each time.

(4) If victim is unconscious, but breathing—

   (a) Keep head and neck aligned with body.

   (b) Roll victim on side (drains the mouth and prevents the tongue from blocking airway).

(5) If breathing difficulty is caused by chest trauma, treat chest injuries. [see below]

> **Caution**
> *Do not* remove an impaled object unless it interferes with the airway. You may cause more tissue damage and increase bleeding. For travel, you may shorten and secure the object.

Control bleeding as follows:

(1) Apply a pressure dressing (figure V-2).

(2) If *still* bleeding—

   (a) Use direct pressure over the wound.

   (b) Elevate the wounded area above the heart.

(3) If *still* bleeding—

   (a) Use a pressure point between the injury and the heart (figure V-3).

   (b) Maintain pressure for 6 to 10 minutes before checking to see if bleeding has stopped.

(4) If a limb wound is *still* bleeding—

> **Caution**
> Use of tourniquet is a last resort measure. Use only when severe, uncontrolled bleeding will cause loss of life. Recognize that long-term use of a tourniquet may cause loss of limb.

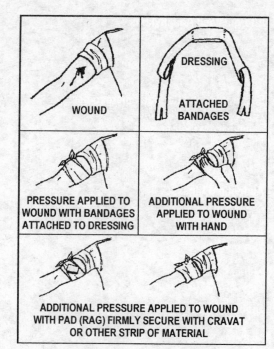

Figure V-2. Application of a Pressure Dressing.

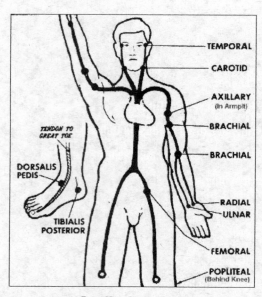

Figure V-3. Pressure Points.

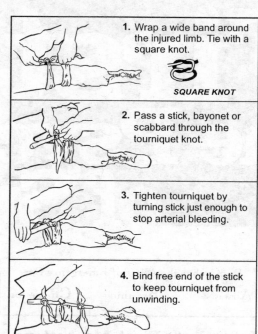

1. Wrap a wide band around the injured limb. Tie with a square knot.

SQUARE KNOT

2. Pass a stick, bayonet or scabbard through the tourniquet knot.

3. Tighten tourniquet by turning stick just enough to stop arterial bleeding.

4. Bind free end of the stick to keep tourniquet from unwinding.

Figure V-4. Application of a Tourniquet.

   (a) Apply tourniquet (TK) band just above bleeding site on limb. A band at least 3 inches (7.5 cm) or wider is best.

   (b) Follow steps illustrated in figure V-4.

   (c) Use a stick at least 6 inches (15 cm) long.

   (d) Tighten only enough to stop arterial bleeding.

   (e) Mark a TK on the forehead with the time applied.

   (f) Do *not* cover the tourniquet.

> **Caution**
> The following directions apply only in survival situations where rescue is unlikely and no medical aid is available.

   (g) If rescue or medical aid is not available for over 2 hours, an attempt to slowly loosen the tourniquet may be made 20 minutes after application. Before loosening—

      · Ensure pressure dressing is in place.

      · Ensure bleeding has stopped.

      · Loosen tourniquet slowly to restore circulation.

      · Leave loosened tourniquet in position in case bleeding resumes.

Treat Shock

(Shock is difficult to identify or treat under field conditions. It may be present with or without visible injury.)

(1) Identify by one or more of the following:

   (a) Pale, cool, and sweaty skin.

   (b) Fast breathing and a weak, fast pulse.

   (c) Anxiety or mental confusion.

   (d) Decreased urine output.

(2) Maintain circulation.

(3) Treat underlying injury.

(4) Maintain normal body temperature.

   (a) Remove wet clothing.

   (b) Give warm fluids.

      · *Do not* give fluids to an unconscious victim.

      · *Do not* give fluids if they cause victim to gag.

   (c) Insulate from ground.

   (d) Shelter from the elements.

(5) Place conscious victim on back.

(6) Place very weak or unconscious victim on side, this will—

   (a) Allow mouth to drain.

   (b) Prevent tongue from blocking airway.

Treat Chest Injuries

SUCKING CHEST WOUND

This occurs when chest wall is penetrated; may cause victim to gasp for breath; may cause sucking sound; may create bloody froth as air escapes the chest.

Continued ➡

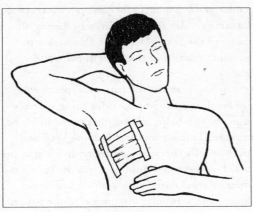

Figure V-5. Sucking Chest Wound Dressing.

(a) Immediately seal wound with hand or airtight material.

(b) Tape airtight material over wound on *3 sides only* (figure V-5) to allow air to escape from the wound but not to enter.

(c) Monitor breathing and check dressing.

(d) Lift untapped side of dressing as victim exhales to allow trapped air to escape, as necessary.

FLAIL CHEST

Results from blunt trauma when 3 or more ribs are broken in 2 or more places. The flail segment is the broken area that moves in a direction opposite to the rest of chest during breathing.

(a) Stabilize the flail segment as follows:

- Place rolled-up clothing or bulky pad over site.

- Tape pad to site.

- *Do not* wrap tape around chest.

(b) Have victim keep segment still with hand pressure.

(c) Roll victim onto side of flail segment injury (as other injuries allow).

FRACTURED RIBS

(a) Encourage deep breathing (painful, but necessary to prevent the possible development of pneumonia).

(b) Do not constrict breathing by taping ribs.

Treat Fractures, Sprains, and Dislocations

(1) Control bleeding.

(2) Remove watches, jewelry, and constrictive clothing.

(3) If fracture penetrates the skin—

(a) Clean wound by gentle irrigation with water.

(b) Apply dressing over wound.

(4) Position limb as normally as possible.

(5) Splint in position found (if unable to straighten limb).

(6) Improvise a splint with available materials:

(a) Sticks or straight, stiff materials from equipment.

(b) Body parts (for example, opposite leg, arm-to-chest).

(7) Attach with strips of cloth, parachute cord, etc.

(8) Keep the fractured bones from moving by immobilizing the joints on both sides of the fracture. If fracture is in a joint, immobilize the bones on both sides of the joint.

(9) Use *RICES* treatment for 72 hours.

Caution

Splint fingers in a slightly flexed position, *not* in straight position. Hand should look like it is grasping an apple.

Rest.
Ice.
Compression.
Elevation.
Stabilization.

(10) Apply cold to acute injuries.

(11) Use 15 to 20 minute periods of cold application.

(a) *Do not* use continuous cold therapy.

(b) Repeat 3 to 4 times per day.

(c) Avoid cooling that can cause frostbite or hypothermia.

(12) Wrap with a compression bandage after cold therapy.

(13) Elevate injured area above heart level to reduce swelling.

(14) Check periodically for a pulse beyond the injury site.

(15) Loosen bandage or reapply splint if no pulse is felt or if swelling occurs because bandage is too tight.

—From *Survival, Evasion, and Recovery (Field Manual 21–76-1)*

Preventing and Treating Shock

U.S. Army

Anticipate shock in all injured personnel. Treat all injured persons as follows, regardless of what symptoms appear:

- If the victim is conscious, place him on a level surface with the lower extremities elevated 15 to 20 centimeters.

- If the victim is unconscious, place him on his side or abdomen with his head turned to one side to prevent choking on vomit, blood, or other fluids.

- If you are unsure of the best position, place the victim perfectly flat. Once the victim is in a shock position, do not move him.

- Maintain body heat by insulating the victim from the surroundings and, in some instances, applying external heat.

- If wet, remove all the victim's wet clothing as soon as possible and replace with dry clothing.

- Improvise a shelter to insulate the victim from the weather.

- Use warm liquids or foods, a prewarmed sleeping bag, another person, warmed water in canteens, hot rocks wrapped in

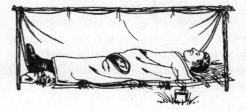

CONSCIOUS VICTIM

- Place on level surface.
- Remove all wet clothing.
- Give warm fluids.
- Allow at least 24 hours rest.
- Insulate from ground.
- Shelter from weather.
- Maintain body heat.
- Elevate lower extremities 15 cm to 20 cm.

UNCONSCIOUS VICTIM

Same as for conscious victim, except—

- Place victim on side and turn head to one side to prevent choking on vomit, blood, or other fluids.
- Do not elevate extremities.
- Do not administer fluids.

Treatment for shock.

clothing, or fires on either side of the victim to provide external warmth.

- If the victim is conscious, slowly administer small doses of a warm salt or sugar solution, if available.

- If the victim is unconscious or has abdominal wounds, do not give fluids by mouth.

- Have the victim rest for at least 24 hours.

- If you are a lone survivor, lie in a depression in the ground, behind a tree, or any other place out of the weather, with your head lower than your feet.

- If you are with a buddy, reassess your patient constantly.

—From *Survival (Field Manual 21–76)*

Patient Assessment

Tod Schimelpfenig

The initial assessment is a ritual performed on every patient to find and treat life-threatening medical problems. Besides attending immediately to vital functions, it provides order during the first frantic minutes of an emergency. You check, stop, and fix problems in the vital respiratory and circulatory systems. You assume disability and protect the spine. You assess and treat for environmental hazards.

Establishing Responsiveness

As you approach the patient, introduce yourself and ask if you may help. You're obtaining consent to treat, being polite, and finding out if the patient is responsive. If there is no response, attempt to arouse the patient by saying hello loudly—the person may just be asleep.

If this fails to arouse the patient, try a painful stimulus—pinch the shoulder or neck muscle or rub the breastbone.

At this point, if there is any mechanism of injury, control the cervical spine (neck). Place

Continued →

hands on the head to prevent unnecessary movement of the neck.

If the patient is awake and talking, the airway is not obstructed; the person is breathing and has a pulse. If the patient is quiet, you need to check the ABCs (airway, breathing, and circulation) immediately. In both responsive and unresponsive patients, you proceed through the entire initial assessment, and make a decision about possible disability, environmental threats, and hidden major injury.

ABCDE

The initial assessment checks the airway, breathing, and circulation, plus possible serious bleeding and shock. The airways are the mouth, nose and throat, and trachea. Oxygen is exchanged between the air and the blood in the lungs. Circulation is a function of the heart, the blood vessels, and the blood, which contains vital oxygen. We use ABCDE (airway, breathing, circulation, disability, environment, expose, examine) as a memory aid for the initial assessment sequence. ABC is familiar as the initial phase of cardiopulmonary resuscitation (CPR).

Airway. The airway is the path air travels from the atmosphere into the lungs. An obstructed airway is a medical emergency because oxygen cannot reach the lungs. If the patient is awake, ask the patient to open his or her mouth and check for anything, such as gum or broken teeth, that could become an airway obstruction. If the patient is unresponsive, assess the airway by opening it with the head-tilt-chin-lift method or the jaw thrust and look inside the mouth. If you see an obvious obstruction—a piece of food, perhaps—take it out.

If you can see, hear, or feel air moving from the lungs to the outside, the airway is open. A patient making sounds is able to move air from the lungs and past the vocal cords. This indicates that the airway is at least partially open.

Signs of an obstructed airway are lack of air movement, labored breathing, use of neck and upper chest muscles to breathe, and pale gray or bluish skin. If you discover an airway obstruction, attempt to clear the airway before proceeding to assess breathing. The appropriate techniques are those taught in CPR for treating a foreign body-obstructed airway.

Breathing. If the patient is awake, ask him or her to take a deep breath. If the patient's breathing is labored or painful, expose the chest and look for life-threatening injuries. If the patient is unresponsive, assess breathing using the "look, listen, and feel" format taught in CPR classes. Look for the rise and fall of the chest as air enters and leaves the lungs. Listen for the sound of air passing through the upper airway. Feel the movement of air from the patient's mouth and nose on your cheek. If the patient is not breathing, give two slow, even breaths, then proceed with a check for a pulse.

Circulation. Check for the presence or absence of a pulse. Place the tips of your middle and index fingers over the carotid artery for at least 10 seconds. The carotid is a large central artery, accessible at the neck. Other possible sites are the femoral artery in the groin and the radial artery in the wrist (preferable for a responsive patient).

It may be difficult to feel a pulse if the patient

has a weak pulse from shock, is cold, or is wearing bulky clothing. Finding a pulse is not always easy. If you are unsure about the presence of the carotid pulse, try the femoral or the radial pulse.

If the patient is moving or moaning, he or she must have a pulse. If there is no pulse, start CPR. If there is a pulse but no breathing, start rescue breathing.

Look for bleeding. Severe bleeding can be fatal within minutes. Look for obvious bleeding or wet places on the patient's clothing. Quickly run your hands over and under the patient's clothing, especially bulky sweaters or parkas, to find moist areas that may be caused by serious bleeding. Look for blood that may be seeping into snow or the ground. Most external bleeding can be controlled with direct pressure and elevation of the wound. Chapter 7 ["Wound Care," pages 431–435] addresses bleeding control in detail.

Disability. Initially assume a spinal injury in any accident victim. Since moving a spine-injured patient poorly can cause paralysis, move the patient only if necessary and as little as possible. An airway opening technique for an unresponsive victim or an accident victim is the jaw thrust. It does not require shifting the neck or spine. See pages 431–435 ("Brain and Spinal Cord Injuries").

Environment/Expose/Examine. Without moving the patient, expose and examine for major injuries, which may be hidden in bulky outdoor clothing. Quickly unzip zippers, open cuffs, and look under parkas.

Assess and manage environmental hazards. It's not uncommon in wilderness medicine to need to protect the patient from extreme environments. You may need to move your patient off snow and onto an insulating pad, or out of a river onto dry ground.

The Focused Exam and History

Now pause a moment to look over the scene. The initial assessment is complete. Immediate threats to life have been addressed. Take a deep breath and consider the patient's and the rescuers' needs. If the location of the incident is unstable—such as on or near loose boulders or a potential avalanche slope—move to a safer position. Provide insulation, adjust clothing, rig a shelter. Assign tasks: boil water for hot drinks, build a litter, set up camp, write down vital signs. Establishing clear delegation of tasks helps the rescuers by giving everyone something to do and helps the patient by creating an atmosphere of order and leadership.

The focused exam and history is done after life-threatening conditions have been stabilized. It consists of doing a complete head-to-toe physical exam, checking vital signs, and taking a thorough medical history.

Head-to-Toe Patient Examination

The head-to-toe exam is a comprehensive physical examination. Begin the head-to-toe examination by first making the patient comfortable. Except in cases of imminent danger, avoid moving an injured patient until after the exam. Your hands should be clean, warm, and gloved. Ideally, the examiner should be of the same

gender as the patient; otherwise, an observer of the same gender should be present during all phases of the exam. Designate a notetaker to record the results of the focused exam and history.

As you examine the patient, explain what you are doing and why. Besides being a simple courtesy, this helps involve the patient in his or her care. This survey starts with the head and systematically checks the entire body down to the toes. One person should perform the survey in order to avoid confusion, provide consistent results, and minimize discomfort to the patient. Also, with a single examiner, the patient will be able to respond to one inquiry at a time.

The examination technique consists of looking, listening, feeling, smelling, and asking. If you are uncertain of what is abnormal, compare the injured extremity with the other side of the body or with a healthy person.

Head. Check the ears and nose for fluid and the mouth for injuries that may affect the airway. Check the face for symmetry; all features should be symmetrical down the midline from the forehead to the chin. The checkbones are usually accurate references for facial symmetry. Feel the entire skull for depressions, tenderness, and irregularity. Run your fingers along the scalp to detect bleeding or cuts. Check the eyes for injuries, pupil abnormalities, and vision disturbances.

Neck. The trachea, or windpipe, should be in the middle of the neck. Feel the entire cervical spine from the base of the skull to the top of the shoulders for pain, tenderness, muscle rigidity, and deformity.

Shoulders. Examine the shoulders and the collarbone for deformity, tenderness, and pain.

Arms. Feel the arms from the armpit to the wrist. Check the pulse in each wrist; it should be equal on both sides. Ask the patient to move his or her fingers, then check grip strength by having the patient squeeze your hands. Check for sensation by gently pinching the fingers or scratching the palm of the hand and fingers. If no injury is apparent, ask the patient to move each arm through its full range of motion.

Chest. Feel the entire chest for deformity or tenderness. Push down from the top and in from the sides. Ask the patient to breathe deeply as you compress the chest. Look for open chest wounds. Observe the rise and fall of the chest for symmetry.

Abdomen. Feel the abdomen for tenderness or muscle rigidity with light pressure. If there is tenderness, localize it into a quadrant. Look for distension, discoloration, and bruising.

Back. Feel the spine. Feel each vertebra from the shoulders to the pelvis. It may be difficult to accomplish this without moving the patient, but it is important to slide your hand as far as possible under the patient. There may be a hidden injury.

Pelvis. Press down on the front of the pelvis and in from the sides. Is there deformity or instability? Does the pressure cause pain?

Legs. Check the legs from the groin to the ankle. Check the pulse in each of the feet; they should be equal. Check for sensation and motor function in the feet by touching the patient's feet and by asking the patient to move his or her

Continued →

The INITIAL ASSESSMENT

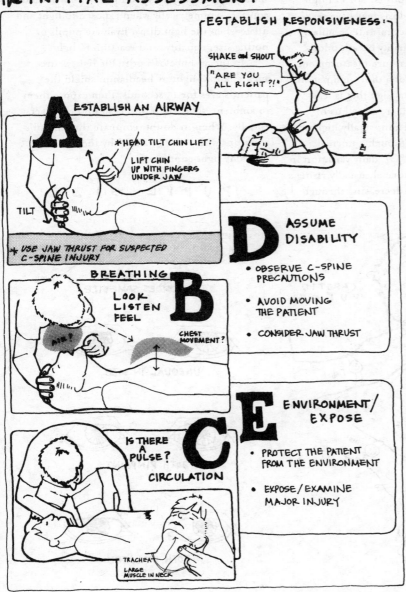

ESTABLISH RESPONSIVENESS:
SHAKE and SHOUT
"ARE YOU ALL RIGHT?!"

A ESTABLISH AN AIRWAY
*HEAD TILT CHIN LIFT:
LIFT CHIN UP WITH FINGERS UNDER JAW
TILT
*USE JAW THRUST FOR SUSPECTED C-SPINE INJURY

B BREATHING
LOOK LISTEN FEEL
AIR?
CHEST MOVEMENT?

D ASSUME DISABILITY
• OBSERVE C-SPINE PRECAUTIONS
• AVOID MOVING THE PATIENT
• CONSIDER JAW THRUST

C CIRCULATION
IS THERE A PULSE?
TRACHEA
LARGE MUSCLE IN NECK

E ENVIRONMENT/ EXPOSE
• PROTECT THE PATIENT FROM THE ENVIRONMENT
• EXPOSE/EXAMINE MAJOR INJURY

FOCUSED ASSESSMENT and HISTORY

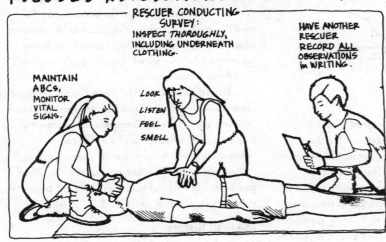

RESCUER CONDUCTING SURVEY:
INSPECT *THOROUGHLY*, INCLUDING UNDERNEATH CLOTHING.

HAVE ANOTHER RESCUER RECORD ALL OBSERVATIONS in WRITING.

MAINTAIN ABCs, MONITOR VITAL SIGNS.

LOOK LISTEN FEEL SMELL

toes and to push his or her feet against your hands.

Vital Signs

Vital signs are objective indicators of respiration, circulation, heart and brain function, blood volume, and body temperature. Checking the vital signs helps further evaluate the ABCs. Airway and breathing are checked by noting skin color and respiratory rate and depth. Good color and easy and regular breathing are signs our airway and lungs are working well. Circulation is evaluated by pulse, skin color, skin temperature, and level of responsiveness. Effective circulation gives us warm, pink skin and enough oxygen to keep our brain alert.

As a general rule, measure and record vital signs every 15 to 20 minutes—more frequently if the patient is seriously ill or injured. The initial set of vitals—responsiveness, pulse, respiration, skin signs, pupils, temperature—provides baseline data on the patient's condition. The changes that occur thereafter provide information on the progress of the patient.

Level of the Responsiveness. Brain function, also known as mental status and reflected in how responsive we are to our environment, may be affected by toxic chemicals such as drugs or alcohol, low blood sugar, abnormally high or low temperature, diseases of the brain such as stroke, circulatory or respiratory shock, or pressure from bleeding or swelling caused by a head injury.

I have chosen to use the term "responsiveness" rather than the more common "consciousness" to describe brain function. Consciousness is a vague term and difficult to measure. The more specific responsiveness is a criterion we can evaluate on every patient and then describe with clarity and specificity.

When you assess responsiveness, first determine the initial state. Begin by approaching the patient, introducing yourself, saying "Hello," and asking if you can help. You're being polite and finding out if the patient is awake, asleep, or possibly unresponsive.

Then describe the stimulus you used to arouse the patient. If the patient opened his or her eyes and responded after a simple "Hello," the person may have been asleep or distracted. If you needed to shout loudly several times to arouse the patient, the person would be described as not awake but responsive to a verbal stimulus. If you needed to use pain to arouse the patient, the person would be described as not awake and responsive only to pain.

Alert. Normally, we are awake (or we wake quickly from sleep), are alert, and know who we are, where we are, the date or time, and recent events. This is described as A (awake/alert) and O (oriented) times 1, 2, 3, or 4, depending on whether the patient knows who he or she is, where he or she is, what date or time it is, and recent events:

- A+O×4   The person knows person, place, time, and event.
- A+O×3   The person knows person, place, and time, but not event.
- A+O×2   The person knows person and place, but not time and event.
- A+O×1   The person knows person, but not place, time, and event.

A patient who is awake but not oriented to person, place, time, or event is described as disoriented. The spoken response may be incoherent, confused, inappropriate, or incomprehensible.

Verbally Responsive. The patient is not awake but responds to a verbal stimulus, such as the rescuer saying, "Hello, how are you?" If the patient does not respond, repeat louder: "Hey! Sir (or Ma'am)! Wake up!" The patient's response may be opening the eyes, grunting, or moving. Higher levels of brain function respond to verbal input, lower levels to pain. Test for responsiveness to verbal stimuli first, painful stimuli second.

Painfully Responsive. The patient is not awake, does not respond to verbal stimuli, but does respond to painful stimuli by moving, opening the eyes, or groaning. To stimulate for pain, pinch the muscle at the back of the shoulder or neck, or rub the sternum.

Unresponsive. The patient is not awake and does not respond to voice or painful stimuli.

Report the patient's initial state, the stimulus you gave, and the response. For example: "This patient is awake, alert, and oriented times four." Or, "This patient is not awake, but can be aroused with a verbal stimulus. When awake, the patient knows his name but is otherwise disoriented."

Heart Rate. Every time the heart beats, a pressure wave is transmitted through the arteries. We feel this pressure wave as the pulse. The pulse rate indicates the number of heartbeats over a period of time. For an adult, the normal range is 60 to 100 beats per minute. A well-conditioned athlete may have a normal pulse rate of 50. Shock, exercise, altitude, illness, emotional stress, or fever can increase the heart rate.

The heart rate can be measured at the radial artery on the thumb side of the wrist or at the carotid artery in the neck. Place the tips of the middle and index fingers over the artery. Count the number of beats for 15 seconds and multiply by four.

In addition to rate, note the rhythm and strength of the pulse. The normal rhythm is regular. Irregular rhythms can be associated with heart disease and are frequently rapid. The strength of the pulse is the amount of pressure you feel against your fingertips. It may be weak or strong.

A standard pulse reading includes the rate, rhythm, and strength of the pulse. For example:

Continued ➡

"The pulse is 110, irregular, and weak." Or, "The pulse is 60, regular, and strong."

Skin Signs. Skin signs indicate the condition of the respiratory and cardiovascular systems. These include skin color, temperature, and moisture, often abbreviated SCTM.

Pinkness. In a light-colored person, normal skin color is pink. In darker-skinned individuals, skin color can be assessed at the nail beds, inside the mouth, palms of the hands, soles of the feet, or lips.

Redness. Redness indicates that the skin is unusually flushed with blood. It is a possible sign of recent exercise, heatstroke, carbon monoxide poisoning, fever, or allergic reaction.

Paleness. Pale skin indicates that blood has withdrawn from the skin. Paleness may be due to fright, shock, fainting, or cooling of the skin.

Cyanosis. Blue skin, or cyanosis, appears when circulation to the skin is reduced or the level of oxygen in the blood falls. Well-oxygenated blood is brighter red than poorly oxygenated blood. Cyanosis indicates that oxygen levels have fallen significantly, or that the patient may be cold.

Jaundice. Yellow skin combined with yellow whites of the eyes—jaundice—is a sign of liver or gallbladder disease. The condition results from excess bile pigments in the blood.

Temperature and Moisture. Quickly assess the temperature and moisture of the skin at several sites, including the forehead, hands, and trunk. In a healthy person, the skin is warm and relatively dry. Skin temperature rises when the body attempts to rid itself of excess heat, as in fever or environmental heat problems. Hot, dry skin can be a sign of fever or heatstroke. Hot, sweaty skin occurs when the body attempts to eliminate excess heat and can also be a sign of fever or heat illness.

Skin temperature falls when the body attempts to conserve heat by constricting blood flow to the skin; for example, during exposure to cold. Cool, moist (clammy) skin is an indicator of extreme stress and a sign of shock.

A report on skin condition should include color, temperature, and moisture. For example: "The patient's skin is pale, cool, and clammy."

Respiration. Respiratory rate is counted in the same manner as the pulse: Each rise of the chest is counted over 15 seconds and multiplied by four, or 30 seconds and multiplied by two. Watch the chest rise and fall, or observe the belly move with each breath. Normal respiration range is 12 to 20 breaths per minute.

The patient's depth and effort of breathing enable you to gauge his or her need for air and the presence or absence of chest injury. In a healthy individual, breathing is relatively effortless.

A patient experiencing breathing difficulty may exhibit air hunger with deep, labored inhaling efforts. A patient with a chest injury may have shallow, rapid respirations accompanied by pain. Irregular respirations are a sign of a brain disorder. Noisy respirations indicate some type of airway obstruction. Assess and, if necessary, clear the airway.

Smell the breath. Fruity, acetone breath can be a sign of diabetic coma. Foul, fecal-smelling breath may indicate a bowel obstruction.

Report respirations by their rate, rhythm, effort, depth, noises, and odors. For example, a patient in diabetic ketoacidosis may have respirations described as "20 per minute, regular, labored, deep. There is a fruity breath odor."

Temperature. Temperature measurement is an important component of a thorough patient assessment, but it is the vital sign that is least often recorded in the field. It can tell us of underlying infection or of abnormally high or low body temperatures. Although a normal temperature is 98.6°F (37°C), daily variation in body temperature is also normal, usually rising a degree during the day and decreasing through the night.

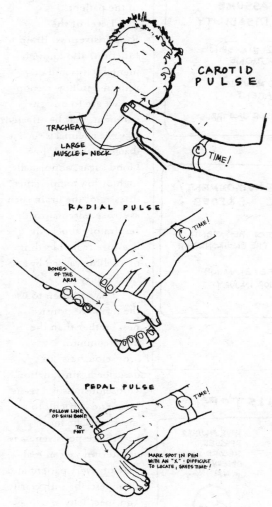

Temperature can be measured orally or rectally. Axillary readings—taken under the armpit—are the least reliable. Rectal temperatures are the most accurate indication of the core temperature available to first responders. Rectal temperature is sometimes considered necessary for suspected hypothermia but is rarely measured due to patient embarrassment and cold exposure. Diagnosis of hypothermia in the outdoors, discussed in pages 451–452 ("Cold Injuries"), is often based on other factors, such as behavior, history, appearance, and mental status.

Before taking a temperature with a mercury thermometer, shake down the thermometer to push the mercury below the degree markings. This is essential for an accurate reading. Place the thermometer under the patient's tongue for at least 3 minutes. The patient should refrain from talking or drinking during this time. A report on temperature should include the method, such as "100°F oral" or "37°C rectal."

Pupils. Pupils are clues to brain function. They can indicate head injury, stroke, drug abuse, or lack of oxygen to the brain. Both pupils should be round and equal in size. They should contract symmetrically when exposed to light and dilate when the light dims. Evaluate pupils by noting size, equality, and reaction to light.

In the absence of a portable light source, such as a flashlight or headlamp, shield the patient's eyes for 15 seconds, then expose them to ambient light. Both pupils should contract equally. When in doubt, compare the patient's reactions with those of a healthy individual in the same light conditions.

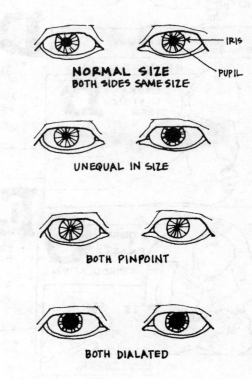

A patient whose brain cells are deficient of oxygen may have equal but slow-to-react pupils. A wide, nonreactive pupil on one side and a small, reactive pupil on the other side indicates brain damage or disease on the side with the larger pupil. Very small, equal pupils may indicate drug intoxication.

Blood Pressure. Although blood pressure is always measured when professional medical care is being administered, accurate measurement requires a stethoscope and a sphygmo-manometer—equipment rarely carried on wilderness trips. Because evacuation decisions can be made without measuring blood pressure, this vital sign is not presented.

Medical History

The patient's medical history provides background that is often relevant to the present problem. Gathering the history is an ongoing process that you typically carry out while measuring vital signs and performing the head-to-toe exam. Obtaining an accurate history depends greatly on the quality of communication between you and the patient. This rapport begins as soon as you approach the scene. Communicating clearly, acting orderly, and appearing to be in control make it easier to obtain an accurate history.

Chief Complaint. Obtain the patient's chief complaint—the problem that caused him or her to solicit help. Pain is a common complaint—for example, abdominal pain or pain in an arm or leg after a fall. In lieu of pain, a

Continued ➡

chief complaint may be nausea or dizziness. A memory aid for investigating the chief complaint is OPQRST.

Onset. Did the chief complaint appear suddenly or gradually?

Provokes. What provoked the injury? If the problem is an illness, under what circumstances did it occur? What makes the problem worse, and what makes it better?

Quality. What qualities describe the pain? Adjectives may include stabbing, cramping, burning, sharp, dull, or aching.

Radiates. Where is the pain? Does it move, or radiate? What causes it to move? Chest pain from a heart attack can radiate from the chest into the neck and jaw. Pain from a spleen injury can be felt in the left shoulder.

Severity. On a scale of 1 to 10 (with 1 being no pain or discomfort and 10 being the worst pain or discomfort the patient has ever experienced), how does the patient rate this pain? This question can reveal the level of discomfort the patient is experiencing.

Time. When did the pain start? How frequently does it occur? How long does it last? Correlate the patient's complaints with the vital signs.

SAMPLE
This is a memory aid for a series of questions that completes the medical history.

Symptoms. What symptoms does the patient have? Nausea? Dizziness? Headache? Ask the patient how he or she is feeling, or if anything is causing discomfort. A symptom is something the patient perceives and must tell you about (e.g., pain). Tenderness, on the other hand, is a sign, something you can find when you touch an injury during a patient exam.

Allergies, Medications. Ask if the patient is currently taking any medications or has any allergies. If so, find out if he or she has been exposed to the allergen and what his or her usual response is. Ask about nonprescription, prescription, and herbal medications, as well as possible alcohol or drug use. Ask whether the patient is allergic to medications or has other environmental allergies to food, insects, or pollen.

Past History. The past history consists of a series of questions you ask the patient to discover any previous and relevant medical problems. (If the patient has a broken leg, for example, it's unlikely we need to know about childhood illness.) First ask these general questions: Has the patient ever been in a hospital? Is the patient currently seeing a physician? Next, ask about specific body systems. Avoid medical jargon. For instance, asking the patient about any previous heart problems is less confusing than asking, "Do you have a cardiac history?"

Additional sources of information may include a medical alert tag or a medical information questionnaire. A medical alert tag is a necklace, bracelet, or wallet card that identifies the patient's medical concerns. It reports a history of diabetes, hemophilia, epilepsy, or other disorders; allergies to medication; and other pertinent information. Medical forms are common to many outdoor schools, camps, and guide services. The NOLS student medical history form is filled out by the student prior to the trip and is available for review by field staff.

Last Intake and Output. Ask the patient when he or she last ate and drank. This information may tell you whether the patient is hydrated or give you important history if, for example, the patient is diabetic. Also find out when the patient last urinated and defecated. Clear, copious urine indicates good hydration; dark, smelly urine suggests dehydration. A patient with diarrhea or vomiting may be dehydrated.

Recent Events. Recent events are unusual circumstances that have occurred within the past few days that may be relevant to the patient's present situation. Recent events might include symptoms of mountain sickness preceding pulmonary edema or changes in diet preceding stomach upset.

The Assessment

The assessment is a review of the information gathered during the initial assessment and the focused exam and history. Examine the records of the head-to-toe examination, the vital signs, and the medical history. Think through OPQRST and SAMPLE.

Rule out possibilities as you assess. Many diagnoses are made by physicians on the basis of what a condition isn't rather than what it could be. Is chest pain a muscle pull or a heart attack? Does the patient have the flu, mountain sickness, or early cerebral edema?

The Plan

Next, prioritize the patient's medical problems and develop a treatment plan for each.

The initial exam provides a baseline. Periodically repeat the exam to judge the patient's response to treatment and any changes for better or worse. If there is any change or deterioration in the patient, return to the beginning and repeat the initial assessment.

—From *NOLS Wildness Medicine*

Injuries to the Head, Spine, Abdomen, and Chest

Greg Davenport

Injuries to the Head

Signs and symptoms of a head injury include bleeding, increasing headache, drowsiness, nausea, vomiting, unequal pupils, and unconsciousness. To treat a suspected head injury, first immobilize the neck if a neck injury is suspected. Then monitor the victim for any change in mental status, and if the victim is conscious, treat him or her for shock by slightly elevating the head and keeping him or her warm. If the victim is unconscious, treat him or her for shock by laying the victim on his or her side to avoid aspiration of vomit.

Injuries to the Spine

Signs and symptoms of a spinal injury include pain, numbness, tingling, decreased sensation or lack of feeling in extremities, and the inability to move the body below the injury site. Be sure to immobilize the neck and body on a firm flat surface, if a spinal injury is suspected, and treat for shock.

Injuries to the Abdomen

Signs and symptoms of an abdominal injury include bleeding, abdominal wall bruising, pain, drowsiness, nausea, and vomiting. An open wound where intestines are exposed should be covered, and care should be taken to prevent drying of the wound. To treat an open intestine wound, rinse away any dirt and debris with a mixture of sterile water and salt (1 quart of sterile water mixed with 1 teaspoon of salt). After cleaning the area, cover it with a clean dressing that is wetted with the above solution. It's extremely important to prevent the intestines from drying out. Both open and closed abdominal injury should be treated for shock.

Injuries to the Chest

Signs and symptoms of a chest injury can vary tremendously, depending on the cause or problem. As a general rule, subject may have pain, coughing and shortness of breath, irregular breathing pattern (rapid or slow), anxiety, and cyanosis. An open chest wound should be covered with a piece of plastic or other airtight material. (While dressing may be used, it is not as effective.) Tape the covering on three sides to allow air to escape but not enter the opening. If the victim's breathing pattern worsens, remove the patch. Both open and closed chest injuries should be treated for shock.

—From *Surviving Coastal and Open Water*

Brain and Spinal Cord Injuries

Tod Schimelpfenig

Brain Injuries

Head injuries include scalp, skull, and brain injuries. Scalp and skull injuries can be serious by themselves, but we're more concerned with possible injury to the brain.

A large blood supply feeds the scalp, causing it to bleed profusely when cut. A bruised or lacerated scalp can mask underlying injury to the skull or brain. Examine scalp injuries carefully to see if bone or brain is exposed or if an indentation, which might be a depressed fracture, is present. Bleeding from the scalp can be controlled by applying gentle pressure on the edges of the wounds, being careful to avoid direct pressure on possibly unstable central areas.

The skull consists of 22 fused bones. The strongest are the bones forming the top and sides of the protective box encasing the brain. Fractures of the skull are not in themselves lifethreatening except when associated with underlying brain injury or spinal cord injury, or when the fracture causes bleeding by tearing the blood vessels between the brain and the skull. Many serious brain injuries occur without skull fractures.

Skull fractures can be open or closed. Open skull fractures expose the brain to infection.

Continued →

Brain injury can be fatal when it disrupts heartbeat and breathing. In the long term, a severe brain injury may leave the patient physically immobile or mentally incompetent, with severely impaired judgment and problem-solving ability or an inability to process or communicate information properly.

The brain can be injured by a direct blow to the head or by twisting forces, which cause deformation and shearing against the inside of the skull. Some movement between brain and skull is possible. A blow to the head can make the brain "rattle" within the skull, tearing blood vessels in the meninges or within the brain itself, stretching and shearing brain cells and the connections between cells.

A mild brain injury (also known as a concussion) is temporary brain dysfunction or loss of responsiveness following a blow to the head. There may be no or only mild brain injury in this case. Contusions (bruising of brain tissue) and hemorrhages or hematomas (bleeding within the brain) are more serious injuries that can lead to increased pressure in the skull. Encased in this rigid box, a swelling or bleeding brain presses against the skull; the body has no mechanism to release such an increase in pressure. As pressure rises, blood supply is shut off by compression of swollen vessels, and brain tissue is deprived of oxygen. The brain stem can be squashed by the pressure, affecting heart and lung function.

Signs and Symptoms of Brain Injury

Signs and symptoms of brain injury depend on the degree and progression of injury. Some indications of brain injury appear immediately from the accident; others develop slowly.

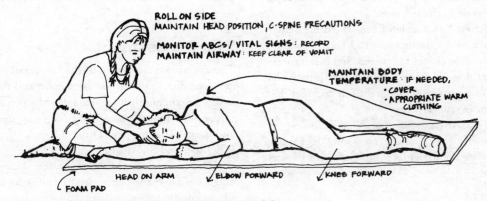

JAW THRUST AIRWAY OPENING FOR SUSPECTED C-SPINE PATIENTS:
- DO NOT MOVE NECK OR SPINE.
- DO NOT TILT HEAD BACK

PLACE FINGERS IN FRONT OF EARLOBE.
PUSH JAW FORWARD AND UP.

ONE HAND ON EACH SIDE OF HEAD:

JAW
EAR

ROLL ON SIDE
MAINTAIN HEAD POSITION, C-SPINE PRECAUTIONS
MONITOR ABCS / VITAL SIGNS: RECORD
MAINTAIN AIRWAY: KEEP CLEAR OF VOMIT
MAINTAIN BODY TEMPERATURE · IF NEEDED,
· COVER
· APPROPRIATE WARM CLOTHING
HEAD ON ARM   ELBOW FORWARD   KNEE FORWARD
FOAM PAD

CARING FOR A BRAIN-INJURED PATIENT

Changes in Level of Responsiveness. Loss of responsiveness may be short or may persist for hours or days. The patient may alternate between periods of responsiveness and unresponsiveness or be responsive but disoriented, confused, and incoherent—exhibiting changes in behavior and personality or verbal or physical combativeness.

Headache, Vision Disturbances, Loss of Balance, Nausea and Vomiting, Paralysis, Seizures. Headache, vision problems, loss of balance, nausea and vomiting, and paralysis may accompany brain injury. In serious cases, the patient may assume abnormal positions, with the legs and arms stiff and extended or the arms clutched across the chest. A brain-injured patient may have seizures.

Combativeness. A brain-injured patient may become combative, striking out randomly and with surprising strength at the nearest person. If the brain is oxygen-deprived, supplemental oxygen and airway maintenance may help alleviate such behavior. Restraint may be necessary to protect the patient and the rescuers.

Blood or CSF Leakage, Soft Tissue Injury to Skull, Obvious Skull Fracture, Raccoon Sign, Battle's Sign. Blood or clear cerebrospinal fluid (CSF) leaking from the ears, mouth, or nose is a sign of a skull fracture, as are pain, tenderness, and swelling at the injury site or obvious penetrating wounds or depressed fractures. Two other signs of skull fracture—bruising around the eyes (called the raccoon sign) and bruising behind the ear (Battle's sign)—usually appear hours after the injury.

Slow Pulse, Rising Blood Pressure, Irregular Respirations. Changes in vital signs that indicate a serious and late stage brain injury are a slow pulse, rising blood pressure, and irregular respiratory rate. These contrast with the rising pulse, falling blood pressure, and rapid, regular respirations seen with shock.

Assessment for Brain Injury

Initial assessment of brain injury can be difficult. The symptoms of a mild brain injury are similar to those seen in more serious injuries. The assessment may also be complicated when the patient's mental status is affected by drugs, alcohol, or other traumatic injuries.

Assessment of brain injury begins by checking the airway, breathing, and circulation (ABC); bleeding; and cervical spine. A patient with a brain injury is at high risk for cervical spine injury. Avoid movement of the neck. If you suspect brain or neck injury, use the jaw thrust to open the airway.

After a thorough physical assessment, including vital signs, evaluate the nervous system. Note the level of responsiveness and the patient's ability to feel and move extremities. Use the AVPU (awake and alert, not awake but responsive to a verbal stimulus, not awake but responsive to pain, or not awake and unresponsive) system to assess mental status. Question the patient or bystanders as to a loss of responsiveness. Was it immediate, or was there a delay before the patient became unresponsive? Has the patient been awake but drowsy, sleepy, confused, or disoriented? Has the patient been going in and out of responsiveness?

Watch any brain-injured patient carefully, even if the injury does not at first appear serious. Let the patient rest, but wake him or her up every couple of hours and assess responsiveness.

Treatment of Brain Injury

Evacuation is required for any patient who has become unresponsive, even for a minute or two, or who exhibits vision or balance disturbances,

Continued ➡

The Concept:

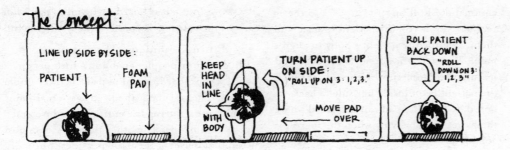

LINE UP SIDE BY SIDE:

PATIENT   FOAM PAD

KEEP HEAD IN LINE WITH BODY

TURN PATIENT UP ON SIDE: "ROLL UP ON 3: 1,2,3."

MOVE PAD OVER

ROLL PATIENT BACK DOWN "ROLL DOWN ON 3: 1,2,3"

Techniques:

RESCUER POSITIONS:

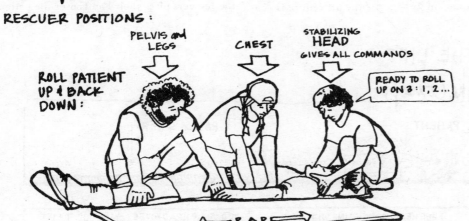

ROLL PATIENT UP & BACK DOWN:

PELVIS and LEGS

CHEST

STABILIZING HEAD GIVES ALL COMMANDS

READY TO ROLL UP ON 3: 1, 2...

PAD

ROLL PATIENT UP ON SIDE:
- TO MOVE PAD
- TO INSPECT PATIENT'S BACK

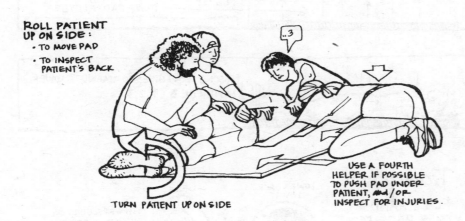

..3

USE A FOURTH HELPER IF POSSIBLE TO PUSH PAD UNDER PATIENT, AND/OR INSPECT FOR INJURIES.

TURN PATIENT UP ON SIDE

IMPROVISED CERVICAL COLLAR

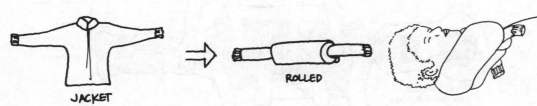

JACKET

ROLLED

STABILIZING THE HEAD:

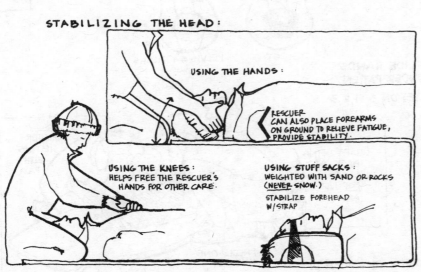

USING THE HANDS:

RESCUER CAN ALSO PLACE FOREARMS ON GROUND TO RELIEVE FATIGUE, PROVIDE STABILITY.

USING THE KNEES: HELPS FREE THE RESCUER'S HANDS FOR OTHER CARE.

USING STUFF SACKS: WEIGHTED WITH SAND OR ROCKS (NEVER SNOW.) STABILIZE FOREHEAD W/STRAP

---

irritability, lethargy, or nausea and vomiting after a blow to the head. A patient who experiences momentary loss of responsiveness but who awakens without any other symptoms may be walked out of the wilderness with a support party capable of quickly evacuating the patient if his or her condition worsens.

ABCs. An injured brain needs oxygen. Ensuring an open airway is the first step in treatment.

If Vomiting, Position Patient on Side. Brain-injured patients have a tendency to vomit. Logrolling the patient onto his or her side while maintaining cervical spine stabilization helps drain vomit while maintaining the airway. Use the jaw thrust to open the airway.

Control Scalp Bleeding. Cover open wounds with bulky sterile dressings as a barrier against infection. Although it is acceptable to clean scalp wounds, cleaning open skull injuries may introduce infection into the brain, so leave them as you find them. Stabilize impaled objects in place.

Do Not Control Internal Bleeding or Drainage. Do not attempt to prevent drainage of blood or clear CSF from the ears or nose. Blocking the flow could increase pressure within the skull.

Elevate head. Keep the patient in a horizontal or slightly head-elevated position. Do not elevate the legs, as this might increase pressure within the skull.

Record Neurological Assessment. Watch the patient closely for any changes in mental status. These observations will be valuable to the receiving physician. Record changes in your patient report.

Spinal Cord Injuries

As with head injuries, spinal cord injuries primarily involve young people, with most cases occurring in men between the ages of 15 and 35. An estimated 10,000 new spinal cord injuries occur each year in the United States, and because central nervous tissue does not regenerate, victims are left permanently disabled—half as paraplegics and half as quadriplegics. Motor vehicle accidents account for the majority of spinal injury cases, followed by falls and sporting injuries.

The spinal cord is the extension of the brain outside the skull. A component of the central nervous system, the spinal cord is the nervous connection between the brain and the rest of the body.

The spinal cord is protected within the vertebrae, 33 of which form the backbone, or spine. A force driving the spine out of its normal alignment can fracture or dislocate the vertebrae, thereby injuring the spinal cord. There can be vertebral fractures or ligament and muscle damage to the backbone, however, without damage to the spinal cord. Fractured or dislocated vertebrae can pinch, bruise, or cut the spinal cord, damaging the nervous connections.

The smallest vertebrae with the greatest range of motion are in the neck—the most vulnerable part of the spine. From there, the vertebrae become progressively larger as they support more weight. The location of damage to

Continued ➡

the spinal cord determines whether the patient may die or be left paralyzed from the neck down (quadriplegia) or the chest down (paraplegia).

Signs and Symptoms of Spinal Cord Injury

Signs and symptoms of spinal cord injury include weakness, loss of sensation or ability to move, numbness and tingling in the hands and feet, incontinence, soft tissue injury over or near the spine, and tenderness in the spine.

Assessment for Spinal Cord Injury

Check for strength, sensation, ability to move, and weakness or numbness in the hands and feet. Ask the patient to wiggle fingers or toes, push his or her feet against your hands, or squeeze your hands with his or hers. Ask the patient to identify which toe or finger you are touching. If the patient is unresponsive, check for sensation by applying a painful stimulus at the toes and fingers (a pinprick or pinch) and watching the patient's face for a grimace.

Treatment of Spinal Cord Injury

Treatment for a spinal cord injury is to stabilize the spine to prevent further damage. Although it may be necessary to move a spine-injured patient, your first choice should be on-scene stabilization.

Stabilize the Spine. If spinal immobilization devices are not available, one person should always be at the head of the patient, controlling the head and maintaining stabilization of the neck. A clothing or blanket roll may be used as an improvised cervical or neck collar to aid in stabilization, freeing rescuers for other tasks. A strap of cloth or bandage across the forehead secured with wrapped clothing stabilizes the head and neck.

Move with Logroll or Lift. Assume that the patient may have to be moved at least twice during the rescue—once to place insulation underneath the body to prevent hypothermia, and a second time to place the patient on a litter or backboard. Two common techniques for moving the patient are the logroll and the lift. Practice these under the guidance of an emergency care instructor.

A patient can be assessed and immobilized while lying facedown or on his or her back or side. Unless airway, breathing, or bleeding problems are present, you should take the time required to carry out the logroll or lift and explain your actions to the patient.

How to Perform a Four-Person Logroll:

1. The rescuers take positions:

   - Rescuer One maintains stabilization of the head throughout the procedure and gives the commands.
   - Rescuer Two kneels beside the patient's chest and reaches across to the patient's shoulder and upper arm.
   - Rescuer Three kneels beside the patient's waist and reaches across to the lower back and pelvis.
   - Rescuer Four kneels beside the patient's thighs and reaches across to support the legs with one hand on the patient's upper thigh, the other behind the knee.

2. The rescuers roll the patient onto his or her side:

   - Rescuer One, at the head, gives the command, "Roll on 3; 1, 2, 3," and the rescuers slowly roll the patient toward them, keeping the patient's body in alignment. Rescuer One supports the head and maintains alignment with the spine. Once the patient is on his or her side, a backboard or foamlite pad can be placed where the patient will be lying when the logroll is complete.

3. The rescuers roll the patient onto his or her back:

   - When Rescuer One gives the command, "Lower on 3; 1, 2, 3," the procedure is reversed, and the patient is slowly lowered onto the backboard or foamlite pad while the rescuers keep the spine in alignment.

Lifting Technique. The patient can be lifted by four people, enabling a fifth person to slide a backboard, foamlite pad, or litter underneath. The rescuer at the head again maintains stabilization during the entire procedure and gives commands. The other three rescuers position themselves at the patient's sides, one kneeling at chest level and another at pelvis level on the same side, while the third rescuer kneels at waist level on the opposite side. Before lifting, the rescuers place their hands over the patient to

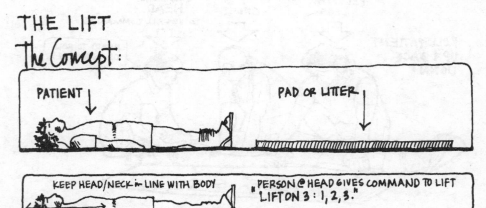

THE LIFT
The Concept:

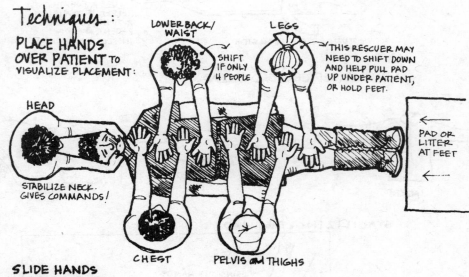

Techniques:

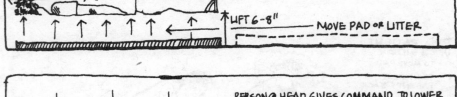

Continued ➡

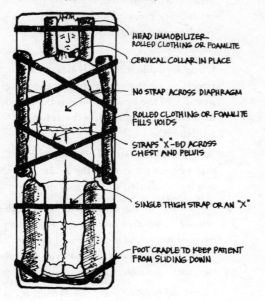

PATIENT PACKAGING POINTS

HEAD IMMOBILIZER
ROLLED CLOTHING OR FOAMLITE

CERVICAL COLLAR IN PLACE

NO STRAP ACROSS DIAPHRAGM

ROLLED CLOTHING OR FOAMLITE
FILLS VOIDS

STRAPS "X"-ED ACROSS
CHEST AND PELVIS

SINGLE THIGH STRAP OR AN "X"

FOOT CRADLE TO KEEP PATIENT
FROM SLIDING DOWN

FILL VOIDS NEXT TO HEAD
WITH ROLLED CLOTHING OR FOAMLITE

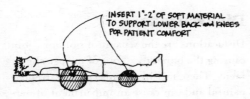

INSERT 1"-2" OF SOFT MATERIAL
TO SUPPORT LOWER BACK AND KNEES
FOR PATIENT COMFORT

visualize their hands in position under the chest, lower back, pelvis, and thighs. They then slide their hands under the patient as far as they can without jostling the patient. On the command, "Lift on 3; 1, 2, 3," rescuers lift the patient to a standing position, then lower him or her onto the pad or litter.

Immobilize the Spine. Ideally, the patient should be moved as few times as possible, and preferably after immobilization on a backboard, Kendrick Extrication Device, SKED litter, or other spine-splinting device, and with a cervical collar and head immobilization. Until such equipment arrives, insulate and shelter the patient.

Wilderness treatment may require caring for a patient during prolonged immobilization. It's uncomfortable to lie still on a hard surface for hours. Current advanced trauma life support (ATLS) curriculum recommends that patients on backboards be logrolled off the backboard approximately every 2 hours to prevent pressure sores on the back. Padding is important. A little bit under the lower back and behind the knees goes a long way to make the patient comfortable. Strapping over bony areas helps tie the patient down, but the straps should be padded and can be loosened when the patient is not being carried.

The Focused Spine Assessment. If a mechanism for a spinal cord injury has occurred, for example, from a fall from a height, a high-velocity skiing fall, a diving accident, or a blow to the head, initially assume the worst and control the head. If the mechanism is severe, or the

patient has signs of a spinal cord injury, immobilize the spine. If the mechanism seems trivial and the patient has no signs of spine injury, you may consider performing a focused spine assessment to gather information to help you decide if immobilizing the spine is necessary.

After a thorough assessment, it is acceptable to consider "clearing" the spine of injury by using a method approved by the Wilderness Medical Society to rule out spine injury. Without this protocol, we would unnecessarily immobilize all patients with insignificant mechanisms for injury. As with all wilderness protocols, support from a physician advisor is recommended.

Making a decision to not immobilize begins with a thorough patient assessment. Then proceed sequentially through this series of steps:

1. Is the patient A+O3/4 and sober?

   —If no, immobilize the spine. If yes, proceed to the next step.

2. Is the patient free from distractions (injuries, emotional distress)?

   —If no, immobilize the spine. If yes, proceed to the next step.

3. Is the patient free of pain, tenderness, tingling, or numbness on the spine?

   —If no, immobilize the spine. If yes, proceed to the next step.

4. Is the patient free of unusual or abnormal sensations in the extremities, such as numbness or tingling? Do extremities have normal circulation and movement?

   —If no, immobilize the spine. If yes, you can make a decision to not immobilize the spine.

If the patient fails any step in this process, or you're uncertain about the results of your exam, immobilize the spine. If at any time you're uncomfortable with this process, you can choose a conservative plan and immobilize the patient.

—From *NOLS Wilderness Medicine*

Chest Injuries

Tod Schimelpfenig

Rib Fractures

The most commonly fractured ribs are ribs five through ten. Ribs one through four are protected by the shoulder girdle and are rarely fractured. The floating ribs—ribs eleven and twelve—are more flexible and will give before breaking.

Signs and Symptoms. Rib fractures cause deformity and/or discoloration over the injured area. The patient complains of tenderness over the fracture (point tenderness) when touched. Breathing or coughing causes sharp, stabbing pain at the site of the fracture. Respiratory rate increases as the patient breathes shallowly in an attempt to decrease the pain. The patient may clutch the chest on the fractured side in an attempt to splint it. Carefully observe rib fracture victims for other injuries.

Treatment. A single fractured rib that is not displaced (simple rib fracture) does not

require splinting. Non-narcotic pain medication (acetaminophen or ibuprofen) may be all the treatment necessary.

Tape the Fracture Site on One Side of Chest. If the pain is severe, tape the fractured side from sternum to spine with four or five pieces of 1- to 2-inch adhesive tape. This decreases movement at the fracture site and diminishes pain. Tape should never be wrapped completely around the chest, as this can restrict breathing. You may also find that a simple sling and swathe on the arm on the injured side limits movement and provides comfort. If the patient is not in respiratory distress, he or she may be able to walk out.

Flail Chest

A flail chest occurs when 3 or more adjacent ribs are broken in two or more places, loosening a segment of the chest wall. When the patient breathes in, the increased negative pressure pulls the flail segment inward, and the lung does not fill with air as it should. When the patient breathes out, the opposite occurs, and the flail segment may be pushed outward. The flail segment moves in a direction opposite of normal breathing, thus the term "paradoxical respirations."

Signs and Symptoms. A flail chest develops only with a significant chest injury, such as a heavy fall against a rock. The patient may be in respiratory distress. Put your hands under the patient's shirt, and you may feel a part of the chest moving in while the opposite part of the chest is moving out. This may also be visible upon inspection.

Treatment. Stabilize the flail chest:

- Position the patient on the injured side with a rolled-up piece of clothing underneath the flailed segment.

- Apply pressure with your hand to the flailed area. This works only as a temporary measure, as it is difficult to hold pressure while transporting the patient.

- Tape a large pad firmly over the flail segment (without circling the chest).

Treat the patient for shock and evacuate.

Injuries to Lungs

In addition to injuries to the ribs, the underlying lungs may be damaged. Blood vessels can be ruptured and torn, causing bleeding into the chest, and lungs can be punctured, causing air to leak into the chest.

Pneumothorax. This occurs when air leaks into the pleural space, creating negative pressure that collapses the lung. Pneumothorax can be caused by a fractured rib that lacerates the lung (traumatic pneumothorax), a weak spot on the lung wall that gives way (spontaneous pneumothorax), or an open chest wound.

Hemothorax. This occurs when lacerated blood vessels cause blood to collect in the pleural space. The source can be a fractured rib or lacerated lung. If more than 1 liter of blood leaks into the pleural space, a hemothorax may compress the lung and compromise breathing. The loss of blood may also cause shock.

Continued ➡

First Aid

Spontaneous Pneumothorax. A congenital weak area of the lung may rupture, creating a spontaneous pneumothorax. The highest incidence occurs in tall, thin, healthy men between the ages of 20 and 30. Eighty percent of spontaneous penumothoraxes occur while the person is at rest. The patient complains of a sudden, sharp pain in the chest and increasing shortness of breath.

Tension Pneumothorax. If a hole opening into the pleural space serves as a one-way valve—allowing air to enter but not to escape—a tension pneumothorax develops. With each breath, air enters the pleural space, but it cannot escape with expiration. As pressure in the pleural space increases, the lung collapses. Pressure in the pleural space eventually causes the mediastinum to shift to the unaffected side, putting pressure on the heart and good lung. If the pressure in the pleural space exceeds that in the veins, blood cannot return to the heart, and death occurs.

As pressure builds, you may see the trachea deviate toward the unaffected side, tissue between the ribs bulge, and the neck veins distend. Respirations become increasingly rapid. The pulse is weak and rapid. The pulse is weak and rapid; cyanosis occurs.

Open Chest Wounds

If a wound through the chest wall breaks into the pleural space, air enters, creating a pneumothorax. If the wound remains open, air moves in and out of the pleura, causing a sucking noise.

The goal of treatment is to limit the size of the pneumothorax. Quickly seal the hole with any nonporous material—a plastic bag or petroleum jelly—impregnated gauze, for example. Tape the dressing down on three sides to seal the hole, yet allow excess air pressure in the chest to escape.

Respiratory Distress

Respiratory distress is an overall term that covers any situation in which a patient is having difficulty breathing. Respiratory distress can occur after an injury, during an illness such as pneumonia, during a heart attack or an asthma attack, or after inhalation of a poisonous gas.

Signs and symptoms of respiratory distress are anxiety and restlessness; shortness of breath; rapid respirations and pulse; signs of shock, including pale, cool, and clammy skin and cyanosis of the skin, lips, and fingernail beds; and labored breathing using accessory muscles of the neck, shoulder, and abdomen to achieve maximum effort. The patient is usually more comfortable sitting than lying.

Respiratory distress is a frightening experience for both the patient and the rescuer. If the underlying cause is emotional, as in hyperventilation syndrome (see page 442), reassurance may be all that's needed to alleviate the problem. If a chest injury with underlying lung damage or an illness such as pneumonia or a pulmonary embolus occurs, treatment in the field is difficult. Evacuation is the course of action. The airway can be maintained, the patient placed in the most comfortable position for breathing, the injury splinted or taped, wounds dressed, and the patient treated for shock.

—From *NOLS Wilderness Medicine*

U.S. Army

Fractures

There are basically two types of fractures: open and closed. With an open (or compound) fracture, the bone protrudes through the skin and complicates the actual fracture with an open wound. After setting the fracture, treat the wound as any other open wound.

The closed fracture has no open wounds. Follow the guidelines for immobilization, and set and splint the fracture.

The signs and symptoms of a fracture are pain, tenderness, discoloration, swelling deformity, loss of function, and grating (a sound or feeling that occurs when broken bone ends rub together).

The dangers with a fracture are the severing or the compression of a nerve or blood vessel at the site of fracture. For this reason minimum manipulation should be done, and only very cautiously. If you notice the area below the break becoming numb, swollen, cool to the touch, or turning pale, and the victim shows signs of shock, a major vessel may have been severed. You must control this internal bleeding. Treat the victim for shock, and replace lost fluids.

Often you must maintain traction during the splinting and healing process. You can effectively pull smaller bones such as the arm or lower leg by hand. You can create traction by wedging a hand or foot in the V-notch of a tree and pushing against the tree with the other extremity. You can then splint the break.

Very strong muscles hold a broken thighbone (femur) in place making it difficult to maintain traction during healing. You can make an improvised traction splint using natural material as follows:

- Get two forked branches or saplings at least 5 centimeters in diameter. Measure one from the patient's armpit to 20 to 30 centimeters past his unbroken leg. Measure the other from the groin to 20 to 30 centimeters past the unbroken leg. Ensure that both extend an equal distance beyond the end of the leg.

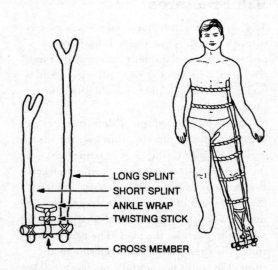

Improvised traction splint.

- Pad the two splints. Notch the ends without forks and lash a 20- to 30-centimeter cross member made from a 5-centimeter diameter branch between them.

- Using available material (vines, cloth, rawhide), tie the splint around the upper portion of the body and down the length of the broken leg. Follow the splinting guidelines.

- With available material, fashion a wrap that will extend around the ankle, with the two free ends tied to the cross member.

- Place a 10- by 2.5-centimeter stick in the middle of the free ends of the ankle wrap between the cross member and the foot. Using the stick, twist the material to make the traction easier.

- Continue twisting until the broken leg is as long or slightly longer than the unbroken leg.

- Lash the stick to maintain traction.

Note: Over time you may lose traction because the material weakened. Check the traction periodically. If you must change or repair the splint, maintain the traction manually for a short time.

Dislocations

Dislocations are the separations of bone joints causing the bones to go out of proper alignment. These misalignments can be extremely painful and can cause an impairment of nerve or circulatory function below the area affected. You must place these joints back into alignment as quickly as possible.

Signs and symptoms of dislocations are joint pain, tenderness, swelling, discoloration, limited range of motion, and deformity of the joint. You treat dislocations by reduction, immobilization, and rehabilitation.

Reduction or "setting" is placing the bones back into their proper alignment. You can use several methods, but manual traction or the use of weights to pull the bones are the safest and easiest. Once performed, reduction decreases the victim's pain and allows for normal function and circulation. Without an X-ray, you can judge proper alignment by the look and feel of the joint and by comparing it to the joint on the opposite side.

Immobilization is nothing more than splinting the dislocation after reduction. You can use any field-expedient material for a splint or you can splint an extremity to the body. The basic guidelines for splinting are—

- Splint above and below the fracture site.

- Pad splints to reduce discomfort.

- Check circulation below the fracture after making each tie on the splint.

To rehabilitate the dislocation, remove the splints after 7 to 14 days. Gradually use the injured joint until fully healed.

—From *Survival* (Field Manual 21–76)

Athletic Injuries

Tod Schimelpfenig

Living and traveling in the wilderness, carrying a pack, hiking long distances, climbing, and paddling can all cause sprains, strains, and tendinitis. Athletic injuries account for 50 percent of injuries on NOLS courses and are a frequent cause of evacuations.

Sprains, or injuries to ligaments, are categorized as grades one, two, or three. With a grade one injury, ligament fibers are stretched but not torn. A partly torn or badly stretched ligament is a grade two injury. Completely torn ligaments are grade three injuries. Strains are injuries to muscles and tendons. A muscle stretched too far is commonly referred to as a "pull." A muscle or tendon with torn fibers is a "tear." A tendon irritated from overuse can become tendinitis.

When faced with an athletic injury, the first responder in the wilderness has to choose between treating the injury in the field—possibly altering the expedition route and timetable to accommodate the patient's loss of mobility—or evacuation.

We don't try to diagnose the injury or grade the sprain or the strain. We decide if an injury is usable or not. If usable, we use RICE therapy and may tape for support. If unusable, we immobilize and evacuate.

The most common athletic injuries on NOLS courses are ankle and knee sprains, Achilles tendinitis, and forearm tendinitis. Most of the athletic injuries we experience are minor, but even a moderate ankle sprain can take a week to heal. It is difficult to rest for 7 days without affecting a wilderness trip.

Common Causes of Athletic Injury on NOLS Courses

- Playing games such as hug tag and hacky sack.
- Tripping while walking in camp.
- Stepping over logs.
- Crossing streams, including shallow rock hops.
- Putting on a backpack.
- Lifting a kayak or raft.
- Falling or misstepping while hiking with a pack (on any terrain).
- Falling while skiing with a pack.
- Shoveling snow.
- Bending over to pick up firewood.

General Treatment for Athletic Injuries (RICE)

Athletic injuries are generally treated with RICE: rest, ice, compression, and elevation. Allowing these injuries to heal until they are free of pain, tenderness, and swelling prevents aggravation of the condition. Gently rub the injured area with ice, wrapped in fabric to prevent frostbite, for 20 to 40 minutes every 2 to 4 hours for the first 24 to 48 hours, then allow it to passively warm. Cooling decreases nerve conduction and pain, constricts blood vessels, limits the inflammatory process, and reduces cellular demand for oxygen.

Compression with an Ace bandage helps reduce swelling. Care must be taken when applying the wrap not to exert pressure on an injury that swells dramatically or to cut off blood flow to the fingers or toes.

Elevating the injury above the level of the heart reduces swelling. Nonprescription pain medications such as acetaminophen and ibuprofen may help as well.

Assessment of Athletic Injuries

A thorough assessment includes an evaluation of the mechanism of injury, as well as the signs and symptoms. Knowing the mechanism helps you determine whether the occurrence was sudden and traumatic, indicating a sprain, or whether it was progressive, suggesting an overuse injury.

Signs and symptoms of a sprain include swelling, pain, and discoloration. Point tenderness and obvious deformity suggest a fracture. Ask the patient to try to move the joint through its full range of motion. Painless movement is a good sign. If the patient is able to use or bear weight on the affected limb, and pain and swelling are not severe, he or she can be treated in the field.

Severe pain, the sound of a pop at the time of injury, immediate swelling, and inability to use the joint are signs of a serious sprain, possibly a fracture. This injury should be immobilized and the patient evacuated from the field.

Ankle Sprains

Uneven ground, whether boulder fields in the backcountry or broken pavement in the city, contributes to the likelihood of ankle sprains. Of all ankle sprains, 85 percent are inversion injuries—those in which the foot turns in to the midline of the body and the ankle turns outward. Inversion injuries usually sprain one or more of the ligaments on the outside of the ankle.

Ankle Anatomy. The bones, ligaments, and tendons of the ankle and foot absorb stress and pressure generated by both body weight and activity. They also allow for flexibility and accommodate surface irregularities so that we don't lose our balance.

Bones. The lower leg bones are the tibia and the fibula. The large bumps on either side of the ankle are the lower ends of these bones—the fibula on the outside, and the tibia on the inside. Immediately under the tibia and fibula lies the talus bone, which sits atop the calcaneus (heel bone). The talus and calcaneus act as a rocker for front-to-back flexibility of the ankle. Without them, we would walk stiff-legged.

In front of the calcaneus lie two smaller bones, the navicular (inside) and the cuboid (outside). They attach to three small bones called the cuneiforms. Anterior to the cuneiforms are five metatarsals, which in turn articulate with the phalanges (toe bones).

Ligaments. Due to the number of bones in the foot, ligaments are many and complex. For simplicity, think of there being a ligament on every exterior surface of every bone, attaching to the adjacent articulating bone.

There are four ligaments commonly associated with ankle sprains. On the inside of the ankle is the large, fan-shaped deltoid ligament jointing the talus, calcaneus, and several of the smaller foot bones to the tibia. Rolling the ankle inward, an eversion sprain, stresses the deltoid ligament. Spraining the deltoid requires considerable force, and due to its size and strength, it is seldom injured. In fact, this ligament is so strong that if a bad twist occurs, it frequently pulls fragments of bone off at its attachment points, causing an avulsion fracture.

On the outside, usually the weaker aspect, three ligaments attach from the fibula to the talus and the calcaneus. Together these three ligaments protect the ankle from turning to the outside.

Muscles and Tendons. Muscles in the lower leg use long tendons to act on the ankle and foot. The calf muscles—the gastrocnemius and soleus—shorten to point the toes. These muscles taper into the largest tendon, the Achilles, which attaches to the back of the calcaneus. The peroneal muscles in the lower leg contract and pull the foot laterally and roll the ankle outward. Muscles in the front of the lower leg turn the foot inward and extend the toes.

Treatment of Ankle Sprains. Sprains should have the standard treatment of rest, ice, compression, and elevation to limit swelling and allow healing. If a severe sprain or a fracture is suspected, immobilize the ankle. Aggressively treating a mild sprain with RICE for the first 24 to 48 hours and letting it rest for a few days may allow a patient to stay in the mountains rather than cut the trip short. A simple method for providing ankle support is to tape the ankle using the basket weave.

Knee Pain

Pain in the knee from overuse can be treated by ceasing the activity causing the discomfort and controlling pain and inflammation with RICE. In the event of a traumatic injury resulting in an unstable knee, splint and evacuate. If the injury is stable and the patient can bear weight, use RICE to control pain and inflammation. If the patient can walk without undue pain, wrap the knee with foamlite for support.

Tendinitis

A tendon is the fibrous cord by which a muscle is attached to a bone. Its construction is similar to that of kernmantle rope, with an outer sheath of tissue enclosing a core of fibers. Some tendons, such as those to the fingers, are long. The activating muscles are in the forearm, but the tendons stretch from the forearm across the wrist to each finger. These tendons are surrounded by a lubricating sheath to assist their movement.

Tendinitis is inflammation of a tendon. When the sheath and the tendon become inflamed, the sheath becomes rough, movement is restricted and painful, and the patient feels a grating of the tendon inside the sheath. Fibers can be torn or, more commonly, irritation from overuse or infection can inflame the sheath, causing pain when the tendon moves. There may be little pain when the tendon is at rest.

Tendons are poorly supplied with blood, so they heal slowly. Tendons are well supplied with

Continued →

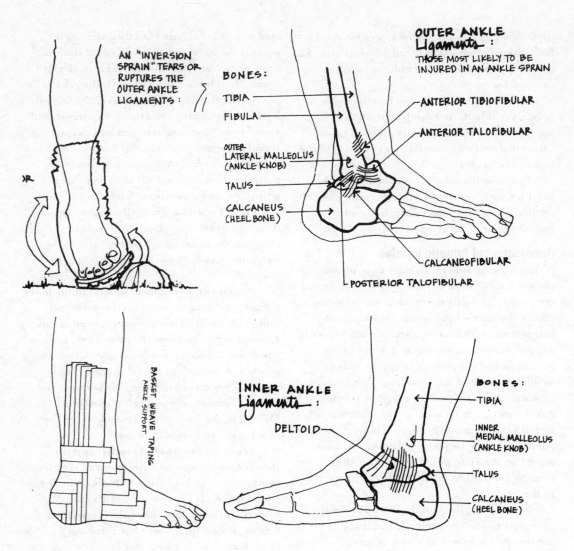

AN "INVERSION SPRAIN" TEARS OR RUPTURES THE OUTER ANKLE LIGAMENTS:

BONES:
TIBIA
FIBULA
OUTER LATERAL MALLEOLUS (ANKLE KNOB)
TALUS
CALCANEUS (HEEL BONE)

OUTER ANKLE Ligaments: THOSE MOST LIKELY TO BE INJURED IN AN ANKLE SPRAIN

ANTERIOR TIBIOFIBULAR
ANTERIOR TALOFIBULAR
CALCANEOFIBULAR
POSTERIOR TALOFIBULAR

BASKET WEAVE TAPING ANKLE SUPPORT

INNER ANKLE Ligaments:
DELTOID

BONES:
TIBIA
INNER MEDIAL MALLEOLUS (ANKLE KNOB)
TALUS
CALCANEUS (HEEL BONE)

nerves, however, which means that an injury will be painful. Tendons can be injured by sudden overloading, but are more frequently injured through overuse. Factors contributing to tendinitis include poor technique, poor equipment, unhealed prior injury, and cool and tight muscles.

Assessment for Tendinitis

Tendinitis, in contrast to ankle sprains, is a progressive overuse injury, not a traumatic injury. Common sites for tendinitis are the Achilles tendon and the tendons of the forearm. The Achilles, the largest tendon in the body, may fatigue and become inflamed during or following lengthy hikes, especially with significant elevation gain. Boots that break down and place pressure on the tendon can provide enough irritation in one day to initiate inflammation.

Forearm tendinitis is common among canoeists and kayakers. Poor technique and inadequate strength and flexibility contribute to the injury. Similar tendinitis comes with repetitive use of ski poles, ice axes, and ice climbing tools.

Tendinitis may also occur on the front of the foot, usually caused by tightly laced boots or stiff mountaineering boots. The tendons extending the toes become irritated and inflamed. Tendinitis causes swelling, redness, warmth, pain to the touch (or pinch), painful movement, and sounds of friction or grinding (crepitus).

Treatment of Tendinitis

Treat tendinitis with RICE: rest, ice, compression, and elevation. It may be necessary to cease the aggravating activity until the inflammation subsides. Prevent or ease tendinitis of anterior muscles by varying boot lacing. Lace boots more

loosely when hiking and more tightly when climbing.

Achilles Tendinitis. To relieve stretch on the Achilles tendon, provide a heel lift. To relieve direct pressure from the boot, place a 6-inch by 1-inch strip of foamlite padding on either side of the Achilles tendon. The placement should take the pressure off without touching the Achilles.

Forearm Tendinitis. Forearm tendinitis is primarily associated with the repetitive motion of paddling. Pay close attention to proper paddling technique. Keep a relaxed, open grip on the paddle. On the forward stroke, keep the wrist in line with the forearm during the pull and push, and avoid crossing the upper arm over the midline of the body.

Other paddling techniques that may help prevent forearm tendinitis include keeping the thumb on the same side of the paddle as the fingers and switching a feathered paddle for an unfeathered paddle. The feathered paddle requires a wrist movement that can sometimes aggravate tendinitis.

Tendinitis of the forearm is treated with RICE. Also, the wrist can be taped to limit movement that aggravates the condition.

Muscle Strains

Muscles can be stretched and torn from overuse or overexertion. Initial treatment is RICE, followed by heat, massage, and gentle stretching. Radiating muscle pain, strong pain at rest, pain secondary to an illness, or pain from a severe trauma mechanism is a reason to evacuate the patient for evaluation by a physician.

Final Thoughts

Errors in technique and inadequate muscular conditioning or warm-up produce injury. Overuse of muscles and joints (when there is no single traumatic event as the cause of injury) generates many of the sprains and strains on NOLS courses.

Jerky movements, excessive force, or an unnecessarily tight grip on the paddle while kayaking contribute to forearm tendinitis. Performing the athletic movements required for difficult rock climbs without warming up or paying attention to balance and form can cause injury. Even the seemingly simple actions of lifting a backpack or boat, stepping over logs, and wading in cold mountain streams can be dangerous.

Steep terrain and wet conditions contribute to injuries. Slippery conditions make it harder to balance and can cause falls. Falls that occur in camp and while hiking are the cause of many athletic injuries. Surprisingly, injuries are just as likely to occur when backcountry travelers are wearing packs as when they are not. Possibly this is because people are more attentive to technique when hiking or skiing with a pack.

You are more likely to be injured when you are tired, cold, dehydrated, rushed, or ill. You're not thinking as clearly, and your muscles are less flexible and responsive. Injuries happen more frequently in late morning and late afternoon, when dehydration and fatigue reduce awareness and increase clumsiness. Shifting from a three-meal-a-day schedule to breakfast and dinner plus three or four light snacks during the day helps keep your food supply constant.

Haste, often the result of unrealistic timetables, is frequently implicated in accidents. Try to negotiate the more difficult terrain in the morning, when you are fresh. Take rest breaks before difficult sections of a hike or paddle. Stop at the base of the pass, the near side of the river, or the beginning of the boulder field. Drink, eat, and stretch tight muscles. Check equipment for loose gaiters that may trip you and for poorly balanced backpacks.

The sustained activity of life in the wilderness and the need for sudden bursts of power when paddling, skiing, or climbing necessitate physical conditioning prior to a wilderness expedition. A regimen of endurance, flexibility, and muscle strength training will help prevent injuries and promote safety and enjoyment of wilderness activity.

—From *NOLS Wilderness Medicine*

Wound Care

Tod Schimelpfenig

Closed Wounds

Closed injuries include contusions (bruises) and hematomas. With both, the tissue and blood vessels beneath the epidermis are damaged. Swelling and discoloration occur because blood and plasma leak out of the damaged blood vessels. With contusions, blood is dispersed within the tissues. Hematomas contain a pool of blood—as much as a pint surrounding a major

Continued

bone fracture. Depending on the amount of blood dispersed, reabsorption can take from 12 hours to several days. In some cases, the blood may have to be drained by a physician to enhance healing.

Treatment for Closed Wounds

A memory aid for treating closed injuries is RICE: rest, ice, compression, and elevation.

Rest. Rest decreases bleeding by allowing clots to form. In the event of a large or deep bruise, extremities can be splinted to decrease motion that may cause newly-formed clots to break away and bleeding to continue.

Ice. Ice causes the blood vessels to constrict, decreasing bleeding. Never apply ice directly to bare skin, as this can cause frostbite. Instead, wrap the ice in fabric of a towel-like thickness before applying to the skin. Ice the wound for 20 to 40 minutes every 2 to 4 hours for the first 24 to 48 hours, then allow the area to passively warm.

Compression. Apply manual pressure or a pressure dressing. When applying a pressure dressing, wrap it snugly enough to stop bleeding but not so tightly that the blood supply is shut off. Check by feeling for a pulse distal to the injured site.

Elevation. Elevate the injury above the level of the heart. Elevation reduces bleeding and swelling by decreasing the blood flow to the injury.

Open Wounds

Open injuries include abrasions, lacerations, puncture wounds, and major traumatic injuries—avulsions, amputations, and crushing wounds.

Abrasions. Abrasions occur when the epidermis and part of the dermis are rubbed off. These injuries are commonly called "road rash" or "rug burns." They usually bleed very little but are painful and may be contaminated with debris.

Abrasions heal more quickly if treated with ointment and covered with a semiocclusive or occlusive dressing.

Lacerations. Lacerations are cuts produced by sharp objects. The cut may penetrate all the layers of the skin, and the edges may be straight or jagged. If long and deep enough to cause the skin to gap more than 1/2 inch (1 cm), lacerations may require sutures. Sutures, a task for a physician, are also indicated if the cut is on the face or hands or over a joint, or if it severs a tendon, ligament, or blood vessel. Tendons and ligaments must be sutured together to heal properly. Lacerations on the hands or over a joint may be sutured to prevent the wound from being continually pulled apart by movement. Lacerations on the face are usually sutured to decrease scarring.

Puncture Wounds. Puncture wounds are caused by pointed objects. Although the skin around a puncture wound remains closed and there is little external bleeding, the object may have penetrated an artery or organ, causing internal bleeding.

If an impaled object is through the cheek and causing an airway obstruction, it must be removed to allow the patient to breathe. Otherwise, leave impalement in place. Removing the object may cause more soft tissue injury and increase bleeding by releasing pressure on compressed blood vessels. Stabilize and prevent movement of impaled objects with protective padding. Some people argue for removal of impaled objects in situations of long or difficult transportation. This advice usually applies to objects in the extremities, not those in the chest, head, abdomen, or eye. Check with your physician advisor for guidance on this question.

Tetanus is a rare but serious complication. Although tetanus may be more likely to occur in a farm or ranch environment than on a "clean" mountainside, it is a good idea to make sure your tetanus booster is up-to-date before you take off into the backcountry. Tetanus boosters should be given at least every 10 years.

Treatment for Open Wounds

The principles for treating open wounds are to control bleeding, clean and dress the wound, and monitor for infection.

Control Bleeding. Controlling bleeding is the first priority when treating open wounds. Death can come quickly to a patient with a tear in a major blood vessel. There are four methods for controlling bleeding. The most effective—direct pressure and elevation—will stop most bleeding when used in combination. Pressure points and tourniquets are also used.

Direct Pressure. The best method for controlling bleeding is to apply pressure over the wound site. Using your hand and a piece of wadded fabric—preferably sterile gauze—apply direct pressure to the wound. Be sure to wear rubber or latex gloves or place your hand in a plastic bag. If the wound is large, you may need to pack the open area with gauze before applying pressure. Maintain pressure for 5 minutes, then slowly release. If the bleeding resumes, apply pressure for 15 minutes.

Elevation. As with closed injuries, the combination of splinting, a pressure dressing, and elevation will help decrease the bleeding. Direct pressure and elevation control almost all bleeding. In fact, it is unusual for a wound to require the first responder to utilize pressure points or a tourniquet.

Pressure Points. Pressure points are areas on the body where arteries lie close to the skin and over bones. Pressure applied to the artery at one of these points can slow or stop the flow of blood in that artery, thereby reducing bleeding at the site of the injury. Pressure on these points is rarely effective by itself and is usually applied in conjunction with other techniques.

Tourniquets. Apply a tourniquet only as a last resort, when no other method will stop the bleeding. Tourniquets completely stop the blood flow, and if the tourniquet is left on for more than a few hours, there is a chance that the tissue distal to the tourniquet will die and the extremity may require amputation.

Clean the Wound. Consider any wound, even a minor finger cut or a blister, as potentially infected. On wilderness expeditions wound cleaning is a priority. When you clean a wound, eliminate as much potentially infectious bacteria and debris as possible without further damaging the skin.

Wash Your Hands and Put on Gloves. Wash your hands. Use soap and water to prevent contamination of the wound. Put on rubber or latex gloves.

Scrub and Irrigate the Wound. Scrub the skin around the wound, being careful not to flush debris into the wound. Clip long hair, but don't shave the skin. Then scrub or irrigate an open wound for at least 3 minutes with water that has been disinfected with chlorination or iodination, filtering, or water that has been boiled and cooled. Many wounds can be cleaned simply by irrigating with clean water. If the wound is obviously dirty or contaminated, a 1 percent povidone-iodine (usually one part 10 percent povidone-iodine diluted with 10 parts water to approximate the color of dark tea) is a suitable irrigation solution. Medical science tells us that the volume of water is the most important factor in cleaning the wound. At NOLS, we carry 35cc syringes in the first aid kit for pressure-irrigating wounds. Plastic bags or water bottles with pinholes can work as improvised irrigation syringes. Try to remove all debris even if this requires some painful scrubbing. Remove large pieces of debris with tweezers that have been boiled or cleaned with povidone-iodine.

Rinse with Disinfected Water. After cleaning the wound, rinse off the solution with liberal amounts of disinfected water. Check for further bleeding—you may need to apply direct pressure again if blood clots were broken loose during the cleaning process.

Dress and Bandage the Wound. Dressings are sterile gauze placed directly over the wound; bandages hold the dressing in place. Both come in many shapes and sizes. Semiocclusive (Telfa) or occlusive (Second Skin, Opsite, Tegaderm) dressings promote healing by keeping the area moist. Ointments (such as Polysporin or Bacitracin) serve the same purpose. Dry dressings that adhere to the wound impede the healing process.

Next, apply an antibiotic ointment. The ointment should be applied to the dressing rather than directly to the wound. This avoids contaminating the remaining antibiotic in the tube or bottle. Apply the bandage neatly and in such a way that blood flow distal to the injured area is not impaired. After applying the bandage, check the pulse distal to the injury.

Do not close wound edges until the wound has been thoroughly cleaned. Generally, the edges of a small wound will come together on their own. If the skin is stretched apart, butterfly bandages or Steri-strips can hold the edges together. If the injury is over a joint, the extremity may require splinting to prevent the edges from pulling apart. Highly contaminated wounds should be packed open.

Physicians don't agree on how long a wound can be kept open until it is stitched. A wound that will not close on its own or with a bandage can usually be stitched even a day or two later. The need to use sutures to close a wound does not, by itself, create an emergency. Reasons to expedite an evacuation for an open wound include obvious dirt or contamination; animal bites; wounds that open joint spaces; established infection; wounds from a crushing mechanism; any laceration to a cosmetic area, especially the face; wounds with a lot of dead tissue on the

Continued ➡

edges or in the wound itself; and wounds that obviously need surgical care, such as open fractures and very deep, gaping lacerations.

Animal bites are a concern for infection because of the bacterial flora in animal mouths and the crushing, penetrating, and tearing mechanism of the wounds. In North America, wild animal attacks, while dramatic and often highlighted in the press, are unusual. Worldwide they are believed to be more common, but the evidence is anecdotal, not scientific.

After the Bandage Is Applied. Check circulation, sensation, and movement of the body part distal to the injury. Can the patient tell you where you are touching? Can he or she flex and extend the extremity? Is the area distal to the injury pink and warm, indicating good blood perfusion? Any negative answers to these questions may indicate nerve, artery, or tendon damage that will require evacuating the patient.

If a dressing becomes soaked with blood, leave it in place and apply additional dressings. Removing the dressing disturbs the blood clots that are forming. After bleeding has been controlled, dressings should be changed daily and the injured area checked for signs of infection.

Infection

The newspapers and television media occasionally tell dramatic tales of aggressive and resistant wound infections and "flesh-eating bacteria." But on a daily basis outside the wilderness, we give little thought to the potential for wounds to be contaminated and colonized by bacteria. Before modern medicine understood infection and practiced clean wound care, infections were common and dangerous. In some environments, such as the tropics, they remain quite common and serious. In the wilderness we have less than ideal circumstances for cleaning wounds, but our efforts are essential in preventing wound infection.

Assessment for Infection. Redness, swelling, pus, heat, and pain at the site; faint red streaks radiating from the site; fever; chills; and swollen lymph nodes are all signs of infection.

It may be difficult to decide if local swelling, without an obvious wound, is due to a muscle strain, bug bite, or infection. The possibility of a deep infection is a concern. History may help rule out the muscle strain.

The four cardinal signs of a soft tissue infection are: redness, swelling, warmth, and local pain. The progression in a wound to increased pain, warmth, increased soft tissue swelling, and expansion of redness over 18 to 24 hours suggests infection. Drawing a circle around the swollen area with a pen will help you determine if the infection is spreading or resolving.

Treatment of Infection. An infection that is localized to the site of the injury can be treated in the field. If the edges of the wound are closed, pull them apart and soak the area in warm antiseptic solution or warm water for 20 to 30 minutes three to four times a day. If the infection starts to spread—as evidenced by fever, chills, swollen lymph nodes, or faint red streaks radiating from the site—or if the wound cannot be opened to drain, evacuate the patient. If you have oral antibiotics and a protocol for their use, start them early in suspected wound infections.

—From *NOLS Wilderness Medicine*

Treatment of Wounds and Skin Ailments

U.S. Army

Open Wounds

Open wounds are serious in a survival situation, not only because of tissue damage and blood loss, but also because they may become infected. Bacteria on the object that made the wound, on the individual's skin and clothing, or on other foreign material or dirt that touches the wound may cause infection.

By taking proper care of the wound you can reduce further contamination and promote healing. Clean the wound as soon as possible after it occurs by—

- Removing or cutting clothing away from the wound.

- Always looking for an exit wound if a sharp object, gun shot, or projectile caused a wound.

- Thoroughly cleaning the skin around the wound.

- Rinsing (not scrubbing) the wound with large amounts of water under pressure. You can use fresh urine if water is not available.

The "open treatment" method is the safest way to manage wounds in survival situations. Do not try to close any wound by suturing or similar procedures. Leave the wound open to allow the drainage of any pus resulting from infection. As long as the wound can drain, it generally will not become life-threatening, regardless of how unpleasant it looks or smells.

Cover the wound with a clean dressing. Place a bandage on the dressing to hold it in place. Change the dressing daily to check for infection.

If a wound is gaping, you can bring the edges together with adhesive tape cut in the form of a "butterfly" or "dumbbell."

In a survival situation, some degree of wound infection is almost inevitable. Pain, swelling, and redness around the wound, increased temperature, and pus in the wound or on the dressing indicate infection is present.

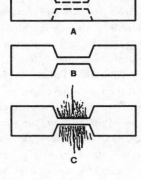

Butterfly closure.

To treat an infected wound—

- Place a warm, moist compress directly on the infected wound. Change the compress when it cools, keeping a warm compress on the wound for a total of 30 minutes. Apply the compresses three or four times daily.

- Drain the wound. Open and gently probe the infected wound with a sterile instrument.

- Dress and bandage the wound.

- Drink a lot of water.

Continue this treatment daily until all signs of infection have disappeared.

If you do not have antibiotics and the wound has become severely infected, does not heal, and ordinary debridement is impossible, consider maggot therapy, despite its hazards:

- Expose the wound to flies for one day and then cover it.

- Check daily for maggots.

- Once maggots develop, keep wound covered but check daily.

- Remove all maggots when they have cleaned out all dead tissue and before they start on healthy tissue. Increased pain and bright red blood in the wound indicate that the maggots have reached healthy tissue.

- Flush the wound repeatedly with sterile water or fresh urine to remove the maggots.

- Check the wound every four hours for several days to ensure all maggots have been removed.

- Bandage the wound and treat it as any other wound. It should heal normally.

Skin Diseases and Ailments

Although boils, fungal infections, and rashes rarely develop into a serious health problem, they cause discomfort and you should treat them.

Boils

Apply warm compresses to bring the boil to a head. Then open the boil using a sterile knife, wire, needle, or similar item. Thoroughly clean out the pus using soap and water. Cover the boil site, checking it periodically to ensure no further infection develops.

Fungal Infections

Keep the skin clean and dry, and expose the infected area to as much sunlight as possible. Do not scratch the affected area. During the Southeast Asian conflict, soldiers used antifungal powders, lye soap, chlorine bleach, alcohol, vinegar, concentrated salt water, and iodine to treat fungal infections with varying degrees of success. *As with any "unorthodox" method of treatment, use it with caution.*

Rashes

To treat a skin rash effectively, first determine what is causing it. This determination may be difficult even in the best of situations. Observe the following rules to treat rashes:

- If it is moist, keep it dry.

- If it is dry, keep it moist.

- Do not scratch it.

Use a compress of vinegar or tannic acid derived from tea or from boiling acorns or the bark of a hardwood tree to dry weeping rashes. Keep dry rashes moist by rubbing a small amount of rendered animal fat or grease on the affected area.

Remember, treat rashes as open wounds and clean and dress them daily. There are many substances available to survivors in the wild or in captivity for use as antiseptics to treat wounds:

Continued ➡

- *Iodine tablets.* Use 5 to 15 tablets in a liter of water to produce a good rinse for wounds during healing.
- *Garlic.* Rub it on a wound or boil it to extract the oils and use the water to rinse the affected area.
- *Salt water.* Use 2 to 3 tablespoons per liter of water to kill bacteria.
- *Bee honey.* Use it straight or dissolved in water.
- *Sphagnum moss.* Found in boggy areas worldwide, it is a natural source of iodine. Use as a dressing.

Again, use noncommercially prepared materials with caution.

—From *Survival (Field Manual 21–76)*

Care for Common Conditions

Greg Davenport

Burns

Burns are rated by depth as first, second, or third degree, each indicating increasingly deeper penetration. A first-degree burn causes superficial tissue damage, sparing the underlying skin, and is similar in appearance to a sunburn. A second-degree burn causes damage into the upper portion of the skin, with resultant blister formation that is surrounded by first-degree burn damage. A third-degree burn causes complete destruction of the skin's full thickness and often beyond. In addition, first- and second-degree burns are usually present.

To treat burns, cool the skin as rapidly as possible and for at least forty-five minutes. This is extremely important, since many burns continue to cause damage for up to forty-five minutes, even after the heat source has been removed. Remove clothing and jewelry as soon as possible, but don't remove any clothing that is stuck in the burn. Never cover the burn with grease or fats, as they will only increase the risk of infection and are of no value in the treatment process. Clean the burn with water (preferably sterile), apply antibiotic ointment, and cover it with a clean, loose dressing. To avoid infections, leave the bandage in place for six to eight days. After that time, change the bandage as necessary. If the victim is conscious, fluids are a must. Major burns cause a significant amount of fluid loss, and ultimately the victim will go into shock unless these fluids are replaced. If pain medications are available, use them. Burns are extremely painful.

Foreign Bodies in the Eye

Most eye injuries encountered in the wilderness are a result of dust, dirt, or sand blown into the eye by the wind. Symptoms include a red and irritated eye, light sensitivity, and pain in the affected eye. To treat, first look for any foreign bodies that might be causing the irritation. The most common site where dirt or dust can be found is just under the upper eyelid. Invert the lid and try to find and remove the irritant. If you're unable to isolate the cause, rinse the affected eye with clean water for at least ten to fifteen minutes. When rinsing, keep the injured eye lower than the uninjured to avoid contaminating the other eye. Apply ophthalmic antibiotic ointment, if available, to the affected eye.

Wounds, Lacerations, and Infections

Clean all wounds, lacerations, and infections, and apply antibiotic ointment, a dressing, and a bandage daily.

Blisters

Blisters result from the constant rubbing of your skin against a sock or boot. The best treatment is prevention. Monitor your feet for hot spots or areas that become red and inflamed. If you develop a hot spot, apply a wide band of adhesive tape across and well beyond the affected area. If you have tincture of benzoin, use it. It will make the tape adhere better, and it also helps toughen the skin. To treat a blister, cut a blister-size hole in the center of a piece of moleskin, and place it so that the hole is directly over the blister. This will take the pressure off the blister and place it on the surrounding moleskin. Avoid popping the blister. If it does break open, treat it as an open wound, applying antibiotic ointment and a bandage.

Thorns, Splinters, and Spines

Thorns and splinters are often easy to remove. Cactus spines, however, hook into the skin, and in most cases you'll need a pair of tweezers or pliers to get them out. If you can't pull out the spines, don't panic. They often come out on their own over a period of several days. Whether or not you remove them, prevent infection and protect the area by applying antibiotic ointment, a dressing, and a bandage.

Sun Blindness

Sun blindness is a result of exposure of the eyes to the sun's ultraviolet rays. It most often occurs in areas where sunlight is reflected off sand, snow, water, or light-colored rocks. The resultant burn to the eyes' surface can be quite debilitating. Symptoms include bloodshot and tearing eyes, a painful and gritty sensation in the eyes, light sensitivity, and headaches. Prevention by wearing 100 percent UV sunglasses is a must. If sun blindness does occur, avoid further exposure, apply a cool wet compress to the eyes, and treat the pain with aspirin as needed. If symptoms are severe, apply an eye patch for twenty-four to forty-eight hours.

Bowel Disturbances

Bowel disturbances in the wilderness are common and include diarrhea and constipation.

Diarrhea

Diarrhea is a very common occurrence in a survival situation. In the desert, diarrhea can lead to dehydration and hyponatremia. Some common causes are changes in water and food consumption, drinking contaminated water, eating spoiled food, eating off dirty dishes, and fatigue or stress. Diarrhea is almost always self-limiting, and unless you have antidiarrhea medications, treatment should consist of supportive care. Consume clear liquids for twenty-four hours, and follow with another twenty-four hours of clear liquids plus bland foods.

Constipation

Constipation is common in a survival setting. To treat, drink fluids and exercise. Laxatives are contraindicated and rarely needed.

—From *Surviving the Desert*

Treating Common Camping Injuries

U.S. Army Corps of Engineers

Burns

Burns may be caused by a variety of agents such as fire, the sun, or any boiling liquid.

There are three degrees of burns:

1. First Degree
2. Second Degree
3. Third Degree

All three require special attention.

FIRST DEGREE BURNS

Symptoms: redness mild swelling pain caused by the sun or heat.

Aid: Submerge in cold water for the length of time the pain persist.

SECOND DEGREE BURNS

Symptoms: redness blisters caused by a severe sun burn, liquid, or fire burn.

Aid: Immerse in cold water for 1–2 hrs. Apply freshly ironed or cleaned bandages, that have been wrung out in ice water, then apply to burn.

THIRD DEGREE BURNS

Symptoms: This degree of burn destroys all layers of the skin, and damages the nerves. May appear white or charred (black). The red blood cells are destroyed. This burn is usually caused by flame, ignited clothing, hot objects, or electricity.

Procedure: Don't remove clothing attached to burn. Cover burned areas with sterile dressings, or freshly ironed or cleaned linens.

If the hands or feet are involved: Keep them above the heart by elevating them with a pillow. If the face is burned: Have the victim sit up.

If medical aid is more than an hour away:
Give the victim a weak solution of:

1 level teaspoon salt
1/2 level teaspoon baking soda
1 quart of water

This should be given: 1/2 glass every 15 minutes. Aspirin may be given for pain.
Seek medical attention immediately!

Choking

Cause: food or other particles in the airway.

Procedure: Grab the victim from behind. Lock your arms around his/her abdominal area just above the belly button and below the rib cage. Jerk your arms into the victim's abdominal area. This should be done in quick thrust to force the food or foreign matter out.

Even though breathing has been restored, foreign matter may still remain, resulting in serious complications. Seek medical attention immediately.

Continued →

Fish Hooks in Hand

If the barb has *not* penetrated the skin: Just back the hook out.

If the barb *has* penetrated the skin: Push the hook on through until the barb comes out the other side. Cut one end of the hook off. Pull the other half on out of the skin, as diagramed:

In any case: *Get a tetanus shot*

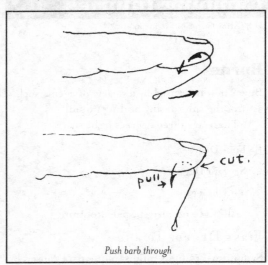

Push barb through

Carbon Monoxide Poisoning

Cause: Using charcoal to dry out a tent.

Symptoms: cherry red color in skin, dizziness, headache

Procedure: Remove victim from hazard, seek medical assistance, loosen clothing, and clear airway. If victim has stopped breathing, begin artificial respiration.

Fainting

Cause: insufficient amount of blood to the brain.

Symptom: paleness, sweating, coldness, dizziness, numbness in the feet and hands, then blackout.

Procedure: Keep the victim down, loosen clothing, bathe face with a cool washcloth. Examine victim for injury from his/her fall.

Unless recovery is prompt, seek medical attention.

—From *Camper's First Aid*

Allergies and Anaphylaxis
Tod Schimelpfenig

Signs and Symptoms of Mild to Moderate Allergic Reactions

Allergic reactions range from mild to severe, and they can be immediate or delayed. For most people, the allergic response is mild, though often irritating. Hay fever is one example of a mild allergic response. Hay fever sufferers complain of a runny nose, sneezing, swollen eyes, itching skin, and possibly hives. An allergic reaction may also be local, the result of insect stings or contact with a plant. The local reaction is red, swollen, and itching, perhaps with hives, but stays near the point of contact.

Treatment for Mild to Moderate Allergic Reactions

First remove the allergen from the patient or the patient from the offending environment. It's hard to treat a pollen reaction standing under a tree shedding millions of pollen grains or to treat an allergy to dust in a dusty cabin. Antihistamines and decongestants are the usual treatment. The antihistamines treat the underlying reaction, the release of too much histamine. Monitor the patient closely for a developing severe reaction.

Signs and Symptoms of Severe Allergic Reactions

An anaphylactic response is a massive, generalized reaction of the immune system that is potentially harmful to the body. Common triggers of anaphylaxis are drugs and some foods; people can also react to bee stings and insect bites. Instead of the mild symptoms of hay fever, anaphylaxis produces asphyxiating swelling of the larynx, rapid pulse, a rapid fall in blood pressure, rash itching, hives, flushed skin, swollen and red eyes, tearing of the eyes, swelling of the feet and hands, nausea, vomiting, and abdominal pain. The airway obstruction and shock may be fatal. Onset usually occurs within a few minutes of contact with the triggering substance, although the reaction may be delayed. Any large areas of swelling, typically involving the face, lips, hands, and feet; respiratory compromise; or shock should be treated with epinephrine.

Treatment of Severe Allergic Reactions

If you catch the allergic reaction while the patient can still swallow, administer oral antihistamines. When the reaction becomes severe, the anaphylaxis is treated with immediate administration of epinephrine, a prescription medication, to counteract the effects of the histamine. Persons who know that they are vulnerable to anaphylactic shock usually carry injectable

---

Blisters
Steven Boga

A "hot spot" is the first sign of a blister. Treat with tape (some people swear by duct tape), Second Skin, Moleskin, or Newskin to protect against further rubbing.

Do not open a blister unless it is the size of a nickel or larger and there is danger of its rupturing or interfering with walking. If you do plan to open a blister, wash your hands and clean the skin with soap and water. Sterilize a pin or needle over a flame, holding the end of the pin with a cloth, then let it cool. Puncture the base of the blister, not the center, and let it drain from the pinprick. Apply an antibiotic ointment, then cover with a light bandage, a piece of gauze, or a thin foam pad with a hole in the center.

Check daily for signs of infection—reddening, swelling, or pus. See a doctor if infection occurs.

—From *Orienteering*

---

epinephrine in an TwinJect or EpiPen. Trip leaders should be familiar with their use and seek the advice of a physician advisor when responding to this emergency.

Use of the EpiPen

1. Unscrew the yellow or green cap off of the EpiPen or EpiPen Jr and remove the auto-injector from its storage tube.

2. Grasp unit with the black tip pointing downward. Form fist around the unit (black tip down).

3. With your other hand, pull off the gray safety release.

4. Swing and jab firmly into outer thigh until it clicks. (Auto-injector is designed to work through clothing.)

5. Hold firmly against thigh for approximately 10 seconds. (The injection is now complete. Window on auto-injector will show red.)

6. Remove unit from thigh and massage injection area for 10 seconds.

7. Carefully place the used auto-injector (without bending the needle), needle-end first, into the storage tube of the carrying case for needle protection after use.

—From *NOLS Wilderness Medicine*

Respiratory and Cardiac Emergencies
Tod Schimelpfenig

A history of asthma, heart disease, or even a heart attack does not, by itself, prevent someone from paddling a river, climbing a peak, or hiking the Wind River Range. The wilderness first responder will see these medical conditions and should be knowledgeable in their assessment and treatment.

Hyperventilation Syndrome

Hyperventilation syndrome is an increased respiratory rate caused by an overwhelming emotional stimulus. The patient becomes apprehensive, nervous, or tense. For example, a person may normally have a fear of heights, and the thought of rock climbing triggers a hyperventilation episode, or a climber may fall and suffer a minor injury but begin to hyperventilate out of fear and anxiety. The hyperventilation can quickly become the major condition affecting the patient.

Signs and Symptoms of Hyperventilation. Signs and symptoms of hyperventilation include a high level of anxiety, a sense of suffocation without apparent physiological basis, rapid and deep respiration, rapid pulse, dizziness and/or faintness, sweating, and dry mouth.

As the syndrome progresses, the patient may complain of numbness or tingling of the hands or around the mouth. Thereafter, painful spasms of the hands and forearms—carpopedal spasms—may occur. The hands curl inward and become immobile. The patient may complain of stabbing chest pain. Rapid respiration increases the loss of carbon dioxide, which causes the

Continued ➡

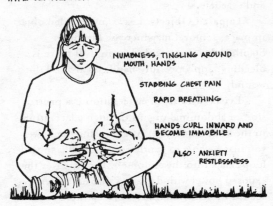

CARPOPEDAL SPASMS
HYPERVENTILATION SYNDROME:

NUMBNESS, TINGLING AROUND
MOUTH, HANDS

STABBING CHEST PAIN

RAPID BREATHING

HANDS CURL INWARD AND
BECOME IMMOBILE.

ALSO: ANXIETY
RESTLESSNESS

blood to become alkaline. The alkaline blood causes the carpopedal spasms.

Treatment for Hyperventilation. To treat hyperventilation syndrome, calm the patient and slow his or her breathing. Coach the patient to breathe slowly. It may take some time before the symptoms resolve. Breathing into a paper bag, once thought to help increase carbon dioxide in the blood, is no longer a recommended treatment.

Pulmonary Embolism

A pulmonary embolism occurs when a clot (usually from a leg vein) breaks loose and lodges in the blood vessels of the lung. Pulmonary embolus is not uncommon outside the wilderness and can be a tough diagnosis. Decreased mobility—lying in a tent waiting out a storm, for example, or long plane flights—may predispose a person to a blood clot. Smoking and a history of recent surgery or illness that kept the patient in bed are also risk factors. There is an increased tendency for blood to clot in arteries and veins at high altitudes. Dehydration, increased red blood cells, cold, constrictive clothing, and immobility during bad weather have been cited as possible causes.

Signs and Symptoms of Pulmonary Embolism. The patient complains of a sudden onset of shortness of breath and pain with inspiration. Respiratory distress may develop, including anxiety and restlessness; shortness of breath; rapid breathing and pulse; signs of shock, including pale, cool, and clammy skin and cyanosis of the skin, lips, and fingernail beds; and labored breathing using accessory muscles of the neck, shoulder, and abdomen to achieve maximum effort.

Treatment for Pulmonary Embolism. First responders can't dissolve the embolism in the field. You can identify the respiratory distress, administer oxygen if it is available, and evacuate the patient promptly.

Pneumonia

Pneumonia is a lung infection that can be caused by bacteria, viruses, fungi, and protozoa. The inflammation of the alveolar spaces causes swelling and fluid accumulation. Difficulty breathing can result. People weakened by an illness, chronic disease, fatigue, or exposure are especially at risk. Pneumonia can be a serious infection and is a leading cause of death.

Signs and Symptoms of Pneumonia. Signs and symptoms of pneumonia are shortness of breath, fever and chills, a productive cough with green-yellow or brown sputum, and pain on inspiration or coughing. The patient may have a recent history of upper respiratory infection and lung sounds, if you can listen with a stethoscope, may be noisy.

Treatment of Pneumonia. Patients with pneumonia should be evacuated. Encourage the patient to cough and breathe deeply to keep the lungs clear. Hydration is important, and oxygen, if available, will be helpful. The patient may be more comfortable sitting up.

Asthma

Asthma is an allergic response characterized by narrowing of the airways, increased mucous production, and bronchial edema. Asthma's exact cause is unknown. We do know that allergy and environmental factors such as molds, cold air, chemical fumes, cigarette smoke, exercise, and infections play a role.

Asthma is usually a reversible condition. The airway narrowing can improve spontaneously or in response to medication. A prolonged, severe asthma attack that is not relieved by treatment is an emergency requiring rapid transport. There are other chronic lung diseases, such as emphysema and bronchitis, in which the breathing impairment is persistent because of destruction of lung tissue and chronic inflammation.

Signs and Symptoms of Asthma. Signs and symptoms of mild to moderate asthma are wheezing, chest tightness, and shortness of breath. The heart and breathing rates are increased. When asthma becomes severe, the patient may be hunched over, bracing the upper body and working to breathe. The patient may be able to speak only in one- or two-word clusters. Lung sounds may be diminished or absent. If the patient becomes sleepy or too fatigued to breathe, the situation is dire.

Treatment of Asthma. Usually the patient treats the asthma by self-administering medication, commonly a bronchodilator, with an inhaler. You may need to help the patient relax and use the inhaler properly; shake it first, hold it in the mouth, exhale, and then depress the device and inhale the mist deeply, holding the breath for 5 to 10 seconds before exhaling. To stabilize the initial exacerbation, aggressive use of the patient's inhaler (3, 4, or 5 treatments) might be needed. Warm, humidified air can help relax airways and clear mucus. Severe asthma episodes may require medications (epinephrine and steroids) usually not available in the wilderness, and such patients should be evacuated promptly.

Chest Pain and Heart Disease

Heart disease is a leading cause of death in the United States. Atherosclerosis, a common form of heart disease, slowly builds deposits on arterial walls that narrow the artery and impede blood flow. The narrowed artery can spasm, constrict, or lodge a clot, depriving tissue of blood. If this happens in the brain, the result may be a stroke. If it happens in the heart, it causes chest pain, also known as angina pectoris,

or a myocardial infarction, a heart attack. Angina is pain from diminished blood flow. A myocardial infarction is heart muscle damage from blocked blood flow. Sudden death from a heart that beats erratically, or not at all, can be a result of this disease.

Signs and Symptoms of Cardiac Chest Pain. Cardiac chest pain is often described as crushing, tight, pressing, viselike, and constricting. It is below the breastbone and can radiate into the left arm and jaw. Shortness of breath, anxiety, pale sweaty skin, nausea, and dizziness are also common complaints. The pulse may be irregular. If the pain is brought on by physical or emotional stress and is relieved by rest, it may be angina. If it is unprovoked and persists, it may be a myocardial infarction.

Treatment for Cardiac Chest Pain. Figuring out whether nontraumatic chest pain is a heart condition can be difficult under the best of circumstances. Inflammation of the stomach or esophagus, chest muscle strains, rib injury, lung problems, bronchitis, and coughing can all cause chest pain. To complicate the situation, cardiac pain does not always fit the classic pattern and description. A patient with chest pain symptoms that cannot be attributed to a chest injury, lung problem, stomach upset, or muscle strain should be given one-half adult aspirin (160mg) every 12 hours and evacuated. Reduce the demands on the heart by calming the patient and making him or her rest. If available, administer oxygen. If your patient has a history of cardiac chest pain, he or she may have nitroglycerin, a medication administered by placing a tablet under the tongue.

—From *NOLS Wilderness Medicine*

Abdominal Illness

Tod Schimelpfenig

There are many, many illnesses that can develop within the abdomen. This section is by no means exhaustive, but it does cover problems that, in our experience, we tend to see in the backcountry. The most important part of this chapter is the final section, which reminds us not to worry about diagnosis, but rather to do a sound assessment and decide if the patient meets the evacuation criteria.

Kidney Stones

Kidney stones occur when minerals precipitate from the urine in the kidney. Approximately three-quarters of kidney stones are crystallized calcium. Predisposing factors for kidney stones include urinary tract infections, dehydration, an increase in dietary calcium, too much vitamin D, and cancer.

Signs and Symptoms of Kidney Stones. As a stone passes down the ureter, the patient experiences excruciating pain that comes and goes with increasing intensity. The pain usually begins at the level of the lowest ribs on the back and radiates to the lower abdomen and/or groin. The patient is pale, sweaty, nauseated, and "writhing" in pain. There may be pain with urination and blood in the urine. Chills and fever are not

Continued →

present. The duration of the pain depends on the location of the stone. Pain is severe while a stone is passing from the kidney to the bladder and stops after the stone has dropped into the bladder. The pain may last as long as 24 hours, but the duration is usually shorter.

Treatment for Kidney Stones. Drinking copious amounts of water may help the patient pass the stone. Pain medication may help. If pain continues for more than 48 hours or if the patient is unable to urinate, evacuate.

Appendicitis

Appendicitis is an inflammation of the appendix, usually caused by a kinking of the appendix or by a hardened stool obstructing the opening. Due to the obstruction, mucus builds within the appendix, causing pressure, swelling, and infection. The highest incidence of appendicitis occurs in males between the ages of 10 and 30.

Signs and Symptoms of Appendicitis. The classic symptoms of appendicitis are pain behind the umbilicus (the navel), anorexia, nausea, and vomiting. The usually develop gradually over 1 to 2 days. The pain then shifts to the lower right quadrant, halfway between the umbilicus and the right hipbone. The patient may have one or two bowel movements but usually does not have diarrhea. When you apply pressure with your hand over the appendix, the patient may complain of pain when you remove your hand. This is called rebound tenderness. A fever and elevated pulse may be present. Due to infection and pain, the patient may lie on his or her side or back with legs tucked onto the abdomen (fetal position). There may also be pain when the patient jumps, walks, or jars his or her right leg or side.

Before the appendix ruptures, the skin over the appendix becomes hypersensitive. If you stroke the skin surface with a pin or grasp the skin between the thumb and forefinger and pull upward, the patient may complain of pain. If the appendix ruptures, the pain temporarily disappears but soon reappears as the abdominal cavity becomes infected (peritonitis). If the infection remains localized (abscess), the patient may only run a low fever and complain of not feeling well. The abscess may not rupture for a week or more.

Treatment for Appendicitis. Appendicitis is a surgical emergency. The patient must be evacuated.

Peritonitis

Peritonitis is an inflammation of the peritoneum. Causes include penetrating abdominal wounds, abdominal bleeding, or ruptured internal organs that spill digestive juices into the abdominal cavity.

Signs and Symptoms of Peritonitis. Signs and symptoms of peritonitis vary, depending on whether the infection is local or general. The patient lies very still, as movement increases the pain. He or she may complain of nausea, vomiting, anorexia, and/or fever. The abdomen is rigid and tender. The infection causes peristaltic activity of the bowel to stop, so the patient has no bowel movements. Shock may be present. The patient appears very sick.

Treatment for Peritonitis. Peritonitis is a severe infection beyond our capability to treat in the wilderness; treat the patient for shock and evacuate.

Hemorrhoids

Hemorrhoids are varicose veins of the anal canal. They may be internal or external. Constipation, straining during elimination, diarrhea, and pregnancy can cause hemorrhoids. External hemorrhoids can be very painful. Internal hemorrhoids tend not to be painful but bleed during bowel movements. The stool may be streaked on the outside with blood. The patient may complain of itching around the anus.

Treatment for Hemorrhoids. Apply moist heat to the anal area. This can be done with a bandanna dipped in warm water. Rest, increased liquid and fruit intake to keep the stools soft, and/or anesthetic ointments (such as dibucaine, Preparation H, or Anusol) help decrease pain and bleeding.

Gastric and Duodenal Ulcers

Decreased resistance of the stomach lining to pepsin and hydrochloric acid, or an increase in the production of these chemicals, may result in ulcers. Stress, smoking, aspirin use, certain bacteria, caffeine or alcohol consumption, and heredity are possible causes.

Signs and Symptoms of Ulcers. The patient complains of a gnawing, aching, or burning in the upper abdomen at the midline 1 to 2 hours after eating or at night, when gastric secretions are at their peak. The pain may radiate from the lowest ribs to the back and frequently disappears if the patient ingests food or antacids.

Is it indigestion, or is it an ulcer? Indigestion symptoms tend to be associated with eating. The patient complains of fullness and heartburn and may belch or vomit small amounts of food. Indigestion worsens when more food is ingested. As time passes and the stomach empties, symptoms disappear. Indigestion tends to be related to a single meal.

Treatment for Ulcers. The primary treatment for ulcers is to take antacids an hour after meals; eat small, frequent meals; and avoid coffee, alcohol, and spicy foods, which increase the secretions of the stomach. Long-term treatment includes rest and counseling to decrease stress. If the ulcer perforates the wall of stomach, symptoms of peritonitis occur.

Abdominal Trauma

Abdominal organs are either solid or hollow. When hollow organs are perforated, they spill their contents into the abdominal cavity. Solid organs tend to bleed when injured. Either bleeding or spillage of digestive juices causes peritonitis.

Blunt Trauma. Inspect the abdomen for bruises; consider how the injury occurred to diagnose what, if any, organs may have been damaged. Pain, signs and symptoms of shock, and a significant mechanism of injury are reasons to initiate an evacuation.

Penetrating Wounds. Assume that any penetrating wound to the abdomen has entered the peritoneal lining. Treat the patient for shock and evacuate.

Impaled Objects. Leave any impaled object in place; removal may increase bleeding. Stabilize the object with dressings. If there is bleeding, apply pressure bandages around the wound.

Evisceration. An evisceration is a protrusion of abdominal organs through a laceration in the abdominal wall. After rinsing the bowel you may be able to gently "tease" small exposed loops back into the abdomen. If not, cover the exposed bowel with dressings that have been soaked in disinfected water. Keep these moist to prevent the exposed loops of bowel from becoming dry. Change the dressings daily. Treat for shock and evacuate the patient.

Abdominal Assessment

The first responder needs a few simple skills to be able to evaluate the condition of a patient with an abdominal problem.

1. Inspect the abdomen. Position the patient in a warm place, lying down. Remove the patient's clothing so that you can see the entire abdomen. A normal abdomen is slightly rounded and symmetrical. Look for old scars, areas of bruising, rashes, impaled objects, eviscerations, and distention. Check the lower back for the same. Look for any movement of the abdomen—wavelike contractions may indicate an abdominal obstruction.

2. Listen to the abdomen in all quadrants. Place your ear on the patient's abdomen and listen for bowel sounds (gurgling noises). An absence of noise indicates an injured or ill bowel. You must listen for at least 2 to 3 minutes in all quadrants before you can properly say that no bowel sounds are present.

3. Palpate the abdomen. With your palms down, apply gentle pressure with the pads of the fingers. Make sure your hands are warm and that you palpate in all the quadrants. Cold fingers or jabbing can cause the patient to tighten the abdominal muscles, thereby impeding the assessment. The abdomen should be soft and not tender. Abnormal signs include localized tenderness, diffuse tenderness, and stiff, rigid muscles ("board-like abdomen").

4. Discuss the patient's condition with him or her. Ask about pain: Where is it located, where does it radiate to, and what is the severity and frequency? What aggravates or alleviates the pain? Are there patterns to the pain (at night, after meals, etc.)? Ask the patient about his or her past medical history. Any past surgery, diagnoses, treatment, or injuries? Any problems with swallowing, digestion, or bowel, bladder, or reproductive organs?

—From *NOLS Wilderness Medicine*

Diabetes, Seizures, and Unresponsive States

Tod Schimelpfenig

Diabetes

Diabetes is a disease of sugar metabolism, affecting, by conservative estimates, 10 million Americans. It is a complex disease characterized by a broad array of physiological disturbances. In the long term, diabetic complications include high blood pressure and heart and blood vessel disease; it can also affect vision, kidneys, and healing of wounds. In the short term, the disturbance in sugar metabolism can manifest itself as too much or too little sugar in the blood.

Diabetes is thought to be caused by genetic defects, infection, autoimmune processes, or direct injury to the pancreas. The pancreas produces the hormones, most notably insulin, that help regulate sugar balance. Insulin facilitates the movement of sugar from the blood into the cells. An excess of insulin promotes the movement of sugar into the cells, lowers the blood sugar level, and deprives the brain cells of a crucial nutrient. This disorder is known as hypoglycemia (low blood sugar).

In contrast, a deficit of insulin results in cells that are starved for sugar and an excess of sugar in the blood, disturbing fluid and electrolyte balance. This disorder is known as hyperglycemia (high blood sugar) or diabetic coma.

A healthy pancreas constantly adjusts the insulin level to the blood sugar level. The pancreas of a person with diabetes produces defective insulin or no insulin. To compensate for this, a diabetic takes medication to stimulate endogenous insulin or takes artificial insulin. Treatment plans for diabetics also include diet and exercise.

Hypoglycemia

Hypoglycemia results from the treatment of diabetes, not the diabetes itself. If a diabetic takes too much insulin or fails to eat sufficient sugar to match the insulin level, the blood sugar level will be insufficient to maintain normal brain function.

Hypoglycemia can occur if the diabetic skips a meal but takes the usual insulin dose, takes more than the normal insulin dose, exercises strenuously and fails to eat, or vomits a meal after taking insulin.

Signs and Symptoms of Hypoglycemia. Hypoglycemia has a rapid onset. The most prominent symptoms are alterations in mental status due to a lack of sugar to the brain. The patient may be irritable, nervous, weak, and uncoordinated; may appear intoxicated; or, in more serious cases, may become unresponsive or have seizures. The pulse is rapid; the skin pale, cool, and clammy.

Treatment for Hypoglycemia. Brain cells need sugar and can suffer permanent damage from low blood sugar levels. The treatment of hypoglycemia is to administer sugar. If the patient is awake, a sugar drink or candy bar can help increase the blood sugar level. If the patient is unresponsive, establish an airway, then place a small paste of sugar between the patient's cheek and gum. Sugar is absorbed through the oral mucosa. Improvement is usually quick after the administration of sugar.

Hyperglycemia

Diabetics who are untreated, who have defective or insufficient insulin, or who become ill may develop a high level of sugar in the blood. Consequences of this may be dehydration and electrolyte disturbances as the kidneys try to eliminate the excess sugar, and acid-base disturbances as cells starved for sugar turn to alternative energy sources.

Signs and Symptoms of Hyperglycemia. Hyperglycemia tends to develop more slowly than hypoglycemia. The first symptoms are often nausea, vomiting, thirst, and increased volume of urine output. The patient's breath may have a fruity odor from the metabolism of fats as an energy source. The patient may also have abdominal cramps or pain and signs of dehydration, including flushed, dry skin and intense thirst. Unresponsiveness is a late and very serious symptom.

Treatment of Hyperglycemia. This patient has a complex physical disturbance and needs the care of a physician. Treatment is supportive: airway maintenance, vital signs, and treatment for shock. Dehydration is a serious complication of hyperglycemia. If the patient is alert, give oral fluids.

Hypoglycemia or Hyperglycemia?

Hypoglycemia usually has a rapid onset; the patient is pale, cool, and clammy and has obvious disturbances in behavior or altered mental status. Hyperglycemia has a gradual onset. Often, the patient is in an unexplained coma, with flushed, dry skin. A fruity breath odor may be present. A patient with hypoglycemia will respond to sugar; a hyperglycemic patient will not, but the extra sugar will cause no harm.

Two questions to ask any diabetic patient are: Have you eaten today? And have you taken your insulin today? If the patient has taken insulin but has not eaten, you should suspect hypoglycemia. The patient will have too much insulin, not enough sugar, and a blood sugar level that is too low to sustain normal brain function. If the patient has eaten but has not taken insulin, hyperglycemia should be suspected. This person has more sugar in the blood than can be transported to the cells.

Most persons with diabetes are very knowledgeable about their reactions and intuitively know if they are getting into trouble. Many diabetics measure their blood sugar levels daily and their urine for ketones. If you're on a wilderness trip with a diabetic, learn his or her medication and eating routines, how he or she measures his or her blood sugar and his or her daily fluctuations in blood sugar level. This can make you familiar with his or her management of diabetes, and helpful if he or she becomes hypo- or hyperglycemic.

When we're sick, we're under stress and we use hormones to fight the infection. Some of these hormones both raise blood sugar and interfere with insulin. The result is that it's more challenging for diabetics to regulate blood sugar when they are sick. A diabetic should have a "sick day" plan, and the trip leader needs to know what that is. The components of a sick day plan include insulin adjustment, food and fluid intake, and decision points for evacuation such as urine ketone, hyperglycemia, and vomiting. Thresholds for evacuation may be: several days of illness without relief; vomiting or diarrhea for more than 6 hours; moderate to large amounts of ketones in urine; blood glucose readings consistently greater than normal despite taking extra insulin; early signs of hyperglycemia; loss of a sense of control of blood sugar levels.

It is important for persons with diabetes to eat at regular intervals. If there is a possibility that a diabetic's insulin could be lost or destroyed—for example, by a boat flipping on the river—make sure that someone else in the group is carrying an extra supply. With control and care, diabetics can participate without problems in any activity.

Seizures

A seizure is a disruption of the brain's normal activity by a massive paroxysmal electrical discharge from brain cells. The seizure begins at a focus of brain cells, then spreads through the brain and to the rest of the body through peripheral nerves. This electrical disturbance may cause violent muscle contractions throughout the body or result in localized motor movement and possible loss of responsiveness.

The causes of seizures include high fever, head injury, low blood sugar, stroke, poisoning, and epilepsy. Low blood sugar is a cause of seizures in diabetics. Brain cells are sensitive to low oxygen and sugar levels, and if these fall below acceptable levels, a seizure may be triggered. The most common cause of seizures is epilepsy, a disease that manifests as recurring seizures.

The onset of epilepsy is not well understood. Often it begins in childhood or adolescence, but it can also be a consequence of a brain injury. Most persons with epilepsy control their seizures with medication. Interruption of the medication or inadequate dosage is frequently the cause of seizures.

At one time, seizures were attributed to mental illness. The source of these misperceptions may have been the dramatic visual impact of a writhing, moaning person having a seizure. Educating bystanders and group members about epilepsy and seizures can help alleviate such misunderstandings.

Signs and Symptoms of Seizures. The typical generalized seizure begins with a short period, usually less than a minute, of muscle rigidity, followed by several minutes of muscle contractions. The patient may feel the seizure approaching and warn bystanders or cry out at the onset of the episode. The patient suddenly falls to the ground, twitching and jerking.

As muscular activity subsides, the patient remains unresponsive but relaxed. He or she may drool, appear cyanotic, and become incontinent. Pulse and respiratory rate may be rapid. The patient may initially be unresponsive or

Continued →

difficult to arouse, but in time—usually within 10 to 15 minutes—the patient becomes awake and oriented.

Treatment of Seizures. When the seizure has subsided, open the airway, assess for injuries, and take vital signs. Place the patient on his or her side during the recovery phase to help maintain an open airway.

Treatment for a seizure is supportive and protective care. You cannot stop the seizure, but you can protect the patient from injury. The violent muscle contractions of a seizure may cause injury to the patient and to well-meaning bystanders who attempt to restrain the patient. Move objects that the patient may hit. Pad or cradle the head if it is bouncing on the ground. A patient in seizure will not swallow the tongue; however, the airway may become obstructed by saliva or secretions, and the patient may bite his or her tongue.

An accurate description of the seizure tells the physician much about the onset and extent of the problem. In most cases, a seizure runs its course in a few minutes. Repeated seizures, especially repeated seizures in which the patient does not regain responsiveness in between, and seizures associated with another medical problem such as diabetes or head injury are serious medical conditions.

An epileptic patient with an isolated seizure requires evaluation by a physician but does not require a rapid evacuation. These occasional seizures are often due to changes in the patient's need for medication or failure to take the medication as prescribed. After recovering from the seizure, the patient should be well fed and hydrated and assessed for any injury that may have occurred during the seizure.

Unresponsive States

A responsive patient can react to the environment and protect himself or herself from sources of pain and injury. An unresponsive patient is in danger. He or she is mute and defenseless, unable to rely on even the gag reflex to protect the airway. Many conditions cause unresponsiveness: head injury, stroke, epilepsy, diabetes, alcohol intoxication, drug overdose, and fever.

A patient who is unresponsive for unexplained reasons poses a difficult diagnostic problem . . . Since obtaining a history of an unresponsive patient is impossible, carefully question bystanders for any background information they may be able to provide.

Often, all you can do is support the patient and transport him or her to a physician for further evaluation. Care for an unresponsive patient includes airway maintenance and cervical spine precautions unless trauma can be ruled out entirely. If you are unsure why a patient is unresponsive, place some sugar between the patient's cheek and gum. This will help a hypoglycemic patient and won't hurt a patient who is unresponsive for any other season.

—From NOLS Wilderness Medicine

Bites and Stings
Greg Davenport

Snakebites

Treat all snakebites as though poisonous unless you can positively identify the snake as nonpoisonous. Of those that are poisonous, few are ever fatal or debilitating with proper medical intervention. Poisonous snakebites are often categorized as hemotoxic, damaging blood vessels and causing hemorrhage, or neurotoxic, paralyzing nerve centers that control respiration and heart action. Common signs that envenomization has occurred include some of the following:

HEMOTOXIC ENVENOMIZATION
(RATTLESNAKE, PUFF ADDER,
SIDEWINTER, SAND VIPER, HORNED
VIPER)

Immediate: one or more fang marks and bite site burning.

5 to 10 minutes: mild to severe swelling at the bite site.

30 to 60 minutes: numbness and tingling of the lips, face, fingers, toes, and scalp. If these symptoms occur immediately following a bite, they are likely due to anxiety and hyperventilation.

30 to 90 minutes: twitching of the mouth, face, neck, eye, and bitten extremity. In addition, the victim may develop a metallic or rubbery taste in the mouth.

1 to 2 hours: sweating weakness, nausea, vomiting, chest tightness, rapid breathing, increased heart rate, palpitations, headache, chills, confusion, and fainting.

2 to 3 hours: the area begins to appear bruised.

6 to 10 hours: large blood blisters often develop.

6 to 12 hours: difficulty breathing, increased internal bleeding, and collapse.

NEUROTOXIC ENVENOMIZATION
(CORAL SNAKE, COBRA, KRAITS,
MAMBAS)

Immediate: bite site burning may or may not occur, and only a small amount of localized bruising and swelling is often noted.

Within 90 minutes: numbness and weakness of the bitten extremity.

1 to 3 hours: twitching, nervousness, drowsiness, giddiness, increased salivation, and drooling.

5 to 10 hours: slurred speech, double vision, difficulty talking and swallowing, and impaired breathing.

10 hours or more: death is often the end result without medical intervention.

Snakebite treatment centers on getting the victim to a medical facility as fast as you safely can. In doing so, follow these basic treatment guidelines to increase survivability:

• Have the victim move out of the snake's range, then stop, lie down, and stay still.

Physical activity will increase the spread of the venom. If you can do so safely, try to identify the kind of snake. If you can kill the snake, do so and bring it along for identification purposes. Protect yourself from accidental poisoning by cutting off the head and burying it.

• Remove the toxin from the wound site as soon as possible using a mechanical suction device, following the manufacturer's instructions, or by squeezing for thirty minutes. Don't cut and suck. This will hasten the spread of the poison and also expose the small blood vessels under the the aid giver's tongue to the venom.

• Remove all jewelry and restrictive clothing from the victim.

• Clean the wound, and apply a dressing and bandage. Do not pour alcoholic beverages on the wound, and do not apply ice. Circulation to the site is already impaired, and applying ice may cause symptoms similar to severe frostbite. If the bite is on an extremity and you are more than two hours from a medical facility, use a pressure dressing over the wound or constrictive band—not a tourniquet—placed 2 inches above the site, between it and the heart. This will help restrict the spread of the poison.

—Pressure dressing. Place a clean dressing over the bite and cover it with an elastic wrap that encircles the extremity. The wrap should be about 10 inches wide and centered firmly on top of the bite site. Although it should be snug, make sure it isn't so tight that it cuts off the circulation to the fingers or toes. Nail bed capillary refill should return with two to three seconds, and the victim should have normal feeling beyond the dressing site. To assess capillary refill, press on the victim's fingernail and count how many seconds it takes for it to resume its pink color once released.

—Constrictive band. A constrictive band is not a tourniquet. It is used to slow down the flow in the superficial veins and lymph system. Use any material that allows you to create a 4-inch-wide band, wrapping it around the extremity so that it is between the bite and the heart. If limb swelling makes the band too tight, it can be moved up the extremity.

• After a dressing or band is applied, splint the extremity. The victim should keep the wound site positioned below the level of the heart.

• Have the victim drink small amounts of water.

• Transport the victim to the nearest hospital.

It's best to take precautions to avoid snakebites in the first place. Avoid known habitats like rocky ledges and woodpiles. If you see a snake, leave it alone unless you intend to kill it for food. Carry a walking stick that can be used for protection, and wear boots and full-length pants.

Continued ➜

Lizard Bites

The Gila monster and its cousin, the Mexican beaded lizard, are the only two known species of venomous lizards. Both are similar in appearance and habits, but the Mexican beaded lizard is slightly larger and darker. The Gila monster averages 18 inches in length and has a large head, stout body, short legs, strong claws, and a thick tail that acts as a food reservoir. Its skin is coarse and beadlike, with a marbled coloring that combines brown or black with orange, pink, yellow, or dull white. Most of the lizard's teeth have two grooves that guide the venom, a neurotoxin that affects the nervous system, from glands in the lower jaw. The venom enters the wound as the lizard chews on its victim. Although a bite can be fatal to humans, it usually isn't. Treatment for lizard bites is the same as that for a snakebite.

Animal Bites

Thoroughly clean the site and treat it as any other open wound.

Insects, Centipedes, Spiders, and Scorpions

Clean any sting or bite that cannot be identified, and use antihistamines when appropriate. Remove any stingers using whatever means are suitable. In most cases, this is done by scraping a knife or similar item 90 degrees across the stinger. Monitor for secondary infection and treat with antibiotics if one occurs.

Bee or Wasp

If stung, immediately remove the stinger by scraping the skin, at a 90-degree angle, with a knife or your fingernail. This will decrease the amount of venom that is absorbed into the skin. Applying cold compresses and/or a cool paste made of mud or ashes will help relieve the itching and pain. To avoid infection, don't scratch the stinger site. Carry along a bee sting kit, and review the procedures of its use prior to departing for the wilderness. If someone has an allergic anaphylactic reaction, it's necessary to act fast. Using the medications in the bee sting kit and following basic first-aid principles will reverse the symptoms associated with this type of reaction in most cases. Regardless of results, it's best to get the victim to the nearest hospital as soon as possible when anaphylaxis occurs.

Kissing Bug (Conenose Bug)

The kissing bug is dark brown to black with reddish-orange spots on the abdomen and measures 1/2 to 1 inch long. It has a cone-shaped head on a long body and three pairs of legs. It usually bites and feeds on the blood of its victim when the victim is asleep. The name kissing bug is derived from the fact that the bug often bites its victims on the lips. These bugs often live inside rodent and birds' nests and are seen in spring and early summer. The bites may be painful and cause redness, swelling, and itching. In some instances, sensitive individuals can have a serious allergic reaction that causes severe itching, rash,

nausea, vomiting, and breathing problems. Anaphylactic reaction can occur in very sensitive people. Treatment involves cleaning the site and using antihistamines when necessary. If allergic, use a bee sting kit and seek immediate medical attention.

Ants

Ants, especially fire ants, can produce very painful bites that often leave small, clear blisters on the skin. The biggest concern aside from pain is avoidance of secondary infection. Clean the bite with soap and water, and use antihistamines if needed. If an infection occurs, treat as any other infection. If allergic, use a bee sting kit and seek immediate medical attention.

Ticks

Remove a tick by grasping it at the base of its body, where its mouth is attached to the skin, and applying gentle backward pressure until it releases its hold. If its head isn't removed, apply antibiotic ointment, bandage, and treat as any other open wound.

Mosquitoes and Flies

To minimize the number of bites you'll experience from these pesky insects, use insect repellent and cover the body's exposed parts with clothing or mud. Insects that carry parasitic, viral, and bacterial agents transmit vector-borne diseases. Common diseases are malaria (in the tropics) and West Nile virus. Since wild and domestic birds carry West Nile virus, it appears to have no boundaries; mosquitoes become carriers when they bite an infected bird. The risk of getting the virus is seasonal, beginning in the spring and reaching its peak in mid-to late August. Approximately 80 percent of those infected will not have any symptoms. When symptoms do occur, they usually only last a few days and include fever, headache, muscle aches, backache, skin rash, and swollen lymph glands. In rare cases the infection can lead to an infection in the brain or its lining. Treatment is supportive and includes rest, fluids, and pain control. If you think you have been infected, you should seek out medical care as soon as possible.

Centipedes and Millipedes

Centipedes inject venom using fanglike front legs. Millipedes have toxins on their bodies that, when touched, are highly irritating. Both can cause redness, swelling, and pain to the bite site. If bitten, clean the area with soap and water. Use a pain medication if needed.

Spiders

Desert spiders avoid the searing heat by taking cover in burrows or under rocks, emerging at night to eat. The most prominent dangerous spiders of the deserts are the black widow, brown recluse, and tarantulas.

BLACK WIDOW

The black widow's venom is fifteen times as toxic as the venom of the prairie rattlesnake, and it is considered the most venomous spider in North America. However, black widow spiders inject only a relatively small amount of venom and are not usually deadly to adults. Only the female spider is venomous. The black widow female is

shiny black and often has a reddish hourglass shape on the underside of her spherical abdomen. Her body is about 1 1/2 inches long. The adult male is harmless, about half the female's size, with a smaller body and longer legs, and usually has yellow and red bands and spots over the back. The black widow's bite may be painless and go unnoticed. Symptoms may include muscle cramps (including the abdomen), sweating, swollen eyelids, nausea, vomiting, headache, and hypertension. To treat, clean the site well with soap and water. Apply a cool compress over the bite location, and keep the affected limb elevated to about heart level. Persons younger than sixteen and older than sixty, especially those with a heart condition, may require hospitalization. Healthy people recover rapidly in two to five days.

BROWN RECLUSE

The brown recluse spider is 1/4 to 1/2 inch long, has a yellowish to brown color, and supports a distinct violin-shaped patch on its head and midregion. Its bite causes a long-lasting sore that involves tissue death and takes months to heal. In some instances, its bite can become life threatening. The bite initially causes mild stinging or burning and is quickly followed by ulcerative necrosis that develops within several hours to weeks. The initial sore is often red, edematous, or blanched, and a blue-gray halo often develops around the puncture. As time passes, the lesion may evolve into ashen pustules or fluid-filled lesions surrounded by red, patchy skin. After several days, the tissue begins to die. Other symptoms include fever, weakness, rash, muscle and joint pain, vomiting, and diarrhea. To treat, clean the site with soap and water, immobilize the site, and apply a local compress. Use a pain medication if needed. The bite site ultimately needs rapid debridement. Transport the victim to a medical facility as soon as possible.

TARANTULAS

Tarantulas have hairy bodies and legs come in a wide range of colors, from a soft tan through reddish brown to dark brown or black. The desert tarantula can grow to be 2 to 3 inches long and is common to the Sonoran, Chihuahuan, and Mojave Deserts of the U.S. Southwest. When confronted, a tarantula will rub its hind legs over its body, brushing off irritating hairs onto its enemy. Skin exposed to this hair is prone to an itching rash. A tarantula bite to humans is rare, and even if venom is injected, it rarely causes more than slight swelling, numbness, and itching. To treat a tarantula bite, clean the site with soap and water, and protect against infection. Treat skin exposures to tarantula hairs by removing the hairs with tape.

Scorpions

Scorpions are among the best-adapted creatures to desert climates. The scorpion has a flat, narrow body, two lobsterlike claws, eight legs, and a segmented abdominal tail. Its upward and forward curved tail has a venomous stinger supplied by a pair of poison glands. Most scorpions are tan to brown in color and range from 1 to 8 inches in length. Their stings are generally painful but not fatal to humans. Other symptoms may include swelling at the site of the sting,

Continued ➡

The female black widow has a reddish hourglass on its abdomen.

The brown recluse has a violin-shaped patch on its head and midregion.

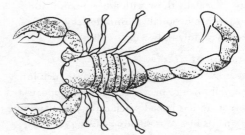

The scorpion has a venomous stinger at the end of its tail.

Mosquito Bites
Steven Boga

Mosquitoes are prolific and voracious, and willing to give their life for one last shot at your juicy self. You have to admire that kind of dedication.

The first rule in mosquito country is to know your limitations. You can't kill or outrun them all. Lured by your warmth and expired carbon dioxide, they move in for the attack. Even if they don't strike (only the females bite), their incessant whining in your ears may drive you to take up indoor sports.

The second rule, for me, is to use a chemical repellent containing DEET (diethyl metatoluamide). The powerful DEET is absorbed through the skin—48 percent of an application is absorbed within six hours. This means it can cause side effects. The most common side effect is a rash, but occasionally anxiety, behavioral changes, lethargy, and mental confusion have been reported. If you agree with me that it's worth the risk, apply it sparingly to skin and liberally on clothes. After applying DEET, wash your hands or keep them away from your eyes and mouth. With young children, don't use a repellent with more than about a 30 percent concentration of DEET. If you prefer an alternative to DEET, try Natrapel, which contains citronella.

If you insist on being bitten, don't scratch. Always an attraction to mosquitoes, I used to be a mad scratcher, which resulted in quarter-size welts followed by hideous scabs followed by scars. Eventually, I learned that if I can get through the first half-hour without scratching, the welt goes away. Anti-itch medicines may help you resist.

—From *Orienteering*

numbness, muscle twitching, difficulties in breathing, and convulsions. Death is rare. There are a few species, some twenty worldwide, whose venom is potentially fatal, but survival rates are generally high. A scorpion's poison is neurotoxic, and treatment should follow that of a neurotoxic snakebite.

—From *Surviving the Desert*

Leeches
U.S. Army

Leeches are blood-sucking creatures with a wormlike appearance. You find them in the tropics and in temperate zones. You will certainly encounter them when swimming in infested waters or making expedient water crossings. You can find them when passing through swampy, tropical vegetation and bogs. You can also find them while cleaning food animals, such as turtles, found in fresh water. Leeches can crawl into small openings; therefore, avoid camping in their habitats when possible. Keep your trousers tucked in your boots. Check yourself frequently for leeches. Swallowed or eaten, leeches can be a great hazard. It is therefore essential to treat water from questionable sources by boiling or using chemical water treatments. Survivors have developed severe infections from wounds inside the throat or nose when sores from swallowed leeches became infected.

—From *Survival (Field Manual 21–76)*

Human or Animal Bites
U.S. Army

Human or other land animal bites may cause lacerations or bruises. In addition to damaging tissue, bites always present the possibility of infection.

Human Bites

Human bites that break the skin may become seriously infected since the mouth is heavily contaminated with bacteria. Medical personnel MUST treat all human bites.

Animal Bites

Land animal bites can result in both infection and disease. Tetanus, rabies, and various types of fevers can follow an untreated animal bite. Because of these possible complications, the animal causing the bite should, if possible, be captured or killed (without damaging its head) so that it can be tested for disease.

First Aid

1. Cleanse the wound thoroughly with soap.

2. Flush it well with water.

3. Cover it with a sterile dressing.

4. Immobilize the injured arm or leg, if appropriate.

5. Transport the casualty immediately to an MTF [medical treatment facility].

Note: If unable to capture or kill the animal, provide medical personnel with any information that will help identify it.

—From *First Aid (Field Manual 4–25.11)*

How to Extract Porcupine Quills
Allan Macfarlan

A dog or a man pierced by quills may die because the barbed quills work their way into the flesh and may ultimately penetrate a vital organ. Get to a veterinarian or a doctor as quickly as you can, but if that is impossible, you must pull the quills out yourself with pliers. A dog should be firmly tied with a stick lashed between his jaws so that he cannot bite before you undertake the painful task. Snip the ends of the hollow quills off so that they deflate slightly and can be yanked out more easily. A good disinfectant should be used afterward since porky picks up a lot of dirt on his barbed quills.

—From *Exploring the Outdoors with Indian Secrets*

Poison Oak/Ivy/Sumac Rashes
Steven Boga

Poison oak, ivy, and sumac contain an irritant called urushiol, a sap found in the roots, stems, and leaves. The plant must be touched, bruised slightly, to release urushiol; you can't get a rash from just being in the neighborhood.

The best way to escape the wrath of urushiol is to know what the plants look like and stay away from them. Keep in mind the ditty "Leaves of three, let it be" (though if you take that too literally, you'll miss out on some good berries). The poison plants may cling to the ground or grow up the trunks of trees or along fences. They may look like shrubs, bushes, small trees, or vines. Leaves may be dull or glossy with sawtoothed or smooth edges. In autumn, the leaves may turn orange; in summer, poison ivy has white berries.

If you think you've touched poison plants, put on clean gloves and carefully remove your clothing. Wash everything in strong detergent. Wipe off your shoes. Wash your body with soap and water. (You might first try rubbing with an anti-poison ivy lotion such as Tecnu.)

If you develop an itchy rash, try not to scratch. Scratching won't cause the rash to spread, but it can lead to infection. The blisters don't contain urushiol, so you can't pass the rash to another person. However, if you have the oil on your body before the rash develops, you can pass it by touching someone.

Cold saltwater compresses, cool baths, calamine, baking soda, and over-the-counter cortisone cream offer relief. The best product I've found for drying up the blisters is Derma Pax. But even if you do nothing, you'll probably be rid of all traces in less than three weeks.

—From *Orienteering*

Continued ➡

Heat Injuries

Greg Davenport

Heat Rash

Heat rashes often occur in moist, covered areas of the body. These bumpy red irritants can be pretty uncomfortable. To treat, keep the area clean and dry, and air it out as much as you can. If you have hydrocortisone 1 percent cream, apply a thin layer to the rash twice a day.

Sunburn

Prevent sunburn by using a strong sunscreen before exposure to the hot sun. If sunburn should occur, apply cool compresses, avoid further exposure, and cover any areas that have or may become burned.

Muscle Cramps

Muscle cramps are a result of excessive salt loss from the body, exposure to a hot climate, or excessive sweating. Painful muscle cramps usually occur in the calf or abdomen while the victim's body temperature is normal. To treat, immediately stretch the affected muscle. The best way to prevent recurrence is to consume 2 to 3 quarts of water per day when engaged in minimal activity, and 4 to 6 quarts per day when in extreme cold or hot environments or perhaps even more during heavy activity.

Heat Exhaustion

Heat exhaustion is a result of physical activity in a hot environment and is usually accompanied by some component of dehydration. Symptoms include feeling faint or weak, cold and clammy skin, headache, nausea, and confusion. To treat, rest in a cool, shady area and drink plenty of water. Since heat exhaustion is a form of shock, you should lie down and elevate your feet 8 to 12 inches.

Heatstroke

Heatstroke occurs when the body is unable to adequately lose its heat. As a result, body temperature rises to such high levels that damage to the brain and vital organs occur. Symptoms include flushed dry skin, headache, weakness, lightheadedness, rapid full pulse, confusion, and in severe cases, unconsciousness and convulsions. Heatstroke is a true emergency and should be avoided at all costs. Immediate treatment is imperative. Immediately cool the victim by removing his or her clothing and covering the body with wet towels or by submersion in water that is cool but not icy. Fanning is also helpful. Be careful to avoid cooling to the point of hypothermia.

Hyponatremia

Hyponatremia is a potentially fatal condition that can occur under extremely hot conditions. It is caused by a lack of sodium in the blood and frequently occurs when someone drinks too much water while losing high levels of body salt through sweating. Symptoms are dizziness, confusion, cramps, nausea, vomiting, fatigue, frequent urination, and in extreme conditions, coma and even death. To treat, stop all activity, move to a shaded area, treat for shock, and have the victim eat salty foods along with small quantities of lightly salted water or sports drinks. If the victim's mental alertness decreases, seek immediate help.

—From *Surviving the Desert*

High-Altitude Illnesses

U.S. Army

Acclimatization

Terrestrial altitude can be classified into five categories. Low altitude is sea level to 5,000 feet. Here, arterial blood is 96 percent saturated with oxygen in most people. Moderate altitude is from 5,000 to 8,000 feet. At these altitudes, arterial blood is greater than 92 percent saturated with oxygen, and effects of altitude are mild and temporary. High altitude extends from 8,000 to 14,000 feet, where arterial blood oxygen saturation ranges from 92 percent down to 80 percent. Altitude illness is common here. Very high altitude is the region from 14,000 to 18,000 feet, where altitude illness is the rule. Areas above 18,000 feet are considered extreme altitudes. ...

Symptoms and Adjustments

A person is said to be acclimatized to high elevations when he can effectively perform physically and mentally. The acclimatization process begins immediately upon arrival at the higher elevation. If the change in elevation is large and abrupt, some soldiers can suffer from acute mountain sickness (AMS), high-altitude pulmonary edema (HAPE), or high-altitude cerebral edema (HACE). Disappearance of the symptoms of acute mountain sickness (from four to seven days) does not indicate complete acclimatization. The process of adjustment continues for weeks or months. The altitude at which complete acclimatization is possible is not a set point but for most soldiers with proper ascent, nutrition and physical activity it is about 14,000 feet.

Immediately upon arrival at high elevations, only minimal physical work can be performed because of physiological changes. The incidence and severity of AMS symptoms vary with initial altitude, the rate of ascent, and the level of exertion and individual susceptibility. Ten to twenty percent of soldiers who ascend rapidly (in less than 24 hours) to altitudes up to 6,000 feet experience some mild symptoms. Rapid ascent to 10,000 feet causes mild symptoms in 75 percent of personnel. Rapid ascent to elevations of 12,000 to 14,000 feet will result in moderate symptoms in over 50 percent of the soldiers and 12 to 18 percent may have severe symptoms. Rapid ascent to 17,500 feet causes severe, incapacitating symptoms in almost all individuals. Vigorous activity during ascent or within the first 24 hours after ascent will increase both the incidence and severity of symptoms. Some of the behavioral effects that will be encountered in unacclimatized personnel include:

- Increased errors in performing simple mental tasks.
- Decreased ability for sustained concentration.
- Deterioration of memory.
- Decreased vigilance or lethargy.
- Increased irritability in some individuals.
- Impairment of night vision and some constriction in peripheral vision (up to 30 percent at 6,000 feet).
- Loss of appetite.
- Sleep disturbances.
- Irregular breathing.
- Slurred speech.
- Headache.

Judgment and self-evaluation are impaired the same as a person who is intoxicated. ...

Acute Mountain Sickness

Acute mountain sickness is a temporary illness that may affect both the beginner and experienced climber. Soldiers are subject to this sickness in altitudes as low as 5,000 feet. Incidence and severity increases with altitude, and when quickly transported to high altitudes. Disability and ineffectiveness can occur in 50 to 80 percent of the troops who are rapidly brought to altitudes above 10,000 feet. At lower altitudes, or where ascent to altitudes is gradual, most personnel can complete assignments with moderate effectiveness and little discomfort.

Personnel arriving at moderate elevations (5,000 to 8,000 feet) usually feel well for the first few hours; a feeling of exhilaration or well-being is not unusual. There may be an initial awareness of breathlessness upon exertion and a need for frequent pauses to rest. Irregular breathing can occur, mainly during sleep; these changes may cause apprehension. Severe symptoms may begin 4 to 12 hours after arrival at higher altitudes with symptoms of nausea, sluggishness, fatigue, headache, dizziness, insomnia, depression, uncaring altitude, rapid and labored breathing, weakness, and loss of appetite.

A headache is the most noticeable symptom and may be severe. Even when a headache is not present, some loss of appetite and a decrease in tolerance for food occurs. Nausea, even without food intake, occurs and leads to less food intake. Vomiting may occur and contribute to dehydration. Despite fatigue, personnel are unable to sleep. The symptoms usually develop and increase to a peak by the second day. They gradually subside over the next several days so that the total course of AMS may extend from five to seven days. In some instances, the headache may become incapacitating and the soldier should be evacuated to a lower elevation.

Treatment for AMS includes the following:

- Oral pain medications such as ibuprofen or aspirin.
- Rest.
- Frequent consumption of liquids and light foods in small amounts.

Continued →

- Movement to lower altitudes (at least 1,000 feet) to alleviate symptoms, which provides for a more gradual acclimatization.

- Realization of physical limitations and slow progression.

- Practice of deep-breathing exercises.

- Use of acetazolamide in the first 24 hours for mild to moderate cases.

AMS is nonfatal, although if left untreated or further ascent is attempted, development of high-altitude pulmonary edema (HAPE) and or high-altitude cerebral edema (HACE) can be seen. A severe persistence of symptoms may identify soldiers who acclimatize poorly and, thus, are more prone to other types of mountain sickness.

Chronic Mountain Sickness

Although not commonly seen in mountaineers, chronic mountain sickness (CMS) (or Monge's disease) can been seen in people who live at sufficiently high altitudes (usually at or above 10,000 feet) over a period of several years. CMS is a right-sided heart failure characterized by chronic pulmonary edema that is caused by years of strain on the right ventricle.

Understanding High-Altitude Illnesses

As altitude increases, the overall atmospheric pressure decreases. Decreased pressure is the underlying source of altitude illnesses. Whether at sea level or 20,000 feet the surrounding atmosphere has the same percentage of oxygen. As pressure decreases the body has a much more difficult time passing oxygen from the lungs to the red blood cells and thus to the tissues of the body. This lower pressure means lower oxygen levels in the blood and increased carbon dioxide levels. Increased carbon dioxide levels in the blood cause a systemic vasodilatation, or expansion of blood vessels. This increased vascular size stretches the vessel walls causing leakage of the fluid portions of the blood into the interstitial spaces, which leads to cerebral edema or HACE. Unless treated, HACE will continue to progress due to the decreased atmospheric pressure of oxygen. Further ascent will hasten the progression of HACE and could possibly cause death.

While the body has an overall systemic vasodilatation, the lungs initially experience pulmonary vasoconstriction. This constricting of the vessels in the lungs causes increased workload on the right ventricle, the chamber of the heart that receives de-oxygenated blood from the right atrium and pushes it to the lungs to be re-oxygenated. As the right ventricle works harder to force blood to the lungs, its overall output is decreased thus decreasing the overall pulmonary perfusion. Decreased pulmonary perfusion causes decreased cellular respiration—the transfer of oxygen from the alveoli to the red blood cells. The body is now experiencing increased carbon dioxide levels due to the decreased oxygen levels, which now causes pulmonary vasodilatation. Just as in HACE, this expanding of the vascular structure causes leakage into interstitial space resulting in pulmonary edema or HAPE. As the edema or fluid in the lungs increases, the capability to pass oxygen to the red blood cells decreases thus creating a vicious cycle, which can quickly become fatal if left untreated.

High-Altitude Pulmonary Edema

HAPE is a swelling and filling of the lungs with fluid, caused by rapid ascent. It occurs at high altitudes and limits the oxygen supply to the body.

HAPE occurs under conditions of low oxygen pressure, is encountered at high elevations (over 8,000 feet), and can occur in healthy soldiers. HAPE may be considered a form of, or manifestation of, AMS since it occurs during the period of susceptibility to this disorder.

HAPE can cause death. Incidence and severity increase with altitude. Except for acclimatization to altitude, no known factors indicate resistance or immunity. Few cases have been reported after 10 days at high altitudes. When remaining at the same altitude, the incidence of HAPE is less frequent than that of AMS. No common indicator dictates how a soldier will react from one exposure to another. Contributing factors are:

- A history of HAPE.

- A rapid or abrupt transition to high altitudes.

- Strenuous physical exertion.

- Exposure to cold.

- Anxiety.

Symptoms of AMS can mask early pulmonary difficulties. Symptoms of HAPE include:

- Progressive dry coughing with frothy white or pink sputum (this is usually a later sign) and then coughing up of blood.

- Cyanosis—a blue color to the face, hands, and feet.

- An increased ill feeling, labored breathing, dizziness, fainting, repeated clearing of the throat, and development of a cough.

- Respiratory difficulty, which may be sudden, accompanied by choking and rapid deterioration.

- Progressive shortness of breath, rapid heartbeat (pulse 120 to 160), and coughing (out of contrast to others who arrived at the same time to that altitude).

- Crackling, cellophane-like noises (rales) in the lungs caused by fluid buildup (a stethoscope is usually needed to hear them).

- Unconsciousness, if left untreated. Bubbles form in the nose and mouth, and death results.

HAPE is prevented by good nutrition, hydration, and gradual ascent to altitude (no more than 1,000 to 2,000 feet per day to an area of sleep). A rest day, with no gain in altitude or heavy physical exertion, is planned for every 3,000 feet of altitude gained. If a soldier develops symptoms despite precautions, immediate descent is mandatory where he receives prompt treatment, rest, warmth, and oxygen. He is quickly evacuated to lower altitudes as a litter patient. A descent of 300 meters may help; manual descent is not delayed to await air evacuation. If untreated, HAPE may become irreversible and cause death. Cases that are recognized early and treated promptly may expect to recover with no aftereffects. Soldiers who have had previous attacks of HAPE are prone to second attacks.

Treatment of HAPE includes:

- Immediate descent (2,000 to 3,000 feet minimum) if possible; if not, then treatment in a monoplace hyperbaric chamber.

- Rest (litter evacuation).

- Supplemental oxygen if available.

- Morphine for the systemic vasodilatation and reduction of preload. This should be carefully considered due to the respiratory depressive properties of the drug.

- Furosemide (Lasix), which is a diuretic; given orally can also be effective.

- The use of mannitol should not be considered due to the fact that it crystallizes at low temperatures. Since almost all high-altitude environments are cold, using mannitol could be fatal.

- Nifidipine (Procardia), which inhibits calcium ion flux across cardiac and smooth muscle cells, decreasing contractility and oxygen demand. It may also dilate coronary arteries and arterioles.

- Diphenhydramine (Benadryl), which can help alleviate the histamine response that increases mucosal secretions.

High-Altitude Cerebral Edema

HACE is the accumulation of fluid in the brain, which results in swelling and a depression of brain function that may result in death. It is caused by a rapid ascent to altitude without progressive acclimatization. Prevention of HACE is the same as for HAPE. HAPE and HACE may occur in experienced, well-acclimated mountaineers without warning or obvious predisposing conditions. They can be fatal; when the first symptoms occur, immediate descent is mandatory.

Contributing factors include rapid ascent to heights over 8,000 feet and aggravation by overexertion.

Symptoms of HACE include mild personality changes, paralysis, stupor, convulsions, coma, inability to concentrate, headaches, vomiting, decrease in urination, and lack of coordination. The main symptom of HACE is a severe headache. A headache combined with any other physical or psychological disturbances should be assumed to be manifestations of HACE. Headaches may be accompanied by a loss of coordination, confusion, hallucinations, and unconsciousness. These may be combined with symptoms of HAPE. The victim is often mistakenly left alone since others may think he is only irritable or temperamental; no one should ever be ignored. The symptoms may rapidly progress to death. Prompt descent to a lower altitude is vital.

Preventive measures include good eating habits, maintaining hydration, and using a

Continued ➡

gradual ascent to altitude. Rest, warmth, and oxygen at lower elevations enhance recovery. Left untreated, HACE can cause death.

Treatment for HACE includes:

- Dexamethasone injection immediately followed by oral dexamethasone.

- Supplemental oxygen.

- Rapid descent and medical attention.

- Use of a hyberbaric chamber if descent is delayed.

Hydration in HAPE and HACE

HAPE and HACE cause increased proteins in the plasma, or the fluid portion of the blood, which in turn increases blood viscosity. Increased viscosity increases vascular pressure. Vascular leakage caused by stretching of the vessel walls is made worse because of this increased vascular pressure. From this, edema, both cerebral and pulmonary, occurs. Hydration simply decreases viscosity.

—From *Military Mountaineering (Field Manual 3—97.61)*

Cold Injuries

U.S. Army

The best way to deal with injuries and sicknesses is to take measures to prevent them from happening in the first place. Treat any injury or sickness that occurs as soon as possible to prevent it from worsening.

The knowledge of signs and symptoms and the use of the buddy system are critical in maintaining health. Following are cold injuries that can occur.

Hypothermia

Hypothermia is the lowering of the body temperature at a rate faster than the body can produce heat. Causes of hypothermia may be general exposure or the sudden wetting of the body by falling into a lake or spraying with fuel or other liquids.

The initial symptom is shivering. This shivering may progress to the point that it is uncontrollable and interferes with an individual's ability to care for himself. This begins when the body's core (rectal) temperature falls to about 35.5 degrees C (96 degrees F). When the core temperature reaches 35 to 32 degrees C (95 to 90 degrees F), sluggish thinking, irrational reasoning, and a false feeling of warmth may occur. Core temperatures of 32 to 30 degrees C (90 to 86 degrees F) and below result in muscle rigidity, unconsciousness, and barely detectable signs of life. If the victim's core temperature falls below 25 degrees C (77 degrees F), death is almost certain.

To treat hypothermia, rewarm the entire body. If there are means available, rewarm the person by first immersing the trunk area only in warm water of 37.7 to 43.3 degrees C (100 to 110 degrees F).

Caution

Rewarming the total body in a warm water bath should be done only in a hospital environment because of the increased risk of cardiac arrest and rewarming shock.

One of the quickest ways to get heat to the inner core is to give warm water enemas. Such an action, however, may not be possible in a survival situation. Another method is to wrap the victim in a warmed sleeping bag with another person who is already warm; both should be naked.

Caution

The individual placed in the sleeping bag with victim could also become a hypothermia victim if left in the bag too long.

If the person is conscious, give him hot, sweetened fluids. One of the best sources of calories is honey or dextrose; if unavailable, use sugar, cocoa, or a similar soluble sweetener.

Caution

Do not force an unconscious person to drink.

There are two dangers in treating hypothermia—rewarming too rapidly and "after drop." Rewarming too rapidly can cause the victim to have circulatory problems, resulting in heart failure. After drop is the sharp body core temperature drop that occurs when taking the victim from the warm water. Its probable cause is the return of previously stagnant limb blood to the core (inner torso) area as recirculation occurs. Concentrating on warming the core area and stimulating peripheral circulation will lessen the effects of after drop. Immersing the torso in a warm bath, if possible, is the best treatment.

Frostbite

This injury is the result of frozen tissues. Light frostbite involves only the skin that takes on a dull whitish pallor. Deep frostbite extends to a depth below the skin. The tissues become solid and immovable. Your feet, hands, and exposed facial areas are particularly vulnerable to frostbite.

The best frostbite prevention, when you are with others, is to use the buddy system. Check your buddy's face often and make sure that he checks yours. If you are alone, periodically cover your nose and lower part of your face with your mittened hand.

The following pointers will aid you in keeping warm and preventing frostbite when it is extremely cold or when you have less than adequate clothing:

- *Face.* Maintain circulation by twitching and wrinkling the skin on your face making faces. Warm with your hands.

- *Ears.* Wiggle and move your ears. Warm with your hands.

- *Hands.* Move your hands inside your gloves. Warm by placing your hands close to your body.

- *Feet.* Move your feet and wiggle your toes inside your boots.

A loss of feeling in your hands and feet is a sign of frostbite. If you have lost feeling for only a short time, the frostbite is probably light. Otherwise, assume the frostbite is deep. To rewarm a light frostbite, use your hands or mittens to warm your face and ears. Place your hands under your armpits. Place your feet next to your buddy's stomach. A deep frostbite injury, if thawed and refrozen, will cause more damage than a nonmedically trained person can handle. The chart below lists some do's and don'ts regarding frostbite.

Trench Foot and Immersion Foot

These conditions result from many hours or days of exposure to wet or damp conditions at a temperature just above freezing. The symptoms are a sensation of pins and needles, tingling, numbness, and then pain. The skin will initially appear wet, soggy, white, and shriveled. As it progresses and damage appears, the skin will take on a red and then a bluish or black discoloration. The feet become cold, swollen, and have a waxy appearance. Walking becomes difficult and the feet feel heavy and numb. The nerves and muscles sustain the main damage, but gangrene can occur. In extreme cases, the flesh dies and it may become necessary to have the foot or leg amputated. The best prevention is to keep your feet dry. Carry extra socks with you in a waterproof packet. You can dry wet socks against your torso (back or chest). Wash your feet and put on dry socks daily.

Dehydration

When bundled up in many layers of clothing during cold weather, you may be unaware that you are losing body moisture. Your heavy clothing absorbs the moisture that evaporates in the air. You must drink water to replace this loss of fluid. Your need for water is as great in a cold environment as it is in a warm environment. One way to tell if you are becoming dehydrated is to check the color of your urine on snow. If your urine makes the snow dark yellow, you are becoming dehydrated and need to replace body fluids. If it makes the snow light yellow to no color, your body fluids have a more normal balance.

Cold Diuresis

Exposure to cold increases urine output. It also decreases body fluids that you must replace.

Sunburn

Exposed skin can become sunburned even when the air temperature is below freezing. The sun's rays reflect at all angles from snow, ice, and water, hitting sensitive areas of skin—lips, nostrils, and eyelids. Exposure to the sun results

Do	Don't
· Periodically check for frostbite. · Rewarm light frostbite.	· Rub injury with snow. · Drink alcoholic beverages.
· Keep injured areas from refreezing.	· Smoke · Try to thaw out a deep frostbite injury if you are away from definitive medical care.

Continued →

451

in sunburn more quickly at high altitudes than at low altitudes. Apply sunburn cream or lip salve to your face when in the sun.

Snow Blindness

The reflection of the sun's ultraviolet rays off a snow-covered area causes this condition. The symptoms of snow blindness are a sensation of grit in the eyes, pain in and over the eyes that increases with eyeball movement, red and teary eyes, and a headache that intensifies with continued exposure to light. Prolonged exposure to these rays can result in permanent eye damage. To treat snow blindness, bandage your eyes until the symptoms disappear.

You can prevent snow blindness by wearing sunglasses. If you don't have sunglasses, improvise. Cut slits in a piece of cardboard, thin wood, tree bark, or other available material. Putting soot under your eyes will help reduce shine and glare.

Constipation

It is very important to relieve yourself when needed. Do not delay because of the cold condition. Delaying relieving yourself because of the cold, eating dehydrated foods, drinking too little liquid, and irregular eating habits can cause you to become constipated. Although not disabling, constipation can cause some discomfort. Increase your fluid intake to at least 2 liters above your normal 2 to 3 liters daily intake and, if available, eat fruit and other foods that will loosen the stool.

—From Survival *(Field Manual 21–76)*

Hypothermia
Cecil Kuhne

Hypothermia refers to a lowering of the body's temperature to a dangerous level. Any boater exposed to cold weather—and especially cold water—can become a victim. Once the body is thrust into cold water, the brain begins to conserve body heat by constricting blood vessels in the arms and legs. Shivering usually (but not always) begins as the body attempts to generate heat. Then the body's core temperature starts to drop. As it falls below 95 degrees F, there is difficulty with speech. Other symptoms of hypothermia typically include fatigue, apathy, forgetfulness, and confusion. Further decreases in temperature bring on muscle stiffness, irrational thinking, amnesia, and unconsciousness. If the victim becomes unconscious, the situation is extremely serious, and hospitalization is required as soon as possible. Death occurs when the body temperature drops below 78 degrees. In near-freezing water, the time from immersion to death can be as short as ten minutes.

Awareness of the causes of hypothermia—and the speed with which death can result—is the most important aspect of prevention. If you dump in very cold water, get out immediately, even if this means abandoning your boat to swim for shore. Even with protective clothing, hypothermia can set in quickly.

Treatment is simple, and the sooner, the better. First, replace wet clothes with dry ones, and then move the person into a warm shelter. If

the person is unable to generate his or her own body heat, rewarming is required. Hot liquids may help, but never give the victim alcoholic drinks, which dilate blood vessels, allowing even greater heat loss. Heat from a supplemental source should also be provided. If it's not possible to build a fire, body heat from others is helpful. They should be lightly clothed for best results.

Hypothermia can be prevented, to a large extent, by adequate clothing, proper food, and good physical conditioning. The best clothing for cold conditions is a wet suit or dry suit. The food you eat is also important. Sugar and carbohydrates are quickly oxidized to provide heat and energy. The physical condition of the boater is also a factor, so it pays to stay in good shape.

Hypothermia Symptoms

99–96 degrees F. The body starts to shiver intensely and cannot be controlled. The victim cannot do complex tasks.

95–91 degrees F. The victim still shivers violently and has trouble speaking clearly.

90–86 degrees F. Shivering decreases or stops, and the victim cannot think clearly. The muscles are stiff, but the victim keeps his posture. Total amnesia may occur. The victim usually can keep in psychological contact with the environment.

85–81 degrees F. The victim becomes irrational, loses contact with the environment, and drifts into stupor.

80–78 degrees F. The victim becomes unconscious and does not respond to the spoken word. The victim's heartbeat becomes irregular, and there are no reflexes.

Below 78 degrees F. Death will occur as the result of complications arising from failure of the cardiac and respiratory centers in the brain. These may include cardiac fibrillation and pulmonary edema. There is hemorrhage in the lungs.

Frostbite and Nonfreezing Cold Injury
Buck Tilton and John Gookin

Frostbite

Frostbite is the localized freezing of tissue, and it often goes hand in hand with hypothermia. Proper treatment of frostbite can save near-frozen tissue and reduce the damage to already frozen tissue.

As with hypothermia, frostbite is progressive. It starts as a superficial problem, with no actual freezing of tissue. Initially, skin is pale and numb, cold to the touch. If you notice it, treat it immediately with passive skin-to-skin contact: cover a nose with your warm hand, stick a cold hand against your warm stomach, or put cold toes against the warm abdomen of a friend. Don't rub the cold skin, and don't place it near a hot heat source, because numb tissue is very susceptible to heat injury. The skin should soon return to normal.

Untreated, the condition progresses to partial-thickness frostbite (partially frozen tissue),

indicated by pale, numb, cold skin. The skin moves when you gently press on it. This problem looks superficial, and you may not know whether it's true frostbite until the skin is warmed. Passive warming should begin immediately. Give ibuprofen, if available, and lots of water to drink. If blisters form after warming, you know that the problem was partial-thickness frostbite, and a physician should be consulted as soon as possible. In the meantime, do two things: (1) Leave the blister bubble intact; it protects the underlying tissue and lessens the chance for infection. (2) Be careful to prevent refreezing. Blisters can refreeze quickly, multiplying the damage.

Skin with full-thickness frostbite is pale, numb, and hard—unmoving to gentle touch. Normal field conditions make the warming of deep frostbite impractical. Often, all you can do is remove the clothing from the frostbitten part (unless it's frozen to the skin), gently bundle the frozen skin in lots of dry insulation, and evacuate the patient. If refreezing is unlikely, however, and you have the means available, full-thickness frostbite is best treated by rapid warming in water of approximately 104 to 108 degrees F (40 to 42 degrees C). Water that is too hot can cause heat damage, and water that is too cold delays warming. Warming is usually accomplished in thirty to forty minutes, but it's better to err on the side of caution and warm longer than necessary. Soft, dry cotton should be placed between thawed digits; otherwise, contact with the frostbitten skin should be avoided. Pain is often intense, and painkillers should be given when available, before thawing. Ibuprofen started as soon as possible seems to reduce the extent of tissue damage. Keep the patient well-hydrated, and prevent refreezing. Find a doctor as soon as possible.

To prevent frostbite, follow the same guidelines for preventing hypothermia. In addition, wear appropriate clothing; avoid snug clothing that restricts circulation, especially on the feet and hands. Take care to protect your skin from wind and from contact with cold metal and gasoline. Avoid alcohol and tobacco, which can impair blood flow. If your toes start to hurt from the cold, rejoice that the nerves are functional, and stop and warm them to prevent permanent injury.

Nonfreezing Cold Injury

Nonfreezing cold injury (NFCI), also known as immersion foot or trenchfoot, is a cold-weather emergency resulting from prolonged contact with cold—and usually moisture—which causes inadequate circulation and results in tissue damage. The foot first shows a bit of swelling and discoloration (usually white or bluish), and the patient may complain of numbness. This may be the only sign, unless the damage is substantial. Then, on warming, the foot swells extensively with excess fluid, and the damaged tissue typically looks red. The patient may complain of tingling pain, often severe, that doesn't let up. Blisters may form, followed by ulcers where the blisters have fallen off, revealing dead tissue underneath. In severe cases, gangrene may result.

If you think that you or a companion is developing NFCI, warm the foot in warm water (as for frostbite), then carefully dry it. You can

Continued ➡

also keep the foot elevated above the level of the heart while you gently warm it with passive skin-to-skin contact. If the foot looks dirty, carefully wash it before drying it. Do not rub the foot or place it near a strong heat source, such as a fire or stove, both of which can damage the tissue. Start the patient on a regimen of over-the-counter anti-inflammatory drugs (aspirin or, even better, ibuprofen), following the label directions. Keep the patient in dry socks at all times. It will probably take twenty-four to forty-eight hours before the severity of the damage is fully apparent. If the foot is hurting or obviously swollen or develops blisters, get the patient to a physician.

NFCI is encouraged by poor nutrition, dehydration, wet socks, inadequate clothing, and the constriction of blood flow by too-tight boots and socks. Make sure that your boots fit, with plenty of room for your socks, and keep a dry pair of socks on hand at all times (preferably packed in a plastic bag). People who sweat heavily are also more susceptible to NFCI, and an antiperspirant spray can reduce sweating and thus reduce the risk. Periodically, preferably twice a day, dry your feet and gently massage them before stuffing them back into your boots. Do not sleep in wet socks.

Once you have suffered NFCI, it can recur after a shorter exposure to cold, wet conditions. The damage is cumulative, and tends to grow worse with each repetition, along with the possibility of permanent consequences.

—From NOLS Winter Camping

Medical Problems Associated with Sea Survival

U.S. Army

At sea, you may become seasick, get saltwater sores, or face some of the same medical problems that occur on land, such as dehydration or sunburn. These problems can become critical if left untreated.

Seasickness

Seasickness is the nausea and vomiting caused by the motion of the raft. It can result in—

- Extreme fluid loss and exhaustion.
- Loss of the will to survive.
- Others becoming seasick.
- Attraction of sharks to the raft.
- Unclean conditions.

To treat seasickness—

- Wash both the patient and the raft to remove the sight and odor of vomit.
- Keep the patient from eating food until his nausea is gone.
- Have the patient lie down and rest.
- Give the patient seasickness pills if available. If the patient is unable to take the pills orally, insert them rectally for absorption by the body.

Note: Some survivors have said that erecting a canopy or using the horizon as a focal point helped overcome seasickness. Others have said that swimming alongside the raft for short periods helped, but extreme care must be taken if swimming.

Saltwater Sores

These sores result from a break in skin exposed to saltwater for an extended period. The sores may form scabs and pus. Do not open or drain. Flush the sores with fresh water, if available, and allow to dry. Apply an antiseptic, if available.

Immersion Foot, Frostbite, and Hypothermia

These problems are similar to those encountered in cold weather environments. Symptoms and treatment are the same as covered on page 451.

Blindness/Headache

If flame, smoke, or other contaminants get in the eyes, flush them immediately with salt water, then with fresh water, if available. Apply ointment, if available. Bandage both eyes 18 to 24 hours, or longer if damage is severe. If the glare from the sky and water causes your eyes to become bloodshot and inflamed, bandage them lightly. Try to prevent this problem by wearing sunglasses. Improvise sunglasses if necessary.

Constipation

This condition is a common problem on a raft. Do not take a laxative, as this will cause further dehydration. Exercise as much as possible and drink an adequate amount of water, if available.

Difficult Urination

This problem is not unusual and is due mainly to dehydration. It is best not to treat it, as it could cause further dehydration.

Sunburn

Sunburn is a serious problem in sea survival. Try to prevent sunburn by staying in shade and keeping your head and skin covered. Use cream or Chap Stick from your first aid kit. Remember, reflection from the water also causes sunburn.

—From Survival (Field Manual 21–76)

Saltwater Boils

Greg Davenport

After a week or two in a life raft, you probably will develop saltwater boils on areas of your skin that are in constant contact with the wet floor of the raft. These include your buttocks, knees, elbows, and hands. Prevention is the key. Try to keep the raft floor dry, and cover your skin with clothes, oils, or barrier creams. If a boil occurs, avoid further contact with the raft floor, and keep the wound clean, dry, and exposed to the air.

—From Surviving Coastal and Open Water

Injuries from Marine Animals

U.S. Army

With the exception of sharks and barracuda, most marine animals will not deliberately attack. The most frequent injuries from marine animals are wounds by biting, stinging, or puncturing. Wounds inflicted by marine animals can be very painful, but are rarely fatal.

Sharks, Barracuda, and Alligators. Wounds from these marine animals can involve major trauma as a result of bites and lacerations. Bites from large marine animals are potentially the most life threatening of all injuries from marine animals. Major wounds from these animals can be treated by controlling the bleeding, preventing shock, giving basic life support, splitting the injury, and by securing prompt medical aid.

Turtles, Moray Eels, and Corals. These animals normally inflict minor wounds. Treat by cleansing the wound(s) thoroughly and by splinting if necessary.

Jellyfish, Portuguese Man-of-War, Anemones, and Others. This group of marine animals inflict injury by means of stinging cells in their tentacles. Contact with the tentacles produces burning pain with a rash and small hemorrhages on the skin. Shock, muscular cramping, nausea, vomiting, and respiratory distress may also occur. Gently remove the clinging tentacles with a towel and wash or treat the area. Use diluted ammonia or alcohol, meat tenderizer, and talcum powder. If symptoms become severe or persist, seek medical assistance.

Spiny Fish, Urchins, Stingrays, and Cone Shells. These animals inject their venom by puncturing the skin with their spines. General signs and symptoms include swelling, nausea, vomiting, generalized cramps, diarrhea, muscular paralysis, and shock. Deaths are rare. Treatment consists of soaking the wounds in hot water (when available) for 30 to 60 minutes. This inactivates the heat sensitive toxin. In addition, further first aid measures (controlling bleeding, applying a dressing, and so forth) should be carried out as necessary.

—From First Aid (Field Manual 4-25.11)

Maintaining Health in Survival Situations

U.S. Army

To survive, you need water and food. You must also have and apply high personal hygiene standards.

Water

Your body loses water through normal body processes (sweating, urinating, and defecating). During average daily exertion when the atmospheric temperature is 20 degrees Celsius (C) (68 degrees Fahrenheit), the average adult loses and therefore requires 2 to 3 liters of water daily. Other factors, such as heat exposure, cold

Continued ➡

exposure, intense activity, high altitude, burns, or illness, can cause your body to lose more water. You must replace this water.

Dehydration results from inadequate replacement of lost body fluids. It decreases your efficiency and, if injured, increases your susceptibility to severe shock. Consider the following results of body fluid loss:

- A 5 percent loss of body fluids results in thirst, irritability, nausea, and weakness.

- A 10 percent loss results in dizziness, headache, inability to walk, and a tingling sensation in the limbs.

- A 15 percent loss results in dim vision, painful urination, swollen tongue, deafness, and a numb feeling in the skin.

- A loss greater than 15 percent of body fluids may result in death.

The most common signs and symptoms of dehydration are—

- Dark urine with a very strong odor.

- Low urine output.

- Dark, sunken eyes.

- Fatigue.

TREATING STINGS, PUNCTURES, AND IRRITANTS: A QUICK GUIDE

U.S. Army

Stings

1. Flush wound with salt water (fresh water stimulates toxin release).

2. Remove jewelry and watches.

3. Remove tentacles and gently scrape or shave skin.

4. Apply a steroid cream (if available).

5. DO NOT rub area with sand.

6. Treat for shock; artificial respiration may be required.

7. DO NOT use urine to flush or treat wounds.

Punctures

1. Immerse affected part in hot water or apply hot compresses for 30-60 minutes (as hot as victim can tolerate).

2. Cover with clean dressing.

3. Treat for shock as needed.

Skin Irritants (includes poison oak and poison ivy)

1. Wash with large amounts of water. Use soap (if available).

2. Keep covered to prevent scratching.

Infection

1. Keep wound clean.

2. Use iodine tablet solution or diluted betadine to prevent or treat infection.

3. Change bandages as needed.

—From *Survival, Evasion, and Recover*
(Field Manual 21-76.1)

- Emotional instability.

- Loss of skin elasticity.

- Delayed capillary refill in fingernail beds.

- Trench line down center of tongue.

- Thirst. Last on the list because you are already 2 percent dehydrated by the time you crave fluids.

You replace the water as you lose it. Trying to make up a deficit is difficult in a survival situation, and thirst is not a sign of how much water you need.

Most people cannot comfortably drink more than 1 liter of water at a time. So, even when not thirsty, drink small amounts of water at regular intervals each hour to prevent dehydration.

If you are under physical and mental stress or subject to severe conditions, increase your water intake. Drink enough liquids to maintain a urine output of at least 0.5 liter every 24 hours.

In any situation where food intake is low, drink 6 to 8 liters of water per day. In an extreme climate, especially an arid one, the average person can lose 2.5 to 3.5 liters of water per hour. In this type of climate, you should drink 14 to 30 liters of water per day.

With the loss of water there is also a loss of electrolytes (body salts). The average diet can usually keep up with these losses but in an extreme situation or illness, additional sources need to be provided. A mixture of 0.25 teaspoon of salt to 1 liter of water will provide a concentration that the body tissues can readily absorb.

Of all the physical problems encountered in a survival situation, the loss of water is the most preventable. The following are basic guidelines for the prevention of dehydration:

- *Always drink water when eating.* Water is used and consumed as a part of the digestion process and can lead to dehydration.

- *Acclimatize.* The body performs more efficiently in extreme conditions when acclimatized.

- *Conserve sweat not water.* Limit sweat-producing activities but drink water.

- *Ration water.* Until you find a suitable source, ration your water sensibly. A daily intake of 500 cubic centimeters (0.5 liter) of a sugar-water mixture (2 teaspoons per liter) will suffice to prevent severe dehydration for at least a week, provided you keep water losses to a minimum by limiting activity and heat gain or loss.

You can estimate fluid loss by several means. A standard field dressing holds about 0.25 liter (one-fourth canteen) of blood. A soaked T-shirt holds 0.5 to 0.75 liter.

- With a 0.75 liter loss the wrist pulse rate will be under 100 beats per minute and the breathing rate 12 to 20 breaths per minute.

- With a 0.75 to 1.5 liter loss the pulse rate will be 100 to 120 beats per minute and 20 to 30 breaths per minute.

- With a 1.5 to 2 liter loss the pulse rate will be 120 to 140 beats per minute and 30 to 40 breaths per minute. Vital signs above these rates require more advanced care.

Food

Although you can live several weeks without food, you need an adequate amount to stay healthy. Without food your mental and physical capabilities will deteriorate rapidly, and you will become weak. Food replenishes the substances that your body burns and provides energy. It provides vitamins, minerals, salts, and other elements essential to good health. Possibly more important, it helps morale.

The two basic sources of food are plants and animals (including fish). In varying degrees both provide the calories, carbohydrates, fats, and proteins needed for normal daily body functions.

Calories are a measure of heat and potential energy. The average person needs 2,000 calories per day to function at a minimum level. An adequate amount of carbohydrates, fats, and proteins without an adequate caloric intake will lead to starvation and cannibalism of the body's own tissue for energy.

Plant Foods

These foods provide carbohydrates—the main source of energy. Many plants provide enough protein to keep the body at normal efficiency. Although plants may not provide a balanced diet, they will sustain you even in the arctic, where meat's heat-producing qualities are normally essential. Many plant foods such as nuts and seeds will give you enough protein and oils for normal efficiency. Roots, green vegetables, and plant food containing natural sugar will provide calories and carbohydrates that give the body natural energy.

The food value of plants becomes more and more important if you are eluding the enemy or if you are in an area where wildlife is scarce. For instance—

- You can dry plants by wind, air, sun, or fire. This retards spoilage so that you can store or carry the plant food with you to use when needed.

- You can obtain plants more easily and more quietly than meat. This is extremely important when the enemy is near.

Animal Foods

Meat is more nourishing than plant food. In fact, it may even be more readily available in some places. However, to get meat, you need to know the habits of, and how to capture, the various wildlife.

To satisfy your immediate food needs, first seek the more abundant and more easily obtained wildlife, such as insects, crustaceans, mollusks, fish, and reptiles. These can satisfy your immediate hunger while you are preparing traps and snares for larger game.

Personal Hygiene

In any situation, cleanliness is an important factor in preventing infection and disease. It becomes even more important in a survival situation. Poor hygiene can reduce your chances of survival.

A daily shower with hot water and soap is ideal, but you can stay clean without this luxury. Use a cloth and soapy water to wash yourself. Pay special attention to the feet, armpits, crotch, hands, and hair as these are prime areas for

Continued ➡

infestation and infection. If water is scarce, take an "air" bath. Remove as much of your clothing as practical and expose your body to the sun and air for at least 1 hour. Be careful not to sunburn.

If you don't have soap, use ashes or sand, or make soap from animal fat and wood ashes, if your situation allows. To make soap—

- Extract grease from animal fat by cutting the fat into small pieces and cooking them in a pot.
- Add enough water to the pot to keep the fat from sticking as it cooks.
- Cook the fat slowly, stirring frequently.
- After the fat is rendered, pour the grease into a container to harden.
- Place ashes in a container with a spout near the bottom.
- Pour water over the ashes and collect the liquid that drips out of the spout in a separate container. This liquid is the potash or lye. Another way to get the lye is to pour the slurry (the mixture of ashes and water) through a straining cloth.
- In a cooking pot, mix two parts grease to one part potash.
- Place this mixture over a fire and boil it until it thickens.

After the mixture—the soap—cools, you can use it in the semiliquid state directly from the pot. You can also pour it into a pan, allow it to harden, and cut it into bars for later use.

Keep Your Hands Clean
Germs on your hands can infect food and wounds. Wash your hands after handling any material that is likely to carry germs, after visiting the latrine, after caring for the sick, and before handling any food, food utensils, or drinking water. Keep your fingernails closely trimmed and clean, and keep your fingers out of your mouth.

Keep Your Hair Clean
Your hair can become a haven for bacteria or fleas, lice, and other parasites. Keeping your hair clean, combed, and trimmed helps you avoid this danger.

Keep Your Clothing Clean
Keep your clothing and bedding as clean as possible to reduce the chance of skin infection as well as to decrease the danger of parasitic infestation. Clean your outer clothing whenever it becomes soiled. Wear clean underclothing and socks each day. If water is scarce, "air" clean your clothing by shaking, airing, and sunning it for 2 hours. If you are using a sleeping bag, turn it inside out after each use, fluff it, and air it.

Keep Your Teeth Clean
Thoroughly clean your mouth and teeth with a toothbrush at least once each day. If you don't have a toothbrush, make a chewing stick. Find a twig about 20 centimeters long and 1 centimeter wide. Chew one end of the stick to separate the fibers. Now brush your teeth thoroughly. Another way is to wrap a clean strip of cloth around your fingers and rub your teeth with it to wipe away food particles. You can also brush your teeth with small amounts of sand, baking soda, salt, or soap. Then rinse your mouth with water, salt water, or willow bark tea. Also, flossing your teeth with string or fiber helps oral hygiene.

If you have cavities, you can make temporary fillings by placing candle wax, tobacco, aspirin, hot pepper, tooth paste or powder, or portions of a ginger root into the cavity. Make sure you clean the cavity by rinsing or picking the particles out of the cavity before placing a filling in the cavity.

Take Care of Your Feet
To prevent serious foot problems, break in your shoes before wearing them on any mission. Wash and massage your feet daily. Trim your toenails straight across. Wear an insole and the proper size of dry socks. Powder and check your feet daily for blisters.

If you get a small blister, do not open it. An intact blister is safe from infection. Apply a padding material around the blister to relieve pressure and reduce friction. If the blister bursts, treat it as an open wound. Clean and dress it daily and pad around it. Leave large blisters intact. To avoid having the blister burst or tear under pressure and cause a painful and open sore, do the following:

- Obtain a sewing-type needle and a clean or sterilized thread.
- Run the needle and thread through the blister after cleaning the blister.
- Detach the needle and leave both ends of the thread hanging out of the blister. The thread will absorb the liquid inside. This reduces the size of the hole and ensures that the hole does not close up.
- Pad around the blister.

Get Sufficient Rest
You need a certain amount of rest to keep going. Plan for regular rest periods of at least 10 minutes per hour during your daily activities. Learn to make yourself comfortable under less than ideal conditions. A change from mental to physical activity or vice versa can be refreshing when time or situation does not permit total relaxation.

Keep Camp Site Clean
Do not soil the ground in the camp site area with urine or feces. Use latrines, if available. When latrines are not available, dig "cat holes" and cover the waste. Collect drinking water upstream from the camp site. Purify all water.

—From *Survival (Field Manual 21–76)*

Survival Stress
Greg Davenport

The effects of stress upon a survival situation cannot be understated. To decrease its magnitude, you must not only understand it but also prevail over it. The most important key to overcoming these survival stresses is the survivor's will. The will or drive to survive is not something that can be taught. However, your will is directly affected by the amount of stress associated with a survival situation.

Survival Stressors
The environment, your condition, and the availability of materials will either raise or decrease the amount of stress you'll experience.

Environmental Influences
Three environmental conditions directly affect your survival: climate (temperature, moisture, and wind); terrain (mountainous, desert, jungle, or arctic); and life forms (plants and animals). Sadly, many people have perished when these influences have been unfavorable. In other situations, however, survivors have been successful in either adapting to the given conditions or traveling to another location that better meets their needs. Understanding how the environment might affect you is the first step to overcoming the unpredictable hardships of nature.

Your Physical and Mental Condition
Both the physical and psychological stresses of survival will directly affect your outlook and may even dictate the order in which you meet your needs. To prioritize your needs properly, it is important to make decisions based on logic and not emotion. Recognizing the physical and psychological stresses of survival is the first step to ensuring that this is done.

Physical Stresses
These stresses are brought about by the physical hardships of survival. Overcoming them requires proper preparation. A good rule for all wilderness travelers is the six Ps of survival: Proper prior preparation prevents poor performance. Properly preparing involves ensuring that your immunizations are up-to-date, staying well hydrated both before and during any outback adventure, and being physically fit prior to traveling into the wilderness.

Psychological Stresses
The amount of time a survivor goes without rescue will have a significant impact upon his will or drive to survive. As time passes, the survivor's hopes of being found ultimately begin to diminish. With decreased hope comes increased psychological stress. The basic stresses that affect the survivor psychologically are pain, hunger and thirst, heat or cold, fatigue, loneliness, and fear.

Availability of Materials
The materials available to meet your needs include both what you have with you and what you can find in the surrounding environment. It's unlikely that a lone survivor will have all the necessary tools and equipment to meet all of his survival needs.

Overcoming Survival Stress
The most important key to surviving is the survivor's will. The will or drive to survive is not something that can be taught. However, your will is directly affected by the amount of stress associated with a survival situation. Prior preparation and using the three-step approach to survival (stop, identify your needs and prioritize them, and improvise) will help alleviate some of this stress.

Continued ➡

Prior Preparation

Take the time to prepare for each outing. Leave a detailed trip outline along with return times with someone you can trust. Carry gear specific to the trip, and make sure your survival kit is adequate. Be fit for the adventure. Failing to prepare is preparing to fail. Keep the odds in your favor by taking a little extra time to think the trip through and develop contingencies should things go wrong.

Stop

Stop what you're doing, clear your thoughts, and focus on the problem. Are you lost? Do you have a physical problem that prevents further movement? No matter what the problem is, stop, clear your thoughts, and begin looking at possible solutions.

Identify and Prioritize Your Needs

Recall the five basic elements of survival: personal protection, signaling, sustenance, travel, and health. Recognizing and prioritizing these essentials will help alleviate many of the fears you may have. The exact order in which they're met will depend upon the effects of the surrounding environment. In addition, your conditions, availability of materials, the expected duration of stay, and the given situation all affect how you meet your needs. For example, shelter is of higher priority in an arctic environment than in a mild climate; in the desert, search for water takes on an especially high priority. Take the time to logically plan how to meet your needs, allowing for adjustments as necessary. Through this process, you can greatly diminish the potentially harmful effects of Mother Nature.

Improvise

Improvising is a method of constructing equipment that can be used to meet your needs. With creativity and imagination, you should be able to improvise the basic survival necessities. This will increase your chances of survival and decrease the amount of stress. For more details on the five-step improvising process refer to page 469.

Survival Tips

If you take care of your five survival essentials, health needs should not be an issue. For example, properly meeting your personal protection needs will decrease the odds of environmental injuries (cold and hot injuries). In addition, using the three-step approach to survival will decrease the effects of psychological stress and make you feel more confident about your outcome.

Faith (perhaps the greatest motivator), fear, and pride are three examples of what people have used to overcome what appeared to be insurmountable. Several years back I met a man who told me that his sole motivation for rescue was that his wife had the checkbook. Although I can't verify the validity of his story, I did find it amusing. What motivates you? Whatever it is, you'll need to learn to harness it and allow it to produce the energy needed to overcome your preconceived limits.

—From *Wilderness Survival*

The Psychology of Survival

U.S. Army

Survival Stressors

Any event can lead to stress and, as everyone has experienced, events don't always come one at a time. Often, stressful events occur simultaneously. These events are not stress, but they produce it and are called "stressors." Stressors are the obvious cause while stress is the response. Once the body recognizes the presence of a stressor, it then begins to act to protect itself.

In response to a stressor, the body prepares either to "fight or flee." This preparation involves an internal SOS sent throughout the body. As the body responds to this SOS, several actions take place. The body releases stored fuels (sugar and fats) to provide quick energy; breathing rate increases to supply more oxygen to the blood; muscle tension increases to prepare for action; blood clotting mechanisms are activated to reduce bleeding from cuts; senses become more acute (hearing becomes more sensitive, eyes become big, smell becomes sharper) so that you are more aware of your surroundings; and heart rate and blood pressure rise to provide more blood to the muscles. This protective posture lets a person cope with potential dangers; however, a person cannot maintain such a level of alertness indefinitely.

Stressors are not courteous; one stressor does not leave because another one arrives. Stressors add up. The cumulative effect of minor stressors can be a major distress if they all happen too close together. As the body's resistance to stress wears down and the sources of stress continue (or increase), eventually a state of exhaustion arrives. At this point, the ability to resist stress or use it in a positive way gives out and signs of distress appear. Anticipating stressors and developing strategies to cope with them are two ingredients in the effective management of stress. It is therefore essential that the soldier in a survival setting be aware of the types of stressors he will encounter. Let's take a look at a few of these.

Injury, Illness, or Death

Injury, illness, and death are real possibilities a survivor has to face. Perhaps nothing is more stressful than being alone in an unfamiliar environment where you could die from hostile action, an accident, or from eating something lethal. Illness and injury can also add to stress by limiting your ability to maneuver, get food and drink, find shelter, and defend yourself. Even if illness and injury don't lead to death, they add to stress through the pain and discomfort they generate. It is only by controlling the stress associated with the vulnerability to injury, illness, and death that a soldier can have the courage to take the risks associated with survival tasks.

Uncertainty and Lack of Control

Some people have trouble operating in settings where everything is not clear-cut. The only guarantee in a survival situation is that nothing is guaranteed. It can be extremely stressful operating on limited information in a setting where you have limited control of your surroundings. This uncertainty and lack of control also add to the stress of being ill, injured, or killed.

Environment

Even under the most ideal circumstances, nature is quite formidable. In survival, a soldier will have to contend with the stressors of weather, terrain, and the variety of creatures inhabiting an area. Heat, cold, rain, winds, mountains, swamps, deserts, insects, dangerous reptiles, and other animals are just a few of the challenges awaiting the soldier working to survive. Depending on how a soldier handles the stress of his environment, his surroundings can be either a source of food and protection or can be a cause of extreme discomfort leading to injury, illness, or death.

Hunger and Thirst

Without food and water a person will weaken and eventually die. Thus, getting and preserving food and water takes on increasing importance as the length of time in a survival setting increases. For a soldier used to having his provisions issued, foraging can be a big source of stress.

Fatigue

Forcing yourself to continue surviving is not easy as you grow more tired. It is possible to become so fatigued that the act of just staying awake is stressful in itself.

Isolation

There are some advantages to facing adversity with others. ... Being in contact with others ... provides a greater sense of security and a feeling someone is available to help if problems occur. A significant stressor in survival situations is that often a person or team has to rely solely on its own resources.

The survival stressors mentioned in this section are by no means the only ones you may face. Remember, what is stressful to one person may not be stressful to another. Your experiences, training, personal outlook on life, physical and mental conditioning, and level of self-confidence contribute to what you will find stressful in a survival environment. The object is not to avoid stress, but rather to manage the stressors of survival and make them work for you.

We now have a general knowledge of stress and the stressors common to survival; the next step is to examine our reactions to the stressors we may face.

Natural Reactions

Man has been able to survive many shifts in his environment throughout the centuries. His ability to adapt physically and mentally to a changing world kept him alive while other species around him gradually died off. The same survival mechanisms that kept our forefathers alive can help keep us alive as well! However, these survival mechanisms that can help us can also work against us if we don't understand and anticipate their presence.

It is not surprising that the average person will have some psychological reactions in a survival situation. We will now examine some of

Continued ➡

the major internal reactions you and anyone with you might experience with the survival stressors addressed in the earlier paragraphs. Let's begin.

Fear

Fear is our emotional response to dangerous circumstances that we believe have the potential to cause death, injury, or illness. This harm is not just limited to physical damage; the threat to one's emotional and mental well-being can generate fear as well. For the soldier trying to survive, fear can have a positive function if it encourages him to be cautious in situations where recklessness could result in injury. Unfortunately, fear can also immobilize a person. It can cause him to become so frightened that he fails to perform activities essential for survival. Most soldiers will have some degree of fear when placed in unfamiliar surroundings under adverse conditions. There is no shame in this! Each soldier must train himself not to be overcome by his fears. Ideally, through realistic training, we can acquire the knowledge and skills needed to increase our confidence and thereby manage our fears.

Anxiety

Associated with fear is anxiety. Because it is natural for us to be afraid, it is also natural for us to experience anxiety. Anxiety can be an uneasy, apprehensive feeling we get when faced with dangerous situations (physical, mental, and emotional). When used in a healthy way, anxiety urges us to act to end, or at least master, the dangers that threaten our existence. If we were never anxious, there would be little motivation to make changes in our lives. The soldier in a survival setting reduces his anxiety by performing those tasks that will ensure his coming through the ordeal alive. As he reduces his anxiety, the soldier is also bringing under control the source of that anxiety—his fears. In this form, anxiety is good; however, anxiety can also have a devastating impact. Anxiety can overwhelm a soldier to the point where he becomes easily confused and has difficulty thinking. Once this happens, it becomes more and more difficult for him to make good judgments and sound decisions. To survive, the soldier must learn techniques to calm his anxieties and keep them in the range where they help, not hurt.

Anger and Frustration

Frustration arises when a person is continually thwarted in his attempts to reach a goal. The goal of survival is to stay alive until you can reach help or until help can reach you. To achieve this goal, the soldier must complete some tasks with minimal resources. It is inevitable, in trying to do these tasks, that something will go wrong; that something will happen beyond the soldier's control; and that with one's life at stake, every mistake is magnified in terms of its importance. Thus, sooner or later, soldiers will have to cope with frustration when a few of their plans run into trouble. One outgrowth of this frustration is anger. There are many events in a survival situation that can frustrate or anger a soldier. Getting lost, damaged or forgotten equipment, the weather, inhospitable terrain, ... and physical limitations are just a few sources of frustration and anger. Frustration and anger encourage

impulsive reactions, irrational behavior, poorly thought-out decisions, and, in some instances, an "I quit" attitude (people sometimes avoid doing something they can't master). If the soldier can harness and properly channel the emotional intensity associated with anger and frustration, he can productively act as he answers the challenges of survival. If the soldier does not properly focus his angry feelings, he can waste much energy in activities that do little to further either his chances of survival or the chances of those around him.

Depression

It would be a rare person indeed who would not get sad, at least momentarily, when faced with the privations of survival. As this sadness deepens, we label the feeling "depression." Depression is closely linked with frustration and anger. The frustrated person becomes more and more angry as he fails to reach his goals. If the anger does not help the person to succeed, then the frustration level goes even higher. A destructive cycle between anger and frustration continues until the person becomes worn down—physically, emotionally, and mentally. When a person reaches this point, he starts to give up, and his focus shifts from "What can I do" to "There is nothing I can do." Depression is an expression of this hopeless, helpless feeling. There is nothing wrong with being sad as you temporarily think about your loved ones and remember what life is like back in "civilization" or "the world." Such thoughts, in fact, can give you the desire to try harder and live one more day. On the other hand, if you allow yourself to sink into a depressed state, then it can sap all your energy and, more important, your will to survive. It is imperative that each soldier resist succumbing to depression.

Loneliness and Boredom

Man is a social animal. This means we, as human beings, enjoy the company of others. Very few people want to be alone all the time! As you are aware, there is a distinct chance of isolation in a survival setting. This is not bad. Loneliness and boredom can bring to the surface qualities you thought only others had. The extent of your imagination and creativity may surprise you. When required to do so, you may discover some hidden talents and abilities. Most of all, you may tap into a reservoir of inner strength and fortitude you never knew you had. Conversely, loneliness and boredom can be another source of depression. As a soldier surviving alone, or with others, you must find ways to keep your mind productively occupied. Additionally, you must develop a degree of self-sufficiency. You must have faith in your capability to "go it alone."

Guilt

The circumstances leading to your being in a survival setting are sometimes dramatic and tragic. It may be the result of an accident or military mission where there was a loss of life. Perhaps you were the only, or one of a few, survivors. While naturally relieved to be alive, you simultaneously may be mourning the deaths of others who were less fortunate. It is not uncommon for survivors to feel guilty about being spared from death while others were not.

This feeling, when used in a positive way, has encouraged people to try harder to survive with the belief they were allowed to live for some greater purpose in life. Sometimes, survivors tried to stay alive so that they could carry on the work of those killed. Whatever reason you give yourself, do not let guilt feelings prevent you from living. The living who abandon their chance to survive accomplish nothing. Such an act would be the greatest tragedy.

Preparing Yourself

Your mission as a soldier in a survival situation is to stay alive. As you can see, you are going to experience an assortment of thoughts and emotions. These can work for you, or they can work to your downfall. Fear, anxiety, anger, frustration, guilt, depression, and loneliness are all possible reactions to the many stresses common to survival. These reactions, when controlled in a healthy way, help to increase a soldier's likelihood of surviving. They prompt the soldier to pay more attention in training, to fight back when scared, to take actions that ensure sustenance and security, to keep faith with his fellow soldiers, and to strive against large odds. When the survivor cannot control these reactions in a healthy way, they can bring him to a standstill. Instead of rallying his internal resources, the soldier listens to his internal fears. This soldier experiences psychological defeat long before he physically succumbs. Remember, survival is natural to everyone; being unexpectedly thrust into the life and death struggle of survival is not. Don't be afraid of your "natural reactions to this unnatural situation." Prepare yourself to rule over these reactions so they serve your ultimate interest. ...

It involves preparation to ensure that your reactions in a survival setting are productive, not destructive. The challenge of survival has produced countless examples of heroism, courage, and self-sacrifice. These are the qualities it can bring out in you if you have prepared yourself. Below are a few tips to help prepare yourself psychologically for survival. Through studying this manual and attending survival training you can develop the *survival attitude*.

Know Yourself

Through training, family, and friends take the time to discover who you are on the inside. Strengthen your stronger qualities and develop the areas that you know are necessary to survive.

Anticipate Fears

Don't pretend that you will have no fears. Begin thinking about what would frighten you the most if forced to survive alone. Train in those areas of concern to you. The goal is not to eliminate the fear, but to build confidence in your ability to function despite your fears.

Be Realistic

Don't be afraid to make an honest appraisal of situations. See circumstances as they are, not as you want them to be. Keep your hopes and expectations within the estimate of the situation. When you go into a survival setting with unrealistic expectations, you may be laying the ground-

Continued ➡

work for bitter disappointment. Follow the adage, "Hope for the best, prepare for the worst." It is much easier to adjust to pleasant surprises about one's unexpected good fortunes than to be upset by one's unexpected harsh circumstances.

Adopt a Positive Attitude

Learn to see the potential good in everything. Looking for the good not only boosts morale, it also is excellent for exercising your imagination and creativity.

Remind Yourself What Is at Stake

Remember, failure to prepare yourself psychologically to cope with survival leads to reactions such as depression, carelessness, inattention, loss of confidence, poor decision-making, and giving up before the body gives in. At stake is your life and the lives of others who are depending on you to do your share.

Learn Stress Management Techniques

People under stress have a potential to panic if they are not well-trained and not prepared psychologically to face whatever the circumstances may be. While we often cannot control the survival circumstances in which we find ourselves, it is within our ability to control our response to those circumstances. Learning stress management techniques can enhance significantly your capability to remain calm and focused as you work to keep yourself and others alive. A few good techniques to develop include relaxation skills, time management skills, assertiveness skills, and cognitive restructuring skills (the ability to control how you view a situation).

Remember, "the will to survive" can also be considered to be "the refusal to give up."

—From *Survival (Field Manual 21–76)*

Survival and Medical Kits

Greg Davenport

A survival and medical kit should be one of the most important items you carry. Sadly, they are often the first item compromised when trying to decrease your pack's load. Better to carry a little extra weight than to have a debilitating blister forming and be without moleskin, or find yourself without a means of starting a fire during harsh wet and cold conditions.

Survival Kit

As a bare minimum a survival kit should carry the ten essentials (see table). I advise, however, that you consider carrying much more. Take the time to review the five survival essentials (covered throughout this book) and consider potential problems when putting your kit together. Try to create a kit that will meet your needs under all situations. Put together several kits: a large one for your pack, a medium-size one for your CamelBak, and a small one that you always have on your person.

The Semiessentials

Other items you might consider in addition to the ten essentials include a tent or shelter mate-

rial, paracord for improvising, signaling devices (signal mirror, ground-to-air panel, flares, etc.), water-purifying system, snare wire and fishing gear, wristwatch, note paper and a pencil, toilet paper, and a plastic bag.

I carry my survival gear using a complete yet scattered design. My pack is filled with items that will meet my everyday and emergency needs. In addition, I carry a smaller yet fairly complete kit in my CamelBak (which goes everywhere with me, including on top of my pack during long trips) and a smaller yet comprehensive kit in the cargo pocket of my pants. When carrying my pack, I have safety gear. If I take my pack off and walk around camp with just the CamelBak on, I am covered. Finally, if for some odd reason I find myself separated from my pack and CamelBak, the kit in my cargo pocket covers me. A list of my smaller cargo pocket kit is provided. Take a look and see how it might work for you.

Medical Kit: Suggested Items

antibiotic ointment	routine medications
antihistamine	scissors
aspirin	snake bite kit
Band-Aids	soap
bee sting kit	sunscreen
Chapstick	tincture of benzoin
matches	triangular bandage
medical tape	tweezers
moleskin	various dressings
roller gauze	water purification tablets

—From *Wilderness Survival*

Survival Planning

U.S. Army

Survival planning is nothing more than realizing something could happen that would put you in a survival situation and, with that in mind, taking steps to increase your chances of survival. Thus, survival planning means preparation.

Preparation means having survival items and knowing how to use them. People who live in snow regions prepare their vehicles for poor road conditions. They put snow tires on their vehicles, add extra weight in the back for traction, and they carry a shovel, salt, and a blanket. Another example of preparation is finding the emergency exits on an aircraft when you board it for a flight. Preparation could also mean knowing your intended route of travel and familiarizing yourself with the area. Finally, emergency planning is essential.

Importance of Planning

Detailed prior planning is essential in potential survival situations. Including survival considerations in mission planning will enhance your chances of survival if an emergency occurs. For example, if your job requires that you work in a small, enclosed area that limits what you can carry on your person, plan where you can put your rucksack or your load-bearing equipment. Put it where it will not prevent you from getting

out of the area quickly, yet where it is readily accessible.

One important aspect of prior planning is preventive medicine. Ensuring that you have no dental problems and that your immunizations are current will help you avoid potential dental or health problems. A dental problem in a survival situation will reduce your ability to cope with other problems that you face. Failure to keep your shots current may mean your body is not immune to diseases that are prevalent in the area.

Preparing and carrying a survival kit is as important as the considerations mentioned above. All Army aircraft normally have survival kits on board for the type area(s) over which they will fly. There are kits for over-water survival, for hot climate survival, and an aviator survival vest. If you are not an aviator, you will probably not have access to the survival vests or survival kits. However, if you know what these kits contain, it will help you to plan and to prepare your own survival kit.

Even the smallest survival kit, if properly prepared, is invaluable when faced with a survival problem. Before making your survival kit, however, consider your unit's mission, the operational environment, and the equipment and vehicles assigned to your unit.

Survival Kits

The environment is the key to the types of items you will need in your survival kit. How much equipment you put in your kit depends on how you will carry the kit. A kit carried on your body will have to be smaller than one carried in a vehicle. Always layer your survival kit, keeping the most important items on your body. For example, your map and compass should always be on your body. Carry less important items on your load-bearing equipment. Place bulky items in the rucksack.

In preparing your survival kit, select items you can use for more than one purpose. If you

Ten Essentials of a Survival Kit	
Essential Items	**Five Survival Essentials Category**
map	navigation
compass	navigation
knife	improvising, fire, etc.
water and food	sustenance
rain gear and proper clothing for warmth	personal protection (clothing)
headlamp or flashlight	health (avoid traumatic injuries at night)
first-aid supplies	health (environmental and traumatic injuries)
matches or spark source	personal protection (fire)
tinder	personal protection (fire)
sunglasses and sunscreen	health (environmental injuries)

Continued ➡

have two items that will serve the same function, pick the one you can use for another function. Do not duplicate items, as this increases your kit's size and weight.

Your survival kit need not be elaborate. You need only functional items that will meet your needs and a case to hold the items. For the case, you might want to use a Band-Aid box, a first aid case, an ammunition pouch, or another suitable case. This case should be—

- Water repellent or waterproof.
- Easy to carry or attach to your body.
- Suitable to accept varisized components.
- Durable.

In your survival kit, you should have—

- First aid items.
- Water purification tablets or drops.
- Fire starting equipment.
- Signaling items.
- Food procurement items.
- Shelter items.

Some examples of these items are—

- Lighter, metal match, waterproof matches.
- Snare wire.
- Signaling mirror.
- Wrist compass.
- Fish and snare line.
- Fishhooks.
- Candle.
- Small hand lens.
- Oxytetracycline tablets (diarrhea or infection).
- Water purification tablets.
- Solar blanket.
- Surgical blades.
- Butterfly sutures.
- Condoms for water storage.
- Chap Stick.
- Needle and thread.
- Knife.

—From *Survival* (Field Manual 21-76)

Three Steps to Wilderness Survival

Greg Davenport
Illustrations by Steven Davenport

The ability for a person to prevail in a survival situation is based on three factors: survival knowledge, equipment, and will to survive. All are important, but the most important is the will to survive. Unfortunately the will to survive cannot be taught in a book. Increasing your knowledge of survival skills and understanding of related gear, on the other hand, can. One method of increasing your skills and knowledge is through others. It's with this end in mind that this book has been written. For most of the last twenty years I have used a simple three-step approach to help overcome most survival scenarios. Understanding and using this

SMALL CARGO POCKET KIT ITEMS

Survival Category	Items	Potential Uses
personal protection	needle	sewing, splinter removal
	dental floss	floss teeth, sewing, gear repair
	duct tape	clothing repair, gear repair, medical tape, signaling, note paper
	knife	cutting applications, metal match striker, screwdriver, digging, skinning
	parachute cord	lashing shelters/tools, gear repair, inner strands for sewing, snares
	vaseline/cotton tinder	tinder, lip balm, moisten dry skin
	metal match	fire starter, nighttime signal device
	candle	match saver/fire starter, light source
	matches	fire starter
signaling	mirror	ground/air signal, ground/ground signal
	whistle	audible signal
	survey tape	ground signal, trail marker, note paper, gear repair
	coins	pay phone, ground/air signal, fishing lure
	marker	note taking, writing messages
sustenance	condoms	water bladder
	water purification tablets	water purification
	water purification container	air/water tight container
	tubing	water bladder hose, sling shot, snare device, tourniquet
	safety pin	secure tubing to clothing, clothing repair, gear repair, splinter removal, secure arm sling
	bread ties	secure top of water bladder, keep small gear organized
	aluminum foil	water scoop for condom, fire base on wet ground, wind block for small fires, cooking, signaling
	snare wire	snares, gear repair
	fishing line	fishing, gear repair, sewing, shelter lashing, all cordage applications
	fishing hooks	fishing, sewing, gear repair
	fishing sinkers	fishing
	fishing float	fishing, trail marker
travel	button compass	
medical	medical tape	secure dressings, gear repair, clothing repair, all tape applications
	Band-Aids	small wound dressings
	antibiotic cream	small wound care, chapped lip/skin balm
	moleskin	blister prevention/repair
	alcohol preps	disinfect skin/needles
	Ziploc bag for picture of loved ones	relieve stress, motivation to succeed
miscellaneous	Ziploc bags	keep small essential dry/organized
	PSK pouch	carry survival gear
	three-step approach card	guidance for a survival scenario

Continued ➔

approach keeps the survivor organized, reduces stress, and ultimately increases the will to survive. It can do the same for you.

Greg Davenport's Three-Step Approach to Wilderness Survival

As an outdoor educator and wilderness survival expert, I believe a survivor's needs remain constant regardless of his or her circumstances (climate, terrain, or health). In fact, the only thing that changes in how these needs are met is how they are prioritized and how well you improvise to meet them. The three steps are stop and recognize the situation for what it is; identify and prioritize your five survival essentials for the situation you are in; and improvise to meet your needs (using man-made and natural resources).

Step 1

Stop and recognize the situation for what it is. If you think you're lost, you probably are. Stop trying to find that familiar road or rock. Walking when lost burns up daylight and moves you beyond the probable search-and-rescue zone. This common scenario often leads to a cold and frustrating night for both you and search-and-rescue teams. Once you recognize that you are lost, stop wandering around! Use your time to identify and meet your five survival essentials, making a safe and rapid rescue more probable.

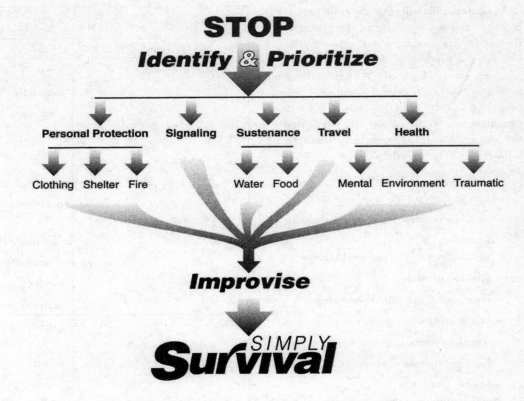

Greg Davenport's three-step approach to global survival.

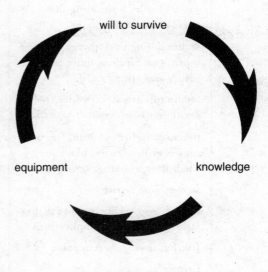

Factors that influence survival.

Step 2

Identify and prioritize your five survival essentials. Once you've recognized the situation for what it is, it's time to identify your five survival essentials and prioritize them in order of importance. Take the time to write down your order of preference and be willing to adjust the order as mandated by your constantly changing scenario. The five survival essentials are:

1. Personal protection (clothing, shelter, fire)

2. Signaling (man-made and improvised)

3. Sustenance (identifying and procuring water and food)

4. Travel (with and without a map and compass)

5. Health (mental, traumatic, and environmental injuries)

Health, personal protection, and sustenance needs relate to maintaining life. Signaling and travel relate to returning home. Although these needs are constant, your situation and the environment will dictate the exact order and method used to meet them.

Step 3

Improvise to meet your needs (using man-made and natural resources). Tap water, refrigerators, heaters, and a nice bed are not part of an outdoor adventure. These needs can often be met, however, with a little imagination, your gear, and what Mother Nature provides.

Since it's unlikely you'll have all the necessary resources in your gear, you'll need to improvise using what you have and what Mother Nature can supply. Sometimes this task is easy, and other times it may stretch your imagination to its limits. Using the following five-step approach to improvising will help in the decision process.

1. Determine your need (shelter, signal, heat, etc.).

2. Inventory your available man-made and natural materials.

3. Consider the different ways you might meet your need (tree-well shelter, snow cave, etc.).

4. Pick the one that best utilizes your time, energy, and materials.

5. Proceed with the plan, ensuring that the final produce is safe and durable.

The only limiting factor is your imagination! Don't let it prevent you from creating a masterpiece that keeps you comfortable while in your survival situation.

No matter what your circumstances, these three steps will help you during a time when you are uncertain of what tomorrow brings. They keep you organized, on task, and focused on a safe return home.

—From *Wilderness Survival*

Miscellaneous

Ways to Improve Night Vision

Allan A. Macfarlan

Sometimes hunters travel at night, and some hunters—coon hunters, for instance—operate at night since the animals are on the move then. Many wildlife photographers like to call varmints at night or sit up for game and take flash pictures. Many game animals and predators come readily to calling in darkness, and the sudden flash of highspeed flash equipment doesn't seem to bother them much.

Don't sit in front of the fire or a light just before you leave your tent or cabin at night. It's best to stay in a dark room for about an hour before you go. That way, your eyes accommodate to darkness before you run the risk of stepping into a hole or off a bluff.

Angle vision works in both daylight and darkness, as the Indians knew, and it's useful when you're trying to distinguish a dimly lit object or estimate range. If you're puzzled about something that you see, move your head slightly from side to side. This allows the eyes to "feel" the object, and the binocular properties of human sight seem to reach out and touch the surface of the object. Perhaps catching the object from a slightly different angle brings out its outline more clearly. When pinpointing a coon high in a tree at night or estimating the range for a long shot at big game in daylight, the intervening objects seem to move as your head moves from side to side. Of course the twigs or other objects that are closest to the observer seem to move the most, and as distance increases away from him, they seem to move less. This illusion enables a human being to estimate distance more accurately. To the unmoving eye, the foreground, middle ground, and background sometimes seem to have no depth at all. Range estimation then is very difficult.

How to Acquire "Owl Eye"

What the Indians sometimes called "owl eye" is achieved by cupping the fingers around each eye so that dim light surrounding a distant object is concentrated in the observer's eyes and distracting light reflected from other objects is excluded. The effect of the concentration is so great that the observed object often seems to increase in size. Owl eye is especially useful at dawn and dusk when light is diffused by dampness.

Resting the Eyes

When your eyes become blurred from gazing too long in the dark or dim light, close them slowly and keep them closed for several minutes. Then open them again very slowly. If that doesn't work, keep your eyes closed while you count slowly to twenty. Then open them and try blinking again. If that does not clear your night vision, you are probably overtired or eyesore, and it is best to return to camp and take a rest.

Silhouette Vision

Indian hunters used silhouette vision to great advantage at night. It's often possible to take up a position so that you focus a dimly seen object against the skyline or against the comparatively luminous glow of a lake or wide river. You can also determine the outline of a distant object by moving it across the stars or moon. When the object blots out light as your eyes move, you get a clearer outline. If the object itself is moving, you can keep track of it by remaining still and watching the stars blink out and then on again as the object obscures the light. If you develop this skill, you'll be able to say exactly what a moving animal is—bear, moose, antelope, coyote, wolf, fox, and so forth.

—From *Exploring the Outdoors with Indian Secrets*

Wilderness Waste Disposal

Back-Country Sanitation

U.S. Forest Service

Sanitation practices in the back country require extra effort. Washing and the disposal of human waste must be done carefully so the environment is not polluted and fish and aquatic life are not injured. Water can become polluted from the runoff of soaps, food waste, and human waste. Toilet paper and other trash also leave an unsightly impact.

Water and Washing: There are *Giardia* bacteria and other contaminants in many streams, springs, and water sources, so plan to filter or boil all drinking water. Wash at least 50 feet away from camp and any water sources. For personal washing, use a container and rinse away from water sources. For kitchen waste, scrape burnable food scraps into the campfire or put it in a plastic bag to be carried out and then wash dishes away from water sources. Use small amounts of biodegradable soap. Washing without soap would be better since any soap can pollute lakes and streams. Pour wash water on the ground at least 50 feet from water sources and the kitchen area.

Human Waste: Use the "cat method" of making a shallow hole and covering it when done. It should be dug in the top 6–8 inches of organic soil and be at least 200 feet away from camp, trails, and water sources. Groups may need to walk well over 200 feet to ensure that catholes are scattered during their stay at that site.

Latrines concentrate impacts and should be used only outside wildernesses when large groups are staying for a long time in popular areas. Locate the latrines at least 200 feet away from camp, trails, and water sources. Dig a hole at least 12 inches deep, add soil after each use, and fill in once it is within 4 inches of being full.

Trash: If your back-country trip has been well planned, there should not be too much trash. Never bury your trash because animals will probably dig it up. While you're hiking, make an effort to pocket all trash, including cigarette butts, and then empty your pockets into a trash bag later. Remember that peanut shells, orange peels, and egg shells are trash. IF YOU PACK IT IN, YOU SHOULD PACK IT OUT.

Remember:

· Do all washing away from camp and water sources.

· Dig catholes 200 feet or more from camp, trails, and streams.

· Burn food scraps completely in the fire or put then in a plastic bag and carry them out.

· Pack it in. Pack it out.

· Obtain special guidelines for grizzly bear country.

—From *Leave No Trace! A Wilderness Ethi*

Continued ➡

Garbage and Human Waste Disposal

Cecil Kuhne

Garbage

In the total scheme of things, what difference does one candy bar wrapper thrown to the wind make? The answer is a lot, especially when the single effect is multiplied, as it invariably is.

The rule for disposal of garbage is simple: Carry it all out. The best method for doing so is a plastic bucket with an airtight lid or perhaps a plastic garbage bag placed inside a more resilient nylon bag. Keep a small bag handy for use during the day, and be careful to collect even the smallest piece of paper.

If you're using a campfire or charcoal briquettes, burn all trash possible, but remember that aluminum foil packets will not burn and that certain foods (such as egg shells) require more time than a short morning fire. If the garbage can't be burned, dispose of it by placing everything except liquids in the garbage bag (grease, in particular, should always be carried out).

Liquid garbage, such as coffee, soup, and dishwater (containing biodegradable soap), should be strained first. The solids remaining can then be thrown into the garbage bag. In wooded areas (which foster quick decomposition), the liquid can be poured into a single hole dug for that purpose (but at least a hundred feet away from any area normally used for camping). In wooded areas that are heavily used, it may be better to pour the liquids into the main current of the river, where they will quickly disperse—but first check with the government agency managing the river. In desert regions (which don't foster quick decomposition), the liquid should always be poured into the main current of the river.

One way to avoid garbage in the first place is to plan ahead: Select foods and packaging that will result in as little trash as possible.

Human Waste Disposal

Solid human waste presents both an environmental impact and a hazard to human health. As a result, many government agencies now require it to be carried out. It's inevitable that the system will be implemented on most government lands, and it's a good idea in all heavily traveled areas. The cheapest, most convenient, and most effective means of containing and transporting this waste is in an airtight toilet box sold by various camping supply companies. The necessary items include the following:

- Metal toilet box approximately 18" x 14" x 8" in size (surplus ammunition boxes work well if they're airtight)
- Toilet seat
- Chemical deodorant or chlorine bleach
- Toilet paper, water dispenser, and hand soap

The system is easy to set up. Pour a small amount of the chemical deodorant or chlorine bleach into the toilet box and place the toilet seat on top (the water dispenser and hand soap can be situated nearby). Plastic bags should not be used with this system because they are not biodegradable.

Chemical deodorant or chlorine bleach is important because it reduces bacterial growth and the production of methane gas. The amount of chemical deodorant needed depends on the type used: A few ounces a day of liquid deodorant is sufficient for six or seven people, whereas approximately twice as much chlorine bleach is required for the same number of people. The number of toilet boxes needed depends on the number of people and the length of the trip; on average, it's possible to containerize a week-long trip for ten people in one box. After the trip, the waste should be deposited in an approved solid-waste landfill.

Side hikes also require sanitary waste disposal, but of a slightly different kind. To reduce impact, bury the waste (after carefully burning the toilet paper) in a hole about six inches deep, the best depth for soil elements that cause rapid decomposition. Carry a small backpacker's trowel, and make the hole at least a hundred feet from the river's high-water line and away from any area normally used for camping.

—From *Paddling Basics: Canoeing*

Winter Wilderness Waste Disposal

Buck Tilton and John Gookin

Dispose of Waste Properly

The familiar expression is worth repeating: Pack it in, pack it out. Always inspect your campsites and your rest-break spots, and leave no waste behind. Carry garbage bags and pack out leftover food as well as your trash, and lend a hand by packing out the refuse discarded by others. In most cases, litter covered by snow will be litter on the surface in a few months or less.

Avoid the thought that it doesn't matter where you defecate in snow. Use trailhead and backcountry toilets whenever they are available. When they're not, defecate at least 200 feet (about 70 adult paces) from any water source and well away from trails and campsites. Whenever possible, defecate at the base of a tree. Dig into the snow close to the trunk of the tree, down to the ground, or into the ground, if you can. Even if you can't, feces near a tree will decompose more quickly than those in the open, encouraged by the heat produced by the tree. In the absence of trees, deposit feces near a boulder. Thoughtful winter campers ski-pack a trail to a satisfactory spot (or more than one spot, to prevent an accumulation of feces) before they need the spot. Whenever possible, choose a spot where sunlight will hasten decomposition. Don't bury feces deeply in snow; a shallow hole, covered when you've finished, allows for a faster decomposition rate while still hiding the waste from sight. Although the melting snow in spring will soften and disperse the nasty mass, sunlight does most of the work of decomposition. Winter also offers the possibility of letting feces freeze, packing the piles in garbage bags, and sledding them out with you.

The use of toilet paper is acceptable, as long as you pack the soiled paper out. Snow makes a very nice natural wipe, if its consistency allows you to mold it into a usable shape.

Urination causes little or no harm to the environment in winter, but designating an appropriate spot eliminates the unsightliness of yellow holes all over the place. Locating that spot near a tree minimizes the possibility of gathering "bad" snow to melt for water.

—From *NOLS Winter Camping*

Bone Collecting

Glenn Searfoss

Bone-Collecting Basics

The collection and study of bones is an important activity for mammalogists and forensic scholars as well as fascinating and enlightening hobby for laymen. This post-postmortem examination allows researchers to determine an animal's physical attributes, probable environmental lifestyle, species rank, and sometimes the probable cause of death. Besides, bones—especially skulls—make great conversation pieces.

So, other than procuring them from a retail outlet such as Skulls Unlimited International, where can bones be found?

Our world is built upon the remains of all the creatures who have ever lived. We find their skeletons fossilized in rock, ground up as sand beneath our feet, and diluted in the air we breathe and the water we drink. More recent casualties lie on or buried just beneath the surface of the ground. Their remains are scattered everywhere: along roads, in fields, and in forests. But just how do you go about collecting them? What precautions should you take? What situations should you avoid?

Successful bone collecting takes patience, practice, and an awareness of your surroundings. Although experience is the best teacher, this chapter should help you get started.

Collection Gear

The right equipment will make bone collecting both easier and safer. A usable outfit for this adventure is simple and inexpensive and should consist of the following five items:

- Brightly colored clothing (hat, shirt, pants, or all three).
- Gloves, either latex or cloth. Latex gloves offer a sure grip, are nonporous, and are impervious to disease, but they retain body heat and make your hands sweat. The main advantage of cloth over latex is that cloth gloves will not cause hands to sweat and are more comfortable to wear over extended periods.
- A container for transporting the bones you find. Plastic heavy-duty trash bags are ideal. They are strong, lightweight, and easy to fold up and carry until needed. If you use cloth bags, wash them after each successful excursion.
- A stick for probing remains.
- Disinfectant to rinse your hands. A small bottle containing a minimum 10 percent solution of bleach and water will suffice.

Continued ➜

The Ethics of Bone Collecting

Before collecting bones, it is important to understand the role they play in an ecosystem. Collectors should question their motives for gathering bones and consider the long-term effects of their removal.

An ecosystem does not waste bones. Rather, they provide food for many creatures. Oils and rancid fats, constantly secreted by bones during decomposition and weathering, supply food immediately for insects and mammals. Long after the oils have been exhausted, bones continue to furnish a source of calcium and minerals to mammals, such as rodents, who gnaw on them. With their final decomposition, much-needed elements and minerals are returned to the earth. The removal of bones from an ecosystem will deprive some organism, animal or vegetable, of an essential source of food.

That leads us to this question: Given their position in the food web, is it ethical to remove bones from their natural setting? If so, under what conditions?

Bones are routinely collected for study by colleges, museums, and nature centers. They are scavenged by amateur naturalists and hobbyists for private collections, as well as by artists who use skeletal structures in their work. Nature warehouses are also known to sell items procured from the wild. Do any of these individuals or organizations have valid reasons for the gathering of bones from their natural setting?

- Institutions, such as nature centers and museums, use bones for study and educational presentations. While these osteology collections are often purchased through biological warehouses, they are still augmented with specimens found in the field. Limiting or eliminating field collection would restrict an important source of specimens.

- Profit is another motive. A business must sell its products. If these products consist of items found in the wild, such as bones, then a constant source of supply must be established and maintained.

- Naturalists may find themselves on the horns of a dilemma, as the inclination to collect conflicts with the awareness of bones' role in nature.

- An artist needs supplies, especially if his or her art involves bones. Art supplies are not cheap, and found materials are the least expensive.

- It is hard to tell a nine- or ten-year-old, let alone an adult, that he or she cannot keep a found skull. For this person a whole new world has opened up.

Many find it difficult to resist the desire to possess, whether for educational, personal economic, or creative reasons. All collectors must face this issue. This book does not attempt to answer this question or impose ethical constraints. These responsibilities lie with the individual collector. To a greater or lesser degree, ethics plays a part in any endeavor. While engaged in bone collecting, you are encouraged to trust your own judgment and empathy for nature.

How to Find Bones

Bones in the wild can usually be spotted by sight if you train yourself to notice unusual shapes and contrasting colors. Once you find a bone, you can launch a search for other skeletal fragments.

Color

There are no colors quite like those of bones in the wild, so noticing color contrasts between them and their surroundings is the first step to locating skeletal remains. Developing an eye for these contrasts takes practice. At first you will investigate every white object you see. From a distance it is easy to confuse a rock, paper, or piece of whitened wood with a real bone. It is also easy to dismiss slight contrasts as not worth examining and thus pass over bones. Don't be discouraged. Practice sharpens and trains the eye at spotting these treasures.

Shapes

Every bone in a skeleton has a unique shape. When clearly seen either from a distance or close up, specific bones, such as scapulas and vertebrae, can be quickly recognized by their profiles. Since complete or partial burial by fallen grasses and other vegetation can obscure identifying contours, however, shape recognition is best utilized as an auxiliary to color contrasts in the initial location of bones. Once located through color contrasts, you can recognize skeletal fragments by shape during the close-up work of pattern searches.

Search Patterns

Two basic search patterns, *spiral* and a *linear zigzag*, are used in the hunt for skeletal remains and can be effectively implemented by individuals or groups. Each pattern has a geographic terrain for which its employment is best suited.

Spiral Pattern

When using a spiral search pattern, slowly wind outward from the first bone discovered. If a major portion of a skeleton is subsequently discovered, begin the pattern again, this time using the new find as the center position. This pattern is best suited for use on open land. Depending on the terrain, one of two spiral patterns may be used.

If you find bones on a slope, such as a gully wall or side hill, use an elliptical spiral pattern—either oval or teardrop shaped—that opens and widens faster downhill than uphill. On this terrain, bone scattering is primarily a function of gravity, as carcasses have a tendency to roll downhill or be pulled there by scavengers.

For bones located in a flat, wide area, such as an open field, use a circular spiral pattern that increases at an even rate in all directions. On this terrain gravity has less effect on skeletal scattering and scavengers are as likely to pull a carcass in one direction as another.

Linear Zigzag Pattern

With a linear zigzag search pattern, move slowly from side to side while advancing in one direction. Once the likelihood of finding bones by traveling farther in that direction has diminished, return to the starting position. Repeat the process in the opposite direction. This search pattern best suits the banks of watercourses and dry streambeds.

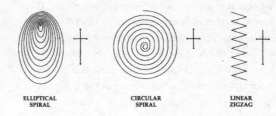

ELLIPTICAL SPIRAL   **CIRCULAR SPIRAL**   **LINEAR ZIGZAG**

Three basic search patterns: elliptical spiral, circular spiral, and linear zigzag. The crossed arrows to the right of each image indicate the relative increase and direction of search pattern expansion.

Where to Find Bones

Bones can be found anywhere, and every place should be investigated. Depending upon your proximity to water, however, some locations may prove more likely prospects than others.

Bones are most often found near water sources. Explore along the edges of large bodies of water such as lakes, ponds, and oceans. Investigate dry hummocks in swampy areas and along the banks of streams and rivers. Seasonal sources of water, like dry streams, riverbeds, and arroyos, should also be considered.

Bones can also be found away from water. Animals often seek shelter and die in places that are protected and out of the wind. Their bones can be found scattered in areas such as depressions in large open fields or woods, the leeward sides of hills, gullies, and ravines.

Locating the bones of small mammals, such as rodents, is difficult. However, if birds of prey inhabit the collecting area, small mammal bones can often be found along cliff bases, under standing dead trees, and beneath telephone poles. These raptors prefer elevated areas with a clear view when consuming their prey. Bones scattered about the ground may be intact or fragmented, but rarely form complete skeletons.

When to Collect Bones

Bone collecting can be done at any time of the year, but some seasons are better suited to this than others. The best season to collect skulls and bones is late spring. After the snows have melted, when the previous year's vegetation is still matted down and before new plant growth has started, bones are easier to spot. Their color contrasts strongly with the darker background of dead vegetation in which they lie. At this time bones are often partially or completely uncovered, allowing their shapes to be more pronounced.

Summer is a difficult time to find bones because the abundance of standing, color-shaded, fully leafed vegetation tends to obscure bones.

Because of the contrast of white bone against rusty leaves and dead grass, fall is also a good bone-collecting season. Because dry, standing vegetation often covers and conceals them, however, bones are more difficult to spot in the fall than in the spring.

Wintertime in northern climates is a bad time for bone collecting. Even a slight dusting of snow can obscure skeletal fragments. Bones are hard to spot in a white-on-white world. If you live where there is no snow you may be in luck, however: The fall- or summerlike conditions in these regions offer some hope for visual bone sightings.

Continued ➡

Although winter is not the best time to find bones, it is a good time to locate carcasses. Then you can return to the remains in the spring to collect the bones, after nature and time have stripped them of flesh.

Searching around such a carcass will often turn up others. During winter everything needs to eat, and carnivores, as well as omnivores, are not apt to pass up an easy meal. Since many animals will be drawn to a carcass, it is not unusual to find the remains of would-be gourmands who were unlucky enough to meet up with larger predators who were staking out the carcass in hopes of finding fresh meat.

Final Notes on Collecting

The hobby of bone collecting develops a crossdisciplinary understanding of geography, mammalogy, physics, behavioral psychology, and ecology. Through such study a person may learn to infer an animal's behavior and general lifestyle and in this way develop tools for understanding nature and its complexity. The hints supplied in this chapter should make the search for bones easier. Hunting of any sort always presents dangers to the hunter, however, and the following sections discuss some of the hazards inherent in bone collecting.

Safety Precautions

Hazards to health and safety are inherent in any expedition. Since knowledge often alleviates fear, collectors will find it important to develop an awareness of the hazards peculiar to bone collecting. The risks of many of the perils discussed in this chapter are low and all can be diminished, if not eliminated, with proper attention to detail.

When in pursuit of bones, safety should be the primary concern. Many dangers can befall unwary and unprepared collectors. Including the standard hazards associated with hiking and climbing, the most likely dangers arise from fellow humans, wild animals, and the weather.

Roadside Safety

Many animals are killed along our nation's major transportation routes. If you insist on examining roadkill, don't be stupid. At all times wear bright clothing, be alert to the sounds of any motorized vehicle, and keep a close watch up and down the road or train tracks.

These precautions will only mitigate the danger. When crouched down looking at a dead animal lying in or along the side of the road or train tracks, a person is difficult to see. Even if you're wearing bright clothing, a driver may not become aware of your presence until it's too late.

The only sure way to not be hit is to stay out of and away from roads. Remember, cars and trains are heavy machines that build up momentum as they move. Often traveling in excess of fifty miles per hour, they take a while to stop when brakes are applied. An automobile may take twenty feet or more to come to a complete stop. Since trains are heavier than cars, a suddenly braking train may slide hundreds of feet along a track before coming to a halt. A screech of rubber on asphalt, or steel on steel, and either you're safe or you're roadkill. Because of the danger presented by motorized vehicles of any kind, leave the remains of road-killed animals alone.

Hunting Season

Searching for bones in the outdoors can be dangerous during hunting season and the best advice is to stay out of the woods and fields at this time. Although many hunters are safe and conscientious, some are not. Unsafe hunters have been known to make "sound shots"—firing a gun in the general vicinity of a sound without actually seeing the target—or fire in rapid succession at an animal without taking sharp aim. Both "hunting techniques" are reckless and dangerous.

Although good hunting practices and techniques mitigate these dangers, even they produce an inevitable stray bullet.

Wild Animals

It is easy to become so engrossed in a search that you are unaware of events going on around you. With the increasing encroachment of humans into the habitat and territories of wild animals, it is not unlikely that a backyard or backcountry bone collector may find himself face to face with a bear or mountain lion.

Usually this isn't a problem, since most animals tend to shy away from humans. This response shouldn't be counted on, however. When faced with such a predicament the better part of valor is recommended. Retreat, but don't act like prey. If additional information is desired, most nature centers provide cautionary brochures on actions a person should take when confronted by aggressive wild animals.

Weather Conditions

Humans often consider themselves superior and invulnerable to natural events. Any number of outdoor casualties can attest that nature is indifferent to our arrogance.

Since many hiking and outdoor books detail effective cautionary tactics, I will just say that on any excursion into the out of doors, be prepared. Each season and geographic region has both predictable and unpredictable weather patterns. Carry gear sufficient for expected as well as inclement weather. But most of all, know your limits. Many people overestimate their physical capabilities and underestimate the forces of nature.

Health Hazards

It should go without saying that you should not collect fresh remains. It takes a while for nature to scour bones clean of flesh and disease. The larger the animal, the longer it takes. Depending on the age of the bones and whether the climate is humid or arid, you may be exposed to several types of viral or bacterial contamination. Therefore, wait until nature has removed the bulk of, if not all, flesh and sinew from the bones, then collect and clean them.

The Dangers of Decomposition

Once dead, all organisms decompose, with muscle and other soft tissues decaying faster than bone. The speed at which this process occurs is directly related to the amount of moisture in the air and on the ground surface. The presence of moisture speeds up decomposition. Humidity keeps flesh somewhat moist, providing an ideal environment for the organisms that cause tissues to break down and rot. An arid climate like a desert inhibits decay but does not stop it. The

bacteria that promote decay, and other organisms, such as flesh-eating insects, are still active.

Decomposition does not happen overnight. Sometimes it takes several years for a carcass to skeletonize. Even after the flesh is removed from the outside of bones, marrow is still sealed inside. A soft fatty connective tissue, marrow usually takes a long time to empty from the hollow center and spongelike areas of a bone. In my backyard, I have ten-year-old elk bones still full of marrow. (See figure below.)

Exposure to rotting flesh presents immediate hazards to health and well-being. Although these risks drop in direct proportion to a bone's cleanliness, they never go away completely. Three major infections may be caused by handling decaying remains without proper precautions: blood poisoning, botulism, and tetanus.

Blood Poisoning

Also called *septicemia*, *blood poisoning* is an infection caused by the invasion of the bloodstream by virulent bacteria. Once introduced through an open wound, such as a cut or deep scratch on your hand, the infection spreads, swelling tissues and sending painful livid red streaks across afflicted body parts. Of the three risks mentioned here, this is the greatest.

Botulism

Also called acute food poisoning, *botulism* is caused by *botulin*, a toxin secreted by the spore-forming bacterium *Clostridium botulinum*. Botulin is

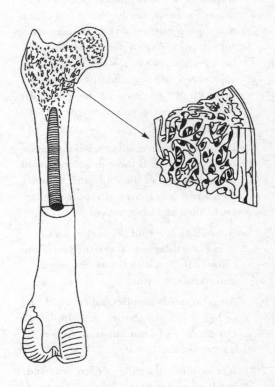

A split section of femur. Fats and marrow fill the center hollow and the spongelike material at the bone ends. The enlarged cutout section on the right illustrates the porous nature of this material.

transmitted through contact with the mucous membranes found in your nose or mouth. You don't have to eat rotten flesh to be affected. All you need to do is pick up a bone that still has some flesh clinging to it or rancid oils oozing from it and, with the hand that touched the rotten flesh, inadvertently wipe your nose or mouth.

Continued ➡

System

Tetanus

An acute infectious disease, *tetanus* is caused by a toxin produced by the bacillus *Clostridium tetani*. The toxin, often introduced through an open wound, causes rapid spasms and prolonged contraction of voluntary muscles. An early symptom of tetanus is characterized by the spasming of the jaw muscles that eventually results in the inability to open the jaw. It is for this reason that advanced tetanus is also referred to as lockjaw.

Contagious Diseases

Death is not always the result of old age or accident. Animals, both domestic and wild, die from disease or fall prey to accidents due to debilitation caused by a disease. Regardless of how an animal dies, a pathogen can cling to decaying flesh, bones, or hair. The fresher the carcass, the greater the danger of contamination to a collector. Four of the most common diseases are discussed here: distemper, rabies, bubonic plague, and anthrax.

Distemper and Rabies

Distemper is a highly contagious virus whose infection is marked by fever and respiratory and nervous symptoms. Rabies is an acute viral disease of the nervous system of warm-blooded animals. These are two of the most prominent diseases among animals. Both can make an animal disoriented, causing it to wander into areas outside its normal territory. If it wanders onto a road, it may be struck and killed by a passing motor vehicle.

These diseases can be contracted or carried through the handling of carcasses. Although rabies is infectious to humans, distemper is not. Pet lovers beware, however, because humans can act as carriers for these diseases and infect pets and livestock.

Bubonic Plague

Also called the Black Death, this plague decimated Europe in the fourteenth century, killing approximately one quarter of its human population. The disease, caused by the bacterium *Pasteurella pestis*, is transmitted through the bites of fleas that live on warm-blooded mammals. In the Middle Ages it was a large rat population that hosted the fleas. Today the disease is still transmitted primarily through large populations of rodents such as squirrels and prairie dogs, but any mammal can be a carrier of plague-infested fleas. Although fleas require a live host to survive and do not live long after a host is dead, do not take the chance of contracting this disease by handling fresh carcasses.

Anthrax

Although controlled, anthrax occasionally flares up in domestic livestock and wild animals. It is an infectious disease of warm-blooded animals caused by the spore-forming bacterium *Bacillus anthracis*. It can be transmitted to humans through the handling of infected products such as hair.

Precautions You can Take

There are a number of simple precautions you can take to guard your health and safety. First, wear brightly colored clothes. The best color is fluorescent orange, also called hunter's orange. This color stands out well against most backgrounds, reflects light, is attention getting, and makes the wearer easy to see.

Next, wear cloth or latex gloves when handling skeletal remains to protect your hands against possible contamination. Latex gloves have the advantage of being nonporous and, as long as they remain undamaged, impervious to disease.

Clean all clothing after each successful collecting excursion. Soak all articles, including gloves, in a bleach-water solution, then wash them in warm soapy water.

After handling remains, avoid touching your eyes; body orifices, such as mouth and nose; and any cuts and abrasions. Prevent contagion by washing your hands with a 10 percent solution of bleach* and water.

Disinfect collected bones by soaking them overnight in a solution of nine parts water to one part bleach. When soaking time is up, remove and, using a scouring pad or old toothbrush, wash them in warm soapy water, then let them air dry. If you can, dry them in the sun, as ultraviolet radiation kills bacteria. If desired, use some form of lacquer, clear spray paint, or floral plastic spray to seal the bones. This will prevent possible infection from future handling. The next section provides details on bone disinfection, preparation, and preservation techniques.

Conclusion

Collecting bones can be fun, but you must be aware of the risks to yourself and others. Play it safe and stay off roads and train tracks. When hunting season comes around, do not go into the woods and fields. When collecting skulls and other bones, take the precautions of wearing gloves and bright clothes. Remember to keep your own life and bones intact.

* The best bleach to use is Clorox. Other bleaches often contain a high percentage of lye.

Bone Preparation and Cleaning

Because of the health risks associated with bones found in the wild, specimens should always be sanitized. In fact, bone cleaning should be considered one of the single most significant tasks undertaken by collectors.

Many bones, even those weathered for several years, may still have remnants of flesh and tendons attached to them. Collectors should remove these tissues to eliminate both possible disease sources and offensive odors. Depending on your intended use, one of two types of cleaning may be undertaken: home quality and museum quality.

Home-Quality Specimens

Most people do not gather bones for scientific purposes but rather for display in homes or private rooms. These collections often consist of loose bones that may be strung together and mounted but more often remain spread out along shelves or stashed in boxes. The primary concerns for cleaning home-quality specimens are hygiene and aesthetics. Home-quality cleaning requires that the following four conditions be met.

- All muscle and ligament tissue must be removed from the bones.
- Bones should be sterilized both inside and out.
- All surface oils must be removed, leaving bones dry, not greasy, to the touch.
- Bones should be white, off-white, or slightly yellow in color.

The Cleaning Kit

The basic components of a home cleaning kit are readily available within most homes, supermarkets, and hardware stores. Depending on the specimens' condition—flesh-free or with flesh still attached—all or some of the following items may be used.

- Safety goggles, to protect your eyes from splattering hot water, caustic chemicals, and chemical solutions.
- Disposable latex gloves, to protect your hands from hot materials and caustic cleaners.
- Old clothes that cover your arms to the wrists and your legs to the ankles.
- A drop cloth or newspapers, used for drying specimens.
- A large pot or five-gallon metal can used exclusively for boiling bones.
- Preferably two, but at least one, three- to five-gallon plastic pails used strictly for soaking and scrubbing bones.
- Several cutting and scraping utensils such as scalpels, paring knives, old steak knives, toothpicks, or thin, flat, narrow-tipped pieces of wood.
- Several soft, abrasive scraping utensils such as a plastic dish-washing pad, plastic vegetable scrubber, or a toothbrush.
- A kitchen stove, a camping stove, or an open fire with a grate, for "cooking" bones. Be aware that boiling bones, especially old ones, can produce noxious, foul-smelling fumes. When cleaning is performed in the house, use of a range hood or exhaust fan is recommended.
- One or all of the following basic household cleaning chemicals: ammonia, Clorox bleach, or a degreaser. During the bone-cleaning process these chemicals must be used outdoors or in well-ventilated areas.

Once this kit has been assembled the cleaning process can begin. Use only those items necessary for the job at hand. Once kit items are used for bone cleaning, they should never be used for any other purpose.

Initial Preparation

No matter how spotless bones may appear when found, they should always be considered possible sources of infection. Therefore, all specimens should be cleaned and disinfected before being brought into your home for display. Although this will not eliminate all infectious agents, it will greatly reduce risks of contagion.

The preparation process discussed in this section assumes relatively flesh-free specimens. If you have fleshed specimens, use a knife or

Continued ➡

your gloved hands to remove as much muscle and ligament material from the bones as possible, being careful not to cut or scratch them.

Next, cover the ground or floor with the drop cloth or newspapers. Then mix a 10 percent disinfectant solution of approximately 1.6 cups bleach or ammonia to 1 gallon of water. Soak the specimens overnight. Wearing gloves and goggles, remove the bones one at a time and gently scrape away as much softened flesh and ligament material as possible. If the bones are already free of ligament and muscle tissue, simply scrub them with a brush. When finished, lay the specimens on the drop cloth to dry.

If you're working with small bones, the above procedure should adequately clear them of fat and grease. If the bones are large, however, the cleaning process will require another step. Once the scrubbed and disinfected bones have dried, the larger leg and hip bones should be drilled at certain positions along their sides and ends. This technique, illustrated below and at right, will help to clear marrow and other fatty substances from the bones.

Skulls require more preparation than other skeletal structures. In addition to the general preparation detailed above, assuring the removal

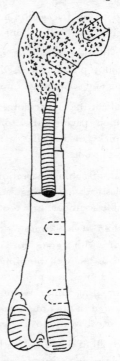

Illustrations of bone-drilling techniques used to evacuate marrow and other fatty substances from large leg bones during the cleaning process.

or absence of brain tissues from the skull is very important. If brains are not removed prior to prolonged soaking or cooking, they may expand and force the brain case apart.

If brains are still in the skull, first soak the skull in warm water and then remove the brains with a bent wire or soft-ended implement. Do this gently, as the divisional plate of bone inside the brain case is fragile. Once the major portion of brain material has been removed, rinse the brain case with warm water to remove any remaining tissue.

CLEANING METHODS

Cleaning bones is a relatively simple process. Two basic methods are discussed here: maceration and boiling. Choose whichever method you

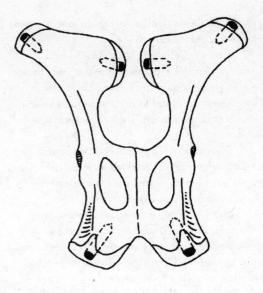

Illustrations of bone-drilling techniques used to evacuate marrow and other fatty substances from large hip bones during the cleaning process.

prefer, depending on available time and materials, as well as your level of patience. You should also consider the sensibilities of your neighbors, parents, or spouse, as bone cleaning can be an odoriferous process.

Maceration

Maceration involves submerging bones in a covered bucket of 1.5 percent ammonia water—in the proportion of two quarts water to one ounce ammonia. Clorox bleach may be substituted for ammonia.* Leave the bones in the solution a few weeks or months until all tissue decays. Then remove the bones from the solution, scrub them gently, rinse with warm water, and allow to dry thoroughly. The soaking process can take weeks or months and generates offensive odors, so it's best done only in rural areas with distant neighbors. Maceration is certainly not the quickest method of cleaning bones, but it is perhaps the best home method for preserving delicate structures in both large and small animals. For example, the most difficult bones to clean and preserve are those in a skull that support the sinus membranes. These waffled, honeycomblike structures are very delicate. In fact, many people, even museum personnel, simply remove these structures to facilitate cleaning. By using maceration, however, they can be nicely preserved.

Boiling

An alternative to maceration is *boiling*, simply cooking bones in water or a weak bleach or ammonia solution. Because bones often smell bad when boiling, it is best to do this outside on a camp stove. You could try it on your kitchen stove, but even if you use an exhaust fan you're likely to drive everyone out of the house.

To prepare bones for boiling, soak them overnight in a 1.5 percent ammonia solution (two quarts water to one ounce ammonia). This solution may be used for cooking the bones the next day. Tie a long string to each specimen

---

* Remember: Bleach and ammonia are extremely caustic. Immersion of specimens in strongly concentrated solutions of these chemicals will result in the deterioration of delicate bone structures such as those of the sinus.

before immersing it so that it can be lifted and examined from time to time during cooking.

When you're ready to cook, add more liquid (water or solution) to the pot if necessary so that the specimens are covered.* Bring the liquid to a rolling boil, then reduce to a gentle boil by lowering the heat. Stirring occasionally, cook the specimens until flesh and ligaments separate easily from the bone. Allow larger bones to cook longer, particularly those that have been drilled.

The basic problem with this cleaning method is that boiling can loosen bone joints, especially those in the skull.

Be very careful when boiling skulls, especially those of juveniles and smaller mammals. If the skull does fall apart, you can reconstruct it by using epoxy glue, superglue, or even liquid solder in a tube. Be careful to position the joints exactly, because once the glue or solder has set you won't get another chance. Do this outdoors or in a well-ventilated area, and wear gloves.

Prolonged cooking of skulls often results in the softening and eventual disintegration of the cartilagelike material that holds teeth in their sockets. Should this occur, carefully gather the teeth and later reset them in their proper position using rubber cement, superglue, or epoxy glue.

Boiling can also crack teeth, especially those of larger mammals. This happens because sudden changes in temperature cause tooth enamel to shrink at a different rate than the tooth's bony center. To minimize tooth-cracking, limit sudden hot-to-cold temperature changes by immersing skulls in a bucket of hot water as soon as you remove them from the pot. If gentle scrubbing is required, do this while the skull is still submerged. When the liquid has cooled, remove the skull and allow it to dry. To further prevent teeth from cracking, coat them with polyurethane, clear fingernail polish, or paraffin wax during the final cleaning, as discussed below.

FINAL CLEANING

The final scraping and probing can be the most tedious part of the bone-cleaning process, but is essential to ensure that all tissue has been removed. With gloved hands, remove specimens from the maceration bucket or use the strings to lift bones one at a time from the boiling pot. Immediately upon removal, use a small, hard instrument to pick or scrape off all extraneous material from each specimen, occasionally rinsing the bones in a bucket of hot water.

When you have removed as much material as possible with the hard scraper, switch to soft scrubbing pads. Immerse the specimen in a bucket of hot water and gently but thoroughly scrub as much of its surface area as you can reach. Then set the specimen aside on the paper or drop cloth and move on to the next.

When you have cleaned all of the bones, you need to degrease them with a final rinse, since you pulled them through a thin layer of oil when removing them from the maceration bucket or

---

* Note: To avoid adverse chemical reactions, do not add bleach solution to ammonia solution when soaking or cooking bones.

Continued ➔

boiling pot. To do this, fill the bucket with a 10 percent solution of hot water and ammonia or bleach (two quarts water to 6.4 ounces ammonia). Immerse the bones in this solution and let stand for one hour, or until the liquid has cooled. Fill another bucket or pot with a 10 percent solution of ammonia or bleach and immerse the bones one at a time. This time scrub them gently but thoroughly with a soft pad or toothbrush. When finished, place the specimens on the paper or cloth and let dry in a well-ventilated area, preferably outside in the sun, for two weeks longer.

If you wish, bones can be whitened by simmering them approximately six hours in a 10 percent solution of water and hydrogen peroxide or bleach. Check the bones frequently, as prolonged submersion can make the bones chalky and cause them to crumble. Also, be careful not to make the solution too strong, as strong solutions can cause severe and rapid bone deterioration.

Sealing Bones

Once cleaned and dried, specimens should be sealed for longer preservation. Sealing home-quality specimens is important because most, if not all, of the bone's natural grease sealant has been removed during the cleaning process, thus leaving bones very porous and subject to crumbling and splitting.

Most hardware stores and home hobby centers carry several commercial sealing products. Use these materials in open, well-ventilated areas. The following five products are easily obtainable and relatively simple to apply.

Bones can be sealed with a later of *clear wax* such as paraffin. A wax coating can be polished, but once it is rubbed in it attracts dust, is difficult to clean, and, like furniture, requires occasional upkeep. Researchers find this sealant a plus because it can be removed, allowing close study of the bone.

Available in most hardware and woodworking stores, the active lifespan of *varnish* is shorter than other lacquer-type sealants and it can be difficult to apply an even coating to specimens. Varnish also tends to crack and yellow with age, but for the short term it provides easy upkeep.

Polyurethane, a permanent sealant, is available in hardware and woodworking stores. With a long active lifespan, it is easy to maintain and has a clear, durable finish that resists cracking with age. If kept in constant sunlight, however, it may yellow.

Available in home hobby centers, hardware stores, and even in large supermarkets, *clear enamel spray paint* combines easy administration and upkeep with long life. The application of a minimum of three coats is recommended on specimens to ensure total coverage.

Clear plastic floral spray is available in home hobby centers and offers the advantages of easy upkeep and simple application with long life. A minimum of three coats should be applied.

—From *Skulls and Bones*

Crafting Stone and Bone Tools

Greg Davenport
Illustrations by Steven Davenport

Stones

Hammers, axes, clubs, mortars, pestles, and arrowheads are just a few examples of how stones have been used throughout time. Through the processes of flint knapping, pecking, and crumbling, most rocks can be transformed into these tools.

Flint Knapping

Flint knapping is the art of making flaked stone tools. Percussion flaking is the process of creating a flake (blank) by striking one stone with another. The resultant black can then be made into a knife or arrow point by using a pressure-flaking technique.

FLINT KNAPPING MATERIALS

- **Safety materials.** The act of flint knapping is not without potential risk and you should always wear leather gloves, eye protection, long plants, leather to cover your legs, and shoes. In addition, working in a well-ventilated area is highly advisable.

- **Hammer stones.** A hammer stone is used to strike the stone. Stream-rounded cobbles are ideal for hard hammer flaking and antler billets are best when using a soft hammer technique. The size of the stone or antler billet will depend on the detail of work you are doing.

- **Pressure flaker.** A pressure flaker is used to create spear tips and similar items. Unlike the hammer that strikes your stone, this tool applies its force by pressing the flaker against the stone. The tine of a deer antler is the most commonly used pressure flaker. Nails, bone, and thick copper wire with improvised handles are other options.

- **Stones.** The most common stones used are obsidian (the easiest to use and recommended for beginners), basalt, rhyolite, chert, and flint. Man-made options can be found in glass and porcelain. The ideal material will be homogeneous, brittle, and elastic. Homogeneous stones are the same consistency throughout, lacking flaws and irregularities. There is a fine balance between rocks that are brittle yet elastic. A rock that is brittle and yet elastic will break easily but if not deformed to its breaking point it will return to its original shape. To understand flint knapping better I'd like to review a stone's nomenclature.

  —*Core.* A core is the piece from which the flakes are removed. It may be used to provide sharp flakes or be turned into a tool itself.
  —*Flake.* A flake is the material removed from the core. The flake is often used to make tools such as arrow points and knife blades.
  —*Striking platform.* The surface (usually flat) on both the core and the flake where the separating force is applied.

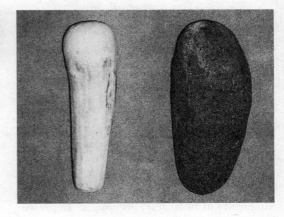

Hard hammer and an antler billet.

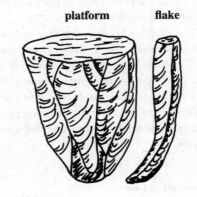

Antler tine and copper wire flakers.

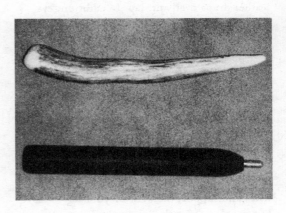

Platform and flake.

PERCUSSION FLAKING

There are four basic methods of percussion flaking:

- **Hammer and anvil.** In this technique, the core's edge is struck against an anvil (large stationary rock) to remove the flake. The biggest problems associated with this method are the lack of control and dangers related to flying flakes.

- **Bipolar.** Similar to the hammer and anvil except with this technique the core is placed on the anvil and struck with a large heavy hammer. This method is most often used on stones that are very difficult to work with. It has the same disadvantages as seen with the hammer and anvil.

- **Hard hammer percussion.** In this technique, the core is held in one hand and struck with the hammer stone. This method allows you to have more control over where the core is struck and how large the flake will be.

Continued ➡

- **Soft hammer percussion.** In this technique, a hammer that is softer than the core is used. Common examples of this are soft limestone, deer antler, and bones. A blow to the core with a soft hammer starts a flake fracture, which it can then tear away from the core.

For our purposes I am going to discuss hard hammer percussion flaking. This method allows you to create both core and flake tools from a rock. Holding the stone in your less dominant hand while striking it with a hammer is a very simple way of visualizing this process. To prevent cuts, be sure to wear leather gloves and to place a leather drape over your lap. In addition, eye protection is advised.

To make tools from the core or resultant flakes, the rock must have a proper platform for you to strike. This platform must provide an angle with fewer than 90 degrees between it and the side of the rock. If the rock does not naturally have this angle, it will be necessary to create it by breaking the stone in half. I normally use a bipolar method to accomplish this.

Once you have a good platform, sit down and hold the stone—platform side up—in your hand and support the wrist on your leg (be sure to wear gloves, goggles, and use a lap mat). Approximately $1/4$ to $1/8$ inch from the edge of the stone, strike the platform with your hammer using a downward angle of fewer than 90 degrees. The distance between the edge of your stone and where you strike determines the size of the flake. Too close to the edge and you only get chips; too far away from the edge and you probably won't even produce a blank. You don't need to hit the core hard. In fact, in most cases you only need to guide the hammer stone down onto the platform.

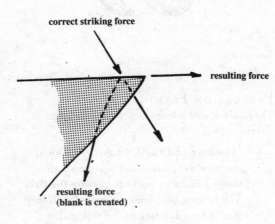

Strike the core at an angle of fewer than 90 degrees.

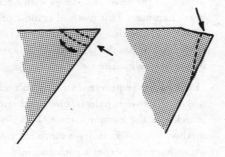

To increase a platform's angle, strike it from the opposite direction first.

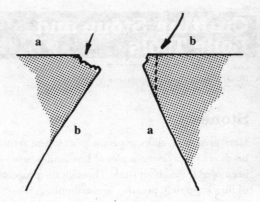

To remove platform irregularities, strike it from the opposite direction first.

On occasion you may have irregularities in your platform or its angle may be more than 90 degrees. Striking the stone form the opposite direction usually corrects this problem. This process is often referred to as faceting.

Depending on your needs, the core and flakes can be used as is or can provide an excellent source from which to improvise. Pressure flaking is the next step.

Pressure Flaking

Pressure flaking is similar to percussion except on a smaller scale and the chips are removed by pressure instead of striking. Holding the flake in one hand and pushing chips off its beveled sides until sharp is a simple way of looking at pressure flaking. To do this you will need your safety gear, an abrader (usually a fine-grained sandstone), and a pressure flaker (antler tine or copper wire flaker). To make a copper flaker, cut a 2-inch piece of large diameter wire, drill a hole in a handle of your choice (slightly smaller diameter), and pound the wire into the hole until only $1/2$ inch is showing.

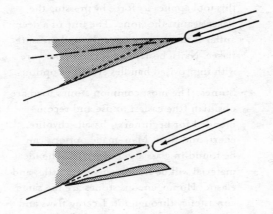

To remove a flake, use an inward and slightly off center force along with a gentle downward motion.

As with hammer percussion, pressure flaking requires a proper platform. In pressure flaking, however, the platform is the edge itself. Ideally, the edge is slightly above the centerline on the side from which you intend to remove the flake. When a flake is removed from one side, the platform (edge) moves toward the other face of the piece. For best results, the platform needs to be sharp enough to dig into the pressure tool and prevent it from slipping off.

When working the blank be sure to wear a leather glove or use a leather pad to protect the hand. Place the flake on the palm of your hand (hold it between your fingertips and the heel of

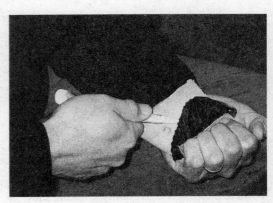

Ray Rickleman shows the proper technique for pressure flaking using an antler tine.

your hand) and support your hand by placing your wrist on your leg. Before starting, remove any thin sharp edges by rubbing your abrader over them toward the interior surface of the flake. This not only helps decrease the chances of cutting yourself but will also create a good

Various arrow and spear tips along with examples of the stone prior to pressure flaking.

platform from which to start. Use your flaker to remove as many flakes as you can before turning the blank over and doing the same on the other side (you should abrade the edge in the same direction as flaking before turning it over).

With pressure flaking the force is applied inward, slightly off the center plane, and in line with the surface of the flake you are removing. As you increase your force, apply a gentle downward motion until the flake breaks free. Too much downward force creates only short chips; too much inward force crushes the edge without removing any flakes. *Note*: If your edge is not bifacial, you will need to use a downward angle and force on the tip until enough short flakes are removed to create a bifacial point. In general, pressure flaking removes short chips from the rock. If you need to thin the blank, apply as much inward pressure as you can with just enough downward pressure to start the flake. If done right it will product the long slender flakes needed to thin the piece. When notching the blank, continually work the area with short controlled strokes, making sure not to compromise the flake's core causing it to break. A few examples of a final produce are an arrowhead, knife blade, or spear tip.

Pecking and Crumbling

Pecking and crumbling is the process of creating grooves and depressions in a rock. In most cases this is done to prepare a rock for a handle. Using a harder rock or hammer stone, repeatedly strike the rock you are working on, breaking

Continued ➡

down its grain until you create the desired result. Applying water to the stone while working on it will speed up the crumbling process.

Bone Tools

An animal provides us with many resources. Clothing and glue are just a few examples. Its bones can be used to make awls, needles, arrowheads, knives, scrapers, punches, spear points, clubs, and many other tools. Bones are hard enough to accomplish many tasks and yet soft enough to easily transform into a workable item. To transform a bone into a tool, I first look at it and try to envision what need it can meet with

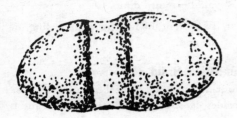

Pecked rock.

the least amount of modification. Sometimes, I will just break it and work with the various sizes created. At other times, I score it—on each side— and use a hammer stone to break it in half. Either way, a sanding stone is used to develop the bone into the desired tool.

Hafting

Hafting is the process of securing your stone or bone to a handle, which is often made out of wood. The two most common types are forked and wrapped (details on hafting arrowheads and spearheads are explained under the construction of each).

Forked Hafting

Cut a 2- to 3-foot branch of straight-grained hardwood (softwood will also work) that is approximately 1 to 2 inches in diameter. Six to 8 inches down from one end of the stick, snugly lash a line around the wood. I often use wet rawhide since it shrinks during the drying process creating a tight bond. With a knife, split the wood down the center and lash your stone between the wood and as close to the lashing as possible. Finally, secure the rock (bone or other material) to the stick with a tight lashing (done above, below, and across it). Using a strong forked branch is another method in which to create the same type of tool. Simply secure the rock between the two forked branches.

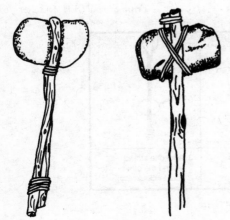

Using a sapling as a handle.   *Hafting a forked branch to an ax.*

Sapling Hafting

This process is simple. Using a slender willow sapling (or similar material), wrap it twice around your pecked stone or bone and secure it in place with buckskin ties. The ties should be placed just below the wrap and at the bottom of the newly formed handle.

—From *Wilderness Living*

Improvising
Greg Davenport

With creativity and imagination, you can improvise the basic survival necessities. The only limiting factor is your imagination.

Five Steps of Improvising

When working through the improvising process, the following five-step guide helps you make the best choice.

1. Determine your need.
2. Inventory your available materials, man-made and natural.
3. Consider the different options of how you might meet your need.
4. Pick one, based on its efficient use of time, energy, and materials.
5. Proceed with the plan, ensuring that the final product is safe and durable.

For example, you're lost in a temperate forest during a cool spring evening, it's 8 P.M., and you're in need of a shelter.

1. Determine your need: You need a shelter.
2. Inventory your available materials:
   a. Man-made: You have line, a tarp, a poncho, and a large plastic bag.
   b. Natural: In the general area, you can see trees, branches, leaves, and cattails.
3. Consider the different options of how you might meet your need:

   a. Construct a tarp shelter.
   b. Construct a poncho shelter.
   c. Construct a shelter using the plastic bag.
   d. Find a good tree well (may even incorporate your tarp into the lower boughs to add to the natural protection).
   e. Construct a natural shelter using cattail leaves to provide the outer covering.
4. Pick one, based on its efficient use of time, energy, and materials:
   a. Time. Options *a* through *d* require little time to construct.
   b. Energy. Options *a* through *d* require very little energy.
   c. Materials. Options *a*, *b*, and *c* would require materials that could be put to better use. Options *d* and *e* are good choices, since they spare your man-made resources. Option *d* would use material in an appropriate fashion, provided the tarp was not necessary to meet any of your other needs.
5. Proceed with the plan, ensuring that the final product is safe and durable: Construct the shelter, ensuring that it meets the criteria in the section on personal protection.

—From *Wilderness Survival*

Improvised Cordage
Greg Davenport
Illustrations by Steven A. Davenport

Improvised cordage (line)—from Mother Nature's resources—expands our ability to meet various daily needs. Fishing line, belts, and rope are just a few examples of the various items you can create. Cordage can be made from various materials such as plants, outer and inner tree bark, animal products (sinew, hide, and so on), and various man-made products (parachute line, twine, and so on). The best rope-making materials have four basic characteristics:

Example	Preparation
Stalks of fibrous plants	Examples include stinging nettle, milkweed, and dogbane. To prepare, pound dry stems, remove woody outer stalks, clean and use remaining fibers. Be careful when removing the outer wood that you don't break the inner fibers.
Cattail and rushes	Pound the leaves between rocks to start the breakdown process. Soak for several days, occasionally working the leaves with your hands. Remove the leaves from the water and if any of the outer cellulose is still present, scrape it off with a knife (use a 90-degree angle).
Yucca leaves	Prepare the same as cattail. Yucca can be used without soaking by simply scraping away the cellulose first.
Grasses and weeds	It is best to use grasses and weeds when they are green.
Trees	Willow, elm, spruce, cedar, and juniper are just a few examples. In most cases the inner bark is what you'd use. It's best when the tree is near dead since in this state much of the inner bark's moisture has dissipated.
Animal products	Hair, wool, sinew, rawhide, and buckskin can all be used. A lot of animal products, however, are not suited for wet conditions. Sinew, rawhide, and buckskin should be wet when used for lashing, but for cordage, make sure they are dry before beginning.

Continued ➡

- Fibers need to be long enough for ease of work.

- Fibers need to be strong enough to pull on without breaking.

- Fibers need to be pliable enough to tie a knot in without breaking.

- Fibers need a grip that allows them to bite into one another when twisted together.

Regardless of what you use, as long as it meets these criteria it should work. Some examples of various options are listed below:

Spinning a Cord

Using any material that meets the characteristic of good cordage, twist it between your thigh and palm. Add additional fibers to the free end as needed to make one continuous cord that can be used to create a two-strand, three-strand, or four-strand braid.

Two-Strand Braid

The two-strand braid is an excellent all-around line that can be used for many improvising tasks. For tasks where a lot of weight will be applied to the line, however, a four-strand braid would be a better option. Use the following steps to make a two-strand braid:

good braid

bad braid

A properly spun two-strand braid will have even tension throughout.

- Using spun cord, grab it between the thumb and forefinger of your left hand so it measures two-thirds of its length on one side and one-third on the other.

- With the thumb and pointer finger of your right hand, grasp the fiber that is farthest away from you. Twist it clockwise until tight and then move it counterclockwise over the other strand. It is now the closer of the two.

- Twist the second strand (which is now the farthest away) clockwise until tight and then move it counterclockwise over the first strand.

- Continue this process until done.

- Splicing will need to be done as you go and this is the reason for the two-thirds and one-third split. Splicing both lines at the same location would significantly compromise that point. Splicing is simply adding line to one side. Make sure to have plenty of overlap between the preceding line and the new one and to use line of similar diameter.

- To prevent the line from unraveling, finish the free end with an overhand knot.

If you are in a hurry—needing a piece of short line right then—there is a quicker alternative:

- Using spun cord, grab one end between the thumb and forefinger of your left hand and roll it in one direction—on the thigh—with your right palm.

- Repeat this process until the whole line is done and is tight.

- Continue holding the line in your left hand and grasp the other end with your right hand.

- Place the middle between your teeth and move your hands so that you have both ends tightly held in one hand.

- Release the line from your mouth. Due to the tension created from rolling the line on your leg, the two strands will spin together.

Three-Strand Braid

A three-strand braid is ideal for making straps and belts. Use the following guidelines to make a three-strand braid:

- Tie the three lines together at one end and lay the lines out so that they are side by side.

- Pass the right-side strand over the middle strand.

- Pass the left-side strand over the newly formed middle strand.

- Repeat this process, alternating from side to side (right over middle; left over middle), until done.

- To prevent the line from unraveling, tie the end.

Four-Strand Braid

A four-strand braid is ideal for use as a rope. It provides the strength and shape desired and is far superior for this purpose to either the two-

LASHING AND CORDAGE
U.S. Army

Many materials are strong enough for use as lashing and cordage. A number of natural and man-made materials are available in a survival situation. For example, you can make a cotton web belt much more useful by unraveling it. You can then use the string for other purposes (fishing line, thread for sewing, and lashing).

Natural Cordage Selection

Before making cordage, there are a few simple tests you can do to determine you material's suitability. First, pull on a length of the material to test for strength. Next, twist it between your fingers and roll the fibers together. If it withstands this handling and does not snap apart, tie an overhand knot with the fibers and gently tighten. If the knot does not break, the material is usable. Figure 12-8 shows various methods of making cordage.

Lashing Material

The best natural material for lashing small objects is sinew. You can make sinew from the tendons of large game, such as deer. Remove the tendons from the game and dry them completely. Smash the dried tendons so that they separate into fibers. Moisten the fibers and twist them into a continuous strand. If you need stronger lashing material, you can braid the strands. When you use sinew for small lashings, you do not need knots as the moistened sinew is sticky and it hardens when dry.

You can shred and braid plant fibers from the inner bark of some trees to make cord. You can use the linden, elm, hickory, white oak, mulberry, chestnut, and red and white cedar trees. After you make the cord, test it to be sure it is strong enough for your purpose. You can make these materials stronger by braiding several strands together.

You can use rawhide for larger lashing jobs. Make rawhide from the skins of medium or large game. After skinning the animal, remove any excess fat and any pieces of meat from the skin. Dry the skin completely. You do not need to stretch it as long as there are no folds to trap moisture. You do not have to remove the hair from the skin. Cut the skin while it is dry. Make cuts about 6 millimeters wide. Start from the center of the hide and make one continuous circular cut, working clockwise to the hide's outer edge. Soak the rawhide for 2 to 4 hours or until it is soft. Use it wet, stretching it as much as possible while applying it. It will be strong and durable when it dries.

—From *Survival (Field Manual 21-76)*

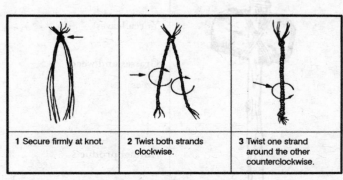

| 1 Secure firmly at knot. | 2 Twist both strands clockwise. | 3 Twist one strand around the other counterclockwise. |

Making lines from plant fibers.

Continued →

Three-strand braid.

strand or three-strand braids. To make a four-strand braid, follow these directions:

- Tie the four lines together at one end and lay the lines out so that they are side by side.

- Pass the right-hand strand over the strand immediately to its left.

- Pass the left-hand strand under the strand directly to its right and over the original right-hand strand.

- Pass the new outside right strand over the strand immediately to its left.

- Pass the new outside left strand under and over the next two strands, respectively, moving to the right.

- Repeat this process (right strand over strand immediately to its left; left strand under and over the two strands immediately to its right).

- Splice as needed.

—From *Wilderness Living*

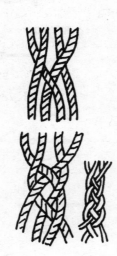

Four-strand braid.

Improvised Backpacks

Improvising a Rucksack
U.S. Army

The materials for constructing a rucksack or pack are almost limitless. You can use wood, bamboo, rope, plant fiber, clothing, animal skins, canvas, and many other materials to make a pack.

There are several construction techniques for rucksacks. Many are very elaborate, but those that are simple and easy are often the most readily made in a survival situation.

Horseshoe Pack
This pack is simple to make and use and relatively comfortable to carry over one shoulder. Lay available square-shaped material, such as poncho, blanket, or canvas, flat on the ground. Lay items on one edge of the material. Pad the hard items. Roll the material (with the items) toward the opposite edge and tie both ends securely. Add extra ties along the length of the bundle. You can drape the pack over one shoulder with a line connecting the two ends (below).

Square pack
This pack is easy to construct if rope or cordage is available. Otherwise, you must first make cordage. To make this pack, construct a square frame from bamboo, limbs, or sticks. Size will vary for each person and the amount of equipment carried (above right).

—From *Survival (Field Manual 21-76)*

Improvised Backpacks
Greg Davenport
Illustration by Steven A. Davenport

To make an improvised backpack, start by finding a forked branch (sapling or bough), and cut it 1 foot below the fork and 3 feet above. Trim off excess twigs, cut notches about 1 inch from each of the three ends, and tie rope or line around the notches of the two forked branches. Bring the two lines down and tie them to the notch on the single end of the sapling to create the pack's shoulder straps. Make sure your shoulders can fit through these loops and that the line is not too tight or too loose. Place your gear inside a waterproof bag and attach it to the forked branch. To carry this pack, create a chest strap that runs through the shoulder straps at armpit height. This line should be long enough that you can hold its free end in your hand to control the amount of pressure exerted by the pack on your armpits and shoulders.

Horseshoe pack.

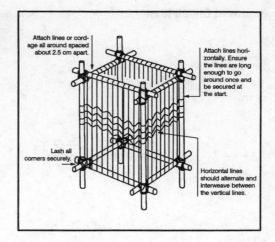

Square pack.

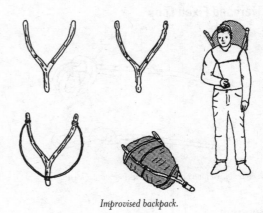

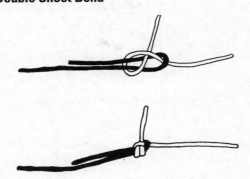

Improvised backpack.

—From *Surviving the Desert*

Common Knots
Greg Davenport
Illustrations by Steven A. Davenport

Square Knot

Square knot connects two ropes of equal diameter together.

Double Sheet Bend

Double sheet bend connects two ropes of different diameters.

Continued →

Improved Clinch Knot

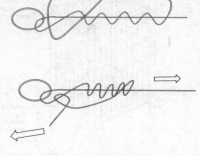

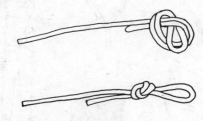

Improved clinch knot is used to attach a hook to a line of different diameters.

Overhand Fixed Loop

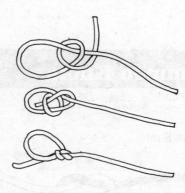

Overhand fixed loop has multiple uses in a survival setting.

Bowline

Unlike the overhand fixed loop, bowline is much easier to untie after you use it.

Double Half Hitch

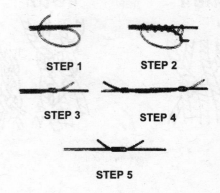

Double half hitch secures a line to a stationary object.

—From *Surviving Coastal and Open Water*

Fishing Knots
Gene Kugach

The following illustrations show how to tie some of the more commonly used fishing knots. Some helpful tips to remember when tying knots are:

1. Use plenty of working line.
2. Tighten knots with a steady, even motion.
3. Pull the knot tight.
4. Don't trim the tag end too close.

Knots are used for various purposes. The type of knot you use will depend on its intended application, such as attaching lures, hooks, sinkers, and so forth.

The following illustrations show a few additional knots to learn. By using them, you can improve your fishing ability.

Clinch knots

BASIC CLINCH KNOT

STEP 1

STEP 2

IMPROVED CLINCH KNOT

DOUBLE CLINCH KNOT

STEP 1   STEP 2

STEP 3   STEP 4

Perfection Loop

STEP 1   STEP 2

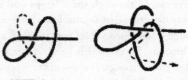

STEP 3   STEP 4

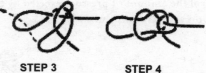

STEP 5

Fisherman's bend   Fly line loop

Palomar knot

STEP 1   STEP 2

STEP 3   STEP 4

Turtle knot

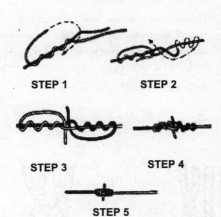

STEP 1   STEP 2

STEP 3   STEP 4

Blood knot

STEP 1   STEP 2

STEP 3   STEP 4

STEP 5

Knot splice

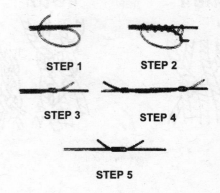

STEP 1   STEP 2

STEP 3   STEP 4

STEP 5

Two-fold open-eye end

STEP 1   STEP 2

Continued

ALBRIGHT KNOT

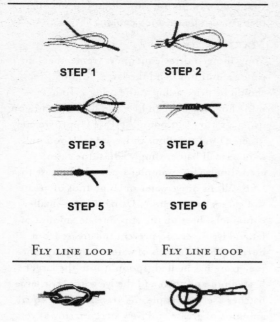

STEP 1   STEP 2

STEP 3   STEP 4

STEP 5   STEP 6

FLY LINE LOOP   FLY LINE LOOP

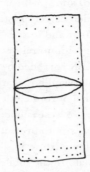

Improvised Containers

Greg Davenport
Illustrations by Steven A. Davenport

Containers provide you with the ability to cook, store, and transport various liquids and solids. They can be created from animal stomachs or rawhide, wood, weaved baskets, or clay.

Containers Created from Animals

Shaping, drying, and using an animal's stomach is the most common example of creating a container from large game. The easiest way to do this is to pour sand into the stomach, shape it, and let it dry. Once dry, simply pour out the sand. These containers hold their shape fairly well and tend to last a long time. In addition to the stomach, rawhide can be shaped using the same sand method. Other options include the animal's skull, hoofs, or pelvis.

Containers Created from Wood

Find a log that when split in half provides the dimensions of the bowl you want to create. Split it in half lengthwise and place a hot red coal in

Using a coal to make a wooden bowl.

the center of the inner surface. Gently blow on the coal until it no longer glows or appears to have stopped burning into the wood. Dump it out, scrape away the char until good wood is exposed again, and place another coal onto the fresh surface. Repeat this process until done. Once you have the shape you want, scrape the bowl's inside surface until it is smooth, and work its outer surface until you achieve the desired shape.

Containers Created from Bark

When making a birch bark container, score the bottom and make holes on the sides and top for your cordage.

Bark is a versatile resource that can be used to meet many of our needs. Maple, willow, birch, cedar, and juniper bark are often used to create a container. Birch bark is probably the easiest to use. It can be gathered from a live tree or one that has recently died. To procure the bark, cut a large rectangular piece (be sure to cut all the way through the bark), pry a corner free, and peel it from the tree. Do not ring the tree when doing this or you may kill it. If you don't intend to work the bark right away, soak it in water until you can get to it. This prevents it from drying out and becoming brittle. Lay the bark side down (side that was not against the inner tree) on a level surface, identify the center between the two ends, and using that as your guide, score (don't cut) two opposing oblique shapes that create an eye shape. (See illustration.) The score should allow the bark to bend but not break. Using the score as your guide, fold the ends together so that the eye-shaped area becomes the bottom of your soon-to-be container. As the sides are brought together the bottom should naturally create a slight upward curve. To make the sewing process easier, go ahead and mark the sides while they are together. The marks should be close to the edge but not so close as to split the bark. Lay the bark flat and drill the holes. To help stabilize the container's opening, it is advisable to wrap a sapling around it. In order to hold the sapling in place, you'll need to drill holes at the top of both ends. These holes need to run in an alternating diagonal sequence with one close to the top edge and one 1/2 inch below. (See illustration.) Once all the holes are drilled, fold the container together and sew the sides together with cordage or rawhide. Wrap the sapling around the top and hold it in place by lacing the cordage or buckskin around it (using the alternating holes). For ease of transport, attach a buckskin or cordage handle to the top.

—From *Wilderness Living*

Making Glues and Soap

Greg Davenport

Improvised Glues

Animal Glue

The effectiveness of animal glue depends on how well it is made, the cleanliness of the wood's surface, and whether you size the wood before applying the glue. Once the wood is cleaned, sizing will help fill the wood's gaps and seal its surface. To clean the material's surface of all oils and debris, use either the lye mixture (discussed on next page) or a soap like Fels-Naptha with warm water and a toothbrush. Sizing is done by simply applying a first coating of glue to the material and letting it dry. I compare this process to using primer before applying paint. The primer protects the wall, providing a better surface for the paint to stick to. Animal glues can be made from sinew, hide, and hide scrapings.

SINEW GLUE

Fill a large pot (or a no. 10 coffee can) two-thirds of the way full of sinew, cover it with water, and bring to a boil for 2 to 3 hours. During this time, stir occasionally and remove any debris that floats to the top. Add water if it looks like the sinew may burn. Next, pour the light syrup (perhaps a little runnier than Elmer's glue) through a fine porous cloth onto a wide tray. Ideally it will be between 1/4 to 1/2 inch thick. Set it in a cool area that provides a breeze (or use a fan) and let it dry. Once it has dried, cut or break it into smaller pieces and store it in a cool dry place that is protected from animals, rodents, and insects.

If you need to use the glue at that moment, just keep it warm. If working with wood or fibers keep it around 140 degrees [F]; if you're working with sinew or other animal parts keep the glue at about 120 degrees. No matter what, don't let it get above 180 degrees. At that high temperature the glue loses a lot of its adhesive qualities. If dried, the glue will need to be reconstituted before using. To do this, place a piece of the glue in a pot, cover with water, and wait several hours until it plumps up. Heat it to around 160 degrees—stirring occasionally—until it reaches a uniform consistency. Lower the temperature of the syrup until it reaches the temperature desired for its use.

HIDE GLUE

The best material for hide glue is obtained from the scrapings created during the tanning process (membraning). If you don't have scrapings, the hide itself can actually be used with or without hair. If you decide to use the hide, however, it's best to clean it of fat and hair first. To turn hide scrapings into glue use the same steps as you did when making glue from sinew except boil it for approximately 1 hour. Pour the thickened syrup through a porous material. Wring the moisture out of the hide and into the same container. If the hide provides a lot of moisture, you may need to boil the liquid for a short time to return it to its syrupy consistency. At this point the

Continued →

temperature can be reduced based on the work you intend to do or the glue can be dried in the same fashion as done with sinew.

Fish Glue

The skin and air bladder of fish can be made into fairly effective glue. When using skin, remove all meat, fat, and scales and wash it thoroughly. Next, cut it into strips and prepare it in the same way that you would sinew or rawhide. The biggest difference is that fish glue will not totally dry. In fact, at best you'll end up with a medium-thick syrup as your final product.

Pitch Glue

Pitch glue is most often made from pine, fir, or spruce, each of which tends to bleed the pitch outside its bark. To make it, try to gather as much pure pitch as you can (dirt will compromise the quality). The hard pitch can be easily placed into a container and wet pitch can be removed with a knife and then scraped into your container. Since pitch becomes brittle if overcooked and it needs to be used when warm, only prepare small amounts at a time (enough for the intended task). Heat the pitch until it turns into a liquid—removing debris as it becomes obvious. If you don't have a container to heat the pitch in, use a dry nonporous rock strategically placed next to the fire. Pitch may flame up if placed too close to the fire, so be careful! Adding powdered eggshells to the liquid pitch will make the glue stronger and more flexible. To use, apply the wet pitch to the object in the same fashion you would any other glue.

Soap

Soap is more than just a nice convenience. It also helps us clean wounds, clothes, eating utensils, and cooking gear.

Plant Soap

There are many plants that have cleansing properties. Most contain a lather-producing substance called saponin. Saponins work by making foam when they are mixed with water and the foam lifts off dirt and grease. The most common of these plants include:

Name	Plant Part
Soapwort (bouncing bet)	Whole plant
Soapbark	Inner bark
Soapberry	Fruit
Soaproot	Bulb
Acacia	Pods
Yucca	Root

To create lathery suds from most soap plants simply crush the plant part, add moisture, and rub it between your hands. To save the plant part for later use, just let it dry.

Lye Soap Made Using Wood Ash

To make soap the old-fashioned way you'll need white ash, water (rain or springwater is best since it won't contain any undesirable minerals), animal fat (grease), plant oil (optional), salt (optional), a wooden container (plastic or stainless steel can also be used), and a wooden stirring stick. Before making the soap itself, you'll need to make lye water and prepare your animal fat.

Making Lye Water

To create this alkaline solution (lye water), mix approximately 2 gallons of hardwood white ash with 1 gallon of water (2:1 ratio) and stir them together. Be sure to use a wooden barrel, plastic bucket, or stainless steel container and to stir with a wooden stick. Do not use aluminum or tin containers since they are badly corroded by the caustic solution. Let sit for several hours and then pour the solution through a porous cloth into another container. Be sure to wear rubber gloves, eye protection, and an apron to protect your clothes. To determine if the mixture is right, place an egg or small potato in the solution (make sure it has enough room to float in the liquid—even if you have to lean the bucket to one side). If it sinks, the solution is too weak; if it floats and turns sideways, it is too strong. When the mixture is just right, the egg will float so that approximately 1/2 to 1 inch of its top is showing above the surface. If the egg sinks, you can boil the lye water down—making it stronger—until it supports the egg correctly. If the egg turns sideways, you can add water (1 cup at a time)—making it weaker—until it supports the egg correctly. CAUTION: THIS SOLUTION CAN AND WILL BURN YOUR SKIN AND YOUR EYES AND IS HARMFUL IF SWALLOWED. THE CONTAINER SHOULD BE COVERED, MARKED, AND KEPT OUT OF ANIMALS' AND CHILDREN'S REACH. If any of the lye solution gets on your skin, wash it off with vinegar. If it gets in your eyes, rinse thoroughly for 20 minutes and seek immediate medical attention.

Preparing the Animal Fat

The fat of most animals can be used for making soap. Remove the fat from the meat, cut it into small cubes, place it in a cast-iron frying pan, and melt it slowly over a low heat source. As a general rule, 1 pound produces about 1 cup of grease. Once melted, pour the grease through a porous cloth. To further clean the grease, mix it with equal amounts of water and bring it to a boil. Next, remove it from the heat and add 1/4 cup of cold water and let it cool. Once the fat has hardened, scrape away anything that looks dirty. Since the hardened fat is sitting on the water, it is best to remove it to a dry container until ready for use. This final product can be put aside for several weeks before using but if this is done be sure to store it in a cool area that

is away from animals, rodents, and insects. If you don't want to use animal fat, use any oils that can also be used for cooking.

Making Soap

You will need three containers (remember, no tin or aluminum) and the largest of the three should be twice as big as the others. To determine how much fat and lye you'll need figure on using a ratio of 12 pounds grease (approximately 30 cups) to 20 gallons of lye water. If you only want a small batch, simply adjust the ratio accordingly (for example: 1 pound of grease to 1.66 gallons of lye water or .6 pounds of grease to 1 gallon of lye water). Using the two smaller containers, heat up the appropriate amount of fat and lye water. To prevent the grease from burning, add 1/2 inch of water to the pot. Once the grease has melted, spoon it into the larger heated pot and then add the lye water. For large batches use two people and transfer small equal amounts of grease and lye water (stirring as you go) until done. Be sure to keep heating the mixture throughout the whole process.

To determine if the mixture is right use the following rule of thumb:

· If a thick film of grease forms on top, you need more lye.

· If the mixture doesn't thicken, you need more grease.

Once the mixture has a creamy, light caramel appearance you can test it to determine if it is done. Place a small amount of the soap on a glass or china plate and let it cool. When cool, if done, it will appear transparent with white streaks and specks throughout. If it is gray and weak looking or has a gray outer margin, it needs more lye. If it cools with a gray skin over it, it needs more fat. If done, you can store the liquid soap in a wooden container and use as needed.

If you want bar soap, you'll need to reduce the soap's water content. Adding a handful of salt will separate the soap and water. Once the salt is added, let the mixture cool. During this time the soap will separate from the water and will float on top of it. Remove the soap, add a small amount of water, heat to a boil for a few minutes, let it cool, and then skim the soap off the top again. At this point you can rewarm the soap and pour it into your awaiting molds to dry (this can be something as simple as a glass cake pan). If you are using a wooden container, soak it overnight in water and then line it with a wet cloth before pouring the soap in. Other containers should be greased (don't use tin or aluminum). Cover the soap and let it dry overnight. Once dry, remove the soap and use a wire cutter to cut it into useful sizes. At this point the soap is still green and needs to air dry for at least one month. Stack it so that it gets good air circulation in an area that is free from sunlight and moisture.

—From *Wilderness Living*

Bibliography

Stackpole Books

Angier, Bradford. *Feasting Free on Wild Edibles*. Mechanicsburg, PA: Stackpole Books, 1966 and 1969.

Angier, Bradford. *Field Guide to Medicinal Plants*. Mechanicsburg, PA: Stackpole Books, 1978.

Bensman, Bobbi. *Bouldering*. Mechanicsburg, PA: Stackpole Books, 1999.

Boga, Steven. *Orienteering*. Mechanicsburg, PA: Stackpole Books, 1997.

Davenport, Gregory J. *Surviving Coastal and Open Water*. Mechanicsburg, PA: Stackpole Books, 2003.

Davenport, Gregory J. *Surviving Cold Weather*. Mechanicsburg, PA: Stackpole Books, 2002.

Davenport, Gregory J. *Surviving the Desert*. Mechanicsburg, PA: Stackpole Books, 2004.

Davenport, Gregory J. *Wilderness Living*. Mechanicsburg, PA: Stackpole Books, 2001.

Davenport, Gregory J. *Wilderness Survival*. Mechanicsburg, PA: Stackpole Books, 2006.

Dickert, Wayne and Jon Rounds (ed). *Basic Kayaking*. Mechanicsburg, PA: Stackpole Books, 2005.

Elliott, Lang. *A Guide to Night Sounds*. Mechanicsburg, PA: Stackpole Books, 2004.

Fergus, Charles. *Bears: Wild Guide*. Mechanicsburg, PA: Stackpole Books, 2005.

Fergus, Charles and C. Leonard Fergus. *Common Edible & Poisonous Mushrooms of the Northeast*. Mechanicsburg, PA: Stackpole Books, 2003.

Forrest, Louise R. *Field Guide to Tracking Animals in Snow*. Mechanicsburg, PA: Stackpole Books, 1988.

Geary, Don. *Using a Map & Compass*. Mechanicsburg, PA: Stackpole Books, 1995.

Gray, Ed. *Track Pack: Animal Tracks in Full Life Size*. Mechanicsburg, PA: Stackpole Books, 2003.

Grimm, William Carey. *The Illustrated Book of Trees*. Revised and updated by John T. Kartesz. Mechanicsburg, PA: Stackpole Books, 1993.

Grimm, William Carey. *The Illustrated Book of Wildflowers and Shrubs*. Revised by John T. Kartesz. Mechanicsburg, PA: Stackpole Books, 2002.

Herd, Tim. *Discover Nature in the Weather*. Mechanicsburg, PA: Stackpole Books, 2001.

Kugach, Gene. *Fishing Basics*. Mechanicsburg, PA: Stackpole Books, 1993.

Kuhne, Cecil. *Paddling Basics: Canoeing*. Mechanicsburg, PA: Stackpole Books, 1998.

Kuhne, Cecil. *Paddling Basics: Kayaking*. Mechanicsburg, PA: Stackpole Books, 1998.

Lawlor, Elizabeth P. *Discover Nature at Sundown*. Mechanicsburg, PA: Stackpole Books, 1995.

Lawlor, Elizabeth P. *Discover Nature at the Seashore*. Mechanicsburg, PA: Stackpole Books, 1992.

Lawlor, Elizabeth P. *Discover Nature in Water & Wetlands*. Mechanicsburg, PA: Stackpole Books, 2000.

Lawlor, Elizabeth P. *Discover Nature in Winter*. Mechanicsburg, PA: Stackpole Books, 1998.

Macfarlan, Allan A. *Exploring the Outdoors with Indian Secrets*. Mechanicsburg, PA: Stackpole Books, 1971.

Pearson, Claudia, ed. *NOLS Cookery*. Mechanicsburg, PA: Stackpole Books, 2004.

Rinehart, Kurt. *Naturalist's Guide to Observing Nature*. Mechanicsburg, PA: Stackpole Books, 2006.

Rounds, Jon, ed, and Wayne Dickert. *Basic Canoeing*. Mechanicsburg, PA: Stackpole Books, 2003.

Schimelpfenig, Tod. *NOLS Wilderness Medicine*. Mechanicsburg, PA: Stackpole Books, 1991 and 2002.

Schuh, Dwight. *Fundamentals of Bowhunting*. Mechanicsburg, PA: Stackpole Books, 1991.

Searfoss, Glenn. *Skulls and Bones*. Mechanicsburg, PA: Stackpole Books, 1995.

Smith, Richard P. *Animal Tracks and Signs of North America*. Mechanicsburg, PA: Stackpole Books, 1982.

Tilton, Buck and John Gookin. *NOLS Winter Camping*. Mechanicsburg, PA: Stackpole Books, 2005.

Van Holt, Tom. *Stargazing*. Mechanicsburg, PA: Stackpole Books, 1999.

Wells, Darran. *NOLS Wilderness Navigation*. Mechanicsburg, PA: Stackpole Books, 2005.

U.S. Army Field Manuals

Basic Cold Weather Manual (Field Manual 31-70). Department of the Army: Washington, DC, 1968.

First Aid (Field Manual 4-25.11). Department of the Army: Washington, DC, 2004.

Military Mountaineering (Field Manual 3-97.61). Department of the Army: Washington, DC, August 26, 2002.

Survival (Field Manual 21-76). Department of the Army: Washington, DC, 1970. [Editor's note: Only artwork from this edition of Survival was used here.]

Survival (Field Manual 21-76). Department of the Army: Washington, DC, ... [Between 1986 and 1998]

Survival, Evasion, and Recovery: Multiservice Tactics, Techniques, and Procedures. U.S. Army, Marine Corps, Navy, Air Force; Air Land Sea Application Center: Washington DC, 1999.

Other U.S. Government Publications

A Pocket Guide to Cold Water Survival. U.S. Dept. of Transportation, U.S. Coast Guard: Washington, DC, 1990.

Camper's First Aid. U.S. Army Corps of Engineers, Louisville District: Louisville, KY, 1988.

Leave No Trace! An Outdoor Ethic. U.S. Dept. of Agriculture, Forest Service: Washington, DC, 1992.

Continued ➜

Index

A

abandon-ship bag, 349–51
abandon ship procedures, 357–59
ABCDE, 428–29
abdominal illness, 443–44
abdominal injury, 431, 444
acacia, 105
acclimatization, 449
achenes, 83
aches, 125
acorns, 84, 107–8, 122–23
acute mountain sickness, 449–50
A-frame, 244–45, 251
agave, 105
aggregate fruits, 84
airway obstruction, 428
Alabama black cherry, 92
Alaskan brown bear, 35
Albright knot, 473
allergic reactions, 442
alligators, 453
Altair, 390
alternating track pattern, 8
altimeter, 286, 411
altitude, 271, 449–51
amanita, 149
amaranth, 105, 126
ambush hunting, 205
amphibians, 168–69
anabatic wind, 382
analog method, 379
anaphylactic shock, 74, 442
anchor, 362, 256
Andromeda, 390–91
animals
    avoiding, 41–44
    birds, 47–57, 207, 211
    bites, 447–48, 453
    calling, 205–7
    communication, 206–7
    dangerous, 65, 69–74
    desert, 262
    fish, 70–73
    as food, 167–72, 454
    frogs, 57–61
    glue, 473
    insects, 73–74
    mammals, 11–47
    snakes, 65–69
    soap, 474
    tracking, 7–11, 203–6
    trapping, 191–98
    turtles, 61–65
    water and, 176, 184
    wounded, 212–13
    See also hunting; tracking; specific animals
ankle, sprained, 437–38
antelope, pronghorn, 32–33
anthrax, 465
antifungal wash, 125
antihemmorhagics, 125
antiseptics, 125
ants, 447
anxiety, 457
Apache foot snare, 194
appendicitis, 444
apple tree, 87, 93

aquatic mammals, 21–23
Aquila, 390
arachnids, 73
arctic
    edible animals in, 170–71
    edible plants in, 125
    foxes, 27
    shelter in, 250–54
    travel in, 283–306
    water in, 184–87
    See also cold weather
Arcturus, 391
armadillos, 40
arrow, handmade, 201–2
arrowhead, 126
arrowroot, 105
arrow-wood, 92, 97
ash trees, 91–92, 96–98
asparagus, 105
aspen, 87, 95–96, 98, 127
asthma, 443
A-tent, 244
athletic injury, 437–38
atlatl, 202–3
attacks
    bear, 36–37
    shark, 70
Auriga, 394
Australian poncho raft, 312–13
avalanches, 271, 306–11
avalanche transceiver, 285, 308
AvaLung, 285
ax, 240, 285, 290–92

B

backpack, 315, 471. *See also* pack
bacteria, 178
badgers, 20
bait, 192, 227–28
Baked Potato Chips, 166
baking, 154, 157, 173
balsam fir, 93
bamboo, 105
bamboo fire saw, 237
Banana Chips, 163
banana tree, 105, 177–78
baobab tree, 188
bark, 85–86, 97–98, 106, 473
barnacles, 172
barometric pressure, 377–78
barracuda, 70–71, 169, 172, 453
Basic Biscuits, 160
basswood, 88, 96
bats, 44–47
battery, 239
bay trees, 88–89, 92
bayberry, 87, 92
beach shade shelter, 249
Bean and Pasta Soup, 163
Bearpaw snowshoes, 298
bears, 34–41
Beaufort wind scale, 377
beavers, 21–23, 41
Beavertail snowshoes, 298
beech, 88, 96, 98
beechnut, 105
Beef Jerky, 163

bees, 73–74, 447
berries, 84, 106
Betelgeuse, 390, 393
big brown bats, 45–46
Big Dipper, 388, 390–92, 395
bighorn sheep, 33–34
bilge pump, 351
binoculars, 412
birch, 87, 93, 97, 98, 108, 126–28
birch bark torch, 242
birds
    birding, 47–52
    calling, 207
    as food, 169, 171
    hunting, 211
    identification of, 51–52
    nests, 53
    predicting weather, 380, 384
    preparing, 215
    tracks, 55–57
    trapping, 194, 197
    water and, 176, 184
    in winter, 53–54
bivouac bag, 255
black ash, 98
black bear, American, 34–35, 37–39, 42
blackberries, 105, 128
black gum tree, 87, 90, 95
blackhaw, 92, 97
black locust, 90, 93, 98
black walnut, 97
black widow, 73, 447–48
black willow, 97
blanket, 256, 422
Blast Match, 233
bleeding, 125, 426, 428
blindness, 441, 451, 453
blisters, 441–42
blood, 175, 212–13
blood knot, 472
blood sausage, 174
blowfish, 169
blueberries, 105
blue grouse, 55
blue-ringed octopus, 71
bobcats, 24
body signals, 423–24
boiling, 173, 178, 180, 466
boils, 440, 453
bola, 202–3
bone collecting, 462–67
boning fish, 215
bone tools, 467, 469
Böotes, 391
bottle purifier, 179
bottle trap, 195
botulism, 464
bouldering, 277–83
bow and drill, 234, 239
bow, handmade, 198–201
bow trap, 195
bowl, improvised, 174
bowline knot, 472
box trap, 194
box turtle, eastern, 63–64
boxing the needle, 407
brace strokes, 333–34

bracken fern, 101–2
brain injury, 431–33
breadfruit, 105
breakfast, 153, 163, 165–66
broiling, 173
brown recluse spider, 73, 447–48
brush raft, 312
bubonic plague, 465
buckeye, 92, 97
buckwheat tree, 89, 90, 92
buds, 85
buffalo, 34
bulk rationing, 151–53, 158
bullfrog, 58–59
bullheads, 230
bully tree, 90, 93
bulrush, 129
buoyant apparatus, 348
buoys, 355
burdock, 105, 108–9, 130
burning glass, 234, 239
burns, 441
bushmaster, 68
butane, 316
butchering game, 213–15
buttercup, 79
butternut, 109

C

cactus, 105, 177, 441
California thrasher, 49
California towhee, 49–50
CamelBak, 186
camellia, 88, 90, 95
campfires, 241–42
camphor tree, 89, 92
candle, 235
canines, 25–28
Canis Major, 392–93
Canis Minor, 392–94
canoeing, 329–34, 339–42, 345–46
canyons, 265
capsules, 84
carbohydrates, 157, 167
carbon dioxide poisoning, 252
carbon monoxide poisoning, 442
cardinal, 53
caribou, 32–33
Carolina false buckthorn, 88, 94–95
Carolina ground cricket, 74
carpopedal spasms, 442–43
cars, 266
cashew nut, 105
Cassiopeia, 390, 392–93, 395
castor bean, 145
catalpa, 91, 96
catawba rosebay, 92
catfish, 230
catholes, 461
cats, 23–26
cattail, 105, 109–10, 127, 129, 123, 125, 314, 469
cattail torch, 242
cave, 246, 251
cedar, 86, 93–94, 125
cellular phones, 421
centipedes, 73, 447

Continued ➜